Microsoft® Exchange Server 2010 Inside Out

Tony Redmond

PUBLISHED BY
Microsoft Press
A Division of Microsoft Corporation
One Microsoft Way
Redmond, Washington 98052-6399

Library of Congress Control Number: 2010935972
ISBN: 978-0-7356-4061-0

Printed and bound in the United States of America.

Microsoft Press books are available through booksellers and distributors worldwide. For further information about international editions, contact your local Microsoft Corporation office or contact Microsoft Press International directly at fax (425) 936-7329. Visit our Web site at www.microsoft.com/mspress. Send comments to mspinput @microsoft.com.

Microsoft and the trademarks listed at http://www.microsoft.com/about/legal/en/us/IntellectualProperty /Trademarks/EN-US.aspx are trademarks of the Microsoft group of companies. All other marks are property of their respective owners.

The example companies, organizations, products, domain names, e-mail addresses, logos, people, places, and events depicted herein are fictitious. No association with any real company, organization, product, domain name, e-mail address, logo, person, place, or event is intended or should be inferred.

This book expresses the author's views and opinions. The information contained in this book is provided without any express, statutory, or implied warranties. Neither the authors, Microsoft Corporation, nor its resellers, or distributors will be held liable for any damages caused or alleged to be caused either directly or indirectly by this book.

Acquisitions Editor: Martin DelRe
Developmental Editor: Karen Szall
Project Editor: Karen Szall
Editorial Production: nSight, Inc.
Technical Reviewer: Paul Robichaux; Technical Review services provided by Content Master, a member of CM Group, Ltd.
Cover: Tom Draper Design

Body Part No. X17-21593

Contents at a Glance

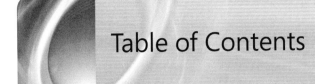

Table of Contents

What do you think of this book? We want to hear from you!

Microsoft is interested in hearing your feedback so we can continually improve our books and learning resources for you. To participate in a brief online survey, please visit:

www.microsoft.com/learning/booksurvey/

What do you think of this book? We want to hear from you!

Microsoft is interested in hearing your feedback so we can continually improve our books and learning resources for you. To participate in a brief online survey, please visit:

www.microsoft.com/learning/booksurvey/

Foreword

I took over the Exchange team in 2008 after 18 years in various roles at Microsoft, and was welcomed to the team appropriately via a post on the "You Had Me at EHLO" Exchange team blog. In November 2009, not too long after taking on this new mantle, I was in Las Vegas preparing to keynote the Exchange Connections conference to celebrate the launch of Exchange Server 2010. Knowing that I'd have some time to get to know members of the much-lauded Exchange community at the event, I reached out to my team for suggestions on which customers to seek out, which partner booths to visit, and any other advice they had. If one thing was universally clear it was that I had to—simply must—meet Tony Redmond.

Tony has been a fixture in the Exchange community for over a decade. Whether it is his advocacy for the Exchange customers or his critical feedback toward improving the product, Tony has played a significant role in the Exchange ecosystem since before the first Exchange Server ever shipped out of Redmond. He is one of the most popular speakers and authors on Exchange and an important voice for every one of the executives who preceded me as leader of Exchange at Microsoft.

It is appropriate that, after 14 years, Tony is publishing a book on Exchange Server 2010 SP1, a release that has so much to do with responding to customer and community feedback through early adopter and beta programs in which he has been so active over the years. Although an important milestone for the server, Exchange 2010 SP1 is also a significant milestone in our cloud strategy. This is the version of Exchange that we carry to our own datacenter as we bring the capabilities of Exchange 2010 to the cloud. It is unprecedented in the industry to provide a product that so comprehensively increases the operational efficiency of IT, makes users more productive in their daily workflow, reduces the risk profile of an organization, and brings this value to customers whether they choose to deploy servers on premises or migrate mailboxes into the cloud.

It is this unprecedented choice and flexibility that makes Exchange so unique and SP1 so important. It is with this focus that my team marches forward as we plan for the next updates to Exchange Online and the next versions of Exchange Server. Exchange 2010 SP1 makes me excited for the future of Exchange and I hope it does the same for you.

On behalf of my entire team, thank you for being part of our Exchange family and enjoy the book!

Rajesh Jha
Corporate Vice-President, Exchange
Microsoft Corporation

Introduction

Welcome to my tenth book covering the technology in Microsoft Exchange Server and its surrounding ecosystem. I seem to have been constantly writing about Exchange since before its introduction as version 4.0 in March 1996 in books and many articles printed in the redoubtable *Windows IT Pro* magazine (*http://www.windowsitpro.com*). All my previous books were published under the Digital Press imprint, which has now disappeared as a result of corporate upheavals. This is my first book working with Microsoft Press and it's been an interesting and productive experience for me to work with the publishing arm of the company that engineers Exchange. I look forward to future collaboration.

No book can cover every aspect of a huge product such as Exchange. To attempt to do so would require a multivolume set spanning many thousands of pages and create something that would probably be too expensive for most administrators to buy. This book covers the topics in Exchange that are most interesting to me and those that I think are most useful to the majority of administrators who need to understand how to manage an Exchange organization. There are some notable omissions, such as Unified Messaging and Exchange's connection to other Microsoft products such as Office Communications Server, which you might find surprising. However, the truth is that there are other books available that do a good job of covering these topics, so I feel able to concentrate on the areas that I think deserve the most investigation (or are most interesting to me). There's also an incredible amount of information posted in blogs and other commentaries available on the Web, so if your interest is piqued by a topic and you want to find more information, plug the topic into your search engine of choice and you're likely to find additional insights and observations. Apart from anything else, you'll discover information that is up to date and reflects advances due to software updates (I predict that Microsoft will continue to upgrade Exchange 2010 after Service Pack 1!) and the knowledge that accumulates over time about any product that's used in production environments.

Exchange 2010 has been an interesting journey because it provoked more new thoughts and ideas for me than any other version released by Microsoft. Although Exchange 2007 laid down much of the architecture that Exchange 2010 exploits, there is a mass of detail in the changes between the two versions. Two of the three big changes effected in Exchange 2007—Windows PowerShell, the transition to a pure SMTP-based transport system, and the introduction of transaction log shipping as the basis for database replication—have been expanded and enhanced in a very effective manner. Remote Windows PowerShell and the Database Availability Group might be what people remember as the big new things that appeared in Exchange 2010, but their foundation was laid many years previously and what we see today is simply the result of a lot of development and hard work since Microsoft finished the development of Exchange 2003. Maybe that's why there is so much to discuss and comment on.

Service Pack 1

I decided to base the book on Exchange 2010 Service Pack 1 (SP1), which Microsoft released to customers in August 2010, because I felt that there were a number of important areas that were incomplete in the original (RTM) version of Exchange 2010 released in October 2009. The fact that Microsoft needed additional time and effort to fully build out the features in Exchange 2010 should come as no surprise to anyone who has any experience with Exchange.

Don't get me wrong: The software that Microsoft shipped to customers in late 2009 was highly functional and had many strong points. However, the nature of software development is that a little extra time always helps to smooth rough edges and deliver the complete plan that the engineers wanted to build when they started to work on Exchange 2010. SP1 had the benefit of nine months' more development, testing, and documentation, plus the invaluable exposure that software receives when customers deploy it into production environments. The experience gained from this time, the feedback from customers and the Microsoft Most Valuable Professional (MVP) community, the insight shared in blogs and forums, and the bugs that were uncovered and fixed made SP1 a better target about which to write. Besides, I hate books that are rushed to market to meet an arbitrary date so that they can be first to market to cover new technology, because I know the dangers involved in writing about beta versions of technology. You can hope that the developers won't change the software between the beta and final version, but all too often a diversion appears between the description on the printed page and what the software actually does. It's safer to wait and see what the experience is with the software after it is released rather than rush to market to sell a few more books.

Many major and minor differences exist between the original version of Exchange 2010 and SP1 and I have attempted to indicate clearly where these differences exist.

Writing style and general approach to content

My writing approach to books is best described as chaotic and not very organized. I don't start with a list of topics and work through from A to Z until the book is done. I think I would find such an approach tiresome and would lose interest halfway through. Instead, I build the book from page to page and split content into chapters as the form of the book develops. Text is added as I discover new and interesting facts about the technology. I make no apologies for this approach, because it has served me well in my previous 12 books. However, I acknowledge that topics that don't interest me are omitted or receive short shrift. Ah well, you can't be brilliant at everything and you have to leave room for others to prosper.

Along these lines, I made some deliberate decisions about topics that I would not cover in this book to concentrate on what I believe are the most important technical and functional changes in Exchange 2010. In effect, I used the 80–20 rule to select topics that I believe are of interest to the vast majority of the Exchange community and omitted others. So, to take two examples, if you are interested in the finer technical points of Unified Messaging or Active Directory Rights Management Services, you'll probably want to buy a different book. I think that these topics deserve specialized in-depth attention that cannot be justified in a book that attempts to cover the fundamental principles of Exchange. The same is true about connecting Exchange organizations with federation or integrating Exchange with various other products such as Microsoft Office Communications Server. These tasks can be done and are often done, and the subjects are explained better elsewhere. Be warned, therefore, that you might be disappointed if your favorite topic is not covered. On the other hand, you might be delighted that a topic of special importance to you is covered across many pages because we share a joint interest in it. In passing, I note that three chapters were removed from the original draft of the book to get the book down to a reasonable size. These chapters covered public folders, hardware planning, and cloud-based Exchange.

I doubt that many will read the book from beginning to end. At least, I have not written the text to flow from one chapter to another in the way that a novel or a history does. I expect most people to plunge into a part that interests them and then discover new topics as the need arises or curiosity takes over. I like technical books where chapters are self-sufficient and I hope that this book meets that goal.

In terms of other sources of technical information about Exchange 2010, I recommend that you download the latest version of the compiled help file (CHM) and keep it close at hand, because it will provide you with an invaluable guide to Exchange 2010 that you can use offline. TechNet provides an online copy, but Microsoft is quite good at updating the downloadable CHM regularly and did an excellent job for SP1. They've also gotten a lot better in terms of the breadth and depth of the content, even if it sometimes leaves gaps in the explanation. Of course, those gaps are exploited by the mass of Exchange 2010 books, magazine articles, and blogs. I particularly like the blogs of my fellow Exchange MVPs, even if it took me a long time before I got around to writing a blog myself. I now blog regularly at *http://thoughtsofanidlemind.wordpress.com/* and hope that I add some value to the Exchange community there.

Examples used in the book

I've tried to include as many examples as I can to illustrate points and show you exactly what you can expect to see when you execute a command. There are three kinds of examples:

- A simple screen shot. Hopefully these are self-evident. I've tried hard to avoid liberally scattering screen shots across the pages of the book because I hate big, thick, technical books that are half composed of screen shots. However, given the graphic nature of Windows and the Exchange management GUI, some screen shots are inevitable! In most cases I have opted to use Outlook Web App to illustrate client functionality simply because you can be guaranteed that Outlook Web App is available within every Exchange 2010 deployment. In addition, huge variation exists in the feature set available in the Outlook versions supported by Exchange 2010; Outlook 2010 is therefore only used to illustrate unique features that are only exposed in this version.

- Illustrative Windows PowerShell (Exchange Management Shell) commands. If only because it is the foundation of Exchange 2010, there are many EMS examples throughout the book. If you don't know how to use EMS to manage Exchange, you miss out on so much of the potential that the product offers. All references to cmdlets in the body of the text plus example commands are shown like this:

```
Get-User -Identity Redmond
```

- Windows PowerShell commands and example output. In some cases I want to show you exactly what you will see when a command is executed. Windows PowerShell output can be pretty ugly and reading it from a screen shot is not always easy, so I show the Windows PowerShell command before and then the output in a separate block immediately following the command:

```
Get-StoreUsageStatistics -Database 'VIP Data'
```

DigestCategory	SampleId	DisplayName	TimeInServer
TimeInServer	0	Mailbox -Redmond, Tony	485

I'm certainly not an elegant or skilled Windows PowerShell coder. Rather, I like to think of myself as a contented hacker who fully buys into the concept that the charm of Windows PowerShell is that you can quickly stitch together snippets of code to do remarkable things. I apologize if I offend any purists with the examples presented in the book. I just do my best to make things happen with the best code I can.

The examples are based on an Exchange organization called contoso.com that runs on my notebook. It's really amazing how notebook technology has evolved to a point where a portable computer can happily support several servers while still allowing you to run client applications such as Word and Outlook that are available through a simple Alt+Tab keystroke.

Thanks

David Espinoza, Senior Product Manager in the Exchange "ship team," has been a delight to work with for many years. The ship team does what its title indicates: It is responsible for the complex choreography involved in shepherding a product from development to a point where it can be used by customers. David's team runs the Technology Adaption Program

(TAP), which puts beta versions of Exchange into customer hands early so that code can be exercised in real-life environments. The ship team organizes regular calls to inform people about new features and development progress, makes new builds available on a regular basis, and acts as the interface for bugs and feature requests that flow back from customers into Microsoft. All in all, the team does a standout job and David and his faithful assistants Robbie Roberts and Kern Hardman deserve my full thanks.

I've also received great advice and information from many individual contributors in the Exchange development group, including Dmitri Gavrilov, Jim Edelen, Kumar Venkateswar, Crystal Flores, William Rall, Julian Zbogar-Smith, Derek Tan, Kamal Janardhan, David Los, Sanjay Ramaswamy, Frank Byrum, Robin Thomas, Yesim Koman, Todd Luttinen, Linden Goffar, Ed Banti, Jim Knibb, Mayerber Carvalho Neto, Greg Taylor, Paul Bowden, and Siddhartha Mathur. I also acknowledge the help that I received from Bill Long to make the ExFolders utility work with beta builds of SP1.

Martin DelRe first contacted me in August 2008 to explore the possibilities of writing a book for Microsoft Press. Exchange 14, which is what Exchange 2010 was known as then, seemed like a good target and there was certainly plenty of new stuff to write about, but I was busy and didn't become enthused about the project until June 2009. Martin guided me through the process of writing for a new publisher (they are all different) and made sure that I didn't have to cope with too much bureaucracy, for which I am very thankful. Karen Szall directed the production of the book from submission through copyediting, technical review, and eventual publication, and did a wonderful job of making everything come together on time, including the ability to manage a constant flow of changes from me as I attempted to update the technical content of the book to match new experiences, insights, and reports of problems and workarounds discovered in the field.

A group of willing volunteers within HP who have enormous experience with enterprise messaging systems reviewed the material as it was under development. I'd like to thank Marc Van Hooste, Kevin Laahs, Andreas Zit, and Mike Ireland for their advice.

HP has one of the largest deployments of Exchange, with more than 350,000 mailboxes supported by a highly centralized datacenter structure centered in the United States. Kathy Pollert, Mike Ireland, and Stan Foster have contributed greatly to my understanding of how Exchange functions in very large environments and I truly appreciate the insight that they have shared with me over the last decade. I'd also like to thank Aric Bernard and Guido Grillenmeier for allowing me to deploy new software into the sandbox environment used by HP consultants on a regular basis. Aric and Guido are Active Directory gurus and would probably prefer that Exchange was kept well away from their nice, clean domain controllers. Into every life a little rain must fall and every Active Directory administrator has to learn that the directory is there to serve applications rather than to explore the wonders of replication. We had fun getting Exchange 2010 to even install into HPQBOX, mostly because a previous deployment of Exchange 2007 had been removed through brutal surgery applied to the directory, leaving many lingering objects that just got in the way. Guido cleaned everything up and Aric made the servers run nicely, and I appreciate their efforts.

Finally, the dedicated effort of Paul Robichaux as technical editor must be acknowledged. Paul read every page, challenged places where I didn't seem to make sense or had misstated something, and ferreted out errors, all to improve the overall quality and content of the book. I owe him a lot.

In conclusion

I hope that you enjoy the book and its contents prove valuable in your understanding of Exchange 2010 as you approach the assessment, design, deployment, operations, and management of the software in production. At the end of the day, Exchange is only software and it's only as good as the people who work with it. To do a good job, you need knowledge about the product and wisdom to know when that knowledge runs out and it's time to look elsewhere for help, whether that's seeking out a Web site or asking someone for an opinion. The key is to realize that best practice is never stagnant and evolves all the time. Assuming that knowledge gained two or three years ago represents the current best advice and guidance is a fool's position. Always be prepared to learn.

Tony Redmond
September 2010

The author can be contacted through his blog at
http://thoughtsofanidlemind.wordpress.com/.

Support for this book

Every effort has been made to ensure the accuracy of this book. As corrections or changes are collected, they will be added the O'Reilly Media Website. To find Microsoft Press book and media corrections:

1. Go to *http://microsoftpress.oreilly.com.*

2. In the Search box, type the ISBN for the book, and click Search.

3. Select the book from the search results, which will take you to the book's catalog page.

4. On the book's catalog page, under the picture of the book cover, click View/Submit Errata.

If you have questions regarding the book or the companion content that are not answered by visiting the book's catalog page, please send them to Microsoft Press by sending an email message to *mspinput@microsoft.com*.

We want to hear from you

We welcome your feedback about this book. Please share your comments and ideas via the following short survey:

http://www.microsoft.com/learning/booksurvey

Your participation will help Microsoft Press create books that better meet your needs and your standards.

> **Note**
> We hope that you will give us detailed feedback via our survey. If you have questions about our publishing program, upcoming titles, or Microsoft Press in general, we encourage you to interact with us via Twitter at *http://twitter.com/MicrosoftPress*. For support issues, use only the email address shown above.

# CHAPTER 1

Introducing Microsoft Exchange 2010

FOR more than 30 years, I have worked with email software. The advent of a new version of a popular software product such as Microsoft Exchange Server 2010 generates different emotions for the different players who participate in the cycle of product development, deployment, operations, and support, not to mention a flurry of excited commentary from those who observe developments in the industry. This book seeks to explain the impact of the release of Exchange 2010 and the subsequent Service Pack 1 update for those who are involved in Exchange deployment, operations, and support. Much of the insight into the product comes from the other key players—the team that develops Exchange and keeps working to improve it on a daily basis. They have their view about what's important; most of the time I agree with their position (if only after arguing until I understand where they are coming from), and sometimes I disagree. You'll see this dichotomy of views presented as you go through the different topics presented in this book. We should begin, though, by presenting the case for Exchange 2010 and exploring just what Microsoft wanted to accomplish in this release of the product.

Microsoft hopes that the quality of Exchange 2010 merits its introduction and that customers consider the new and enhanced features to be compelling enough to warrant a fast upgrade. In addition, Microsoft likes to see an improvement in their competitive situation, something that is especially important in the new era of cloud-based services where Google has taken a lot of mindshare and IBM shows new signs of life with an online version of Domino. Customers want a product that meets their requirements and is easy to deploy and manage, one that isn't too different from previous versions and the deployment of which won't cost an enormous amount in terms of personnel effort and new hardware. Partners hope for new business—whether it's an increase in product sales or an uptick in services revenue—to help customers analyze and assess, then decide how best to use the new software. All of these things are true for Exchange 2010, which sits at the center of a large ecosystem spanning well over 100 million deployed mailboxes that has been growing since 1996.

It's tough to drive innovation into a product that has been around for so long, and it's tough to satisfy all of the different constituencies that use Exchange, from the small business that deploys one or two servers to the world's largest enterprises that support hundreds of thousands of mailboxes. Each time Microsoft releases a new version of Exchange, they have to include enough "new stuff" in the product to create a compelling case for an upgrade. The evolution to the cloud makes this release even more interesting because Microsoft now has to build a product that works equally well for on-premise and hosted deployments. Companies have offered hosted Exchange services for years, so that's not what is different here. The critical changes are the nature of competition and Microsoft's decision to enter the hosted services market in a much more emphatic way than they have in the past.

When briefing customers about the development priorities for Exchange 2010, Microsoft stresses three areas:

1. Increase operational flexibility through easier deployment, higher availability, and simpler administration. Much of the development work occurs in the Store and Client Access Server (CAS) to increase availability through data replication and break the connection between databases and servers. A new ability to delegate administrative tasks through the Exchange Control Panel coupled with the expansion of Windows PowerShell to support remote tasks allows customers to automate common processes.

2. Streamline communications by supporting larger, better-organized mailboxes; investing more into unified communications; and allowing users to work more easily together no matter what device or client they use. The focus here is to support 10 GB mailboxes with the same performance that Microsoft Exchange Server 2007 uses to support 1 GB mailboxes. The user experience is further enhanced with new functionality in Microsoft Outlook 2010, Outlook Web App, and mobile clients. In passing, it's worth noting the name change for OWA (which I will use throughout the book, if only to stop calling the application by its old name). OWA was originally named Outlook Web Access in Microsoft Exchange 5.0. This name reflected the provision of access to a mailbox from a browser (initially only Microsoft Internet Explorer was supported) rather than the full-fledged application into which OWA gradually evolved. Microsoft now regards OWA as a client that delivers functionality comparable with Outlook in most respects. The name change to Outlook Web App reflects this stance and also aligns the name with other Web-based versions of Microsoft Office applications.

3. Deliver greater visibility and control with protected communications, built-in compliance and archiving functionality, and better reporting and management alerts. Exchange has supported message journaling since Microsoft Exchange Server 2003 and Microsoft Exchange Server 2007 introduced features such as managed folders

and transport rules. Exchange 2010 takes a much more comprehensive approach to the problem posed by legal requirements to meet regulations, comply with discovery actions, and handle situations such as sexual harassment.

Microsoft makes a fair point that these areas of investment have to work as well for hosted environments as they do when deployed onsite. Security is obviously a big challenge for hosted environments, as all communications have to be routed from a customer's own network across the Internet to a datacenter hosted by Microsoft or another provider. It's not just a matter of transporting messages anymore; directory synchronization and administrative commands have to flow as easily as messages, and everything has to work in dedicated environments as well as the multitenant shared environments that are becoming more common because of their cost efficiencies.

At the time of writing, Exchange has been under development for more than 16 years, and its source code encompasses some 21 million lines of code. No engineering group stays constant over such an extended period. Different engineering managers, internal Microsoft politics, and competitive pressure have all contributed to different priorities for the product over the years. The initial thrust in 1996 through 1998 to provide a migration path for Microsoft Mail and to take market share from other email systems evolved into a head-on fight with Lotus Notes, from which Microsoft emerged triumphant at the start of the 21st century. Since then, the focus has been on making Exchange easier to manage, cheaper to deploy, and better resistant to failure. Much of this work can be seen in Exchange 2007 and 2010 in features such as the use of Windows PowerShell as the basis for administration, a steady reduction in I/O demands, and the introduction of different flavors of continuous log replication. Cloud-based services represent the latest competitive threat through offerings such as Gmail.

Microsoft now has a somewhat bifurcated set of development priorities that must continue to satisfy the requirements of customers who deploy "on premise" while also serving the needs of Microsoft's own hosted service that operates in mammoth multitenant datacenters. Exchange 2010 is the first version to be developed under this regime, and it will be interesting to see how Microsoft's focus will move between the hosted and on-premise worlds over the next few years.

The motivation to upgrade

The first point in a deployment project is to understand why you want to deploy Exchange 2010. Different circumstances dictate the ability and willingness of companies to move forward with the deployment of a new version of Exchange, including these common scenarios:

- They currently run a very old version of Exchange, including Exchange 5.5 (released in 1997).

- They might have declined to upgrade from Exchange 2003 to Exchange 2007 because their current infrastructure meets their needs. They might have wanted to avoid the need to buy new hardware to deploy Exchange 2007 or did not want to grapple with the need to understand the new architecture, perhaps because of other priorities within their overall IT infrastructure. Like all new software versions, another reason for not upgrading is that Exchange 2007 did not deliver sufficient or relevant new functionality to justify the cost.

- They might run another mail system and now want to move to Exchange. The vast bulk of these migrations are from Lotus Notes, which continues to lose market share to Exchange. Some migrations from Novell GroupWise from a very small installed base are still seen.

Believe it or not, there are companies that still operate very old Exchange servers. Because it is relatively simple when compared to today's software, Exchange 5.5 is very stable. Although its use has declined over the last few years, there are still some companies that aren't interested in running the latest version and continue to use servers commissioned between 1999 and 2002. Their logic is impeccable and follows the old adage that you shouldn't attempt to fix something that isn't broken. However, although software bits don't degrade over time, hardware does, and the older servers that support versions like Exchange 5.5 or Exchange 2000 are becoming obsolete, as replacement parts become harder to source and replacement servers are so cheap that it's more cost effective to throw the old hardware away if it fails. Hardware is actually a small part of the overall upgrade cost, as new software licenses and the time required to migrate data to a newly installed Exchange 2010 organization will be far more expensive.

Moving from Exchange 2003 or Exchange 2007

Exchange 2003 is another stable platform that has served customers well. Like Exchange 5.5, it has benefited from the work done in previous versions to fix bugs and complete functionality. Faced with the need to buy new hardware and to deploy new 64-bit versions of Windows and other associated applications before they could move to Exchange 2007, many companies opted to stay with Exchange 2003. Although server hardware has been 64-bit capable for a long time, the move to use a 64-bit platform for an operating system and applications introduces some instability and "newness" into the infrastructure. If the infrastructure is reliable, the servers are not due to be replaced, and there is no good business reason to upgrade, then it's easy to understand why people chose to leave things alone. In addition to the hardware refresh, the need to upgrade administrator knowledge to cope with the Exchange 2007 architecture, change operational procedures, and perhaps rewrite some code to use Windows PowerShell instead of Windows Management Instrumentation (WMI) scripts all contributed to the disruption and cost of the migration.

If you run Exchange 2007 today, you may experience less fear of the unknown elements of a new version because much of the Exchange 2010 architecture is an enhancement of Exchange 2007 and is therefore not as new and unknown as it would be if you approach Exchange 2010 from a deployment based on Exchange 2003. Features that made their debut in Exchange 2007—such as continuous log replication—are in their second iteration, and there's a mass of published information from Microsoft and third parties covering topics from basic design approaches to Windows PowerShell code examples that help bridge the knowledge gap.

Some observers referred to the original release of Exchange 2010 as "Exchange 2007 finished," a comment that is underlined by the completion of the management user interface to support the deployment of features such as retention tags in Exchange 2010 SP1. There's some truth in this view insofar as it is the nature of server software used by a huge variety of companies to constantly evolve and there's no doubt that some of the features introduced in Exchange 2007 have matured further in Exchange 2010. The best example is high availability, but there are others, such as Unified Messaging, where features such as voice mail transcription make Exchange a much more user-friendly platform for voice mail, and the changes made to allow organizations to deploy policy-driven compliance for messaging. Some of these changes rely on additional Microsoft components such as Active Directory Rights Management and won't be as valuable to companies that operate in a heterogeneous IT environment, but they are all signs of building out functionality to meet different needs.

Of course, you now have the choice between running Exchange 2010 on premises or in the cloud, or even in a hybrid configuration where some users are hosted internally and some have their mailboxes in the cloud. The option to adopt an "evergreen" approach to messaging and have Microsoft take care of running Exchange for you will be attractive to some companies and less so to others, but at least the choice now exists.

Companies that do not currently operate Exchange and want to migrate from another email system often have the easiest transition because they have already decided to move to Exchange and the decision now is which version to deploy. Based on current support policies and previous practice, you can expect that Microsoft will provide mainstream support for Exchange 2007 (assuming the latest service pack is deployed) until at least November 2012, so there's plenty of time available to deploy and use what is now well-understood technology.

A move to Exchange is usually combined with a deployment of Microsoft Office on the desktop, and the combination of the latest versions of Exchange 2007 and Office 2007 delivers solid results in most cases. The same is true of Exchange 2003, as this product has been around so long that all of its original flaws have now been eradicated or at least brought to the point where they are well understood and can be avoided in production environments. Depending on how long after the product is released the decision is made and the availability of fixes included in a roll-up release or a service pack, the deployment team might worry that they have to face unknown product limitations or bugs similar to the CAS scalability issues that some early Exchange 2007 deployments faced.

Testing and beta versions

Microsoft goes to great lengths to run beta versions of Exchange internally to validate that it works in enterprise environments. However, someone once observed that running code inside Microsoft isn't really a fair test because users are supported by the massed ranks of the Windows, Exchange, Outlook, and other associated engineering groups. On the other hand, Microsoft will say that their users are among the most demanding on the planet and will find problems where no one else will. To cover the world outside Microsoft, they also have an extensive Technology Adoption Program (TAP) that allows customers early access to code for testing. The companies that participate in the TAP are committed to dedicating considerable resources to installing and testing successive beta versions of Exchange and to using the test software to host real-life production mailboxes. However, no matter how extensive the tests that are performed through these programs, it is unreasonable to expect that Microsoft will discover all of the potential issues that customers will face when software is deployed across a base that spans well over 100 million mailboxes in circumstances from small 50-user systems serving a single office to massive hosting environments.

The problem gets even larger when you consider that Exchange 2010 introduces some major new code, such as the components that support the Database Availability Group, role-based access control, and compliance features. The difficulty of testing new functionality for major products underpins the mantra that you should never deploy Microsoft software until the first service pack is available: It's best to leave others to endure the horror stories experienced in early deployments. Although better testing and programs such as the TAP have improved the situation dramatically in terms of finding bugs and usability issues much sooner in the development process, Microsoft can't shake this perception among the customer base.

From a user perspective, the most obvious gain in moving to a new version of Exchange is the availability of a more functional user interface for Outlook Web App. The last major change that fundamentally improved the Outlook user experience came in Exchange 2003 with cached Exchange mode because it removed a lot of hassle that users experienced in previous versions waiting for messages to synchronize over patchy network connections. Exchange 2010 offers the promise of huge mailboxes and better Outlook performance (available from Outlook 2007 SP2 onward) together with features such as MailTips and archive mailboxes.

Fundamental questions before you upgrade

No matter what the situation is, companies have to answer some fundamental questions about why they want to deploy Exchange 2010 before they can proceed:

- Will Exchange 2010 lead to a reduction in existing operational costs?

  - Consolidation might result in fewer servers, leading to cheaper support and administration costs.

  - Virtualization might reduce the number of physical servers that need to be deployed.

  - Cheaper storage might replace storage area network (SAN) technology.

  - Add-on software might be eliminated because the desired features are now included in Exchange 2010. For example, third-party data replication products can be replaced with Database Availability Groups.

  - Clusters can be replaced with standard servers to remove complexity from the operational environment.

  - Other reasons might also exist.

- What new costs will the company take on to move to Exchange 2010?

  - New servers might be needed.

  - New or upgraded software licenses for Windows Server 2008 or Windows Server 2008 R2, Exchange 2010, and any associated products (third party and Microsoft) are required. To access specific functionality, you might have to purchase enterprise Client Access Licenses (CALs).

  - Replacement of code that depends on deprecated application programming interfaces (APIs) is necessary.

  - Client upgrades (Windows Mobile devices, Outlook 2010, and so on) need to be made.

  - Training for administrators, help desk personnel, and users must be provided.

  - Consulting will be advisable to help to make the transition.

- Apart from basic email functionality, what features in Exchange 2010 does the business need?

  - Will you use Unified Messaging (including integration with other Microsoft products such as Office Communications Server)?

  - Is better high availability required?

  - Will you use archiving and compliance?

- What are the major roadblocks to deployment?

  - The need to upgrade other applications, including rewriting code that depends on now unsupported APIs such as Web Distributed Authoring and Versioning (WebDAV), could cause difficulty.

  - There is also a need to test third-party applications that integrate with Exchange or wait for vendors to release new versions of their applications that are certified to work with Exchange 2010.

  - A new version of Outlook must be deployed to take full advantage of the features of Exchange 2010.

- Can I get the same functionality at the same price point elsewhere?

  - Microsoft's Business Productivity Online Suite (BPOS) includes the option to run a hybrid model, where some mailboxes are supported on classic on-premise servers and some run in the cloud. Moving to the cloud seems like a simple decision, but considerable complexity lurks under the surface.

  - A different email platform might be selected, although this introduces additional work items in terms of platform selection, clients, and migration.

After you understand the full context of your current situation and know what the motivation is to deploy Exchange 2010, you can proceed to the planning phase.

No in-place upgrades

Microsoft chose not to engineer the code to allow administrators to upgrade a server from Exchange Server 2003 to Exchange Server 2007, and they have gone along the same route for Exchange 2010. The logic was that it is just too difficult to create software that can perform a reliable upgrade from a 32-bit platform of Windows Server 2003 and Exchange Server 2003 to a 64-bit platform of Windows Server 2003 and Exchange Server 2007, even if Windows and Exchange run the latest service pack. There are just too many edge cases that Microsoft won't know about until they are encountered in the field. All of the

Exchange code base and associated products such as Microsoft ForeFront run on the 64-bit platform today, so that's not the major engineering concern.

The problem now is how to accomplish a dual in-place upgrade of operating system and mail server to get to the desired Windows 2008/Exchange 2010 configuration. This is far less of a problem than when the underlying platform changes, as in the case of going from a 32-bit to a 64-bit platform, but it still would require substantial engineering effort to write and then test the code to perform a complete upgrade.

Microsoft's view is that the experience of Exchange Server 2007 deployments proved that it is far easier to introduce new servers and move mailboxes to those servers when you are ready. Such an approach avoids the need to perform in-place database upgrades that would otherwise be required to support the database schema changes such as the major upgrade applied in Exchange 2010. It also eliminates the need to test the installation (setup) program to make sure that it can accommodate the multitude of scenarios that Exchange is deployed into for production.

CAUTION

The problem with in-place database upgrades is that they are usually slow because every page in the database has to be processed to upgrade it to a new version. The need to process databases introduces a period of vulnerability during the installation process. For example, if your server supports a mailbox database of 100 GB and the data can be upgraded at the rate of 10 GB/hour, you can look forward to a 10-hour period during the installation when the server is fully occupied with the database upgrade. Not only must this processing occur when all users are blocked from using their mailboxes, but if anything happens during the upgrade, you'll have to restart after you fix the problem. Building this kind of data upgrade into upgrades introduces too much risk. From an engineering perspective, it is far better to require customers to install new servers with clean databases and then gradually move users over to the new platform. Although the "no upgrade" approach means that new servers are required for Exchange 2010, it might be possible to align the upgrade with a hardware refresh cycle or to reuse some older servers.

Although customers might incur some extra cost to achieve the upgrade, Microsoft will argue that the time they save from not having to figure out how to make in-place upgrades work (even partially) allows their engineering teams to dedicate time to solving other problems, such as making mailbox moves work more efficiently (which occurs in Exchange 2010), improving the quality and features of the installation program, and upgrading tools such as the Exchange Best Practice Analyzer to help administrators understand any issues that might exist in their infrastructure that must be resolved before an Exchange 2010 upgrade can proceed. In addition, users typically experience less downtime when new servers are introduced because they don't depend on complex upgrade processes. On balance, it's hard to argue against Microsoft's decision, and in any case, we can't do anything about it except order the new hardware to allow the upgrade to Exchange 2010 to proceed.

What version of Windows?

Microsoft supports the deployment of Exchange 2010 on either Windows Server 2008 SP2 or Windows Server 2008 R2 Standard or Enterprise editions. Exchange 2010 is not certified for deployment on Windows Server 2008 Datacenter edition (see *http://www. windowsservercert.com*), and Microsoft initially would not support Exchange 2010 on this platform. Lacking certification doesn't mean that software won't function on a specific version of Windows; instead, it means that the software has not been put through the certification process.

Microsoft reversed their position in early 2010, and you can safely use Windows Server 2008 Datacenter even if Exchange 2010 doesn't boast the official certified logo. It remains doubtful whether the additional features of the Windows Server 2008 Datacenter edition make it an attractive platform for Exchange 2010 because few companies will need to exploit 256 processor cores or hot-add or hot-replace CPUs, especially when these features come with a hefty increase in the cost of the software license. By comparison, Windows Server 2008 R2 Enterprise supports a maximum of 32 processor cores and won't allow a CPU to be replaced or added while the server is running. However, there are bound to be a few companies that will want to explore the Datacenter edition, and it's good that Microsoft will support the deployment of Exchange 2010 on the platform.

The Windows Server 2008 Core, Web, or Foundation server editions remain unsupported and are unlikely to ever be supported given that they are essentially cut-down versions of Windows designed to be deployed to meet specific needs. (It's possible to make some Exchange 2010 roles install on Server Core, but they don't work once installed, so it's not just a matter of Microsoft arbitrarily deciding to block those versions.) No support exists for Exchange 2010 to run on the Itanium (IA64) version of Windows.

Selecting the version of Windows Server 2008 for deployment is a critical decision, as Microsoft does not support in-place server upgrades (with Exchange 2010) from Windows Server 2008 SP2 to Windows Server 2008 R2. Given the relative age of the operating systems, you are likely to use Windows Server 2008 R2 sometime in the next couple of years. Therefore, it is an excellent idea to consider using Windows Server 2008 R2 as the basic operating system for your Exchange 2010 deployment. This is much better than creating a situation in which the only way that you can upgrade to Windows Server 2008 R2 is by deploying a set of new Exchange servers on new Windows Server 2008 R2 and moving mailboxes over to them and then decommissioning the old Windows Server 2008 SP2 servers. It also makes sense to run the same version of the operating system and Exchange on every server in the organization, as this makes support and administration much easier.

Another point to take into consideration is that Windows engineering has made improvements in some of the critical components affecting Exchange that make Windows Server 2008 R2 the best choice for specific servers. For example, testing done by the Exchange development group demonstrates that Remote Procedure Call (RPC) over HTTP performance is better in Windows 2008 R2 than in Windows Server 2008 SP2. This has a direct influence on the ability of a CAS server to handle Outlook Anywhere connections and means that Windows Server 2008 R2 is a better platform for Internet-facing CAS servers. See *http://msexchangeteam.com/archive/2010/04/30/454805.aspx* for details of the performance tests that make this point.

INSIDE OUT   Upgrading workstations used for management

The Exchange 2010 administration tools can run on either Vista SP2 (x64) or Windows 7 (x64) workstations, so you might need to upgrade workstations that you want to use for management. You can run the Exchange 2007 SP2 administration tools on the same workstation, provided that you install the Exchange 2007 tools first and then install the Exchange 2010 administration tools. Alternatively, you can simply use Windows terminal services to connect to the servers that you want to manage from Vista or Windows 7 workstations.

Preparing for Exchange 2010

Apart from deciding on the operating system, what actions can you take to prepare for an eventual deployment of Exchange 2010, assuming that you run an earlier version of Exchange today? The following is a non-exhaustive list that should be supplemented with details of your particular environment, including items such as applications that depend on Exchange.

- If you already operate an earlier version of Exchange, you should run the Exchange Best Practice Analyzer (ExBPA) tool regularly to identify any problems that can be found by validating the details of your infrastructure against Microsoft's best practice database.

- Be sure to check for required upgrades and hot fixes before you install servers. Exchange affects many parts of the operating system and has a track record of exposing weaknesses. Microsoft IT discovered a problem with NTFS deadlocks on heavily loaded mailbox servers soon after they deployed Exchange 2010 internally. This problem is specific to Windows 2008 SP2 and required administrators to kill Store.exe to free the deadlock condition, so it was pretty serious. Microsoft fixed the problem quickly (see KB974646 for details), but it's a good example of the kind of problem that comes to light when new combinations of operating system and applications go into production.

- If you haven't already done so, you should move your Active Directory to Windows 2003 forest functional mode (or higher). Exchange 2007 shares the same requirement and there is no good reason to keep Active Directory at a lower functional level. Deploy Active Directory domain controllers and global catalog servers on 64-bit Windows Server 2003 SP2 or, even better, on Windows 2008 SP2 or R2. Note that Exchange does not support domains that have an underscore in their name because of an internal dependency on X.509 certificates, which cannot contain this character.

- Remove any Exchange server that runs Exchange 2000 or earlier versions as they cannot be installed in a forest that supports Exchange 2010. If you still run Exchange 2003, make sure that these servers run SP2 as this is the version that can coexist with Exchange 2010 inside an organization.

- Exchange 2007 servers must be upgraded to SP2 (or later releases). We'll discuss this topic in more detail in just a little while.

- Decide on the version of Exchange 2010 you will use. The choice is between the standard edition and the enterprise edition. See "Exchange 2010 Editions" later in this chapter for more information on the features supported by each version. Note that you can upgrade from the standard to enterprise edition but you can't downgrade from enterprise to standard. If you intend to use the new Database Availability Group high availability feature, you need to run the enterprise edition of either Windows Server 2008 SP2 or R2; bear in mind that you can't upgrade an existing Windows installation from the standard to the enterprise edition without a reinstall.

- CALs are also required for every user who connects to Exchange 2010. Standard and enterprise versions are available. The enterprise version is additive, meaning that you also have to buy a standard CAL for each user. You need the enterprise CAL to be able to use features such as Unified Messaging, advanced journaling, and archive mailboxes.

The test plan

Successful preparation always involves dedicated effort to test and test again to ensure that new software works well in the environment run by a specific company. Microsoft cannot be expected to test for every possible condition that software encounters in the wild, so you have to protect yourself by designing and executing a comprehensive test plan. The plan should address these points:

- All clients used by your company (in all versions) have to be verified against Exchange 2010. The list might include:

  - All versions of Outlook that you currently use. Note that no version prior to Outlook 2003 SP2 is supported by Exchange 2010.

  - The features and functionality available in Outlook Web App 2010 for the browsers that you use (Internet Explorer, Chrome, Opera, Firefox, Safari), including the various platforms that these browsers run on, such as Windows, Linux, UNIX, and Apple Mac.

  - Internet Messaging Access Protocol 4 (IMAP4) and Post Office Protocol 3 (POP3) clients (Eudora, Thunderbird, and so on) on whatever operating system platforms you use.

  - Entourage and other Mac solutions. If you are using Office 2008, you need the Exchange Web Services version of Entourage 2008 to connect Entourage to Exchange 2010. In late 2010, Microsoft shipped a new client, Outlook for Mac, as part of Office 2011. It is a worthwhile upgrade if you have Mac users currently running Entourage.

  - Mobile clients (Windows Mobile, other ActiveSync clients, Apple iPhone, Palm Pre, Android devices, and so on).

- The outcome of the client test plan might result in a number of steps that you have to take before or during the Exchange 2010 deployment, including:

  - Consider the deployment of Outlook 2007 SP2 (or later) as soon as possible to benefit from better support for large mailboxes and improved overall performance. Exchange 2010 does not support versions before Outlook 2003, and it's really best to upgrade to Outlook 2007 to get other features such as Autodiscover.

  - Some Exchange 2010 features (such as MailTips) do not work with Outlook unless you deploy Outlook 2010, so consider how your plans (if any) to deploy Office 2010 might influence your plans to introduce Exchange 2010.

  - Opt for Windows Mobile devices that run at least version 6.0 (Windows Mobile 6.5 or Windows Phone 7 devices are preferred). If you don't use Windows Mobile, select devices that support ActiveSync rather than depend on the IMAP or POP3 protocols to support mobile access to mailboxes.

Testing for operational processes

Apart from the purely functional testing, you should also test how well Exchange 2010 will function in your operational environment. There are many changes in the software that will cause you to change operational processes and procedures in different areas. For example:

- Unless you plan to use Exchange 2007 for an extended period, do not deploy additional single copy cluster (SCC) or local continuous replication (LCR) instances for high availability solutions as both features are deprecated in Exchange 2010. Use cluster continuous replication (CCR) or standby continuous replication (SCR) instead, as these are closer to the technology used in the new Database Availability Group that replaces both CCR and SCR in Exchange 2010.

- If you use a third-party data replication solution to protect mailbox data, consider whether the new replication features of Exchange 2010 will replace or complement your existing solution.

- If you use tape-based backup solutions for Exchange, you need to consider how to use a solution based on Volume ShadowCopy Services (VSS) instead. Exchange 2010 no longer supports backups made with the streaming backup APIs that have been around since Exchange 5.0, and that means no tape backups. Do not underestimate the work required to move from tape-based backups to VSS-based backups, especially in terms of complying with auditing requirements, off-site storage, and so on.

- If you use a third-party archiving and compliance solution, have a discussion with the vendor to understand their go-forward plan to work with or move to the archiving and compliance functionality that is in Exchange 2010. The ideal situation is that the third-party solution will interoperate seamlessly with the base features built into Exchange. If you don't use archiving today, you might want to consider increasing mailbox quotas so that users can keep more information in their mailboxes that is eventually archived by Exchange 2010. Note that this approach has consequences for storage and backup operations.

- Discuss the permissions model used in your company to control access to Windows resources and applications to ensure that the role-based access control model introduced by Exchange 2010 meets the company's security and organizational needs. Exchange 2010 SP1 includes support for a split permissions model (see Chapter 4, "Role-Based Access Control") that will interest companies that like to keep a clear and distinct separation between Windows and Exchange administration.

Testing for programming and customizations

Not everyone wants to exploit the range of APIs and programmable interfaces available to access Exchange data, but you might be surprised when you start to analyze the range of features that people use to work with Exchange in your company and see that different ways of accessing information are important to different groups. You should test to ensure that you will be able to continue to deliver the same degree of service to end users after Exchange 2010 is deployed, no matter how they access data. End users include administrators, so interfaces between Exchange and other products (both Microsoft and third party) are important areas to explore and understand. Some items to keep in mind include the following:

- Understand what customizations you have applied to Exchange 2007 to ensure that everything is transferred over to Exchange 2010. Microsoft makes sure that customizations such as transport and journal rules are transferred on the deployment of the first Exchange 2010 server in an organization, but you should know what you have so that you know what to check is still working for Exchange 2010. You will have to reapply customizations such as changes to OWA themes or front-end logon screens manually. Exchange holds most of its administrative settings in Active Directory so these are always available, even if a server suffers a catastrophic failure. However, some settings and data objects, such as Secure Sockets Layers (SSL) certificates and Microsoft Internet Information Services (IIS) settings, are stored outside Active Directory and must be manually updated for Exchange 2010.

- Understand what use is made of older Exchange APIs such as WebDAV, which Exchange 2010 replaces with Exchange Web Services (EWS). You will probably have to rewrite any custom code using EWS or look for another solution that can be used with Exchange 2010, such as a Windows PowerShell script. Alternatively, you can consider keeping an Exchange 2007 server around to support an application that uses a deprecated API until you have the chance to rewrite the code.

- Check any code that uses Windows PowerShell to perform tasks such as system monitoring or account maintenance to ensure that it will continue to work with remote PowerShell and Exchange 2010. For example, Microsoft Identity Lifecycle Management (ILM) V1 includes the option to "enable Exchange 2007 provisioning" to allow administrators to update Exchange data as part of the provisioning process.

> **Note**
>
> Behind the scenes, ILM requires administrators to install the Exchange Management Shell on the same server to be able to call the Update-Recipient cmdlet. However, ILM V1 is a 32-bit product that depends on the ability to use 32-bit Windows PowerShell for its integration with Exchange. Microsoft has updated Forefront Identity Manager 2010 (the successor to ILM) to allow it to call remote PowerShell on an Exchange 2010 server, so if you're using ILM, you should move to FIM 2010 as part of your Exchange 2010 migration.

- Prepare a deployment plan to introduce Exchange 2010 servers into the organization, taking into account restrictions such as the inability of OWA clients to open public folder replicas that reside on Exchange 2007 servers (OWA 2010 can only open public folder replicas on Exchange 2010 servers). The suggested order of deployment is CAS servers, then Edge and hub transport servers, and finally mailbox servers (and Unified Messaging servers, if you use Unified Messaging). Smaller deployments might find that their needs are best met by running Exchange 2010 on one or more multirole servers.

Of course, the prospect of going through a migration from one version of an email server to another is never appealing. Depending on your requirements, it might be better to plan for a totally different approach such as outsourcing Exchange to a third party using either a traditional on-premise deployment or a cloud-based approach through Microsoft BPOS.

Bringing Exchange 2007 up to speed

If you run Exchange 2007 today, it's likely that you have deployed SP2 or SP3. Microsoft released SP2 in August 2009 and SP3 in mid-2010. These releases are part of Microsoft's regular release schedule to provide bug fixes and enhancements to customers. SP2 is also an important stepping stone to Exchange 2010 because it upgrades the Active Directory schema to the revision level required by Exchange 2010. The schema upgrade allows Exchange 2010 and Exchange 2007 servers to coexist within the same organization. Schema upgrades have to be replicated around the complete Active Directory forest, so this task has to be factored into your deployment plans.

Another advantage of deploying Exchange 2007 SP2 or SP3 is that these versions support Windows PowerShell 2.0, which means that you can use the same version of Windows PowerShell to work with both Exchange Server 2007 and Exchange Server 2010. If you want to deploy Exchange 2007 on Windows 2008 R2, you need to deploy Exchange 2007 SP3. It is not a requirement to deploy Exchange 2007 SP3 to support Exchange 2010 SP1, as Exchange 2010 is quite happy to work alongside Exchange 2007 SP2 or SP3. This being said, Exchange 2007 SP3 supports Windows 2008 R2, and is therefore the natural partner to deploy alongside Exchange 2010 SP1.

Moving to a new service pack for Exchange 2007 might also require you to upgrade other products. For example, if you use Microsoft Forefront Security for Exchange Server for antivirus and anti-spam protection, you need to deploy its SP2 release alongside Exchange 2007 SP2. The need to coordinate upgrades for different products adds some time and complexity to the upgrade project. Additional downtime should also be factored into your plans if you run clustered Exchange 2007 servers (SCC or CCR) that need to be upgraded.

INSIDE OUT   A general rule

The general rule is that all Exchange 2007 servers in the Active Directory site in which you first introduce Exchange 2010 must run SP2 (or later), as must all CAS and Unified Messaging servers in the entire forest. You also need to install SP2 or SP3 on Exchange 2007 mailbox servers from which you intend to move mailboxes to Exchange 2010.

Deploying earlier versions of Exchange servers alongside Exchange 2010

The possibility exists that you might want to deploy some Exchange 2007 servers inside a brand new Exchange 2010 organization. On the surface, this shouldn't be a problem because Exchange 2010 can coexist with Exchange 2007 in the same organization. However, the order in which you deploy servers is important. If you begin an organization with an Exchange 2010 server, you will only be able to install Exchange 2010 servers in that organization because beginning with Exchange 2010 will mark the organization as incapable of supporting earlier versions. Therefore, if you think that you will need to use Exchange 2007, you should start by installing an Exchange 2007 server first, then adding Exchange 2010 servers as required. The Exchange 2007 server doesn't have to be active. It simply has to exist in the organization to create the conditions to permit support of a hybrid organization.

The same situation exists if you are running Exchange 2003 today and want to deploy Exchange 2010. If you go ahead and deploy an Exchange 2010 server into the organization, you will never be able to deploy an Exchange 2007 server into that organization; a side effect of installing Exchange 2010 server is a block on the deployment of anything else but an Exchange 2003 or Exchange 2010 server into the organization.

If you think that you might need to use Exchange 2007 in the future (perhaps to support an application that has not yet been upgraded to support Exchange 2010), you need to install an Exchange 2007 multirole server (everything except Unified Messaging). However, you don't need to ever use the Exchange 2007 server, and it can exist as a virtual server that does nothing except provide evidence to the Exchange 2010 setup program that Exchange 2007 is present.

Once you reach the point when Exchange 2007 will never be required again, you can remove the server, but be sure before you proceed, because if you remove the Exchange 2007 server from the organization and then install a new Exchange 2010 server, the setup program will block future deployment of Exchange 2007.

Web-based Deployment Assistant

There's a lot of new technology in Exchange 2010 and system administrators sometimes need help to know how best to approach a deployment. You can employ consultants to help, and this is certainly a recommended option for large or complex deployments. Microsoft has been working on tools to help customers manage and optimize Exchange. The latest is the Exchange 2010 Deployment Assistant, which is available online at *http://technet.microsoft.com/exdeploy2010*.

The Deployment Assistant is based on a lot of real-world feedback from experts and customers. It allows you to explore the recommended steps to deploy Exchange 2010 in different scenarios, including upgrades from Exchange 2003 and Exchange 2007 and a green-field deployment. The idea is that you answer a few questions to set the basic context for the deployment and the assistant then generates a recommended set of steps in a PDF file that you can download.

> **Note**
>
> The output generated by the Deployment Assistant contains a lot of good information about the work activities that have to be performed to deploy Exchange 2010, but it should be regarded as no more than a first draft. Automated tools can't be expected to know everything that might influence your organization, so you have to be prepared to add detail to provide the necessary depth for a fully developed deployment plan.

Exchange 2010 editions

Exchange 2010 is available in three editions. The standard edition is the most common, as it contains all of the necessary functionality required by an email server. It is limited to five databases (including a public folder database if deployed). If you attempt to mount a sixth database, Exchange 2010 Standard Edition will gracefully refuse and issue event 9591: Exceeded the max numbers of 5 MDBs on this server. You also have to operate under the same restriction if you install a trial version of Exchange 2010. The standard version of Exchange 2010 supports the new Database Availability Group (DAG) high availability feature. Microsoft made the decision to include DAG support in Exchange 2010 standard edition very late in the development cycle to allow all sizes of customers to deploy high availability solutions. However, to use a DAG, you need to deploy Exchange on the Enterprise edition of Windows Server 2008 SP2 or R2 to provide the Windows Failover Clustering feature that underpins the DAG.

Exchange 2010 Enterprise edition is designed to meet the needs of large enterprises. You can mount up to 100 databases on a server running the Enterprise edition, so it is the obvious choice for large-scale deployments. The Coexistence edition (also known as the gateway edition) is only used to facilitate connectivity and migration from previous versions of Exchange to the Microsoft BPOS-managed version of Exchange 2010; you aren't supposed to deploy it for normal production use even though there are no technical blocks that prevent you from doing so.

Apart from deciding on the version of Exchange to deploy, you'll also need to be sure that you buy the right user CALs. Use of some Exchange features such as archive mailboxes requires an enterprise CAL per mailbox, as does voice mail integration, the discovery and retention features, extended Exchange ActiveSync policies, and use of Microsoft's Forefront anti-spam protection for Exchange 2010. The enterprise CAL is additive in that you first buy a standard CAL to license the standard features and then purchase an enterprise CAL if you need to use the extended features. U.S. list prices at product announcement were $55 for the standard CAL and $35 (additive) for the enterprise CAL, $550 for Exchange 2010 Standard edition, and $3,200 for Exchange 2010 Enterprise edition. However, these are very much guide prices and are subject to volume discounts and other negotiations; you should refer to the Exchange 2010 licensing page at *http://www.microsoft.com/exchange/2010 /en/us/licensing.aspx* to get an idea of what licenses are required for the specific features you want to use.

INSIDE OUT   How many enterprise CALs do you need?

The Exchange 2010 version of Exchange Management Console (EMC) has been updated to report the number of standard and enterprise CALs that you need to support users, and it now highlights features that trigger the need for an enterprise CAL. For example, if you create a new mailbox that has an associated archive, EMC flags that the archive requires an enterprise CAL. The RTM version sometimes produced CAL counts that were just plain wrong. The code used by SP1 is better, but you are still advised to check its CAL count to make sure that it is right.

Active Directory

The successful deployment and management of Active Directory has been a fundamental prerequisite for Exchange since Exchange dropped its own directory service in Exchange 2000. In fact, Active Directory shares many of the characteristics of the older Exchange directory services, and there is no doubt that Microsoft learned a lot about how to design and operate directories from the experience gained with Exchange 4.0 to Exchange 5.5.

The strong link between Exchange and Active Directory

By any measure, Exchange makes the most extensive use of Active Directory of any Microsoft application. The Exchange installation procedure does the following:

- Extends the Active Directory schema to add a large number of new objects and attributes to support Exchange features and to allow the creation of objects such as connectors in Active Directory. New attributes such as email addresses extend existing objects such as users, contacts, and groups to allow them to work with Exchange. Other attributes are created for new objects and are only used for those objects. For example, the ability to define a maximum number of active databases that a server can support is dependent on the *msExchMaxActiveMailboxDatabases* (almost all of the objects that belong to Exchange are prefixed with "msExch") attribute that Exchange 2010 adds when preparing Active Directory for deployment.

  Most of the attributes are single valued, such as the database that hosts a mailbox. Others are multivalued, such as the email addresses for a mailbox. *LegacyExchangeDN* is the most famous attribute added by Exchange, as it has served as an X.500-based identifier for Exchange objects since the first version of the product and now provides backward compatibility for applications that rely on it to identify objects such as mailboxes. Today, Exchange relies on globally unique identifiers (GUIDs), 16-byte numbers, to identify objects.

- Creates a container called Microsoft Exchange under the Services root in the Configuration Naming Context. All the configuration data about objects managed by Exchange are located here (Figure 1-1). The objects include servers, policies, address lists, connectors, and so on. Data about mail-enabled objects are not held in this container. Instead, they are stored as attributes on the mail-enabled objects themselves, which means they will normally be found in the organizational units in the default naming context. Mail-enabled objects use the extended schema to populate attributes such as email addresses. EMC relies heavily on data fetched from the Exchange container. The data are replicated around the forest to ensure that a common and consistent view of the Exchange organization is available everywhere. This fact underlines how Active Directory replication supports Exchange operations.

- Adds a set of attributes to the Partial Attribute Set (PAS), which is the subset of Active Directory data that is replicated to global catalog servers and are available to every domain within the forest. For example, Exchange adds many mailbox attributes, such as the database and server that currently hosts a mailbox or the full set of Simple Mail Transfer Protocol (SMTP) addresses for a mailbox, to ensure that message routing works throughout the forest. Other user data form the basis of the Global Address List (GAL) and is added to the PAS so that it is available everywhere.

- Adds a set of extended rights (permissions) to allow administrators to manage objects such as databases.

- Adds and extends the set of Active Directory property sets (groups of properties) to make management easier by managing sets of properties as single entities rather than having to deal with each of the individual properties that make up a set. For example, the Exchange Personal Information property set contains all of the attributes that Exchange holds about individual users, such as their phone numbers.

The following table summarizes the position by showing where Exchange stores the data that it relies on within Active Directory.

Table 1-1 Where Exchange stores information in Active Directory

Partition	Active Directory Location	Exchange data stored	Replication scope
Domain	Dc=domain, DC=parent domain	Mail-enabled recipients (groups, contacts, accounts)	Every domain controller in the domain
Configuration	CN=Microsoft Exchange, CN=Services, CN=Configuration, DC = domainroot	Exchange configuration objects such as policies, global settings, address lists, templates, and connectors	Every domain controller in the forest
Schema	CN=Schema, CN=Configuration, DC= domain root	Exchange-specific classes and attributes	Every domain controller in the forest

INSIDE OUT   Coming to terms with Active Directory schema upgrades

Active Directory schema upgrades are not popular with Active Directory administrators because once a domain controller learns that a schema update is in progress, it halts all other forms of Active Directory replication until its schema is upgraded. The fear is that schema upgrades will interfere with the normal work of Active Directory and affect other applications, a feeling that can be compounded when the scale of the upgrade required for Exchange 2010 is revealed.

This fear can be addressed by understanding that schema updates will replicate quickly throughout a forest if Active Directory replication is healthy. The risk to other applications can be reduced by scheduling the schema upgrade for a time of low user demand. For this reason, many companies schedule Active Directory upgrades over holiday weekends. It's a good idea for you to validate that Active Directory replication is healthy with the RepAdmin utility before you commence the upgrade, just in case some problems have crept into the forest unnoticed.

ADSIEdit

ADSIEdit has proven its worth to Exchange administrators time after time to fix problems with Active Directory objects or simply to help them understand the complex relationship between Exchange and Active Directory. Figure 1-1 illustrates the utility in use to browse the Microsoft Exchange container and review the values of properties of an object. (In this case, details of the administrative audit policy for the organization; see Chapter 15, "Compliance," for more information.) Microsoft refers to ADSIEdit as a Lightweight Directory Access Protocol (LDAP) editor to manage attributes in Active Directory. It is installed on Windows 2008 servers along with the Active Directory Domain Services role, after which you can access ADSIEdit through the Start menu Administrative Tools option. Once you start ADSIEdit, you need to connect it to the Configuration Naming Context to be able to access Exchange data.

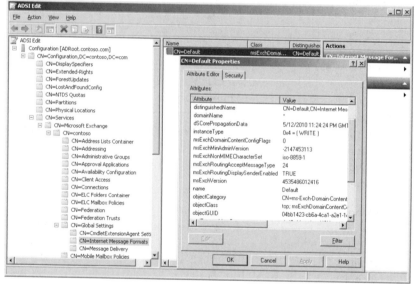

Figure 1-1 Exchange 2010 objects in Active Directory.

ADSIEdit started life in Windows 2000 as an add-in for Microsoft Management Console (MMC) that Microsoft didn't really support, probably because they didn't want administrators to have the ability to mess up Active Directory by editing objects and properties. If you've used ADSIEdit with previous versions of Windows, you'll see that work has been done in Windows 2008 to polish the program. However, you still work with raw data and a user interface that doesn't attempt to do much to protect you with warnings about the potential consequences of certain actions, such as editing an attribute.

CAUTION

There is no doubt that you can do great harm with ADSIEdit if you don't know what you are doing. It's best to be cautious and use ADSIEdit to gain an insight into the internal working of applications such as Exchange that depend on Active Directory to hold their configuration data.

Types of Active Directory deployments that support Exchange

Active Directory implementations in use today extend from a single forest to multiple forests with many variations in between. Some companies deployed Active Directory early and have an implementation that features a root domain which contains a small number of servers such as the schema master, with applications and users deployed into a set of geographic or business-centric domains. Others have deployed multiple Active Directory forests because separate security contexts are required by different businesses. Others have acquired multiple forests through buying companies and are in the process of merging applications, domains, and forests into a more streamlined design. Some companies have deployed a single domain forest that supports everything. In large companies it is quite common to find that Active Directory is under the control of a separate team from the group that manages Exchange. It's obvious from the previous discussion about how Exchange leverages Active Directory that close coordination is required from all concerned to achieve a smooth deployment.

Exchange supports three basic Active Directory designs. Apart from understanding that a forest can only support a single Exchange organization (there is always a one-to-one mapping between a forest and an Exchange organization), the biggest thing to remember is that a forest (and not a domain) is the security boundary for Active Directory. Thus, once you deploy multiple forests, you have to make sure servers and user accounts are able to access the resources that they need to do work, no matter in what forest the resource is located.

- Single forest: This is the simplest design and the one that is normally most appropriate for small to medium deployments as it removes a great deal of complexity. All servers in the forest share the same schema and configuration, even if multiple domains are deployed, and no difficulties are usually encountered with security and permissions, as all objects operate within a single security context.

- Multiforest: Sometimes referred to as cross-forest implementation, this deployment features two or more forests that operate independently from each other in terms of the accounts and applications that are deployed inside each forest. It is possible to synchronize user account information between each forest so that users can access a common directory that includes everyone. Exchange can be deployed in one or more forests.

When Exchange is deployed in multiple forests, the organizations have different names, SMTP addresses, configurations, and so on, and a messaging flow between the organizations can be established by SMTP connections to complement the common directory. Multiforest deployments usually occur as the result of company acquisitions. Less commonly, companies have deployed Exchange in multiple forests because of the need to satisfy particular requirements for specific parts of the company that were inconsistent with the needs of other parts. Exchange 2010 supports the ability to move mailboxes between organizations, so this is not an obstacle. It's also possible to use the Exchange 2010 management console to access multiple organizations at one time. However, the different security contexts created by multiple forests make management more difficult and complex than in a single forest.

- Resource forest: In this scenario, user accounts and groups are deployed in a root forest, and applications such as Exchange are deployed in a special resource forest. Exchange mailboxes exist in the resource forest and use disabled user accounts that belong to the resource forest. Users who log on to the root forest gain access to their mailboxes in the resource forest through an association with the mailboxes.

  Resource forests have some attraction because they allow a very clear separation of administrative responsibilities between Windows (the root domain) and applications, each of which is assigned its own resource domain. Resource domains are often used in a hosting environment where the hosting provider creates a resource domain to host and manage Exchange. A one-way trust is usually used to connect the resource forest with the root forest, as this allows the hosting provider to manage Exchange without having any control over Active Directory.

There are many variations on these three basic themes in production today. For example, a design composed of root and resource forests is often referred to as a hybrid forest if mail-enabled accounts exist in both forests. You then get into the discussion about whether to deploy one domain per forest, multiple domains per forest, or a mixture of both. Multiple domains are commonly used to isolate Exchange management and operations or to distribute administrative activity across business units or geographic regions. Cost is another factor to include in the planning debate. Additional domains normally imply the need to deploy extra servers as domain controllers. Extra servers increase the complexity of the environment that you have to manage, monitor, and operate and drive cost in terms of hardware (servers and storage), datacenter power and cooling, network bandwidth, and software licenses.

INSIDE OUT   Think before you leap

It is important to settle on the most appropriate design for your company *before* you begin to deploy Exchange because it is very difficult to change the basic shape of an Active Directory forest after it has been deployed. If you're unsure about how to proceed, it's sound advice to start simple and deploy a single forest to support Exchange. The old KISS ("Keep it simple, Stupid") adage comes to mind here! Later on, if you find that this model does not meet business requirements, you can evolve it by adding additional forests or even additional Exchange organizations. Remember that every additional domain and forest adds complexity and therefore cost to your implementation, so think long and hard before you venture away from a single forest.

The role of ADAccess

Operational Exchange servers make constant connections with Active Directory to retrieve directory information that is then loaded into on-server caches and used for many purposes that we explore throughout this book. A component called ADAccess, which runs as part of the System Attendant service, is responsible for providing all other Exchange services with a consistent, common view of the Active Directory topology as well as the population and maintenance of a cache that the services can consult when they need to retrieve information about the Active Directory topology.

ADAccess also performs tests to ensure that servers that are indicated to be domain controllers and global catalog servers are functional enough to be used by Exchange, as there is no point in Exchange attempting to read configuration data or to make a routing decision based on data from a barely functional or uncontactable Active Directory server. ADAccess monitors the availability of Active Directory servers within the local site and will instruct Exchange to failover from one server to another if an Active Directory server goes offline, including situations when all of the Active Directory servers in the local site are unavailable and Exchange needs to contact a domain controller in a remote site. In this scenario, ADAccess will make the decision about what server to contact based on Windows site link connection costs. ADAccess detects when the local Active Directory servers come online again and will redirect Exchange to a local server as soon as one is available.

If you examine the properties of a server and open the System Settings tab (Figure 1-2), you'll see the set of domain controllers and global catalog servers used by Exchange. Domain controllers are used to provide configuration data to Exchange, and global catalog servers are the source of directory information about mail-enabled objects from anywhere in the forest. As you can see from Figure 1-2, the same server can perform both roles.

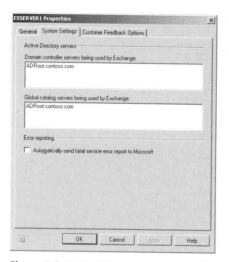

Figure 1-2 Active Directory servers used by Exchange.

Every 15 minutes, ADAccess runs the Topology Discovery process on Exchange servers to discover the domain controllers and global catalog servers that are available. Topology Discovery checks what Active Directory servers are available within the local site and those that are available outside the site (local servers are always used whenever possible). Event 2080 is logged after each discovery, and you can discover some additional detail about the servers by examining the data reported in the event log. By comparison, Exchange logs event 2070 when ADAccess cannot locate any suitable global catalogs during its attempts to discover the Active Directory topology.

The results reported in Figure 1-3 show that only one in-site server has been found. Apart from the fully qualified domain name (FQDN) of the server, ADAccess reports a cryptic set of letters and numbers for each server that it discovers. The letters indicate what role the server can play for Exchange. D indicates that the server is a domain controller; G means that it is a global catalog; C means that the server is acting as the Configuration domain controller.

In Figure 1-3, we see that Topology Discovery reports "CDG" for both servers, meaning that each is able to act as the Configuration domain controller, a regular domain controller, and a global catalog server. Exchange inserts a hyphen in the position when a server cannot be used for a particular purpose. For example, a server listed as "CD-" is a domain controller but not a global catalog. Table 1-2 shows how you can interpret the numeric values reported by ADAccess. Note that Exchange 2010 does not support read-only domain controllers (RODCs). These servers can exist in your Active Directory, but Exchange needs to connect to a writable domain controller.

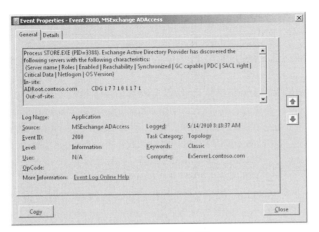

Figure 1-3 ADAccess discovers Active Directory servers.

Table 1-2 Interpreting ADAccess flags

Position	Use	Meaning
1	Availability	1 indicates that the server is available.
2	Port access	Bit mask indicating what ports are available for LDAP access via a Transmission Control Protocol (TCP) connection. 1 means that LDAP access for global catalog requests is possible through port 3268; 2 means that the server is reachable for domain controller requests through port 389; and 4 means that the server can act as the configuration domain controller. 7 indicates that the server is available for all necessary ports. 0 means that the server is unreachable and not usable by ADAccess.
3	Synchronization status	Bit mask indicating the Active Directory synchronization status of the server as indicated by the isSynchronized flag on the rootDSE object. 1 indicates that the global catalog is synchronized; 2 that the domain controller is synchronized; and 4 that the configuration domain controller is synchronized. 7 means that the server is completely synchronized in terms of Active Directory.
4	Global catalog flag	1 indicates that the server is a global catalog server; 0 means that it is a domain controller.
5	PDC flag	1 indicates that the server is the primary domain controller (PDC) for the domain; 0 means that it is not.

6	SACL test flag	1 indicates that ADAccess has the necessary security permission (via the system access control list [SACL]) to read Exchange information from the directory; 0 means that it does not.
7	Critical data flag	1 indicates that ADAccess located the Exchange server that it is running on in the configuration naming context of the domain controller. This container stores critical data such as the names of Exchange servers, the roles installed on each server, routing data, and so on. ADAccess only selects a domain controller if it hosts this container.
8	Netlogon	Bit mask indicating the success of ADAccess in connecting to the NetLogon service running on the domain controller using RPC. Similar to the results reported for LDAP access, 7 means that all attempts to connect were successful.
9	OS Version flag	1 indicates that the domain controller runs a version of Windows that supports Exchange 2010 (Windows Server 2003 SP1 or higher, SP2 recommended); 0 indicates that it does not.

INSIDE OUT   Monitoring SACL

The SACL flag is worthy of further comment. If the SACL for the Exchange Servers group is removed from a domain controller, many Exchange services, including the Information Store, will refuse to start. Many support calls were generated as a result of overeager administrators cleaning up Active Directory and removing the SACL with unfortunate results the next time Exchange started. Microsoft added code called the SACL Watcher to Exchange 2010 SP1 to monitor the presence of the SACL. Every 10 minutes, the watcher code runs to check the SACL and if it is missing, the watcher adds the SACL back.

Exchange 2010 caches configuration data from Active Directory in memory and shares the data with all the services that need to use it. However, unlike some previous versions of Exchange, it does not cache recipient data, as the belief is that it is better to fetch the definitive version of data from the Active Directory rather than run the risk that cached data might be outdated.

TROUBLESHOOTING

EMC can't contact a domain controller

Errors occur with computers and systems sometimes go offline. Unless it is the only domain controller or global catalog in a site, it shouldn't matter too much if you need to take an Active Directory server offline to apply a hot fix or other upgrade, as Exchange will quickly detect that the server is offline and switch its attention to another server. In some circumstances, the point at which a server goes offline could interfere with EMC and cause a slight hiccup. For example, Figure 1-4 shows a problem that occurred when EMC attempted to create a new mailbox. The domain controller to which EMC was connected when the administrator began to run the New Mailbox Wizard was taken offline, and the operation failed after a timeout (which accounts for the 21 seconds reported for the attempt). The usual solution is to exit EMC to force it to connect to a new global catalog server and try again.

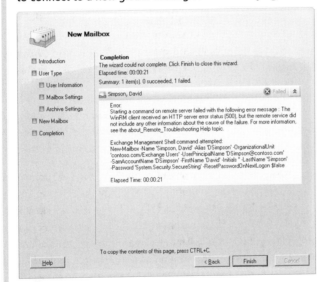

Figure 1-4 An Active Directory error occurs when creating a new mailbox.

Planning for global catalogs

The basic rule is to place at least one global catalog server in each site that hosts an Exchange server. This is probably sufficient for small sites that host one or two Exchange servers, but as the number of Exchange servers grows and the need to ensure availability increases, you will need to position more global catalog servers to handle the load generated by users and Exchange and to ensure that service continues even if one of the global catalog servers fails. This then raises the question of just how many global catalog servers are needed within a site.

Global catalog servers are critical to Exchange. For example, the transport system cannot expand a distribution group's membership or execute a query to determine the membership of a dynamic distribution group if a global catalog is unavailable. Thus, if you don't provide sufficient global catalog capacity within a site, your Exchange servers won't function smoothly, no matter how powerful and well configured they are. The classic trap that people fall into is to assume that the relatively light load exerted on global catalogs by standard Windows processing (client logins and so on) persists after Exchange comes on the scene. This could not be further from the truth, as demand on a global catalog expands dramatically once Exchange is active. The general rule of thumb is therefore to follow these recommendations:

- Servers running a 32-bit operating system: Provide one global catalog processor core for every four processors dedicated to Exchange.

- Servers running a 64-bit operating system: Provide one global catalog processor core for every eight processors dedicated to Exchange.

In other words, in a site supporting four Exchange servers, each equipped with four-way processor cores, you have 16 processors dedicated to Exchange and therefore need to deploy two 64-bit processor cores (or four 32-bit cores) for global catalogs. Two servers equipped with two-way processor cores would be a good solution in this case. Dividing the load across two servers means that Exchange will be able to continue working even if one global catalog is unavailable, and most servers have at least two processor cores today. An investment in global catalogs is a good thing, as there is nothing quite as good at stopping Exchange dead as the unavailability of a global catalog.

Servers running Windows 2008 are a better choice for global catalogs and should be the basic choice for deployment. Apart from being a more modern platform than the 32-bit Windows Server 2003 alternative, the servers will be able to address more memory and load more of the Active Directory into memory for speedier access. In all but the largest deployments, you can easily equip the server with sufficient memory to cache the entire Active Directory, which is the ideal situation.

Another issue that you need to consider is how to position global catalogs alongside Exchange servers. Again, we have a simple rule of thumb to follow: You need a global catalog on every wide area network (WAN) segment that supports an Exchange server. In other words, you must ensure that you position global catalogs so that any network outage has a minimal effect on Exchange. Satisfying the rule might not always be possible, especially if you feel that you have to place an Exchange server in a branch office (to speed up email for local users) and cannot afford to add a global catalog.

CAUTION

Exchange does not support Windows 2008 RODCs that are often recommended for branch deployments. In this case, you might consider directing Active Directory lookups to a global catalog server across a WAN link. However, although it seems an attractive option to use the network in this way, this approach inevitably leads to outages and user dissatisfaction. The better option is either to follow the rule of thumb and deploy a local global catalog in each site or to centralize Exchange and global catalog servers together in a single datacenter and use clients such as Outlook running in cached Exchange mode to connect over the WAN.

Exchange 2010 does not support Windows 2008 RODCs. You can still deploy RODCs in your infrastructure, but you have to make writeable domain controllers and global catalog servers within the Active Directory sites that host Exchange servers. Any RODC will be ignored by Exchange.

Preparing Active Directory for Exchange

Out of the box, Active Directory knows nothing about Exchange, so you have to prepare Active Directory to support the deployment of your Exchange organization. The basic framework for preparation is as follows:

1. Make sure that the forest runs in Windows Server 2003 functional mode. The computers used for domain controllers and global catalog servers should run Windows Server 2003 SP2 at a minimum, with Windows Server 2008 the preferred operating system for Active Directory.

2. Prepare the forest by adding or modifying elements in the Active Directory schema to support Exchange. This operation has to be done once for the forest and should be run in the domain that contains the schema master for the forest. You can do this by running the Exchange setup program with the /PrepareSchema or /PS switch. After this command completes, the Active Directory schema contains all of the classes and attributes required to support Exchange.

3. Introduce Exchange configuration data into the forest by running the Exchange setup program with the /PrepareAD /OrganizationName switches. After this command completes, you will find a Microsoft Exchange container created to hold details of the organization from servers to databases to connectors. This process also creates the universal groups required to manage Exchange and sets appropriate permissions on objects to allow them to be managed.

4. Prepare every domain that will contain an Exchange server *or* an Outlook client by running the Exchange setup program with the /PrepareDomain switch. You can also run setup with the /PrepareAllDomains switch to prepare all of the domains in the forest.

You cannot perform these operations unless your account has administrator permission for the target forest or domain. You'll also need to be a member of the Schema Administrators or Enterprise Administrators group to have sufficient permission to be able modify the schema before you can run the installation procedure with the /PrepareSchema switch. In addition, your account needs to be a member of the Exchange Organization Administrators security group (which is created when you prepare the organization) to be able to prepare a domain. Replication has to occur after each step to ensure that all domain controllers are at the same level, so it's wise to leave an interval between each step to allow this process to complete.

INSIDE OUT   Schema upgrades and replication activity

Schema upgrades might take some time to perform, and you probably don't want a lot of replication activity going on while you upgrade the schema master. You can disable replication on the schema master while the upgrade progresses and then start replication after all the upgrades have been applied. This is done with the RepAdmin utility. For example, to disable replication:

```
RepAdmin /Options Schema-Master.contoso.com +Disable_Outbound_Repl
+Disable_Inbound_Repl
```

If the upgrade is successful, you can then restart replication with:

```
RepAdmin /Options Schema-Master.contoso.com-Disable_Outbound_Repl
-Disable_Inbound_Repl
```

The joys of command-line utilities and their wonderful syntax!

Although the most common need for schema extensions arises when Exchange 2010 is first deployed for an organization, it's also important to recognize that schema updates might be required before a build-to-build upgrade can be performed. For example, Exchange 2010 SP1 introduces some new schema upgrades that must be applied to Active Directory before you can deploy the first Exchange 2010 SP1 server.

If you are installing Exchange from scratch to build a brand new organization, it is sufficient to run the installation procedure because it will do all the work to extend the Active Directory schema, add the necessary Exchange objects to instantiate the new organization to the Configuration Naming Context, and then proceed to install the new server. Subsequent server installations add their own objects to the organization data. Software upgrades such as the deployment of a service pack or set of roll-up fixes can also affect the information held in Active Directory.

One way to check the current version is to examine the value of the *objectVersion* property of the Microsoft Exchange System Objects (MESO) object. This is a container that holds objects that Exchange uses for internal processing. The value of the *objectVersion* property is usually increased following a successful software upgrade. The value of the *objectVersion* property for the Exchange 2010 RTM version is 12639 (build 639.21), while Exchange 2010 SP1 (build 218.15) displays 13214.

Another check that is often performed is to look at the *rangeUpper* property of the *Ms-Exch-Schema-Version-Pt object*. The value of this property for the RTM release of Exchange 2010 is 14622. Table 1-3 lists the relevant values for each version of Exchange that has required an Active Directory schema upgrade since the original extension occurred for Exchange 2000. See Chapter 2, "Installing Exchange 2010," for more information about how you can interpret Exchange version numbers.

Table 1-3 **Exchange versions and schema upgrades**

Value of rangeUpper	Exchange Version
14726	Exchange 2010 SP1
14622	Exchange 2010 RTM or Exchange 2007 SP2
11116	Exchange 2007 SP1
10628	Exchange 2007 RTM
6870	Exchange 2003 RTM
4406	Exchange 2000 SP3
4397	Exchange 2000 RTM

Microsoft recommends that you do not install Exchange on a domain controller. This is good advice and it is wise to maintain as much separation as possible between Exchange and Active Directory, even in small installations where extra servers impose a significant cost in terms of the overall deployment. The logic is that having Active Directory on the same server as Exchange creates additional complications in case the server experiences an outage and has to be rebuilt. At worst, if one server supports Active Directory and Exchange and is the only server in use, any outage creates an immediate disaster, where you can expect that the server will be unavailable to users for a significant time and some data are likely to be lost. It can take significant time and error to recover from situations like this, so it is best to be safe and maintain separation if at all possible.

As is obvious from Table 1-3, Exchange 2007 SP2 uses the same schema version as the RTM version of Exchange 2010. However, a caveat exists that governs the existence of down-level (Exchange 2007 and Exchange 2003) servers in an organization where Exchange 2010 is present. The general rule is that the installation of Exchange 2010 server as the first server in the organization blocks the installation of any down-level server thereafter. Therefore, if you want to install an Exchange 2003 SP2 or Exchange 2007 SP2 server in the organization to support something like an old email connector, you have to make sure that the down-level version is present before you deploy the first Exchange 2010 server. Once Exchange 2010 recognizes the existence of the down-level servers, it will "tolerate" their existence and you can continue to deploy more instances of these servers thereafter for as long as they are needed.

> **Tip**
>
> Deploying legacy servers is not the ideal situation because it is preferable to concentrate on the newer technology, but it is possible that you'll need additional Exchange 2007 servers to meet the needs of applications that might not have been upgraded for Exchange 2010.

The joys of a customizable schema

Active Directory boasts a customizable schema that is used by applications like Exchange to extend the underpinning database for their own purposes. Exchange adds just over 3,000 attributes to Active Directory as part of its installation process before you can install the first server in an organization. This number has increased ever since Exchange first began to use Active Directory in Exchange 2000, and every new version of Exchange continues to tweak the Active Directory schema to accommodate new features. For example, Exchange 2007 was the first version to support unified messaging, so it created a batch of new attributes to sort information about things like phone dialing plans. In its turn, an example of how Exchange 2010 extends the schema is the addition of new attributes to support the DAG. The total impact of the extensions is a growth of approximately 6 MB in the Active Directory database (.dit file).

Ideally, you should run process schema updates before you start to deploy any Exchange 2010 servers by running the Exchange installation procedure with the /preparead or /prepareschema switch (depending on whether you are installing a new organization or updating an existing organization). The best approach is to run the installation procedure "close" (in network terms) to the schema master for the forest. The computer used must be a member of the same domain and Active Directory site as the schema master. The procedure unpacks the set of .ldf files included in the Exchange kit and then calls the Ldifde.exe utility to process the schema updates that these files contain. Afterward, Active Directory replicates the updated schema to all domain controllers in the forest.

TROUBLESHOOTING

I changed the schema and now Exchange isn't synchronized with Active Directory

Sometimes Exchange and Active Directory become unsynchronized as the result of a change made to the schema for other purposes. For example, KB951710 (fixed in Exchange 2007 SP1 roll-up update 5) describes the problem that occurred when an organization extended the "Company" attribute in the schema to accommodate more than 64 characters. All versions up to and including Exchange 2007 SP1 have code that expects the company attribute to be no more than 64 characters, so any attempt to write more than this amount through EMC or Exchange Management Shell (EMS) results in an error. You can use other tools (like ADSIEdit) to update Active Directory through LDAP and write more than 64 characters into the attribute only to risk a potential corruption when Exchange subsequently attempts to retrieve or set the value.

The same situation is known to have occurred with changes to other attributes such as "Title" and "Initials," and although the Exchange engineering team is willing to consider changing their code to accommodate customer requirements to store more information in Active Directory, there will always be a time lag before Microsoft can issue new code. The moral of the story is that you need to carefully consider the impact of any schema update you make to Active Directory and test it thoroughly against all of the applications that use Active Directory before you apply the change in production.

Finally, if you are moving from Exchange 2003 to Exchange 2010, you must run Setup.com /PrepareLegacyExchangePermissions in every domain that supports Exchange 2003 servers. This action makes sure that the Exchange 2003 Recipient Update Service (RUS) continues to function after the Active Directory schema is updated for Exchange 2010. The new schema introduces a new property set called the Exchange-Information property set that the role-based access control model in Exchange 2010 uses to grant permission to users to manage recipient information. Running /PrepareLegacyExchangePermissions in the domain allows the RUS to continue to have permissions to update properties on user objects that it needs to stamp new email addresses and other attributes.

Ready-to-go custom attributes

Even when the product included its own directory, Exchange has provided a set of custom attributes that you can use to store information about mailboxes, contacts, and groups. The logic here is that it is impossible for the designer of any general-purpose directory to include all of the attributes required by every company that might use the directory and that it's easier to provide a set of custom attributes than to go into the potential support nightmare that might occur if everyone attempted to extend the schema to add their own set.

To access the custom properties in Exchange 2007 and Exchange 2010, select an object in EMC, view its properties, and click Custom Properties. Figure 1-5 shows the set of custom attributes for a mailbox. It's common to use attributes to store employee identifiers, department codes, job codes, identifiers for synchronization with other email directories, and an indicator whether the mailbox is used by a permanent employee.

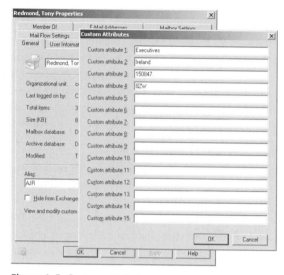

Figure 1-5 Custom attributes.

CAUTION

Be careful to ensure that the data that you hold about people in Active Directory comply with applicable privacy laws in any jurisdiction in which you operate.

The custom attributes are also accessible through EMS. For example:

```
Get-Mailbox -Identity 'EPR' | Select Name, Custom*
Set-Mailbox -Identity 'EPR' -CustomAttribute1 '8ZW' -CustomAttribute12 'Temporary
Assignment'
Set-DistributionGroup -Identity 'Sales' -CustomAttribute10 'Synchronized 10-Dec-2010'
Set-DynamicDistributionGroup -Identity 'Texas Users' -CustomAttribute3 'Dallas'
Set-MailContact -Identity 'Ruth, Andy' -CustomAttribute1 'Lotus Notes User'
```

Based on operational experience, you can write values of up to at least 600 characters into the custom attributes.

Let's install

We now know the landscape for Exchange 2010, how to prepare for deployment, the operating system to use, the versions that are available, and how Exchange relies on Active Directory to provide its foundation. The next step is to actually install the software on a server, which is where we go in Chapter 2.

Chapter 1

Installing Microsoft Exchange 2010

NSTALLING Exchange 2010 is not a particularly difficult operation, provided you do the necessary work to prepare. A test server can be installed and configured in well under an hour; production-class servers take longer because of the additional care that administrators must exert when they work in an environment where a mistake can impact the service delivered to users. Whatever the circumstances, the fundamental steps to install Exchange 2010 are very similar. We have to prepare Active Directory, install prerequisite software, and then deploy the required Exchange server roles on target computers. This chapter covers all these topics and discusses the next step in a server's evolution, which is when a service pack or upgrade comes along.

Approaching the installation

If you have done the work to prepare the environment by installing the various prerequisites on the servers that will host Exchange (see Chapter 1, "Introducing Microsoft Exchange 2010"), the Exchange installation process is straightforward and painless. The steps that you'll take include the following:

- If you are deploying Exchange for the first time, you have to select a name for the organization. An organization name can be up to 64 characters and obviously cannot be blank. You can include spaces in the name; if this is the case and you install Exchange from the command line, enclose the name in quotes. You don't need to enclose the name in quotes if you install with the graphical user interface (GUI). Users don't see the organization name. Usually, the organization is named after the company that owns the system. However, this is not compulsory. Indeed, because of the number of corporate mergers, some consultants recommend that it's best to choose a nonspecific name such as "Email" or "Exchange."

- Identify the target servers on which to install Exchange and the roles that each server will support.

- Decide on a name for each server. A good naming convention is one that conveys the purpose and use of a server without forcing the administrator to examine server properties to discover its purpose. For example, Ex-HT-Dublin01 might be a good name if you know that "Ex" prefixes all Exchange servers, "HT" indicates a hub transport server, and "Dublin01" shows that the server is the first server installed in the Dublin Active Directory site or datacenter. On the other hand, the name "XYZ-Server-1234" poses a comprehension challenge for administrators unless they can learn all the server names by heart. Table 2-1 provides a set of codes that you could use in a server naming convention.

- Install prerequisite components such as Microsoft .NET Framework 3.5, Windows PowerShell 2.0, Windows Remote Management (WinRM), and Active Directory remote management tools on the servers on which you want to install Exchange 2010. Windows 2008 R2 servers include Windows PowerShell 2.0 and Windows Remote Management, but it is always a good idea to consult TechNet to validate the current list of prerequisite features. For this purpose, *http://www.microsoft.com /exchange/2010/en/us/system-requirements.aspx* is a good starting point. As discussed later in this chapter, Exchange 2010 SP1 is able to install prerequisite software when you install a server.

- Remove or upgrade any servers that run unsupported versions of Exchange, as these will stop the Exchange 2010 installation program. Exchange 2010 will not install if it detects an Exchange 2000 server or an Exchange 2003 server that is not running SP2 or later. Exchange 2007 servers must run SP2 or later.

Table 2-1 Codes for server naming

Server role designator	Server role
DC	Domain controller
GC	Global catalog server
MB	Mailbox server
HT	Hub transport server
ED	Edge transport server
CAS	Client Access server
ESV	Exchange multirole server
UM	Unified Messaging server

Unless it's for a test environment, it is not a good idea to install Exchange 2010 on a domain controller and the Exchange setup program will issue a warning to this effect if it detects that it is running on a domain controller. The presence of Exchange 2010 on a domain controller has the side effect of elevating the privileges of domain administrators through the Exchange Trusted Subsystem. In effect, domain administrators will then have full read-write control over every object in Active Directory. This may be the situation anyway, but it's not good to distribute permissions without reason.

Running /PrepareAD

The final step is to prepare Active Directory by installing the necessary schema extensions to support Exchange 2010. To do this, run the Setup program with the */PrepareAD* switch (Figure 2-1). Setup reads the instructions contained in an LDF file to extend the Active Directory schema and creates the security groups that the Exchange installation process will use to create the organization and install servers.

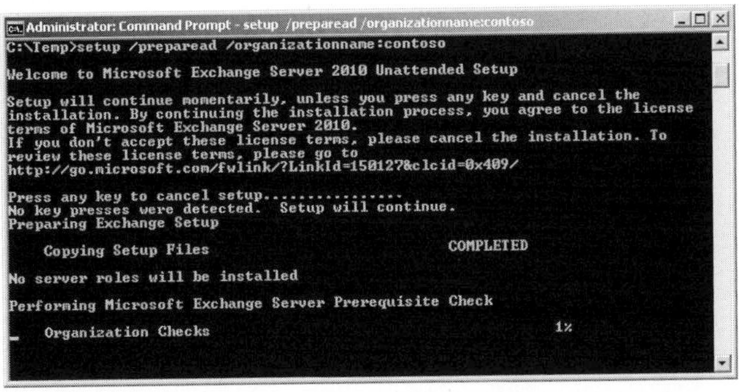

Figure 2-1 Running command-line setup to prepare Active Directory.

The Exchange installation kit contains a number of different sets of LDF files to cater for the various conditions that occur on a server. You can explore the LDF files in the Setup \ServerRoles\Common\Setup\Data and Setup\Data folders in the installation kit to see how Exchange extends the schema in different situations. For example, the set of files named PostWindows2003_schema0.ldf to PostWindows2003_schema99.ldf are used to update a forest where Windows 2003 has been installed but Exchange has never been deployed.

See the section "Preparing Active Directory for Exchange" in Chapter 1 for a more comprehensive discussion about the steps required to prepare Active Directory for Exchange 2010.

Exchange 2010 SP1 builds on the schema extensions implemented by Exchange 2010 and extends the schema further to support the introduction of new features such as the hierarchical address book and the group naming policy. You therefore need to include the schema extension as part of the planning for the deployment of SP1. Of course, if you plan to use Exchange 2010 SP1 for the initial deployment, you only need to extend the schema once as the SP1 version includes all of the previous extensions.

It's not a disaster if you forget to run Setup /PrepareAD and then proceed to run Setup to install the first Exchange 2010 server in the organization. Setup will detect that the organization has not been prepared beforehand and is able to execute /PrepareAD as part of the steps it takes to prepare and then install the first Exchange server as long as you use an account that is part of the Schema Admins group to run Setup.

Figure 2-2 shows what happens when Setup detects that /PrepareAD has not been run. You can also see that Setup is warning that additional Exchange 2007 servers cannot be installed into the organization once Setup prepares Active Directory. This is because no Exchange 2007 server is present in the brand new organization. However, even if Setup is smart enough to run /PrepareAD for you, the nature of schema extensions and the require-ment for the new schema to replicate throughout the forest means that it's still a much better idea to schedule this task separately well in advance of the deployment of the new organization. This approach allows you to ensure that the schema has replicated correctly and that Active Directory is truly ready for Exchange.

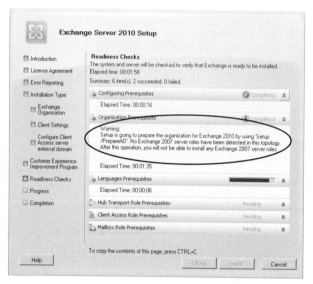

Figure 2-2 Setup runs /PrepareAD when installing the first Exchange server in an organization.

Installing prerequisite system components

A set of prerequisite software must be installed on a server before you can deploy Exchange 2010. Windows 2008 R2 servers are easier to prepare for Exchange 2010 because the .NET Framework 3.51, Windows Remote Management, and Windows PowerShell 2.0 are included in the operating system. To prepare Windows 2008 SP2 servers, you have to copy and install these components as the first step in the deployment process.

If the .NET Framework, Windows Remote Management, and Windows PowerShell 2.0 are installed on a server, both the GUI and command-line versions of the Exchange 2010 SP1 installation program offer the option to automatically configure all the remaining prereq-uisites thereafter. Figure 2-3 shows how the GUI version of Setup offers the option to install any required Windows roles and features. As you can see, you'll be prompted if any of the roles and features that are installed by Setup require a server reboot. (In particular, the

Windows Desktop Experience feature, which is required on Exchange Unified Messaging [UM] servers, will force a reboot.) In case a Windows hotfix or something else is missing that Setup can't install, you have the opportunity to install the missing item and then retry, or if you have to exit Setup, you can restart from the place where you left off.

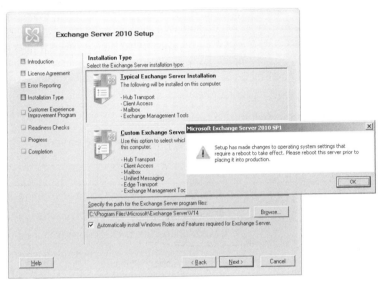

Figure 2-3 Exchange 2010 SP1 setup program offers to install required roles and features.

By comparison, to run setup.com to install a typical Exchange 2010 SP1 server including any required Windows server roles and features, type this command into a CMD session:

```
Setup.com /Mode:Install /roles:"C,H,T" /InstallWindowsComponents
```

The Exchange 2010 installation procedure requires that you configure the features manually. You can add all the necessary features by:

- Selecting and installing each feature with Windows Server Manager

- Running one of the installation configuration files provided with Exchange

- Installing each feature with the Add-WindowsFeature cmdlet in Windows PowerShell 2.0

Microsoft includes a set of Extensible Markup Language (XML) configuration files in the \Scripts directory under the Exchange installation directory that you can run to configure a server. These files can be used on both Windows 2008 R2 and SP2 servers, and the commands that they contain are directives for the ServerManagerCmd command that install the required Windows features. Although the ServerManagerCmd command is still present in Windows 2008 R2, Microsoft has deprecated ServerManagerCmd, and the long-term direction is to use Windows PowerShell to configure software instead. However, the command works today.

To configure the required features with one of the provided XML files, run PowerShell as the Administrator and use the Import-Module ServerManager cmdlet to add the *ServerManager* module to the set of cmdlets available to the session. You can then select the most appropriate XML file from those provided in the \Scripts directory and input that to the ServerManagerCmd cmdlet. Table 2-2 lists the available files. For example, the command to configure a typical Exchange server (one that hosts the Client Access Server [CAS], hub transport, and mailbox server roles) is:

```
ServerManagerCmd –ip \Scripts\Exchange-Typical.xml
```

Table 2-2 XML configuration files to prepare Exchange 2010 servers

Server roles	Script
CAS, HT, MBX (typical server)	ServerManagerCmd –ip \Scripts\Exchange-Typical.xml
CAS	ServerManagerCmd –ip \Scripts\Exchange-CAS.xml
HT	ServerManagerCmd –ip \Scripts\Exchange-Hub.xml
MBX	ServerManagerCmd –ip \Scripts\Exchange-MBX.xml
UM	ServerManagerCmd –ip \Scripts\Exchange-UM.xml
Edge	ServerManagerCmd –ip \Scripts\Exchange-Edge.xml

ServerManagerCmd installs the features specified in the configuration file. Any features that are already configured will be ignored. Table 2-3 lists the features that are configured for each role. If you want, you can create your own scripts to automate the deployment process and use the Add-WindowsFeature cmdlet to add the different components for the server roles that you require. Some idea of the close relationship that exists between Exchange 2010 and Microsoft Internet Information Services (IIS) is shown by the number of IIS features that must be installed before you can deploy Exchange. These extensions support critical components such as remote PowerShell, Outlook Web App, and the Exchange Control Panel application.

Table 2-3 Windows PowerShell commands to add Windows features

Server roles	Windows PowerShell command
CAS, HT, MBX	Add-WindowsFeature NET-Framework,RSAT-ADDS,Web-Server,Web-Basic-Auth,Web-Windows-Auth,Web-Metabase,Web-Net-Ext,Web-Lgcy-Mgmt-Console,WAS-Process-Model,RSAT-Web-Server,Web-ISAPI-Ext,Web-Digest-Auth,Web-Dyn-Compression,NET-HTTP-Activation,RPC-Over-HTTP-Proxy

Server roles	Windows PowerShell command
CAS	Add-WindowsFeature NET-Framework,RSAT-ADDS,Web-Server,Web-Basic-Auth,Web-Windows-Auth,Web-Metabase,Web-Net-Ext,Web-Lgcy-Mgmt-Console,WAS-Process-Model,RSAT-Web-Server,Web-ISAPI-Ext,Web-Digest-Auth,Web-Dyn-Compression,NET-HTTP-Activation,RPC-Over-HTTP-Proxy
HT or MBX	Add-WindowsFeature NET-Framework,RSAT-ADDS,Web-Server,Web-Basic-Auth,Web-Windows-Auth,Web-Metabase,Web-Net-Ext,Web-Lgcy-Mgmt-Console,WAS-Process-Model,RSAT-Web-Server
UM	Add-WindowsFeature NET-Framework,RSAT-ADDS,Web-Server,Web-Basic-Auth,Web-Windows-Auth,Web-Metabase,Web-Net-Ext,Web-Lgcy-Mgmt-Console,WAS-Process-Model,RSAT-Web-Server,Desktop-Experience
Edge	Add-WindowsFeature NET-Framework,RSAT-ADDS,ADLDS

Although it's easy to fire up a Windows PowerShell session, import the *ServerManager* module, and install the necessary components (Figure 2-4), there are several good Windows PowerShell scripts available on the Internet that can help you automate the installation of prerequisite components.

For example, some of the Exchange Most Valuable Professionals (MVPs) have collaborated to create the *Set-Exchange2010Prereqs.ps1* script that can be found and downloaded from a number of sites such as *http://www.ucblogs.net/files/folders/powershell/entry125.aspx*. The code in the script presents a menu to allow you to select various server configurations and then installs the necessary features. Its authors have done an excellent job of keeping the script updated to take account of new software such as Exchange roll-up releases and SP1. Of course, before you run any code downloaded from the Internet, you should run it on a test server to validate that the code doesn't do anything inappropriate and then make whatever changes are necessary to meet your requirements. For example, you might check that there's sufficient disk space available to install Exchange. To run the script, open a standard Windows PowerShell session and then set the script execution policy to be unrestricted, as otherwise Windows PowerShell will block the execution of any unsigned scripts. Remember to set the execution policy back to its original value after you are finished.

Figure 2-4 Installing Windows components with Windows PowerShell.

In addition to installing prerequisite software, before you run the installation program for a new Exchange CAS server, you have to update the properties of the .NET TCP Port Sharing service so that it starts automatically. CAS servers use the .NET TCP Port Sharing service to allow Exchange to multiplex communications through a single TCP port instead of requiring separate ports to be assigned to each service, specifically by the Mailbox Replication Service when it processes requests to move mailboxes or import and export data from mailboxes. The setup process checks that the .NET TCP Port Sharing service is started and its startup state is Automatic rather than the default (Manual). You can configure the service by executing this command from the CMD prompt:

```
Set-Service NetTcpPortSharing -StartupType Automatic
```

Installing the Microsoft Filter Pack

Before you can install the mailbox and hub transport roles, you must first install the Microsoft filter pack. Exchange uses the filters in the pack (referred to as IFilters) to be able to include attachments of various formats in its content indexes and to allow the hub transport service to apply transport rules that search attachments for specific words or phrases. The filter pack is available from the Microsoft Web site. If you deployed Exchange 2007 or the RTM version of Exchange 2010, you probably installed version 1.0 of the filter pack. Microsoft has updated the filter pack for Office 2010, and this version is the prerequisite for Exchange 2010 SP1. You can upgrade a server with the new filter pack and Exchange will update its content indexes as necessary.

The installation of the filter pack makes its filters available to Windows Search. After you install Exchange 2010, you need to take the steps described in *http://technet.microsoft.com /en-us/library/ee732397.aspx* to enable Exchange Search to use the filters. This should be done on all mailbox and hub transport servers. Because of the widespread use of Adobe's PDF format, you should also download and install the Adobe 64-bit PDF IFilter from *http://www.adobe.com/support/downloads/detail.jsp?ftpID=4025* to allow Exchange Search to include PDF documents in its content indexes. (Note that Adobe's filter has problems with some types of PDF files, so don't be surprised if your PDF searches don't find every possible match!) If you are unsure about how to enable these filters for Exchange Search, you can investigate Pat Richard's script at *http://www.ucblogs.net/files/folders/powershell /entry122.aspx*, which provides a very nice way to install the Microsoft Filter Pack, the Adobe PDF filter, or both.

Running Setup

Once Active Directory is prepared and you have installed the necessary prerequisite software and features, you can proceed to install Exchange. This can be done using the GUI version of the setup program, or you can use the command-line version.

Exchange 2010 setup supports four distinct modes:

- Installation of a new server, including the option to install a new role on an existing server.

> ### Note
>
> If you use a service pack to install Exchange on a new server, setup performs a complete installation from scratch. You do not have to apply the service pack separately after the base installation finishes.
>
> You can install the language pack (see next section) if it is available or go ahead with just English, the default language. Make sure that you install your preferred language to manage Exchange on Windows before you install Exchange so that Exchange Management Console (EMC) runs in that language rather than English.

- Uninstall, including the option to remove a specific role from a server.

- B2B (build to build), the installation of a new build of Exchange on top of an existing server. This mode is used to apply service packs and roll-up updates; it's also used extensively during the development phase of the product when the engineering group generates a new build nightly. All server roles are upgraded at one time during a B2B run; due to the dependency between various shared components, you cannot apply a new software build to just one role on a server. The command-line switch to apply a B2B update is Setup.com /M:Upgrade.

- Disaster recovery, which rebuilds a server based on its configuration data stored in Active Directory. It does not recover any of the mailbox or public folder databases that might have been present on the server: These have to be restored separately. The command-line switch for this mode is Setup /m:RecoverServer.

INSIDE OUT   Command-line vs. a GUI version setup

The command-line version is most often used to execute an unattended installation, but experienced administrators who have installed Exchange many times usually prefer the brevity and simplicity of the command-line setup, whereas those who are less experienced or want a little more guidance through the various steps prefer the GUI. Another tip is to always perform installations (initial and subsequent upgrades) with elevated permissions, as this avoids running into any potential problems with Windows 2008 User Account Control (UAC).

Chapter 2

As an example of using the command-line version of setup, this command installs a new CAS server:

```
Setup /Mode:install /Roles:ClientAccess
```

Command-line switches can be reduced to just the few characters required to make the switches unique. For example, the previous command can also be passed as:

```
Setup/m:i/r:cas
```

The GUI version of the installation program boots into an entry screen that Microsoft refers to as the "Can Opener" internally, perhaps because it opens all the possibilities that exist when Exchange is deployed correctly. Some might argue that it also opens up a can of worms, but that's another day's work! This version of the setup program depends on the .NET Framework and Windows PowerShell, which is the reason these components must be installed on a server before you can even attempt to run the program.

After initialization, the setup program takes you through multiple stages to gather information about the environment and to validate that all of the necessary prerequisites exist to allow the installation to proceed before creating the files on disk to build the chosen roles for the new server. You can get some idea of the amount of prerequisite checking that the setup program performs by browsing the contents of ExBPA.PrePreqs.xml. As the name suggests, setup leverages the framework used by the Exchange Best Practice Analyzer (ExBPA) to perform these checks. As mentioned earlier, the SP1 version of Setup will install any missing Windows server roles and features required by Exchange if you allow it to do so.

The GUI used by the setup program is adaptable in that it will ask for different information depending on the options that you choose. For example, if you install a CAS server that supports email connections from outside your network, you'll be asked for the names of the external Uniform Resource Locators (URLs) that clients will use to access the service. If you install a hub transport server that will connect to Exchange 2003, you'll be asked to nominate the Exchange 2003 bridgehead server that will link that infrastructure to Exchange 2010.

The time required to install a brand new server from start to finish varies according to server size and configuration, but you can certainly expect to be finished in well under an hour, especially if you only install a single role on a server. All of the steps to deploy prerequisite software and to then install Exchange can be scripted for unattended installs. Installing Exchange on a virtual server (Hyper-V or VMware) follows the same course as on a physical computer, assuming that you have done the necessary work to prepare the virtualization platform for Exchange by configuring the virtual servers with appropriate CPU, disk, and memory resources as per the recommendations published by the virtualiza-tion platform vendor.

Setup captures details of its progress in a watermark stored in the system registry to allow it to restart from the point of failure. The SP1 version also captures state information such as the options that you selected for the installation, meaning that you can restart Setup and won't have to input all your options again (Figure 2-5).

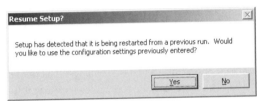

Figure 2-5 Setup offers to resume at the place it left off.

TROUBLESHOOTING

A failure occurs during setup
If a failure occurs, you will not be able to run setup in a different mode until you complete the process that you started in the original mode. For example, if a server fails in the middle of installing a new role, you have to go back and complete or undo the installation before you can execute setup in another mode (such as applying an upgrade).

Following a successful installation, you can then apply the latest roll-up updates and any hot fixes that Microsoft has made available for Exchange 2010 to bring the server up to the latest software revision. Installing a roll-up update is straightforward (but should always be tested first) and should proceed smoothly as long as you run the update procedure with elevated permissions.

Setup logs

If any problems occur during the installation, you can normally find the reason why in the files that the installation procedure places in the \ExchangeSetupLogs folder. The contents of the main installation log, ExchangeSetup.log, are quite interesting to review because you can find details there of all of the commands used to install Exchange on a server, includ-ing the changes applied to Active Directory. Exchange is tremendously verbose in terms of the information written into the setup log (SP1 is a little less verbose as it removes some of the messages output by the RTM version). The log is broken into major activities, which are indicated by a long line of asterisks, and minor activities, indicated by a shorter line. Initialization of the installation process is a major activity; running a Windows PowerShell script to perform a single task is a minor activity.

As a glance at Figure 2-6 reveals, there's a mass of data within the setup log. Most of the data captured in the logs are of no use unless you encounter a problem during an installation and need to find out why the problem occurred. Even so, most of the information that you'll need is right at the end of the log, where you'll see details of the problem experienced by the setup program and the actions that it took to unwind the installation. The remainder of the data in the log is interesting but is unlikely to be looked at by anyone except a Microsoft support specialist who's trying to track down an elusive problem.

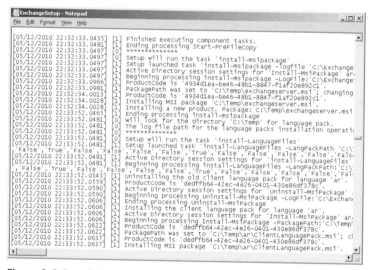

Figure 2-6 Examining the contents of ExchangeSetup.log.

In addition to the setup logs, the ExchangeSetupLogs folder contains a number of Windows PowerShell scripts that the installation procedure generates to perform different steps, including the configuration of the various server roles installed on the server. The fact that Exchange uses Windows PowerShell in this manner underscores the importance of scripting to the product, as do the many examples of scripts built to perform uninstalled installations.

If problems persist and you can't install Exchange or Exchange doesn't work as expected after the installation, Microsoft support is likely to ask you to provide information such as the installation logs and the application event log to enable the support team to understand what happened and how to set about fixing any problems. They might also ask you to run the Exchange Trace Analyzer utility (ExTRA) to gather debugging information.

ExTRA runs in the background to gather information about Windows and Exchange at an additional level of detail.

> **Tip**
>
> One minor event that occurs during an installation is that the path for executables is updated with the location of the Exchange binaries. This is a nice feature because it avoids the need for administrators to play around with file locations when they want to run Exchange utilities such as Eseutil.exe.

Uninstalling Exchange

Of course, no one would ever remove Exchange from a computer unless it was a test box or it was time to decommission the server after you upgrade to a new release. If you need to remove Exchange, however, two methods are available to uninstall a single role, multiple roles, or a complete Exchange server:

- Run Setup.com from the command line. For example, to remove the hub transport role from a server, the command Setup.com /Mode:Uninstall /Roles:HT will do the trick.

- Go to Control Panel, click Uninstall A Program, and then select Exchange 2010 from the list of programs. This invokes the GUI setup program in uninstall mode. You can then select the roles that you want to remove from the computer.

When the time comes to remove roles or a complete server, the first step is to ensure that data is transferred off the server before you run Setup. Although this is not a comprehensive checklist, these steps are among those that you should review before you decommission a server:

- Move mailboxes to databases on other servers (or move complete databases if the server is a member of a Database Availability Group [DAG]).

- Exclude the mailbox databases on the server from automatic provisioning so that an administrator does not inadvertently create new mailboxes in those servers (see Chapter 6, "Managing Mail-Enabled Recipients").

- Dismount and remove databases.

- Remove the server from its DAG, if it is a member.

- Clear any outstanding move requests for databases hosted by the server.

Chapter 2

- Move public folder replicas from a public folder database, if hosted by the server.

- Move the responsibility for Offline Address Book (OAB) generation and distribution, if hosted by the server.

- Disable group metrics generation and make sure that another server in the organization takes on this task.

- Remove the server from any send connectors for which it is a source.

- If the server being removed is a CAS, ensure that connectivity (external and internal) for all supported client types will continue to function.

After you relocate mailboxes and move responsibilities such as OAB generation, it's wise to leave the server in place for a couple of days to check that everything continues to run smoothly. You should check the event logs on the server to be decommissioned and the servers to which you have transferred work to ensure that no problems are flagged. You could then take the server offline for another period to see if anything breaks. Finally, after you are sure that everything is ready to proceed and no lurking problems exist, you can run Setup in removal mode. As an added protection, Setup will check that all prerequisites are satisfied before it will proceed. Figure 2-7 shows what happens when Setup encounters issues that an administrator needs to resolve.

Usually, issues reported can be resolved quickly with the steps suggested by Setup.

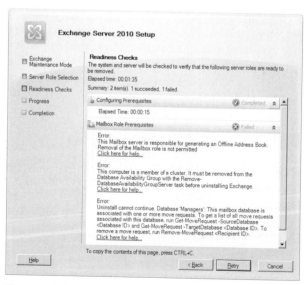

Figure 2-7 Setup reports errors during its prerequisite checks before a server can be uninstalled.

INSIDE OUT   Entering the dark zone

We enter Exchange's dark zone if the suggested resolution does not work. The dark zone is where a problem exists that cannot be resolved with an option available through EMC, a Windows PowerShell command, or some other common utility. It might be that a software or hardware bug has caused incorrect data to be written into Exchange's configuration data in Active Directory or that an administrator has updated a program and caused a conflict with Exchange. Whatever the case, it is a bad situation to be in when Setup won't proceed and you've tried all suggestions, including those found on the Internet.

It's at this point that some advocate using the ADSIEdit utility (see Chapter 1, "Introducing Exchange 2010"), in an attempt to edit or remove Active Directory that is inaccessible through other means. For example, if Setup is unable to remove Exchange from a server and you really want to remove it from the organization, you could use ADSIEdit to remove the server object from Active Directory and then delete the computer account. Of course, this is a radical step and certainly not something to attempt without a clear and comprehensive understanding of what you're about to do, but it is a method that has often been used to remove a stubborn server.

Perhaps the Exchange development group will help by providing a new Setup mode in the future, giving us a command something like this:

```
Setup /m:Remove /YesIReallyMeanIt /TakeNoExcuses /BlowitAwayServerName
```

Repairing Exchange

The Setup program for Exchange 2010 does not support a repair mode. In other words, you cannot run Setup in a repair mode to have it scan a server for any missing files, registry keys, Active Directory objects, or other elements that might be affecting the ability of the server to run properly. If you get into a situation where a server is not functioning correctly and nothing you do seems to make any difference (and there's no help to be gained by searching the Internet), you might be forced to deinstall all of the roles from the server to remove Exchange and then reinstall the server from the beginning. This is not so bad, as experience with broken software demonstrates that a "flatten and rebuild" approach usually delivers a more robust solution than attempting to repair individual flaws that might be hiding other problems which then only appear once you repair the apparent problem.

An alternative approach is to wait for Microsoft to provide a service pack or roll-up update and install it as an upgrade to a more recent build. This will usually fix any problems caused by a missing component, if only because a build-to-build upgrade includes code that will create objects such as a missing registry key or permission which it detects as the server is upgraded.

Installing an edge server

An edge server is a specialized version of Exchange designed to reside in a perimeter network to handle incoming messages from the Internet. The server is not part of the Exchange organization, nor does it belong to the same Active Directory forest into which you install Exchange. However, an edge server can be installed in a separate Active Directory forest, perhaps one that you use to control all of the servers installed into the perimeter network. The isolation of the edge server from the other Exchange servers and Active Directory ensures that they remain protected even if the edge server is compromised by a hacker or other attack on security.

An edge server can only support that role. You cannot install the mailbox, CAS, or hub transport roles on the same server. Running setup proceeds in much the same way as a normal server except that you select the option for a custom server installation. Setup will only allow you to select the edge server role, and the management tools (EMC and Exchange Management Shell [EMS]) will be included automatically. Before installing Exchange you need to install the components that the setup program depends on, including the .NET Framework 3.51 and Windows PowerShell 2.0 (this is included in the operating system if you deploy the edge server with Windows 2008 R2).

You also need to install Active Directory Lightweight Directory Services (AD LDS) and the Remote Server Administrative Tools Active Directory Management Tools (RSAT-ADDS) before you install the edge role on a computer. AD LDS is a special version of Active Directory designed to provide directory storage and access for applications. It is a replacement for Active Directory Application Mode (ADAM) for Windows 2003 and used by Exchange 2007 edge servers. When you install the Exchange 2010 edge server, the setup program configures AD LDS to support Exchange. Somewhat confusingly, the service that manages the interaction between Exchange and AD LDS is still called Microsoft Exchange ADAM. The contents of the AD LDS directory are populated through a process called edge synchronization that we discuss in Chapter 14, "Message Hygiene."

Language packs

The first corporate email systems were determinedly monolingual. Systems such as IBM PROFS and Digital's ALL-IN-1 were splendid in U.S. English, but struggled to deal with anything else. The first email system to accommodate multiple languages was the ALL-IN-1 Basic European Edition (BEV), introduced by Digital in 1986 to support languages such as French, German, Hebrew, and Dutch. Great strides have been made to make software more international in the quarter-century since based on the principle of separating language-dependent strings from the underlying code, even if disagreement occurs between applications about some of the more esoteric details.

Exchange and its clients have always supported multiple languages. Exchange 2010 uses a language-neutral model for the product. This approach is also used by Windows 2008 and Vista and means that Microsoft provides an installation kit for the base product and a separate language pack that contains all of the elements required for every supported language. The separation of the language pack from the product distribution allows Microsoft to update languages without impacting Exchange. They can add new languages or simply improve the quality of the translation to address local idioms or nomenclature identified by users. You can find the current list of languages supported by Exchange at *http://technet .microsoft.com/en-us/library/dd298152.aspx*.

The language pack can be installed during the setup of an Exchange server or afterward (you need to download the language pack from Microsoft's Web site first). You can install it with the GUI or using the */LanguagePack* parameter with the command-line setup program. The command-line program supports fresh installations, installations after initial server deployment, and language pack updates.

> **Tip**
>
> If you install Exchange without the language pack, the Exchange management tools and clients will only run in English, no matter what language is used to install Windows on the server. This is why it's a good idea to install Windows in the language with which you want to administer Exchange before you apply the language pack.

A separate language pack is available for UM. This language pack includes elements such as the prerecorded prompts used by UM, automatic speech recognition files, and support for voice preview and text-to-speech translation to allow content to be read to users in different languages.

Recovering a failed server

If you're unfortunate enough to suffer a catastrophic hardware failure that renders a computer completely unusable, you can recover the configuration for the server from Active Directory to rebuild Exchange. To do this, you first have to provide new hardware that runs the same operating system as the failed server and has the same drive letters available for the databases that the server supports. The new server should be as powerful in terms of its ability to support user load as the failed computer. Given that new hardware usually has improved performance, it shouldn't be a problem to replace the failed computer with new hardware, but it might be problematic to replace it with older hardware if the configuration of that computer isn't as capable and is therefore less likely to be able to support the same load.

Once the new hardware is installed, you will need to do the following:

- Reset the Active Directory computer account for the failed server.

- Install and configure Windows with the prerequisite roles and features including any hot fixes required by Exchange; the Setup program does not have the ability to install any required software when it runs in recovery mode.

- Ensure that network connectivity works properly and that the new computer is con-figured with the correct IP addresses and other settings.

- Join the replacement computer to the domain hosting Exchange with the same name as the failed server.

- Authenticate the Windows server license.

You can then run Setup.com with the **/m:recoverserver** option. In this mode, the instal-lation procedure reads the details of the server configuration from Active Directory and reconstructs an exact replica of the failed server. Figure 2-8 shows a recovery operation in progress.

Figure 2-8 Running Setup.com in recovery mode.

Exchange keeps details of the software versions installed on a computer in the system reg-istry, and the setup program will only recover a server to the same version of Exchange that was installed on it before it failed. In other words, you cannot recover and upgrade at the same time; for instance, it's not possible to recover a failed Exchange 2010 server with an Exchange 2010 SP1 software kit, so be sure you keep a share or DVD with the version of Exchange that you've actually installed.

After the recovery is complete, all of the server roles defined in Active Directory will be operational on the replacement server. In the case of a failed mailbox server, you will still have to restore databases to their location on disk. The fully up-to-date database and transaction logs might be accessible from the disks used by the failed server. If not, you'll have to recover from backup and replay whatever transaction logs are available to bring the databases as up-to-date as possible. Some data loss is inevitable in this case. In the case of nonmailbox servers, you might also have to restore configuration files that are not included in Active Directory. For example, if you update the transport configuration file for some reason, you will have to either:

- Copy the updated configuration file from another hub transport server (if available) in the organization. All configuration updates should be applied consistently across the organization.

- Recover the configuration file from another backup.

- Manually apply the update again. This assumes that you have details of the edits that should be applied to the configuration file, which underlines the need for careful documentation of these types of changes.

Special steps are required for failed servers that are members of a DAG. The installation procedure won't allow you to run /m:recoverserver if it detects that the server is a member of a DAG. To proceed, you first have to remove database copies and then evict the failed server from the DAG before you can run the steps described earlier. After the server is restored to full health, you can bring it back into the DAG and create new database copies. See *http://technet.microsoft.com/en-us/library/dd638206.aspx* for more information about the steps required to restore a failed DAG member server.

Remember that the operation you've just performed is a recovery of Exchange based on information in Active Directory. Any information or configuration setting that is stored outside Active Directory, such as customizations made to configuration files, will need to be restored separately.

INSIDE OUT   Delegated setup

Exchange 2010 supports the ability for an administrator to delegate setup activity for a server to a nonprivileged user. This can be done for any server after the first Exchange server is installed in an organization. In outline, this is done by running the Exchange setup program in a special mode that creates the server object in Active Directory and prepares it for completion at some point in the future. You then delegate the completion task to another user, and he can then run the Exchange setup program to complete the installation.

The first task is to run Setup to create the server object in Active Directory and prepare the server for future completion.

```
Setup.com /NewProvisionedServer:ExServer7.contoso.com
```

The physical server must exist and be properly prepared for Exchange to be installed. After a successful Setup run, you can check Active Directory, and you'll see that the new server is listed along with the other Exchange servers.

To complete server provisioning, the user's account must be a member of the Delegated Setup role group. We'll get to discuss Exchange's role-based access control system and the various role groups that are defined in later chapters. For now, it's suffi-cient to know that you have to run an EMS command to add the mailbox to which you want to delegate the server completion task. You can only delegate roles to mailboxes or universal security groups, so the user has to have a mailbox or be a member of a uni-versal security group before you can delegate a role. For example, to assign the task of performing the delegated setup to the user who owns the mailbox named Redmond, we open EMS and type this command:

```
Add-RoleGroupMember –Identity 'Delegated Setup' –Member 'Redmond'
```

Afterward, this user will be able to run Setup on the provisioned server to complete the installation, provided of course that she holds local administrator permission for the server.

Customer Experience Improvement Program

The Exchange 2010 Setup program offers you the chance to join Microsoft's Customer Experience Improvement Program (CEIP). This is a program that gathers data from opera-tional Exchange servers to allow Microsoft to understand how Exchange is used in produc-tion. Microsoft then uses the data to decide how to develop Exchange over the next few releases. In short, this ensures that their engineering effort is business-driven and focused in areas that deliver a real customer impact rather than being based on interesting tech-nology challenges. The kind of questions that Microsoft hopes will be answered by the CEIP data includes the following:

- How many users turn on Short Message Service (SMS) notification for their mailboxes?

- How many non-delivery reports (NDRs) are generated by the transport system, and for what reason?

- How much latency exists between the time a user sends an SMS and the time the mobile device picks up the SMS message from Outbox?

- What are the most frequently observed cmdlet errors?

- What Exchange server roles are most often installed in virtualized (VMware, Hyper-V) environments?

Enabling a server to provide CEIP data requires a deliberate opt in. You can opt in by selecting the option when you run the GUI version of Setup to install an Exchange server. Alternatively, you can enable CEIP reporting by doing either of the following:

- Going to the Microsoft Exchange On-Premise node in EMC and accessing the Customer Feedback page (Figure 2-9).

- Running two EMS commands to enable CEIP reporting for the organization and then for the servers that you'd like to provide data. For example, these commands enable the organization to provide CEIP data from server ExServer1. The *–Industry* parameter is optional and is used to categorize the results by industry. If set, it must be one of the values defined by Microsoft such as Manufacturing, Transportation, Finance, or Agriculture. If you are unsure, enter Unspecified:

```
Set-OrganizationConfig –CustomerFeedbackEnabled $True –Industry "NonProfit"

Set-ExchangeServer –Identity ExServer1 –CustomerFeedbackEnabled $True
```

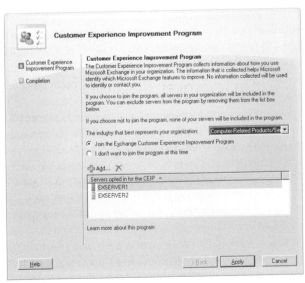

Figure 2-9 Enabling CEIP for the organization.

The effect of enabling CEIP is to create a registry value called HKEY_Local_Machine \Software\Microsoft\SQMClient\Windows\CEIPEnable and set it to 1 (one). The presence of this registry value instructs a Windows component called Software Quality Metrics (SQM) to record and then upload CEIP data on a regular basis. SQM gathers information from applications that register for CEIP, such as Exchange, on a per-session basis and stores these data in memory to a threshold of approximately 15 KB. According to the SQM engineers, 15 KB is sufficient to hold roughly 4,000 datapoints gathered about how an application functions. When the threshold is reached or the session terminates, SQM writes the data to a file on disk and uploads the file to Microsoft the next time that a new session is initialized. This approach is taken to ensure that an application shutdown is not delayed by the need to transmit data to Microsoft.

It's natural to worry that data about operational environments might be reused for purposes that you don't approve. In this case, the CEIP data gathered by Microsoft is governed by the privacy guidelines described at *http://www.microsoft.com/products/ceip/en-us /privacypolicy.mspx*. Microsoft does not store information that can be identifiable to a specific customer. However, before you enable CEIP for Exchange, it's a good idea to verify that your company's privacy and security teams review the Microsoft privacy guidelines and support the transmission of CEIP data from your organization to Microsoft.

The services of Exchange

Once upon a time, email servers were engineered and delivered as a single monolithic process. The Information Store process captures the imagination as the single most obvious embodiment of Exchange with its seeming ability to occupy huge amounts of memory, but in reality, the Exchange code base is spread across a series of interconnecting services that collectively deliver all of the product's functionality. Not all services run on all servers, as some are only required for specific activities. For example, you don't need to run the Internet Messaging Access Protocol 4 (IMAP4) or Post Office Protocol 3 (POP3) services unless you need to support clients that connect to Exchange using these protocols. Some services have dependencies on other Exchange services or base Windows services (such as the Net TCP Port Sharing service).

Table 2-4 lists the details of the sets of services that you can expect to see on a multirole server together with their internal names and any dependency that exists. You can see that the majority of Exchange services depend on the Active Directory Topology service. This is not surprising because Exchange stores so much information about its own configuration in Active Directory and makes use of other data such as users and groups. If this service isn't running, then Exchange doesn't know about the Active Directory site topology that exists or the domain controllers that are available, so it can't fetch the data necessary to start up services such as Transport, nor does it know what user accounts are mail-enabled, what database holds their mailboxes, or even what their email addresses are.

Table 2-4 **Exchange 2010 services**

Service Name	Use	Dependencies	New in Exchange 2010
Active Directory Topology (MSExchangeADTopology)	Computes the current Active Directory site topology and makes these data available to other services		
Address Book (MSExchangeAB)	Generates the OAB and other address book views	AD Topology	
Anti-spam update (MSExchangeAnti-spamUpdate)	Applies updates to Microsoft Forefront anti-spam services	AD Topology	
Edgesync (MSExchangeEdgeSync)	Synchronizes information between the Exchange organization and standalone edge servers	AD Topology	
File Distribution (MSExchangeFDS)	Distributes files such as OAB updates to servers within the organization	AD Topology Workstation	
Forms-based Authentication (MSExchangeFBA)	Manages forms-based authentication process executed on CAS servers to allow access to OWA and ECP		
IMAP4 (MSExchangeIMAP4)	Provides access to mailboxes for IMAP4 clients	AD Topology	
Information Store (MSExchangeIS)	Manages the internal operations (including memory management) for mailbox and public folder databases	RPC Server Event Log Workstation	
Mail Submission (MSExchangeMailSubmission)	Submits messages from the Information Store to the Transport service	AD Topology	
Mailbox Assistants (MSExchangeMailboxAssistants)	Performs background maintenance operations on mailboxes such as auctioning calendar requests and automatic message archiving	AD Topology	
Mailbox Replication (MSExchangeMailboxReplication)	Replicates mailbox contents to target servers during mailbox moves performed by the Mailbox Replication Service (MRS)	AD Topology Net .TCP Port Sharing	Yes
Monitoring (MSExchangeMonitoring)	Allows applications to call the Exchange diagnostic commands		
POP3 (MSExchangePop3)	Provides access to mailboxes for POP3 clients	AD Topology	
Protected Service Host (MSExchangeProtectedServiceHost)	Provides a secure host for internal Exchange services that need to be protected from other services	AD Topology	Yes
Replication (MSExchangeRepl)	Manages the replication of transaction logs to target mailbox servers within a DAG	AD Topology	

Chapter 2

Service Name	Use	Dependencies	New in Exchange 2010
RPC Client Access (MSExchangeRPC)	Manages incoming RPC client (Outlook) connection requests and directs clients to server holding target mailbox	AD Topology	Yes
Search Indexer (MSExchangeSearch)	Generates content indexes of data held in mailbox and public folder databases	AD Topology Microsoft Search (Exchange)	
Server Extension for Windows Backup (WsbExchange)	Permits Windows 2008 Backup utility to take online backups of Exchange databases		
Service Host (MSExchangeServiceHost)	Provides an internal host for Exchange services; for example, this service generates group metrics data for mail tips	AD Topology	
System Attendant (MSExchangeSA)	Performs background monitoring and maintenance functions such as the application of email address policies to objects; some of the functions served by the System Attendant process in previous versions of Exchange have moved to the Service Host process	RPC Server Event Log Workstation	
Throttling (MSExchangeThrottling)	Provides throttling function to limit the ability of user actions to swamp system resources	AD Topology	Yes
Transport (MSExchangeTransport)	Manages Transport system to move messages between Exchange servers and connectors	AD Topology	
Transport Log Search (MSExchangeTransportLogSearch)	Executes search requests through message tracking logs on mailbox and hub transport servers	AD Topology	
Microsoft Search (Exchange) (MSFTESQL-Exchange)	A version of the SQL-based search process tailored to produce content indexes from Exchange mailbox and public folder data	RPC	
Microsoft Exchange ADAM (ADAM_MSExchange) (only on edge servers)	Controls the interaction between an Exchange 2010 edge server and the AD LDS instance that stores configuration and other data used to process incoming messages	COM+	
Microsoft Exchange Credential (MSExchangeEdgeCredential)	Manages the shared credentials required to synchronize data between an edge server and hub transport servers in a connected Active Directory site	ADAM	

> **Note**
>
> On a side note, as Windows PowerShell is a big part of the future for Windows manage-
> ment, you can examine details of a service through Windows PowerShell. For example,
> to see what service dependencies exist for the Information Store service, you can use a
> command like this:
>
> ```
> Get-service MSExchangeIS | Select Name, ServicesDependedOn|Format-List
> ```
>
> **The output is:**
>
> ```
> Name               : MSExchangeIS
> ServicesDependedOn : {RPCSS, EventLog, LanmanServer, LanmanWorkstation}
> ```

Other services run on servers that host the UM role, and others are present if you deploy
Microsoft Forefront antivirus and anti-spam services (at additional cost). Of course, if you
choose to deploy third-party technology for functions such as anti-spam, monitoring,
backup, or archiving, those services will be present and have to be managed.

Versions, roll-up updates, and service packs

Exchange 2007 marked a new approach to support delivered in the form of updated code.
Previous versions of Exchange focused on regular service packs, which became very large
updates similar in many respects to the release of a brand new version of the product. The
current approach divides updates into two different kinds of releases that you can plan for:

- Service packs (SP): Microsoft releases a new service pack for Exchange on average
  once a year, so it came as no surprise to see Exchange 2010 SP1 appear in June 2010.
  A service pack typically includes new functionality as well as fixes. It is common to
  find that the first service pack completes functionality that could not be finished in
  time to allow the product to meet its planned release date. This factor, plus a feeling
  that no one really wants to live on the bleeding edge of new technology, is usually
  cited as the reason why companies delay upgrades until Microsoft has released the
  first service pack for a new product.

- Roll-up updates (RU): Roll-up updates appear roughly every three months and are
  cumulative in that RU3 includes all of the fixes issued in RU1 and RU2. Therefore, you
  can apply the latest RU to update a product with all of the current released fixes. Roll-
  up fixes are issued on the Web and different versions are available for each version
  of Exchange (including service packs) that Microsoft supports, so you have to be sure
  that you download and install the right RU for the version of Exchange that you use.
  Some hot fixes that pertain to specific situations might also be available separately,

and it's worth checking with Microsoft whether any important hot fixes exist for functionality that are important to your deployment before you plan to deploy a roll-up update.

Testing roll-up updates

Make sure that you test roll-up updates before you deploy into production as there have been cases for both Exchange 2007 and Exchange 2010 where problems occurred during or after the installation of the update. For example, Microsoft published the first roll-up update for Exchange 2010 on December 9, 2009. After deploying RU1, some customers reported that their users couldn't access the OWA logon page because of a JavaScript syntax error. The problem was easily fixed by removing and recreating the OWA virtual directory, but it serves to demonstrate that your servers might present a different environment to those used by Microsoft to test new releases, so predeployment testing is an absolute necessity. It's also important to install roll-up updates with accounts that have full administrator permissions to ensure that all files are properly updated.

It is sometimes difficult to understand the difference between a roll-up release, a service pack, and a new version of a Microsoft server product. My view is that a roll-up release helps you keep servers running the latest possible code so that you run a lower risk of encountering a known bug. Of course, roll-up releases have been known to introduce their own problems in the past, and the regular cadence of releases means that you have yet another task to fit into a maintenance schedule. Nevertheless, Microsoft's approach of delivering a flow of fixes through roll-up releases has worked well for Exchange 2007 as it allows administrators to plan scheduled software maintenance on a consistent basis. The same approach applies for Exchange 2010, and I anticipate that it will be equally valuable.

INSIDE OUT A best practice for server software levels

It is best practice to ensure that all servers in an organization run at the same software level, including roll-up releases. There is no good logic to allow servers to run at different software levels for any sustained period. This is especially important when the Active Directory schema is updated by a service pack to introduce new properties for objects used by Exchange. In some cases, feature changes or bug fixes in service packs require you to upgrade all servers to the same service pack level; Microsoft does a good job of documenting these requirements, and you should follow them.

A service pack is a more definitive point in a product's development cycle. It includes fixes and will bring software to a patch level to at least the same degree as the most recent roll-up release, and it usually adds some value in terms of improvements to product features. The improvements might be in the form of completing functionality that couldn't be finished or were simply too buggy before Microsoft shipped the previous version of the software or simply refining features in the light of customer feedback. For example, the release to manufacturing (RTM) version of Exchange 2007 didn't include Standby Cluster Replication because the work required to ensure that log replication would work across two datacenters was incomplete when the cut-off came to build the RTM software, so it appeared in Exchange 2007 SP1. Similarly, ActiveSync made its appearance in Exchange 2003 SP2. Microsoft used to have a rule that no new feature could be added to a service pack that caused a user interface change. Thankfully, this rule has long been ignored, as all it did was introduce badly wanted features that had no administrative interface except registry changes or command-line utilities. Microsoft introduced a lot of new functionality in Exchange 2010 and made many changes in SP1 to improve the functionality of features such as personal archives, move requests, and retention policies.

A new version of Exchange can be a more refined release of an existing architecture as the result of a couple of additional years in development, or it can be a brand new architecture that seeks to meet different customer challenges. Exchange 2003 was a development of Exchange 2000. Exchange 2007 was a brand new architecture. Some will argue that Exchange 2010 is a refinement and expansion of the architecture laid down in Exchange 2007, but I consider that the amount of change to the Store in terms of the new schema, the requirement to move to Windows 2008, and the introduction of native high availability features within the product mark Exchange 2010 as a new architecture. This means that the deployment of Exchange 2010 requires the same degree of attention and planning as the move from Exchange 2003 to Exchange 2007 (or even from Exchange 5.5 to Exchange 2000).

Exchange 2010 Service Pack 1

It's fair to say that the first release of Exchange 2010 was feature-rich, but had some rough edges that required further work to bring it up to the standard required to convince large enterprises that the software was ready to deploy. As we will see throughout the remainder of this book, Exchange 2010 introduced fundamental change in areas such as authorization and control (role-based access control), compliance (personal archives, retention tags and policies, and discovery searches), high availability (DAGs), and a brand new management application (Exchange Control Panel). Unsurprisingly, although these features worked, the engineers could do far more to round out the product once they were given more time to refine and smooth the functionality, which is exactly what happened in Exchange 2010 SP1.

Table 2-5 lists the most important areas of improvement in Exchange 2010 SP1, together with the chapter in which the improvements are discussed in some detail.

Table 2-5 **Areas of improvement in Exchange 2010 SP1**

Improvement in Exchange 2010 SP1	Chapter
Installation of required Windows features by Setup (Windows 2008 R2 servers only)	1
More comprehensive user interface provided in ECP to manage RBAC roles, role groups, and assignments	4
Increased range of management options available in ECP	5
Store driver fault isolation	7
New mailbox repair requests	7
Granular transaction replication for DAGs	8
New scripts to help manage DAGs	8
Upgrades to the Public Folder management console	9
Outlook Web App user interface improvements and new features	12
Mailbox import and export requests	14
Hierarchical address book	14
Flexibility to place personal archive in a different database than the primary mailbox	17
User interface in EMC to define retention tags and policies	17
Discovery searches initial scans and deduplication of results	17

Version numbers

Exchange's build numbers tell you the exact version of the software. The format used is:

<product version>.<service pack number>.<major build number>.<minor build number>

A version number such as 14.00.0639.021 means:

- Product version 14: Exchange 2010 is a component of the "Office 14" wave of products. Exchange 2007 was version 12 and there is no version 13.

- Service pack 00: No service packs have been applied, so you know that this is the original version of the product.

- Major build 639: Microsoft builds new versions of the product on an almost daily basis and the build number increments sequentially, so this is build 639, the build used for the RTM version of Exchange 2010.

- Minor build 021: Twenty-one minor updates have been applied to major build 639. The number of minor updates is accounted by the way that Microsoft tweaked the last major build of Exchange 2010 with a series of minor fixes as they drove to complete the product.

You can find the version information in the "Help About Exchange Server 2010" option of the EMC. Another way is to open the Server Configuration node of EMC where you can see the version number of every server in the organization. This is broadly equivalent to executing the following EMS command:

```
Get-ExchangeServer | Select Name, ServerRole, AdminDisplayVersion
```

For administrative purposes, you might want to capture the software edition that's installed on each server and output this information to a comma-separated-value (CSV)-formatted file that you can later analyze with Microsoft Excel, Microsoft Access, or another program that is capable of reading CSV data:

```
Get-ExchangeServer | Select Name, Edition, AdminDisplayVersion, ServerRole | Export-
CSV C:\TEMP\Servers.CSV
```

The data exported should look similar to this:

```
#TYPE Selected.Microsoft.Exchange.Data.Directory.Management.ExchangeServer

"Name","Edition","AdminDisplayVersion","ServerRole"

"EXCH-SVR1","Enterprise","Version 14.0 (Build 639.21)","Mailbox, ClientAccess,
HubTransport"

"EXCH-DUBLIN","Enterprise","Version 14.0 (Build 639.21)","Mailbox, ClientAccess,
HubTransport"
```

Version 639.21 is the RTM release of Exchange 2010. The development team released this version to manufacturing on October 8, 2009. The first production customer deployments were already in progress before this time as part of Microsoft's Technology Adoption Program. General deployments in the wider customer base started in November 2009. Exchange 2010 SP1 is version 218.15 and was released to manufacturing on Build 218.15 and August 23, 2010.

Exchange also writes information about version numbers into the system registry as shown in the following example. You can retrieve this information with some Windows PowerShell code (see Figure 2-10 Installation information in the system registry) to identify the major and minor builds that are installed on a server. In this instance, MsiBuildMajor is 639 and MsiBuildMinor is 21, so this server runs version 639.21 or the RTM release of Exchange 2010. The following example shows Windows PowerShell code you can use to fetch the Exchange version information from the system registry.

```
$RegExSetup = 'Software\\Microsoft\\ExchangeServer\\v14\\Setup'
$Server = (Get-Content env:ComputerName)
$Registry = [Microsoft.Win32.RegistryKey]::OpenRemoteBaseKey('LocalMachine', $Server)

$RegKey = $Registry.OpenSubKey($RegExSetup)
$V1 = "MsiBuildMajor"
$V2 = "MsiBuildMinor"
```

```
$BuildMajor = ($RegKey.GetValue($V1)) -as [String]
$BuildMinor = ($RegKey.GetValue($V2)) -as [String]
$ExVersion = $BuildMajor + ";" + $BuildMinor
Write-Host $Server "runs version" $ExVersion
```

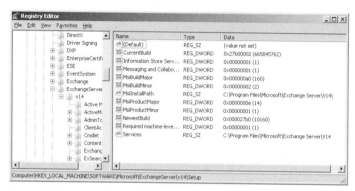

Figure 2-10 Installation information in the system registry.

Exchange also stores information in the system registry about roll-up updates that are installed on a server. These data are held in a series of entries (one for each update) at HKLM\Software\Microsoft\Windows\CurrentVersion\Installer\UserData\S-1-5-18\Products \AE1D439464EB1B8488741FFA028E291C\Patches. The subkeys that provide information about each roll-up update are called DisplayName (the name of the patch) and InstallDate (the date it was installed on a server).

Object versions

Every object belonging to Exchange is also assigned a version number, which is used to determine the minimum version of the management tools that can manage the object. For example, if you use the Get-Mailbox cmdlet through the EMS to view the properties of a mailbox object, you should see the version reported as shown here:

```
Get-Mailbox -identity "Redmond, Tony" | Select ExchangeVersion
```

```
ExchangeVersion
0.10 (14.0.100.0)
```

We can see that version 14 is listed, so we know that this object should be managed through Exchange 2010 management tools. We can also see that the minor version is 100 and we know that the minor build number for the RTM release is 639, so any build of Exchange 2010 can manage mailbox objects. Mailboxes certainly exist in previous versions of Exchange, and the fact that the version number specifies that Exchange 2010 must be used indicates that mailbox objects have been upgraded for Exchange 2010. We know this is true because new attributes have been added to mailbox objects for features such as archive mailboxes. If you look at the version numbers for other objects that are introduced in Exchange 2010, like management roles, you'll see even higher version numbers such as 14.0.451.0. However, because the minor build number (451) is under the RTM build number, these objects can be managed by any release of Exchange 2010. By comparison, if we look at a send connector and do the same thing, we see a different version number:

```
Get-SendConnector | Select ExchangeVersion
```

```
ExchangeVersion
(8.0.535.0)
```

In this context, version 8 indicates Exchange 2007 (this is despite the fact that Exchange 2007 was codenamed Exchange 12 like Exchange 14 became Exchange 2010). As it happens, build 535 for Exchange 2007 was the original RTM release, so this version indicates that any management tool issued with Exchange 2007 onward can manage the object.

An excellent article on the Exchange development team blog (*http://msexchangeteam .com/archive/2010/01/08/453722.aspx*) gives guidance as to what version of objects can be managed by the different versions of EMC and EMS.

Reporting licenses

Just like Exchange 2007, EMC also reports any unlicensed servers in the organization (Figure 2-11) that it detects when it starts up and reads in the Exchange configuration data. Microsoft regards these servers as being in a trial status. In other words, you've installed Exchange to kick the tires and see what the server can do. Servers in trial status are not eligible to receive support from Microsoft.

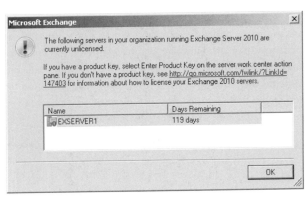

Figure 2-11 EMC reports an unlicensed Exchange server.

You can view the current licensing situation by clicking the Server Configuration node of EMC to display a list of servers in the organization. EMC uses different icons to mark licensed and unlicensed servers.

At first glance the icon's purpose is not immediately obvious, but there is one licensed and one unlicensed server in the set of servers shown in Figure 2-12. The second server is the unlicensed variety.

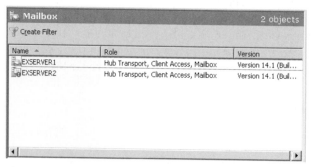

Figure 2-12 Viewing license status for servers.

To resolve this problem, select the unlicensed server, and then select the Enter Product Key option in the action pane. This invokes the wizard that accepts a valid product key and generates a product identifier for the server. The change will not be active until the next time that the Information Store service is restarted. The alternative is to use the shell with a command like this:

```
Set-ExchangeServer -Identity 'ExServer6' -ProductKey '25-Char-Product-Key-Value'
```

> **Tip**
>
> Exchange does not terminate abruptly once the warning period elapses. All of its func-
> tionality continues as before, and you can even upgrade a server that has exceeded its
> trial period to Exchange 2010 SP1. However, you have entered the twilight zone where
> you might be guilty of running unlicensed software, and Exchange will continue to
> nag you until you enter the required license. This is not a great situation to be in as it
> exposes your company to large fines in most jurisdictions, so it's best not to go there
> unless the servers are used in labs or for other test purposes.

Security groups and accounts created by Exchange

As discussed in Chapter 1, Exchange depends on Active Directory and fully exploits the extendable schema to add a set of objects and properties that enable the Exchange components to work. Alongside the schema changes, the Exchange installation procedure creates a number of security groups and mail-enabled accounts that Exchange uses for different purposes. Table 2-6 lists the security groups that Exchange creates in Active Directory and their purposes. Most are universal security groups (USGs), which are created in a new organizational unit (OU) called Microsoft Exchange Security Groups in the root domain of the forest. As indicated in Table 2-6, many are used to hold the security principals required to enable users to perform the tasks assigned to role groups defined in Exchange's new role-based access control mechanism (see Chapter 5, "Exchange Management Console and Control Panel").

Table 2-6 Exchange USGs created in Active Direct

Group	Purpose	RBAC
Delegated Setup	Administrative role group for accounts who complete the setup for an Exchange server after it has been provisioned by an organization administrator.	Yes
Discovery Management	Administrative role group for accounts who perform discovery searches and retrieval of discovered information from user accounts.	Yes
Exchange All Hosted Organizations	Global group. This group holds mailboxes hosted on off-premise servers and is used to apply password setting objects on those mailboxes.	
Exchange Servers	Every Exchange 2007 and Exchange 2010 server in the organization is a member of this group and is used to allow the servers to mutually authenticate against each other.	
Exchange Trusted Subsystem	A highly privileged group that has read-write access to every object in the Exchange organization. Unless the Active Directory split permissions model is used, this group is a member of the Administrators local group and the Exchange Windows Permissions group and can create and update Active Directory objects. Exchange system components such as the System Attendant and Information Store processes use the access granted through this group to perform tasks. Removal of this group from other groups or access control lists (ACLs) will invariably cause Exchange to malfunction. If you deploy Exchange 2007 SP2, you'll find that the Exchange Trusted Subsystem group is created in the Microsoft Exchange Security Groups OU to support interoperability between Exchange 2007 and Exchange 2010.	
Exchange Windows Permissions	A privileged group used by Exchange to manipulate Windows permissions and Active Directory objects.	
Exchange LegacyInterOp	A group used by Exchange to perform privileged operations with legacy servers in the same organization.	
Hygiene Management	Administrative role group to manage tasks to cleanse the email stream such as anti-spam and antivirus.	Yes

Group	Purpose	RBAC
Organization Management	Administrative role group for accounts that have permission to manage objects at an organization level such as create new connectors or transport rules. Members have full control over any object in the Microsoft Exchange container in Active Directory. The account used to install the first Exchange server in an organization automatically belongs to this group.	Yes
Public Folder Management	Administrative role group for accounts that have permission to manage (add, modify, delete) public folders and their settings (quotas, expiration periods, and so on). However, although these accounts can mail-enable a public folder, they cannot change mail-enabled attributes for a folder (such as an email address), as this requires recipient management status.	Yes
Recipient Management	Administrative role group for accounts that have permission to manage mailboxes, distribution groups, and other recipient types.	Yes
Records Management	Administrative role group for accounts that need to perform records management tasks such as the definition of a managed folder mailbox policy.	Yes
Server Management	Administrative role group for accounts that need to perform server-specific management tasks such as monitoring messaging queues, configuring virtual directories, and so on.	Yes
UM Management	Administrative role group for accounts that can manage Unified Messaging.	Yes
View-Only Organization Management	Administrative role group for accounts that have permission to view details of the Exchange configuration.	Yes

In addition to the groups listed in Table 2-6, a group called Exchange Install Domain Servers is created in each domain that supports an Exchange server. This group is created during the installation of the first Exchange server in a domain and is added to the membership of the Exchange Servers USG in the Microsoft Exchange Security Groups OU. It is used by the setup program to ensure that it can complete even if Active Directory replication has not yet populated details of the USG in the local domain. Clearly it is best to wait for replication to finish before you attempt to install a server.

As shown in Figure 2-13, Exchange creates a small number of mail-enabled accounts in the default Users OU of the root domain in the Active Directory forest. Microsoft could have created these accounts in a special OU but preferred to exploit the fact that you can usually guarantee that the Users OU is always available unless it has been removed for some reason by an administrator, so using this eliminated the need to create an additional OU. If you want, you can move these accounts to another OU. The accounts are named in such a way that it's obvious that they are intended for system rather than human use:

- *SystemMailbox{e0dc1c29-89c3-4034-b678-e6c29d823ed9}*: Used to hold metadata about discovery searches. The display name for this account is Microsoft Exchange. This mailbox is also used to hold administrator audit log reports from Exchange 2010

SP1 onward. See Chapter 15, "Compliance," for more information on how to configure the auditing of administrator actions.

- *SystemMailbox{1f05a927-xxxx-xxxx-xxxx-xxxxxxxxxxxx}*, where x is a randomly assigned number: Used for message moderation, to store details of move requests that are currently in progress, and for testing mail flow and Messaging Application Programming Interface (MAPI) connectivity. The display name for this account is Microsoft Exchange Approval Assistant.

- *FederatedEmail.4c1f4d8b-8179-4148-93bf-00a95fa1e042*: Used for federation operations between different Exchange organizations and for Rights Management operations. This account also has a display name of Microsoft Exchange Approval Assistant.

- *DiscoverySearchMailbox{D919BA05-46A6-415f-80AD-7E09334BB852}*: Used for storing the results of discovery searches so that these items can be retrieved by administrators. Exchange creates the default discovery mailbox in with the name just shown. The mailbox is created in the mailbox database of the first Exchange 2010 server in the organization. You can create other discovery mailboxes to use with searches. For example, in a large distributed organization, you might have separate discovery mailboxes for every country or region.

CAUTION

Apart from accessing the discovery mailbox to access the results of discovery searches (see Chapter 15) you should not attempt to log onto these accounts or use the mailboxes for anything other than management purposes. If you need to remove a server or database that hosts any of these mailboxes, you should move the mailboxes to another database first.

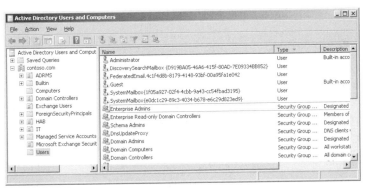

Figure 2-13 Mail-enabled Active Directory accounts created by Exchange 2010.

Two scenarios and the Exchange Trusted Subsystem USG

The Exchange Trusted Subsystem USG is interesting from many perspectives. It is a highly permissioned USG that allows Exchange services read and write access to any object owned by Exchange. Normally you won't need to touch the Exchange Trusted Subsystem group, but there are two known circumstances when you might need to add it explicitly to an object. The first is when you configure the file share witness for a DAG to be on a server that does not have Exchange 2010 installed on it. In this scenario, you need to add the Exchange Trusted Subsystem group to the local Administrators group on the server that holds the file share witness to enable that server to participate within the DAG. See Chapter 11, "Client Access Server," for more information on this topic.

The second situation is where you want to manage Exchange 2007 servers using an Exchange 2010 management console or EMS. Exchange 2007 servers have no knowledge of the Exchange Trusted Subsystem so a management operation attempted from Exchange 2010 will probably result in an "access denied" error. The solution is once again to add Exchange Trusted Subsystem to the local Administrators group on the Exchange 2007 server.

Contemplating management

Now that we've installed Exchange 2010 after making sure that our Active Directory was ready to support its deployment, we are ready to contemplate the challenge of understanding the management of Exchange. Both Exchange 2007 and Exchange 2010 are built on the foundation of Windows PowerShell, so that's the next logical step in our odyssey.

# CHAPTER 3

The Exchange Management Shell

M ICROSOFT Windows PowerShell is an extensible automation engine consisting of a command-line shell and a scripting language. Originally code-named Monad, Windows PowerShell 1.0 debuted in 2006. Microsoft Exchange Server 2007 was the first major Microsoft application to support Windows PowerShell in a comprehensive manner. Although not every administrator welcomed the opportunity to learn a new scripting language, the overall impact was extremely positive, as evident by the many code snippets for Exchange administration that are distributed on the Internet. The role of Windows PowerShell continues to expand across Microsoft products, and it now extends itself into Microsoft's newest offerings, including the deployment and management of applications on the Azure cloud computing platform.

Windows PowerShell is built on top of the Microsoft .NET Framework and is implemented in the form of cmdlets, specialized .NET classes that contain the code to implement a particular operation, such as the creation of a new mailbox or the enumeration of the processes that are currently active on a server. Applications implement Windows PowerShell support by providing sets of application-specific cmdlets that collectively represent the functionality required to fully support the application, or they can be used to access different data stores such as the file system or system registry. Cmdlets can be run separately or combined together by piping the output generated by one cmdlet to become the input of the next. Cmdlets can also be combined into scripts (with a .ps1 file extension) to provide more comprehensive processing and logic or included in executables when the need exists to launch a stand-alone application. Many scripts are available on different Internet sites to assist with Exchange management.

How Exchange leverages Windows PowerShell

From an Exchange perspective, Windows PowerShell provides a way to perform tasks quickly and simply in a variety of manners, from one-off interventions that process one or more Exchange objects to complex scripts that perform tasks such as mailbox provisioning. Most administrators cut their teeth with PowerShell by using the Exchange Management Shell (EMS) to do simple things, like using Get-Mailbox to report on a mailbox's properties and Set-Mailbox or Set-CASMailbox to set a property, before moving on to the more esoteric commands to manipulate connectors, control ActiveSync, update Active Directory with user safe lists, and so on. The saying is that almost anything is possible with Windows PowerShell, and this is certainly true when you dedicate enough energy and time to mastering the language, not to mention the time necessary to scan the Internet for useful examples of scripts that can be adapted to meet your needs.

Prior to Exchange Server 2007, business logic was scattered in components throughout the product. The management console did things—even simple things like setting a property on a server—using different code and logic than in the setup program, and the application programming interfaces (APIs) included in the product usually provided a third way to approach a problem. The result was a total lack of consistency, duplication of code, and a tremendous opportunity to create bugs in multiple places. In addition, there was no way for administrators to automate common tasks to meet the needs of their organization; essentially, if an Exchange engineer didn't code something into the product, it couldn't be done.

Figure 3-1 illustrates the central role that Windows PowerShell now plays in the Exchange architecture and how it provides a central place to encapsulate business logic that underpins the Exchange setup program, the Exchange Management Console (EMC), the Exchange Control Panel (ECP), and the EMS.

Exchange's use of Windows PowerShell to implement functionality presented by the graphical user interface (GUI) of EMC and the setup program is probably the most extensive of any Microsoft application. As explored throughout this book, the options presented by EMC to work with mailboxes, connectors, servers, and other objects invariably result in a call to one or more PowerShell cmdlets that actually do the work. It's also worth emphasizing that the functionality presented to administrators, specialist users (those who perform a subset of administrative tasks such as maintaining user details), and normal users is all based on PowerShell.

The exact scope and range of the functionality presented to any individual user is determined by the permissions granted to them through role-based access control (RBAC). RBAC is a huge shift in the way that Exchange manages and grants permissions to users that is designed to function across a range of different environments, from a single-server organization to an organization composed of a mixture of on-premise and hosted servers. The need to accommodate such a wide range of environments is also the reason

Microsoft has moved from local PowerShell (where all commands are executed on a local server) to remote PowerShell (where commands are redirected through Microsoft Internet Information Services [IIS] for execution on a target server). We'll get to the details of just how remote PowerShell and RBAC work together in the Exchange Server 2010 version of EMS shortly.

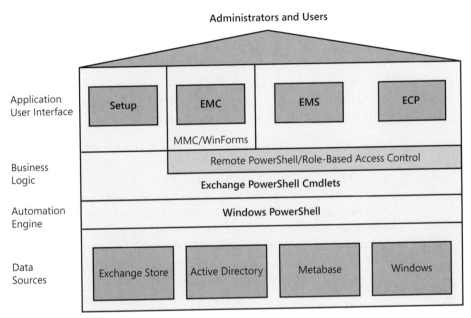

Figure 3-1 Windows PowerShell at the heart of Exchange.

Simplifying the implementation of new functionality

The critical point is that the four major administrative interfaces in Exchange all lead to the same place and execute the same business logic. Apart from removing redundant and overlapping code, having a single place to implement business logic allows the Exchange engineers to concentrate on implementing new functionality rather than reimplementing features specifically for use by EMC, EMS, or the setup program. This approach allows Exchange to deliver a more consistent administrative environment and a comprehensive method to automate tasks to deal with mailboxes, databases, connectors, and all the other components that collectively make up an Exchange organization.

The RTM release of Exchange 2010 includes 584 cmdlets that are added by EMS to join the standard set of Windows PowerShell cmdlets, including cmdlets to work with the system registry, the file system, variables (including environmental variables), and so on. The number of cmdlets grows again to 619 in Exchange 2010 SP1. For example, the Export-Mailbox and Import-Mailbox cmdlets that are used to export and import mailbox data from Outlook personal storage (PST) files are replaced by the New-MailboxExportRequest and New-MailboxImportRequest cmdlets and other associated cmdlets used to control the requests.

For more information about these cmdlets, refer to Chapter 12, "Mailbox Support Services."

Collectively, the set of EMS cmdlets manages objects and the properties of those objects that form Exchange. Objects include mailboxes, servers, transport rules, connectors, and so on. You can determine the exact number of cmdlets owned by Exchange with the following command:

```
Get-ExCommand | Measure-Object | Select Count
```

INSIDE OUT   Finding the cmdlets available to you

Of course, as you will learn when we discuss RBAC in Chapter 4, "Role-Based Access Control," an EMS session in Exchange 2010 only allows you access to the cmdlets and parameters that are defined in the roles included in the role groups of which your account is a member. Accounts that are highly permissioned, such as those belonging to the Organization Management role group, can use many more cmdlets than those that belong to a lesser permissioned role group, such as Help Desk or Recipient Management. You can use this command to generate a full list of all of the Exchange 2010 cmdlets that your account can access:

```
Get-ExCommand > C:\Temp\ExCommands.txt
```

By comparison, Exchange 2007 includes 394 cmdlets, 26 of which are removed in Exchange 2010 (largely because of the demise of storage groups). The 216 new cmdlets provided in Exchange 2010 reflect the new functionality in the product, such as the introduction of the RBAC model, mailbox archives, and the Database Availability Group (DAG), along with the expansion of existing functionality such as messaging records management.

Windows PowerShell has been at the heart of Exchange since Exchange 2007, and its use and syntax are fundamental skills for administrators to master. In fact, many of the more hardcore Exchange administrators prefer EMS to EMC because of the additional flexibility that EMS provides. This chapter lays out the basics of Windows PowerShell and sets the stage for the examples of Windows PowerShell found in other chapters. To begin, let's review the biggest change that Microsoft has made to EMS in Exchange 2010: the transition from a purely local implementation to remote PowerShell and its associated technology.

Once we understand how to connect to EMS, we'll go on to review how to use cmdlets to get work done.

Remote PowerShell

Exchange Server 2007 was the first major Microsoft server product to embrace Windows PowerShell extensively. Windows PowerShell has a relatively short history, and its 1.0 release exhibited some of the flaws that you'd expect. Inconsistencies in syntax are easily overcome, but the lack of remote capability was more serious because it required the installation of Windows PowerShell and its snap-in (set of cmdlets) for Exchange on any workstation or server from which you wanted to perform management tasks. In reality, this shortcoming is often overlooked because Exchange administrators are accustomed to having to install software before they can operate. Installing software is an acceptable requirement in environments where all the servers are under your control and within your own network, but it causes problems when you want to manage servers remotely. The Microsoft introduction of online services where companies will be able to run their Exchange environments inside large Microsoft datacenters means that remote management has taken on new importance. Exchange 2010 includes many new features designed to ease the transition to online services, and remote PowerShell provides the fundamental building block for management. The combination of remote PowerShell with RBAC allows administrators to manage objects residing on a server in a remote datacenter as easily as you can manage objects on a local server.

> **Note**
>
> You can think of Windows PowerShell as implemented in Exchange Server 2007 as "local PowerShell" because cmdlets are executed in a local process. The only element of remote access in Exchange 2007 is if you pass the *–Server* parameter to identify a server against which to execute a command. Even so, if data are needed from a remote server, such as fetching a set of mailbox objects, they are retrieved across the network and processed locally.

Exchange 2010 extends the concept of remote management to support the remote execution of commands in a secure manner using HTTPS and a Kerberos-based encryption mechanism that is easily manageable through firewalls (assuming that port 80 is open). Remote PowerShell is used for all EMS sessions in Exchange 2010. Even if you are logged on to an Exchange server and want to use EMS to change a property of that server, EMS still creates a remote session to the local server to do the work. The same applies for EMC, because Exchange creates a remote session when you log on to connect to a server in the local Active Directory site to retrieve information about the organization and then display it in the console. In effect, remote PowerShell replaces local PowerShell in Exchange 2010 for all server roles except Edge servers. The sole exception is for commands used during setup, which continue to execute locally. The removal of local PowerShell and the concentration on the combination of remote PowerShell and RBAC as the basis for administrative control over Exchange components is a major change in the product.

The implementation of remote PowerShell for Exchange 2010 separates business logic into code that runs on the client and code that runs on the Exchange server. It is based on common Windows components such as Windows PowerShell 2.0 and the WS Management model (WS-Man and Windows Remote Management, WinRM). The discussion at *http:// blogs.msdn.com/powershell/archive/2009/01/06/manage-winrm-settings-with-wsman -provider.aspx* provides useful background about how Windows PowerShell remoting is built on top of WinRM. Collectively, the Windows components combine to provide an effective ability to perform Exchange management operations remotely.

The logic for replacing local PowerShell with the remote model is simple. Just like the change in Exchange 2007 to force all messages to flow through the transport system so that a single common place existed to apply features such as transport rules, remote PowerShell forces Exchange administration to flow through RBAC so that a PowerShell session will only ever include the cmdlets necessary to do the job. The logic for keeping local PowerShell on Edge servers is simple, too. These servers are isolated from the rest of the organization so they do not have access to the RBAC roles. Anyone who logs onto an Edge server as an administrator operates in a management context of just that server and has complete control over that server. However, he cannot affect any other server or object in the Exchange organization.

The need to support hosting platforms such as Microsoft Business Productivity Online Services (BPOS) was a major influence on Exchange's move to remote PowerShell. Providing a secure and controllable mechanism that permits administrators to execute privileged commands to control the subset of objects that they own inside an infrastructure that is controlled and managed by someone else is always a difficult task, especially when all the data have to pass across the Internet. Exchange 2007 controls access to its management cmdlets through access control lists (ACLs) that are linked to Active Directory accounts. If the ACLs on your account mark you as an Exchange administrator, you can use Windows PowerShell to manage Exchange; if not, you can't. However, in an online services environment where many different companies share the same multitenant server and storage infrastructure, it is highly unlikely that you will share the same Active Directory. Trust relationships and directory synchronization provide answers that have been used in hosting environments, but these solutions often require a good deal of effort to set up and maintain. Microsoft takes a new approach to the management of permissions in Exchange 2010 with the introduction of RBAC. The concept is not new and has been used in previous authentication or identity management systems on UNIX and other platforms. What's different here is its application to provide Exchange with a method to extend RBAC so that roles apply remotely.

> **CAUTION!**
>
> Until Microsoft removes the functionality, it is possible to use local PowerShell with the Exchange 2010 snap-in to perform management operations on a server. However, Microsoft is not testing local PowerShell with Exchange anymore, and it is entirely possible that problems will appear in local PowerShell that will never be resolved. Given the engineering and strategic focus on remote PowerShell, it makes sense for everyone to make the transition now and embrace this platform as the future of command-line Exchange management.

Flowing remotely

To understand how remote PowerShell and RBAC work together, let's examine how an administrator might create a new mailbox on a remote server. In this example, the administrator works on a help desk and has been assigned a role that allows her to create new mailboxes and update the properties of existing mailboxes. We also assume that the user's account is enabled to use remote PowerShell. In many cases, people in specialist roles such as help desk personnel will use the EMC or the ECP to perform tasks, but an experienced Exchange administrator might prefer to use a command-line interface because of its power and flexibility when compared to either EMC or ECP.

Figure 3-2 lays out the various components used by remote PowerShell from the local PowerShell host on a workstation or server across the network to IIS and the PowerShell application running there. The other components are the PowerShell engine and the complete set of cmdlets available to Exchange 2010, the Exchange authorization library that handles the interpretation of roles in terms of the cmdlets that each RBAC role can use, and the Active Directory driver used to read data from Active Directory. For the purpose of this discussion we'll assume that the account used has been assigned a role such as Recipient Management and is enabled for remote PowerShell. If you are unsure about the account's status, you can enable it to use remote PowerShell as follows:

```
Set-User -IdentityAccountName -RemotePowerShellEnabled $True
```

All PowerShell sessions flow through IIS because even a local connection goes through *localhost*. All Exchange 2010 servers support IIS and the PowerShell virtual directory, or vdir, and all are members of the Exchange Trusted Subsystem security group and therefore can manipulate any object in the organization.

Chapter 3

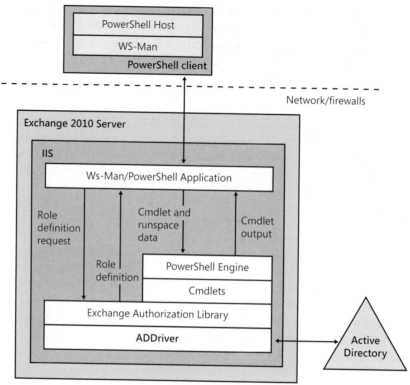

Figure 3-2 Remote PowerShell architecture.

If you run EMS on a workstation or server that has the Exchange management components installed, EMS creates a remote session automatically as part of its initialization process. If you run PowerShell on a workstation that doesn't have the Exchange management components installed, you will have to specify the name of the server with which you want to work. This is done with the New-PSSession cmdlet, passing the name of the server to which to connect in the form *https://fqdn/PowerShell/*. This cmdlet creates a secure authenticated connection to IIS running on the target server and begins a session there by checking the role held by the account that initiates the connection.

How the initialization script finds a server

When a user creates a remote PowerShell session on an Exchange server, the initialization script attempts to connect him to the same server. If the attempt to establish a connection with the local server fails for some reason (later we discuss some of the issues that might interfere with a connection), the initialization script then enumerates the full set of Exchange servers in the local site and attempts to make a connection to one of the servers chosen at random. If this attempt fails, the script moves on to the next server and continues until a successful connection is established or all available servers have been attempted and have failed. The initialization script works in the same way when executed on a workstation that has the Exchange management components installed on it, except that the initialization begins by randomly selecting one of the servers from the site.

IIS uses the RBAC mechanism to check the user's role and associated permissions via the Exchange Authorization Library (a new component in Exchange 2010). The Exchange Authorization Library (or ADDriver) connects to Active Directory to use it as the definitive source of information about accounts and supplements these data with its knowledge about the Exchange-specific roles that administrators have assigned to users. During a PowerShell session, ADDriver connects to a domain controller in the local site to fetch data from Active Directory and keeps this connection throughout the session (something referred to as DC affinity). This is different from the behavior that exists in Exchange 2007 because all PowerShell sessions on a server run in the same process, so you cannot have a static setting because it might be inappropriate for some sessions. In Exchange 2007, each PowerShell session functions in its own process and you have complete control over the Active Directory settings. Many PowerShell cmdlets support the –*DomainController* parameter to allow you to connect to a specific domain controller (specifying the fully qualified domain name [FQDN]) should the need arise.

Things are a little more complicated in a hosted environment where you are connected to your local network but need to work with Exchange data in a forest maintained by the hosting provider. In this instance, a directory synchronization process occurs to synchronize the basic account information from the local Active Directory forest and the data held in the Active Directory forest managed by the hosting provider.

A role group defines the set of administrative actions that a user is allowed to perform inside Exchange and can be resolved into a set of PowerShell cmdlets that the user is allowed to use within her PowerShell session. Because our user works with mailboxes as defined by the Recipient Management role group, the set of cmdlets that she can use includes commands with easily identified purposes such as New-Mailbox, Set-Mailbox, Get-Mailbox, and so on. Unlike the situation with Exchange 2007, where the complete set of cmdlets is available after you load the Exchange snap-in to a PowerShell session, RBAC ensures that the user can execute only the cmdlets required to perform her role. If you are an Exchange administrator who holds the Organization Management role, you'll have access to almost the full set of cmdlets (to gain access to the full set, you have to grant your account access to some minor roles). However, if your account has been assigned only the roles necessary to be able to work with recipients, you'll see just the cmdlets covered by the roles assigned to you.

Chapter 3

> **Tip**
>
> Permissions granted through RBAC are evaluated during session initialization. If you are assigned a new role, you have to create a new session with EMS, EMC, or ECP before you can access the cmdlets made available through the newly assigned role.

Users are not normally aware that they are restricted in terms of available cmdlets unless they attempt to use one to which they do not have access. The point is that they shouldn't care that they can't use hundreds of cmdlets, many of which do obscure things like setting properties on messaging connectors or one-off operations such as creating a new DAG. Instead, RBAC makes sure that users can only access the cmdlets that they need to get their job done.

Connecting to remote PowerShell

When you run EMS on a server that has the Exchange 2010 management components installed, the EMS initialization script creates an environment that is roughly equivalent to an Exchange 2007 EMS session. The code in the RemoteExchange.ps1 script attempts to create a remote session with the local host. If successful, it then proceeds to identify your account to Exchange and uses RBAC to determine the cmdlet set that you are allowed to use, and so on.

There's no obvious evidence given to a user that his role has forced RBAC to restrict the cmdlet set or parameters that he can use with cmdlets, because the initialization of a session progresses just like it would for a fully privileged user. However, once you start to execute cmdlets, you quickly realize that you can't do as much as you'd like to. For instance, if you log on with a restricted user account and attempt to use the Get-Mailbox cmdlet to fetch a list of mailboxes, all you'll see is your own mailbox. This is logical because your role allows you to see details of your own mailbox but not others. In the same way, if you then attempt to use the Set-Mailbox cmdlet to update a property that only administrators can access, you won't be able to even use tab completion (we discuss this in a little while) to reveal a restricted property. On the other hand, you will be able to use the Set-Mailbox cmdlet to update properties that are generally exposed for user update through ECP, so (assuming *JSmith* is the alias for your mailbox) you'll be able to do things like this:

```
Set-Mailbox -Identity JSmith -MailTip 'Hello World'
```

or this:

```
Set-Mailbox -Identity JSmith -Languages 'EN-US', 'EN-IE'
```

INSIDE OUT   You can do some things; you can't do others

Somewhat strangely, you'll also be able to execute Get-MailboxStatistics to report the number of items in your mailbox but not Get-MailboxFolderStatistics to report the folders and the items that each contains. All of this is controlled by RBAC, the roles that your account holds, and the scope for the roles in terms of the cmdlets and parameters defined in the role. From this discussion, you should now understand how critical RBAC is to remote PowerShell and by extension to every aspect of the Exchange 2010 management toolset.

If EMS can't connect to the local host, it attempts to connect to a server in the local Active Directory site. If no server in the local site responds, EMS attempts to connect to an Exchange server in a remote Active Directory site selected at random. The problem here is that EMS could select an Exchange server in the worst possible site at the end of an extended network connection. However, if you're in this situation, you have other problems to solve. It is not a sign of good Exchange server health if a server in the local site doesn't respond to a connection request from EMS.

The Exchange help file contains details of some of the errors that can occur during initialization of a remote PowerShell session, including the following:

- Attempting to connect without using Secure Sockets Layer (SSL; http rather than https).

- Specifying an incorrect virtual directory name (see the section "A more complex environment to manage" later in this chapter).

- Attempting to connect to an Exchange server that doesn't exist (or is offline).

- Various network errors.

- Trying to connect with an account that is not enabled for remote PowerShell (the administrator account is automatically enabled, but you might have to enable other accounts specifically with the Set-User cmdlet). This information is stored in the *protocolsetting* attribute of the user's account. For example, this command enables Windows PowerShell for the account Redmond:

```
Set-User -Identity Redmond-RemotePowerShellEnabled $True
```

- The Windows PowerShell initialization script can't be executed because of the server's execution policy.

Assuming all is well, you should be able to proceed. When connected, you should then be able to work in much the same manner as when you connect to Windows PowerShell remotely with EMS in Exchange Server 2007, subject to the limitation that the role group to which you belong might restrict the set of available cmdlets. The time required to set up a new session is longer than in Exchange 2007 because of the way that the session is set up, but once EMS is fully initialized it should be very familiar to anyone who has worked with EMS in Exchange 2007. To get some idea of how much work is done to create a new EMS session, use a text editor to review the code in the RemoteExchange.ps1 and ConnectFunctions.ps1 scripts in the Exchange binaries folder.

Be careful where you execute

One interesting aspect of connecting to a server to instantiate a Remote PowerShell session is that sometimes you end up executing commands on a server that you don't expect. For example, if you start EMS on a server in a site and EMS cannot connect to the local server for some reason, you might end up being connected to another server without noticing that this has happened. The EMS initialization script puts the server name in the title bar of the window for the EMS session so the server name to which you are connected is pretty obvious. However, it's amazing how many people don't notice this small but important fact.

As explained earlier, being connected to one server rather than another isn't usually an issue when high-performance links connect the servers. However, if the command generates a log, it will be created on the server to which you're connected, which might cause you to scratch your head if you go looking for a log on the local server. For example, if you recover a mailbox from a recovery database (refer to Chapter 9, "Backups and Restores," for more information on this topic), the log file is created in the \Logging\MigrationLogs directory on the server where the command executes. It can be quite frustrating to search for a log on a local server when Exchange has quite correctly created it elsewhere! If you need to connect to a specific server, you can run the Connect-ExchangeServer cmdlet after you initialize a session.

A more complex environment to manage

There's no doubt that EMS operates within a far more complex environment in Exchange 2010 than it did in Exchange 2007. Apart from the extra cmdlets to know and master, and some changes in syntax for older cmdlets such as the addition of new parameters and the deprecation of a small number of cmdlets, the way that Microsoft has implemented remote PowerShell creates a number of dependencies that must be present before EMS functions correctly. The major dependencies are as follows:

- Active Directory

- Windows PowerShell

- IIS 7.0

- Windows Remote Management (WinRM)

- Exchange RBAC

Figure 3-3 illustrates one of the symptoms that you might see when a remote PowerShell session aborts due to one of the most common problems reported to Microsoft. Essentially, software versions must be correct; WinRM, IIS, and the authorization and other settings on several virtual directories have to be configured correctly; and all components must be able to connect together. To make the point, it's worthwhile to discuss some common issues and their underlying causes. Apart from an inability to contact a domain controller to authorize a session, there are three known causes for this symptom:

1. The KerbAuth module (used by remote PowerShell to authenticate user connections) is not registered as a native module for the PowerShell virtual directory.

2. The WSMan module (used for Windows Remote Management functions) is not registered correctly for PowerShell because its entry is missing from the Application Host configuration file.

3. The user attempting to connect is not enabled for remote PowerShell. This is rarely the cause because most administrators run EMS when they are logged onto a mail-enabled account that is also enabled for PowerShell. To check that this is the case, you can use the Get-User cmdlet to validate that the account's *RemotePowerShellEnabled* property is set to $True.

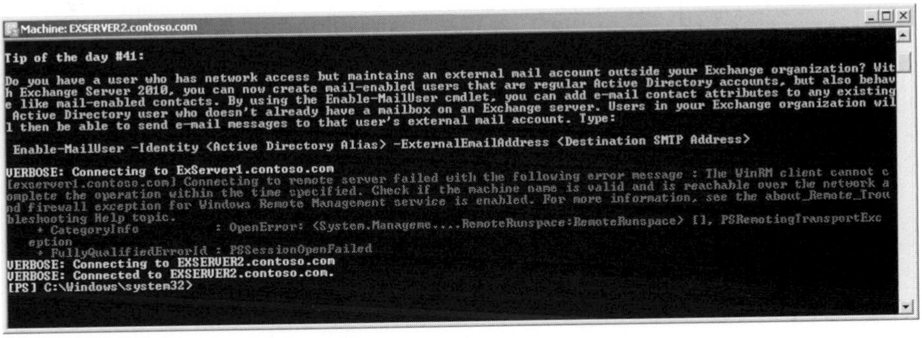

Figure 3-3 EMS fails to connect to a server.

You can check for the underlying problems in the first two cases by using the IIS Manager to view the modules registered for the PowerShell virtual directory. In Figure 3-4, we can see that the KerbAuth module is registered as a Native type enabled directly for the directory (entry type is Local). These are the correct values. The code points to the KerbAuth.DLL module in the Exchange binary directory, which is also correct.

Chapter 3

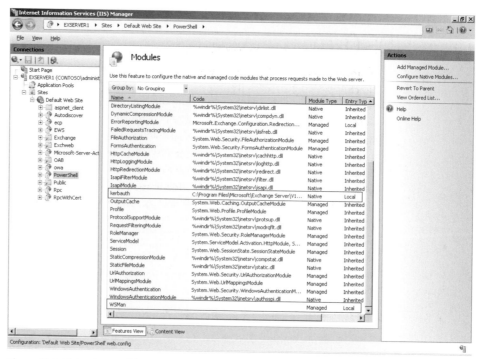

Figure 3-4 Detecting problems with IIS modules registered for PowerShell.

Often the problem lies with the WSMan module at the bottom of the list of modules. First, there's no value for "code," so IIS can't load anything. Second, the module type is set to Managed, whereas it should be Native. To fix this problem, we have to update the %Windir%\System32\Inetsrv\Config\ApplicationHost.config file and register the WSMan module in the global modules section. Open the file with a text editor and look for the section:

```
<globalModules>
```

Then add a new line in the set of global modules:

```
<add name="WSMan" image="C:\Windows\system32\wsmsvc.dll" />
```

You don't have to restart IIS to make the change effective because EMS will use the updated information about the WSMan module the next time it initializes a session.

INSIDE OUT   Accounts need to be mail-enabled

In previous versions of Exchange you didn't need a mail-enabled account (an Active Directory account that is linked to an Exchange mailbox) to run EMS or EMC as long as the account was sufficiently permissioned to access the Exchange objects. RBAC relies on mail-enabled accounts to manage its role definitions, which is why the account that you use to install the first mailbox server in an Exchange 2010 organization is automatically mail-enabled. Any attempt to use an account that is not mail-enabled or has something wrong with its mailbox (for example, it was on a server that has subsequently been removed from the organization but lingering traces remain in Active Directory) will cause RBAC to fail and you won't be able to use EMS or EMC. This issue is addressed in Exchange 2010 SP1; this version allows accounts that are not mail-enabled to use ECP to perform administrative actions. However, accounts that are not mail-enabled still cannot run EMS or EMC. Chapter 5, "Exchange Management Console and Control Panel," contains more information about how to grant ECP access to an account that is not mail-enabled.

TROUBLESHOOTING

Can't connect to the remote host because WS-Management service is not running

If you encounter a problem where EMS reports that the connection to the remote host was refused because the WS-Management service is not running, the cause could be either that the service is indeed not started or it is not configured to support remote access requests via HTTP. You can run the WinRM utility to check and update the server's configuration with the necessary settings to allow these requests. To do this, run Windows command shell (CMD) as the Administrator and then issue the WinRM QuickConfig command. If missing, this command will create the listener processes on which WinRM depends.

EMC issues the Discover-ExchangeServer command during its initialization to begin the process of connecting to a Client Access Server (CAS) server and reading information about the organization to display in the console. Figure 3-5 illustrates a common problem caused by the account being used to run EMC not having sufficient Exchange permissions to be able to execute the task. The same problem causes the error message "Starting a command on remote server failed with the following error message: access is denied" when EMS initializes and no Exchange cmdlets are available in the EMS session.

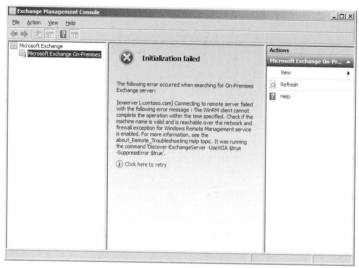

Figure 3-5 A problem with permissions causes EMC to fail.

RBAC dictates what the account with which you have logged in is able to do with Exchange. If you see an error like this, it's a good indication that something's wrong with permissions. The fix might be as simple as logging out and reusing a properly permissioned account (for example, one that holds the Organization Management role), or it could be a more sinister cause such as a build-to-build upgrade that has failed to update the default RBAC role groups properly. The solution is to rerun the part of the installation process to update the role groups, but this should only be done after you establish that this is indeed the root cause. For example, if you can't run EMC or EMS with the account that you used to perform a build-to-build upgrade following an apparent successful completion, it's a good indicator that something's gone wrong with the role groups and they need to be reapplied.

Among the less common problems reported by administrators are the following:

- The WinRM IIS extension (a server feature) is missing for some reason. The usual solution is to install the WinRM IIS feature with Server Manager and reboot the server.

- WinRM is unable to load the Exchange authorization dynamic-link library (DLL) because the environment variable pointing to the Exchange installation path (the directory where the DLL is located) is missing. The solution is to add the *ExchangeInstallPath* variable (and make sure that it points to the right place).

- The computer clock on a server is not fully synchronized with domain controllers. Among other things, the EMC initialization process validates that the server to which you connect is a member of the Exchange Servers universal security group. If the system clock on the Exchange server differs from the domain time by more than five minutes, the Kerberos ticket presented by the computer to an Active Directory domain controller will be invalid. The lack of clock synchronization will prevent any access to Active Directory so the check fails because the computer won't be able to read the group membership. To avoid this problem, make sure that the clocks on all Exchange servers are synchronized with the domain.

All of this goes to prove that the interaction among Exchange 2010, IIS, WinRM, and Windows PowerShell collectively forms a complex mechanism where everything has to function properly before administrators can do their work.

Advantages of remote PowerShell

Microsoft doesn't make changes to products like Exchange without seeing some clear advantage. In this case, three potential advantages are available. First, separating client and server processing and using IIS as the mechanism to route remote traffic allows communication through a well-understood route that can flow across firewalls and so accommodate both Microsoft Online Services and enterprise customers that operate multiple Active Directory forests.

Second, creating the ability for administrators to delegate tasks to other users on the basis of well-defined roles adds to overall system security and prevents inadvertent mistakes that can affect essential data. For example, an administrator who can amend mailbox details might not be able to add new mailboxes or affect other parts of the messaging infrastructure such as deleting the subscription that connects an Exchange Edge server to the rest of the organization.

Third, remote capability means that you can perform Exchange management tasks from a workstation without installing the Exchange management tools, meaning that you should be able to manage Exchange from just about any workstation that's connected to your network. Of course, you still need to install Windows PowerShell and any prerequisite software such as the latest version of the .NET Framework, but these components are more likely to be part of a corporate build for an administrator workstation (or integrated into the base operating system) than Exchange-specific code.

Chapter 3

INSIDE OUT A disadvantage is a slower startup

One disadvantage of remote PowerShell is that it is slower to start up than local PowerShell. On a cold server (one where the IIS worker process has not been started for Windows PowerShell), it can take 20 to 30 seconds before EMS is fully initialized. You can measure the startup performance of EMS on your server by feeding its initialization script to the Measure-Command cmdlet. Achieving the fastest server in terms of EMS startup became quite a challenge in terms of gaining bragging rights for many of the participants in Microsoft's Exchange 2010 Technology Adoption Program (TAP). The fastest startup reported was 1.54 seconds.

```
Measure-Command {.'C:\Program Files\Microsoft\Exchange
Server\V14\bin\RemoteExchange.ps1'; Connect-ExchangeServer -auto}
```

The output:

```
Days              : 0
Hours             : 0
Minutes           : 0
Seconds           : 4
Milliseconds      : 553
Ticks             : 45537444
TotalDays         : 5.2705375E-05
TotalHours        : 0.001264929
TotalMinutes      : 0.07589574
TotalSeconds      : 4.5537444
TotalMilliseconds : 4553.7444
```

Another way of measuring the performance of remote PowerShell is with the Test-PowerShellConnectivity cmdlet. In this example run the New-TestCASConnectivity.ps1script from the \Scripts directory (see Figure 3-6) to create a synthetic test account to be used for the connection and then execute the test cmdlet. The script creates the test user account in the Users organizational unit (OU) of Active Directory. If you have multiple OUs beginning with "Users," the script will fail to create the mailbox. You can fix the problem by editing the script and updating the variable that holds the OU name.

```
.\New-TestCASConnectivityUser.ps1
Test-PowerShellConnectivity -ClientAccessServer ExServer1 -VirtualDirectoryName
'PowerShell (Default Web Site)' -TrustAnySSLCertificate
```

Once a server has been running for a while, starting a new EMS session is much faster because IIS is warmed up. You can measure the difference by using Measure-Command again. However, even on the fastest server with a fully warmed IIS, remote PowerShell will never match the immediacy of a local PowerShell session simply because of the extra layers that have to be connected to make everything work.

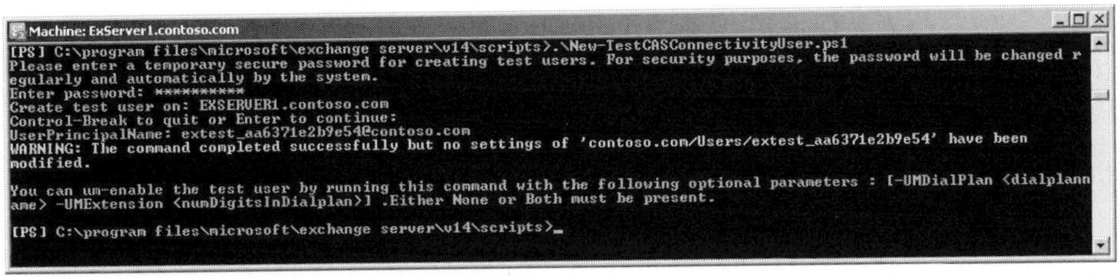

Figure 3-6 Running the New-TestCASConnectivityUser script.

INSIDE OUT   Help isn't as extensive in remote PowerShell

Another disadvantage is that remote PowerShell does not support the same kind of help that local PowerShell does. In EMS in Exchange 2007, you can use wildcards to locate help for a group of cmdlets, as in Get-Help *Exchange. This won't work in Exchange 2010 on Microsoft Windows 2008 SP2 or R2 because of some limitations in remote PowerShell, but the feature reappears when you deploy Windows 2008 R2 SP1.

With all of these caveats in mind, let's explore what happens when a new EMS session starts to understand why things might be a tad slower.

EMS basics

There are more than 600 cmdlets in the set available to Exchange 2010 SP1, but you're not likely to use the vast majority of these simply because many are designed for one-time use. For example, after you configure a receive connector, you're probably not going to revisit the Set-ReceiveConnector cmdlet very often once the connector is working. On the other hand, there are cmdlets such as Get-Mailbox that you'll use daily. Some examples (in no particular order) of frequently used Exchange cmdlets include the following:

- **Get-ExchangeServer**   Return a list of Exchange servers in the organization

- **Disable-Mailbox**   Disable a user's mailbox

- **Add-DistributionGroupMember**   Add a new member to a distribution group

- **Set-Mailbox**   Set a property of a user's mailbox

- **New-MoveRequest**   Set up a request to move a mailbox to another database

- **Get-MailboxDatabase**   Retrieve properties of a mailbox database

- **Get-MailboxStatistics**   Return statistics about user mailboxes such as the total item count, quota used, and so on

- **Get-TransportConfig**   Return properties that control how the transport service processes messages

- **Get-ExBlog**   Launches a browser to bring you to the Exchange development team's blog

Note the consistent syntax of verb (Get, Set, Move, Remove, or Disable) and noun (Mailbox, User, and so on). Along with commands that operate on objects, you find commands that help you to work with data, such as Where-Object, Sort-Object, and Group-Object. Where-Object, Sort-Object, and Group-Object are commonly shortened by using their aliases of Where, Sort, and Group. You can type **Help** followed by a cmdlet name at any time to get help on the syntax of the command. As discussed previously, unlike Exchange 2007, you cannot use wildcards with Get-Help to retrieve information about a set of similar cmdlets.

> ### Tip
> When you start to write scripts, consider spelling out cmdlet names completely and avoiding the use of aliases. This is important because you can never know in what environment a script will be run and cannot, therefore, assume that an alias will be defined and available for use in your code.

The Exchange developers have provided very accessible help for the EMS cmdlets. Apart from using the Help cmdlet, there are other ways of seeking help. In Exchange 2007, when you look for help, EMS displays help for the complete set of cmdlets available to it. In Exchange 2010, RBAC controls limit help content so that you see help only for the set of cmdlets available to the roles that a user holds.

One side effect of this change is that wildcard searches using the Get-Help cmdlet are no longer possible to look for help in the set of Exchange cmdlets. For example, you can't use a command like Get-Help *Exchange* to retrieve information about any cmdlet that includes "Exchange" in its name. This is an unfortunate reduction of functionality that

Microsoft plans to address in a future release of PowerShell. However, you can still do the following:

- Use the Get-Command cmdlet to list the cmdlets that you can use with different objects. The set of cmdlets will be limited to whatever is permitted by the RBAC roles held by your account. For example, **Get-Command *contact*** lists all of the cmdlets available to work with contacts (shown in the following example). You can also use the shortened alias of *gcm* for Get-Command. This is one way to work around the loss of functionality in the Get-Help cmdlet.

```
CommandType       Name                        Definition
-----------       ----                        ------
Function          Disable-MailContact         ...
Function          Enable-MailContact          ...
Function          Get-Contact                 ...
Function          Get-MailContact             ...
Function          New-MailContact             ...
Function          Remove-MailContact          ...
Function          Set-Contact                 ...
Function          Set-MailContact             ...
```

- Use the –Detailed switch to get more detailed help about a cmdlet. For example: Get-Help Get-CASMailbox –Detailed.

- Use the –Full switch to have EMS return every bit of information it knows about a cmdlet: Get-Help Get-DistributionGroup –Full.

- Use the –Examples switch to see whatever examples of a cmdlet in use EMS help includes: Get-Help Get-MailboxServer –Examples.

- Use the –Parameter switch to get information about a selected parameter for a cmdlet: Get-Help Get-Mailbox –Parameter Server. This switch supports wildcards, so you can do something like **Get-Help Set-Mailbox –Parameter *Quota***.

INSIDE OUT   Getting to know the cmdlets

You will probably begin by using the –Full switch to retrieve all available help for a cmdlet to get to know what each cmdlet does. After you learn more about the cmdlet, you can move on to the default view once you become more accustomed to working with EMS. Remember that the Exchange help file contains information about all the EMS cmdlets. The advantage of using the help file (which is always present on a server) is that you can use the help file's index and search for specific entries.

Chapter 3

Most of the time, you will probably work with commands by invoking EMS interactively and then typing whatever individual commands or scripts are necessary to get something done. The user interface of EMS is based on the Win32 console with the addition of features such as customizable tab completion for commands. After you become accustomed to working with EMS, things flow smoothly and it is easy to get work done. It is then usually faster to start EMS and issue the necessary code to change a property on a mailbox or a server than to start EMC and navigate to the right place to make the change through the GUI.

> **Tip**
>
> Working through EMS is especially valuable if you have to perform management operations across an extended network link when waiting for the GUI to display can be painful. If you have a programmatic mind, you can also call EMS cmdlets through C# code, which is how Microsoft invokes them in the EMC and other places throughout Exchange, such as setting up servers and databases in the setup program (the blog written by Glen Scales at *http://gsexdev.blogspot.com/* provides many good examples of how to call EMS cmdlets). In the past, the different groups that contributed to Exchange had to build their own programming interfaces, whereas now everyone uses PowerShell.

You can see that EMS focuses on performing tasks rather than taking the more object-focused approach implemented in the GUI, something that reflects a desire to accommodate administrators who think about how to do things rather than how to work with objects. After all, it is human nature to think in terms of the task of moving a mailbox to a different server rather than thinking about how to manipulate the properties of a mailbox object to reflect its new location.

Cmdlets accept structured pipelined input from each other in a common manner to allow them to process data in a consistent manner, no matter what cmdlet provides the data. Programmers therefore do not have to worry about reformatting data for input to specific cmdlets, so the task of assembling different cmdlets together into a script to do a job is much easier. Microsoft built Windows PowerShell around the concept of objects, so objects are accepted as input, and the output is in the form of objects that you can then pipe to other cmdlets. Even if the output from a cmdlet looks like plain text, what you see is one or more objects that you can manipulate in a much more powerful manner than you can ever work with text output. The implementation is really very elegant.

Command editing

It should already be obvious that you could do a lot of typing to enter commands into Windows PowerShell, make the inevitable mistakes, correct, and try again. To make life a little easier, PowerShell supports the same kind of command-line editing as CMD does. Some of the more important keys that you can use are described in Table 3-1.

Table 3-1 Command editing keystrokes for Windows PowerShell

Keyboard command	Effect
F2	Create a new command based on your last command. A pop-up screen appears to allow you to enter a character. PowerShell then creates a new command using the last entered command up to the character that you specify. For example, if the last command is Get-MailboxStatistics –Identity TRedmond and you press F2 followed by **c**, PowerShell inserts "Get-MailboxStatistic". You can then complete the command as you like.
F4	Deletes characters in the current command up to a specified position. For example, if the cursor is located at the "M" of Get-MailboxStatistics and you press F4 followed by **x**, PowerShell deletes "Mailbo" and the result is "Get-xStatistics". Although this example wouldn't result in a useful command, F4 is useful when you need to edit a lot of parameters in a complex command.
F7	Pops up a list of the last 50 commands used in the current session to allow you to select a command for reuse.
F8	Moves backward through the command history.
Tab	Requests PowerShell to attempt to complete a command based on what you've typed.
Left/Right arrows	Move the cursor left and right through the current command line.
Up/Down arrows	Move up and down through the history of previous commands.
Delete key	Deletes the character under the cursor.
Insert key	Toggles between character insert and character overwrite mode.
Backspace key	Deletes the character before the cursor.

Most of these keys are pretty basic and straightforward. The two most interesting keys are F7 and Tab. F7 pops up a list of the last 50 commands that you have run in the current session (Figure 3-7) so that you can both see what you've done in the immediate past and select one of the commands to reexecute. You can type a couple of characters into the F7 list and EMS will look for the first matching command or you can use the Up and Down arrow keys to navigate through the command history. At times it's more convenient to use Up and Down arrows because you can retrieve more commands and edit a command before executing it (F7 selects the command and executes it immediately).

Chapter 3

Figure 3-7 Using the F7 key to recall EMS commands.

INSIDE OUT   An easy way to type a command

Tab completion is a wonderful feature that Windows PowerShell inherited from CMD. Tab completion means that you can partially enter a command and then press the Tab key to have PowerShell try to fill in the rest of the cmdlet name followed by its parameters. For example, type:

```
Get-Dist
```

This isn't the name of a valid cmdlet, but it is the root of several cmdlets, so when you press Tab, PowerShell completes the first valid cmdlet that matches and inserts:

```
Get-DistributionGroup
```

If you press Tab again, PowerShell moves to the next cmdlet that matches and inserts:

```
Get-DistributionGroupMember
```

If you press Tab again, PowerShell returns to Get-DistributionGroup because there are only two valid matches. However, things get even better because PowerShell supports completion for parameters as well. If you insert "–" to indicate a parameter value after Get-DistributionGroup and press Tab, PowerShell starts with the first parameter and will continue through all valid parameters. If you press Tab too many times and pass by the parameter that you want to use, you can use Shift+Tab to go back through the parameter list. If you add some characters to help PowerShell identify the parameter, it attempts to complete using that value. For example: PowerShell completes Get-DistributionGroup –Ma into the command Get-DistributionGroup –ManagedBy.

Chapter 3

Even better, tab completion is context-sensitive, so it understands the structure of the object that you are navigating. For example, if you want to move through the system registry, tab completion understands the hive structure, so you can type a location in the registry and then use the Tab key to move through the available choices from that point. For example, type:

```
CD HKLM:\Software\Microsoft\Exchange
```

Now press Tab and PowerShell will lead you through all of the registry locations used by Exchange.

Windows PowerShell supports both named and positional parameters. Identifiers are a good example of a positional parameter. For example, if you enter **Get-Mailbox Tony**, PowerShell assumes that "Tony" is the value for the –*identity* parameter.

Finally, PowerShell will complete variables and even the properties of variables (such as their length) in a way similar to how the Microsoft Visual Studio IntelliSense feature works. If you type the incomplete name of a variable and press Tab, PowerShell will attempt to complete it from the list of known variables. For example, if you fill a variable with details of a mailbox like so:

```
$Mailbox = Get-Mailbox –Identity Redmond
```

and then type **$Ma** and press Tab, PowerShell will complete and return $Mailbox. This is a very useful feature if you forget the names of variables that you've defined. To see how properties are completed, type:

```
$Mailbox.Di
```

Pressing Tab now will request PowerShell to go through the list of properties beginning with "Di". For a mailbox, the list is DistinguishedName and DisplayName.

Handling information returned by EMS

Any cmdlet such as Get-EventLog that retrieves some information about an object will output a default set of properties about the object (or references to an object). Sometimes those properties are not the exact ones that you want to examine, so you will inevitably end up using the Format-List and Format-Table cmdlets to expand the set of properties returned by a command. For example, if you use the Get-Mailbox cmdlet to view the properties of a mailbox, the information returned isn't all that interesting:

Chapter 3

```
Get-Mailbox -Identity TRedmond
```

Name	Alias	ServerName	ProhibitSendQuota
Tony Redmond	TRedmond	ExServer1	unlimited

However, if you pipe the output to Format-List, you see a lot more information—far too much to review comfortably on screen—so it's better to pipe the output to a text file and compare it at your leisure.

If you compare the properties and values output for an Exchange 2010 mailbox with the set returned by Get-Mailbox on an Exchange 2007 server, you will notice that there are numerous new properties that are used for new functionality such as litigation hold, MailTips, and the new mailbox move process. In its turn, Exchange 2010 SP1 introduces some new mailbox properties to support features such as mailbox auditing. We discuss the use of these properties as we meet the new features in the remainder of the book.

```
Get-Mailbox -Identity TRedmond | Format-List
```

The Get-Mailbox cmdlet does not return every property that you can set on a user object because EMS differentiates between general Active Directory properties for a user object and those that are specific to Exchange. For example, Get-Mailbox does not list the Office property for a user because every user object in Active Directory has this property whether they are mail-enabled or not. Thus, if you want to retrieve or update the Office property, you have to use the Get-User and Set-User cmdlets, respectively. The same differentiation exists for groups and contacts, where the Get-Group/Set-Group and Get-Contact/Set-Contact cmdlets are available.

Selective output

It is easy to list every property, but when you have limited screen space, you need to be more selective about the properties that you want to output, and that's why it's often a good idea to use the Select-Object cmdlet to select the data that you really need before you pipe to Format-Table. In this case, we use the Select alias for Select-Object, just because this cmdlet is used so often and it is nice to have the chance to use shorthand.

```
Get-Mailbox -Identity Pelton | Select Name, PrimarySmtpAddress, Database
```

Name	PrimarySmtpAddress	Database
David Pelton	David.Pelton@contoso.com	ExServe1\DB1

PowerShell output can obscure data because it contains too many spaces. For example:

```
Get-ExchangeServer
```

```
Name        Site              ServerRole    Edition     AdminDisplayVersion
----        ----              ----------    -------     -------------------
ExServer1   contoso.com/Conf....  Mailbox,...  Enterprise  Version 14.0 (Bu...
ExServer2   contoso.com/Conf....  Mailbox      Enterprise  Version 14.0 (Bu...
ExServer3   contoso.com/Conf....  Mailbox,...  Enterprise  Version 14.0 (Bu...
ExServer4   contoso.com/Conf....  Mailbox      Enterprise  Version 14.0 (Bu...
```

To force PowerShell to remove spaces and display more useful data, pipe the output to the Format-Table cmdlet and use the –*AutoSize* parameter to fit the output columns into the available space:

```
Get-ExchangeServer | Format-Table -AutoSize
```

```
Name      Site                         ServerRole                             Edition     AdminDisplay
                                                                                           Version
-------   -----                        -------------                          ---------   ------------
ExServer1 contoso.com/Configuration/S...  Mailbox, ClientAccess, HubTransport  Enterprise  Version...
ExServer2 contoso.com/Configuration/S...  Mailbox                              Enterprise  Version...
ExServer3 contoso.com/Configuration/S...  Mailbox, ClientAccess, HubTransport  Enterprise  Version...
ExServer4 contoso.com/Configuration/S...  Mailbox                              Enterprise  Version...
```

Another way of extracting and then working with data is to direct the output of a command into a variable, in which case you have a complete picture of the object's properties in the variable. For example, this command loads all of the available information about the server called ExchMbxSvr1 into the *$Server* variable:

```
$Server = Get-ExchangeServer -Identity 'ExchMbxSvr1' -Status
```

You can extract additional information about the server to use by including the name of the property that you're interested in (specifying the –*Status* parameter requests Get-ExchangeServer to provide some additional information about the current domain controller and global catalog that the server is using). You can also use a variable as an array and populate the array with a call to a command.

In this example, we populate an array called $Mailboxes with a call to Get-Mailbox, using a filter to ensure that we only include actual mailboxes (and not room or equipment mailboxes). Legacy mailboxes (those that have not yet moved to Exchange 2010 servers) are included. This output is a good example of how cmdlets can generate individual objects or an array of objects with each object being individually accessible within the array.

```
$Mailboxes = Get-Mailbox -Filter {RecipientTypeDetails -eq 'UserMailbox'}
```

Chapter 3

Once populated, you can then navigate through the array as follows:

```
$Mailboxes[0]
$Mailboxes[1]
$Mailboxes[2] etc.
```

You can reference specific properties of the objects using the "." operator.

```
$Mailbox[2].Name
$Mailbox[53].PrimarySmtpAddress
```

INSIDE OUT   Finding what you want when there's a lot of output

The output from a cmdlet like Get-Mailbox can easily result in a lot of data that make it difficult to find the piece of information in which you are really interested. One technique that helps is to pipe the output to the Out-String cmdlet and then use the FindStr cmdlet to search the output for a particular term. For example, here's how to use the two cmdlets to search the output from Get-Mailbox to find a particular term. In this instance, EMS will list any occurrence of the word "Tony" if it exists in the list of mailbox names returned by Get-Mailbox:

```
Get-Mailbox | Out-String | FindStr 'Tony'
```

By default, EMS truncates the output of multivalue properties after 16 values. For example:

```
Get-Mailbox –Identity 'Pelton, David' | Format-List Name, EmailAddresses
```

```
Name           : Pelton, David
EmailAddresses : {smtp:dp12@contoso.com, smtp:dp11@contoso.com,
smtp:dp10@contoso.com, smtp:dp9@contoso.com, smtp:dp8@contoso.com,
smtp:dp7@contoso.com, smtp:dp6@contoso.com, smtp:dp4@contoso.com,
smtp:dp5@contoso.com, smtp:dp3@contoso.com, smtp:dp2@contoso.com,
smtp:dp1@contoso.com...}
```

Truncation can hide some valuable data. In the preceding example, we can see many of the email addresses defined for a mailbox, but the default Simple Mail Transfer Protocol (SMTP) address is not shown. If this limitation becomes a concern, you can force EMS to output more values for a property by amending a variable called *$FormatEnumerationLimit*. This variable is defined in the EMS initialization script (\bin\Exchange.ps1) and the default value of 16 is normally more than sufficient. If you want to see more variables, you can set the variable to be a different limit or set it to –1 to instruct EMS that it can enumerate as many values as are available for any property. For example:

```
$FormatEnumerationLimit = -1
Get-Mailbox -Identity 'Pelton, David' | Format-List Name, EmailAddresses
```

```
Name          : Pelton, David
EmailAddresses : {smtp:dp12@contoso.com, smtp:dp11@contoso.com,
smtp:dp10@contoso.com, smtp:dp9@contoso.com, smtp:dp8@contoso.com,
smtp:dp7@contoso.com, smtp:dp6@contoso.com, smtp:dp4@contoso.com,
smtp:dp5@contoso.com, smtp:dp3@contoso.com, smtp:dp2@contoso.com,
smtp:dp1@contoso.com, smtp:dp@contoso.com, smtp:dp16@contoso.com,
smtp:dp15@contoso.com, smtp:dp14@contoso.com, smtp:dp13@contoso.com,
smtp:Pelton@contoso.com, SMTP:David.Pelton@contoso.com}
```

Using common and user-defined variables

PowerShell includes a number of variables that you will use frequently. *$True* and *$False* are variables that you can pass to shell commands and scripts to check for true and false conditions. Usually, *$True* is equivalent to setting a check box for an option in EMC and *$False* is equivalent to clearing a check box. If you prefer numeric values, you can replace *$True* and *$False* with 1 (one) and 0 (zero). Other global variables that you commonly meet as you work with PowerShell include *$Null* (no value), *$home*, which returns the user's home folder, and *$pwd*, which returns the current working folder. Important Exchange 2010 (and 2007) variables include the following:

- *$ExBin*: Points to the directory where Exchange binaries and other important files are kept. On an Exchange 2010 server, this variable normally resolves to disk:\Program Files\Microsoft\Exchange Server\V14\bin.

- *$ExScripts*: Points to the directory where important Exchange .ps1 scripts are kept. On an Exchange 2010 server, this variable resolves to disk:\Program Files\Microsoft \Exchange Server\V14\Scripts.

- *$ExInstall*: Points to the root directory for Exchange. On an Exchange 2010 server this variable resolves to disk:\Program Files\Microsoft\Exchange Server\V14.

You can use these variables to access files in these directories. For example, to see a list of scripts provided by Exchange, type **Dir $ExScripts.**

Checking that a value is *$True* or *$False* is a common occurrence. For positive conditions, you can shorten the check by just passing the property to check against, and PowerShell will assume that you want to check whether it is true. For example, let's assume that we want to find out what mailboxes are enabled to use Outlook Web App (OWA). We can use this command and as you can see, there is no mention of *$True*, but it works:

```
Get-CASMailbox | Where-Object {$_.OWAEnabled} | Select Name
```

Chapter 3

Note the use of *$_* in the last command. *$_* is a very important variable because it points to the current object in the pipeline. Scripting languages on other platforms such as UNIX and Linux also support pipelines, which are used to compose complex commands by allowing the output of one command to be passed as the input to another. The "|" operator indicates that a pipeline is in place. Data are passed as fully formed objects rather than a text stream. This allows PowerShell to operate on the full structure of data that are pipelined, including the attributes and types used to define the objects piped from one cmdlet to another.

For example, if you create a filter to look for people in a certain department because you want to update the name of the department, you might do something like this:

```
Get-User | Where-Object {$_.Department -eq 'Legal'} | Set-User -Department 'Law'
```

Notice that the Department property is prefixed with *$_* to indicate that we want to check this property for every object that the call to Get-User passes through the pipeline. We actually use *$_.* as the prefix because it includes the "." operator to specify that we want to access a property. If we just passed *$_*, then the comparison would not work because PowerShell would compare "Legal" against the complete object.

User-defined variables can be integer, decimal, or string—you decide by passing a value to the variable you want to use. For example:

```
$Tony = 'Tony Redmond'
$Figure = 15.16
```

This obviously creates a string variable and the second variable holds a decimal value. Variables are case insensitive and case preserving. Using the preceding example, I can refer to *$Tony* as *$TONY* or *$tony* or even *$ToNY* and PowerShell will refer to the same variable. Variables are local unless you declare them to be global by prefixing them with Global, as in:

```
$Global:Tony = 'Tony Redmond'
```

Once a variable is global, you can reference it interactively and in scripts that you can call from anywhere.

A word of caution about PowerShell and quotation marks

Be careful how you use quotation marks in Windows PowerShell because, although it might appear that double and single quotes are interchangeable, there is a subtle difference that might catch you. Single quotes represent a literal string, one that PowerShell will use exactly as you provide it. Double quotes mean that PowerShell should examine the string and resolve any variable that it finds inside through a process called variable expansion. Consider this example:

```
$n = Date
$n1 = 'Right now, it is $n'
```

```
$n1
Right now it is $n
$n2 = "Right now, it is $n"
$n2
Right now, it is Tue Jan 16 17:59:54 2010
```

Can you see the difference a little quotation mark makes? Best practice is to use single quotes whenever you are sure that you want a string variable to stay exactly as you have typed it and to use double quotes elsewhere. Be careful about using editors that insert "smart quote marks" because PowerShell cannot deal with them; it is best to use a simple text editor whenever you create or edit a script. You cannot mix and match the different types of quotation marks to enclose a variable because PowerShell will refuse to accept the command if you try. You will not do any great harm if you use double quotes instead of single quotes, but it is best to use single quotes as the default.

Moving away from strings, the following creates an integer:

```
$Tony = 1
```

To create a decimal variable, we can do something like this:

```
$Tony = 17.55
```

You can easily assign a variable a value for kilobytes, gigabytes, and so on by appending the suffix to the value. For example:

```
$MaxMailboxSize = 500MB
```

You can even perform calculation, as in $C = 17*5 or $Sum = (2*7.15)/4.

> **Tip**
>
> Do not include hyphens when you name variables because PowerShell will interpret the hyphens as parameters. In other words, $ServerName is a good name for a variable, but $Server-Name is not.

Like any good scripting language, Windows PowerShell supports conditional checking with IF and ELSEIF that you will mostly use in scripts. It's easy to generate code that goes through a certain number of iterations with constructs such as 1..100 | ForEach-Object <command...>. We will go through examples of these constructs as we use more sophisticated PowerShell code in later chapters.

INSIDE OUT   Debugging PowerShell scripts

One of the few things that PowerShell misses is comprehensive debugging capabilities. About the only thing that you can do is use the Set-PSDebug cmdlet before you run a script to step through code. Don't get too excited, because if you've been used to setting debug points in programs or stepping back and forward through instructions to examine the results of commands, change the value of variables, and so on, you'll be disappointed with what you can do to debug PowerShell scripts during development. In some respects, writing a PowerShell script is a matter of trial and error. See the help file for more details about the Set-PSDebug cmdlet. For now, I use it as follows:

```
Set-PSDebug -Trace 2 -Step
```

Because Exchange 2010 EMS runs in a remote session, you will see more output debug information for interactive commands than you see in Exchange 2007. To turn debugging off, type:

```
Set-PSDebug -Off
```

The nature of PowerShell means that it is very extendable, so it should come as no surprise to find that you can install software to help create a programming environment tailored to your needs. Two tools that help are the PowerShell Debug Virtualizer (*http://poshdebugvisualizer.codeplex.com/*) and PowerGUI (*http://www.powergui.org /index.jspa*).

Identities

You might have noticed the *–Identity* parameter in use in some of the cmdlets that we have explored so far. In many cases, a call to an Exchange cmdlet results in a set of objects being returned (for example, all the mailboxes on a server). In these instances, you might need to identify a specific object within the chosen set to work with (think of a pointer to an item in an array). For example, if you issue the Get-ExchangeServer cmdlet, you retrieve a list of all of the Exchange servers in the organization. If you want to work with one server, you have to tell EMS what server you want to select by passing its identity. For example, to work with just the server named ExchMbxSvr1:

```
Get-ExchangeServer -Identity 'ExchMbxSvr1'
```

Apart from its obvious use to identify the object with which you want to work, *–Identity* has a special meaning within PowerShell because it is a positional parameter. In other words, you can specify the parameter's value without specifying the parameter's name, so the example just used is just as valid if you use:

```
Get-ExchangeServer 'ExServer1'
```

INSIDE OUT   Best practice to include the *Identity* parameter

Although you might find it faster to omit the *Identity* parameter when you're working interactively with EMS, it is best practice to always include the *Identity* parameter when you write code for reusable scripts because this ensures that there is no possibility that another administrator or programmer will mistake the value passed as the identity for anything else.

If you want to, you can retrieve a list of objects and store them in a variable and retrieve the values as you wish. The variable holds the objects as an array. For example, to populate a variable with a set of mailboxes hosted by a server:

```
$Mbx= Get-Mailbox -Server 'ExServer1'
```

To retrieve the different objects in the array, pass the number of the object that you want to work with, starting from zero. For example, to fetch the first mailbox in the array:

```
$Mbx[0]
```

If you are more specific, you can ask for one of the object's properties. For example, to get the identity of the first mailbox in the array:

```
$Mbx[0].Identity
```

```
IsDeleted           : False
Rdn                 : CN=Eoin P. Redmond
Parent              : contoso.com/Exchange Mailboxes
Depth               : 3
DistinguishedName   : CN=Eoin P. Redmond,OU=Exchange Mailboxes,DC=contoso,DC=com
IsRelativeDn        : False
DomainId            : contoso.com
ObjectGuid          : 0bcd15b3-c418-43be-b678-2658614f732b
Name                : Eoin P. Redmond
```

You might be surprised by the amount of information returned here for the mailbox's identity (it's all defined in the schema), but it contains all of the ways that you can navigate to this object via its relative distinguished name (shown here as the "rdn" property), distinguished name, globally unique identifier (GUID), and name. Normally, you'll just use the name of a mailbox to find it, but you can use the other methods and Exchange will find the mailbox. There is no requirement to parse out a specific piece of the identity that you want to use or to trim values, as PowerShell does it all for you. For example, you can use an identity to discover the groups to which a user belongs. Here's the code:

```
$U = (Get-User -Identity TRedmond).Identity; Get-Group | Where-Object {$_.Members -eq
$U}
```

Chapter 3

The Get-User cmdlet loads the user's identity into a variable, then the Get-Group and the Where-Object cmdlets scan through all groups to discover any that include the user in their membership. Scanning the membership list of groups to discover string matches is never going to be as quick (and will get slower and slower as the number of groups in the forest grows) because a string compare will never get close to the backward pointers that consoles such as Active Directory Users and Computers or EMC use to display group membership when it comes to speed of access, so don't be surprised if scanning for group membership in this way takes some time to complete.

If you don't like user-friendly forms such as email addresses or mailbox names, Exchange also allows you to use GUIDs as identifiers. Because they are obscure and long, GUIDs are difficult to type, but you can still use them. One slightly complicating factor is to know which GUID to use where. You might want the GUID that points to a user's mailbox, the GUID pointing to her Active Directory account, or even the one pointing to her archive mailbox. For example, this command displays all GUIDs registered for a mailbox:

```
Get-Mailbox -Identity 'Tony Redmond' | Format-List *Guid*
```

```
ExchangeGuid  : c2c4a3b5-c1a6-5a17-971d-8549123a78d0
ArchiveGuid   : 00000000-0000-0000-0000-000000000000
Guid          : 288617d1-4592-4211-bb20-26ab755458c8
```

The ExchangeGuid property points to the user's mailbox. The logic here might be that the GUID is the entity that ties a user account object to Exchange. However, if you use the Get-MailboxStatistics cmdlet to retrieve some statistics about the mailbox, EMS reports the same GUID as the MailboxGuid property. The two values are the same, and the difference in naming is just a little confusing. The Guid property identifies the user's Active Directory account. In this case, the ArchiveGuid is shown as all zeros, which means that no archive mailbox is associated with this mailbox. Now that you know what the GUIDs are, you could use them to reference a mailbox. For example:

```
$MBX = Get-Mailbox -Identity 'Tony Redmond'
$GUID = $MBX.ExchangeGuid
Get-Mailbox -id $GUID
```

The great thing about identities is that sometimes you don't need to bother using them! This situation occurs when you pipe information from one cmdlet for processing by another because the shell understands that it needs to operate on the current object that has been fetched through the pipe. For example, this command takes a list of mailbox identities passed in strings and pipes them to the Set-Mailbox cmdlet:

```
"TRedmond", "JSmith", "JDoe" | Set-Mailbox -Office "Dublin"
```

Piping

Piping output from one cmdlet to another is something you'll do frequently as you work with Exchange data. The important thing to remember is that Windows PowerShell outputs fully formed objects that can be manipulated when fed as input to other cmdlets through the pipeline. This wouldn't be possible if PowerShell output text strings. For example, let's assume that you want to change the value of the Office property for a set of users who have moved to a new building. It would be tedious if you had to fetch the identity of each user individually, determine the identity for each user, and then pass the value to make the change to each user's properties. A simple pipe does the trick because PowerShell knows that it can use the stream of data from one command to identify the objects that it has to process with another. Here's how you might update the Office property for a complete set of users without any mention of an identity. You'll see that the two cmdlets used to do the work are separated by the pipe character "|". This is the character that tells PowerShell to pipe the output from the first cmdlet to become the input to the second.

```
Get-User -Filter {Office -eq 'Building A'} | Set-User -Office "Building B"
```

Because it's natural for Exchange administrators to want to know what's happening on their servers, they use cmdlets like Get-MailboxStatistics (report statistics for a mailbox) and Get-MailboxFolderStatistics (report statistics for an individual folder) extensively. Here's another example of piping in action. In this case, we want to find out how many mailboxes on a server have more than a certain number of items in their Inboxes. The logic for examining data like this is that a large number of items in a folder often leads to poor client performance. As discussed in Chapter 7, "The Exchange 2010 Store," Exchange 2010 makes some fundamental changes to its database schema to improve the number of items it can deal with in an individual folder, but even so, it's good to know who the pack rats are in the company. The code fetches a list of mailboxes from a server and pipes them into the Get-MailboxFolderStatistics cmdlet. This generates a set of objects that represents the folders in all the mailboxes, which we then pipe into the Where-Object cmdlet to look for Inbox folders with more than 2,500 items. Finally, we select a couple of properties to output so that we know the name of the mailboxes with the large Inbox folders and the count of items in each folder.

```
Get-Mailbox -Server 'ExServer1' | Get-MailboxFolderStatistics | Where-Object
{$_.Name -eq 'Inbox' -and $_.ItemsInFolder -gt 2500} | Select Identity, ItemsInFolder
```

Identity	ItemsInFolder
contoso.com/Exchange Mailboxes/VIPs/Redmond, Deirdre P\Inbox	3572
contoso.com/Exchange Mailboxes/Ruth, Andy\Inbox	3711
contoso.com/Exchange Mailboxes/Pelton, David\Inbox	4910
contoso.com/Exchange Mailboxes/EMEA/Redmond, Eoin\Inbox	3318
contoso.com/Exchange Mailboxes/VIPs/Redmond, Tony\Inbox	2751

Of course, it would be impolite to send a note to these users to remind them that good filing practices lead to clean mailboxes, but you can still think about it!

When piping information generates errors

Occasionally EMS will complain when it's asked to pipe information from one cmdlet to another. The typical error is shown here:

```
Pipeline not executed because a pipeline is already executing. Pipelines cannot
be executed concurrently.
    + CategoryInfo : OperationStopped:
(Microsoft.Power...tHelperRunspace:ExecutionCmdletHelperRunspace) [],
PSInvalidOperationException
    + FullyQualifiedErrorId : RemotePipelineExecutionFailed
```

This doesn't seem like a good error and it stops the pipeline immediately. It's frustrating, too, because it normally occurs with code that worked perfectly well in Exchange 2007. The root cause is the changeover to remote PowerShell.

Local PowerShell, which is what we used in Exchange 2007, includes a mechanism to let pipelines communicate with some perceived concurrency. This is done to get around the single-threaded nature of PowerShell. The mechanism essentially holds outputs from a pipeline until a cmdlet is ready to process them and creates a very effective impression of bidirectional communication. However, no amount of smart buffer management can do everything, and a new challenge arises when remote PowerShell comes into play. Exchange 2010 uses remote PowerShell more extensively than any other product, so it's hardly surprising that we'd see some problems like this in the first implementation of remote management. Remote PowerShell can't play some of the same fancy memory management tricks that are possible when everything happens locally, and the net effect is that sometimes EMS runs headlong into an inability to manage more than a few items in the pipeline. It's hard to predict when this might happen. Sometimes code to cycle through many objects will complete successfully. For example:

```
Get-Mailbox | Set-Mailbox –CustomAttribute15 'Exchange User'
```

Other times, EMS will complain immediately and nothing in the pipeline is processed. One example that causes an immediate halt is when you incorporate a ForEach cmdlet to process many objects. For example, if I change the preceding code to:

```
Get-Mailbox | ForEach {Set-Mailbox –Identity $_.Identity –CustomAttribute15 'Exchange User'}
```

EMS immediately complains that it can't execute concurrent pipelines. I know that this isn't the most efficient code, but it illustrates that you will usually run into trouble if you attempt to pipeline more than a few objects into a ForEach that calls another cmdlet. Microsoft has admitted that this is a problem that should be solved in a future version of PowerShell. In the interim there's an easy workaround. All you need to do is force the operations to be processed sequentially rather than have EMS attempt any concurrency. To do this, enclose the first command (that creates the set of pipelined objects) in parentheses. The code that works even with remote PowerShell is shown here (again, not efficient, but good enough to illustrate the point):

```
(Get-Mailbox) | ForEach {Set-Mailbox -Identity $_.Identity -CustomAttribute15
'Exchange User'}
```

Everything goes a tad more slowly, but the code will work and we can all get on with our lives.

Adding recipient photos

Now that you've spent some time learning more about EMS in Exchange 2010, let's take a look at something tangible that you can do with it: add contact pictures to your users in the Global Address List (GAL).

The Import-RecipientDataProperty cmdlet is a little gem that's been added to Exchange 2010. You can use this cmdlet to import an audio file or picture for a recipient. If present, these data are made available through the GAL, the reading pane, contact details, and other places in Microsoft Outlook 2010 that support these properties. The audio file is intended to contain the spoken name of a recipient so that you know how to pronounce it, and the picture is obviously to allow you to know what the recipient looks like. To restrict the impact on Active Directory, an audio file is limited to 25 KB and a picture file to 10 KB.

Here's an example of how to import a photo for a recipient (mailbox, distribution group, or contact). The syntax is slightly complicated by the need to specify the type of data that is being provided and to stream the data in using the Get-Content cmdlet.

```
Import-RecipientDataProperty -Identity 'Tony Redmond' -Picture -FileData
([Byte[]]$(Get-Content -Path 'C:\Temp\TR.jpg' -Encoding Byte -ReadCount 0))
```

After a successful import, the *ThumbnailPhoto* attribute of the recipient's Active Directory object is populated with the picture data. You can see this with the ADSIEdit utility (Figure 3-8).

Before these data are visible to users, you have to make sure that they are published to global catalog servers. By default, the *ThumbnailPhoto* attribute is not in the partial attribute set (PAS) that domain controllers replicate to global catalogs. Unless another administrator has included the *ThumbnailPhoto* attribute in the PAS, you will have to update the Active Directory schema to include it in replication. *http://en.wikipedia.org/wiki /Active_Directory* contains a good discussion of how to extend the PAS.

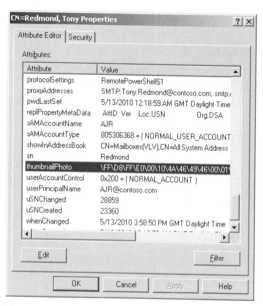

Figure 3-8 A populated *ThumbnailPhoto* property.

CAUTION

Adding new attributes to the PAS is not something that you want to do without careful planning because of the possible impact on the network, because it replicates all of the additional data that you add to Active Directory to every global catalog.

After replication has taken place, clients should be able to access and display the photos alongside other user data. In addition, before users are able to view thumbnails offline, you need to update the Offline Address Book (OAB) attributes to force Outlook to download the data from Active Directory. Before you rush to do this, be sure to read the discussion in the section "Creating and using customized OABs" in Chapter 12.

If necessary, you can subsequently remove picture data from a mailbox with the Set-Mailbox cmdlet. For example:

```
Set-Mailbox -Identity 'Tony Redmond' -RemovePicture
```

Too many objects

By default, EMS returns up to 1,000 objects in response to cmdlets (the value in Exchange 2007 is 5,000). Therefore, if you run a cmdlet like Get-Mailbox, Exchange will return up to 1,000 mailboxes if they are available. If you work in a small Exchange organization that supports fewer than 1,000 mailboxes, you don't need to worry too much about the number of objects you have to deal with, as PowerShell will likely return relatively few objects and things usually progress quickly. However, it's a different situation in large organizations where you have to pay attention to the filters you specify to retrieve data or override the default limit for returned objects by specifying the *ResultSize* parameter for cmdlets. For example, to let EMS return as many mailboxes as it can find, you could use a command like this:

```
Get-Mailbox -ResultSize Unlimited
```

This command will work, but it will be very slow because EMS has to read every single mailbox in the organization. Think about how long this might take to execute in an organization that supports more than 300,000 mailboxes. In these situations it's always better to specify a filter to restrict the number of objects that EMS looks for and returns.

OPATH filters

OPATH is the basic syntax used for PowerShell queries. It is similar in concept but uses different syntax than Lightweight Directory Access Protocol (LDAP) queries. Dynamic distribution groups (see Chapter 6, "Managing Mail-Enabled Recipients") also use OPATH queries to locate objects in Active Directory when the transport system builds addressee lists to deliver message addresses to these groups.

Some base guidelines about the syntax OPATH queries are as follows:

- OPATH requires a hyphen before –and, –or, and –not operators.

- Comparison operators include –eq (equal), –ne (not equal), –lt (less than), –gt (greater than), –like (like), –ilike, and –notlike. –Like and –notlike are wildcard string compares. –iLike and –inotlike are case insensitive.

- Filters should be expressed within braces; for example, {Office –eq 'London'}.

You'll see many more examples of OPATH queries in the remainder of this book.

Server-side and client-side filters

Windows PowerShell supports server-side and client-side filters. There's a big difference in performance between the two types of filters, especially when you have to process more than a hundred objects.

Client-side filters are the default; any code that uses the Where cmdlet executes a client-side filter. Client-side filters request data from a server and then perform the filtering on the client. This is an effective approach if you only have 10 or 15 objects to process, but it obviously doesn't scale too well as the number of objects increases.

Server-side filters have better scalability because the request for data forces the server to return a filtered data set to the client. Because Exchange servers often have to deal with tens of thousands of objects, a number of the Exchange cmdlets support server-side filters. If a cmdlet supports the –*Filter* parameter, it supports server-side filters. In most cases, these are cmdlets that deal with objects where you can expect large numbers, such as mail-enabled recipients or message queues. All of the precanned filters generated for dynamic distribution groups, address lists, and email address policies use server-side filters.

As an example of server- and client-side filtering in action, two methods are available to find all the mailboxes with "James" in their names, as demonstrated in these commands:

```
Get-Mailbox –Filter {Name –like '*James*'} –ResultSize 5000

Get-Mailbox –ResultSize 5000 | Where {$_.Name –like '*James*'}
```

On the surface, these two pieces of code seem reasonably similar, but they are very different in reality. The first code example uses a server-side filter and the second uses a client-side filter. The second difference is that the two filter types can generate very different results because of the way that the filters operate. If we omit the –*ResultSize* parameter, the same query is generated: Find all the mailboxes with a name that contains "James" (the –*ResultSize* parameter in the first example limits the total objects returned to 5,000). However, if you time both queries, you will find that the server-side filter invariably executes faster than the client-side filter, largely because fewer data are transferred between server and client. To understand why the filters generate different results, we have to appreciate how the filters work:

- The server-side filter returns the first 5,000 mailboxes it finds that include James in the mailbox name.

- The client-side filter fetches data for the first 5,000 mailboxes and then applies the filter to find the mailboxes that include James in the name. However, the filter only applies to the set that the client fetched and might not find all of the mailboxes that we actually want to discover.

Even though we ask the server-side filter to do more work (working with any reasonably sized set of mailboxes, the server-side filter will have to process significantly more data to find the first 5,000 mailboxes that match), it still executes faster. For example, when I executed similar commands within a very large Exchange organization (170,000 mailboxes), the server-side filter completed processing in 43 seconds, whereas the client-side filter completed in 81 seconds. The rule here is that the effect of server-side filtering gets better and better as the number of objects increases.

INSIDE OUT   PowerShell and memory limits

Another aspect to consider is that PowerShell does not have the ability to fetch and cache data on disk temporarily in the way that a database might. This is not an issue if you want to process only a few objects, but it can lead to memory issues if you attempt to process tens of thousands of mailboxes at one time, especially if you use client-side filters and want to pipeline the output to another command. In this case, you ask PowerShell to find all the objects that match the specified filter, store the data in memory, process the data, and pipe the matching objects to the second command. Experience shows that these operations can cause PowerShell to complain that it is running out of memory. This is likely to be one of the growing pains that all software goes through and apart from using loops to process data there is not a good solution to the memory exhaustion problem available today.

Sometimes people make the mistake of assuming that the client-side filter is faster because server-side filters provide the data in one motion after the server processes all the data. You therefore wait for a while without seeing anything and then see all the filtered records at one time. By comparison, the client-side filter fetches and filters data continuously and so you see output as the command finds each matching record. However, the important indicator of performance is how long each type of filter takes to complete and server-side filters are always faster.

The commands that you are most likely to use with server-side filters are as follows:

- **Get-User**   Retrieve basic Active Directory properties for any user account, including mail-enabled accounts.

- **Get-Mailbox**   Retrieve Exchange-specific properties for mailboxes.

- **Get-MailContact**   Retrieve Exchange-specific properties for mail-enabled contacts.

- **Get-DistributionGroup**   Retrieve Exchange-specific properties for mail-enabled groups.

Each of the commands that you can use to work with user accounts, groups, and mailboxes supports a different set of filterable properties. To discover what properties are available for filtering, you can use PowerShell to query the properties of a returned object. For example:

```
Get-Mailbox -Identity Redmond | Get-Member | Where-Object {$_.MemberType -eq
'Property'} | Sort-Object Name | Format-Table Name
```

This set of commands calls a command to return some information about an object. It then pipes the information returned by the first command to the Get-Member cmdlet, which extracts information about the properties. We sort the properties by name and output them in table format. The output looks like this:

```
Name
----
AcceptMessagesOnlyFrom
AcceptMessagesOnlyFromDLMembers
AddressListMembership
Alias
AntispamBypassEnabled
CustomAttribute1
CustomAttribute10
CustomAttribute11
CustomAttribute12
CustomAttribute13
CustomAttribute14
...
WindowsEmailAddress
```

This method works for the Get-Mailbox, Get-CASMailbox, Get-User, Get-Recipient, Get-DistributionGroup, and Get-DynamicDistributionGroup cmdlets. You can use any of the values reported in a –*Filter* statement. For instance, the call that we just made to Get-Mailbox reports that the custom attributes are available, so to find all mailboxes that have a value in the CustomAttribute10 property, we can generate a command like this:

```
Get-Mailbox -Filter {CustomAttribute10 -ne $Null}
```

If you look at the filterable properties reported by the Get-DynamicDistributionGroup cmdlet, you can see that the ManagedBy property is available for this dynamic distribution group, whereas it is not for mailboxes. Hence, we can execute a filter like this:

```
Get-DynamicDistributionGroup -Filter {ManagedBy -ne $Null}
```

When you create a filter, it is best to be specific as possible. You can state several conditions within a filter. Another example of a server-side filter that returns all the mailboxes in the Dublin office where the user name contains "Tony" is shown next. The Get-User cmdlet also works with this filter, but Get-Mailbox executes more quickly because the server does not have to process accounts that are not mail-enabled.

```
Get-Mailbox -Filter {Office -eq 'Dublin' -and Name -like '*Tony*'}
```

After you have mastered server-side filtering, you will find that you use it all the time to work with sets of users. For example, let's assume that you want to give a new mailbox quota to members of a certain department but no one else.

```
Get-User -Filter {Department -Eq 'Advanced Technology'} |

Set-Mailbox -UseDatabaseQuotaDefaults:$False -IssueWarningQuota 5000MB
-ProhibitSendQuota 5050MB
-ProhibitSendReceiveQuota 5075MB
```

Transcripts

If you encounter a problem executing some EMS commands and need to produce some debug information to give to your support team or Microsoft, you can do this by generating a transcript. A transcript captures details of all commands executed in a session and is useful in terms of capturing the steps necessary to solve a problem or documenting steps to expose an issue that you want to report to Microsoft. You can combine this by adding the –*Verbose* parameter to most commands to gather a lot of information about what you've tried to do and what happened when you tried it. Use the Start-Transcript cmdlet to force EMS to capture debug information. For example:

```
Start-Transcript c:\Temp\Transcript.txt
```

All commands and output will be captured until you stop the transcript with the Stop-Transcript cmdlet. At this point, you can examine the output with any text editor and you'll see something like the output shown in the following example.

```
*************************
Windows PowerShell Transcript Start
Start time: 20100313093116
Username  : CONTOSO\e14admin
Machine   : ExServer1 (Microsoft Windows NT 6.1.7600.0)
*************************
PS C:\temp> $env:path
C:\Windows\system32\WindowsPowerShell\v1.0\;C:\Windows\system32;C:\Windows;
C:\Windows\System32\Wbem;C:\Windows\System32\WindowsPowerShell\v1.0\;
C:\Windows\idmu\common;C:\Program Files\System Center Operations Manager 2007\;
C:\Program Files\Microsoft\Exchange Server\V14\bin;c:\temp
```

Bulk updates

Those faced with the task of bulk updates (either to create a lot of new mailboxes or other objects, or to modify many existing objects) in Exchange 2000 or Exchange 2003 had quite a lot of work ahead of them because Exchange offered no good way to perform the work. You could create comma-separated value (CSV) or other load files and use utilities such as CSVDE or LDIFDE to process data in the files against Active Directory, or you could write your own code to use CDOEXM or ADSI to update Active Directory. Either approach involved a lot of detailed work where it was quite easy to make a mistake. The alternative (to use the ESM or Active Directory Users and Computers consoles to make the necessary changes through a GUI) was boring and an invitation to make a mistake. The root cause of Exchange's problems with bulk changes was the lack of a programmable way to automate common management operations, something that changed with the arrival of EMS.

You can combine the Get-User and Set-Mailbox cmdlets effectively to solve many problems. Here is an example where you need to update the send quota property on every mailbox for a set of users whose business group has decided to fund additional storage. You can identify these users by their department, which always starts with "Advanced Tech" but sometimes varies in spellings such as "Advanced Technology" and "Advanced Technology Group." Conceptually, the problem is easy to solve.

1. Look for all users who have a department name beginning with "Advanced Tech."

2. Update the send quota property for each user.

With Exchange 2000 and Exchange 2003, we can use the Find option in Active Directory Users and Computers to build a suitable filter to establish the set of users. The problem here is that you then have to open each user located by Active Directory Users and Computers to update their quota through the GUI, something that could become very boring after several accounts. You could also export a CSV-formatted list of users to a text file, manipulate the file to find the desired users, and then process that list through CSVDE to make the changes, but you have to search for all matching users across the complete directory first. There is a lot of work to do.

The process is easier in EMS. First, you use the Get-User cmdlet with a suitable filter to establish the collection of mailboxes that you want to change. The following command returns all users who have a department name that begins with "Advanced Tech" and then updates the ProhibitSendQuota property to the desired amount (let's say 1000 MB). Because we have a collection of user objects established, we can use the Set-Mailbox cmdlet to perform the update. Note that some of these users might not be mail-enabled, but error handling is another day's work.

```
Get-User | Where {$_.Department –like '*Advanced Tech*'} | Set-Mailbox
–ProhibitSendQuota 1000MB –UseDatabaseQuotaDefaults $False
```

Mergers, acquisitions, and internal reorganizations pose all sorts of problems for email administrators. EMS will not solve the big problems, but it can automate many of the mundane tasks that occur. For example, department names tend to change during these events. EMS makes it easy to find all users who belong to a specific department and update their properties to reflect the new organizational naming conventions. If only executing organizational change was as easy as this one-line command, which transforms everyone who works for the "Old Designs" department over to the "Cutting Edge Design" department, things would be much easier:

```
Get-User | Where {$_.Department -eq 'Old Designs'} | Set-User
-Department 'Cutting Edge Design'
```

Note the use of *$_.Department*; this indicates a value fetched from the current pipeline object. In this case, it is the department property of the current user object fetched by Get-User. To verify that we have updated all the users that we wanted to (and maybe provide a report to human resources or management), we can use some code like this:

```
Get-User | Where {$_.Department -eq 'Cutting Edge Design'} | Select Name,
Department | Sort Name | Format-Table > c:\temp\Cutting-Edge.tmp
```

A variation on this theme is to output the data to a CSV file to make the data easier to work with in Microsoft Excel, Microsoft Access, or another tool that can read CSV data.

```
Get-User | Where {$_.Department -eq 'Cutting Edge Design'} | Select Name,
Department | Sort Name | Export-CSV c:\temp\Cutting-Edge.CSV
```

Things are even easier if you just need to change everyone's company name after your company is acquired.

```
Get-User | Set-User -Company 'New Company'
```

You can even do things like only alter the users whose mailbox belongs to a particular database:

```
Get-Mailbox -Database 'VIP Mailboxes' | Set-User -company 'Big Bucks'
-Department 'Executives'
```

> **Tip**
>
> All of the examples discussed so far depend on you being able to identify some property that you can use as the basis for a filter. But what about a situation in which you do not have a common property value to check for? In this case, you can build a simple list of mailbox names (or any other format that the *–identity* parameter will accept such as a Universal Principal Name [UPN]) and use the Get-Content cmdlet to read the names one by one and pipe these values to whatever other command you need to use. For example, here is how we can use that trick to enable ActiveSync access for a set

of users. In this example, the Get-Content cmdlet is used to read lines containing the identities of the mailboxes that we want to change from a text file and pipe them as input to the Set-CASMailbox cmdlet:

```
Get-Content c:\temp\Users.txt | Set-CASMailbox –ActiveSyncEnabled $True
```

Another place where EMS excels is where you want to apply a common setting across all servers in your organization. For example, let's assume that you want to apply a new retention limit for items of 60 days (perhaps mandated by the legal department) to all servers:

```
Get-MailboxDatabase | Set-MailboxDatabase –ItemRetention 60.00:00:00
```

These simple examples demonstrate the value of having a scripting language that supports automation of common management tasks.

Code changes required by remote PowerShell

As we have discussed, one of the joys of Windows PowerShell is its ability to pipe the output of one cmdlet to become the input for another. For example, you might do this to fetch a list of mailboxes from a server called "ExServer1" and pipe that list to the Set-Mailbox cmdlet to set a new limit on each mailbox:

```
Get-Mailbox –Server 'ExServer1' | Set-Mailbox –IssueWarningQuota 5000MB
```

This all works nicely when you use verbs with similar nouns (both verbs use the "mailbox" noun in this example) or when Microsoft has optimized cmdlets with different nouns (server and mailbox, for instance) so that they can work with each other. In other instances where the verbs are dissimilar and not optimized, you can use the ForEach cmdlet as an intermediate step. Here's the previous cmdlet restated:

```
Get-Mailbox –Server 'ExServer1' | ForEach {Set-Mailbox –IssueWarningQuota 5000MB}
```

This approach worked nicely in Exchange 2007, but the change to use remote PowerShell means that some code that works on Exchange 2007 doesn't work on Exchange 2010. It's hard to be definitive on this point because Microsoft is constantly tweaking remote PowerShell and EMS to improve matters, but most of the problems seem to be in piping data between cmdlets. Figure 3-9 shows the kind of error condition you might encounter.

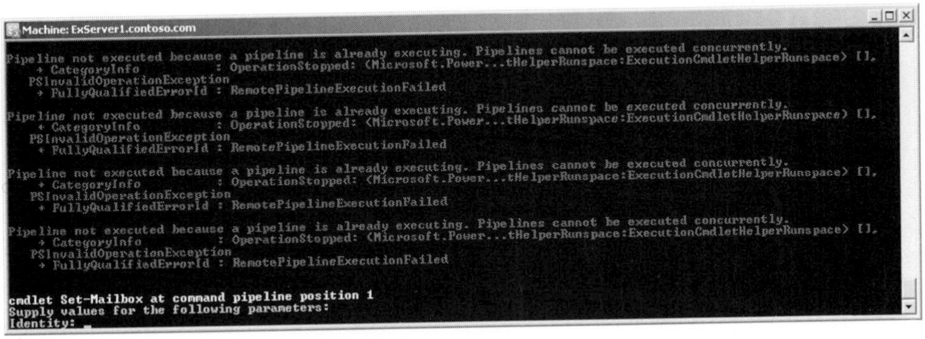

Figure 3-9 Problems with PowerShell piping.

In this case, the code gets a list of mailboxes from a database and then checks the size of each mailbox against a variable to see if it exceeds a limit (500 MB in this case) and then reports the mailboxes that do. One fix is to make the first part of the pipeline into a subexpression like this:

```
$MaxSize = 500MB
(Get-Mailbox -Database 'VIP Mailboxes') | ?{ (Get-MailboxStatistics $_).TotalItemSize
-gt $MaxSize } | Select Name
```

Another workaround is to take a three-part approach using variables to act as pipe intermediaries:

```
$Mb1 = Get-Mailbox -Database 'VIP Mailboxes'
$Mb2 = $Mb1 |?{ (Get-MailboxStatistics $_).TotalItemSize -gt $maxsize }
$Mb2 | Format-List Name, DisplayName
```

Another problem area is with multivalued attributes such as email addresses. In Exchange 2007, you can add another email address to a mailbox with code like this:

```
$Addr = Get-Mailbox -id 'Redmond, Tony'
$Addr.EmailAddresses += 'TR@contoso.com'
$Addr | Set-Mailbox
```

These commands first fetch the properties of a mailbox and store them in a variable. The value of the email address property is then updated with a new SMTP address, and we then update the mailbox with the Set-Mailbox cmdlet, pipelining the new values from the variable. PowerShell seems happy with the syntax and informs us that the Set-Mailbox cmdlet completed successfully, but the mailbox properties are not updated. The problem seems to be with the way that remote PowerShell handles pipelined input. To update the email address with remote PowerShell, we need code like this:

```
(Get-Mailbox -Identity 'Redmond, Tony') | %{ Set-Mailbox -Identity $_ -EmailAddresses
($_.EmailAddresses + 'TR@contoso.com')}
```

This version of the code is more specific in its use of the current pipeline object (indicated with $_.) and works with remote PowerShell.

You can argue that syntax change between versions is merely the consequence of development in PowerShell and the same type of change that forced code upgrades has been seen in many other programming languages. This is true, but it is a side effect of the evolution of Exchange to use remote PowerShell that has to be taken into account in deployment plans, because you will have to validate every piece of script code that you wrote for Exchange 2007 to ensure that it will work for Exchange 2010.

Command line versus Integrated Scripting Environment

Windows PowerShell 1.0 only supports a command-line interface, but PowerShell 2.0 introduces an Integrated Scripting Environment (ISE) or GUI for developers to create and test scripts. You can use the ISE (Figure 3-10) to develop and test Exchange scripts. Traditionalists will prefer to handcraft their scripts with NotePad—why would anyone need an editor that uses different colors?—and test the results interactively from the command line. Developers who are more used to ISE-type environments will like the more visually rewarding interface. Either option is valid.

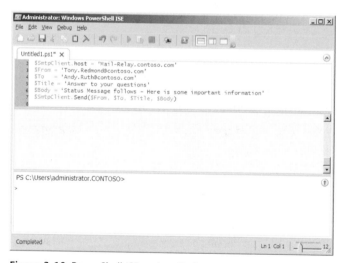

Figure 3-10 PowerShell ISE and an Exchange script.

> **Note**
>
> Remember that before you can use the PowerShell ISE on a server you have to install it using the Add Feature option to add the Windows PowerShell Integrated Scripting Environment. PowerShell ISE is installed by default on Microsoft Windows 7 workstations.

> **Tip**
>
> In addition, before you can access any of the Exchange 2010 cmdlets, you have to create a remote PowerShell session to an Exchange 2010 server. The easiest way to do this is to add a new menu item for ISE in your profile to invoke the necessary code to connect to Exchange 2010 and load the cmdlets permitted by RBAC. Use these steps to add the new menu item to ISE:
>
> 1. Start ISE.
>
> 2. Follow the steps in *http://technet.microsoft.com/en-us/library/dd819492.aspx* to create and edit your ISE profile.
>
> 3. Add the following code to the profile to define a new Ctrl+E command to connect to Exchange 2010, replacing the hardcoded server name shown here with the server to which you want to connect:
>
> ```
> $psISE.CurrentPowerShellTab.AddOnsMenu.SubMenus.Add(
>     "Load Exchange 2010",
>     {
>         $Session = New-PSSession -ConfigurationName Microsoft.Exchange `
>         -ConnectionUri
> http://exserver1.contoso.com/PowerShell/?SerializationLevel=Full `
>         -Authentication Kerberos
>
>         Import-PSSession $Session
>     },
>       "Control+E"
> )
> ```
>
> 4. Restart ISE. The new item should be available under the Add-ons menu and can be invoked there or with the Ctrl+E key combination.

Calling scripts

After you have written a script, you have to decide where to keep it. You could put the new script in the directory that stores the Exchange binaries, but this is a bad idea for many reasons, not least because your script could be overwritten by the installation of a future Exchange service pack, roll-up update, or even a completely new version.

INSIDE OUT   A wise practice

It is wise to maintain a clear separation between the code for which you are responsible and the code that Microsoft distributes with Exchange. Therefore, you should create a directory to hold all of the scripts that you use to work with Exchange. You can then call your scripts in the knowledge that they will be available.

The basic rule of calling a script is that if the script is in the working directory (the directory that you are currently in), you prefix the name with ".\"

```
C:>.\Get-All-Users.ps1
```

If you're not in the right directory, you can move to where you want to be with the cd command:

```
C:> cd c:\Scripts\
```

Alternatively, you can supply the full path to where the script is located:

```
C:>c:\Scripts\Get-All-Users.ps1
```

If there are spaces in the directory names, then you need to enclose the path in single or double quotes:

```
C: '\Program Files\Microsoft\Exchange Server\V14\Scripts\CollectOverMetrics.ps1'
```

Even better, you can amend the path used by PowerShell to look for scripts and add your directory to it. For example, running this command adds the C:\MyScripts directory to the path:

```
$env:path = $env:path + ";c:\MyScripts'
```

Once a script is in a directory that's included in the path, you can invoke it by just typing its name.

Profiles

When you start EMS, Windows PowerShell runs a script called Bin\Exchange.ps1 to initialize EMS by loading the Exchange snap-in and defining a set of variables that are used by EMS such as the default scope for Active Directory queries. The script also prints out some welcome information for EMS.

If you make frequent use of EMS, you should consider creating a profile that EMS can load when it initializes a new session. If it finds a profile, PowerShell will execute the commands in it before it runs Exchange.ps1 to create the EMS session. This order is used to ensure that you can't interfere with the creation of the EMS session.

I like profiles because they remind me of the convoluted login command procedures that I used to create for OpenVMS. Typical examples of commands included in profiles are the following:

- Definition of aliases (shorthand for commands): For example, you could do Set-Alias gmbx Get-Mailbox to allow you to use gmbx any time you want to run the Get-Mailbox cmdlet.

- As discussed earlier, you can add one or more directories containing scripts to the path.

- Position your session in a specific directory where you prefer to work.

PowerShell defines a global variable called *$Profile* to hold the location of your profile. The exact location varies across different versions of Windows. The profile doesn't exist by default and you might have to create it before you can edit it to add some commands. First, let's see whether a profile is available for the account that you use:

```
Test-Path $Profile
```

If the response is $True, you know that a profile exists. If not, you have to create it with:

```
New-Item -Path $Profile -Type File -Force
```

After you have a profile, you can edit it as follows:

```
Notepad $Profile
```

Here's a really simple profile with which you could begin:

```
$env:path = $env:path + ";c:\Scripts"

'You are now entering PowerShell: ' + $env:Username
$StartTime = (Get-Date)
Write-Host "Session starting at $StartTime"
Set-Location c:\temp
```

After you finish updating the profile, save the file and then restart EMS to see whether your changes are effective. As you can imagine, there are endless possibilities for inventive code to run within a profile.

Script initialization

As you write scripts to use with Exchange, you should include some code in the scripts to ensure that they can only run on Exchange servers and that the servers have access to the Exchange cmdlets. Here are two snippets that do the trick. The first checks that the set of Exchange snap-ins are loaded.

```
Get-PSSnapin Microsoft.Exchange.* -Registered -ea SilentlyContinue | Out-Null
  If (!$?)
    {
       Write-Host "Exchange cmdlets are not available on this server."
       Return $False
    }
```

If we didn't suppress the output, we should see that three snap-ins are loaded and registered for Exchange:

```
Name         : Microsoft.Exchange.Management.PowerShell.E2010
PSVersion    : 1.0
Description  : Admin Tasks for the Exchange Server

Name         : Microsoft.Exchange.Management.PowerShell.Setup
PSVersion    : 1.0
Description  : Setup Tasks for the Exchange Server

Name         : Microsoft.Exchange.Management.Powershell.Support
PSVersion    : 1.0
Description  : Support Tasks for the Exchange Server
```

The next code snippet retrieves the computer name with the Get-Content cmdlet and feeds it to the Get-ExchangeServer cmdlet to validate that the server has at least one Exchange role installed. This code does not validate that the server supports a specific role, although you could modify the code to use Get-MailboxServer, Get-ClientAccessServer, Get-TransportServer, or Get-UMServer to check whether the server supports the mailbox, CAS, hub transport, or Unified Messaging roles.

```
Get-ExchangeServer (Get-Content env:ComputerName) –ea SilentlyContinue | Out-Null
  If (!$?)
    {
       Write-Host "Microsoft Exchange is not installed on this server."
       Return $False
    }
       Return $True
    }
```

Active Directory for PowerShell

Active Directory is a huge dependency for Exchange. Although Exchange 2007 did a great job of supporting Windows PowerShell, the application had to run on Windows Server 2003 servers, and the Active Directory engineering team did not do the work to support PowerShell for Active Directory for that version of the operating system.

The situation is different for Exchange 2010, because Microsoft has done the work to support Active Directory for PowerShell 2.0 on Windows Server 2008 R2 servers and Windows 7 clients. Active Directory Web Services and the PowerShell module are installed by default on all Windows Server 2008 R2 domain controllers. If you want to manage pre-Windows Server 2008 R2 Active Directory domains, you can use the Active Directory Management Gateway Service (*http://www.microsoft.com/downloads/details.aspx?FamilyID=008940c6 -0296-4597-be3e-1d24c1cf0dda&displaylang=en*). However, there is no way to run the Active Directory PowerShell cmdlets directly on a Windows Server 2008 SP2 server.

To install the Active Directory module on a non-domain controller Windows Server 2008 SP2 server or client, use PowerShell from an administrator's account and execute the following code:

```
PS C:\> Import-Module ServerManager
PS C:\> Add-WindowsFeature -Name "RSAT-AD-PowerShell" —IncludeAllSubFeature
```

Things are even easier on Windows Server 2008 R2 servers, as all you need to do is fire up the Active Directory Module for PowerShell that's installed under Administrative Tools. Assuming that the Active Directory module is available on a server or client, you can load it into any PowerShell session with the following command:

```
PS C:\> Import-Module ActiveDirectory
```

Active Directory is represented to PowerShell like files on a hard drive reference through as the AD: drive. To get a list of the new Active Directory cmdlets, type:

```
PS AD:\> Get-Help *-AD*
```

If your system is joined to a domain, you can then navigate Active Directory. For example, here's how to create a new OU called Sales after navigating to the desired location in Active Directory:

```
PS C:\> CD AD:
PS AD:\> CD "DC=abc,DC=com"
PS AD:\DC=abc, DC=com> MD "OU=Sales"
```

To compare how much easier it is to access Active Directory data with the new module, the command to retrieve a list of domain controllers is:

```
PS C:\> Get-ADDomainController  | Format-Table Name, OperatingSystem
```

```
Name                        Operatingsystem
----                        ---------------
CONTOSO-DC07                Windows Server 2003
CONTOSO-DC01                Windows Server® 2008 Enterprise
CONTOSO-DC02                Windows Server 2008 R2 Enterprise
```

Setting the right scope for objects in a multidomain forest

When you start EMS, Exchange sets the default scope for queries performed against Active Directory to the domain to which the server belongs. This is fine if you operate a single domain forest, but it is definitely not if you have to manage objects in a multidomain forest because it means that any query that you perform will only return objects from the local domain.

Chapter 3

Exchange 2007 uses the *ViewEntireForest* property of the *$ADminSessionADSettings* global variable defined in the Exchange.PS1 file in the \Bin directory of the location where you installed Exchange to set the scope for Active Directory queries. You can edit the *ViewEntireForest* property of the *$AdminSettingADSettings* variable to set the scope to view the entire forest as follows:

```
## Reset the Default Domain
$Global:AdminSessionADSettings.ViewEntireForest = $True
```

Microsoft decided to deprecate the *AdminSessionADSettings* property for Exchange 2010. In an Exchange 2010 environment, you use the new Set-ADServerSettings command instead and set the *–ViewEntireForest* parameter to be $True (to see the entire forest) or $False (to see just the objects owned by the default domain). The logical place to do this is in your personal PowerShell profile. For example:

```
Set-ADServerSettings -ViewEntireForest $True
```

You can also use this command to point to a particular domain controller to retrieve Active Directory data. For example:

```
Set-ADServerSettings –PreferredServer 'DC1.contoso.com'
```

If you do not want to set your scope to the entire forest, a partial workaround is to specify a global catalog server in the remote domain to use for the query. Another way of forcing EMS to operate on a forest-wide basis is to specify the *–IgnoreDefaultScope* parameter for cmdlets such as Get-Mailbox. This parameter tells EMS to ignore the default recipient scope setting for EMC (typically the domain into which a server is installed) and use the entire forest instead. For example, if we wanted to set up a batch of mailboxes to move from an Exchange 2003 server to Exchange 2010 that used accounts in multiple domains, we could use a command like this:

```
Get-Mailbox –Server 'Exch2003' –ResultSize Unlimited –IgnoreDefaultScope | New-
MoveRequest –TargetDatabase 'Mailbox Database 1002' –BatchName 'Move Group from
Exchange 2003'
```

The natural question at this point is whether changing the scope for Active Directory queries will affect how you work with EMS. The answer is yes, because when you set a forest-wide scope, EMS fetches data from across the forest rather than the local domain. Unless you use parameters to focus in on particular groups of objects, such as specifying that you want to work with the mailboxes from one server, you will probably have to wait longer for a response. This is because you will ask EMS to process cmdlets that deal with servers, mailboxes, databases, or other objects across a complete forest rather than just one domain, but in most cases, the wait is worthwhile because you see the big picture and do not run the risk of missing something.

Some useful EMS snippets

A scan of the Internet results in many interesting EMS code snippets that can be usefully employed by an Exchange administrator. In this section we discuss some good examples. The idea is not to present complete solutions; rather, I hope to inspire you to experiment with EMS to see just how much value you can get from a few lines of reasonably straightforward code. After all, if you can do a lot of work in a couple of lines that take just a few minutes to type in and get running, think of how much you can do if you really set your mind to exploiting EMS!

Looking for large folders

The first example shows how to discover users who might be suffering from performance problems because they have very large folders in their mailboxes. The number of items that cause problems has grown as Microsoft tuned the database schema. With Exchange 2000 or Exchange 2003, the danger mark is around 5,000 items. The threshold increases to 20,000 with Exchange 2007 and leaps to 100,000 for Exchange 2010. Of course, the client used is also important, because Outlook 2010 is better at dealing with large folders than Outook 2003 is. Having more than 20,000 items in a folder is evidence of solid pack-rat behavior by anyone, and it marks a folder that will probably never be cleaned out simply because it takes too much effort to explore the contents and decide what should be kept and what should be deleted. In any case, let's assume that you want to flag potential issues to users who have more than 5,000 items in a folder. We can use code like this:

```
Get-Mailbox –Server ExServer1 | Get-MailboxFolderStatistics | Where {$_.ItemsInFolder
–GT 5000} | Sort ItemsInFolder –Descending | Format-Table Identity, ItemsInFolder
–AutoSize
```

Identity	ItemsInFolder
contoso.com/Exchange Users/Redmond, Eoin\Inbox	5271
contoso.com/Exchange Users/Ruth, Andy\Inbox	5265
contoso.com/Exchange Users/Andrews, Ben\Inbox	5263
contoso.com/Exchange Users/Pelton, David\Inbox	5230
contoso.com/Exchange Users/Simpson, David\Inbox	5218
contoso.com/Exchange Users/Redmond, Tony\Sent Items	5215

This code does the following:

- Calls Get-Mailbox to generate a list of all mailboxes located on databases hosted by a server. It is possible to process all mailboxes in an organization by changing the code to Get-Mailbox –ResultSize Unlimited, but such a command will take a long time to process in any organization with more than a few thousand mailboxes (although you could use a server-side filter where appropriate).

Chapter 3

- Calls Get-MailboxFolderStatistics to extract a count of items in each folder.
- Filters any folder with more than 5,000 items.
- Sorts the filtered folders by descending order.
- Outputs the information.

Note that an Exchange 2010 server even reports details of the folders in the dumpster (for example, "Deletions") that are not reported by an Exchange 2007 server.

Outputting a CSV file

Another variant of code that reports on user mailboxes is our next example. This script creates a CSV file that we can use to analyze mailbox usage with Excel or another tool (Figure 3-11). Again, this script could take quite some time to finish in a medium to large organization, so be sure to test it on perhaps just one server before you launch it to process mailboxes from all servers.


```
$ExchangeServers = Get-MailboxServer
$AllUsers = @()
ForEach ($Server in $ExchangeServers)
{$AllUsers += Get-Mailbox -Server $Server | Get-MailboxStatistics | Select
ServerName, DisplayName, Itemcount, TotalItemSize}
$AllUsers | Export-CSV c:\temp\MailboxList.csv -NoTypeInformation
```

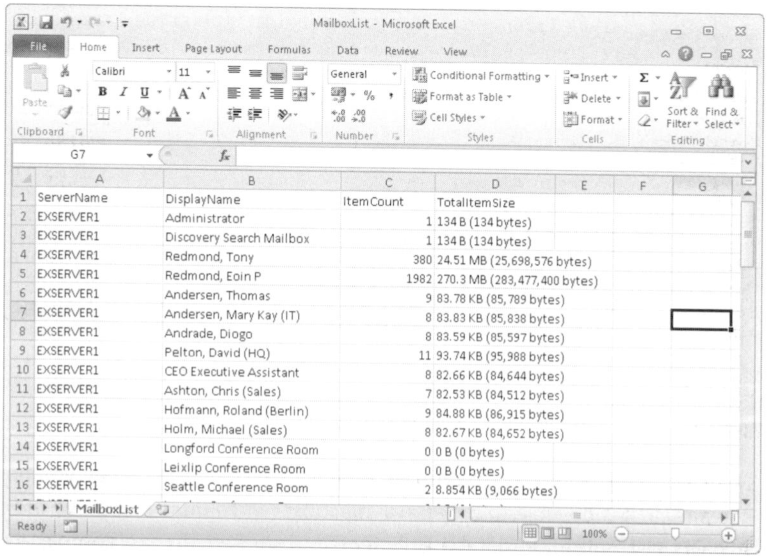

	A	B	C	D
1	ServerName	DisplayName	ItemCount	TotalItemSize
2	EXSERVER1	Administrator	1	134 B (134 bytes)
3	EXSERVER1	Discovery Search Mailbox	1	134 B (134 bytes)
4	EXSERVER1	Redmond, Tony	380	24.51 MB (25,698,576 bytes)
5	EXSERVER1	Redmond, Eoin P	1982	270.3 MB (283,477,400 bytes)
6	EXSERVER1	Andersen, Thomas	9	83.78 KB (85,789 bytes)
7	EXSERVER1	Andersen, Mary Kay (IT)	8	83.83 KB (85,838 bytes)
8	EXSERVER1	Andrade, Diogo	8	83.59 KB (85,597 bytes)
9	EXSERVER1	Pelton, David (HQ)	11	93.74 KB (95,988 bytes)
10	EXSERVER1	CEO Executive Assistant	8	82.66 KB (84,644 bytes)
11	EXSERVER1	Ashton, Chris (Sales)	7	82.53 KB (84,512 bytes)
12	EXSERVER1	Hofmann, Roland (Berlin)	9	84.88 KB (86,915 bytes)
13	EXSERVER1	Holm, Michael (Sales)	8	82.67 KB (84,652 bytes)
14	EXSERVER1	Longford Conference Room	0	0 B (0 bytes)
15	EXSERVER1	Leixlip Conference Room	0	0 B (0 bytes)
16	EXSERVER1	Seattle Conference Room	2	8.854 KB (9,066 bytes)

Figure 3-11 User mailbox report.

Creating a report in HTML

PowerShell is pretty flexible in terms of processing output. Generated reports can to show management and others the kind of work that servers do. The typical reports generated by EMS are plain text. We can also generate HTML reports by piping objects through the ConvertTo-HTML cmdlet (the Out-HTML cmdlet at *http://poshcode.org/1612* is also useful for generating HTML content). This example explores how to generate a useful report that shows mailboxes that have exceeded their storage quota. You could use a report like this to proactively check for users who are experiencing problems with their quota and perhaps allocate them some additional quota to allow them to resume working. The output is shown in Figure 3-12.

```
Get-MailboxDatabase | Get-MailboxStatistics | Sort StorageLimitStatus, TotalItemSize
-Descending | ConvertTo-HTML DisplayName, StorageLimitStatus, Database, ItemCount,
TotalItemSize > C:\Temp\Mbxs.html
```

You can enhance the output further by formatting the HTML with a style sheet or adding other information such as the date and time of the report. We leave that as an exercise for the reader.

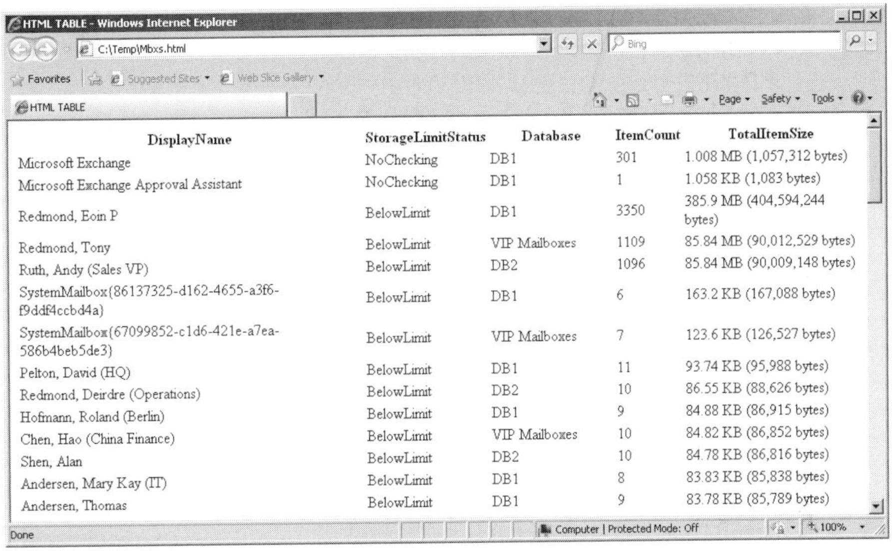

DisplayName	StorageLimitStatus	Database	ItemCount	TotalItemSize
Microsoft Exchange	NoChecking	DB1	301	1.008 MB (1,057,312 bytes)
Microsoft Exchange Approval Assistant	NoChecking	DB1	1	1.058 KB (1,083 bytes)
Redmond, Eoin P	BelowLimit	DB1	3350	385.9 MB (404,594,244 bytes)
Redmond, Tony	BelowLimit	VIP Mailboxes	1109	85.84 MB (90,012,529 bytes)
Ruth, Andy (Sales VP)	BelowLimit	DB2	1096	85.84 MB (90,009,148 bytes)
SystemMailbox{86137325-d162-4655-a3f6-f9ddf4ccbd4a}	BelowLimit	DB1	6	163.2 KB (167,088 bytes)
SystemMailbox{67099852-c1d6-421e-a7ea-586b4beb5de3}	BelowLimit	VIP Mailboxes	7	123.6 KB (126,527 bytes)
Pelton, David (HQ)	BelowLimit	DB1	11	93.74 KB (95,988 bytes)
Redmond, Deirdre (Operations)	BelowLimit	DB2	10	86.55 KB (88,626 bytes)
Hofmann, Roland (Berlin)	BelowLimit	DB1	9	84.88 KB (86,915 bytes)
Chen, Hao (China Finance)	BelowLimit	VIP Mailboxes	10	84.82 KB (86,852 bytes)
Shen, Alan	BelowLimit	DB2	10	84.78 KB (86,816 bytes)
Andersen, Mary Kay (IT)	BelowLimit	DB1	8	83.83 KB (85,838 bytes)
Andersen, Thomas	BelowLimit	DB1	9	83.78 KB (85,789 bytes)

Figure 3-12 Viewing the HTML version of the mailbox report.

It's worth noting that when you run the Get-MailboxStatistics cmdlet, you force EMS to make a remote procedure call (RPC) to the Information Store to retrieve the latest data for the mailboxes (individual, database, or server). The information is completely up to date and reflects the exact state of the mailbox rather than cached data that could be a couple of hours old. The Store caches information about mailbox quotas and updates the cache every two hours to avoid the overhead of the I/O that it would need to otherwise generate to check quotas every time a user attempts to send a message or to check that a mailbox can accept a new message.

TROUBLESHOOTING

Users report they've deleted messages but still exceed quota
Given the dynamic flow of messages in and out of mailboxes, it's likely that a small difference exists between the cached data and the actual state. This sometimes causes confusion when a user reports that she has exceeded quota and can't send mail even though she has deleted many messages and has to wait until the Store refreshes its cache to determine the new mailbox size and respect the fact that she has reduced the size to under quota. If this becomes a problem and users complain that Exchange takes too long before it allows them to resume email activity, you can amend the system registry to force Exchange to refresh the cache more often with the caveat that more frequent refreshes impose an extra overhead on the server. See *http://technet.microsoft .com/en-us/library/aa996988(EXCHG.80).aspx* for details.

Finding disconnected mailboxes

Disconnected mailboxes are mailboxes that exist in databases but aren't connected to Active Directory accounts. Obviously we want to remove any disconnected mailboxes that aren't required, but first we have to discover whether any exist. This code does the trick and is another example of collecting a list of objects, using it to generate some data, and then filtering it to locate the information that we need:

```
Get-MailboxServer | Get-MailboxStatistics | Where {$_.DisconnectDate -ne $Null} |
Format-Table DisplayName, OriginatingServer
```

Creating and sending messages from the shell

Although EMS includes a New-MailMessage cmdlet to create a new message in the Drafts folder of a user's mailbox, it does not include a complementary cmdlet to send the newly created message, and it's left to the user to rescue the message from the drafts folder, address it properly (because you can't add addresses with New-MailMessage), and send it.

Windows PowerShell 2.0 includes the Send-MailMessage cmdlet, which is able to create and send an SMTP message (including attachments), and this might be a solution for the problem. If it doesn't meet your needs, investigate the Send-SMTPMail cmdlet from the PowerShell Community Extensions (pscx.codeplex.com) project. Alternatively, you can assemble a mail message from its individual elements and send it as follows:

```
$SmtpClient = New-Object System.Net.Mail.SmtpClient
$SmtpClient.host = 'Mail-Relay.contoso.com'
$From = 'Tony.Redmond@contoso.com'
$To   = 'Andy.Ruth@contoso.com'
$Title = 'Answer to your questions'
$Body = 'Status Message follows - Here is some important information'
$SmtpClient.Send($From, $To, $Title, $Body)
```

These commands work if you point them to an SMTP server that is willing to relay messages for clients. Most Exchange servers and especially Exchange hub transport servers restrict the ability of clients to relay messages, especially unauthenticated clients. You can allow anonymous clients to connect and relay messages. See the section "Receive connectors" in Chapter 13, "The Exchange Transport System," for details about how to amend the properties of a receive connector to allow anonymous submission.

If your mail server doesn't allow anonymous connections, you can pass credentials by either setting the *UseDefaultCredentials* property to $True (the default is $False), which tells Windows to fetch whatever default network credentials are cached for the current logged-on user, or you can pass explicit credentials by setting the property with the necessary values for username and password. For example:

```
$SmtpClient.UseDefaultCredentials = $True
```

or

```
$Credentials = New-Object
System.Net.NetworkCredential('Tony.Redmond@contoso.com', 'Password')
SmtpClient.Credentials = $Credentials
```

Including credentials in plain text in a script isn't very secure. You can do a much better job by prompting the user for credentials to use:

```
$Credentials = Get-Credential
```

This command displays a standard Windows login dialog box for the user to input his username and password. We can then fetch the data and store it as follows:

```
$Username = $Credentials.Username
$Password =$Credentials.GetNetworkCredential().Password
$Credentials2 = New-Object System.Net.NetworkCredential($UserName,
$Password)
SmtpClient.Credentials = $Credentials2
```

So far, we've sent a pretty simple message. What if we want to read addresses for all the mailboxes in a container and send a message to them? We can use a container such as a

Chapter 3

distribution group (in which case you'd use the Get-DistributionGroupMember cmdlet to fetch the names) or from an OU as shown in the next example.

Reporting database size and mailbox count via email

This script (a variation of one discussed on *http://www.powershellcommunity.org*) looks for Exchange 2010 mailbox servers and extracts some data about the size of the mailbox databases on those servers and the number of mailboxes in each database. The script then creates and sends a message similar to the note shown in Figure 3-13.

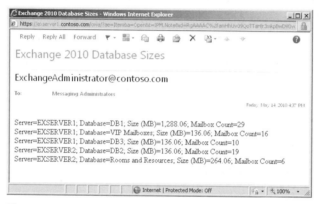

Figure 3-13 Output from database report script.

> **Note**
>
> If you run a report like this against databases that have multiple copies as part of a DAG, you'll see an entry for each database copy, so it will seem like some duplication is present.

The data in the message aren't particularly pretty but are a good example of how you can use PowerShell to very quickly extract and distribute data that are useful to administrators, especially if you leverage the power of the cloud and use scripts that are available on the Internet as the starting point. Of course, if you build on a script to create something that could be useful to others, you should consider sharing your work so that others in the community can benefit.

```
$BodyText = ""

$ExchangeServers = Get-ExchangeServer |
 Where-object {$_.AdminDisplayVersion.major -eq 14 -and $_.IsMailboxServer
-eq $True}
   ForEach ($Server in $ExchangeServers)
```

```
{
$db = Get-MailboxDatabase -server $server
ForEach ($objItem in $db)
    {
    $edbfilepath = $objItem.edbfilepath
         $path = "'\'\" + $server + "'\'\" +
    $objItem.EdbFilePath.DriveName.Remove(1).ToString() + "$"+
    $objItem.EdbFilePath.PathName.Remove(0,2)
    $dbsize = Get-ChildItem $path
         $dbpath =
    $EdbFilePath.PathName.Remove(0,2).remove($EdbFilePath.PathName.length-6)
    $mailboxcount = Get-MailboxStatistics -database $objitem | Measure-Object
    $ReturnedObj = New-Object PSObject
    $ReturnedObj | Add-Member NoteProperty -Name "Server" -Value $Server
    $ReturnedObj | Add-Member NoteProperty -Name "Database" -Value
$objItem.Identity
    $ReturnedObj | Add-Member NoteProperty -Name "Size (MB)" -Value ("{0:n2}" -
f ($dbsize.Length/1024KB))
    $ReturnedObj | Add-Member NoteProperty -Name "Mailbox Count" -Value
$mailboxcount.count
    $BodyText += $ReturnedObj
    $BodyText +="<p>"
    }
 }
$BodyText = $BodyText.Replace("@{","")
$BodyText = $BodyText.Replace("}","'n")

$MailMessage = New-Object System.Net.Mail.Mailmessage
$MailMessage.From = 'ExchangeAdministrator@contoso.com'
$MailMessage.To.Add('MailAdmins@contoso.com')
$MailMessage.Subject = "Exchange 2010 Database Sizes"
$MailMessage.IsBodyHtml = $True
$MailMessage.Body = $BodyText

$SmtpClient = New-object System.Net.Mail.SmtpClient
$SmtpClient.Host = 'exserver1.contoso.com'
$SmtpClient.Send($MailMessage)
```

The same technique can be used to create scripts that generate and send a wide variety of messages to report details of the system (not limited to Exchange; more components support PowerShell all the time) or for other housekeeping functions. For example, you could send a message to the proud owners of new mailboxes to welcome them to the email system and to inform them about different aspects of the environment, such as where to go to find more information, how to report problems, where to go to download programs, how to access internal Web sites, and so on. Such a script would have to locate new mailboxes with a loop by checking their creation date and then compose the message using commands similar to those shown earlier. Alternatively, you can explore the possibilities of a cmdlet extension agent (see *http://technet.microsoft.com/en-us/library/dd335067.aspx*) to add your own code to perform some additional actions when a cmdlet is called. For example, you could create an extension for the New-Mailbox cmdlet so that a message is automatically sent to the new mailbox after it is created.

Verbose PowerShell

Usually EMS performs whatever you ask it to do and doesn't give any indication of the processing that it performs in the background. You ask for a new mailbox to be created, and it's either created or some problem occurs that stops the command executing. If the problem is ignorance on the part of the user, such as an error in syntax or attempting to do something that doesn't make sense like creating a mailbox in a database that doesn't exist, you can simply fix the problem and try again.

Sometimes you need to know exactly what EMS does to help track down a problem, perhaps to provide information to Microsoft support to help them figure out what's going on in your Exchange deployment. You might just want to know what's happening when you execute a command. In either case, you can add the *–Verbose* parameter to a command to have PowerShell generate details of exactly what it does as it proceeds. Figure 3-14 shows some of the output when the New-MailboxDatabase cmdlet is used to create a new mailbox database. You can see how EMS validates the context that it is executing within, including checks to locate a global catalog server, validate RBAC authorization, and check that the mailbox database doesn't already exist.

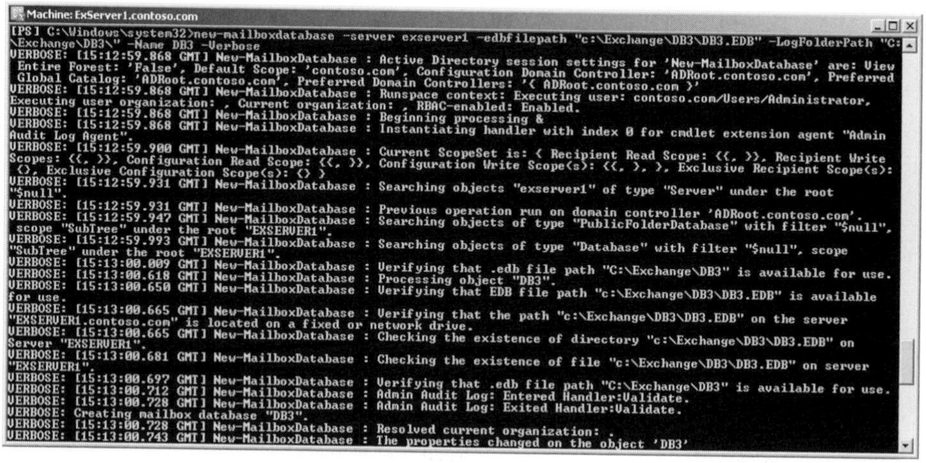

Figure 3-14 Examining some verbose PowerShell output.

Setting language values

There are many EMS cmdlets that allow you to set translated or localized values for strings. For example, if you create a MailTip, you can create localized text in different languages. The same is true when you create message classifications, retention policy tags, and so on. The question then is how Exchange decides whether to display a localized value. In general, here is what happens.

Every mailbox is assigned one or more language values. We'll discuss how this is done in Chapter 6. You can find out what languages are assigned to a mailbox with this command:

```
Get-Mailbox -Identity <mailbox> | Select Languages
```

Which languages are supported?

The languages supported by the mailbox (or, perhaps more correctly, spoken by the user who owns the mailbox) are listed in the international codes for languages. For example, EN-US indicates the English (EN) language as spoken in the United States, whereas EN-CA is English in Canada, EN-GB is English in Great Britain, and EN-IE is English in Ireland. English isn't the only language supported by Exchange, and you'll find other language codes such as ES-MX (Spanish in Mexico) or NL-NL (Dutch in Holland).

The first step is to retrieve the languages supported by the mailbox. Once this is known, Exchange can compare the supported languages against the localized values that are available; if a match is found, that localized value is provided to the client. An exact match for language and country (for example, ES-MX) is attempted first and if this doesn't work, a match is tried for just the language (ES). It might be that the languages supported by the mailbox contain multiple matches (for example, EN-US and EN-IE). In this case, Exchange selects the closest match in the order in which the languages are listed.

If no match is found, the default value is used. Typically this is the language used to install the server. OWA and Outlook 2010 both support localized values for features such as MailTips. Other clients or older versions of these clients might not.

Execution policies

EMS is pretty powerful, and just a few cmdlets can have a tremendous effect on many objects throughout Exchange. Some questions might have crossed your mind about how to control the ability of users to execute EMS commands.

The first line of protection is provided by RBAC. As you recall, users are only permitted access to the set of cmdlets and parameters available to the roles that each user holds. Even though trusted users will be assigned the roles that they need to get their work done, you still don't want them to execute scripts that they download from the Internet or obtain elsewhere.

A second line of defense is therefore provided by Execution Policies, which define the conditions under which PowerShell loads files for execution. There are four policies: *Restricted, AllSigned, RemoteSigned,* and *Unrestricted.* You configure the execution policy used for a server with the Set-ExecutionPolicy cmdlet. The default is RemoteSigned, which you can verify with the Get-ExecutionPolicy cmdlet. In this mode, EMS permits the execution of any script created locally, providing the script contains cmdlets that are supported by the role held by the user who invokes the script. Table 3-2 lists the alternate modes together with the potential trade-off in security that you might have to make for each mode.

Table 3-2 **PowerShell execution policies**

Execution Policy mode	Meaning
Restricted	No scripts can be run, even if they are signed by a trusted publisher.
AllSigned	Scripts must be digitally signed by a trusted partner before EMS will run them.
RemoteSigned	EMS will run any script created locally. Scripts that originate outside the system (such as those downloaded from the Internet) cannot run.
Unrestricted	EMS will run any script. This mode should only be used for test environments.

If you attempt to run an unsigned script that doesn't comply with policy, PowerShell signals that it cannot load the script. Scripts are signed with the Set-AuthenticodeSignature cmdlet, but you need to get a valid certificate first. The certificate can be one that you generate yourself or one that you buy from a commercial vendor, such as VeriSign. See *http://technet .microsoft.com/en-us/library/bb125017.aspx* for further details of how to generate and apply certificates to sign scripts.

CAUTION

Obviously, running an Exchange server with an unrestricted execution policy is a horrible idea. In fact, you should avoid any deviation from the default policy unless you have an excellent reason why you need to change. To change the policy, use the Set-ExecutionPolicy command to update the default execution policy on an Exchange 2010 server. For example:

```
Set-ExecutionPolicy -ExecutionPolicy Unrestricted
```

The change to the execution policy is effective immediately. Be sure to test any change that you want to make before putting the change into production, because it might break scripts that you or applications depend on. Execution policy is a server-specific setting. However, its setting is recorded in the system registry, and it is possible to use a group policy to apply the same setting to every server within the organization. To do this, configure a group policy to set the value of the ExecutionPolicy value to the desired execution mode. The key is located under:

```
HKLM\Software\Microsoft\PowerShell\1\ShellIds\Microsoft\PowerShell
```

Note that because the setting for the execution policy is held in the system registry, Windows will deny any attempt to update the value unless your account has the privilege to change the system registry.

Testing cmdlets

Exchange 2010 includes a set of test cmdlets that you can use to verify that different aspects of servers are working correctly. The cmdlets were first introduced in Exchange 2007 and have been updated to take account of changes in Exchange 2010. For example, the Test-SystemHealth cmdlet doesn't complain about circular logging if it detects that this is enabled for a database because the impact of circular logging is very different in Exchange 2010, especially when databases are protected by multiple copies. There's no need to run these cmdlets unless some suspicion exists that a server is not performing as expected or there is evidence that some problems exist, such as user complaints about server responsiveness when using an online client.

Some of these cmdlets, such as Test-MailFlow, are used by Microsoft Systems Center Operations Manager when it monitors Exchange servers. Like many other cmdlets, if you add the *–Verbose* parameter to any command, you'll see fuller details of what actually goes on as Exchange processes the command.

Test-SystemHealth

The Test-SystemHealth cmdlet is designed to validate the configuration of an Exchange server. When executed, the first step is to check with the Microsoft Web site for any available updates for the configuration data and settings that should be validated. The command then proceeds to check system settings in an attempt to detect obvious errors or variations from what Microsoft believes are appropriate settings for a production Exchange server. Essentially, these are many of the settings recommended by the Exchange Best Practice Analyzer. As shown in Figure 3-15, you can execute the command interactively with:

```
Test-SystemHealth
```

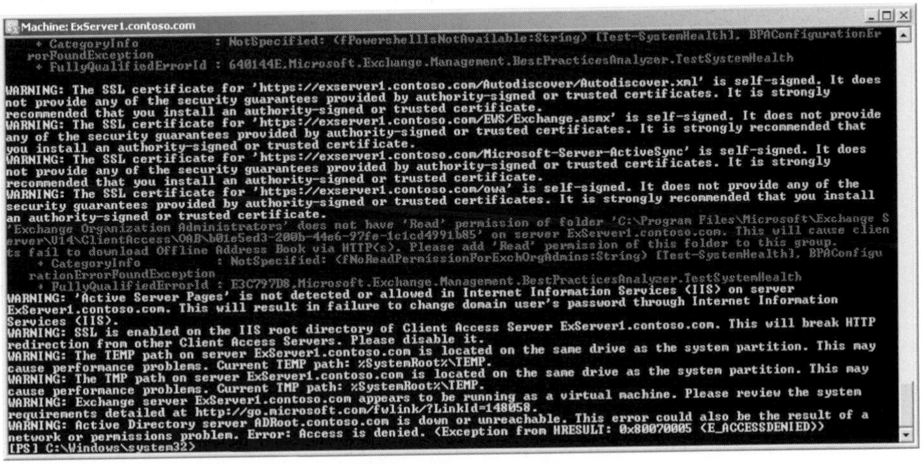

Figure 3-15 Running Test-SystemHealth.

By default, the credentials of the account that you use to run the command are used to access Exchange. You can provide explicit credentials by passing them in the *–ExchangeCredentials* parameter. You can also specify a different Active Directory account to log onto the server with the *–ADCredentials* parameter. In both cases, the Get-Credential cmdlet can be used to gather the necessary credentials.

Test-SystemHealth outputs details as it encounters potential problems. Figure 3-15 is the result of running the command on a multirole server hosted on VMware. The flagged issues aren't particularly serious but deserve attention from an administrator just in case any of them could prevent all aspects of the server from functioning properly. Following the details of the issues detected by the Test-SystemHealth cmdlet on a screen can be a challenge if more than a few issues are detected. However, you can capture additional details by specifying the name of an output file as follows:

```
Test-SystemHealth –OutFileLocation 'C:\Temp\Test-SystemHealth.log'
```

A text summary file that details the checks that were performed and a file in Extensible Markup Language (XML) format that contains much more detail about the checks and the results are generated. These files can serve to identify system issues, and I haven't seen any reason to suppress the output as support personnel invariably need this kind of data to resolve problems.

Test-ServiceHealth

The Test-ServiceHealth cmdlet validates that all of the Windows services on which Exchange depends are available. A check is performed for each role installed on a server and the output is similar to the following:

```
Test-ServiceHealth
```

```
Role                     : Mailbox Server Role
RequiredServicesRunning  : True
ServicesRunning          : {IISAdmin, MSExchangeADTopology, MSExchangeIS,
MSExchangeMailboxAssistants, MSExchangeMailSubmission, MSExchangeRepl,
MSExchangeRPC, MSExchangeSA, MSExchangeSearch, MSExchangeServiceHost,
MSExchangeThrottling, MSExchangeTransportLogSearch, W3Svc, WinRM}
ServicesNotRunning       : {}

Role                     : Client Access Server Role
RequiredServicesRunning  : True
ServicesRunning          : {IISAdmin, MSExchangeAB, MSExchangeADTopology,
MSExchangeFBA, MSExchangeFDS, MSExchangeMailboxReplication,
MSExchangeProtectedServiceHost, MSExchangeRPC, MSExchangeServiceHost, W3Svc,
WinRM}
ServicesNotRunning       : {}

Role                     : Hub Transport Server Role
```

```
RequiredServicesRunning  : True
ServicesRunning          : {IISAdmin, MSExchangeADTopology, MSExchangeEdgeSync,
MSExchangeServiceHost, MSExchangeTransport, MSExchangeTransportLogSearch,
W3Svc, WinRM}
ServicesNotRunning       : {}
```

Test-MAPIConnectivity

The Test-MAPIConnectivity cmdlet verifies that Messaging Application Programming Interface (MAPI) clients can connect to a database by logging on to a mailbox in the database and retrieving a list of items in the Inbox. If a mailbox is not specified, the cmdlet uses the system mailbox in the target database instead. For example, the following command connects to my mailbox. The latency is reported in "ticks." In this case, the reported latency is approximately 11 milliseconds. Exchange will drop an attempt to connect if it doesn't receive a response within 10 seconds. If required, you can alter this timeout value, but a lack of response within 10 seconds is a sure sign that a server is under enormous strain.

```
Test-MAPIConnectivity –Identity 'Tony.Redmond@contoso.com'
```

```
RunspaceId  : 8795186d-ef1e-4f19-a4aa-f8d8d9967e9f
Server      : London-EX1
Database    : VIP Data
Mailbox     : Redmond, Tony
Result      : Success
Latency     : 00:00:00.0114335
Error       :
Identity    :
IsValid     : True
```

If you add the –*MonitoringContext* parameter to the cmdlet and set its value to $True, you'll also receive some information about relevant system events and performance monitor counters. Normally you don't need to see this information.

Administrators sometimes use Test-MAPIConnectivity to validate that a server is operating properly and responding to users within a reasonable time. Here's a one-line script that tests connectivity to all of the databases on a server and outputs the connect time in milliseconds.

```
Test-MAPIConnectivity –Server 'ExServer1' | % {Write-Host "Database:" $_.Server "\"
$_.Database "Result:" $_.Result "Milliseconds:" $_.Latency.Milliseconds $_.Error}
```

Test-ReplicationHealth

The Test-ReplicationHealth cmdlet was originally introduced in Exchange 2007 SP1 to test the working of the cluster continuous replication (CCR) and standby continuous replication

Chapter 3

(SCR) features and is updated for Exchange 2010 to test all of the aspects of log replication within a DAG. You can execute this command by selecting a mailbox server that is a DAG member as follows:

```
Test-ReplicationHealth -id ExServer1
```

Server	Check	Result	Error
ExServer1	ClusterService	Passed	
ExServer1	ReplayService	Passed	
ExServer1	ActiveManager	Passed	
ExServer1	TasksRpcListener	Passed	
ExServer1	TcpListener	Passed	
ExServer1	DagMembersUp	Passed	
ExServer1	ClusterNetwork	Passed	
ExServer1	QuorumGroup	Passed	
ExServer1	FileShareQuorum	Passed	
ExServer1	DBCopySuspended	Passed	
ExServer1	DBCopyFailed	Passed	
ExServer1	DBInitializing	Passed	
ExServer1	DBDisconnected	Passed	
ExServer1	DBLogCopyKeepingUp	Passed	
ExServer1	DBLogReplayKeepingUp	Passed	

Test-ExchangeSearch

The Test-ExchangeSearch cmdlet validates that content indexing and search is working properly. You can execute a test for a specified mailbox database or mailbox. In both cases, Exchange creates some simple items in the target database and checks that indexing has occurred and then cleans up by removing the test data. It does not check items that require an IFilter to be indexed, such as PDF or other complex formats. To test search for a mailbox database (the system mailbox in the database is used for this test):

```
Test-ExchangeSearch -MailboxDatabase 'VIP Data'
```

To test search for a specific mailbox:

```
Test-ExchangeSearch -Identity 'David.Simpson@contoso.com'
```

Database	Server	Mailbox	ResultFound	SearchTime	Error
DB2	ExServer2	DSimpson	True	2	

Test-OWAConnectivity

The Test-OWAConnectivity cmdlet tests that connectivity is available to the OWA application. You can test a CAS server or on the basis of a specific Uniform Resource Locator (URL). For example, to test that connectivity works for all virtual directories used by OWA on a CAS server:

```
Test-OWAConnectivity –ClientAccessServer ExServer4
```

ClientAccessServer	MailboxServer	URL	Scenario	Result	Latency (ms)	Error
ExServer4.contoso.	ExServer4.	https://ExServer4.	Logon	Success	112.66	

To test that connectivity works for a specific URL (typically the URL used to access OWA), we can amend the command as follows. In this case, we also pass the credentials of a user mailbox to use during the connectivity test. The mailbox must be located on a mailbox server in the same Active Directory site as the CAS server. We also specify that the test accepts any SSL certificate. This might be the case when you're testing OWA connectivity after you set up a new CAS server. Later on, when you have installed the necessary certificates, you can test that the certificates work by dropping the –*TrustAnySSLCertificate* parameter:

```
Test-OWAConnectivity –URL https://ExServer2.contoso.com/owa –MailboxCredential
(Get-Credential contoso\TRedmond) –TrustAnySSLCertificate
```

Test-ECPConnectivity

The Test-ECPConnectivity cmdlet is new for Exchange 2010. It tests that connectivity can be established to the ECP application through a nominated CAS server. The test performs a test logon using the system mailbox and then executes an Exchange Web Services call to test that ECP is functioning properly. The result is reported as a pass or failure together with the latency of the calls.

A high latency such as the one reported here is a matter of concern unless it is the first attempt to access ECP since a server was booted, in which case it could be that the application needs to "warm up" within IIS. You should run the test several times again and observe whether the latency reduces as ECP is accessed. If not, check that the server is performing normally and validate that the application functions properly by logging on to ECP as a user.

```
Test-ECPConnectivity –Identity ExServer1
```

Chapter 3

```
CasServer    LocalSite    Scenario         Result     Latency(MS)    Error
---------    ---------    ----------       --------    -----------    -----
ExServer1    Dublin       Logon            Success        237.70
ExServer1    Dublin       WebServiceCall   Success          0.00
```

Test-MRSHealth

The Test-MRSHealth cmdlet validates that the Mailbox Replication Service (MRS) is functioning properly on a CAS server. This cmdlet is new to Exchange 2010. Three aspects are tested: that the MRS service is running, that the service responds to an RPC ping, and that MRS is scanning for queued move requests. In this example, we test that MRS is running on a server called ExServer2. The results show that everything is normal.

```
Test-MRSHealth -Identity ExServer2
```

```
Check          : ServiceCheck
Passed         : True
Message        : The Mailbox Replication Service is running.
Identity       : ExServer2
IsValid        : True

Check          : RPCPingCheck
Passed         : True
Message        : The Mailbox Replication Service is responding to RPC ping.
Server version: 14.0.682.0 caps:01.
Identity       : ExServer2
IsValid        : True

Check          : QueueScanCheck
Passed         : True
Message        : The Mailbox Replication Service is scanning MDB queues for
jobs. Last scan age: 00:08:49.1792211.
Identity       : ExServer2
IsValid        : True
```

Testing POP3 and IMAP4 Connectivity

The Test-POP3Connectivity and Test-IMAP4Connectivity cmdlets validate that the Post Office Protocol 3 (POP3) and Internet Message Access Protocol 4 (IMAP4) services are running normally and that a mailbox can log on and create and send messages using the POP3 and IMAP4 protocols. The basic command to perform a check against a specific CAS server using the credentials of a user account is as follows:

```
Test-IMAP4Connectivity -ClientAccessServer ExServer1 -MailboxCredential
(Get-Credential Contoso\TRedmond)
```

```
CasServer   LocalSite    Scenario        Result      Latency(MS)    Error
---------   ---------    -----------     --------    -----------    -------
ExServer1   Dublin       Test IMAP4 C... Success        385.62
```

Use the same syntax with the Test-POP3Connectivity cmdlet to validate that all is well for POP3 connections.

Testing mail flow

The Test-MailFlow cmdlet validates that mail submission, transport, and delivery are working properly. You can test by sending system-generated messages from one mailbox server to another, to a specific mailbox database, or to a remote email address. Test messages are sent with delivery receipt requests so that Exchange has some way to measure the end-to-end delivery time. The output of a successful test is a measurement of the latency of the overall operation expressed in seconds.

To test the delivery of messages from a mailbox server, you can simply type **Test-MailFlow** when logged on to that server. In this instance, Exchange connects to the system mailbox in the databases located on the server and attempts to send messages using the system mailbox. A better test is to allow Exchange to discover available mailbox servers and use them as targets for the test. This is done as follows:

```
Test-MailFlow –AutoDiscoverTargetMailboxServer
```

```
TestMailflowResult      : Success
MessageLatencyTime      : 00:00:02.4773026
IsRemoteTest            : True
```

If you're having problems with a specific server, you can identify it as the target:

```
Test-Mailflow –TargetMailboxServer 'ExServer1'
```

It's possible to be even more specific and test that mail submission and delivery are functioning correctly for a mailbox database:

```
Test-MailFlow –TargetDatabase 'VIP Mailboxes'
```

All of the commands explored to date cause messages to flow to and from the system mailboxes located in the databases that are involved in the tests. You can also test mail delivery to a remote email address by providing Exchange with an SMTP address, to which it can send a test message similar to the one illustrated in Figure 3-16.

```
Test-MailFlow –TargetEmailAddress 'Tony.Redmond@contoso.com'
```

Chapter 3

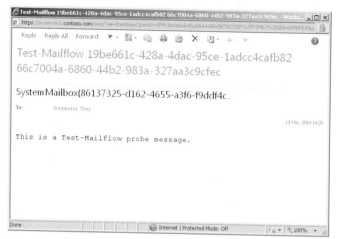

Figure 3-16 Test message sent by the Test-MailFlow cmdlet.

Note that Exchange might report tests to remote email domains as failures. This occurs when it cannot confirm the successful delivery of the message because of the length of time that the remote email server takes to respond to the delivery receipt request. It's also possible that the remote email system will suppress delivery service messages. On the other hand, if you use a local SMTP address as the target mailbox, you'll invariability receive a success status because all of the processing occurs within the same Exchange organization. If your test fails within an Exchange organization, it's evidence that something pretty serious is going on within the transport system. You can adjust the latency setting that governs the threshold to regard a test as a "success" or "failure" with the –*ErrorLatency* parameter. The default setting is 15 seconds for local test and 180 seconds for a remote test. The –*ExecutionTimeOut* parameter is also involved, as it sets a limit for the total amount of time that a test can run before it exits. The default is 240 seconds, so it's also possible that a remote email server might not respond before the total test time expires.

But we need some control

EMS is a great way to get work done with Exchange as long as you don't mind grappling with the command-line interface. If no control were exerted, you could do massive damage to an Exchange organization with EMS, such as selecting all the mailboxes in a database and removing them with a single line of code. Of course, only the people who need to control the full scope of the organization should be able to take such drastic action. Traditionally, control is given through permissions and privileges. Exchange 2010 takes a different approach and adopts the RBAC model. All administrators need a solid grounding in RBAC and its implementation in Exchange, so that's where our journey leads us next.

# CHAPTER 4

Role-Based Access Control

WHEREAS the introduction of the Database Availability Group (DAG) is the most technologically interesting advance in Microsoft Exchange Server 2010, the implementation of a new permissions model based on the concept of role-based access control (RBAC) exerts the most pervasive influence across all parts of the product. RBAC is therefore the most important element for administrators to master.

Taken as a whole, RBAC is an approach to restricting access to systems and data based on the need of administrators and users to do their jobs. In other words, you should only have access to information that you need rather than access to a lot of data that you really don't. RBAC is not a new concept, and it has been implemented in other operating systems and applications including HP-UX, Linux, Oracle DBMS, SAP R/3, and others.

Previous versions of Exchange use Windows access control lists (ACLs) to grant permissions to users and administrators to allow them to do their work. ACLs are an effective way to manage permissions for environments that are well structured and do not tend to change much over time. Windows itself and many of the applications that run on Windows fall into this category. Exchange is a little more dynamic and spans hundreds of thousands of objects in its largest deployments. Tracking and updating ACLs across such a dynamic environment for so many objects is a real challenge, and the real-world experience revealed that ACLs are often updated incorrectly, can be difficult to understand and therefore debug when things go wrong, and are prone to disruption through changes applied by software upgrades or patches. Another issue is that the conventional model of creating, updating, and setting permissions on objects often doesn't translate well into the task-driven environment that exists within an application such as Exchange where permissions have to support scenarios such as permitting help desk personnel to reset a user's password without being able to affect any other setting of the user's account. The granularity available in RBAC addresses this need.

Even if some problems are encountered as administrators learn about RBAC and make the transition from the previous permissions model, Microsoft believes that Exchange's implementation of RBAC will avoid complexity and ease management over time. In addition, RBAC should simplify matters for administrators enormously by removing the need to grapple with ACLs on a daily basis. Instead, administrators should be able to assign the ability to perform tasks by adding users to role groups, leaving RBAC to do all the necessary ACL maintenance in the background.

It is impossible to understate the influence of RBAC throughout Exchange 2010. It would require a 300-page book to cover every aspect of RBAC in depth. This chapter does not attempt to present such comprehensive coverage. Instead, the basics are set out to get you started and encourage you to investigate further to determine how best to apply RBAC to help you manage your organization.

RBAC basics

When Microsoft discusses RBAC in Exchange 2010, they often describe it in the form of a triangle (Figure 4-1) to show how roles, role groups, scopes, and assignments fit together.

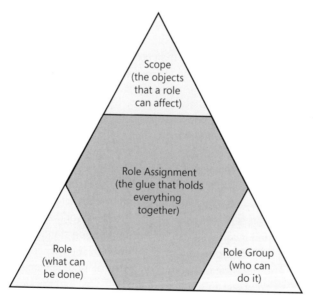

Figure 4-1 The RBAC triangle.

These are the major elements of RBAC as implemented in Exchange 2010:

- **Management role**   A collection of role entries that define the set of cmdlets and parameters that a user can run.

- **Management role group**   A container for a group of management roles that collectively allow a user to function in a role such as recipient management. Exchange 2010 includes a default set of management role groups, and you can define new management role groups to meet specific needs that are not served by a default role group.

- **Management role assignment**   The ability to assign a management role to an individual user or to the members of a role group (universal security group).

- **Management role assignment policies**   Management role groups are primarily intended for use by administrators to enable them to perform administrative tasks such as recipient management. The ability of users to work with personal data is controlled by management role assignment policies. Out of the box, Exchange 2010 provides a default role assignment policy that defines how users can update the information in their profiles (contact phone numbers, display name, and so on) and distribution group membership. The default role assignment policy is automatically assigned to users when their mailbox is created or moved to an Exchange 2010 server unless another role assignment policy is explicitly assigned. A mailbox can only be assigned a single role assignment policy at a time.

- **Management role scope**   The definition of the scope or the collection of objects that a management role can work with. A role such as Organization Management has a scope of the complete organization because the users who hold this role have to be able to manage any object in the entire organization. Other roles might be restricted to a particular scope such as an organizational unit (OU) in Active Directory to allow a fine granularity of management operations, such as the ability to manage mailboxes that belong to a certain region.

- **Management role entries**   Permit access to one or more cmdlets to enable a user to perform a certain task. For example, access to the New-Mailbox cmdlet allows a user to create a new mailbox. It is possible to restrict role entries to selected parameters for a cmdlet.

Another way of understanding RBAC is to look at it from the perspective of the work that someone does with Exchange. This will be either as an administrator or as an end user. The methods used by RBAC to associate the rights that the two groups need to do their work are as follows:

- Administrators and other specialist users who have to perform operational tasks with an Exchange server gain the rights to do their work through membership in appropriate role groups. Each role group consists of a number of roles. To give administrators permission to do something, simply assign them the correct management role by putting them into the appropriate role group.

Chapter 4

> **Note**
>
> The Organization Management role group is the most powerful because it includes practically every role available to Exchange (there are some exceptions).

- Users don't need to be granted membership in role groups to be able to interact with Exchange because control of their data (mailbox and mailbox settings) is granted through the default management role assignment policy. That's a long and complicated term to explain "default settings."

Before we plunge into the details of what roles, assignments, and policies mean in detail, Table 4-1 helps establish a context for the discussion by associating various tasks that are performed by different individuals in an Exchange organization with the role group that provides access to the permissions required to execute each task.

Table 4-1 **Linking role groups to tasks**

Task	Role Group required	Notes
I want to be the all-powerful manager of the complete Exchange organization.	Organization Management	Some roles have to be explicitly delegated before even a member of the Organization Management group can perform a task. The need to assign the mailbox import-export role to an account to gain access to the cmdlets to import or export mailbox data is the best example.
I want to be able to see the objects in the Exchange organization, but I don't need to edit anything.	View-Only Organization Management	This role allows its holders to view details of configuration objects (servers, connectors, and so on) plus recipients anywhere in the organization.
I want to be able to manage mailboxes and distribution groups.	Recipient Management	Members of this role group can create, edit, and delete any mail-enabled object except public folders.
I want to be able to help users maintain the settings for their mailboxes.	Help Desk	The Help Desk role group includes the User Options and View-Only Recipients roles. This set of roles might limit the effectiveness of the Help Desk role group in some companies, which is why you can modify role groups to add new roles to expand what the role group members are allowed to do.
I want to be able to manage Exchange server configuration settings.	Server Management	Members of this role group will not be able to manage recipient objects unless they are also members of the Recipient Management role group. Customizations are possible to restrict the ability to manage specific servers or databases.

I need to be able to per-form discovery searches and respond to legal actions.	Discovery Management	This role group also allows its members to manage the process of putting mailboxes on litigation hold.
I need to be able to man-age public folders.	Public Folder Management	Members of this group can use the Public Folder management console (available in the Exchange Management Console [EMC] toolbox) to manage public folders.
I need to manage differ-ent aspects of compliance across the organization.	Records Management	This role group allows its members to manage admin-istrative auditing, message tracking, journaling, reten-tion policies and tags, message classifications, and transport rules.
I need to manage the Unified Messaging servers and set up objects such as dial plans.	UM Management	This role group allows administrators to manage the Exchange Unified Messaging application (if deployed within the organization).

Now that we have some idea of how RBAC might affect the work that administrators do and we've given the formal definitions of the different terms that we'll meet, let's consider what these entities mean in practical terms.

Roles

Exchange 2010 SP1 includes 69 built-in roles that are designed to cover the vast majority of administrative and user tasks performed in Exchange organizations. The majority of the roles cover administrative tasks, from taking care of address lists to managing public fold-ers, and there is a small set of roles (all prefixed with "My") that are used to assign rights to users to maintain their mailbox settings and other options. You can see the complete col-lection of roles with the command:

```
Get-ManagementRole
```

When you break it down, a role can be decomposed into a set of cmdlets and parameters that Exchange makes available to anyone who holds the role. For example, if we look at the Message Tracking role, you find that it includes the six cmdlets that you need to be able to search through message tracking logs. This is revealed as follows:

```
Get-ManagementRoleEntry 'Message Tracking\*'
```

```
Name                          Role               Parameters
-------                       -----              ---------------
Set-ADServerSettings          Message Tracking   {ConfigurationDomainController, Confirm, Debug,.
Get-Recipient                 Message Tracking   {Anr, BookmarkDisplayName, Credential, Debug,
New-OrganizationRelationship  Message Tracking   {DeliveryReportEnabled, DomainNames, Name}
```

```
Write-AdminAuditLog            Message Tracking   {Comment, Confirm, Debug, DomainController,
Get-MessageTrackingReport      Message Tracking   {BypassDelegateChecking, Debug, DetailLevel,
Get-Mailbox                    Message Tracking   {Anr, Arbitration, Archive, Credential, Database,
Search-MessageTrackingReport   Message Tracking   {BypassDelegateChecking, Confirm, Debug,
Set-OrganizationRelationship   Message Tracking   {DeliveryReportEnabled, Identity}
Get-MessageTrackingLog         Message Tracking   {Debug, DomainController, End, ErrorAction,
Get-ExchangeServer             Message Tracking   {Debug, Domain, DomainController, ErrorAction,
Get-DomainController           Message Tracking   {Credential, Debug, DomainName, ErrorAction,
```

If you recall the discussion about how the Exchange Management Shell (EMS) and its relationship with RBAC in Chapter 3, "The Exchange Management Shell," it should now be clear
how cmdlets are made available to users and loaded into an EMS session during initialization. In this case, if a user holds the Message Tracking role through membership of a role
group, EMS will load the 11 cmdlets and their available parameter set as listed earlier to
make them available during the session (you'll see only six cmdlets listed on an Exchange
2010 server).

Role entries are named through a combination of the role group name and the cmdlet, so
including the asterisk wildcard character in the command instructs Exchange to return all of
the cmdlets assigned to the role group. To return details of a specific cmdlet, including the
parameters that can be used, we include the cmdlet name:

```
Get-ManagementRoleEntry 'Move Mailboxes\Get-Recipient' | Format-List
```

You can also find the list of roles that a specific cmdlet is assigned to with the Get-
ManagementRole cmdlet. For example, to list all roles that can update mailbox information
with the Set-Mailbox cmdlet:

```
Get-ManagementRole -cmdlet 'Set-Mailbox'
```

Using role assignment policy to limit access

Role assignments can limit access down to the parameter level for a cmdlet. Exchange uses
this capability to restrict users from being able to write to specific data items within a larger
set. For example, the default role assignment policy allows users to update their contact
details, but not their display name, through Exchange Control Panel (ECP). You can interrogate Exchange to discover the role assignments that underpin this capability by looking for
the assignments that control the ability to use the Set-User cmdlet to update their mobile
phone number (one of the data items permitted by the default role assignment policy) as
follows:

```
Get-ManagementRole -Cmdlet Set-User -CmdletParametersMobilePhone| Get-ManagementRoleAssignment
 -GetEffectiveUsers -Delegating $False | Where-Object {$_.Effectiveusername -ne "All Group Members"}
| Format-Table Role, RoleAssigneeName, EffectiveUserName
```

If we explore this code, we see that it does the following:

- Look for all roles that permit access to the *MobilePhone* property through Set-User.

- Pipe the roles to Get-ManagementRoleAssignment to return a list of users who have been delegated access through a role assignment (if the *–Delegating* parameter is set to *$True*, you will see a list of users who can delegate access to others).

- Filter the list to remove "All Group Members" because we only want to see individual users.

- Output the role, assignee name, and user name.

The output:

```
Role                    RoleAssigneeName                    EffectiveUserName
----                    ----------------                    -----------------
Mail Recipients         Organization Management             Administrator
Mail Recipients         Organization Management             Halstead, Dean
Mail Recipients         Help Desk Level 2 Support           Ruth, Andy
Mail Recipients         EMEA Help Desk                      Pelton, David
Mail Recipients         EMEA Help Desk                      Smith, John
Mail Recipients         APJ Help Desk                       Akers, Kim
User Options            Organization Management             Administrator
User Options            Organization Management             Redmond, Tony
MyContactInformation    Default Role Assignment Policy      All Policy Assignees
```

CAUTION

RBAC currently allows restrictions to be placed on cmdlets that write data (cmdlets beginning with New- and Set-). It does not support restrictions on the Get- cmdlets that allow users to retrieve the properties of an object. This means that restricted users can read all of the data for an object, even though they might not be able to update some or even all of the attributes.

Chapter 4

INSIDE OUT   Controlling access to Remove-Mailbox

Some organizations do not like the fact that Exchange administrators can remove a mailbox and the underlying Active Directory account using the Remove Mailbox option in EMC or the Remove-Mailbox cmdlet in EMS. The same argument can be advanced for the Remove-MailContact cmdlet, but most of the focus is on the ability to remove a user account from Active Directory. Exchange doesn't allow you to remove role entries from its built-in roles, so you can't remove the Remove-Mailbox entry to solve the problem. Instead, you have to make sure that no one except organization administrators has access to the Mail Recipient Creation role because it is the only role that includes access to Remove-Mailbox. You can use this code to check who has received delegated access to the Mail Recipient Creation role and then remove it:

```
Get-ManagementRoleAssignment -Role "Mail Recipient Creation" -Delegating $False
| Remove-ManagementRoleAssignment
```

Creating roles for specific tasks

It is entirely possible that your deployment might require a new role to perform very specific tasks. You can create a new role for this purpose using the following rules:

- Custom roles have to be created using one of the built-in roles as a parent; they cannot be created from another custom role.

- A child role cannot hold more rights than its parent.

- The set of cmdlets that are included in a role must include a "Get" cmdlet to match every "Set" or "Remove" cmdlet. For example, if you look at the MyProfileInformation role that allows users to update their own personal contact data through ECP, you'll see that it includes entries for the Get-Mailbox cmdlet to retrieve the current personal data and Set-Mailbox and Set-User cmdlets to allow the user to update the data. If you look at the details of the individual role entries for Set-Mailbox and Set-User, you will see that the parameters are restricted to a limited set including the display name, first name, initials, and so on.

As an example, assume that we want our Help Desk staff to be able to update the personal information for recipients because we really don't want users doing this through ECP. The first step is to figure out what built-in role to use as the parent. We could pick MyProfileInformation or Mail Recipients because both roles allow access to user properties. In this case, we'll base our custom role on Mail Recipients.

```
New-ManagementRole -Name 'Help Desk User Updates' -Parent 'Mail Recipients'
```

The built-in Mail Recipients role includes a very large number of cmdlets that we don't want to make available to the role holders, so we will remove everything except the Get-Mailbox cmdlet, because it's easier to put back the few cmdlets that we need rather than editing them in place.

```
Get-ManagementRoleEntry –Identity 'Help Desk User Updates\*' | Where {$_.Name –ne
'Get-Mailbox'} | Remove-ManagementRoleEntry –Confirm:$False
```

We can now add the cmdlets to our role and specify the parameters that we'll allow with each cmdlet. We want to allow the Help Desk to update a number of different user settings, so we need to permit access to six cmdlets in all (five in addition to the one left after we remove the set inherited from the parent role—some trial and error might be necessary before you determine the exact cmdlet set you require):

```
Add-ManagementRoleEntry 'Help Desk User Updates\Set-Mailbox' –Parameters Identity,
DisplayName, SimpleDisplayName
Add-ManagementRoleEntry 'Help Desk User Updates\Get-User'
Add-ManagementRoleEntry 'Help Desk User Updates\Set-User' –Parameters Identity,
FirstName, LastName, Initials, Office, Phone, MobilePhone, Department, Manager
Add-ManagementRoleEntry 'Help Desk User Updates\Get-CASMailbox'
Add-ManagementRoleEntry 'Help Desk User Updates\Set-CASMailbox' –Parameters Identity,
IMAPEnabled, OWAEnabled, OWAMailboxPolicy
```

We can now check that the custom Help Desk User Updates role includes the correct cmdlets and parameters with:

```
Get-ManagementRoleEntry 'Help Desk User Updates\*' | Format-List
```

Assuming everything checks out, we are now ready to assign the new role to users.

Scopes

All RBAC roles have a scope that tells Exchange what objects they can access and update. You can refine a scope considerably so that a role is scoped on just the objects in an OU, a group of specific users, or everything in the Exchange configuration container. You can also create scopes that restrict users to managing a server or group of servers. Exchange 2010 SP1 adds a new scope to allow you to control access to specific databases. See the section "RBAC enhancements in SP1" later in this chapter for more information.

In this example, we look at the scope of the Move Mailboxes role, which is required by anyone who wants to move a mailbox between databases:

```
Get-ManagementRole 'Move Mailboxes' | Format-List *Scope*
```

```
ImplicitRecipientReadScope  : Organization
ImplicitRecipientWriteScope : Organization
ImplicitConfigReadScope     : OrganizationConfig
ImplicitConfigWriteScope    : OrganizationConfig
```

The most important scopes are the implicit write scopes because these define the objects that the cmdlets covered by the role can update. In this case, to move mailboxes, we need the ability to update the mailbox object afterward, so the recipient write scope is organization-wide. You'll also see that the role has the ability to read information from the organization's configuration so that we can select any database in the organization as a target for the mailbox move.

If you create a new RBAC role, it has to be the child of an existing RBAC role, and it automatically inherits the scope of the parent role unless you define a new scope. We'll see how this happens in Chapter 5, "Exchange Management Console and Control Panel," when we look at how to create a new role to allow users to update distribution groups that they own without the ability to create new groups. You can create new scopes as you create new roles, but a better technique is to define a scope once so that it is available to multiple roles. Exchange provides the New-ManagementScope cmdlet for this purpose. Scopes can be created so that roles operate on specific servers, an OU, or even the members of a distribution group. For example, this command creates a new scope based on a distribution group called Company Officers. You can even use a dynamic distribution group for this purpose.

```
New-ManagementScope -Name 'Company Officers' -RecipientRestrictionFilter
{MemberOfGroup -eq "cn=Company Officers,ou=Exchange Users,dc=contoso,dc=com"}
Get-ManagementScope 'Company Officers'
```

```
RecipientFilter        :MemberOfGroup -eq 'CN=Company Officers,OU=Exchange
Users,Dc=contoso,dc=com'
ScopeRestrictionType : RecipientScope
Exclusive            : False
ExchangeVersion      : 0.10 (14.0.100.0)
Name                 : Company Officers
DistinguishedName    : CN=Company Officers,CN=Scopes,CN=RBAC,CN=Microsoft
Exchange,CN=Services,CN=Configuration,DC=contoso,DC=com
Identity             : Company Officers
ObjectClass          : {top, msExchScope}
```

Once created, scopes can be assigned to role groups using the *–CustomConfigWriteScope* (for server and database scopes) and *–CustomRecipientWriteScope* parameters (for recipient-based scopes).

Role groups

Roles can be assigned on an individual basis or on a group basis. Although roles provide the granularity necessary to break down all the different tasks performed by a typical Exchange administrator, it would be far too complex to assign tasks through individual roles. Role groups provide a convenient method to gather together the roles necessary to perform higher level tasks such as "Mailbox Search" and avoid the need to assign the 11 separate roles that would otherwise be required. It's much easier to manage the assignment of a single role group than it is to manage 11 separate role assignments, and it's also less likely that administrators will make mistakes and create security problems when they manage RBAC through role groups.

Users are assigned roles by making them members of role groups. In effect, a role group describes a high-level set of tasks that you expect a certain type of administrator to perform. For example, someone working on a help desk needs to be able to view and update details of recipients, but you probably don't want them to mess with a send connector or transport rule. The role group defined for Help Desk contains all of the roles (and therefore access to all of the cmdlets) that are necessary to do the work required by this role and no more.

Role groups provide much of the foundation of the RBAC implementation in Exchange 2010. You can see the built-in role groups (and any that you have subsequently created) with:

```
Get-RoleGroup
```

Behind the scenes, every role group is represented by a Universal Security Group (USG) held in the Microsoft Exchange Security Groups OU in Active Directory (Figure 4-2). The USGs are flagged to Exchange so that it knows that these groups are used by RBAC. Where necessary, the existing Exchange 2007 ACLs are copied to a role group when the first Exchange 2010 server is installed into an organization that contains Exchange 2007 servers to allow the role group to perform its management function.

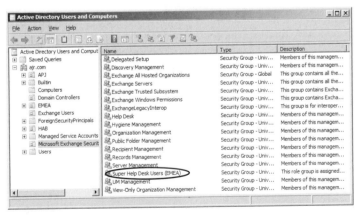

Figure 4-2 The USGs used by RBAC.

A key difference between the USGs used to instantiate role groups and other USGs is that you can manage role groups (and by default, their underlying USGs) from EMC, EMS, and ECP. The "Super Help Desk Users (EMEA)" USG shown in Figure 4-2 is not one of the

Chapter 4

standard USGs created during the installation of Exchange 2010 for RBAC. You won't see it in your Exchange deployment because it's a USG created by Exchange when I created a new role group for my organization. This underlines the point that there is a one-to-one mapping between role groups and USGs.

INSIDE OUT   Delegating roles that are not assigned by default

Apart from having access to the vast majority of roles defined in an organization, users in the Organization Management role group have the ability to delegate the roles that they don't possess by default. The Mailbox Import Export role is the best example of a role that is not held by users who are part of the Organization Management role group but can be delegated to them if required. The reason Mailbox Import Export is not held by members of the Organization Management role group is simple: User mailbox contents should be protected against unnecessary access, so you have to take a deliberate step to grant access to mailboxes before you are allowed to run the cmdlets to export or import mailbox data.

Despite the fact that USGs underpin roles, it is a mistake to assume that you could simply use the Active Directory Users and Computers console to add user accounts to the USGs to assign roles. Behind the scenes, Exchange notes the role assignments, and adding a user to a USG is not sufficient and will cause unpredictable results in the future. The Organization Management and Delegated Setup roles are also unique in that they are assigned Active Directory ACLs in addition to Exchange permissions because of the need to have these ACLs to perform tasks such as installing servers. The vast majority of the work done by users holding roles to manage the various aspects of Exchange is facilitated by RBAC, so they don't need to be assigned ACLs. See Chapter 3 for more information about how RBAC functions to control the cmdlets available to a user when they initialize an EMS session.

You can find information about the the set of default role groups and role assignments included in Exchange 2010 at *http://technet.microsoft.com/en-us/library/dd638077.aspx*.

Role groups and assignments might change over time as Microsoft tweaks RBAC through service packs and new versions of Exchange. Each role group spans a number of different administrative roles that provide granularity for task assignment. The names of the role groups are reasonably descriptive of the tasks that you could expect someone assigned to the role group to undertake. Microsoft's goal for Exchange 2010 was to provide a set of role groups that meet the needs of the majority of customers, but you can customize a role group (for example, to remove or add a task) or create a new role group if the default set doesn't meet your requirements. Again taking the default Help Desk role, you might decide that you want these users to have some visibility into message queues and to perform message tracking. In this case, you could customize the Help Desk role group to add the "transport queues" and "message tracking" roles.

It is also possible to assign a specific role to a user or group without placing them in a role group. However, as mentioned earlier, Microsoft doesn't recommend that you take this approach because you are likely to end up with a proliferation of role assignments that become difficult to monitor and manage.

INSIDE OUT   Reviewing Exchange 2007 delegations

One consequence of the change from the Exchange 2007 model for delegated administration to the RBAC implemented in Exchange 2010 is the need to review the delegations that were in place within an organization for Exchange 2007 to ensure that users who had been delegated some access (such as View-Only Administrators) are assigned the correct role groups to allow them to continue working as before following the deployment of Exchange 2010. Note that the Get-ExchangeAdministrator cmdlet that is used to report Exchange administrative assignments in Exchange 2007 is removed in Exchange 2010.

Creating a new role group

Now that we understand the connections among roles, role groups, and assignments, we can consider how to create a new role group and see what happens to instantiate the new role group. The first thing to do is figure out if we actually need a new role group. The general approach to creating a new role group is as follows:

1. Write down the need for the new role group and why none of the out-of-the-box role groups are appropriate. It's always preferable to use one of the default role groups as creation of new role groups increases the level of complexity within the organization.

2. Create the new role group with the New-RoleGroup cmdlet and assign the roles incorporated into the role group.

3. Assign users to the new role group.

Chapter 4

Most companies have help desks that need access to certain functionality to do their work. In this example, we create a new role group that includes the necessary roles required to perform Level 2 support tasks in a Help Desk:

```
New-RoleGroup 'Help Desk Level 2' –Roles 'Message Tracking', 'Mail Recipients',
'Move Mailboxes' –Members 'Eoin.Redmond@contoso.com', 'Hao.Chen@contoso.com'
–ManagedBy 'Nancy.Anderson@contoso.com', 'David.Jones@contoso.com' –Description
'This group is used by Level 2 support personnel'
```

At least one role must be assigned to a new role group when it is created. If you do not assign a scope to the role group, it takes the default scope of the roles included in the group, which is usually organization-wide. As explained earlier, when Exchange creates the new role group, it also creates a USG in the Microsoft Exchange Security GroupsOU in Active Directory. The users specified in the *–ManagedBy* parameter are allowed to manage the group, but they are not members of the group and don't possess the role yet. Users not included when the role group is created can be added afterward with the Add-RoleGroupMember cmdlet and can be subsequently removed with the Remove-RoleGroupMember cmdlet. Users join the security group as you add them as members to the role group.

```
Add-RoleGroupMember –Identity 'Help Desk Level 2' –Member 'Tony Redmond'
Remove-RoleGroupMember –Identity 'Help Desk Level 2' –Member 'Tony Redmond'
```

In addition, Exchange creates three role assignments to match the three roles specified in the New-RoleGroup cmdlet. Exchange uses a naming convention of *Role Name-Role Group Name*, so we end up with role assignments such as "Mail Recipients-Help Desk Level 2." You can see these role assignments with the Get-ManagementRoleAssignment cmdlet as follows:

```
Get-ManagementRoleAssignment –RoleAssignee "Help Desk Level 2"
```

Role assignment

To summarize so far, we have defined scopes to say what objects a role can access and update, a role to say what cmdlets and parameters are made available to the holders of the role, and role groups to help manage who can do what. Role assignments provide what Microsoft refers to as the glue for RBAC in that they link roles and their scope to users or groups. To see the complete set of role assignments in the organization, type:

```
Get-ManagementRoleAssignment
```

Exchange 2010 SP1 includes 176 role assignments ordered by assignee name. In other words, all of the roles assigned to the Organization Management role group are found together, as are all of the roles assigned to the other role groups such as Hygiene Management, Discovery Management, Move Mailboxes, and so on. Naturally, because it is the most powerful and functional role group, Organization Management has the most role assignments. At the bottom of the list you'll find the roles assigned to the default role assignment, which is what Exchange assigns automatically to every user when his mailbox is created. These assignments include MyBaseOptions and MyContactInformation, which are the assignments necessary to allow a user to be able to edit her own personal information through ECP. Custom role assignments are found at the end of the list.

Role assignments are named using a convention of *Role-Role Group*, so we end up with names such as "Message Tracking-Records Management" and "Transport Queues-Organization Management." To examine a specific role assignment, we pass the name of the assignment to the Get-ManagementRoleAssignment cmdlet:

```
Get-ManagementRoleAssignment –Identity 'Exchange Servers-Server Management' | Format-List
```

```
User                            : contoso.com/Microsoft Exchange Security Groups/Server Management
AssignmentMethod                : Direct
Identity                        : Exchange Servers-Server Management
EffectiveUserName               : All Group Members
AssignmentChain                 :
RoleAssigneeType                : RoleGroup
RoleAssignee                    : contoso.com/Microsoft Exchange Security Groups/Server Management
Role                            : Exchange Servers
RoleAssignmentDelegationType    : Regular
CustomRecipientWriteScope       :
CustomConfigWriteScope          :
RecipientReadScope              : Organization
ConfigReadScope                 : OrganizationConfig
RecipientWriteScope             : Organization
ConfigWriteScope                : OrganizationConfig
Enabled                         : True
RoleAssigneeName                : Server Management
IsValid                         : True
ExchangeVersion                 : 0.11 (14.0.550.0)
Name                            : Exchange Servers-Server Management
```

RBAC does not function in the same way as regular security permissions, where the most restrictive permission is what the operating system uses. Instead, RBAC operates on the principle that it provides users with the combination of all of the roles that have been assigned to them. This allows them to accomplish any of the tasks covered by those roles. Consider when you make an account a domain administrator: Immediately the account gains a great deal of power within the domain, and there is a huge difference in the capabilities of that account and another "standard" user account. Now consider what happens when you add an account to a role group: It gains the ability to run any of the cmdlets covered by the role. Gradually, as you add the account to other role groups, it gains access to more cmdlets until we arrive at the Organization Management level—which is really an accumulation of nearly every role available to Exchange—and you begin to realize how roles build on roles to create a highly customizable framework that enables all kinds of users to get their work done. Unity through role accumulation delivers a more granular security assignment mechanism than any of the previous Exchange ACL-based authorization schemes, even if there is no explicit deny mechanism available to positively block someone from doing something.

INSIDE OUT   Controlling role assignments

Each role assigned to a user provides cmdlets and parameters that the user is authorized to run. The total set of roles that a user holds creates the complete set of cmdlets and parameters that the user can run. Because users gain the ability to run an increasing set of cmdlets through role assignment, you should only assign to users the precise roles that you want them to have; otherwise you run the risk of users gaining the ability to run a cmdlet or use a parameter because they are assigned a role that they don't really need to have. As we have seen, you can tailor the roles by adding or removing cmdlets. You can also tailor a role group by removing or adding a role assignment to reduce or add the functionality available to the members of the role group.

Specific scopes for role groups

As discussed earlier, Exchange supports the concept of scoping for a role group. In other words, when you set a scope for a role group, members of the role group are only able to manage the objects covered by the defined scope. The most common scope is set by an OU in Active Directory, meaning that a role assignment made with this scope is able to process any object in the OU. You can create the scope in three ways:

- **RecipientOrganizationalUnitScope parameter**   Specify an explicit OU in Active Directory.

- **CustomRecipientWriteScope parameter**   Create a management scope with the New-ManagementScope cmdlet that points to an OU in Active Directory. This approach is preferable if you will reuse the scope several times. It also allows you to give the scope a human-friendly name that might be more recognizable than the name of the OU.

- **Database name**   Exchange 2010 SP1 allows you to create scopes based on database names.

For example, a large organization might have a distributed help desk with different teams located in regions around the world to support local user communities. You might not want the American help desk to be able to manage European users and vice versa. In this case, you could create two role groups for the American and European help desks and set the appropriate scope so that the two role groups only have access to the users that they support.

TROUBLESHOOTING

You can't add a scope to an existing role group using Set-RoleGroup

The Set-RoleGroup cmdlet doesn't allow for a scope to be retrospectively added to a role group. If you need to set a scope on a role group after it is created, use the Get-ManagementRoleAssignment cmdlet to fetch details of all of the role assignments for the role group and then pipe this information to the Set-ManagementRoleAssignment cmdlet to set the new scope for each role assignment. For example:

```
Get-ManagementRoleAssignment –RoleAssignee 'Help Desk Level 2' | Set-
ManagementRoleAssignment –RecipientOrganizationalUnitScope
'contoso.com/Exchange Users'
```

In this example, we create a new role group with a scope set to allow the members of the role group to manage European mailboxes.

```
New-RoleGroup 'European Help Desk' –Roles 'Message Tracking', 'Mail Recipients',
'Move Mailboxes' –Members 'Luka.Abrus@contoso.com', 'Mark.Harrington@contoso.com'
–ManagedBy 'Darren.Parker@contoso.com', 'Ellen.Adams@contoso.com' –Description 'This
group is used to manage European mailboxes'
–RecipientOrganizationalUnitScope 'contoso.com/EMEA Mailboxes'
```

Alternatively, we could create the management scope beforehand to point to the name of the OU and then use it with the New-RoleGroup cmdlet.

```
New-ManagementScope –Name 'European Mailboxes' –RecipientRoot 'contoso.com/Exchange
Mailboxes/EMEA' –RecipientRestrictionFilter {RecipientType –eq "UserMailbox}
```

```
New-RoleGroup 'European Help Desk' –Roles 'Message Tracking', 'Mail Recipients',
'Move Mailboxes' –Members 'Luka.Abrus@contoso.com', 'Mark.Harrington@contoso.com'
–ManagedBy 'Darren.Parker@contoso.com', 'Ellen.Adams@contoso.com' –Description
'This group is used to manage European mailboxes' –CustomRecipientWriteScope
'European Mailboxes'
```

Further information about how to define and use database scopes is available in the section "Database scoping" later in this chapter.

Chapter 4

Special roles

The list of roles included in the Organization Management role group includes the following five special roles that have to be delegated before they can be used:

- **ApplicationImpersonation**   This is a special-purpose role intended primarily for use by Service Accounts that need to take on the persona of a user to accomplish a task.

- **Mailbox Import Export**   This role allows a user to import or export data into or from a mailbox.

- **Mailbox Search**   This role allows a user to search mailbox contents. The role is assigned to the Discovery Management role group, but the role group has no default members and needs to be populated before searches can be performed.

- **Support diagnostics**   This role allows access to diagnostic cmdlets such as Test-ReplicationHealth that are intended for use by Microsoft or other support personnel to retrieve diagnostic information from an Exchange server or organization. The role is not assigned to any user by default.

- **Unscoped role management**   This role permits unscoped roles to be created and managed. Unscoped roles are used to authorize access to custom scripts and cmdlets. The role is not assigned to any user by default but it can be delegated to users by holders of the Organization Management role.

The inclusion in this list of the role that enables a user to import data into a mailbox or export data out of a mailbox might be surprising, but it is entirely justified if you consider that you probably want the ability to export mailbox data to be explicitly assigned to specific individuals on an as-needed basis. The last thing that anyone wants is to run the risk that a user might be inadvertently given the ability to export mailbox data belonging to another user. When this access is required, you can assign it to a user who needs the role as follows:

```
New-ManagementRoleAssignment -Role 'Mailbox Import Export' -User
'Darren.Parker@contoso.com'
```

It might be more convenient to assign the role to a distribution group, as it is often easier to maintain membership of a group than to perform individual role assignments. The group has to be a USG rather than a universal distribution group or a dynamic distribution group.

```
New-ManagementRoleAssignment -Role 'Mailbox Import Export' -SecurityGroup 'Mailbox
Import-Export Team'
```

After the role is assigned, assignees are able to use the Export mailbox option in EMC and the Export-Mailbox and Import-Mailbox cmdlets (Exchange 2010) and

New-MailboxImportRequest and New-MailboxExportRequest cmdlets (Exchange 2010 SP1) in EMS. The SP1 version of EMC does not offer options to import or export mailboxes, as Microsoft did not have the time to update the EMC wizard for these actions to use the replacement cmdlets introduced in SP1. Users need to restart EMC/EMS after they have been assigned the role to force a refresh of the RBAC data and to allow the new assignment to become effective.

See Chapter 14, "Message Hygiene," for more information about the new set of cmdlets introduced in SP1 to implement mailbox import and export operations.

Unscoped roles

Unscoped management roles are interesting because they allow you to create tailored roles for administrative purposes. I suspect that this area will receive little attention initially as deployment teams grapple with the initial implementation of RBAC within a company. As administrators become more comfortable with RBAC over time, it's likely that the notion of being able to create and assign custom-built roles will become more interesting.

The basic idea behind a custom unscoped role is that it is a mechanism that allows administrators to grant access to non-Exchange cmdlets or Windows PowerShell scripts to management role groups, individual users, or USGs. For example, let's assume that you have written some PowerShell scripts that can be used to extract data from Exchange for reporting purposes and want to assign access to those scripts to people who work on the help desk so that they can generate the reports. Granting access to the ability to perform specific work without the need to grant access to a particular role or cmdlet is another reason why you might create a custom role. For example, you might want to allow the help desk to create mailboxes but only in a specific OU following a structured naming guideline and populating mailbox properties in a certain manner. You could do this by writing a script that encodes all of the business logic necessary to create the mailboxes and grant access to the script. The help desk users who receive the custom role can run the script but they can't run the New-Mailbox cmdlet in any other manner.

To begin, you have to delegate the ability to create unscoped roles to an account. This ability is not granted by default, even to accounts that hold the Organization Management role. However, accounts that hold the Organization Management role can delegate the Unscoped Role Management role to themselves or other accounts with the New-ManagementRoleAssignment cmdlet. This command assigns the role to a USG called "Exchange Admins," which obviously has to exist before you attempt to assign a role to it:

```
New-ManagementRoleAssignment –Role 'Unscoped Role Management' –SecurityGroup
'Exchange Admins'
```

Providing the account you use is a member of the Exchange Admins group, you can now create an unscoped top-level management role. Remember that you have to reinitialize a new EMS session after your account is assigned the Unscoped Role Management role to allow RBAC to make the *–UnscopedTopLevel* parameter available for the New-ManagementRole cmdlet. If you don't do this, EMS will report an error when you run the New-ManagementRole cmdlet and pass it the *–UnscopedTopLevel* parameter.

```
New-ManagementRole –Name 'Exchange Admin Scripts' –UnscopedTopLevel
```

Name	RoleType
Exchange Admin Scripts	UnScoped

The management role is empty and now needs to be populated with the scripts that we want to make available to the users to whom we will eventually assign the role. The scripts need to be copied to the default remote script directory on every server (\Program Files\ Microsoft\Exchange Server\V14\RemoteScripts\). Scripts are placed here rather than in the default scripts directory to create a clear separation between scripts that are run locally and those that can be run remotely. Thereafter, you can add a role entry for each script. For example:

```
Add-ManagementRoleEntry 'Exchange Admin Scripts\DBReportMail.PS1' –Type Script
–UnscopedTopLevel
```

This command associates the script named DBReportMail.PS1 with the custom role and allows the holders of the role to run the script. We can assign the custom role to the users who need it as normal:

```
New-ManagementRoleAssignment –Role 'Exchange Admin Scripts' –User 'Help Desk'
```

After the assignment is made, the users will be able to run the script the next time that they log into EMS.

What role groups do I belong to?

A simple question that administrators often ask is what role groups they— or someone else— have been assigned. Assignment information is held in the membership of the different role groups, so that's what we have to investigate to determine what roles a user possesses.

In this example, we run the Get-RoleGroup cmdlet and pipe its output to the Where-Object cmdlet to look for any entry in the membership of a role group that has a partial match with a user called "Redmond":

```
Get-RoleGroup | Where-Object {$_.Members –Like '*Redmond*'} | Format-List Name,
Members
```

```
Name    : Organization Management
Members : {contoso.com/Exchange Users/Redmond, Eoin P, contoso.com/Exchange Users/Redmond,
Tony, contoso.com/Users/Administrator}

Name    : Discovery Management
Members : {contoso.com/Exchange Users/Redmond, Tony, contoso.com/Users/Administrator}
```

The output shows that a partial match for "Redmond" is discovered in the membership of the Organization Management and Discovery Management role groups. We can then scan the membership information that's returned to find the user we are interested in.

Of course, if you just want to check the membership of a role group to see the list of users, the Get-ManagementRoleAssignment cmdlet is the right tool. In this example, we retrieve the list of users who have an assignment for the Mailbox Import Export role group.

```
Get-ManagementRoleAssignment –Role 'Mailbox Import Export' | Format-Table
RoleAssigneeName, RoleAssignmentDelegationType, RoleAssigneeType
```

RoleAssigneeName	RoleAssignmentDelegation	TypeRoleAssigneeType
Organization Management	DelegatingOrgWide	RoleGroup
Administrator	Regular	User

We can see two different types of assignments reported here:

- Members of the Organization Management role group are allowed to delegate access to the Mailbox Import Export role group, but they are not granted the permissions assigned to a regular member. In other words, members of the Organization Management role group can assign the role group to others, but they are not allowed access to the functions made available to role group members.

- The Administrator user account is a regular member. This is the result of a specific assignment. In fact, because the Administrator account is usually a member of the Organization Management role group, Administrators can assign themselves membership of Mailbox Import Export.

The Get-ManagementRoleAssignment cmdlet is very useful in terms of finding out who can do what to an object. For example, you can use it to determine who has the ability to write to different objects:

- A user mailbox:

```
Get-ManagementRoleAssignment –WritableRecipient "Akers, Kim" –GetEffectiveUsers
```

Chapter 4

- A server object:

```
Get-ManagementRoleAssignment -WritableServer 'ExServer1'
-GetEffectiveUsers
```

- A mailbox or public folder database:

```
Get-ManagementRoleAssignment -WritableDatabase 'DB1'
```

If you use the *–GetEffectiveUsers* parameter, all of the users who can modify the object indirectly through membership of role groups and USGs are returned. If you omit this parameter, only the role groups, users, and USGs that are directly assigned the role are returned.

Assignment policies

So far in our discussion we have looked at direct assignment of roles to role groups where users receive rights through their membership of the group to enable them to perform administrative operations such as viewing transport queues or conducting discovery searches. Every RBAC system needs a default policy to provide a basic set of functions that users can run. Exchange 2010 includes the concept of a management role assignment policy to enable users to perform certain functions that have to be performed by administrators in previous versions of Exchange. The default management role assignment policy that is assigned automatically to mailboxes as they are created is called the Default Role Assignment Policy and includes a number of roles specifically designed for end users. Table 4-2 lists the roles covered by the default role assignment policy.

> **Note**
>
> End-user roles are different from management roles in that they only affect data relating to the end users such as their personal information or the distribution groups that include the end users. By comparison, management roles have a much broader scope in that they can affect data relating to other users or other components of Exchange.

A mailbox can have only one management role assignment policy. Individual mailboxes or groups of mailboxes can be assigned different management role assignment policies. You can use the following command to see the roles included in the default role assignment policy:

```
Get-ManagementRoleAssignment -RoleAssignee 'Default Role Assignment Policy'
```

Or, if you want to check the roles assigned to a specific user through a role assignment policy, you can substitute his name for the name of the assignment policy. For example:

```
Get-ManagementRoleAssignment -RoleAssignee 'Akers, Kim'
```

Table 4-2 **User roles in Default Role Assignment Policy**

Role	Use	Enabled by default
MyBaseOptions	Base option to allow user to access ECP	Y
MyContactInformation	Allows end users to update their phone and contact information	Y
MyProfileInformation	Allows end users to update their first name, last name, initials, and display name	N
MyVoiceMail	Allows end users to manage their voice mail options such as greetings	N
MyTextMessaging	Allows end users to manage options for text messaging	N
MyDistributionGroupMembership	Allows end users to manage their membership of distribution groups (list groups, leave, join new groups)	Y
MyDistributionGroups	Allows end users to create new groups and to manage the membership of groups that they own	N

You can remove any of these roles from the default role assignment policy and thus make them unavailable to users through ECP. For example, to remove the text messaging options from ECP:

```
Remove-ManagementRoleAssignment 'MyTextMessaging-Default Role Assignment Policy'
```

As we'll see when we discuss ECP in just a few pages, administrators can also change the default role assignment policy to make other options available to users. In addition, you have the flexibility to create a new role assignment policy and apply it to selected users to allow them access to a different set of tasks than is available to "standard" users. To set a new default role assignment policy:

```
Set-RoleAssignmentPolicy 'New End-User Default Role Assignment Policy' –IsDefault
```

Management role assignment policies are assigned with the New-Mailbox cmdlet or Enable-Mailbox cmdlet when you create a new user account, or enable an existing account with a mailbox or with the Set-Mailbox cmdlet to change the policy for an existing mailbox. These assignments are explicit, whereas the assignment of the default policy is implicit. An explicit assignment always takes precedence over an implicit assignment. Here's how we would assign an explicit policy to a mailbox:

```
Set-Mailbox –Identity 'David Jones' –RoleAssignmentPolicy 'VIP Users'
```

Sometimes it is useful to be able to process a group of users. For example, let's assume that you want to run a Unified Messaging pilot in just one office and enable the users in that office to be able to update their voice mail settings through ECP. The Voicemail options

Chapter 4

are not enabled in the default policy, so we need to create a new policy, assign the Voice-mail options to the policy, and then enable the policy for the mailboxes in the specific office. This set of commands does the trick. We create the policy, assign the necessary roles including voice mail and the other roles that users need to be able to update their contact and personal information through ECP, and then assign the new role to all mailboxes that belong to the Chicago office:

```
New-RoleAssignmentPolicy -Name 'VoiceMail Pilot Users'
New-ManagementRoleAssignment -Role 'MyBaseOptions' -Policy 'VoiceMail Pilot Users'
New-ManagementRoleAssignment -Role 'MyVoiceMail' -Policy 'VoiceMail Pilot Users'
New-ManagementRoleAssignment -Role 'MyProfileInformation' -Policy 'VoiceMail Pilot
Users'
New-ManagementRoleAssignment -Role 'MyContactInformation' -Policy 'VoiceMail Pilot
Users'
Get-Mailbox -Filter {Office -eq 'Chicago'} | Set-Mailbox -RoleAssignmentPolicy
'VoiceMail Pilot Users'
```

Users will pick up the new management role assignment policy the next time they log in to ECP.

RBAC enhancements in SP1

Given the fundamental nature of the transition from the older permissions model to RBAC in Exchange 2010, it should come as no surprise that Microsoft found some improvements to make to RBAC in Exchange 2010 SP1. The updates provide a complete overhaul of the user interface (UI) to manage RBAC in ECP and functionality changes broken down into four broad categories:

1. Database scoping

2. Support for the deployment of an Active Directory split permissions model

3. Provision of a number of RBAC reports in the Exchange Best Practices Analyzer

4. RBAC validation rules

You can also consider the radical overhaul of the ECP UI to support far broader and more comprehensive access to roles, role groups, and role group assignments to be a fifth area of improvement. We discuss all of these areas in the coming sections.

Managing role groups through ECP

All of the discussion about how to manage roles, role groups, and role assignments through EMS remains valid for Exchange 2010 SP1. However, we can now perform day-to-day RBAC management through ECP. To illustrate the new interface, let's explore the steps to accomplish some real-life tasks.

Our first task is to amend the Help Desk role group so that its members are allowed to manage ActiveSync policies because the SP1 version of ECP supports access to these policies. The first thing we need to know is what roles include access to the cmdlets that manipulate ActiveSync policies. It is logical that an ActiveSync policy is created with the New-ActiveSyncMailboxPolicy cmdlet, so we can find out the role that supports it with:

```
Get-ManagementRole –Cmdlet 'New-ActiveSyncMailboxPolicy'
```

```
Name                                      RoleType
-------                                   --------
Recipient Policies                        RecipientPolicies
```

The output shows that the Help Desk role group must be assigned the Recipient Policies role before they can manage ActiveSync policies. We can now open ECP with an account that is a member of the Organization Management role group and go to the Administrator Roles section under Users and Groups (Figure 4-3). We can see from the description of the Help Desk role group that it only has two roles assigned by default: User Options and View-Only Recipients. These roles allow members of the Help Desk role group to view recipients and manage mailbox options.

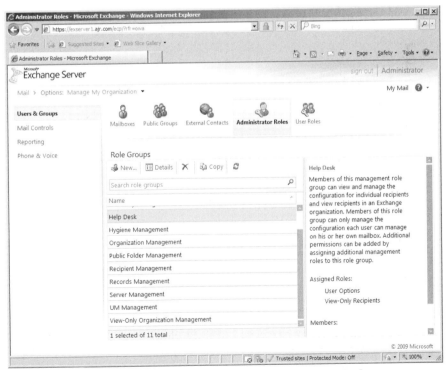

Figure 4-3 Viewing role groups with the SP1 version of ECP.

Click Details to view the current properties of the Help Desk role group. Move down to the Roles section, which lists the two roles currently in the role group. Click Add to expose the set of available roles that can be added to the role group (Figure 4-4). All of the roles known to Exchange are exposed in the list, but you have to remember that some of the roles are not used with ECP. For example, the Database Availability Groups role allows administrators to work with the servers and databases within a DAG but only with EMC or EMS, because ECP doesn't support the necessary UI. The same is true for other roles such as Edge Subscriptions, Email Address Policies, and Mailbox Import Export. You can certainly add these roles to a role group as long as you understand that users will only be able to make use of the cmdlets exposed by access to the roles if they run EMC or EMS.

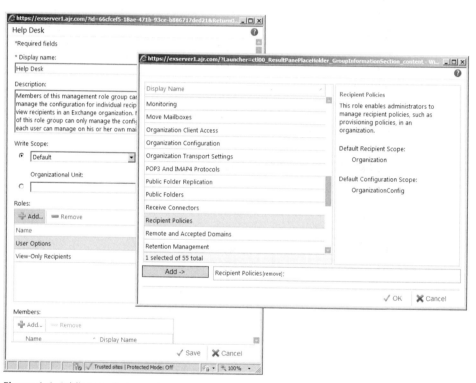

Figure 4-4 Adding a role to a role group.

To complete our task, scroll down to find the Recipient Policies role and click it to select the role. Once the role is selected, click Add and then click OK to exit the dialog box and return to the properties of the Help Desk role group. Recipient Policies should now be listed in the set of assigned roles. Click Save to update the role group definition and return to ECP. Any user who is assigned to the Help Desk role group will be able to access ActiveSync policies the next time that she starts ECP.

Amending an existing role group is now very easy with ECP. To move on, our next task is to create a new role group for Level 2 help desk support staff who operate in just one region (EMEA). The IT managers in EMEA have decided that their most senior support people should be able to perform a range of administrative tasks including mailbox searches and updating mailbox information. A new role group is needed because we want to restrict the ability of the members of the role group to be able to update objects in a specific OU. This can be done by setting the scope of the role group to the OU rather than using the default scope that allows organization-wide access.

There are two ways to accomplish the goal. We can create a new role group from scratch, or we can select an existing role group that possesses many of the characteristics of the role group that we want to create and make a copy of it to use as the basis of the new role group. If you're familiar with functions made available through the set of role groups supported by Exchange, you'll probably want to create the new role group from scratch. If not, it's best to copy the existing group that is closest in terms of permissions to the new role group that you want to create. To copy a group, select it in the Role Groups section of ECP and click Copy. After ECP copies the group, you can give the copy a new name to reflect its purpose. In either case, you'll eventually end up editing the properties of the new role group as illustrated in Figure 4-5.

Figure 4-5 Creating a new role group with ECP.

Apart from the roles assigned to the role group, the most important thing shown here is the write scope, which is set to "contoso.com/EMEA". In other words, the members of this role group will be able to view information about objects stored elsewhere in Active Directory, but they will only be able to create or update objects stored in the EMEA OU. Because ECP doesn't support the ability to create new mailboxes, members of the role group will only be able to update the properties of existing mailboxes in the EMEA OU. They will be able to create new groups, but only if the default location for new groups is the EMEA OU.

See Chapter 5 for information about how to define a default location for groups.

When you've added all the necessary roles to the role group, you can then add the members. When you click Save, the new role group and the underlying security group will be created and assigned to the users you nominate as members.

Database scoping

Exchange 2010 supports the creation of scopes to restrict management access to recipients or servers. Two scopes did not prove flexible enough to address the needs of customer deployments, so SP1 adds a third scope based on databases or groups of databases.

> **Note**
>
> A scope based on databases will only be respected by SP1 (or later) servers, so if you want to use database scoping you can only deploy and implement it reliably after all mailbox servers run SP1.

To create a database scope, you define a new management scope based on a database list or a database filter. A database list contains the names of specific databases separated by commas and is an appropriate scope when you need to assign management responsibility to a fixed set of databases that you don't think will change often. For example, this command creates a database scope that is limited to two named databases:

```
New-ManagementScope -Name 'CEO Databases' -DatabaseList 'CEO-Database1,
CEO-StaffDatabase'
```

A database filter establishes a condition that Exchange can use to identify a set of databases. This is the most appropriate choice when you want a scope that is flexible enough to accommodate a changing set of databases, assuming that you can create a filter that identifies the databases. This example creates a filter that selects databases with a name that matches a prefix of "DUB-":

```
New-ManagementScope –Name 'Dublin Databases' –DatabaseRestrictionFilter {Name    –
Like 'DUB-*'}
```

INSIDE OUT   Using database names to create filters

Names are likely to be the basis for most database filters, but you can create filters based on other properties including the database description. Filters that are not based on the database name (for example, using properties such as the database description or distinguished name) require a certain discipline in maintaining those properties or else the scope is unlikely to locate the desired databases. Note that database scopes are only effective on servers running Exchange 2010 SP1 or later. See the section "Understanding Management Role Scope Filters" in the Exchange Help file for a full list of the supported properties that can be included in database filters.

When you create a database scope, you permit access to the cmdlets that are used to manipulate databases such as Set-MailboxDatabaseCopy. However, you have to be careful not to overlap with server scopes because some operations are permitted by either a database or a server scope and some depend on a specific scope. For example, a database scope will control the ability to create a new mailbox with the New-Mailbox cmdlet or to move a mailbox with New-MoveRequest if the target database falls under its scope. This is logical because a server scope cannot apply in this case because databases are not tied to servers.

Implementing a split permissions model

Exchange uses two very important security groups to gain access to Active Directory information. These two groups provide the control over Active Directory objects that is implemented through cmdlets and made available to administrators and users through the role groups managed by RBAC.

- The Exchange Trusted Subsystem group allows Exchange services and cmdlets to manipulate objects that are exclusively owned by Exchange, such as servers, connectors, and the properties that make an object mail-enabled.

- The Exchange Windows Permissions group allows Exchange services and cmdlets to manipulate objects that are often controlled by Active Directory administrators such as the creation of user and group objects.

Chapter 4

The default Exchange installation ties the two together by making the Exchange Trusted Subsystem group a member of the Exchange Windows Permissions group. This arrangement allows Exchange services and cmdlets to have full access to anything held in Active Directory. For many companies the unification of Exchange and Windows administrative permissions in a security model that permits administrators to control both Exchange and Active Directory works well, especially when no great differentiation exists between the administrators who look after Exchange and those who manage Active Directory and Windows. However, other companies have clearly delineated responsibilities between the two sets of administrators, and the default RBAC implementation in Exchange 2010 doesn't meet their needs as well.

The shared administrative model remains the default for Exchange 2010 SP1, and you have to explicitly choose to implement a clear division between Exchange and Windows. If desired, you can decide to institute either of two split-mode permissions models. These are an Active Directory–based permissions model and an RBAC-based permissions model. The Active Directory split permissions model is the more restrictive because it means that the ability to manipulate security principals is completely removed from Exchange; the RBAC-based split permissions model is preferable because it takes advantage of RBAC capabilities to restrict permissions at a highly granular level to a small number of accounts represented by a role group containing the accounts that you want to allow to create or remove security principals such as user accounts. In addition, the RBAC-based split permissions model allows Exchange administrators to continue to work with Exchange-specific objects such as distribution groups in Active Directory.

If you want to utilize the Active Directory split permissions model, you have to choose this option when you run Setup to install the Exchange 2010 organization. This can be done through the GUI version of Setup (Figure 4-6) or by running Setup.com to prepare Active Directory for Exchange. This is done by launching Setup in a command box with elevated permissions with the following parameters:

```
C:> Setup /PrepareAD /ActiveDirectorySplitPermissions:True
```

It is possible to revert to the normal permissions model by running Setup again to reverse the changes that it made to groups and role assignments. This is done with the following command:

```
C:> Setup /PrepareAD /ActiveDirectorySplitPermissions:False
```

Behind the scenes, the division is affected by removing the Exchange Trusted Subsystem group from the Exchange Windows Permissions group. Because all Exchange servers are members of the Exchange Trusted Subsystem group, this has the effect of removing the ability of Exchange servers to manipulate many Active Directory objects unless code (such as cmdlets) is run by an account that has sufficient Windows permissions to update Active

Directory. In addition, role assignments are modified to remove the ability of Exchange administrators to perform actions such as the creation of a new mail-enabled account.

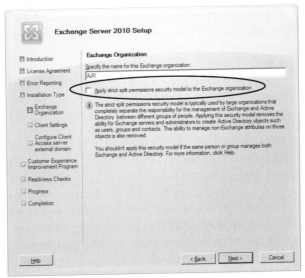

Figure 4-6 Applying the Setup option to apply the Active Directory split permissions model to Exchange.

You do not need to make any changes with Setup to implement the RBAC-based split permissions model. Instead, you create a new role group to contain the accounts that will be allowed to manipulate security principals and assign the mail recipient creation, security group creation, and membership roles to the group. Usually, the members of the new role group will be Active Directory administrators. You add delegating role assignments so that the members of the new role group will be able to assign the role to other users. You then remove the current role assignments that allow users to perform actions such as creating new mailboxes so that only members of the new restricted group are able to take these actions.

Chapter 4

INSIDE OUT   Start with a test organization

The Exchange documentation contains all the necessary information to guide you through the process of implementing either the Active Directory or the RBAC-based split-mode permissions models, including how to upgrade an Exchange 2010 RTM organization to use your selected model as part of the deployment of SP1. Like anything else to do with permissions, this is not an exercise to go through without careful planning and testing, so the first step is to try it out in a test organization to see whether the new model meets your needs. In addition, it is common sense to sit down with the Active Directory administrators to determine the optimal permissions environment that meets security, operational, and business requirements before making any changes to the organization. Finally, make sure that any changes made to permissions don't interfere with other applications that might interact with Exchange, such as account provisioning or identity management systems.

RBAC reports in ExBPA

By now you should be convinced that RBAC is important to Exchange. Including an analysis of RBAC within an organization that reports issues that have to be resolved in the Exchange Best Practice Analyzer (ExBPA) is therefore a good idea. You might ask why RBAC wasn't analyzed by ExBPA before SP1. The answer is simple: There wasn't enough evidence of best practice or potential problem areas based on hard experience gathered from real-life deployments to be able to build the ExBPA rule set to check for problems and make recommendations.

The errors reported by ExBPA include the following:

- Missing RBAC containers (a very basic problem)

- Missing precanned role types and role groups (possibly deleted by an administrator experimenting with the RBAC cmdlets)

- Multiple default role assignment policies

Advisory warnings are issued for problems such as these:

- No assignments exist for a given role management group

- An empty Organization Management role group (who's managing the organization?)

- No default role assignment policies (users won't be able to access ECP without a default role assignment policy)

- A default role assignment policy that's missing the MyBaseOptions role (users won't be able to update mailbox settings)

- Mailboxes that aren't assigned the default role assignment policy (these mailboxes won't be able to update their settings)

- An exclusive scope that doesn't have any role assignments (this could cause problems with access to data)

These issues are a good starting point and contain most of the obvious problems that can occur for RBAC. It's likely that additional experience with RBAC in production environments will bring other problems to light that will be incorporated into ExBPA reports in the future.

RBAC validation rules

Microsoft designed validation rules mostly for their online hosted environment. Essentially, these are data-driven rules set by Microsoft that cannot be edited; they dictate how RBAC behaves in certain well-bounded circumstances. The best example of their use in the enterprise version of Exchange is the control placed on resource mailboxes when they are opened through ECP. You might want to open a mailbox for a conference room to view its calendar and resolve some scheduling conflicts, but some of the elements in the UI presented by ECP don't make much sense when you are working with a room mailbox. For example, you are unlikely to want to manage ActiveSync data because the room mailbox doesn't use mobile devices, so the RBAC validation rules that run inside Exchange 2010 SP1 remove some of the UI elements that are presented for "normal" mailboxes.

Most administrators will not be aware of RBAC validation rules, nor will they care that Microsoft has implemented these rules within the product. However, it's nice to know what kind of magic customizes the UI for different mailbox types. Another one of the great mysteries of the age is now explained.

Exchange Control Panel and roles

Curiously, apart from a link to ECP in the Toolbox, EMC includes no UI to deal with roles, role groups, assignments, and policies. Everything to do with RBAC in terms of end users (and their roles) is processed through ECP and anything else has to be done with EMS. The logic for this decision might be that Microsoft believes that EMC is concerned with day-to-day management operations that occur frequently and it is unlikely that administrators will want to change roles or role group definitions very often. Indeed, if Microsoft's design works, most deployments are likely to accept the default set of definitions and never make a change.

The Exchange 2010 version of ECP allows administrators to assign roles to users and supports some customization of the default role assignment policy.

Figuring out RBAC

RBAC probably won't make much of a difference to the way that the administrator of a small Exchange deployment approaches her work. If you log into the Administrator account and perform all tasks from there, the default assignment of the Organization Management role to the Administrator account means that the account is all powerful and has full read and write access to any object in the Exchange organization, much in the same way that the Administrator account can do anything with Active Directory. RBAC is much more interesting and useful within larger deployments where finer granularity is often required for administrator roles.

INSIDE OUT   Heed good advice

Although you can go to extremes in defining exactly what someone can do, Microsoft offers some good advice: You should avoid special role assignments to individual users because this can create a very complicated security environment that becomes hard to manage as people leave or join the organization.

Sorting out the connections among roles, role groups, role assignments, scopes, and users can be complex when you start to use the Exchange implementation of RBAC. It is wise to take some time to get to know how the different parts fit together before you begin to change the default assignments or add your own role groups and assignments to meet the needs of your organization. Sit down with a test server and see what you can discover about RBAC. Try some of the commands that we have investigated in this section to become accustomed to the concepts and how they are implemented in Exchange 2010. Eventually it will all make sense!

On to management

Exchange boasts other management tools with which administrators will spend a lot of time, so it's important that we get comfortable with the EMC and ECP as well as the role-based authorization model that now determines the access that administrators have to different areas of the product. The next port of call is therefore EMC and the many options it provides for user management.

Exchange Management Console and Control Panel

T HERE'S not much point in running an email system unless people can use it to communicate. Learning how to use the tools available to manage these objects is a fundamental first step in this process. Microsoft has justifiably been criticized in the past for making Exchange complex to manage, largely through the use of badly documented and archaic registry settings to enable or manage features. In addition, customers have asked for tools that are flexible enough to accommodate the needs of a range of administrative personnel, from local administrators who take care of tasks for just one server to help desk personnel to organization administrators. For example, in Exchange Server 2003 or Exchange Server 2007, if you want to give someone the ability to maintain user properties such as the Office in which they work, you must give that person access to the full-blown management console. In addition to the tools, granting and maintaining permissions to let people work with Exchange is complicated, creating the potential for error in granting permissions that could expose data to unintended manipulation by untrained users. There is also no good way of auditing what happens to an Exchange server through the administrative tools.

Using the administrative model as implemented in previous versions of Exchange meant that administrators spent far too much time doing mundane things to keep an Exchange organization healthy when they could be more productive elsewhere.

In addition to its investment in remote PowerShell and the huge increase in the number of cmdlets available through Exchange Management Shell (EMS), Microsoft's response in Exchange 2010 is to deploy a three-pronged approach to administration:

1. The Exchange Management Console (EMC) is designed for use by full-time administrators who need access to the broadest set of options to work with all aspects of an organization. The concept and implementation of a management console for Exchange is familiar to anyone who has ever attempted to keep an Exchange server going.

2. Microsoft Exchange Server 2010 introduces a new Web-based component called the Exchange Control Panel (ECP) for part-time administrators who only need access to specific objects, such as help desk personnel who look after user account maintenance. ECP is tightly associated with role-based access control (RBAC) and the new RBAC model that we discuss in the section "Auto-generated PowerShell commands" later in this chapter. The big advantage of a role-based approach is that authorization is now focused on the tasks that users have to perform rather than the underlying Active Directory directory service objects involved in the tasks. It is easier to understand the roles and assign the right roles to individuals instead of grappling with the complexities of Active Directory permissions.

3. Users shouldn't have to go to administrators or the help desk to maintain options that do not impact system operation or performance. Exchange 2010 includes a much wider range of user-settable options through Outlook Web App (OWA) as "self-service for users." For instance, users are able to join or leave distribution groups, assuming that group properties are configured to permit these operations.

In this chapter, we review the changes made to EMC in Exchange 2010 and go on to discuss RBAC, the new RBAC model, and ECP before going into the details of the different types of mailboxes and groups.

Exchange Management Console

Exchange has always included a management console. The first generation of Exchange included the ADMIN program; the second had the Exchange System Manager (ESM); and Exchange 2007 introduced the EMC. Both ESM and EMC are snap-ins for the Microsoft Management Console (MMC). EMC leverages Microsoft .NET Windows Forms extensively for other elements of its graphical user interface (GUI) such as the many wizards used to create and configure objects.

Changes to EMC in Exchange 2010

Overall, the version of EMC used by Exchange 2010 (Figure 5-1) presents a familiar environment for an administrator accustomed to Exchange 2007. Even though it is different than the Exchange 2003 ESM console, its layout is understandable because it splits the different objects that have to be managed in an Exchange organization into logical chunks. You sometimes have to think about where exactly a particular setting is manipulated, but generally things are easily found.

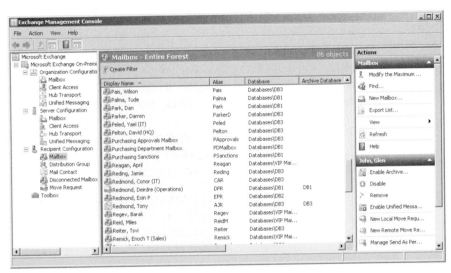

Figure 5-1 The Exchange 2010 Management Console.

Starting from the top of the console, the information about the Exchange organization is divided into the following major parts:

- Organization Configuration: Allows administrators to work with settings that are in effect across the entire organization. For example, this is where you set up email address policies that create new email addresses for recipients or create new transport rules that are applied to every outgoing message. This is also the location where you manage the new Database Availability Groups (DAGs), including database copies.

- Server Configuration: Allows administrators to work with configuration details specific to mailbox, client access, and hub transport servers, including the certificates used by Exchange. Unified Messaging servers are managed here if your organization uses this functionality. For example, this section is where you would configure, send, and receive connectors for a hub transport server or configure how Outlook offline address book (OAB) files are distributed by client access servers.

- Recipient Configuration: Allows administrators to work with all types of mail-enabled recipients: mailboxes (including linked, room, and equipment mailboxes), groups (normal and dynamic), and contacts (including mail users). This section of EMC also supports move requests, the new method of moving mailboxes within an Exchange organization and between Exchange organizations.

- Toolbox: Like Exchange 2007, this section of EMC provides access to a collection of useful Microsoft-provided utilities that execute outside EMC. We will discuss the contents of the toolbox in more detail in Chapter 17, "The Exchange Toolbox."

Chapter 5

- Mailbox – Entire Forest: Incorporation of "Exchange Forests" into EMC allows the administration of up to ten Exchange organizations from a single console. An Exchange forest is simply an Exchange organization that belongs to an Active Directory forest. An Active Directory forest can only support a single Exchange organization. This change also allows EMC to deal with a mixture of objects running in an on-premise Exchange organization and a hosted Exchange organization.

Exchange 2010 adds a number of interesting features to EMC, including the following:

- Addition of the Organizational Health feature provides administrators with a snapshot of essential data (mailboxes, servers, and so on) about an organization.

- A log of PowerShell commands executed during an EMC session can be created and exported for review.

- Commands can be executed for a selected group of objects rather than having to select and update objects individually.

- Diagnostic levels can be set for Exchange components. In Exchange 2007 you have to do this through EMS.

- There is a user interface (UI) for new features, such as the DAG and the Connectivity test in the toolbox.

- The associated UI that was used to create and manage storage groups has been removed.

- Pointers to Exchange community resources allow administrators to easily find external help and information about the product.

- There are other various updates and enhancements (and a few bug fixes). For example, when you create a new mailbox, you can assign a User Principal Name (UPN) from any of the UPN suffixes known to the Active Directory forest.

> **Tip**
> You can use the Get-UserPrincipalNameSuffix cmdlet to discover the set of suffixes that exist.

INSIDE OUT   Behind the scenes

Two major changes are made behind the scenes for EMC.

- First, like all other management components, EMC is dependent on remote PowerShell, and the console has to connect to an Exchange 2010 server when it initializes. If EMC cannot create a remote PowerShell session, it cannot access the Active Directory to fetch Exchange configuration data.

- Second, all permissions in Exchange are now based on RBAC and EMC checks for the roles that users hold when they start the console so that it displays only the options that the role permits.

These changes come with a performance penalty and the Exchange 2010 version of EMC does not start as quickly as its Exchange 2007 counterpart. In addition, the need to channel everything through remote PowerShell often slows the refresh or retrieval of data, as indicated by the Refresh: In Progress message displayed in the lower left section of the EMC window. Microsoft improved EMC startup in SP1 by preloading remote PowerShell, optimizing its use of RBAC, and using new cmdlets such as Get-OrganizationalUnit to accelerate retrieval of data from Active Directory, but its performance is still slightly slower than in Exchange 2007.

EMC includes an interesting new option to allow the administrator to send email to a user. Before you can use this option, you have to configure an email client on the machine where EMC runs. This is acceptable on a workstation, but might be less so on a server.

Like all other parts of Exchange, EMC supports multiple languages and will output localized strings based on the Windows UI language selected for the account used to run EMC. However, you will need to install the correct Exchange language pack on the workstation before you can select a particular language. If a selected language is unavailable, Exchange defaults to English. In multilingual deployments. It is a good idea to install the same set of language packs on all servers and workstations used for administration. Most companies that operate in this situation will simply install the Exchange language pack to have access to all supported languages. Apart from a small amount of storage, this doesn't place any additional load on the server, because the language packs contain localized strings that are only used when required.

A different console philosophy from Exchange 2003

If you're upgrading to Exchange 2010 from Exchange 2003, you'll notice a major change in the way that Exchange deals with Active Directory objects. Mail-enabled recipients are

Chapter 5

Active Directory objects and appear in the Active Directory Users and Computers console, and if you are moving from Exchange 2003, you'll be accustomed to managing recipients through Active Directory Users and Computers. In fact, a clear split in management tools exists in Exchange 2003: Recipient properties are created and managed through Active Directory Users and Computers, whereas Exchange-specific objects such as servers and connectors are created and managed through the ESM console. ESM can certainly access the objects created by Active Directory Users and Computers (because otherwise you could never manage mailboxes), but it's a secondary and largely read-only relationship.

When Microsoft replaced ESM in Exchange 2007, a fundamental change was made to integrate the functionality required to allow EMC full management access to mail-enabled recipients. The PowerShell cmdlets that underpin the Exchange 2007 and Exchange 2010 management consoles incorporate all of the code required to manipulate Active Directory objects, and Exchange administrators hold the permissions necessary to update the Active Directory. Because everything can be done through one console, Exchange now delivers a much cleaner and straightforward management environment and administrators are not forced to move between consoles to work. Another advantage is that a clear division of responsibilities is now possible among the administrators who are responsible for Active Directory and those who are responsible for Exchange. Of course, in smaller deployments the same people probably have both responsibilities, but the ability to maintain separation between administrative responsibilities is important to those with large deployments.

This change in approach means that Exchange no longer installs any add-in code for the Active Directory Users and Computers console so you cannot mail-enable users, contacts, or groups, or create new mailboxes from this console. Likewise, although you can create groups from Active Directory Users and Computers, you cannot use this console to mail-enable a group or create dynamic distribution groups. You can still see Exchange objects through Active Directory Users and Computers and you can update the set of properties that are general to Active Directory rather than specific to Exchange.

> **Tip**
>
> One way to think about the division between Active Directory Users and Computers and EMC is that any property exposed by the Set-User cmdlet is available to Active Directory Users and Computers and any exposed to the Exchange recipient cmdlets like Set-Mailbox and Set-DistributionGroup are accessible through EMC.

Figure 5-2 provides a good example of the division of responsibilities in action. The Active Directory Users and Computers console is able to list all of the recipients stored in an organizational unit (OU), so you can see contacts, distribution groups, and users. The distribution groups include mail-enabled universal distribution and security groups, as well as "query-based distribution groups," the name that Active Directory Users and Computers uses for dynamic distribution groups (the link is logical because this is what Exchange called these groups when they were first introduced in Exchange 2003). Even though these objects are visible, you won't be able to access their properties. The Exchange-related information that was previously available to Active Directory Users and Computers through the installation of some add-in code that Exchange loaded into the console is no longer provided with Exchange.

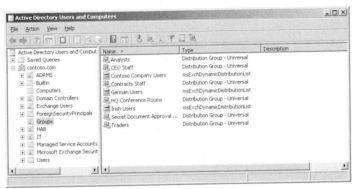

Figure 5-2 Dynamic group properties as viewed through Active Directory Users and Computers.

Managing objects across Exchange 2010 and Exchange 2007

As discussed in Chapter 2, "Installing Exchange 2010," Exchange stamps objects such as mailboxes and connectors with version numbers that allow the management tools to understand which objects they can and cannot manage. It is still advised that you use the version of management tools that originally created an object. If this isn't available, then you can generally use the latest version of the management tools to work with objects because it's far more likely that the latest version includes backward compatibility with earlier versions. Achieving forward compatibility with objects that can change radically across versions is a trick not often mastered in software.

However, there are exceptions to the general guideline that result when underlying change is too major to be coded around. These are as follows:

- You can view Exchange 2007 mailbox databases with the Exchange 2010 EMC, but you can't manage these databases because Exchange 2010 has no knowledge of the storage groups to which Exchange 2007 mailbox databases are tied.

- The Exchange 2010 EMC cannot enable or disable Exchange 2007 mailboxes for Unified Messaging (UM), nor can it manage mobile devices that synchronized with mailboxes on Exchange 2007 servers. These limitations are a result of the changes to UM and ActiveSync in Exchange 2010.

Chapter 5

- The Exchange 2010 queue viewer cannot connect to an Exchange 2007 hub transport server to retrieve information about messages on its queues.

- Because of their different structure and vastly increased rule capabilities, Exchange 2010 transport rules can only be viewed from the Exchange 2010 EMC.

- Exchange 2010 mailbox servers have many different properties to support DAGs and have also dropped some properties (such as those associated with storage groups). Thus, you can only manage Exchange 2007 servers through the Exchange 2007 EMC and Exchange 2010 servers through its version of EMC.

- Despite the fact that they appear to contain similar data, you cannot perform messaging tracking from Exchange 2010 to Exchange 2007 or vice versa. Instead, you must track the path of a message on one set of servers and then switch to the other version to complete the process, if required.

Other minor glitches might appear as you use the Exchange 2010 EMC. When in doubt, you should use the version of the management tools that created the object.

EMC startup

Like EMS, the Exchange 2010 version of EMC is based on remote PowerShell and RBAC. When EMC starts, it contacts a server to initialize a remote PowerShell session. Usually, EMC selects the computer on which it is running if it is an Exchange 2010 server, but you can select a specific server by clicking the Microsoft Exchange (On-Premises) root and then right-clicking to access properties. The properties show the server to which you are currently connected and present the option to select automatic connection to a server or to browse for a specific server (Figure 5-3).

After EMC has established a remote PowerShell session, it begins to retrieve the data necessary to fill in the UI. You know EMC is fetching data when you see the Refresh: In Progress message in the lower left corner of the console. During initialization, EMC executes the cmdlets permitted by RBAC (for the account used to run EMC) to discover information about the organization, servers, and so on in order to build its cache with essential data about the Exchange organization. Later, EMC might execute other cmdlets to retrieve information about specific objects as the user navigates from node to node. For example, if the user moves to Server Configuration and clicks Client Access Servers, EMC executes cmdlets such as Get-OWAVirtualDirectory, Get-OABVirtualDirectory, and Get-ActiveSyncVirtualDirectory. Another example is when the user moves to the Recipient Configuration section, EMC executes the following command to fetch details of all mail-enabled recipients subject to the constraint set by the maximum number of objects to retrieve from Active Directory. It also sorts the fetched objects.

```
Get-Recipient -PropertySet ConsoleLargeSet  -ResultSize '500' -SortBy DisplayName
-RecipientType 'DynamicDistributionGroup','UserMailbox','MailContact','MailUser',
'MailUniversalDistributionGroup','MailUniversalSecurityGroup','MailNonUniversalGroup'
```

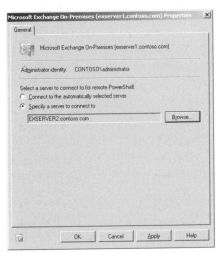

Figure 5-3 Selecting a server for an EMC connection.

When EMC cannot access a server

It's possible that EMC will not be able to access a server to retrieve some data. As we know, remote PowerShell requires a complex set of connections involving the network, Windows Remote Management, Microsoft Internet Information Services (IIS), and Active Directory before commands complete successfully. If any hiccups occur, EMC will not be able to display data and could also experience delays of several minutes during which EMC is unresponsive. This is especially obvious in organizations that contain legacy Exchange servers, in which cases you could see errors of the type shown here:

```
The task wasn't able to connect to IIS on the server 'cas1.contoso.com'. Make
sure that the server exists and can be reached from this computer: The RPC
server is unavailable. It was running the command 'Get-OwaVirtualDirectory'.
```

Microsoft is aware of the problem and is working on a fix.

Another part of the initialization process is to retrieve the RBAC role assignments for the user. A user should possess a management role to use EMC. If he doesn't possess a management role, he will be restricted as to what he can do with EMC. EMC uses RBAC metadata maintained in its cache to ensure that a user only sees the options that are available to him. For example, if a user is assigned the View-Only Management role, he will be unable to make any change to objects. EMC signals this fact by graying out fields and displaying a small yellow lock icon next to each unavailable field (Figure 5-4).

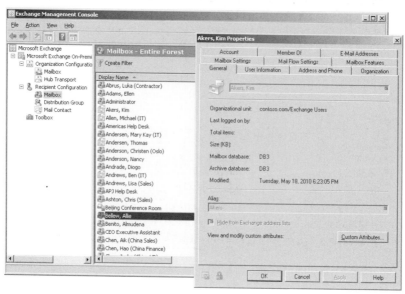

Figure 5-4 Restricted access to EMC.

Building a customized UI based on a user's role is a good idea because it stops the frustration that results when someone attempts to take an action that she doesn't have the necessary permission to perform, even if the customized UIs create some new questions when users ask why their version of EMC is different from someone else's (or different from what they read about in books or online materials). However, once loaded during the EMC initialization process, the RBAC data are inflexible in that if a change is made to a user's role, EMC will not reflect the change until the next time it loads and rebuilds its cache by reading RBAC information from the Active Directory.

How EMC accesses Exchange data

EMC has an absolute dependency on Active Directory. Throughout a session, EMC reads and writes data about objects that it fetches from the Microsoft Exchange organization container in the Configuration Naming context. Other data come from mailbox and public folder databases, but the vast majority of information displayed by EMC is sourced from Active Directory.

The information contained in Active Directory is static and is not intended to reflect information that changes in real time, because this would generate constant replication requests to keep pace with status updates for Exchange objects. Even if Active Directory could keep up with the replication, it's likely that the activity would swamp networks and prevent other useful work. The dependency on Active Directory is the reason there are times when EMS exposes transient data that you never see in EMC. For example, you can use the Get-MoveRequestStatistics cmdlet to view the percentage of a mailbox move that is complete and the current rate of data transfer between source and target server, but you will never see this level of detail in EMC. Instead, EMC displays the status of a move request from start to in progress to complete, but only if you refresh the display.

INSIDE OUT   Getting the latest information

Because EMC essentially gives only a static snapshot of the set of objects that you are looking at, it is wise to use the refresh option before you start to do anything with EMC to make sure that you are dealing with the latest information rather than stale data. For instance, refreshing the set of mailboxes picks up new mailboxes that have been added and updates mailboxes that have had status changes, such as those that are being moved to a different server or those that have just been given an archive.

Another example of how the dependency on Active Directory can be slightly frustrating is that EMC does not show the amount of storage used by mailboxes as one of the data items displayed when it lists mailboxes. The amount of current storage used by a mailbox is not maintained in Active Directory with the majority of the other mailbox properties, so if EMC were to list this information, it would have to make a call to the Information Store service to retrieve storage data for each mailbox. This might be an acceptable overhead for a small installation where all the mailboxes are in the same database, but you can appreciate the likely performance implications of attempting to fetch data about 30 mailboxes scattered over 15 different databases on 10 servers.

EMC does display the storage currently used by a mailbox if you view its properties (Figure 5-5). Usually there is a small but noticeable delay while this information is retrieved because the underlying call to the Get-Mailbox cmdlet has to access Active Directory information from a domain controller in the user's domain to ensure that all of the information is up to date. Going to a specific domain controller avoids the potential of retrieving outdated information from a global catalog server. EMC also makes a call to the Get-MailboxStatistics cmdlet to retrieve information from the Store. The two commands that are used to complete the picture are therefore:

```
Get-Mailbox -Identity 'Akers, Kim' -ReadFromDomainController
Get-MailboxStatistics -Identity 'Akers, Kim'
```

Chapter 5

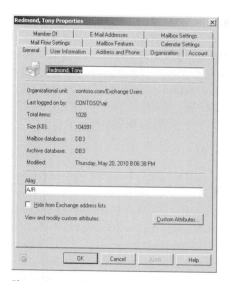

Figure 5-5 Mailbox properties showing current storage used.

Figure 5-5 also shows a change made in Exchange 2010 SP1 that allows a user's mailbox and personal archive to be separated in two different databases.

> **Note**
>
> When you view mailbox properties, you might see that a mailbox has been last logged into by an account that doesn't own the mailbox. This occurs when another user has logged into the mailbox using delegated permissions that he has been granted.

Two important settings control how EMC displays data. The first is the domain controller from which EMC reads configuration data. A domain controller from the current site is selected automatically during EMC initialization but you can tell EMC to use a different controller if you want. To do this, select the Organization Configuration node and then right-click. Select the Modify Configuration Domain Controller option (Figure 5-6) and then select the domain controller that you want using the server picker.

Of course, you can use the Get-ExchangeServer cmdlet to retrieve the Active Directory configuration (the Status parameter is required to force EMS to query Active Directory for this information) and the Set-ExchangeServer cmdlet to tell Exchange to use a preferred domain controller:

```
Get-ExchangeServer -Identity 'ExServer1' -Status
Set-ExchangeServer -Identity 'ExServer1' -DomainController 'dc1.contoso.com'
```

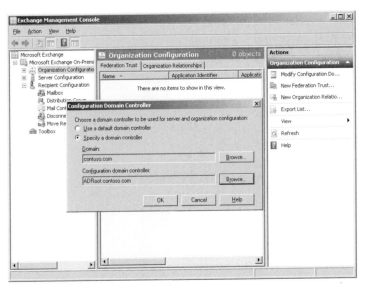

Figure 5-6 Selecting a configuration domain controller for EMC to use.

The second setting is the number of objects that EMC displays in the result pane at one time. For performance reasons, EMC limits the amount of data fetched from Active Directory to 1,000 objects. Small installations will most likely not need to change this value because it should be sufficient for EMC to display everything that you need to see about the organization. The situation is different in large organizations, because you probably want to display more than 1,000 objects from time to time. For example, 1,000 is a restrictive limit where you might have 10,000 mailboxes on a server. To change this setting, select the Modify The Maximum Number Of Objects option in the action pane (the pane listing available options for the selected option to the right of the console) and set the required value (Figure 5-7).

The recipient scope also affects data displayed by EMC. This setting establishes the size of the net cast into Active Directory to fetch recipient information for EMC to display. The default values are to view all objects in the forest that supports the Exchange organization.

Viewing every recipient in the forest is impossible in very large organizations, if only because the maximum number of items will be exceeded and it would be far too slow to retrieve them all. You can therefore provide a filter for EMC by instructing it to select users from just one OU. Depending on the layout of your Active Directory, this can be an effective way of focusing in on the set of users with whom you need to work on a site, country, or regional basis. Of course, if you store all your mail-enabled objects in a single OU, this won't be much of a filter and you'll end up attempting to fetch all the recipients, which demonstrates the worth of considering how you store mail-enabled objects in Active Directory before you begin a deployment.

Chapter 5

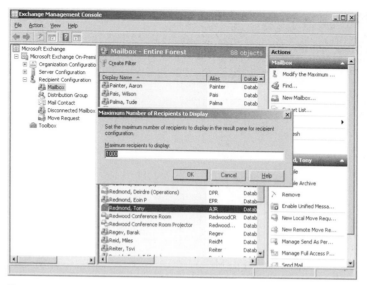

Figure 5-7 Modifying the maximum number of objects displayed by EMC.

Changing EMC columns

Like any MMC, you can use the Add/Remove option on the View menu to change the columns that you see when you access different types of objects. Figure 5-8 shows the process in action. We begin with the default columns, which are Display Name, Alias, Organizational Unit, Recipient Type Details, and Primary SMTP Address. Unless you maximize the EMC window on a large screen you can usually only see the first three of these columns due to limited screen real estate, but EMC would display them if enough space were available.

> **Note**
>
> The database that hosts a mailbox is often of interest to administrators, so we've made a change to add Database to the list and placed it in third position. Some administrators prefer other arrangements, such as listing the department to allow them to click the department heading and sort the mailboxes into department order. You can sort on any available column by clicking its heading.

Of course, EMC deals with different types of objects, depending on whether you work with organization, server, or recipient configurations. It is therefore logical that different columns are available to reflect the current EMC context. For example, if EMC is positioned in Organization Configuration to show details about mailbox servers, the columns available for display are the properties of mailbox servers.

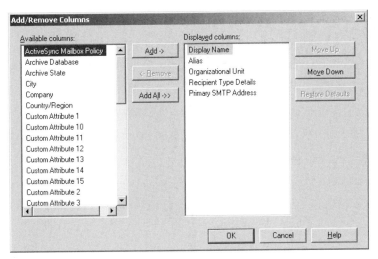

Figure 5-8 Selecting columns for EMC to display.

Auto-generated PowerShell commands

Just like in Exchange 2007, every time an EMC wizard executes a command, it displays the underlying EMS code and allows you to use Ctrl+C to copy the code for reuse. This feature helps administrators learn how to use EMS and to begin to master Exchange cmdlets to build scripts that automate common administrative operations.

Microsoft developed this capability in Exchange 2010 to add EMS command logging in other places where commands are executed, such as updating the properties of an object. In Figure 5-9, a mailbox is selected for update. Once you update a field, EMC activates the small EMS icon on the lower left corner of the Mailbox Properties dialog box. Clicking the icon reveals the code that EMC will execute to apply the change. Reviewing the code, we learn that Exchange prefers to use the canonical (domain and account) name for the mailbox as the identity parameter. The canonical name is the distinguished name of the object in Active Directory and is guaranteed to be unique, which is probably why Exchange uses it. Most administrators use the alias, display name, or Simple Mail Transfer Protocol (SMTP) address to identify mailboxes when they write EMS code because these names are usually shorter to type or easier to understand.

The same feature can be combined with another new feature of Exchange 2010 EMC: multiple object editing, also known as bulk editing. The previous version of EMC allows you to select and edit a single object, but bulk edits (for example, to change everyone's postal address because you've moved to a new office) can only be done with EMS. Although this is a nice opportunity to practice scripting skills, it can also be a nuisance.

Chapter 5

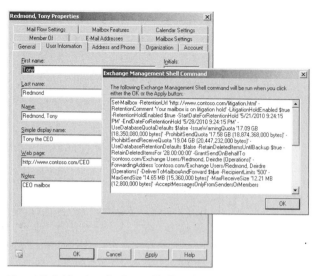

Figure 5-9 Viewing the PowerShell code to update a mailbox object.

Figure 5-10 illustrates this point. We use EMC to select three mailboxes and then click Properties in the action pane. EMC then displays the normal Mailbox Properties dialog box and populates editable fields with "<current values>" to indicate that these fields probably have different values for each of the selected objects. You can then enter new values and click the EMS icon to reveal the code. Once again, we learn something about how EMS works behind the scenes because we can see how to input a list of values for EMS to process (each mailbox is identified with its canonical name). Additionally, we see that we need to use the Set-User cmdlet rather than the Set-Mailbox cmdlet to set address and phone properties because these properties are for the Active Directory user object rather than the mailbox. Likewise, if we want to view the updated properties to verify that the change has been applied correctly, we have to use the Get-User cmdlet instead of Get-Mailbox.

After clicking OK to proceed, EMC warns you that the changes will be applied to multiple objects. This extra check stops administrators from making mistakes and lets them know just how many objects will be updated if they proceed. You might have selected 3,000 objects by accident and don't really want to update them all!

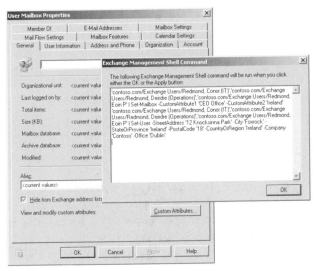

Figure 5-10 Viewing PowerShell code for a bulk mailbox edit.

Using EMS command logs

EMC also includes the ability to capture details of all of the EMS commands executed during a session. This is a very useful facility for many purposes, including auditing of administrator commands on sensitive systems and the ability to send a complete record of all commands required to replicate a problem that can then be sent to Microsoft or another support organization. You can also use the information captured in the log to understand how the Exchange cmdlets work and how to pass properly formatted values to parameters. Capturing commands into the EMS log is enabled by default.

To view the entries in the command log, on the View menu, select View Exchange Management Shell Command Log. EMC then displays a separate window (Figure 5-11) that displays any commands that have been logged and allows you to turn logging on or off, to write the contents of the log to a comma-delimited text file, to clear an existing log, and so on.

Chapter 5

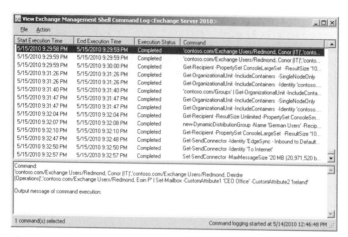

Figure 5-11 Viewing entries in the EMS command log.

Figure 5-11 illustrates how EMS command logging works. Details of the EMS cmdlets and parameters are captured in the background. The command log provides an interesting insight into how EMC works and demonstrates just how tight the connection between it and EMS is. You can pick up a lot of tips about how to formulate EMS commands and how to pass correct values to cmdlet parameters by browsing through the command log. In this case, we can see that the following steps are executed (when relevant, the code executed is shown underneath the step):

1. A bulk update is applied to two mailboxes (the command used is selected in the bottom pane of the command viewer). EMC then refreshes its display with:

   ```
   Get-Recipient -PropertySet ConsoleLargeSet -ResultSize '1000'
   -SortBy DisplayName -RecipientType 'UserMailbox'
   ```

2. The administrator moves from the Mailbox node under Recipient Configuration to Distribution Groups. EMC therefore fetches details of distribution groups from Active Directory. The filter used differs in Exchange 2010 SP1, because EMC now uses a call to the Get-OrganizationalUnit cmdlet, which is faster than the calls used in Exchange 2010.

   ```
   Get-OrganizationalUnit -IncludeContainers -Identity 'contoso.com'
   -SingleNodeOnly
   ```

3. The administrator begins to create a new dynamic distribution group. Part of this process is the creation of a filter for Exchange to use to determine group membership. The administrator uses the Preview feature to see whether the filter entered generates the correct group membership (the filter is passed in the –*RecipientPreviewFilter* parameter at the end of the command).

```
Get-Recipient -ResultSize Unlimited -PropertySet ConsoleSmallSet
-RecipientTypeDetails RemoteUserMailbox,RemoteRoomMailbox,RemoteEquipmentMailbox,
RemoteSharedMailbox,
MailUser,UserMailbox,LinkedMailbox,SharedMailbox,LegacyMailbox,RoomMailbox,
EquipmentMailbox,PublicFolder,MailContact,MailForestContact,
MailUniversalDistributionGroup,MailUniversalSecurityGroup,MailNonUniversalGroup,
DynamicDistributionGroup
-OrganizationalUnit 'contoso.com/Exchange Users'
-RecipientPreviewFilter '(&(st=Berlin)'
```

4. The filter must be satisfactory when the administrator proceeds to create the new
    dynamic distribution group. When instantiated, the filter uses one of the special
    conditional properties. See Chapter 6, "Managing Mail-Enabled Recipients," for more
    information about dynamic distribution groups.

```
New-DynamicDistributionGroup -Name 'German Users' -RecipientContainer
'contoso.com/Exchange Users' -IncludedRecipients 'MailboxUsers'
-ConditionalStateOrProvince 'Berlin','Germany' -OrganizationalUnit
'contoso.com/Exchange Users' -Alias 'GermanUsers'
```

5. The administrator navigates to the Organization Configuration node. This action
    forces EMC to refresh the data that it displays and requires the execution of a
    number of cmdlets to fetch information about organization-level components such
    as mailbox and public folder databases (Exchange 2010 holds these objects at the
    organization level rather than at the server level, as previous versions do).

6. The administrator moves to the Hub Transport node and updates the properties of a
    send connector. The first cmdlet fetches the properties of the connector so that they
    can be displayed, the second updates the MaxMessageSize property to 20 MB, and
    the third refreshes the connector information in EMC's display. Note the interesting
    use of the globally unique identifier (GUID) to identify the connector, whereas the
    first use of the Get-SendConnector cmdlet uses the display name.

```
Get-SendConnector -Identity 'To Internet'
Set-SendConnector -MaxMessageSize '20 MB (20,971,520 bytes)' -Identity 'To
Internet
Get-SendConnector -Identity 'ee1a81fc-7427-4191-8677-5a091a2d0a16'
```

The addition of bulk edits and the command log gives administrators new ways to understand and use EMS for their own purposes.

Naming conventions

The topic of naming conventions should be covered when you plan for deployment. We've
already touched on server naming conventions in Chapter 2. It's important that a server
be assigned a name that make sense and conveys some information about its purpose,
because this will make it much easier for administrators to manage the organization. Other
important objects to consider when naming include the following:

Chapter 5

- User mailboxes: My strong preference for many years has been to use the Last Name, First Name convention as the convention mimics the way that telephone directories work and it makes it easier to navigate the large groups of users in the Global Address List (GAL) who share common surnames (like Smith or Ng). The convention also works well for multinational companies that have to accommodate non-European surnames. We'll discuss this topic in greater depth in Chapter 6.

- Room and equipment mailboxes: Most companies have already named rooms in buildings so it makes sense to follow the established convention. When rooms exist in multiple buildings, you might want to prefix the room name with a building identifier. For example, the Leixlip conference room in Building 43-1 might be called B43-1-Leixlip. Building names tend to be well understood by users so you can afford to be a little cryptic in the names for these mailboxes.

- Distribution groups: Ideally, general-purpose distribution groups should convey the use of the group ("Exchange 2010 Interest List") and those intended for business-linked communication should indicate the business group and purpose ("Finance Department Planning Group"). Common sense and consultation with the group owners about the purpose of the group should lead to a sensible and easily understood name.

- Mail-enabled contacts: These objects should use the same naming convention as user mailboxes.

- Public folders: Use the same approach to naming as for distribution groups. Above all, avoid the temptation to be cryptic because it can be hard enough to navigate the public folder hierarchy without creating another obstacle to user comprehension.

- DAG: These objects are only visible to administrators, but it's still important to use a convention that informs administrators about the DAG's purpose.

- Databases: Unlike any previous version, Exchange 2010 requires that databases have names that are unique within the entire organization. Previous versions of Exchange also assigned unique names to databases but did so by combining the name of the storage group and the database. Now that storage groups have been removed, you have to assign a name to each database that is unique across the organization. The simplest convention is to assign names that indicate what mailboxes exist in the database. This could be the department name if you group mailboxes by department. Some companies indicate the mailbox size in the name so that the administrators know where to put mailboxes of a particular type and size when they are created. For example, "UK Sales-1GB" indicates users who belong to the U.K. sales department who have 1 GB mailboxes. Descriptive database names certainly work, but it becomes more difficult to think of good names to use once you have more than 20 or 30 databases to manage. See Chapter 8, "Exchange's Search for High Availability," for a more comprehensive discussion on how to name databases in large-scale deployments.

- Connectors: Messaging connectors should have names that clearly indicate their purpose and the type of traffic that they support. For example, "SMTP to Internet" or "SMTP to Lotus Notes."

INSIDE OUT   Avoid retroactive naming policies

Don't create a heap of objects and then attempt to apply a retroactive naming policy, as it is dreadfully boring to go through objects and rename them. Take the time early on to decide on a naming convention and then communicate the convention, with some examples, to any administrator who has the permission to create objects in the organization.

Organizational health data

If you click the root of an organization, EMC displays some statistics about the organization such as the number of databases, users, servers, and so on (Figure 5-12). This information must be gathered before it can be displayed. This is a new feature of Exchange 2010. Invoke the gathering process by selecting the Collect Organization Health Data option in the action pane or by choosing to access the latest data at the bottom of the information screen. Both options invoke the wizard to collect information about the organization.

The wizard begins by reading in configuration data held in the ExBPA.StayingInformed .Config.xml file. Microsoft has used the Exchange Best Practice Analyzer (ExBPA) since 2006 to help organizations validate their infrastructures against what Microsoft considers to be best practice. Essentially, ExBPA gathers data, checks them against a set of rules to identify likely problem conditions, and then issues recommendations to address the issues. The Organizational Health Gathering Wizard is only concerned with fetching data and does not attempt to analyze the data in any way. Instead, Exchange stores the data in Active Directory using the Set-OrganizationConfig cmdlet. Logically, the collection phase takes the longest because the wizard has to access information about servers and databases, and then count mailboxes and calculate which mailboxes require enterprise Client Access Licenses (CALs). Table 5-1 lists the features that are licensed for a mailbox through standard and enterprise CALs. Remember that CALs are additive, so the enterprise CAL incorporates all the features licensed by the standard CAL, even if you still have to buy both CALs.

Chapter 5

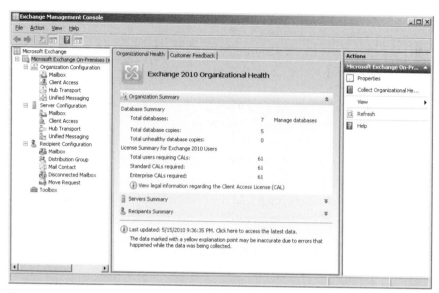

Figure 5-12 Organizational health statistics displayed by EMC.

Table 5-1 Determining the requirement for enterprise CALs

Feature set	Standard CAL required	Enterprise CAL required
Standard email functionality with Outlook, OWA, or other clients including calendar, journal, notes, and contacts	X	
Advanced ActiveSync policies for mobile devices		X
Journaling on a database basis	X	
Journaling on a selective basis (per-user or other criteria)		X
Unified Messaging		X
Retention policies (if configured with a personal tag)		X
Personal archive		X
Retention or litigation hold		X
Discovery searches across multiple mailboxes		X
Information Protection, including journal and transport rule decryption, Outlook Protection Rules, and search of protected content		X
Use of Forefront Protection 2010 for Exchange for antivirus and anti-spam protection		X

INSIDE OUT   Be patient; counting mailboxes takes time

Counting mailboxes is the longest part of the process and can take many minutes to complete in a large organization. It's an example of a feature that is easy and quick to demonstrate but can take forever (or seem to take forever) in a production environment. If the wizard is unable to collect some data (for example, because a mailbox database was not mounted), it indicates this with an exclamation mark.

As you can see from Figure 5-13 the data gathered are saved as properties of the *msExchOrganizationSummary* attribute of the root object for the Exchange organization. You can retrieve the data with the Get-OrganizationConfig cmdlet. However, because the data are stored in an array, you have to parse the values out before they are useful. The easiest way to do this is to store the values in a variable and then fetch the data that you want. Each of the different values is stored using an offset into the array. For example, to retrieve the number of standard CALs required, take the following steps:

```
$Config = Get-OrganizationConfig
$Cals = $Config.OrganizationSummary[10].Value
```

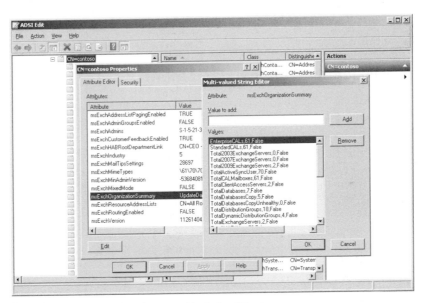

Figure 5-13 Organization data saved in Active Directory.

The total mailboxes in the organization can be retrieved with:

```
$Mbx = $Config.OrganizationSummary[5].Value
```

Dynamic distribution lists use offset 3, standard distribution lists use offset 4, and so on.

Remember that the organization data are only accurate immediately after generated and will change over time. You should refresh the data before using them as the basis for any decision.

> ## Useful information for administrators—if you have SP1
>
> Data are only good if they are gathered accurately. Unfortunately, the original Exchange 2010 version included some significant errors in the way the organizational health data were gathered because the calculation of the requirement for enterprise CALs was flawed. As you probably know, an enterprise CAL is additive, meaning that you pay more on top of a standard CAL to access additional Exchange 2010 features such as archiving. The scan for enterprise CALs certainly does some things correctly, such as not counting discovery, room, and equipment mailboxes, but it makes some errors, too. For example, it thinks that every mailbox enabled with the default ActiveSync policy requires an enterprise CAL. It also counts the mailbox for the account that is used to install Exchange, even though this account is usually only used for administrative purposes and is only mail-enabled because of the way that RBAC is enabled in Exchange 2010. Microsoft recognized the problem and has adjusted the code used to calculate the requirement for enterprise CALs in SP1. The report is now accurate and provides a useful set of data for any administrator.

Managing multiple organizations

All previous Exchange consoles manage just one organization. Some companies operate two or more organizations in different Active Directory forests. There are different reasons this is the case. Perhaps the company wants to assign different user communities to different versions of Exchange; perhaps it wants to maintain different security contexts or impose ethical firewalls between different parts of the company; or perhaps the company has simply acquired multiple implementations of Exchange along with businesses that they have purchased.

It's reasonably easy to manage multiple Exchange organizations (all versions) with Remote Desktop Connection. However, it's even easier when all of the Exchange organizations are displayed in a single console. You can add another Exchange 2010 organization (or an Exchange forest) to EMC by clicking the Microsoft Exchange root in the leftmost pane and then selecting Add Exchange Forest from the action pane. Obviously, because you will be sharing information and performing administrative actions that affect objects in the other Exchange organization, an Active Directory trust or federated trust must exist between the two forests before you can connect the organizations. You'll also need to have an account that holds the necessary privileges to be able to administer the other Exchange organization (ideally, one that holds the Organization Management role). If you synchronize account information between the forests, it might be possible to use the same account everywhere. Figure 5-14 illustrates the process. You'll be asked to provide a "friendly name" (something that makes sense to you) for the other organization and the fully qualified domain name (FQDN) for an Exchange server that runs remote PowerShell and effectively acts as a gateway into the organization for you. If you click Logon With Remote Credential, it means that you want to use the credentials of the account that you used to log in. If not, you have to provide credentials for an administrative account in the other organization.

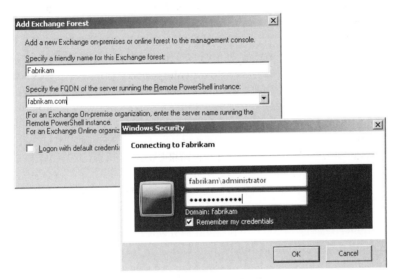

Figure 5-14 Adding a new Exchange forest to EMC.

Once connected, the details of the other organization are listed in EMC and you can work with the objects based on the role that you hold within that organization. In other words, if you only have view access, you can see but can't touch.

Sharing policies

Sharing policies are the mechanism used by Exchange 2010 to control how users share data between organizations. In the first release of Exchange 2010, sharing is restricted to calendar and contact information between organizations that enjoy a federated trust relationship created with the New-OrganizationRelationship cmdlet. Federation between two Exchange organizations requires the deployment of the Microsoft Federation Gateway, which acts as a trusted broker between the two organizations to ensure that data can pass between them in a safe and secure manner. The Microsoft Federation Gateway is part of the Active Directory Federation Services role that can be installed on a Microsoft Windows 2008 server. After Active Directory Federation Services is installed, you can use the New Federation Trust Wizard in EMC or the New-FederationTrust cmdlet to establish the necessary connection with another organization. Detailed steps describing how to use the wizard and cmdlet are provided in the Exchange 2010 help file.

See *http://technet.microsoft.com/en-us/library/dd727938(WS.10).aspx* for more information about the deployment of Active Directory Federation Services.

Exchange 2010 SP1 adds the ability to dictate a sharing policy to control how users share calendar data (but not contacts) with Internet recipients, and it is possible that Microsoft will expand sharing policies to control more aspects of sharing in the future. More information on this topic is presented in Chapter 10, "Clients."

Sharing policies are accessed through the Mailbox section of Organization Configuration in EMC. Exchange provides a default sharing policy that is empty until an administrator updates it with details of the organizations with which they want to allow users to share data. The default sharing policy is assigned to all mailboxes. You can create different sharing policies within an organization and assign these policies to different groups of mailboxes if you want to differentiate sharing capabilities. For example, you might want the default sharing policy to remain empty and then create a different sharing policy to enable sharing with one or more organizations or Internet users and then assign that policy to the users who are allowed to share their data.

The New Sharing Policy Wizard (Figure 5-15) is invoked when you click New Sharing Policy. A sharing policy is built from domain name and action pairs, where the domain name is the SMTP domain name for the organization with which you want to share data and the action defines the level of data sharing for that domain. The available options for data sharing are described in Table 5-2.

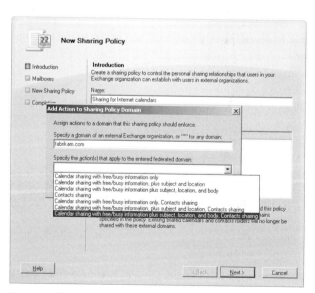

Figure 5-15 New Sharing Policy Wizard.

Table 5-2 **Levels of data sharing assigned through sharing policies**

Sharing	Settings that control data shared
Federated Organization	Calendar sharing with free/busy information only Calendar sharing with free/busy information, plus subject and location Calendar sharing with free/busy information plus subject, location, and body Contacts sharing Calendar sharing with free/busy information only, Contacts sharing Calendar sharing with free/busy information, plus subject and location, Contacts sharing Calendar sharing with free/busy information plus subject, location, and body, Contacts sharing
Internet calendars	Calendar sharing with free/busy information only Calendar sharing with free/busy information, plus subject and location Calendar sharing with free/busy information plus subject, location, and body

It's important to realize that a sharing policy can be composed of entries for multiple domains, each of which might have a different action assigned to it. Thus, you could create a sharing policy that looks like the example illustrated in Figure 5-16.

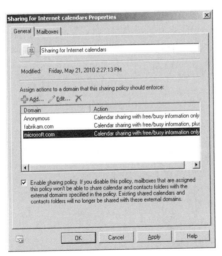

Figure 5-16 Details of a multientry sharing policy.

After you have defined the domains and actions included in the sharing policy, the wizard allows you to assign the policy to selected mailboxes. You don't have to assign the policy at this point; it can be assigned to one or more mailboxes at any time. To assign a sharing policy to a mailbox, use the Set-Mailbox cmdlet. For example:

```
Set-Mailbox -Identity 'Akers, Kim' -SharingPolicy 'Sharing policy for Internet
calendars'
```

Chapter 5

Certificate management

X.509 certificates are important to Exchange because they underpin the Secure Sockets Layer (SSL)-based secure communications between clients and servers, including SMTP conversations (secured with Transport Layer Security [TLS]) to transfer email between servers. Certificates can also be used for federation between Exchange organizations. The certificates authenticate that their holders are who they claim to be and are used to create the secure channels used to transfer data. Exchange 2010 supports three kinds of certificates:

- Self-signed certificates. A self-signed certificate is one that is generated by the application that wishes to use it. It is not signed by a certification authority (CA), and other applications or computers might not trust it because it doesn't have a certificate path that includes a trusted CA.

- Certificates issued by a Windows CA (Windows Certificate Services).

- Certificates issued by a commercial SSL vendor such as Thawte or VeriSign.

Table 5-3 lists the different protocols used by Exchange to communicate and the types of certificates that can be used to secure these connections. As you can see, third-party certificates are most useful and are an absolute requirement to secure external communications. Certificates are also used to secure communications between a reverse proxy server and Exchange if you deploy such a server in the perimeter network for external communications.

Table 5-3 Protocols and required certificates

Server role	Protocols requiring certificate	Required level of certificates
Client Access Server	OWA Exchange Web Services Outlook Anywhere ActiveSync POP3 and IMAP4 AutoDiscover	Third-party (recommended) or Windows public key infrastructure (PKI). Include the FQDN of the server and the Uniform Resource Locators (URLs) for applications such as Outlook Anywhere, Outlook Web App, and Office Communications Server.
Mailbox	Outlook (MAPI) OWA (HTTPS)	Self-signed
Unified Messaging	None	Self-signed
Hub transport	SMTP over TLS	Third party (recommended) or Windows PKI for external; self-signed for internal hub transport to hub transport communications. Include the FQDN of the server and the domain name.
Edge transport	SMTP over TLS	Third-party (recommended) or Windows PKI. Include the FQDN of the server and the domain name.

When you install Exchange on a server, Exchange automatically creates a self-signed certificate to enable the server to communicate with other servers and clients within the organization. However, only other Exchange servers in the organization automatically trust the self-signed certificates presented by a server. Self-signed certificates created by Exchange include the server name and its FDQN in the Subject Alternate Name field and last for five years. The biggest advantage of a self-signed certificate is that it is free.

Security alert: Limitations with self-signed certificates

A self-signed certificate can be used for all Exchange communications within the firewall and also supports some external connections (OWA and ActiveSync) after the certificate has been copied into the trusted root certificate store on the client computer. Some mobile devices don't permit this, so you can't use these devices with self-signed certificates. Additionally, these certificates are not able to secure Outlook Anywhere connections. Microsoft Outlook 2003 and Outlook 2007 accept self-signed certificates used for internal communications "quietly" in that they do not display any errors when they connect to an Exchange 2010 server. Outlook 2010 is more cautious and signals a potential problem to a user (Figure 5-17).

Figure 5-17 Outlook 2010 flags a problem with a self-signed certificate.

In most cases, because of the limitations imposed on the supported functionality and the difficulty of managing the certificates over time, self-signed certificates are only used for test deployments or deployments that do not support external client connectivity.

Windows Certificate Services provides a PKI to allow organizations to publish their own certificates. The certificates are more manageable because a complete Windows PKI is available to control the issuing, renewal, and revocation of certificates. Before they can be used to enable secure connections, these certificates have to be installed in the trusted

Chapter 5

root certificate store of computers that are not part of Active Directory and that need to communicate with Exchange. Windows PKI certificates are more manageable than self-signed certificates and are also free, so they are an acceptable solution for small to medium deployments.

From this discussion, you can see that the best solution for almost all deployments is to use a commercial certificate bought from a reputable, third-party trusted, CA that takes the responsibility to issue and ensure the validity of certificates. These certificates are obviously more expensive, but they offer a major advantage because the issuer's CA certificates are usually already installed in the trusted root certificate store of client computers, meaning that you don't have to install certificates manually before devices can connect.

The Exchange 2007 version of EMC doesn't provide any UI to deal with certificates, so EMS is required whenever you need to work with certificates. This isn't a problem if you're used to the nomenclature and parameters used with certificates, but can be offputting if you don't work with certificates often. Exchange 2010 provides the UI to view the certificates assigned to servers and wizards to create new certificates and assign the certificates to Exchange services (OWA, ActiveSync, and so on) with the Exchange Certificate Wizard. Click the Server Configuration node and select a server to see the certificates that are assigned to the server. In the example shown in Figure 5-18, you can see that the certificate is self-signed, meaning that this is the certificate that Exchange automatically generates when a server is installed.

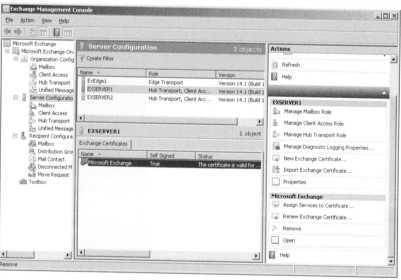

Figure 5-18 Viewing the certificate installed on a server.

There are a number of ways to work with certificates. You can do any of the following:

- Assign services to a certificate: This option allows you to assign one or more services to a certificate. The Assign Services to Certificate Wizard (Figure 5-19) presents the set of services that already use the selected certificate and allows the administrator to assign the certificate to any other service that does not already use the certificate. As you can see, in this case, Unified Messaging is the only service that can be assigned to the certificate.

- Renew an Exchange certificate: This option renews a self-signed certificate for a further five-year period and assigns it to the services that use the existing certificate. Clients will have to import the newly extended certificate to avoid seeing prompts about its potentially untrusted status.

- Request a new Exchange certificate: This option allows you to create a request that is later sent to a Windows or commercial third-party CA that will generate the necessary certificate to meet the requirements gathered by the wizard. The certificate is brought into Exchange with the Complete Pending Request option, where you give Exchange the name of the certificate file generated by the CA to allow it to import the certificate.

- Import an Exchange certificate: This option is used when a company has general certificates that are used for other services in addition to Exchange. You provide the name of the file containing the certificate and its private key and Exchange imports it.

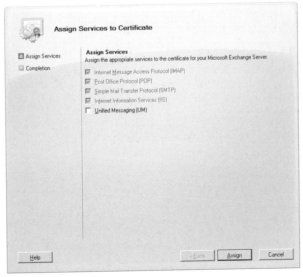

Figure 5-19 Assigning a certificate to services.

The New Certificate option invokes a wizard (Figure 5-20) to do all of the work to gather requirements for a new certificate that can be used by the Exchange services and generates a certificate request in the form of an encoded file that can be provided to a CA. After the new certificate is available (Figure 5-21), it can be imported into Exchange with the Complete Pending Request option and then assigned to the services that need to use it.

Planning for the deployment and use of certificates is a complex task that requires an understanding of how certificates are created and managed, the services that use certificates, what function the certificates service, the needs of other applications, and how to minimize the expenditure on commercial certificates by only purchasing certificates that cover multiple hostnames. You should understand this information and plan how to meet your requirements before deploying anything.

Figure 5-20 Defining requirements with the New Exchange Certificate Wizard.

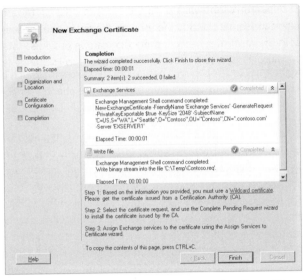

Figure 5-21 Completing the New Exchange Certificate Wizard.

Microsoft provides good information on these topics in TechNet. Another source is the book *Microsoft Exchange 2010 Best Practices* by Sigfried Jagott and Joel Stidley (2010, Microsoft Press).

Exchange Control Panel

ECP is a browser-based administrative interface that is designed to serve a number of purposes:

- User self-service: The simplified management interface allows users who don't have Exchange administration knowledge and skills to perform many of the day-to-day tasks that have stolen so much time from administrators in previous versions of Exchange. Users can configure their mailboxes to meet their own needs without asking an administrator to update their Active Directory account or use EMC to update a mailbox setting. This ability alone addresses a major bugbear and cost point for Exchange.

- Delegation of tasks to specialized staff: ECP supports a range of tasks that can be assigned to specialized staff. For example, help desk personnel can update and maintain user accounts and groups and legal staff can perform discovery searches and place users on litigation hold.

- Provide the interface to specific tasks: EMC is the entry point to a lot of different management tasks but it doesn't support the UI to access everything that an

Chapter 5

Exchange administrator might want to do. ECP provides the UI for tasks such as roles and role group management and ActiveSync device policy management that don't exist in EMC.

- Tenant management: The Web-based nature of ECP makes it a much easier administrative tool to deploy for customers who use hosted Exchange services such as Microsoft Business Productivity Online Services (Exchange Online – BPOS).

ECP can be accessed directly through its own virtual directory by typing a URL of the form *https://ExServer1.contoso.com/ecp*. Exchange 2010 originally required all users who accessed ECP to have mail-enabled accounts. This restriction was removed in Exchange 2010 SP1 and administrators who don't have an Exchange mailbox can access ECP by typing in the direct URL. Microsoft estimates that 99 percent of all of the ECP functions are available to accounts that are not mail-enabled, with the obvious exceptions being features such as the ability to receive a notification email when a discovery search is finished. Users whose accounts are mail-enabled can access ECP directory or via OWA (click the Options button) and they can switch back to OWA from ECP. All of the options presented through OWA in Exchange 2007 are now integrated into ECP.

You only see the tasks allowed for your role

Like EMS, ECP utilizes RBAC to ensure that users will only see the tasks that their role allows them to perform. In other words, ECP modifies the options that it displays to reflect the roles that a user holds. Administrators who hold the Organization Management role see all options and can work with user data; users who hold the default role see a limited set of options and can only work with data that belong to them.

If you were to use the version of ECP intended for hosted deployments, you would notice that ECP exposes the UI to allow administrators to create transport rules. This is interesting because it's attractive to be able to perform administrative tasks without having to install any software, but you can't use ECP to maintain transport rules for on-premise deployments. Microsoft believes that hosted deployments have simpler requirements for features like transport rules and that they can accommodate the need to construct and deploy basic transport rules in the current version of ECP. The EMC Transport Rule Wizard supports the creation and editing of rules based on a far more comprehensive set of predicates and conditions. Together with the ability to script and automate deployment through EMS, EMC is deemed to be better suited to the needs of on-premise deployments. Over time, Microsoft will have the opportunity to observe the practical day-to-day needs of hosted deployments in production and is likely to make adjustments to bring ECP closer to the rule functionality available in EMC today.

Chapter 5

SP1 updates for ECP

Microsoft enhanced ECP considerably in Exchange 2010 SP1. Apart from the general makeover and improved performance that was also applied to OWA (for example, the breadcrumb navigation to lead users back through options), the feature set available to administrators through ECP is expanded considerably to include the ability to manage the following:

- Journal and transport rules

- ActiveSync device policies (also manageable through EMC) and device access rules (only manageable through ECP)

- Litigation hold for mailboxes

- Room mailboxes

- Role groups and role assignments (see Chapter 4, "Role-Based Access Control")

- Access to common auditing reports

- Definition of group naming policy

- Access to ECP for accounts that don't have an Exchange mailbox

- Ability to select personal tags to use to mark items for retention

- Unified Messaging options (if UM is deployed)

Other minor updates include the ability to manage security groups and to hide a group from the GAL. The support for security groups is limited to the ability to make a distribution group into a security group. After this is done, the security group is managed in the same way as any other group. I should note here that ECP refers to distribution groups known as "public groups."

Exchange 2010 does not allow you to apply your own customized theme to the ECP UI, as it does for OWA. Being able to customize the appearance of user-viewable pages by adding corporate logos or incorporating new options is a popular request from administrators that Microsoft might facilitate in a future release.

An overview of the ECP application

ECP is built as an ASP.NET application that you can use with any of the browsers that support the premium version of OWA. You can use ECP with other browsers but might not be able to perform all of the tasks. For example, although Firefox 3+ is fully supported on

Windows, it might not function as well for ECP when used on a Linux platform. Behind the scenes, ECP is implemented as an IIS virtual directory that runs on Exchange 2010 CAS servers. Exchange installs the virtual directory automatically when you add the CAS role to a server. Like the OWA virtual directory, ECP settings are stored in Active Directory and the IIS metabase and managed through a set of cmdlets:

- New-ECPVirtualDirectory: Used by the Exchange setup program to create a new IIS virtual directory for ECP. It is unlikely that you will ever need to use this command outside the setup program.

- Set-ECPVirtualDirectory: Sets properties of the ECP virtual directory such as the authentication setting to use.

- Get-ECPVirtualDirectory: Retrieves values for the properties of the ECP virtual directory.

- Remove-ECPVirtualDirectory: Removes an ECP virtual directory.

- Test-ECPConnectivity: Tests that ECP is functioning normally and can be accessed by Web clients.

Exchange 2010 allows you to connect to ECP if you log on with an account that has a mailbox on an Exchange 2010 server. The logic is that any account that you want to use to perform administrative operations with Exchange must be mail-enabled to allow Exchange to assign the necessary roles to the accounts through RBAC. There must be some technical connection between ECP and OWA because ECP uses the OWA authorization module, which is designed to authorize accounts that have Exchange mailboxes.

> **Tip**
>
> ECP displays a maximum of 500 objects at one time. If there are more than 500 objects available for mailboxes, groups, or other kinds of objects, you will have to select the object you want to work with by typing part of its name into the search box to allow ECP to retrieve a partial set of matching objects.

Basic ECP user options

When you open ECP (Figure 5-22), you can select what you want to manage: your own account, another user, or elements of the organization as permitted by your role. Myself is the pointer to view and change settings for the user's own mailbox, the groups he belongs to and might like to join, and junk email filter options. Only administrators (any user who has been assigned an administration role) see My Organization and Another User. The My

Organization entry point allows you to manage items such as discovery searches, transport and journal rules, and role assignments. The Another User entry point allows access to the settings for another user's mailbox.

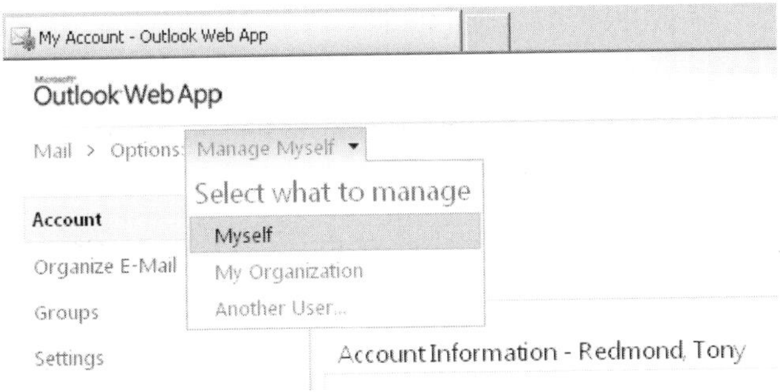

Figure 5-22 Selecting what to manage with ECP.

RBAC controls the options that are presented to users when they open ECP. For example, the option to work with the settings for another user's mailbox is only visible if your account holds the Recipient Management role. Because ECP uses RBAC to decide whether to reveal an option to a user, you can therefore determine the options that are displayed to a user by modifying role assignments.

The Exchange team posted a good description of how ECP uses RBAC on their blog at *http://msexchangeteam.com/archive/2010/03/04/454148.aspx.*

Essentially, the steps are as follows:

1. Determine the cmdlets that are associated with a particular option. As we know from the discussion about RBAC in Chapter 4, users are assigned role groups to provide them with the permission to execute actions. Role groups contain roles that define the cmdlets and parameters that can be executed through the role. We therefore start by examining the Web.config file in the \Program Files\Microsoft\Exchange Server\V14 \ClientAccess\ecp\Reporting directory to locate the entry for the functionality we are interested in, which then reveals the cmdlets.

2. Run the Get-ManagementRole cmdlet to find the roles that include the cmdlet. Some cmdlets are in just one role, and others feature in many roles.

3. Run the Get-ManagementRoleAssignment cmdlet to find out the roles that are assigned to the users for whom we want to customize ECP. This might be a specific user or a group of users. Compare the output with the roles discovered with Get-ManagementRole in step 2 to find a match between role and role group. Some knowledge of how Exchange works is necessary to make this deduction! Failing this, some trial and error will bring you to the right answer.

4. Create a new role assignment policy with the New-ManagementRoleAssignment cmdlet. We will use this policy to replace the existing default role assignment policy that the users hold. All of the basic options exposed to a user through ECP are revealed through the roles included in the default role assignment policy.

5. We eventually want to remove some options from the role assignment policy so that users aren't able to see them through ECP. However, we do want them to be able to use some options, so the roles that enable these options must be added to the new role assignment policy. For example, to allow users to see and update their contact information, we have to include the MyContactInformation role.

6. The option that we want to remove is likely included in one of the base roles. We can make a copy of the role by running the New-Management Role cmdlet and specifying the existing base role as the parent. This action creates a replica of the existing base role. We can then edit the new role that we've just created to remove whatever cmdlet is used for the option that we want to block. Once we have edited the new base role, we can add it to the role assignment policy that we created in step 4.

7. We now have a new role assignment policy that contains the necessary roles to allow the user to see the options we want to reveal but lacks the options we want to block. To implement the block, we run the New-ManagementRoleAssignment cmdlet to assign the role assignment policy to the user. The next time that the user starts ECP, RBAC will inform ECP of the new set of roles that the user possesses and ECP will then tailor its UI to reflect what the user can and cannot see.

This all seems very complex because there are a number of steps to work through and you have to understand that roles are based on cmdlets, collected into role groups to enable access to features, and assigned to users by policy. ECP in Exchange 2010 SP1 makes everything much simpler by allowing you to do all the work through the browser interface without resorting to EMS. However, it's good to understand the concepts and know what happens behind the scenes.

Most users will reach ECP by selecting the Options choice when working in OWA because this causes OWA to make a referral to the ECP application. Figure 5-23 illustrates the basic view that nonpermissioned standard users see. All they can manage through this view are personal mailbox settings such as their phone numbers.

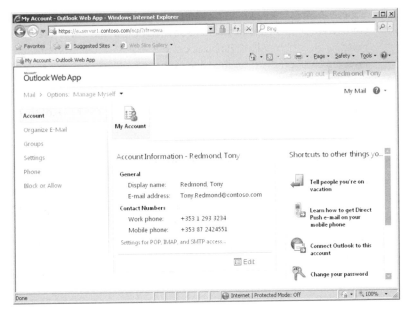

Figure 5-23 Basic ECP options presented to users.

Different screens reveal user-settable options such as creating an autosignature (Figure 5-24). Other options on this screen include reading behavior, the format for new messages (the default is HTML), and the font used when creating text in new messages. You can also choose whether to show the From and BCC fields in message headers. The From field is useful when composing messages on behalf of other users. However, a side effect is that you can't encrypt messages using the OWA Secure Multipurpose Internet Mail Extensions (S/MIME) control when the From field is exposed in the message header. The other options include the following:

- Spelling: Select whether to ignore words in uppercase and containing numbers, whether to spell check new messages before they are sent, and what language dictionary to use with OWA. You cannot alter words in the spell-check dictionary used by OWA.

- Calendar: Determine the days and hours for your working week and what automatic processing Exchange performs for your calendar (for example, automatically placing new meeting requests on your calendar). There's a useful option here to help troubleshoot calendar issues that a user might have that sends calendar log information to Microsoft. This section is also the place where users can configure their text messaging settings.

Chapter 5

- General: Decide whether recipient information in new messages is resolved against the GAL or your contacts. You can also elect to use the low-vision version of OWA here.

- Regional: Select the language used for the mailbox and the date and time format. You can only select from the languages installed on the CAS server to which ECP is connected.

- Password: Set a new password for your Windows account.

- S/MIME: Download the S/MIME control that allows OWA to encrypt and digitally sign outgoing messages.

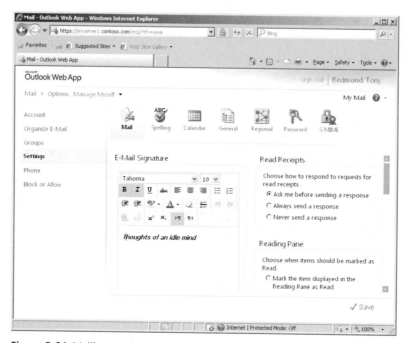

Figure 5-24 Mailbox settings available in ECP.

Many of these options are user settings that were available through OWA in previous versions of Exchange; indeed, if you select Options when working with OWA 2010, the browser session is referred to a customized version of ECP that only shows user options.

Inbox rules

Rules can be a confusing topic. There is one set of rules that is owned and maintained by Exchange and another set that Outlook owns. The rules feature exposed in Outlook could be considered a superset of Exchange's because the Outlook rule editor has traditionally been superior and more functional than the version supplied with Exchange for use with OWA. However, the superiority only really exists in terms of the user interface to rules. Behind the scenes, Exchange performs the majority of the processing on incoming items and leaves Outlook to perform only the steps that have to be executed on a client.

INSIDE OUT   Separate rules functionality

There's a good reason Exchange has separate rules functionality. Without it, rules processing would be unavailable to users who cannot use Outlook, but it is inconsistent and ineffective for two rule sets to exist. Exchange cannot manipulate a rule owned by Outlook and vice versa and attempts to synchronize the two sets of rules. Another potential point of confusion is the difference in operation between client-side and server-side rules. Client-side rules imply some action is required that can only be performed by a client, whereas server-side rules can be executed by the server independent of any client interaction. The outcome of server-side rule processing applies to all clients and items have to pass through server-side rules before they can be processed by client-side rules. Junk mail processing is an example of server-side processing. Exchange cleans up the mail stream by removing unwanted spam before passing messages to clients. An example of a client-side rule is one that checks incoming messages for any item that has "Important" in the subject and moves it into a special folder within a .pst file. Another example is a rule that looks for messages and signals an alert whenever a message from a specific user arrives. My personal favorite is a rule that delays all outgoing messages (except those marked with high importance) by two minutes to allow the sender to rescue a message that has been incorrectly addressed, doesn't have the right attachment, or has simply been sent in a moment of great passion and contains some inappropriate words. None of these rules can be processed by the server because they require Outlook to perform an action.

Exchange and Outlook work to process messages through all applicable rules. Exchange executes all the rule processing that is possible on the server and then, if further client-side processing is necessary, it creates a special message in the Deferred Actions folder. These messages are called deferred action messages (DAMs), and tell Outlook that it has to complete processing of a message. Outlook reads and executes the DAMs as they are created by Exchange. Any DAMs that are accumulated when Outlook is offline are cleared the next time that the client initializes. You never see this activity because the folder and the messages are hidden from any client view, although they can be seen using a debug utility such as MFCMAPI.

In previous versions of Exchange, users maintain rules through Outlook or OWA. This is also the situation with Exchange 2010, but the big change is that users can now create, modify, and delete their server-side rules through ECP. Administrators can also maintain rules for users through ECP or EMS. Previously, administrators never had any level of access to user rules and users were 100 percent responsible for their maintenance. Access through ECP is through the Inbox Rules tab of the Organize Email section, which displays all of the server-side rules that are currently held as hidden items in the mailbox root (Figure 5-25). Administrators continue to have no access to the client-side rules executed by Outlook.

Similar to the Outlook Rules Wizard, ECP offers reasonable flexibility when it comes to choosing conditions for a new rule. There are four basic things that you have to figure out for a rule: what criteria the server has to look for in new messages to determine whether to apply a rule, what action should be taken, whether any exceptions to the rule exist, and finally, whether Exchange should stop processing other rules after a rule is executed. ECP allows you to move rules up and down in order of priority so you can easily define your most important rule and the order of processing for subsequent rules.

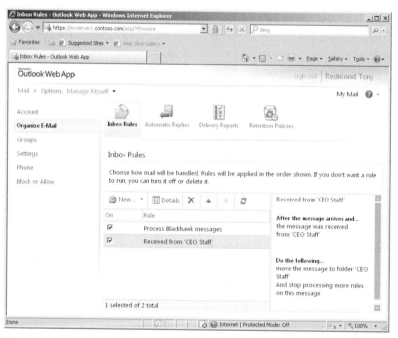

Figure 5-25 Viewing Inbox rules.

Although there are some users who create a set of very convoluted and complicated rules to manage their inboxes to a high degree, the vast majority of users are probably satisfied with a few simple rules that move messages into different folders based on the author or subject together with another criterion such as whether the user is a TO or CC recipient. Although the Outlook user interface might be a better choice for users who want to fine-tune complicated rules, ECP does a good job for the basic rules used by the majority of people.

As shown in Figure 5-26, ECP organizes the rule definition into the three major sections. Drop-down lists provide you with the different conditions for each section and you can use the mailbox/group picker to select names as required. The rule is very simple in this example: Move any message that contains a specified word in the message subject or body into a selected folder unless the message contains "Failure" in its subject. The rule is marked to stop further processing because if the message has been moved into the right folder by this rule, there's really nothing else that we want to do with it with another rule.

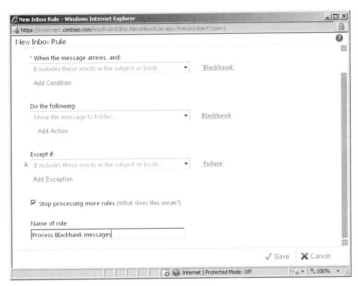

Figure 5-26 Creating a new Inbox rule.

Behind the scenes, rules are more complex than the simple example we've just discussed. You can get some idea of the degree of complexity that a rule can have by reviewing the many parameters of the New-InboxRule and Set-InboxRule cmdlets that control how the criteria and actions are set. For example, the code to create a trivial rule for a mailbox that looks for the word "Hello" in either the body of the text or the message subject and then sets the message status to Read and stops further processing of rules is as follows:

```
New-InboxRule 'Stop Hello spam' -Mailbox 'Kim.Akers@contoso.com'
-BodyContainsWords 'Hello' -SubjectContainsWords 'Hello' -StopProcessingRules $True
-MarkAsRead $True
```

Chapter 5

> ### A security check on administrators
>
> Although it's possible for an administrator to set up a trivial rule for a user like the one just shown , administrators cannot create rules that move items from one folder to another, even within the same mailbox. Administrators should not know what folders exist in user mailboxes and it would be inconsistent and a potential security breach if they were able to create a rule that moved items for a user, potentially without that user's knowledge. For example, it would be a problem if an administrator created a rule in the CEO's mailbox that refiled any new message including a key phrase into a folder in the administrator's mailbox.

You can certainly use EMS to create a rule for your mailbox to move messages into a folder after they arrive. For example, this rule looks for any message sent to a group (identified with its SMTP address) and moves it to a folder. The folder is identified using a scheme that ensures uniqueness, if not ease of use. You can use the Get-MailboxFolder -Recurse | Format-List Name, Identity command to see the list of folders in your mailbox.

```
New-InboxRule -Name "Exchange Discussion Group messages" -SentTo
'ExchangeDiscussions@contoso.com' -MoveToFolder "contoso.com/Users/Akers,
Kim:\Inbox\Exchange Discussions"
```

The most recently added rule always moves to the top of the priority order. We can use Get-InboxRule to retrieve details of the rules set on a particular mailbox. The rules are listed in priority order.

```
Get-InboxRule -Mailbox 'Kim.Akers@contoso.com' | Format-List
```

As mentioned earlier, Exchange and Outlook maintain different rule sets in a user mailbox. If you attempt to make a change to an inbox rule through ECP or EMS, Exchange will flag a potential problem if you go ahead because it will have to delete any deleted rules or "execute on send" rules belonging to Outlook. In other words, Exchange will only save the rules that it knows about (the ones that are displayed by ECP). Microsoft is aware that this is a less than acceptable situation and intends to improve it in the future. In the interim, the best advice is to always use the same client to work with inbox rules because any attempt at cross-platform rules maintenance is likely to result in trouble.

Delivery reports

Hearing from users that an email was never delivered is a pretty common experience for administrators. From time to time, it's true that problems cause Exchange to stop working and messages don't get delivered, but in most situations the problem that stops a message from getting to its final destination is simple user error. Typical reasons include messages being addressed incorrectly (sent to the wrong person), messages queued to be sent in the future, or messages in the Drafts folders waiting to be sent. You can also find information about received messages such as the membership of groups in the recipient list and whether a rule operated on a message.

Although it's satisfying for an administrator to eventually figure out what the problem was, it can also take a lot of time. Delivery reports allow users to interrogate Exchange to discover what happened to a message that they sent. If they can't figure things out, a user or an administrator can search for the specific message and generate a comprehensive delivery report that explains exactly what happened.

Users can generate delivery report information (Figure 5-27) for messages that they send, providing they use one of the following:

- OWA: Access the Delivery Reports option by selecting a message, right-clicking, and selecting Open Delivery Report.

- Outlook 2010: Access delivery reports in the backstage area.

- ECP: Available through the Organize Email section.

If they use another client, an administrator will have to generate a delivery report for them.

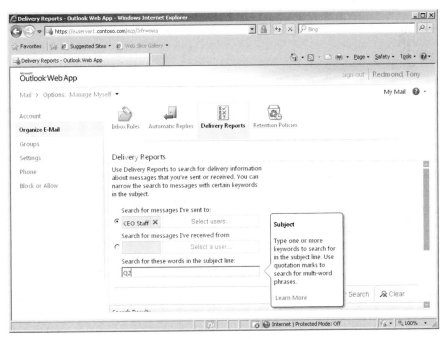

Figure 5-27 A user creates a delivery report search.

To begin a search, click Delivery Reports and then complete the basic parameters for the search. These are as follows:

- Either: Search for messages that the user has sent OR messages that she has received

- AND words in the message subject line

After the search executes, ECP displays any matching messages that it can find in the results pane below the search criteria (Figure 5-28). You can then select one of the messages to view details (Figure 5-29).

Figure 5-28 Delivery report search results.

Figure 5-29 Viewing the details of a delivery report.

A user is connected to a CAS server when he tracks a message and is therefore not limited to accessing delivery report information for the server where his mailbox is currently located. He can generate a delivery report for a message even if the mailbox has been moved between databases on the same mailbox server because they sent the message or if the database has been activated on another server within a DAG.

ECP administrator options

When a user who has been assigned some capabilities gained by membership of a management role group starts up ECP, she sees additional options and capabilities linked to the cmdlets and parameters permitted by the role group. Figure 5-30 illustrates the UI displayed to a user who holds the Recipient Management role. In addition to the options to work with her personal settings for her mailbox, she can choose to manage My Organization, which permits her access to whatever objects she is allowed to manage. In this case, the user is able to work with distribution groups and the group naming policy for the organization.

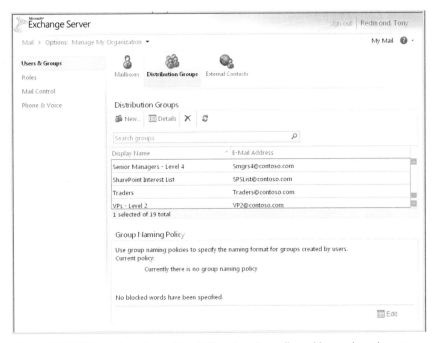

Figure 5-30 ECP user interface with additional options allowed by a role assignment.

Holders of the Recipient Management role can work with mailboxes, groups, and contacts. They can create new groups and contacts but they are limited to updating the properties of existing mailboxes. The reason is that creating a new mailbox often involves creating a new

Active Directory account. Microsoft did not have the time to do the engineering to cater to the many different scenarios that occur around account creation, including the selection of the host OU, delegated administration, and so on. Although mailbox creation appeared in some early builds of Exchange 2010, it was removed when these problems became apparent. For now, you have to create new mailboxes through EMC or EMS, but it would not be a surprise to see a "create new mailbox" feature reappear in a future version of ECP.

INSIDE OUT   Who will use ECP?

Because ECP is designed to address the needs of administrative staff who don't need to be exposed to the guts of an Exchange organization and the complexity sometimes revealed through EMC, it should come as no surprise that experienced administrators are unlikely to want to do much in ECP. There are options that deal with roles and delivery reports that are not in EMC that will force administrators to use ECP (or EMS). Staff such as help desk personnel, who aren't necessarily experienced with Exchange administration, will be relieved that they don't have to go through EMC or EMS to perform tasks such as updating the properties of groups, including the message approval settings. As mentioned earlier, ECP doesn't support the creation or maintenance of dynamic distribution groups, possibly because of the complex nature of the OPATH filters that underpin these groups.

Administrator searches for delivery reports

Users can search their own delivery reports but sometimes need a little help. They might not even know that they can search delivery reports and create help desk requests such as "I sent a note to someone in another company about an important contract and need to know that the message was delivered!" The help desk can talk the user through the process of conducting his own search but sometimes it's easier to perform the search for him. Out of the box, administrators can perform a search on behalf of a user as long as they possess one of the following roles:

- Organization Management

- Recipient Management

- Records Management

You can add the ability to perform delivery report searches by adding the Message Tracking role to a user or group. For example, this command adds the role to a security group called the "Central Help Desk." Any user who is a member of the group will be able to search delivery reports on behalf of another user, provided that they also hold the right to be able to view information about other users through another role such as View-only Organization.

```
New-ManagementRoleAssignment "Message Tracking and Delivery Reports" -Role "Message
Tracking" -SecurityGroup 'Central Help Desk'
```

Before starting, it's good to understand where the data that underpin delivery reports come from. Exchange maintains message tracking logs to trace the progress of messages from the time that they are submitted from a mailbox to the Store to a hub transport server and so on, until the message exits Exchange through a connector or is delivered to one or more recipient mailboxes. Message tracking logs have been around for many versions to allow administrators to track messages or to analyze message volumes and patterns of use. Exchange 2010 expands the use of the data to allow users to track the progress of their own messages through the Delivery Reports option. Administrators can continue to access message tracking logs through the Tracking Log Explorer option in the EMC toolbox and will do so for many purposes such as traffic analysis or message forensics. You can find a full description of how to use the Tracking Log Explorer and its cmdlets in Chapter 17.

The Delivery Reports option is valuable because it allows administrators to assign the ability to retrieve details of a message's progress and then send those details to the person who requested them to prove that the message was processed properly as far as Exchange can report. Usually this means the boundary of the organization because Exchange can't report the progress of a message through foreign email systems or even into other Exchange systems that don't run Exchange 2010.

Despite the fact that Exchange can keep many weeks of message tracking logs, Delivery Reports only work for the past two weeks, because this is the time that Exchange maintains special indexes that it uses for searches.

TROUBLESHOOTING

Why isn't a delivery report available for a mailbox that has been moved?
Because message tracking logs are specific to a server, it follows that some delivery reports do not work after a mailbox is moved from one server to another. Delivery reports for messages sent or received after the mailbox has been moved onto a server are available because the message tracking logs that contain the necessary information are present on the same server. Any request for a delivery report for a message sent or received before the mailbox was moved will fail because the necessary data are unavailable.

Chapter 5

Two configuration settings control the amount of data that can be included in delivery reports. Subject logging determines whether you can see the subject of messages when you search. Obviously it is a lot easier to locate a specific message if you know its subject and can see it in the set of results after a search. Message subjects are logged on mailbox and hub transport servers and if you want to disable the collection of these data, you have to do this with the Set-MailboxServer and Set-TransportServer cmdlets. The setting only applies to a single server, so if you want to do this for all servers in an organization, you have to first fetch details of all mailbox or transport servers and then pipe the set of servers into the appropriate cmdlet. For example:

```
Get-TransportServer |Set-TransportServer –MessageTrackingLogSubjectLoggingEnabled
$False
```

INSIDE OUT   Message subject logging and confidential information

Some companies disable message subject logging in an attempt to preserve employee privacy on the basis that giving administrators the ability to see message subjects might expose information that users would prefer not to share. For example, if an administrator performs a delivery report search against the CEO's mailbox and finds a message from the CEO to the CFO with the subject "Merger with Fabrikam Corp.," she has probably discovered something that she should not have. Eliminating message subject logging certainly stops administrators from stumbling onto sensitive information through delivery reports and message tracking, but it also makes it much more difficult for users or administrators to locate messages. All things considered, it is best to retain message subject logging on the assumption that administrators should know that if they make an unauthorized search for confidential or sensitive information, they must be prepared to deal with the consequences of their action.

Read status tracking controls whether you can see if the status of a message has been changed from unread to read. Clients change this status when a user opens a new message or the message is viewed through a preview pane for a set time (configurable on the client). Exchange 2010 disables read status tracking by default, so if you want to see read status reported, you will have to enable it as follows:

```
Set-OrganizationConfig –ReadTrackingEnabled $True
```

Read tracking is configured at the organization level, so if you enable the feature, Exchange tracks read status for every mailbox in the organization. You might not want to do this for specific sensitive users, such as executives or other users who have confidential positions. In this case, you can disable read status tracking selectively on a per-user basis:

```
Set-Mailbox –Identity 'Samantha Smith' –MessageTrackingReadStatusEnable $False
```

Access to delivery reports is available through the Reporting node of ECP. Users can search for information about messages that they sent and administrators can select a mailbox to search for. Administrators access delivery reports through the Reporting tab in ECP. Users can perform a search through their messages to generate a delivery report through the Organize E-Mail tab. Users can also generate a delivery report for a specific message with OWA. To do this for an outgoing message, select it in the Sent Items folder, right-click, and then select Open Delivery Report. For received messages, select the message and use the same option through the shortcut menu or select the Delivery Report option displayed in the message header.

User-generated delivery reports only show information relevant to the delivery of a message to that mailbox. For example, you can see whether a group was expanded to address a message to the mailbox or if a rule processed the message after Exchange delivered it to the mailbox, but you cannot see what happened when Exchange delivered the message to the other recipients.

To begin a search of delivery reports for another user, opt to manage My Organization and then go to the Mail Control section. You can then input the search criteria. The first step is to select the mailbox to search, followed by the message recipients (for outgoing messages) or people who sent email to the mailbox, and words that appeared in the message subject. If the message was sent to or received from an external correspondent, you can enter her SMTP address. While you don't have to include any subject information, it is a good idea because it will improve the effectiveness and speed of the search. When you execute the search, Exchange looks through its message tracking log data and locates any messages that match the search criteria (Figure 5-31).

Search Results			
🔲 Details ⟳			
From	To	Subject	Sent Time ▾
Smith, Samantha	Exchange 2010 Interest List;jsmith@fab...	The Fabrikam contract	20/05/2010 12:25
Smith, Samantha	jsmith@fabrikam.com;Akers, Kim	Fabrikam contract	20/05/2010 12:23
Smith, Samantha	jsmith@fabrikam.com	RE: Fabrikam contract	20/05/2010 12:16
1 selected of 3 total			

Figure 5-31 Results of the delivery report search.

Behind the scenes, ECP calls the Search-MessageTrackingReport cmdlet and provides it with the search parameters entered by the user who initiates the request. We'll explain how to execute searches with EMS shortly. CAS servers manage delivery report searches, so the first port of call is to contact a CAS server in the site. If we are looking for messages sent from a mailbox, the CAS server will begin the search on the mailbox server that currently hosts the database where the mailbox is located. On the other hand, if we're looking for evidence of messages coming from an external sender, the search has to begin with the hub transport servers in the site because that will be the first place a message enters. Once the starting point is determined, Exchange contacts the Log Search service running on the server and

Chapter 5

queries it using the search criteria. When a message is found, its path can be tracked from server to server until its final disposition is known. This might be delivery to a mailbox or exiting the organization across a connector. Exchange is able to track messages across sites by sending queries using Exchange Web Services to CAS servers in another site. Those CAS servers then perform queries against the hub transport and mailbox servers in their site, collate the details, and send them back to the requesting server. All of the data accumulated during a search are then formatted and displayed (Figure 5-32) to the user through ECP or EMS.

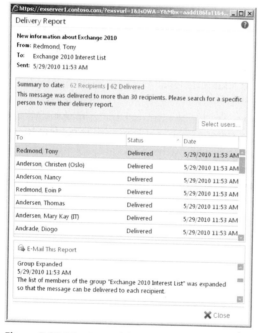

Figure 5-32 Viewing a delivery report for a message sent to a large distribution group.

You can browse the set of delivery reports that are found and select any that seem to match. If you click an item in the list, ECP displays basic information about the message including the full recipient list, the count of the number of recipients, and the number of successful deliveries. You can get a full report of all of the known steps that the message took from sending through processing by the transport system to final delivery by clicking on any of the recipients. For example, the delivery report shown in Figure 5-32 is for a message sent to a large distribution group whose membership has been resolved into a total of 62 recipients.

> **Tip**
>
> Like all groups, Exchange has to resolve the membership before it can route a message, so the membership of any group addressed in a message, including dynamic distribution groups, is listed in a delivery report. ECP displays 30 recipients at a time, so if a message was delivered to more than 30 recipients, you will have to search the recipient list to find the person in whom you're interested before you can view full details of the delivery report for his mailbox.

Figure 5-33 illustrates the kind of information that the help desk might need to satisfy a user request. We can see the list of recipients for the message and a summary of their disposition. One message was delivered successfully within the organization and the other was transferred because it was addressed to an external recipient. By clicking the external recipient, we see the details of its transit and can confirm that the message was successfully sent from our organization to the recipient's email domain. We don't have any control over what happened to the message afterward, but at least we can confirm to the user that all seems well.

Figure 5-33 Validating that a message has been transferred to its final destination.

Once you are satisfied that a message was delivered successfully, you can click the EMail This Report link to email a copy to the user who reported the problem to prove that the message got through. At the same time, you might allow yourself a small amount of satisfaction that you have proved to a user that the email system really does work—this time.

The implementation of delivery report searches in Exchange 2010 satisfies two major user queries: Did a message that I sent arrive at its destination, and why did I not receive a particular message? If you want to execute searches and retrieve more comprehensive information about the path a message took, you can use the Tracking Log Explorer from the EMC toolbox (see Chapter 17 for more information).

Using EMS to search delivery reports

Behind the scenes, Exchange uses the Search-MessageTrackingReport cmdlet to execute delivery report searches. For example, a search of Samantha Smith's mailbox for messages received from Tony Redmond might use a command like the one shown next. Note that unlike message tracking log searches, you cannot state a date range. All delivery report searches look back two weeks. Two other points are, first, that the *–ByPassDelegateChecking* parameter is used to tell Exchange that you're performing a search of a mailbox that is not your own and therefore depend on the roles assigned to you to perform delivery report searches. The second is the use of the *–ResultSize* parameter to tell Exchange that we want to find all matching messages. Up to 1,000 entries are returned if you omit this parameter.

```
Search-MessageTrackingReport –Identity 'Smith, Samantha' –Sender 'Redmond, Tony'
–Subject 'Exchange' –ByPassDelegateChecking –ResultSize Unlimited | Select
FromDisplayName, Subject, SubmittedDateTime
```

FromDisplayName	Subject	SubmittedDateTime
Redmond, Tony	For you to review (Exchange)	2/10/2010 4:44:48 PM
Redmond, Tony	Exchange design document	2/10/2010 11:49:06 AM
Redmond, Tony	Exchange Budget for 2010	2/10/2010 11:15:49 AM

Any user can conduct a search for delivery reports for items in her mailbox. You use the same syntax for searches, provide the identifier of your mailbox, and omit the *–ByPassDelegateChecking* parameter.

Each of the messages retrieved by a search has a unique identifier provided in the *MessageTrackingReportId* property. You can use this value to retrieve full details of a selected delivery report. This operation can be a tad complicated if you have to search a large number of delivery reports, but here's the essential operation. First, we will search for any message sent by a user to a distribution group. The command looks very much like our previous search except that we're looking for messages sent from a mailbox to a particular recipient (the SMTP address of the distribution group):

```
Search-MessageTrackingReport –Identity 'Tony Redmond' –Recipients 'E14InterestList'
–ByPassDelegateChecking –ResultSize Unlimited
```

Exchange fetches all delivery reports that match our search. We're interested in information about a particular recipient, so we need to go down through the delivery reports and filter out the data about the recipient. A ForEach loop that processes the output of the search does the trick:

```
ForEach {Get-MessageTrackingLog –Identity $_.MessageTrackingReportId
–ByPassDelegateChecking –DetailLevel Verbose –RecipientPathFilter
'Tony.Redmond@contoso.com' –ReportTemplate RecipientPath}
```

This code examines the delivery reports for any detail concerning the recipient specified in the –*RecipientPathFilter* parameter. Again, we use the SMTP address of the recipient. The output isn't as pretty as what ECP provides, but it does show what happened to get the message to the recipient.

For more information about delivery reports, the Exchange development group has blogged on this topic at *http://msexchangeteam.com/archive/2010/01/13/453792.aspx*.

Transport and journal rules

Exchange 2010 SP1 allows you to create and manipulate transport and journal rules through ECP. All of the predicates, conditions, and exceptions for rules that are supported by EMC can be accessed through ECP. Some users might find that ECP is easier to work with and it's certainly good that you don't need to install the Exchange management tools on a workstation to be able to work with rules. This is an especially important development for the hosted version of Exchange because it allows administrators to manage rules for their hosted organization via HTTPS.

For on-premise deployments, I suspect that transport and journal rules will continue to be managed through EMC in the majority of cases simply because it is the tool that has always been used and is therefore better documented and known to the administrators who work with rules. Transport and journal rules are explored in detail in Chapter 16, "Rules and Journals."

Running ECP without an Exchange mailbox

Exchange 2010 SP1 allows you to grant access to the ECP application to accounts that do not have an Exchange mailbox. Many companies have security guidelines that prohibit administrators from using their personal accounts (those that they use to access applications such as email and other resources) when they manage computers. The idea is to force administrators into a certain state of mind when they work in privileged environments so that a clear sense of separation exists between work performed as a system administrator and work performed as a normal user.

Exchange 2010 forces every administrator account to be mail-enabled, which means that companies who want to enforce the separation can not do so unless they create two accounts for administrators, one for normal use and one with administrative permissions. SP1 extends the RBAC mechanism to allow an administrator to select a non-mail-enabled account and make it a member of a role group. Figure 5-34 shows an account called "Computer Administrator" added as a member of a role group. You can add non-mail-enabled accounts to role groups as powerful as Organization Management or to more restricted role groups such as Help Desk.

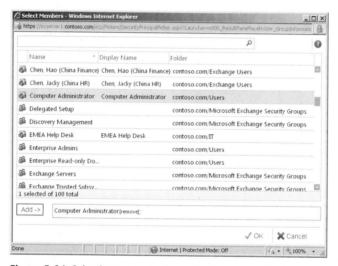

Figure 5-34 Selecting a non-mail-enabled account to include it in the membership of a role group.

To access ECP, the account owner logs in as usual and accesses ECP with the URL *https://server-name/ECP*. Naturally, because he doesn't have a mailbox, any attempt to use OWA will be politely refused with the error that Exchange can't find a mailbox for the account.

Managing the settings for another user's mailbox

When you work with the mailbox settings of another user, ECP makes this obvious by displaying a warning banner at the top of the page (Figure 5-35). You clearly want administrators to remain logged on to another user's mailbox for only as long as it takes to do a job and the warning indicates the need to close the window to remove ECP's connection to the mailbox once the task is complete. Before an administrator can open another user's mailbox, she has to be allowed full access to the mailbox. See Chapter 6 for more information.

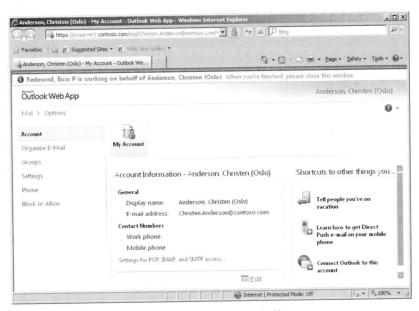

Figure 5-35 Working with ECP on another user's behalf.

Managing groups with ECP

Distribution groups have long been a fundamental part of a messaging system. Tradition-ally, Exchange has allowed administrators to create and manage groups, including group membership, through its administration console. Users access groups through clients such as Outlook. However, the interaction that users have with groups is largely read-only and only a relatively small proportion of users have reason to maintain group membership. In the past, this function has largely been carried out through Outlook. Outlook is an accept-able tool for group maintenance when the group is owned by the same domain as the account that attempts to update it, but it has proven problematic in multidomain deploy-ments if Outlook does not connect to a domain controller that holds a writeable copy of the group. This issue is addressed in Exchange 2010 as part of the relocation of the code that controls group updates from the mailbox server to the CAS, provided that the user is a nominated owner for the group.

Given the fact that Outlook is not designed to be a directory maintenance tool, many com-panies have created self-service Web-based portals based on the Lightweight Directory Access Protocol (LDAP) to allow users to manage groups. These portals allow users to cre-ate, manage, and delete groups and are often found in environments where multiple email systems share a common directory.

ECP presents two different views of groups: Users have access to "public" groups that they either own (are a registered manager of the group) or of which they are a member, whereas

Chapter 5

administrators can create, manage, or delete groups on behalf of the organization as a whole. Apart from the different labels used in the ECP UI, there are some subtle differences between the two types. A public group is one that is visible to end users. Other groups exist in Exchange that a user will never see:

1. Groups that are marked as hidden from Exchange address lists and therefore don't appear in the GAL. End users will never see these lists.

2. Dynamic distribution groups. The membership of these lists is controlled by the OPATH filter in each group that the transport system evaluates whenever a message addressed to a dynamic distribution group passes through its categorizer. End users cannot edit or view the OPATH filters (and probably don't want to), so it doesn't make sense for ECP to reveal these groups.

3. Room lists. These are distribution groups with membership that is entirely composed of room mailboxes and are used by Outlook 2010 to make it easier for a user to find a suitable conference room when scheduling a meeting. There is no sense in end users interacting with these groups because they serve an internal purpose, so they are hidden by ECP. Room lists are explained in more detail in Chapter 6.

ECP does not allow administrators to work with the full set of groups, nor does it reveal the full set of properties that Exchange supports for groups. To some degree, this reflects the fact that ECP is only in its second iteration in Exchange 2010 SP1 and Microsoft has not yet expended the same development time or effort to build the same rich set of capabilities into ECP as exist in EMC or EMS. However, it's also fair to say that ECP is designed to allow access to the most common management tasks and that in the immediate future this interface will probably not offer the ability to accomplish the most complex tasks that an Exchange administrator might perform. We cover the topic of distribution groups in more detail in the next chapter when we discuss how to work with them using EMC and EMS.

Defining a default group location and group naming policy

If you allow administrators and users free rein to create groups, it's likely that a wide variety of names will be used. It's important that groups have names that are appropriate and easy for users to find when they go looking for the right group to which to send a message. We can't do much about the intended use of a group because this varies from groups that reflect organizational structure (the members of a department) or users at the same level (all the VPs in the company) to the banal but much-used (the company softball team), but we can make sure that the groups follow a naming convention that allows users to find them in a logical place in the GAL.

Exchange 2010 SP1 includes the ability for an administrator to control two important aspects of group creation through ECP.

- The location in Active Directory where new groups are created

- The naming policy that is applied to new groups

If you use ECP to create a new group with Exchange 2010, the group is automatically placed in the Users OU. This OU has the advantage that it is guaranteed to be present because it's one of the default OUs created when you install Active Directory. Few administrators delete OUs without good reason, but if you do remove the Users OU then users won't be able to create new groups with ECP. No restrictions exist on OU location when you create new groups through EMC or EMS because you can specify exactly which OU you want to use.

INSIDE OUT   You can define where a new group is located

Administrators asked for the ability to control where new groups are created. Exchange 2010 SP1 includes the ability to define the location for all new groups created within the organization. To define where new groups are placed, use a command like this:

```
Set-OrganizationConfig -DistributionGroupDefaultOU 'contoso.com/Exchange
Groups'
```

Exchange will continue to create new groups in the default Users OU if you don't define another location.

You can only create a single OU for the organization so this is very much a one-size-fits-all solution to the problem that works well for small deployments but isn't flexible enough for large organizations, which might want to distribute groups across a number of OUs. Stuffing thousands of groups into one OU is not always the best approach but it's understandable that Microsoft took this approach because no one really wants to expose the Active Directory OU structure to users through ECP to allow them to select where a new group should be created. The upshot is that you might have to move groups around to put them into more appropriate OUs after they have been created by users. Relocating a group to another OU does not affect the ability of group owners to manage it or other users to see it in the GAL.

No naming policy can completely prevent users from giving silly or inappropriate names to new groups. It would be unreasonable to expect such an intelligent policy as parsing group names to determine their worth, because that would require a good deal of artificial intelligence and knowledge about company culture. One company's silly name is another company's code name for a breakthrough product. The intention behind the ability to create a group naming policy through ECP is to do no more than to allow new groups to be clearly identified in the GAL through the application of a suitable prefix or suffix. The naming policy applies to groups created by users through ECP; it is not applied to groups that are created by administrators through ECP or EMC. Administrators can also use the *IgnoreNamingPolicy* parameter when they create a new group with EMS. For example:

```
New-DistributionGroup -Name 'Senior Executives' -Type Security
-IgnoreNamingPolicy -SAMAccountName 'SeniorExec' -OrganizationUnit
'contoso.com/Groups'
```

> **Note**
>
> A single group naming policy applies across the organization. You cannot have granular naming policies based on business structure or other filters.

To create a group naming policy for the organization, open ECP and select Manage My Organization, then Users and Groups, and then Distribution Groups. The option to create the naming policy is under the list of groups. Details of the naming policy, if it is already defined, will be listed here. Click Edit to edit the policy and you'll be presented with a screen similar to that shown in Figure 5-36, where you can define what prefix or suffix should be applied to new groups along with any words that users are not allowed to include in group names. These words might include inappropriate words that are offensive or not suitable for business purposes.

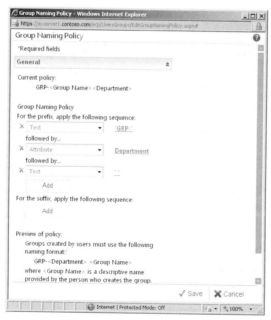

Figure 5-36 Defining a group naming policy for the organization.

When you define the prefix or suffix, you can instruct Exchange to use a text string or an Active Directory attribute or a mixture of both combined in whatever order you choose. In this context, the Active Directory attribute is determined from the account of the user who creates the new group and Exchange won't include the value in the group name if the attribute is not populated.

Prefixes are used most often to identify groups simply because all groups are then listed together in the GAL. Figure 5-36 specifies that a prefix is created from three parts: a text string (GRP-), followed by an Active Directory attribute (Department), and then a blank space. Thus, if the user specifies that the group name is Dublin Users and the value of their Department attribute is Admin, the resulting group name is GRP-Admin Dublin Users. If the Department attribute is blank, the group name will be GRP Dublin Users. ECP informs users about the effect of the naming policy after they create new groups with a pop-up message similar to that shown in Figure 5-37.

Information   ×

   ⓘ In accordance with the group naming policy for your organization,
     this group has been created with the following name: GRP-Sales
     Athena Project.

                                                    [Close]

Figure 5-37 A user is advised of the effect of the group naming policy.

When you have selected the right combination of text and Active Directory attributes to form group names, click Save to write the new policy into the organization settings. Exchange stores the group naming policy in the *DistributionGroupNamingPolicy* property of the organization configuration. You can access the properties that control how users create groups with the Get-OrganizationConfig cmdlet. For example:

```
Get-OrganizationConfig | Select Distr*
```

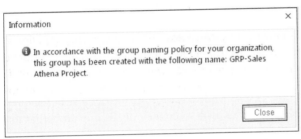

```
DistributionGroupDefaultOU    DistributionGroupNameBlockedWordsList    DistributionGroupNamingPolicy
--------------------------    -------------------------------------    -----------------------------
contoso.com/Exchange Users    {Cake, Pizza}                            GRP-<Department><GroupName>
```

> **Tip**
>
> It's possible to update the group naming policy with the Set-OrganizationConfig cmdlet, but it's easier to update the policy with ECP and you are less likely to make a mistake.

From a computer point of view, group names that are generated according to a policy are useful because they ensure that groups are all arranged neatly in the GAL. From a human perspective, an administrator might still need to review and possibly amend group names slightly to make them more aesthetically pleasing. Of course, your users might be fully prepared to accept computer-friendly rather than user-friendly group names, in which case you won't have to make any changes.

Creating new groups

ECP uses a simple and straightforward process to create a new group. Figure 5-38 shows the basic elements of a group being populated. The following information can be input:

- The group name (mandatory): An organization group naming policy can provide a prefix or suffix to identify the new object as a group. This name is descriptive and should indicate who will receive messages sent to the new group. The name of the group must be unique.

- The group alias (mandatory): An alias to identify the group. It is best practice for the alias for any object to be unique, but the alias does not have to be unique for a group.

- Description: Some descriptive text to indicate the purpose of the new group. This information is displayed to users when they view group properties through the GAL.

- Ownership: A list of one or more users who are entitled to manage the properties of the group including its membership. ECP automatically adds the user who creates the new group as an owner.

- Membership: The list of mail-enabled objects that will receive messages sent to the group. The managers of the group are added as members.

- Membership Approval: A set of properties that control whether users can join or leave the group without administrator intervention, as follows:

  ○ The *MemberJoinRestriction* property controls how an end user can join a group.

  ○ The *MemberDepartRestriction* property controls how an end user can leave a group.

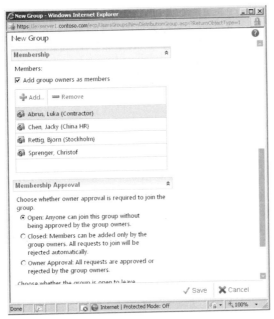

Figure 5-38 Creating a new group with ECP.

> **Note**
>
> The same values are used to control exit and join requests. These are as follows:
>
> - Open: An end user can join or leave this group at any time without permission.
>
> - Closed: An end user cannot join or leave this group because its membership is controlled. Members have to be added or removed by an administrator.
>
> - ApprovalRequired: An end user can apply for membership in the group. Exchange will route the request to the group managers, one of whom must approve the request to add the end user to the group's membership.

More advanced elements, such as MailTips, can be added to the group by editing its properties with ECP or EMS after it is created.

Creating security groups with ECP

The default type for a new group is a mail-enabled universal distribution group. If you need a group to be a mail-enabled security group (one that holds a security principal), you need to mark it as such when you create the group (Figure 5-39). This is a new feature introduced in Exchange 2010 SP1 and only administrators can create a security group (the check box is disabled when users who aren't administrators create new groups).

In addition, security groups don't support the ability of users to join or leave the group without administrator permission. This restriction is quite logical. A security group is a security principal used to permit access to some kind of resource. It wouldn't make for a very secure situation if users could gain access to a security principal without some form of oversight.

Figure 5-39 Making a group a security group.

Because it's not supported by the Set-DistributionGroup cmdlet, you can't use any Exchange management tool to modify the properties of a mail-enabled distribution group to make it into a mail-enabled security group after it is created. However, you can change a group's properties through the Active Directory Users and Computers console to make it a mail-enabled security group.

Users and groups

For many companies, giving users the ability to know what groups they belong to, to know what groups are available to join, and to join and leave groups without administrator intervention is perhaps the most interesting administrative feature delivered in ECP. With ECP, users can do the following:

- View the public groups to which they belong

- Update the membership of the public groups of which they are a registered manager

- Delete groups that they own

- Create new groups

- Join or leave open groups that someone else has created

Like everything else in ECP, the ability of users to perform these tasks is controlled by the Default Role Assignment Policy (Figure 5-40). Every Exchange mailbox has a role assignment policy that provides it with the ability to call cmdlets to work with objects such as groups. All mailboxes start out with the Default Role Assignment Policy but you can create and assign new policies to mailboxes as required.

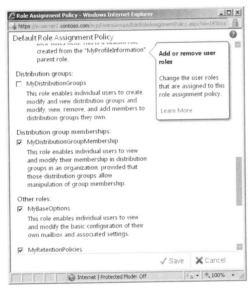

Figure 5-40 The Default Role Assignment Policy.

When ECP initializes, it checks the role assignment policy applied to the mailbox to discover what UI it is allowed to display. Figure 5-40 shows the role assignments included in the Default Role Assignment Policy that control what users can do with groups. As you can see, the set of roles included in this role assignment policy includes *MyDistributionGroupMembership*, so ECP allows users to view and modify their membership in groups. We can also see that the check box for the *MyDistributionGroups* role is not selected, so this role will not be assigned to users through the role assignment policy and ECP won't display the UI to allow users to create new groups. The net effect of these role assignments is that when users access the Groups section of ECP, they will only see a list of groups called Public Groups I Belong To (Figure 5-41). These are the groups of which the user is a member. If the user is a member of many groups, she can use the Search Groups option to search through the groups to find the group with which she wants to work.

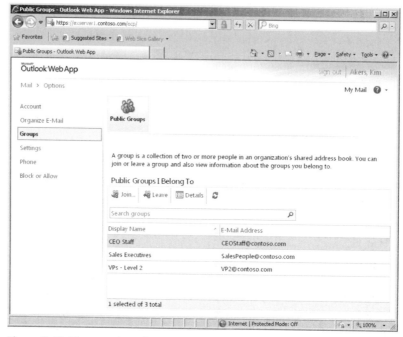

Figure 5-41 The user view of public groups presented by ECP.

Figure 5-42 shows the properties of a group as viewed through ECP. Membership requests are under the control of an administrator as requests to join are automatically rejected, so we know that the *MemberJoinRestriction* property is set to ApprovalRequired. You can edit the properties of a distribution group with EMC to set the exit and join properties (on the Membership Approval tab) or use the Set-DistributionGroup cmdlet. For example:

```
Set-DistributionGroup -Identity 'SharePoint Interest List' -MemberJoinRestriction
'ApprovalRequired' -MemberDepartRestriction 'Open'
```

Figure 5-42 Viewing group properties.

The concept of self-maintaining groups that use this feature is explored in more detail in Chapter 6.

Allowing users to create new groups through ECP

If you decide to permit users to create groups by changing the Default Role Assignment Policy to include the *MyDistributionGroups* role, you'll see the first effect of the policy change when users open the Groups section in ECP. As shown in Figure 5-43, because of the assignment of the *MyDistributionGroups* role, ECP now displays a new list of groups called Public Groups I Own, along with options to create a new group or to update the details of an existing group. The groups shown in this list are those for which the user is listed as one of the group managers. You can discover which users are the managers of a group by viewing its properties through EMC. Alternatively, you can use the Get-DistributionGroup cmdlet in EMS.

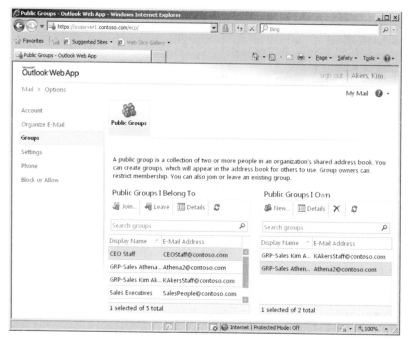

Figure 5-43 ECP after the *MyDistributionGroups* role is assigned.

In this example, we discover the users registered as managers of the CEO Staff group and see that there are two users listed. If either of these users accesses ECP, he will see the CEO Staff group listed in the set of groups that he owns.

```
Get-DistributionGroup -Identity 'CEO Staff' | Format-Table ManagedBy
```

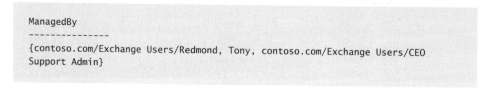

```
ManagedBy
---------------
{contoso.com/Exchange Users/Redmond, Tony, contoso.com/Exchange Users/CEO
Support Admin}
```

If this doesn't seem like a good idea, we can change the policy to remove the ability to create new groups.

Planning for user-created groups

Before you allow users to create groups, you should consider the consequences that might flow from this decision:

- Users don't typically plan how to best create groups and are prone to create groups without checking to see whether a comparable group already exists. They are unlikely to follow any naming conventions. You could therefore end up with duplicated groups scattered throughout the GAL. Exchange 2010 SP1 supports the creation of a naming policy for groups.

- In the same light, apart from occasionally updating group membership, users are unlikely to maintain groups. Orphan groups will occur after users leave the organization. The result is the accumulation of many outdated and unwanted zombie groups that linger in the GAL until an administrator deletes them.

- Users can create mail-enabled universal groups; they cannot create mail-enabled universal security groups. If a user needs a mail-enabled universal security group, she can create a group and then ask an administrator to upgrade it to become a universal security group.

- Consider the appropriate location in Active Directory for user-created groups. For more information about how to configure the default organization unit for group creation, refer to the section "Defining a default group location and group naming policy" earlier in this chapter.

These issues escalate in importance as the organization grows. Allowing users to create their own groups in a small organization where it's easy to keep track of what's happening in the GAL is one thing; allowing 100,000 users to create groups and ending up with 250,000 extra groups in the GAL is quite another. Users will find it difficult to find recipients in the GAL and OAB file downloads will become larger and larger. Even worse, the thought of cleaning up tens of thousands of unwanted or unused groups on a regular basis is numbing.

Maintain groups but don't create!

In Exchange 2010, the Default Role Assignment Policy is not granular enough to block users from creating new groups while allowing them to manage groups that they own. However, you can create a new customized management role and add it to the default role assignment policy to replace the existing role assignment that allows users to create their own groups. The new management role is based on the old role, but we remove the cmdlet that allows users to create new groups so that all that remains are the cmdlets that allow users to update the existing groups that they own. The procedure to create the new management role and add it to the Default Role Assignment Policy is as follows:

1. Define a new customized management role based on the existing *MyDistributionGroups* role.

    ```
    New-ManagementRole –Name MyGroupsMaintain –Parent MyDistributionGroups
    ```

2. Remove the New-DistributionGroup cmdlet from the new customized management role that you just created. The other cmdlets that interact with distribution groups such as Add-DistributionGroupMember (to add a recipient to a group) are maintained in the role.

```
Remove-ManagementRoleEntry MyGroupsMaintain\New-DistributionGroup
–Confirm:$False
```

3. Remove the standard MyDistributionGroups role from the Default Role Assignment Policy. The first command captures a pointer of the unwanted role assignment into a variable and the second removes the role assignment from the Default Role Assignment Policy.

```
$OldAssignment = Get-ManagementRoleAssignment –RoleAssignee 'Default Role
Assignment Policy' –Role 'MyDistributionGroups'
Remove-ManagementRoleAssignment $OldAssignment –Confirm:$False
```

4. Assign the new customized management role to the Default Role Assignment Policy. Essentially, our new role takes the place of the standard *MyDistributionGroups* role. The only difference between the two is that our new role doesn't allow users to access the New-DistributionGroup cmdlet so they will never be able to create new groups.

```
New-ManagementRoleAssignment –Name 'MyGroupsMaintain-Default Role Assignment
Policy' –Role MyGroupsMaintain –Policy 'Default Role Assignment Policy'
```

5. We now validate that the new role has been assigned to the Default Role Assignment Policy. You'll notice that the *MyDistributionGroups* role assignment is no longer included in the policy.

```
Get-ManagementRoleAssignment –RoleAssignee 'Default Role Assignment Policy' |
Select Name, Role
```

```
Name                                                   Role
-------                                                ----
MyDistributionGroupMembership-Default Role Assignment Po...   MyDistributionGroupMembership
MyBaseOptions-Default Role Assignment Policy          MyBaseOptions
MyContactInformation-Default Role Assignment Policy   MyContactInformation
MyTextMessaging-Default Role Assignment Policy        MyTextMessaging
MyVoiceMail-Default Role Assignment Policy            MyVoiceMail
MyProfileInformation-Default Role Assignment Policy   MyProfileInformation
MyGroupsMaintain-Default Role Assignment Policy       MyGroupsMaintain
```

After we have verified that the correct role assignments are in place, we can open ECP to see whether the change that has been made to the Default Role Assignment Policy is effective. Figure 5-44 illustrates what we expect. The user can see all of the groups that he owns and can manage group membership, update group details, and even delete a group. However, if you compare this screen to the equivalent before the change was made to the Default Role Assignment Policy (Figure 5-41), you'll see that the New option is not available so the user cannot create a new group.

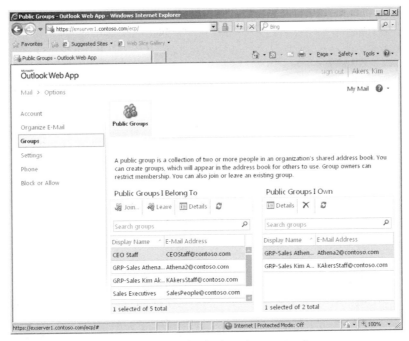

Figure5-44 The effect of the customized role assignment policy.

It's also possible that you might want to remove the ability to delete groups, just in case a user makes a horrible mistake and gives you the opportunity to reconstruct a large distribution group. In this scenario, you can simply remove the Remove-DistributionGroup cmdlet in the same way as the New-DistributionGroup cmdlet was removed (see step 2 in the process described earlier).

On the other hand, if you prefer not to grapple with the finer details of roles, assignments, and policies, Microsoft has published a script to do the work for you on the Exchange blog at *http://msexchangeteam.com/* (search for a reference to *ManageGroupManagementRole.ps1*). You can grab the script and run it to make the necessary assignments.

Setting diagnostics for Exchange servers

The ability to set diagnostics at different levels for the various components that function on an Exchange server has always existed. From Exchange 4.0 to Exchange 2003 you set diagnostic levels through the management console by selecting the component (for example, MSExchange ActiveSync) and the level that you wanted to apply. Once a new level is set, Exchange complies by outputting more or less detail about its operations as events written into the Application Event Log. This mechanism worked well until Exchange 2007 appeared and administrators discovered that the new Exchange 2007 management console had no GUI to deal with diagnostics, meaning that they had to set diagnostic levels through PowerShell. For example, to set the diagnostic level to High for the public store, you type:

```
Set-EventLogLevel "MSExchangeIS\9001 Public\General" –Level High
```

Microsoft addressed the problem in Exchange 2007 SP2 when they included the ability for EMC to set server diagnostics as properties of a server (Figure 5-45) in addition to manipulation through PowerShell. The same behavior exists in Exchange 2010.

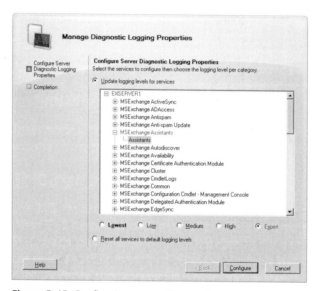

Figure 5-45 Configuring server diagnostics.

As shown in Table 5-4, Exchange supports five levels of diagnostic logging based on the level assigned to events recorded by the application. Critical events and those assigned a level of zero are always written into the event log. Events with a higher level are captured if an elevated diagnostic level is chosen.

Table 5-4 Diagnostic levels for Exchange 2010

Level	Description
Expert	Highly verbose: Essentially Exchange documents everything it does
High	Quite verbose: Exchange logs any event with a level of five or lower
Medium	Fairly detailed: Exchange logs any event with a level of three or lower
Low	Reasonable detail: Exchange logs any event with a level of one or lower
Lowest	Only critical events or errors with a logging level of zero are captured; this is the default level used for all Exchange services.

CAUTION

Be careful about setting diagnostic levels to Medium or higher. Exchange is quite happy to provide a vast amount of diagnostic information by writing events into the Application Event Log, but you run the risk that you won't be able to see the forest for the trees and some essential piece of information will be overlooked simply because so much data are available. To prevent the Application Event Log from being clogged up with an excessive number of events, make sure that you reset the diagnostic level to Lowest when you've completed troubleshooting the problem that caused you to elevate the level.

You can use the Get-EventLogLevel cmdlet to return the current diagnostic levels for a server. This cmdlet doesn't support any filter function so the easiest way to check that all the levels are correct is to capture the output into a text file for easier examination. For example:

```
Get-EventLogLevel –Server ExServer1 > C:\Temp\EventLevels.txt
```

But what will we manage?

All of the Exchange management tools—EMS, EMC, and ECP—have now been described and we have probed some of the detail about the objects that they manage. It's time now to move onto the objects that make a messaging system come alive: mailboxes.

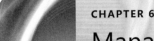
Managing Mail-Enabled Recipients

N ow that we have mastered the tools that are available to manage Exchange, we can proceed to create some mailboxes, groups, and contacts and discuss how we might successfully manage these objects. A reasonable amount of change takes place in Microsoft Exchange Server 2010 in areas such as moderated recipients, but there are still some foundational topics that we need to review first. Let's start by discussing how to name mailboxes so that administrators and users alike can find the people with whom they want to communicate.

Stop and think

Managing a successful Exchange deployment is not determined by the number of mailboxes in the organization. Before you rush to create any mailboxes, you should lay out some guidelines for when mailboxes are created and when they are removed. Best practice for mailbox maintenance includes these important points:

- Applications don't need mailboxes. Some administrators assume that it is a good thing to assign mailboxes for use by applications that need to create and send messages, usually by submitting a text message to a Simple Mail Transfer Protocol (SMTP) server. Applications do not need mailboxes for this purpose because they can create and submit messages to an SMTP server that supports submission from anonymous senders. The easiest way to support email submission for applications is to use the transport pickup directory (see Chapter 13, "The Exchange Transport System"). If you do create mailboxes for application use, make sure that you secure the accounts associated with the mailboxes so that they are restricted.

- There are different types of mailboxes for a reason. Although it might seem fine to use "normal" mailboxes for resources (rooms and equipment), Exchange has a purpose behind the differentiation that it supports across mailbox types. Resource mailboxes are tied to disabled Windows accounts and user mailboxes are not. Once you start to use normal mailboxes for resources, you create a potential security issue. Always assign the right mailbox type when you create a mailbox.

- Mailboxes shouldn't be kept forever. The information in a mailbox belonging to someone who leaves the company is probably of some interest, but interest wanes over time and the information contained in most such mailboxes is probably useless after three months. Of course, there will be exceptions, including mailboxes belonging to executives, which might be needed should a discovery search be required for local information to respond to a legal action. Nevertheless, you should agree on guidelines to govern when mailboxes can be removed and make sure that old mailboxes and old Windows accounts don't linger past their "best by" date (see Chapter 15, "Compliance").

> **Note**
>
> Apart from anything else, old mailboxes and accounts could represent a security weakness that a hacker can exploit. Some companies move all mailboxes belonging to departed employees to a special database so that they are grouped together and are obviously different from "live" mailboxes.

- Audit mailboxes regularly. You don't want to pay Microsoft any more for Client Access Licenses (CALs) than you have to. CALs are calculated on the basis of mailbox numbers so it follows that keeping unnecessary mailboxes costs money. You should audit the mailboxes that exist in the organization at least every six months and remove any unused mailboxes. It's easy to take a list of mailboxes in a database and report the last time that they were logged on to detect potentially unused mailboxes. For example, this command fetches details of all user mailboxes in a database and sorts them according to the last time a user logged onto the mailbox. Other information that might indicate an unused mailbox, such as the total number of items in the mailbox, is also included. This report shows that approximately two months separates the most recent logon (my mailbox) and the oldest. It's reasonable to suspect that the mailboxes that have not been accessed in two months are no longer needed.

```
Get-Mailbox –Database DB1 –RecipientTypeDetails UserMailbox | Get-MailboxStatistics
| Sort-Object LastLogonTime | Format-Table DisplayName, LastLogonTime, ItemCount,
TotalItemSize
```

```
DisplayName            LastLogonTime          ItemCount   TotalItemSize
-----------            -------------          ---------   -------------
Holm, Michael          5/20/2010 12:08:43 PM         81   170.3 MB (178,611,937 bytes)
Chen, Jacky            5/21/2010 10:46:29 AM         33   161 KB (164,888 bytes)
Palma, Tude            5/26/2010 4:23:28 PM          34   41.07 MB (43,064,720 bytes)
Ruth, Andy (Sales VP)  5/26/2010 5:24:37 PM        1089   145.9 MB (153,019,826 bytes)
Smith, Samantha        5/26/2010 5:40:33 PM          57   60.79 MB (63,744,292 bytes)
```

With these points in mind, we can proceed to create and manage some mailboxes.

Mailbox naming conventions

Although email Address policies allow you to define and apply different patterns for SMTP addresses, Exchange 2010 does not provide policies to control the generation of display names, which is the attribute that Exchange uses to sort objects in the Global Address List (GAL) and Exchange Management Console (EMC) and also for recipients and authors in message headers.

Table 6-1 lists the different attributes for the various names or name components used by Exchange that are stored in the Active Directory directory service. The default pattern for display names is *%g %s* – in other words, *first name*<space>*last name*, or in my case, "Tony Redmond." This is an acceptable naming convention for small implementations where everyone knows everyone else and it is easy to find the correct recipient by browsing the GAL, but it becomes increasingly difficult to find people as the number of directory entries increases. The question, therefore, is what naming convention to use that is efficient and logical for users when they search for an object in the GAL. More variation occurs in surnames than in given names. Common given names like John or Mary occur thousands of times in a large GAL, so if the GAL is sorted by given name, you might have a tiresome search before you locate the right recipient. It is easier to search using a surname, even with common surnames, like Smith, Chan, or Ng. Telephone directories are organized by surname, so it makes sense to carry the analogy forward and do the same thing for the GAL.

Table 6-1 **Mailbox attributes and names**

Attribute	Meaning
Alias	Unique name for the object
Name	Full name of the object composed of first name and last name
FirstName	First name of the user

Chapter 6

LastName	Surname of the user
DisplayName	Name used to sort the GAL and for other display purposes (such as EMC and in message headers)
DistinguishedName	Name used to identify object in Active Directory
PrimarySMTPAddress	Primary SMTP email address (often *first name.last name@ domain*)
UPN	User Principal Name or the name of a user in email format that can be used to log on to a Windows server; usually the same value as the primary SMTP email address

EMC includes logic to respect locales so that name-related edit boxes are reordered to reflect language-specific naming conventions. The language that you use determines the fields that are exposed when you create new objects and the order in which the fields are used. For example, EMC doesn't display the initials field in the French version. If you create users in the Chinese version, the boxes are presented by EMC in surname, initials, and first name order, which is exactly what some organizations that run everything in English would like to use. However, you can't force this order to occur in other locales because the ordering is hard-coded in EMC.

INSIDE OUT   Applying a different naming convention

Although the sequence used in naming conventions is hard-coded in EMC, it is possible to alter a convention. If you want to apply a different naming convention, the usual approach is to either:

- Allow EMC to create the mailboxes and contacts as usual and subsequently edit the Display Name.

- Create mailboxes and other mail-enabled recipients using shell scripts so that you have complete control over the format used for display names.

There mightbe other circumstances in which you have mailboxes that you don't want to name using the last name, first name convention, such as those used for discovery results, but these can be dealt with on an exception basis. Figure 6-1 shows a GAL where the mailboxes use the Last Name, First Name convention. As you can see, some of the entries have additional information to identify individuals who share common names. It is common to use department names, locations, or job titles to help users identify the correct recipient.

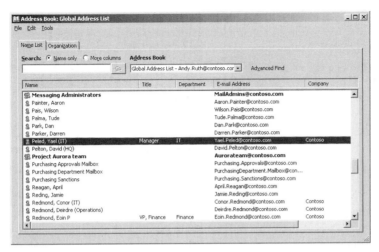

Figure 6-1 A well-ordered GAL.

Some companies like to impose a special naming convention for distribution groups so that users know when they are sending a message to a group rather than to an individual recipient. The Exchange 2010 MailTips feature helps here; it can either warn users when they address a message to a large group or display a tailored tip to indicate the purpose of the group. One solution is to prefix groups with some characters. For example, you could use "DG:" as a prefix so that your groups would have names such as "DG: Sales Executives" and "DG: IT Department". The advantage of this approach is that all of the groups are found in a single location in the GAL. Some take the idea further and use a prefix such as "##" that places all groups at the start of the GAL. You then end up with names like "## Sales Executives". This approach works but is not as user friendly as the other option.

Creating new mailboxes

Creating a new mailbox with EMC is easy. Click the New Mailbox option and EMC launches the New Mailbox Wizard to gather the information that it needs to create the mailbox. Figure 6-2 shows the initial screen used by the wizard.

Exchange 2010 supports the following mailbox types:

- User mailboxes: The standard full-function mailboxes used by Exchange. EMC can create a mailbox in any database in the organization.

- Room mailboxes: Used to represent conference rooms so that users can book them for meetings through calendar requests.

Chapter 6

- Resource mailboxes: Used to represent other items of equipment (such as projectors, communication equipment, or whiteboards) that users might need to reserve for a meeting.

- Linked mailboxes: Mailboxes that are linked to a user account in a separate, trusted forest.

The New Mailbox Wizard can create any of these mailbox types.

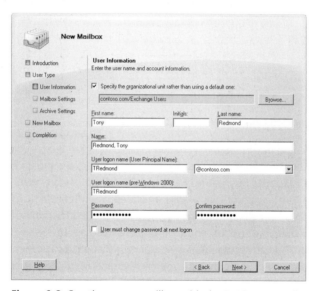

Figure 6-2 Creating a new mailbox with the EMC New Mailbox Wizard.

Integrating mailbox creation into overall company policy

Before plunging into the details of how to use the wizard to create a new mailbox, it's important to recognize that creating a mailbox might be only one small part of a complete user on-boarding process that covers multiple activities including:

- HR provisioning: Allocation of employee number, creation of employee record in human resources (HR) system, generation of identity badge, application for corporate credit card, and so on.

- IT provisioning: Allowing access to operating systems (Windows might be only one of the operating systems used by the company), applications including email and Web repositories or document management systems, allocation of mobile devices, and provision of security tokens or keys necessary to allow virtual private network (VPN) access to the company network from the Internet.

- Facilities provisioning: Assigning office space and physical items the employee requires, including PC and printer.

Many large companies operate sophisticated workflow applications that take care of many of these activities. A similar workflow is usually present to remove access and "deprovision" an employee who leaves the company. Because the on-boarding process can be so complicated and require interaction with so many different applications, it's wise to consider how you will integrate the creation of an Exchange mailbox into the process. For example, will you build a step into the workflow to create a mailbox automatically and have the characteristics of the mailbox (quota, personal archive, retention policy) preset depending on the employee's level and job code, or will you have a request generated and sent by email to the help desk?

The most common problems encountered by administrators when they attempt to create mailboxes with EMC's New Mailbox Wizard are the following:

- Failure to provide a unique alias or UPN: The wizard does not check whether the values assigned to the alias or UPN have already been used by an existing Active Directory object until it attempts to create the new mailbox, at which time you'll see an error similar to that shown in Figure 6-3. The management consoles in Exchange Server 2003 and Exchange Server 2007 both populate the alias field with a suggested value determined through a background call to Active Directory. For some reason, the security model used by Exchange 2010 forced Microsoft to remove this call, so the administrator has to determine a unique alias. Fixing the problem is easy for an administrator—simply go back through the screens and input a unique alias—but it can be frustrating to do this because it's impossible to know what might be a unique alias unless you check Active Directory first. Your company might have rules that determine how to create new aliases that help you figure out what the value should be.

> **Note**
>
> This problem doesn't exist in Exchange 2010 SP1 because Microsoft includes code in the New Mailbox Wizard to calculate a unique alias based on the name properties of the mailbox. However, you might still want to adjust the alias that is automatically generated by the wizard to satisfy naming guidelines.

- Failure to provide a password for a new account that meets Windows requirements: If you input a password that does not meet the policy implemented for Windows (for example, one that contains the name of the user), the wizard will not be able to create the new account when it attempts to create the new mailbox.

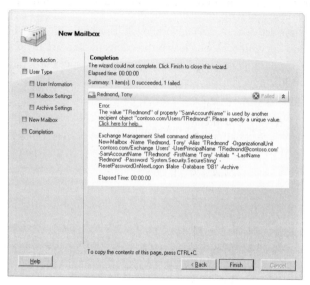

Figure 6-3 Error in mailbox creation:Duplicate UPN detected.

- Inadvertent selection of features that require an enterprise CAL: Features such as managed folder policies and archive mailboxes increase the number of enterprise CALs that your organization requires. The wizard indicates that these features require enterprise CALs but it's easy to miss the warnings (or not understand the consequences of opting for the feature; not every administrator understands the cost difference between standard and enterprise CALs). Unlike the other cases, selecting a feature that requires an enterprise CAL does not prevent the mailbox from being created.

Using a wizard is great if you have only a few mailboxes to create. Once the load increases, it's time to master the intricacies of the cmdlets that are used, especially if you need to integrate mailbox creation with another process, such as that used by the HR department to introduce a new employee to the company. As in many cases, the code generated by EMC to perform an action is a good starting point. The code necessary to create a new mailbox with a new Windows account is shown next. Table 6-2 lists the most common parameters to use when creating a new user mailbox complete with a Windows account. As you will see later, other types such as room and equipment mailboxes use different parameters:

```
New-Mailbox -Name 'Eoin P. Redmond' -Alias 'epr' -UserPrincipalName 'epr@contoso.com'
 -SamAccountName 'epr' -FirstName 'Eoin' -Initials 'P' -LastName 'Redmond' -Password
 'System.Security.SecureString' -ResetPasswordOnNextLogon $True -Database 'DB1'
```

Because this code was copied from EMC, it contains 'System.Security.SecureString' for the password value. If you create a script to create new mailboxes, you can use the ConvertTo-SecureString cmdlet to convert a predetermined value into a suitable secure string for the password. For example:

```
-Password (ConvertTo-SecureString 'Exchange2010!' -AsPlainText -Force)
```

Creating a mailbox is only the start of the process to build out a mailbox that is fully ready to use. The code that you've just looked at doesn't exploit the ability to assign special mailbox quotas, set up moderation for the mailbox, apply ActiveSync or Outlook Web App (OWA) policies, or create an archive mailbox. All of these settings can be enforced as you create the new mailbox with the New-Mailbox cmdlet or immediately afterward with the Set-Mailbox cmdlet. In addition, Exchange 2010 provides a new set of cmdlets to manipulate settings such as language and regional settings, as well as autoreply and calendar settings. See the section "Manipulating mailbox settings" later in this chapter for more information on this topic.

Table 6-2 Properties used to create a new mailbox with New-Mailbox

Property	Use	Mandatory
Name	Name of the mailbox.	N
Alias	Unique identifier for the mailbox. This value can contain no special characters.	Y
UserPrincipalName	UPN; an identifier for the mailbox in SMTP format.	Y
FirstName	First name for the mailbox owner	N
Initials	Initials for the mailbox owner	N
Last Name	Surname for the mailbox owner	N
DisplayName	Display name for the mailbox as used in the GAL and message header. If omitted, Exchange creates a display name based on the language used to run EMC. For example, English language variants of EMC create display names from the first name and last name.	N
Password	Password for the Windows account. If omitted, Exchange prompts for a password for the new account.	Y
ResetPasswordOnNextLogon	Flag to indicate whether user will be forced to reset his Windows password the next time he logs on.	Y
Database	Database where the new mailbox will be created.	N
OrganizationalUnit	Active Directory organizational unit (OU) in which to create the new Windows account. If omitted, Exchange uses the default OU.	N
ActiveSyncMailboxPolicy	The name of the ActiveSync policy to apply to the new mailbox. If omitted, Exchange applies the default ActiveSync policy.	N

Chapter 6

| Archive | Flag to indicate whether an archive mailbox is created. | N |
| ManagedFolderMailboxPolicy | The name of the Managed Folder policy to apply to the mailbox. | N |

If you select the option to create a mailbox for a Windows account that already exists, EMC uses the Enable-Mailbox cmdlet to create a new mailbox and associate it with the Windows account that you select. The code is much simpler because the Windows account already has many established properties that you'd otherwise have to provide. All you need to state for the new mailbox is an identity, an alias, and a target database. For example:

```
Enable-Mailbox -Identity 'contoso.com/Exchange Mailboxes/Akers,Kim' -Alias 'KAkers'
-Database 'DB2'
```

Immediately after the new mailbox is created, Exchange applies the appropriate email address policy to create a suitable email address for the mailbox and updates Active Directory with this value. See the section "Email address policies" later in this chapter for more information about how to create email address policies.

Completing the new mailbox setup

You now have a new mailbox, but it is hardly complete. Many different operations might be performed to a new mailbox before it is completely ready to be handed over to its owner. Tasks that might be performed include the following:

- Add the new mailbox to distribution groups. For example:

  ```
  Add-DistributionGroupMember -Identity Sales Executives' -Member Akers, Kim'
  -BypassSecurityGroupManagerCheck
  ```

- Update mailbox properties so that the new mailbox is discovered by the queries used to determine the membership of dynamic distribution groups. In this example we put a value into one of the customized attributes:

  ```
  Set-Mailbox -CustomAttribute1 'Sales' -Identity 'Akers, Kim'
  ```

- Update other mailbox properties that are not revealed by the New Mailbox Wizard. Many of the properties that people associate with a mailbox are actually updated with the Set-User cmdlet rather than the Set-Mailbox cmdlet because they belong to the base Active Directory user object rather than the mailbox. In this example, we update a number of properties with the Set-User cmdlet to fill out the directory information for the new mailbox. We discuss some other examples of mailbox properties (language settings and so on) that you might consider manipulating later on in this chapter.

  ```
  Set-User -City 'Sydney' -Company 'Contoso' -CountryOrRegion 'Australia'
  -Department 'Sales' -Manager 'Redmond, Tony' -Office 'Sydney'
  ```

```
-Phone '8170-19944'
-Title 'VP APJ' -Identity ' Akers, Kim'
```

- Enable a personal archive for the mailbox (this can be done during the initial creation, but some administrators prefer to wait to enable this action until the user confirms that she wants an archive).

```
Enable-Mailbox -Archive -Identity 'Akers, Kim'
```

It can take quite a long time to complete all of the properties for a new mailbox. For this
reason, many administrators script the process of creating a new mailbox and only use the
New Mailbox Wizard for one-off mailbox creation. The scripts used to create a mailbox
range from moderately simple (basically a collection of one-line Exchange Management
Shell [EMS] commands) to very complex. In the latter case, the scripts usually accept a feed
from an identity provisioning or HR management system that maintains information about
employees and output the necessary commands to create a ready-to-go mailbox.

Creating new room and resource mailboxes

The code to create a new room mailbox is similar to that used to create a user mailbox,
except that we use the *–Room* parameter to mark it as a room mailbox. For example:

```
New-Mailbox -Name 'Conference Room A' -Alias 'Confa' -OrganizationalUnit
'contoso.com/Exchange Mailboxes' -UserPrincipalName 'confa@contoso.com'
-SamAccountName 'Confa' -FirstName 'Conference' -Initials ''
-LastName 'Room A' -Database 'DB1' -Room
```

The code to create a new equipment mailbox is also similar. In this case, the *–Equipment*
parameter is used to mark the mailbox as an equipment mailbox. For example:

```
New-Mailbox -Name 'Projector Conference A' -Alias 'ProjConfA' -OrganizationalUnit
'contoso.com/Exchange Mailboxes' -UserPrincipalName 'ProjConfA@contoso.com'
-SamAccountName 'ProjConfA' -FirstName 'Projector' -Initials ''
-LastName 'Conference A' -Database 'DB1' -Equipment
```

Room and equipment mailboxes are created with disabled Windows accounts. It is a good
idea to group these accounts into their own OU and to consider assigning these mailboxes
to their own database to clearly isolate them from regular mailboxes.

Mailbox provisioning agent and database allocation

Exchange 2010 includes a mailbox provisioning agent whose purpose is to assign new
mailboxes to available databases. The mailbox provisioning agent is one of the standard
set of cmdlet extension agents provided with Exchange 2010. Its purpose is to look for new
mailbox creation requests that do not specify a database where the new mailbox should be
created. Once it detects such a request, the mailbox provisioning agent scans for all healthy
databases within the same Active Directory site as the server or workstation on which the

Exchange management tools are running, omitting any databases that are explicitly marked to be excluded from provisioning on a permanent or temporary basis. A healthy database is one that is online and operational. The provisioning agent exhibits no great intelligence and selects a database for the new mailbox on a random basis from the set of available databases.

CAUTION !

If you want to create a mailbox for an account that belongs to a remote site, you should connect to a server in the site that you want to own the mailbox before you create it; otherwise, the mailbox will be created in a database in the local site.

The mailbox provisioning agent does not take the current number of mailboxes in a database into account when it selects a target database. If you allow Exchange to allocate mailboxes to available databases, you will likely need to rebalance load from time to time by moving mailboxes around. You can find out just how many mailboxes are assigned to the different databases with a simple EMS command, albeit one that will take some time to complete in a large organization due to the need to contact every database to count the mailboxes:

```
Get-Mailbox | Group-Object database | Sort Count -Descending | Format-Table Count,
Name -AutoSize
```

```
Name              Count
----              -----
DB3                252
IT Department      222
DB1                217
DB2                210
VIP Data           117
Sales              101
```

Equipped with this kind of information, you can redistribute some mailboxes to the databases that are not heavily populated or suspend some databases from automatic provisioning so that they don't accept new mailboxes.

When you use EMC to create a new mailbox and elect to allow Exchange to select the database to host the new mailbox (Figure 6-4), the only indication that the new mailbox is created on a remote server is a slight delay when the new mailbox is created that would not occur when a mailbox is created locally.

Two flags are available to help you control the databases that are available for automatic provisioning. One flag (IsExcludedFromProvisioning) is intended to mark a database for permanent exclusion and the other (IsSuspendedFromProvisioning) marks a database that is excluded temporarily. If either flag is set to True, the database is excluded from provisioning and will remain in that state until both flags are reset to False. Both flags have the same practical effect of stopping Exchange from using a database for provisioning. The difference between them is how long the provisioning block will exist. Excluded means "never use this database for provisioning"; suspended means "don't use this database for provisioning until I tell you that it's okay to do so." Let's explore how these circumstances might arise.

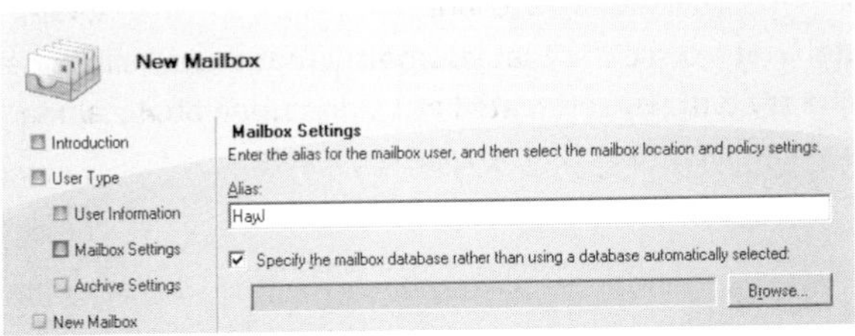

Figure 6-4 Specifying a database for a new mailbox.

You might want to exclude a database from mailbox provisioning on a permanent basis if it is reserved for a particular purpose. For example, you might want to assign a database that has elevated quotas to a certain class of user or users that belong to a particular department. You might also decide that automatic mailbox provisioning is a bad idea and that you'd prefer to assign new mailboxes to specific databases manually. In either case, you can use a command like this to exclude the database from provisioning:

```
Set-MailboxDatabase –Identity 'VIP Mailboxes' –IsExcludedFromProvisioning $True
```

A temporary exclusion might be invoked when you know that a database should not be assigned new mailboxes for a certain period of time. For example, the database might be due for a move to a new disk that allows it to grow to a larger size and you don't want to add any more mailboxes until the new storage is available. In this case, you can block provisioning temporarily with a command like this:

```
Set-MailboxDatabase –Identity 'DB1' –IsSuspendedFromProvisioning $True
```

When you are ready to allow the database to be assigned new mailboxes on an automatic basis, you set the flag back to $False.

```
Set-MailboxDatabase –Identity 'DB1' –IsSuspendedFromProvisioning $False
```

Unlike many other properties that are stored in the Active Directory, a change to a flag to suspend or include a database in automatic provisioning is immediately respected by the mailbox provisioning agent.

By default, new mailbox databases created using EMC are added to automatic mailbox provisioning. Databases that are made available for automatic provisioning also become

Chapter 6

candidates for selection as targets for mailbox moves and personal archives if the locations for these operations are not specified by administrators. In other words, if you don't specify a target database when you move a mailbox or create a personal archive for a mailbox, the mailbox provisioning agent will select a target from a list of available databases. In SP1, my tests show that Exchange usually picks the same database as the primary mailbox to hold an archive, even if you don't select a specific target database. I also found that if you issue a New-MoveRequest command to move a mailbox that has an archive, MRS will move the primary and archive mailboxes together to a target database that it automatically selects.

If you create new databases from EMS, you can specify that the database is excluded on a permanent or temporary basis by setting the flags described above when you run the New-MailboxDatabase cmdlet.

TROUBLESHOOTING

A valid mailbox wasn't found and mailbox creation failed

You can go too far and exclude all available databases from automatic provisioning. In this situation, you'll see the error shown in Figure 6-5 when the mailbox provisioning agent scans for databases and discovers that none are available.

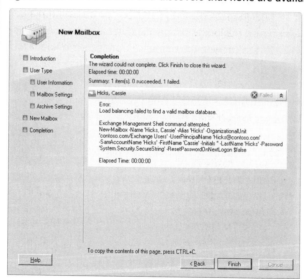

Figure 6-5 No databases available for load balancing.

The fix is simple: Either reset the flag on a database to make it available or go back to the Mailbox Settings screen and select a database. The explicit selection of a database tells the mailbox provisioning agent that it doesn't have to make a selection so the error will be avoided.

Of course, the problem with automatically assigning mailboxes to databases, rather than asking administrators to think about what database is the best host, is that it ignores any consideration of with whom the owner of the new mailbox is likely to correspond. For years, it has been best practice to keep the mailboxes for people who share a common work-group together in the same database to minimize the use of system resources to transport messages between members of the workgroup. Advances in technology have reduced the importance of this principle. Exchange 2010 has eliminated single-instance storage within databases and Exchange 2007 began forcing all messages to move through a hub trans-port server, even when they are addressed to a recipient in the same database. Even so, it's still good to consider mailbox placement from a wider perspective than a simple distribu-tion across available mailboxes and retain some administrator involvement in the process instead of leaving all decisions up to a computer.

Languages and folders

Once the language pack is installed on a CAS server, users have the option to select to run OWA in their preferred language by making the choice through their mailbox settings. Administrators are limited in that they can only run EMC in the language used to install Windows. It's important that you install the language pack on all Client Access Server (CAS) servers so that users can access their preferred language when they connect. It is confus-ing for a user to connect to one CAS server and be able to use French and then connect to another CAS server in the site (perhaps one in the same CAS array) and see OWA rendered in English, which is the default when no other language pack is available. Another impor-tant point is that the logon screen for OWA uses the default language installed on the server, so even if a user has selected French as her preferred language, she'll see a logon screen in English unless French is the default language installed on the server or the user has selected French as a supported language for her browser.

Creating a mailbox populates the set of properties in Active Directory that are required to mail-enable the account. Exchange does not create the actual mailbox in the assigned database until the user first logs onto the mailbox or it is required to deliver a message to the new mailbox. At this point, Exchange creates the various special folders that it needs to process email, including the Inbox, Sent Items, and Deleted Items. If the user selects another language to run OWA, the language pack provides the translated strings to display these folders through OWA but the contents of the folders remain untouched.

For instance, if a user selects Polish as his preferred language, the Inbox is then displayed as "Skrzynka odbiorcza," Sent Items becomes "Elementy wyslane," and Deleted Items is "Elementy usunięte," whereas switching to Portuguese produces "A Receber," "Itens Envia-dos," and "Itens Eliminados." The only folder name that seems to persist across multiple languages is the Unread Mail search folder. For example, if you start off in French, this folder remains displayed as "Courrier non lu" no matter how many languages you use when starting OWA. Behind the scenes, if a mailbox uses OWA in multiple languages, Exchange records the fact in the Languages property of the mailbox. For example:

```
Get-Mailbox -Identity JSmith | Select Languages
```

```
Languages
---------
<pt-PT, pl-PL, en-GB, en-IE, fr-FR, en-US>
```

Languages are appended to the leftmost side of the list as they are accessed, so we can tell that Portuguese was the last language used by this mailbox and that the previous languages were Polish, English (UK), English (Ireland), French, and English (US).

The initial language for a mailbox is taken from the default locale installed on the server where it is created. If this is incorrect or you prefer to use a different language, you can tell Exchange to use your preferred language with the Set-Mailbox cmdlet. For example, to set the mailbox of a user called Geert Camelbeke to use the Dutch language special folder names, do the following:

```
Set-Mailbox -Identity'Camelbeke, Geert' -Languages 'nl-NL'
```

Outlook and other clients that run locally on PCs pick up regional and time zone settings from the PC and use these settings to present elements of the user interface (UI) such as the time zone used in the calendar. Figure 6-6 shows OWA running in Polish and ECP in Dutch. The layout of the client interfaces is the same as the English version, but the language strings, variables, and local settings such as date format differ.

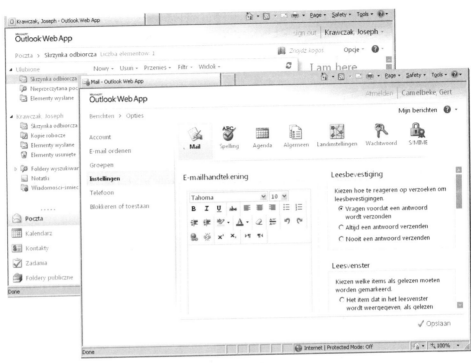

Figure 6-6 Using OWA and ECP in French and Dutch.

INSIDE OUT   Switching from language to language

It's easy for an OWA user to switch from language to language if the language packs are installed and available on a CAS server. However, be aware that some values are persistent. For example, if you start off with French and move to English, all of the default folder names will change to properly translated values such as "Inbox," "Sent Items," and "Deleted Items," but the names of search folders will not be translated, so you end up with "Courrier non lu" where you'd expect to see Unread Mail. This is a known bug that isn't fixed in Exchange 2010 SP1.

As an online application that depends on the server, OWA takes a different approach. Each time OWA starts, it checks whether the time zone and preferred language is set for a mailbox whenever a user logs on and presents a screen to allow the user to select her preferred time zone and language if these settings are missing. You can prevent the user from seeing the dialog box (and potentially avoid help desk calls) by configuring the OWA virtual directory with a default language code. For example, the following command sets "English (Ireland)" as the default language code for OWA for both the client language and the text used for logon and error dialog boxes. The default value for this setting is 0, which is why the language selection screen is presented to users who don't have a preferred language set for their mailbox.

```
Set-OWAVirtualDirectory -Identity 'OWA (default web site)' -DefaultClientLanguage
6153 -LogonAndErrorLanguage 6153
```

See TechNet for a full list of supported regional codes.

It makes sense to apply the same setting on all CAS servers in the organization. To do this on a remote server, you include the name of the server in the Web site:

```
Set-OWAVirtualDirectory -Identity 'ExServer2\OWA (default web site)'
-DefaultClientLanguage 6153 -LogonAndErrorLanguage 6153
```

Setting a default language code for the OWA virtual directory allows users to connect without being bothered by OWA to select their preferred language, but it is incomplete because it doesn't configure the mailbox with a time zone setting. This is not a problem if all of the mailboxes share the default time zone configured for the server, but it is an issue when servers support mailboxes that operate in multiple time zones. Another issue is that the user might be prompted to select a language when they access ECP through OWA if Exchange can't determine what time zone is assigned to the mailbox.

It is therefore much better to complete the job by using the Set-MailboxRegionalConfiguration cmdlet to provide a full set of regional information for a mailbox. This example sets my mailbox to use the Ireland variant of English as the mailbox language together with the appropriate time zone, date format, and time format for the region:

```
Set-MailboxRegionalConfiguration -Identity 'Tony Redmond' -Language 'en-IE'
-TimeZone 'GMT Standard Time' -DateFormat 'dd/MM/yyyy' -TimeFormat 'H:mm'
```

INSIDE OUT   Date and time formats are case sensitive

Be careful with the format used to specify dates and times because Exchange will reject a setting if it is inappropriate for the selected time zone or doesn't match the required mask. Uppercase and lowercase characters are important. For example, "d/M/YY" will be rejected as a valid date format for the "en-IE" locale, whereas "d/M/yy" is acceptable. EMS will tell you the values that you can use when it signals the error. Alternatively, you can use ECP to set the regional options for a mailbox (see Chapter 5, "Exchange Management Console and Control Panel") and then use the Get-MailboxRegionalConfiguration cmdlet to check the values written to the mailbox properties and then replicate those properties for other mailboxes as they are created.

PST files are a special case

Note that Exchange does not respect the locale of a Personal Storage (PST) file if you use the Import-Mailbox cmdlet to import content from it to populate items into a new mailbox. For instance, a PST that has been used with the French version of Outlook will have French folder names. If you now use Import-Mailbox to import the items from the PST into a new mailbox created on an English language Exchange server, Exchange will create English language special folders before it imports data from the PST. You will therefore end up with two sets of special folders, one set in French and one in English. For this reason, it's best to be explicit with Exchange and tell it what the preferred language should be for a mailbox before you import any data into it.

Exchange Server 2007 supports the –*TemplateInstance* parameter for the New-Mailbox cmdlet. This parameter instructs Exchange to copy values from an existing object to create a new object and it is a useful way to ensure that the new object has its properties populated with correct values. Microsoft has deprecated the parameter in Exchange 2010. Any scripts that depend on the creation of mailboxes based on templates will have to be adjusted so that any required values such as policies are applied appropriately when a new mailbox is created.

Manipulating mailbox settings

Exchange 2010 provides a set of new cmdlets to allow administrators to query and set properties of mailboxes. You can think of this as administrative access to the options that users have to configure their mailboxes through Outlook or OWA. These properties are stored as hidden items in the root of user mailboxes and are not accessible to administrators in previous versions of Exchange. Table 6-3 lists the elements of mailbox configuration that can be manipulated by administrators and the cmdlets used for this purpose.

Table 6-3 **Mailbox configuration cmdlets**

Purpose	Cmdlets
Change regional preferences (language, date format, time zone)	Get-MailboxRegionalConfiguration Set-MailboxRegionalConfiguration
Change the auto reply settings	Get-MailboxAutoReplyConfiguration Set-MailboxAutoReplyConfiguration
Change mailbox calendar settings and how the Calendar Assistant processes incoming requests	Get-MailboxCalendarConfiguration Set-MailboxCalendarConfiguration Get-CalendarProcessing Set-CalendarProcessing
List or add mailbox folders	Get-MailboxFolder New-MailboxFolder

Chapter 6

Change general mailbox settings	Get-MailboxMessageConfiguration Set-MailboxMessageConfiguration
Change spelling settings	Get-MailboxSpellingConfiguration Set-MailboxSpellingConfiguration
Change junk mail settings	Get-MailboxJunkEMailConfiguration Set-MailboxJunkEMailConfiguration

Before you attempt to query or set the properties of a mailbox, make sure that you have the necessary access rights to the mailbox. The Add-MailboxPermission cmdlet can be used as follows:

```
Add-MailboxPermission -Identity 'John Smith' -User 'Europe Help Desk'
-AccessRights FullAccess
```

Mailboxes assume a default regional configuration based on the language and regional settings of the server where they are created. If your server runs the U.S. English version of Exchange in the Pacific Time Zone, any mailboxes that you create on that server will inherit these settings along with other associated settings such as date and time format. Users can change these settings with a client by, for example, using the options presented by OWA to select a language the first time a user logs into her mailbox. To retrieve the regional configuration for a mailbox:

```
Get-MailboxRegionalConfiguration -Identity 'John Smith'
```

The Set-MailboxRegionalConfiguration cmdlet allows you to tweak the regional settings. In this example, we set the mailbox language, time zone, and date format:

```
Set-MailboxRegionalConfiguration -Identity 'John Smith' -Language 'Es-es'
-TimeZone 'Eastern Time Zone' -DateFormat 'dd-mmm-yyyy'
```

Get-MailboxAutoReplyConfiguration/Set-MailboxAutoReplyConfiguration query and set the auto reply settings for a mailbox. For example, to find out the mailboxes in a database that have autoreply currently set and the time that the autoreply lapses, we can use the following command:

```
Get-Mailbox -Database 'VIP Data' | Get-MailboxAutoReplyConfiguration | Where
{$_.AutoReplyState -eq 'Scheduled'} | Select MailboxOwnerId, EndTime
```

```
MailboxOwnerId                                   EndTime
--------------                                   -------
contoso.com/Exchange Users/Akers, Kim            11/18/2010 2:00:00 AM
```

If you dump all of the autoreply data maintained for a mailbox, you can see the autoreply text that the user has created to send to internal and external recipients:

```
Get-MailboxAutoReplyConfiguration -id 'Kim Akers'
```

```
AutoReplyState       : Scheduled
EndTime              : 11/18/2010 2:00:00 AM
ExternalAudience     : Known
ExternalMessage      : <html dir="ltr">
                        <head>
                        <style type="text/css" id="owaTempEditStyle"></
style><style type="text/css" id="owaParaStyle"></style>
                        </head>
                        <body><div style="font-family:Tahoma; font-size:13px">I
am away and will reply when I return. <div style="font-family:Tahoma; font-
size:13px"></div>/div>
                        </body>
                        </html>
InternalMessage      : <html dir="ltr">
                        <head>
                        <style type="text/css" id="owaTempEditStyle"></
style><style type="text/css" id="owaParaStyle"></style>
                        </head>
                        <body><div style="font-family:Tahoma; font-size:13px">I
am away and am not able to reply. Please contact Phyllis Harris, my assistant,
at &#43;1 650 561 4136, who may be able to help you. Phyllis is also available
at Phyllis.Harris@contoso.com.
                        <div style="font-family:Tahoma; font-size:13px"></div></
div>
                        </body>
                        </html>
StartTime            : 1/14/2010 2:00:00 AM
MailboxOwnerId       : contoso.com/Exchange Users/Akers, Kim
Identity             : contoso.com/Exchange Users/Akers, Kim
```

You can also set up a new autoreply for a user who has gone on vacation and has forgotten to let anyone know. In this instance, you enable autoreply, set a time limit, and create separate messages for internal and external audiences. You also tell Exchange that autoreplies only go to external correspondents who are known contacts of the recipient.

```
Set-MailboxAutoReplyConfiguration -Identity 'Kim Akers' -StartTime '12/10/2010 19:30'
-AutoReplyState Enabled -EndTime '12/15/2010 07:00' -InternalMessage 'Kim Akers is on
vacation and will respond to your message after she returns on December 15'
-ExternalMessage 'Kim Akers is on vacation' -ExternalAudience 'Known'
```

To turn off autoreply for a user:

```
Set-MailboxAutoReplyConfiguration -Identity 'Kim Akers' -AutoReplyState Disabled
```

TheGet-MailboxCalendarConfiguration/Set-MailboxCalendarConfiguration cmdlets query and set the properties of calendar settings. For example, this command configures the calendar to use GMT as the time zone with a starting time for the workday of 8:30 A.M.:

```
Set-MailboxCalendarConfiguration -Identity 'John Smith' -WorkingHoursTimeZone 'GMT
Standard Time' -WorkingHoursStartTime 08:30:00
```

Chapter 6

The Set-CalendarProcessing cmdlet is used to determine how the Calendar Assistant processes calendar requests that arrive into mailboxes. If you access mailbox properties through EMC, you can access these settings through the Calendar Settings tab. The same can be done with EMS. For example, this command sets the first and fourth setting shown in Figure 6-7:

```
Set-CalendarProcessing -Identity 'Redmond, Tony'
-RemoveForwardedMeetingNotifications $True -ProcessExternalMeetingMessages $True
```

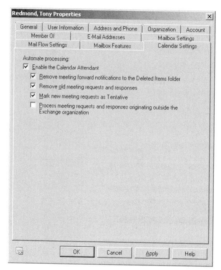

Figure 6-7   Changing automated calendar settings for a mailbox.

Users can manipulate these settings through the Automatic Processing section of OWA options. See Chapter 10, "Clients," for more details. It's worth noting that the Set-Calendar-Processing cmdlet is capable of doing much more than manipulating the limited set of properties revealed through EMC, especially for resource mailboxes. See the Exchange help file for more information.

The Get-MailboxFolder and New-MailboxFolder cmdlets retrieve a list of folders in a mailbox and create a new folder. You can decide to retrieve just top-level folders, the complete set, or look for specific details about a folder and its children. Here's the command to retrieve a complete list from a mailbox:

```
Get-MailboxFolder -Identity 'John Smith\'-Recurse -MailFolderOnly
```

To create a new folder called "Exchange 2010" in the top level of the mailbox:

```
New-MailboxFolder -Parent 'John Smith' -Name 'Exchange 2010'
```

Get-MailboxMessageConfiguration and Set-MailboxMessageConfiguration retrieve and set general properties of a mailbox. For example, to define that Exchange should append an autosignature to every outgoing message and to provide the text for the autosignature:

```
Set-MailboxMessageConfiguration -Identity 'John Smith' -AutoAddSignature $True
-SignatureText 'From the desk of John Smith'
```

Get-MailboxSpellingConfiguration and Set-MailboxSpellingConfiguration query and set the properties that control how a user performs spell checking of messages. This example tells Exchange to perform spell checking for any message before it is sent, ignore words that contain mixed digits and uppercase characters (usually technical terms), and to use the Finnish language dictionary:

```
Set-MailboxSpellingConfiguration -Identity 'John Smith' -CheckBeforeSend $True
-IgnoreMixedDigits $True -IgnoreUpperCase $True -DictionaryLanguage 'Finnish'
```

Get-MailboxJunkEmailConfiguration and Set-MailboxJunkEmailConfiguration query and set the properties that control a user's junk mail settings. The most noteworthy of these properties are the trusted senders and blocked sender lists. Both are multivalued properties, so you have to manipulate them in a variable before updating the property with new values. For example, to add the cohowinery.com domain to the blocked senders list:

```
$List = Get-MailboxJunkEMailConfiguration -Identity 'John Smith'
$List.BlockedSendersAndDomain += 'cohowinery.com'
Set-MailboxJunkEMailConfiguration -Identity 'John Smith' -BlockedSendersAndDomain
$List.BlockedSendersAndDomain
```

Of course, users can overwrite these settings using Outlook or OWA after you've updated any of their mailbox settings. If you have given your account the permission to access a mailbox, make sure that you remove the access after you've adjusted all of the required regional settings. In this example, we use the Remove-MailboxPermission cmdlet to remove the full access rights to the mailbox that we have been working with from the "Europe Help Desk" account.

```
Remove-MailboxPermission -Identity 'John Smith' -User 'Europe Help Desk'
-AccessRights FullAccess
```

Bulk mailbox creation

The methods used to create new mailboxes range from one-off operations to sophisticated scripts used to generate hundreds or thousands of mailboxes following a company merger. Some companies write code to integrate mailbox creation into their new employee onboarding process, whereas others are happy to send support tickets to their administrators to request new mailboxes on an on-demand basis. Using EMC to create a bunch of mailboxes isn't much fun, because navigating multiple pages generated by the New Mailbox Wizard rapidly becomes a tedious slog after you've done it once or twice.

It's worth taking the time to introduce some automation through EMS code if you're in a situation where you need to create more than a few mailboxes. Here's some code that does the trick by reading in data about the new mailboxes from a comma-separated value (CSV) file and then calling some cmdlets to create the new mailbox, adding the new mailbox to a distribution group, updating Active Directory attributes on the new account, and finally updating the mailbox regional data. The code also makes sure that the *Last name, First Name* naming convention is followed for mailbox names. Unlike scripts that you might use with Exchange 2007, this version doesn't need to specify a database because the mailbox provisioning agent will assign each mailbox to a database. Of course, it would be easy to amend the input file to include a database and to change the script to pass the database in the *–Database* parameter in the New-Mailbox command.

The input CSV file is similar to that shown in Figure 6-8. The first line of the file contains the field headings used to reference the data in the array loaded with the Import-CSV cmdlet. Assuming that the script is called Bulk-Mailbox-Load.ps1 and the input file is Users.csv, we invoke it with:

```
C:> .\Bulk-Mailbox-Load.PS1 Users.CSV
```

Figure 6-8 Checking a CSV file to use as input for a bulk mailbox load.

The code follows:

```
## Import data from the input CSV file and store it in variable 'data'
$Data = Import-CSV $args[0]
$CurrentDate = "Created on " + (Get-Date)

ForEach ($i in $Data)
{
##Convert the plain text password to a secure string
  $PW = ConvertTo-SecureString $i.Password -AsPlainText -Force
## Populate some variables that we want to use
  $UPN = $i.FirstName + "." + $i.LastName + '@' + $i.FQDN
  $FullName = $i.LastName + ', ' + $i.FirstName
  $Alias = $i.LastName + $i.FirstName
## Create the new mailbox
  New-Mailbox -Password $PW -UserPrincipalName $UPN -Name $FullName
-OrganizationalUnit $i.OU -Database $i.Database -Alias $Alias
-FirstName $i.FirstName -LastName $i.LastName
## Add the new mailbox to the distribution group
  Add-DistributionGroupMember -Identity $i.DL -Member $UPN
## Update some Active Directory attributes for the new account
```

```
  Set-User -Identity $UPN -Office $i.Office -Company $i.Organization
-Phone $i.Phone -Title $i.Title -Notes $CurrentDate
## Update the mailbox regional settings with the language and time zone
  Set-MailboxRegionalConfiguration -Identity $UPN -Language $i.Language -TimeZone
$i.TimeZone
}
```

This script is by no means perfect and it will need to be amended before it can be used in a production environment. For instance, you might want to populate more mailbox or user account properties or remove the step to add the mailbox to a distribution group because you have dynamic distribution groups that automatically incorporate new mailboxes based on their office, database, or other criteria. You might want to set ActiveSync or OWA policies for the new mailboxes or assign different storage quotas. The joy of EMS and Windows PowerShell in general is that it is very easy to make these changes and create a bulk load script that's appropriate for your organization.

Setting quotas

Three mailbox properties combine to control the quota available to the mailbox.

- *IssueWarningQuota*: This value determines when Exchange starts to issue warning messages to the user that he is approaching the point when he will exceed his mailbox quota. Typically, this value is placed between 10 and 20 MB short of the point where the user will no longer be able to send mail.

- *ProhibitSendQuota*: This value determines when Exchange stops the user from sending any new messages. When users refer to their mailbox quota, they usually refer to this value. Mailbox quotas vary enormously from deployment to deployment and based on the work that users do. A factory worker might need a quota of only 50 MB to be able to receive workplace notices and announcements, whereas an executive in an information-rich company could require a quota of 10 GB or higher. The vast majority of users in large corporations have a mailbox quota of between 100 MB and 500 MB. This might change over time as Exchange 2010 replaces legacy versions and companies realize the benefits of being able to use cheaper storage. In fact, some companies that have already deployed Exchange 2010 have established mailbox quotas of between 5 GB and 10 GB.

- *ProhibitSendReceiveQuota*: This value determines the point when Exchange refuses to accept new messages in the mailbox. Messages arriving past this point are returned to the originator with an error indicating that the target mailbox is full. Typically, this value is placed between 100 MB and 200 MB higher than the *ProhibitSendQuota* value to allow for situations such as vacations, when users might inadvertently leave their mailboxes almost full. The buffer established by the difference between the *ProhibitSendQuota* and *ProhibitSendReceiveQuota* values allows the mailbox to con-

Chapter 6

tinue to accept new messages until users return and are able to delete old items from their mailboxes and restore full operation.

Exchange sends messages to warn users of approaching quota thresholds or to tell them that they have exceeded their mailbox quota according to a schedule maintained in the *QuotaNotificationSchedule* property that is set on every mailbox database. For example:

```
Get-MailboxDatabase -Identity 'DB1' | Format-List Name, QuotaNotificationSchedule
```

```
Name                      : DB1
QuotaNotificationSchedule : {Sun.1:00 AM-Sun.1:15 AM, Mon.1:00 AM-Mon.1:15 AM,
Tue.1:00 AM-Tue.1:15 AM, Wed.1:00 AM-Wed.1:15 AM, Thu.1:00 AM-Thu.1:15 AM,
Fri.1:00 AM-Fri.1:15 AM, Sat.1:00 AM-Sat.1:15 AM}
```

When a new mailbox is created with EMC or EMS, it takes its quota settings from those assigned to the database where it is created. For example, any mailbox created in the database shown in Figure 6-9 starts to receive warning messages at 1.9 GB, stops being able to send new messages at 2 GB (the mailbox quota), and is unable to receive any more new mail at 2.3 GB. These are the default values assigned to new mailbox databases created by Exchange 2010. If these values don't work for your installation, you need to update database properties to create whatever values you want to use. After you update the database properties, you might need to review mailboxes that already exist in the database to determine whether their quotas need to be adjusted.

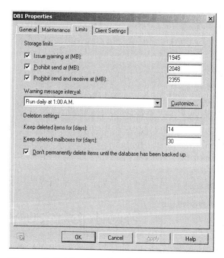

Figure 6-9 Viewing the default storage quotas for a mailbox database.

After they are created, individual mailboxes can be assigned specific quotas to meet their business needs. To update quotas with EMC, select the mailbox, view its properties, click the

Mailbox Settings tab, and click Storage Quotas (Figure 6-10). Clear the Use Mailbox Database Defaults check box to make the three quota fields active.

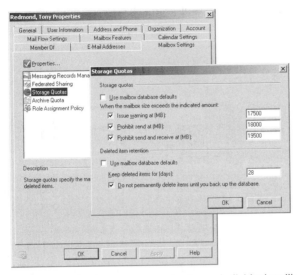

Figure 6-10 Setting storage quotas for an individual mailbox.

You can also use the Set-Mailbox cmdlet to assign new quota values to mailboxes. For example:

```
Set-Mailbox –Identity 'Redmond, Tony' –UseDatabaseQuotaDefaults $False
–IssueWarningQuota 500MB –ProhibitSendQuota 520MB –ProhibitSendReceiveQuota 540MB
```

Quota values can be expressed in KB, MB, or GB. A one-line EMS command is a great way to set the same quota on a group of mailboxes. For example, you could set the same quota values for every mailbox in an OU:

```
Get-Mailbox –OrganizationalUnit 'contoso.com/Exchange Users' | Set-Mailbox
–UseDatabaseQuotaDefaults $False –IssueWarningQuota 500MB
–ProhibitSendQuota 520MB –ProhibitSendReceiveQuota 540MB
```

The same approach can be used to assign quotas to every member of a distribution group. In this case, the command to give members of the IT department the quotas that they need is:

```
Get-DistributionGroupMember –Identity 'IT Department' | Set-Mailbox
–UseDatabaseQuotaDefaults $False –IssueWarningQuota 985MB
–ProhibitSendQuota 1GB –ProhibitSendReceiveQuota 1.1GB
```

To check that the right quotas are in place, we can do something like this:

```
Get-Mailbox –Identity 'Redmond, Tony' | Select *quota*
```

```
ProhibitSendQuota                            : 2.949 GB (3,166,699,520 bytes)
ProhibitSendReceiveQuota                     : 3 GB (3,221,225,472 bytes)
RecoverableItemsQuota                        : unlimited
RecoverableItemsWarningQuota                 : unlimited
UseDatabaseQuotaDefaults                     : False
IssueWarningQuota                            : 2.93 GB (3,145,728,000 bytes)
RulesQuota                                   : 64 KB (65,536 bytes)
ArchiveQuota                                 : 50 GB (53,687,091,200 bytes)
ArchiveWarningQuota                          : 45 GB (48,318,382,080 bytes)
```

As you can see, Exchange maintains several other quota settings for mailboxes. The *RecoverableItemsQuota* and *RecoverableItemsWarningQuota* settings are roughly equivalent to the *ProhibitSendQuota* and *IssueWarningQuota* settings, except that they control the amount of data that a mailbox can store in the recoverable items folder (the "dumpster"). By default, Exchange 2010 allows an unlimited amount of data to be held in the dumpster. See Chapter 16, "Rules and Journals," for more information about the dumpster. The *RulesQuota* setting limits the amount of rules data that a mailbox can hold, and 64 KB is the default. The *ArchiveQuota* and *ArchiveWarningQuota* settings control how much information can be held in an associated personal archive if this feature is enabled. Exchange allows an unlimited quota for the archive so in this case the quota has been set back to a hard limit of 50 GB (still more than enough).

New quotas are not immediately effective, because the Store first has to refresh the cached data that it holds about mailbox settings. The cache is refreshed every two hours, so it is possible that you could have to wait this long before the new quota settings are in place. You can update a registry setting called "Reread Logon Quotas Interval" to force more frequent refreshes of these data at the expense of additional system overhead (refreshing the data every five minutes would definitely be a bad idea; every hour or so should be acceptable). The DWORD value is set in seconds (the default value is 7,200 seconds, or two hours). This value depends on other values that control how often Exchange retrieves information from Active Directory. Another option is to restart the Information Store process to force a cache refresh. This approach is acceptable on a test server but probably not on a production server.

Details of how to alter the values in the Reread Logon Quotas Interval registry setting can be found at *http://technet.microsoft.com/en-us/library/bb684892(EXCHG.80).aspx.*

Estimating database size

From a planning perspective, it's important to realize that the simple calculation of

*(number of mailboxes * quota) = database size on disk*

is highly unlikely to be accurate. There are other factors to take into account to determine the likely size of a database.

1. A quota is a maximum value allowed to a mailbox. Unless the quota is very small, users will take some time to fill their quota. A 2 GB quota might take a user two years to fill.

2. The dumpster requires further space in the database. If you allow users to retain deleted items for 21 days, you'll use up to 10 percent additional space. This storage is not charged to the user's quota.

3. Personal archives will occupy further space if they are stored in the same database as their primary mailbox (or even if they are not, primary mailboxes from one database will be stored alongside mailboxes in another).

4. White space will exist within the database. These are database pages that were previously used to store items that have been deleted and are available for reuse by Exchange to store new items and attachments. Exchange is very efficient at reusing deleted pages, but, even so, the nature of email is that new items arrive on an ongoing basis, some of which are deleted and some of which are kept. The flow of creates and deletes within the database results in a churn of pages, so you can estimate that another 10 percent of mailbox sizes might be occupied by white space.

There is a better calculation to use to attempt to estimate the maximum predicted size to which a database might grow in order to place the database on a disk that has sufficient space. By adding 20 percent to the previous calculation, we can estimate the database to be:

*(number of mailboxes * quota) * 1.2 = database size on disk*

Tip

Don't forget to reserve some additional disk space to accommodate expected database growth over the next year or so and to allow for temporary space required by activities such as mailbox moves or offline database maintenance.

Chapter 6

What's in a mailbox?

After we assign quotas to mailboxes, users will start to populate the mailboxes with various items. The Get-MailboxStatistics cmdlet provides a snapshot of what's in a mailbox and what types of items are stored. For example:

```
Get-MailboxStatistics -Identity 'Redmond, Tony' | Select DisplayName, ServerName,
Database, LastLogonTime, ItemCount, DeletedItemCount, AssociatedItemCount,
TotalItemSize, TotalDeletedItemSize
```

```
DisplayName               : Redmond, Tony
ServerName                : ExServer1
Database                  : DB1
LastLogonTime             : 12/30/2010 4:31:28 AM
ItemCount                 : 38176
DeletedItemCount          : 8281
AssociatedItemCount       : 52
TotalItemSize             : 2.247GB (2,412,430,212 bytes)
TotalDeletedItemSize      : 26.81 MB (28,112,322 bytes)
```

Among the interesting information that we find here is the following:

- The item count is the total number of items that are in folders in the mailbox. The *TotalItemSize* is the size of those items as calculated by the Store.

- The deleted item count is the total number of items that are in the dumpster (see Chapter 15, "Compliance," for more information about the dumpster). The *TotalDeletedItemSize* is the size of those items.

- The associated items (sometimes called FAI messages) are hidden items used by Exchange and Outlook to store configuration data about the mailbox. For example, if you change a mailbox setting through OWA, this information is written to a hidden item in the mailbox. The number of associated items varies from mailbox to mailbox and is dependent on user activity, but it is commonly a range of 10 to 60 items. The lower end of the range is for mailboxes that are relatively new and the upper end is typical of mailboxes that have been in use for some time.

You can also generate data for all mailboxes in a database or on a specific server with the Get-MailboxStatistics cmdlet. The second example pipes the output in CSV format to a file that you can open with Microsoft Excel or Microsoft Access and use for reporting purposes.

```
Get-MailboxStatistics -Database 'DB1'
Get-MailboxStatistics -Server 'ExServer1' | Export-CSV 'C:\Temp\Mailboxes.CSV'
```

If you use Get-MailboxStatistics with the *–Server* parameter on a server that hosts database copies from a Database Availability Group (DAG), you'll see an error for the database copies that tells you that they are not mounted or unavailable. This is because the cmdlet can't open these databases to read mailbox data because the databases are mounted in a special way that allows replication to occur but blocks other access.

Removing or disabling mailboxes

Mailboxes don't last forever and eventually you will want to remove some from Exchange, usually after users leave the company. You'll probably want to keep a mailbox for some time after a user leaves so that its contents are not immediately lost and they remain accessible to other users or for legal purposes. EMC provides two options for mailbox removal: You can either disable or remove a mailbox. The words "disable" and "remove" seem similar, but there's a huge difference in what happens behind the scenes in each of these operations.

When you disable a mailbox, Exchange removes all of the properties from the underlying Windows user account in Active Directory that associates the user with the mailbox. The contents of the mailbox will be purged from its database after the deleted mailbox retention period expires. Once Exchange purges a deleted mailbox from a database, the only way that you can retrieve the mailbox afterward is to retrieve it from a backup.

The equivalent EMS command to disable a mailbox is:

```
Disable-Mailbox -Identity 'Redmond, Tony'
```

When you remove a mailbox, in addition to marking the mailbox for purging after its retention period expires, you also remove the Windows user account from Active Directory. The EMS command used by EMC is:

```
Remove-Mailbox -Identity 'Redmond, Tony'
```

As with disabled mailboxes, Exchange retains the content of removed mailboxes in their original databases until their retention period expires. If you want, you can force Exchange to remove the Active Directory user account and mailbox contents immediately by setting the *–Permanent* parameter to $True. For example:

```
Remove-Mailbox -Identity 'Redmond, Tony' -Permanent $True
```

Before disabling or removing a mailbox, EMC warns about the consequences of taking the action. Although the result seems dire, you can reconnect a mailbox to an Active Directory account as long as the mailbox is available in the database. If the mailbox has a personal archive, you'll be told about this in the warning message.

Chapter 6

INSIDE OUT
Preparing for the future with Remove-Mailbox and Remove-StoreMailbox cmdlets

Exchange 2010 SP1 still includes the Remove-Mailbox cmdlet. However, SP1 also includes the Remove-StoreMailbox cmdlet, and over the next few releases Microsoft will gradually emphasize that:

- Remove-Mailbox should be used to remove the Active Directory account for the user and mark the mailbox for deletion after its retention period expires.

- Remove-StoreMailbox is used when you want to remove the mailbox from its database immediately. In effect, this new cmdlet will replace the Remove-Mailbox cmdlet when it is used with the *–Permanent* and *–StoreMailboxIdentity* parameters.

Why create a brand new cmdlet to do a job that is already possible with an existing cmdlet? The answer is that it forces administrators to make a distinct choice to remove a mailbox permanently. With Remove-Mailbox it's easy for an administrator to overlook the *–Permanent* parameter and so end up with mailboxes lingering in the database until their retention period expires. The purpose of Remove-StoreMailbox should be very easy to understand. It also makes the task of auditing easier because, if the need arises, an auditor can simply search for all uses of Remove-StoreMailbox rather than going through each instance of Remove-Mailbox to determine whether the *–Permanent* parameter was used. More information about how to audit administrator actions is available in Chapter 15.

Reconnecting mailboxes

When Exchange disconnects a mailbox after running either the Disable-Mailbox or Remove-Mailbox cmdlet, it stamps the current date and time in the mailbox's *DisconnectDate* property. This marks the start of the clock that ticks down until the retention time expires. The retention time for deleted mailboxes is a property of a mailbox database and can differ from the default 30 days. For example, for legal reasons you might want to remove or retain mailboxes for some classes of employees for different lengths of time. This is easily achieved by placing the employee mailboxes into databases that are configured with different retention periods. You can use this command to see the current deleted mailbox retention period for all the databases in the organization:

```
Get-MailboxDatabase | Select Name, MailboxRetention
```

Setting a different retention period is a matter of using Set-MailboxDatabase to set the desired value. For example, to set a mailbox retention period of 60 days for the "VIP Data" database, we would use this command:

```
Set-MailboxDatabase -Identity 'VIP Data' -MailboxRetention 60
```

The Disconnected Mailbox section of Recipient Configuration lists all of the current disconnected mailboxes that exist in every mounted database on a server (Figure 6-11). EMC uses a command like this to fetch information about disconnected mailboxes:

```
Get-MailboxStatistics -Server 'ExServer1.contoso.com' | Filter-PropertyNotEqualTo
DisconnectDate
```

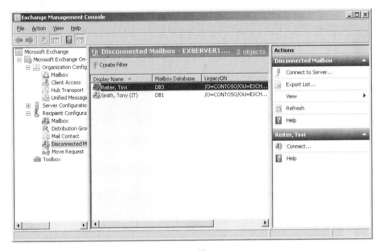

Figure 6-11 Viewing disconnected mailboxes.

If you need to check another server, select Connect To Server in the action pane and input the name of the desired server. EMC might report errors when it scans the databases on a server that prevent it from showing all disconnected mailboxes. For instance, there's no way to extract mailbox information from a database that isn't mounted.

Sometimes it can take a little while after a mailbox is disabled or removed before it shows up on the list of disconnected mailboxes. This might occur because Active Directory hasn't replicated the disconnected status for the mailbox to the domain controller that EMC is using. It might also be that the Store has not yet stamped a disconnected date on the mailbox so it isn't picked up by the filter that EMC uses to find disconnected mailboxes. If you notice that a mailbox hasn't appeared in the list, you can force Exchange to scan for disconnected mailboxes that exist in a database with the Clean-MailboxDatabase cmdlet. For example:

```
Clean-MailboxDatabase -Identity 'DB1'
```

Chapter 6

Afterward, you could check the database to see if anything has changed. I usually do something like this:

```
Get-MailboxStatistics –Database 'DB1' | Where {$_.DisconnectDate –ne $Null} | Select
DisplayName, DisconnectDate
```

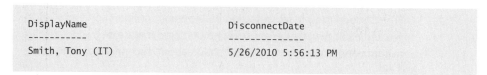

```
DisplayName                          DisconnectDate
-----------                          --------------
Smith, Tony (IT)                     5/26/2010 5:56:13 PM
```

Once you've found a disconnected mailbox that you want to bring back online, you can select the Connect option from the action pane to invoke the Connect Mailbox Wizard (Figure 6-12) to guide you through the necessary steps.

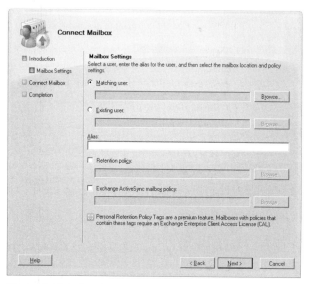

Figure 6-12 Using the Connect Mailbox Wizard.

The wizard has two ways to reconnect a mailbox.

1. If the original Active Directory account still exists, the Matching User option will be able to find and select the original account.

2. If you deleted the original Active Directory account by either using the Remove-Mailbox cmdlet or deleting the account separately after disabling the mailbox, the Existing User option allows you to select an Active Directory account to connect the mailbox. This could be a new account that you create for the original mailbox owner or a completely different account. The account cannot already be linked to another

mailbox, and if you click Browse to search for available accounts, the picker only displays accounts that aren't associated with a mailbox. The only other requirement is to make sure that you input a unique alias.

EMC uses the Connect-Mailbox cmdlet to reconnect a mailbox. In this example, you see that EMC uses the globally unique identifier (GUID) to identify the mailbox in the database. The selected Active Directory account is specified in the –*User* parameter.

```
Connect-Mailbox -Identity '50e2778f-e8ae-40d7-9dd8-bb22a101e8e5' -Database 'DB1'
-User 'contoso.com/AJR' -Alias 'AJR'
```

EMC tends to favor GUIDs because they are the most precise method of identifying an Exchange object. However, you can also use the mailbox display name to identify the mailbox to reconnect. If unsure about the display name, you can discover its exact value by running the Get-MailboxStatistics cmdlet against the database as described earlier.

```
Connect-Mailbox -Identity 'Redmond, Tony' -Database 'DB1' -Alias AJR
```

The mailbox GUID is useful if you want to delete a mailbox from a database before its retention period expires. This code scans a database for a particular mailbox, saves its GUID in a variable, and then removes the contents using the Remove-Mailbox cmdlet. Note the use of the –*StoreMailboxIdentity* parameter in this command.

```
$Mbx = Get-MailboxStatistics -Database 'DB1' | Where {$_.DisplayName -eq 'Redmond,
Tony'}
Remove-Mailbox -Database 'DB1' -StoreMailboxIdentity $mbx.MailboxGuid
```

When you delete mailbox contents like this, you will have to use a backup to retrieve them if necessary afterward.

INSIDE OUT   Avoiding errors

You might be concerned about the potential for error that can occur if an administrator uses the Remove Mailbox option instead of disabling a mailbox and discovers that he has just deleted the user's Active Directory account. To avoid problems and to make sure that mailboxes are kept as long as they are required, many companies have adopted a simple process where they do the following:

1. Disable the Windows account to prevent any further access to the account.

2. Hide the mailbox from the GAL.

3. Change the SMTP email address to make it invalid and stop new messages from arriving in the mailbox.

Chapter 6

4. Set up a suitable autoreply message for the mailbox so that anyone who sends to the new SMTP address is told that their message won't be read.

5. Keep the mailbox online and accessible for up to 90 days.

Between 45 and 60 days is usually sufficient to establish whether the mailbox contents are required. When the mailbox is no longer required, you can safely eliminate both the account and mailbox.

Email address policies

Email address policies define the format of email addresses that Exchange creates for mail-enabled objects. The combination of email address policies and the cmdlets that maintain and apply the policies replace the processing performed by the recipient policies and the Recipient Update Service (RUS) in Exchange Server 2000 and Exchange Server 2003. Unlike in earlier versions of Exchange, email address policies are applied in a consistent and immediate manner because EMC and the underlying EMS cmdlets that create or update mail-enabled recipients call a common set of business logic. The only way to stop Exchange from applying an email address policy to an object is to explicitly exclude it from these updates. For example:

```
Set-Mailbox -Identity 'David Pelton' -EmailAddressPolicyEnabled $False
```

Typically, the effect of an email address policy is felt when a new mail-enabled object is created or updated or after an administrator makes a change to a policy that creates a new email address type or format. After you install Exchange for the first time, you will find that the installation has created a policy called "default policy" under the Hub Transport section of the Organization configuration. This policy creates email addresses using the alias assigned to the object plus the SMTP domain of the Exchange organization, and is applied to every mail-enabled object until another email address policy with a higher priority is created. For example, an object with an alias of "TR" in the organization "contoso.com" will receive an SMTP address of "TR@contoso.com".

Behind the scenes, each email address policy uses a recipient filter to determine the objects that come within the scope of the policy. Logically, the default email address policy must have a very broad recipient filter because it has to apply to any object for which Exchange can find no other matching email address policy. The recipient filter for the default email address policy is very simple, because the filter catches everything. You can see details of the policy with the Get-EmailAddressPolicy cmdlet:

```
Get-EmailAddressPolicy –Identity 'Default Policy' | Select Name, *Filter*, *Exch*
```

```
Name                          : Default Policy
RecipientFilter               : Alias -ne $null
LdapRecipientFilter           : (mailNickname=*)
LastUpdatedRecipientFilter    : Alias -ne $null
RecipientFilterApplied        : True
RecipientFilterType           : Precanned
ExchangeVersion               : 0.1 (8.0.535.0)
```

The recipient filter ensures a match against all recipients that have an alias. It uses a filter that is preset within Exchange rather than a custom-coded filter that is designed to select a specific group of recipients. We discuss the topic of precanned and custom filters later on when we consider how they underpin dynamic distribution groups (see the section "OPATH queries" later in this chapter). The Lightweight Directory Access Protocol (LDAP) version of the filter is present to allow the RUS running on Exchange 2003 servers to understand the policy and use it to stamp correct email addresses on objects created on those servers. However, the ExchangeVersion only allows Exchange 2007 servers or later to manage the policy.

Legacy email address policies that were created with Exchange 2003 only include LDAP-based filters and do not have the recipient filters used by Exchange 2007 and Exchange 2010. You can locate these policies as follows, to look for any email address policy that has an Exchange version corresponding to Exchange 2003.

```
Get-EmailAddressPolicy | Where {$_.ExchangeVersion –Like '*6.5*'} | Select Name,
*Filter*
```

> **Note**
> All legacy policies need to be upgraded or removed. You cannot use the wizard for this purpose because EMC will flag an error if you attempt to edit a legacy email address policy.

You have two choices about how to handle these policies if you want to use them with Exchange 2010:

- Delete the old email address policies and recreate them using the Exchange 2010 Wizard. Although this approach ensures that resulting policies are totally suited to Exchange 2010, don't delete anything until you are sure that a newly created policy is available.

Chapter 6

● Upgrade the existing email address policy with the Set-EmailAddressPolicy cmdlet. To do this, you must prepare the recipient filter to insert into the policy. For example, the legacy LDAP policy has a filter of (mailNickname=*). The equivalent precoded query is "AllRecipients," so you can upgrade the policy to insert the recipient filter required by Exchange 2010 with the following command:

```
Set-EmailAddressPolicy –Identity 'Default Policy' –IncludedRecipients
'AllRecipients' –ForceUpgrade
```

Of course, upgrading a filter that looks for all recipients is easy, especially when the commands are documented in help files and books. It takes more work to figure out the translation of an LDAP custom filter into a suitable recipient filter. We discuss how to create custom recipient filters shortly.

Email policy priority

Several email address policies can exist within an organization (Figure 6-13). Generally it is a good idea to restrict the number of email address policies that are in use to the minimum possible because it can become complicated to understand where email addresses originate, especially when policies are based on different recipient properties. Each policy is assigned a priority order (one is the highest priority) and Exchange searches the policies in priority order to find the highest rated policy to use when it needs to apply a policy to an object. When you create the first custom email policy within an organization, it is automatically assigned a priority of one and the default policy is moved down to a special priority of "lowest" to ensure that any custom email address policy takes precedence.

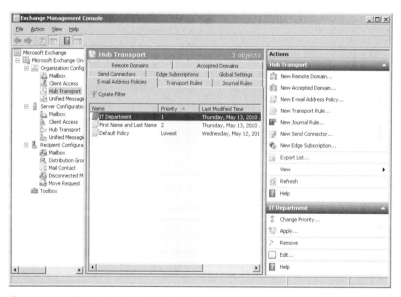

Figure 6-13 The email address policies for an organization listed in priority order.

Creating a new email address policy

Exchange operates quite happily with only the default email address policy in place because the unique alias assigned to each new object ensures that the resulting email address is also unique. However, most companies use different conventions for generating email addresses that are shared across all email systems in use within the company. Exchange provides the flexibility to create and apply suitable email addresses through custom email address policies that you can apply to some or all of the organization. By default, email address policies create SMTP format addresses, but you can also configure addresses for many other email systems, such as Lotus Notes and Novell GroupWise.

To begin, click the New E-Mail Address Policy option in the action pane. Exchange launches the New E-Mail Address Policy Wizard (Figure 6-14).

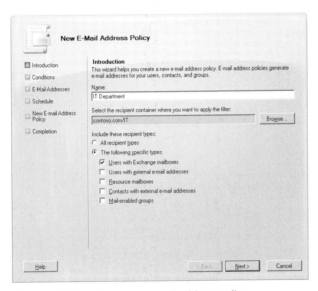

Figure 6-14 Creating a new email address policy.

Begin by naming the policy and deciding the scope of objects to which the policy will apply. The scope is established in three ways.

1. You can select an OU in Active Directory that Exchange will use as the root of the search to find matching objects to apply the policy. If you leave the recipient container blank, Exchange applies the policy to every matching object in the organization. In this case, we've selected an OU called "IT," which is logical because we're creating an email address policy to apply to members of the IT department.

2. You can limit the policy to selected recipient types from mailboxes to groups or even resource mailboxes.

3. When we move to the second screen of the New E-Mail Address Policy Wizard, you can establish additional search conditions for Exchange to locate the target object set (Figure 6-15). In this example, we've decided to use one of the 15 custom attributes that you can populate for mail-enabled objects and search for any object that has "IT" in CustomAttribute6. The conditions available here are the same set that you use with dynamic distribution groups (see the section "Dynamic distribution groups" later in this chapter) with one difference: You cannot create your own LDAP-based query using other object properties outside the conditions presented by the wizard. In practice, this is not a limitation because there is more than enough flexibility in the set that is available.

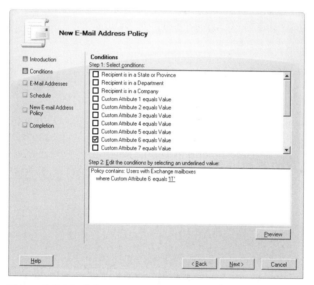

Figure 6-15 Defining criteria for a new email address policy.

The next step in the wizard is to decide on the format of email addresses that the policy will create for the set of objects located using the search criteria. You can elect to add one or more email addresses. For example, you might decide to add an email address that is user-friendly, such as Kim.Akers@contoso.com, and have another address that is used for internal routing purposes. This is a relatively common arrangement when companies support several different email systems and use front-end "bastion" servers to cleanse the incoming email stream arriving from the Internet and then route messages to the appropriate hub server for the addressee's email system. Another scenario is when users are assigned both a user-friendly email address designed for external publication and another that is used internally. For example, you might have Tony.Redmond@contoso.com and TRedmond@IT.EMEA.contoso.com. The first address works well for business cards; the second address contains some internal information that we might not want to share outside the company.

Mergers and acquisitions or company renaming situations create other scenarios in which multiple email addresses might be required.

> **Tip**
>
> An email address policy is perfectly capable of accommodating these and other scenarios. The only issue that you have to take care of beforehand is to create an accepted domain record for every domain that you want to use in email addresses. For example, if you want to use contoso.com and contoso-europe.com, both must be known to Exchange as accepted domains before they can be used in email addresses. You don't have to make the domain that you use when you install Exchange known an accepted domain because this is done as part of the installation process.

Figure 6-16 illustrates the options that exist to compose the format for the email addresses. These options are perfectly acceptable for addresses composed of English first and last names, but might struggle to cope with names from other languages. The non-English versions of Exchange offer other alternatives and you can also create a custom mask for the address using the variables described in Table 6-4. If you want to create a custom mask, you can do so through EMS by either specifying it when you create a new email address policy with the New-EmailAddressPolicy cmdlet or by updating an existing email address policy with the Set-EmailAddressPolicy cmdlet.

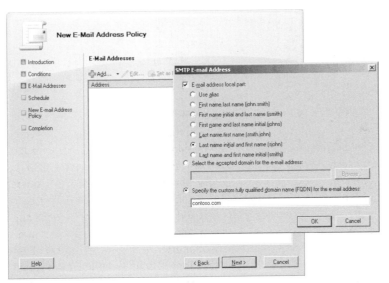

Figure 6-16 Creating the address format to apply to mail-enabled objects.

Table 6-4 **Email address policy mask variables**

Variable	Value
%g	Given name (first name)
%i	Middle Initial
%s	Surname (last name)
%d	Display name
%m	Exchange alias
%xs	Uses "x" number of letters of the surname; for example, if the surname is Smith and the variable is %2s, Exchange inserts "Sm"
%xg	Uses "x" number of letters from the given name; for example, if the given name is "Jane" and the variable is %3g, Exchange inserts "Jan"

The EMS command to create the new email address policy that we have just gone through is shown next. The filter specifies that we want to apply the policy to any user who has a mailbox. The email address format selected in Figure 6-16 is set in the *–EnabledEmailAddressTemplates* parameter. The value is prefixed with "SMTP" so we know that the address is of this type.

```
New-EmailAddressPolicy -Name 'IT Department' -RecipientContainer 'contoso.com/IT'
-IncludedRecipients 'MailboxUsers' -ConditionalCustomAttribute6 'IT'
-Priority '1' -EnabledEmailAddressTemplates 'SMTP:%g.%s@contoso.com'
```

The resulting filter that is stored in the policy is shown here. It is still a precanned filter because it is based on a limited set of properties.

```
Name                          : IT Department
RecipientFilter               : ((CustomAttribute6 -eq 'IT') -and (RecipientType
-eq 'UserMailbox'))
LdapRecipientFilter           : (&(extensionAttribute6=IT)(objectClass=user)
(objectCategory=person)(mailNickname=*)
                                (msExchHomeServerName=*))
LastUpdatedRecipientFilter    : ((CustomAttribute6 -eq 'IT') -and (RecipientType
-eq 'UserMailbox'))
RecipientFilterApplied        : True
RecipientContainer            : contoso.com/IT
RecipientFilterType           : Precanned
ExchangeVersion               : 0.1 (8.0.535.0)
```

The filter matches what we would expect from our interaction with the wizard and looks for any mailbox where the value of the "CustomAttribute6" property is "IT" that is stored in the "IT" OU (or any child OU).

Creating email address policies with custom filters

If the wizard is not capable of creating a sufficiently exact filter for an email address policy, you can create an email address policy with a custom filter using the New-EmailAddressPolicy cmdlet. In this situation, the syntax rules are the same as those used to specify recipient filters for dynamic distribution groups, so the filters you can create are very flexible. As an example, let's assume that you want to create an email address policy that only applies to mailbox users in the Dublin office. You could use New-EmailAddressPolicy to create the new policy and then immediately apply it with Update-EmailAddressPolicy. Note that before Exchange will accept the value used here for the primary SMTP address template (@dublin.contoso.com) this domain must be created as an accepted domain for the organization.

```
New-EmailAddressPolicy -Name 'Dublin Office Users' -RecipientFilter {Office
-eq 'Dublin' -and RecipientTypeDetails -eq 'UserMailbox'}
-EnabledPrimarySMTPAddressTemplate 'SMTP:@dublin.contoso.com'
Update-EmailAddressPolicy -id 'Dublin Office Users'
```

Unlike the email address policies that we have considered up to this point, policies created in this manner have a custom recipient filter. You cannot edit these policies with the EMC wizard afterward, so if you need to subsequently update the recipient filter, you will have to do it by writing a new recipient filter with the Set-EmailAddressPolicy command. It's useful to look at a custom email address policy to figure out the differences between custom and "normal" polices. When we view the details of the policy that we just created, we can see that Exchange has generated the appropriate LDAP filter and that the RecipientFilterType is now "Custom."

```
Get-EmailAddressPolicy -Identity 'Dublin Office Users' | Select Name, *Filter*
```

```
Name                        : Dublin Office users
RecipientFilter             : (Office -eq 'Dublin' -and RecipientTypeDetails -eq
'UserMailbox')
LdapRecipientFilter         : (&(physicalDeliveryOfficeName=Dublin)
(objectClass=user)(objectCategory=person)(mailNickname=*)
(msExchHomeServerName=*)(msExchRecipientTypeDetails=1))
LastUpdatedRecipientFilter  : (Office -eq 'Dublin' -and RecipientTypeDetails -eq
'UserMailbox')
RecipientFilterApplied      : True
RecipientFilterType         : Custom
```

Setting priority for an email address policy

Once you create a new email address policy, it automatically assumes the highest priority. This might not be correct, because you generally want policies assigned on the basis of selective criteria to be applied before any catch-all or default policy. You can move the new email address policy to the correct priority by selecting it and then clicking Change Priority in the action pane (Figure 6-17).

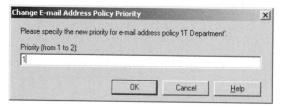

Figure 6-17 Changing the priority of an email address policy.

You can then assign a value within the range of available choices. For example, if three custom policies are available, you can assign a priority from 1 to 3; if there are six, you'll be able to assign a priority from 1 to 6. You cannot select "lowest," because this priority is reserved for the default policy. After you decide on the new priority, Exchange moves the policy into the correct position and rearranges the other policies accordingly. The equivalent EMS command is:

```
Set-EmailAddressPolicy -Identity 'IT Department' -Priority '1'
```

After changing the priority of a policy, you should click Apply on the action pane to force Exchange to search for objects that come within the scope of the policy and create new email addresses for these objects (if such addresses does not already exist). If created, the new email addresses are made the primary addresses for the object and all previous email addresses are preserved so that Exchange can deliver messages sent to these addresses.

You can opt to have Exchange apply the new email address policy immediately or wait for a suitable time, in which case EMC will pause and wait for the appointed time before it executes the command. Applying a new email address policy to thousands of objects can take a long time to complete and generate many Active Directory transactions, and also force a complete Outlook Address Book (OAB) download for all clients due to the number of updates in the directory, so it is wise to create any required mail address policies early in a deployment and avoid the effect of a widespread update later on in the production cycle.

Sometimes you are forced to update many recipients to ensure that they receive email addresses of the right type. The example email address policy that we created for the IT department will only be applied to recipients that are stored in the "IT" OU. Exchange will apply the policy after we create it to the recipients that already exist in the OU, but if we move recipients into the OU later on (perhaps after they join the IT department), we need to update their addresses. If you prefer, you can start the update process through EMS with a command such as the one shown next. Note that the Update-EmailAddressPolicy cmdlet does not include the ability to schedule the update for a future time and date. You can combine this cmdlet with a suitable scheduling utility if you want to apply the update at a particular time in the future.

```
Update-EmailAddressPolicy -Identity 'IT Department'
```

Virtual list view (VLV) for Exchange address lists

Exchange 2010 introduces virtual list view (VLV) support for address lists. Active Directory also supports VLV for its searches beginning with Windows Server 2003. The idea behind VLV is that it helps applications such as directory services to respond to client requests that generate very large result sets more efficiently by enabling the application to display a sub-set of the total result set without having to retrieve every matching entry. For example, if you search Active Directory for every recipient in a large organization, the result set is likely to contain thousands of entries. VLV allows the application to browse the first group of matching entries (maybe 100 or so) and then page forward and move to the next set if the client needs more data. Exchange 2010 uses VLV to provide more efficient access to recipient data sets.

By default, Exchange sets an attribute called *IsAddressListPagingEnabled* in its organization configuration to indicate that it can use VLV. You can check this attribute as follows:

```
Get-OrganizationConfig | Select IsAddressListPagingEnabled
```

If the attribute is set to true, Exchange uses VLV in the code that underpins the Get-Recipient cmdlet. EMC makes extensive use of this cmdlet to fetch recipient data to display details about mailboxes, distribution groups, and so on. Although it's unlikely that you would ever want to do this, you can disable VLV by running the Disable-AddressListPaging cmdlet. In this case, Exchange reverts to the behavior used in Exchange 2007 and fetches complete result sets, which can slow things down a little. You can reset the attribute by running the Enable-AddressListPaging cmdlet. In addition to resetting the *IsAddressListPagingEnabled* attribute to True, running the Enable-AddressListPaging cmdlet also recreates the precoded system address lists such as "All Rooms" and "All Recipients," so it is possible to fix these address lists by running the cmdlet if they ever become corrupted.

Behind the scenes, the *IsAddressListPagingEnabled* attribute is represented by a Boolean value called *msExchAddressListPagingEnabled* set on the *msExchOrganizationContainer* object.

Discovery mailboxes

Discovery mailboxes are used as the repository for the metadata that drives discovery searches and the output that the searches generate from user mailboxes. We'll discuss how searches are executed in Chapter 15. Discovery mailboxes cannot receive email. Two different discovery mailboxes are created by the Exchange 2010 installation procedure.

The first is the discovery metadata mailbox that holds information about completed and pending searches. You will not be able to perform discovery searches unless this mailbox is online and available. It has the fixed name "*SystemMailbox{e0dc1c29-89c3-4034-b678-e6c29d823ed9}*". This mailbox is created as an arbitration mailbox and you can locate it with:

```
Get-Mailbox -Arbitration
```

The second type of arbitration mailbox is a discovery search mailbox, which is used to store the items copied as a result of discovery searches for later access and review by users who have been granted permission to open the mailbox. A single discovery search mailbox is created by the installation procedure and should be accessible by users who are members of the Discovery Management role group. As such, these users should be able to open the default Discovery Mailbox to be able to peruse its contents. If you create additional discovery mailboxes, you will have to assign full access to the accounts that will use these mailboxes for mailbox searches.

As explained next, you can create other discovery mailboxes as required. Discovery mailboxes are visible through EMC, so you can examine their properties (Figure 6-18) and perform other mailbox-related operations such as moving them between databases. The Hide From Exchange Address Lists check box should be selected because it's a good idea to hide discovery mailboxes from the GAL to stop users from attempting to send email to them.

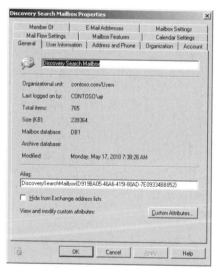

Figure 6-18 Properties of the default discovery mailbox.

You can locate all of the discovery mailboxes that exist in the organization with EMS by using the following command:

```
Get-Mailbox -RecipientTypeDetails DiscoveryMailbox
```

Name	Alias	ServerName	ProhibitSendQuota
----	-----	----------	-----------------
DiscoverySearchMailbox...	DiscoverySearchMa...	ExServer1	50 GB (53,687,091,200 bytes)
EMEA Legal Searches	EMEASearches	ExServer2	50 GB (53,687,091,200 bytes)

Note that the server name reported isn't actually the server that hosts the mailbox. Instead, it's the server that hosted the database where the mailbox was originally created. To discover the server that currently hosts the discovery mailbox, you'll have to retrieve the database name using Get-Mailbox and then the current server using Get-MailboxDatabase.

The Exchange installation procedure creates the default arbitration mailboxes in the Users OU of the root domain. For this reason, unless you are logged into the root domain, you might have to establish the correct Active Directory scope to find these mailboxes.

```
Set-ADServerSettings -ViewEntireForest:$True
Get-Mailbox -Arbitration
```

Creating additional discovery mailboxes

Exchange creates the default discovery mailbox in the mailbox database of the first Exchange 2010 mailbox server that you deploy. This is an acceptable configuration for small deployments, but might prove problematic for larger organizations where the sheer volume of data uncovered by a discovery search could be very large in terms of the number of items and the size of the storage required. Storage should not be an issue because the default quota assigned to the discovery mailbox is 50 GB. However, you do have to remember that the mailbox server that holds the database where the discovery mailbox is located has to do a lot of work to copy items that are unearthed by a search. For example, if a search locates 10,000 items that occupy 6 GB, the server has to be able to accept the workload necessary to copy and store these items. The workload is composed of the CPU consumed during the search, the storage for the discovered items, and the transaction logs generated as the discovered items are created in the discovery mailbox. A search might be performed several times before the final information is captured and each time the server will be stressed. For this reason, you need to think about the following:

1. The number of discovery mailboxes that are created and available within the organization. One will suffice for small organizations, but perhaps it is better to create a number of discovery mailboxes on different servers for use by the teams who perform searches.

2. The location of the discovery mailboxes. The ideal situation is that the mailboxes being searched, the users who perform the search, and the database hosting the target discovery mailbox should be in the same site, because this eliminates any need for extended network connections to search, store, and review information. In any case, you need to consider whether the server hosting the database that contains the discovery mailbox has sufficient capacity to handle the load generated by searches.

Users in the Discovery Management role group are able to perform searches. We'll cover this topic in detail in Chapter 15. Part of creating a new search request is the selection of the discovery mailbox that is used to hold the result of the search. The need to hold potentially huge amounts of data uncovered by searches is the reason why discovery mailboxes are assigned a 50 GB storage quota. Once data are captured by a search, users have to be granted full access to the discovery mailbox if they want to be able to open the mailbox and access the search results. See the section "Managing full access permission" later in this chapter for information about how to grant full access to a mailbox.

You can create additional discovery mailboxes by using the New-Mailbox cmdlet with the –Discovery switch. For example:

```
New-Mailbox 'Legal Action Discovery Mailbox' –UserPrincipalName
'LegalDiscovery@contoso.com' –Discovery
```

> **Tip**
>
> After you create a new discovery mailbox, make sure that you assign Full Access permission to the mailbox to the groups that need to access the search results that it stores. By default, the default discovery mailbox can be opened by the Administrator account, but permission to access this mailbox also needs to be granted to anyone who needs to access it.

If you attempt to delete a mailbox database that holds discovery mailboxes, Exchange will report an error and you will need to move these mailboxes before you can delete the database. To do this, use the New-MoveRequest cmdlet to move the discovery arbitration mailbox and EMC to move the discovery metadata mailbox. The reason why you need to split the operations between EMC and EMS is that you can see the discovery metadata mailbox in EMC but you can't see the discovery arbitration mailbox. Here's a sample command that moves the discovery arbitration mailbox to another database:

```
New-MoveRequest -Identity 'SystemMailbox{e0dc1c29-89c3-4034-b678-e6c29d823ed9}'
-TargetDatabase 'DB1'
```

Setting mailbox permissions

The ability to change the way that messages are processed in a mailbox became a fundamental part of email system functionality a long time ago. Exchange allows you to assign different levels of control over mailboxes to influence the way that messages are delivered to the mailbox, who has the right to send messages from or on behalf of the mailbox (there is a difference), or who has complete control over the mailbox. These assignments can be made by changing mailbox properties through Mail Flow Settings or by assigning different Active Directory permissions to allow other accounts to impersonate or access contents in the mailbox.

Mail flow settings

- EMC provides three settings under the Mail Flow Settings tab of a mailbox's properties (Figure 6-19): Grant Send On Behalf Of permission. This feature allows another user to send a message on behalf of a mailbox's owner. Exchange clearly indicates that the message is generated by one user on behalf of another and so these messages are clearly different than those sent using the Send As permission. Outlook users can delegate the same permission to other users. The feature is commonly used by personal assistants who support other users.

> **Tip**
> Once set, allow an hour or so before you attempt to use the new permission to enable Exchange to refresh its Store cache from Active Directory, because you won't be able to use the Send As permission until it is acknowledged by the Store.

- Set a forwarding address: You can redirect incoming messages and tell Exchange to deliver them to another mailbox. Optionally, you can have Exchange deliver copies of incoming messages to both the original and redirected mailbox.

- Set maximum recipients: You can limit the number of recipients that a user can add to messages. A group counts as a single recipient. This setting overrides any recipient limit set on hub transport servers.

Chapter 6

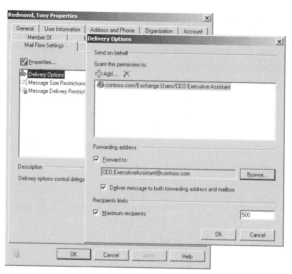

Figure 6-19 Changing mail flow settings for a mailbox.

The equivalent EMS command to apply the settings shown in Figure 6-19 is:

```
Set-Mailbox -Identity 'Redmond, Tony'-ForwardingAddress 'CEO Executive Assistant'
-GrantSendOnBehalfTo 'CEO Executive Assistant' -RecipientLimits 500
```

If you need to grant the Send on Behalf of permission to several mailboxes at one time, you can simply input a list of the desired mailboxes to the *–GrantSendOnBehalfTo* parameter. For example:

```
Set-Mailbox -Identity 'Redmond, Tony' -GrantSendOnBehalfTo 'CEO Executive Assistant',
'Pelton, David', 'Akers, Kim'
```

Apart from mailboxes, you can grant the ability to send messages on behalf of distribution groups, dynamic distribution groups, and mail-enabled contacts. This has to be done through EMS, because EMC doesn't present the option for these recipient types. For example:

```
Set-DistributionGroup -Identity 'Legal Department' -GrantSendOnBehalfTo 'Pelton,
David'
```

The difference between Send on Behalf and Send As

The difference between the Send on Behalf and Send As features is the degree of impersonation used when a message is sent. When you use the Send on Behalf feature, the messages that are delivered clearly indicate that you have sent a message on behalf of someone else. This option is most useful when it's important to show that someone is assisting another user to deal with her email. When you use the Send As feature, the recipient gets no indication that you sent the message, because it appears to come from the person that you impersonate. Usually, the Send As feature is used for functional mail- boxes that are shared by groups of users, such as a mailbox dedicated to handling help desk queries.

Behind the scenes, the Send on Behalf feature only requires Exchange to transport some additional information in the message header so that clients can display the name of the user who actually generated the message when it is viewed by the recipient. By compari- son, the Send As feature requires a user to possess the Active Directory permission to impersonate someone else to send a message using his identity.

Normally, Send As permission is assigned by using an EMC wizard. Select the mailbox to which you want to assign the permission and then select the Manage Send As Permission option in the action pane. The wizard then presents a dialog box to allow the administrator to select the users who will be allowed to impersonate the mailbox (Figure 6-20). You can add or delete as many users as you need through one wizard session. Exchange caches per- missions and it might take up to an hour before the new permission is effective. In addition, the users who receive the permission will have to start a new client session before they can send messages on behalf of the mailbox.

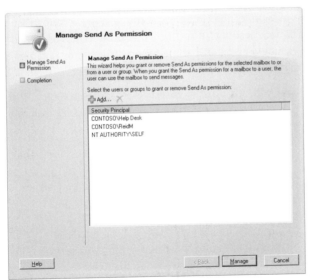

Figure 6-20 Assigning Send As permission to a mailbox.

The process used to send messages with Send As permission varies from client to client. The same approach is taken with OWA when it is used to send a message on behalf of another user with the difference that no trace of the originator's name is shown in the message

Chapter 6

header (Figure 6-21). In effect, the Send As feature allows you to effectively impersonate another user for the purpose of sending email.

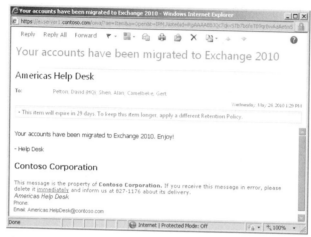

Figure 6-21 A message sent on behalf of the help desk.

Naturally, we can assign the Send As permission to an account with EMS. The following code assigns the permission for the Help Desk account to my account. Distinguished names are used to reference both accounts. It is critical that these values are typed in correctly, because any error, including an extra space between the surname and first name, will cause EMS to be unable to locate the relevant Active Directory object.

```
Add-AdPermission -Identity 'Help.Desk@contoso.com' -ExtendedRights 'Send-As'
-User 'Tony.Redmond@contoso.com'
```

To revoke the permission, we can use a command like this:

```
Remove-ADPermission -Identity 'Help.Desk@contoso.com' -User
'Tony.Redmond@contoso.com' -InheritanceType 'All' -ExtendedRights 'Send-As'
-ChildObjectTypes $Null -InheritedObjectType $Null -Properties $Null
```

Managing full access permission

Assigning Send As permission for a mailbox allows a user to impersonate someone else, but apart from being able to create and send messages, the Send As permission does not grant any further access to mailbox contents. You need Full Access permission to be able to open a mailbox and peruse its contents. One obvious example of when users need this facility is when they perform discovery searches (see Chapter 15), because Exchange places the output from these searches into discovery mailboxes (selected individually for each search) that the investigators have to open to review the results. Before the investigators can open the discovery mailbox, an administrator has to assign them full access permission to the discovery mailbox.

As we learned earlier in this part of the book, an Exchange organization can have multiple discovery mailboxes. Select the mailbox to which you want to assign permission and select the Manage Full Access Permission option in the action pane. EMC launches a wizard (Figure 6-22) where you can pick the accounts or groups that need the permission. Notice that the Exchange Servers and Exchange Trusted Subsystem groups are already included in the list of users and groups. This is to allow Exchange access to the discovery mailbox so that it can store search results in it.

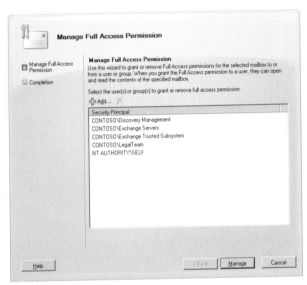

Figure 6-22 Managing Full Access permission for a mailbox.

In this case, we're adding permissions for a new discovery mailbox, so we add the names of individual investigators and the Discovery Management group. The latter will allow users who are members of the Discovery Management role group to access the mailbox. After the set of users to receive Full Access is complete, click Manage.

Behind the scenes: When EMC assigns permissions

Behind the scenes, the Add-MailboxPermission cmdlet makes the assignment. This cmdlet requires you to pass the name of the mailbox to which you want to assign full access. You can use any of the valid identifiers for this purpose. When EMC assigns permissions, it uses the full distinguished name of the mailbox. The advantage of using a distinguished name is that you can be absolutely certain that you are working with the correct mailbox, which is always important when you deal with permissions. The disadvantage is that you have to be very careful about typing in a distinguished name because they can be quite verbose or complicated (for instance, the distinguished name for the default discovery mailbox is pretty long).

If you set up other discovery mailboxes it's likely that you will give them names that are a little less obscure and are therefore easier to input. In this example, we assign Full Access permission for a new discovery mailbox to the members of the Discovery Management group:

```
Add-MailboxPermission -Identity 'CN=Legal Action Discovery
Mailbox,CN=Users,DC=contoso,DC=com' -User 'CONTOSO\Discovery Management'
-AccessRights 'FullAccess'
```

When you assign permissions to multiple mailboxes or groups, you have to use multiple Add-MailboxPermission commands. After all the permissions are assigned, we can check the permissions on the mailbox as follows. This output shows what we expect. The Discovery Management group is in the list of permissions, and we can also see that another account called "LegalTeam" has been assigned access. A user who receives Full Access permission can then open the mailbox with OWA.

```
Get-Mailbox -Identity 'Legal Action Discovery Mailbox' | Get-MailboxPermission | ?
{$_.AccessRights -Like "FullAccess"} | Sort-Object Deny | Format-Table User,
AccessRights, Deny, IsInherited -AutoSize
```

User	AccessRights	Deny	IsInherited
CONTOSO\Exchange Servers	{FullAccess}	False	True
CONTOSO\Discovery Management	{FullAccess}	False	False
CONTOSO\LegalTeam	{FullAccess}	False	False
CONTOSO\Enterprise Admins	{FullAccess}	True	True
CONTOSO\Domain Admins	{FullAccess}	True	True
CONTOSO\Organization Management	{FullAccess}	True	True

Apart from the need to open and access content in discovery mailboxes, Full Access permission is commonly required in other scenarios, such as when several users share a functional mailbox. For example, if you want to allow a group of users to open a mailbox belonging to a help desk so that they can see the problems and issues reported to the help desk, you will need to assign Full Access permission for the help desk mailbox to each user who needs access. Obviously, granting access to a group rather than individual user accounts makes this process a lot easier to manage.

INSIDE OUT   What does Full Access really mean?

Full Access permission allows users to access all of the content in a mailbox, as well as the ability to create and save draft messages or add other content to the mailbox. However, Full Access permission does not allow the holder to assume the identity of the mailbox and use it to send messages, because this could create a situation where someone accesses a shared mailbox and uses those permissions to send insulting or other inappropriate messages that could not be traced back to an individual. The term "Full Access" often creates an expectation that you can do everything with a mailbox that its owner can, but the reality is that you need to hold the Send As permission to be able to send messages using the mailbox's identity.

Remember that the Information Store caches permissions for mailboxes to improve performance. This means that it could take up to two hours before a permission change to allow Full Access or Send As for a mailbox becomes effective. Unfortunately, there are only two ways around this problem. You can either restart the Information Store service to force it to reload its cache or you can reduce the interval that the Store uses to reload its cache. The first solution forces all clients to disconnect and isn't a good thing to do during the working day; the second imposes an extra performance penalty on the server when it reloads the cache. Although some experienced administrators have reported good results when they reduced the logon cache interval to between 15 and 20 minutes, neither option is particularly attractive. The best idea might be to be patient and wait for Exchange to take its own good time to discover the amended permissions before attempting to use them, or, if possible, update permissions at a time (like midnight) when the delay enforced by caching won't impact users.

See *http://technet.microsoft.com/en-us/library/bb684892(EXCHG.80).aspx* for information about how to change the Reread Logon Quotas Interval registry entry to adjust the logon cache interval.

Sending messages on behalf of other users

If you plan to send messages on behalf of other users, you should enable the From field in the client interface so that users can select the mailbox from which they want to send the message. In OWA, the From field is enabled in Mail Options in the Sections setting of Mail group, by selecting Message Format. If you've downloaded the Secure Multipurpose Internet Mail Extensions (S/MIME) control, you'll see a warning that S/MIME messages cannot be sent when this option is used. This is because S/MIME operates on the basis of personal digital signatures that cannot be shared or reused by other users, so if you send a message on behalf of someone else, you can't apply a digital signature to a message or encrypt it.

Chapter 6

When the From field is enabled, the user can select the email account from which they want to send by clicking the arrow to the right of the label. This action reveals a drop-down list where the user's own account is first (Figure 6-23). The user can then select Other Email Address to have OWA display the Account Picker dialog box to allow another mailbox to be selected. It's also possible to input the name directly into the From field of a mail-enabled recipient on behalf of whom they have the right to send mail. If a mailbox is selected for which the user doesn't have the permission to send mail, OWA will flag the problem with an error message and won't send the message. When a recipient replies to a message that was sent on behalf of a user, Exchange delivers the response to the mailbox of the user for whom the message was sent.

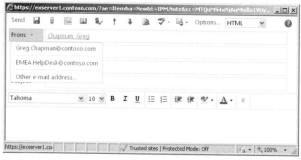

Figure 6-23 Selecting a mailbox on behalf of which to send a message.

The process to enable the From field to send messages on behalf of another user varies across Outlook versions, so you should consult the documentation for your version to determine the necessary steps. Other email clients might not support the send on behalf of another user feature.

Opening another user's mailbox

Once you have been granted the Full Access permission to another mailbox you can add it to your Outlook profile to have Outlook open the mailbox alongside your own. Alternatively, if you want a clear separation between the two mailboxes, you can configure a separate profile that points to the target mailbox and select that profile when you open Outlook.

OWA doesn't use profiles, but it does support three methods to access content in another user's mailbox:

- Open just the Inbox folder from another mailbox: This option is useful for people who need access to messages that arrive in a shared mailbox used for a function such as a help desk. The steps from selecting the option to inputting the mailbox name (you can use the Ctrl+K combination to validate the name of the mailbox that you want to select) to the Inbox appearing under the normal folder list are as follows:

1. Open your mailbox as normal with OWA, right-click the root of your mailbox, and then select Open Other User's Inbox.

2. You can then input the name of the other mailbox into the Open Other User's Inbox dialog box.

3. If you have the permission, OWA will list the other mailbox and its Inbox under the list of folders for your own mailbox (and personal archive, if you have one).

4. The option to open another user's Inbox is persistent and lasts across OWA sessions. If you want to remove the other Inbox, you have to select it and then select the Remove From View option.

- Open the complete mailbox of another user: This option allows complete access to all folders in another user's mailbox, including archive folders, and is appropriate for use by support staff that monitor and process incoming messages for another user. It's also useful for people who perform discovery searches and need to open the discovery search mailbox to access the results of the searches (see Chapter 15). Access is one-time and does not persist across OWA sessions, so you have to open the other user's mailbox each time you want access. To open another user's mailbox, click the down arrow shown beside the name of your mailbox on the far right side of the screen and then input the name of the mailbox that you want to open in the Open Other Mailbox dialog box. OWA attempts to autocomplete the mailbox name as you type based on email addresses that you have used before. You can input the display name, alias, or SMTP address of the mailbox that you want to open and use Ctrl+K to validate what you've entered. When complete, click OK to have OWA attempt to open the mailbox. If you have permission, OWA will grant complete access to every item in every folder.

- Include the name of the mailbox that you want to open in the URL that you use to invoke OWA: This is a variation of option 2 that allows you to go directly to the selected mailbox without going through the intermediate phase of opening your own mailbox. Simply append the SMTP address of the mailbox in the Uniform Resource Locator (URL) that you type into the browser. For example, if you usually type **https://webmail.contoso.com/owa**, you could open the mailbox for Kim. Akers@contoso.com by typing **https://webmail.contoso.com/owa/Kim.Akers@ contoso.com**

Chapter 6

Auditing mailboxes

You can audit the actions taken by a user (including an administrator) who opens another user's mailbox by enabling auditing on the mailbox (see Chapter 15) to capture details of actions such as hard and soft deletes, emptying the Deleted Items folder, and so on. You can also audit actions taken by mailbox owners when they are connected to the mailbox.

Enabling mailbox auditing is a good option to consider for sensitive mailboxes like those belonging to high-level executives or others in positions where you mighthave to provide data in response to discovery actions to demonstrate compliance with regulatory or legal requirements. Administrators can then run audit reports with EMS to retrieve details of actions taken by the different users who worked with the mailbox and have the reports mailed to a compliance officer or other user for review.

Distribution groups

Every Exchange organization supports distribution groups and the largest deployments usually include tens of thousands of groups. It is certainly useful to be able to address many different recipients through one common address. However, distribution groups are seldom managed as well as mailboxes and tend to linger in the directory long after they have ceased to be used. I worked at Hewlett-Packard until 2010 and, even then, I could find groups called the "Windows 2000 Launch Team" and "Windows NT Forum" in the GAL, both of which were artefacts of work done in the past.

Windows supports four different types of groups. Exchange really has use for only two of these: universal groups and dynamic or query-based groups. Universal groups are available anywhere within the forest, because their membership is published to global catalog servers. From an Exchange perspective, this means that you can be sure that everyone in the group will receive messages addressed to the group because every hub transport server can expand the group's membership in the same way when they route messages sent to the group.

Universal groups can hold security principals and be used as the basis for access control as well as communication, so they are very useful objects. The Exchange recipient type for mail-enabled universal groups is *MailUniversalDistributionGroup,* unless the group is created as a security group, in which case it is of type *MailUniversalSecurityGroup.*

Like other Exchange objects, groups have a version number that indicates the version of Exchange that created (or last edited) the object. If you have groups created on previous versions of Exchange, their versions will be updated to version 14 the first time that you edit any metadata (but not membership) with Exchange 2010.

A new distribution group is devoid of members. Before it is useful, you have to populate the group with members, and the maintenance of group membership is an ongoing activity for the group owners. Dynamic distribution groups score on this point because their membership is evaluated by the transport system each time the group is included in an email header. A dynamic distribution group does not have the membership list found in normal distribution groups. Instead, it includes an OPATH query that the transport system runs against Active Directory to determine the current group membership. Mail-enabled objects leave and join dynamic distribution groups based on their Active Directory properties. For example, if the query looks for every user with an Exchange mailbox who is located in Texas, then the transport system will send a copy of a message addressed to this group to every user that it can find in Active Directory whose state or province attribute is set to Texas. The advantage of dynamic distribution groups is that their membership always returns the most up-to-date information available in Active Directory. The disadvantage is much the same, because if you don't populate Active Directory with accurate data then a query won't return the membership that you expect or need.

Returning to our previous example, a query to find everyone in a specific country will succeed if the Active Directory objects that you want to locate all have the same values in the country attribute but will fail if administrators use different spellings or ways to identify a country when they populate user accounts. "US" and "U.S." are completely different values, as are "UK," "U.K.," and "United Kingdom." Because the membership of dynamic distribution groups is only evaluated when required and is not represented by links to other Active Directory objects, these groups can't hold security principals.

Now that the difference between normal distribution groups and dynamic distribution groups has been established, we leave further discussion about this topic until later in this chapter.

Behind the scenes, Windows holds the membership for distribution groups as a set of backward pointers to the objects that represent the members of the group. These objects can be mail-enabled accounts, contacts, public folders, or other groups. In technical terms, the membership is stored in a single multivalued attribute called "Member" that contains the pointers. Figure 6-24 shows the membership of a group displayed through EMC (left) and ADSIEdit (right). In the past, the way that Active Directory held group membership in a single multivalued attribute placed a practical restriction on the number of objects that could be members of a group. This limitation was removed with the introduction of linked value replication (LVR) in Windows 2003 and you can now store well over 5,000 members in a group. However, maintaining the membership of very large groups can be a real pain and most administrators try to keep groups under 1,000 members. Exchange 2010 introduces the ability for users to join and leave groups through the ECP, which will relieve some work for administrators.

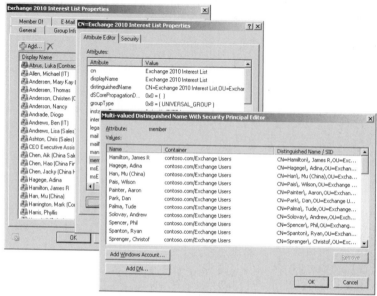

Figure 6-24 Group membership as shown by EMC and ADSIEdit.

Room lists

Managing or finding a suitable conference room for a meeting can be quite a hassle at times. Exchange 2010 attempts to facilitate this process by introducing the concept of a room list. This is a distribution group whose membership is composed entirely of room mailboxes and is marked with a special property so that Outlook 2010 (the only client that currently supports room lists) can recognize that it can use the room list group. The intention is that you would create room list groups to help users navigate the full collection of rooms available within a company. This is more important in large companies that might have hundreds of rooms spread across multiple buildings in multiple locations. In such a scenario, you might create a room list for each company building. The feature is obviously less interesting for smaller companies that might have only one or two rooms to manage.

To create a room list group, you can either:

- Create a distribution group as normal with EMC and then mark it as a room list with EMS.

- Create the distribution group with EMS and mark it as a room list when it is created.

To create a new room list group with EMS, you use the New-DistributionGroup cmdlet as normal and include the *–RoomList* parameter. For example:

```
New-DistributionGroup –Name 'HQ Conference Rooms' –OrganizationalUnit
'contoso.com/Groups' –RoomList
```

To mark an existing group (one created with EMC), you use the Set-DistributionGroup cmdlet:

```
Set-DistributionGroup –Identity 'Building 2 Rooms' –RoomList
```

After you have created the room list groups, you can proceed to populate their membership with room mailboxes. EMC marks room list groups with a special icon to let you know that you can only add room mailboxes to their membership, but if you make a mistake and attempt to add a normal mailbox to the membership, you'll see the error shown in Figure 6-25.

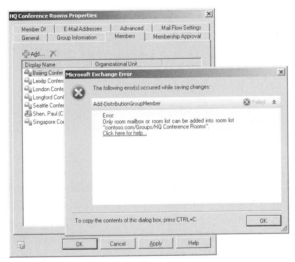

Figure 6-25 Error populating the membership of a room list distribution group.

Outlook 2010 uses room list groups when users set up meetings. The room list finder allows users to select a particular room list group (for instance, the room list group that contains the rooms of the building where they want to hold the meeting). Outlook then loads the room mailboxes from the group and retrieves the free/busy data for the rooms to show the user when the rooms are free. The user can then select the most appropriate room and add it to the meeting. This feature does not override any restrictions imposed by the Resource Booking Attendant (see the section "Processing meeting requests according to policy" later in this chapter for more information); it simply provides an easier way for users to locate suitable conference rooms for their meetings.

Chapter 6

Figure 6-26 shows a room list group in action. You can see that the HQ Conference Rooms list has been selected in the Show A Room List drop-down box. Selecting the group reveals all the rooms that it includes and the user can then select the room that he'd like to book.

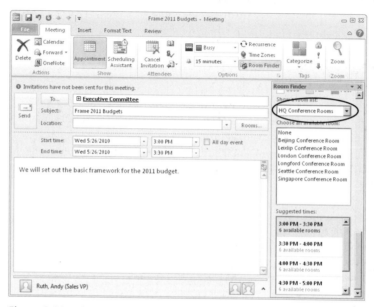

Figure 6-26 Using a room list with Outlook 2010.

Group owners

When a group is created, Exchange assigns the account that was used to create it as the group's owner. This really doesn't matter if group membership is always maintained by administrators, but it can be useful to assign the ability to manage groups to individual users. Outlook was the only tool for this purpose that was available in previous versions of Exchange. If you own a group, you can use Outlook to select the group from the GAL and update its membership (Figure 6-27). This wasn't always possible with previous versions of Exchange, especially when the group was owned by one domain and your account was in another.

As discussed in Chapter 5, you can modify the Default Role Assignment Policy to allow users to maintain group membership through ECP. If you do this, you might also need to update groups to assign ownership to users. This is easily done by selecting a group, view-ing its properties, and clicking the Group Membership tab. You can then add or remove users as group owners. However, unlike in Exchange Server 2003 and Exchange Server 2007, you cannot add a group as the owner of another group. This change in behavior is due to the introduction of role-based access control (RBAC) as the central authorization authority for all Exchange 2010 actions. Channeling authorization requests through RBAC ensures that a user who attempts to update group membership has the authority to do so. RBAC doesn't support the assignment of group management to another group in Exchange 2010 (including SP1) and insists that every user who needs to be able to manage a group be listed individually as a group manager. Figure 6-28 shows that the Exchange 2010 Interest List group is managed by three users.

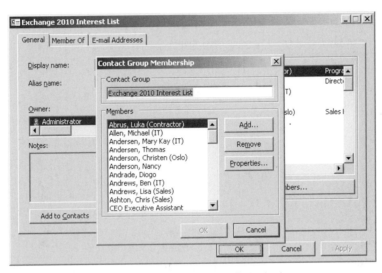

Figure 6-27 Editing group membership through Outlook.

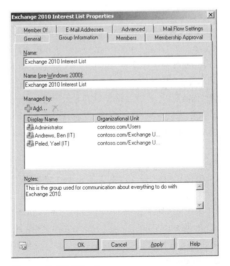

Figure 6-28 Viewing group ownership.

You can also use theSet-DistributionGroup cmdlet to update the management list for a group. The input to the *–ManagedBy* parameter is a comma-separated list of identifiers to the mailboxes of the users who you want to be group managers. The identifiers can be email addresses, names, aliases, or even distinguished names, whatever format pleases you, as long as Exchange can uniquely identify the intended group owner. Although you can assign many managers to a group, it's usually best to keep the set limited to between two and six because more than this creates the potential for confusion if several managers attempt to update the group membership at one time.

```
Set-DistributionGroup -Identity 'Exchange 2010 Interest List'
-BypassSecurityGroupManagerCheck -ManagedBy 'Administrator', 'Andrews, Ben (IT)',
'Peled, Yael (IT)'
```

You can use a command like this to check that the right owners have been assigned to the group:

```
Get-DistributionGroup -Identity 'Exchange 2010 Interest List' | Select Name,
ManagedBy | Format-List
```

Group expansion

Exchange expands the membership of groups included in message headers when the messages pass through a hub transport server. The default is to let any hub transport server expand a group, but you can assign this task to a specific server if you want (Figure 6-29). The downside of defining a specific server to expand a group is that any messages addressed to the group can only be routed as long as the server is online, which creates a single point of potential failure (or delay) within your messaging environment.

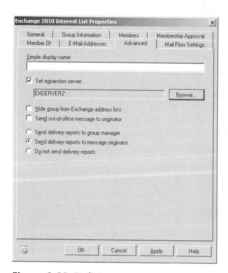

Figure 6-29 Defining an expansion server for a group.

When a hub transport server expands a group, it builds a list of the individual group members in memory and uses the list to send the message along the most efficient route. The expanded membership is not added to the message header, because this would increase the size of the message. Each address adds between 1 KB and 2 KB to the size of a header, so it doesn't make much sense to take on this overhead, especially when some groups could have thousands of members.

> **Tip**
>
> **Keeping just the group name in the header allows recipients to respond to the message and be sure that Exchange will deliver it to the current membership. It also avoids problems with replies going to nonexistent addresses.**

Protected groups

A protected group is one that is restricted in terms of the users who can send messages. As we have discussed, you can use moderation to protect groups, but you can also restrict from whom a group is willing to accept messages. Figure 6-30 shows the basic approach. Select the group and edit its properties. Go to the Mail Flow Settings property page and select Message Delivery Restrictions. You can then select the users who are allowed to send messages to the group, as well as those who will be explicitly blocked.

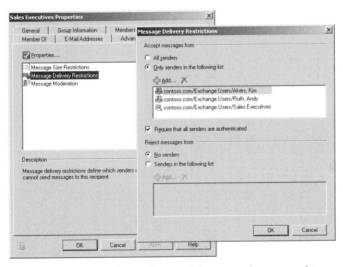

Figure 6-30 Limiting the mailboxes and groups who can send to a group.

Exactly the same step can be taken with EMS using the Set-DistributionGroup cmdlet.

```
Set-DistributionGroup -Identity 'contoso.com/Exchange Users/Sales Executives'
-BypassSecurityGroupManagerCheck -AcceptMessagesOnlyFromSendersOrMembers 'Ruth,
Andy', 'Akers, Kim', 'Sales Executives'
```

You'll notice that in both instances I made sure to allow the members of the group to send messages to the group. Although it is conceivable that you might set up a security group to protect some resource and prevent the group members from being able to send messages to the group, in most cases it is desirable to allow the members to email the group.

Anyone who then attempts to send messages to the protected group will receive a message delivery report (DSN error code 5.7.1) similar to that shown in Figure 6-31. Anyone using a client that supports MailTips will also see a notice appear telling her that she isn't allowed to send messages to the group; however, she can attempt to send the message, and Exchange will duly block the email. Hopefully the text included in the message delivery report is clear enough so that anyone receiving such a response will understand the reason why delivery failed and won't bother the help desk with a request to be able to send email to the protected group.

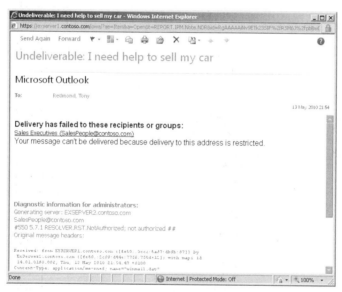

Figure 6-31 Message delivery report for a message sent to a restricted group.

The same error is seen if an external user attempts to send messages to a distribution group that requires sender authentication. By default, Exchange 2010 groups require sender authentication, which means that the sender must be known to the organization before the hub transport service will route incoming messages to the group. If you want to allow external users (perhaps from another Exchange organization in your company) to send messages to a group, you can turn off the authentication requirement by clearing the Require That All Senders Are Authenticated check box under Message Delivery Restrictions for the group, or with a command similar to this:

```
Set-DistributionGroup -Identity 'Exchange 2010 Interest List'
-RequireSenderAuthenticationEnabled $False
```

Self-maintaining groups

In previous books on Exchange, I made the point that group maintenance presented a number of issues for administrators, especially in large organizations where there is a constant flow of demands from users to join or leave groups, or to understand why they couldn't find a particular group or send a message to a group, or even to know the membership of a group. Exchange 2010 still has some deficiencies (how hard would it be to create some UI to generate a nicely formatted report about group membership?) but it has improved the situation with the introduction of MailTips (see Chapter 12, "Mailbox Support Services"), which help stop people from sending messages to very large groups and self-maintaining groups, and which allow you to configure a group's properties so that users can join or leave the group through ECP. As you can see from Figure 6-32, you can also configure the group to be:

- Open: Exchange will honor all requests by users to join or leave the group without question. Universal security groups (USGs) cannot be set to be open because they also hold a security principal that can control access to resources.

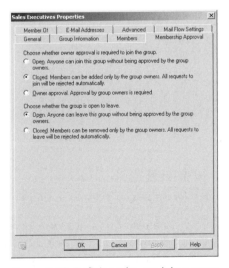

Figure 6-32 Defining who can join a group.

- Closed: Only the group owners can add or delete members from the group. This is the default value and should be set on any USG.

- Approval required: Users can apply to join the group, but the request will only be executed after approval is received from a group owner. The approval process is similar to that used for moderated groups.

Naturally, these criteria can be set through EMS. For example:

```
Set-DistributionGroup –Identity 'Sales Executives' –MemberJoinRestriction 'Closed'
–MemberDepartRestriction 'Open' –AcceptMessagesOnlyFromDLMembers 'Sales Executives'
–Notes 'The Sales Executive group is restricted' –ManagedBy 'Andrews, Ben (IT)'
```

In this case, we set the flags on the Sales Executives group so that its membership is closed for new members (owners can always add new members), that requests to leave the group will receive automatic approval, and that only members of the group are allowed to send messages to the group. Finally, a note is added to tell users that the group is restricted. This note is visible when users view group properties through the GAL.

Viewing group members

The next question that arises after you've populated a group is how to be sure that the right members have been added. It's easy to review the membership of a small group by looking at the group properties with Outlook or OWA, but this approach fails once you have more than 50 members, because the client interface is not really suitable for browsing large groups. It would be nice to find a button that generates a formatted listing of group members, but no client includes this feature and neither does ECP or EMC. If you need to create a list of group members you have to do it with EMS. Here's a one-liner to fetch the membership of a group, select two properties, and pipe the output to a text file:

```
Get-DistributionGroupMember –Identity 'Sales Executives' | Select Name, DisplayName >
C:\TEMP\Sales.txt
```

A variation on the theme would be to pipe the output to a CSV file with the Export-CSV cmdlet that you can then manipulate with Excel to pretty up the report. Sometimes you want to find out how many members are in a distribution group quickly. You can do this as follows:

```
(Get-DistributionGroupMember –Identity 'Sales Executives').Count
```

Some companies don't like the fact that Outlook reveals group membership so easily. They want the ability to stop users from being able to see group members either through the GAL or by expanding the membership of a group after adding it to the header of a message. Common examples of groups that administrators are asked to suppress include confidential senior management teams, external advisors, or members of board committees.

It is possible to set access control lists (ACLs) on groups to block access to all but selected users. However, this arrangement is administratively difficult to control for all but a few groups. A better solution is to create a dummy distribution group that points to the real distribution group, which is marked as hidden from the GAL. In Figure 6-33, we see a group called "GRP-Super Secret Group" that users can see in the GAL. If they look at group membership, they see a pointer to "GRP-Real Secret Group." This group is hidden, so even if users can see it listed as a member of another group, they can't see the membership.

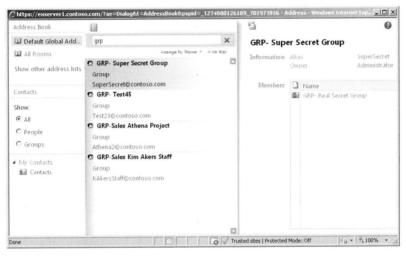

Figure 6-33 Stopping users from viewing group membership.

Using a dynamic distribution group is an even better solution because no client ever exposes the membership of a dynamic group. You can exploit the 15 custom attributes available for mail-enabled objects to assign values that are then used by the filters for dynamic groups. Thus, you could create mail-enabled contacts for the external advisors that you want to hide and put "EXADV" in one of the custom attributes; the board committees might use another attribute, and so on. This is a valuable approach because it can be easily implemented through the existing management tools (EMC and EMS) and doesn't depend on some black magic such as manipulation of ACLs that could be affected by a change in a future version of Windows or Exchange.

INSIDE OUT   An additional control through Outlook 2010

Outlook 2010 imposes an additional control over moderated groups (those that require approval before messages can be sent to them). If you add a moderated group to a message header, right-click and select Expand Group, Outlook will refuse to insert the addresses of individual members of the group into the message header.

Tracking group usage

Groups are very easy to create, are a powerful method to address many recipients at one time, and are reasonably easy to maintain. The only downside is that groups tend to linger in Active Directory well past their "best by" date. It's common to create groups to assist with communication for an event or some other specific purpose. The group is used for many messages in the time leading up to the event. Afterward, it sits in the GAL waiting to be used again and will stay there until an administrator concludes that the group is no longer used and puts it out of its misery. Two questions arise from this scenario. The first is how to know whether groups are being used. The second is what to do with groups that are no longer used.

```
Name                        Count
----                        -----
Sales@contoso.com           12
Marketing@contoso.com       11
Management@contoso.com      9
IT@contoso.com              1
```

There are many ways that you can build on this code. For example, you can check for usage in a particular date range or output data in a form that you can collect from all hub transport servers over time to provide an organization-wide view.

Now that we know how to identify the usage of groups, we can review the groups in the GAL and determine the groups that no one ever uses. If a group hasn't been used in a couple of months, it's a good candidate to be removed—or at least hidden—from the GAL for a month or so to see whether anyone notices. If no one does, then you can safely delete the group.

Dynamic distribution groups

Keeping track of people is generally difficult in large companies, which is why they invest so much money in HR systems. The same challenge exists for messaging administrators and help desk personnel, who can spend a lot of time maintaining the membership of groups as new people join the company, others leave, and others take on new roles and responsibilities. As we have just discussed, populating and maintaining the membership of large distribution groups can be a nuisance for Exchange administrators.

Dynamic distribution groups offer a solution to this problem by allowing groups to be based on a query that Exchange can execute against Active Directory to determine the latest membership every time a message is sent to a group. The success and failure of dynamic distribution groups is entirely dependent on the accuracy of the data held in

Active Directory. A dynamic distribution groups is successful when messages are delivered to the right people all the time, and you can expect success if the properties of mail-enabled objects are maintained in a consistent manner. On the other hand, if the data are inconsistent or not maintained you can expect some "interesting" results when the transport system expands the group to address a message.

It's also fair to say that dynamic distribution groups generate a higher load on hub transport servers than normal groups. Instead of reading group membership when a message is routed, the hub transport server has additional processing to execute the query to determine group membership before a message can be routed. Although most queries are simple and execute quickly, especially on the high-powered server technology in use today, it's also possible to create queries that return thousands of recipients such as "All users in the United States," which will impose some strain as messages are processed. Even so, it's unlikely these groups will be used more than a few times per day and this should not impose too high a performance penalty on any server.

From a user perspective, the only difference between a normal group and a dynamic group is that you cannot view the membership list of a dynamic group by looking at the group properties through the GAL. Dynamic groups don't hold security principals, so they cannot be used to secure objects. Apart from these minor differences, dynamic groups appear very similar to normal groups.

OPATH queries

Behind the scenes, every time a hub transport server processes a message addressed to a dynamic distribution group, it uses the query stored in the group's properties to search Active Directory and expand the group membership into a list of addresses that match the query. Queries are stored in OPATH format. Earlier versions used LDAP queries but OPATH is the default query syntax for Windows PowerShell, so Exchange Server 2007 adopted it as the standard.

A dynamic distribution group stores its query in the *MSExchQueryFilter* property, where you'll find something like this:

```
((RecipientType -eq 'UserMailbox' -and Department -eq 'Sales') -and -not (Name -like
'SystemMailbox{*'))
```

This query looks for all mailboxes that have Sales as the value in their *Department* property. The last part of the query excludes system mailboxes. It is obvious that this query will only work if the value of the *Department* property is maintained. The query won't find mailboxes that belong to the department if the value is left blank or not spelled correctly. In other words, don't expect dynamic distribution lists to be able to understand what Active Directory should contact. These queries operate on precise data.

> **Tip**
>
> Queries used for dynamic distribution groups are scoped to establish what Active Directory objects should be included when the query is evaluated. The scope is stored in the *RecipientContainer* property for the query. It's important to establish the correct scope because this has a dramatic effect on the objects that the query returns and, therefore, on who will receive messages addressed to the group. If the scope is set incorrectly, you might end up with no objects being found, meaning that a message will not reach any recipients. On the other hand, if the scope is set too broadly, a message could be delivered to tens of thousands of mailboxes when you really intended it to go to just a few.

If you're moving from Exchange Server 2003, you might have some of the older LDAP-based query-based distribution groups. You can upgrade these groups to become dynamic distribution groups with the Set-DynamicDistributionGroup cmdlet by specifying the *–ForceUpgrade* parameter. This will upgrade the version of the group and make it manageable by Exchange 2010 and translate the old LDAP query into OPATH format. Both LDAP and OPATH format queries are kept in the group properties to ensure backward compatibility and to ensure that the query is understood by Exchange 2003 transport servers. For example:

```
Set-DynamicDistributionGroup –Identity 'Old Exchange 2003 Users' –ForceUpgrade
```

It is possible that the cmdlet will be unable to translate the LDAP query into OPATH, especially if you built a highly customized LDAP query to use with Exchange Server 2003. In this instance, Exchange will flag an error and you will have to create a new dynamic distribution group to use with Exchange 2010 and replace the older group.

Creating new dynamic distribution groups

You can create precanned or custom OPATH queries for dynamic distribution groups. Precanned queries are the most common but also the most limited, because they are based on restricted criteria. The advantage of precanned queries is that they can be quickly built using an EMC wizard that builds the OPATH query for you. Because they are based on a limited set of criteria, precanned queries are tuned for performance. Custom queries are more flexible because you essentially roll your own OPATH query and add it to the group through EMS. On the other hand, custom queries are harder to build and maintain and usually run a little more slowly than precanned queries.

Before starting the wizard, take the time to figure out three key characteristics of the new group:

- The scope for the query: Active Directory can only return recipients based on the scope of the query that you use. The scope is established by an OU and its children within a single domain; it cannot span multiple OUs. If the recipients that you want to find are in multiple OUs (or domains), you will need to create separate dynamic distribution groups for each OU and then combine the groups together into one "supergroup."

- The recipients: You can include all types of mail-enabled recipients or just a particular type, such as recipients that have Exchange mailboxes.

- Criteria for selection: Precanned queries allow you to filter against the following Active Directory properties:

  - State or Province (StateOrProvince)

  - Department

  - Company

  - Custom Attributes (CustomAttribute1 through CustomAttribute15)

You can specify multiple values for the properties stated in the criteria. For example, you can look for users in the "Sales" and "Marketing" departments that work in the "Coho" or "Coho Winery" company.

The EMC wizard leads you through the selection of the criteria that you want to use plus the values used for any filters. Figure 6-34 shows the set of properties that can be selected for precanned filters.

> **Note**
>
> You have to provide values for Exchange to check against. In this case, we want to find users who are located in Ireland. It's inconvenient that you can't use the *Country* property for this purpose because it seems likely that this property would be one of the more commonly used. However, Microsoft didn't select it, so we've used the *State or Province* property instead. Of course, for the group to be successful, the *State or Province* property will have to be populated with the values for which we are checking.

Figure 6-34 Defining the filter conditions for a dynamic distribution group.

The Preview button in the lower right of Figure 6-34 is tremendously useful because it allows you to test the effectiveness of the filter that you've just created. If Active Directory is populated with the correct values that you've selected, you should see results similar to those shown in Figure 6-35.

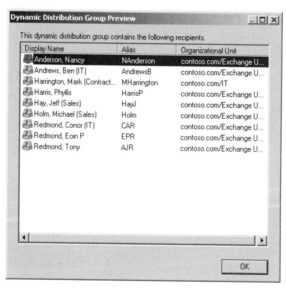

Figure 6-35 Previewing the result of a filter.

> **Tip**
>
> It's a good idea to scan the list of recipients found by the filter to confirm that the right recipients are present and that the list doesn't include a recipient that shouldn't be there. After bad or missing Active Directory data, the most common problem in finding recipients with filters is an incorrect scope. Remember, the filter that Exchange generates will start at a certain OU in Active Directory and find objects in that point and child OUs. It won't find objects elsewhere.

Once you're satisfied that the filter generates the correct result set, you can go ahead and finish the wizard and allow Exchange to create the new dynamic distribution group (Figure 6-36).

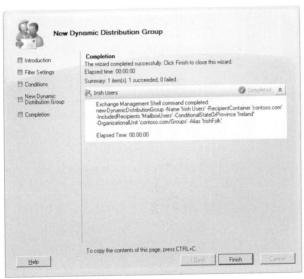

Figure 6-36 Completing the New Dynamic Distribution Group Wizard.

When Exchange saves the new group, it generates the OPATH query and stores it in both OPATH and LDAP format. You can see these queries with the Get-DynamicDistributionGroup cmdlet.

Creating dynamic groups using custom filters

You cannot create a dynamic distribution group through EMC that is based on a custom filter. Instead, you use the New-DynamicDistributionGroup cmdlet in EMS to create the new group and specify the OPATH query that you want to use. For example, here is the one-line command to create a group that contains a recipient filter that includes anyone who works for the Contoso company:

```
New-DynamicDistributionGroup -Alias 'ContosoDynamicDL' -Name 'Contoso Company Users'
-IncludedRecipients 'MailboxUsers' -RecipientContainer 'contoso.com'
-OrganizationalUnit 'contoso.com/Groups'-Managedby 'Administrator'
```

In fact, this is not a very complex filter and it could easily have been generated by the EMC wizard. Note that the *–RecipientContainer* parameter specifies the objects that will form part of the dynamic group based on their place within Active Directory. In this case, we specify the root of the "contoso.com" domain, meaning that any object under this point will be included. After creating the new dynamic distribution group, you can determine whether the filter is precanned or custom with the Get-DynamicDistributionGroup command:

```
Get-DynamicDistributionGroup -Identity 'Contoso Company Users' | Format-List Display-
Name, RecipientFilterType, RecipientFilter, LDAPRecipientFilter
```

```
DisplayName              : Contoso Company Users
RecipientFilterType      : Precanned

RecipientFilter          : ((RecipientType -eq 'UserMailbox') -and
(-not(Name -like 'SystemMailbox{*')) -and (-not(Name -like
'CAS_{*')) -and (-not(RecipientTypeDetailsValue -eq 'MailboxPlan')) -and
(-not(RecipientTypeDetailsValue -eq 'DiscoveryMailbox')) -and
(-not(RecipientTypeDetailsValue -eq 'ArbitrationMailbox') ))

LdapRecipientFilter      : (&(objectClass=user)(objectCategory=person)
(mailNickname=*)(msExchHomeServerName=*)(!(name=System

Mailbox{*))(!(name=CAS_{*))(!(msExchRecipientTypeDetails=16777216))(!(msExchRe-
cipientTypeDetails

=536870912))(!(msExchRecipientTypeDetails=8388608)))
```

Even though we created this dynamic distribution group through EMS, it looks like a pre-canned query, very similar to the filters generated by the EMC wizard. The reason is that Exchange optimizes filters as much as possible when they are created. The examination decided that this filter is really a precanned filter because it does not use any properties outside the set of conditional properties on which precanned filters are based. As you will recall from our earlier discussion, the conditional properties that are available for filtering when you create dynamic distribution groups with EMC are as follows:

- ConditionalDepartment

- ConditionalCompany

- ConditionalStateOrProvince

- The 15 custom attributes (*ConditionalCustomAttribute1* to *ConditionalCustomAttribute15*)

Why have special conditional properties?

The reason this set of special conditional properties exists is very simple. A dynamic distribution group is a recipient object. You can set properties for recipient objects, including the properties that you might want to use when you create a filter. The potential for confusion when setting properties of the group itself and the properties used by the filter that generates the group membership is obvious, so the Exchange developers added the special filtering properties to make it obvious when you want to set a property of the group and when you want to set the value of a property used in a filter.

If the set of special filter properties don't suffice for the filter that you want to create, you can create a custom filter using other properties of recipient objects and store it in the *RecipientFilter* property. Note that if you create a custom filter, you cannot combine it with a precanned filter. The rules of thumb for building filters for dynamic distribution groups are therefore:

- Precanned filters are easiest to build but you are limited to a restricted set of special conditional properties. For example:

```
Set-DynamicDistributionGroup –Identity 'UK Employees'
-ConditionalStateOrProvince 'England', 'Wales', 'Scotland'
-ConditionalCompany ''Contoso', 'Contoso UK',
-ConditionalCustomAttribute1 'Employee'
-IncludedRecipients 'MailboxUsers'
```

In this example, the filter that Exchange uses to build the dynamic group is: Any account from England, Wales, or Scotland that belongs to the company called Contoso or Contoso UK and that has the value "Employee" in custom attribute 1. Any filter that has to check multiple values for a property is evidence of a certain lack of standards in the population of mailbox data. Remember the caveat that although dynamic distribution groups are great ways to address changing populations, they can be slow for the transport service to resolve against Active Directory if more than a few hundred addresses result or if you add many conditions. This is one case where simpler is better.

- As shown in the last example, you can restrict a dynamic distribution group to send messages to a certain set of recipient types by specifying the *–IncludedRecipients* parameter. You can then select from one or more of the following values: AllRecipients, MailboxUsers, Resources, MailContacts, MailGroups, MailUsers, or even None (which would be a kind of non-op).

- If a precanned filter doesn't suffice, you can create a filter query based on a broader range of recipient properties and store it in the –*RecipientFilter* property. You can combine properties to create a filter that is as complex as you like. For example:

```
-RecipientFilter {Company -eq 'Contoso' -and Office -eq 'Dublin' -and
Department ne 'Sales' -and ServerName -eq 'ExServer1' -and CustomAttribute15
-eq 'Employee'}
```

- You cannot combine precanned and custom filters in a dynamic distribution group.

To illustrate the point, let's create a dynamic distribution group that is useful to administrators. In previous versions of Exchange, it was common to manage users on a server basis, so it's a good idea to have a dynamic group that sends messages to everyone whose mailbox is on a specific server so that we can advise them about important issues such as server outages for planned maintenance. The command to create a new dynamic distribution group with a recipient filter that includes all the mailboxes on an Exchange server is shown next. We have to use a custom filter in this case because 'ServerName' is not one of the set of special properties supported by precanned filters.

```
New-DynamicDistributionGroup -Name 'Mailboxes on ExServer1'
-Alias MbxSvr1 -RecipientContainer 'contoso.com' -OrganizationalUnit Groups
-RecipientFilter {ServerName -eq 'ExServer1'}
```

This code works superbly for Exchange 2007, but poses a problem for Exchange 2010, because you cannot predict what Exchange 2010 server hosts a mailbox because the connection between database and server is broken as part of the introduction of the DAG feature (see Chapter 8, "Exchange's Search for High Availability," for more information). The dynamic group created with the preceding code still works on Exchange 2010, but there is no guarantee that we can communicate with the desired target audience if the database that holds their mailboxes has moved to a different server. Therefore, we need to create a dynamic group that addresses messages to all of the mailboxes in a database rather than one that addresses them to all of the mailboxes on a server. This is slightly more difficult because Exchange requires you to pass the full distinguished name of the target mailbox database as part of the filter rather than a simple display name. The logic is probably that the full distinguished name ensures that you always use the right database. In any case, the command to create a new dynamic group to address mailboxes in the VIP Mailboxes database is as follows:

```
New-DynamicDistributionGroup -Name 'VIP Mailboxes' -Alias 'VIPList'
-RecipientContainer 'contoso.com' -OrganizationalUnit 'Exchange Groups'
-RecipientFilter {(RecipientType -eq 'UserMailbox' -and Database -eq "CN=VIP
```

```
Mailboxes,CN=Databases,CN=Exchange Administrative Group (FYDIBOHF23SPDLT),
CN=Administrative Groups,CN=contoso,CN=Microsoft Exchange,CN=Services,
CN=Configuration,DC=contoso,DC=com")}
```

Being forced to use the full distinguished name for the target mailbox database makes the command more complicated than before because the distinguished names for any Exchange object contain some historical elements that make the name longer than it needs to be. You can use the Get-MailboxDatabase cmdlet to find the full distinguished name of a mailbox database as follows. When the commands execute, the $DN variable contains the distinguished name. Be sure to use the exact value in the filter and don't insert any additional spaces between the components of the distinguished name.

```
$DB = Get-MailboxDatabase -Identity 'VIP Mailboxes'; $DN = $DB.DistinguishedName
```

Before you create the new group, you can test the effectiveness of the filter by passing it to the Get-Mailbox cmdlet. If the filter works with Get-Mailbox, it will work as a custom recipient filter for a dynamic group. For example:

```
Get-Mailbox -Filter {(RecipientType -eq 'UserMailbox' -and Database -eq "CN=VIP
Mailboxes,CN=Databases,CN=Exchange Administrative Group (FYDIBOHF23SPDLT),
CN=Administrative Groups,CN=contoso,CN=Microsoft Exchange,CN=Services,
CN=Configuration,DC=contoso,DC=com")}
```

Once the new group is created, you can review its properties, including the custom filter, through EMC (Figure 6-37).

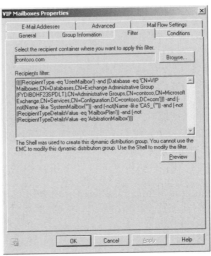

Figure 6-37 Viewing a custom filter used for a dynamic distribution group.

INSIDE OUT Changes to recipient types for custom filters

The recipient filter shown in EMC has been amended by Exchange to exclude some special recipient types. The Preview button works in the same way as for precanned filters, so you can test the effectiveness of your custom filter. You cannot use EMC to edit a custom recipient filter created for a dynamic distribution group. The only way to edit a custom filter is to create a new recipient filter and update the group with the Set-DynamicDistributionGroup cmdlet.

There is no equivalent to the Get-DistributionGroupMember cmdlet available to list the membership of dynamic distribution groups. You can use the EMC Preview option to view group membership or pass the filter to the Get-Mailbox or Get-Recipient cmdlets as described earlier to generate the recipient set. If desired, you can pipe the output from either cmdlet to a text file for easy review.

Moderated recipients

Exchange 2010 allows you to apply moderation to mailboxes, contacts, and distribution groups. When moderation is enabled, it means that any message addressed to the recipient must first pass through a moderation phase to approve or reject the message. Rejected messages are returned to the sender and approved messages are allowed through for delivery to the original recipient. Moderation occurs in the transport service as a form of rule applied to messages after they are submitted by the Store Driver on a mailbox server. Scenarios in which moderation is useful include the protection of sensitive mailboxes (such as those of executives) by forcing communications to be moderated by someone like an administrator, or external contacts that might be published in the GAL to which you want to restrict communication from specific people who represent your company. Because they are often used to debate issues and post information that is of wide interest to many people, groups are possibly the most obvious target for moderation, so we will begin this discussion by looking at how to protect groups as an example of how the feature works.

Many companies use distribution groups as a convenient way of communicating with large audiences. It is very convenient to be able to send a message and have it delivered to many people, but sometimes you want to ensure that only appropriate content is sent to large distributions. Moderation is a very effective way of restricting the mailboxes and groups that can send new messages to a group. Figure 6-38 shows the properties of a group as it is enabled for moderation. In this case we've created a group to facilitate discussion about Exchange 2010.

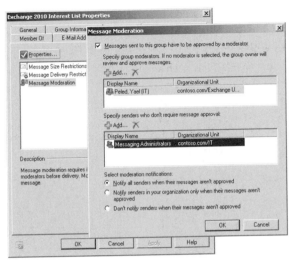

Figure 6-38 Setting the moderation properties for a group.

It's possible that members might send inappropriate messages to the group (such as advertisements for products or other services). We want to keep the discussion focused so we nominate a moderator to review all of the messages sent to the group. You can also see that we can exclude some senders from moderation, meaning that any messages that they send will be posted without checking. The IT department will probably know something about Exchange 2010 so we'll let the messaging administrators post directly to the list. We also configure the properties so that only internal users receive notifications if their messages are declined. It is a bad idea to send these notifications to "everyone" because spammers could end up receiving a confirmation that they have sent a message to a valid email address.

The EMS code to set the same properties to moderate messages going to the group is as follows:

```
Set-DistributionGroup –Identity 'Exchange 2010 Interest List' –ModerationEnabled
$True –ModeratedBy 'Peled, Yael (IT)' –ByPassModerationFromSendersOrMembers
'Messaging Administrators' –ByPassNestedModerationEnabled $True
–SendModerationNotifications Internal
```

Note the use of the *–ByPassNestedModerationEnabled* parameter. When set to $True, any nested groups that also require moderation are governed by the decision of the moderator of the group to which the message is addressed. In other words, if you send a message to a group called Investment Approvals that contains another moderated group called Management Committee, Exchange first sends the message to the moderator of Investment Approvals. If approval is received, Exchange then validates whether nested moderation is enabled. If yes (the flag is True), Exchange distributes the message to nongroup recipients

Chapter 6

of Investment Approval and sends an approval request to the moderator of the Management Committee group, who can approve or reject the request for distribution to the members of this group.

> **Tip**
>
> To avoid excessive delays for messages (and create less work for moderators), it's a good idea to enable nested moderation for all but the most sensitive groups.

After a group is set up for moderation, Exchange automatically displays a MailTip to warn users when they address a message to the group. The warning tells the user that his message might not be delivered immediately because it has to go through a moderation process to gain approval before final delivery (Figure 6-39).

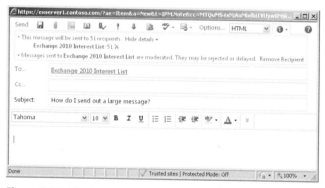

Figure 6-39 Viewing the MailTip that warns about a moderated group.

> **Tip**
>
> Moderation is a new Exchange 2010 feature so it won't work if a legacy Exchange server expands group membership when a message is processed by the transport system. To avoid this problem, you can set the properties of moderated groups so that they are always expanded by an Exchange 2010 hub transport server. See the "Group expansion" section earlier in this chapter for information how to define an explicit hub transport server to be used for group expansion.

How to enable moderation for dynamic distribution groups

Dynamic distribution groups support moderation; However, you cannot enable moderation for these groups through EMC because the EMC UI does not support this feature. You can enable moderation of a dynamic group through EMS but the range of parameters is a little less functional than is supported for normal groups. For example, the discussion about moderation of messages sent to nested groups is moot because dynamic distribution groups don't support this feature, so any message sent to a dynamic group whose resolved membership includes other moderated groups will require separate approvals for each group.

To enable moderation for a dynamic distribution group, we need code like this:

```
Set-DynamicDistributionGroup -Identity 'Sales Users' -ModerationEnabled $True
-ModeratedBy 'Redmond, Tony' -ByPassModerationFromSendersOrMembers 'Sales
Department' -SendModerationNotifications Internal
```

Apart from the missing UI in EMC, moderation for dynamic distribution groups works in the same way as for other moderated recipients.

Moderation requests

Moderators receive messages similar to the one shown in Figure 6-40 to allow them to approve or reject a message. The process is very straightforward and only requires a simple click from the moderator to allow the message to proceed. When multiple users are assigned to be moderators for mail-enabled objects, Exchange delivers copies of messages for moderation to every moderator. The first moderator who processes the request determines its outcome. In other words, if moderation requests go to two moderators and the first moderator approves the request, Exchange will respect that decision even if the second moderator attempts to decline the request a few seconds later. Once a response is received, Exchange removes the moderation request from the mailboxes of the other moderators.

Logically, moderators are automatically excluded from moderation because a moderator is always regarded to be a "trusted sender." Group owners are also excluded from moderation on the basis that if someone owns a group, she should be able to send to the group membership without hindrance. Also, if you don't assign a moderator to a group, the group owner automatically fulfills the moderation role and receives the requests for approval to send to the group.

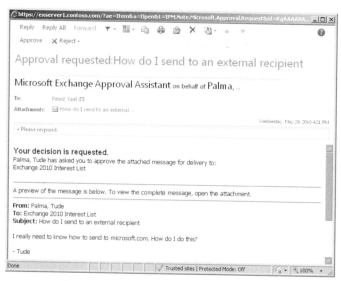

Figure 6-40 A request to approve a message posted to a moderated group.

Behind the scenes, the transport service is responsible for detecting when a message is sent to a moderated recipient. Previous versions of Exchange do not support moderated recipients, so moderation does not occur if a message sent to a group is processed by an Exchange 2007 hub transport server. The solution to this problem is to configure the moderated group to always use an Exchange 2010 hub transport server. For example:

```
Set-DistributionGroup -Identity 'Exchange 2010 Interest List' -ExpansionServer
'ExServer3'
```

Of course, mailboxes and mail-enabled contacts don't use expansion servers, so this solution is not available for these objects. Instead, the hub transport servers in the sites that host these objects should be running Exchange 2010 (hub transport servers are usually deployed before mailbox servers) and this will take care of the problem.

When the categorizer running on a hub transport server detects a moderated recipient, it routes the message to an arbitration mailbox. This is a temporary holding location where the Store keeps moderated messages until they can be processed by a human. In this case, messages remain in the arbitration mailbox until they are approved or rejected by the group moderator who receives the requests for approval in her mailbox alongside regular messages.

Approved messages are then rerouted to the group and delivered as normal, while declined messages are returned to the original sender. A process called the Information Assistant is responsible for monitoring messages in the arbitration mailbox and routing them after approvals or rejections are received from a moderator. The Information Assistant also cleans up the arbitration mailbox by removing old or orphaned requests that can accumulate there.

> **Note**
> The default expiry time for moderated messages is five days; this interval cannot be configured in Exchange 2010. Once a message expires, Exchange returns it to the originator with a note indicating that delivery didn't occur because the moderator failed to make a decision.

Users can see the current status of a message awaiting moderator approval through delivery or message tracking reports but cannot do anything to encourage moderators to take action except to send them a message (which they might ignore) or to phone them.

Exchange does not maintain a special queue for messages awaiting moderation that an administrator can view to prompt a moderator to take action or to redirect a message if a moderator is unavailable for any reason. In addition, an administrator cannot log onto the arbitration mailbox to action a message awaiting approval. Everything awaits moderator approval and, if it doesn't come and a message expires, the moderator cannot take further action. The message is returned to the originator with a reject status.

Messages can be sent to recipient lists that include moderated and nonmoderated recipients. In this case, the transport service bifurcates the message and delivers a copy immediately to the nonmoderated recipients. A separate copy is delivered to the arbitration mailbox to await attention from a moderator. It's possible that a moderated group can contain subgroups, some of which also require moderation. You can allow a separate moderation process to occur for each group or you can mark the group to allow automatic approval for all subgroups by setting its *–AutoApproveNestedDLEnabled* flag. For example:

```
Set-DistributionGroup -Identity 'Exchange 2010 Interest List'
 -AutoApproveNestedDLEnabled $True
```

> **Journaling messages**
> If you enable journaling, Exchange journals the messages as they pass through the arbitration mailbox. The following stages are captured:
>
> - The approval request from the arbitration mailbox to the moderator. The original message is captured as an attachment to this message.
>
> - The approval or reject decision from the moderator to the arbitration mailbox.
>
> - If the message is approved, journaling captures the final message sent to the members of the distribution group.

An arbitration mailbox is created automatically when you install Exchange. Apart from other functions such as storing mailbox search metadata, this mailbox is used to process moderated messages for every moderated object unless you decide to create and use additional arbitration mailboxes. You are unlikely to need additional arbitration mailboxes unless you need to spread the processing load across multiple sites because you make heavy use of moderated recipients. Exchange does not load-balance moderated recipients across available arbitration mailboxes; you will have to do this manually by setting the *ArbitrationMailbox* property on the recipient to force it to use a specific arbitration mailbox. For example:

```
Set-DistributionGroup –Identity 'Exchange 2010 Interest List' –ArbitrationMailbox
'ArbMbx London'
```

Moderated mailboxes

Moderated mailboxes are another common scenario in many Exchange deployments where the need exists to protect mailboxes that the company might deem sensitive. Moderation provides an effective solution to this problem, but you can only set up moderation for mailboxes through EMS. In this example, we set moderation for the CEO's mailbox where the processing of incoming messages is done by the executive assistant. As you can see in Figure 6-41, a MailTip is displayed when users address email to the CEO's mailbox. You can see that Exchange also displays a default MailTip because the mailbox is moderated to tell users of a potential delay in delivery, but it is good to provide an additional level of detail in a custom MailTip to emphasize the point.

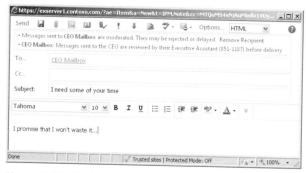

Figure 6-41 Viewing MailTips information for a moderated mailbox.

We discuss how Exchange 2010 implements mail tips and the clients that support this feature in Chapter 12. In the meantime, this command sets up moderation for the CEO mailbox, establishes a list of users whose messages will bypass moderation, and creates the customized MailTip.

```
Set-Mailbox –Identity 'CEO Mailbox' –ModeratedBy 'CEO Executive Assistant'
–ModerationEnabled $True –ByPassModerationFromSendersOrMembers 'Executive Committee'
```

```
-MailTip 'Messages sent to the CEO are reviewed by their Executive Assistant
(851-1187) before delivery'
```

You can only assign the responsibility for moderation to other mailboxes and cannot assign this task to a distribution group, even a security group. Instead, if you want to assign moderation to multiple users, you have to specify each mailbox individually. For example:

```
Set-Mailbox -Identity 'CEO Mailbox' -ModerationEnabled $True -ModeratedBy 'CEO
Executive Assistant', 'CEO Support Team'
```

Finally, we can protect mail-enabled contacts. This command shows how we might apply moderation to a mail contact that points to an external recipient for our public relations (PR) agency. We don't want everyone in the company to communicate with the agency, so we apply moderation and set up a bypass for the members of the marketing department.

```
Set-MailContact -Identity 'PR Agency' -ModeratedBy 'PR Administrator'
-ModerationEnabled $True -ByPassModerationFromSendersOrMembers 'Marketing Dept'
```

Mail-enabled contacts

Mail-enabled contacts are a convenient way to add external correspondents to the GAL. Typically, contacts represent people working in other companies to whom a number of users need to send messages on a frequent basis. They are commonly used to facilitate contact with specific individuals or utility mailboxes for external vendors such as PR agencies. To create a new contact, under Recipient Configuration, go to the Mail Contact section and click New Mail Contact in the action pane. The wizard is very straightforward, because essentially all you're doing is creating an Active Directory object to hold some details of the contact including her email address.

Creating a mail contact with EMS is more interesting because more options are exposed. Here's an example of a command that creates a new mail-enabled contact. Note that the email address must be unique.

```
New-MailContact -ExternalEmailAddress 'SMTP:JackJones@gmail.com' -Name 'Jones, Jack'
-Alias 'JackJones' -FirstName 'Jack' -Initials '' -LastName 'Jones'
-OrganizationalUnit 'contoso.com/Exchange Contacts'
```

This command uses only a small subset of available parameters to manage the new mail contact. For example, you can define that the mail contact should only receive messages in plain text format of a maximum message size.

```
Set-MailContact -Identity 'Jones, David' -MessageFormat 'Text' -MessageBodyFormat
'Text' -MaxReceiveSize 200KB -UsePreferMessageFormat $False
```

Like other mail-enabled objects, contacts support moderation, so you can assign a moderator for the contact so that any messages sent to it will be redirected to another user for approval before they are transmitted to the contact by Exchange. Let's assume that we have a contact for a PR agency but don't want everyone in the organization to send requests for interviews, new advertising campaigns, and other requests to the agency. You could channel these messages to a moderator with a command like this. You'll notice that I like to use the new MailTips feature (see Chapter 12) to provide users with an immediate indication that sending to a contact might not result in immediate delivery.

```
Set-MailContact -Identity 'PR Agency' -ModeratedBy 'Cook, Kevin'
-ModerationEnabled $True SendModeratorNotifications 'Always' -MailTip 'Messages to
the PR Agency are moderated by Kevin Cook'
```

Another way of putting a block on users sending to a contact is to set it up so that Exchange will only allow messages sent by specific users. Using a group for this purpose is the most convenient method from an administration perspective.

```
Set-MailContact -Identity 'PR Agency' -AcceptMessagesOnlyFromSendersOrMembers
'PR Department' -MailTip 'Only members of the PR department are allowed to
communicate with our PR agency'
```

Mail users

Mail users are much like contacts in that both object types have external email addresses. However, there is one important difference: Contacts are usually linked to people who have no relationship with your organization, but mail users are linked to Active Directory accounts. You can therefore think of mail contacts as being most suitable for people who work outside your company, whereas mail users are often the most appropriate choice for those who work inside the company.

INSIDE OUT   Mail users and security groups

In essence, Exchange supports this recipient type to enable you to incorporate users in the GAL even when they use a different email system. Because mail users are linked to Active Directory accounts, they are also security principals and can therefore be added to security distribution groups that grant access to resources. You can add contacts to security groups, too, but this has no effect other than allowing the contacts to receive any messages sent to the group.

Mail users don't have their own section in EMC, because they are treated as a form of contacts. Go to contacts and click New Mail User in the action pane to start the New Mail User Wizard. When you create a mail user, you associate it with an existing Active Directory account or create a new account. In the latter case, you have to provide details for the account in much the same way as you do when you create a new account for a mailbox. The first screen of the wizard collects information such as the first and last name. The second (Figure 6-42) then collects the email address for the user.

The code generated by EMC to create a new mail user looks very similar to the code used to create a new mailbox:

```
New-MailUser -Name 'Hamlin, Jay' -Alias 'HamlinJay' -OrganizationalUnit
'contoso.com/Users' -UserPrincipalName 'Hamlin@contoso.com' -SamAccountName 'Hamlin'
-FirstName 'Jay' -Initials '' -LastName 'Hamlin' -Password
'System.Security.SecureString' -ResetPasswordOnNextLogon $True
-ExternalEmailAddress 'SMTP:Jay.Hamlin@sendmail.contoso.com'
```

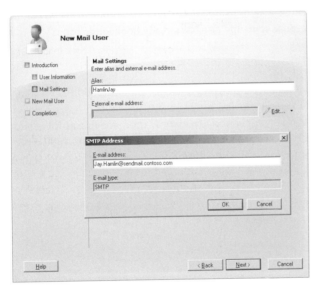

Figure 6-42 Creating a new mail user.

Like contacts, mail users support moderation and MailTips. However, EMS is a little inconsistent in its cmdlets because you cannot set up a MailTip with the New-MailUser cmdlet. Instead, you have to apply the MailTip after the mail user is created with the Set-MailUser cmdlet. For example:

```
Set-MailUser -Identity 'Hamlin, Jay' -MailTip 'Messages sent to this address only
support plain text messages'
```

Resource mailboxes

Exchange 2010 and Exchange 2007 support mailboxes that are configured to represent rooms that can be added to meeting requests. Equipment mailboxes are a further mailbox variation that can be attached to rooms to represent the various items that support meetings in the room such as whiteboards, projectors, and tables. Although all mailboxes occupy space in databases, room and equipment mailboxes are differentiated through the type assigned to the mailboxes and the properties that you can set on the mailboxes. Collectively, room and equipment mailboxes are referred to as resource mailboxes.

> **Note**
>
> Resource mailboxes have disabled Windows accounts. To create a separation between normal user accounts and resource mailboxes, it's a good idea to place these accounts in a separate Active Directory OU. No one ever needs to log onto a room or equipment mailbox to process the meeting requests that they receive. As we'll see, the Resource Booking Attendant is able to handle these requests automatically to confirm the booking or deny it because someone else has already booked the room.

Despite the fact that Exchange provides a useful All Rooms address list that you can use to filter out room mailboxes when you browse the GAL (Figure 6-43), it's still important that you use a suitable naming convention to identify room mailboxes for users. Some companies name their rooms after cities, others after important or well-known people, and others after scientific inventions. Whatever convention you adopt, make sure that it is used consistently to help users find rooms easily.

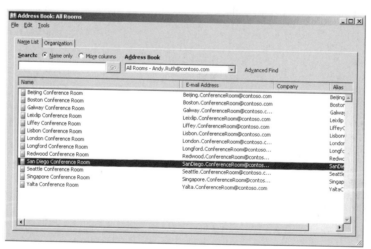

Figure 6-43 Viewing room mailboxes in the GAL.

Outlook and OWA clients can include room mailboxes in calendar requests. As shown in Figure 6-44, the OWA scheduling assistant makes a clear distinction between meeting attendees and the room selected for the meeting when a user creates a meeting. The Outlook version of the scheduling assistant allows you to input the name of a room into the attendee list or pick a room by clicking Add Room.

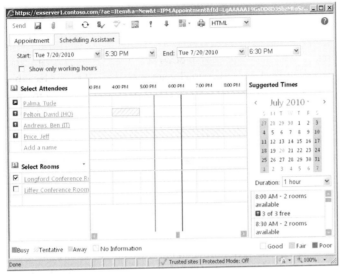

Figure 6-44 Including rooms in an OWA meeting request.

You can discover the current set of room mailboxes with this command:

```
Get-Mailbox –Filter {ResourceType –eq 'Room'} | Format-Table Name, Res* -AutoSize
```

Name	ResourceCapacity	ResourceCustom	ResourceType
----	----------------	--------------	------------
Conference Room 14341		{}	Room
Executive Conference Room		{}	Room
Preston Conference Room		{}	Room
Liffey Conference Room		{}	Room
London Conference Room	16	{Concall}	Room
Lisbon Conference Room	24	{Concall}	Room
Longford Conference Room		{}	Room
Leitrim Conference Room	24	{Concall}	Room
Liverpool Conference Room	50	{Whiteboard, Concall, HALO}	Room
Leixlip Conference Room	100	{TV}	Room

Defining custom properties for resource mailboxes

We see two properties listed that can be used to communicate details about the rooms to users when they decide which room they'd like to book. The *ResourceCapacity* property is used to state the number of people that can fit in the room. This is purely advisory because Exchange doesn't apply any intelligence to meeting requests to check that the number of attendees listed doesn't exceed the capacity of the selected room. The *ResourceCustom* property allows administrators to indicate whether anything special is available in the room. Before you can populate any value into the *ResourceCustom* property, you have to create a set of custom properties for the resource configuration with the Set-ResourceConfig cmdlet. For example, this command creates a basic set of different items that you might find in a room:

```
Set-ResourceConfig -ResourcePropertySchema ("Room/TV", "Room/Concall", "Room/HALO",
"Room/Whiteboard", "Room/Video", "Room/ComfortableChairs")
```

You'll note that the resource values can't have spaces. There is no UI in EMC or ECP to manage the set of custom properties. If you need to update the set of custom properties you can either rewrite the complete set or update the current set with a few lines of EMS code. For example:

```
$CurrentConfig = Get-ResourceConfig
$CurrentConfig.ResourcePropertySchema+="Room/PictureWindow"
Set-ResourceConfig -ResourcePropertySchema $CurrentConfig.ResourcePropertySchema
```

Note that the set of custom properties can also contain properties that are used to differentiate equipment mailboxes. All of the entries in the set that we have seen so far are prefixed with "Room/" so Exchange knows that these properties only apply to room mailboxes. Properties used with equipment mailboxes are prefixed with "Equipment/" and can be added as described earlier. Once the resource configuration is populated, if a room is equipped with the HP Halo Communications System, this could be indicated as such by setting the property as follows:

```
Set-Mailbox -Identity 'Liverpool Conference Room' -ResourceCustom ('HALO')
```

This command will overwrite any existing custom properties that exist for the mailbox. If multiple custom resources are available in a room, you can populate them like this:

```
Set-Mailbox -Identity 'Liverpool Conference Room' -ResourceCustom ('HALO', 'Concall')
```

Of course, you can also set these properties through EMC by selecting the mailbox and then going to the Resource General tab. Figure 6-45 shows the custom property picker that exposes the set of properties defined with the Set-ResourceConfig cmdlet. Because we've selected a room mailbox, it follows that Exchange has applied a filter so that the picker only displays the custom properties applicable to room mailboxes.

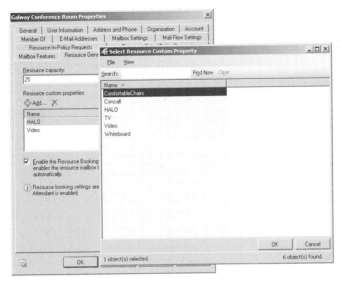

Figure 6-45 Setting custom properties for a room mailbox.

Providing policy direction to the Resource Booking Attendant

Another important property is shown on the Resource General tab. When you enable the Resource Booking Attendant, you instruct Exchange that the attendant should monitor incoming meeting requests for the room to decide whether or not the requests should be accepted. The policy set for the room mailbox determines the action that the Resource Booking Attendant takes. Each room mailbox can have a distinct booking policy that you can see through the Resource Policy tab.

Figure 6-46 illustrates two important property tabs that provide the direction to the Resource Booking Attendant: the Resource Information tab and the Resource Policy tab.

The Resource Information tab defines how the attendant handles items that it adds to the calendar of the room mailbox. This information is exposed if a user browses the room's calendar to look for a suitable time to schedule a meeting. Attachments, comments, and subjects for meetings are removed because they often contain confidential information that you don't want all to see if they look for a meeting slot. You can also see that a property governs how noncalendar items are processed when they are delivered to the mailbox. Room mailboxes have SMTP addresses and can be sent normal email like any other mailbox. Telling Exchange to remove noncalendar items as they arrive keeps the mailbox from filling up with unwanted material. The Calendar Assistant can be configured to remove old meeting requests and responses from a room mailbox, but you can also apply a retention policy to room mailboxes to have old items cleaned up from their calendar after a suitable period (maybe two years).

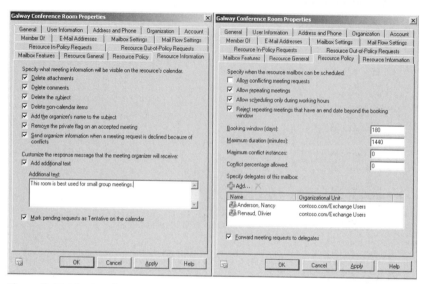

Figure 6-46 Viewing the resource information and booking policy for a room mailbox.

At the bottom of the Resource Information tab, you can see that an administrator can provide some additional text that the attendant inserts into messages that confirm and deny meeting requests. Administrators often use this property to describe the room or provide some information about how people can find the room if it's located in one of the cube-filled labyrinths favored by large corporations. You can see how this text appears to users in the example illustrated in Figure 6-47.

The Resource Policy tab defines basic rules for the Resource Booking Attendant to follow when it examines incoming meeting requests. Basic conditions include items such as whether the room is available outside normal working hours, how long meetings can last (the default is 1,440 minutes, or 24 hours; while this allows for all-day meetings, you might want to shorten the value), and whether to accept requests to schedule repeated meetings such as a team meeting that occurs at the same time every week. It's also possible to prevent people from booking rooms too far in advance (180 days is the default) and to apply some level of automation to the resolution of conflicting requests. For example, the Conflict Percentage Allowed property is used to set a threshold for the instances of a recurring meeting that create conflicts. For example, if this property is set to 20, then any request for a recurring meeting will be declined if more than 20 percent of the meeting instances cause a conflict.

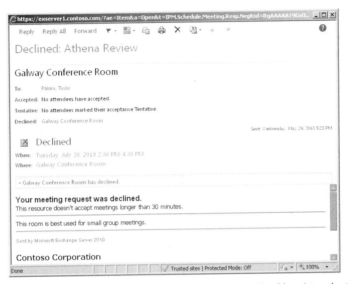

Figure 6-47 A meeting is declined by the Resource Booking Attendant.

INSIDE OUT   Meeting room conflicts

In reality, the most senior person will get to hold his meeting in the room, but because Exchange is unaware of company structure and politics all it can do is allow you to define whether conflicting requests are accepted or immediately declined and, if accepted, how many conflict instances are permitted for a time slot. It would be silly to allow an unlimited number of conflicts to be scheduled, because this would create some aggravating situations when multiple teams turn up in the same place at the same time for their meetings. However, it may be acceptable to allow one or two conflicts if you have someone who checks the room's calendar from time to time to introduce some human intelligence to the conflict resolution algorithm.

To allow access to the calendar of a room mailbox, you use the Add-MailboxPermission cmdlet to assign the *ChangePermission* right to the user to whom you want to grant access to the calendar.

```
Add-MailboxPermission -AccessRights FullAccess -User 'Smith, Samantha' -Identity
'Galway Conference Room'
```

Once the permission to access the calendar is assigned, the assignee can open the calendar just like any other shared calendar and browse the entries to resolve conflicts (Figure 6-48).

Chapter 6

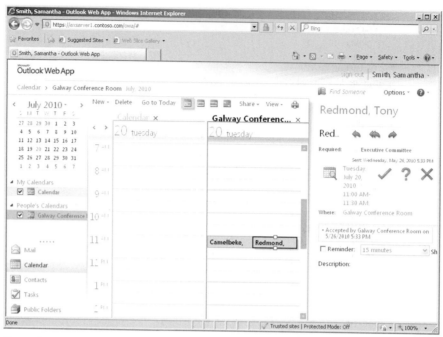

Figure 6-48 Accessing a room's calendar to resolve conflicts.

The calendar properties that influence policy can be accessed with the Get-Calendar-Processing cmdlet. Note that these properties are present for all mailboxes and not just room mailboxes. For now, we'll examine the calendar processing properties for a room:

```
Get-CalendarProcessing –Identity 'Leixlip Conference Room' | Format-Table
```

```
AutomateProcessing              : AutoAccept
AllowConflicts                  : False
BookingWindowInDays             : 180
MaximumDurationInMinutes        : 60
AllowRecurringMeetings          : True
EnforceSchedulingHorizon        : True
ScheduleOnlyDuringWorkHours     : True
ConflictPercentageAllowed       : 0
MaximumConflictInstances        : 20
ForwardRequestsToDelegates      : True
DeleteAttachments               : True
DeleteComments                  : True
RemovePrivateProperty           : True
DeleteSubject                   : True
AddOrganizerToSubject           : True
DeleteNonCalendarItems          : True
TentativePendingApproval        : True
```

```
EnableResponseDetails                      : True
OrganizerInfo                              : True
ResourceDelegates                          : {contoso.com/Exchange Users/Smith,
Samantha}
RequestOutOfPolicy                         : {contoso/Exchange Users/VIP-Con-
tracts Staff}
AllRequestOutOfPolicy                      : False
BookInPolicy                               :
AllBookInPolicy                            : True
RequestInPolicy                            :
AllRequestInPolicy                         : False
AddAdditionalResponse                      : True
AdditionalResponse                         : This room is best suited for IT
department meetings.
RemoveOldMeetingMessages                   : True
AddNewRequestsTentatively                  : True
ProcessExternalMeetingMessages             : False
RemoveForwardedMeetingNotifications        : False
Identity                                   : contoso.com/Exchange Users/Leixlip
Conference Room
```

Properties can be updated with the Set-CalendarProcessing cmdlet. For example, to restrict booking slots to 45 minutes and to only accept booking requests up to 120 days in advance:

```
Set-CalendarProcessing –Identity 'Leixlip Conference Room'
–MaximumDurationInMinutes 45 –BookingWindowInDays 120
```

> **Note**
>
> The Get-CalendarProcessing and Set-CalendarProcessing cmdlets replace the Get-MailboxCalendarSettings and Set-MailboxCalendarSetting cmdlets used in Exchange 2007, so you will have to update code if you have any scripts that use these cmdlets.

You can set the available hours for a room mailbox with the Set-MailboxCalendarConfiguration cmdlet. First, let's find out what the current settings are with the Get-MailboxCalendarConfiguration cmdlet. An edited version of its output is shown here:

```
Get-MailboxCalendarConfiguration –Identity 'Leixlip Conference Room' | Format-List
```

```
WorkDays                 : Weekdays
WorkingHoursStartTime    : 08:00:00
WorkingHoursEndTime      : 17:00:00
WorkingHoursTimeZone     : Pacific Standard Time
WeekStartDay             : Sunday
```

Because booking meeting rooms is a time-sensitive activity, it's important to set the mailbox's time zone correctly so that it corresponds to the location of the meeting room. The default time zone is inherited from the server where the mailbox is created. In this case, we know that PST is inappropriate because our room is located in Dublin, so we update the time zone property as follows:

```
Set-MailboxCalendarConfiguration –Identity Leixlip 'Conference Room'
–WorkingHoursTimeZone 'GMT Standard Time'
```

Processing meeting requests according to policy

The *AutomateProcessing* property of a room mailbox tells the Resource Booking Assistant how to handle incoming meeting requests within the structure established by the booking policy for the mailbox. Three values can be present:

- *None*: Exchange does not process incoming meeting requests

- *AutoUpdate*: This is the default setting for all mailboxes (including room mailboxes) and it allows the Calendar Assistant to place tentative meeting requests into user calendars without any intervention on the part of the user. The user has to open and respond to the meeting request before it is confirmed or rejected.

- *AutoAccept*: This is the value set when you enable the Resource Booking Assistant for a room mailbox. The Resource Booking Assistant is able to process incoming requests and accept or reject them according to policy.

Requests to include room mailboxes in meetings will be either in-policy or out-of-policy. In-policy means that the request complies with the policy because it's inside the time permitted to book the room, is a suitable length, doesn't conflict with other requests, and so on. Table 6-5 lists the properties that influence how the Resource Booking Assistant applies policy to incoming meeting requests for a room. You can see how these properties are shown for a mailbox in Figure 6-49.

Table 6-5 Properties that influence processing of room bookings

Property	Meaning
AllBookInPolicy	If $True, the assistant automatically approves in-policy requests to book the room from all users.
AllRequestInPolicy	If $True, the assistant tentatively accepts in-policy requests to book the room from all users. Requests will have to be approved by a room delegate unless the *AllBookInPolicy* property is $True.
AllRequestOutofPolicy	Governs whether out-of-policy requests are acceptable for the room. All such requests have to be approved by a room delegate.

BookInPolicy	Lists the users whose requests to book the room are automatically accepted.
RequestInPolicy	Lists the users who are allowed to submit in-policy requests to book the room. All requests have to be approved by a room delegate.
RequestOutOfPolicy	Lists the users who are allowed to submit out-of-policy requests to book the room. All requests have to be approved by a room delegate.
ProcessExternalMeetingMessages	Determines whether meeting requests will be accepted from users outside the Exchange organization.

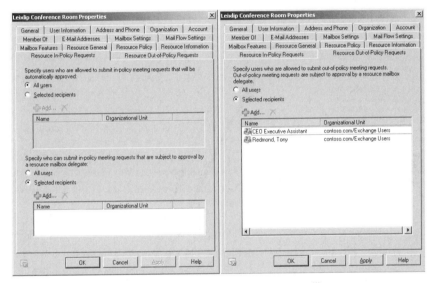

Figure 6-49 Viewing booking policy properties for a room mailbox.

Examining the properties illustrated in Figure 6-50, we see the following:

- All users are allowed to send in-policy requests to book the room (*AllBookInPolicy* and *AllRequestInPolicy* are $True). No special restriction is in place for approving requests from any particular user (the *BookInPolicy* and *RequestInPolicy* properties are empty).

- Out-of-policy requests are accepted from the "CEO Executive Assistant" mailbox and my mailbox for approval by a room delegate (the *RequestOutofPolicy* property is populated with this information).

No user interface exposes the *ProcessExternalMeetingMessages* property. By default, this is set to $False so incoming room requests from external senders will be ignored. If set to

Chapter 6

$True, the Resource Booking Assistant applies the same policy conditions that exist for internal requests.

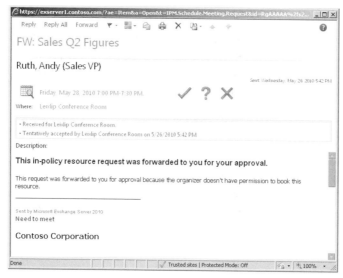

Figure 6-50 Viewing a room request sent to a delegate.

Naturally, you can manipulate all of these properties through EMS. For example, if you want to route all meeting requests for a room received from any user to a delegate for approval, you could use a command like this:

```
Set-CalendarProcessing -Identity 'Leixlip Conference Room' -AllRequestInPolicy $True
-AllBookInPolicy $False
```

No exceptions are stated in the *BookInPolicy* property, so every request to book the room is channeled to the room delegate (or delegates, if multiple users are defined). The request is noted as tentative in the room's calendar until a delegate decides to accept or reject the request by responding to the message requesting a decision that the Resource Booking Assistant sends to him (Figure 6-50). The meeting will remain in a tentative state if no delegate is defined for the mailbox. Note that a delegate cannot approve her own request for a room. To avoid this problem, you should add room delegates to the list of users whose requests to book a room will be automatically approved.

To allow an exception to the rule and permit someone to book a room without going through the delegate approval process, we simply put his name into the *BookInPolicy* list. For example, this command adds JSmith to the BookInPolicy list. You can identify users or groups by name, alias, UPN, or SMTP address:

```
Set-CalendarProcessing -Identity 'Leitrim Conference Room' -BookInPolicy JSmith
```

To add several users or groups to the exception list, add their names separated by a comma.

Equipment mailboxes

Equipment mailboxes are very similar to room mailboxes in the properties that you can assign to set a policy for their booking and the way that the Resource Booking Assistant is able to monitor and process incoming requests. Use this command to find the equipment mailboxes within your organization:

```
Get-Mailbox -Filter {ResourceType -eq 'Equipment'}
```

From a user perspective, equipment mailboxes are added to meetings like any other recipient. Unlike room mailboxes, neither OWA nor Outlook provides a specific picker to allow users to select equipment to include in meetings, nor is there an "All equipment" address list to browse through to find equipment. For this reason, it's important that the naming convention applied to equipment mailboxes clearly identifies these mailboxes in the GAL.

Data, data, everywhere

We know how to create and manage users, groups, and contacts. Now we need to understand the heart of Exchange and investigate the basics of the Information Store and how it has evolved in Exchange 2010 to answer the changing demands of email. On to the Store!

# CHAPTER 7

The Exchange 2010 Store

MAINTAINING and evolving a database isn't an easy engineering challenge, especially when the database has to deal with transactions that vary widely from a simple 10 KB message sent to a single recipient, to a message sent to a large distribution (with each address individually expanded in the header) accompanied by a 10 MB Microsoft PowerPoint attachment. Microsoft has always spent energy to tweak the Extensible Storage Engine (ESE) database, its schema, and the Store as new versions of Exchange rolled out but never really began to evolve it until work began on Exchange Server 2007. Perhaps less work was required on the Store when Microsoft's major competition was Lotus Notes, mailboxes were relatively small, and storage was expensive. At that point, it was sufficient to make the Store more efficient in background maintenance operations and to include new features like the dumpster. Today's competitive environment is different, and there is a real need to support very large mailboxes to compete with low-cost online services as well as to answer the continuing demands of the corporate sector for improvements in areas such as high availability. Microsoft might well have invested more engineering in the Store even if Google hadn't come along, but there is no doubt that competition can have a stunning effect on innovation.

The overall goals that Microsoft engineering took on to enhance the Store in Microsoft Exchange Server 2010 were the following:

- Improve I/O performance, reduce the cost and complexity of storage, and increase the flexibility available to storage architects when laying out storage designs for Exchange.

- Make 10 GB mailboxes work as well in Exchange 2010 as 1 GB mailboxes work in Exchange 2007.

- Improve mailbox availability and resilience through increased use of the data replication techniques first seen in the continuous log replication features in Exchange 2007. This work marks a new approach to high availability within the product, and the previous single-copy cluster-based approach that started with the "Wolfpack" technology and Exchange 5.5 is no longer used. Some associated work is done in the transport system to increase the chance that a message can never be lost, no matter what type of catastrophic failure occurs.

Whenever you think about the Exchange Store, you consider three major components:

1. The ESE, the database engine that organizes the contents of mailbox and public folder databases at page level.

2. The Information Store, which lays down a logical schema that defines the contents of mailboxes and public folders and how those contents are organized.

3. The EDB and transaction logs. The EDB is the database file on disk. The transaction logs record any change made to a page within a database (adds, modifies, deletes) and provide the ability for Exchange to recover from a database failure by replaying transactions recorded in the logs. The transaction logs are also used to replicate data between servers and so keep database copies synchronized so that copies can be quickly switched in to provide continuous service to users if the primary (active) database fails.

In this chapter, we review the major changes that Microsoft has engineered into the Exchange 2010 Store and discuss some of their motivations and logic behind the changes.

Long live Jet!

Exchange 2010 continues to use ESE, its version of the Microsoft Jet database engine that is shared with other Microsoft products such as Access. Of course, ESE is very different than other Jet databases, because it has been highly optimized over the years for Exchange—a process that continues with the new schema introduced with Exchange 2010. Some are surprised that Microsoft persists with ESE as the platform for Exchange when they seem to have another perfectly good enterprise-class, high-performance database engine in SQL. On the surface, it's an attractive notion to unify all database development activities into a common platform that Microsoft and third-party developers can support. Money would be saved on engineering, testing, and support activities, and everyone could leverage a single target platform through a unified set of application programming interfaces (APIs). Microsoft has investigated the effort required to move Exchange to SQL on a number of different occasions, including the ill-fated Kodiak project prior to Exchange 2007. However, apart from the sheer engineering effort, a number of technical and nontechnical challenges would have to be overcome before Exchange could use SQL.

The demands on the two database engines are very different: ESE is optimized to process messaging transactions that vary from a one-line message sent between two people to a message sent to a very large distribution complete with a multigigabyte attachment (your favorite communication from the marketing department). SQL is optimized to handle structured transactions that do not tend to be highly variable. Could performance and scalability be maintained in a single database that attempts to serve both demands?

ESE allows users to create their own indexes (views) on the fly with a simple click on a column heading in Outlook. The result is a colossal number of temporary views that differ from database to database that ESE manages in an elegant manner. SQL doesn't tend to be so accommodating. Again, SQL could provide the functionality, but would it take away from database performance?

SQL is designed to be a platform for applications. Exchange has experienced many attempts to become a platform for different types of applications, such as workflow routing, but is now simply a messaging server. Microsoft SharePoint (which uses SQL) has supplanted Exchange as the cornerstone of Microsoft's collaboration applications strategy. If Exchange used SQL, would Microsoft still be able to sell SharePoint as successfully as they do today?

Both SQL and Exchange have developed third-party ecosystems around their platforms that add enormous value to anyone who wants to deploy these products. Given that most partners who support Exchange today do not use ESE to access the Store, there shouldn't be a problem moving them to SQL, but there might be some who do have a problem. These issues can be overcome in time, but it might slow adoption of whatever new version of Exchange embraces SQL.

In any case, who really cares what database engine powers an application as long as it does the job and delivers robust and scalable performance in a reliable manner? Do people ask what database Google uses for Gmail or Yahoo! uses for Zimbra? This really shouldn't be an issue as long as Microsoft ensures that no functionality is lost when the transition occurs, if that's what happens in the future.

Maximum database size

With Exchange 2010, Microsoft has increased its recommended maximum database size to 2 TB instead of the 250 GB that most administrators considered the practical maximum in Exchange 2007. The increase in database page size to 64 KB has moved the maximum theoretical size of a database to the NTFS limit (16 TB–64 KB). To be safe, the absolute limit for an Exchange 2010 database is 16,000 GB, just below the NTFS theoretical limit. Few customers are likely to operate databases that are anywhere near this value in the next decade, especially when they consider just how long it will take to restore such a monster database, should that need arise.

An eight-fold to ten-fold increase in recommended database size in one software version seems startling on the surface, but it can be justified by three major technical and operational factors.

- First, streaming tape backups are not supported by Exchange 2010, and you are forced to use Volume ShadowCopy Services (VSS) disk-based backups instead. VSS backups are faster and more capable of dealing with huge volumes of data. Think of a server that supports ten 1 GB databases. If you use the fastest available tapes (LTO-4 class today), you will be lucky to complete a backup operation in 12 hours. Taking a snapshot is a lot faster, and if you need to create a copy on tape to satisfy off-site archival procedures, you can do this after the VSS backup is available. The classic tape backup is no longer available to Exchange, so part of the planning process for the introduction of Exchange 2010 is the determination of how to deploy a VSS-based backup solution if you haven't already done this.

> **Tip**
>
> VSS is no longer the fastest method to restore a database and bring it back into production. You can certainly recover a database from a snapshot or cloned copy, but it is much faster to use a DAG with Exchange 2010 and depend on its high availability capabilities to replace a failed active copy with a passive copy.

- Exchange 2010 supports a more extensive replication model. You can have up to 16 copies of a database instead of the single copy supported by the Cluster Continuous Replication (CCR) and Standby Continous Replication (SCR) features in Exchange 2007. Few companies will create 16 copies of a database unless they are completely paranoid, but it's nice to know that this possibility exists. If you create three or more copies of a database, it's fair to argue that backup operations become less important than they were in the past because you are able to recover more quickly and more simply from a passive copy instead of reaching for the most current backup. This fact does not eliminate the need for backups completely, as legal and other requirements might mandate backup copies for off-site storage. See Chapter 8, "Exchange's Search for High Availability," for a discussion about the Database Availability Group (DAG) and how Exchange 2010 handles multicopy database replication.

- Microsoft has made many changes in the Store at the ESE layer to improve performance and reduce management operations that could often not be completed for large databases. Exchange 2007 performs online defragmentation during a scheduled maintenance period that typically begins around midnight. As databases grow, it becomes harder and harder to scan all the pages in the database and achieve online defragmentation. Exchange 2010 takes a different approach to maintain contiguity within the database.

Defragmentation occurs all the time as pages flow into the database, so there is no need to fit within a limited maintenance window or worry about the size of the database. The additional CPU cycles required to process pages as they are added to the database are released by improvements made elsewhere, especially in operations that generated a lot of I/O activity in the past, such as index creation and restricted views. Note that a large database really doesn't take longer to mount and make available to users; the primary consideration in terms of mount time is the number of transaction logs that need to be replayed to bring the database up to date during the mount operation. Larger databases might have more transaction logs to replay, but the net impact probably won't be noticed.

You can add other elements to the mix such as the fixes made to Outlook 2007 SP2 to address the performance problems when OST and PST files grew past 2 GB in size. Without such a fix on the client side, it would be impossible to consider the support of very large mailboxes. Although the largest known production Exchange mailboxes today (in the 100 GB range) are uncommon, the influence of free consumer email systems like Gmail and Windows Live Mail that offer mailboxes of between 7 GB and 25 GB increases the pressure on Exchange administrators to provide similar capacity for business use. It's a world removed from the original 25 MB quotas of Exchange 4.0.

Database limits for the standard edition

The discussion about maximum database size so far is largely theoretical because most deployments will never even contemplate operating a database that is larger than a few hundred gigabytes. The standard edition of Exchange 2010 is designed for smaller deployments, so it flags informational messages in the application event log to advise administrators that there is a limit of 1,024 GB (1 TB) for databases and inform them how large their database currently is. For example, you might see a message like this logged as event 1216 in the Application Event Log:

```
The Exchange store DB1 is limited to 1024 GB. The current physical size of this
database (the .edb file) is 173 GB. If the physical size of this database minus its
logical free space exceeds the limit of 1024 GB, the database will be dismounted on a
regular basis.
```

In the normal course of events you won't worry too much about this advice because you probably will act well in advance to restrict database growth before the file reaches 1 TB, and there should be sufficient room for mailbox growth in the database before the restriction kicks in. However, it is possible to increase the maximum file size for a database mounted on servers running the Exchange 2010 standard edition by following these steps:

1. Discover the globally unique identifier (GUID) of the database for which you want to increase the maximum permitted size. To do this, run the Exchange Management Shell (EMS) command:

```
Get-MailboxDatabase | Format-Table Name, GUID - AutoSize
```

```
Name       Guid
-------    ------
DB1        3a8b2dad-7f50-4168-9b17-bed403ac0230
DB2        f9d1c326-bfd0-41bd-90a5-1ac9ed4383e4
```

Let's assume that you want to increase the maximum size of database DB2. Record the GUID that is reported by EMS.

2. Run Regedit (system registry editor) on the mailbox server where the database is currently mounted.

3. Navigate to HKEY_LOCAL_MACHINE\SYSTEM\CurrentControlSet\Services \MSExchangeIS\<SERVER NAME>\Private-<database GUID>. For example, if the server is ExServer1, we want to go to the key HKEY_LOCAL_MACHINE\SYSTEM \CurrentControlSet\Services\MSExchangeIS\ExServer1 \Private-f9d1c326-bfd0-41bd-90a5-1ac9ed4383e4

4. Check whether a value called Database Size Limit in GB exists under the key. If it does, you can enter the new maximum size in this value. If not, create a new DWORD value called Database Size Limit in GB and then enter the desired value. You can input any value up to 16,000, so it is also possible to reduce the maximum supported database size on a server using this method.

The Store will respect the new limit as soon as the registry is updated.

Mailboxes per database (or per server)

Given that we have larger mailboxes, does it follow that more mailboxes can be supported per database and that, indeed, Exchange 2010 will support more users per server than Exchange 2003 or Exchange 2007? The classic way of approaching the question is to figure out the maximum size of database that you want to operate based on available disk space, I/O patterns, backup regime, and so on, and then use that to calculate how many mailboxes of a certain quota can be accommodated by the database. Thus, a 100 GB database can handle 200 * 500 MB mailboxes. You then assign databases to servers based on available disk space and I/O capability. As we'll discuss soon, the I/O profile of Exchange 2010 is very different from that of its predecessors.

Calculating database size by multiplying the number of users by the mailbox quotas is still a valid way to approach the problem of what size database you are able to support, and it's certainly one that works in small to medium deployments. However, email systems have become more complex in the last few years, and there are other factors that have to be taken into account. You might ask some or all of the following questions to help frame the discussion.

- Are any legal or regulatory conditions in place that force retention of mailbox data for a specified period?

- What is the company's backup regime? Will we use DAGs to achieve higher availability and protection with Exchange 2010?

- How are users coping with current mailbox quotas? Are most within limits, or do we see a constant stream of requests for additional space? Are we happy to have users spend time juggling mailbox contents to keep under their quota?

- What deleted items retention policy do we operate? Is it sufficient, or should it be extended? How often do we have to restore a backup to recover user data?

- Do we force automatic deletion of items in mailboxes? If not, should we do so by using a retention policy?

- Do we use an archiving product with Exchange? Will Exchange 2010 personal archives replace or complement this product? Will personal archives be co-located in the same database as the primary mailboxes or in another database?

- Do we need to journal messages? How often do we have to perform legal discovery searches or otherwise react to complaints where email is essential evidence that has to be found and retained?

- Has the messaging profile of our users changed in the last few years? Are they sending and receiving more email? What is the average size of the messages? Are they making more use of calendars and other mail-enabled applications?

These questions address a mixture of technical and business requirements and lead to an understanding of how users generate and use mailbox data. There's no simple formula to turn the responses into an answer of the mailbox quota you should provide and how many databases of a particular size will be required. Instead, you're more likely to end up with a realization that you have to deliver a mixture of differentiated services to various categories of users. Executives and other "high-impact" staff will have different quotas, retention periods, and archiving and legal requirements than factory workers, and their mailboxes will probably be in databases located on the most highly available servers. These servers might use different hardware configurations, be operated by dedicated staff, and have to support access through a variety of devices (mobile, Outlook, and Outlook Web App [OWA]) rather than the more limited variety that might be allowed to less important users.

INSIDE OUT The assumptions behind capacity planning

Considerations such as availability, recovery, and business requirements must be factored into server planning. Tools such as the Microsoft Exchange 2010 Mailbox Server Role Requirements Calculator (*http://msexchangeteam.com/archive/2010/01/22 /453859.aspx*) help to determine the basic technical design for Exchange 2010, but be prepared to hand-tailor the resulting output as you incorporate other needs that cannot be easily input into a spreadsheet before you arrive at the final design. All sizing tools make assumptions such as the default client type, user profile, and concurrency ratio, and the recommendations that they make will be most satisfactory when your situation closely matches these assumptions. In other circumstances, your users might be busier than the assumption, or they don't use Outlook and OWA, or they don't connect as often as you'd expect (a hosting environment matches these conditions with Internet Message Access Protocol [IMAP] and Post Office Protocol 3 [POP3] clients and very low user concurrency ratios) and therefore the results generated by a sizing tool will need to be adjusted before they make sense for you.

Dealing with I/O

Even though the type and volume of email had changed dramatically since Microsoft first laid out Exchange's database schema in 1996, Exchange Server 2000, 2003, and 2007 use the same schema that emphasizes efficient storage over utility. Cheaper storage makes it less attractive to focus on storage efficiency. To achieve a reduction in I/O, the Store had to move away from forcing disks to do many small random I/Os to fetch data, instead using larger sequential I/Os. The physical performance difference between random and sequential I/O almost guarantees better performance and lower I/O activity for any application if the code is written to move away from random I/O. To make the change, Exchange 2010 introduces a new schema (discussed in the section "A new database schema" later in this chapter) that generates fewer I/Os by emphasizing contiguity over storage, essentially by keeping mailbox content together. Because more data are contiguous, the Store can read data out in large sequential chunks rather than in many random and smaller chunks.

A side effect of the new Exchange 2010 schema is that the concept of single-instance storage is consigned to Exchange's wastebasket. You might assume that Exchange 2010 databases will grow larger because mailboxes hold their own copies of messages. In fact, this isn't true because of other changes in the Exchange 2010 Store, such as the way that it compresses message content. However, a side effect of the elimination of single-instance storage is that more transaction logs are generated to capture the insertion of individual copies of items into the table for each mailbox. For example, if you send a message with a 1 MB attachment to 10 mailboxes in the same database, the Store has to create at least 10 transaction logs.

Views (or secondary indexes) are a very valuable user feature. Outlook allows users to sort items within folders using a wide variety of properties (author, date received, subject, and so on). Every time a user opts for a different sort order, the Store creates a new view. Thereafter, as new items arrive into the Store, a lot of work occurs to update the views. Eventually, if a view is not used, it expires and is removed by the Store.

Large mailboxes tend to have many views, and those views are usually for the default folders (Inbox, Sent Items, and Deleted Items). Many people don't like the work involved in filing email into different folders and are happy to let messages build up in the default folders, only taking action when prompted to by quota exhaustion. Human behavior results in folders that hold many thousands of items, and in earlier versions of Exchange, the Store generated more I/O when it had to access large folders. This prompted Microsoft to recommend that the largest folder should hold fewer than 5,000 items in Exchange 2007. The combination of superior OST performance delivered from Outlook 2007 SP2 onward coupled with the improvements delivered by the enhancements made to the Exchange 2010 Store means that Microsoft's new recommendation for the maximum number of items in a folder is now 20,000.

Nontechnical users were seldom aware of any limitation and carried on using the Inbox as a convenient dumping ground for messages. Better search technology within Outlook compounded the problem because there was now no penalty for messy or nonexistent filing, and you could find any item you needed quickly, even within a cluttered Inbox.

The combination of an inefficient schema and the way the Store created views caused many I/O operations. I/Os are random because the pages that represent the contents of a mailbox were usually not contiguous within the database. This factor and the 8 KB page size resulted in many small I/Os whenever a client requested data. For competitive reasons, Microsoft wanted to efficiently support very large mailboxes in Exchange 2010. The tweaking that they had done in Exchange 2007 had helped a bit, but a more fundamental overhaul was necessary.

How Exchange 2010 supports large mailboxes

- Introduces a new Store schema that is designed to deal with large mailboxes more efficiently.

- Forces pages within the Store to be laid out contiguously rather than having pages scattered around the database.

- Expands the default page size from 8 KB to 32 KB and ensures that the Store allocates pages in large contiguous chunks rather than randomly within the database.

- Moves away from many random small-sized disk I/Os to fewer sequential larger I/Os. The logic here is very simple: Today's disks are capable of providing data at up to 300 sequential I/O operations per second (IOPS), whereas their ability to handle random I/O remains constrained at around 50 IOPS. Given that disks can provide sequential data six times faster than random data, it makes perfect sense for Microsoft to focus their engineering investment on moving activity within the Store from random to sequential. Apart from the performance benefit, this step enables a wider range of storage designs to support Exchange.

- Increases the cache size for the Store from 20 MB to 100 MB for mailbox databases that have copies in a DAG. This step enables the Store to keep more dirty pages in memory. This cache size (basically the number of uncommitted log files) is referred to as the checkpoint depth, and it controls the amount of data in the cache waiting to be committed to the database on disk. Increasing the cache improves the chance that Exchange can update a page in memory rather than having to generate an I/O to retrieve it from disk. There are risks in increasing the cache, including longer shutdown times as the cache needs to be flushed to disk and longer recovery times from crashes as more transactions have to be replayed from transaction logs. However, the overall benefit in I/O improvement is worth taking these risks.

- Introduces data compression of some object types within the Store.

Table 7-1 lists the three major ways that Microsoft changed elements of contiguity at the physical (ESE database) and logical (Store) levels to reduce the number of small I/Os generated as the result of normal client operations such as accessing mailboxes to send and receive messages.

Table 7-1 Improving the I/O characteristics of Exchange 2010

Element	Exchange 2007	Exchange 2010
Page contiguity (ESE)	Databases have poor page contiguity as 8 KB pages that compose messages and attachments are arranged randomly around the database. Many small I/Os are required to retrieve data.	Databases exhibit much better contiguity as 32 KB pages are allocated in contiguous ranges to allow the Store to retrieve data in fewer, larger I/Os that span up to 100 pages.
Logical contiguity (Store)	Message headers for each folder are kept in a separate table. Many small I/Os are generated to fetch headers to provide to clients.	All of the headers for a mailbox are kept in a single folder so it is easier for the Store to fetch headers in a single large I/O.
Dynamic contiguity (views)	The Store updates views and indexes every time a new item arrives. This activity generates a lot of small I/Os to maintain the indexes in the database.	The Store only updates views and indexes when they are accessed by a client. Fewer, larger I/Os are generated as a result.

You can see that the work to tune the Store was taken from a very foundational level in a fundamental shift away from the way that Exchange has organized database pages since its first version. Inside a reasonably small database, it's probably acceptable to assign pages to store new items in whatever pages are free within the database. For a 20 KB message this meant that you might have the item placed in five pages (4 KB each) scattered in different locations within the database. From a logical perspective, the database can find the five pages and provide their locations to the Store whenever a client requests the item, but this activity generates a lot of very small I/Os. Matters improved somewhat when Microsoft increased the default page size from 4 KB to 8 KB in Exchange 2007, but the internal organization remained as before. Exchange 2010 increases the page size to 32 KB so that it is more likely that a single item will fit in one page and makes the more important change to take care that pages required to hold new items are assigned contiguously in large chunks.

When clients need to access an item, the Store uses a technique called *gap coalescing* to read in a range of pages in a single large I/O rather than hunting around the database for individual pages. The Store also writes pages in contiguous chunks to smooth I/O. Consider the situation where four pages in a contiguous set of six pages are updated in the cache and need to be written to disk. Exchange 2007 writes each of the four dirty pages in individual I/Os. Exchange 2010 writes the six (dirty and clean) pages out in one large I/O and ESE discards the unchanged pages as it updates the database. Using gap coalescing reduces the overall I/O demand exerted by Exchange and increases overall data throughput.

The change that updates views on demand rather than after every change is also important in terms of I/O reduction. Microsoft refers to this as a change from a "nickel and dime" approach, where the Store is in a state of constant turmoil as views are updated after the arrival of new items, to a "pay to play" approach, where the Store only updates a view when a client wants to use it. Consider the situation where a user creates a view through OWA (Outlook clients that work in online mode also create views in this manner; when Outlook works in cached Exchange mode it creates views on the client) to look at items in her inbox sorted by author (sender) rather than the default sort order (received date/time). Such a view is normally created to allow a user to look for items sent by a specific individual— when a view sorted by author is much more useful than the default view sorted by the time an item is received. However, let's assume that the user then switches back to the default view and doesn't look at a view by author for another week. Even though the client has no intention of accessing the view, the Store keeps updating it just in case. This might be good because a view is immediately available, but it incurs a horrible overhead for the Store to keep track of all the views and to update views as new items arrive. The resulting updates generate I/O activity because the changed views have to be written back into the database. Eliminating these updates and using an on-demand model is a very intelligent change, especially as the multicore servers used today are very capable of handling the small extra demand for the processor to compute a view when required.

In their efforts to improve I/O performance, Microsoft also paid attention to the concept of database write smoothing. Every disk has its performance limitations that restrict the amount of data that it can handle at any time. If you attempt to write too much data to disk at one time, the disk will be swamped and a disk contention condition occurs. The application is not able to write its data as quickly as it wants and everything halts until the disk is able to accept more data and the contention condition is relieved. Write smoothing means that the application is intelligent enough to detect when disks are approaching the limits of their performance and is able to throttle back its demand to allow the disk to continue to process data at a consistent rate.

Exchange 2010 uses the checkpoint depth as its measure to determine when it should throttle database writes. This approach has the advantage in that it works for all disks. When the checkpoint depth is between 1.0 and 1.24 of the checkpoint target, the Store limits the outstanding write operations for each logical unit number (LUN) to one until the condition improves. If the checkpoint depth goes past 1.25 of the target, further throttling is imposed by increasing the maximum number of outstanding write operations per LUN until a balance is attained and the depth begins to reduce. Pending writes remain in the cache until they can be written to disk.

Table 7-2 summarizes the respective I/O characteristics of Exchange 2007 and Exchange 2010. The data demonstrate the effect of moving from I/Os of a largely random nature to more sequential access together with increasing the average I/O size.

Table 7-2 I/O characteristics of Exchange 2007 and Exchange 2010

Database I/O characteristic	Exchange 2007	Exchange 2010
I/O type	Random	Mostly sequential
Read-write ratio	1:1	3:2
Average read I/O size	12 KB	52 KB
Average write I/O size	8 KB	60 KB

Microsoft made many other tweaks to the Exchange 2010 Store based on the experience of Exchange 2007. Page coalescing is improved, data are written to disk in larger chunks including pages that are not dirty (these updates are discarded), page caching is more efficient, content search is better, and so on. Despite incurring some additional overhead to support new Store features such as data compression, the net effect is that Microsoft believes that customers will see up to an additional 70 percent drop in I/O requirements over Exchange 2007, which in turn featured I/O reductions of up to 70 percent over Exchange 2003. This actual gain must be measured in your own specific hardware environment and might be better or worse depending on server and storage configurations, user workloads, and types of clients. In any case, the changes that Microsoft has made to the Exchange 2010 Store are positive because they focus on how to handle the large mailboxes and content types that exist today rather than the smaller mailboxes and messages that Exchange 4.0 dealt with in 1996.

INSIDE OUT   When are large mailboxes justified?

Many Exchange deployments started with mailbox quotas of 50 MB to 100 MB and have gradually increased over time to a range of 250 MB to 500 MB, with some select mailboxes being allocated a higher quota. Usually these mailboxes are owned by executives or other users who have a business need for higher email volumes or to hold data for longer periods. The other users resort to PSTs to hold messages that they want to keep so that they stay within their allocated quota.

Microsoft designed Exchange 2010 to support larger mailboxes. In reality, this means a mailbox size of 5 GB to 10 GB. A mailbox quota of 5 GB is sufficient to store approximately 100,000 items with a 50 KB average size. For most people, it will take five years to accumulate that much mail, and it is possible that the company's legal team would prefer that users not store quite so much mail!

Before we all rush out to enable 5 GB mailbox quotas, it's wise to reflect on the business requirements that we might meet with large mailboxes. These reasons might be valid for your company:

- Reduction in unproductive time spent by users who struggle to stay within lower quotas. How much does it cost if a message containing some time-critical information cannot be delivered to a mailbox because its quota is exhausted?

- Elimination of PSTs through the deployment of archive mailboxes.

- Elimination of expensive deleted item recovery from backups through the deployment of an extended deleted items retention period (more than 60 days).

- Ability to conduct online searches through all email available to the company rather than the subset that is available in online mailboxes.

- Protection of all email rather than just the items in the Exchange database.

- Provision of all mailbox content to multiple clients (OWA and mobile devices cannot access PSTs).

Once you have a set of reasons to justify the deployment of larger quotas, you can begin to figure out how to deploy the servers and storage necessary to support large mailboxes.

Maintaining contiguity

Microsoft has taken enormous care to allocate contiguous space within Store databases. However, this is not the end of the story, because pages have a lifetime that begins with their creation and extends through modifications and deletes.

Given that Microsoft's maximum recommended database size for Exchange 2010 is now counted in terabytes, it's obvious that the old way of maintaining contiguity through scheduled background maintenance would not work. Table 7-3 lists the major changes that Exchange 2010 makes to ensure that contiguity is maintained inside databases no matter how large they become.

Table 7-3 **Changes in background database maintenance operations**

ESE function	Exchange 2007 SP1 (and later)	Exchange 2010
Cleanup	Deleted items and mailboxes are removed from the database after their retention time expires during online background maintenance.	Deleted items and mailboxes are removed from the database immediately their retention period expires. Deleted pages are zeroized by default.
Compaction	Pages freed by deleted items and mailboxes are recycled during online background maintenance.	Pages freed by deleted items are recycled immediately. This activity is auto-throttled to prevent interference with database responsiveness.
Contiguity/ Defragmentation	The recycling of deleted pages does not take contiguity into account and recycled pages are used randomly.	ESE analyzes the database for contiguity and free space at run time to ensure that contiguity is maintained as defragmentation occurs. This activity is also auto-throttled.
Checksum	When configured, the checksums in database pages are verified during background maintenance.	The default is to run checksum validation continuously in the background on both active and passive database copies to detect potential corruptions immediately. Administrators can opt to run this check during scheduled background maintenance instead.

Essentially, the Store checks each transaction to ensure that maximum contiguity is maintained and that it is using available space efficiently. If necessary, a background thread is created to address any problems—perhaps it will shuffle some pages so that they are more contiguous or to free up space in the database. All of this work is throttled automatically so that background operations never interfere with the ability of the Store to service user requests, just like Windows Desktop Search only indexes items on a PC's hard disk when the PC is inactive.

The result of these operations is that Exchange 2010 databases start out and remain more contiguous than their predecessors. Of course, some extra CPU resources are consumed to perform run-time processing, but this should not be a problem in most situations because the normal bottleneck for Exchange has been I/O rather than CPU for the last decade.

As you read the discussion about contiguity and about the larger 32 KB page size used by Exchange 2010, the thought might run through your mind that larger pages arrayed in bigger chunks might increase the overall on-disk size of a database. This conclusion is correct, but it is offset by the introduction of data compression within the database.

Microsoft believes that the potential extra growth in database size is fully mitigated by the way that they compress message headers and HTML and text body parts. Their tests show that a database might grow 20 percent compared to its Exchange 2007 equivalent without compression but that it remains the same size once data are compressed. Of course, the exact ratio of compression will vary depending on the mix of content within a database (Rich Text Format [RTF], text, HTML, different types of attachments). For example, RTF messages are already compressed and are therefore not compressed again when they are written into a database. Outlook 2010 generates HTML format messages by default, so databases that support these clients get more value from compression than databases that support earlier clients such as Outlook 2003, where the default message format is likely to be RTF. Exchange 2010 SP1 achieves more efficiency by first clustering records and tags into contiguous chunks within a page before attempting to compress the data.

INSIDE OUT   Data compression doesn't include attachments

Although great value is attained by compressing message bodies, Exchange doesn't attempt to compress attachments. Tests by the Exchange development team demonstrate that most attachment types that circulate with messages, such as newer versions of Word documents and Excel worksheets, don't compress well because they are already stored in a compressed format. The same is true of other attachment types that you might not want to see circulated via email including JPEG, PNG, MP3, and WMA. Some older formats such as Word 2003 do compress well, but as these versions are being rapidly replaced their attachments will form a decreasing percentage of the overall attachment volume. The decision was therefore made to avoid incurring the CPU overhead of compression to achieve what might be a marginal decrease in overall storage requirement, especially at a time when storage costs are declining rapidly. The same logic was used when the decision was made not to attempt to compress RTF message bodies.

In terms of assessing the practical impact of the change, it is impossible to compare anything other than two databases populated with the same test data. You could take an Exchange 2003 database and move all the mailboxes to Exchange 2010 to gauge the impact and use that as a benchmark, but the very nature of this exercise is flawed because the content in email databases is in a state of constant change. You might get a certain result on one day and see a very different result a week later. It is fair to say that companies who have deployed Exchange 2010 have not reported a massive difference in database sizes. The signs are therefore encouraging, and the introduction of compression at this point illustrates the comprehensive nature of the overhaul of core components delivered in Exchange 2010.

A new database schema

The schema sets out how data are physically and logically organized within a database. Apart from some minor tweaking, Microsoft has used the same schema from Exchange 4.0 through Exchange 2007, but the schema used in Exchange 2010 introduces some major changes, the biggest of which is the way that the contents of mailboxes and folders are organized.

Prior to Exchange 2010, the basic layout of a mailbox database was as follows:

- A mailbox table containing a pointer to every mailbox in the database.

- A folders table containing a pointer to every folder in every mailbox in the database.

- A message table containing an entry for every message in every folder in the database.

- An attachments table containing an entry for every attachment in the database.

- A message/folder table maintained for every folder that lists all the messages in a specific folder. For example, the message/folder table for your Inbox contains pointers to every message in your Inbox.

In essence, you have four big tables shared by every mailbox in the database and a set of message/folder tables for all the different folders. This schema, shown in Figure 7-1, obviously works successfully, but ESE generates more I/O than necessary to navigate through the tables in response to user requests, especially as some of the tables become very large in databases that support thousands of mailboxes. For example, a database supporting 4,000 mailboxes, each of which has 150 folders containing 20,000 items, has a folders table with 600,000 rows and a messages table with 80,000,000 rows. The message/folder tables aren't so much of a problem because most users have noted the advice given over the years to restrict the number of items within a folder to less than 5,000.

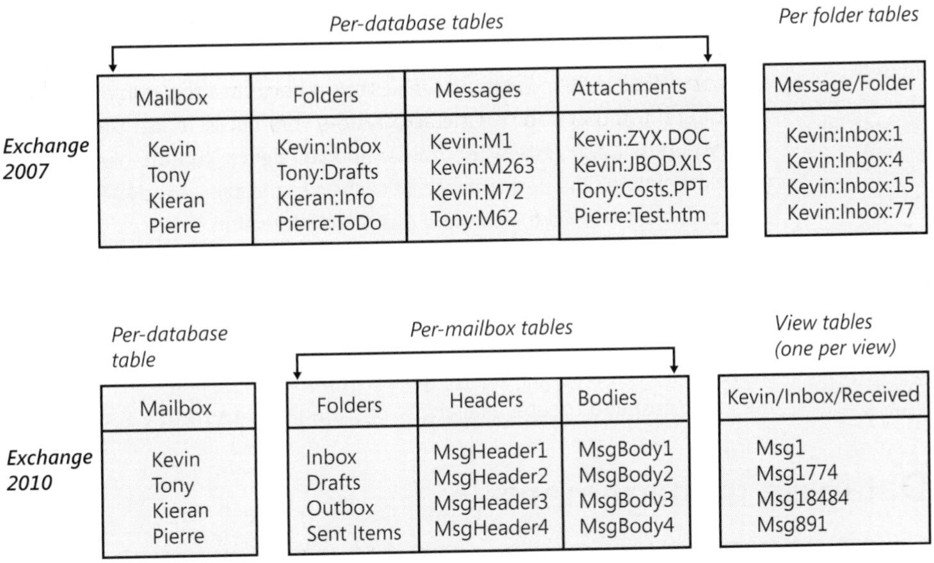

Per-database tables				Per folder tables

	Mailbox	Folders	Messages	Attachments	Message/Folder
Exchange 2007	Kevin Tony Kieran Pierre	Kevin:Inbox Tony:Drafts Kieran:Info Pierre:ToDo	Kevin:M1 Kevin:M263 Kevin:M72 Tony:M62	Kevin:ZYX.DOC Kevin:JBOD.XLS Tony:Costs.PPT Pierre:Test.htm	Kevin:Inbox:1 Kevin:Inbox:4 Kevin:Inbox:15 Kevin:Inbox:77

Per-database table		Per-mailbox tables			View tables (one per view)

	Mailbox	Folders	Headers	Bodies	Kevin/Inbox/Received
Exchange 2010	Kevin Tony Kieran Pierre	Inbox Drafts Outbox Sent Items	MsgHeader1 MsgHeader2 MsgHeader3 MsgHeader4	MsgBody1 MsgBody2 MsgBody3 MsgBody4	Msg1 Msg1774 Msg18484 Msg891

Figure 7-1 Difference between Exchange 2007 and Exchange 2010 database schemas.

As shown in Figure 7-1, the layout imposed by the Exchange 2010 schema is as follows:

- A mailbox table containing a pointer to every mailbox in the database (as before).

- A folders table for each mailbox in the database. Although there are many more folders tables, the size of each is much smaller. Taking the example cited earlier, there are now 4,000 folders tables (one for each mailbox), each of which holds 150 rows.

- A message header table for each mailbox in the database. The message header table holds all the Messaging Application Programming Interface (MAPI) properties (subject, address list, priority, and so on) for the messages in a mailbox. Again, we have 4,000 message header tables, but the maximum size of a table is set by the number of items in the largest mailbox, or around 20,000 rows in our example.

- A message body table for each mailbox in the database. The message body table holds the message content (the body text), including attachments. Again, you have 4,000 message body tables for our example database and the maximum size of the table is determined by the number of items in the largest mailbox.

- In addition, ESE maintains view tables on an as-required basis. A view is an ordering of a folder (for example, the Inbox ordered by date received). Previous versions of Exchange use secondary indexes to populate views. Exchange 2010 holds views as tables. Although there can be many views (more than the number of folders because users can create multiple views per folder), the maximum size of a view table is determined by the number of items in the largest folder.

In summary, Exchange 2010 changes its database storage schema to move from a focus on tables that store data for a complete database to tables that occur for each mailbox. This approach allows ESE to be more efficient as it navigates through a database and generates fewer I/O transactions for the storage system to process. It also allows Exchange 2010 to support up to 100,000 items per folder and still deliver reasonable responsiveness to clients that work online. The performance of cached mode clients is dependent on other factors, such as the speed of the local hard disk and the version of the client (Outlook 2007 SP2 or later is best).

On the downside, the new schema eliminates any possibility of single-instance storage because the focus is now on per-mailbox tables rather than tables that exist on a per-database basis. Given the much reduced importance of single-instance storage because of the lower cost and greater availability of storage, its loss is not a reason for mourning.

Database management

Database management covers many different topics. We start with a discussion about the basic files that constitute an Exchange mailbox database (see Figure 7-2) and then go on to discuss some of the finer details about how transaction logs and the other files are used.

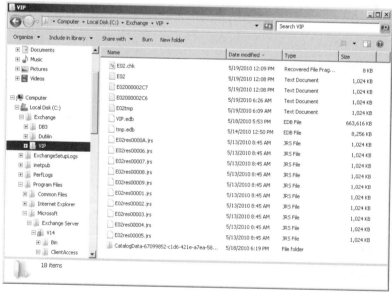

Figure 7-2 Files for a mailbox database.

The most important files that you will see in the directory used to hold an Exchange database are the following:

- Database file: For example, Vip.edb. All of the tables and data required to provide content to clients are held in the database.

- Current transaction log: For example, E02.log. This log file is the one into which the Store is currently writing active transactional data.

- Previous transaction logs: The remainder of the transaction log set that holds previously captured transactions. These log files are removed automatically by the Store on a regular basis (if circular logging is enabled) or following a successful full backup. The transaction log set forms the basis for replication of data between servers to keep database copies updated within a DAG. In Figure 7-2, the transaction log set goes from E0200002C6 to E0200002C7 (generations 710 to 711, indicating that the current log is generation 712).

- Checkpoint file: For example, E01.chk. The checkpoint file tracks the progress of the Store in writing logged transactions (those captured in transaction logs) into the database.

- Reserved logs: For example, E00res00001.jrs. Exchange uses these files to provide some additional space for the database to flush transactions into if the need arises. SP1 increases the number of JRS files to 10 per database.

- Some data about active database transactions might be stored in Tmp.edb. This file is usually only a few megabytes in size and is deleted whenever the database is dismounted or when the Information Store service stops. The Store logs transactions for this database in Exxtmp.log (E01tmp.log in this example).

Because databases are no longer directly associated with servers (except that they are hosted by servers), database management is performed at the organization level in Exchange 2010. Figure 7-3 illustrates a typical view of Exchange Management Console (EMC) for a small organization positioned in the Database Management section of the console. The data are split into individual databases (top) and the copies of the databases (bottom). The presence of multiple copies indicates that some of the databases belong to a DAG.

Administrators in larger organizations that encompass hundreds or thousands of databases spread over servers installed around the world will probably find that they get better response from EMC by creating a filter to focus on the databases about which an individual administrator is concerned. To apply a filter, click Create Filter and then select the filter that you want to use. Common filters include the databases that are mounted on a particular server or the databases that belong to a specific DAG. You can combine conditions to create very specific filter criteria. When you have selected the filter to use, click Apply Filter to have EMC select the databases that meet the criteria. Figure 7-4 shows a filter that first selects databases that belong to a specific DAG.

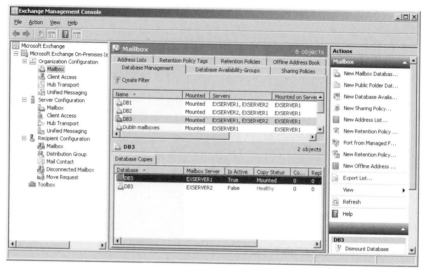

Figure 7-3 The EMC Database Management option.

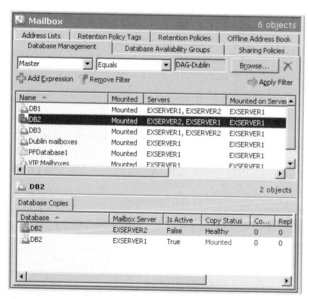

Figure 7-4 Using a filter to locate databases.

Creating new mailbox databases

New databases are created at the organization configuration level of EMC. It's always a good idea to create new mailbox databases on the server that will initially host them, because this avoids the potential for any errors due to network connectivity. Navigate to the Mailbox node under Organization Configuration and then click New Mailbox Database in the action pane to launch the New Mailbox Database Wizard. Figure 7-5 shows the first step in the wizard when you choose the name of the new database and the server where Exchange will initially mount the new database.

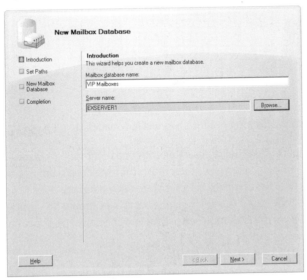

Figure 7-5 Choosing the name and server for a new mailbox database.

The next step in the process is to select the storage locations for the database and transaction log files (Figure 7-6). Both locations for the new database file and the transaction logs must be on a fixed drive (one with a drive letter that does not change). When you create a new mailbox database with EMC, Exchange reads the value of the *DataPath* property of the server that will host the new database to discover the default database location. You can find out this value with a command like this:

```
Get-ExchangeServer -Identity 'ExServer1' | Select Name, DataPath
```

```
Name                         DataPath
-------                      --------
ExServer1                    C:\Program Files\Microsoft\ExchangeServer\V14\Mailbox
```

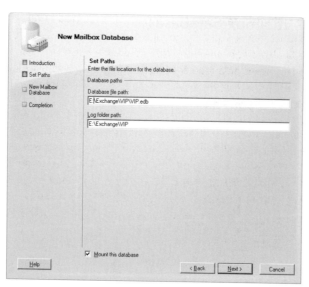

Figure 7-6 Selecting the file locations for a new mailbox database.

Creating new databases and their transaction logs in a common location under the Exchange root directory is a convenient approach for test servers, but it is not recommended in production. Best practice is to separate each database by placing it in its own directory. The directories used to store mailbox databases should be outside the C:\Program Files\Microsoft\Exchange Server structure because this should be used only for program binaries and other associated files.

> **Note**
>
> You cannot update the *DataPath* property for a server with EMS because this property is not exposed to the Set-ExchangeServer cmdlet. However, you can modify the default path using ADSIEdit by editing the *MsExchDataPath* attribute for the Exchange server object. No side effects appear to be caused by making this change, and if you decide to do this, it is best to be consistent and make the same change on all mailbox servers.

In the example shown in Figure 7-6, the transaction logs are placed on the same drive as the database. Except on test systems, this would never have been done in previous versions of Exchange because a hardware failure that affected the database could also impact the transaction logs and potentially remove the ability to recover data into a restored database. The need to protect database contents still exists in Exchange 2010, and you should place databases and transaction logs on different physical drives—preferably using different controllers—unless the database is part of a DAG and is protected through replication. Even with DAG-protected databases, you need to take operational considerations into account before making the final decision where to place transaction logs. For example, if you think that you will move mailboxes on a regular basis, you might want to place transaction logs on a separate drive to ensure that there is sufficient space for the transaction logs that Exchange generates as mailboxes move between databases.

Once you create a new mailbox database, you must mount it before it can be used. In Figure 7-6, you can see that the Mount This Database check box is selected, which is intended to instruct EMC to go ahead and issue a **Mount-Database** command after the new database is successfully created. However, experience with both the RTM and the SP1 versions of Exchange 2010 shows that if you attempt to mount the new database immediately, the potential exists for the database to fail to mount with an error similar to this:

```
Couldn't mount the database that you specified. Specified database: Mailbox
Database 03; Error code: An Active Manager operation failed. Error: The database
action failed. Error: Operation failed with message: MapiExceptionNotFound: Unable to
mount database.
```

CAUTION

The error is more common when a server is under load than when a server (such as a test server) is lightly loaded. In short, the meaning of this error is that you need to pause before you proceed to mount the database to give Exchange time to update itself about the availability of the new database. To proceed to have the database mounted, you can either wait for about 30 seconds (the interval seems to vary from organization to organization) and then attempt to mount the database with EMC or EMS, or leave the database in its dismounted state. In this case, the Active Manager component will attempt to mount the database automatically after its retry interval lapses (four minutes). We discuss Active Manager in more detail in Chapter 8, when we review how the Exchange 2010 DAG works.

Most administrators want to get on with life and use the new database, so they'll wait for 30 seconds and then mount it. The issue is mitigated in SP1 and new databases usually mount smoothly immediately after creation.

An example of typical EMS code that creates a new mailbox database is:

```
New-MailboxDatabase -Server 'ExServer1' -Name 'Sales' -EdbFilePath
'e:\E2010\Sales.edb' -LogFolderPath 'e:\E2010'
```

After the database is successfully created, we can proceed to mount it and make the database available to host new mailboxes:

```
Mount-Database -Identity 'Sales'
```

Exchange doesn't assign an Offline Address Book (OAB) to a new database. This isn't an issue as Exchange will use the Default Offline Address Book if no other OAB is assigned. However, it can be a problem if you create multiple OABs for use by different parts of the company and want to assign specific OABs to certain user communities. In such a scenario, it is common to create a mailbox database for each community and assign the correct OAB to the database. You can check the current OAB that is assigned to a database by selecting it and then viewing the Client Settings property tab (Figure 7-7). If the OAB property is blank, it means that Exchange will use the default OAB. If this isn't correct, click Browse and select an OAB to use and apply the change.

You can check for mailbox databases that don't have assigned OABs with the following command. The databases with a blank value returned for the *OfflineAddressBook* property need to be updated.

```
Get-MailboxDatabase | Select Name, OfflineAddressBook
```

You can update any database that doesn't have an assigned OAB to use the default OAB with this command:

```
Get-MailboxDatabase | Where {$_.OfflineAddressBook -eq $Null} | Set-MailboxDatabase
-OfflineAddressBook '\Default Offline Address Book'
```

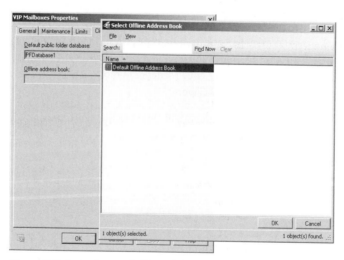

Figure 7-7 Assigning an Offline Address Book to a new mailbox database.

New mailbox databases automatically become available as targets for the automatic mailbox provisioning system, meaning that new mailboxes can be immediately created in these databases by the EMC wizard. This might not be what you intended, especially if you create a new database with specific characteristics to support the needs of a particular user community and want to reserve this database for that community. In this case, you need to block the new database from the automatic provisioning process. See Chapter 6, "Managing Mail-Enabled Recipients," for details about how to exclude or suspend databases from automatic mailbox provisioning.

A final point to consider is whether any third-party product requires permission to access the new mailbox database. Research in Motion's BlackBerry Enterprise Server is an example that needs to be assigned permission to access mailboxes so that it can update those mailboxes with messages for BlackBerry mobile devices. All of this goes to prove that it is a good idea to create your own checklist for creating new mailbox databases so that all necessary steps are taken to bring them properly into production.

Updating mailbox databases after installation

When you install an Exchange 2010 mailbox server, the Setup program will create a default mailbox database for that server and place the new database, its transaction logs, and its search catalog in a directory under the Exchange installation directory. A unique name is assigned to the database to ensure that it will not clash with any other mailbox database within the organization, so you end up with a database placed in a location such as:

C:\Program Files\Microsoft\Exchange Server\V14\Mailbox\Mailbox Database 2136564033 \Mailbox Database 2136564033.edb

The location and name of the database are probably not optimal for a production server, so there are a number of tasks that you should consider once the server is up and running properly. These tasks are also relevant for public folder databases:

1. Rename the database so that it complies with the organizational naming standard for databases. The name must still be unique, so you have to determine what it should be and then check that the name is unique.

2. Mailbox and public folder databases are created with circular logging disabled. You might wish to enable circular logging, especially if the database is going to be used within a DAG. See the section "The question of circular logging" later in this chapter for more information about circular logging.

3. Move the database and transaction log files to a more suitable location away from the disk where the Exchange binaries and other system files are installed.

4. If required, assign an OAB to the database.

Renaming a database is easy. Select the database, view its properties, and then type the new name as shown in Figure 7-8. Alternatively, you can use the Set-MailboxDatabase cmdlet to do the job. For example:

```
Set-MailboxDatabase -Identity 'Mailbox Database 2136564033'-Name 'DB2'
```

Figure 7-8 Changing a database name.

Circular logging is enabled (or disabled) on the Limits tab of the database properties. Again, this property can be easily manipulated with EMS, as shown next. Note that the database must be dismounted and remounted before the Store will implement circular logging, so the appropriate commands are included:

```
Set-MailboxDatabase -Identity 'DB4' -CircularLoggingEnabled $True
Dismount-Database -Identity 'DB4' -Confirm:$False
Mount-Database -Identity 'DB4'
```

To move a database to a more appropriate location, click the database and select the Move Database Path option. EMC displays the Move Database Path Wizard shown in Figure 7-9.

> **Note**
>
> This operation should only be attempted when you are connected to the server where the database is currently mounted; if you attempt to perform it from a remote node, EMC will not allow you to input new disk locations for the database and transaction logs.

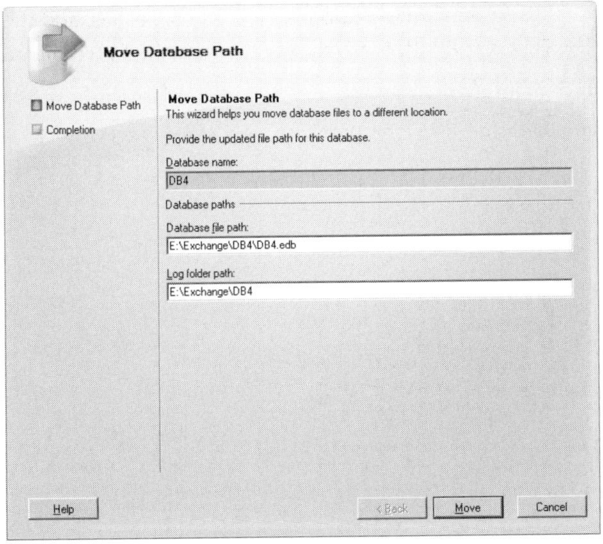

Figure 7-9 Moving a mailbox database to a new location.

To execute the move, simply type the name of the new locations for the database and transaction logs (they do not have to be on the same disk) and click Move. EMC will inform you that the database must be temporarily dismounted before it can be moved. Click OK to confirm that the move should proceed and Exchange will move all of the database files to the new location and then remount the database to restore service to users.

Databases can also be moved using the Move-DatabasePath cmdlet. For example:

```
Move-DatabasePath -Identity 'DB4' -EdbFilePath 'E:\Exchange\DB4\DB4.edb'
-LogFolderPath 'E:\Exchange\DB4'
```

Moving database locations inside a DAG is more complicated because multiple copies might exist for a database, and it is required that the copies are kept in the same location on all servers. See Chapter 8 for more information on this topic.

Background maintenance

All databases have internal structures that require some degree of maintenance to ensure logical consistency, and Exchange is no different. You can take a database offline to rebuild it with the ESEUTIL utility or verify its internal structures with the ISINTEG utility (in previous versions of Exchange; see the section "Protection against excessive database or log growth" later in this chapter), but these operations require you to deprive users of access to their mailboxes. Microsoft designed Exchange to be highly available with as little downtime as possible, and online maintenance is necessary to tune the databases while allowing users to continue working. On Exchange 2010 servers, the Store performs 11 nightly online maintenance tasks (see Table 7-4).

Table 7-4 **Background maintenance tasks**

Task	Mailbox Store	Public Store
Purge indexes	Yes	Yes
Perform tombstone maintenance	Yes	Yes
Purge the deleted items cache	Yes	Yes
Expire outdated public folder content	No	Yes
Remove public folders that exceed tombstone lifetime	No	Yes
Clean up public folder conflicts	No	Yes
Update server versions	No	Yes
Clean up reliable event tables	Yes	No
Purge deleted mailboxes	Yes	No
Check for orphaned messages	Yes	Yes
Check Free/Busy and OAB folders	No	Yes

Online maintenance focuses on content maintenance, meaning that the tasks are to purge the database of unwanted content or to ensure that the content are as accurate as possible. Content maintenance usually completes in under an hour on even the largest servers. Previous versions of Exchange also performed ESE maintenance as part of nightly background maintenance. ESE maintenance focuses on the physical structure of the database to ensure that it is as efficient as possible. ESE maintenance is far more I/O intense than content maintenance and can take many hours to complete. These tasks are:

- Online defragmentation

- Page checksum checks

Online defragmentation (known as OLD) reorganizes pages within the database so that they are in the most efficient structure. As the size of Exchange databases grew, the time required to defragment databases swelled to a point where it became increasingly difficult to finish online defragmentation within the allocated time window. Exchange 2010 therefore runs online defragmentation on a 24x7 basis rather than as part of the nightly background maintenance tasks. You can't alter this setting because the Store is designed to run in this mode. You can track the work that is done with Performance Monitor using the *MsExchange Database/Defragmentation Tasks* counters.

If you look at the Maintenance tab of the properties for a mailbox database (Figure 7-10), you see a reference to 24x7 ESE scanning. This does not refer to online defragmentation. Instead, it controls how the Store validates page checksums. A page checksum indicates whether the contents of a page are valid. The feature reads and then checksums database pages sequentially from first to last to detect corruption. Any single-bit errors that the Store detects in pages are fixed during the scan. Exchange also checksums pages as they are accessed from databases, but there is no guarantee that every page will be accessed over time, so this change was intended to process every page to proactively identify any lingering corruption.

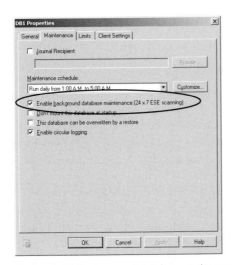

Figure 7-10 Background database maintenance.

Microsoft introduced database page checksum checks in Exchange 2007 SP1 as part of their work to make databases more self-maintaining. In its first iteration (Exchange 2007), page checksum validation was performed at the end of the set of background maintenance tasks. This approach worked, but it affected the continuous replication process. Microsoft therefore upgraded checksum validation in Exchange 2007 SP1 to allow the work to be done in the background. On most systems, pages are processed at a rate of about 5 MB/sec, or roughly 18 GB/hour, so it is relatively easy for Exchange to go through every page in a database at least once every three or four days.

Exchange 2010 allows you to run background checksum checks (or Online Database Scanning) in two ways:

- The default for Exchange 2010 mailbox databases is to scan a database continuously. You will see a warning in the error log if the Store cannot complete checksum validation for an entire database in three days. Within a DAG, the passive database copies run background checksum validation automatically to ensure that database copies are not corrupt. This is the best approach for large databases (anything over 500 GB), as it ensures that all pages will be checked regularly.

- Clear the check box that controls 24x7 operations to instruct the Store to validate page checksums only as the last part of the background maintenance process. You can adjust the schedule to allocate more time to checksum validation by increasing the size of the maintenance window. The other content checking tasks should take less than an hour so you can assume that the remainder of the window is available for checksum validation. This method is recommended for databases smaller than 500 GB.

INSIDE OUT   So many pages, so little time

The reason for introducing 24x7 checking is simple. Confining the work to a set period at night is not a problem with small databases because you can be reasonably confident that Exchange will be able to process all the pages in a database during the maintenance period. However, as databases become larger and larger, more pages must be processed. The Store processes pages sequentially from the start of the database to the end, and as the number of pages to be validated grew, it became harder and harder for the Store to complete the task within the allocated maintenance window. Hence the need for Exchange to be able to accommodate a 24x7 processing cycle. Another reason is that Exchange 2010 is able to patch single corrupt pages in databases when it operates within a Database Availability Group. If checksum validation occurs continuously, Exchange is able to patch problem pages on an ongoing basis. See the section "Incremental Synchronization" in Chapter 8 for more information about single page patching.

You can also control the way that background maintenance works through EMS. For example, to enable continuous background processing for page checksums, you set the properties of a mailbox database as follows:

```
Set-MailboxDatabase –Identity 'DB1' –BackgroundDatabaseMaintenance $True
```

If the value of the *BackgroundDatabaseMaintenance* property is set to $False, the Store validates page checksums only during the background maintenance window. The default maintenance window is between 1:00 A.M. and 5:00 A.M. each morning. We'll discuss how to change the maintenance window shortly.

Checksum validation is throttled automatically so that it does not affect responsiveness to client requests. You can monitor activity by enabling ESE advanced counters in the system registry and then using Performance Monitor to review the MSExchange Database Defragmentation performance counters.

See "Extended ESE performance counters are enabled" at *http://technet.microsoft.com/en-us /library/aa997394.aspx* for more information.

Scheduling background maintenance

Background maintenance takes place during a time window that you configure on servers. Ideally, this time should be when there is a low level of user activity and other operations such as backups are not running. By default, Exchange schedules maintenance for between midnight and 5:00 A.M. Most companies allocate between five and six hours to background maintenance, usually commencing at midnight. Another common option for installations that provide a service to users in different time zones when there is consistent user demand throughout the day is to allow a larger maintenance window over the weekend and shorten it during the work week.

If the Store cannot finish all its tasks during the allocated time window, it will complete the current task and restart from the next task when the next time window begins. You can set up a separate custom schedule for a database by selecting the database properties through EMC, and then set the maintenance window as shown in Figure 7-11.

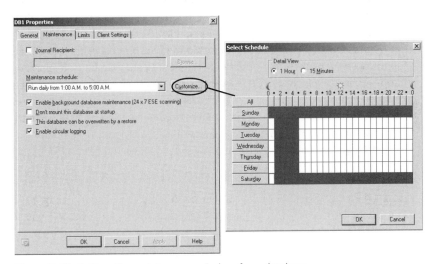

Figure 7-11 Setting the maintenance window for a database.

You can also use the Get-MailboxDatabase or Get-PublicFolderDatabase cmdlets to retrieve the current maintenance schedule for a database. For example:

```
Get-MailboxDatabase -Identity 'DB1' | Format-Table Name, MaintenanceSchedule
-AutoSize
Name MaintenanceSchedule
DB1  {Mon.1:00 AM-Mon.5:00 AM, Tue.1:00 AM-Tue.5:00 AM, Wed.1:00 AM-Wed.5:00 AM,
Thu.1:00 AM-Thu.5:00 AM, Fri.1:00 AM-Fri.5:00 AM, Sat.1:00 AM-Mon.12:00 AM}
```

If you want to apply the same maintenance schedule to a set of mailbox or public folder databases, you have to use the Set-MailboxDatabase and Set-PublicFolderDatabase cmdlets. For example, to set the maintenance window to between 1:00 A.M. and 7:00 A.M. daily for a group of databases on a server, you can use a command like this:

```
Get-MailboxDatabase -Server 'ExServer1' | Set-MailboxDatabase
-MaintenanceSchedule 'Sun.1:00 AM-Sun.7:00 AM, Mon.1:00 AM-Mon.7:00 AM,
Tue.1:00 AM-Tue.7:00 AM, Wed.1:00 AM-Wed.7:00 AM, Thu.1:00 AM-Thu.7:00 AM,
Fri.1:00 AM-Fri.7.00 AM, Sat.1:00 AM-Sat.7.00 AM, Sun.1:00 AM-Sun.7:00 AM'
```

This syntax is useful because it allows you to be extremely precise about the exact time when maintenance can occur. However, the syntax used to specify the date/time settings is a little fussy. Always leave a space between the minutes and "AM" (as in 7:00 AM) and have a hyphen between the first time and the day for the second time (as in AM-Wed). If in doubt, you can always use EMC to set the maintenance schedule on a database and then review the EMS command log to see the syntax used to set a schedule by EMC.

Content maintenance tasks

Now that we understand what happens during background maintenance and when it happens, we can consider some of the details. Clients like Outlook make extensive use of the Store's ability to generate indexes or views on a dynamic basis. For example, if you decide that you want to view your Inbox by author rather than by date, Outlook asks the Store for this view. If the Store has previously generated the view and has it cached, the response is very quick, but the Store is able to process quickly a request for a brand new view. Over time, the Store accumulates large numbers of views; each folder in every mailbox can have several views.

Expiry dates control the accumulation of views in the database

It is not desirable to retain all of the views because each view occupies space within the database. In addition, users might not require a view after its first use. The Store assigns an expiry time to each view and monitors these data in an internal table called the *index-aging table*. When background maintenance runs, the Store scans the index-aging table to discover views that are older than 40 days and removes any view that has expired. Of course, if a client accesses a view, the Store resets its expiry time.

The next task is to perform tombstone maintenance. The Store maintains a list of deleted messages for each folder and a list of "tombstones" to indicate that a message was deleted. The tombstone list is most important for replicated folders, such as public folders, because it provides the Store with a list of message delete operations that it must replicate to every server that holds a replica of the folder. After successful replication, the Store can clear the entries from the tombstone list. Background maintenance ensures that the lists are accurate.

TROUBLESHOOTING

I need a deleted message

When a client deletes a message, the Store sets a flag to hide the message from the mailbox (a soft delete). A hard delete means that an item is permanently removed from the database and cannot be recovered, which is what eventually happens when Exchange removes items after they exceed their deleted retention period. Clients can retrieve messages from the deleted items cache by clearing the flag, thus causing the message to reappear in the mailbox. (This is essentially what happens when you use the Recover Deleted Items feature in Outlook or OWA.)

During background maintenance, the Store examines every message that has the deleted flag set (if enough time is available in the maintenance window, the Store processes the entire contents of the deleted items cache) to determine whether its retention period has expired. If this is true, the Store removes the message from the Store (a hard delete) and makes the pages used to hold the message available for reuse. You can set retention periods on a per-mailbox, per-database, or per-public-folder basis and can control these settings through EMC or EMS.

The usual deleted item retention time is set at 14 days. Exchange also allows you to set a retention period for content in a public folder either per database or per folder. The idea here is that you might use some public folders to hold content that ages out in a systematic way, such as an RSS feed. By aging out content from a public folder, you impose a check on how large the folder grows. To set a new age limit for a public folder database to 365 days:

```
Set-PublicFolderDatabase -Identity 'PFDatabase1' -ItemRetentionPeriod 365.00:00:00
```

To set a specific age limit for a public folder:

```
Set-PublicFolder -Identity '\Exchange 2010\Admin Discussions' -AgeLimit
'365.00:00:00' -UseDatabaseAgeDefaults $False
```

If you want to set an age limit for a set of public folders from a known root, you can use a combination of the Get-PublicFolder and the Set-PublicFolder cmdlets.

```
Get-PublicFolder -Identity '\Exchange 2010' -Recurse | Set-PublicFolder
-AgeLimit '365.00:00:00' -UseDatabaseAgeDefaults $False
```

Chapter 7

> **Tip**
>
> Use the *–Recurse* parameter to walk down through the child folders.

Background maintenance checks for deleted public folders and system messages that have exceeded their retention period and then removes them. The Store also checks for deleted mailboxes, which have a default retention period of 30 days, and removes any that have expired. Removing obsolete folders and mailboxes cleans up the internal table structure of the database and increases efficiency.

The next check is for deleted public folders that have expired. By default, if you delete a public folder, the Store creates a tombstone for the folder. This allows the replication mechanism to propagate the deletion properly to servers that hold replicas. Because replication might not occur quickly in some circumstances, the Store retains the tombstone for 180 days (default value). If replication has not propagated the tombstone in 180 days, your organization is experiencing fundamental replication difficulties, and a few erroneous tombstones are of little concern. During background maintenance, the Store checks for folder tombstones that have expired and removes them. However, the Store only removes a maximum of 500 tombstones per 24-hour period.

Public folder replication is something of a black art, and it is easy for conflicts to occur. For example, multiple users modify the same item in different replicas of a public folder, or multiple users might attempt to simultaneously save an item in the same replica. When a conflict happens, the Store sends a conflict resolution message to the users who provoked the problem to ask them to resolve the issue. It is easier for people to decide which change is more important and so resolve the conflict. While the people decide what to do, the Store maintains the different versions of the items in conflict. However, if the users fail to respond, the Store examines each item in conflict and resolves them automatically, usually by accepting the most recent version.

The next task is to update server versions for the public stores. This process updates any version information that is necessary to maintain the system configuration folder. The Store incurs no great overhead and you cannot control the process.

The Store checks that the system folders that hold the free/busy data and OAB files exist and that there are no duplicates.

Tracking background maintenance

The Store logs events in the Application Event Log as it performs background maintenance. Like elsewhere in Exchange, the selected level of diagnostics logging determines how much information the Store writes about maintenance operations into the Application Event

Log. You set the level for diagnostic logging using the Set-EventLogLevel cmdlet for the 'MSExchangeIS\9000 Private\Background Cleanup' and 'MSExchangeIS\9001 Public \Background Cleanup' settings. Change the value from "Lowest" to "Expert." For example:

```
Set-EventLogLevel -Identity 'MSExchangeIS\9000 Private\Background Cleanup'
-Level 'Expert'
```

After applying the new setting, the Store begins to generate events the next time it runs background maintenance. Except on very large or heavily loaded servers, many of these tasks complete quickly. The obvious exception is background defragmentation. This is the most intense activity and can last a number of hours depending on whatever other load the server is under, hardware configuration, and the size of the databases that the Store processes.

Corrupt item detection and isolation

Bad items or messages that contain some corruption such as a malformed header have a nasty habit of causing extreme difficulty for an Exchange administrator. Exchange 2007 introduced the ability to detect and isolate corrupt messages in the transport system. Essentially, if the transport system thinks that a message is corrupt and likely to cause problems such as provoking a software crash, it considers the message to be "poison" and isolates it in a queue that the administrator can examine to decide whether the message really is a problem. Exchange 2010 applies the same concept to the Store to address situations where a mailbox that contains one or more corrupt items can cause the Information Store process to terminate abnormally when a client attempts to access a corrupt item.

As you know, the Information Store process is multithreaded. The threads are connected to mailboxes to do work and the Store detects a problem mailbox when:

- The Store has more than five threads connected to a mailbox that have been "frozen" for 60 seconds or more.

- One of the threads connected to a mailbox crashes abnormally. The nature of software is that crashes do occur, so Exchange allows for up to three crashes within a two-hour period before it regards a mailbox to have exceeded the acceptable threshold for crashes.

When the Store identifies a problem mailbox, it writes details about the mailbox into the system registry. These details include the mailbox GUID (to identify the mailbox), the time that a crash occurred, and the number of times that the problem has occurred. This information is stored under the root for the mailbox database that contains the mailbox in two entries written for a problem mailbox. The first entry captures the last crash time, the second the count of crashes.

- HKLM\System\CurrentControlSet\Services\MSExchangeIS\Server Name \Private-{Database GUID}\QuarantinedMailboxes\{Mailbox GUID}\LastCrashTime

- HKLM\System\CurrentControlSet\Services\MSExchangeIS\Server Name \Private-{Database GUID}\QuarantinedMailboxes\{Mailbox GUID}\CrashCount

When a mailbox exceeds the crash threshold or the Store considers that threads are being blocked by corrupt content, the Store puts the mailbox into quarantine. This means that normal client interaction, including access by Exchange mailbox assistants, is blocked. If you check the Application Event Log, you'll find a 10018 event from MSExchangeIS logged for each problem mailbox. The text of the event tells you the distinguished name of the problem mailbox and looks like this:

```
The mailbox for user /o=TonyR/ou=Exchange Administrative Group (FYDIBOHF23SPDLT)
/cn=Recipients/cn=TRedmond has been quarantined. Access to this mailbox will be
restricted to administrative logons for the next 6 hours.
```

A quarantined mailbox cannot be logged onto, nor will Exchange deliver messages to it (the messages remain on the transport queues). The only operation that you can perform against a quarantined mailbox is to move it to another database. By default, Exchange maintains a mailbox in quarantine for up to six hours (21,600 seconds). You can change the quarantine period and the threshold for crashes by entering two new registry keys. These are specific to a mailbox database and are read when the database is mounted. The first key is in seconds and sets the quarantine period; the second sets the threshold for thread crashes that Exchange will tolerate before considering a mailbox to contain some corrupt items.

- HKLM\System\CurrentControlSet\Services\MSExchangeIS\Server Name\Private-{Database GUID}\QuarantinedMailboxes}\MailboxQuarantineDurationInSeconds

- HKLM\System\CurrentControlSet\Services\MSExchangeIS\Server Name\Private-{Database GUID}\QuarantinedMailboxes}\MailboxQuarantineCrashThreshold

INSIDE OUT An EMS command to identify quarantined mailboxes

An administrator probably is not going to be aware of a quarantined mailbox until a user complains that he cannot access his mailbox, in which case a check against the registry might reveal that the mailbox is in quarantine. In Exchange 2010, the Get-MailboxStatistics cmdlet is updated so that you can use it to check for quarantined mailboxes. This command lists all mailboxes currently in quarantine.

```
Get-MailboxStatistics | Where {$_.IsQuarantine -eq $True}
```

You can access a quarantined mailbox with a utility such as MFCMAPI (available from *http://mfcmapi.codeplex.com/*) and use it to remove any corrupt items that you detect. However, determining that an item is corrupt requires a deep knowledge of MAPI and how it expects data to be organized and is probably far beyond the capabilities of the normal Exchange administrator. SP1 allows for a better solution by permitting quarantined mailboxes to be moved to a different database. Two good things can result from moving the mailbox. First, you can isolate the mailbox to a database where crashing will not impact service to other users. Second, the act of moving the mailbox can remove problems such as consolidating the named properties used by items in the mailbox or dropping corrupt (bad) items as the Mailbox Replication Service transfers items from the source to the target mailbox. See Chapter 12, "Mailbox Support Services," for more information about how mailbox moves are performed.

The Store keeps the problem mailbox in quarantine until the quarantine duration elapses and then releases it by removing the registry keys for last crash time and crash count. The registry keys are also removed by the Store if they are more than two hours old when a database is mounted. The logic here is that dismounting and remounting the database might well have cleared any lurking problem that caused problems with Store threads. Of course, releasing a mailbox that contains corrupt data from quarantine could set off a new cycle of crashes, leading to further quarantine.

TROUBLESHOOTING

How do I deal with a mailbox stuck in a quarantine cycle?
If a mailbox goes into a cycle of constant quarantining, it's an indication that some deep problem exists that you might be able to resolve by moving the mailbox to another database. In this instance, you instruct Exchange to ignore any corrupt items that it detects during the move operation so that the mailbox is as clean as possible after the move. If this doesn't work and the mailbox continues to cause problems, the only route open to you is to export as much information as possible to a PST and then delete the mailbox. If the export operation fails because of corruption, you might be able to recover data through a database restore as described in Chapter 9, "Backups and Restores."

The Store periodically monitors mailboxes that have caused thread crashes. If no further crashes occur in a two-hour period, the Store concludes that whatever problem existed was transient and removes the mailbox from the list of quarantined mailboxes in the system registry. Obviously, an administrator can decide to remove a mailbox from the list, too, by manually deleting the entry in the system registry. This is not recommended unless you know that the underlying problem no longer exists or you want to restore client access to a mailbox to allow the user to recover as much data as she can from the mailbox before you delete and re-create the mailbox.

If you don't see the QuarantinedMailboxes entry under a database root in the registry, you know that the Store has never detected a problem mailbox for that database. Note that Exchange replicates mailbox quarantine data from the registry to other servers in a DAG via the failover cluster service to ensure that a failover retains knowledge of problem mailboxes.

Backups and permanent removal

You can stop the Store from permanently removing items from databases until a successful backup has been performed. You control this stage of deletion by setting a property of a database (Figure 7-12). The equivalent EMS command is:

```
Set-MailboxDatabase -Identity 'Sales'-RetainDeletedItemsUntilBackup $True
```

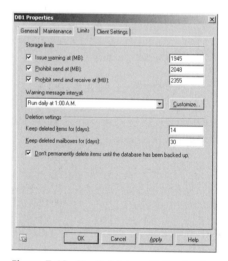

Figure 7-12   Don't delete until the database has been backed up.

When this property is set, items remain in the dumpster until a successful backup is performed, even if they exceed the retention period. You do not want to get into a position where items expire from the dumpster, are removed by background maintenance, and cannot be recovered from a backup because there was a failure to make a backup or a failure occurred during processing rendering a backup invalid. It is best practice to set the property on all mailbox databases except those that use circular logging, which are usually intended to store transient data that do not need the same degree of protection as user mailboxes.

Protection against high latency

Store databases can suffer from high latency for a number of reasons. A disk might be failing and is responding to requests in seconds rather than milliseconds, or the server might be under extreme demand for CPU or suffering from memory shortage. Then it's possible that a mailbox could be causing an issue caused by a client-side bug or other problem.

Exchange 2010 SP1 includes a new script called Troubleshoot-DatabaseLatency.ps1 that you can run if a server seems to be under strain to attempt to determine the root cause of excessive latency. For example, to check the latency of a database called DB1, the syntax of the script is:

```
Troubleshoot-DatabaseLatency.ps1 –Database "DB1" –LatencyThreshold 60
–TimeInServerThreshold 10 –Quarantine $True –MonitoringContext $True
```

The parameters that can be supplied to the script are as follows:

- *LatencyThreshold* is the threshold for latency and is 70 milliseconds by default. Normally you won't need to amend this threshold unless you want to experiment to see what results are returned in your environment under different conditions or you are advised to do so by Microsoft CSS as part of a troubleshooting exercise.

- *TimeInServerThreshold* indicates the number of seconds of work per minute that can be performed on behalf of a single mailbox before the mailbox is considered hazardous to the health of the database. The number of seconds of work is measured by aggregating the time spent inside Store (CPU, waiting for I/O and other operations) by all threads working on behalf of the mailbox over the period reported by the Get-StoreUsageStatistics cmdlet. The number of seconds of work per minute is calculated by dividing the aggregate number by the measurement period used by the Get-StoreUsageStatistics cmdlet (10 minutes). By default, the threshold is 60 seconds.

- *Quarantine* should be set to $True if you want mailboxes that are observed to be the cause of high server demand to be placed into quarantine.

- *MonitoringContext* determines whether the script is running on a server that is monitored by a system such as Microsoft System Center Operations Manager (SCOM). If this is the case, set the property to $True to force the script to write events to the Application Event Log.

If the problem is caused by a mailbox that occupies more than one CPU thread over a 10-minute period, Exchange will put the mailbox into quarantine and keep it there for the default quarantine period unless it is moved to a different database. The same mechanism is used as for corrupt item detection (see earlier) with the crash count set to three to force immediate quarantine. A mailbox is also put into quarantine if it peaks close to the 1 thread/10 minute threshold three times in a two-hour period.

Protection against excessive database or log growth

Many situations have been observed over the years when a mailbox server seems to grow the size of a database excessively or generate a very large number of transaction logs. Databases usually grow at a rate consistent with the growth of the mailboxes that the database holds. The same is true of transaction logs, although you can see a spurt in transaction log generation with no increase in database size if there is a lot of white space available in the database that can be filled by new transactions or if other activities, like deleting a large number of mailboxes, cause a spike in transaction log growth.

For instance, if a database grows at the rate of 100 MB/month and suddenly expands by 1 GB overnight with the attendant increase in transaction logs, it might be due to legitimate activity or a software bug. Legitimate activity includes the movement of many mailboxes into a database or the import of data from PSTs. Known bugs in the past include the submission of messages by Outlook that go into a loop and continually generate new transactions. The problem therefore is to determine whether database growth is due to a problem or administrative activity. The former might not go away and could need a patch to fix a bug; the latter will subside over time.

Microsoft provides a troubleshooter script in Exchange 2010 SP1 called Troubleshoot-DatabaseSpace.ps1 that you can run against a mailbox server that is currently experiencing excessive database or log growth. The script takes a reasonably hands-off approach to problems in that it doesn't rush to conclusions. Instead, it lets the potential problem go until available space on the disk that hosts the database or the transaction logs falls below a threshold where it will be exhausted within a configurable time period at the current rate of growth. At this point, the script determines the mailboxes that are responsible for the growth and quarantines them to throttle back growth. If the current rate of growth will not exhaust available space within the period, Exchange logs an event that describes the potential for disk exhaustion due to database or log growth in the Application Event Log or, if SCOM is installed, an SCOM alert is raised.

The script is run as follows:

```
Troubleshoot-DatabaseSpace.ps1 –DatabaseIdentityDB1
-PercentEdbFreeSpaceThreshold 29 -PercentLogFreeSpaceThreshold 20 –HourThreshold 6
-Quarantine:$True
```

The parameters are the following:

- *–PercentEdbFreeSpaceThreshold* sets the threshold for the percentage of free space available on the disk that holds the database. Exchange takes available white space in the database into account when it calculates how much free space exists on the disk.

- *–PercentLogFreeSpaceThreshold* sets the threshold for the percentage of free space available on the disk that holds the database's transaction logs.

- *–HourThreshold* sets the threshold for the number of hours worth of free space that must be available if the database continues to grow its size or transaction logs. In this example, the troubleshooter script will respond (and quarantine mailboxes determined to be causing excessive growth) if disk space will be exhausted in six hours or less based on the current rate of consumption. If sufficient space exists to allow the database to grow for the specified period, the script logs an event and leaves it to the administrator to take the necessary action to restrict further growth.

- *–Quarantine* determines whether the troubleshooter is allowed to quarantine mailboxes. If set to false, the script will not attempt to quarantine problematic mailboxes.

Store driver fault isolation

As we'll discuss in some depth when we discuss Exchange's message transport service in Chapter 15, "Compliance," the Store Driver is a very important component that runs on a hub transport server and provides the mechanism to deliver inbound messages to mailbox databases. Exchange 2010 SP1 includes code to manage connections from the Store Driver as it delivers messages in such a way that allows Exchange to isolate and limit the effect of any faults that occur. Table 7-5 lists the Store Driver limits that are in place for Exchange 2010 SP1.

Table 7-5 Connection limits imposed by Exchange on the Store Driver

Connection	Limit
Hub transport server to mailbox server	Concurrent delivery to a mailbox: Only one message can be delivered concurrently to the same mailbox. This limit is in place to ensure that all the mailboxes in a database receive a similar speed and quality of service.
	Concurrent delivery to a database: Only two messages can be delivered concurrently to the same mailbox database. This limit prevents a problem with one database from affecting all the other mailbox databases on a server. The problem can be caused by an underlying hardware issue such as a failing disk or storage controller or a software bug. Exchange might reduce this limit automatically if it senses that the performance of a mailbox database is lower than normal.
	Concurrent delivery to a mailbox server: Only 24 messages can be delivered concurrently to the same mailbox server. A hub transport server can deliver to any mailbox server in the site. This limit prevents a problem with one mailbox server (that might be experiencing heavy load) from affecting delivery to all other mailbox servers in the site.
	Concurrent delivery per message across all mailbox servers: Only 12 concurrent deliveries per individual message can be attempted to all mailbox servers in the site. This limit prevents a problem with a corrupt or expensive message (such as one with a number of large attachments or several hundred recipients in the message header) from absorbing all available connections and therefore stopping or slowing down delivery from a hub transport server to the mailbox server within a site.

Mailbox server to hub transport server	Concurrent submission to a hub transport server: The limit for the maximum number of connections is calculated as five times the number of available mailbox processor cores.This limit controls how many concurrent submissions can be made from a mailbox server to all hub transport servers in the site.
	Concurrent submission from a mailbox database: Only four connections can be performed concurrently from a mailbox database.
	Concurrent submissions from a single mailbox server: A hub transport server will only process at most 12 concurrent submissions from any single mailbox server.
	Concurrent submissions to a hub transport server: A mailbox server will only make a maximum of 15 concurrent submissions to any single hub transport server.
Site-wide hub transport to mailbox server	The upper limit for the number of connections from hub transport servers to mailbox servers across the site is 20 times the total number of hub processor cores in the site. For example, if there are two hub transport servers in the site, each equipped with four processor cores, the limit is 160 connections.
Site-wide mailbox servers to hub transport servers	The upper limit for the number of connections from mailbox servers to hub transport servers across the site is five times the total number of mailbox processor cores. For example, if there are six mailbox servers in the site, each equipped with four processor cores, the limit is 120 connections.

The death of ISINTEG

ISINTEG is the Information Store Integrity maintenance utility provided by Microsoft to address problems that occurred in the logical structure of Exchange databases (by comparison, ESEUTIL handles problems that cause physical corruption at a much lower level). It has been present in every version of Exchange. ISINTEG exists in Exchange 2010 but it's a shell utility that does nothing. There are two reasons why ISINTEG is neutered in Exchange 2010. First, the radical schema updates for the database created a whole new set of potential scenarios where corruption might occur. At the same time, it's also fair to say that the new schema nullified the root cause for many corruptions that occur in databases prior to Exchange 2010. Second, Microsoft just didn't have the time to do the work to create an upgraded ISINTEG for Exchange 2010.

The previous database schema uses a lot of tables that are maintained at database level. A corruption that occurs in a table can therefore affect all the mailboxes in a database. The Exchange 2010 schema changes the focus for data partitioning from database tables to mailbox tables, and Microsoft now expects database-level corruptions to be very rare. Although the likelihood of corruptions is greatly lowered by the new schema, it's also true that new mailbox-level corruptions are possible. However, because most data are now stored in mailbox tables, the simple act of moving a mailbox from one database to another is sufficient to clean out many problems that might exist in these tables. Bad items are dropped en route from the source to target database and problems that might exist in views and item counts are fixed as the new mailbox is built in the target database.

Given the new situation, Microsoft decided to take a different approach to ISINTEG. Instead of providing a utility that forces you to take a database offline for potentially several hours to perform maintenance, Microsoft introduced a new set of mailbox repair cmdlets in Exchange 2010 SP1 to allow administrators to create repair requests for mailboxes that address the most common causes of corruption for views and item counts. These include the following:

- Search folder corruptions (mailbox)

- Incorrect aggregate counts on folders (mailbox)

- Incorrect contents returned by folder views (mailbox)

- Public Folder replication state

- Public Folder view verification

- Public Folder physical corruption

The repair cmdlets use roughly the same model as mailbox move, import, and export requests in that an administrator creates a repair request that is queued for processing by the Store, which then performs whatever repairs are required asynchronously with the database online, so there's no need for the user to log out of her mailbox while the Store examines and adjusts internal mailbox structures. The New-MailboxRepairRequest cmdlet creates a repair request for a mailbox and the New-PublicFolderDatabaseRepairRequest cmdlet creates a repair request for a public folder database. For example:

```
New-MailboxRepairRequest –Mailbox JSmith –CorruptionType Folder View
```

If you add the –*DetectOnly* parameter to the request, Exchange will report any corruption that it finds but won't repair it. The other corruption types that can be fixed in a mailbox are *SearchFolder*, *AggregateCounts*, and *ProvisonedFolder*. These repairs fix problems with search folders, counts on folders, and provisioned fields. You can perform several repairs at one time by specifying a list of the fixes that you want to make. For example:

```
New-MailboxRepairRequest –Mailbox JSmith –CorruptionType FolderView, AggregrateCounts
```

You can also scan all of the mailboxes in a database at one time to fix any corruptions that are found in any mailbox. For example:

```
New-MailboxRepairRequest –Database DB1 –CorruptionType FolderView, SearchFolder,
AggregateCounts
```

Only one type of corruption can be fixed for a public folder database. This is the replica list and is fixed as follows:

```
New-PublicFolderDatabaseRepairRequest –Identity 'PFDatabase1'-CorruptionType
ReplicaList
```

When you submit a new mailbox repair request, Exchange responds with a task identifier and the name of the server that will handle the request. This is the mailbox server that currently hosts the active copy of the database. The only evidence that Exchange has progressed the repair exists in the application event log, which captures event 10047 (Figure 7-13) when a mailbox repair request is initiated and event 10048 when the repair completes successfully and no corruption is in the mailbox. Event 10059 is logged when a database repair starts. Event 10062 is logged when a corruption is found and a fix is made (if the –DetectOnly parameter is not specified). You may need to run several mailbox repairs before all corruptions are eliminated and event 10048 is reported. All of the events are logged on the server that processes the repair request.

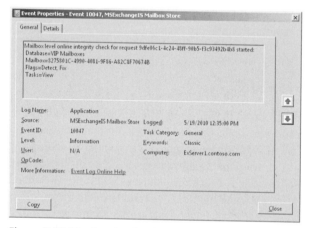

Figure 7-13 Viewing details of a mailbox repair request logged into the event log.

INSIDE OUT   Canceling a repair job

You can't cancel or review the current status of a repair job. This functionality is likely to be added by Microsoft in a future release. For now, the only way to terminate a repair job is to dismount a database or move the database to another server (or if the database crashes due to a software bug). These actions clear out any pending or active repair jobs within the database.

To ensure that performance is not impacted, you can only run a single repair against a complete database on a server at one time. However, you can run up to 100 individual mailbox repairs concurrently on a server (spread across multiple databases).

If the database has copies within a DAG, the results of any repairs made to fix problems found in the tables within the mailbox are replicated along with other transactions to the database copies and are logged as events in the Application Event Log on the server where the repair is performed. Much the same happens when repairs are applied to a public folder database, with the exception that the repair occurs on a specified public folder database and any changes to items resulting from the repairs are replicated using the public folder replication mechanism.

INSIDE OUT   Database encryption

Windows Server 2008 supports BitLocker, the standard Windows encryption mechanism, so is it possible to put Exchange databases on a BitLocker-protected device? You can put databases on a device that is protected by BitLocker, but this only provides a certain level of protection in that it stops someone from copying a database and moving it to another system before attempting to break into the database and access its content.

Microsoft will support a database that is encrypted with BitLocker as per *http://technet .microsoft.com/en-us/library/dd421859.aspx*.

Exchange can still continue to read and write data into a database on a BitLocker-protected device because it accesses the device through Windows and Windows is able to access the protected data. However, you have to question the usefulness of the protection in most real-world scenarios. I cannot think of an instance of someone stealing an Exchange database to gain access to information. If someone did steal a disk that contained an Exchange database, BitLocker would do an excellent job of protecting the data. On the other hand, I know of plenty of situations when Exchange administrators have used their privileges to open another user's mailbox to browse its contents with Outlook or another client. Placing databases on an encrypted drive will not prevent this kind of access. In addition, Windows 2008 (and 2008 R2) contains a bug that causes Windows to incorrectly report that WFC volumes used by a DAG are shared volumes, so BitLocker won't encrypt disks that contain DAG databases. This will hopefully be fixed in a forthcoming service pack.

Controlling named properties

Exchange is based on MAPI and MAPI treats everything about a message as a property. The subject is a property, as are the recipients, date and time sent, and so on. Exchange supports a maximum of 64 KB worth of known properties, each of which is assigned a name and a value. A property name can be a string or a numeric value. It doesn't really matter what the name is because properties are designed for internal use and aren't exposed by clients to people. You can, of course, use a program such as MFCMAPI to see the internal property names and their associated values. Outlook generates an enormous number of properties for its messages because it is a highly functional client that needs to use properties to hold the data on which its features depend.

MAPI splits the available range of properties into three sections. Some are used for MAPI named properties (such as those assigned by Outlook), some are used for replication, and 8 KB of properties are reserved as non-MAPI named properties. The original intention for these named properties was that they could be requested by developers who wanted to store some application-specific data along with a message. For example, if you wrote a workflow application, you could transfer the data required by the application, such as a workflow item's approval status, as a property of the item. This design made perfect sense in the early days of Exchange when tools such as the Electronic Forms Designer were shipped with the product.

Named properties were largely a slumbering side alley until Exchange 2000 appeared and introduced the STM (streaming file), a complementary file to the JET EDB database that stored non-MAPI or Multipurpose Internet Mail Extensions (MIME) data that flowed into Exchange from the Internet. The idea was that keeping the MIME content in a separate file would allow Exchange to deal with it more efficiently when required by clients. A component called IMAIL processed Internet content and split it into properties that were stored in the EDB and the MIME content, which went into the STM. The properties were derived from the normal properties that you'd expect to find on messages plus any x-headers that were present.

This mechanism worked well for some time. The STM disappeared in Exchange 2007 but IMAIL remained to promote x-headers into named properties. No real problems appeared until the growing use of x-headers created strain on Exchange's ability to assign these headers to named properties. Remember that no control exists over x-headers; anyone can create an x-header for their own purposes and send it off on messages to all across the Internet, so you end up with headers like *x-myapplication-data*. Exchange would do its best to process these x-headers as they arrived on a server and stored them as named properties, but an obvious problem now became very apparent: Anyone could create a message that included 8 KB or more x-headers and send it to an Exchange recipient to cause the Store to exceed its limit of named properties. The result was that Exchange would bounce subsequent messages that included new x-headers with an error because it couldn't promote the new headers to become named properties. The problem report in the nondelivery report (NDR) looks like this:

```
#550 5.2.0 STOREDRV.Deliver: The Microsoft Exchange Information Store service
reported an error. The following information should help identify the cause of this
error: "MapiExceptionNamedPropsQuotaExceeded:16.18969:3D010000,
```

In addition, errors 9666, 9667, 9668, and 9669 charted the problems in the Application Event Log as Exchange approached and then exceeded the named property limit.

Further problems were seen with journaling, because the Exchange 2007 journal databases had to cope with messages coming from many different databases within the organization, each of which might introduce new named properties. Exchange 2007 stores named properties on a per-database basis, so you can see how a single journal database might be quickly overwhelmed. At its worst, exceeding the named properties quota could cause problems with database replication in Exchange 2007 CCR clusters and force database reseeding as a result.

A number of solutions were tried, the most common of which are the following:

- Update the system registry to increase the range assigned to named properties up to the Exchange 2007 maximum of 32 KB.

- Install a transport agent called *HeaderFilterAgent* (details available on *http://headerfilteragent.codeplex.com/Wikipage*) that would remove any x-header from incoming messages that didn't appear in an "approved list" and so prevent the problem ever getting to crisis point.

- Force Exchange to reset its named property range by creating new mailbox databases and move mailboxes to those databases.

All these are short-term tactical solutions. The real solution was to stamp down hard on the ability of any random unauthenticated correspondent anywhere in the Internet to consume valuable server resources, and that's just what Microsoft did in Exchange 2007 SP1 RU9 (and later) and then in Exchange 2010.

The solution is to limit the creation of named properties to authenticated senders and MAPI applications that obey the rules for property creation. In addition, Exchange 2010 stores named properties at a mailbox level rather than for a database, so if a problem ever occurred with a quota you can address it by moving the mailbox to another database. The move mailbox request will rebuild the named property range for the mailbox and likely fix any lurking problems.

> **Note**
>
> It's possible that the stricter regime imposed by Exchange 2007 SP2 and Exchange 2010 might break some existing applications that depend on their ability to transmit x-header information or other properties. If this is the case, you will have to rewrite the application so that it creates the property according to the new rules using MAPI or Exchange Web Services.

Database defragmentation

As we know, Exchange 2010 performs ongoing online defragmentation to achieve maximum page contiguity and space utilization within the database. The overall size of the database is not affected by online defragmentation as pages freed by processing are recycled and made available to the Store to hold new items. Offline defragmentation or a database rebuild is accomplished by taking the database offline and then running the ESEUTIL utility in /D mode to build a new copy of the database by reading all of the pages out of the old database and writing them into the new. Depending on system performance and the size of the database, an offline rebuild can take a long time, and the only thing that it accomplishes is the return of unused space to the file system. In the days of Exchange 5.5 and Exchange 2000, when background defragmentation was inefficient and ineffective, it was deemed best practice to perform an offline rebuild for databases on a regular basis to prevent them from swelling to obscene sizes.

Microsoft has improved the effectiveness of background defragmentation significantly and you should never have to take a database offline to rebuild it except in exceptional circumstances. For example, mailboxes allocated to students while they attend universities are more transient than mailboxes used in corporate email systems because there is typically a very large turnover of the student body annually. If you had to delete 10,000 student mailboxes from a database, performing a rebuild would shrink the database dramatically and make backups faster. On the other hand, you could argue that VSS-based backups are much faster than tape-based backups and the size of the database is much less relevant now, so you could leave the database online and let it fill up with new mailboxes.

Another example of where a rebuild might be required in previous versions of Exchange is when the window assigned for background maintenance operation is not sufficient to allow defragmentation to complete so over time the database bloats with unused pages. However, given that Exchange 2010 performs online defragmentation on an ongoing basis, this argument to justify an offline rebuild does not hold water now.

Unlike previous versions of Exchange, you won't see events logged to indicate when background maintenance has started and finished online defragmentation, nor will you see any reports of the white space that's available in a database following a defragmentation pass. This is quite logical because the continuous nature of Exchange 2010 online defragmentation means that it starts when the Information Store mounts a database and finishes when the Store service shuts down. The loss of events to log the start and finish of defragmentation does not mean that you cannot see evidence that defragmentation is proceeding. Microsoft has added a new set of counters to the system Performance Monitor, so you can start the PerfMon utility and add the MSExchange Database/Instances/DB Maintenance IO Reads/sec counter to the set being monitored. The level of activity varies with system load, and you should see more activity when the system is lightly loaded and less when users are active.

You can still gain a sense of the amount of white space available in a database with the Get-MailboxDatabase cmdlet. Normally, to avoid any performance impact, a call to this cmdlet only reports the static information about a database that is held in Active Directory. In this case, we need to force EMS to make a call to the Store to retrieve internal database data, so we pass the –*Status* parameter to retrieve the necessary data:

```
Get-MailboxDatabase -Identity 'DB1' -Status | Select Name, DatabaseSize,
AvailableNewMailboxSpace
```

You can also perform the same check for all the mailbox databases in use within the organization. This command can take some time to complete because it requires EMS to check the status for each database on every server. In this case, we'll fetch the data and sort it by database size.

```
Get-MailboxDatabase -Status | Sort-Object DatabaseSize -Descending | Format-Table
Name, DatabaseSize, AvailableNewMailboxSpace
```

Name	DatabaseSize	AvailableNewMailboxSpace
MBDatabase3	1.57 GB (1,686,175,744 bytes)	121.1 MB (126,943,232 bytes)
MBDatabase1	1.195 GB (1,283,522,560 bytes)	69.44 MB (72,810,496 bytes)
IT Department	936.1 MB (981,532,672 bytes)	6.063 MB (6,356,992 bytes)
VIP Data	856.1 MB (897,646,592 bytes)	176.1 MB (184,647,680 bytes)
MBDatabase2	736.1 MB (771,817,472 bytes)	628.4 MB (658,931,712 bytes)
Dublin Users	384.1 MB (402,718,720 bytes)	90.22 MB (94,601,216 bytes)
Sales	352.1 MB (369,164,288 bytes)	83.59 MB (87,654,400 bytes)
PR	264.1 MB (276,889,600 bytes)	108 MB (113,278,976 bytes)
Operations	264.1 MB (276,889,600 bytes)	117.5 MB (123,207,680 bytes)

The reported database size should be pretty close to the actual file size on disk. The figure for available new mailbox space gives an indication of the available white space in the database and, as you can see, the percentage of free space varies from database to database depending on recent activity in the database. For example, a database that hosts a set of mailboxes that has remained constant over time will have a lower amount of free space than a database that has had some mailboxes move out to another database. This is obvious when you compare the data reported for the "IT Department" (0.64 percent free) and "MBDatabase2" (85.3 percent free) databases. Over time the percentages for the two databases will come much closer together as user activity consumes space. If there is more than 15 percent available space in a database, it might be due to incomplete maintenance or another reason, such as the recent deletion of many mailboxes.

The available new mailbox space value is a fair approximation

The value reported for available new mailbox space is not a totally accurate indication of available white space because it only includes pages that are immediately available to be assigned to new mailboxes, which use space from the root tree within the database. It does not include free pages that exist in mailbox or index tables. However, it's a good approximation of how much white space exists in the database.

Moving away from internal structures, at the level of the database file Exchange 2010 uses an 8 MB default file extent whenever it requests more disk space from Windows. Exchange 2010 SP1 increases the extent to 128 MB and changes the extent used by passive database copies in a DAG so that they also use 128 MB. This is a bigger change in some respects, as passive copies don't use a fixed extent in RTM. Instead, they grow the database by the minimum amount required. The change to use a larger file extent and coordination between active and passive copies reduces the potential for on-disk fragmentation of databases.

Using ESEUTIL

ESEUTIL is a useful but dangerous utility. It's useful because it can fix some low-level problems in a database (however, it won't be able to fix fundamental corruption caused by hardware failures). It's dangerous because some administrators and other commentators consider it to be a good thing to run ESEUTIL against Exchange databases on a regular basis "just in case." Such an attitude is firmly entrenched in the 1990s when, to be blunt, the Exchange database wasn't as robust and reliable as it is today—and has been since Exchange 2003.

In the early days, the predominant reason for running ESEUTIL was to recover disk space from the database. Exchange was like a swollen pig when it came to growing its database and wasn't very good at reusing database pages after they were released when messages were deleted. A 10 GB database (big in those days) might only contain 7 GB of mailbox data; you had to rebuild the database with ESEUTIL to return the 3 GB of unused storage to the system. Of course, disks were expensive and small, so recovering 3 GB was a big thing, making the exercise usually worthwhile, even if you had to take the database offline over the weekend to perform the rebuild.

It's a different situation today. Disks are larger, they are radically less expensive, and Exchange is much better at recovering and reusing pages within its databases. It's true that software bugs occasionally cause excessive growth in the size of a database, but the software bugs are being closed off one by one and additional safeguards are being added to Exchange to prevent a database from suddenly swelling.

I don't cover the correct use of ESEUTIL in detail in this book. The utility has been around since the earliest days of Exchange and is well covered in other books, blogs, and TechNet. Instead, I refer to ESEUTIL in the places where it is needed, such as validating a recovery database before it is mounted in Chapter 9.

INSIDE OUT   Don't use ESEUTIL to rebuild a database

The upshot is that you should not have to rebuild a database with ESEUTIL unless advised to do so by Microsoft Support. If anyone tells you that running ESEUTIL to rebuild databases regularly is good for Exchange, you should treat them with the same look as you'd give someone who told you to have a monthly colonic irrigation to improve your complexion.

Those considering using ESEUTIL to rebuild a database simply to return some disk space to Windows need to remember that a database rebuild renders the current set of its transaction logs invalid. Essentially, the rebuild transforms the internal structure of the database, so any of the transactions in the logs cannot be applied if the need occurs to recover transactions through log replay. This situation is not a problem on a standard server because you can make a full backup immediately after the rebuild to establish a new secure baseline for the database. It's different when a DAG is involved because the transaction logs provide the replication mechanism for the database copies, and if you rebuild an active database, you essentially reset the database and you will have to reseed all the database copies after the rebuild is complete. Not recommended!

Database usage statistics

The Get-StoreUsageStatistics cmdlet is new to Exchange 2010 and is designed to be a diagnostic aid for administrators who are concerned about Store performance for a particular mailbox, database, or server. The cmdlet retrieves data about Store activity for an individual mailbox or for all the mailboxes in a database or server to report the amount of server time executed for Store operations over the last 10 minutes. The cmdlet analyzes the mailboxes with the highest TimeInServer value over the last 10 minutes using performance data sampled every second.

The following example retrieves data for the activity in a specific database. In this instance, we see that the time of highest demand was during the "3" sample (three minutes ago) as there is activity for three separate mailboxes noted during this time. The "TimeInServer" field provides a relative measurement of the demand that a mailbox exerts on the server. It is calculated from the total time spent processing synchronous and asynchronous requests sent to the Store for a mailbox, so it is a pretty good catch-all metric that loosely encapsulates the performance indicated by the other metrics. For example, if the activity for a mailbox is I/O intensive, then the latencies for that mailbox tend to be higher and this increases the TimeInServer figure. Heavy demand for the CPU also increases the TimeInServer figure because the Store has to spend more time processing requests on behalf of the mailbox. Looking at the following data, we can also see that the user who generated the most activity was "Akers, Kim" in the fourth sample, as her TimeinServer rating of 3235 was roughly twice as high as any other mailbox during the 10-minute duration of the sample.

```
Get-StoreUsageStatistics -Database 'VIP Data'
```

DigestCategory	SampleId	DisplayName	TimeInServer
TimeInServer	0	Mailbox - Akers,Kim	485
TimeInServer	1	Mailbox - Smith, John ...	32
TimeInServer	1	Mailbox - Online Archi...	0
TimeInServer	2	Mailbox - EMEA Help Desk.	1163
TimeInServer	3	Mailbox - Ruth, Andy	16
TimeInServer	3	Mailbox - Andersen, Ch...	94
TimeInServer	3	Mailbox - Online Archi...	16
TimeInServer	4	Mailbox - Akers, Kim	3235
TimeInServer	5	Mailbox - Redmond, Tony	1657
TimeInServer	6	Mailbox - Shen, Alan	1510
TimeInServer	7	Mailbox - Sousa, Luis	391
TimeInServer	8	Mailbox - Redmond, Tony	905
TimeInServer	9	Mailbox - Park, Dan	297

To access statistics for all the databases on a server, you'd use a command like this:

```
Get-StoreUsageStatistics -Server 'ExServer1'
```

Note that Exchange only returns statistics for mounted databases. Database copies are noted but you won't see any statistics. This is logical because no mailboxes can connect to these database copies. An individual mailbox can appear multiple times in the output for a database or a server. To drill down on the activity for a mailbox, you can retrieve more detailed statistics for a specific mailbox by passing its name to the cmdlet.

```
Get-StoreUsageStatistics -Identity 'Akers, Kim'
```

```
DigestCategory       : TimeInServer
SampleId             : 1
SampleTime           : 5/23/2010 2:39:10 AM
DisplayName          : Mailbox - Akers, Kim
TimeInServer         : 424
TimeInCPU            : 79
```

```
ROPCount          : 222
PageRead          : 0
PagePreread       : 0
LogRecordCount    : 975
LogRecordBytes    : 467303
LdapReads         : 1
LdapSearches      : 0
ServerName        : ExServer1
DatabaseName      : VIP Data
```

Apart from the TimeInServer metric, the data include:

- TimeInCPU: The number of milliseconds of CPU time used for operations for this mailbox. Samples are taken on a one-minute basis, and, if the server has multiple processors, this number can exceed 60 seconds. The timer is very simple and is triggered whenever the CPU dedicates time to the thread handling operations for the mailbox.

- ROPCount: The number of remote (client) operations performed on the mailbox during the sample period.

- PageRead: The number of noncached page reads required by the mailbox.

- PagePreRead: The number of preread pages required by the mailbox.

- LogRecordCount: The number of log records written out for this mailbox during the sample period. Together with TimeInServer, this is a good indication of the amount of activity performed by the Store to handle mailbox operations.

- LogRecordBytes: LogRecordCount converted to bytes.

- LDAPReads: The number of asynchronous Lightweight Directory Access Protocol (LDAP) reads required by mailbox operations.

- LDAPSearches: The number of LDAP searches performed on behalf of the mailbox.

The measurement data are cleared out after 10 minutes. This means that Get-StoreUsageStatistics returns blank results if you look for data 10 minutes after the last mailbox activity was recorded. If fewer than 25 users have been active during the last 10 minutes, only these users will be listed in the summary.

Transaction logs

Transaction logs are the basic mechanism to capture and record transactions that occur for an ESE database. ESE uses a dual-phase commit for transactions to meet the Atomicity, Consistency, Isolation, and Durability (ACID) test. A transaction is defined as a series of database page modifications that ESE considers to be a single logical unit. All of the modifications must be permanently saved before a transaction is complete and held in the database. For example, the arrival of a new message into a user's Inbox is represented by a number of different page modifications. The message header might occupy one page, the contents could be held in other pages, and the message might be shared with a number of different users including the originator, so it appears in different folders within the database. ESE has to be able to perform all the updates to modify all pages affected by the transaction to save the transaction. If it does not, ESE discards the transaction.

All transactions that occur in a mailbox database are captured in transaction logs, including system transactions generated as a result of housekeeping or other background maintenance operations. Because of the asynchronous way that the Store saves transactions to the log while batching transactions for efficient committal to the database, it is entirely possible for users to read and write messages in memory without the Store ever going to disk to fetch data.

> **Note**
>
> Fast, efficient, and secure access to data is the major advantage delivered by the write-ahead logging model used by Exchange, and it is important that every administrator understands how the model works.

Log sets

ESE deals with transaction logs as if they formed one very large logical log, which the Store divides into a set of generations to be more convenient to manage. Each log represents a single generation within the log set and is assigned a sequential generation number for identification purposes. Obviously, a single message that has a number of large attachments can easily span many log files. ESE manages the split of data across the logs automatically and is able to retrieve data from several logs to form the single message and its attachment if the need arises to replay the transaction into a database. On a busy server, millions of transactions might flow through the logs daily, and it is common to see hundreds if not thousands of logs created each day.

Apart from the activity generated by users, transaction logs capture background and maintenance activity such as the generation of NDRs, mailbox moves, the import of mailbox data from other messaging systems, and so on. Any operation that causes data to flow in and out of a database is captured in a transaction log, as is any operation that changes data in place within the database. If you want to estimate the number of transaction logs that a server will generate daily, you can use the rule of thumb of 25 MB of data (or 25 logs) per active user per eight-hour working day. The Exchange team's blog asserts that the number of logs per user per day varies from 7 to 42, depending on the average size of message and the number of messages that users send and receive, so taking 25 logs is a reasonable middle value that has stood the test of time. This rule assumes that you remove transaction logs from servers by taking daily full backups.

INSIDE OUT   Transaction logs should be 1 MB

Transaction logs are 1 MB, a size reduced from the 5 MB logs generated by every other version of Exchange except Exchange 2007. The 1 MB size was selected to facilitate easy replication between servers and to ensure that Exchange can quickly resolve any data divergence that might occur due to an interruption in replication. Choosing a small log size also makes it less likely that data will be lost if a log file cannot be copied or is corrupted due to a storage or other hardware failure. Any variation from the expected 1 MB file size is an indication that the file might be corrupt for some reason. If you see unexpected log sizes, you should stop the Information Store service and check the event log, database, and disks for errors.

The transaction log set for a database is assigned a prefix followed by an eight-digit hex number representing the generation number of the log. Over 4 billion log files can be created for a database before the Store has to reuse file names. The prefix for the first database created on a server is E00, the prefix for the second is E01, the third E02, and so on, so the current transaction log for the first database is E00.log. The same log prefix is used for the transaction logs for all database copies within in a DAG. Thus, you might have multiple log sets with the same prefix on the same server.

Tip

It is quite safe to have files that share the same file name because the log sets are placed into separate directories. There is no danger that Exchange will ever be confused as to what log belongs to what database because the header of every transaction log contains an identifier that associates it with the correct database.

Public folder databases also maintain their own set of transaction logs. These logs capture the same kind of add, change, and delete transactions that occur for items in mailbox databases but are maintained as quite separate entities.

Every time the Information Store service starts up, the Store automatically checks the databases as it mounts them to verify that the databases are consistent. A flag in the database header indicates whether the database is consistent or inconsistent, depending on whether the Store was able to shut the database down cleanly the last time it shut down. A clean shutdown flushes all data from the Store's cache and commits any outstanding transactions into the database to make the database consistent.

An inconsistent database is one that has some outstanding transactions that the Store has not yet committed. If the Store detects that a database is inconsistent, it attempts to read the outstanding transactions from the transaction logs to replay the transactions into the database and so make the database consistent. This operation is referred to as a soft recovery and, although it happens less frequently today than with earlier versions of Exchange, soft recoveries occur from time to time, usually after a software or hardware failure has caused Exchange to terminate abruptly. In most instances, you are unaware that the Store has performed a soft recovery, and you will not find out unless you check the event log to see whether the Store replayed any transactions after it mounted a database. If you are unsure whether a database is consistent, you can run the ESEUTIL utility with the /MH parameter to check the database header.

The only way that you can be sure that a database is consistent is to perform a controlled shutdown of the Information Store service (which makes all databases consistent) or to use EMC or the Dismount-Database cmdlet to dismount a specific database. At this point, the Store makes sure that it commits any outstanding transactions that exist within its cache before it shuts down the database. Making a full backup creates a somewhat similar situation in that the database after the backup is consistent. However, because the database is still online, the Store will continue to commit transactions immediately after the backup finishes, so the database is only consistent for a very short time.

Transaction logs are tied to their databases in two ways. First, ESE writes a unique identifier (or signature) into each log as it creates the file. The log signature must match the signature of the corresponding database before ESE can use the contents of a log to recover transactions. Second, ESE records the path to the directory where the database is located in the transaction logs. You can find information about identifiers and locations by running the ESEUTIL utility with the /ML parameter to dump the header information from a transaction log as shown in the following sample.

```
Extensible Storage Engine Utilities for Microsoft(R) Exchange Server
Version 14.00
Copyright (C) Microsoft Corporation. All Rights Reserved.

Initiating FILE DUMP mode...

      Base name: e01
      Log file: e0100000736.log
      lGeneration: 1846 (0x736)
            Checkpoint: NOT AVAILABLE
      creation time: 11/20/2009 01:03:23
```

```
prev gen time: 11/20/2009 00:26:26
Format LGVersion: (7.3704.16.1)
Engine LGVersion: (7.3704.16.1)
Signature: Create time:11/06/2009 00:06:00 Rand:466930790 Computer:
EnvSystemPath: C:\Exchange\VIP\
EnvLogFilePath: C:\Exchange\VIP\
Env Log Sec size: 512
Env (CircLog,Session,Opentbl,VerPage,Cursors,LogBufs,LogFile,Buffers)
  (    off,    552,  27600,  15960,  27600,    2048,    2048,   24572)
Using Reserved Log File: false
Circular Logging Flag (current file): off
Circular Logging Flag (past files): off
Checkpoint at log creation time: : (0x733,8,0)
1 C:\Exchange\VIP\VIP.edb
      dbtime: 823366 (0-823366)
      objidLast: 4116
      Signature: Create time:11/06/2010 00:06:00 Rand:466892842 Computer:
      MaxDbSize: 0 pages
      Last Attach: (0x4CF,9,86)
      Last Consistent: (0x4CE,8,1F)

    Last Lgpos: (0x736,34,0)

Number of database page references:   304

Integrity check passed for log file: e0100000736.log
Operation completed successfully in 0.156 seconds.
```

Transactions, buffers, and commitment

After a client submits a message to the Store, an ESE session that is responsible for the transaction follows a well-defined order to apply the transaction to commit the new message to the Store. The same order is followed for other transactions such as deletes and moves. First, ESE obtains a timestamp using the internal time (called a "db-time" held in an 8-byte value) maintained in the database header. To modify a page, ESE must calculate a new db-time based on the current value in the header. Once it has calculated the new db-time, ESE writes the records that make up the transaction into the current transaction log. After this operation completes, the session can go ahead and modify the appropriate pages in the database. Page modifications occur in an in-memory cache of "dirty pages," so ESE might first have to fetch the necessary pages off the on-disk database.

When a client performs an operation that modifies a database page, ESE follows this sequence:

- The database page is fetched from the ESE in-memory cache. If the page is not cached, ESE fetches it from disk.

- A log record is generated to describe the page fetch and update the cache.

- The database page is modified and ESE marks the page as "dirty." The page is not written immediately to disk as it might be modified by subsequent transactions. The version store tracks dirty pages to make sure that they are accounted for in case the database session is terminated abnormally. The version store is an internal component that keeps an in-memory list of modifications made to the database that the Store uses for purposes such as transaction rollback or to resolve attempts to apply multiple modifications to the same page.

- The database page is linked to the record in the cache to prevent ESE from flushing the page to disk before the transaction log record is written. ESE always commits pages to the database after it is sure that the pages have been successfully captured in a transaction log.

- Once the log buffer (1 MB) is full or a commit record is recorded for the transaction, ESE commits the changed page by recording it into the current transaction log. This operation might require a "log roll" (the creation of a new log generation). If a database is replicated, Exchange 2010 SP1 implements "block replication" at this point. See Chapter 8 for more information about how block replication works.

- Eventually, the dirty pages are flushed from memory and written into the database.

- The checkpoint is advanced.

To ensure that data are always protected, it is a cardinal rule for ESE that database writes cannot occur before their transactions are first committed into a transaction log. If you look at the steps that make up a complete transaction, you see that the last step is to commit the transaction to disk. For example, the last step shown in Figure 7-14 is a commit command for the transaction identified as ESE session 8. Other prior steps in session 8 begin a transaction and insert some data to replace an existing page. The commit is a synchronous operation, so no other transaction can occur for that session until the write to disk is complete. Enabling write-back caching on the disk that holds the transaction logs improves performance by allowing the write to complete in the controller's memory and so release the synchronous wait. The controller is then responsible for writing the data to disk.

Each log record represents an individual page modification. Transactions start with a Begin transaction record and proceed with the individual operations until the transaction is complete, a Commit transaction record is added, and the transaction is committed to the transaction log. The sequence of transaction records allows ESE to replay complete transactions into databases when it needs to recover data. If ESE reads in a transaction and cannot find a commit record, it considers the transaction to be incomplete and will not replay it into a database.

Chapter 7

```
          Session #    Page   Page Offset   Length    Data

Begin     (8)
Replace   27223(8,[1477:6],8,8,8)01 00 00 00 70 03 00 00
Delete    27150(8,[992:0])
Insert    27224(9,[1095:7],255)7F 14 2F 6F A8 1C ...
Insert    27225(5,[702:8],255)80 D7 74 C9 68 6C ...
Insert    27226(8,[696:1],255)80 94 26 BC B5 9B B5 ...
Insert    27227(8,[735:8],255)80 D7 74 C9 68 6C 17 ...
Commit    (8)

          Timestamp
```

Figure 7-14 Data in a transaction log.

The delivery of a single new message causes ESE to modify many different pages because many tables might need to be updated. ESE also updates the index for each table and, if the message contains a large attachment, its content will be broken up into several long value chunks, all of which generate log records. All of these transactions are captured in log files. If you monitor the log file directory for a database when a large message is delivered to multiple mailboxes in that database, you will observe a spurt of log generation activity. For example, a 1 MB message sent to 10 mailboxes will generate at least 10 transaction logs.

On the other hand, if you delete an item that has a very large attachment, Exchange only needs to capture the page numbers of the pages that now contain deleted data, and the actual content does not appear in the logs. As you can see from Figure 7-14, the entries in a log represent low-level physical modifications to the database and records for differ-ent transactions are interspersed throughout a log file. Replaying a transaction is therefore quite a complex matter. Each transaction log contains a sequential list of operations that the Store has performed on pages in memory. The log captures details of when a transac-tion begins, when it is committed, and if the Store needs to roll it back for some reason.

Each record in the log is of a certain type. Record types include Begin (a transaction is start-ing), Replace (some data in a page are being updated), Delete (data are removed), Insert (data are added), and Commit. Transactions from multiple sessions are interleaved through-out a transaction log. This means that the Begin record type also identifies the session that performed a transaction. You can think of a session as a thread running within the Store process. The session forms the context within which ESE manages the transaction and all of the associated database modifications. Each session could be tied back to a particular cli-ent, but the database has no knowledge of individual clients (MAPI or otherwise), as all it sees are the threads that operate on its contents.

Regretfully, there is no tool provided to interpret a log file. Figure 7-14 illustrates how a set of transactions might appear in a log. In this example, the first transaction in session 8 (or thread 8) is replacing a record in the database. Every physical modification to a database is time stamped. ESE uses timestamps later if it has to replay transactions from a particular point in time. The page number and an offset within the page are also recorded. The length of the data to be replaced is then noted and is followed with the actual binary data that are inserted into the page. The next transaction is a record delete. The set of insert transactions demonstrates that transactions from multiple sessions are intermingled within a log. Sessions write data into the log file as they process transactions. Any dump of a log file from even a moderately busy server will record transactions from scores of sessions.

When the Store replays transactions from logs to make a database consistent, it has to interpret the contents of all the different transaction logs that have accumulated since the last good backup to find the transactions that it requires and then assemble the different records for those transactions from the logs and replay them into the database.

Dirty pages in the cache are flushed to disk every 30 seconds. Pages are not necessarily flushed in order, as they might be modified several times during their life in the cache. Along with flushing, ESE calculates a checkpoint to mark the current recovery point so that it knows what transaction logs are required to update a database and make it current should it need to replay logs in case of an outage. Each transaction log has a generation number that is incremented by 1 as each 1 MB transaction log file is closed off. The log generation number tracks the position and sequencing of transactions in a log file in the log stream. ESE uses the generation numbers to determine the exact log files that it needs for any recovery operation. The generation number of the last committed log file is also written into the checkpoint to allow ESE to calculate the required log files. For example, let's assume that the current log file generation is 0x36b0 (14,000) and the log file generation written into the checkpoint file is 0x3683 (13,955). In simple terms, using these values we can say that:

- Any log files with a generation value less than 0x3683 that contain complete transactions (begin and commit records) have had their transactions written into the database.

- Any log files between the checkpoint value (0x3683) and the current generation (0x36b0) might have some of their transactions written to the database, but as we cannot be sure of what these transactions are, all of the transaction logs between 0x3683 and 0x36b0 are required for replay purposes if we have an outage and need to recover the database. The last generation number required is called the waypoint, so we can say that the difference (in generation numbers) between the checkpoint and the waypoint represents the set of transaction logs required for recovery.

Transaction logs only hold 1 MB of data. On heavily loaded systems when new transaction logs are being created all the time, it is possible that new generations of logs exist past the waypoint. These logs contain transactions that have not been committed into the database. The transactions could be incomplete (no commit record exists) or are in the process of being written when the failure occurs. For whatever reason, these logs are not required for recovery purposes. However, if a failure occurs and the database is updated, the transactions in these log files will be ignored and lost.

From this description you'll realize that transaction logs are critical to the good health of any Exchange server. Transaction logs are also the key to database replication in both Exchange 2007 and Exchange 2010 as these are the files that Exchange copies and replays to keep database copies synchronized.

> ## Checkpoint file
>
> The checkpoint file allows the Store to know what transaction logs are required should it need to perform a recovery. The Store updates the checkpoint file every 30 seconds when it flushes dirty pages into the database.
>
> There is always a separate checkpoint file for a set of transaction logs (otherwise known as a log stream) and because Exchange 2010 maintains a set of transaction logs per database, it follows that there's a separate checkpoint file per database.
>
> When a database is mounted, Exchange reads the checkpoint file to determine whether there are any outstanding transaction logs that it should process to bring the database completely up to date. This is known as a soft recovery and it happens every time a database is mounted to ensure that an inconsistent database (one that has outstanding transactions) is restored to full health even if it has been shut down unexpectedly due to a computer failure or software bug. Unless tens of thousands of logs are necessary to update a database, a set of transaction logs usually doesn't take long to replay because the checkpoint file allows Exchange to quickly identify the point at which the last written transaction occurred and avoid the overhead of examining all available transaction logs and assessing whether the transactions they contain are in the database.
>
> However, if the checkpoint file is lost for some reason, Exchange will examine all available transaction logs to determine whether any transactions exist in the logs that have not been committed into the database. If some transaction logs are unavailable due to storage failure or another reason, you will have to run the ESEUTIL utility with the /P switch to make the database consistent again and allow Exchange to mount it. In this situation, it is more than likely that users will experience some data loss as there is no way to recover the transactions in the lost logs.

Transaction log checksum

Every transaction log contains a checksum that Exchange validates to ensure that the log data are consistent and valid. Microsoft introduced the checksum to prevent logical corruption occurring as the Store replays transactions into a database during a recovery process.

Exchange uses a type of "sliding window" algorithm called LRCK (Log Record Checksum) to validate checksums for a selected group of records in a log to ensure log integrity. The Store reads and verifies these checksums during backup and recovery operations to ensure that invalid data are not used. If the Store detects invalid data through a checksum failure, it logs a 463 error in the system event log. If the Store fails to read the header of a transaction log and is unable to validate the checksum, it signals error 412 in the Application Event Log. Transaction log failure inevitably leads to data loss, as the only way to recover from this error is to restore the last good backup. All of the transactions since that backup will be lost.

Transaction log I/O

The Store always writes transactions in sequential order and appends the data to the end of the current transaction log. All of the I/O activity is generated by writes, so it is logical to assume that the disk where the logs are located must be capable of supporting a reasonably heavy I/O write load. In comparison, the disks where the databases are located experience read and write activity as users access items held in their mailboxes.

On large servers, the classic approach to managing the I/O activity generated by transaction logs is by placing the logs on a dedicated drive or LUN. This solves two problems. First, the size of the disk (today, usually 500 GB or greater) means that free space should always be available. If you accumulate 500 GB of logs (500,000 individual log files), it means that either your server is under a tremendous load or you haven't made a full online backup in the recent past. Full online backups remove the transaction logs when they successfully complete. Second, in all but extreme circumstances, a dedicated drive is capable of handling the I/O load generated by transaction logs. I cannot think of a reason why a dedicated drive could become swamped with I/O requests from log activity. In any case, if such a load was ever generated on a server, the I/O activity to the databases is probably going to be of more concern than the log disk.

INSIDE OUT Applying some logic

Of course, having a dedicated drive for log files is a luxury that you might not be able to afford. But the logic applied to justify the drive—reserve enough space for log file growth and keep an eye on I/O activity—should be remembered when you decide where the logs should be stored on your system. For example, it's a bad idea to locate the logs on the same drive as other "hot" files, such as a Windows page file.

As noted in our earlier discussion about creating a new mailbox database, another classic best practice is to never place the logs on the same drive as a database. The logic is that keeping the logs with their database might seem like a good idea, but like keeping all of your eggs in one basket, if a problem afflicts the disk holding the database, the same problem will strike down the transaction logs and you will lose data. This advice still holds for databases that are not replicated, but it becomes less valuable the more database copies you have within a DAG. If you only have two database copies, then database and log isolation across different disks is still a good idea because your tolerance to failure is limited to one copy. On the other hand, if you have three or more database copies, then you can co-locate databases and transaction logs because any failure will still result in the availability of at least two databases.

The question of circular logging

Circular logging means that the Store generates a limited number of transaction logs by reusing logs as their contents are committed into the database. This feature was originally introduced into Exchange as a mechanism to restrict disk usage on low-end servers because storage was an expensive commodity. Circular logging is also common on test servers and edge transport servers where data are transient and don't usually need to be captured for a permanent record. From an operation perspective, at low periods of demand the Store uses a relatively small set of between four and eight logs to capture transactions. However, this figure depends on system load and how quickly the Store can commit transactions to the database. It is quite common to see thousands of transaction logs created for a database that is under heavy load (for example, when many mailboxes are being moved into the database), and these logs might persist for some time, especially if they are being replicated to other servers. Eventually, as system load decreases and replication occurs, the Store will truncate the set of logs used for circular logging back to a minimal set and keep it at this level until system load grows again.

In the past, except on very small servers, administrators always configured production databases not to use circular logging. There were just too many things that could and did go wrong, from hardware failures to administrative errors, to want to remove the safety blanket that transaction logs provide. After all, if problems occurred, you could always restore a good copy of a database and replay transactions from logs generated since the backup to bring a database up to date. This wasn't possible with circular logging because the transaction logs are reused.

Exchange 2010 presents different arguments for whether or not circular logging is a viable approach for production servers. We now have the ability to configure multiple database copies in a DAG, and we can configure substantial lag times to ensure that a database copy is isolated from potential corruption, so there are situations when circular logging is a good approach to take for mailbox databases with the very strong caveat that you have to think through all the potential scenarios that you might have to deal with before you take the plunge. It's also true that you need to understand how circular logging could impact other components such as your backup regime, as explained in the Microsoft blog at *http:// msexchangeteam.com/archive/2010/08/18/455857.aspx*. Some companies will always need the ability to replay transaction logs, so they will want to keep transaction logs. Some will use DAGs to move away from the need to ever make backups. Most companies will fall somewhere in the spectrum between these limits and have to figure out what is the best approach to satisfy their business needs and objectives.

> **Note**
>
> By default, new mailbox databases do not use circular logging, so if you want to enable circular logging to save disk space, you have to update the database properties after it is created. The new logging behavior becomes effective the next time the database is mounted.

Figure 7-15 shows how to enable circular logging on a mailbox database. The equivalent EMS command is:

```
Set-MailboxDatabase –Identity 'DB1' –CircularLoggingEnabled $True
```

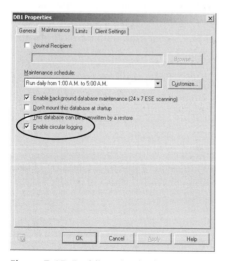

Figure 7-15 Enabling circular logging on a mailbox database.

Circular logging will not prevent disk space exhaustion, and disks still need to be carefully monitored to ensure that sufficient storage is available to accommodate logs even if they have to be retained for an unexpected period. In a DAG, Exchange keeps transaction logs until their content has been applied to all database copies. If one database copy is down, Exchange will keep the transaction logs on the servers that host the other copies until the offline copy comes back online and the Store is able to replay the outstanding logs success-fully to update that database copy. This process occurs to mitigate the chance of data loss even when circular logging is enabled. For this reason, it is wise to keep a substantial buffer of available disk space on disks that host transaction logs, just in case. This topic is explored in more detail in Chapter 8.

Noncircular logging

Noncircular logging means that the Store generates as many transaction logs as required to store all of the transactions generated for a database and only removes these logs after a backup is performed. Obviously, noncircular logging consumes far more disk space than circular logging because even a medium-sized Exchange server can generate gigabytes of 1 MB transaction logs daily.

When circular logging is disabled, the Store continuously creates new transaction logs as it fills the current log with data. The Store performs the following steps to create a new log and switch it to become the current log. First, the Store advances the checkpoint in the checkpoint file to indicate that it has committed the transactions in the oldest log into the database. Next, the Store creates a temporary file called *<database prefix>*tmp.log, or E00tmp.log for the first database created on a server. The Store switches this file into use to become the current log when it closes off the current log to ensure that transactions can be continually written into a log without pausing.

> **Note**
> If the Store fails to create the temporary file, it usually means that no more disk space is available on the disk that holds the transaction logs. In this case, the Store will proceed to an orderly shutdown of the Information Store service and uses the two reserved log files to hold transaction data that it flushes from its cache during the shutdown.

When the temporary log file is created, the Store initializes its log header with the genera-tion number, database signature, and timestamp information. When the current log file is full, the Store stops writing transactional data and renames the current log file to incorpo-rate the generation number in its file name (for example, E000007E71.log). The Store then renames the temporary log file to be E00.log to make it the current transaction log and then resumes writing transaction data into the current log file, flushing any transactions that have accumulated in the short time required to switch logs.

The Store continues with the process of creating the temporary log file and switching it to take the place of the current log file until the Information Store service shuts down. The number of logs created on a server varies according to message traffic and other activity, such as mailbox moves and public folder replication. Busy and large servers can generate tens of gigabytes of transaction logs daily, so this is obviously an important factor to take into account when you size storage for servers. However, the space occupied by transaction logs is released when the files are truncated following a successful full backup. The logic here is that you do not need the transaction logs any more if you have a full backup. The database is consistent after the backup and you have a backup copy if a problem arises. The backup copy also contains the transaction logs that are necessary to allow the Store to make the database consistent if you need to restore it.

Reserved logs

In Exchange Server 2000 and Exchange 2003, every storage group is assigned two special log files called Res1.log and Res2.log to provide the Store with some emergency storage in case it is unable to create new transaction logs for any reason. The only time that I have seen these files used is when space is exhausted on the disk that holds the transaction logs. Running out of disk space was a reasonably common occurrence in the early days of Exchange because disks were small and expensive, but such an event is much less common today. Most administrators now monitor free disk space on all disks used by Exchange and take action to release space if less than 1 GB is available.

Exchange 2007 and Exchange 2010 use different names for the reserved logs (which now only occupy 1 MB each). These files are *databaseprefix*res00001.jrs and *databaseprefix*res00002.jrs. For example, E00res00001.jrs is the first reserved log file for the first database created on a server. Exchange 2010 SP1 increases the number of JRS files to 10 to reflect the increasing amount of data that databases have to handle.

You should never get close to the point where the reserved logs are called into play. First, you should ensure that all the disks that hold mailbox databases or transaction logs are sufficiently large to accommodate normal operation and any expected growth over the next year or so. Second, you should monitor available space on all relevant disks on an ongoing basis. Third, if your monitoring fails or you haven't provided sufficient space to cater for an expected spurt in growth (for instance, a database and its set of transaction logs might grow considerably if you move many mailboxes to the database), Exchange includes a self-protection mechanism known as backpressure that prevents the transport service from delivering new messages to the mailboxes in a database if the available space on a disk used to hold a mailbox database or transaction log falls below 1 GB. This step prevents new messages from causing a problem, but it might not stop other procedures (such as

mailbox moves) from grabbing some more space. Exchange releases the block on new message deliveries once the available space on the disk grows past 1.5 GB. The additional space
could be released by Exchange as a result of removing transaction logs after their contents
are committed into the database or through administrator intervention.

INSIDE OUT   Less than 1 GB of free space requires action

In either case, the fact that free space is reduced to less than 1 GB is a danger signal
that warrants immediate and proactive attention from the administrator to take the
necessary steps to free space on the disk so that the situation cannot reoccur.

Exchange logs event 10014 whenever a low space condition exists on a disk holding transaction logs and event 10015 when the same problem occurs on a disk holding a mailbox
database. The problem is also recorded in the PerfMon counters *MSExchangeIS Mailbox
\Delivery Blocked: Low Database Space* and *MSExchangeIS Mailbox\Delivery Blocked: Low
Log space*.

And now for something completely different

Much of the technology discussed so far has existed in one form or another for at least
several versions of Exchange. The Store is powered by a database engine, and its physical
instantiation is a set of databases on disk. The interesting subject is to discuss just what can
be done with those databases using the new technology in Exchange 2010, which is where
we go next.

# CHAPTER 8

Exchange's Search for High Availability

F OR many companies, their email system is a mission-critical application. Microsoft has
invested much engineering talent and finance over the years to provide Microsoft
Exchange Server with the ability to resist different types of failure and deliver a
highly available service. The investment has spanned software engineering to improve
the quality of the Exchange code base, especially in the Store and Transport subsystems,
through making better use of hardware by reducing the requirement for expensive storage
through leveraging other technology as it became available, such as Windows clusters and
asynchronous data replication. Microsoft Exchange Server 2007 was a watershed for high
availability in many ways because of the introduction of continuous log replication technology (also known as log shipping). Local Continuous Replication (LCR) is available to copy
transaction logs and then replay them into a database copy on the same server; Cluster
Continuous Replication (CCR) uses the same approach but in the context of a two-node
Windows cluster; and Standby Cluster Replication (SCR from Exchange 2007 SP1 onward)
provides a solution between servers in different datacenters.

The implementation of log replication in Exchange 2007 is a little immature, and its deployment can be complex. Having three different solutions to select can be confusing—the lack
of automatic failover, together with the lack of a graphical user interface (GUI) management interface to control end-to-end operations from creation to failover and some other
minor glitches, are hallmarks of a V1.0 implementation. These limitations aside, you cannot
argue that the basic technology involved in closing transaction logs, copying them from a
source to a target server, validating their content, and then using that content to update
passive copies of databases by replaying the transactions in the logs works. Microsoft's
decision to focus on continuous log replication as the basis for high availability is therefore
very understandable, especially as they have eliminated the multiple log replication options
presented by Exchange 2007 and delivered a single, more manageable, and complete solu-

tion in Microsoft Exchange Server 2010. LCR, CCR, and SCR are no more, but as we will see, the new Database Availability Group (DAG) feature is more than an adequate replacement.

Microsoft also wanted Exchange 2010 to include sufficient functionality to allow customers to build highly available Exchange infrastructures without having to invest in expensive third-party add-on products. There is no doubt that third-party technology boasts its own set of availability features, especially when coupled with high-end storage systems, but Microsoft has a very large and diverse customer base that uses Exchange, not all of which can afford the financial and administrative costs of deploying add-on technology. Having a solid set of high-availability features built into the product and administered through the standard management interfaces (Exchange Management Console [EMC] and Exchange Management Shell [EMS]) increases the attractiveness of Exchange as a platform, removes complexity, and avoids cost for customers in the small to medium segment and for a large number of enterprise customers.

Finally, Microsoft wanted to allow customers to deploy highly available servers in an incremental fashion. In previous versions of Exchange, you have to do a considerable amount of work to prepare to deploy a highly available solution. For example, if you want to deploy clustered Exchange servers, you have to ensure that suitable hardware is available, then install a Windows cluster, then install Exchange with the correct switches to create virtual Exchange servers running on the cluster and connected to cluster resources such as shared storage. This isn't something that you do without planning and a lot of specialized knowledge. The concept of incremental deployment as implemented in Exchange 2010 is that you can deploy "normal" Exchange mailbox servers first and then decide to include those servers into a DAG as the need arises to incorporate more high availability into the environment. You also have the ability to gradually expand the DAG to include more servers or more database copies to add resilience against different failure scenarios as time, money, and hardware allows.

Breaking the link between database and server

Even though it was flawed in places, the introduction of continuous replication in Exchange 2007 was a big step forward to achieving in-product high availability. The final piece in the jigsaw came with removing the historical tight connection between server and mailbox database. If you look at the configuration data for Exchange 2007 in Active Directory directory service, you see a structure of Organization–Administrative Groups–Servers–Databases. In other words, databases are a child of servers and each database is owned by a server. The situation is completely different in Exchange 2010, where the structure is Organization–Database Availability Groups/Servers/Databases. Now DAGs, servers, and databases are held at the same level within the Exchange organization, and links connect these objects to establish the servers and databases that are in a DAG. Other links connect database copies to databases and the servers that host the copies. A new system management component called *Active Manager* uses this information to understand what database copy is currently active on what server and what available passive copies exist. The link between database and server is broken and no longer exists.

Exchange Server 2007 also introduced the concept of database portability, which means that you can take a mailbox database from one server and mount it on another server. In Exchange 2010, Microsoft refers to this capability as *database mobility.* The major difference between portability and mobility is that you are not moving a database from server to server. Instead, you move the active focus for client connections and workload between copies of a database. All of the copies of a database share the same globally unique identifier (GUID) or identity, so each is able to function as the active master no matter what server it is currently located on. Database copies also must have the same path on the server for database and log files. The ability to move databases around servers within a DAG is fundamental to the ability to manage database-level failures and achieve high availability within Exchange and without recourse to third-party software as previously required.

Exchange 2010 treats a mailbox database as a unit of failover in that it can be moved between servers in a DAG as problems occur. Of course, you do not need to define DAGs within your organization, and you can run Exchange as before with databases that never move off their host server. If you elect to deploy a DAG, servers become members of the DAG and are able to host active and passive copies of mailbox databases that are hosted by the DAG. All of the services that you expect to run on a mailbox server still exist (the Information Store service, and so on) and operate on the mailbox databases that are currently hosted by a server, including running the Replication Service to process incoming copies of transaction logs to update passive copies of mailbox databases whose active copies exist on other servers elsewhere in the DAG.

INSIDE OUT   The advantages to multiple passive database copies

Just like log replication in Exchange 2007, a database only ever has one active copy at a given time, but in Exchange 2010 you can create multiple passive copies up to the number of available servers in the DAG. The more copies that exist for a database, the more likely it is that you can quickly recover from an outage that affects a server or some storage attached to a server and the less likely that your infrastructure has a single point of failure. The reduction in disk I/O in Exchange 2010 and the ability to use cheaper disk technology to host databases mean that you can afford to maintain more database copies. Of course, you have to maintain a reasonable balance here to ensure that you don't create more database copies than you really require.

For example, in a DAG that spans 10 servers, a database can be active on one server and you can have its contents replicated to passive copies that are managed on the 9 other servers in the DAG. This is a rather extreme example and it's more likely that databases will have three passive copies to achieve a good balance between the ability to recover from different outage scenarios and the amount of data replication that is required to keep the passive copies updated. In a situation where the DAG stretches across multiple datacenters or a need exists for a lagged copy, the number of passive copies might be increased to four. The point is that system designers now have great flexibility in terms of the way that they protect data in different circumstances.

As you would expect, the active copy of a database can be mounted or dismounted. If mounted, the database is generating transactions that Exchange replicates to the target servers that host copies of the database. Nothing much happens for dismounted databases.

Apart from its mounted state, Exchange 2010 defines a database to be either the source for replication or the target for replication. A database copy can act as the source or target but cannot function as both at the same time. In much the same manner, a database copy can be active, meaning that it is available to service incoming connections from email clients, or passive, meaning that it is available to be switched into active mode to take over service, but it cannot be both active and passive at the same time. Only one copy of a database can be active within the DAG at any time, and a server cannot host more than one copy of a database. All of this is quite logical and provides the framework within which replication and database transition from active to passive and back again occurs.

Introducing Database Availability Groups

Microsoft introduced storage groups as the basis for database management in Exchange 2000. Databases fit inside storage groups, which in turn belonged to servers. All of the databases in a storage group shared a common set of transaction logs, and transactions from all of the databases in the storage group are interleaved in the transaction logs. From Exchange 2003 onward, if you had a problem with a database, you could use the Recovery Storage Group to access a recovered copy of a database and retrieve mailbox data. However, although it was sometimes convenient to use storage groups for management, eventually Microsoft determined that they introduced an extra layer of complication for administrators and the process to back storage groups out of the product began in Exchange 2007, in which the continuous log replication feature works only for storage groups that hosted just one database. You could still put more databases in a storage group, including public folder databases, but Microsoft gave a clear indication that they preferred single database storage groups, especially if you wanted to exploit their investment in Exchange's high-availability features. It therefore comes as no surprise that storage groups have disappeared in Exchange 2010.

Removing storage groups simplifies administration but doesn't help with high availability. Log replication in Exchange 2007 helps to deliver more highly available messaging, but it is limited to one source server and one target server. Exchange 2007 CCR and SCR deployments proved that the mechanism of shipping transaction logs to target systems where the Replication Service replayed the contents of the log to update a passive copy of the source database to keep it updated and ready to switch in case of problems with the original database worked. Exchange 2010 builds on Exchange 2007 to allow a single database to have multiple copies that are tied together into a new structure called a Database Availability Group (DAG). The term is new to Exchange and it has an unfortunate definition in other places. Wikipedia mentions that a dag is a clump of dung stuck to the wool of a sheep.

Fundamentally, a DAG is a collection of databases and copies that are shared across up to 16 servers. Although 16 might seem an arbitrary figure to use as the limit of the servers that a DAG can support, in fact, it's a limit imposed by Windows Failover Clustering, which can only support 16 nodes in its clusters. As Windows Failover Clustering underpins the DAG, the restriction flows through to the DAG.

In any case, 16 seems like a number that should be sufficient for most deployments and is certainly enough to explore just how far Microsoft can push the envelope for the combination of technologies that constitute a DAG. These include the following:

- Log replication (the technology to implement transfer and replay plus the network load to support replication)

- Networks

- Windows Failover Clustering

- Monitoring and management tools

- Server and storage hardware

After all, if we look at the previous generation of single-copy clusters, aside from Microsoft's own internal implementation, relatively few customers ever went past four servers in a cluster so there is no obvious demand for megaclusters spanning hundreds of servers. This is the first implementation of the DAG and it is possible that Microsoft will consider whether it is feasible and advantageous to increase the number of servers that a single DAG can support in future versions of Exchange or to leverage new features delivered in a new version of Windows. For now, we remain at 16. The simple answer of putting individual servers in multiple DAGs is available if you need to protect databases on more than 16 servers.

The DAG implements the concept of an active (or primary) database—the one to which users currently connect—and its copies on other servers that can be swapped into place to become the active database. The database copies are kept updated through log replication

Chapter 8

and replay. If a problem occurs on a server that renders the databases running on the server inaccessible, the DAG can activate a copy and make it the active copy. The new remote procedure call (RPC) Client Access Layer redirects client connections seamlessly to the newly activated copy (see Chapter 11, "Client Access Server"). Databases cannot be swapped around between servers if the product architecture demands that databases are firmly attached to servers, which is the traditional approach taken by all previous versions of Exchange. The introduction of the DAG smashes the link between a database and the owning server to make portable databases the basic building block for high availability in Exchange 2010. This is probably the most fundamental architectural change that Microsoft makes in Exchange 2010. The servers within a DAG can support other roles, but each DAG member must have the mailbox role installed because it has to be able to host a mailbox database.

The servers in a DAG can be on different subnets and span different Active Directory sites as long as the underlying network infrastructure supports sufficient bandwidth to transfer the expected volume of transaction log files between the different servers. To ensure smooth operation, Microsoft recommends that mailbox servers in a DAG are connected with a network that accommodates a round-trip latency of 250 milliseconds or less. In addition, Microsoft recommends that you block cross-network traffic between the datacenters to avoid excessive heartbeat traffic across the cluster and so conserve available bandwidth for more important activities such as log replication. There are other issues to consider when a DAG stretches across two datacenters, including the assignment of IP addresses for the networks, using appropriate Domain Name System (DNS) time to live (TTL) settings to ensure that clients pick up network changes quickly in the event of failovers, and the provision of suitable names for all of the services offered to clients by Exchange from both datacenters.

> **Tip**
>
> An in-depth discussion of these issues is impossible in the context of a book that attempts to cover the wide horizon presented by Exchange. If you are considering a stretched DAG, you should sit down with an Exchange consultant who has considerable experience with DAGs to chart out the current situation, your business needs, and a suitable design for the DAG.

An Exchange 2010 server running the enterprise edition can support up to 100 active databases. This number is increased when you include passive database copies that a server hosts for other servers to a combination of up to 100 databases with a continuing limit of up to 100 databases owned by the server. Even though Exchange 2007 servers include an earlier version of log replication technology, you cannot include Exchange 2007 servers within a DAG.

Determining the MAPI endpoint

Messaging Application Programming Interface (MAPI) clients connecting to servers running Exchange 2007 or an earlier version know that their endpoint is a mailbox in a database on a particular server. The *msExchHomeServerName* property of the user's Active Directory account points to the server and the *HomeMDB* property points to the database. Exchange 2010 breaks the connection between server and database so a new scheme is required to determine the endpoint for MAPI clients. Exchange 2010 does not use the *msExchHomeServerName* value because it would be too expensive to apply updates to potentially thousands of Active Directory objects during a database transition within a DAG. Instead, the following algorithm is used:

- Fetch the *homeMDB* property for the user object in Active Directory. The full value of the property is shown here. The first CN in the property ("Dublin Users") identifies the database that holds the user's mailbox.

  `CN=Dublin Users,CN=Databases,CN=Exchange Administrative Group`
  `(FYDIBOHF23SPDLT),CN=Administrative Groups,CN=contoso,`
  `CN=Microsoft Exchange,CN=Services,CN=Configuration,DC=contoso,DC=com`

- Truncate the value of the database's *legacyExchangeDN* property to determine the server *legacyExchangeDN*. This isn't the actual server that hosts the database. Instead, it is the Client Access Server (CAS) server that currently provides the RPC Client Access service for the database.

  `/o=contoso/ou=Exchange Administrative Group (FYDIBOHF23SPDLT)`
  `/cn=Configuration/cn=Servers/cn=ExServer2/cn=Microsoft Private MDB`

- Use the server *LegacyExchangeDN* to determine where the active copy of the mailbox database (MDB) is currently mounted. This value is available in the *msExchOwningServer* property of the database object.

- Connect to the MAPI endpoint provided by the CAS server. The CAS server will handle communications with the mailbox server.

This is just one example of how the code base in Exchange has changed to accommodate the introduction of the DAG.

The dependency on Windows clustering

Underneath the hood, the DAG uses Windows Failover Clustering technology to manage server membership within the DAG, to monitor server heartbeats to know what servers in the DAG are healthy, and to maintain a quorum. The big difference from clustering as implemented in other versions of Exchange is that there is no concept of an Exchange virtual machine or a clustered mailbox server, nor are there any cluster resources allocated to Exchange apart from an IP address and network name. Windows Failover Clustering uses the network name to update the password for the Computer Name Object for the cluster. The Primary Active Manager (see the next section) also uses the list of possible owners of the cluster's File Share Witness (FSW) resource as the candidate servers when it needs to transition due to a server outage. However, apart from these small points, there's no practical dependency on the network name as Exchange reverts to server names if the cluster name is unavailable. In fact, you never need to manage cluster resources such as nodes, network, or storage using the Windows Failover Cluster Manager because everything is managed through Exchange—and if you attempt to change the cluster settings with Cluster Manager, there's a fair chance that you could end up breaking something on which Exchange depends. In effect, Exchange provides a blanket that hides the complexity of cluster technology from system administrators.

INSIDE OUT   Operating system requirements

Even though Exchange uses a bare minimum of cluster technology, the dependency on Windows clustering means that you can only add mailbox servers to a DAG if they are running on Exchange 2010 Enterprise on Microsoft Windows Server 2008 (SP2 or R2) Enterprise edition. It also means that all of the DAG member servers must be part of the same domain. You should also run the same version of the operating system on all of the DAG member servers; you definitely cannot mix Windows Server 2008 SP2 and Windows Server 2008 R2, and it just makes good sense to keep the servers at the same software level. Exchange 2010 SP1 demonstrates that it is wise to keep all software at the same revisions on all DAG members; you can activate a database copy by moving it from a server running the RTM version of Exchange 2010, but you cannot perform the reverse operation and move the active database copy from a server running SP1 to one running RTM.

Despite its name, Windows Failover Clustering takes no part in the failover of Exchange mailbox databases. This functionality is provided by a new system management component within Exchange called the Active Manager, which maintains visibility of server conditions and the current state of databases, and is responsible for instructing servers to move database copies from active to passive and passive to active as required. Even better, an Exchange administrator doesn't have to be concerned with the complexities of Windows clustering, as Exchange configures the limited clustering features that it needs (cluster heartbeat and quorum) when it adds the first mailbox server to a DAG. Some of the information relating to the DAG is held in Active Directory. This information tends to be static and doesn't change very often, such as the name of the DAG. Other information that is more dynamic and prone to change quickly, such as database mount status (active or passive), is held in the cluster database.

Active Manager

Active Manager runs as part of the Microsoft Exchange Replication Service (MSExchangeRepl, not to be confused with the Mailbox Replication Service) on every server within a DAG. Conceptually, Active Manager is the orchestrator for native-mode high availability in Exchange because it decides which database copies are active and which are passive, taking into account administrator preferences such as the database activation preference order. You can regard Active Manager as the successor of the resource management model used by previous iterations of Exchange clustering technology.

Active Manager can operate in two roles. One server in the DAG takes on the Primary Active Manager (PAM) role and the others operate in a Standby Active Manager (SAM) role. Whether in PAM or SAM mode, servers continually monitor databases at both the Information Store and Extensible Storage Engine (ESE) levels to be able to detect failures. However, it is the PAM that determines which database copies are currently active and those that are passive; the SAM concentrates on monitoring the health of the Information Store process and the databases that run on the local server. Once it detects a failure of the Information Store or a database, the SAM on that server asks the PAM to initiate a failover, providing that the databases affected by the failure are replicated and a copy exists that the failover can make active. A failure might be caused by a storage failure that takes one or more disks offline or a problem that causes the ESE database engine to consider that a disk is unresponsive. If the server hosting the PAM is still online, it initiates the failover. If this server has been taken offline by a failure, another server in the DAG seizes the PAM role and begins to bring any necessary database copies online to restore service.

The server that holds the PAM role is responsible for processing topology changes that occur within the DAG and making decisions about how to react to server failures, such as deciding to perform an automatic transition of a passive copy of a database to become active because the server that currently hosts the active copy is unavailable for some reason. The PAM server owns the cluster quorum resource for the default cluster group that underpins the DAG. If the server that owns the cluster quorum resource fails, the PAM role moves to the server that takes ownership of the cluster quorum resource. We will discuss the criteria used by the PAM to select the database copy to activate shortly. Once a new database copy has been successfully mounted, the PAM updates the RPC Client Access service with details of the server that hosts the newly activated copy so that client connections can be directed to the correct server.

The active copy of a database is referred to as the *mailbox database master*. Its copies can be moved from active to passive state through a *switchover*, which is a change initiated by an administrator, perhaps in preparation to take a server offline to apply a service pack or other software upgrade, or a *failover*, which is the result of a hardware or software outage that prevents a database from functioning properly. In either case, Active Manager is responsible for selecting and enabling a new copy to accept incoming client traffic and is the definitive source of information about what server has mounted the currently active copy of a database. Configuration information is written back into the cluster database and updated there by Active Manager, but transient information relating to current database status is held in memory. You can view information about a DAG, including information about the names of the servers in the DAG and the current Active Manager, with the Get-DatabaseAvailabilityGroup cmdlet.

The following output is an edited version of the properties of a DAG returned by the Get-DatabaseAvailabilityGroup cmdlet. You can see that the DAG is composed of two servers (ExServer1 and ExServer2), that ExServer1 is currently serving as the PAM, and that a server called adroot.contoso.com hosts the FSW.

```
Get-DatabaseAvailabilityGroup -Identity 'DAG-Dublin' -Status | Format-List
```

```
Name                                       : DAG-Dublin
Servers                                    : {EXSERVER2, EXSERVER1}
WitnessServer                              : adroot.contoso.com
WitnessDirectory                           : C:\DAG-Dublin\FSW
AlternateWitnessServer                     :
AlternateWitnessDirectory                  :
NetworkCompression                         : InterSubnetOnly
NetworkEncryption                          : InterSubnetOnly
DatacenterActivationMode                   : Off
StoppedMailboxServers                      : {}
StartedMailboxServers                      : {}
DatabaseAvailabilityGroupIpv4Addresses     : {}
DatabaseAvailabilityGroupIpAddresses       : {}
AllowCrossSiteRpcClientAccess              : False
OperationalServers                         : {EXSERVER1, EXSERVER2}
PrimaryActiveManager                       : EXSERVER1
ServersInMaintenance                       : {}
ThirdPartyReplication                      : Disabled
ReplicationPort                            : 64327
NetworkNames                               : {DAGNetwork01}
WitnessShareInUse                          : Primary
AdminDisplayName                           :
ExchangeVersion                            : 0.10 (14.0.100.0)
DistinguishedName                          : CN=DAG-Dublin,CN=Database Availability
Groups,CN=Exchange Administrative Group (FYDIBOHF23SPDLT),CN=Administrative
Groups,CN=contoso,CN=Microsoft Exchange,CN=Services,CN=Configuration,
DC=contoso,DC=com
Identity                                   : DAG-Dublin
ObjectCategory                             : contoso.com/Configuration/Schema/
ms-Exch-MDB-Availability-
ObjectClass                                : {top, msExchMDBAvailabilityGroup}
OriginatingServer                          : ADRoot.contoso.com
```

If the PAM fails, its functions automatically pass to another server in the DAG that takes over ownership of the cluster quorum resource. You can also move the cluster quorum resource to another server to transfer the PAM role if you want to take the server that holds the role offline for some reason, such as to apply a software upgrade or patch.

One interesting aspect of the introduction of Active Manager is that the internal working of Active Manager and its ability to perform database transitions remains confidential within Microsoft. Third-party clustering or high-availability solutions that work with Exchange can upgrade their products to accept a direction from Active Manager to perform a transition, but they cannot integrate at a lower level.

Automatic database transitions

Figure 8-1 illustrates an example of a DAG containing three servers, each hosting two databases. Each of the databases is replicated to another server to provide a basic level of robustness to a server outage. If server 1 fails, which hosts the active copies of databases 1 and 2, the Active Manager process will reroute user connections to pick up the copies of the databases on servers 2 and 3. Users connected to database 1 will be redirected to server 2 and those connected to database 2 will go to server 3. Similarly, if the disk holding database 2 on server 1 fails, Active Manager will detect the problem and reroute traffic to server 3.

In this scenario, each database has just one copy and you might decide that the probability that more than one server will ever fail at one time is negligible, so it is sufficient to rely on the single additional copy. However, if the DAG extended across more than one datacenter you would probably configure every database to be replicated to all servers. In this scenario, copies of databases 1 and 2 would be present on server 3, meaning that if servers 1 and 2 were both unavailable, users could still get to their data using the copies hosted on server 3.

The number of copies you can create for an individual database is limited only by the number of available servers in the DAG, disk space, and available bandwidth. The high-capacity bandwidth available within a datacenter means that the availability of sufficient disk space to hold replicated databases and transaction logs is likely to be more of an issue. This issue is somewhat negated by the ability to deploy databases on low-cost drives, providing there is sufficient rack space, power, and cooling within the datacenter to support the disks. One sample environment has 15 servers in a DAG. There are 110 active databases and each database has two passive copies, so there's a total of 330 databases in the environment. Each server supports 22 databases (a mixture of active and passive) and dedicates 18 TB of storage for mailbox databases. Having three copies of each database is a reasonable approach to ensuring high resilience against a wide range of failures, including an interesting design point of planning database copies so that a failure that affects a rack cannot prevent service to a database. In other words, you should not put all the servers that host a database and all of its copies in the same rack.

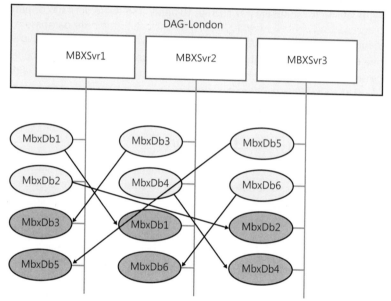

Figure 8-1 Databases and copies within a Database Availability Group.

The Microsoft Exchange Replication Service monitors database health on each DAG member to ensure that active databases are properly mounted and available and that ESE has signaled no I/O or corruption errors on a server. If an error is detected, the Replication Service notifies Active Manager, which then begins the process of selecting the best possible available copy and then making that copy of the database active to take the place of the failed database.

INSIDE OUT Dismounting an active database is not a failover

Before discussing the details of how automatic database transitions occur, it's worth making the point that Exchange does not invoke a transition when an administrator dismounts an active database. This action is deemed to be one that the administrator has taken deliberately, possibly to allow maintenance to proceed or even for something more prosaic such as enabling circular logging for a database. Exchange therefore has no reason to consider a failover because these are designed to occur automatically as a result of change in the operating environment that is not caused by an administrator.

Best copy selection

To make the choice to replace a failed copy of a replicated database, Active Manager runs a process called *best copy selection* (BCS). The aim of BCS is to take all possible complications and administrative blocks into account when selecting the right database copy to transfer service to, as it's obviously not a good thing to attempt to transfer service to a database that is failing in its own right. BCS works by creating a sorted list of available database copies after ignoring any database copies that are:

- On servers that are currently unreachable for some reason (network failure, maintenance, or other conditions).

- Administratively blocked from activation because the *DatabaseCopyAutoActivationPolicy* property of the database has been set to Blocked using the Set-MailboxDatabaseServer cmdlet.

Hopefully, the resulting list after exclusions has at least one copy. If only one database copy is available, Active Manager runs the attempt copy last logs (ACLL) process to bring that database copy up to date. If more than one database copy is available, Active Manager proceeds with the BCS process by sorting the list according to the copy queue length, with the copy with the fewest outstanding logs to copy at the top of the list. The actual sort is performed using the value of the *LastLogInspected* property. This property contains the date and time that the last transaction log file was inspected for the database copy. The end result is that the database copy that needs the least work to update after activation is at the top of the list.

Administrators are able to indicate a preference for a database copy to be activated in case of failure by setting the *ActivationPreference* property on a database copy with the Set-MailboxDatabaseCopy cmdlet. For example, in a DAG where database copies are maintained in two datacenters, it would be normal to set the activation preference so that the copies in the local datacenter are activated ahead of those in the remote datacenter. In this scenario, you can run this command to assign an activation preference value of 2 to the database copy DB1 on server ExServer1:

```
Set-MailboxDatabaseCopy -Identity 'DB1\ExServer1' -ActivationPreference 2
```

You don't want to get into a situation where a database copy that is less preferred for activation is brought online ahead of a more preferred copy, but the only way Exchange knows your preferences for activation is if you set them. To respect administrator choice, Active Manager sorts the list by Activation Preference. Active Manager now knows the state of health of the database copies that are available to it sorted in activation preference.

It's possible that the state of health of the copies might not be as good as we'd like, so Active Manager now reviews the state of health of each database copy more thoroughly using criteria such as the following:

- Database status: *Healthy* is best because it means that the database copy is ready to go. The other status values are *DisconnectedAndHealthy*, *DisconnectedAndResynchronizing*, or *SeedingSource*. All of these status values indicate that more work is required to bring the database copy online.

- Content index: Once again, a healthy status is best because it indicates that all of the content in the database has been indexed. A status of crawling indicates that Exchange is still indexing the content of the database copy.

- Copy queue length: It is best when the queue contains 10 transaction logs or fewer, as this means that the database copy has been copying logs from the active database to keep up to date.

- Replay queue length: Once again we want to see a moderate queue length of less than 50 logs awaiting replay. More than this number indicates more work is required to bring the database copy online.

Active Manager goes through its list sorted by activation preference and will select a database copy that is healthy, has a copy queue length of less than 10, and has a replay queue length of less than 50 If it can't find a database copy that matches these criteria, it reduces the standard for activation and looks for a database copy with a content index of "Crawling." If this doesn't work, it reduces its standard further until it can find a database copy that matches. Of course, it is possible that Active Manager will have to significantly reduce its selection standard before it can find a matching database copy, and that copy might have a low activation preference and be in the process of reseeding. Therefore, it's going to take a considerable effort to bring the copy online and restore service.

It's also possible that no database copy will meet even a reduced standard for activation. For example, if all of the other database copies are offline, Active Manager won't be able to activate any database copy automatically and reports failure. In this case, the administrator has to either fix the problem with the original database copy and bring it back online or address the issues that prevent Active Manager from bringing one of the other copies online.

The full set of criteria for the standard for activation is described in "Understanding Active Manager" at *http://technet.microsoft.com/en-us/library/dd776123.aspx*.

Note that Microsoft tweaked the best copy selection policy in SP1 so that if the AutoDatabaseMountDial property of a database is set to "Lossless", Active Manager uses the activation preference as the primary sort key when it selects a database copy to activate. This change reinforces the importance of activation preference in environments where data loss is not tolerated during failovers.

ACLL: Attempt copy last logs

Assuming that Active Manager can determine a suitable database copy to activate, it instructs the Replication Service on that server to run the ACLL process to copy any missing transaction logs from the server that hosts the failed database copy. Exchange 2010 obviously faces additional complexity over the log shipping scenario in Exchange 2007 in that copies of transaction logs that might be required to bring a database up to date can exist in many more servers than before.

The purpose of ACLL is to assemble all available data in the form of transaction logs to allow the Replication Service to update the database copy before it is mounted and made available to users. The best outcome is when all outstanding transaction logs can be copied from the server that hosted the failed database copy because the Replication Service will then be able to replay all the logs and the database copy will be completely up to date and a lossless failover is successful.

Of course, the nature of failure is that a database is most often taken offline because of a storage outage. In this case the disk holding the transaction logs might also be affected and the Replication Service won't be able to copy any logs. In this scenario, the *AutoDatabaseMountDial* property of the mailbox server is consulted to establish the tolerance for data loss caused by missing logs.

> **CAUTION**
>
> The default value for the *AutoDatabaseMountDial* setting on an Exchange 2010 mailbox server is *BestAvailability*, meaning that the mailbox server is happy to mount a database if up to 12 transaction logs are missing. This represents a potential data loss of 12 MB. Much of these data are probably messages that Exchange can recover from the transport dumpster, so it is acceptable to go ahead and mount the database and run the risk of a small data loss. Other values are *GoodAvailability*, representing a tolerance of 6 transaction logs, and *Lossless*, meaning that no data loss is tolerated.

Exchange will not mount a database automatically if the number of missing transaction logs exceeds the limit set by *AutoDatabaseMountDial*. Two actions can be taken from this point. The administrator can decide that she wants to force the database to mount and accept whatever data loss is incurred or she can locate the missing transaction logs from a backup (if one is available that has these logs) or a server that hosts another copy of the database.

If the ACLL process completes successfully, Active Manager has a database copy that is up to date and ready to mount. It therefore goes ahead and issues a mount request to bring the selected database copy online and make it available to clients. However, further checks occur to ensure that mounting the database will not exceed the maximum number of active databases configured for the server or that the database copy is suspended for activation. We discuss how to configure these settings later on in this chapter. Either of these issues will block activation.

If ACLL does not complete successfully, Active Manager selects another database copy and starts the process again. This cycle continues until a database copy is successfully activated and mounted or Active Manager reaches the end of the list of available copies and has to declare failure.

Transaction log replay: The foundation for DAG replication

Within a DAG, the transaction logs that are generated on the active server are pushed by the Replication Service to each of the servers that maintain passive mailbox database copies, where the logs are then validated and then replayed to update the passive copies. The DAG is the boundary of data replication for transaction logs. In other words, you cannot replicate logs to a server in a different DAG and have Exchange replay the logs into a database replica there. It then follows that before you can create a copy of a database, it must reside in a DAG and the target server must be part of the same DAG. The DAG is also the boundary for failover insofar as failovers only occur within the DAG.

A number of major differences in the log replication process exist between Exchange 2007 and Exchange 2010. The first is how data flows between servers. Exchange 2010 uses the ESE streaming application programming interface (API) to seed a database and raw Transmission Control Protocol (TCP) sockets to transfer logs between source and target servers instead of the Server Message Block (SMB) transfers used by Exchange 2007. In addition, Exchange 2007 uses one SMB session for all databases on a server, whereas Exchange 2010 uses one TCP socket per database. Although this change is largely mandated by the need to accommodate multiple copies per database, it obviously assists in scalability. When you create a DAG, you have the option to select the TCP port to use and can decide to use IPsec to protect the data and compression to reduce the amount of data transferred between servers. This change is intended to improve efficiency. IPsec must be configured through Windows rather than Exchange.

The second change is that the server hosting the active copy of the database now pushes transaction logs to the servers that host copies. In Exchange 2007, only one server holds a copy and it is logical for it to pull the transaction logs.

The third change is that the Information Store replays transaction logs instead of the Microsoft Exchange Replication Service to ensure that databases are immediately ready to accept a full client load if a transition is required. Transactions are replayed effectively in

Exchange 2007 but because the replay happens outside the Information Store process the transactions cannot populate the in-memory cache used for recent transactions. The net effect is that the cache is "cold" rather than "warm," which means that if a client requests data, it is likely that the Store will have to read the data from disk and incur an I/O cost rather than being able to read the data from its cache. Therefore, when a transition occurs, it will take some time before the Store is able to serve clients as efficiently as it can with a fully populated cache.

These differences aside, the basic process of transaction log replication and replay is essentially the same in Exchange 2010 as it was in Exchange 2007. The Microsoft Exchange Replication Service is composed of a set of components that interact to keep replication and replay flowing.

- The copier on the active server copies closed log files from the database to the inspector location on each server that hosts a database copy. This process is asynchronous and occurs on a continual basis as new logs are created. A log file is available to be copied when the Store closes off the current log file, renames it, and creates a new current log.

- The inspector on the copy server checks its directory regularly to detect new logs and then verifies that each of the logs is valid. If valid, the inspector moves the log file to the replay directory. If a log fails validation, the inspector copies it again to ensure that temporary conditions (such as a network glitch) do not stop continuous replication from working. If Exchange cannot recopy a log, then the passive copy of the database will have to be reseeded.

- The log replayer replays the contents of the copied logs to update the database copy using the same kind of processing that the Store executes for soft database recoveries following an unexpected server outage. The Store replays logs every 60 seconds or after 10 new logs become available.

- The truncate deletor deletes log files that the log replayer has successfully used to update the database copy. Full online backups of Exchange databases have traditionally removed log files, but when continuous replication is used, the truncate deletor makes sure that the log files that have not yet been replayed are not deleted.

- The incremental seeder component is responsible for ensuring that the database copies are not in a diverged state after a restore has been performed or after a database failover.

If you use EMC to look at a database that has copies (Figure 8-2), you'll see an immediate indication of whether replication is flowing smoothly. In this instance, you can see that the active copy of the database is on server ExServer1 and that another copy is hosted on server ExServer2, where the copy is marked "healthy," meaning that Exchange believes that it is a candidate to be activated if required. You can see that the database copy has a copy queue length of one transaction log and a replay queue length of six logs. The copy queue is the number of logs that are waiting to be copied from the active server to the one holding the copy. The replay queue is the number of logs that are waiting to be replayed into the copy database.

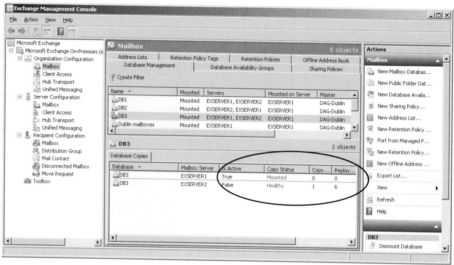

Figure 8-2 Viewing database copy status in a DAG.

INSIDE OUT   Fluctuations in the number of logs

The number of logs in the replay and copy queues fluctuates in line with the activity generated by clients. Relatively low numbers such as those shown here are of no concern. You should only become worried if you see the number of logs in the queues growing over time and failing to decrease even as the load eases on the server. This kind of situation indicates that something is interfering with log replication or replay or that some source of abnormal load exists. For example, it is possible to generate a very high load on a database when you move mailboxes around. Moving a large 2 GB mailbox generates at least 2,000 transaction logs. The Mailbox Replication Service (MRS) processes up to five mailbox moves concurrently, so if you move five large mailboxes to a single target database that has copies in a DAG you immediately generate an enormous load for the CPU (to process the incoming data, including updating the content index) and the storage subsystem. Replication activity is driven by the volume of transaction logs and large queues are likely.

INSIDE OUT   Consequences and how to deal with them

Two consequences usually result from the heavy load generated on the target server. First, all of the servers that host copies of the target database will be very busy and users might experience performance degradation until the mailbox moves taper off toward the end. Second, Exchange might put the mailbox move requests into a StalledDueToHA status and not resume the moves until server load decreases and the replication queues clear. You can see the StalledDueToHA status by using the Get-MoveRequestStatistics cmdlet to interrogate the current move queue. The stalled status indicates that Exchange has had to back off processing of move requests until the replay queue clears to reduce the number of outstanding transaction logs and ensure the preservation of high availability. For these reasons, it is important to schedule mailbox moves at a time when server load is light and the servers are able to cope with the demand generated by moving data from source to target servers. In addition, you should spread the load of mailbox move requests so that no one database becomes the target of more than three or four concurrent moves.

It's important to know that EMC shows a static snapshot of replication activity that is valid only for the time that EMC last fetched information about a database. To know what the current activity is, you have to click the Refresh option to force EMC to execute the Get-MailboxDatabase –Status command and retrieve updated status information about the selected database. Sometimes it is more convenient to see what's happening with replication using the Get-MailboxDatabaseCopyStatus cmdlet.

```
Get-MailboxDatabaseCopyStatus –Identity 'DB1\ExServer2'
```

Name	Status	CopyQueue Length	ReplayQueue Length	LastInspectedLogTime	ContentIndex State
DB1\ExServer2	Healthy	1	3	3/15/2010 9:23:10 AM	Healthy

Apart from noting that the copy and replay queue lengths are within acceptable limits and that the last inspected log is reasonably recent (at times of low user activity, replication activity can be limited to the log files generated every 15 minutes as a result of "log roll"), the other interesting item that we see from this output is that the content index is functioning properly for the copy. This indicates that items are being properly indexed as transaction logs are replayed into the database copy. It's important that context indexing works as the Active Manager takes the health of the index into account when it considers which copies are candidates for activation following an outage.

Chapter 8

Before the Information Store replays transaction logs into a database copy, it verifies the checksum and database signature of the logs to ensure that they are valid. This is equivalent to running the ESEUTIL against the log using the /K switch. If the checksum fails, Exchange recopies that log. If Exchange fails to copy and validate the log a third time, it is an indication that something very bad is happening within the storage subsystem to cause a physical corruption and you might need to reseed the database.

Many problems will be limited to a single mailbox

It's worth emphasizing at this point that the way Exchange 2010 performs continuous background maintenance to fix problematic pages in the database coupled with the validation of transaction logs during the replication process does a good job of preventing physical corruption arising from storage problems from infecting multiple database copies. If a page becomes corrupt and cannot be fixed by background maintenance, it will be detected when the replication process attempts to validate the transaction log that contains the corrupted page. It's possible that logical corruption caused by a software bug might sneak through, as this might not result in a bad checksum. If this happens, the new schema makes it likely that the problem will affect a single mailbox (in the past, a logical corruption in a table could affect many mailboxes) and you can recover from a backup or a lagged database copy.

Once the Replication Service has verified a transaction log, it moves the log into the log directory. The Store then replays the log to update the database copy using a process similar to the soft recovery process that occurs when Exchange needs to update a database whenever it is mounted. The log replay is also similar to the processing performed when you run ESEUTIL /R to replay logs to a database, but it is faster because Exchange attempts to batch log files together to stream transactions into the database. A separate instance of ESE that runs inside the Information Store process is responsible for log replay. The Store replays logs in generation order. For example, if the Replication Service copies log generation 1876 and the Store is replaying log generation 1873, it is logical that generation 1876 has to wait until the Store has replayed logs 1874 and 1875. If this did not happen then transactions that span several log generations could not be replayed accurately.

Tip

Transient network conditions could cause the network link between servers to have reduced capacity or be unavailable for a period. When this happens, the queues of transaction logs waiting to be replicated to servers that cannot be reached will grow. Once the network is restored to good health, normal replication activity will clear the backlog and the database copies on the other servers will be brought up to date. There is no need for a reseed in these situations.

The Replication Service might detect logs that it ignores for updates. For example, for some reason, a copied log file might be too old to apply to the database copy or it might be corrupt. These logs are moved into the IgnoredLogs directory and can be deleted. The IgnoredLogs directory can have two subdirectories—E00OutOfDate and InspectionFailed. The first directory holds any E00.log file that is present in the replica directory when a failover occurs. The file was probably created because the replica copy was previously run as the active copy. When a failure occurs, the Store creates a new E00.log file to act as the current transaction log, so if it finds an E00.log file in place, it simply moves it into the E00OutOfDate directory to get the old file out of the way. The InspectionFailed directory is there to hold log files that the inspector rejects for some reason, perhaps because the Store cannot read the file or believes that the signature in the header is invalid.

Transaction log compression

From the description so far, it is obvious that Exchange ships a great number of transaction logs around between servers in a DAG to keep all the databases synchronized. To minimize the network impact, Microsoft made some changes to the way that data are written to transaction logs. The order of processing is now as follows:

1. ESE compresses all message headers and HTML/text bodies before writing these data to the transaction logs.

2. The 1 MB transaction logs are compressed as they are replicated to servers within the DAG.

3. The transaction logs are decompressed before they are written to the replication target disk.

4. The compressed message headers and bodies are decompressed when clients request the Store to access the data.

Microsoft believes that this processing reduces transaction log traffic by approximately 20 percent (this might vary across different environments). Microsoft also changed the way that Exchange performs "log rolls," essentially the generation of a transaction log after a set period. The idea behind log roll is to keep replication ticking over and ensure that the databases are synchronized. Every 90 seconds on an Exchange 2007 server, a timer expires and the Store checks to see if any dirty pages have been generated in that period. These pages might be generated by user activity or server processes (such as background maintenance). If database activity has occurred, the Store creates a new transaction log (the "log roll"), even if there are not enough dirty pages to fill a complete transaction log. Using a 90-second timer means that an inactive server could generate a maximum of 960 log rolls daily (per storage group) that have to be replicated to target servers in CCR or SCR configurations. In some situations, up to 10 percent of total transaction log replication traffic was generated by empty logs.

Clearly any reduction in traffic will only occur for inactive servers and won't do anything for servers that are used on a 24x7 basis, but it is an indication of how Microsoft has tweaked log replication to be more efficient based on the experience gained from Exchange 2007.

Block replication

Block replication is a new feature introduced in Exchange 2010 SP1 to minimize the delay between a transaction occurring in an active database and when it is copied and replayed to all of the database copies. The idea is that speeding up replication reduces the potential exposure to data loss in the case of failure caused when a transaction log is corrupted between the times that it is generated and copied. In this respect, a transaction log can be considered a potential single point of failure that Exchange needed to address to achieve true high availability.

Exchange 2010 depends on the replication and replay of complete transaction logs to keep database copies updated. The current transaction log file is locked and the data that it holds are unavailable when it is in use. Exchange 2010 SP1 still uses transaction log replication but the log copier component includes some new code that monitors the state of replication to understand when it is safe enough to begin replication at the block level as data are flushed to disk. In this context, "safe" means that file-level replication is proceeding without problems and the database copies are all healthy.

The following approach is taken by Exchange 2010 SP1 mailbox servers:

- All replication begins in file mode. When a server comes online, it contacts the servers that host the active copies of any of its databases to request replication of any log generations that it has not yet seen.

- The servers that host the active databases respond with copies of any outstanding logs.

- The server replays the logs and brings its database copies up to date.

- Once a database copy is current (in other words, the next transaction log it needs is the current transaction log), Exchange can switch over to block mode.

- In block mode, as transactions are written into the ESE log buffer (the 1 MB cache used to accumulate transactions to be written into a transaction log), the log copier copies the data in parallel to all of the servers that hold a database copy. The data are written into a similar log buffer on these servers.

- When the log buffer on the receiving servers is full, the complete buffer is written out as a transaction log. The new log is inspected to ensure that it is not corrupt, and if this check passes, the log is inserted into the log stream to be replayed into the passive database.

- Replication continues in block mode until a replay queue of four logs accumulates on a server. At this point, Exchange automatically switches back into file mode and replication continues in this mode until the replay queue is cleared and the next log required is once again the current transaction log. Exchange then transfers back into block mode.

The same data paths are used for block replication and copying transaction logs, which are still copied to servers that host database copies to ensure that the copies have complete data sets available to them. The advantage of block mode is that transactions are dispatched immediately when they are available to the log buffer of the active database. No log roll is required and transaction data arrive to the servers that hold passive databases as quickly as the server hosting the active database can dispatch data across the network.

> **Note**
>
> Because log file replication continues and the logs are verified both on the sending and receiving servers (a verification failure causes a log rewrite), the previous potential for failure caused by a corrupt transaction log is removed.

An individual transaction might fit into a single 32 KB database page. New data obviously reach the servers that host database copies faster if the log copier only has to wait for and then copy a 32 KB page instead of a complete 1 MB transaction log. The case is less obvious for transactions generated by large multimegabyte messages as these require the replication of a number of transaction logs. However, sufficient small transactions fit into single pages to make block replication very attractive in terms of its ability to dramatically reduce overall replication latency.

Block replication also changes the activation process when Exchange has to bring a passive database copy online. If a copy was using block replication when the failure occurred, Exchange uses whatever partial log content is available to create a complete transaction log that it uses to bring the passive copy up to date as it is activated. This step ensures that the newly activated database will have all available data in it when it is brought online. Later on, when the failed server comes back online, the incremental reseeding code is able to resolve any divergence that exists between the data in the fragment used to update the activated database and the data that it might have received had replication been complete. The normal resolution to any divergence is a request to recopy the complete log generation represented by the fragment that arrived from the database that has all the information. Once the missing log is distributed, it can be replayed into the other database copies to make sure that all copies contain the same information.

Chapter 8

Transaction log truncation

Busy mailbox servers generate a lot of transaction logs. If circular logging is not enabled on a database, its transaction logs will continue to accumulate until they are truncated by the Store or manually deleted by an administrator. Log truncation for databases that do not use circular logging typically occurs when a successful backup occurs as the Store is able to remove all of the transaction logs that are no longer required because their contents are safely committed within the backed up copy of the database.

When circular logging is enabled, the Store uses a much smaller set of transaction logs to hold transactions that are pending commitment into the database. Once the transactions in a log are committed and the checkpoint has been advanced past the log generation, the Store can delete the log file. This mechanism allows the Store to operate with a set of between five and ten transaction logs depending on the activity of the database.

Things are slightly different when circular logging is used for databases within a DAG. Several copies of a database can exist within a DAG and it's important that the Store takes no action that might expose a database to data loss. Deleting a transaction log on one server cannot proceed without being sure that the log might not be required by another database copy. For example, one copy of the database might be offline because its server is down for maintenance. To allow for circumstances like this, the Store keeps the transaction logs until it is quite sure that they will never be required again. The following checklist is used.

Truncation occurs for transaction logs for databases without lagged copies (we'll discuss where lagged database copies are useful in the section "Using a lagged database" later in this chapter):

- Has the log file been backed up or is circular logging enabled?

- Is the log file generation less than the database's checkpoint?

- Has the log file been replayed successfully for all other database copies?

- Has the log file been inspected by servers that host lagged copies?

If the database has a lagged copy, it uses this variation:

- Is the log file generation less than the database's checkpoint?

- Is the log file older than the replay lag time and truncation lag time configured for the lagged copies?

- Has the log file been deleted on the active copy?

After all checks are met, the Store knows that it no longer needs a transaction log and it proceeds to delete it. If not, the log is retained until all conditions are satisfied. Note that a lagged copy creates the need to ensure that sufficient storage is available to hold all of the logs generated in this period. If you set the lagged copy to keep logs for 14 days or longer it is conceivable that you might have to set aside several gigabytes of storage for this purpose.

The set of transaction logs maintained for any copy of a database depends on how quickly the transaction logs are replicated within the DAG and then replayed into all copies of a database. You shouldn't be concerned if you see a temporary accumulation of transaction logs for a database copy, as the database might be waiting for an update from the other copies to allow it to truncate the log set, which might not happen for several hours. On the other hand, you should investigate to determine the underlying reason if you see the log set steadily grow over time, especially if no reduction occurs during off-peak times when fewer logs are being generated.

Incremental resynchronization

Although you'd like to imagine that things will always progress smoothly when transaction logs are copied around between servers and replayed to update database copies, the potential for some interruption always exists. Exchange 2007 includes the lost log resilience (LLR) and incremental reseed features to help Exchange keep database copies available even if one or more recent transaction logs are lost, damaged, or otherwise unavailable. LLR allows Exchange to mount a database even if it is not completely updated because of missing logs and works by delaying writes to the database until the missing log generations are created. Exchange 2007 allows you to vary the number of logs but Exchange 2010 hard-codes this value to 1, which is one of the reasons Exchange 2010 has reduced the number of empty transaction logs that it generates. Incremental reseed allows the Store to correct divergences in the transaction log stream between the active and passive database copies.

These features proved valuable in production, albeit with some problems. For example, incremental reseed depends on the delayed replay capabilities of LLR so it couldn't patch a passive database copy once any divergent logs were replayed, which meant that you would have to reseed the complete database. Administrators didn't consider this to be a good option for large databases.

Exchange 2010 introduces a modified and improved feature called *incremental resynchronization* to automatically correct divergences in database copies. However, an automatic correction can only occur under certain conditions when Exchange can be reasonably sure that it has access to enough data to enable it to correct matters. These are as follows:

- Following an automatic failover of a database, Exchange checks all the copies of a database to ensure they are consistent.

- If you create a new copy of a database and some files (database and/or log files) already exist at the copy location on the target server. This might happen if you enable and disable a database copy, and stops you from having to reseed the database each time.

- Following resumption of replication activity if you stop the Replication Service for any reason.

Whenever the Store detects a divergence condition between an active database and one of its copies, it looks in the available transaction logs to determine where the divergence took place. It then locates the relevant pages in the problem database copy, reads the changed pages from the active database, and copies any necessary log files from the active server. The update or patch information for the problem pages is then applied from the copied transaction logs into the diverged database copy to synchronize it with the active copy.

Exchange 2010 also includes the ability to patch individual pages within a database. In previous versions of Exchange, especially those prior to Exchange 2007, administrators hated seeing events -1018 or -1022 logged in the Application Event Log because these events indicate that the Store had detected a page-level corruption in a database. Corruptions usually occurred as the result of some hardware problem, often in storage controllers, and although a database could continue to run with the corruption, the problem was that the only way to fix a database that contained a corruption was to restore from the last good backup. Given that some databases were well over 100 GB, this wasn't a popular option with administrators.

A page corruption in a single-copy database is a severe problem. Replicating the corruption to many database copies creates a problem with a whole new dimension. For this reason, Exchange 2010 is able to detect and fix page-level corruptions that occur in active or passive database copies.

If the Store detects a problem page in the active database, it places a marker in the log stream (in the current transaction log) that acts as a request for a valid copy of the corrupted page. The request is sent to all database copies where it is inspected and processed along with other log content. When the Information Store replays data for the passive copy, it notices the marker and responds to the request by invoking a "replication service callback" to ship a copy of the page to the server that hosts the active database. When this server receives the replicated page, the Store patches it back into the active database to remove the corruption. Other servers that host passive copies might also respond with pages, but these are ignored once the active database has been restored to good health.

The process to fix a corrupted page in a passive database copy is slightly different. In this case, the server that hosts the passive copy immediately pauses log replay. Log copying continues, to ensure that all of the transaction logs that will eventually be required to bring the database completely up to date are available on the server. The server then requests a copy of the corrupted page from the server that hosts the active database using the internal ESE seeding mechanism. The active server responds with the page data. The passive server then waits until all the log files necessary to bring it up to date past the point where the active server provided the page (as indicated by the maximum required generation) have been copied and inspected. When it is sure that all the required data are available, the passive server then restores the corrupt page and resumes log replay to clear the backlog of transaction logs that have accumulated since the corruption was first detected.

Seeding a database

Seeding a database is the process that Exchange uses to create an initial database copy or to re-create a database copy if the current copy cannot be updated through log replay. Exchange 2007 also uses database seeding for CCR and SCR implementations. During a seed, Exchange copies the database from source to target and then updates the copy by replaying the transaction logs that have accrued since the copy operation started. One difference between the two versions is that Exchange 2010 copies the search catalog from the source to the target server to avoid the need to re-create the catalog on the target server. Another is that Exchange 2010 is able to use a passive copy of a database as the source for a copy. The CCR and SCR features of Exchange 2007 only support two copies of a database so it always has to seed a copy from the active database.

The time required to seed a database depends on the network speed between the two servers and the current workload that each server is under. Given the wide variation in environments, it is hard to give a definitive figure for the expected throughput, but you should expect to achieve a copy rate of up to 50 GB/hour if you use a 100 Mbps network. In other words, if you have a 1 TB database and need to reseed it, you can expect that this operation will take more than 20 hours to complete. You might consider this an unacceptable length of time to reseed a database, but the only real solution is to increase capacity for the replication network. Obviously, reseeding a 1 TB database is much faster on a 1 gigabit network. Even though Microsoft has attempted to minimize the need for reseeding, the potential always exists that this might be necessary, so if you plan to use very large databases, you also need to consider fast replication networks.

Unique database names

Because databases are no longer tied to servers, it follows that database names are now unique in Exchange 2010. The old default database names assigned by legacy versions of Exchange (such as "First Mailbox Database") that are the same on all servers (unless you rename the databases) are replaced by a naming scheme that assigns unique visible names to databases. The naming convention that generates uniqueness creates names such as Mailbox Database 1236069237. Although these names are certainly unique, they are difficult to remember and to use to reference databases from EMS. In most cases, you will consider renaming the database to reflect its location or use. For example, if a problem affects a server that hosts a database called Executive Mailboxes, there's a fair chance that this outage will draw more management attention and concern than a similar outage that affects a server hosting a database called Resource Mailboxes. In this instance, the database name flags a certain importance that might prompt a faster response from administrators that avoids other problems down the line. You'd hope that administrators always respond quickly to failure conditions, but sometimes a little hint helps everyone do the right thing.

You do not have to worry about creating unique names for existing databases on legacy servers because only Exchange 2010 servers can function in a DAG and Exchange will create unique names as you install new servers. You don't have control over the name given to the default database that the Exchange installation program creates for a new mailbox server unless you specify a name using the *–mdbname* parameter for the setup program running in command mode. You can also specify the path for the transaction logs with the *–LogFolderPath* parameter and the path for the database files with the *–DBFilePath* parameter. For example:

```
Setup.com /Roles:MB,CAS,HT /Targetdir:D:\Exchange /MdbName:DB1 /DbFilePath:F:
\Exchange\DB1\DB1.EDB /LogFolderPath:L:\Exchange\DB1Logs"
```

This command instructs Setup to install three server roles into the D:\Exchange directory and to create a new mailbox database called DB1 with the database file in F:\Exchange\DB1 and its transaction logs in L:\Exchange\DB1Logs.

If you make a mistake and the server installation creates a database with a default name, you can rename it afterward. At one point in time during development, Microsoft considered removing the ability to rename a database (because of a potential performance impact caused by the need to fetch data from Active Directory whenever the Get-MailboxDatabaseCopyStatus cmdlet was executed). Caching the database names seemed like a good solution at the expense of removing the ability to rename databases. After receiving a huge amount of pushback from customers in the early adopters' program, Microsoft wisely backtracked and restored the ability to rename databases.

To rename a database, select it in EMC, open its Properties dialog box, and input a new name on the General tab (Figure 8-3). Clearly you have to choose a new name that is unique.

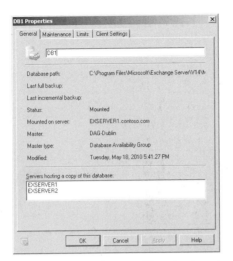

Figure 8-3 Renaming a mailbox database in a DAG.

You can also rename a database using EMS with the Set-MailboxDatabase cmdlet. For example:

```
Set-MailboxDatabase –Identity 'ExServer1\Mailbox Database 1236069237' –Name 'DB5'
```

The Information Store or any other Exchange component never uses display names to reference databases (the internal GUID is used for this purpose), so you can safely rename a database as many times as you want until you're happy. However, Exchange does update the distinguished name of the database and if you've used this name to reference the database in a script or other code, you will have to update the code to point to the new name. For example, if you created a dynamic distribution group with a custom filter to address all of the mailboxes in a particular database as described in Chapter 6, "Managing Mail-Enabled Recipients," the custom filter won't work after you rename the database because the distinguished name is different.

When you rename a database, you do not rename the underlying database files and these retain their original name. For example, when we renamed Mailbox Database 1236069237, Exchange simply updated the display name for the database and the underlying files remained intact. This fact becomes apparent if you access the files for any reason. For example, if you move the database and log paths away from the default location where Exchange places them during an installation to another disk, you'll see the original file names (Figure 8-4). Because replicated databases share the same location on all servers, EMC will flag an error to inform you that you cannot use this wizard if you attempt to move the path for a replicated database. (For more about how to move replicated databases, see the section "Moving database locations within a DAG" later in this chapter.) Continuing to use the original file names should not cause a problem unless you prefer to use file names that match the database name, in which case you should avoid using default databases and create the desired file names when you create new databases.

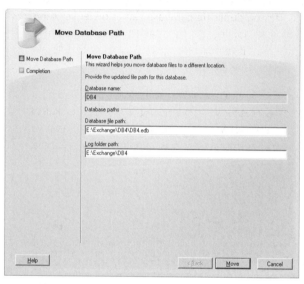

Figure 8-4 Moving the location of a database and its transaction logs.

Small to medium deployments probably don't have to worry too much about how their databases are named because only a relatively small number of databases will be in use. In these deployments it is certainly appropriate to use descriptive database names such as "VIP Mailboxes," "New York Mailboxes," or even "Critical Mailboxes" because it is less likely that these deployments will implement sufficient databases to run the risk of losing track of what a database is used for. However, larger deployments might have to manage several hundred databases distributed across multiple physical locations and organized into several DAGs. In this situation, it is worth thinking about whether your organization needs to use a specific database naming scheme before you begin to deploy servers.

INSIDE OUT How Exchange refers to databases

Behind the scenes, Exchange continues to assign unique GUIDs to databases and uses these GUIDs instead of the visible names whenever it needs to refer to a database. Apart from the GUID and visible name, other important database properties maintained in Active Directory include the EdbFilePath (the path to the database files) and the list of servers that host copies of the database. In fact, all of the copies of a database in a DAG must share the same path.

If you upgrade from Exchange Server 2003 or Exchange Server 2007, you are likely to have a number of duplicate mailbox database names distributed around the organization. Both versions use a combination of server name, storage group name, and database name to establish uniqueness. Having duplicate database names on legacy servers will not be a problem if you always move mailboxes to Exchange 2010, but you might run into some minor issues if you want to move mailboxes from Exchange 2010 to a legacy server because Exchange 2010 relies on unique database names.

To remove the ambiguity for EMC, when you select the target database for the move, you have to filter target databases by server name in the database picker to find the right database. If you prefer to use the New-MoveRequest cmdlet in EMS, you have to be sure to include the server name in the target database parameter. For example:

```
New-MoveRequest -Identity 'EPR' -TargetDatabase
'E2007Server\StorageGroupName\MbxDatabaseName'
```

Changes in message submission within a DAG

Transport processing changes slightly within a DAG to achieve better high availability for multirole servers. Normally, the mail submission service will use the closest hub transport server to submit new outgoing messages (and will use the hub transport service running on the local server if this role is active). Within a DAG, the mail submission service will round-robin between hub transport servers within the same Active Directory site and will failback to a local instance if no remote servers are available. In addition, the transport system attempts to route a message via a server other than the one that hosts the mailbox database from where the message originated. These steps are taken to save a copy of the message in the transport dumpster so that it can be recovered following an outage.

Day-to-day DAG management and operations

Setting up a new DAG is not something to do on a whim, nor is it something that you should attempt unless you have sufficient knowledge of all of the technologies that are involved. These include:

- Exchange 2010

- Windows Server 2008 and Failover Clustering

- Networks

Exchange hides most of the details of dealing with Windows Failover Clustering from the administrator when it builds and maintains a DAG and you should never have to look at the cluster details unless a problem occurs and you have to carry out some investigation to retrieve information, probably under the direction of Microsoft Support. Even so, it's still a good idea to know the nature of the beast with which you are dealing, if only at a reasonably high level.

In addition, the account that you use needs to have sufficient permissions to be able to install all of the necessary components or to make changes to the Exchange organization or the Windows system. Setting up a new DAG for a test environment is an interesting exercise in the application of a combination of computer software and hardware to solve a problem and it's something that you need to go through several times before you deploy a DAG into production. When that time comes, you need to understand what form the DAG will take and what purpose it will serve. For example, important considerations include what servers will participate in the DAG, how the servers will communicate to replicate transaction logs, what mailbox databases will be replicated to what servers, where the FSW for the DAG is located, and how the overall design will operate under different circumstances such as an individual or multiserver outage. These details should be written down and validated before any step is taken to create a production-quality DAG. Assuming that all the up-front work is done, you can create a new DAG by running the New Database Availability Group Wizard through EMC or by using the New-DatabaseAvailabilityGroup cmdlet through EMS. Either approach works well, the only major difference being that a DAG created through EMC will use Dynamic Host Configuration Protocol (DHCP) IP addresses for its networks, whereas you have the option to provide static IP addresses for a DAG created with EMS. At least, that's the way things work in the original version of Exchange 2010.

Microsoft's thought process was that EMC is designed to provide a very simple administrative experience to encourage use of DAG features in even the smallest sites, so they decided to remove some complexity from the DAG creation wizard. You can always assign static IP addresses for DAG communications by updating the DAG properties after it is created. Administrators protested and wanted maximum flexibility through EMC, too, so Microsoft changed EMC in SP1 to allow the assignment of static IP addresses there as well.

You only have to provide a name for the DAG when you use the wizard to create a new DAG. The name must be unique in the forest and can be up to 15 characters in length. You can also complete the fields to specify the names of the witness server and the directory on the server to hold the share. However, if you leave these fields blank, the wizard will fill them in by searching for a hub transport server in the local site that doesn't have the mailbox role installed and then create the default directory and share on that server to use.

Figure 8-5 illustrates the creation of a new DAG through EMC. The operation is extremely simple and the only likely mistake at this stage is the placement of the FSW on a server that might be part of the DAG in the future. If you make a mistake at this point, you can simply update the properties of the DAG to reassign the FSW to a different server (Figure 8-6).

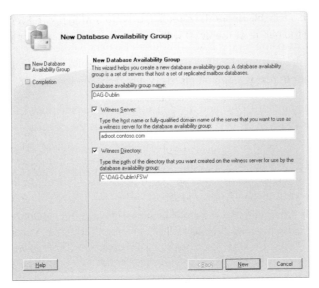

Figure 8-5 Creating a new DAG with EMC.

As part of creating the DAG on an Exchange 2010 server, you have to provide a universal naming convention (UNC) share path and directory for use by the FSW for the cluster. This directory can be on a Windows Server 2003 or Windows Server 2008 (SP2 or R2) server and Exchange will create the physical directory as it sets up the DAG. The server that hosts the FSW must be in the same forest as the DAG, but it cannot be a member of the DAG. You can specify a UNC and directory for an alternate file share for the cluster to use if the server that hosts the primary FSW is unavailable.

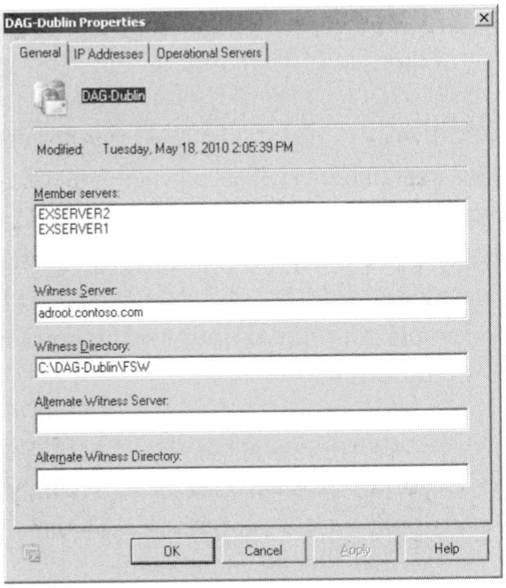

Figure 8-6 Viewing DAG properties.

Exchange 2010 SP1 is more flexible and you can do the following:

1. Only specify the name for the DAG: This forces Exchange to look for a hub transport server in the site that doesn't have the mailbox role installed. If a suitable server is found, Exchange creates a default directory and file share for the FSW on that server.

2. Specify the name of the DAG and the directory to use for the FSW: The same search for a hub transport server occurs and Exchange creates the directory and the file share there.

3. Specify the name of the DAG and the FSW server: Exchange creates a default directory for the FSW on the specified server.

4. Specify all the parameters for the DAG: Exchange creates the FSW directory with the specified name on the target server.

> **Note**
>
> A single server can host the FSW for multiple DAGs as long as each DAG is assigned its own unique directory. Microsoft recommends that the easiest way to meet these requirements is to locate the FSW on a hub transport server in the same Active Directory site that hosts the DAG (a DAG can span multiple Active Directory sites, so in this instance you select a hub transport server in one of the sites to host the FSW). One good reason for placing the FSW on an Exchange server is that you can then be sure that an Exchange administrator will be able to manage all of the DAG components.

Because the FSW does not have to be placed on an Exchange server, EMC doesn't monitor whether the FSW is available. It is also entirely possible for an administrator to remove or wipe a server that is acting as the FSW for one or more DAGs with no complaint from Exchange until the next time that a DAG needs to use the FSW. At that time, Exchange will discover that the server is no longer available and any command that depends on the FSW will fail. Fortunately, the simple fix is to edit the DAG properties with EMC or use the Set-DatabaseAvailabilityGroup cmdlet to move the FSW to another server. In scenarios that stretch a DAG across multiple datacenters, you should locate the FSW in the primary datacenter so that a network interruption between the primary and secondary datacenter doesn't trigger a failover or halt DAG operations.

If you opt to place the FSW on a server that doesn't have Exchange 2010 installed, you should first add the Exchange Trusted Subsystem universal security group (USG) to the local Administrators group on the target server before you create the DAG. This step ensures that Exchange is able to create and manage the directory and share on that server. You do not have to take any other step to allow Exchange to manage the FSW; some commentators have blogged that you should add the machine account for the server that hosts the FSW to the Exchange Trusted Subsystem group. Such advice should be ignored because you have to take extreme care when you allow access to the Exchange Trusted Subsystem group. This group permits access to any Exchange object in Active Directory and you need to keep it as restricted as possible. Because it's really only creating an object in Active Directory to prepare for servers to join the DAG, Exchange can still create the DAG object even if it cannot create the FSW on the nominated server. In this case you'll see an error similar to that shown in Figure 8-7. To fix the problem of an uncreated FSW, you will have to use the Set-DatabaseAvailabilityGroup cmdlet to update the DAG properties with the name of the server hosting the FSW and the directory where the FSW resource is located after you add the Exchange Trusted Subsystem USG to the local Administrators group.

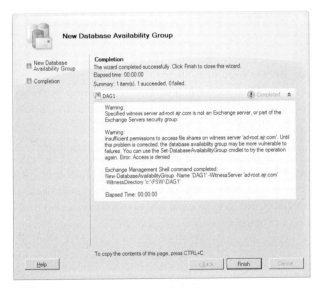

Figure 8-7 Error creating the FSW during DAG creation.

You'll see a similar warning about the server hosting the FSW not being an Exchange server even if Exchange is able to create the FSW on a server where the Exchange Trusted Subsystem has been added to the local Administrators group (Figure 8-8). Providing that this is what you intended, you can ignore this warning.

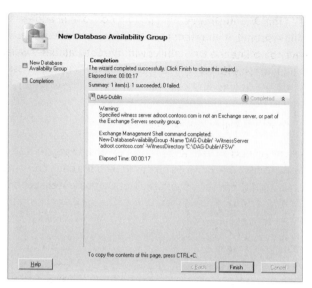

Figure 8-8 DAG created, but with a warning.

INSIDE OUT   Create a firewall rule for remote management

Firewalls can get in the way of communications—even legitimate communications—so, if the Windows firewall is enabled on the target server, you should create a firewall rule to allow remote management so as to avoid RPC access errors during DAG communications. A rule such as the one shown here is appropriate:

```
NetshAdvfirewall Firewall set rule group="Remote Administration" new enable=yes
```

You can also create a DAG through EMS. The following example creates a new DAG called LondonDAG and assigns a static IP address to the DAG. As discussed earlier, you don't have to register an IP address at this point and indeed, if you create a DAG with EMC, no IP address is registered and Exchange leases an address using DHCP (Microsoft does not support Automatic Private IP Addressing [APIPA] for DAG networks). You can assign an IPv6 address for the DAG, but only if you simultaneously assign an IPv4 address. IPv6 is still unknown territory for most Windows administrators, though, so you should probably plan on using IPv4 only for your DAG deployments until the IPv6 world is a bit more mature.

Windows Failover Clustering registers the IP address as a network resource for the Windows cluster resource that underpins the DAG. Essentially, you can think of the IP resource as a pointer that identifies the DAG in DNS. As we'll see later on, one IP address is enough for a DAG that spans a single subnet. If you want to add servers to the DAG that span different subnets, you will have to update the DAG object with the Set-DatabaseAvailabilityGroup cmdlet to add new IP addresses for each of the subnets that you want to use. Most companies prefer to use static IP addresses for server resources, so that's what we will do:

```
New-DatabaseAvailabilityGroup -Name 'DAG-Dublin'
-DatabaseAvailabilityGroupIPAddresses 192.165.1.8
```

If you don't assign an IP address or set the value to 0.0.0.0, Exchange will attempt to lease an address using DHCP. If you use DHCP, Exchange will report the IP address as 0.0.0.0 any time that you look at the DAG properties with the Get-DatabaseAvailabilityGroup cmdlet.

> **Note**
> Get-DatabaseAvailabilityGroup only reports the static properties that are stored in Active Directory. If you want to see the full properties for the DAG, including the properties maintained by Exchange, use Get-DatabaseAvailabilityGroup –Status.

DAGs use Majority Node Set clusters, as do Exchange 2007 CCR and SCR clusters. This means that at least half of the votes that exist within the cluster must be available for the cluster to run. Each server node has a vote, as does the FSW. The cluster adjusts itself automatically to maintain quorum as member servers are joined and leave. After the new DAG is created, it is an empty cluster with no member servers, so the cluster operates in node majority quorum mode with the only vote belonging to the FSW. This is okay as one valid vote out of one is available. As you add mailbox servers to the DAG, the cluster automatically changes to use a node and file share majority quorum and the DAG begins to use the witness server to maintain the quorum. Inside a fullyformed DAG that has all its member servers online, the vote of the FSW is not required to maintain quorum. However, if member servers fail or are taken offline, the vote of the FSW becomes more important. For example, in a four-node DAG, the quorum is three (> 50 percent of four member servers). If half the servers fail, the vote of the FSW is needed to maintain quorum and to keep the cluster online. When it is created, the new DAG is also represented as an empty object in Active Directory (Figure 8-9). We'll see how server objects are linked to the DAG object as you add servers to build out the DAG.

If you're in a situation where active users are spread across two datacenters it is better to run two DAGs rather than attempt to run a single DAG with servers in both datacenters. The logic is that a DAG has a single FSW, so if you operate a single DAG, its FSW must be located in one of the datacenters, which in turn creates a potential single point of failure for the users located on servers in the other datacenter. Any network outage that removes access to the FSW from the other datacenter creates a condition where the FSW is inaccessible and cannot be used to maintain quorum. It is therefore better to create two DAGs and locate an FSW in each datacenter.

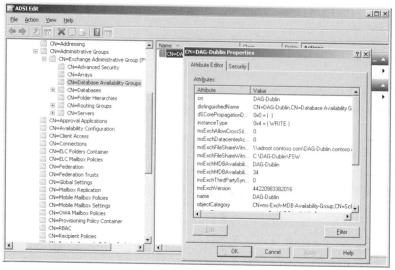

Figure 8-9   Viewing a DAG object in Active Directory.

Microsoft's preferred approach is that you use its continuous replication technology to maintain database copies within a DAG. They also support a replication API to allow other vendors to build DAG solutions with their own feature set. Assuming the third-party solution is installed and available, these DAGs are created with the New-DatabaseAvailabilityGroup cmdlet using the *–ThirdPartyReplication* parameter. Once a DAG is created based on a third-party solution, it cannot be changed. If you want to revert to use the Exchange technology, you have to remove all servers from the DAG, remove the DAG, and then re-create it.

See the Microsoft Web site for a current list of approved third-party replication solutions for Exchange 2010.

Building the DAG

Immediately after creation, a new DAG is an empty container that is waiting to be filled with mailbox servers and their databases that bring functionality to the DAG. Being able to construct a DAG gradually over time is one of the advantages that the implementation brings to Exchange. The alternative, which we see in the implementation of clustered mailbox servers in Exchange 2007, is to install all of the servers in the cluster at one time. After the DAG is created and its properties verified, you can start to add mailbox servers to the DAG before creating new database copies that will be managed by the servers. This process doesn't have to begin immediately and you can keep an empty DAG in the organization for as long as you need to before you begin to add servers.

Servers are added and removed from the DAG using the Manage Database Availability Group Wizard through EMC or by using the Add-DatabaseAvailabilityGroupServer and Remove-DatabaseAvailabilityGroupServer cmdlets. To begin to manage DAG membership with EMC, go to the Mailbox section of the Organizational Configuration node and select the DAG from the Database Availability Groups tab, then right-click to reveal the menu options for DAG management (Figure 8-10).

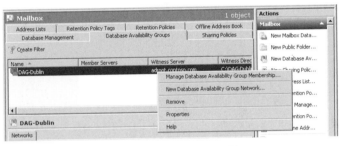

Figure 8-10 Option to manage DAG membership.

CAUTION

> Microsoft recommends that you don't install Exchange on a domain controller. It therefore follows that they're not particularly excited if you add a mailbox server that happens to run on a domain controller to a DAG. Exchange doesn't block this action and you can go ahead and use a domain controller if you really must; hopefully, you will only do this in a test configuration and not in production use.

After a mailbox server is added to a DAG, you can manage its membership in the DAG from another Exchange server. Some administrators prefer to use Server Manager to install the Windows Failover Clustering feature (Figure 8-11) before they attempt to add a server to a DAG because they prefer to make sure that all of the prerequisites are in place before they proceed.

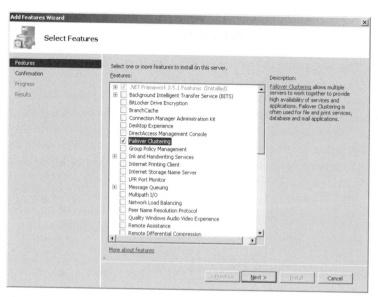

Figure 8-11 Installing Windows Failover Clustering.

Figure 8-12 illustrates the EMC Wizard adding a new server to a DAG.

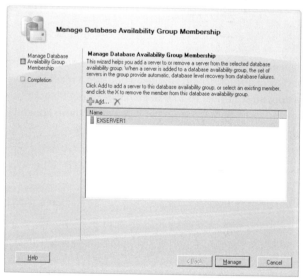

Figure 8-12 Adding a new server to a DAG.

The following steps occur to instantiate a DAG with the addition of the first mailbox server. Exchange has to do quite a lot of work to bring a server into a DAG, especially if it has to install Windows Clustering, so this process does not happen quickly.

1. Exchange validates that the server has the mailbox server role installed and does not host the FSW resource for the DAG.

2. If not present, Exchange installs Windows Failover Clustering on the mailbox server.

3. A failover cluster is created using the name of the DAG.

4. A cluster network object (CNO) is created in the Computers organizational unit (OU) in Active Directory (Figure 8-13).

5. The name and IP address of the DAG is registered in DNS as a Host (A) record.

6. The mailbox server is linked to the DAG object by populating the *MSExchMDBAvailabilityGroupLink* property on the server object in Active Directory.

7. The cluster database is updated with information about the databases hosted by the newly added server. These databases remain as standalone active copies until you create additional passive copies through replication to other servers in the DAG.

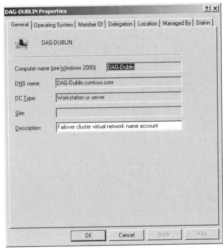

Figure 8-13 Properties of the DAG object added to the Computers OU.

Although it is easiest to add servers using EMC, you can also do this through EMS. For example:

```
Add-DatabaseAvailabilityGroupServer –Identity 'DAG-Dublin' –MailboxServer 'ExServer2'
```

When you add additional mailbox servers to the DAG, Exchange does the following:

- Validates that the server has the mailbox role installed.

- Joins the server to the cluster.

- Adjusts the quorum model. A node majority model is used for DAGs with an odd number of members, whereas a node and file share majority model is used for DAGs with an even number of members. The quorum model is automatically adjusted as servers join and leave the DAG, including when they are taken offline for maintenance or suffer a failure. The adjustment occurs in the background and does not require any administrator intervention.

- Links the server to the DAG object in Active Directory.

- Updates the cluster database with information about the databases hosted by the newly added server.

Figure 8-14 shows details of a DAG with two member servers as viewed through the Windows Failover Cluster Manager. The networks have been configured automatically using DHCP and the cluster is configured to use a node and file share majority quorum (because the cluster is formed by an even number of servers). In this case, the FSW is hosted on a server that doesn't run Exchange, so we had to add the Exchange Trusted Subsystem to the local Administrators group on the server before using it to host the FSW. As you can see, there is no obvious indication that the FSW is on a non-Exchange server.

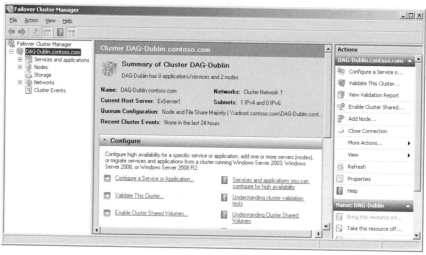

Figure 8-14 DAG details seen through Failover Cluster Manager and EMC.

INSIDE OUT
Do not manage DAG resources through Failover Cluster Manager

Although a DAG is visible to the Failover Cluster Manager, you should never attempt to manage any of the resources used by the DAG through this console. If you do, don't expect much sympathy from Microsoft Support if one of your changes compromises the integrity of the DAG. Exchange stores many important properties for a DAG in Active Directory and the only way that you can manipulate DAG settings properly is through EMC or EMS. If necessary, the underlying code in the DAG management cmdlets will update the settings of the Windows cluster.

I've already stated that the more developed state of Windows Server 2008 R2 makes it my preferred platform for Exchange 2010. Development occurs over time in response to real-life operational experience and Windows clustering is no different. An example is the design change in Windows Server 2008 R2 to handle situations where clusters could enter a lost quorum state because the FSW resource was in a failed state even though the witness directory was available. Microsoft provides a retrofit update in KB978790 that you can apply to Windows 2008 servers. The change kicks in when the cluster determines that it is necessary to use the FSW to maintain quorum. If the FSW resource is failed, the cluster attempts to kickstart it back into action by bringing the resource online. If the server that hosts the FSW is available, it can respond and report that the FSW is available and accessible and the cluster can maintain quorum. However, if the FSW cannot be brought online, the cluster is in a lost quorum condition that has to be resolved by an administrator.

Before a server can join a DAG, it must be able to communicate with the cluster service running on every other member server that is currently in the DAG. In other words, you cannot expect to populate a DAG if some servers are offline or experiencing network problems. There are a number of reasons why communication might not be possible, including the following:

- Servers are powered off or otherwise unavailable.

- The cluster service is not running on a server.

- Firewall rules on a server are blocking communication to the cluster service.

- The DNS service is unavailable.

- Authentication problems (Kerberos, Active Directory, or NTLM) are interfering with secure server-to-server communications.

Production servers should have two network interface cards (NICs) to allow them to isolate MAPI traffic (interaction with other servers including CAS and Active Directory) and replication traffic (log shipping and database seeding). This is not a hard technical requirement from an Exchange perspective because it is perfectly feasible to have all traffic routed across a single NIC, assuming that the NIC has sufficient capacity to handle the network traffic (Microsoft recommends Gigabit Ethernet for single NICs). However, Windows Failover Clustering also has a dependency on a solid network and because dependable replication is so important to the smooth operation of the DAG, it's really best if you deploy servers equipped with dual NICs for DAGs. Additional replication networks can be added as required and you can take advantage of techniques such as NIC teaming to improve overall network resilience against failure. (See the section "DAG networks" later in this chapter.) You can also consult TechNet to determine how to best to configure network settings for DAG operations.

Investigating DAG problems

All of the activities performed by DAG maintenance operations are captured in log files stored in the \ExchangeSetupLogs\Dagtasks directory. Each log file is named "DagTask" plus the date and time when the task was performed, so it's easy to find the relevant file. Take a look at the following two extracts of example DAG log files. The first reports the creation of a new DAG.

```
new-databaseavailabiltygroup started on machine EXSERVER1.
[2009-10-07T09:16:10] new-dag started
[2009-10-07T09:16:10] commandline:      $scriptCmd = {& $wrappedCmd
@PSBoundParameters }
[2009-10-07T09:16:10] Option 'Name' = ''.
[2009-10-07T09:16:10] Option 'WitnessServer' = 'AD-SERVER12.CONTOSO.COM'.
[2009-10-07T09:16:10] Option 'WitnessDirectory' = 'c:\FSW\DublinDag'.
[2009-10-07T09:16:10] Option 'WhatIf' = ''.
[2009-10-07T09:16:21] New-DatabaseAvailabilityGroup passed the initial checks.
[2009-10-07T09:16:22] New-DatabaseAvailabilityGroup completed successfully.
new-databaseavailabiltygroup explicitly called CloseTempLogFile().
```

The second shows that Exchange detected that Windows Failover Clustering was not installed on a server when it was added to a DAG, so Exchange went ahead and installed the component on the server.

```
[2009-10-07T09:57:49] Updated Progress 'Adding server 'EXSERVER1' to database
    availability group 'DAG-Dublin'.' 6%.
[2009-10-07T09:57:49] Working
[2009-10-07T09:57:49] Updated Progress 'The task is installing the Windows
    Failover Clustering component on the server EXSERVER1.' 8%.
[2009-10-07T09:57:49] Working
```

```
[2009-10-07T10:06:37] The following log entry comes from a different process,
    run on machine EXSERVER1'. BEGIN
[2009-10-07T10:06:37] [2009-10-07T09:57:50] Updated Progress 'The task is
    installing the Windows Failover Clustering component on the server
    exserver1.' 2%.
[2009-10-07T09:57:50] Working
[2009-10-07T10:06:36] Updated Progress 'The task has installed the Windows
    Failover Clustering component.' 4%.
```

The system event log is also a useful source of information if you need to track down the source of a problem and in particular, the crimson events logged for the high-availability channel are often revealing about what happens in terms of Active Manager (see the section "Crimson events" later in this chapter). More detailed cluster-related logging is captured in the Windows\Cluster\Reports directory. This information is pretty verbose but could hold the key to some of the more esoteric issues that occur from time to time. One way to limit the mass of data in the logs that you have to review is to attempt to correlate it with any event log entries that seem to be related to the problem.

Managing DAG properties

After the DAG is created, you can alter its properties to meet operational requirements using EMC or the shell. You need to be a member of the Organization Management role group to be able to modify DAG properties, which are listed in Table 8-1.

Table 8-1 **DAG properties**

Property	Use
FSW share (WitnessServer)	Path for the share used by the FSW
FSW directory (WitnessDirectory)	Name of the directory used by the FSW
Alternate FSW share (AlternateWitnessServer)	Path for an alternate FSW
Alternate FSW directory (AlternateWitnessDirectory)	Name of an alternate directory used by the FSW
Network encryption (NetworkEncryption)	Disabled: No encryption of data on the DAG network Enabled: Encryption used for replication and seeding InterSubnetOnly: Encryption used on DAG networks in the same subnet SeedOnly: Encryption only used for database seeding
Network compression (NetworkCompression)	Disabled: No compression Enabled: Compression used for replication and seeding InterSubnetOnly: Compression used for DAG networks on the same subnet SeedOnly: Compression only used for database seeding

Replication port (ReplicationPort)	TCP port used for replication activity; if you change this value from the default (64327), make sure that you also make the necessary change on any firewall that is in place to allow replication traffic to pass through the open port
IP addresses (DatabaseAvailabilityGroupIpAddresses)	IP addresses for the subnets used by the Windows failover cluster that underpins the DAG

You can use the Set-DatabaseAvailabilityGroup cmdlet to update DAG properties through EMS (only some of these properties are available through EMC). For example, this command manipulates a number of DAG properties:

```
Set-DatabaseAvailabilityGroup –Identity 'DAG-Dublin' –WitnessServer
'ExHT1.contoso.com' –WitnessDirectory 'D:\DUBDAG' –AlternativeWitnessServer
'ExHT22.contoso.com' –AlternativeWitnessDirectory 'D:\DUBDAG'
–ReplicationPort 33998 –NetworkEncryption SeedOnly –NetworkCompression Disabled
–DatacenterActivationMode Disabled
```

Note that the two alternate FSW properties are only required when a DAG extends across multiple datacenters. We'll discuss how a DAG transition occurs between multiple datacenters in the section "Planning for datacenter resilience" later in this chapter.

By default, DAG network traffic is not encrypted or compressed unless it is replicating across different subnets. The *NetworkCompression* and *NetworkEncryption* properties of the DAG are therefore set to InterSubNetOnly. It's easy to change these values, as they are both properties of the DAG. As such, the values that you assign apply to all traffic between all members and cannot be altered for individual servers. Table 8-1 includes the available options that you can set for DAG encryption. For example, this command enables compression and encryption for all traffic within a DAG:

```
Set-DatabaseAvailabilityGroup –Identity 'DAG-Dublin' –NetworkCompression Enabled
–NetworkEncryption Enabled
```

Exchange uses existing code for intra-DAG communications

Exchange doesn't introduce any new code to encrypt its intra-DAG communications. Instead, it uses the facilities made available in Windows, specifically the Windows Kerberos security support provider (SSP). This module contains routines that allow applications to encrypt, decrypt, sign, and verify the data contained in messages sent between application components such as DAG members. When two DAG members communicate, they each act as an endpoint and begin the connection with a handshake and key exchange. Once the connection is set up, encrypted traffic flows across it that can be decrypted by both members.

Exchange 2010 also supports compression for intra-DAG communications based on the LZ77 algorithm. Once again, a familiar algorithm is reused as LZ77 (otherwise known as XPRESS) is deployed to protect MAPI RPCs flowing between Outlook and Exchange.

You can use the Get-DatabaseAvailabilityGroup cmdlet to review the properties of a DAG. For example:

```
Get-DatabaseAvailabilityGroup –Identity 'DAG-Dublin' | Format-List
```

You might arrive at a situation where you want to change the location of the FSW. Perhaps the server is unavailable for some reason or it is more productive to relocate the FSW to another server. In this case, you can use the Set-DatabaseAvailabilityGroup cmdlet to update the properties for the FSW. This example command moves the FSW to a server called ExServer22 (which cannot be a member of the DAG) and specifies a directory on that server to host the resource:

```
Set-DatabaseAvailabilityGroup –Identity 'DAG-Dublin' –WitnessServer
'ExServer22.contoso.com' –WitnessDirectory 'C:\FSW\DublinDAG'
```

Moving the FSW should only ever be attempted when the DAG is healthy and the FSW is not actively in use to maintain quorum.

DAG networks

A simple DAG composed of two or three mailbox servers such as the one that we have discussed so far has relatively basic network requirements. The DAG has to be able to replicate transaction logs between the mailbox servers and the network has to be able to carry the replication load as well as any other network load generated by other activities such as message transport. A single NIC could be capable of handling the load, albeit with the understanding that a single NIC might also represent a potential single point of failure for the DAG. However, for test and other environments that do not need to operate at the level required for large production systems, a single NIC is often sufficient. At one point in the development of Exchange 2010, Microsoft considered making multiple NICs mandatory for DAG member servers. They pulled back from this position because it meant that low-end servers might not be able to participate within a DAG. Instead, the position is that you can deploy servers equipped with a single NIC as long as you are happy that the solution is robust enough for your purpose.

Figure 8-15 shows a basic DAG made up of two mailbox servers, each of which has one NIC. The details of the networks assigned to the DAG are exposed in the lower pane. Each network used by a DAG must have a subnet. Exchange creates the initial subnet automatically when the DAG is created. We can also see the IP addresses for the NICs used by the two servers. The preferred approach for larger DAGs is to split network traffic across two networks:

- The MAPI network takes care of client connections. This network is also used for database seeding. There is always a MAPI network within a DAG.

- The replication network is used for database seeding and transaction log replication. You don't have to run a replication network. On the other hand, high-end Exchange mailbox servers that have to handle a substantial replication load can be configured with multiple replication networks.

You can also use the Get-DatabaseAvailabilityGroupNetwork cmdlet to view the network information for a DAG. For example:

```
Get-DatabaseAvailabilityGroupNetwork –Identity 'DAG-Dublin' | Format-List
```

```
Name                 : DAGNetwork01
Description          :
Subnets             : {{192.165.65.0/24,Up}}
Interfaces          : {{ExServer1,Up,192.165.65.50}, {EXSERVER2,Up,192.165.65.60}}
MapiAccessEnabled   : True
ReplicationEnabled  : True
IgnoreNetwork       : False
Identity            : DAG-Dublin\DAGNetwork01
IsValid             : True
```

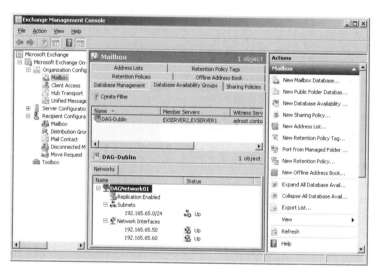

Figure 8-15 Viewing the network used by a simple DAG.

When you use two NICs, the MAPI network is assigned to one network and the replication network is assigned to the other NIC. As you add more NICs, you increase the network capability for the replication network. When a server is configured with more than one replication network, Exchange attempts to direct traffic across the least used network to maximize available network resources. Microsoft recommends that you use Gigabit Ethernet NICs in production Exchange 2010 mailbox servers.

If you elect to use multiple networks, the same configuration must be used for every server in the DAG. Using multiple NICs provides better resilience against failure: If the replication network becomes unavailable for some reason, Exchange will automatically revert to using the MAPI network for both sets of network traffic and you won't have to deal with a server outage. Once the replication network is restored to health, Exchange will automatically start to use it again. However, the server won't be able to function as a member of the DAG if the MAPI network fails and, in this case, Exchange will failover the active databases from the server to other members of the DAG.

As previously discussed, when we created the DAG with the New-DatabaseAvailabilityGroup cmdlet, we specified an IP address to use to identify the Windows cluster resource that underpins the DAG (we could also have leased an address using DHCP). This IP address is registered in DNS and is the one used by the MAPI network. Assigning a single IP address to the DAG is sufficient as long as all the mailbox servers within the DAG share the same subnet. However, if the DAG spans several IP subnets, you must specify an IP address in each subnet for the cluster resource to allow servers in that subnet to participate in the DAG. Apart from MAPI communications, the IP address is needed to allow the cluster group to move between the servers within the DAG. This cannot happen if the cluster doesn't know about all of the IP subnets used by DAG members.

INSIDE OUT   A note about latency

The existence of multiple subnets implies different geographic locations and the sole requirement is that the round-trip network latency between member servers in the DAG must be less than 250 milliseconds. This isn't a difficult requirement in that your DAG will immediately fail once latency exceeds the limit. Instead, if your latency exceeds 250 milliseconds, you can expect that queues of transaction logs will accumulate during peak production hours and that any network outage or other operation that generates a lot of network activity will result in even larger queues that Exchange has to clear to bring database copies up to date. In some instances, large queues can build up even when latency is less than 250 milliseconds and you might need to increase network capacity so that logs are replicated quickly.

Multiple subnets are also required if you deploy a DAG across multiple Active Directory sites. This is not an issue providing that the network requirements are met and that Active Directory replication is functioning normally. After you create the DAG, make sure that its object has been replicated to the domain controllers in the remote site before you attempt to add subnets or servers in that site.

A default gateway must exist for all networks if you specify an IP address for the DAG. In addition, if you use Microsoft Internet Security and Acceleration Server (ISA) or a similar solution to control traffic between the two subnets, turn off strict RPC for the publishing rules to ensure that log replication traffic can flow between the two sites. If you're unsure about connectivity between two sites, it's a good idea to run the Exchange Best Practices Analyzer (ExBPA) on a server in one site and attempt to analyze a server in the other. If ExBPA works, it's a good indication that sufficient connectivity is in place to allow the DAG to function.

As a practical example, let's assume that we want to add a second server to our DAG. This server is in subnet 192.168.66.x. Code similar to that shown here will add the new server to the DAG and specify the IP addresses for all of the subnets now in use for the DAG.

```
Add-DatabaseAvailabilityGroupServer -Identity 'DAG-Dublin' -MailboxServer 'ExServer2'
Set-DatabaseAvailabilityGroupServer -Identity 'DAG-Dublin'
-DatabaseAvailabilityGroupIPAddresses 192.168.65.1, 192.168.66.1
```

If you then went on to add a third server in yet another subnet to the DAG, you would have to provide a third IP address. In effect, you build up a complete picture for the DAG across all of the involved subnets as you build out the DAG by adding servers. It is conceivable that a DAG might be composed of 16 servers, each in a different subnet. If this is the case, you would have to specify an IP address for each of the 16 subnets when you added the last server to the DAG.

Every network used in a DAG has a unique name of up to 128 characters, a descriptive name of up to 256 characters that you can use to indicate the purpose and use of the network, one or more subnets defined in IP address/bitmask format, and a flag indicating whether the network is dedicated to log replication. An example of using the New-DatabaseAvailabilityGroupNetwork cmdlet to create a DAG network is:

```
New-DatabaseAvailabilityGroupNetwork -DatabaseAvailabilityGroup 'DAG-Dublin'
-Name 'DAG-Dublin LS' -Description 'Network used for log shipping in the Dublin DAG'
-Subnets 10.0.0.0/8 -ReplicationEnabled:$False
```

You can use the Get-DatabaseAvailabilityGroupNetwork cmdlet to view the networks that are available to a DAG. If, as in our previous example, you had added servers from multiple subnets to the DAG, you will see the IP addresses specified for those subnets in the information returned here. Use the Set-DatabaseAvailabilityGroupNetwork cmdlet to change parameters for a DAG network. In this case, we change the properties of the network to restrict it to log replication.

```
Set-DatabaseAvailabilityGroupNetwork -Identity 'DAG-Dublin\DAG-Dublin LS'
-ReplicationEnabled:$True
```

The –IgnoreNetwork parameter is available to instruct a DAG not to use a network, usually on a temporary basis. For example:

```
Set-DatabaseAvailabilityGroupNetwork -Identity 'DAG-Dublin\DAG-Dublin LS'
-IgnoreNetwork:$True
```

The Remove-DatabaseAvailabilityGroupNetwork cmdlet is available to remove a network from a DAG. If you remove a network, traffic will flow across the remaining networks that are available to the DAG. You aren't able to run this cmdlet to remove the last remaining network in a DAG.

```
Remove-DatabaseAvailabilityGroupNetwork –Identity 'DAG-Dublin\DAG-Dublin LS'
```

DAGs and IPv6

Windows Failover Clustering seems to require IPv6 to be enabled and the DAG uses components of Windows Failover Clustering for functions such as tracking membership. Can you therefore implement a DAG using only IPv6 networks and move away from IPv4? The answer is no, not yet. Microsoft has built Exchange 2010 to use IPv4 but acknowledge the existence of IPv6. This means that the DAG uses IPv4, so it must be available on all servers that participate in a DAG and a DAG is not supported in pure IPv6 environments. You'll certainly see IPv6 addresses reported for a DAG but you cannot use IPv6 for management of a DAG.

Exchange 2010 has several other restrictions in other areas that prevent the operation of a pure IPv6 environment, including Unified Messaging (UM) where the server must have an IPv4 address to function, and Exchange Web Services and the Autodiscover feature, both of which depend on Windows Communications Framework (WCF), which doesn't support IPv6.

Using circular logging with database copies

Best practice for all previous versions of Exchange dictates that circular logging is never enabled for production databases. However, this practice is based on only ever having a single copy of a database available and depending on backups for protection; it does not take database copies into account. Microsoft now recommends that circular logging be enabled for databases that are protected by at least three copies as the availability of multiple copies ensures that you should be protected from failure and won't need all the transaction logs to replay transactions during the recovery from failure. Microsoft's recommendation does not mean that you always have to have three copies of every database in a DAG; three copies are only required if your DAG design calls for such a number with good reason for each copy, such as a decision to use low-end disks that might be more prone to failure and thus require more protection through copies. In other words, you should be able to justify the extra overhead required to support each copy. Enabling circular logging is interesting, but it's probably an insufficient reason to create an additional copy if that's the only reason to have three database copies.

The basic steps to enable circular logging for database copies within a DAG are to first create the database, then set up its copies, and finally enable circular logging. Exchange will signal an error if circular logging is enabled when you attempt to add a database copy (Figure 8-16). This is not an intuitive process because of some subtle differences in the way that circular logging works for databases that are not in a DAG and those that are in a DAG. As you'll recall, inside a DAG, transaction logs are shipped between servers that host database copies, so turning circular logging on and off could confuse matters, especially for lagged copies (see the section "Using a lagged database" later in this chapter for more information). In addition, the behavior of circular logging differs when a database has one copy and when it has more than one copy and the code is not designed to handle common DAG situations such as increasing or decreasing the number of database copies. The upshot is that you should make a decision about circular logging for databases in a DAG early in the deployment and stay with that configuration from that point onward.

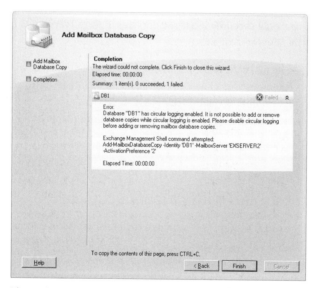

Figure 8-16 Error because circular logging is enabled.

To enable circular logging from EMC, select the database, click Properties, and select the Enable Circular Logging option. Remember to dismount and remount the database to make the setting effective. The EMS commands to enable circular logging and then dismount and remount the database to enable circular logging for a selected database are:

```
Set-MailboxDatabase -Identity 'DB1' -CircularLoggingEnabled $True
Dismount-Database -Identity 'DB1'
Mount-Database -Identity 'DB1'
```

The nature of circular logging is that transaction logs are discarded regularly as transactions are committed to the database, but when you create new database copies in a DAG, you want to be sure that all possible transaction logs that might be required are available, so turning circular logging on is not a good idea until the database copy is up and running. In addition, as we discuss in the section "Removing database copies" later in this chapter, you cannot remove database copies from a DAG if circular logging is enabled on a database, so you need to take this requirement into account as you approach database management.

Adding new database copies to a DAG

You cannot create a new database copy on the same mailbox server that hosts the active copy. In other words, you cannot have two copies (active and passive) of a database on the same server. You also cannot have two passive copies of a database hosted by the same server. This restriction aside, you can create a new copy with the Add New Database Copy Wizard or by using the Add-MailboxDatabaseCopy cmdlet. Either method requires you to determine some settings in advance:

- The database that you want to copy: Remember that you can only copy a database that exists within the DAG.

- The mailbox server in the DAG that will host the new database copy.

- The activation preference number (or preferred list sequence number) for the new copy. Each copy in a DAG has a number that dictates the order in which Exchange will attempt to use the copy after an outage. The active database has preference 1 and the copy database with preference 2 will be used before the copy with preference 3, and so on. When you add a new copy, Exchange sets its activation number one higher than the current highest activation value. Accept this value unless you have good reason not to. If you make a mistake with the activation order you can change its value by selecting the copy from the list of database copies and updating its properties. Exchange will then reorder the other database copies to fit the new activation number that you assign.

To begin the process of creating a new database copy with EMC, select the database that you want to copy listed on the Database Management tab in the Mailbox section of Organization Configuration and then click Add Mailbox Database Copy in the action pane. The Add Mailbox Database Copy Wizard then invites you to select the mailbox server to host the new copy (Figure 8-17). When you have selected the target server, click Add and Exchange will begin to seed the new copy on that server by copying the database. The time taken to seed the new copy depends on the size of the database files (EDB and transaction logs) and the network speed between the two servers. It is a good idea to schedule the seeding of large database copies (> 100 GB) at times of low network demand such as outside normal working hours.

Chapter 8

After the new database copy is seeded, the Store begins the process of resynchronizing it with the active copy. Exchange will copy the EDB and transaction log files from the server that hosts the active copy and you should see the copy status change to Healthy when seeding is complete. During this period the copy queue length decreases first, followed by a decrease in the replay queue length as Exchange synchronizes the new database copy. Eventually, the two queues will reduce to zero and the new database copy is fully up to date.

Databases that do not use circular logging could have thousands of log files that the Store on the receiving server has to copy, inspect, and potentially replay to fully synchronize the new server. If you monitor the status of the database copy, you'll see that the copy queue length will increase as the logs are replicated from the active copy to the new copy and then decrease after all the current logs have been copied. You will then see an increase in the replay queue followed by a reduction to zero as the database copy becomes fully resynchronized and moves into a healthy state. This process is easier if you reduce the number of transaction logs that are involved by creating the new database copy soon after a full backup is taken of the active database. Successful completion of a full backup truncates the log set and reduces the synchronization requirement.

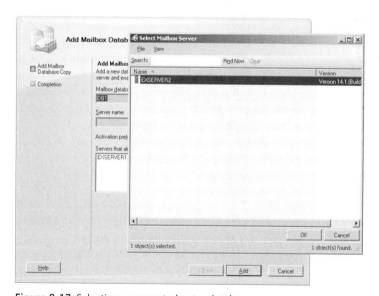

Figure 8-17 Selecting a server to host a database copy.

Handling initial seeding errors

It is possible that a seeding error will occur when you attempt to create a new database copy. Typically, this occurs when Exchange attempts to copy the EDB file from the server that hosts the active database copy to the server where you want to host the new copy.

The first thing to do after such an error is to check that the servers are online and working as normal. The next is to check the errors recorded by Exchange when it attempted to create the database copy. To do this, select the database and view its properties. On the Status tab, click View Errors as shown in Figure 8-18. In this instance, we can see that the problem caused the database copy not to be created on the host server because its corresponding EDB file cannot be found. You can attempt to update the database copy but this is unlikely to succeed if the basic database files do not exist. The solution is therefore to remove the database copy (which only exists as an entry in the Exchange configuration in Active Directory) and restart the process to add a new database copy.

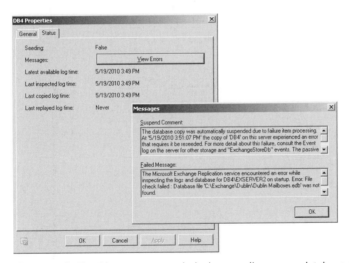

Figure 8-18 Checking errors recorded when seeding a new database copy.

If the database files exist for the new copy it's possible that some transient error interrupted seeding. In these instances, you can resume replication. Select the database copy and then select the Resume Database Copy option to instruct Exchange to recommence replication. EMC will warn you with an explanation of why replication was suspended and request confirmation to proceed (Figure 8-19). Click OK to resume replication and check that the new database copy moves to a healthy state as the transaction logs are replicated from the active copy and replayed into the passive.

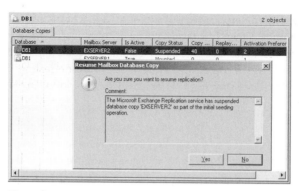

Figure 8-19 Resume a seeding operation.

Monitoring database copies

On an ongoing basis you can browse the set of databases with EMC to check that all data-bases and their copies are in good health. Alternatively, it's much faster to use the Get-MailboxDatabaseCopyStatus cmdlet to report the current replication status of databases. For example, here's the output returned from scanning for replication status for all mailbox servers in a DAG:

```
Get-MailboxServer | Where {$_.DatabaseAvailabilityGroup -eq "DAG1"} |
Get-MailboxDatabaseCopyStatus
```

Name	Status	CopyQueue Length	ReplayQueue Length	LastInspectedLogTime	ContentIndex State
DAG1-DB1\ExServer1	Mounted	0	0		Healthy
VIP Data\ExServer1	Mounted	0	0		Healthy
IT Department\ExServer1	Mounted	0	0		Healthy
DAG1-DB3\ExServer1	Healthy	0	0	2/23/2010 5:11:10 AM	Healthy
PR\ExServer1	Healthy	0	0	2/23/2010 5:09:52 AM	Healthy
ITOPS_DB1\ExServer1	Mounted	0	0		Healthy
ITOPS_DB2\ExServer1	Mounted	0	0		Healthy
DAG1-DB3\ExServer3	Mounted	0	0		Healthy
IT Department\ExServer3	Healthy	0	0	2/23/2010 6:04:12 AM	Healthy
DAG1-DB2\ExServer3	Mounted	0	0		Healthy
Dublin Users\ExServer3	Healthy	0	0	2/23/2010 5:09:52 AM	Healthy
Sales\ExServer3	Healthy	0	0	2/23/2010 4:59:50 AM	Healthy
Operations\ExServer3	Healthy	0	0	2/23/2010 5:09:52 AM	Healthy
DAG1-DB2\ExServer2	Healthy	0	0	2/23/2010 5:11:10 AM	Healthy
DAG1-DB1\ExServer2	Healthy	0	0	2/23/2010 6:19:18 AM	Healthy
VIP Data\ExServer2	Healthy	0	0	2/23/2010 6:19:18 AM	Healthy
IT Department\ExServer2	Healthy	0	0	2/23/2010 6:04:12 AM	Healthy
DAG1-DB3\ExServer2	Healthy	0	0	2/23/2010 5:11:10 AM	Healthy

All database copies are listed here. The copies shown as Mounted in the Status column are those that are currently active. The passive copies are all shown as Healthy, indicating that replication is progressing normally. The State column indicates that there are no errors with any of the active or passive copies, as they all have a status of Healthy. You can find a list of the valid database copy status codes that you will see reported in EMC or by the Get-MailboxDatabaseCopyStatus cmdlet at *http://technet.microsoft.com/en-us/library /dd351258.aspx*.

Reseeding a database copy

A database copy might need to be reseeded after a failure because too many transaction logs are missing to allow Exchange to patch and mend the database copy or following a failure to seed properly when the new copy is created. I find it best to always create a new database copy on the server that will host the copy, as I've experienced some problems creating copies from remote servers. Perhaps it is just luck or it's because when you are logged onto a server you know it is functioning correctly and have the opportunity to take immediate action to rectify any apparent problems before starting the copy.

A reseed means that you select a good database copy on a running server and then copy the database and its transaction logs to the target server to allow the new database copy to become active there. Obviously this can take some time to accomplish if the database is larger than a few gigabytes, so it's best to select the failed database copy (shown with a Failed status) and first attempt to use the Resume Database Copy option to restart synchronization by copying and replaying transaction logs from the source database to bring the failed copy up to date. If this doesn't work, you will have to reseed, so you should select the Update Database Copy option.

The Update Database Copy option launches a wizard to present the options for the reseed (Figure 8-20), the most important of which is the source server to be used to provide the database and transaction logs. This server should be in close proximity to the target server to avoid any network latency problems.

Chapter 8

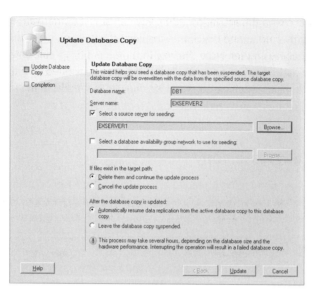

Figure 8-20 Update Database Copy Wizard.

The underlying EMS command to reseed the Sales database on server ExServer4 using ExServer1 as the source server is:

```
Update-MailboxDatabaseCopy -Identity 'Sales\ExServer4' -SourceServer 'ExServer1'
-DeleteExistingFiles -Network $null
```

If you attempt to reseed a database within 15 minutes of a failed seed operation, Exchange will ask you to confirm that the reseed should proceed. Exchange tracks seeding operations ("update requests") to ensure that they don't happen too close together because this might create a scenario where one reseed operation is not complete when another starts, perhaps because two reseeds are launched by administrators on two different servers at roughly the same time. If you see this prompt, you should validate that everything is OK before proceeding. Exchange clears update requests 15 minutes after they have been made.

Adding database copies with EMS

The EMS command to create a new copy of the London-DB1 database on the LondonDAG2 server with an activation preference of 2 is shown here. You don't have to select an activation number; Exchange will determine it for you by adding one to the current highest value. If you do decide to select an activation value, make sure that it does not clash with a value that already exists.

```
Add-MailboxDatabaseCopy -Identity 'DB1' -MailboxServer 'ExServer2'
-ActivationPreference '2'
```

If you make a mistake with the activation value, you can adjust it afterward with the Set-MailboxDatabaseCopy cmdlet and check that the correct activation order is in place with the Get-MailboxDatabase cmdlet. Note the way that we identify specific database copies using the database name and server name. This is the syntax required by many of the EMS cmdlets used to work with database copies; this syntax largely replaces the long distinguished names required in older versions.

```
Set-MailboxDatabaseCopy –Identity 'DB1\ExServer2' –ActivationPreference '1'
Get-MailboxDatabase -Identity 'DB1' | Select ActivationPreference
```

> **Note**
>
> The way that EMC refreshes information about database copies means that it doesn't show the updated activation preference order until the next time you restart the console.

After adding the new database copy, you can check the Mailbox node of Organization Configuration in EMC to get a view of the current mailbox databases that are deployed within the organization. Figure 8-21 shows what you might see in an environment where some databases in the servers in a DAG have copies and some do not. All of the databases, including a public folder database, are managed by a DAG called DAG-Dublin. Public folder databases do not use database replication as they have their own item-based replication mechanism. The only reason that the public folder database appears to be in the DAG is that the server by which it is hosted is part of the DAG.

All of the copies of a database share the same path for database files and transaction logs so you do not have to determine these values on the target server. However, you should make sure that these settings do not create a conflict with existing files that might already be in place on the target server. The section "Activation blocks" later in this chapter offers more details about how to manipulate database locations when databases operate within a DAG.

Chapter 8

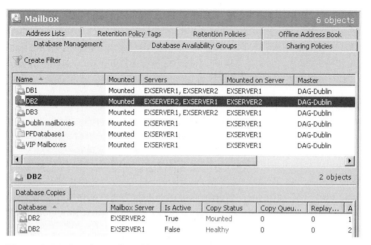

Figure 8-21 Databases listed by EMC.

Earlier we discussed a problem with seeding a new database copy and how you could get around the issue by resuming the seed operation when system conditions improve. EMS offers some additional flexibility over EMC in that you can add a new database copy in anticipation that you will not be able to seed for some reason, such as an expected network outage. Or perhaps you operate in a multiple-datacenter environment and you decide that it would be better to seed using a local passive copy rather than the remote active copy. In this example, we add a new database copy to server ExServer3 with seeding suspended and then force the seeding using server ExServer2 as the source:

```
Add-MailboxDatabaseCopy -Identity 'DB1' -MailboxServer 'ExServer3'
-SeedingPostponed
Update-MailboxDatabaseCopy -Identity 'DB1\ExServer3' -SourceServer 'ExServer2'
```

Using a lagged database

DAGs support lagged database copies. A lagged database copy is one that is not updated by replaying transactions as they become available. Instead, the transaction logs are kept for a certain period and are then replayed. The lagged database copy is therefore maintained at a certain remove to the active database and the other nonlagged database copies.

The primary reason to use lagged database copies (7 and 14 days are common intervals) is to provide you with the ability to go back to a point in time when you are sure that a database is in a good state. By delaying the replay of replicated transaction logs into a database copy, you always have the ability to go to that copy and know that it represents a point in time in the past when the database was in a certain condition. In an Exchange context, logical corruption can mean two things:

1. Database logical corruption: A database page has a valid checksum but the data in the page are incorrect. Typically this occurs when ESE attempts to write a page and receives a success status from Windows but the data are never actually written to disk or are written to the wrong place in the database. Microsoft refers to this as a "lost flush." The version of ESE in Exchange 2010 includes a lost flush detection mechanism to avoid these problems.

2. Store logical corruption: It is possible that an application writes data into a database in a way that generates items that are deemed to be corrupt. Messages migrated from other messaging systems through third-party applications or gateways can sometimes generate corrupt items. If this happens, sufficient corrupt items might be introduced into a database to make a recovery from a lagged copy the only way to restore a database to good health.

When you recover using a lagged database, you essentially roll back the database to a point in time before it experienced a logical corruption problem that has since been replicated to the other nonlagged database copies. This work can take many hours because you have to isolate the database copy, identify the transaction logs that are required to bring it to the point in time before corruption occurred, replay those logs to update the database and bring it to a clean state, and then use it to restart service. Another point to consider is that a large amount of storage might be required to hold all of the transaction logs for the lag period. For example, if the lag period is seven days, then the server that hosts the lagged database copy must be able to store all of the transaction logs for seven days. This could be many gigabytes of logs for even a moderately busy database.

> **Note**
> Because of the manual nature of the work and the time required to perform these activities, lagged copies can never be considered a high-availability option for databases. They certainly help and provide a valuable feature, but not high availability.

If you use a comprehensive backup solution that supports DAGs such as Microsoft System Center Data Protection Manager 2010, that software probably has the capability to restore a database to a particular point in time. This is the purpose of a lagged database copy, so it therefore follows that the deployment of a comprehensive backup solution reduces the need to keep a lagged database copy. You can certainly keep the lagged copy as an extra protection against data loss, but this could be considered overkill, as the correct operation of a backup regime should provide you with sufficient protection against operator failure, storage corruption, or any of the other issues that might cause you to resort to using a lagged database copy. Lagged databases are also less interesting if you use storage technology which supports the ability to take snapshots of databases and transaction logs that

Chapter 8

you can use for restores. Some of the sophisticated storage technology available today includes GUIs that make a database restore to a particular point in time very easy and fast. If you can restore a database at different points such as four hours ago, eight hours ago, and so on, you probably don't need to incur the expense and complexity required to maintain a lagged database copy.

Two advanced properties of mailbox databases that govern lagged log replay and truncation times can only be manipulated through EMS. Originally, these properties were available through EMC but Microsoft removed the UI from EMC on the basis that it has the potential to confuse administrators who are unfamiliar with the way Exchange replays transaction logs. The feeling is that these properties really only concern administrators who manage complex DAGs and that it was therefore best to keep EMC focused on meeting the needs of the majority. If necessary, you can use the Add-MailboxDatabaseCopy or Set-MailboxDatabaseCopy cmdlets to set these properties:

- *ReplayLagTime*: The time (in minutes) governing the delay that Exchange applies to log replays for database copies (replay lag time). Setting this value to zero means that Exchange should replay new transaction logs immediately when they are copied to servers that host database copies. The intention is that you have the chance to keep a server running in a state slightly behind the active copy so that if a problem occurs on the active server that results in database corruption, you will be able to stop replication and prevent the corruption occurring in database copies. Typically, DAGs that use a lagged copy are configured so that there are two or three database copies kept up to date and one (usually in a disaster recovery site) that is configured with a time lag. The maximum lag time is 14 days.

- *TruncationLagTime*: The time (in minutes) governing log truncation delay. Again, you can set this value to zero to instruct Exchange to remove transaction logs immediately after their content has been replayed into a database copy, but most sites keep transaction logs around for at least 15 minutes to ensure that they are available if required to bring a database copy up to date should an outage occur. The maximum truncation lag time is seven days.

Lagged settings are maintained for every database copy. This command shows how to view these settings for a database.

```
Get-MailboxDatabase -Identity 'DB1' | Format-List DatabaseCopies, ReplayLagTimes,
TruncationLagTimes
```

```
DatabaseCopies         : {DB1\EXSERVER1, DB1\EXSERVER2}
ReplayLagTimes         : {[EXSERVER1, 00:00:00], [EXSERVER2, 00:00:00]}
TruncationLagTimes     : {[EXSERVER1, 00:00:00], [EXSERVER2, 00:00:00]}
```

Both the replay lag times and truncation lag times on the two servers that maintain copies of this database are set to 00:00:00 (which is what we expect because these are the default values). These values mean that transaction logs are replayed immediately and no delay occurs for log truncation. We can change the situation by updating the property of one of the copies. For instance, this command sets a replay lag time of seven days on the mailbox database DB1 on server ExServer2:

```
Set-MailboxDatabaseCopy –Identity 'DB1\ExServer2' -ReplayLagTime 7.0:0:0
```

The output of the Get-MailboxDatabase command now shows:

```
ReplayLagTimes        : {[EXSERVER1, 00:00:00], [EXSERVER2, 7.00:00:00]}
TruncationLagTimes    : {[EXSERVER1, 00:00:00], [EXSERVER2, 00:00:00]}
```

Immediately after you set a lagged time on a database copy, you should notice that the replay queue length for the lagged copy begins to grow. This is quite normal and is due to the accumulation of transaction logs after the imposition of the replay lag time. The replay queue length will grow until logs begin to age out past the replay lag time and are replayed into the database. Over time, the replay queue length will stabilize into a range that reflects the average transaction load during the lag period. Depending on the size of the database and the workload that it handles, this range could extend well into the tens of thousands of logs (be sure that you allocate sufficient storage to accommodate the lagged transaction logs). You can monitor the replay queue length with the Get-MailboxDatabaseCopyStatus cmdlet. For example:

```
Get-MailboxDatabaseCopyStatus –Identity 'DB1\ExServer2'
```

Name	Status	CopyQueue Length	ReplayQueue Length	LastInspectedLogTime	ContentIndex State
DB1\EXSERVER2	Healthy	0	7911	6/1/2010 4:15:23 PM	Healthy

If you adjust the lag period for a database copy, the replay queue length will move in line with the adjustment. The queue will grow if you increase the lag period and will reduce if you decrease the lag period, as Exchange will begin to replay queued transaction logs that are now inside the lag period.

In most instances, you probably want to block the activation of a lagged database copy so that the Active Manager doesn't consider the copy to be a viable candidate for activation in case the other copies fail. You can do this with the Suspend-MailboxDatabaseCopy cmdlet. Normally this cmdlet is used to suspend replication for a copy. In this situation, we use the –*ActivationOnly* parameter to tell Exchange that replication can proceed but we never want to automatically activate the lagged copy. This command applies the block to the copy of the DB1 database on server ExServer2:

```
Suspend-MailboxDatabaseCopy –Identity 'DB1\ExServer2' –ActivationOnly
```

If an event occurs that forces you to make the copy a viable target for activation, you can do this with the Resume-MailboxDatabaseCopy cmdlet:

```
Resume-MailboxDatabaseCopy –Identity 'DB1\ExServer2'
```

INSIDE OUT Lagged copies as a disaster recovery mechanism

Lagged databases are a disaster recovery mechanism that should only be implemented as a last option to recover a good copy of a database when all other routes have failed. Despite some overenthusiastic commentary by advocates that lagged copies make obsolete the need to make backups because you can always recover data from a point in time using the lagged copy, this idea is misguided because most system administrators don't have sufficient experience in running production-quality DAGs including lagged copies over an extended period and, therefore, probably haven't had the chance to develop the skills to execute data recovery using lagged copies. In addition, lagged copies cannot provide the truly granular restore capabilities required to put a database back to a specific point in time. You cannot tell Exchange to roll back to "4:23 P.M. on August 27, 2010," for example.

It is a bad idea to discard the warm blanket feeling that a well-designed and oft-practiced backup regime gives to administrators because they know their data are safe and that they can recover. This requires a leap of faith that will likely take several more versions of Exchange to achieve. In the meantime, those who want to live on the jagged edge of new techniques to protect data can depend on lagged copies and the rest of us will use traditional backups for a little while yet.

Activating a mailbox database copy

An administrative move of an active mailbox database so that a passive copy becomes active is called a switchover. It is usually performed when an administrator wants to redirect clients to a copy located on a different server to allow the original server to be taken offline for maintenance. To activate a database copy on another server, go to the Mailbox section under Organization Configuration, select the mailbox database that you want to work with, and then select the Move Active Mailbox Database option in the action pane. EMC then presents the Activate A Database Copy Wizard (Figure 8-22) to allow you to select the mailbox server that hosts the copy to become the active database.

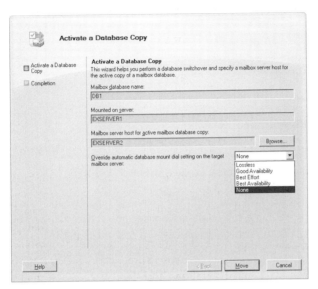

Figure 8-22 Activate a database copy.

The wizard lists all servers that currently have an available copy in alphabetical order. In other words, even though you might have assigned activation numbers to each copy to indicate the preferred order for activation, the wizard does not take the activation number into account when it lists the available servers. In addition, the wizard does not flag an issue if you select the copy with the lowest activation number because an assumption is made that you know what you're doing when you make an explicit selection of the copy to become active. Activation numbers are used, but only when the PAM is forced to make a transition due to a server or storage outage that makes the active database inaccessible.

Alternatively, you can avoid the wizard by selecting a server from the list of database copies, right-clicking to select the Activate Database Copy option from the shortcut menu, and then clicking OK (see Figure 8-23). This approach offers fewer options but it gets the job done a little faster. In either case, assuming that the database copy is healthy and that any transaction logs that are required to bring the copy up to date are available, the Store on the selected server can bring the database online and begin to accept client connections. This process happens very quickly, as all Exchange has to do is switch internal pointers to indicate that a different database copy is now active. No files have to be moved, copied, or otherwise manipulated in a way that would slow things down. Once the selected copy is activated the other copies will briefly resynchronize to take account of the new situation and normal operation resumes.

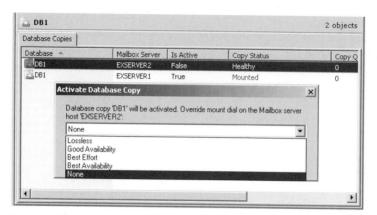

Figure 8-23 Fast activation of a database copy with EMC.

Immediately after a switchover, you might see Exchange report an increase in the copy queue length for the database copy that has just become active, followed by a rapid decrease to zero. Part of the switchover process is a pass through the transaction log set to validate the logs that are present. The pass completes quickly and the high copy queue length is not a problem provided it does not persist past a minute or so.

Of course, administrators are not required to perform failovers, as Exchange does this automatically if a server or disk goes offline and affects an active database. Exchange uses the activation preference order for a database to decide on which server it should activate a copy (if available). Activation preference numbers are assigned when a database copy is created and can be modified afterward with the Set-MailboxDatabase cmdlet. To see the full list of databases and their activation preferences, we can use a command like this:

```
Get-MailboxDatabase | Select Name, ActivationPreference, Server | Sort Name |
Format-Table -AutoSize
```

Name	ActivationPreference	Server
Dublin Users	{[ExServer3, 1], [ExServer4, 2]}	ExServer3
DB1	{[ExServer1, 1], [ExServer2, 2]}	ExServer1
DB2	{[ExServer2, 1], [ExServer3, 2]}	ExServer2
DB3	{[ExServer3, 1], [ExServer1, 2], [ExServer2, 3]}	ExServer1
IT Department	{[ExServer1, 1], [ExServer2, 2], [ExServer3, 3]}	ExServer1
Operations	{[ExServer4, 1], [ExServer3, 2]}	ExServer4
PR	{[ExServer1, 1], [ExServer4, 2]}	ExServer1
Sales	{[ExServer4, 1], [ExServer3, 2]}	ExServer3
VIP Data	{[ExServer1, 1], [ExServer2, 2]}	ExServer1

This output only tells us what the preferred activation order is and the server that currently hosts the database. We can see that two databases are not running on their preferred server: DB3 is active on ExServer1 and Sales is active on ExServer3. There doesn't seem to be a reason why they are not on their preferred server because both servers are hosting other databases, so this might be a pointer to check out why the situation exists and either adjust the activation preference to reflect the current situation or move the databases around so that they are on their preferred server. We can also see that the ExServer1 server is hosting five of the nine databases in a four-server DAG. This is an abnormal disruption of load that deserves further investigation and rebalancing.

Some scripting can help us to discover whether databases are mounted on the preferred server. The following script, composed by Paul Flaherty, was found on the Web. The result can be seen in Figure 8-24. Other scripts are available to move databases back to the server with an activation preference of 1. I'll leave the research on this point to the reader.

```
Get-MailboxDatabase | Sort Name | ForEach {$db=$_.Name; $xNow=$_.Server.Name
;$dbown=$_.ActivationPreference| Where {$_.Value -eq 1};  Write-Host $db "on" $xNow
"Should be on" $dbOwn.Key -NoNewLine; If ( $xNow -ne $dbOwn.Key){Write-host " WRONG"
-ForegroundColor Red; }ELSE {Write-Host " OK" -Foregroundcolor Green}}
```

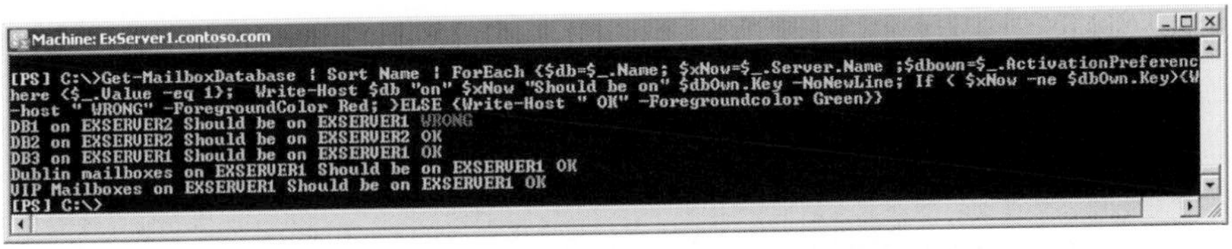

Figure 8-24 Checking databases against their activation preference.

Microsoft provides a script called RedistributeActiveDatabases.ps1 (in the default scripts directory) with Exchange 2010 SP1 to help administrators rebalance databases after a server outage. The script operates in two modes.

- *BalanceDbsByActivationPreference*: This mode attempts to move databases to the most preferred copy without attempting to balance databases across Active Directory sites. This mode is likely to be the most commonly used as a DAG is usually restricted to one site.

- *BalanceDbsBySiteAndActivationPreference*: This mode also attempts to move databases to the most preferred copy while taking account of Active Directory sites. For example, if databases in a DAG are spread across three sites, the script will attempt to activate a third of the total databases on servers in each site. This mode is obviously more complex because of the multisite aspect and should be carefully tested before you use it in production.

For example, to rebalance databases by activation preference for the DAG called "DAG1," you'd type this command. The *–ShowFinalDatabaseDistribution* parameter instructs the script to report on the final disposition of the databases:

```
RedistributeActiveDatabases.ps1 –DAGName DAG1 –BalanceDbsByActivationPreference
–ShowFinalDatabaseDistribution
```

Applying updates to DAG servers

It's a fact of administrator life that software updates will become available on a regular basis for Exchange, Windows, and other products. Although you don't have to apply the regular roll-up updates and service packs that Microsoft releases for Exchange 2010, it's a good idea to do so to ensure that you run the latest software that contains all the fixes to known problems, including security fixes for vulnerabilities that are discovered and fixed on an ongoing basis. Earlier in this chapter we saw that SP1 DAG members can transition database copies to servers running RTM software but the reverse is unsupported. This fact alone underlines the need to keep all of the member servers in a DAG running the latest version of Exchange.

Exchange 2010 includes a lot of new technology and it's inevitable that some bugs will be encountered, so it makes sense to keep up to date with software fixes as Microsoft releases them. This is not a call to install patches immediately as they become available. You should take the time to test any new software before installing it into a production environment. Software testing is a well-developed art these days and Microsoft and other vendors put enormous effort into testing patches against many different configurations, including regression testing to ensure that a fix doesn't reveal another problem, but it is possible that there's something unique in your deployment that could cause a problem for a roll-up upgrade or service pack.

All of the usual caveats about software upgrades are valid for DAG servers. Make sure that you have a backup, that you've run the procedure on a test server that accurately represents the production environment, that you have all the software and licenses that might be required, and that you've allowed enough time to perform the work and have scheduled it to be done at a time when any outage will not severely inconvenience users. The particular issues that we have to take care of with DAG servers are the following:

- Block the server that is being upgraded from activation attempts. You do not want other servers attempting to transfer databases to a server when it is being worked on.

- Switch over the active databases from the server to other servers in the DAG before starting the upgrade.

- Check that all of the transferred databases are active on other servers and that users have not been affected by the switchover.

- Perform the upgrade and check that the server functions properly after it is complete. The server might need to be rebooted, and if this is necessary, we need to validate that everything works properly after the reboot.

- Resume normal copy processing for the databases that we previously blocked.

- Transfer databases from other servers back to the upgraded servers, making sure that we check that users are working normally as each database is transferred.

- Go on to the next server in the DAG and repeat.

To block the activation of databases on a server so that Exchange does not attempt to use the databases during the upgrade, use the Suspend-MailboxDatabaseCopy cmdlet. This cmdlet needs to be run for every database that is active on a server, so we can use the Get-MailboxDatabaseCopyStatus cmdlet to provide us with a list to pipe into Suspend-MailboxDatabaseCopy. This command doesn't suspend any processing; it simply tells Exchange that we don't want to activate any copy of the databases on this server.

```
Get-MailboxDatabaseCopyStatus | Suspend-MailboxDatabaseCopy -ActivationOnly
-Confirm:$False
```

To transfer the databases, we can either have Exchange decide how best to distribute the databases across the available servers in the DAG or choose a target server. To have Exchange reassign all databases from a server, use a command like this:

```
Move-ActiveMailboxDatabase -Server ExServer4
```

Alternatively, you can select a target server:

```
Move-ActiveMailboxDatabase -Server ExServer4 -ActivateOnServer ExServer2
```

Or, you can move each mailbox database and allocate them onto servers as you desire:

```
Move-ActiveMailboxDatabase -Identity 'Sales' -ActivateOnServer ExServer3
```

After the update is applied and tested to ensure that it worked, you can release the activation block previously put in place as follows:

```
Get-MailboxDatabaseCopyStatus | Resume-MailboxDatabaseCopy
```

Again, this command doesn't actually resume any processing. Instead, it informs Exchange that the server is open for business and ready to accept the activation of any database copy.

Dealing with a failed server

It would be nice if we never had to deal with a failed server, but life, software, and hardware don't quite cooperate to make this possible. We therefore have to be prepared to deal with the problem by relocating all of the databases that are mounted on a failed server. This is done with the Switchover Server option shown in Figure 8-25. You can see that we have a problem on server ExServer2 because all three of the databases that should be mounted on the server have a copy status of ServiceDown. Clearly flagging a service down condition is a strong indication that a problem exists on the server. It's not necessarily true that the problem is solely associated with Exchange, but we still have an issue to solve because we have some failed databases to deal with.

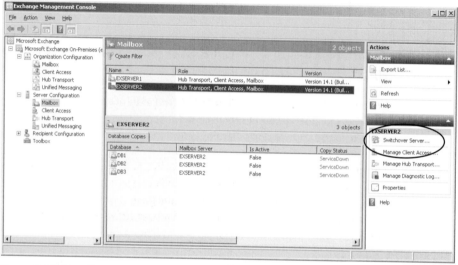

Figure 8-25 Identifying failed databases in a DAG.

Once you select the Switchover Server option, Exchange presents the options shown in Figure 8-26. You can opt to move the active databases from the failed server to a server that you select, or have Exchange select the target server for each database automatically. With the latter option, Exchange looks at the databases that are mounted on the other servers in the DAG and attempts to balance the set of databases supported by each server.

> ## Tip
> The best option is to have Exchange automatically select a target server because this gets databases online quickly without too much thought on the part of the administrator. You can always adjust matters afterward by moving one or more databases to a different server.

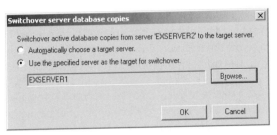

Figure 8-26 Options for server switchover.

AutoDatabaseMountDial and potential issues moving databases

We encountered the *AutoDatabaseMountDial* setting for a mailbox database earlier when we discussed how the ACLL process works when Active Manager attempts to perform an automatic database failover. The *AutoDatabaseMountDial* setting tells Exchange what, if any, data loss is acceptable following a database transition. Hopefully, all of the database copies will be fully synchronized with the active database and the copy that you want to bring online is fully up to date, so the default override setting for automatic database mount on the target server is None, meaning that the Store will apply whatever the *AutoDatabaseMountDial* setting is on that server. However, these are ideal circumstances and it is possible that some condition might have occurred to prevent full synchronization of the database copy on the target server. For example, a network outage might have prevented the most recent set of transaction logs from being copied to the target server. In situations like this, you can instruct the Store to override the *AutoDatabaseMountDial* setting for the database to decide whether it can mount the database. *AutoDatabaseMountDial* is also used by Exchange 2007 CCR or SCR clusters. It is set with the Set-MailboxServer cmdlet and the same value applies to all databases hosted by the server. For example:

```
Set-MailboxServer –Identity 'ExServer2' –AutoDatabaseMountDial 'LossLess'
```

The default value for the *AutoDatabaseMountDial* setting on a server is *BestAvailability*, meaning that a database can be automatically mounted if the copy queue length (the number of logs waiting to be replicated) is less than or equal to 12 transaction logs. The other values are *GoodAvailability*, meaning that the database will mount if the copy queue length is less than or equal to six, and *Lossless*, meaning that the database will only mount if *all* logs generated on the active server have been replicated to the server hosting the passive copy. Lossless clearly ensures that no data are lost following a failover because all logs are available. Varying degrees of data loss could be encountered with the other settings, as up to 12 MB of transaction log data might be missing. It's difficult to quantify what this loss means in practical terms as it depends on the transactions that exist in the missing logs. You might be lucky in that the missing data are for updates such as users responding to meeting requests or you might be unlucky and lose some important messages. However, the transport dumpster might recover some of these data by resubmitting messages that were in transit when the failover occurred. See Chapter 13, "The Exchange Transport System," for more detail about how the transport dumpster protects messages that are in transit between servers.

An administrator can mount a database that cannot be mounted automatically by Active Manager because its *AutoDatabaseMountDial* requirement cannot be met or for another reason. For example, it might be that the content index of a database copy is incomplete so that Active Manager ignores it. You can override this situation and force Exchange to activate the database copy with the Move-ActiveMailboxDatabase cmdlet. For example, this command moves a single database and activates it on server ExServer2.

```
Move-ActiveMailboxDatabase –Identity 'DB1' –ActivateOnServer 'ExServer2'
–MountDialOverrideBestEffort
```

In the example command we use *BestEffort* as the value to override the *AutoDatabaseMountDial* settings. You won't find this value documented, but it is shown by the EMC Activate Database Copy Wizard (Figure 8-22). This value means that Exchange can mount the database with any value for the copy queue length. In other words, you don't care how many transaction logs might not have been copied, as all you want is to get the database online. You might use this override setting in situations where a catastrophic outage has occurred in one datacenter that renders that datacenter inaccessible and you want to activate databases in a secondary datacenter.

CAUTION !

Be careful when using the *BestEffort* override; you are almost certain to lose data. Because of the potential for data loss, Microsoft doesn't allow you to set *AutoDatabaseMountDial* to *BestEffort* with the Set-MailboxServer cmdlet.

In this example, we use the Move-ActiveMailboxDatabase cmdlet to select a database and move it to the ExServer2 server. Specifying $False to the *–Confirm* parameter stops Exchange prompting you to proceed with the move.

```
Move-ActiveMailboxDatabase –Identity 'DB2'–ActivateOnServer 'ExServer2'
–Confirm $False
```

The activation will fail if the search catalog on the target server is not in a healthy state (in other words, the catalog is incomplete for some reason). This is by design to ensure that clients can continue search operations on the newly activated database.

Ignoring the search catalog

You can force Exchange to ignore the search catalog by including the *SkipClientExperienceChecks* parameter. You might ask why Microsoft has given a param- eter a name like *SkipClientExperienceChecks*. It has to do with Microsoft's view that the lack of a content index degrades the client experience. Ignoring the search catalog is quite safe and will not impact users unduly until they attempt online searches and find that the catalog will be unavailable or partially complete. The effect of an incomplete catalog tends to be felt by Outlook Web App (OWA), Exchange Web Services clients, and mobile clients rather than Outlook because when you configure Outlook in cached Exchange mode, it performs searches of the primary mailbox on the client rather than the server, meaning that the impact is only felt for searches of archive mailboxes. The complete code to activate the database in this instance is:

```
Move-ActiveMailboxDatabase -Identity 'DB2'-SkipClientExperienceChecks
-ActivateOnServer ExServer2 -Confirm $False
```

Later on, when client connections have been reestablished to the newly activated data- base, you can force Exchange to update the catalog. The most efficient way to do this is to ask Exchange to reseed a catalog from another online instance. Assuming that an online instance is available, you can use a command like this:

```
Update-MailboxDatabaseCopy -Identity 'DB2' -CatalogOnly
```

Alternatively, if you have the time, you can wait for the catalog to reseed and then activate the database. The problem here is that activations are often forced by operational necessity, meaning that it's more important to have mailboxes online and available to users instead of waiting until everything is perfect, so you might not have the time to reseed the catalog before you are forced to bring the database online.

You can also use the Move-ActiveMailboxDatabase cmdlet to move all of the databases on a server to other servers that host copies of these databases. In effect, this action performs a complete server switchover. For example, this command tells Exchange to switch over all databases from server ExServer2. Active Manager will select the most appropriate database copies to activate based on the copies available in the DAG.

```
Move-ActiveMailboxDatabase -Server 'ExServer2'
```

A server running the enterprise edition of Exchange 2010 can mount up to 100 databases (not including a recovery database). The standard edition of Exchange 2010 is limited to five mounted databases. These figures include both active and passive database copies. Exchange 2010 will allow you to create up to 257 mailbox databases on a server, but only 100 of these can be mounted on a server running the enterprise edition.

INSIDE OUT Preventing performance problems

Every mounted database occupies some system resource. You might not want to have Active Manager activate databases in such a way that a server ends up hosting so many databases that its performance suffers. You can use the Set-MailboxServer cmdlet to set a limit for the number of mounted databases that a server will support. For example, to set a limit of 20 mounted databases:

```
Set-MailboxServer -Identity 'ExServer1' -MaximumActivateDatabases 20
```

If an administrator or Active Manager attempts to mount a database that exceeds the limit set on a server, the Store refuses to mount the database and issues an "ecTooManyMountedDatabases" error in the Application Event Log.

As soon as the RPC Client Access Layer is aware of the transition, it begins to redirect clients to the newly activated database. Exchange 2010 uses cache warming to make sure that the newly activated database copy is not in a cold state, as this would slow down responsiveness to clients. The Store on the server that hosts the newly activated database is replaying transactions as logs arrive and maintains a cache of recently used pages. Cache warming means that the Store retains the cache created through transaction replay instead of discarding it and rebuilding the cache with pages requested by clients. The logic here is that clients are likely to want to use pages that exist in the cache because those pages belong to recent transactions that clients might want to access after they reconnect to the database.

Client response to a transition is dependent on the client platform and version. Outlook clients working in cached Exchange mode will issue a notification that they have lost connectivity and then reconnect when the database is back online. Outlook 2010 is slightly different as it suppresses messages about lost connectivity for what are regarded as trivial reasons such as a network glitch, so you only see a notification when connectivity is reestablished.

Following a successful database mount, the Store requests the Transport Dumpster to recover any messages that were in transit and exist in the dumpster. Active Manager also notifies the RPC Client Access service that a different copy of the database is now active so that it can begin to reroute client connections to that database.

When the fault is repaired on the original server and it comes back online, its copy of the database is passive and is obviously behind the other copies. The Store on that server runs through a divergence detection process and then performs an incremental reseed to bring its database up to date. The first step is to determine the divergence point, which is done by comparing the transaction logs on the server with the logs on a server that hosts a copy that is up to date. The Store can work out what database pages have changed after the divergence point and then request copies of the changed pages from a copy on another server. These pages are replayed back until the failed copy is synchronized with the other copies. The goal is to have all of this work happen and restore service to users within 30 seconds.

In some cases it might not be possible to perform an incremental reseed because the database is so different from the other copies, perhaps because it was offline for an extended period. In these situations, Exchange will prompt you that a full reseed is necessary to create an up-to-date copy of the database.

Activation blocks

Sometimes you might want to block a database copy from being activated as the result of an outage. For example, you probably don't want to have Active Manager activate a copy on a server when you are upgrading or applying a patch to Exchange. To stop automatic activations on a server, use the Set-MailboxServer cmdlet to set the *DatabaseCopyAutoActivationPolicy* property to Blocked. For example:

```
Set-MailboxServer –Identity 'ExServer1' –DatabaseCopyAutoActivationPolicy 'Blocked'
```

To restore the automatic activation setting, use something like this:

```
Set-MailboxServer –Identity 'ExServer1' –DatabaseCopyAutoActivationPolicy
'Unrestricted'
```

Some companies like to deploy a special server that receives copies of transaction logs to replay into a database copy but are never actually used in production. The server might be underconfigured in terms of hardware but is able to support tasks such as offloading backup operations from active servers, recovery of data from backups, legal discovery searches, and so on. A similar technique was used with Exchange Server 2003 and Exchange Server 2007 in multinode clusters where one node was dedicated to backups and other maintenance operations.

If you deploy a server for this purpose, you should use a server activation policy to block activation because the server will be unable to handle the load imposed by a database transition. In the event that you need to make a database copy active on the server, you can amend the server activation policy or activate the database copy explicitly with the Move-ActiveMailboxDatabase cmdlet.

You can also set a maximum value for the number of databases that Exchange is allowed to activate on a server. This is important when you want to be sure that a server will not be swamped with demand for CPU, storage, or memory resources that it cannot handle. For example, you might have a relatively small server within a DAG that hosts the databases for VIP users. Let's assume that the server hosts five active databases and five passive databases

Chapter 8

and has the capacity to handle the load generated by eight active databases. We can use the Set-MailboxServer cmdlet to declare this limit to Active Manager as follows:

```
Set-MailboxServer -Identity 'LondonVIP' -MaximumActiveDatabases 8
```

With this value in place Active Manager will be able to activate three of the five passive databases following outages on other servers. The same approach can be useful to ensure that activation is balanced across multiple servers in a DAG. It's usual practice to balance the number of active (and passive) databases across all available servers in the DAG and you can determine the value for maximum databases in such a way that load should be evenly distributed after an outage and no server is swamped by additional load.

Finally, it's also important to understand that limiting the number of databases that a server can support might cause Active Manager to override the activation preference for a database. Because the number of mounted databases can change all the time through administrator intervention or failovers, Active Manager does not validate the current number of mounted databases on a server against its *MaximumActiveDatabases* property when it reviews database copies to determine their acceptability to become the active copy. Let's take a situation where a database has three copies. The copy on the active server fails because of a disk outage and causes Active Manager to look for the first healthy database with the lowest activation number and then attempt to mount this copy to restore service. The mount attempt will fail if the server that holds that copy is constrained in terms of the number of active databases. This will force Active Manager to go to the next healthy copy. Assuming that no limitation exists, the copy will be mounted even though it has a higher activation preference. All of this goes to show that you need to think through activation scenarios before you apply database limitations to servers.

Moving database locations within a DAG

It is possible that you won't pick the optimal path for database files and transaction logs when you first create a database, especially for the default database that is created when you install Exchange on a new mailbox server. You can easily relocate the database files to a better location with EMC as long as there are no copies, but once you begin to replicate a database within a DAG, you run into the requirement that all copies of a database have identical paths for database files and the transaction logs. Therefore, moving a database to another location is an operation that requires a little planning. The following are the basic steps recommended by Microsoft:

1. Record the full set of properties for the database that you want to move with the Get-MailboxDatabase cmdlet.

2. Turn circular logging off (this step assumes that you follow Microsoft's advice to use circular logging for databases protected by multiple DAG copies). This step ensures

that all of the transaction logs are maintained for the active database during the time when its copies are not available within the DAG.

3. Remove the passive database copies from the other servers in the DAG with the Remove-MailboxDatabaseCopy cmdlet.

4. Use the Move-DatabasePath cmdlet to change the database's path and copy the database files to the new location. The database will be dismounted and then remounted as part of this operation.

5. Create the equivalent location on the servers that will host the database copies.

6. Move the database files on the other servers to the new location and remount the copies. Perform this operation on the server where the database is currently mounted.

7. Add the database copies back to the DAG with the Add-MailboxDatabaseCopy cmdlet. Remember to set the correct activation order for the copies as you add them.

8. Validate database properties and make adjustments as required. For example, you might need to change the lag replay time or truncation lag time on a database copy.

9. Turn circular logging back on if required.

10. Use the Get-MailboxDatabaseCopyStatus and Test-ReplicationHealth cmdlets to validate that replication is proceeding as normal within the DAG. Unless the database copies have been offline for an extended period during which the active database was very busy, you should not need to reseed the database copies because normal replication processing will perform an incremental reseed to bring the passive databases up to date.

An alternative and simpler approach that has been used effectively is as follows:

1. Dismount the database and suspend its copies on all DAG nodes. You can suspend replication to a database with the Suspend-MailboxDatabaseCopy cmdlet. For example:

    ```
    Suspend-MailboxDatabaseCopy -Identity 'VIP Data\ExServer1' -SuspendComment
    'Move database file locations'
    ```

2. Create the new location (database and/or transaction logs) on the server that hosts the database and the servers that host the copies.

3. Copy the files to the new locations.

Chapter 8

4. Move the database files using the Move-DatabasePath cmdlet and the *ConfigurationOnly* switch so that Exchange only updates Active Directory with the new location data. For example:

```
Move-DatabasePath –Identity 'VIP Data' –EDBFilePath 'G:\DAG\Data\DUBMBX01.EDB'
–LogFolderPath 'G:\DAG\Logs\' –ConfigurationOnly
```

5. Verify that the file locations have been updated in Active Directory.

```
Get-MailboxDatabase –Identity 'VIP Data' | Select Name, *Path* | Format-List
```

6. Mount the database and resume replication to allow the database copies to resynchronize. You can use the Resume-MailboxDatabaseCopy cmdlet for this purpose:

```
Resume-MailboxDatabaseCopy –Identity 'VIP Data\ExServer1'
```

7. Check that email is being delivered to mailboxes in the database.

8. Check that replication queues are not building to ensure that replication is proceeding normally and that the state of all the database copies is Healthy. Do this with EMC or by using the Get-MailboxDatabaseCopyStatus cmdlet.

```
Get-MailboxDatabaseCopyStatus –Identity 'VIP Data\ExServer1'
```

As every organization will be slightly different in its implementation of a DAG, it is strongly suggested that you test these procedures thoroughly before you attempt to use one of them in your production environment.

Removing database copies

Adding new database copies is all very well but there will be times when you need to reverse course and remove a copy. You cannot remove the active copy of the database until all passive copies are removed. If you need to remove a database copy that is currently active, you have to force a transition to another copy, wait for the switchover to be successful, and then proceed to remove the now passive database copy. To remove a complete set of database copies, you must delete each passive copy until you reach a point where only the active copy remains, at which point you can use the normal Remove Database option to delete it.

To remove a database copy, first check that replication is healthy and that no network issues exist within the DAG. This is to ensure that all the servers that host copies are aware of the update that you are about to make. Second, because it needs to be sure that no potential exists for data loss, Exchange will only remove a database copy if circular logging is disabled (Figure 8-27). If circular logging is enabled, you have to disable the setting. Then dismount and mount the database and let replication between the copies settle down.

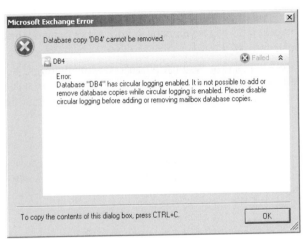

Figure 8-27 A database copy cannot be removed because circular logging is enabled.

When everything is ready, select the passive database that you want to remove from the list of copies, right-click, and select Remove from the shortcut menu (Figure 8-28). The subsequent confirmation message is a little confusing as it asks Do You Want To Remove *<database name>* instead of Do You Want To Remove The Copy Of *<database name>*On*<server>*, but it's safe to click Yes to proceed.

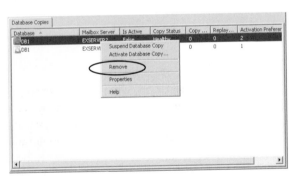

Figure 8-28 Removing a database copy.

The nature of computer software is that we expect occasional glitches to occur and the most common issue that you're likely to see is when Exchange can remove the database copy object from Active Directory but is unable to delete the underlying files. This can occur when a transient error interrupts communication between the workstation on which you are running the Exchange Management tools and the server that hosts the database that you are attempting to remove.

Chapter 8

If Exchange reports an error when it removes a database copy, you can confirm that the reference to the database copy has been removed from Active Directory by running the Get-MailboxDatabase cmdlet to return the list of servers and database copies that Exchange knows about. In this case, the problem was encountered when an attempt was made to delete the copy of database DB4 from server ExServer4. After seeing the error, we want to be sure that this copy has been removed from the database copy list. We can check by retrieving the list of database copies as follows:

```
Get-MailboxDatabase –Identity DB3 | Select Servers, DatabaseCopies
```

```
Servers          : {ExServer1, ExServer2, ExServer3}
DatabaseCopies   : {DB4\ExServer1, DB4\ExServer2, DB4\ExServer3}
```

There's no evidence that a copy of the DB4 database still exists on ExServer4 so we know that the entry was removed from Active Directory. We can therefore proceed to clean up by deleting the database files from the server. Make sure that you select the correct set of files on the right server!

Even after Exchange successfully removes a database copy, it will remind you to check the server that hosted the now removed copy to complete the cleanup by deleting any vestiges of the database files that have been left behind (Figure 8-29).

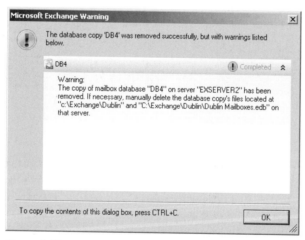

Figure 8-29 Warning that some database files might need to be removed.

If you want to remove a database completely, you have to remove all of the database copies. Naturally, before you remove the last copy of a database, you need to transfer all of the mailboxes that it hosts to another database. This is extremely important for mailboxes that are used for Exchange features such as arbitration and search mailboxes. If you attempt to delete a database that still contains mailboxes, you'll see the error illustrated in Figure 8-30.

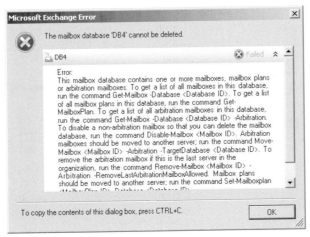

Figure 8-30 Error because mailboxes still exist in a database.

Before proceeding to remove the database, you can use the Get-MailboxStatistics or Get-Mailbox cmdlet to check that no mailboxes are present. For example:

```
Get-MailboxStatistics -Database 'DB4'
```

```
DisplayName                 ItemCount     StorageLimitStatus
-------------------         -----------   --------------------------
SystemMailbox{51eb7f9d...   1             BelowLimit
```

Or:

```
Get-Mailbox -Database 'DB4'
```

All of the mailboxes in the database are listed and we can see that the only mailbox that is present is the default system mailbox, so we know that it is quite safe to go ahead and remove the database. We can do this with EMC by selecting the database and then clicking the Remove option in the action pane (Figure 8-31). Click OK to confirm that the removal should proceed and Exchange will remove the database object from Active Directory. You might have to clean up by deleting the database and transaction log files to complete the process.

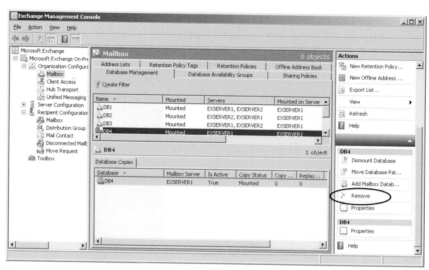

Figure 8-31 Removing the last copy of a mailbox database.

The EMS commands to remove a database copy are as follows. First, let's perform the same task as we did with EMC and remove the database copy for DB4 from server ExServer2. The command is:

```
Remove-MailboxDatabaseCopy -Identity 'DB4\ExServer2'
```

After all but the last database copy are removed, you can run the Remove-MailboxDatabase cmdlet to remove the database from the organization:

```
Remove-MailboxDatabase -Identity 'DB4'
```

Removing servers from a DAG

Before you can remove a server from a DAG, you must remove any database copies from the server by following the process discussed in the last section. We can check for the presence of database copies with the Get-MailboxDatabase cmdlet. In this case, we check the mailbox databases that exist on the ExServer1 server:

```
Get-MailboxDatabase -Server ExServer1
```

Name	Server	Recovery	ReplicationType
Sales	ExServer1	False	None
VIP Data	ExServer1	False	Remote

The output reveals that we have one copy of a replicated database (VIP Data) that is currently mounted on server ExServer1. The first step is to remove the copy of this database from ExServer1. You can leave the nonreplicated database (Sales) intact as it does not affect the server's membership of the DAG.

Once you are sure that all replicated databases are removed, select the Manage Database Availability Group Wizard in EMC or use the Remove-DatabaseAvailabilityGroupServer cmdlet to evict the server from the DAG. For example, to remove the server called ExServer1 from the DAG named DAG-Dublin:

```
Remove-DatabaseAvailabilityGroupServer –Identity 'DAG-Dublin' –MailboxServer
'ExServer1'
```

Chapter 8

INSIDE OUT   To remove a server, the add-a-server process is reversed

The process of removing a server from a DAG essentially reverses the steps performed to add a server to the DAG. The server is evicted from the cluster, the quorum model is adjusted to take account of the reduced number of cluster members, the server is removed from the DAG object in Active Directory, and the databases hosted by the server are removed from the quorum database. Fortunately, Exchange manages these steps automatically so you don't have to do them yourself.

Sometimes you need to remove a server when the server is physically unavailable or cannot be brought online for some reason, perhaps following a hardware outage. You can leave the server in the DAG but this might affect the ability of the cluster to maintain a quorum. As the server cannot be brought online, you cannot run the Remove-DatabaseAvailabilityGroupServer cmdlet in the normal manner. Instead, you can use the cmdlet to simply remove all traces of the server from the DAG configuration data held in Active Directory. The –ConfigurationOnly parameter does the trick. For example:

```
Remove-DatabaseAvailabilityGroupServer –Identity 'DAG-Dublin' –MailboxServer
'Exserver2' –ConfigurationOnly
```

This command will remove the server called ExServer2 from the DAG-Dublin DAG. Later on, when the server is restored to full health, you can reintroduce it into the DAG.

Handling storage hangs

Storage "hangs" occur when an application like Exchange issues an I/O request that cannot be satisfied by the I/O subsystem for some reason, usually when a bug is encountered in either the storage software or hardware. Exchange 2010 SP1 includes some code to handle these conditions more effectively to improve its high-availability capabilities. I originally wrote "elegantly" but then decided that the solution used is better described as effective in the same way that an axe is an effective tool to lop branches off trees.

Exchange 2010 SP1 periodically checks for storage hangs that occur in two ways:

- ESE or the Information Store detects a data drive hang. The process attempts to read or write to a data drive and no response is received. Once a sufficient period has elapsed (a couple of minutes) to ensure that the drive should have been able to respond and the same problem is observed on multiple data drives, ESE concludes that the server is suffering from a problem from which it is unlikely to recover; to restore service ESE therefore raises a failure item. In turn, the Windows Failure Item Manager notices that a failure item has been raised and proceeds to force a server halt through a bugcheck (blue screen of death).

- The replay service (running in a DAG) detects that the operating system is not responding to its requests. This quickly becomes an issue that can compromise high availability, so the solution is blunt and rapid: Exchange forces the server to stop with a bugcheck and reboot. This step is important because the cluster heartbeat service might still function. Administrator action is usually required to discover why the operating system has failed and to address any lurking problems that might exist. Once the failed server is brought back online, the incremental reseed process will restore its database copies to a healthy state.

In both cases, the logic is that it is better to reboot a failing server, as this will restore service as quickly as possible to clients. If the server is standalone, the hope is that the reboot will bring a fully functional server back online and the databases will be remounted and become available for connections. If not, the administrator needs to investigate why the issue occurred. Usually the root cause lies in some hardware failure.

If the server is inside a DAG, forcing it to reboot will cause Exchange to transfer the active databases from the now failed server to other copies within the DAG and so resume service to users as quickly as possible.The normal server failover mechanism then determines that the databases hosted on the failed server are offline and brings the database copy with the lowest activation number online to restore service to users.

Upgrading servers in a DAG

Just as with older clusters, you have to take a certain amount of care when you apply patches and other upgrades to servers in a DAG. The general approach is to remove the target server from the DAG in a way that maintains user service, apply the upgrade, and then reintroduce the server. Two usual scenarios occur: multirole servers and dedicated mailbox servers.

Multirole servers usually support the mailbox and CAS roles, although in smaller deployments they might support mailbox, CAS, and hub transport. It will be difficult to maintain service if the target server is the only one that supports the CAS and hub transport roles, so we will assume that other servers (in or outside the DAG) provide these services. The steps to execute a smooth upgrade are as follows:

1. Move all active databases to another mailbox server in the DAG.

2. Stop the CAS and hub transport services and check that traffic continues to flow using the other servers. If you use a load balancer to route traffic to the CAS on the target server, you will have to remove the server from the array used by the load balancer.

3. Set the activation block on the databases hosted by the server to prevent Active Manager from attempting to activate the databases in case of an outage on another server.

4. Perform the software upgrade and test it afterward. You might need a reboot to bring the server online after installing the patch.

5. Remove the activation block and transition databases back to the server.

6. Restart CAS and hub transport activity.

You can continue with these steps until you have applied the upgrades to every server in the DAG.

> **Tip**
> Remember, it is best practice to maintain consistent software versions across all servers.

The steps necessary to upgrade a dedicated mailbox server are simpler because you do not have to deal with CAS or hub transport services:

1. Move all active databases to another mailbox server in the DAG.

2. Set the activation block on the databases hosted by the server to prevent Active Manager from attempting to activate the databases in case of an outage on another server.

3. Perform the software upgrade and test it afterward.

4. Remove the activation block and transition databases back to the server.

INSIDE OUT   Automate with Windows PowerShell scripts

To make things easier for all concerned, Microsoft provides the Start-DAGServerMaintenance.ps1 script and Stop-DAGServerMaintenance.ps1 scripts in Exchange 2010 SP1. These scripts are designed to automate taking a server out of a DAG to allow an administrator to patch them and then reintroduce the newly upgraded server back into the DAG. You can use these scripts or amend them to meet your operational needs, or write your own version! Just be sure to test them so that you understand how the scripts work before you depend on them for actual maintenance.

System shutdowns

The Exchange 2007 high availability features are not integrated with Windows Server 2003 shutdown code. Microsoft released Exchange 2007 after Windows Server 2003 so there was no opportunity to integrate the requirements of Exchange log replication into the Windows shutdown. In other words, if you shut down an Exchange 2007 server that is part of a CCR cluster, the Exchange Information Store process is shut down without taking any steps to gracefully transition work to a passive member of the cluster. Ideally, an administrator would transfer work to the passive member of the cluster before shutting anything down, but if he forgot, users would experience an interruption of service in the time required to bring the passive copy online.

Exchange 2010 is different, as it was released well after Windows Server 2008 and the work could be done to create a more elegant shutdown process for servers that operate within a DAG. When you shut down a server that hosts databases with copies on other servers in the DAG, Exchange will attempt to transfer the work to another server before allowing the shutdown to proceed. This approach allows users to continue working, assuming that the databases can be transitioned to another server.

Datacenter Activation Coordination

Some DAGs will be deployed across datacenters in multiple sites. These environments create a specific problem when catastrophic hardware failures occur that knock several servers out across multiple datacenters. Normally, when multiple servers in a DAG are affected, the DAG stays offline until the majority of the servers are restored to good health and come online again and the cluster is able to establish a quorum. At this point, Active Manager attempts to restart DAG operations and mount databases to recover from the failure.

If all goes well, the databases will come back online and all the servers will be able to communicate with each other. However, if communications between the datacenters are not available, it is possible to provoke a condition known as *split brain syndrome* because the DAG members will not be able to receive heartbeat signals from the other members. You can think of split brain syndrome as having two parts of a cluster that can't talk to each other; both consider themselves to be authoritative for the cluster, or, in this case, the DAG. If split brain syndrome is allowed to persist, you could end up in a situation where copies of the same databases are activated on servers in two different datacenters and both start to provide service to users. It's obvious what a mess this could cause.

To avoid this problem, you can configure a DAG to use a Datacenter Activation Protocol (DAP) to achieve a state called Datacenter Activation Coordination (DAC). The original intention was that DAC would be used for situations in which there are three or more members in a DAG that spans multiple datacenters. Microsoft tuned DAP in Exchange 2010 SP1 to support two-server DAGs. This is a supported configuration, albeit likely to be unusual, only deployed by small organizations that want to achieve high availability using a minimum number of servers.

When a DAG includes enough servers to allow it to be configured to use DAP, Active Manager maintains an in-memory flag (called the DACP bit) to inform the DAG whether it can mount local databases on the server. When Active Manager starts on a server, the bit is set to 0, meaning that Exchange cannot mount local databases. Active Manager then communicates with Active Manager running on the other members of the DAG to determine to what value their DACP flag is set. If any server responds with a DACP value of 1, it means that local mounts are possible and the server where Active Manager is starting changes its DACP bit to 1 and proceeds to mount its databases. When a DAG has only two members, it uses the boot time of the FSW server as the DACP bit. Active Manager periodically reads and saves this value to be able to use it for arbitration purposes. Because the DACP bit from the FSW is nonzero, the first server starting up in the DAG will be able to mount its databases if the FSW is available.

You configure DAP for a DAG by using the Set-DatabaseAvailabilityGroup cmdlet to set the *DatacenterActivationMode* property. The default is that DAP is off and this value should be left unless you have good reason to change it.

```
Set-DatabaseAvailabilityGroup -id 'DistributedDAG' -DatacenterActivationMode
'Enabled'
```

Planning for datacenter resilience

Planning for resilience against failures that take a complete datacenter out is a complex business. DAGs and DAC provide fundamental building blocks to help address the problem, but they don't provide automatic transitions. Solid, well-planned operational procedures and knowledgeable people leverage the technology to complete the solution. As an example, let's review the high-level steps that are necessary to move a DAG to a secondary datacenter after the primary datacenter fails. In this scenario, London hosts the primary datacenter and Dublin hosts the secondary. We have a DAG called "Production" that stretches across the two datacenters. All of the active database copies are hosted in London and copied to servers in Dublin. Each geographic location forms its own Active Directory site. We assume that sufficient server capacity is available in both datacenters to handle the transport, CAS, and mailbox loads.

Suppose that a failure occurs in London that renders the datacenter inaccessible to client connections. The following steps are taken to redirect traffic to Dublin:

1. Update DNS records for all of the Exchange services (SMTP (MX), HTTP, CAS arrays, Autodiscover, and so on) to point to appropriate servers in Dublin. Any load balancer or other network devices are reconfigured to redirect client connections.

2. In both datacenters, update Active Directory to mark the DAG as "stopped" in the London site. It's obvious that this command depends on the ability to access Active Directory:

   ```
   Stop-DatabaseAvailabilityGroup –Identity 'Production' –ActiveDirectorySite
   'London'
   –ConfigurationOnly
   ```

3. Stop the cluster service on all nodes in the London site.

4. In both datacenters, update Active Directory to activate the DAG member servers in the Dublin site. The example code assumes that you have configured an alternate FSW server and directory in the Dublin site. If not, you can pass values for these properties in the same command:

   ```
   Restore-DatabaseAvailabilityGroup –Identity 'Production'
   –ActiveDirectorySite 'Dublin'
   ```

5. Ensure that the passive copies of the databases hosted by the servers in Dublin are mounted and activated. Client connections should then be established and normal function resumed.

After the problem in the London datacenter is fixed, you might want to transition the workload back from Dublin. The following steps can be used:

1. Verify that the London datacenter is capable of hosting the workload.

2. Add the London servers back into the DAG. This step will reenable the cluster service in London:

   ```
   Start-DatabaseAvailabilityGroup –Identity 'Production' –ActiveDirectorySite
   'London'
   ```

3. Update the DAG properties to transfer the FSW server and directory from a server in the Dublin datacenter (we assume that the FSW was transferred during the previous transition) to a server in London:

```
Set-DatabaseAvailabilityGroup –Identity 'Production' –WitnessServer'LondonHT1'
–WitnessDirectory 'C:\DAG\Production'
```

4. Allow sufficient time for the passive database copies in London to be brought up to date by replaying replicated translation logs from Dublin (a reseed might be required for some databases).

5. Dismount all databases to free client connections and ensure that proper redirection occurs to the London datacenter when it comes online.

6. Update DNS records to move Simple Mail Transfer Protocol (SMTP) and other services back to the London datacenter.

7. Update and mount databases to activate the copies in the London datacenter. Each database has to be moved individually. The *–SkipClientExperienceChecks* parameter allows the Store to move the database even if the search catalog is not up to date.

```
Move-ActiveMailboxDatabase –Identity 'Mailbox DB1' –ActivateOnServer
'LondonMBX2'
-SkipClientExperienceChecks
Mount-Database –Identity 'Mailbox DB1'
```

If you need to reseed a database, you'll notice that EMC does not seem to display the current status as the reseed operation proceeds. In fact, the console does have a progress bar, but you have to set the console window to be more than 80 characters to see it. Even revealed, the progress bar is not helpful, as no indication is given of the scale used. Not knowing how a seed operation is progressing is fine if the database is small because the operation usually completes in a short time; it is more of a problem with large databases (more than 3 GB or so) because you are left guessing as to how long it will take for the reseed to complete. The fact that it does comes as a welcome revelation when it happens.

Datacenter designs differ dramatically so it is impossible to give anything more than a high-level description. The steps outlined here have to be validated and tested based on the details of a specific datacenter to arrive at a fully workable plan for resilience.

Managing cross-site connections

The Autodiscover process directs MAPI clients to connect to a CAS server or array, which acts as the MAPI endpoint for Exchange 2010. The CAS subsequently connects to the mailbox servers that host the active copy of the databases holding the mailboxes required by the clients. When a cross-site failover occurs clients might end up in a situation where the clients and the CAS are in one Active Directory site and the mailbox servers hosting the active databases are in another site. The question then is how to manage the cross-site connections and the data flowing between CAS and mailbox servers.

Allowing cross-site connections to occur is usually sufficient in situations when the mailbox servers in the primary datacenter are likely to come back online in a short period to allow the active databases to be transferred back to their preferred servers. However, the situation is different when the outage for the mailbox servers is expected to last for an extended period or the complete primary datacenter is unavailable for some reason. In these scenarios, you have to redirect clients to a CAS array or server in the secondary datacenter.

Because it means that Outlook profiles don't have to be updated with the name of a new CAS array, the easiest and quickest method to reroute connections is to update DNS to reassign the IP address for the CAS array used by the clients to the array in that site. The alternative is to update the *RpcClientAccessServer* property of the databases that have moved to the secondary Active Directory site to point to a CAS array in that site. This is not a great experience for Outlook users because their client connections fail when it attempts to contact the CAS server in the primary site and they have to wait for administrative actions to complete before connections are possible.

Microsoft considered deploying a new cross-site management mechanism in SP1 with a DAG setting to indicate whether cross-site connections were permitted or not. However, when Microsoft reviewed how the mechanism worked in practice, they concluded that it required further development and withdrew it from the code base for the final release of SP1. It is entirely possible that a more elegant and automated arrangement to manage client connections for DAGs that extend across sites will appear in a future product release.

Crimson events

If you've been a Windows administrator for any period of time, it's likely that you are very familiar with the event log. Windows Server 2008 provides two sets of logs. The Windows Logs are those that feature in previous versions of Windows (Application, Security, and System) and are intended to capture events that apply to the entire system. A separate category of logs called Application and Services Logs capture "crimson channel" or application-level events. Figure 8-32 shows an example of how Exchange 2010 uses these events to capture operational and debug details of high-availability events, in this instance the transition of a database copy to a healthy state.

Exchange 2010 uses the *HighAvailability* channel to capture startup and shutdown events for the Microsoft Exchange Replication Service and the various components that run within this service such as Active Manager, replication operations, the TCP listener, and the VSS writer used for backups. As you can see from Figure 8-32, this channel also captures events relating to database health and transitions as well as anything to do with a DAG's underlying cluster. On the other hand, the *MailboxDatabaseFailureItems* channel captures information about failures that affect normal operation of a replicated mailbox database.

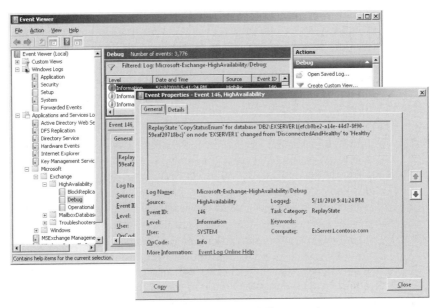

Figure 8-32 Viewing a debug event for High Availability operations.

INSIDE OUT   This isn't a starting place

These events probably won't be the first place that you look if you have to resolve a database failure. More obvious issues such as a storage failure or a network outage are more likely to seize your attention. However, they are an interesting and valuable source of background data that you might be asked to consult if you work with Microsoft Support to resolve a particularly complex issue with a DAG.

Approaching DAG designs

Any technology only moves out of the "interesting" category to become valuable when it can be applied to solve real-life operational problems in production environments. We've already looked at how we might calculate the raw storage requirement for a deployment. In this section, we take a different view and see how to use DAG technology to address the high-availability requirements for a fictional company.

Like all technologies, the Exchange 2010 implementation of the DAG includes various constraints and limitations that system designers have to take into account before they can deploy a DAG. To begin, let's list the most important constraints that we have to take into account when we consider the kind of DAG that we can create:

- No more than 16 servers can exist in a DAG. The general rule is that a DAG becomes more resilient as the number of servers in the DAG increases. This is because the DAG can host more database copies spread across more servers; the increased number of servers provides additional robustness against losing a server; and the increased number of members in the underlying cluster means that it is less likely that a quorum failure will occur and render the cluster useless. These are important points that should be taken into account as you consider whether to build a single DAG or split servers across multiple DAGs. There is no practical limitation that governs the number of DAGs that can exist within a single Exchange organization.

- The normal situation is that all of the servers are in the same Active Directory site. However, if necessary, a DAG can be stretched across multiple datacenters and multiple Active Directory sites as long as the necessary high-quality network connectivity (round-trip latency of less than 250 milliseconds) exists between the two datacenters.

- Sufficient network capacity must exist to support the log replication with latency of no more than 250 milliseconds.

- The dependency on Windows Failover Clustering means that all servers within the DAG must run the enterprise edition of the same version of the operating system (Windows Server 2008 SP2 or R2). The servers should also be patched to the same software level for the operating system and any application, including Exchange 2010.

- You can deploy a DAG with the standard or enterprise version of Exchange 2010. The standard edition is limited to five databases, whereas the enterprise edition allows a single server to support up to a maximum of 100 databases. It is unlikely that any server will support 100 active databases, as this will create a very heavy demand for I/O and memory.

- Two copies of the same database cannot be on the same server.

- Microsoft's recommendation for the maximum size of a database is 2 TB, assuming that the database is protected by at least two copies. Many system designers are uncomfortable with the idea of running such large databases, even when protected by replication, so 1 TB might be a better design point until the Exchange community gains more operational experience with very large Exchange databases running within a DAG.

- Circular logging is supported for databases that are protected by at least two copies. In this situation, the transaction logs and the Content Indexing (CI) catalog can be placed on the same drive as the database.

- Microsoft's performance tests indicate that active users generate approximately 0.2 I/O operations per second. The storage infrastructure must be able to support the I/O demand generated by database operations.

With a full understanding of DAG design principles and limitations in mind, we can discuss how to apply the technology to meet common requirements for high availability and disaster recovery that are found in enterprise deployments. Let's assume that our fictional company wishes to meet these requirements:

1. Host 25,000 mailboxes with 2 GB quota. This is a good figure for the purpose of the design exercise because the needs of most enterprises can be satisfied with 25,000 mailboxes. Larger enterprises can scale up the numbers outlined in this design until they hit the limits of 16 servers in a DAG or 100 active databases mounted on a single server, in which case they can deploy multiple DAGs to meet their needs. Smaller enterprises can scale down the numbers of servers and databases.

2. Deploy across a primary and a secondary datacenter to ensure the ability to resist a complete datacenter outage. If the primary datacenter is inoperative due to an outage, service must be transferred seamlessly to the secondary datacenter.

3. Provide resilience against a storage failure on a single server within the primary datacenter. Provide the same resilience within the secondary datacenter if service is transferred there.

4. Handle multiple storage failures on different servers in each datacenter without losing all online copies of a database. VSS backups to disk followed by copies to tape are used to provide archival copies and to satisfy audit requirements.

5. Have a maximum of 5,000 mailboxes on a server during normal operations and maintain sufficient capacity for servers to be able to handle the redistributed mailbox load following the failure of a complete server or during times when a server is taken offline for scheduled maintenance.

The first implication that arises from these requirements is that we have to create a design that employs two datacenters to ensure continued service following an outage that removes the primary datacenter from service. To satisfy the requirement, the DAG will be stretched across both datacenters within a single Active Directory site and sufficient servers will be placed in both datacenters to be able to handle the complete load generated by 25,000 mailboxes. We will also create sufficient database copies in both datacenters to ensure that we can handle the various storage outage scenarios envisaged in the requirements. The need to accommodate the database copies drives the need for sufficient high-quality bandwidth to connect the two datacenters to handle the log replication traffic. The database copies on the servers in the secondary datacenter will have higher activation preference so that the databases in the primary datacenter are always used first. Sufficient CAS and hub transport servers will be deployed in both datacenters so that the servers in one datacenter are capable of handling the complete connectivity and transport load.

The second implication is that we must have at least two database copies in the primary datacenter. One of these copies is the active database and the second will provide the in-site resilience against a storage failure on a drive that hosts a database. Two copies are also required in the secondary datacenter to provide the same resilience if a storage failure affects a database following the transfer of service to the secondary datacenter. Our design therefore features four copies of every database. Every transaction log generated on the active database has to be replicated and replayed on three other servers, so all of the servers will be reasonably busy as they update their database copies.

The third implication is that we require at least five mailbox servers in both sites to satisfy the requirement to have no more than 5,000 mailboxes on a server. If one server fails or needs to be taken offline for maintenance, the remaining servers will have to be able to handle the load generated by 6,250 mailboxes (5,000 original plus 1,250 from the failed server). Ten mailbox servers fit quite comfortably into a single DAG and allow for six additional servers to be added if load increases through additional mailboxes or an increase in mailbox quota.

All servers will run Windows Server 2008 R2 enterprise edition. We could deploy Windows Server 2008 SP2 but we will not be able to perform in-place upgrades to Windows Server 2008 R2, so there is no point in deploying an operating system version that might be outdated soon. All servers will run Exchange 2010 with the latest roll-up patch release.

25,000 × 2 GB mailboxes results in roughly 50 TB of mailbox database. Microsoft recommends that a mailbox database can be a maximum of 2 TB if it is protected by multiple copies within a DAG. We could distribute the 50 TB of mailbox quota into 25 databases and place five active databases on each server. However, this would mean that each database would hold 1,000 mailboxes. Two issues could result. First, the I/O load generated by such a database under full load is likely to be (1,000 × 0.25) 250 I/O operations per second, which is quite heavy. Second, if a server outage happened, the workload represented by the five databases from the failed server would be distributed across the other four servers in the datacenter. One of the servers would have to take two additional databases, or the load of 2,000 mailboxes, which exceeds the requirement to restrict the maximum load to 6,250 mailboxes following a server outage.

Today, not many people have much operational experience with running 2 TB mailbox databases, so perhaps we don't want to use databases that are quite so large. A server running Exchange 2010 Enterprise Edition can accommodate many more than five active databases, and a larger number of smaller databases allows more flexibility in distributing I/O load across available disks and transferring load following a server outage. In addition, smaller databases allow us to grow if necessary to accommodate larger mailbox quotas or archive mailboxes without creating the requirement to move mailboxes around. We will therefore set our maximum database size to 500 GB (250 mailboxes) and decide that the server will host 20 active databases. Each server will also host 20 copy databases from other servers. In the event of a server failure, the work for five databases (1,250 mailboxes) will be transferred to each of the four remaining servers. We will configure the DAG to limit the number of active databases per server to 25 to enforce the desired 6,250 mailbox limit.

If the primary datacenter suffers a complete failure, the workload will be transferred automatically to the secondary datacenter and the RPC Client Access Layer on the CAS servers in the secondary datacenter will take on transferred client connections and redirect the connections to the database copies on the servers in the secondary center. This might not be the desired behavior, as the available network might not be sufficient to handle client traffic in addition to replication traffic and any other application load generated between the two datacenters. In this case, we can activation block the databases in the secondary datacenter and accept that a delay will occur before we can reactivate a database copy should both copies of a database in the primary datacenter fail. Two database copies are still available in the secondary datacenter, so a further storage failure can still be tolerated, including a failure that takes out a complete server. If more than one storage failure is experienced, it could remove service to one or more databases depending on the distribution of the database copies. However, such a series of failures following a complete datacenter outage is highly unlikely and could only be considered to be the height of bad luck.

In addition to the 50 TB space needed for mailbox databases, we should add 40 percent to account for the CI catalogs and transaction logs for the databases plus associated headroom for growth, maintenance, and to ensure that no disk is ever completely full. The design goal is therefore 70 TB × 4 copies, or 280 TB. Note that this figure accounts for mailboxes that are completely full. It is unlikely that a production environment will operate in a state where all mailboxes are full, especially with a generous 2 GB quota. An average mailbox might be half full, so you could plan to provide 140 TB of storage initially and then grow over time. Archive mailboxes are a complicating factor, as they can be held in the same database as the primary mailbox and could therefore double the storage requirement. Of course, SP1 allows you to split primary and archive mailboxes across different databases, so it is possible that your design might use dedicated databases for archive mailboxes that are managed in a different manner from the databases that hold primary mailboxes.

Each of the mailbox databases is a maximum of 500 GB. Adding 20 percent for the CI catalog and transaction logs gives 700 GB, which means that a single database and its associated files will fit comfortably on a single 1 TB disk and also allow space for growth.

However, this is a simplistic calculation as the storage has to be able to satisfy the I/O demand as well. Microsoft's performance guidelines use 0.2 I/O operations per second per mailbox. This figure is highly dependent on user work habits and is influenced by the number of items and folders in user mailboxes. To be safe, we can use a figure of 0.25 I/O operations per second, so a mailbox database with 250 mailboxes generates a demand of 62.5 I/O operations per second at peak load, assuming that all of the users are concurrently active.

The calculations do not take archive mailboxes or features such as an extended deleted items retention period or litigation hold into account. The exact storage design that is implemented will have to take these factors into account. On a pragmatic level, the storage design will be highly influenced by the existing storage architecture, current available storage products, and other requirements such as the backup regime. For example, an organization that uses storage area network (SAN) storage for Exchange 2007 might want to extend its use for Exchange 2010 and will therefore make the necessary adjustments to accommodate the storage and I/O requirements of 100 active databases and 100 copy databases plus the demands of other applications that are run on the mailbox and other servers in each datacenter. On the other hand, an organization might want to take advantage of the lower I/O demand of Exchange 2010 to move to a lower cost JBOD (just a bunch of disks)-based storage design, especially if they have an eye on expanding mailbox quota from 2 GB to a higher value in future.

The storage calculators and other sizing tools that are available from hardware vendors and Microsoft provide invaluable assistance to system designers, as they calculate the basic foundation for a storage design that has to deliver a certain amount of raw storage and I/O capabilities. In any but the simplest deployment, you shouldn't expect these calculators to provide the most effective and cost-efficient storage design. Instead, treat the output from the sizing tools as a good starting point and then give the data to a storage expert to have her fine-tune the design to meet your exact requirements. One idea is to provide the output from the sizing tools to storage vendors and invite them to state how their products will deliver the necessary performance, capacity, security, and resilience. Apart from the potential of getting some free advice from vendor storage specialists in the responses that you receive, you might benefit from competitively priced storage packages specially designed for Exchange 2010 that might be an off-the-shelf solution for many designs. In addition, the vendors can brief you on new storage and other technology with capabilities that might not be captured in the current generation of sizing tools.

Scripts to help with DAG management

The Exchange development group provides several scripts in the installation kit that are of interest for DAG management, some of which we have already encountered earlier in this chapter. You can find the scripts in the Bin\Scripts directory.

Further documentation about command-line switches and how to run the monitoring scripts on a continuous basis is available on TechNet at *http://technet.microsoft.com/en-us/library /dd351258.aspx.*

The remaining scripts are:

- RedistributeActiveDatabases.ps1: This script is provided in Exchange 2010 SP1 to perform automatic rebalance of a DAG. For example, if you run it with the *–BalanceDbsByActivationPreference* parameter, the script attempts to balance databases by activation preference. See the earlier section "Activating a mailbox database copy" for more information.

- CheckDatabaseRedundancy.ps1: This script checks a mailbox database to validate that it has at least two valid and healthy copies. In this case, the database is considered to possess sufficient redundancy. This example shows the kind of output that you'd expect. In this instance, the database has two copies, so the script considers its current state to be "green." The script is capable of being used by a management framework such as SCOM, in which case its data can be used to monitor the health of replicated databases on an ongoing basis.

```
.\CheckDatabaseRedundancy.ps1 –MailboxDatabaseName 'DB1'
```

```
DatabaseName               : DB1
LastRedundancyCount        : 0
CurrentRedundancyCount     : 2
LastState                  : Unknown
CurrentState               : Green
LastStateTransitionUtc     : 5/21/2010 8:12:17 PM
LastGreenTransitionUtc     : 5/21/2010 8:12:17 PM
LastRedTransitionUtc       :
LastGreenReportedUtc       : 5/21/2010 8:12:17 PM
LastRedReportedUtc         :
PreviousTotalRedDuration   : 00:00:00
TotalRedDuration           : 00:00:00
IsTransitioningState       : True
HasErrorsInHistory         : False
CurrentErrorMessages       :
ErrorHistory               :
```

You can also run the script to check all of the mailbox databases on a server. In this case, simply pass the name of the server as a parameter to the script. Here's an example of running the script for a server. The edited output is for a mailbox database that has only one copy, so it cannot be regarded as redundant. We can also see that this database had a "red" event in the recent past. A red event is something that an administrator might have to look into, such as a storage glitch.

Chapter 8

```
.\CheckDatabaseRedundancy.ps1 'ExServer1'
```

```
DatabaseName              : DB4
LastRedundancyCount       : 0
CurrentRedundancyCount    : 1
LastState                 : Unknown
CurrentState              : Red
LastStateTransitionUtc    : 5/21/2010 8:16:56 PM
LastGreenTransitionUtc    :
LastRedTransitionUtc      : 5/21/2010 8:16:56 PM
LastGreenReportedUtc      :
LastRedReportedUtc        : 5/21/2010 8:16:56 PM
PreviousTotalRedDuration  : 00:00:00
TotalRedDuration          : 00:00:00.0468756
IsTransitioningState      : True
HasErrorsInHistory        : True
CurrentErrorMessages      : {The number of configured copies for database 'DB4' (1) is less
than the required redundancy count (2).,
Name            Status        RealCopyQueue    InspectorQueue    ReplayQueue    CIState
--------        --------      -------------    --------------    -----------    -------
DB4\EXSERVER1   Mounted       0                0                 0              Healthy}
ErrorHistory              : {CheckHADatabaseRedundancy.DatabaseRedundancyEntry+ErrorRecord}
```

Behind the scenes, the Microsoft Exchange Replication Service runs the CheckDatabaseRedundancy script on DAG member servers hourly to report whether databases are sufficiently protected with copies. If a database is found to have just one copy for more than 20 minutes in an hour, the Replication Service reports the results in event 4113 written into the Application Event Log and continues to flag this issue with a new event every 20 minutes until a second copy is available for the database. Event 4114 is written if the database has sufficient copies.

- StartDagServerMaintenance.ps1: This script is designed to prepare a server within a DAG for maintenance by taking it offline in a controlled manner after transitioning all active databases to other servers within the DAG. It also pauses the node in the Windows Failover Cluster for the DAG so that it cannot become the PAM, suspends database activation for mailbox databases, and blocks the DatabaseCopyAutoActivationPolicy for the server so that databases cannot be moved to it during maintenance.

- StopDagServerMaintenance.ps1: This script reintroduces a server into a DAG after it has been maintained. All of the suspended operations are resumed and the server becomes a valid target for database activation again. However, resources are not moved back to the server, as this operation must be performed by an administrator.

- CollectOverMetrics.ps1: This script analyzes the events logged about DAG operations in a specified period (by default, the last day is used). The events logged in the crimson channel discussed previously provide the input data and its output is an HTML format report that lists important transition events that occur for databases within the DAG during the report period.

- CollectReplicationMetrics.ps1: This script collects data about replication operations in real time by contacting servers within a DAG to capture current replication statistics on a regular basis over a measurement period. The data are then analyzed and reported in a .csv file that can be opened and analyzed with Microsoft Excel. Figure 8-33 illustrates typical output for a 10-minute measurement period. The interesting data include the rate at which transaction logs are generated, copied, and replayed for the various databases.

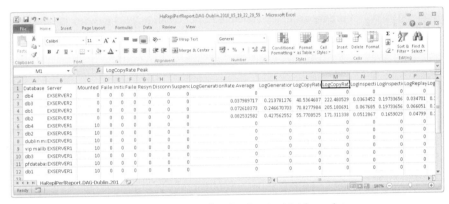

Figure 8-33 Viewing output from the CollectReplicationMetrics script.

INSIDE OUT   These are worth another look

It's fair to say that the original versions of the CollectOverMetrics and CollectReplicationMetrics scripts exhibited many rough edges and some of the documented parameters simply didn't work. Part of this was due to the lack of experience of DAG operations in many diverse environments; part of it was because the developers didn't understand exactly what data would be of most use to administrators to understand the functioning of their DAGs. These scripts received a complete overhaul for SP1 and are now more robust and useful, so you should give them another try if you attempted to use the RTM versions and concluded that they just didn't work.

You can find details about the available parameters and other important information about the scripts on TechNet. Apart from their intended purpose, scripts like this are great learning tools for administrators who want to develop their own scripts to automate monitoring and operations.

Classic clusters are no more

Microsoft has removed support for classic clusters in Exchange 2010 and now focuses firmly on continuous log replication within a DAG as the best approach to achieve high availability within the product. Exchange first supported clusters through the "Wolfpack" technology in Exchange 5.5 in 1997 and since that time clusters (referred to as Single Copy Clusters, or SCC in Exchange 2007) have had a checkered history. On the one hand, clusters were the only game in town in terms of high-availability Exchange servers for a long time until third-party asynchronous data replication solutions became generally available from Exchange 2003 onward. On the other hand, clusters are complex and expensive and have always been so. Extra hardware is required, special procedures are used to install Windows and Exchange on clusters, not all software operates smoothly (or at all) on clusters, and administrators need to have familiarity with cluster operations before they can work effectively. Furthermore, critics of clusters observe the following drawbacks:

- If the Store process fails on a cluster, the cluster restarts the process on the same physical server and no failover occurs. Thus, if the problem exists on that physical server, the problem will persist until an administrator intervenes to solve it.

- Clusters do not solve the problem of storage failures either in the dedicated storage used for the operating system and other important files or the shared storage used by the cluster nodes. If a catastrophic failure occurs in the shared storage, it can knock out the complete cluster as Exchange will not be able to transition storage groups from one node to another.

- Because clusters do not protect against storage failures, they cannot protect mailbox and public folder databases, the heart of Exchange and the most important data used by the messaging system. To protect these data, you have to invest in other technology (such as asynchronous data replication) to ensure that they will be available even if a catastrophic storage failure occurs.

- Third-party additions are required to implement cluster failover across multiple sites.

- SCC clusters require shared SAN storage and cannot operate on lower-cost disks.

Critics acknowledge that clusters do provide some value by protecting against a server failure such as a system "bluescreen," but point out that these failures are now relatively uncommon and that this kind of failure is easy to recover through a server reboot.

Other value is gained by the ability of administrators to apply patches or upgrades to a passive node in the cluster and then move the patched node to become the active node, which is then upgraded. Finally, clusters provide value in some backup solutions as passive nodes can perform backup operations without interfering with the active nodes. Worthy as they are, these advantages could not deliver sufficient advantage in Microsoft's eyes to continue with classic Exchange clusters, especially in view of the engineering investment required to continue the development of Exchange (including service packs, hot fixes, and roll-up releases) on clusters and to support customers who deployed them.

The success of log replication in Exchange 2007 provided Microsoft with a way to increase Exchange's high availability by leveraging native product features that the Exchange engineering team could control and develop through initiatives such as the DAG. From an engineering perspective, this approach is very logical because the Exchange engineering team now has control over the full solution rather than having to rely on other groups to deliver major components. Exchange still relies on Windows Failover Cluster technology and Active Directory, but all of the basic building blocks for high availability are now owned by a single engineering group. The loss of classic clusters will be lamented by customers who have invested in this technology, but it is a logical consequence of Microsoft's decision to refocus their investment in their own technology.

Chapter 8

On to protecting data

We've spent a lot of time discussing how to store information in mailbox and public folder databases. The nature of IT is that accidents happen and hardware fails in even the most well-managed environments. Because these unfortunate events happen, we have to protect ourselves with backup copies, even if our data are replicated to many places around the world. After all, there's nothing like a nice, warm, successful backup to make an administrator feel safe.

Backups and Restores

B ACKUPS have been an integral part of a system administrator's life for as long as I can remember, and although that's a long time, backups have been around for even longer. Faulty disks, server outages, administrative hiccups, software and hardware bugs, and other glitches raise the potential to lose data on any computer system. If data loss is in the air, you need a backup to have a secure feeling that you can recover without breaking a sweat. The advent of the Database Availability Group (DAG) and other developments in Exchange 2010 creates some new and interesting aspects that you have to consider as you lay out your backup strategy. Maybe we shall arrive at a point where backups are less necessary than they once were, or maybe we will have to continue making backups but in a slightly different way. Then there's the question of restores. There is much to discuss, so let's get down to business.

An interesting philosophical question

If DAGs work the way that Microsoft expects them to and deliver a robust high availability environment for Exchange, the theory is that we will be able to change the attitude toward backup and restore that has existed since the first version of Microsoft Exchange. Backups have been the administrator's solution to logical and physical database corruptions that enable a system to be returned to a particular point in time or to recover data when items in mailboxes or complete mailboxes are deleted in error. Microsoft Exchange Server 2010 creates a new scenario where:

- Databases can have many copies, so a failure on one server does not render a database inaccessible.

- Larger mailboxes (protected by replicated databases), retention holds, and deleted item recovery make it more likely that users can recover their own data if they delete items in error.

- Lagged copies of databases offer protection against logical database corruption.

Do we need traditional backups?

With a DAG in place and multiple copies replicating for all important mailbox data-bases, do you need to make the same kind of traditional backups of Exchange data on a daily and weekly cycle? Many companies make daily full backups to simplify restore operations by avoiding the need to restore incremental backups. To comply with audit requirements, after a couple of days, the backup tapes are commonly sent to offsite storage and can be retained there for an extended period. This kind of backup cycle has existed since the first mainframes, and in the era of multicopy replication it is fair to ask whether this is the most effective way to protect critical data so as to be able to recover from catastrophic failures and restore to a certain point in time to respond to legal dis-covery requests or to recover data for users.

Some installations will always need to make backups because of legal or other reasons. For the others, it will be interesting to see how backup regimes change as DAGs are deployed. I suspect that backups will continue to provide a safety blanket until admin-istrators have had the time to become accustomed to how DAGs work. Confidence will increase over time, especially as administrators go through some outages and have the opportunity to see how DAGs cope. We might then see an increasing number of Exchange installations go "backup-less" and depend completely on DAG protection.

The initial response of most administrators is that backups work, so why change? This is a fair position to take until you realize that technology is all about change and the ways of working that were appropriate and delivered cost-effective results yesterday might not be the same today. Exchange 2010 is the first version to support multicopy replication; it is also the first version to have the I/O characteristics to be able to leverage Serial ATA (SATA) stor-age effectively. Technology has improved to a point where cheap disks provide reasonable storage for data, especially when it exists in multiple other locations, and network band-width is cheap enough to allow for replication over multiple sites. We are therefore at a point where the technology has changed to such a degree that we should analyze existing operational procedures to determine whether a better job is possible. This analysis needs to take into account the following factors:

- The legal and audit requirements for the preservation of data with which your orga-nization must comply.

- The cost of recovery from traditional backups versus keeping deleted data in an extended dumpster or from an archive mailbox. Exchange 2007 deployments typi-cally have the vast majority of their data in the active database with some percentage in the dumpster. With the ability to deploy very large mailboxes, the ability to store many weeks or even months of deleted items in the dumpster, and the use of archive mailboxes that are integrated into the client interface, the need to recover offline or deleted data should not arise as often as before.

- The cost of recovery of a complete database from tape backups (or Volume ShadowCopy Services [VSS] snapshots or clones) rather than from a passive copy of the database.

- The cost of tapes, drives, and onsite and offsite storage and the equivalent costs of storing VSS-based backups—do you need as many backups, what rotation is used, and so on.

- The ability to retrieve data from outside the normal backup cycle. For example, assume that your company has to answer a sexual harassment claim where the evidence might reside in messages sent six months ago. What steps are necessary to retrieve these data?

- The test and validation of the operational steps required to recover from different types of outages ranging from a storage failure that affects one database to the loss of servers that host multiple database copies. Apart from anything else, knowing exactly what to do to restore service and access to data quickly and effectively is an absolute prerequisite to convince management that change is possible.

The answers to these questions will guide you to a cost–benefit assessment of whether your organization is ready to operate without backups of Exchange data (you might still need traditional backups for other applications) and how soon you would be able to make the switch after your deployment of Exchange 2010 is complete.

Obviously, each of the points raised has to be argued within the operational context of the company that deploys Exchange 2010. The dumpster is a good example. It has existed in Exchange for about 10 years and serves as an excellent way to allow users to recover items that they have deleted in error without administrative support. Typically, organizations configure the dumpster to store between 7 and 14 days of deleted items to allow users sufficient time to realize that they have deleted something that they really need and recover it before the Store removes the item from the database. Longer retention periods, perhaps up to six months, are often configured for specific mailboxes such as those used by executives. Items in the dumpster do not count against a mailbox quota, and—depending on how active a user is in terms of receiving, generating, and deleting email—the dumpster might be about 10 percent of the size of the mailbox. Some organizations use retention periods of up to two months and the dumpster then adds about 25 percent overhead. However, this overhead is a small price to pay because the dumpster saves a huge amount time for administrators by avoiding the need for single item restores. Ten percent of a 1 GB mailbox is 100 MB.

If you increase mailbox sizes to 10 GB you could have a dumpster of 1 GB. Is that acceptable? Well, if you have to back up those data every day it will certainly add to the time required for backups and restores. However, if you keep everything online and use database replication to protect data, then the 1 GB overhead doesn't sound quite so bad, and there is a huge cost savings in operator time if some or all backup operations can be avoided. This discussion is an example of how new technology and new features will provoke a review of how operations occur today in an attempt to exploit the new technology and arrive at a cost-efficient balance that meets the requirements of the organization.

The Windows Server Backup plug-in for Exchange

Over many years of Exchange, you were able to use the standard NTBACKUP utility to back up databases to disk or tape. The backups were based on an Extensible Storage Engine (ESE) application programming interface (API) that backed up or restored data as a stream to tape or disk, rather than the VSS snapshot-based backups that are used today. Although tape backups were certainly effective, the growing size of databases meant that it took longer and longer to perform backups, even with faster tapes and sophisticated tape libraries. When they first supported Exchange 2007 SP1 on Windows Server 2008, Microsoft decided to remove the ability to make streaming backups for Exchange databases when they decided on an exclusive focus on VSS-based backups for applications. This development caused a big problem for small to medium companies as they tended to be the group that used streaming backups. Larger companies had larger databases and usually had more sophisticated backup solutions that had evolved to use VSS and so were not as heavily affected.

Microsoft's response was to provide a VSS plug-in for Windows Server Backup called WSBExchange.exe that is installed on a server with the installation of the mailbox role for Exchange 2007 SP2 and Exchange 2010. A number of differences exist in the way that Windows Server Backup works compared to NTBACKUP, and there are a few limitations that you have to consider as you plan for backups, so it's worth taking some time to play with Windows Server Backup to perform some backup and restore some databases on a test server. Here are the major points that you need to be aware of:

- The original version of Windows Server Backup could only take VSS-based backups of complete volumes. Exchange databases are included along with all the other data on the volume if they are present. You cannot isolate a single database to be backed up as all databases that exist on the volume will be processed. This issue is addressed with the combination of Windows Server 2008 R2 and Exchange 2010 SP1, where you can select individual directories such as those that contain Exchange mailbox databases for Windows Server Backup to copy.

- You have the choice of making full VSS backups or copy VSS backups. The difference is that transaction logs are truncated following a successful full backup, whereas they are not truncated following a copy backup. In this context, successful means that the consistency check performed against the databases is valid and the volume is fully copied.

- To restore a mailbox or a single database, you restore the database from the backup to a different volume and then use the files to constitute a recovery database.

- Remote backups are not supported. You have to run the backup job on the server that hosts the databases.

- The backup files can be created on a local drive or on a remote network share. You cannot back up directly to tape, so if you have a requirement such as the need to create backup tapes for storage at a remote archival facility, you have to back up to disk first and then move the backup files to tape.

- You can restore a database to the original location or to a different disk. Restoring to the original location overwrites any files that exist in that place. All of the databases backed up in a volume must be restored together. The process is automatic, and you don't need to dismount the database or select the database property *This Database Can Be Overwritten By A Restore* as was the case in previous version of Exchange. An automatic overwrite is a scary prospect as it creates the potential for inadvertent problems if you make a mistake. For example, you might have a problem with one database on a logical unit number (LUN) and want to restore from backup, but you forget that there are two other databases on the LUN that have no problems. When you restore, you overwrite all three databases! You are better off restoring a database to a different location and validating that the correct restore has occurred and then copying files manually. A database restored to a different location can also be mounted by Exchange and used as a recovery database.

- Mount points are only supported when Exchange 2010 is deployed on Windows Server 2008 R2. If you run Exchange 2010 on Windows Server 2008 SP2, you must use drive letters for the volumes that hold the Exchange databases.

Now that we understand how Windows Server Backup works with Exchange databases, let's clarify some points about VSS.

Exchange and Volume ShadowCopy Services

Microsoft introduced VSS in Windows Server 2003. Exchange 2003 was the first version to support VSS for the backup and restore of databases, and after some inevitable problems (caused by lack of knowledge in the administrator community as well as software glitches), its implementation in both Windows and Exchange has gradually evolved and improved. VSS has three major components:

- The *requester* is a backup application such as Backup Exec or Microsoft System Center Data Protection Manager (DPM).

- The *provider* is a Windows component that mediates access to a VSS copy.

- The *writer* is an application-specific component that prepares data for backup. For example, the Exchange writer has to tell ESE to flush its memory cache to disk to ensure that a complete backup is taken.

The exact details of what occurs when you run a VSS backup for Exchange depend on the backup application that you use. You can follow how the backup progresses by looking at the events logged in the Application Event Log. The general flow is as follows:

- The backup application (the requester) contacts VSS (the provider) to indicate that it wishes to access an Exchange database. The user interface (UI) of the backup application allows administrators to state what databases they want to include and this information is passed to the provider.

- VSS calls the Exchange writer to indicate that a backup has been requested. This is the PrepareBackup stage and it forces ESE to flush data, close off the current transaction log, and pause the Lazy Writer and Log Writer processes that take care of writing data into the cache and into transaction logs.

- VSS then tells the Exchange writer to "freeze" the target databases to create a point in time for the backup. A database won't accept new write requests while it is frozen.

- ESE waits until its data are flushed and processes are paused before signaling the requestor that the target databases are frozen.

- Once everything is frozen, VSS creates a snapshot, which is placed on another disk.

- After the snapshot is complete, VSS "thaws" Exchange to allow normal Store processing to restart. The Lazy Writer and Log Writer processes resume. Users are usually unaware that a pause has occurred, especially if they use Outlook in cached Exchange mode.

- The backup application performs a consistency check to ensure that it has good copies of the database files and transaction logs and then removes (truncates) the backed up transaction logs from disk.

- The backup application signals success and disconnects from VSS.

After a snapshot is taken, it is common practice to run another job to move to the snapshot from disk to tape so that it can be taken offsite for archival or business continuity purposes.

Making an Exchange 2010 backup

Although the arguments advanced by some observers that you can operate a backup-less regime for Exchange 2010 if you deploy sufficient database copies within a well-designed DAG are interesting, few administrators are yet at the point where they trust software and hardware enough to accept the premise. Thankfully, making a backup with Windows Server Backup is reasonably painless, as long as you don't have passive database copies on a server. We'll get to that topic in due course, but for now let's consider how to make a simple backup on a server that only hosts active databases. This server could be a standalone server or be in a DAG. Public folder databases cannot have copies and are always in an active state, so they pose no problems for backups and are included if present on a server.

Windows Server Backup presents a number of options through a wizard that works through some steps to create a backup job. Once it starts to process the databases, you don't need to keep the backup application open; it's quite happy to proceed to completion in the background if you close the wizard page. You can check the event log or Windows Server Backup later on to determine whether the backup was successful.

1. Start Windows Server Backup. Select the option to make a backup now.

2. Select Different Options to allow you to add the volumes that you want to back up. Then select Custom to select the volumes. Remember that any and all Exchange databases on these volumes will be included in the backup. Make sure that you include all relevant volumes if databases and transaction logs are located on different volumes.

3. Click Advanced and then select VSS Full Copy to make sure that the transaction logs are truncated following a successful backup.

4. Select the destination for the backup. This can be a local disk or a remote network share. Clearly a local disk will be faster. Windows Server Backup will validate that you have the permission to write to the selected destination. Make sure that you have sufficient free disk space in the destination. Windows Server Backup will write a set of XML files containing backup metadata and the Virtual Hard Disk (VHD) files for each volume to this location.

5. Validate the backup options that you have selected and proceed to the backup.

    Windows Server Backup sets up the necessary files and folders in the backup destination.

Chapter 9

Windows Server Backup then requests that Exchange perform a consistency check on the databases to ensure that they are suitable for backup (Figure 9-1). Each database is checked separately. If the consistency check fails, Windows Server Backup flags the problem in the Application Event Log but continues the backup. However, although the Exchange databases and transaction logs will be on the backup copy, they cannot be used for restores.

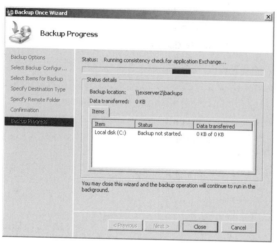

Figure 9-1 Windows Server Backup performs an Exchange consistency check.

Windows Server Backup copies the volumes to the selected destination (Figure 9-2).

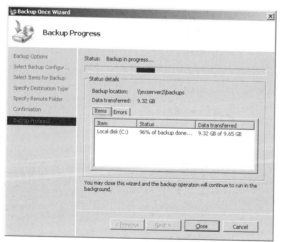

Figure 9-2 Windows Server Backup copies Exchange data.

After all volumes are processed, Windows Server Backup exits and updates the backup history for the local server.

The different steps taken by the backup job can be traced by examining the events logged in the Application Event Log. Table 9-1 lists a sample set of events logged during a backup operation for a DAG member node that hosts several databases. The databases might have multiple copies on other servers. If the databases use circular logging, Exchange might not perform log truncation, especially if the backup is made at times of low user demand when logs are not being produced. Event 9827 is logged when log truncation is not required. On the other hand, if the database does not use circular logging, Exchange will proceed to truncate logs following a successful full backup and will log event 9780 instead.

> **Note**
>
> Several events with the same identifier are generated for some of these steps. For example, event 2001 is logged for each database as ESE freezes it in preparation to make the backup.

Table 9-1 **Backup events**

Event id	Source	Event
9606	MSExchangeIS	VSS writer is prepared to process databases.
2005	ESE	Shadow copy starting; ESE creates an instance to allow it to access the databases.
9811	MSExchangeIS	The database engine prepares each database mounted on server for the backup.
2001	ESE	ESE freezes each database.
9610	MSExchangeIS	Freeze successful.
2003	ESE	Freeze ends.
9612	MSExchangeIS	Databases are thawed successfully.
3156	MSExchangeIS	Databases are mounted for the ESE instance that will make the backup.
224 or 225	ESE	ESE reports log truncation status. Event 224 is logged when log truncation occurs (and notes the file names of the truncated logs); event 225 is logged when log truncation is not required.
9827 or 9780	MSExchangeIS	Both events indicate that the backup is successful. Event 9827 is logged when no log files are truncated; 9780 when log files have been truncated.
2006	ESE	ESE concurs that the full backup is successful.

| 9618 | MSExchangeIS | Exchange VSS writer closes down. |
| 9648 | MSExchangeIS | Backup closes down. |

Following a successful full backup, Windows Server Backup truncates the transaction logs for the databases and updates the Last Good Backup date on the database properties. You can check this date by selecting a database with Exchange Management Console (EMC) and viewing its properties (Figure 9-3). Alternatively, use this command to view the backup status for a server:

```
Get-MailboxDatabase -Server 'ServerName' -Status | Select Name, LastFullBackup
```

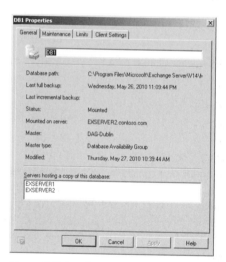

Figure 9-3 Database properties reveal the date of the last successful backup.

A variation on the theme is to scan for all mailbox databases in the organization that have never been backed up. The *–Status* parameter is important because it forces Exchange to retrieve information about backup dates. If you don't specify the *–Status* parameter, all databases will be listed because Exchange will have null values for backup dates:

```
Get-MailboxDatabase -Status | Where {$_.LastFullBackup -eq $Null} | Select Name
```

If a public folder database exists on a server, you will have to issue a separate command:

```
Get-PublicFolderDatabase -Status | Where {$_.LastFullBackup -eq $Null} | Select Name
```

INSIDE OUT   Test your backups to make sure that restores work!

The operations performed by more sophisticated backup applications such as Microsoft System Center DPM, Symantec Backup Exec, or HP Data Protector differ in detail but are similar in concept and flow. All of the major backup products have now been updated to support Exchange 2010, including the ability to make backups of active and passive databases managed by a DAG. Even so, it is a good idea to consult with your backup vendor to determine whether any special steps have to be taken to ensure that you operate a solid backup regime that reliably restores data if necessary.

The backup complexities posed by passive database copies

The Exchange plug-in for the Windows Server Backup utility supports online backups for mailbox databases, but it is not designed to support the backup of database copies in a DAG. The utility works and will take a backup of a DAG member, but only if all database copies on the server are active. If passive copies exist on a server, the backup will proceed and copy the data, but the consistency check fails and the backups therefore cannot be used for a subsequent restore operation. The problem here is that passive database copies are not mounted by the Store in the same way as active databases. Instead, the passive copies are accessed by the Microsoft Exchange Replication Service to replay transaction logs replicated from the servers that host the active copies. A separate VSS writer is required to allow Windows Server Backup to access the passive databases through the Microsoft Exchange Replication Service.

> ### Tip
> It is entirely possible that Microsoft will update the Windows Server Backup utility over time to cope more elegantly with the complexities posed by active and passive database copies within a DAG, so this is a good area to test using the latest software before you go into production. The results reported here were observed using Exchange 2010 SP1 running on Windows Server 2008 R2 servers.

As production DAG members are likely to host both active and passive copies, a more sophisticated solution such as the Microsoft System Center DPM is usually deployed to make backups in most DAG environments. If you really don't want to pay for additional backup software, you could come up with a scheme of moving active databases between servers so that they can be backed up with Windows Server Backup. The idea is that you have to move all the active databases to a server and all the passive databases off that

Chapter 9

server before you proceed to take a backup. This is possible, but it's obvious that such a scheme is intensely manual, prone to error, and likely to cause disruption for users. It's a better idea to bite the bullet and invest in backup software that can handle the complete set of configurations that can exist in a DAG, including the potential need to back up public folder databases along with active and passive copies of mailbox databases. Check with your current backup software provider to ensure that the current version of your backup software is qualified to support DAG operations, heeding any advice that he might have about how to perform efficient backups and restores within a DAG.

INSIDE OUT Passive database copies and active server load

It can be desirable to make backups of passive database copies to relieve load off the active server. Some deployments group passive copies on a dedicated server that is only used for administrative operations and make backups only on that server, but this might not be possible depending on the number of passive copies that have to be deployed across the available servers in the DAG.

As we discussed in the section covering Windows Server Backup, the truncation or deletion of transaction logs that are no longer required occurs following a successful full backup of an active database. After you complete a backup of an active database copy, the Replication service on the server hosting the active database communicates with the Information Store service to update it with the backup status. The Information Store notes that a successful backup has been performed and updates the header of the database with the information about the backup status, date and time, and so on. The header data are replicated along with other database updates to all the servers that host copies. Code in Eseback.dll then calculates which transaction logs are no longer required after the backup and removes them from the server where the backup occurred. The removal of these transaction logs on the active server is signaled to the Replication service on the servers that host database copies to allow the local Replication service to truncate the same logs on those servers.

Restoring to a recovery database

If you operate a DAG and experience a server or storage outage, you should be able to switch over to a database copy and continue to serve users while you work on the problem. The value of DAGs is expressed in that short sentence: Service continues despite a storage or server outage. Of course, this assumes that you have sufficient database copies in place to cope with the failure and that the failure doesn't knock out multiple database copies. If you don't operate a DAG and suffer a storage failure, you might need to revert to a recovery from backup.

INSIDE OUT The realities of deleted items recovery

Even within a DAG, you might still need to access a backup to recover data that are inaccessible any other way. Extended deleted item recovery periods help to push the work down to users who delete something and then find that they really need the item back in their mailbox, but Murphy's Law dictates that administrators only consider changing the default 14-day deleted items retention period immediately after they have been contacted by a user who deleted an important item 15 days ago. You might be able to deflect the recovery request by citing the high cost and manual work involved in retrieving the item, but you might be forced to do the work anyway, especially if the requester is an executive.

Windows Server Backup supports the recovery of Exchange 2010 databases to the same location from which they were originally backed up or to a different location. All of the databases and their transaction logs found on a complete volume are restored in both cases. Recovery to the same location is the approach to use when a disk has had to be replaced and you want to restore matters back to a point in time state. Recovery to a different location is the approach taken when you want to be able to access and retrieve data in one or more mailboxes in a backup set. This approach leverages a recovery database, the successor to the Recovery Storage Group (RSG) used in Exchange 2003 and Exchange 2007. A recovery database is a database that has been recovered from a backup to a location where it is accessible to Exchange. The recovery database contains disconnected mailboxes because they are not connected to Active Directory user accounts, but you can connect to the mailboxes to fetch data and move the data into mailboxes in regular databases to make the data available to users.

Note
You cannot restore a public folder database to a recovery database, which is designed only to accommodate restores of mailbox databases.

> ## Performing a dial-tone database recovery operation
>
> Recovery databases are also used in a *dial-tone database recovery* operation. In this scenario, you have a database that is inaccessible due to a failure, and you want to get users back online as quickly as possible while you work behind the scenes to fix the underlying problem and recover data from backup. *Dial-tone* refers to the restoration of service as a priority. The first step is to create a new database, followed by reassigning the user mailboxes affected by the failure to the empty database. Users can now send and receive new mail but have no access to the content in their original mailboxes. These data are retrieved by restoring a backup of the database to a different location and then swapping the restored database back into production. It might take several hours to fix the problem, restore the original database, and bring it back online. During this time the users will be sending and receiving messages that are stored in the dial-tone database. The magic occurs when you mount the dial-tone database as a recovery database and merge the messages held in it with the content in the production database to create a complete set of user data.

Performing a restore

To begin the restore, you have to identify the following:

- Where the backup set is located

- The date of the backup that we want to restore

- The location to which it will be restored

- What you will do with the restored database afterward

Assuming you have a plan that addresses these questions, you begin by starting the Windows Server Backup utility and pointing it to the location on the same server or in a remote folder where the backup set is located. You can then select the files that you want to recover. Figure 9-4 shows what you can expect to see. In this case, there are three separate mailbox databases available to recover and one has been selected (DB3).

Figure 9-5 shows the next step when you select the recovery location (the folder must already exist and you should make sure that sufficient space is available on the disk) and confirm the parameters for the restore to proceed. If you recover databases to their original location, Exchange will automatically dismount the databases that are currently in that location, perform the restore, and then automatically mount the restored databases to bring them online. Any transaction logs that need to be replayed will then be processed.

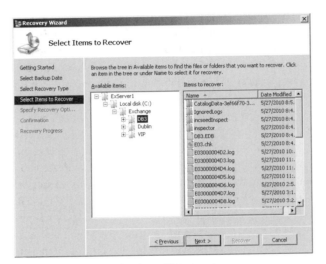

Figure 9-4 Selecting database files to restore.

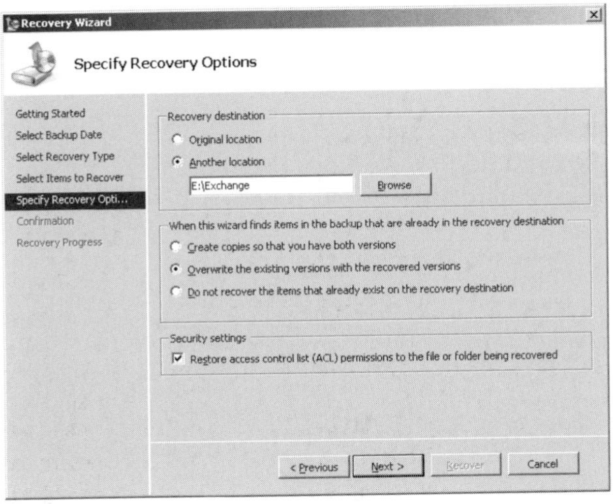

Figure 9-5 Setting the parameters for the restore operation.

Restoring databases is likely to progress faster than the original backup because you usually only need to restore a subset of the data from the complete volume that is in the backup. In Figure 9-6 you can see that several files have been restored and Windows Server Backup is currently processing the DB3 database file. The time required for a restore depends on the speed of the storage subsystem, other server load, and the size of the databases, but you can anticipate that even the slowest server will perform a disk-based restore at more than 300 MB per minute.

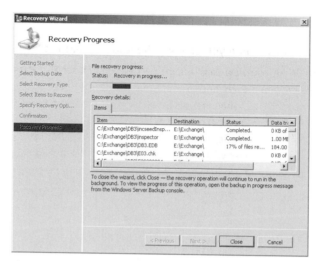

Figure 9-6 Restoring the files for an Exchange database.

After the restore, you will find the databases, transaction logs, and checkpoint files in the restore location. As you can see in Figure 9-7, all the database files and content index catalog folders seem to be in place as you'd expected.

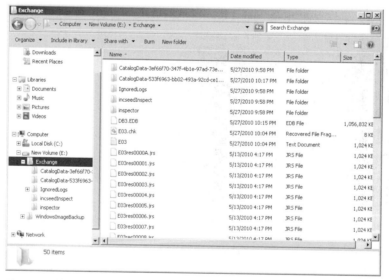

Figure 9-7 Database files after restore.

INSIDE OUT   Know when you can use the Allow Backups to Overwrite flag

One small point: When you view database properties, you will see that databases have a property that allows Exchange to overwrite them during restore operations. This property is meaningless when you use Windows Server Backup because backups and restores are performed on a per-volume basis. When you perform a restore, the Exchange plug-in for Windows Server Backup takes care of dismounting the copy that is in place to allow it to be overwritten. However, the Allow Backups to Overwrite flag is still valid for other backup products that are able to perform more granular restores.

Validating the recovered database

The necessary files are on disk, but we cannot yet connect the database to Exchange to retrieve data. First, we have to check that the database is in a state where it can be mounted on a server as a recovery database. To do this, we run the ESEUTIL program to check the database header. In our case, we want to check the header of DB3.edb, so the command we use is:

```
ESEUTIL/MH DB3.edb
```

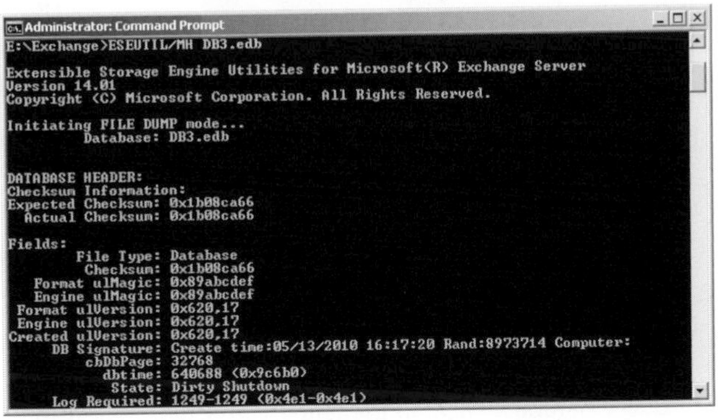

Figure 9-8 Checking a database header with ESEUTIL after it has been restored.

In the output from ESEUTIL (Figure 9-8), we can see that the database state is Dirty Shutdown. Exchange won't let us mount a database while it is in this state, so we need to run ESEUTIL again to replay any outstanding transactions that might exist in the transaction logs that have been restored to bring the database thoroughly up to date. We run the following command:

```
ESEUTIL/R E03 /i /d
```

Chapter 9

/R means that we run ESEUTIL in recovery mode. E03 is the transaction log prefix for the database that we want to recover. We know this by looking for the last transaction log or checkpoint file. You can see that E00.chk is the checkpoint file listed in Figure 9-7, so we know that E00 is the correct prefix. The /i switch means that ESEUTIL will ignore any missing files, and /d is used to indicate the path for the transaction logs. Because we're already positioned in the directory that holds the restored database and its transaction logs, we can leave this value blank. ESEUTIL first reads the checkpoint file to see what transactions are committed in the database and then runs through the outstanding transaction logs to replay their data into the database (Figure 9-9). This process runs quite quickly unless there are thousands of transaction logs to read. Databases that have circular logging enabled that are protected by membership of a DAG will typically have far fewer logs than a database that does not use circular logging.

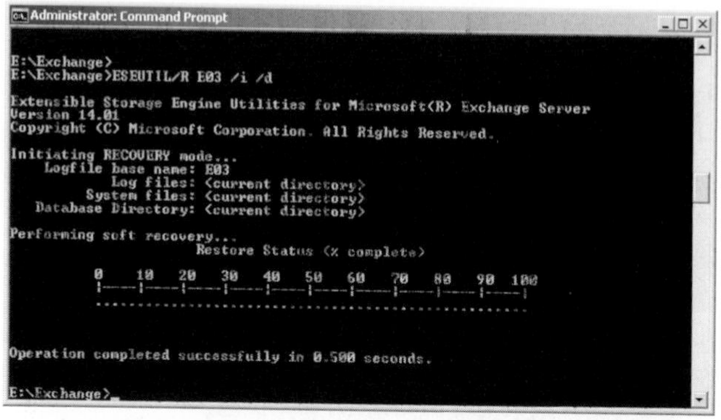

Figure 9-9   ESEUTIL updates the recovered database with transaction log data.

After ESEUTIL has finished recovering the database, we can run ESEUTIL with the /MH switch once more to validate that the database is now in a Clean Shutdown state.

Mounting a recovery database

We now have a database that has been recovered and validated, but it is still not available to Exchange. To allow this to happen, we have to create a pointer to the database and mark it as a recovery database (RDB in Exchange vernacular). This can only be done through Exchange Management Shell (EMS). First, we create the pointer (in Exchange's configuration data in Active Directory) to the database that we have restored using the New-MailboxDatabase cmdlet. The trick here is to specify the *–Recovery* parameter so that Exchange knows that this database will be used for recovery purposes:

```
New-MailboxDatabase –Name 'DB3 Recovery Database' –Server ExServer1 –Recovery
–EDBFilePath 'E:\Exchange\db3.edb' –LogFolderPath 'E:\Exchange'
```

Figure 9-10 Making the recovered database known to Exchange.

As you can see from Figure 9-10, Exchange will let you know that the recovery database can only be mounted if it is in a clean shutdown state. We've already addressed this issue by running ESEUTIL to recover the database and put it into the desired state, so we can proceed. If we view databases through EMC, we can see that the recovery database has now appeared and can be managed in much the same way as any other database (Figure 9-11).

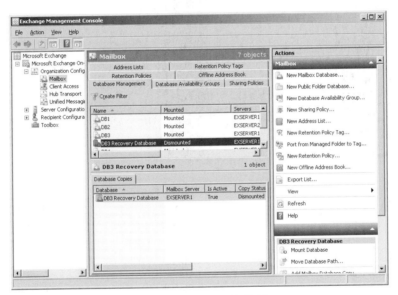

Figure 9-11 The recovery database shows up in EMC.

The next step is to mount the database, which can be done through EMS or EMC. Let's go with the shell:

```
Mount-Database -Identity 'DB3 Recovery Database'
```

> **Note**
>
> If you attempt to mount a database and some of its files are missing, Exchange will warn you that it can't locate some files and offer to go ahead and create a new database and mount it. If you allow Exchange to proceed, you'll end up with a beautiful new and completely empty database, which is what you want sometimes (as in the case of a dial-tone recovery), but not if you intended to restore a complete set of database and log files.

When the database mounts, it creates a new checkpoint file and transaction log set to capture any changes made to the database while it serves in recovery mode. Now that the database is mounted, we can access it with some of the mailbox database cmdlets. For example, to discover the names of the mailboxes and the number of items that each mailbox holds in the database, we could use a command like this.

```
Get-MailboxStatistics –Database 'DB3 Recovery Database' | Select DisplayName,
ItemCount | Format-Table –AutoSize
```

DisplayName	ItemCount
Pelton, David (HQ)	74
Shen, Alan	41
Shah, Niraj (China HQ)	37
Online Archive - Redmond, Tony	126
Camelbeke, Geert	11
Akers, Kim	100
Online Archive - Akers, Kim	7
Smits, Guntars	31
Redmond, Conor (IT)	43
Shen, Paul (China HQ)	39
Peled, Yael (IT)	26
Solovay, Andrew	30
Galway Conference Room	17
Parker, Darren	20
Redmond, Tony	1053
Simpson, David (Sales)	39
Pais, Wilson	21
SystemMailbox{3ef66f70-347f-4b1e-97ad-73e9ff908d0e}	1

This information is useful because it tells us what is in the database. However, we can't use cmdlets such as Get-Mailbox to retrieve information about an individual mailbox in the recovery database. We have to use the Restore-Mailbox cmdlet to get information from a mailbox in a recovery mailbox and move it back into another online database where users can access the recovered data.

Restoring mailbox data

Restore-Mailbox and New-MailboxRestoreRequest (introduced in SP1) are both interesting cmdlets that can be used in a number of different ways to merge information taken from a recovery database into a target mailbox in another database. The target mailbox must be connected to a user account. However, you can direct data taken from a mailbox in the recovery database and move it into a mailbox that has a different name in the target database. Merging means that Exchange doesn't overwrite messages that already exist in the target mailbox; the process is additive and nondestructive. The time required to scan a mailbox and recover items depends on the number of items in the mailbox, server configuration, and system load, but you should be able to scan several hundred items per minute. Exchange keeps you updated with progress as the scan proceeds (Figure 9-12).

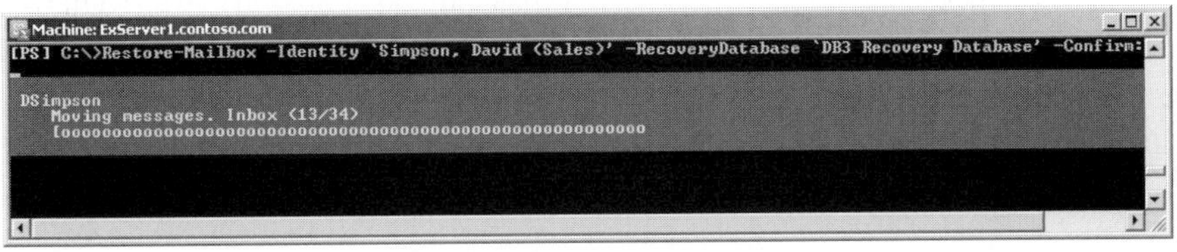

Figure 9-12 Recovering items for a mailbox.

Among the options made available through Restore-Mailbox are the following:

- Recover the data for all mailboxes discovered in the recovery database and restore them into an online database. For example, this command retrieves a list of mailboxes from the DB3 database and restores any mailbox found in the DB3 Recovery Database.

  ```
  Get-Mailbox -Database 'DB3' | Restore-Mailbox -RecoveryDatabase 'DB3 Recovery
  Database'
  ```

- Recover the data for selected mailboxes from the recovery database and restore them into an online database. This example command restores the complete contents of the mailbox for a user called "Simpson, David (Sales)" from the recovery database. We'll include *–Confirm:$False* to prevent Exchange from prompting us whether the command should proceed, as we think we know what we are doing.

  ```
  Restore-Mailbox -Identity 'Simpson, David (Sales)' -RecoveryDatabase 'DB3
  Recovery Database' -Confirm:$False
  ```

- Recover selected data from mailboxes in the recovery database and restore them to an online mailbox. For example, let's assume that user Kim Akers tells you that she has deleted a number of items that she can't recover from the dumpster, but she is really only interested in an item named "Confidential" that was deleted from the Inbox. You can recover the desired item with a command like this:

```
Restore-Mailbox -Identity 'Akers, Kim' -RecoveryDatabase 'DB3 Recovery
Database'
-IncludeFolders '\Inbox' -SubjectKeywords 'Confidential'
-Confirm:$False
```

- Recover selected data and store it in a new folder in a different mailbox. This is a useful technique to recover information from a backup when required by an investigation and the data cannot be located by a discovery search because it has expired and been removed from the database. In this example, we look for information about a project code-named "Athena" in Kim Akers's mailbox and export any matches to the Recovery folder in the mailbox used by the Legal Investigators. Two things are notable in this example. First, specifying the –*ContentKeywords* parameter forces Exchange to search the content of items and attachments, so this can slow things down if there are many large attachments to scan. Second, although you can use any of the regular identifiers (alias, name, and so on) with the –*Identity* parameter to indicate the source mailbox, you have to provide the mailbox name as the value of the –*RecoveryMailbox* parameter. The output of the search is placed in a set of folders under the root folder specified in the command and is identified with the name of the source mailbox and the date and time of the recovery. Figure 9-13 shows how the recovered items appear in the target mailbox.

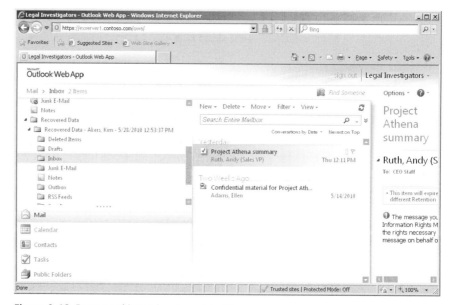

Figure 9-13 Recovered items in a target mailbox.

```
Restore-Mailbox -Identity 'Legal  Investigators' -RecoveryDatabase
'DB3 Recovery Database' -SubjectKeywords 'Athena' -ContentKeywords 'Athena'
-TargetFolder 'Recovered Data' -RecoveryMailbox 'Akers, Kim' -Confirm:$False
```

In all cases, Exchange generates two log files containing details of the operations per-formed by Restore-Mailbox: one is in text format, the other in XML format. Both logs are stored in the \Logging\MigrationLogs directory under the Exchange root directory on the server that processes the restore. The following sample contains a slightly edited version of a text log file.

```
[05/28/2010 11:39:19.0431] [0] Processing object "contoso.com/Exchange
Users/Simpson, David (Sales)".
[05/28/2010 11:39:19.0478] [0] Searching objects "DB3" of type
"MailboxDatabase" under the root "$null".
[05/28/2010 11:39:19.0509] [0] Searching objects "b9f054d2-896f-4207-a9e0-
db1ef3120c52" of type "MailboxStatistics" under the root "DB3 Recovery
Database".
[05/28/2010 11:39:20.0274] [0] [DSimpson] The operation has started.
[05/28/2010 11:39:20.0274] [0] [DSimpson] Approving object.
[05/28/2010 11:39:20.0431] [0] [DSimpson] Opening source mailbox.
[05/28/2010 11:39:20.0446] [0] [DSimpson] Trying to open mailbox by GUID:
       szServerLegacyDN: /o=contoso/ou=Exchange Administrative Group
(FYDIBOHF23SPDLT)/cn=Configuration/cn=Servers/cn=EXSERVER1
       pguidMdb: {533F6963-BB02-493A-92CD-CE1783155B75}
       pguidMailbox: {B9F054D2-896F-4207-A9E0-DB1EF3120C52}
       szServer: EXSERVER1.contoso.com
[05/28/2010 11:39:20.0446] [0] [DSimpson] Open mailbox succeeded.
[05/28/2010 11:39:20.0446] [0] [DSimpson] Opening destination mailbox.
[05/28/2010 11:39:20.0446] [0] [DSimpson] Trying to open mailbox by GUID:
       szServerLegacyDN: /o=contoso/ou=Exchange Administrative Group
(FYDIBOHF23SPDLT)/cn=Configuration/cn=Servers/cn=EXSERVER2
       pguidMdb: {3EF66F70-347F-4B1E-97AD-73E9FF908D0E}
       pguidMailbox: {B9F054D2-896F-4207-A9E0-DB1EF3120C52}
       szServer: EXSERVER2.contoso.com
[05/28/2010 11:39:20.0446] [0] [DSimpson] Open mailbox succeeded.
[05/28/2010 11:39:20.0446] [0] [DSimpson] Moving messages.
[05/28/2010 11:39:20.0446] [0] [DSimpson] Recovering messages.
[05/28/2010 11:39:20.0446] [0] [DSimpson] Merging messages.
[05/28/2010 11:40:27.0259] [0] [DSimpson] 0 items couldn't be moved to the
target mailbox.
[05/28/2010 11:40:27.0259] [0] [DSimpson] Messages moved. Closing connections.
[05/28/2010 11:40:27.0337] [0] [DSimpson] The operation has finished.
```

With Exchange 2010 SP1, you also have the option to use the New-MailboxRestoreRequest cmdlet to recover mailbox data from disconnected mailboxes or those that are in recovery databases. New-MailboxRestoreRequest leverages the asynchronous request model used for mailbox moves, mailbox imports, and mailbox exports that are managed by the Mailbox Replication Service (MRS) and accommodates the need created by SP1 to be able to recover data from a soft deleted mailbox created by a mailbox move operation. The cmdlet is also able to recover data to an archive mailbox. The asynchronous nature of MRS operations means that you don't have to wait for data to be recovered; simply run the command to create a new restore request and go on to do other things while you wait for the request to complete.

This example creates a new mailbox restore request with the New-MailboxRestoreRequest cmdlet. The restore request will read data from the Inbox folder in the mailbox called Akers, Kim from the DB3 Recovery Database and write it into a folder called Recovered Items in a mailbox called Legal Investigators:

```
New-MailboxRestoreRequest –TargetMailbox 'Legal Investigators' –SourceDatabase 'DB3
RecoveryDatabase' –SourceStoreMailbox 'Akers, Kim' –BadItemLimit 5 –TargetRootFolder
'Recovered Items' –SourceRootFolder 'Inbox'  –Name 'Legal Recovery Ref 104'
```

The result is a restore job queued with MRS called "Legal Investigators'\Legal Recovery Ref 104". You can check its progress with the Get-MailboxRestoreRequest cmdlet:

```
Get-MailboxRestoreRequest –Identity 'Legal Investigators'\Legal Recovery Ref 104'
```

Once the job is complete, you can check what it did with the Get-MailboxRestoreRequestStatistics cmdlet:

```
Get-MailboxRestoreRequestStatistics –Identity 'Legal Investigators'\Legal Recovery
Ref 104' | Format-List
```

```
Name                    : Legal Recovery Ref 104
Status                  : Completed
StatusDetail            : Completed
SyncStage               : SyncFinished
Flags                   : IntraOrg, Pull
RequestStyle            : IntraOrg
Direction               : Pull
Protect                 : False
Suspend                 : False
SourceExchangeGuid      : d8f7a889-b430-4791-ad8c-360310f74b1c
SourceRootFolder        : Inbox
SourceVersion           : Version 14.1 (Build 218.5)
SourceDatabase          : DB3 Recovery Database
MailboxRestoreFlags     : Disabled, Recovery
TargetAlias             : LegalInvestigators
TargetIsArchive         : False
TargetExchangeGuid      : 73d598ff-a7ce-4542-8740-b6509424f139
TargetRootFolder        : Recovered Data
TargetVersion           : Version 14.1 (Build 218.5)
TargetDatabase          : DB3
TargetMailboxIdentity   : contoso.com/Exchange Users/Legal Investigators
IncludeFolders          : {}
```

```
ExcludeFolders                   : {}
ExcludeDumpster                  : False
ConflictResolutionOption         : KeepSourceItem
AssociatedMessagesCopyOption     : DoNotCopy
BadItemLimit                     : 5
BadItemsEncountered              : 0
QueuedTimestamp                  : 6/3/2010 10:08:16 PM
StartTimestamp                   : 6/3/2010 10:08:20 PM
LastUpdateTimestamp              : 6/3/2010 10:08:26 PM
CompletionTimestamp              : 6/3/2010 10:08:26 PM
TotalQueuedDuration              : 00:00:04
TotalInProgressDuration          : 00:00:05
MRSServerName                    : ExServer1.contoso.com
EstimatedTransferSize            : 2.414 MB (2,531,099 bytes)
EstimatedTransferItemCount       : 62
BytesTransferred                 : 2.881 MB (3,020,719 bytes)
ItemsTransferred                 : 62
PercentComplete                  : 100
```

INSIDE OUT   Cleaning up after recovery

It is unwise to leave a recovery database in place connected to Exchange or with its files available on disk and potentially accessible to a rogue administrator who holds the necessary permissions and wishes to investigate the contents of the mailboxes in the database. After performing whatever recovery operations are required, you should remove the recovery database and delete the files from disk.

The steps are as follows:

1. Dismount the recovery database.

   ```
   Dismount-Database –Identity 'Sales Recovery Database' –Confirm:$False
   ```

2. Remove the recovery database from Exchange (EMC or EMS).

   ```
   Remove-MailboxDatabase –Identity 'Sales Recovery Database' –Confirm:$False
   ```

3. Delete the database files from the recovery location.

The New-MailboxRestoreRequest cmdlet is not an exact swap for the Restore-Mailbox cmdlet, because it does not boast the same subject and content filtering capabilities that permit the extraction of specific data from a recovery database. Between them, the two cmdlets offer the options of operating interactively or in the background, and over time it's likely that Microsoft will add the missing features to the New-MailboxRestoreRequest cmdlet to allow Restore-Mailbox to be retired.

Complete server backups

Microsoft's focus on database mobility and the break in the link between database and mailbox server has some consequences for backups. In effect:

- Backups are taken on a per-volume level. All databases and transaction logs found on the volume are included in the backup.

- The backups are intended to recover a database or databases following a disk or server failure. In the case of server failure, the Exchange-related configuration data are recovered from Active Directory by running the Exchange Setup program in recovery mode (see Chapter 2, "Installing Exchange 2010"). Separate steps are then taken to recover the data hosted on the server; only one of these steps involves the restore of databases.

- There is no concept of "system state" being included in the Exchange backups. Separate arrangements must be made to secure the Windows configuration for a server. Separate backups are also required for any other application that is installed onto an Exchange server.

- From an Exchange perspective, backups of Exchange servers that do not host the mailbox role only need to focus on configuration data that are not held in Active Directory. For example, if you customize some of the OWA.asp files, you need to make copies of these changes as a server recovery of a Client Access Server (CAS) server will not recover these files. The same is true for changes made to the transport configuration file on hub transport servers.

> **Note**
>
> The obvious issue for administrators that is created by the changes in Exchange 2010 and in the way that Windows System Backup works is that there is no out-of-the-box way to recover a complete server in a single integrated operation. Recovery of an Exchange 2010 mailbox server therefore requires different planning than in previous versions.

Edits to configuration files on hub transport and CAS servers tend to be done once and are then left alone until the next software upgrade comes along, so you don't need to back up these files regularly. However, you do need to make a copy of any updated Exchange configuration or other file that you manually edit and keep it in a safe place to allow for easy access and reapplication in the case of a server restore. In addition, any change made to an Exchange file needs to be documented thoroughly so that other administrators will understand the reason for the change and be able to assess whether the change should be reapplied after a new version, service pack, or roll-up update is installed on a server.

Clients

Now that we have the right hardware in place to have Exchange run smoothly, we can move on to discuss how clients can take advantage of the superb infrastructure that's been created for them to exploit. On to Outlook, Outlook Web App, and the other clients that can connect to Exchange.

MICROSOFT has pursued a multiple client access strategy for Exchange since it first introduced Web access and Post Office Protocol 3 (POP3) support in Microsoft Exchange 5.0. The first browser client was introduced at a time when the set of supported clients was very limited and largely centered on the existing "fat" client (the original Exchange Messaging Application Programming Interface [MAPI] viewer) and Microsoft Outlook 97. Although it could connect to Exchange, the browser interface was slow, only supported Internet Explorer, couldn't scale because it depended on MAPI, and lacked significant functionality, yet it proved that a Web-based interface was viable and laid the basis for a client that has become more and more popular in each new version. Microsoft established the third leg in their client access strategy with the introduction of server-based ActiveSync in Microsoft Exchange 2003 to allow Exchange to deal with an increasing demand for mobile access to mailbox, calendar, and contact information. Of course, RIM's BlackBerry had satisfied the same demand for some years beforehand, but somehow the requirement for mobile access seemed to be more legitimate (at least, for Exchange administrators) when Microsoft delivered ActiveSync. It also made it far cheaper to support mobile clients because ActiveSync is part of the base server and didn't require expensive software licenses or the deployment of additional servers.

Despite some early problems and a Windows Mobile client that continues to lag behind its competitors in terms of usability and features, the level of integration with Exchange that ActiveSync boasts, together with its unbeatable price point (zero extra cost), means that it has had a huge impact in driving mobile access for Exchange.

Microsoft's client access strategy supports the connection of a huge array of clients to Exchange 2010. Exchange Server 2010 supports a variety of different client types.

- Maximum functionality and features are available in Microsoft's own "fat" clients for Windows and Apple Mac that are part of the Office family. Microsoft doesn't support connecting very old versions of Outlook to Exchange 2010, so you'll need to deploy at least Outlook 2003 before you can connect to Exchange 2010. If you don't like buying client software from Microsoft, you can use the Internet Message Access Protocol 4 (IMAP4) or POP3 protocols to connect anything from a free Microsoft client (like Windows Mail) to a mobile device that doesn't support ActiveSync.

- If you decide to use Outlook Web App (OWA), you have a range of supported Web browsers from Internet Explorer to Firefox, Safari, and Chrome. As you'd expect, versions 7 and 8 of Internet Explorer deliver maximum functionality, and you can get the same experience (OWA Premium) if you use Firefox or Safari. However, OWA Premium is supported only when Safari runs on Apple Mac OS X. Other browsers, including Opera, can use the downgraded OWA Basic or light version, which is still highly functional, if not quite as flashy as the premium edition. The full matrix of supported browsers for different versions of Exchange is available at *http://technet .microsoft.com/en-us/library/ff728623.aspx*.

- In the past, Microsoft's strategy for mobile clients has been centered on the partnership of server-based ActiveSync and Windows Mobile clients that run Outlook Mobile. Even today, you need to run Windows Mobile 6.5 or later for clients to enjoy the latest experience, but you can upgrade the Outlook Mobile application on Windows Mobile 6.1 to access the enhanced features delivered by Exchange 2010. I expect that Microsoft mobile clients will continue to deliver highly functional new versions of Outlook Mobile. However, the push to expand the set of available ActiveSync clients has gathered momentum over the last few years, and Microsoft has been very successful in licensing ActiveSync to companies that build mobile clients and mobile applications—from Apple to Google to Nokia to Palm—so it is not difficult to find suitable devices; in fact, restricting the number of device types that connect to Exchange is often a challenge for administrators. If you are among the millions of corporate email users who depend on their BlackBerry, you can continue to use the latest version of RIM's BlackBerry Enterprise Server (BES) to connect BlackBerry devices to Exchange 2010 (an upgrade for BES is necessary to deal with the new application programming interfaces [APIs] introduced in Exchange 2010).

The interesting thing about Microsoft's client access strategy is how much improvement has been made in the Web and mobile platforms in the last few releases. New APIs for browsers, general availability across an extremely wide range of mobile devices, smarter networking, and hard engineering effort has enabled Microsoft to get to a point where they can credibly claim to have delivered on "three screens."

The Outlook question

The perennial issue that comes to mind once Microsoft ships a new version of Exchange is what you should do with Outlook. In the past, Outlook and Exchange had a tenuous relationship. For whatever reasons in the depths of Microsoft politics, the two product groups didn't work together particularly well, and despite the fact that Exchange was easily the most functional and powerful mail server to which Outlook could connect, the focus of the Outlook development group seemed to be far more on Internet mail servers. In some respects, this was natural because far more people use Outlook as part of the Microsoft Office suite in non-Exchange environments (home, college, and connecting to other email systems, including Gmail and Lotus Notes), but it was puzzling at the same time, especially because Outlook's support for IMAP seems weaker than other clients such as Thunderbird or Eudora. Things began to improve in Outlook 2003 when Microsoft did the work to introduce cached Exchange mode and made many changes to improve Outlook's networking demands. Cached Exchange mode has proven to be fundamental for Exchange because without it Microsoft's foray into hosted Exchange online services would be much more difficult. It's also fair to say that the ability of cached Exchange mode to isolate users from network failures has greatly improved the user experience.

Further improvements occurred in Outlook 2007, which was released alongside Exchange 2007, and the two product groups seemed to share a common approach to solving the problems of large-scale enterprise-class deployments. Alas, the release of Exchange 2010 marks a divergence, as Outlook 2010 was released sometime after Exchange appeared to raise the inevitable issue of whether to wait to deploy the latest generations of server and client together or to go ahead with Exchange and deploy Outlook afterward. As we will see, the question isn't simply a matter of deployment timing, because some functionality in Exchange 2010 is dependent on client-side code incorporated in Outlook 2010 or simply works better with Outlook 2010.

Answering this question is easier for small companies than it is for large ones. The law of numbers conspires to create much greater complexity when a new application must be distributed to tens of thousands of desktops and issues such as user training, preparing the help desk to support the rollout, and the cost of new software licenses and potential hardware upgrades are considered. This is the reason so many companies continue to run Outlook 2003 or even earlier clients; they see no logic in going forward with an upgrade that promises great cost for new licenses and deployment while offering little obvious return in the form of user productivity, lower support costs, or anything else. The fact that the Exchange server CALs no longer include a license for Outlook will also make it harder for companies to justify an early upgrade.

However, there is no doubt that Outlook 2010 brings some interesting new functionality to the equation. Whether the new features are worthwhile enough to consider an upgrade is different for every company. To begin the debate, Table 10-1 provides a quick summary of the benefits included in the Outlook versions that you can deploy with Exchange 2010.

Table 10-1 **Comparing different versions of Outlook**

Outlook version	Major benefits for Exchange deployments
Outlook 2003	Introduction of cached Exchange mode and smarter networking to enable faster and more efficient synchronization between server folders and local replicas. Exchange 2010 requires Outlook 2003 SP2.
Outlook 2007	Introduction of AutoDiscover functionality to enable automatic configuration of user profiles. Movement away from public folders as the repository for shared data such as free/busy and Offline Address Book to use Web-based distribution instead. First implementation for managed mail and retention policies.
Outlook 2010	The first 64-bit version of Outlook (also available for 32-bit platforms). Supports features such as MailTips and message tracking from within Outlook. Far more developed and feature-complete version of messaging record management (document retention) policies. Supports cross-organization calendar sharing to help customers deploy in mixed on-premise/hosted deployments. Supports conversation view of email threads (also works with earlier versions of Exchange) as well as the ability to ignore threads you're not interested in. Outlook 2010 also supports personal archives located on Exchange 2010 servers and has the ability to open up to 15 Exchange mailboxes in addition to the primary mailbox.

Outlook 2010 is able to open up to 15 Exchange mailboxes concurrently, not all of which have to belong to the same Exchange organization. By default, Outlook imposes a limit of four mailboxes. This is deliberately set to prevent Outlook from taking up huge amounts of system resources, which would occur if someone attempted to open 10 or 20 mailboxes. However, you can increase the limit for concurrent open mailboxes to 15 by updating the value held in the system registry at HKCU\Software\Microsoft\Exchange\MaxNumExchange.

INSIDE OUT   How the new shared mailbox auto-mapping feature works

Exchange 2010 SP1 includes the ability to auto-map shared mailboxes for Outlook 2010 clients. If you assign Full Access permission to a mailbox using the EMC wizard or the Add-AdPermission cmdlet, Exchange updates the *MsExchDelegateListLink* attribute for the shared mailbox with the distinguished name of the mailbox that is now allowed to open the shared mailbox. When Outlook 2010 connects to Exchange, it receives details of the shared mailbox in the manifest provided by the Autodiscover service and is able to open the shared mailbox underneath the user's primary mailbox. This feature to configure Outlook profiles to include shared mailboxes. However, it depends on the population of the *MsExchDelegateListLink* attribute and any permissions set before the deployment of Exchange 2010 SP1 will not be reflected in the attribute. You therefore have to remove and reassign Full Access permission to shared mailboxes before they automatically appear in Outlook.

Missing functionality when using earlier versions of Outlook

Outlook 2007 and Outlook 2003 are happy to connect to Exchange 2010 but were obviously designed and engineered to operate against previous versions of Exchange and therefore do not include the code necessary to deal with some of the enhancements incorporated in Outlook 2010. To illustrate the point, after you connect Outlook 2007 to Exchange 2010, a number of features are unavailable, including the following:

- No user interface is available to display the MailTips provided by the server.

- Conversation views. Outlook 2007 doesn't understand the internal identifiers that Exchange uses to connect related items into a conversation. The ability to clean up a conversation and remove obsolete items is also missing, as is the Ignore button.

- Integration with Exchange Control Panel (ECP) to access group information, newer Unified Messaging (UM) settings (such as call answering rules), and so on. However, users can still open ECP to access these options.

- Microsoft has announced that they will release code to allow Outlook 2007 to connect to personal archives. This code has not yet been made available to customers at the time of writing.

- Outlook 2007 is able to render voice mail previews as plain HTML in the message body but lacks the control used to play the voice content if you click part of the voice mail preview; Outlook 2007 also cannot process protected voice mail.

- You cannot send Short Message Service (SMS) messages from Outlook 2007.

- There is no user interface to support retention tags and polices. However, Exchange will apply the actions required by retention policies to user mailboxes even if they use Outlook 2007.

If they are configured to use encrypted remote procedure calls (RPCs), Outlook 2003 SP2 clients can connect to Exchange 2010. However, the elimination of User Datagram Protocol (UDP) support in Exchange 2010 causes a problem for Outlook 2003. Outlook 2003 depends on UDP packets for new mail notifications and to update folders in user

Chapter 10

mailboxes. UDP notifications were an appropriate mechanism for this work when clients had to connect over a corporate network (or with a virtual private network [VPN]) to access mailboxes, but they are less useful as connectivity has moved toward a model where pervasive access across the Internet becomes the preferred model. Outlook 2003 supports a polling mechanism as a backup when UDP is not supported. The polling mechanism was provided to support the first Outlook clients that connected to Exchange 2003 servers using RPC over HTTP, but it does lead to a delay of up to one minute before the UDP notification fails and polling delivers notification that a new message has arrived. The problem is less noticeable when Outlook works in cached Exchange mode because of the asynchronous nature of operations, but it still exists. Thus, although you can connect Outlook 2003 SP2 clients to Exchange 2010, users might notice that notifications aren't as snappy as they were before. In order of attractiveness, the available options to address the issue are as follows:

1. Upgrade clients to Outlook 2007 or greater to remove UDP from the equation.

2. Reconfigure Outlook 2003 clients that work in online mode to work in cached Exchange mode (this is always recommended; there are many other advantages to be gained when clients are deployed in cached Exchange mode).

3. Change the polling interval so that notifications arrive faster. By default, Outlook 2003 clients poll every 60 seconds. You can reduce this interval to 10 seconds (Outlook ignores smaller intervals) by updating the system registry on Client Access Server (CAS) servers as described in *http://technet.microsoft.com/en-us/library /aa996515(EXCHG.80).aspx*. A reduced polling interval inevitably generates some increased load on the server, so this is not something to do on a whim.

There are other issues with Outlook 2003 that make this client a less than optimum client for Exchange 2010. The Exchange development group has described the most important issues that affect Outlook 2003 when it connects to Exchange 2010 at *http://msexchangeteam.com/archive/2010/04/23/454711.aspx*. The fact that such a long list of potential problems exists does not make Outlook 2003 bad software, because it was an excellent client when Microsoft first released it in 2003. However, the degree of change that has taken place since in databases, connectivity, and environments has made it difficult for Outlook 2003 to remain as usable as it once was, and it's probably time to refocus efforts on upgrading to a newer client in conjunction with Exchange 2010 deployments.

INSIDE OUT   What is the significance of the UDP problem?

The UDP problem or the list of features only available to Outlook 2010 clients is not mission critical, nor is it sufficient to justify an upgrade for thousands of desktops to Outlook 2010. On the other hand, this list does underscore the close development relationship between client and server and the fact that if you want to achieve maximum functionality from a server, you need to deploy a client that understands how to exploit all of the functionality that the server can offer.

Why new mail notifications seem slower on Outlook

As we've just discussed, Outlook began to transition from using UDP notifications after the introduction of RPC over HTTP. Outlook 2007 and Outlook 2010 use asynchronous RPC notifications because these notifications work through firewalls, whereas UDP usually does not.

Notifications tell Outlook that a change has occurred, such as the arrival of a new message in the mailbox on the server to which it is connected. Outlook still has to fetch details of the change to be able to display it to the user, but processing might be inefficient if Outlook leapt into action immediately. The nature of email is that several changes might occur rapidly at times of peak demand. For example, morning sessions are often marked by flurries of email as users come into work and process their Inboxes before setting out to address the other challenges of the day. If Outlook responded to a notification immediately, it would run the risk that several other new messages might arrive while it is processing the first, which would then force Outlook to engage in a back-and-forth conversation with the server. It is more efficient to batch changes and process them at the same time, which accounts for why you sometimes see several new messages appearing in your Inbox at once when other clients such as Outlook running on a Windows Mobile device display the arrival of individual messages.

When Outlook receives a notification, it sets off a 5-second timer. If no further notification occurs before the timer elapses, Outlook fetches and processes the change. If another notification arrives before the timer expires, Outlook resets the timer and waits again. If the second timer expires, Outlook batches the two notifications and processes them in one operation. However, if continuous changes are detected and the timer keeps being reset, Outlook waits for 60 seconds to let everything settle down on the server and then retrieves whatever is queued and processes these items.

Chapter 10

> **Note**
>
> This mechanism is much more efficient in terms of bytes passing over the wire and in the use of system resources; it avoids a continual dialog between clients and servers during a time when the server is already busy (because it's dealing with a lot of new messages). The mechanism also works well over high-latency networks and is an appropriate way of dealing with the transient interruptions that these networks often experience.

The article at *http://technet.microsoft.com/en-us/library/cc179175.aspx* describes how to configure Outlook 2007 and Outlook 2010 clients to operate in cached mode, including how to alter the 5-second timer interval and the 60-second interval for batched changes. Reducing the timer to, say, 2 seconds will accelerate delivery of new mail at the expense of consuming more system resources to deal with additional synchronization requests. As pointed out earlier, this could have an impact at times of peak demand because you'll force the server to respond to additional requests from clients. For this reason, the wisdom of making a change in this area is unproven. In any case, the only people who are likely to realize that Outlook is slightly slower at announcing the arrival of new messages are (a) those who carry multiple devices and can measure the arrival of a new message on each device, and (b) personnel who insist on being able to access new mail within the nearest nanosecond of its arrival. In most cases, normal human beings don't care very much.

Forcing faster Outlook Anywhere connections

Outlook clients use RPCs to connect to Exchange. The RPCs can flow over TCP or HTTP. Clients seldom need to use HTTP in an environment where clients predominantly connect using an internal network (including VPNs), but an increasing number of connections now occur across the Internet in a mode referred to as Outlook Anywhere. This mode suits users who connect using wireless networks at home or in public places. If a deployment supports many clients who use Outlook Anywhere, you can configure Exchange to force Outlook 2010 clients to attempt to make HTTP connections before they use TCP. This is the reverse of the norm that has applied to date, and its value is that it avoids the need for Outlook to fail in an attempt to connect using TCP before it connects with HTTP, and thus speeds up the time before a client is online. Use this command to make HTTP connections the default mode:

```
Set-OutlookProvider EXPR -OutlookProviderFlags ServerExclusiveConnect
```

This command only affects Outlook 2010 clients. Outlook 2003 and Outlook 2007 clients will continue to operate as before.

To reverse the change:

```
Set-OutlookProvider EXPR -OutlookProviderFlags None
```

Conversation views

Earlier versions of email never included the text of previous messages in replies because doing so would add too much overhead to messages, an issue that was important in the days of dial-up connections and expensive disks. Incorporating all previous replies into messages only became common after PC clients such as Microsoft Mail introduced it as a "feature." Today, including the text of previous messages is default behavior for most email clients and it has become a blight. Although it is sometimes useful to understand the context of a conversation, this extra information is usually unwanted, unnecessary, and the occupant of millions of wasted gigabytes of data that have to be managed and backed up daily.

Most email conversations result in a series of messages with some new information being added in every response. The challenge is to see the valuable information while not being exposed to all the content that you've seen in previous contributions. Exchange 2010 (including OWA) and Outlook 2010 combine in a solution called conversation views. Previous versions of Outlook allow you to click the subject heading to build a primitive form of conversation views in that all of the messages that share a common subject are grouped together. Microsoft also developed some customized Outlook code in the past (used mostly internally within Microsoft) to implement better forms of conversation views, but this code never showed up in any released product.

The new solution compresses conversations into a view where the unique content from each message is shown in the reading pane as the message is selected in the conversation. To do this, new algorithms are used to detect and suppress redundant content from the view displayed to the user. Exchange uses some message properties to decide which messages are actually part of the same conversation. The message properties include the following:

- InternetMessageId

- In-Reply-To

- References

- Subject Prefix

- Normalized Subject

Exchange also maintains a new set of conversation-specific properties to track the items in a conversation. These properties are as follows:

- Conversation Topic

- Conversation Index

- Conversation Index Tracking

- Conversation Identity

For example, if you reply to a message, Exchange knows that the original message and the reply are linked and part of the same conversation and will note this fact, which means that the entire conversation can be viewed as a whole for as long as the items exist in any folder in the mailbox. Figure 10-1 illustrates a conversation that spans five items, one of which is in the Deleted Items folder (and indicated with strikethrough).

Figure 10-1 A threaded conversation shown in OWA.

INSIDE OUT   Conversation views on various platforms

The implementation of conversation views differs slightly across platforms to take account of the different storage and user interface capabilities of each platform. For example, Outlook 2010 is capable of including items that are stored in PSTs in conversations and can therefore do a good job of creating conversation views when connected to servers other than Exchange, including Gmail and Hotmail; OWA can only include items that are available within a mailbox (including the archive mailbox); and Windows Mobile can only show items from the currently selected folder. User interface differences across different client platforms are an inevitable fact of computer life. This is one reason you should be sure to check new platforms to detect possible opportunities for user confusion before introducing a new platform into production.

Older items that have been in mailboxes for a long time or those that originate in non-Exchange systems present a challenge for conversation views because all of their attributes might not be populated in the same way as are newly created items. To get around the problem, Exchange determines the items that form a conversation by using message subjects.

> ## CAUTION!
>
> Sometimes this technique—associating conversations by using message subjects—can associate items that are not part of the same conversation together because they share the same subject. This is one reason to be careful with the Ignore feature in Outlook, which moves a selected item and all other current and future items in the same conversation to the Deleted Items folder.

Exchange attempts to avoid problems caused by older messages that share the same subject with a more recent message by only adding items to conversations if they are within 72 hours of each other, on the basis that the accuracy of including items in conversations based on message subject degrades over time. If you change the subject on a message before you send a reply, you effectively create a new conversation. There is one exception to this rule, and that's when a user starts off a conversation with a message with a blank subject and someone subsequently updates the subject.

Outlook 2010 includes additional code to allow it to implement conversation views when connected to older Exchange servers and non-Exchange servers. This code works, but because it has to function without any help from the server, it is slower and less accurate in terms of linking items together in a conversation than when Exchange 2010 and Outlook 2010 work together. In addition, the client has to process all actions for a conversation. For example, you can decide to "ignore" a conversation, which means that Outlook will automatically move any messages in that conversation into the Deleted Items folder. If Outlook 2010 is connected to a legacy Exchange server, it has to process new items as they arrive to decide whether they belong to the conversation that you've just ignored. Outlook then has to suppress the items that it determines to be in the conversation.

To improve efficiency of conversation processing, Exchange 2010 stores details of actions to apply to conversations in a hidden folder called Conversation Action Settings. The advantage of this approach is that the data are available to the server rather than being limited to Outlook. Thus, if you decide that you want to ignore a conversation, Exchange processes new items as they arrive into the mailbox and all clients see the same effect.

Because some limitations exist in applying conversation views to folders hosted on non-Exchange 2010 servers, Outlook 2010 allows you to suppress conversation views for selected or all folders. From the View menu, select the Show As Conversations check box. Outlook then asks whether to suppress conversations for just the currently selected folder or for all folders. Later on, after you move the mailbox to an Exchange 2010 server, you can reverse the operation and re-enable conversations (Figure 10-2).

Figure 10-2 Enabling conversations in Outlook 2010.

Outlook doesn't provide an option to allow users to become engaged in a conversation after they ignore it, so if you make a mistake and decide that an ignored conversation really is important, the only way to reverse the action is to select an item from the conversation in the Deleted Items folder, open it, and then click the highlighted Ignore button. Outlook then prompts you to verify that you really want to stop ignoring the conversation (Figure 10-3). If you click Stop Ignoring Conversation, all of the items for the conversation will be moved back into the Inbox.

Figure 10-3 Option to stop ignoring a conversation.

INSIDE OUT Control conversation size in Outlook 2010

You can expand and collapse the view to see the hidden content, but most of the time you'll want to see just what's new in the conversation. Outlook 2010 also includes a useful Clean Up Conversation option that removes redundant items from an email thread. These are great ways to keep a growing mailbox under control.

The user options available in Outlook 2010 and OWA to process conversations are shown in Figure 10-4. OWA doesn't support the ability to clean up a conversation, so its options are limited to how conversations are displayed in the user interface. Outlook 2010 allows you to control what messages are cleaned up from conversations and where the removed messages are placed. It also supports a more sophisticated set of conversation views than OWA.

Of course, the notion of conversation views is not new and you might wonder why it has taken Microsoft more than 12 years of development to implement a feature that simply makes good sense, but at least it's available now.

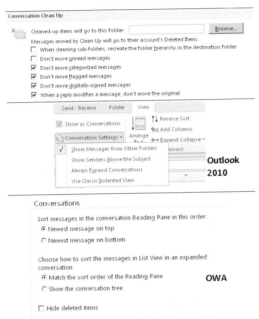

Figure 10-4 Outlook (top) and OWA (bottom) options to control conversation views.

Conflict resolution

Synchronization of items between clients and servers sometimes results in different versions of items in one place or the other. For example, a user works with Outlook offline and modifies an item in the cached version of her mailbox. Later on, she connects to Exchange online using OWA, reads the same item again, and takes an action to modify it, such as clearing an event flag. She then connects Outlook to Exchange and synchronizes, and a conflict results because different versions of the same item now exist. This is a somewhat convoluted example, but given the many ways that people interact with mailboxes through Outlook, OWA, BlackBerries, and Windows Mobile devices, such conflicts occur all the time, especially with calendar items.

All Outlook clients since Outlook 2003 use a conflict resolution engine designed to resolve conflicts automatically. The engine quickly resolves spurious conflicts (two versions exist, but they are identical) and presents a more elegant interface for users to track and resolve conflicts that require user intervention. In these cases, the engine uses an algorithm to determine which copy of the item is most likely to be the version to keep, and Outlook retains this version in the original folder. Outlook moves the other versions into the Conflicts folder, which is a subfolder of the Sync Issues folder in the user's mailbox.

> **Note**
>
> You have to click the Folder List shortcut to have Outlook reveal the Sync Issues folder in the folder tree view.

You can review the contents of the Sync Issues folder from time to time to see what items Outlook has moved there. There are three subfolders: Conflicts, Local Failures, and Server Failures. Outlook uses the Conflicts folder to store all the items that Outlook believes to be in conflict. You can review these items individually and decide whether you want to keep the version in the Conflicts folder by replacing the version that Outlook has retained in the original folder, or you can delete the version in the Conflicts folder, which is an emphatic way of resolving the conflict. Alternatively, you can leave conflicts alone unless Outlook prompts you to resolve a conflict when you access an item. At this time, Outlook displays a conflict resolution band in the message header to present the options that a user can take. You can decide what version to keep and Outlook will update the folder with this version.

> ## Local Failures and Server Failures folders
>
> The Local Failures folder holds copies of items that Outlook was unable to synchronize with the server. Usually the problem that caused the failure is transient (such as a network interruption) and Outlook subsequently synchronized successfully. The Server Failures folder holds items that Exchange was unable to synchronize down to Outlook, and again, the failure condition is usually transient. You can delete the items that you find in the Local Failures and Server Failures folders—I do this on a regular basis to free up a small amount of space in my mailbox.
>
> It is not a sign of good synchronization health if you find more than a few items in the Local Failures and Server Failures folders, and it could be an indication of an underlying problem that you need to address. If such a condition occurs, you can turn on email logging by selecting Tools, Options, Other, and then Advanced to force Outlook to begin logging more detailed results for synchronization operations, which it stores as items in the Sync Issues folder. Note that you have to restart Outlook before detailed logging begins. Some of the information that Outlook logs could help you understand why problems occur, but it is more likely that a Microsoft Customer Service and Support (CSS) specialist will be able to decipher the data, because the information is useful but a tad cryptic.

Listing client connections

You can see details of the clients that are currently connected to a mailbox server with this command:

```
Get-MailboxServer -Identity ServerName | Get-LogonStatistics | Format-List UserName, ApplicationId, ClientVersion
```

The output will include information like this:

```
UserName            : SystemMailbox{dc877527-83e9-4c13-a50c-b4beda917ce3}


ApplicationId     : Client=EventBased
MSExchangeMailboxAssistants;Action=CalendarNotificationAssistant
ClientVersion     : 3585.0.32903.3

UserName          : Redmond, Eoin P.
ApplicationId     : Client=OWA
ClientVersion     : 3585.0.32903.3
UserName          : Redmond, Eoin P.
ApplicationId     : Client=WebServices;UserAgent=[NoUserAgent]
ClientVersion     : 3585.0.32903.3

UserName          : Clark, Molly (IT)
ApplicationId     : Client=MSExchangeRPC
ClientVersion     : 3585.0.32903.3
```

Some of the connections reported here will be internal server-side connections created by Exchange (for example, connections from the Store Driver to deliver messages to a mailbox), but it is easy to identify those which belong to real users. You'll see some interesting things:

- Outlook users are shown with an application identifier of *MSExchangeRPC*, which is the value used to identify connections handled by the RPC Client Access layer. Each Outlook client that is configured in cached Exchange mode generates at least five connections. Four of these are used by the threads that perform "drizzle-mode" background synchronization to maintain the folder replicas in the client OST; the other is used by the thread responsible for sending messages.

- OWA users have two types of connections. The connections with an application identifier of *OWA* are used to maintain connectivity with the server to perform tasks such as listing the contents of a folder or reading a message. The connections shown as *WebServices* are generated to send messages.

Chapter 10

- Background Exchange tasks are identified with the mailbox assistant name. In the preceding example, the connection is for the calendar assistant that notifies users when calendar appointments are due.

- Connections created by the Store Driver to deliver messages from the transport system to mailboxes in a database show the database name as the user name.

- For Exchange 2010 SP1, the client version is the same for all connections. This can be regarded as a bug because it's obvious that client software comes in many different versions. Microsoft is aware of the issue and might address it in a future release.

Blocking client connections to a mailbox

Exchange allows you to disable any or all client connection protocols, including MAPI, on a per-user basis by amending the protocols that the mailbox can access on the Mailbox Features tab (Figure 10-5). If you disable MAPI, a user cannot use Outlook to connect to his mailbox. This option is often taken for mailboxes that use OWA exclusively and never need to use Outlook.

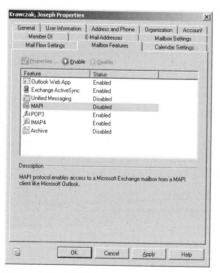

Figure 10-5 Disabling MAPI access for a user.

The Set-CASMailbox cmdlet supports a number of parameters to control how an individual mailbox can use MAPI to connect to a mailbox on an Exchange server:

- –*MAPIBlockOutlookRpcHTTP*: Allows you to determine whether you allow Outlook clients to connect over RPC over HTTP via Outlook Anywhere. Set the parameter to $True to block RPC over HTTP access and $False to allow access.

- *–MAPIBlockOutlookVersions*: Allows you to control what versions of Outlook can connect to Exchange. You might use this setting to force users to upgrade to a more modern version of Outlook such as Outlook 2007 because these clients are able to make efficient use of server resources. If a user attempts to use a blocked version of Outlook, the user will see the error message shown in Figure 10-6. Outlook clients configured for cached Exchange mode continue to work offline, but they cannot connect to the server until an administrator lifts the block.

Figure 10-6 A user discovers that he can't use this version of Outlook to connect to Exchange.

- *–MAPIBlockOutlookNonCachedMode*: Allows you to determine whether you allow Outlook clients to connect in online mode to the server. Set this parameter to $True to allow online access and to $False to force clients to connect in cached Exchange mode. Somewhat confusingly, users blocked from online access also see the same message shown in Figure 10-6, followed by another error message to tell them that Outlook is unable to open their default email folders. Pointing to the version of Outlook rather than the need to use cached Exchange mode might confuse the help desk when users report their problem.

Microsoft identifies Outlook builds using a scheme of *major release, minor release, build number*. The *major release* number is shared across all the Office applications. The Office 12 suite includes Outlook 2007, Office 14 includes Outlook 2010, and so on (Microsoft did not produce an Office 13 suite). The *minor release* indicates whether the build is in the original RTM build, a service pack, or a cumulative update, and the *build number* is incremented daily to include code and fixes checked in by engineers. Here are the build numbers for some recent Outlook versions:

- Outlook 2007: 12.4518.1014

- Outlook 2007 SP1: 12.6425.1000

- Outlook 2010: 14.0.4760.1000

To discover the client version to specify in the *–MAPIBlockOutlookVersions* parameter, you can use the Help/About option with Outlook or check with the useful list of client versions that Microsoft maintains at *http://technet.microsoft.com/en-us/library/aa996848.aspx*.

Chapter 10

As an example, here are two commands. The first restricts access so that the user must use Outlook 2003 or newer; the second restricts access to Outlook 2007 or later. In both cases, an explicit "allow" is included for version 6.0.0 to support Exchange server-side MAPI connections (server connections always use MAPI version 6.0).

```
Set-CASMailbox –Identity'Akers, Kim' –MAPIBlockOutlookVersions
'-6.0.0;10.0.0- 11.5603.0'
Set-CASMailbox –Identity'Akers, Kim' –MAPIBlockOutlookVersions
'-6.0.0;10.0.0-12.4406.0'
```

You have to wait up to 120 minutes for the cached information about the mailbox to expire from the Store's cache. Alternatively, you can restart the Information Store service, but apart from test situations, this is definitely not the best approach because it will affect all the other mailboxes connected to the server.

You can check to see if any restrictions are in place for any protocols on a server by using the Get-Mailbox cmdlet to examine the *ProtocolSettings* property of each mailbox. If a restriction is in place for a specific client version, you will see that version number listed. If an administrator has completely disabled MAPI access for the mailbox, you will see "MAPI" and no version number. For example:

```
Get-Mailbox –Server ExchServer1 | Where {$_.ProtocolSettings –ne $Null} | Select
Name, ProtocolSettings
```

```
Name                          ProtocolSettings
--------                      ----------------
Redmond, Tony                 {MAPI§§§§-6.0.0;10.0.0-11.5603.0§§§§}
Ruth, Andy                    {MAPI§0§§§§§§§§}
Smith, John                   {OWA§1, IMAP4§0§§§§§§§§, POP3§0§§§§§...
```

You can also use the Get-CASMailbox cmdlet to check for MAPI blocks. On the one hand, Get-CASMailbox is more interesting because it also allows you to return the value of the *MAPIEnabled* property (this will be False if the user is completely blocked from using MAPI) and to see the details of all of the protocol settings that you can set on a mailbox. On the other hand, you cannot specify a server name to check against, so Get-CASMailbox will be less efficient, because it will scan the entire organization unless you restrict its scope by using a server-side filter to focus in on one server:

```
Get-CASMailbox –Filter {ServerName –eq'ExchServer1'} | Where {$_.ProtocolSettings
–ne $Null} | Select Name, ProtocolSettings, MapiEnabled
```

```
Name                  ProtocolSettings                 MAPIEnabled
--------              ----------------------           -----------------
Redmond, Tony         {MAPI§§§§-6.0.0;10.0.0-...        True
Ruth, Andy            {MAPI§0§§§§§§§§}                  False
Smith, John           {OWA§1, IMAP4§0§§§§§§§§...        True
```

In addition to imposing blocks on MAPI connections, you can use the Set-CASMailbox cmdlet to disable client access to other protocols. For example:

- To disable access to POP3: Set-CASMailbox –Identity Bond –PopEnabled $False

- To disable access to IMAP4: Set-CASMailbox –Identity Bond –ImapEnabled $False

- To disable access to Outlook Web Access: Set-CASMailbox –Identity Bond –OWAEnabled $False

- To disable access to ActiveSync: Set-CASMailbox –Identity Bond –ActiveSyncEnabled $False

Blocking client access to a mailbox server

Implementing blocks on a mailbox basis is useful, but sometimes you want to block all access to a mailbox server. For example, you might want to update the server with some software or apply a patch without having users impose load on the server or potentially interfere with the upgrade. You could apply such a block with EMS by searching for all mailboxes hosted in active databases on the server and using the Set-CASMailbox cmdlet to disable MAPI access, but it is more convenient to be able to apply the block centrally. For all versions from Exchange 2000 to Exchange 2007, you can block MAPI clients from connecting to a mailbox server by configuring the Disable MAPI Clients key in the registry. This key is intended to allow administrators to require the deployment of a base-level version of Outlook. Put another way, it stops users from attempting to connect with earlier versions that might not meet your company's security requirements because the earlier software doesn't include recent anti-spam and antivirus features such as beacon blocking.

The registry key is set on a mailbox server so that it can be effective only if the mailbox server is responsible for handling client connections, which is the case from Exchange 2000 to Exchange 2007. The RPC Client Access layer running on CAS servers handles MAPI client connections for Exchange 2010, so the old registry key method doesn't work. In fact, because a CAS server can handle MAPI connections for multiple mailbox servers, no one-step mechanism exists in Exchange 2010 to block MAPI connections to a designated mailbox server. Two approaches can be taken if you need to block connections to a mailbox server.

1. Use the Set-RPCClientAccess cmdlet. This cmdlet allows you to block all MAPI connections coming from specific versions. For example, this command blocks access to any version of Outlook prior to Outlook 2007 (major release 12).

```
Set-RPCClientAccess -Server ExCAS01 -BlockedClientVersions
"0.0.0-5.65535.65535; 7.0.0-11.99999.99999"
```

The problem is that all connections to all mailbox servers supported by the CAS server will be blocked. This might be an effective method to use in small sites where you have just one CAS server and one mailbox server.

2. In larger sites that support multiple CAS and mailbox servers, you can set a per-mailbox block with the Set-CASMailbox cmdlet for every mailbox on the server that you want to maintain. For example:

```
Get-Mailbox -Server ExServer1 | Set-CASMailbox -MAPIBlockOutlookVersions
'-6.0.0;10.0.0-12.4406.0'
```

The RPC Client Access layer verifies whether a client can connect using MAPI by checking the server and mailbox blocks set by the Set-RPCClientAccess and Set-CASMailbox cmdlets before it allows a connection to pass from the CAS server to the mailbox server. Either mechanism is equally effective as a block. The choice between the two therefore comes down to whether you can block all connections flowing through a CAS server, no matter what mailbox server they are destined for, or you need to block connections to just one specific mailbox server.

Of course, if you run mailbox servers in a Database Availability Group (DAG), you can use the StartDAGServerMaintenance.ps1 script (see Chapter 8, "Exchange's Search for High Availability") to move all the active mailboxes off a server and block further activation. This step effectively prepares a mailbox server for maintenance operations.

Outlook Web App

After a shaky start when the browser interface could only be politely called clunky and slow, Microsoft has poured development effort into OWA with an eye to creating a browser client that is broadly equivalent in feature set and functionality to Outlook. "Broadly equivalent" is important because Outlook has many advantages due to its key position in the Office suite and the resources dedicated to its development since 1996. At the same time, other browser clients advance the state of the science and give Microsoft a challenge for each new release. Gmail moved away from the classic folder-centric user interface paradigm into a world of conversations; Zimbra and other Web-based email applications have developed snappy, well-built interfaces that are a pleasure to use. Even Microsoft's own free Hotmail browser interface has improved substantially in the last few years.

Even with the best intentions in the world, there are two basic reasons why OWA will never completely match Outlook.

- Microsoft is unlikely to stop development of Outlook, so there will always be a feature race where OWA will have to keep up with Outlook. Outlook 2010 sets a new bar for OWA 2010 to be judged against and there are some places where OWA misses a feature. For example, you can't create a reply and have OWA automatically insert the text of the original message as you can with Outlook. Outlook supports an expanded set of the sort options available to OWA (such as sort by day). OWA doesn't have the same abilities to manage conversations that Outlook 2010 introduces, nor can it undo actions such as deletes or moves in the same way that Outlook can. Finally, there are some browser limitations that OWA has to cope with, such as the inability to save more than one attachment to the file system in a single operation. You can save multiple attachments, but you have to do them individually.

- Outlook's ability to work offline is unlikely to be matched by OWA unless Microsoft implements something similar to Google Gears (which allows Gmail and other Google applications to work offline). Interestingly, Google announced in February 2010 that they had stopped the development of Gears to focus on moving the Gears capabilities to an HTML 5–based solution. Microsoft could certainly build on the work done to provide a similar capability based on HTML 5 in Internet Explorer to add the ability to work offline. Of course, such a solution might not be appreciated in the Outlook development group, because it would remove one of the prime differentiators between the two clients.

Another factor that has to be taken into consideration is that OWA and Outlook are developed by different engineering groups that are under different market pressures. OWA is a client of Exchange and exclusively serves Exchange, so in that respect OWA will always be closer to Exchange. Outlook is regarded as the premier client for Exchange but only because it exposes most functionality. Outlook is part of the Microsoft Office suite and has to be a highly functional client for other email servers, including Hotmail (using an excellent Hotmail connector) and Gmail and other servers through IMAP4. Outlook cannot afford to ignore Exchange, but it cannot afford to be too focused on Exchange, either.

At the end of the day, if you compare the two clients on a feature-by-feature basis, OWA doesn't completely match Outlook, but it does a very good job of getting close. The question is whether the missing features are important to users and whether those missing features stop users from being productive. The answer is that OWA 2010 is highly usable and will meet the needs of the majority of those who use it. The SP1 version improves the responsiveness of OWA by caching and using data more intelligently to eliminate the slight sluggishness that some users experienced with the RTM version. Even so, there are some points that administrators need to know, and that's what we cover in this section.

A refresh for OWA provided by Exchange 2010 SP1

Although there is no doubt that the OWA application in Exchange 2010 is an improvement over its Exchange 2007 predecessor, Microsoft took the opportunity to smooth some rough edges and add some additional functionality in SP1. Part of this work was driven by user feedback received after Exchange 2010 moved into production; part came about simply because the developers had extra time to complete features for inclusion in SP1.

Figure 10-7 illustrates the major features of the new OWA interface in Exchange 2010 SP1. A number of visual differences are immediately apparent.

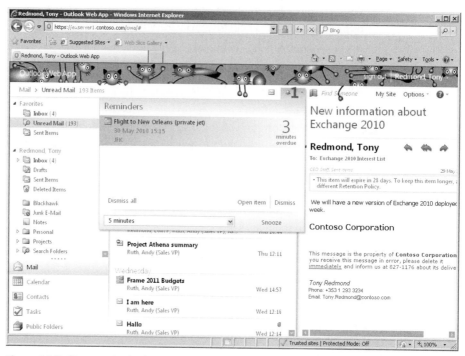

Figure 10-7 The new Outlook Web App user interface introduced in Exchange 2010 SP1.

- User-selectable themes have been reintroduced. My personal favorite (as illustrated in Figure 10-7) is the Herding Cats theme. The themes packaged with Exchange 2010 SP1 cover a reasonable variety of possible choices from the coolness of the Arctic theme to the splurge of colors in the Fingerpaints theme. I am less sure about the Cupcake theme. Microsoft also supports customers who want to customize OWA to apply corporate branding, colors, and icons.

- The typefaces used by OWA are larger to make information clearer and more accessible. The currently selected item is more obvious and now boasts a checkmark to indicate its status.

- Navigation is improved through what the Microsoft UI designers believe is a better use of screen real estate that reveals more content. Further improvement comes through the introduction of a breadcrumb trail to show users where they are and how they got there, plus redesigned icons for major options such as Reply (a change provoked because testing revealed that users made mistakes when they replied to messages). Some unnecessary elements (like the Exchange icon at the top of the mailbox) are removed to declutter the interface.

- Pop-ups to notify users of situations such as an impending meeting are more obvi-ous. Larger typefaces help to convey essential information—in this case, that the meeting is 3 minutes overdue.

- It's also easier to get to common options such as change password without having to navigate from OWA to ECP and back again (Figure 10-8).

> **Note**
> Although at first glance the changes to OWA's screen design might seem cosmetic, they have a real impact on PCs that have small screens, such as netbooks.

Figure 10-8 Enabling easier access to common user options.

Behind the scenes, Microsoft tweaked OWA performance to make the processing of large folders faster. Exchange 2010 moved to use "endless" views to better support folders that hold thousands of items by prefetching items as you scroll. This simulates the scrolling behavior of Outlook, where you get all messages in one continuous list, instead of the paged view used in OWA 2007. Navigation through views is now faster, especially when using conversation views. In SP1, the attention to performance focused on prefetching content to update views. In all previous versions of OWA, operations such as deleting items or marking an item as read are performed synchronously, and OWA waits for the server to confirm the operation as complete before it updates the view. In SP1, actions occur asyn-chronously and appear far more quickly because OWA updates the view without waiting for a response from the server.

> **Note**
>
> There's an obvious danger here that a server problem could invalidate a client action, but this doesn't happen in the vast majority of cases, so it's a worthwhile shortcut to provide better user perception of performance.

A further improvement is made in the way that OWA uploads attachments to make sure that an upload of even a very large file (more than 5 MB) doesn't block other actions. Notifications also receive a makeover to make them less obtrusive by using in-line notifications rather than modal pop-ups.

Apart from user-selectable themes, other features that make a reappearance in SP1 include OWA Web parts, the ability to print several different views of the calendar (a somewhat strange omission in Exchange 2010), and the option to use a reading pane at the bottom of the screen rather than at the side. Web-ready document viewing now supports documents protected with Active Directory Rights Management Services (AD RMS) on Internet Explorer, Firefox, and Chrome on Windows and Safari on a Mac. Many minor bugs in specific browsers—such as the inability to drag and drop between folders using Chrome—are fixed, although some restrictions remain, such as the need to load the optional Secure Multipurpose Internet Mail Extensions (S/MIME) control if you want to be able to drag and drop attachments into a message. Because the S/MIME control is only supported by Internet Explorer, it follows that other browsers can't perform this trick.

Overall, the Microsoft developers aimed to create an interface that is both rich and simple with the major features exposed and easily accessible. The changes made in SP1 are not a radical overhaul of the basic framework established for OWA in Exchange 2010. Instead, they are more like a tune-up to reveal the true potential of the application.

OWA functionality deprecated in Exchange 2010

OWA 2010 boasts a shiny new interface and includes many new features that we review in due course. On the downside, Microsoft has deprecated a number of features that appeared in previous versions because they didn't have the engineering time to upgrade the features to work with Exchange 2010, they felt that the feature wasn't used in the way or as much as they anticipated when they did the work, or for some other reason, including security concerns. Among the best examples of deprecated features are the following:

- Web parts: Exchange 2003 and Exchange 2007 allow you to specify a Web part in a URL to access that Web part directly. For example, you can go directly to a specific view of a folder in a user's mailbox, such as opening a user calendar in the week view. This feature could reappear in a service pack for Exchange 2010.

See *http://msexchangeteam.com/archive/2006/10/26/429362.aspx* for full details about Web parts in Exchange 2007.

- Document access: This feature was introduced in Exchange 2007 and allows OWA users to access documents in a Microsoft SharePoint site and to file shares pointed to through universal naming conventions (UNCs).

If a now-deprecated OWA feature is important to your deployment, you should work with your Microsoft account team to provide this feedback to the Exchange development team so that it can be taken into account when Microsoft draws up the feature list and work commitment for a future service pack or version of Exchange. The development team does listen, as is evident in the list of features that reappear in SP1.

Different browsers, different experiences

OWA is available in two versions: Premium and Light. The CAS server makes a decision about what version of OWA to provide to a client based on the value of the user agent string submitted by the browser when it connects to Exchange. The official Microsoft stance is that you must use Internet Explorer 7 (or later) or Firefox 3.0 (or later) on a supported operating system if you want to use the premium version of OWA with Exchange 2010. Earlier versions of Internet Explorer and Firefox cannot use the premium version and are automatically downgraded to the light version. Along the same lines, you can use OWA Premium with the Safari browser, but only when it is version 3 or later running on a system using the Leopard (10.5) or Snow Leopard (10.6) versions of the Mac X operating system. Other versions of Safari, such as those running on Windows, the iPad, or the iPhone, are only capable of supporting the light version of OWA.

It might seem strange that a browser is capable of supporting the premium version of OWA on one platform and not another, but a mixture of subtle and not-so-subtle rendering differences exist across platforms. Microsoft has to decide where to invest engineering resources to develop, test, and support a specific browser configuration, especially in situations where they depend on engineering groups in other companies to fix bugs and help address issues reported by customers. If Microsoft doesn't see sufficient customer demand to warrant the necessary investment to support the initial engineering for making a browser work well with OWA Premium, the testing to validate the engineering work, and the long-term sustaining support to fix any problems reported by customers and keep pace with new software releases from the browser vendor, they just don't do it. Each browser has its own unique challenges. Safari on iPad, for instance, is the first full-screen browser running on a tablet device that depends exclusively on a virtual keyboard for input (you can, of course, connect a hardware keyboard to an iPad).

The browser/operating system combinations listed in the Tier 1 and Tier 2 categories in Table 10-2 can run the premium version of OWA. For example, I commonly use Google's

Chrome browser with OWA (Figure 10-9). This screen shot used Chrome version 4.0.249.78 connected to Exchange 2010 SP1 complete with my favorite Herding Cats theme. Despite the fact that Microsoft doesn't test Chrome with OWA as thoroughly as it tests Internet Explorer and that Google's iterative development philosophy for their programs generates regular updates for Chrome, everything works pretty smoothly.

Table 10-2 **Microsoft support for browser/operating system combinations**

Microsoft Support Level	Browsers and Platform
Tier 1: Fully tested and supported by the product group	Internet Explorer 7+: Windows XP, Vista, Windows 7, Windows 2003, Windows 2008 Firefox 3+: Windows XP, Vista, Windows 7, Windows 2003, Windows 2008, Mac OS 10.5 and above Safari 3.1+: Mac OS 10.5 and above
Tier 2: Supported but with limited testing	Firefox 3.0 on Linux platforms Chrome on Windows Vista and Windows 7
Tier 3: Supported but only with OWA Light	Internet Explorer 6 Safari on Windows Other browser/operating system combinations (Opera, Safari for iPad, and so on)

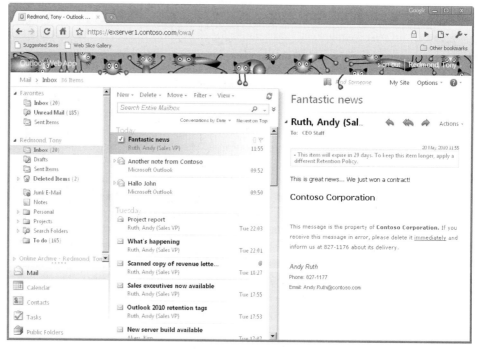

Figure 10-9 Using the premium version of OWA with the Chrome browser.

INSIDE OUT
A couple of OWA features that don't work with Chrome

The only consistent problem that I have discovered with Chrome is that I cannot drag and drop items from one folder to another. Chrome stubbornly refuses to perform this operation, but it will allow you to drag and drop an item into a draft email to add it as an attachment. By comparison, Internet Explorer moves items between folders quite elegantly. Sometimes Chrome fails to signal notifications of new messages or upcoming appointments, but most of the time these work. Another small irritation is that the availability information for users isn't displayed when you browse the Global Address List (GAL) with Chrome where it is with Internet Explorer (Figure 10-10). All of this goes to prove what "supported but with limited testing" means in practice.

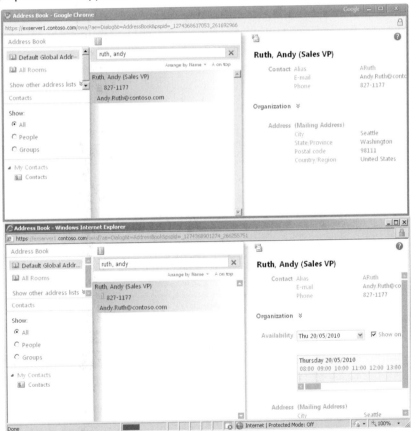

Figure 10-10 Spot the difference! Chrome and Internet Explorer display details of a user from the GAL.

OWA Light

OWA Light is designed to support many different browsers—from those that Microsoft doesn't test (like Opera) to earlier versions of those that they do test (like Firefox)—running on anything from Linux workstations to laptops. It is also designed to accommodate a wide range of screens, from netbooks with relatively low resolution to high-end workstations. Because of the range of capabilities found across different browsers and different versions of browsers, Microsoft limited the amount of "intelligence" in the form of code such as JavaScript that OWA Light runs on the browser. This ensures that OWA Light has a very good chance of working on any browser that it meets, but it does impose some limitations. For example, you might notice that column widths do not dynamically resize to match screen resolution; no matter what size screen you use, the column for message sender is always sized at 16 characters (see Figure 10-11). OWA Premium includes logic to detect the screen resolution and window width and resizes columns to display more or less information based on the current configuration.

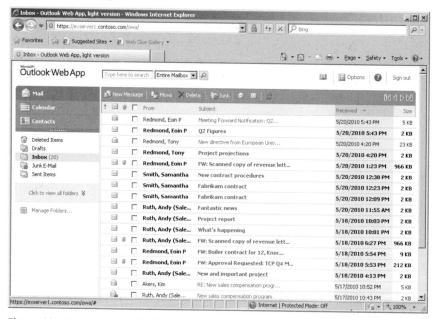

Figure 10-11 Using the OWA Light version.

Spell checking is another example of feature differences between browsers. OWA only supports the integrated spell checker for Internet Explorer. The logic here is that Firefox, Safari, and other browsers offer their own spell-checking capability and it is difficult to engineer the same kind of spell check feature that Microsoft can include in Internet Explorer when they have full control over the interface. It's also fair to say that Internet Explorer doesn't come with an integrated spell checker, so Microsoft had to include one for OWA to achieve parity with Outlook. Taking all factors into account, Microsoft felt that users might be confused if they had to make a choice between the browser's own spell checker and one that they provided for OWA, so if a non–Internet Explorer browser is detected, OWA automatically disables its own spell checker, including the option for users to decide to spell check messages before sending.

INSIDE OUT   Multiple sessions

Modern browsers support tabbed interfaces to allow users to move quickly between different Web sites. On the surface, you'd expect to be able to use the same facility to establish multiple connections to Exchange and be able to open multiple mailboxes with OWA. Unfortunately, this isn't possible because browsers share connections within the same process. OWA requires a relatively large number of connections for mailbox and directory information, so if you opened multiple mailboxes, the browser wouldn't be able support all of the necessary connections and one or both sessions would fail, specifically in the mechanism used to keep OWA updated with new information as the different sessions would block each other's connections.

The workaround is to use the File/New Session (in Internet Explorer 8) or File /New Window (in Internet Explorer 7) commands to create a brand new session complete with its own set of connections. You won't be able to use tabs to move between the sessions within a single browser instance, but you will be able to use Alt+Tab to navigate between the two windows to move between the two sessions.

Chapter 10

OWA configuration file

Exchange stores many configuration settings for OWA in the Active Directory directory service. On the client side, OWA is an ASP.NET application that maintains another group of settings in an application configuration file called Web.config.xml that is located in the \ClientAccess\OWA folder under the Exchange root. These settings affect how OWA runs in a browser. You can edit the OWA configuration file with any text editor as long as you're careful to preserve the XML syntax. Each CAS server has its own OWA configuration file, so you need to apply any changes that you want to make separately on each server. You also need to check the settings after you apply a roll-up update or service pack for Exchange because there is no guarantee that Microsoft will not overwrite the configuration file during an update.

OWA also uses system registry entries to control some settings. In terms of administrator interest, the timeout for a session is probably the most popular of these settings. There are two values: One controls how long OWA will run without terminating a session when a user logs onto a public computer (or clicks the Public check box when they connect to OWA); the other controls the private timeout. The two values are as follows:

Public (15 minutes by default)

HKEY_LOCAL_MACHINE\SYSTEM\CurrentControlSet\Services\MSExchangeOWA
Name: PublicTimeout
Type: DWORD

Private (8 hours by default [640 minutes])

HKEY_LOCAL_MACHINE\SYSTEM\CurrentControlSet\Services\MSExchangeOWA
Name: PrivateTimeout
Type: DWORD

Missing favorites

Some users love to create Favorites folders, and some leave the default set alone (Inbox, Unread, Outbox). Users in the latter category won't care that OWA 2010 is not 100 percent compatible with any version of Outlook 2010 when it comes to Favorites folders. In effect, this means that you can create a new Favorites folder in Outlook 2007, but it might not turn up in the list of folders displayed by OWA. Likewise, you can create a new Favorites folder in OWA 2010 and not see it in Outlook 2007. Even stranger, sort orders vary between versions so that a set of folders enumerates differently in OWA 2010 than they do in Outlook 2007. The reason is that all versions of Outlook prior to Outlook 2010 save data about favorites locally, whereas Outlook 2010 saves the information in the user's mailbox on the server. For historical reasons, different clients store user data in a variety of places. MAPI profiles are in the system registry, whereas Outlook holds many of its settings in hidden items in the root folder of a user's mailbox as well as files such as the nickname cache (.nk2 file). Because OWA is designed for browsers that can run on many different computers, it normally stores its settings in the root of the user's mailbox.

The advantage of having all clients share a common repository is that they will show the same set of folders sorted in the same order. However, during the period when Exchange 2010 is used with older clients, some users might scratch their heads as they wonder where a Favorites folder has gone. Another difference between OWA and Outlook is that OWA does not display special folders that it doesn't need, whereas Outlook always does. For example, the Outbox folder is never used by OWA, so the premium version never displays it in the folder list (curiously, the light version of OWA does show the Outbox folder). The logic here is that you cannot send deferred mail with OWA in the same way that you can with Outlook, so there is no need to show the Outbox (which is where Exchange holds deferred messages).

Forwarding meeting requests

Exchange 2007 introduced a feature to inform meeting organizers when an attendee forwarded the meeting request to another recipient. The Calendar Attendant generates these notifications after they process the meeting forward. Figure 10-12 shows a typical example of a meeting forward notification. In this case, probably no great harm to the organization is done when details of a meeting to celebrate someone's birthday are forwarded to another user; the situation might be very different for meetings to discuss sensitive topics such as budgets, corporate reorganizations and restructuring, and plans to introduce new products.

It might be interesting to know that someone else has been informed about a meeting that you've set up, but it can also be irritating to receive a whole batch of notifications, especially when you organize frequent meetings attended by lots of people. You can have Exchange delete the notifications automatically on a per-mailbox basis using the Set-CalendarProcessing cmdlet.

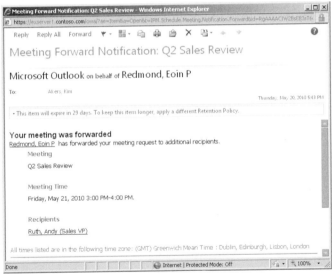

Figure 10-12 How a user knows that his meeting has been forwarded.

OWA also allows users to delete these notifications automatically by selecting the Delete Notifications About Forwarded Meetings check box in the Automatic Processing section of Calendar Options (Figure 10-13), which is an option that is not available in the Outlook UI.

In this example, we force Exchange to move any notification message to the Deleted Items folder for the nominated user:

```
Set-CalendarProcessing –id 'EPR' –RemoveForwardedMeetingNotifications $True
```

It's also possible to do the same thing with Exchange 2007, but you need to use the Set-MailboxCalendarSettings cmdlet, which is deprecated in Exchange 2010. It's also possible to suppress notifications going to external domains after meetings have been forwarded within your organization. This command blocks all meeting forward notifications to every domain. If you just want this to be done for a specific domain, you pass the identifier for that domain.

```
Set-RemoteDomain –MeetingForwardNotificationEnabled $False
```

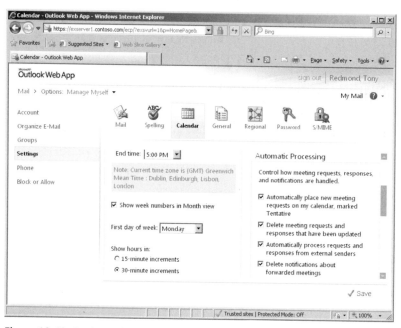

Figure 10-13 Opting to have Exchange automatically delete notifications about forwarded meetings.

OWA Web parts

Web parts refer to the different components used by OWA to assemble its UI. The value of making individual Web parts usable by other browser applications is that you can expose different parts of OWA functionality within those applications. This capability is not supported in Exchange 2010, but is supported with SP1.

The set of Web parts supported by Exchange 2010 and their command format is the same as for Exchange 2007 OWA and is described at *http://technet.microsoft.com/en-us/library /bb232199(EXCHG.80).aspx*. The only difference is that the *f* parameter used in Exchange 2007 to determine the folder to be displayed in the Web part is replaced by *fpath* in Exchange 2010.

Long signatures

If you're migrating from Exchange 2003, you might have configured a value called *SignatureMaxLength* in the system registry to increase the maximum size of signature text that OWA can apply to outgoing messages from the default 4 KB to an upper limit of 16 KB. This ability was often exploited by companies that wanted to append substantial multiparagraph disclaimers to protect themselves.

Exchange 2007 and Exchange 2010 increased the default size of an OWA signature to 8 KB but removed the ability to increase it any further. OWA flags the errors shown in Figure 10-14 if you attempt to input more text than fits into the 8 KB maximum.

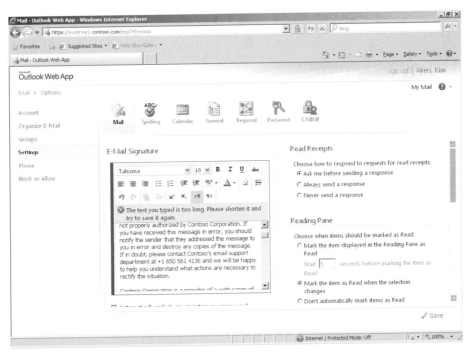

Figure 10-14 Problems adding a very long company disclaimer.

The reason you can't increase the size is that it's much more efficient to apply a company disclaimer to outgoing messages with a transport rule because a transport rule guarantees that a disclaimer will be applied, whereas asking users to configure a disclaimer on an individual basis is prone to fail. The steps to create a transport rule to apply a company disclaimer are described in Chapter 16, "Rules and Journals." It's best to ask users to remove company disclaimer text from their signatures and restrain themselves to personal information that is not included in the disclaimer that the transport rule applies. Because transport rules can now fetch data such as names, telephone numbers, and email addresses from Active Directory to include in a disclaimer, the text that remains to be included in a personal signature is limited to items such as department-specific text or a personal "thought of the day." We'll describe how to create a transport rule that incorporates Active Directory data in a disclaimer in the section "Creating a corporate disclaimer" in Chapter 16.

Sharing calendars

The requirement to share calendars with co-workers is a common collaborative need. OWA allows you to share your calendar with other users and to add their calendars to your view. Everything works on the basis that a user sends an invitation to share her calendar to those with whom she wants to share. Go to the calendar and click the Share icon and then select Share Calendar. OWA creates a message (the top item in Figure 10-15) to inform recipients that you want to share your calendar.

INSIDE OUT   How much are you willing to share?

An important point here is the degree of sharing that you're willing to do. The options are to show everything, in which case people will see whatever you've entered into your calendar except for items that you mark as private; free and busy information, including subject and location, which means that people see the time slices that are taken up in your calendar together with basic information about what you're doing; and just the free and busy information, which displays just the time slots when you are occupied but provides no indication of whether you're on the golf course or engaged in something more productive. You also have the option of requesting reciprocal access to the other person's calendar.

The bottom item in Figure 10-15 shows an invitation to share someone else's calendar. The text giving instructions to go to Microsoft.com for instructions about how to view shared folders is inserted automatically by Exchange but isn't really necessary, because all the recipient has to do is to click the Add To Calendar icon to have OWA do the work to add the shared calendar.

The calendar sharing functionality in OWA is designed to allow users to view calendars belonging to others, so when you share a calendar with another user, Exchange assigns the

Reviewer permission to that user. This permission is sufficient to permit read-only access to your calendar. A user who holds *Reviewer* permission for a calendar cannot update events or add new events, which is the level of access that is usually required by users such as executive assistants. Behind the scenes, Exchange uses the Add-MailboxFolderPermission cmdlet to assign permissions, but there is no user interface provided in OWA to allow another user write access to the calendar. However, an administrator can run the Add-MailboxFolderPermission cmdlet to assign *Editor* permission for a calendar to a user to allow them write access or run the Set-MailboxFolderPermission cmdlet to upgrade an existing *Reviewer* permission to *Editor*.

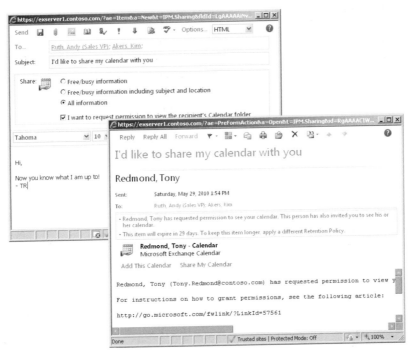

Figure 10-15 Sharing calendars with OWA.

These examples show how the cmdlets are used. The first command assigns the *Editor* permission for the calendar folder owned by Akers to another user called "Pelton, David". The second command upgrades the permission for the same calendar for a different user:

```
Add-MailboxFolderPermission -Identity 'Akers:\Calendar' -User 'Pelton, David'
-AccessRights Editor
```

```
Set-MailboxFolderPermission -Identity 'Akers:\Calendar' -User 'Smith' -AccessRights
Editor
```

Chapter 10

You can add as many shared calendars as you like to your calendar list. However, all computer screens have limited real estate, and it gets very complex for developers to figure out how to squeeze information about all the calendars into the display. Some users run OWA on computers that have reasonably low-fidelity screens (think of a low-end notebook or netbook computer) that only support a screen definition of 1024×760, and OWA has to be able to cope with these situations as well as the extra-large screens that fill half a desk. There's always a trade-off, and in this case it's a limitation to be able to show a maximum of five calendars (your own calendar and four shared calendars). If you attempt to add another calendar, you'll run into the situation illustrated in Figure 10-16. There's no workaround or registry hack that forces OWA to fit more calendars onto the screen, even if the screen definition will support it, so you have to decide which calendars are most important to display and move others in and out of the display set as the need arises.

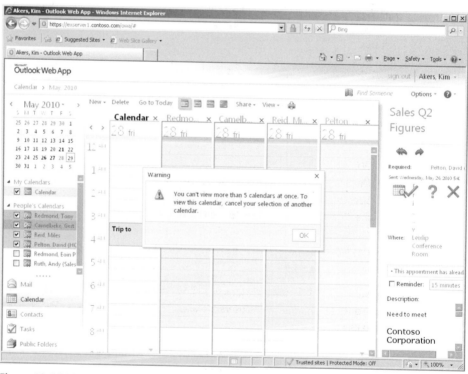

Figure 10-16 Viewing multiple calendars with OWA.

Sharing calendars with Internet users

Exchange 2010 SP1 introduces the ability to share or publish calendars to the Internet. This feature is intended to allow Exchange to offer the same facility that exists in other Web-based calendaring software such as Google Calendar and Yahoo! Calendar.

The feature leverages the work done to introduce federated calendar sharing between Exchange organizations while understanding that the intended target is quite different. Calendar sharing depends on a high level of trust between the participating organizations, whereas sharing calendars with Internet users is obviously a much looser arrangement, because no one manages the Internet and there's no notion of credentials being required to look at calendar data that a user has decided to publish. On the other hand, the Internet does encourage the development and implementation of standard protocols that can be used to share data, and in this case the protocol is iCal, or iCalendar.

Even though Exchange users can now share their calendars with Internet users, the operative word is "can." Sharing does not happen automatically. Exchange 2010 SP1 does not suddenly tear down the shutters and publish every user calendar as widely as possible. Instead, administrators and users alike must both take deliberate and planned actions to first create the conditions where calendar sharing is possible and then to make the decisions about with whom to share calendar data and what level of transparency or access to support.

The basis for calendar sharing is a vdir called /calendar that is underneath the /owavdir. To allow open sharing with the widest possible set of clients, the calendar vdir supports HTTP access. HTTPS connections will not be rejected, but HTTP is all that you need to share a calendar with an Exchange user.

> **Note**
>
> The calendar vdir is serviced by a separate application pool to isolate it from OWA operations, so the fact that HTTP access is supported should not be a concern because there's no way for hackers to break into OWA just because they can get to a user's calendar.

By default, Exchange 2010 does not allow calendar sharing, and the administrator must configure Exchange before users are allowed to share calendars. The following steps must be taken:

1. The OWA vdir must have an *ExternalURL* property set. Typically this is something like *https://mail.contoso.com/owa*.

2. The *InternetWebProxy* property of all of the mailbox servers that host mailboxes containing the calendars that will be shared with Internet users must be populated with the name of the CAS server in the Internet-facing site through which connections will be channelled. For example:

```
Set-ExchangeServer -Identity 'ExServer1' -InternetWebProxy
'http://ExCASInternet.contoso.com'
```

3. The OWA vdir of the CAS server must have its *CalendarPublishingEnabled* property set to $True:

```
Set-OWAVirtualDirectory -Identity "ExServer1\owa (default web site)"
-CalendarPublishingEnabled $True
```

4. A sharing policy must be configured to allow anonymous access to calendars. You can do this by amending the default sharing policy, or you can create a new sharing policy and apply that policy to the select group of mailboxes that you want to allow to share calendars. In this example, we set the default sharing policy to allow users to share calendar data at the level of free and busy information plus detail (the body of the appointment item) about appointments.

```
Set-SharingPolicy -Identity 'Default Sharing Policy' -Domains "Anonymous:
CalendarSharingFreeBusyDetail"
```

> **Note**
>
> Attendee lists or attachments are never shared for meetings. Sharing policies are discussed in more detail in Chapter 5, "Exchange Management Console and Control Panel."

If you create a new sharing policy, you will have to apply it to mailboxes using the Set-Mailbox cmdlet. For example:

```
Set-Mailbox -Identity 'Redmond, Tony' -SharingPolicy 'Internet Calendar Sharing
Policy'
```

Once the administrator has configured Exchange to allow calendar sharing to the Internet, users can publish calendars using the Publish This Calendar option available in the OWA calendar. Outlook doesn't support the same publishing feature directly, so when a user shares his calendar with an Internet correspondent through Outlook, he is redirected to the Web sharing page to execute the option.

Figure 10-17 shows the publication process to make calendars available to Internet users. On the left, the user selects the Publish This Calendar option. This causes OWA to display the dialog box shown in the middle to collect details about how the calendar should be published. The user controls:

- How much detail is revealed about appointments (the options are Availability Only, Limited Details, or Full Details). OWA will flag a warning if the user selects an option that is not allowed by the sharing policy that applies to the user's mailbox.

- How much calendar data are published. You can select to publish anything from one year to one day in advance of and before today.

- Whether the calendar is restricted or public. Restricted calendars have a GUID-based obfuscated URL that is extremely difficult to guess. A sample URL is:

http://mail.contoso.com/owa/calendar/a6cc8807ab2e4e9385ced83564dc56c3 @contoso.com/1f5d738f17aa4700a6469aa9428556b9164533516351988862711 /calendar.html

In addition, Exchange does not allow restricted calendars to be indexed by search engines. Public calendars receive URLs of the type shown in the email at the bottom of Figure 10-17. You can see that the URL is reasonably straightforward and based on the user's alias. A user can switch between public and restricted by changing the publishing settings for the calendar. She can also stop publishing her calendar at any time.

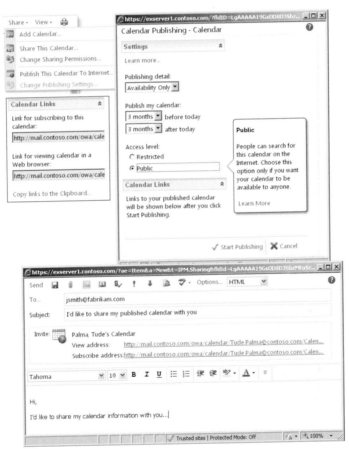

Figure 10-17 The OWA process to enable and then publish calendar information to Internet recipients.

- Who is advised about the availability of his calendar. A user could wait for his public calendar to be discovered by interested parties, but in most cases he will want to inform others that his calendar is now available from the Internet. OWA provides a Send Links To This Calendar option that generates an email for this purpose. Two URLs are included. The HTML link is to allow an Internet recipient to view details of your calendar as a simple Web page. The ICS (Internet Calendar Sharing) link is to allow others to add your calendar to a set of calendars (including presumably their own) that they need to reference on a frequent basis. The exact functionality that is enabled through the ICS link varies according to the client software used.

An administrator can also retrieve calendar settings for a mailbox with the Get-MailboxCalendarFolder cmdlet and configure calendar sharing with the Set-MailboxCalendarFolder cmdlet. For example, to retrieve the calendar settings for my mailbox, I'd use this command:

```
Get-MailboxCalendarFolder -Identity 'TRedmond:\Calendar'
```

```
Identity                 : contoso.com/Exchange Users/Redmond, Tony:\calendar
PublishEnabled           : True
PublishDateRangeFrom     : ThreeMonths
PublishDateRangeTo       : ThreeMonths
DetailLevel              : LimitedDetails
SearchableUrlEnabled     : True
PublishedCalendarUrl     : http://mail.contoso.com/owa/calendar
/TRedmond@contoso.com/Calendar/calendar.html
PublishedICalUrl         : http://mail.contoso.com/owa/calendar
/TRedmond@contoso.com/Calendar/calendar.ics
IsValid                  : True
```

To change the published date range to one year before and after today's date and to change my calendar from public to restricted, I can use the following command:

```
Set-MailboxCalendarFolder -Identity 'Tredmond:\Calendar' -PublishDateRangeFrom
'OneYear' -PublishDateRangeTo 'OneYear' -SearchableUrlEnabled $False
```

Mailbox quota exceeded

OWA displays an indicator at the top of the folder list to show how much storage quota is available in the mailbox. Once the mailbox quota passes the warning limit, OWA changes the display to warn the user that she is running out of storage (Figure 10-18). She will also receive a message from the System Attendant to advise that items have to be removed from the mailbox before she can process more email. Separate storage quotas are maintained for the personal archive (if the mailbox has one), but OWA doesn't display any indication of how much space remains in the archive.

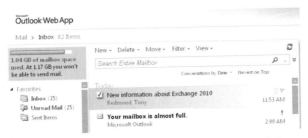

Figure 10-18 OWA signals that a mailbox is getting full.

All of this is very much what you'd expect Exchange to do when a mailbox is full, and you can leave the users to clean up their mailboxes to release some space. However, there are other consequences. When there is no space available, Exchange cannot update items in the mailbox—including hidden items that are used to hold mailbox settings. For example, if you go to Options and attempt to update any setting, OWA will display the error shown in Figure 10-19 when you attempt to save the mailbox settings. The solution is to free some space up in the mailbox to allow OWA to save items.

Figure 10-19 OWA can't save an item.

As discussed in Chapter 6, "Managing Mail-Enabled Recipients," another solution is for an administrator to assign additional quota to the affected mailbox. Because it caches information about mailbox settings for better performance, Exchange can take up to two hours to respect the new quota. However, once the change is effective, users will be able to create and update items in their mailboxes.

Handling attachments

A setting called *maxRequestLength* in Web.config.xml, the OWA configuration file, governs the maximum amount of data that a client can upload to a CAS. The default value for this setting is 30,000. The value is in kilobytes, and, in practical terms, it means that you can upload a 30 MB attachment to OWA or submit a message that is up to 30 MB (for instance, a message with several attachments that cumulatively amount to 30 MB). Of course, being able to attach a very large file and being able to send it are two very different things, and other limits placed on the organization, connectors, or a mailbox could interfere with the ability to actually deliver a large message.

Chapter 10

INSIDE OUT   Setting values and user expectations

Figure 10-20 illustrates how you can edit the OWA configuration file with Notepad. In this case, we change the maximum file size that the browser can upload to 4800, or 4.8 MB. The trick is to set the value so that it aligns with the maximum size supported by connectors so that users don't get into the situation where OWA allows them to create and upload a message only for it to be rejected by a connector. It's also important to inform users about the limitation so that they are not surprised if OWA refuses to upload a large file. Ideally, this should be communicated in the context of explaining how to use Exchange effectively and setting expectations about the size of messages that users can send and receive.

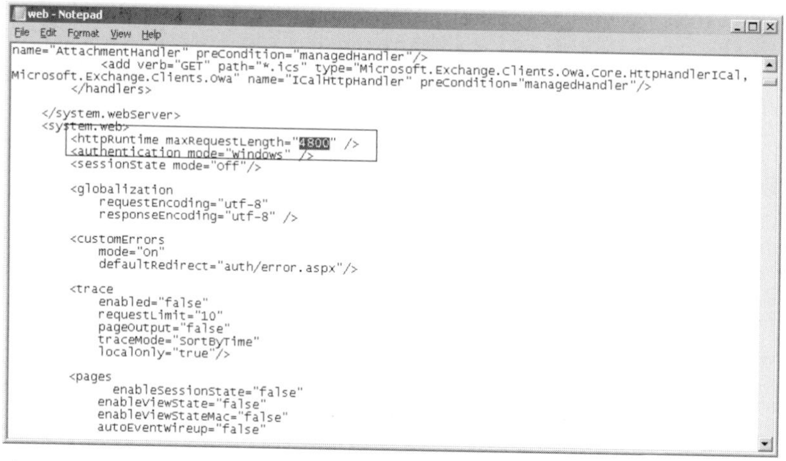

Figure 10-20 Editing the OWA configuration file.

When you attach a document to a message, OWA presents the Attach Files dialog box shown on the right side of Figure 10-21. This dialog box is reasonably effective, but it can be improved with the SP1 version of OWA by installing the latest version of Microsoft's Silverlight development platform on client computers. If OWA detects that Silverlight is available, it opens the normal file Open dialog box that is used elsewhere in Windows. This dialog box, shown on the left side of Figure 10-21, allows you to browse a directory and select multiple files in one operation. (In this case, I've selected some of the draft files for this book.) Due to its increasing popularity with Web developers, Silverlight is likely to be installed on client computers, but if not, you should add it to the list of updates that you consider adding to clients during deployment.

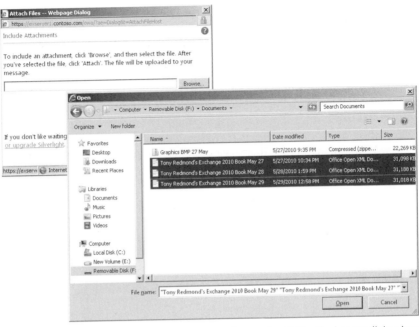

Figure 10-21 The difference that Silverlight makes to the OWA attachment dialog box.

OWA themes and customizations

A theme defines the color scheme and graphic elements used for OWA. Exchange 2007 supports customizable OWA themes and ships a number of different themes, including themes based on Microsoft Zune and Xbox products. You can also create your own theme and include corporate logos, color schemes, and so on. Users select from the range of themes through OWA options. Exchange 2010 still uses themes, but the RTM version doesn't support theme selection and everyone uses the same default theme. Exchange 2010 SP1 addresses the issue by providing a set of 27 themes from which users can select. Administrators don't have control over user choice and cannot impose a theme on users.

Creating a complete theme is a very extensive customization of the OWA UI. Many companies liked the idea of incorporating some aspect of their corporate identity into OWA without doing the work to create a theme. The complete source code of the OWA application is distributed with the Exchange kit, and the classic solution to the problem is to customize some of the files used for the default theme. However, because of the extensive upgrade that Microsoft has applied to the OWA UI in Exchange 2010, you cannot port changes made to the files used by Exchange 2007 directly to their Exchange 2010 equivalents. Instead, you have to redevelop any customization done for Exchange 2007 by reapplying the changes to the Exchange 2010 image and Cascading Style Sheets (CSS) files. The good

Chapter 10

news is that Microsoft supports the customization of the OWA login page and documents what needs to be done to accomplish this task in the Exchange 2010 help file.

The most common customizations are applied to the OWA login pages to update the color scheme and logos to match corporate branding. TechNet contains a section dedicated to this topic that describes the names of the CSS and graphic files that OWA uses, how the components fit together to form the pages viewed by users, and how colors are assigned to the various text sections in the pages. Figure 10-22 shows a useful illustration from TechNet that shows the graphic files that OWA combines to present a customized log-in dialog box. You can use this information to develop the necessary customizations to comply with corporate branding.

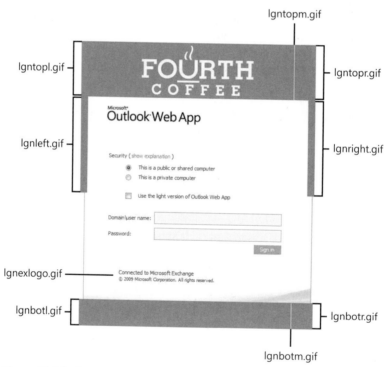

Figure 10-22 Components of OWA customization (source: TechNet).

An easy customization that you can accomplish in a couple of minutes is to add some text to the OWA log-in screen. This is commonly done to provide some guidance to users about how they should seek help in case of problems. Figure 10-23 shows how some text has been added for the contoso.com deployment and how it appears when a user logs into OWA.

To customize the log-in screen with some new text, you do the following:

1. Create a file containing the HTML formatting instructions for the text that you want to display. You can call the file anything you like as long as you store it in the \Program Files\Microsoft\Exchange Server\V14\Client Access Server\OWA\Auth directory. For the purpose of this explanation, let's call the file contoso-disclaimer.inc.

2. Copy the \Program Files\Microsoft\Exchange Server\V14\Client Access Server\OWA \Auth\Logon.aspx file. This is the file that contains all the instructions used by OWA when it logs on a user.

3. Open the Logon.aspx file with a text editor and search for the string "mid tblConn." Right below it, insert a line to instruct OWA to read and display the text contained in the contoso-disclaimer.inc file that we created in step 1. The code in Logon.aspx will then look something like this:

```
<table class="mid tblConn">
<!-- #include file="contoso-disclaimer.inc" -->
```

4. Save Logon.aspx and restart an OWA session (you don't have to restart Microsoft Internet Information Services [IIS] or any of the Exchange services). You should see your text displayed similar to Figure 10-23.

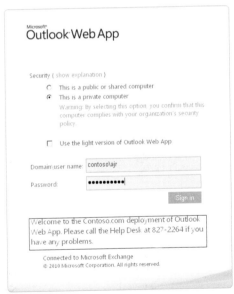

Figure 10-23 Updating the OWA log-in screen with some customized text.

5. The same approach can be taken to update Logoff.aspx if you want users to see a customized message when they sign off from OWA.

6. Once you are happy with the customization, you can apply it on all CAS servers by copying your modified files. There is no automatic mechanism to apply this kind of customization on every CAS server in an organization.

INSIDE OUT Customizations could be overwritten by future product updates

The other thing to remember is that any customization to one of the OWA components is a candidate to be overwritten by a new Microsoft version of the component in a new service pack, hot fix, or roll-up update. That's why you keep careful documentation about any customization that you apply to OWA—to make it easier to apply it after you upgrade Exchange. You should also keep a copy of both the original and the customized versions of any file that you change so that you can review them in the future. It's also fair to say that there is no guarantee that Microsoft will not change the way that OWA works in a future version and render this method of customization—or any method of customization—invalid, so be prepared to build some time to test and perhaps do a little recoding for OWA customizations into every deployment plan.

OWA mailbox policies and feature segmentation

Exchange 2010 supports the ability to allocate different levels of functionality to OWA users through policies. Although Exchange 2010 includes a default OWA policy, it is not actually applied to mailboxes unless you explicitly select the mailbox and apply the policy to it. Otherwise access to OWA features is controlled by the segmentation properties defined for the OWA virtual directory on each CAS server (Figure 10-24). OWA mailbox policies didn't exist in Exchange 2007, and the only way that you could segment functionality was through the properties of the OWA Web site. The problem with this approach is that any change applies to all mailboxes that connect to that CAS. Using policies allows more granular control because you can apply different policies at the level of an individual mailbox. In addition to their ability to segment features presented through OWA, OWA mailbox policies control some of the user-controllable settings available through ECP.

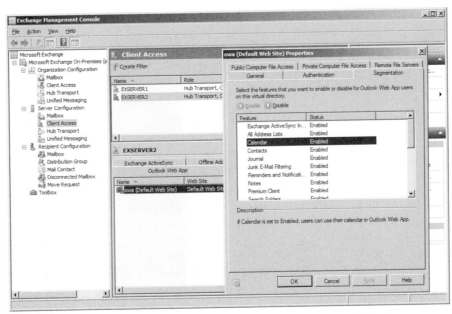

Figure 10-24 Viewing the segmentation properties of the default OWA Web site.

The easiest way to apply any OWA policy, including the default policy, to a set of mailboxes is with the Set-CASMailbox cmdlet. For example, this command fetches all the mailboxes that belong to the Exchange Users organizational unit (OU) and pipes them to Set-CASMailbox to apply the default OWA mailbox policy:

```
Get-Mailbox –OrganizationalUnit 'Exchange Users' | Set-CASMailbox
-OwaMailboxPolicy 'Default'
```

The default OWA policy typically duplicates the default out-of-the-box segmentation properties of the OWA default Web site as installed on a CAS server and permits access to all OWA features, including the premium client. To create a new policy, go to the Organization Configuration section of EMC, select Client Access, then on the Outlook Web App Mailbox Policies tab, and select the New Outlook Web App Mailbox Policy option in the action pane. A wizard then allows you to select which features you want users to access (Figure 10-25). In this case, we create a policy to restrict access to the OWA Light version that also selectively disables some OWA features.

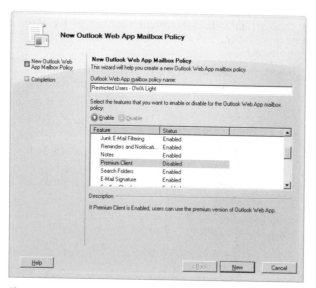

Figure 10-25 Creating a new OWA mailbox policy.

Table 10-3 lists the features that you can control in an OWA mailbox policy. Some of these features depend on other components (text messaging, public folders, and instant messaging), and others require a really good reason before you disable them. For example, it usually doesn't make much sense to disable the Change Password feature because handling user requests to change their passwords creates extra work for help desks.

Table 10-3 OWA features controllable through OWA mailbox policies

Feature	Meaning	Available through
Exchange ActiveSync Integration	If enabled, users can access details of the mobile devices that they have synchronized, including the ability to wipe devices if they are lost and retrieve logs containing details of synchronization operations. If disabled, the option is removed from ECP.	ECP
All Address Lists	If enabled, a user can see all defined address lists in the directory. If disabled, they can only see the GAL.	OWA
Calendar	If enabled, users can access the Calendar application. If disabled, the icon is removed from OWA.	OWA
Contacts	If enabled, users can access the Contacts application. If disabled, the icon is removed from OWA.	OWA
Journal	If enabled, users can see the Journal folder in their folder list. If disabled, OWA hides the folder.	OWA
Junk E-mail Filtering	If enabled, users can access the options to control junk mail processing such as blocked and safe user lists. If disabled, the option is removed from ECP.	ECP

Reminders and Notifications	If enabled, OWA will provide users with notifications of new messages, meeting reminders, and so on. If disabled, these notifications are suppressed.	OWA
Notes	If enabled, users can access the Notes application. If disabled, the icon is removed from OWA.	OWA
Premium Client	If enabled, users are able to use the premium client with a browser that supports this client. If disabled, users are forced to use the standard client no matter which browser they use.	OWA
Search Folders	If enabled, users can access search folders created by Outlook. If disabled, these folders are suppressed.	OWA
E-Mail Signature	If enabled, users can access the option to create or modify email signatures and apply them to outgoing messages. If disabled, the option is removed from ECP.	ECP
Spelling Checker	If enabled, users can spell check the content of messages. If disabled, the option is removed from OWA. Even when enabled, users do not have the option to customize their spelling dictionary.	OWA
Tasks	If enabled, users can create and manage tasks in OWA. If disabled, the option is suppressed.	OWA
Theme Selection	If enabled, users can select a theme other than the default and apply itto OWA and ECP. If disabled, the option is suppressed.	OWA/ECP
Unified Messaging Integration	If this feature is enabled and the mailbox is enabled for UM, users areable to access and manage their UM settings through ECP. If disabled, the option is removed.	ECP
Change Password	If this feature is enabled, users can change their account password from OWA. If disabled, OWA will not prompt users when their password is approaching its expiry date (prompts start 14 days in advance) and they will not be able to see the option to change their password in ECP.	OWA/ECP
Rules	If enabled, users will be able to create and modify rules through ECP. If disabled, the option is suppressed. However, any rules created with Outlook will continue to be respected by Exchange.	ECP
Public Folders	If enabled, users will be able to access and work with public folders. If disabled, the icon is removed from OWA.	OWA
S/MIME	If enabled, users can download the optional S/MIME control and then use it to apply digital signatures to messages and encrypt messages. If disabled, users are not able to create or read opaque-signed or encrypted messages. Messages that are clear-signed can be read (but not composed) and any digital signatures on the message will not be validated. Also, the option to download the S/MIME control is removed from ECP.	OWA/ECP
Recover Deleted Items	If enabled, users can recover deleted items. If disabled, users won't be able to recover deleted items with OWA, but Exchange will continue to preserve these items in the dumpster.	OWA

Chapter 10

Instant Messaging	If enabled and an Instant Messaging (IM) integration is available, users will be able to access IM functionality from within OWA, including the ability to view presence information. If disabled, these features are unavailable.	OWA
Text Messaging	If enabled, users will be able to create and send text (SMS) messages from OWA. If disabled, this feature is removed.	OWA

A new policy can also be created with EMS. For whatever reason, this is a two-step process. First, you create the new policy with the New-OWAMailboxPolicy cmdlet, and then you use the Set-OWAMailboxPolicy cmdlet to define what features are enabled or disabled by the policy. For example, here's a policy that allows users to use the premium client while removing some of the more esoteric features:

```
New-OWAMailboxPolicy -Name 'Limited OWA features'
Set-OWAMailboxPolicy -Identity 'Limited OWA features'
-ActiveSyncIntegrationEnabled $True -AllAddressListsEnabled $True
-CalendarEnabled $True -ContactsEnabled $True -JournalEnabled $True
-JunkEmailEnabled $True -RemindersAndNotificationsEnabled $True
-NotesEnabled $True -PremiumClientEnabled $True -SearchFoldersEnabled $False
-SignaturesEnabled $True -SpellCheckerEnabled $True -TasksEnabled $True
-ThemeSelectionEnabled $False -UMIntegrationEnabled $False
-ChangePasswordEnabled $True -RulesEnabled $True -PublicFoldersEnabled $False
-SMimeEnabled $True -RecoverDeletedItemsEnabled $True
-InstantMessagingEnabled $False -TextMessagingEnabled $False
```

More than just segmentation

Although feature segmentation is the most obvious use of OWA mailbox policies and receives the most attention, you can also control other aspects of how users work with OWA through these policies. After you create a new OWA mailbox policy, you are able to define rules for file access and download when OWA is run on private and public computers. Click the policy with which you want to work and then select Properties. You can then access the properties that control feature segmentation and two other tabs for Public Computer File Access and Private Computer File Access (Figure 10-26).

> **Note**
>
> In this context, Public and Private refer to the access mode chosen by the user when he starts OWA and indicate whether the browser runs on a public computer such as a kiosk or a private computer such as his own laptop.

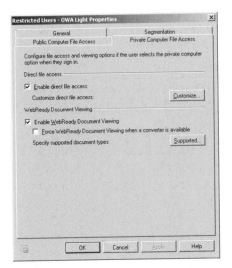

Figure 10-26 OWA Policy File Access options.

The Direct File Access settings (Figure 10-27) allow you to control how various file types are opened by users through OWA. The default option for both public and private computers is to allow direct access, meaning that users are able to open files. However, all types of files are not treated equally, as there are some file types that pose a potential risk of infection because they are often used as threat vectors by hackers who wish to infiltrate a computer. Files are therefore grouped into four categories:

- Always Allow: These files are deemed to be innocuous and safe to open on the client computer. The list includes types such as Word documents (.doc and .docx extensions) and Windows bitmaps (.bmp extension) that you can be reasonably sure will not contain malicious code.

- Always Block: These files pose a significant risk to a computer when they are opened by a user because they contain executable code. These files include types such as Windows batch files (.bat extension) and Windows command files (.cmd extension).

- Force Save: These are files that users cannot open directly and must save to disk before they can access the content. These types include Windows compiled help files (.chm extension).

- All others (unknown files that are not included in the other lists): The policy states what should be done if an unknown file type is detected. The default is to force a save to disk.

Chapter 10

The priority given to action is from top to bottom. In other words, if a file type is on both the Always Block and the Force Save lists, it will be blocked.

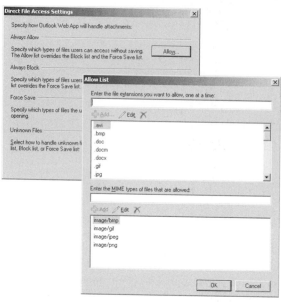

Figure 10-27 Configuring the file access allow list for an OWA mailbox policy.

If you prefer to have users open a viewer to access files rather than running the native application, you can select the Force WebReady Document Viewing When A Converter Is Available option. The effect is to force OWA to check documents as they are opened to see whether a WebReady converter is available and, if so, to always use the converter to open the file rather than calling the application. The idea is to eliminate any potential risk from macros or other code that could be carried around in the common file formats supported by WebReady, such as Microsoft Word and Microsoft Excel. In truth, the antivirus software that runs on today's PCs will usually catch any malicious code, so forcing WebReady viewing for OWA when it is run on a private computer could be considered overkill. Figure 10-28 shows how to access the list of file formats supported by WebReady converters. This list has been augmented over the last few years and supports a reasonably full set of the most common file formats that users will need to open in office environments.

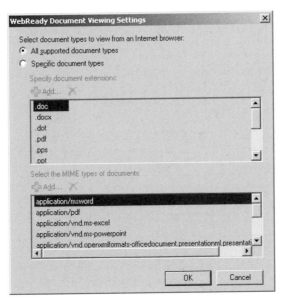

Figure 10-28 Viewing the list of WebReady supported document types.

It might be safe to allow users to open documents with applications on private computers, but it's a different matter on computers that are used for public access. In this scenario, it is reasonably common to block access to attachments to avoid the risk that users might download and leave sensitive files on a computer that can be accessed by an unauthorized individual. You can do this by clearing the option through EMC or by running the Set-OWAMailboxPolicy cmdlet. Settings applied through an OWA mailbox policy override those set through the properties of the OWA virtual directory. For example:

```
Set-OWAMailboxPolicy -id 'Restricted Users - OWA Light'
-DirectFileAccessOnPublicComputersEnabled $False
-ForceWebReadyDocumentViewingFirstOnPublicComputers $True
```

When this policy is applied, users will not be able to open or download and save files on public computers, but they will be able to access the content if a WebReady viewer is available. Web links that are included in messages are still active. Exchange 2010 includes viewers for Microsoft Office documents (see Figure 10-29), RTF, and PDF files.

Chapter 10

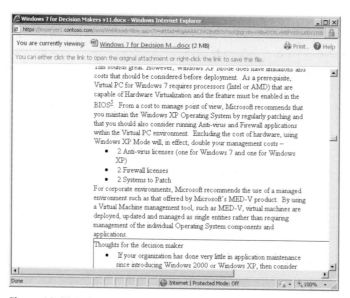

Figure 10-29 Using a WebReady viewer to read a Word document.

INSIDE OUT   A note on document access

Exchange 2007 introduced the ability for OWA users to access documents through UNC paths (typically to a file share) or on SharePoint sites. This feature is deprecated in Exchange 2010, possibly because it is not used extensively but also because of the potential security concerns in accessing documents from unknown or untrusted locations.

Attachment processing

Administrators control how OWA handles attachments by creating a list of attachment types and marking each as blocked, allowed, or "force to save." Obviously, *blocked* means that users cannot open or download an attachment of this type to their PC, normally because the file type is likely to contain a virus or some other dangerous content. *Allowed* means the opposite, as there is a high degree of confidence that these attachments are safe.

OWA performs special processing for attachments marked as *force to save*. This means that the user has to save the attachment to his local disk before he can view its contents. As OWA downloads the attachment from the server, it checks to see whether it is XML or

HTML. In this case, OWA runs some code called Safe HTML to strip out any malicious XML or HTML code. If the attachment is another type, OWA examines the content to see if it actually contains XML or HTML code. This check is performed to ensure that no attachment is ever downloaded that contains malicious code, which could introduce a virus or another dangerous program onto the PC. If hidden XML or HTML code is detected, OWA strips the attachment and replaces it with a text file to tell the user that the attachment was removed.

INSIDE OUT
A high level of protection on OWA prevents the receipt of code in text files

The level of protection supplied by OWA is very high and reflects the experience of PCs being infected by attachments. However, it also means that you cannot send HTML code in a text file to an OWA user because it will be stripped.

Applying an OWA mailbox policy

After the new policy is created, to apply it, you switch to Recipient Configuration and select one or more mailboxes and then Properties from the action pane. Click the Mailbox Features tab, select Outlook Web App, and then select Properties. You can then select an Outlook Web App mailbox policy and apply it to the mailbox (Figure 10-30).

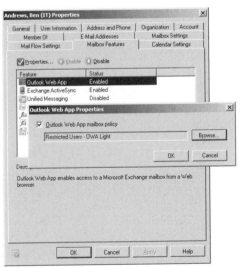

Figure 10-30 Applying an Outlook Web App mailbox policy.

Chapter 10

Exchange enforces the new policy the next time that the user logs into her mailbox. If everything works as expected, the user will be presented with a restricted version of OWA Light. Of course, you can also apply an OWA mailbox policy to a mailbox with EMS:

```
Set-CASMailbox -Identity 'Andrews, Ben (IT)' -OWAMailboxPolicy 'Restricted Users
-OWA Light'
```

INSIDE OUT Integrating OWA and OCS

One small glitch might creep in with the instant messaging section of the policy. OWA 2010 supports a nice integration with Office Communications Server (OCS), but if you want to create the link between the two products, you have to ensure that the OWA mailbox policy that is applied to mailboxes that want to use OCS specifies "OCS" in the *InstantMessagingType* attribute. For example:

```
Set-OWAMailboxPolicy -Identity 'OCS Integration Enabled' -InstantMessagingType
'OCS'
-InstantMessagingEnabled $True
Set-CASMailbox -Identity 'Akers, Kim' -OWAMailboxPolicy 'OCS Integration
Enabled'
```

You can find more information about the integration between OWA and OCS, including some important changes made in Exchange 2010 SP1 to improve how the integration is accomplished, at *http://msexchangeteam.com/archive/2010/09/27/456446.aspx*.

POP3 and IMAP4 clients

POP3 and IMAP4 are Internet email protocols that are supported by a wide variety of clients and servers. Fans of these protocols love the lightweight nature of their connections, which is one of the reasons they are the protocols of choice for most consumer free email services such as Hotmail and Gmail (Hotmail supports POP3; Gmail supports both protocols). POP3 is the older and less functional protocol. IMAP4 is more functional than POP3, but less functional than MAPI. Nevertheless, modern IMAP4 clients, including Outlook, can build a rich range of features around the rudimentary but superefficient communications to download messages from a server. Of course, unlike MAPI, POP3 and IMAP4 are both protocols that clients use to retrieve messages from a server. Apart from age, the fundamental differences between the two protocols are as follows:

- POP3 downloads messages to a client and removes them from the server.

- POP3 supports a very limited set of folders on the server (essentially, the Inbox).

- IMAP4 can leave copies of downloaded messages on the server.

- IMAP4 can access any folder that a server exposes and download messages from the folders to client-side replicas.

- IMAP4 allows a "live sync" mode in which the client holds open a connection to the server; this provides a more Outlook-like sync experience in which messages trickle in to the Inbox as they arrive instead of arriving in batches when a POP3 connection is made.

The vast bulk of clients that connect to Exchange 2010 via POP3 and IMAP4 belong to four categories:

- Users in an educational establishment such as a university.

- Users who access an Exchange mailbox running as a hosted service when Outlook is not provided to restrict costs.

- Users who consider Outlook to be overfeatured, bloated software. Often, these users have used a client such as Eudora or Thunderbird for many years and don't see a reason to change.

- Users who run an operating system that doesn't support the premium version of OWA or who simply prefer to use IMAP. Many Linux users are in this category.

The attraction of using free POP3 or IMAP4 clients is the avoidance of Outlook license fees. This is less of an issue in large corporations that conclude enterprise licensing agreements with Microsoft that include the entire Office application suite. For this reason, relatively few users in large corporate deployments use POP3 or IMAP4 clients. OWA is available if they don't want to use Outlook, and it's easier for the help desk if a limited number of clients are in use. Another reason is that POP3 and IMAP4 clients are purposely designed to work across any server that supports these protocols. They therefore do not support features that are specific to Exchange, such as:

- Display of MailTips

- Organization of message threads into conversation views

- Display of retention tag information

- Display of protected content such as items that require licenses from Active Directory Rights Management Services

For the remainder of this discussion, I focus on setting up the Exchange 2010 IMAP4 server and configuring clients to connect to the IMAP4 server. The steps to set up and configure POP3 access are similar in concept if different in detail but not covered here. Copious detail on this topic is available on the Internet.

Chapter 10

Configuring the IMAP4 server

When you install the CAS role on a server, the setup program creates the Microsoft Exchange POP3 and Microsoft Exchange IMAP4 services to support client connections via these protocols, but does not start the services. Therefore, the first step to support POP3 or IMAP4 clients is to start these services. In addition, you should change the startup state for the services from Manual to Automatic so that Windows will start them every time the server is booted. These Windows PowerShell commands serve the purpose:

```
Set-Service msExchangeImap4 -StartupType Automatic
Start-Service -Service msExchangeImap4
```

Once the IMAP4 service is started, the CAS server runs a virtual IMAP4 server that monitors incoming client connections on port 143 (Transport Layer Security [TLS] or unencrypted connections) and 993 (Secure Sockets Layer [SSL] secured connections). Figure 10-31 shows the properties that are usually of most interest to administrators when they configure IMAP connectivity for Exchange 2010. The *Binding* properties define the ports that the IMAP4 server monitors and the set of IP addresses that clients can use to connect to the IMAP4 server. The *Connection* properties define various limits that the server uses to control client connections. See TechNet for detailed information on these settings.

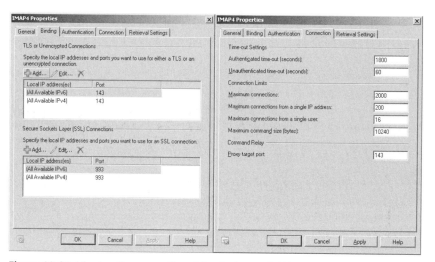

Figure 10-31 Viewing the properties of the Exchange IMAP4 server.

Exchange 2010 SP1 allows you to use basic authentication, Integrated Windows Authentication, and TLS-secured logons (the default) to connect POP3 or IMAP4 clients. As shown in Figure 10-32, you can select the authentication method that you want to use through the Authentication tab of the IMAP4 server Properties dialog box.

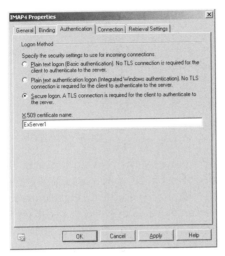

Figure 10-32 Authentication properties for the IMAP4 server.

The Get-IMAPSettings and Set-IMAPSettings cmdlets are used to retrieve and set configuration settings for the IMAP4 server. The equivalent cmdlets for POP3 are Get-POPSettings and Set-POPSettings. For example, to retrieve the current configuration for a CAS server called ExServer1, we use the following command:

```
Get-IMAPSettings –Server ExServer1Protocol
```

```
Name                              : IMAP4
Name                              : 1
MaxCommandSize                    : 10240
ShowHiddenFoldersEnabled          : False
UnencryptedOrTLSBindings          : {:::143, 0.0.0.0:143}
SSLBindings                       : {:::993, 0.0.0.0:993}
InternalConnectionSettings        : {ExServer1.contoso.com:993:SSL, ExServer1.contoso.com:143:TLS}
ExternalConnectionSettings        : {}
X509CertificateName               : ExServer1
Banner                            : The Microsoft Exchange IMAP4 service is ready.
LoginType                         : PlainTextAuthentication
AuthenticatedConnectionTimeout    : 00:30:00
PreAuthenticatedConnectionTimeout : 00:01:00
MaxConnections                    : 2000
MaxConnectionFromSingleIP         : 2000
MaxConnectionsPerUser             : 16
MessageRetrievalMimeFormat        : BestBodyFormat
ProxyTargetPort                   : 143
CalendarItemRetrievalOption       : iCalendar
OwaServerUrl                      :
EnableExactRFC822Size             : False
LiveIdBasicAuthReplacement        : False
```

Chapter 10

```
SuppressReadReceipt            : False
ProtocolLogEnabled             : False
EnforceCertificateErrors       : False
LogFileLocation                : C:\LOGS\IMAP4
LogFileRollOverSettings        : Daily
LogPerFileSizeQuota            : unlimited
Server                         : EXSERVER1
Identity                       : EXSERVER1\1
```

Note that the *ExternalConnectionSettings* property listed has a blank value. This property is displayed by the Account Information page of ECP when a user clicks Settings For POP, IMAP, And SMTP Access. The intention is to provide users with the information that they need to input into clients that use these protocols so that they can connect to Exchange. Unfortunately, if you leave the default settings in place, users will see blank values when they access the page. Users need to know the name of the CAS server to which to connect, the port number for the protocol, and the encryption type security setting. We can set these values with the Set-POPSettings and Set-IMAPSettings cmdlets. To provide the information, you have to take these steps:

- Provide details for POP3 access:

  Set-POPSettings –ExternalConnectionSettings ExServer1.contoso.com:995:SSL –Server ExServer1

- Provide details for IMAP4 access:

  Set-IMAPSettings –ExternalConnectionSettings ExServer1.contoso.com:993:SSL –Server ExServer1

- Publish information about the connector:

Most companies provide a receive connector on a hub transport server that POP3 and IMAP4 clients can use to relay their outgoing messages. To make users aware of which server to use, you publish information about the connector by setting its *AdvertiseClientSetting* property to $True. In this case, I'm telling users to connect to the default receive connector on a hub transport server, but in production circumstances you'd be more likely to create a specific receive connector that is dedicated and configured to act as a client relay.

```
Set-ReceiveConnector –Identity 'ExServer1\Default ExServer1' –AdvertiseClientSettings
$True
```

Remember that the POP3 and IMAP4 settings are server-specific, so you have to set the values on each of the CAS servers that you want to use for this purpose. A restart of IIS on the CAS server might be necessary to make the new values available to clients.

If you change any of the configuration settings for the IMAP4 server, you have to restart the Microsoft Exchange IMAP4 service. It's common to find that you want to turn on protocol logging to help debug connections from a particular client. To enable protocol logging for IMAP4 clients, you need to enable logging and tell Exchange where it should create the log. Enabling logging in Exchange 2007 requires you to edit a configuration file, but Exchange 2010 allows you to enable logging with the Set-IMAPSettings cmdlet. For example:

```
Set-IMAPSettings —Server ExServer1 —ProtocolLogEnabled $True —LogFileLocation
'C:\Logs\'
```

Logging generates a mass of data on the server, some of which is fairly obtuse if you are not familiar with debugging IMAP connections. Clients can also generate logs, and if you need to provide data to help a support representative solve a problem, you should generate server and client logs to ensure that they have full knowledge of what the client is sending and how the server is responding.

Configuring IMAP4 client access

From a user perspective, it is easy to configure a POP3 or IMAP4 client to connect to Exchange 2010. For my example, I chose the Thunderbird free IMAP4 client that you can download from *http://www.mozillamessaging.com/en-US/thunderbird/*. Two separate connections must be configured before an IMAP4 client can download and send messages.

1. An IMAP4 server hosted by a CAS server must be ready to accept client connections so that IMAP4 clients can access mailboxes and download folders and items.

2. A Simple Mail Transfer Protocol (SMTP) receive connector hosted by a hub transport server must be ready to accept client connections to allow IMAP4 clients to relay outgoing messages via SMTP.

Note that the CAS blocks POP3 and IMAP4 from the Anonymous and Guest accounts. Additionally, the Administrator account cannot be used to connect to Exchange via these protocols either. To access the Administrator mailbox, you must use Outlook or OWA.

The steps required to configure the client to connect to Exchange 2010 are as follows:

1. Set the authentication setting to Basic for the IMAP4 server on the CAS to which you want to connect the client. This is sufficient for testing purposes because it ensures that just about any IMAP4 client will be able to connect. Once you have established that connections work freely, you can increase the level of security by moving to Integrated Windows Authentication or Secure Logon, depending on what authentication mechanisms are supported by the client.

2. Restart the IMAP4 server to effect the change in the authentication setting.

3.   Configure the client with the name of the CAS server and the user name in domain name\account name format. Figure 10-33 shows the server settings as input into Thunderbird.

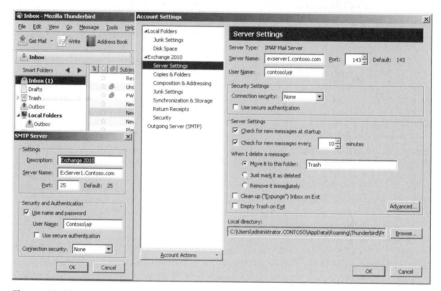

Figure 10-33 Connecting the Thunderbird IMAP4 email client to Exchange 2010.

4.   Connect the client to prove that messages can be downloaded.

5.   Check that the Permission Groups assigned to the default client receive connector on the hub transport server that you want to use for sending outbound messages allows anonymous connections. Again, this is the easiest setting to use to test outgoing message connectivity and should ensure that all types of clients are able to connect to send messages. Once you know that messages are flowing, you can increase the security. As you can see in Figure 10-33, the Thunderbird client supports STARTTLS security with username and password credentials, so this means that the receive connector doesn't need to allow anonymous connections because these connections will be regarded as "Exchange users."

Once messages are being downloaded and sent freely, the next step is to configure Lightweight Directory Access Protocol (LDAP) access to Active Directory so that we can use Active Directory as an address book. The details of how to configure a connection to Active Directory vary from client to client, as does the ability of the client to use the data fetched from Active Directory. Some clients are only able to browse Active Directory, whereas others, like Thunderbird, are able to validate email addresses against Active Directory as they are entered into message headers. Figure 10-34 shows the settings that I used to define Active Directory as an address book for Thunderbird.

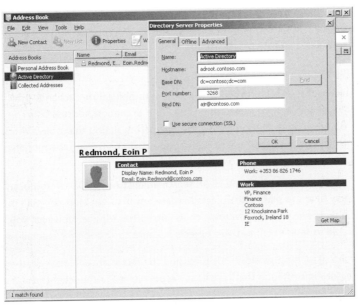

Figure 10-34 Configuring the Thunderbird address book to connect to Active Directory.

The following settings are used:

1. The name is set to Active Directory, but it can be anything that you like, because this serves purely as an illustrative name and has no other function.

2. The hostname is set to the fully qualified domain name (FQDN) of a global catalog server that provides access to Active Directory. Ideally, this should be a global catalog server in the same site as the CAS server.

3. The base DN provides a starting point for LDAP searches in the directory. In this instance, we provide the root of the directory to ensure that searches can find any mail-enabled object in contoso.com.

4. The port number is set to 3268 rather than the standard port (389) used by LDAP.

5. The bind DN is set to my SMTP address.

To test the connection, open the client address book and attempt to search for some mailboxes that you know exist. You should be able to see mailboxes, contacts, and distribution groups.

Chapter 10

INSIDE OUT Only minor issues

Two small issues are the following:

1. The LDAP searches executed by a client might ignore Exchange-specific filters. For example, if you select the Hide From Exchange Address Lists check box for an object, it stops Outlook and OWA users from seeing that object through the GAL. However, this block means nothing to other clients, and the hidden objects will probably be revealed to users.

2. Along the same lines, an LDAP search against Active Directory doesn't impose any filters to eliminate objects that are not mail-enabled, so you'll probably be able to see security groups such as Enterprise Admins. However, you won't be able to send email to these objects because they don't have email addresses.

These are small hiccups along the road, and the fact that users have read-only access to directory information that reveals some objects that other clients don't show isn't really very serious.

Exchange ActiveSync

Microsoft added server-based ActiveSync to Exchange with the release of Exchange 2003 SP2. Exchange 2007 marked a major upgrade for ActiveSync. The version of ActiveSync provided with Exchange 2010 is much less of a change because it's mostly a case of tweaking existing functionality to improve support for clients. It might be the case that ActiveSync is now "competitive enough," and Microsoft is concentrating on licensing ActiveSync as widely as possible. Certainly the licensing activity is progressing in leaps and bounds, because all major smartphone vendors now license ActiveSync, including Apple for iPhone and Google for Android-based devices. The attractiveness of ActiveSync is strongly linked to the success of Exchange as the de facto corporate email platform. Although Windows Mobile has not evolved to match the capabilities of other mobile platforms, Microsoft has experienced increasing success due to the growing number of Exchange mailboxes allied to greater availability of ActiveSync-enabled devices.

Among the major functionality changes in Exchange 2010 ActiveSync that upgraded clients can use are the following:

- Like Outlook and OWA 2010, messages can be grouped in conversations so that all of the items relating to a topic can be handled at a single time. You can deal with a conversation by reading the latest item, deleting one item or the complete conversation, or moving everything in one operation. The most interesting aspect is the way that

Exchange maintains metadata on the server to handle ongoing processing of conversations as new items arrive. The metadata lets Exchange take care of operations such as "delete any further items in this conversation" or "move items as they arrive into this folder."

- You have the ability to fetch free/busy information from the server for contacts to determine if they are available at a certain time. This is a great feature when you attempt to set up a meeting on a mobile device.

- If you deploy Exchange 2010 Unified Messaging, voice mail messages are now played directly within Outlook Mobile (because they are encoded as MP3 files) rather than having to export the voice attachment to be played through Windows Media Player or another audio player. In addition, voice mails are delivered with a transcription of the message in the body so you can get an idea of what the message is about without having to open the voice mail attachment.

- Outlook Mobile stores details of recent email addresses in a nicknames cache in a hidden item in the mailbox root that it shares with OWA and Outlook so that you can see a suggested list of recipients as you enter a new address.

- You can use your phone to send and receive Short Message Service or text messages. You can use OWA or Outlook to compose and send new messages and ActiveSync then synchronizes the SMS messages down to the mobile device, which then transmits the message like any other SMS. The reverse also works, and incoming SMS messages are downloaded to the device and then synchronized by ActiveSync into your mailbox where they can be processed using OWA or Outlook. Text messages are stored like any other message in the Inbox and Sent Items folders and can be operated on like any other item. For example, you can flag a text message for follow-up or forward it to another user.

> **Note**
> Anyone who despairs at the limited keyboards available on many mobile devices will delight in the ability to create and send SMS messages using their computer keyboard. Using ActiveSync to synchronize text messages with Exchange is a simple, brilliant idea. The only complaint that you could make is to ask why this feature hasn't appeared before now, and the answer is probably that although text messaging has been enormously popular in Europe and Asia for years, it's only recently that SMS communications have become popular in the United States.

- Similar to Outlook, an icon to indicate that you have already replied to or forwarded a message is now shown.

Phones running Windows Mobile 6.1 can install a CAB update to upgrade Outlook Mobile to access the new features available in ActiveSync in Exchange 2010. Exchange 2010 users whose mailboxes are enabled for ActiveSync and who access their mailboxes with a suitable device will receive a message inviting them to download an over-the-air (OTA) upgrade to apply to their device (Figure 10-35). The upgrade is downloaded from Microsoft's Web site. When applied, it adds Outlook Mobile to the device and allows the user to access features such as SMS synchronization and conversations. Phones running Windows Mobile 6.5 or greater already have the code necessary to access these features. This is a long-overdue improvement to the situation that existed where companies were essentially forced to upgrade Windows Mobile devices to be able to utilize any features introduced in a new version of ActiveSync, and it might represent a realization within Microsoft that enterprises don't discard mobile devices used for business purposes quite as quickly as consumers do when they pursue the latest fashion device.

Figure 10-35 The invitation to use integrated text messaging.

Setting ActiveSync policies

Unless you specify a different policy, Exchange applies the default ActiveSync policy to mailboxes when they are enabled for ActiveSync. Policies defined on Exchange 2007 are upgraded to be used by Exchange 2010 by the addition of a new capability to allow or block specific applications on a mobile device. This capability is revealed on the Other tab of a policy's Properties dialog box (Figure 10-36). Note that use of this capability requires an upgrade to the enterprise Client Access License (CAL). The properties revealed through the other tabs remain the same, because Exchange 2007 and control settings such as whether a password is required to access the device and what type of password should be used, what size of messages and attachments are to be synchronized, whether nonprovisionable devices (those that do not respect policies) are allowed, and what device capabilities (camera, removable storage, Wi-Fi, and Bluetooth) are supported.

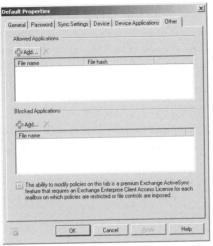

Figure 10-36 Editing an ActiveSync policy to allow or block applications for mobile devices.

INSIDE OUT   Mailbox policy and ActiveSync client–server partnership

Although you can collect all these settings into a policy and apply that policy to mailboxes, it is important to realize that ActiveSync is based on a client–server partnership. The server might insist on some settings, but the client can blithely ignore the demands of the server if the client operating system has never implemented the code to apply the policy fully. ActiveSync makes a clear differentiation among fully compliant devices, partially compliant devices, and noncompliant devices. A *fully compliant* device is one that implements all of the settings specified by a policy. A *partially compliant* device applies some but not all of the settings in a policy, probably because the necessary code to apply one or more settings is not implemented in the operating system. A *noncompliant* device can synchronize with Exchange but essentially ignores policy settings because it does not recognize or will not accept a policy provided to it by the server. For example, you can create a policy that blocks the use of a camera in mobile devices, and this policy will be effective for Windows Mobile devices where the operating system understands how to disable the camera after the policy is applied. However, an Apple iPhone will ignore the policy and the camera can still be used. The reason is that the iPhone includes a partial implementation of ActiveSync, certainly enough to do the basics of email, calendar, and contact synchronization, but missing some important management details.

You can change the policy that is applied to a mailbox at any time. For example:

```
Set-CASMailbox -Identity 'Ruth, Andy' -ActiveSyncMailboxPolicy "Executives"
```

Exchange 2010 SP1 allows you to create and maintain ActiveSync policies through the Phone And Voice section of ECP. Exactly the same parameters are exposed as in EMC. Figure 10-37 illustrates how the creation of a new ActiveSync policy appears in ECP.

Figure 10-37 Creating a new ActiveSync policy with ECP.

Generating ActiveSync reports

All of the transactional information about communications between ActiveSync clients and Exchange is recorded in IIS logs. Here you'll find information such as the protocol version of the devices that communicate with Exchange, the type of synchronization performed (mail, calendar, contacts, everything), statistics about the number of operations performed (adds, changes, deletes), and specific operations such as out-of-office (OOF) message creation. Although all this is available, it is buried in the mass of other data recorded in the IIS logs, and some help is therefore required to retrieve the correct data and interpret it in a human-friendly manner. The Export-ActiveSyncLog cmdlet is designed for just this purpose.

Export-ActiveSyncLog is run on a CAS server. The cmdlet scans the IIS logs to filter data relating to ActiveSync operations and uses these data to generate a set of reports. These are:

- Usage report (Users.csv): A summary of the total items sent and received (number of items and bytes) broken down by item type (email, calendar, etc.).

- Servers report (Servers.csv): A summary of the servers hosting the mailboxes that are associated with ActiveSync requests.

- Hits report (Hourly.csv): The total number of synchronization requests processed per hour plus the total number of unique devices that initiate synchronization requests each hour.

- HTTP status report (StatusCodes.csv): A summary of the different HTTP error response codes and the percentage of the time that each code was encountered. The intention of the report is to give an indication of the overall performance of the server.

- Policy Compliance report (PolicyCompliance.csv): A summary of the number of devices that are compliant, partially compliant, and noncompliant.

- User Agent list (UserAgents.csv): A summary of the total number of unique users who have connected to ActiveSync during the report period, organized by mobile device operating system (different versions of Windows Mobile, iPhone, Android, and so on).

Because the output files are in CSV format, you can open and interpret them to meet your own needs. You can open the files with Microsoft Excel or Microsoft Access or import them into a database to allow more sophisticated analysis and reporting based on data collated over an extended period.

Reporting synchronized devices

The Get-ActiveSyncDeviceStatistics cmdlet provides information about the synchronization status for a mailbox. For example, here's an edited version of the information reported for a mailbox:

```
Get-ActiveSyncDeviceStatistics -id JSmith
```

```
FirstSyncTime           : 2/24/2010 7:00:01 PM
LastPolicyUpdateTime    : 3/3/2010 7:30:22 PM
LastSyncAttemptTime     : 3/4/2010 6:06:18 PM
LastSuccessSync         : 3/4/2010 6:06:18 PM
DeviceType              : PocketPC
DeviceID                : 5ECE2DBB684616DD07FB173DF09254B5
DeviceUserAgent         : MSFT-PPC/5.2.5070
DeviceWipeSentTime      :
```

```
DeviceWipeRequestTime           :
DeviceWipeAckTime               :
LastPingHeartbeat               :
RecoveryPassword                : ********
DeviceModel                     : HP_KB1
DeviceImei                      : ******
DeviceFriendlyName              : HP_iPAQ_Glisten
DeviceOS                        : Windows CE 5.2.21871
DeviceOSLanguage                : English
DevicePhoneNumber               : *******7701
MailboxLogReport                :
DeviceEnableOutboundSMS         : True
DeviceMobileOperator            : AT&T
Identity                        : contoso.com/Exchange users/JSmith
/ExchangeActiveSyncDevices/PocketPC§5ECE2DBB684616DD07FB173DF09254B5
Guid                            : 8fb8848c-8c65-4f43-bb1e-450e582e1622
IsRemoteWipeSupported           : True
Status                          : DeviceOk
StatusNote                      :
DeviceAccessState               : Allowed
DeviceAccessStateReason         : Global
DeviceAccessControlRule         :
DevicePolicyApplied             : Mobile Policy (default)
DevicePolicyApplicationStatus   : AppliedInFull
LastDeviceWipeRequestor         :
DeviceActiveSyncVersion         : 14.0
NumberOfFoldersSynced           : 7
SyncStateUpgradeTime            :
```

INSIDE OUT   It's actually useful data

Some interesting data are revealed here because you can see which devices have synchronized with the mailbox, when they synchronized, and even the mobile operator. These data can provide the basis of some management reports, such as the number of mailboxes that use mobile devices, an analysis of the devices being used, and the distribution of users across mobile operators. You could use these data for multiple purposes such as negotiating a better corporate deal with a mobile operator or planning a replacement strategy for old devices.

The problem with the Get-ActiveSyncDeviceStatistics cmdlet is that it functions on the level of a mailbox, and there's no cmdlet available to provide aggregate data of the type that is useful for analysis. Clearly you don't want to review synchronization data for thousands of mailboxes to gain some understanding of what's happening on a server, so some code is required to fetch the necessary data and store them in a format that permits analysis.

This code uses the Get-CASMailbox cmdlet to fetch information about any mailbox with an ActiveSync partnership that's connected to an Exchange 2010 mailbox server. The Get-ActiveSyncDeviceStatistics cmdlet then extracts statistics for each device (remember, someone can create partnerships with several mobile devices) and writes out these data to a variable. Eventually, after data have been fetched from all the mailboxes, the aggregated data are written into a CSV format file that can be used for later analysis.

```
$Devices = $Null
$Mbx = Get-CASMailbox -ResultSize Unlimited |
Where {$_.HasActiveSyncDevicePartnership -eq $True -and
$_.ExchangeVersion.ExchangeBuild -ilike "14*"}

ForEach ($m in $Mbx)
{
$Devices += Get-ActiveSyncDeviceStatistics -Mailbox $m.Identity
}

$Devices | Export-CSV ExServer1ActiveSync.csv
```

The code works, but it's really only appropriate for use in small deployments of less than 1,000 mailboxes where you won't run into problems processing a lot of data in memory after it's fetched from mailboxes. Another way of doing much the same thing is to use two separate loops. The first processes the list of mailboxes that have ActiveSync partnerships, and the second fetches information for each device that has synchronized with the mailbox. The resulting data are written out in a less verbose manner into a simple text file. The code has been used to generate monthly management reports in organizations supporting more than 30,000 mobile devices:

```
$Date = Get-Date -uformat "%Y%m%d"
$Logfile = "C:\Logs\ActiveSync-all-$date.txt"

$Lst = Get-CASMailbox -ResultSize Unlimited | Where
{$_.HasActiveSyncDevicePartnership -eq $True}

ForEach ($CASMbx in $lst) {
$Devices=$Null
$Devices= @Get-ActiveSyncDeviceStatistics -Mailbox $CASMbx.name)
ForEach ($device in $devices) {
$DeviceModel = $Device.DeviceModel
$DeviceType = $Device.DeviceType
$LastSyncTime = $Device.LastSuccessSync
$PhoneNumber = $Device.DevicePhonenumber
```

```
$UserAgent = $Device.DeviceUserAgent
Add-Content -path $Logfile "$casmbx.name
|$DeviceModel|$DeviceType|$UserAgent|$LastSyncTime|$PhoneNumber|"

    }
}
```

Whatever approach to reporting you take, the important point is that you capture data that make sense for your organization and use them to build a solid and practical ActiveSync policy for your company.

Blocking types of mobile devices

New mobile devices appear all the time, and users are tempted to buy these devices and then attempt to connect the devices to their mailboxes. Often, these connections occur without the knowledge or the intervention of an administrator. This isn't a problem if everything works and the device connects the first time and continues to synchronize mailbox contents perfectly, but it can become a problem when a user attempts to introduce a new device that doesn't comply with corporate security guidelines or runs an operating system that the help desk isn't able to support. For example, the original ActiveSync implementation on the Palm Pre did not enforce the PIN locking feature, which is a pretty big security issue for many companies, so users were told not to use these devices until Palm fixed the problem. The original Apple iPhone also caused some heartburn for some companies because its implementation of all ActiveSync security features was not as complete as found in Windows Mobile. If you enable support for "nonprovisionable devices" by allowing an open connect policy, essentially you allow any device that supports ActiveSync to connect to Exchange and run the risk that the policies to enforce desired security behavior will never reach the device (or that the device will ignore them altogether).

To solve the problem, Exchange 2010 introduces the Set-ActiveSyncOrganizationSettings cmdlet to allow you to exert more control over what happens when users attempt to synchronize new mobile devices for the first time. In this context, a new mobile device is a device with a type for which Exchange has not defined an access policy. You can opt to block synchronization completely, quarantine the device, or allow it. When a device is quarantined, its information is sent to a set of nominated administrators who can decide whether to allow the device to synchronize or continue to block its access to Exchange. For example, the following code sets the default access level to Blocked and sends a note to the HelpDeskAgents@contoso.com email address any time a user attempts to connect a new device. It's more convenient when this address points to a distribution group as this usually ensures a faster response. The *–UserMailInsert* parameter specifies a text string that Exchange includes in the message sent to the user to inform him that his device has been quarantined.

```
Set-ActiveSyncOrganizationSettings –AdminMailRecipients 'HelpDeskAgents@contoso.com'
–DefaultAccessLevel 'Quarantine' –UserMailInsert 'Device quarantined. Please call the
Help Desk to unblock the device'
```

The Get-ActiveSyncOrganizationSettings cmdlet reveals the current policy for new device connections. From this output, we can see that the default ActiveSync policy for the organization allows any device to connect:

```
Get-ActiveSyncOrganizationSettings
```

```
DefaultAccessLevel          : Allow
UserMailInsert              :
AdminMailRecipients         : {}
Name                        : Mobile Mailbox Settings
OtherWellKnownObjects       : {}
AdminDisplayName            :
ExchangeVersion             : 0.10 (14.0.100.0)
Identity                    : Mobile Mailbox Settings
```

Let's assume that the help desk receives notification that a user has attempted to synchronize with a new device called Whiz-Bang01. The administrators should now make the decision about how to deal with these devices. They can allow, block, or continue to quarantine. In view of the fact that users are already attempting to connect, the decision really lies between block and allow. Once the decision is made, it is implemented with a new ActiveSync device access rule. These rules give Exchange the ability to block devices selectively by device type or model. If we want to allow access, we can do this with an access rule like this:

```
New-ActiveSyncDeviceAccessRule –QueryString 'Whiz-Bang01' –Characteristic DeviceModel
–AccessLevel Allow
```

The question now arises about determining the correct values to use to identify a new mobile device when you create a new ActiveSync access rule. One simple way is to examine the characteristics reported in ECP for an ActiveSync partnership established with a mailbox. Go to the Phone section of ECP, select Mobile Phones, and then select the device that you want to check from the list of known devices that have synchronized with the mailbox. Click the Details icon and you'll see the kind of information shown in Figure 10-38.

Figure 10-38 Viewing mobile device characteristics reported by ECP.

You can create access rules based on the device type, model, user agent, or operating system. In this example, we see that the characteristics of the device are as follows:

- Device name: iPAQ_900_Phone

- Device model: HP iPAQ Mobile Messenger 910

- Device type: PocketPC

- Device operating system: Windows CE 5.2.19202

Clearly some of these characteristics are broader than others. For example, if you create an access rule that allows any device of type PocketPC, you allow for a huge variety of Pocket PC devices from many different manufacturers.

Another way to discover the characteristics of devices that connect to ActiveSync is to scan the ActiveSync entries in the IIS logs on the CAS server. The entries are pretty obvious. For example, here's one that shows a user connected with a PocketPC device.

```
2010-03-04 17:27:39 16.234.42.1 POST /Microsoft-Server-ActiveSync/default.eas
Cmd=Sync&DeviceId=5ECE2DBB684616DD07FB173DF09254B5&DeviceType=PocketPC
```

And here's an iPhone entry:

```
2010-03-04 00:03:49 16.234.42.1 POST /Microsoft-Server-ActiveSync/default.eas
User=blackadder&DeviceId=Appl87945RZ53NP&DeviceType=iPhone&Cmd=Sync&Log
```

Android phones show up with a device type of Android.

To block iPhones, we could use the following access rule:

```
New-ActiveSyncDeviceAccessRule -QueryString 'iPhone' -Characteristic DeviceType
-AccessLevel Block
```

After creating the necessary ActiveSync device access rules, we can check them with the Get-ActiveSyncDeviceAccessRule cmdlet. For example, this output shows that the organization has three device access rules in place. All Pocket PCs are allowed to connect as are the Whiz-Bang01 devices, but SmartPhones are blocked.

```
Get-ActiveSyncDeviceAccessRule | Format-Table Name, Characteristic, QueryString,
AccessLevel -AutoSize
```

Name	Characteristic	QueryString	AccessLevel
Whiz-Bang01 (DeviceModel)	DeviceModel	Whiz-Bang01	Allow
PocketPC (DeviceType)	DeviceType	PocketPC	Allow
SmartPhone (DeviceType)	DeviceType	SmartPhone	Block

Once a user's device is blocked by a device access rule, the device will not be allowed to synchronize. It might also be the case that a new device access rule causes a device to be temporarily quarantined while Exchange awaits a human's decision on whether to permit the device to synchronize. In either case, the user will receive an email to tell her what the problem is and what she should do. The information contained in the message will help an administrator to understand what the issue is if the user seeks help. Of course, the user will have to read the message using another client and might decide not to contact the administrator if he realizes that he's using an unapproved device.

> **Note**
> Temporary device quarantine can take up to 90 minutes to resolve for servers running the original version of Exchange 2010; this period is reduced to about 15 minutes for SP1 servers.

Chapter 10

An example of text that a user might receive during a period of temporary quarantine is as follows:

```
Your phone can't synchronize with the server via Exchange ActiveSync until it's
identified and its compliance with the access policies is verified.
You may see synchronization errors on your phone while your phone is being
recognized. If you see this sort of error, select mail as the only content to
synchronize with Exchange and start synchronization from your mobile phone.

Information about your mobile phone:

Device type                  : iPhone
Device ID                    : Appl5K2373BX7TR
Device user agent            : Apple-iPhone2C1/801.26000002
Exchange ActiveSync version  : 14.0
Device access state          : DeviceDiscovery
Device access state reason   : DeviceRule

Sent at 5/10/2010 11:18:53 AM to TRedmond@contoso.com.
```

Exchange 2010 SP1 allows you to manage ActiveSync device access rules through ECP. Figure 10-39 shows the set of rules that we've been working on together with an additional rule to block iPhone access. Apple iPhones have taken an increasing share of the mobile device market since they were first released in 2007. I happen to like the iPhone and use one on a daily basis, so there's no bias against the device here. Apple licenses ActiveSync, which means that you can readily connect an iPhone to Exchange. However, the exact details of the implementation of ActiveSync on a device are entirely the prerogative of the device manufacturer, and the Apple implementation for the iPhone does not create quite as secure an infrastructure as can be attained with Windows Mobile devices, which is why some companies choose to block iPhone access.

In mitigation, Apple offers its Enterprise Deployment Guide to help companies deploy iPhones, and there are other sources that you can consult to find out how companies are managing iPhones. For example, Exchange MVP Jeff Guillet has written an excellent discussion of the strategy used to achieve secure iPhone connectivity to Exchange in one project; see *http://www.expta.com/2010/02/how-to-securely-deploy-iphones-with.html*. There are other examples in blogs and Web sites that you can review to determine whether any of the suggestions and tactics described offer some value to your project.

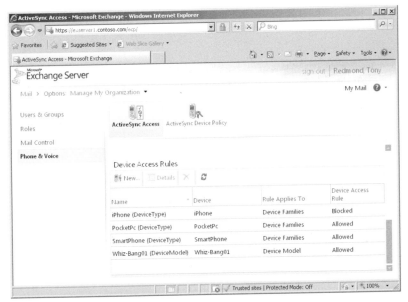

Figure 10-39 Viewing ActiveSync device access rules with ECP.

Blocking devices on a per-user basis

In addition to creating device access rules to control the types of devices that can be connected to ActiveSync, you can use the Set-CASMailbox cmdlet to set the *–ActiveSyncAllowedDeviceIDs* parameter with a list of device identifiers that are allowed to connect to a mailbox. The default value for this parameter is null, meaning that any device can synchronize with a mailbox.

The first step in blocking devices on a per-user basis is to determine the device identifier. The easiest way to discover a device's identifier is to connect it to Exchange. Afterward, you can use the Get-ActiveSyncDeviceStatistics cmdlet to retrieve details about users' ActiveSync activity, including the identifiers for each mobile device that they have connected to Exchange. For example:

```
Get-ActiveSyncDeviceStatistics –Mailbox 'Pelton, David'
```

You can add multiple device identifiers to the list, separating each identifier with a semi-colon. For example, this command allows just one specific device to synchronize with John Smith's mailbox.

```
Set-CASMailbox -Identity 'Pelton, David' -ActiveSyncAllowedDeviceIDs
'4B9207650054671AD0AEE83A424BCD7F'
```

To clear the device identifier to allow any device to connect to the mailbox:

```
Set-CASMailbox -Identity 'Pelton, David' -ActiveSyncAllowedDeviceIDs $Null
```

If we have a list of devices and only want to remove a single device from the list, we can do it by exporting the list to a variable, updating the list in the variable, and then writing it back with Set-CASMailbox:

```
$Devices = Get-CASMailbox -Identity 'Pelton, David'
$Devices.ActiveSyncAllowedDeviceIDs -= '4B9207650054671AD0AEE83A424BCD7F'
Set-CASMailbox -Identity 'Pelton, David' -ActiveSyncAllowedDeviceIDs
$Devices.ActiveSyncAllowedDeviceIDs
```

The same techniques can be used to block devices. In this case, we update the –ActiveSyncBlockedDeviceIds parameter with Set-CASMailbox. For example, you might make a corporate decision to block Android-powered devices and then discover that some-one is using one of these devices to access Exchange. A quick retrieval of the device identi-fier followed by input to Set-CASMailbox will block further synchronization.

Wiping lost devices

It is the nature of mobile devices that some will be lost in airports, taxis, shops, and other places. In the same way, it's almost inevitable that some devices will never be recovered. Being able to wipe the device through an over-the-air command is therefore a necessity to protect the data held on the device. Administrators can wipe a mobile device by selecting the mailbox in EMC and then selecting the Manage Mobile Device option or by running the Clear-ActiveSyncDevice cmdlet. Users can wipe a device by selecting it through the Mobile Phones option of ECP (Figure 10-40). Naturally, these options are only available if a user has first synchronized a device with her mailbox to make the device known to Exchange.

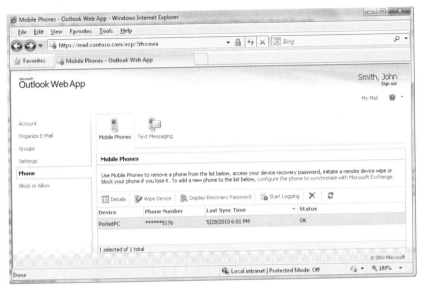

Figure 10-40 ECP option to wipe a mobile device.

When a remote wipe is initiated by an administrator or user, ActiveSync sends a wipe command to the device, which then executes the appropriate command locally. The client then acknowledges the wipe command back to the server together with an indication of success or failure. The following steps happen:

1. Client connects to ActiveSync.

2. Client provides its DeviceID.

3. Exchange queries device for account credentials.

4. Client authenticates with username and password.

5. Exchange checks its ActiveSync block lists to see whether DeviceID is allowed to connect (other things happen at this stage, including a check to see whether the policy that applies to the device has to be refreshed).

6. Exchange checks whether a wipe command is queued for the device and issues command if found.

7. Device acknowledges wipe command and reports status.

Note that if you send a remote wipe request to a device that doesn't support the wipe function, the device will not be able to execute the request and the data will remain. However, synchronization of future data will fail, so you can at least prevent any more sensitive data going to the device. The different degrees of support offered by various device types for remote wipe functionality are a good reason for you to test this feature before approving a device type for deployment. ActiveSync issues a confirmation message when a device acknowledges a wipe request. If a user issues the command through OWA, he receives the confirmation message, and if an administrator issues the request, the administrator and the user associated with the device both receive confirmation messages.

CAUTION!

It's important to realize that a remote wipe command will not erase data on any storage card in the mobile device—the only data removed by a "wipe device" command is that known to ActiveSync. Another thing to think about is that a device must authenticate before Exchange is able to send it a wipe command. In other words, there's no way that you can wipe a device that is stolen unless the thief attempts to connect to Exchange to download new mail. This is one reason why strong passwords and maybe even encryption should be used to protect sensitive corporate information that's stored on mobile devices.

The fact that a device must authenticate before any ActiveSync communication concerning policies (including device wipe commands) is possible introduces the issue of how to deal with people who leave the company. Most companies have well-developed procedures that the IT department uses when they are notified that someone is leaving, and the usual first step that IT takes is to disable the employee's account or change her password so that she can no longer log on to any corporate system. This is a good way to protect confidential information that's held in corporate systems, but it does nothing to remove the information that the employee has on her mobile device. The departure process might require the employee to hand in her mobile device on the day that her employment finishes, but what happens if the device is owned by the employee? The immediate answer is that you should issue a wipe command to remove at least all the email from the device, but this step is impossible if you disable the account, because the device will never be able to authenticate. The lesson here, therefore, is that you need to issue the wipe command and make sure that it is acknowledged before the employee's account is disabled.

Debugging ActiveSync

Understanding what's happening as a mobile device synchronizes with an Exchange mailbox is simple in concept and complex in execution. Much can go wrong between the point where a message is created in Outlook Mobile and the time it is submitted for sending on the server. When problems arise and the user calls the help desk, an administrator can work though the basic problem-solving steps with the user to ensure that the connection is working and nothing else obvious is awry. After that, it can be a challenge to understand what might be going wrong.

To address the problem, Exchange maintains ActiveSync logs to capture details of the interaction between mobile device and Exchange. The contents of these logs describe the events that occur as the device connects and retrieves information. Logging is off by default, so if a problem occurs with a device, the user must click Start Logging in the Mobile Phones options to instruct Exchange to begin to capture the events. Once he has worked through the steps to re-create the problem, the user can stop logging and Exchange sends him the ActiveSync log as an attachment to a message (Figure 10-41).

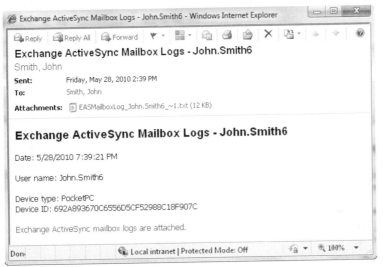

Figure 10-41 Exchange delivers an ActiveSync mailbox log for a mobile device.

ActiveSync logs are in XML format (Figure 10-42), and their contents take some time to interpret. However, these logs are not really designed to be used by administrators. Instead, they are a diagnostic tool for Microsoft support personnel who have access to all of the coded information that might appear in a log and who can therefore figure out what happened between a device and Exchange during a connection.

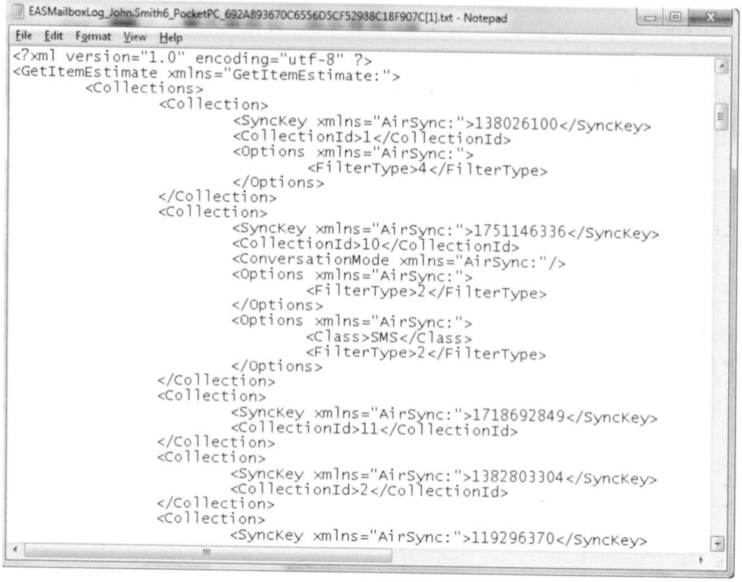

```
EASMailboxLog_John.Smith6_PocketPC_692A893670C6556D5CF52988C18F907C[1].txt - Notepad
File Edit Format View Help
<?xml version="1.0" encoding="utf-8" ?>
<GetItemEstimate xmlns="GetItemEstimate:">
        <Collections>
                <Collection>
                        <SyncKey xmlns="AirSync:">138026100</SyncKey>
                        <CollectionId>1</CollectionId>
                        <Options xmlns="AirSync:">
                                <FilterType>4</FilterType>
                        </Options>
                </Collection>
                <Collection>
                        <SyncKey xmlns="AirSync:">1751146336</SyncKey>
                        <CollectionId>10</CollectionId>
                        <ConversationMode xmlns="AirSync:"/>
                        <Options xmlns="AirSync:">
                                <FilterType>2</FilterType>
                        </Options>
                        <Options xmlns="AirSync:">
                                <Class>SMS</Class>
                                <FilterType>2</FilterType>
                        </Options>
                </Collection>
                <Collection>
                        <SyncKey xmlns="AirSync:">1718692849</SyncKey>
                        <CollectionId>11</CollectionId>
                </Collection>
                <Collection>
                        <SyncKey xmlns="AirSync:">1382803304</SyncKey>
                        <CollectionId>2</CollectionId>
                </Collection>
                <Collection>
                        <SyncKey xmlns="AirSync:">119296370</SyncKey>
```

Figure 10-42 Viewing an ActiveSync mailbox log.

Testing mobile connectivity

Microsoft provides a set of emulator images for Windows Mobile 6.1 and Windows Mobile 6.5 devices that you can download to test connectivity for mobile devices (search for "Windows Mobile Emulator Images"). An emulator is not yet available for Windows Phone 7 (released to manufacturing in September 2010), but should appear in due course. These emulators can be loaded into Microsoft Virtual PC and connected to your network to test that ActiveSync works as expected. If you run a large ActiveSync deployment, it's a good idea to set up these emulators to test against new roll-up releases and service packs of Exchange to ensure that no problem is introduced with the new server software.

ActiveSync for BlackBerry

The traditional method to connect BlackBerry mobile devices to Exchange is to deploy RIM's BES. Although there is no doubt that BES works, it is usually expensive to license and requires a separate server infrastructure. In addition, BES defaults to using MAPI to access Exchange mailboxes and directory information and can generate a significant load on a mailbox server when it connects to fetch and send messages. In some scenarios, the load generated by a BlackBerry user can be three times or more that of an Outlook user. (Newer versions of BES support using Exchange Web Services instead, which helps performance at the cost of a bit more setup work for the BES administrator.)

Technology changes all the time, and solutions are now available (for example, *www.astrasync.com*) that use the ActiveSync protocol to connect BlackBerry devices to Exchange. ActiveSync is included in Exchange, so there is no need to license additional BES software or to deploy more hardware. The performance profile of an ActiveSync client is less than a BlackBerry, so if performance is an issue, a transition to ActiveSync might address the problem. Another advantage is that replacing BES with ActiveSync removes complexity from the infrastructure because all mobile devices will then use a single protocol that can be managed through Exchange. For example, you can enable or disable a mailbox to use ActiveSync through EMS or EMC, whereas a separate management utility is required for BES. The potential savings are somewhat offset by the need to buy and deploy ActiveSync client software, but these costs are usually dwarfed by the savings.

INSIDE OUT   Do the cost–benefit analysis for an upgrade

No one should move away from a working solution without good reason. Administrators who know how BES works and have the necessary skills to manage the full end-to-end client-to-server communications, perhaps using tools such as Zenprise's MobileManager, might be unwilling to consider a move when faced with the challenge of upgrading to Exchange 2010. However, given that a new version of BES must be deployed to support Exchange 2010, and most users refresh their mobile devices regularly, it is a good idea to use the opportunity presented by an Exchange 2010 upgrade project to run a cost–benefit exercise that captures all of the pros and cons of a transition to ActiveSync.

Client throttling

Clients can occasionally create an excessive load on an Exchange server. The reasons this happens are many and varied but usually involve some form of software bug that causes the client to communicate in an unpredictable manner and so creates an out-of-the-ordinary load. The usual corrective action taken in previous versions is to first identify the errant client with the Exchange User Monitor (ExMon) utility and then terminate its connection to relieve the strain on the server and restore normal levels of responsiveness to other clients. You can then figure out what action the client was taking to cause the problem and resolve the situation.

ExMon is one of those invaluable utilities developed by Microsoft engineers that should really be included in the formal product as one of the utilities presented in the Toolbox. For now, you have to download it from Microsoft's Web site. ExMon works against

Exchange 2003, Exchange 2007, and Exchange 2010 servers and allows administrators to view details of the clients that are currently connected to the server, including IP address and software versions.

Exchange 2010 introduces the concept of client throttling to allow administrators to take a more proactive approach to resource management by defining and applying policies to users to control the resources that they can consume for these categories:

- ActiveSync (EAS)

- RPC Client Access(RCA; used for MAPI clients such as Outlook)

- Outlook Web App (OWA)

- POP3

- IMAP4

- Exchange Web Services (EWS; this category includes Unified Messaging users and users running Entourage or Outlook for Mac OS X)

- Windows PowerShell

A default policy is automatically created and enforced within the organization when you install Exchange 2010. The policy comes into effect when the percentage of CPU utilization by Exchange exceeds the threshold defined in the *CPUStartPercent* property of the default policy. This setting is applied on a per-service basis. The default value for *CPUStartPercent* is 75, so when one of the Exchange services monitored for client throttling reaches this threshold, Exchange begins to apply any throttling restrictions that are defined in the default policy or on a per-mailbox basis to ensure that the server can continue to provide a reasonably smooth service to all clients.

Throttling policies can only be managed through EMS. You can view details of the default policy with this command:

```
Get-ThrottlingPolicy | Where {$_.IsDefault -eq $True} | Format-Table
```

A lot of data are output when you examine the attributes of a throttling policy. However, you can break them down into the categories listed earlier. The first six categories correspond to client protocols and are identified with the prefix shown in parentheses. Thus, we can retrieve the settings that govern MAPI clients with:

```
Get-ThrottlingPolicy | Select RCA* | Format-List
```

```
RCAMaxConcurrency            : 20
RCAPercentTimeInAD           :
```

```
RCAPercentTimeInCAS                      :
RCAPercentTimeInMailboxRPC               :
```

The output for the RCA parameters indicates that only one threshold currently is in place to control user workload within the RCA layer: The maximum concurrency for any user is set to 20 (the range is from 0 to 100), meaning that a user can have up to 20 active sessions with a CAS. A connection is maintained from the time a request is made to establish it until the connection is closed or otherwise disconnected by a user action (logging off). If a user attempts to establish more than the allowed maximum, that connection attempt will fail. The other limits are set to null, indicating that no limit is in place. Essentially, this means that a user can continue to use these resources until they are exhausted.

These settings control the amount of time a client can use to execute LDAP requests against Active Directory, run CAS code, and execute mailbox RPC requests. The values can range from 0 to 100 and represent the percentage of a one-minute window that a client can spend in the mode. It is possible to exceed 100 percent because a client can issue concurrent requests, each of which makes a heavy demand. The cumulative load would force Exchange to throttle the load for this client. Because mailbox RPC and LDAP requests flow through the CAS and therefore consume CAS resources, it follows that the CAS setting (*PercentTimeinCAS*) is an overlapping superset of the mailbox and Active Directory settings, so the value for the CAS setting should always be larger than the mailbox and Active Directory settings.

Similar groups of settings are available for the other client categories. For example, you can find those applying to Exchange Web Services with:

```
Get-ThrottlingPolicy | Select EWS* | Format-List
```

TROUBLESHOOTING

Exchange is throttling BES activities

Introducing client throttling had an unfortunate side effect on some applications that impose heavy demands on Exchange. The BES provided the best example, because the account that it uses essentially mimics a hyperactive user that accesses multiple mailboxes to fetch and send messages to mobile devices. The usual problem was that Exchange throttled BES activities because it exceeded the RCA maximum concurrency threshold. The solution was to create a new throttling policy that set the value of the *–RCAMaxConcurrency* parameter to $Null and then assign the new policy to the BES account. This is a step that the administrator can perform after installing BES.

A number of specific parameters are available to control workload generated through Windows PowerShell:

- *–PowerShellMaxConcurrency* (default value 18): This constraint is applied in two different ways. It defines the maximum number of remote Windows PowerShell sessions that a user can have open on a server at one time. It also defines the maximum number of cmdlets that EMS can execute concurrently.

- *–PowerShellMaxCmdlets* (default no limit): Sets the number of cmdlets that a user can execute within the time period specified by *–PowerShellMaxCmdletsTimePeriod*. After the value is exceeded, no future cmdlets can be run until the period expires.

- *–PowerShellMaxCmdletsTimePeriod* (default no limit): The period in seconds that Exchange uses to determine whether the maximum number of cmdlets constraint has been exceeded.

- *–ExchangeMaxCmdlets* (default no limit): Specifies the number of cmdlets that a user can execute within the time period set by *–PowerShellMaxCmdletsTimePeriod*. After the constraint is exceeded, Exchange slows down the execution of other cmdlets.

- *–PowerShellMaxCmdletQueueDepth* (default no limit): Specifies the number of operations that Exchange will allow a user to execute. Operations are consumed by cmdlets as they run. They are also consumed by internal operations (for example, the *–PowerShellMaxCurrency* operation uses two operations). Microsoft recommends that, if set, the value of *–PowerShellMaxCmdletQueueDepth* is set to three times the value of *–PowerShellMaxConcurrency*. Exchange does not apply this constraint to the code run by ECP or EWS.

Three additional settings can be used to constrain the consumption of general resources:

- *–MessageRateLimit* (default no limit): Governs the number of messages per minute that a user can submit to the transport system for processing. Messages over the limit are placed in the user's Outbox until the server is able to accept them. The exception is for clients such as POP3 and IMAP4 that submit directly to the transport system using SMTP. If these clients attempt to submit too many messages, their request is declined and they will be forced to reattempt later.

- *–RecipientRateLimit* (default no limit): Specifies the number of recipients that can be addressed in a 24-hour period. For example, if this value is set to 1,000, it means that the user is allowed to address messages to up to 1,000 recipients daily. Messages that exceed this limit are rejected.

- *–ForwardeeLimit* (default no limit): Specifies a limit for the number of recipients that can be configured in Inbox Rules for the forward or redirect action.

INSIDE OUT   Storing the default throttling identifier in a variable

You'll note that the default throttling policy has a value like
DefaultThrottlingPolicy_dade6c60-e9cc-4692-bc6a-71771158a82f given to its name and
identifier. I suspect that this is a joke played on us by the Microsoft engineers, because
no sensible human being could think that such a name is understandable. If you plan
to work with a policy, you might want to store the identifier in a variable so that you
can use it to refer to the policy that you want to work with. For example:

```
$TP = (Get-ThrottlingPolicy).Identifier
Set-ThrottlingPolicy -Identity $TP -EWSPercentTimeInCAS 80
```

If you create a new policy with the New-ThrottlingPolicy cmdlet, the values from the default
policy are inherited. All you have to do is to state values for the settings that you want to
change. Thus, we can do:

```
New-ThrottlingPolicy -Name 'Restricted CAS Access' -RCAMaxConcurrency 10
```

To apply the new policy, we can either make it the default:

```
Set-ThrottlingPolicy -Identity 'Restricted CAS Access' -IsDefault $True
```

Or, we can apply it selectively to users:

```
Set-Mailbox -Identity 'David Jones' -ThrottlingPolicy 'Restricted CAS Access'
```

Exchange 2010 SP1 improves the way that client throttling works based on feedback from
production deployments. In RTM, if a client is throttled, the result is one or more failed
requests for server data, which can lead to a bad user experience because something will
not work properly or as expected. In SP1, requests that the server throttles are added to a
queue to delay but not fail processing. The requests are backed off by being forced to wait
for a few milliseconds before the server attempts to process them again. Hopefully, when
the wait time elapses, the need to throttle will have passed and the client requests can be
processed normally.

Unified Messaging

UM is a topic that deserves a complete book in its own right to cover the many issues that
have to be considered in implementing Exchange-based voice mail as a replacement for a
traditional voice mail system that is tightly associated with a private branch exchange (PBX).
A great deal of negotiation and coordination normally has to occur between the teams
responsible for telecommunications and messaging within the company to ensure that

Chapter 10

issues such as dial plans are addressed. Companies such as Nortel and Cisco had offered voice mail integration for Exchange in previous versions, but Exchange 2007 marked Microsoft's first integrated version purpose-built to work with Exchange, Outlook, and OWA and to fit into an overall Unified Communications strategy. Microsoft's software-driven approach is different from the hardware-centric approach taken by traditional telecommunications vendors and is centered on TCP/IP communications and open standards. The result is lower cost and a more open platform than has been possible for voice mail systems in the past.

Microsoft has upgraded many aspects of UM in Exchange 2010 to take into account customer experience in deploying Exchange 2007–based UM. Two major advances are also incorporated. First, Exchange 2007 Unified Messaging supports three different audio codecs: WMA, GSM 06.10, and GSM G.711. You could pick a codec for individual users, but none of the codecs were a great solution for non-Windows Mobile devices. Exchange 2010 updates the range of audio codecs to support MP3 and uses MP3 as the default codec for voice messages. The idea behind the change is that MP3 is supported by so many different devices and applications that using MP3 as the default will improve the ability of users to work with voice messages across multiple devices.

The second major enhancement in Exchange 2010 is the introduction of voice mail preview. This is an exciting attempt to make voice content more accessible to users when they cannot replay a message. The challenge of transcribing voice messages into text poses challenges in computer science, language, and culture. It is therefore worthy of comment.

Voice mail preview

Voice mail preview is the ability to transcribe voice messages to text so that the messages can be read on a screen. This feature is especially useful to read voice messages on a mobile device to understand whether you have to respond to the sender quickly. The only problem is that the transcription algorithms sometimes generate text that doesn't quite convey the meaning or intent of the message. All systems that integrate voice face the challenge of comprehending the meaning of voices that share a common language but use different tones, accents, and word patterns, and even mix in words or phrases from other languages. Names can often be a particular challenge, especially if they are "foreign" to the expected language. The code does attempt to clean up the spoken word by eliminating pauses and terms like "ugh" that people often use when they are speaking.

Clearly there's no point in shipping voice preview if every second word is not recognized. However, different languages vary in how recognizable machine-generated text is in terms of the recipient being able to understand the nature and content of the message. English is full of slang; English terms and slang are finding their way into daily use for more languages, so moving the spoken form of a language from a point where 50 percent of words are recognized by automated transcribers (at this level a somewhat accurate version of the message is generated) to 80 percent or higher (where an almost accurate message is generated) relies heavily on testing the results of real-life messages that users attempt to understand. User perception of accuracy varies with the usability of the text generated by the computer; if the text is sufficiently accurate for the user to understand the meaning and importance of its content, the user will probably think that the transcription is pretty accurate. On the other hand, once important words are dropped or mangled, user perception diminishes and even an 85 percent accuracy rate (measured in the number of words that are accurately transcribed) might be considered utterly unusable.

> **Note**
> The word "preview" in the feature name is important; it is unreasonable for a general-purpose email system to provide an absolutely accurate rendition of message contents. Voice mail preview provides a quick way for a user to understand the gist of a message without having to listen to the whole thing.

It's no excuse for technology, but it is true that it is often difficult for humans to understand the content of a voice mail received from someone that has a strange accent or who uses unfamiliar slang or technical terms—imagine how difficult it must be to build code to interpret exactly what someone says. Another difficulty is that there's no way that a general-purpose computer running Windows can determine the language used by the person who leaves a voice mail. An assumption can be made, but it might not be accurate.

Before a computer has any chance of understanding what a human has said in a voice message, a huge amount of analysis and interpretation has to be performed against a vast number of actual messages to comprehend how human beings communicate with each other. The more messages and the more topics that these messages cover, the higher the accuracy of the voice mail preview will be. Getting the required volume and variety of messages to be able to transcribe the contents and use them to validate the computer-generated output is the key limiting factor that prevented Microsoft from supporting more languages for voice preview. A terrific amount of testing and validation must occur before voice preview can support a language. The following factors influence Microsoft's decision to ship a language:

- Has sufficient testing been done to assure a high rate of accuracy for voice transcription?

- How usable is the text generated in the voice preview?

- How sensitive is a culture or language to machine transcription?

Chapter 10

The following languages are supported for voice mail preview in Exchange 2010 RTM:

- English (U.S. English and Canadian English, but not Australian English or other local dialects)

- French

- Italian

- Portuguese

- Polish

Exchange 2010 SP1 adds Spanish (as spoken in Spain rather than in Latin America).

Assuming that your language is on the supported list for voice mail preview, you will probably find that the algorithm used by Exchange to interpret voice messages generates text with a reasonably high degree of fidelity. Your experience will vary from the high 90 percentile accuracy downward to much lower, depending on how clearly users speak when they leave voice mail, the devices that they use, whether there's wind or other noise in the background, and a myriad of other influences. Sometimes the text generated is comical, but most of the time it's acceptable even if a couple of errors creep in. No algorithm can process Klingon or other esoteric languages, but you will get good results if you guide people to be as clear as they can when they leave voice mail. Of course, if people ignore the advice, you can run a competition to find the funniest voice mail preview generated by Exchange. If you really cannot cope with the feature, UM-enabled users can turn off voice mail preview through the options available through OWA.

Voice mail previews are generated as messages arrive. Creating the preview at this point instead of later on through background processing delivers a number of advantages. The preview is immediately available when a message arrives in a user mailbox and can be viewed through a number of interfaces, including mobile devices, to allow users to decide whether the message is important. Microsoft believes that some 90 percent of the value provided by previews is delivered because the preview is immediately available. Because the preview becomes part of the inbound message, its text can be used in notifications and processed by rules. Background processing to locate voice mail and generate previews would work, but this would impose a huge additional load on mailbox servers.

The computational load to generate voice mail previews in real time forces some compromises in how transcription occurs. Transcription is a CPU-intense activity that requires roughly one second of CPU core processing for every second of spoken content. To stop an individual message from soaking up excessive processor resources, Exchange won't attempt to transcribe a message that is longer than 75 seconds. It therefore pays for senders to keep their messages brief and to the point.

Taking the rule of one second of core processing per second of voice mail, we can therefore calculate that a four-core server is capable of transcribing four 60-second messages per minute over a sustained period. During peak periods of user activity during the day, it is likely that more voice mails will arrive for processing than Exchange can transcribe to create previews, so Exchange throttles back its transcription activities whenever a UM server comes under heavy load to avoid the creation of backlogs and to ensure that users get their voice mail as quickly as possible. For example, Microsoft IT runs four UM servers that have 24 cores among them. During one five-day week, the Exchange team found that some 236,269 voice mails were processed by the servers. Taking an eight-hour working day, this works out at about 100 incoming voice mails per minute or around four messages for each of the available cores. Within Microsoft, an average voice mail is around 30 seconds, so only two of these can be transcribed, leaving two to be delivered without preview. Of course, these are average values, and all voice mails are delivered complete with preview during some hours, whereas fewer than half will arrive with preview at peak times.

The settings used to control transcription are contained in the MSExchangeUM.config configuration file, where you'll find values such as *TranscriptionMaximumMessageLength* (the longest message that UM will transcribe) and *TranscriptionMaximumBacklogPerCore* (the maximum number of messages that Exchange will allow to be queued for transcription; the default is 5). You could update the values in the configuration file to alter the way that UM works, but you should understand the following:

- Microsoft doesn't support changes, so if you do alter the values and encounter problems, you'll have to revert to the original values to see if the problem still occurs before you can call Microsoft for support.

- There is no replication of configuration updates between UM servers, so any changes have to be applied manually to all UM servers.

- The next upgrade of Exchange is likely to overwrite the changed values.

- The changes might affect the performance of the UM servers in unpredictable ways (see the previous discussion).

- Microsoft has done a lot of testing to determine the optimal settings. For example, a typical voice mail lasts between 25 and 30 seconds, so one that lasts 75 seconds is likely to be rambling, possibly incoherent, and probably includes some non-business-critical information such as an enquiry about the health of the recipient's partner. Do you therefore need to encourage users to waste computer resources to process and store verbal outpourings of no great import?

Chapter 10

Some companies won't care that some messages arrive without previews. If you're in this category, you can deploy sufficient capacity to handle the average UM load. On the other hand, if you want to ensure that every voice mail arrives with a preview, you have to deploy sufficient processor capacity to handle the expected peak load plus a percentage to allow for higher peaks and growth. The computer-intense nature of transcription makes Exchange 2010 UM servers a poor choice for virtualization, which is why Microsoft recommends that you use standard computers for these servers.

After transcription, Exchange stores voice mail preview content as an XML property for the message. The XML content contains information such as timing (the length of the voice mail), the confidence level for the transcription (how accurate Exchange thinks the preview content is), and phone numbers. If Exchange can recognize the sender, it captures information about the sender for Outlook to display.

Figure 10-43 shows a good example of how voice mail preview appears for a user. This shows a real message that I left for a co-worker after listening to a call run by the Exchange development team to discuss some technical background about voice mail transcription. I attempted to convey some important points about the meeting, but some of the words were lost in the transcription, possibly due to my accent (an Irish accent moderated by spending a lot of time in the United States is a real challenge for the U.S. English transcriber). For example, "Unified Messaging people at Microsoft" becomes "you know five messaging people at Microsoft," which isn't quite what I meant. Nevertheless, the text is good enough to attract the attention of the reader and perhaps get him to call me back, which is what I want to accomplish as the caller.

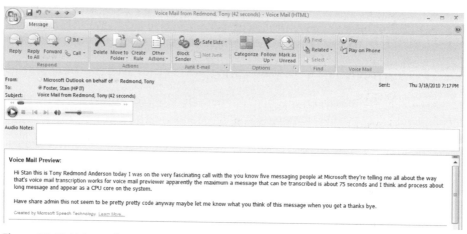

Figure 10-43 Voice mail preview in action.

Fax integration

Unlike Exchange 2007, there is no support for the ability to create new messages from incoming fax calls in Exchange 2010, because Microsoft determined that this was a feature that wasn't used by many customers and so decided to leave this area of functionality to third parties. If Exchange 2007 UM was used, its fax configuration properties are retained and the server is still capable of responding to fax tones for incoming calls. If a fax tone is detected, Exchange looks for the value of the *FaxServerURI* property on the UM Mailbox policy to determine whether a third-party fax solution is available. This value provides a path to the third-party solution and allows Exchange UM to hand off the call in progress to that product, which is then responsible for establishing a session with the sender, creating a new fax message, and sending the message to the user's mailbox. Fax messages in the Inbox still look the same as they did in Exchange 2007 UM; the sole difference is that Exchange UM has no part in their creation or processing. The bottom line, therefore, is that customers who want to integrate fax into Exchange 2010 UM (for example, by allowing a single number to be used for incoming fax and voice calls) need to buy and integrate a suitable third-party solution.

Exchange 2010 APIs

Exchange's history with APIs is checkered at best and poor at worst. APIs have appeared in one release and disappeared in the next, and developers have been unable to depend on an API lasting more than a couple of releases, which is not a good basis on which to plan for a project that wishes to leverage Exchange data. MAPI is the ever-present API in both server and client versions, but it's a difficult API to master as the documentation is sparse and most of the expertise exists within Microsoft. Other APIs such as Web Distributed Authoring and Versioning (WebDAV) were hailed with great anticipation as the "next great thing" when they appeared and have slowly decreased in importance, and others such as Exchange Routing Objects were launched, were rejected by the development community, and sank without trace.

Having inconsistent or incomplete APIs after so many releases is an embarrassment for Exchange—especially when email is the foundation of a collaboration platform—and Lotus Domino, Exchange's major rival, has always excelled in this domain. Exchange 2010 sets out a new beginning that focuses on three APIs. The hope is that these represent the future development platform for the product. Time will tell. Table 10-4 lists the major APIs used by recent Exchange versions and the option presented by Exchange 2010. In most cases, the focus is firmly on EWS, a Simple Object Access Protocol (SOAP)-based interface. Note that some of these APIs (like WebDAV) do not exist in the Exchange 2010 code base, whereas others are outside the direct control of Exchange (Windows Management Instrumentation [WMI]) and will persist for a while longer. Of course, anything that Microsoft decides to deprecate is a bad choice for you to invest in as a development option.

Table 10-4 **Old Exchange APIs and Exchange 2010 options**

API	Used for	Exchange 2010 option
CDOEX	Mailbox access	EWS
WebDAV	Remote Mailbox access	EWS
ExOLEDB	Mailbox access	EWS
OWAURLs	Free/busy access and name resolution	EWS
Store events	Asynchronous and synchronous events	Transport delivery events and EWS
WMI	Management	Windows PowerShell
Collaboration Data Objects (CDO 1.2.1)	Access to Outlook objects through a COM-based interface to MAPI	Will continue to work

In addition, Microsoft has announced that Collaboration Data Objects (CDO) version 1.2.x is going into extended support, meaning that it is now in life support and is no longer a good option for future projects.

You might ask why Microsoft is changing the API landscape again. There is some logic in asserting that the product has changed dramatically in Exchange 2007 and Exchange 2010 and it's time to refocus on a set of APIs that developers can use with confidence. Microsoft wants developers to leverage the .NET Framework, and some of the older APIs (CDOEX, ExOLEDB, MAPI) are difficult to use from managed code. Some of these APIs also depend on redundant code that Microsoft wanted to remove from the code base to reduce maintenance costs and the possibility that a security breach might arise through old code that's subjected to a new style of attack. In addition, Microsoft began a fundamental shift away from monolithic product architecture in Exchange 2007 by encapsulating business logic in a set of Windows PowerShell commands that are called from multiple interfaces. This process continues in Exchange 2010 to create a more scalable and robust product, so it's logical that older interfaces that don't leverage the common set of business logic are removed.

Exchange Web Services

Apart from Windows PowerShell, the big focus for most developers is now on EWS, which was first introduced in Exchange 2007. EWS is an API that is hosted on the CAS server role and exposed as a Windows Communication Foundation (WCF) Web service. Platforms that cannot use the managed WCF API can use the raw SOAP-based functions, which is how EWS is used for platforms such as the Apple Macintosh, iPhone/iPad, and Linux.

You can download a copy of EWS from the Microsoft Web site, and its license allows third-party developers to distribute EWS along with their own code. However, you should resist the temptation to install EWS into the Global Assembly Cache (GAC). Because Microsoft allows developers to include EWS with their code, the danger of installing any particular copy of EWS into the GAC is that you might create a condition similar to "DLL hell" when a function in the version of EWS in the GAC doesn't support a third-party application. You can download a copy of EWS from MSDN.

EWS allows developers to create code to leverage Exchange core functionality (create and send messages, update mailboxes, delete items, and perform searches) while working with a complete set of Store items from messages to appointments to tasks. EWS can work with the GAL, expand distribution lists, access free and busy data, and handle delegate access to mailboxes. It can access search and public folders and manipulate the permissions on folders. The Exchange 2010 version of EWS can access the dumpster and deal with attachments and personal distribution lists, and it can even impersonate users for role-based access control (RBAC) purposes. Windows developers use EWS through a client-side .NET API that provides object-oriented access to the items and structures that they need to deal with. Because EWS is "fully baked" in Exchange 2010, Microsoft has moved away from WebDAV, the API that underpinned recent versions of their Entourage client for Exchange so that the latest version of Entourage is now totally based on EWS.

If you're looking for a good example of how to approach the application of EWS, the simple Exchange mailbox client built by Exchange MVP Glen Scales (*http://gsexdev .blogspot.com/2009/06/simple-exchange-email-client-for.html*) provides an excellent starting point because it's written in the form of a Windows PowerShell script. The script (Figure 10-44) demonstrates how to use AutoDiscover to locate a mailbox, connect to a mailbox, enumerate the folders in the mailbox, create and send messages, and view the contents of message bodies and headers. It's a great example of EWS in action that you can use to discover how to apply EWS to access many Exchange functions.

Although Microsoft positions EWS as the API of choice for developers, it is not used within the product. Instead, Microsoft builds many of the Exchange components that need to work with mailboxes, including EWS, RCA, ActiveSync, and UM, on top of an internal API called XSO. Server-side MAPI is still used within the product, but XSO has taken center stage recently.

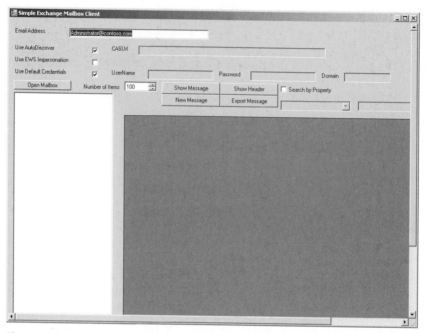

Figure 10-44 The Simple Exchange Mailbox client written in Windows PowerShell.

Windows PowerShell remains the top choice for any server-focused management or administrative process that you need to automate, including when you need to invoke a Windows PowerShell cmdlet from within a .NET language. Remote Windows PowerShell allows administrators to execute cmdlets from workstations that have no Exchange code installed (naturally, the latest version of Windows PowerShell must be installed) and complies with the RBAC model so that administrators can only manage the objects that they have been granted permission to manage.

A common connection point

Having clients is all very well, but we've got to connect them to Exchange to be able to do some work. The CAS is the common connection point where everything comes together in Exchange 2010, so logically it's where our story takes us next, even if, as we discuss, deploying an Exchange 2010 CAS is one of the first steps in many deployments.

Client Access Server

T HE Client Access Server (CAS) is possibly the most misunderstood server role in Exchange Server 2010, perhaps because it is essentially a black box that processes connections coming in from clients and sends those connections on to mailbox servers to permit client access to data. It's very different from a mailbox server, where you can almost visualize the flow of messages and exert great control over databases through Exchange Management Console (EMC) and Exchange Management Shell (EMS). It's also different from hub transport servers, where you can monitor the progress of messages through queues and examine message tracking logs to identify every step that occurs as a message is processed. The CAS doesn't include a management interface to depict a graphical representation of the connections that pass through. The lack of feedback about server functions often makes CAS processing difficult to understand. Even so, the CAS is right at the center of Exchange, and it is a critical server role to appreciate.

There are many white papers available from Microsoft and other parties that provide detailed guidance about how to handle CAS placement and configuration in different scenarios. For example, a particularly good blog post is available at *http://msexchangeteam.com /archive/2009/11/20/453272.aspx*, which describes how to approach the transition of an existing Exchange deployment to introduce Exchange 2010 CAS servers.

It is not my intention to walk through multiple scenarios in this chapter. Instead, I want to look at the basic technology in the CAS and how it serves the role laid out for it within an Exchange organization.

The CAS role

Microsoft introduced the CAS server role in Exchange 2007 to begin the process of moving the responsibility for client connections away from the Store. This was part of the effort to decompose Exchange into a set of server roles that can be individually deployed and managed. The CAS is designed to handle three different kinds of traffic:

- External connections from Internet clients: Traffic that flows into an organization generated by clients using different protocols, including Outlook Anywhere, Outlook Web App (OWA), Internet Message Access Protocol version 4 (IMAP4), Post Office Protocol version 3 (POP3), and ActiveSync clients, as well as clients that use Exchange Web Services (EWS), such as the latest version of Microsoft Entourage and Outlook for Mac.

- Internal connections from intranet clients: Traffic from Messaging Application Programming Interface (MAPI) and other clients.

- Proxied connections from other CAS servers, or traffic redirected by one CAS to another: For example, from a CAS server in one Active Directory site to a CAS server in another site, or when a CAS server does not run the right Exchange version required to access a user's mailbox (this occurs when traffic comes into an Exchange 2010 CAS and needs to go to an Exchange 2007 CAS to access a mailbox on an Exchange 2007 server).

Table 11-1 lists the services that are provided by the CAS server role. Some of these services support access to Exchange through different client protocols, and some deliver significant functionality that improves the client experience. Two are full-fledged applications that serve the needs of users (OWA) and administrators (Exchange Control Panel [ECP]).

Table 11-1 **Services provided by the CAS role**

Service	Functionality
ActiveSync	Access to Exchange mailbox data for any mobile device that licenses the Exchange ActiveSync protocol.
Address Book	Handles client requests for directory information.
Autodiscover	Retrieves required settings to allow supported clients (Outlook 2007 and Outlook 2010, Windows Mobile 6.1 and above) to automatically configure their email profiles and discover the connection points for Exchange services.
Availability	Queries free and busy information for clients to use when scheduling meetings.
Exchange Control Panel (ECP)	Web application that provides a browser interface to Exchange administration options.

Exchange Web Services (EWS)	Provides an Extensible Markup Language/Simple Object Access Protocol (XML/SOAP) interface to Exchange services.
IMAP4	Supports IMAP4 protocol access to Exchange mailboxes.
MailTips	Generates warnings based on the header contents of new messages to help users avoid mistakes such as participating in a Reply All mail storm.
Outlook Anywhere	Enables Outlook 2003, Outlook 2007, and Outlook 2010 clients to connect to Exchange from the Internet using remote procedure calls (RPCs) wrapped in HTTPS.
Outlook Web App	Web application that provides a browser-based client for Exchange mailbox and calendar functionality.
POP3	Supports POP3 protocol access to Exchange mailboxes.
RPC Client Access	Provides MAPI access to Exchange mailboxes.

The single point of contact

The biggest change in the Exchange 2010 CAS is its evolution to become a single point of contact for all connections (except for public folders) through an overhaul of how Exchange deals with MAPI client connections. The Exchange 2007 CAS handles client connections for IMAP, POP3, ActiveSync, OWA, and Outlook Anywhere. It does not handle MAPI connections from Outlook clients; these still go directly to the Store process running on mailbox servers.

Exchange 2010 expands the work of the CAS by completing the relocation of client connections from the Store and provides a new MAPI endpoint to which clients can connect before being proxied by the RPC Client Access (RCA) layer to the mailbox database that hosts the target mailbox. This change is a fundamental part of breaking the link between mailbox and server that allows Exchange 2010 to introduce mailbox database mobility between servers. The Autodiscover feature provides the necessary "magic" to allow Outlook clients to continue to locate their mailboxes after the transition to Exchange 2010. Transferring the MAPI endpoint from mailbox servers to the CAS means that the Exchange 2010 version of the CAS handles more workload than ever before and that the CAS becomes even more essential to the overall health of an Exchange infrastructure. MAPI connections to public folder servers from Outlook are not handled by the CAS and continue to go directly from client to server.

Benefits of relocating the MAPI endpoint

Although relocating MAPI connectivity to the CAS might seem to be simple housekeeping—completing the task of bringing all protocol access together—it also delivers five real benefits to Exchange. First, all protocols now flow through a common code path. This makes it much easier for Exchange developers to implement consistent processing of data across all clients. In the past, it was entirely possible for different clients to process information generated by clients in different ways because the code was implemented in the CAS or mailbox server. Second, because all of the protocol and client access code is now located within the CAS, the vast bulk of the code that handled MAPI client connectivity could be removed from the mailbox server; the only vestige that remains is the code that handles public folder connections. Server-to-server MAPI connectivity code also remains within Exchange, but is never exposed to MAPI clients such as Outlook.

> **Note**
>
> The removal of layers of code, some of which dated back to the earliest Exchange versions, makes it easier for developers to tune mailbox servers to support higher loads and improves the overall stability of the server because there is less code to run and fewer places for bugs to lurk.

The third benefit is a more scalable and streamlined approach to the way that client connections are processed. Exchange 2007 maintains a more complicated set of connections between clients and servers than Exchange 2010 does. An Outlook client connected to Exchange 2007 maintains persistent connections (connections that don't drop) to the mailbox server and global catalog server (for DSProxy access to directory information). This works well except when the servers are called on to handle a heavy load of TCP connections that have to flow through the CAS, such as when Outlook Anywhere is used. Now, the initial connection has to flow from Outlook to the CAS, and then the CAS makes connections on behalf of Outlook to the mailbox server and global catalog. The persistent nature of the connections caused bottlenecks to occur under conditions of heavy load. Exchange 2010 doesn't use persistent connections. Instead, it recognizes an Outlook Anywhere connection and saves its session state information in memory. The CAS has a shared pool of 100 connections with mailbox servers that it can use for active connections. If a user doesn't need to do anything, her connection can remain inactive. Once she wants data, the client can use one of the shared connections and then release it afterward. By using the shared pool of constantly reused connections, the CAS scales better than it can when faced with the need to manage an escalating demand for persistent connections.

The fourth benefit is the introduction of the address book service to replace the older DSProxy service's connection (used since Exchange 2000) to the global catalog to retrieve directory information. The address book service on the CAS is a true endpoint that serves clients as the definitive reference for directory data instead of just acting as an intermediate proxy. The code is simpler, resolves the issue of split connections that arose with Outlook Anywhere clients, and fixes a lingering problem for address book updates in multidomain deployments. These problems occurred when a client attempted to update a group. For example, an Outlook client might select a group from the Global Address List (GAL) and then attempt to amend its membership. Everything worked if DSProxy had connected the client to a global catalog that held a writable copy of the group. It didn't work when the global catalog belonged to a different domain from the group and so only held a read-only copy. The address book service now detects when problems might occur with group updates and routes the update to a suitable global catalog to make the change. Similar code handles other similar issues that used to occur with delegates and certificates, proving the value of being able to implement business logic in a single consistent place.

Last, because Exchange 2010 manages client connectivity at the CAS rather than dividing it between CAS and mailbox server, the time required for a client to transition to a moved database following a failover is much improved. Sorting out the connections for a transition to a new mailbox copy running in an Exchange 2007 Local Continuous Replication (LCR) or Standby Cluster Replication (SCR) configuration can take a couple of minutes before service is fully restored to clients. It's true that Outlook clients configured in cached Exchange mode won't be aware of the nature of the interruption, but it still exists, and OWA and other clients experience the full duration of the outage. The Exchange 2010 CAS is better able to manage these transitions, and the target failover time is now 30 seconds or less.

CAS installation priority

The installation of CAS servers should be the first practical step in your deployment of Exchange 2010. An Exchange 2010 CAS can handle all of the different client connections to both Exchange 2007 and Exchange 2010. It can proxy connections to an Exchange 2007 CAS and make sure that clients that need to connect to a mailbox on an Exchange 2003 or Exchange 2007 server will get there. However, an Exchange 2007 CAS can't perform the same trick, because it obviously does not include the code to allow it to deal with new features such as the CAS hosting the MAPI endpoint for clients and CAS arrays. The recommended order for deployment is therefore as follows:

- If you have an Internet-facing Active Directory site to support external client access (OWA, Outlook Anywhere, ActiveSync), make sure that all of the servers in this site run Exchange 2007 SP2 or Exchange 2003 SP2 so that they can interact with Exchange 2010.

- Begin to deploy Exchange 2010 by introducing CAS servers into the Internet-facing Active Directory site first, and then Edge and Hub transport servers. Prepare for the transfer of incoming client connections from the old environment to the new by configuring Secure Sockets Layer (SSL) certificates to allow Exchange 2010 CAS servers to provide Autodiscover service to Exchange 2007 mailbox servers.

- Move the Internet namespace for the organization to Exchange 2010 by updating the external URLs to redirect traffic to the Exchange 2010 CAS, Edge/Hub transport, and Unified Messaging (UM) servers.

Chapter 11

- Install Exchange 2010 mailbox servers and start to move user mailboxes from legacy servers.

- Remove older CAS and Hub transport servers.

- Remove old UM servers.

- Remove old mailbox servers. Some legacy mailbox servers might be required to support applications that depend on older application programming interfaces (APIs), such as Web Distributed Authoring and Versioning (WebDAV), which are not supported by Exchange 2010.

Outlook traditionally attempts to connect to Exchange using TCP first and then reverts to an RPC over HTTPS connection (Outlook Anywhere) if the TCP connection fails. This is the most appropriate setup for standard corporate clients that spend most of their time working on the internal network. However, if you have many clients that work remotely and usually connect using Outlook Anywhere, you can change the behavior so that Outlook attempts to use RPC rather than HTTPS first. Only Outlook 2010 clients support this recalibration, which possibly reflects the growing popularity of Outlook Anywhere and its ability to connect to Exchange without the need to use a virtual private network (VPN). If you want to make Outlook Anywhere the default, run the Set-OutlookProvider cmdlet as follows:

```
Set-OutlookProvider -id EXPR -OutlookProviderFlags:ServerExclusiveConnect
```

This is a global change, so it will be respected by all Outlook 2010 clients—even if they connect to an Exchange 2007 mailbox—if they connect through an Exchange 2010 CAS. Use this command to revert to previous behavior:

```
Set-OutlookProvider -id EXPR -OutlookProviderFlags:None
```

The Set-OutlookProvider cmdlet defines global settings for the AutoDiscover object. If a change is made to the provider flags properties, Exchange will provide these values to a client with AutoDiscover for its use. Outlook 2007 and Outlook 2010 clients can select particular connection behavior in their profiles and, if selected, this behavior is used in preference to the global setting.

The RPC Client Access layer

Chapter 8, "Exchange's Search for High Availability," discusses how the introduction of the Database Availability Group (DAG) enables Exchange to support multiple copies of a database. Establishing the ability to have multiple database copies adds substantially to the system designer's ability to construct solutions that resist server outages, but the real magic is not in the replication of log files between servers. After all, Exchange 2007 also supports log shipping. Instead, the big breakthrough that enables DAG technology to work is the relocation of the connection point for MAPI clients away from the mailbox server to the CAS. In the past, Outlook clients expected to know which server hosts the database that holds the mailbox they want to access by reference to the mailbox information held in the user's Active Directory account. Equipped with this knowledge, Outlook can make a direct connection to the mailbox server. This mechanism obviously works well, but it copperfastens the tight connection between mailbox database and server.

Figure 11-1 illustrates the Exchange 2010 CAS architecture. The big difference from Exchange 2007 is that all connections from all clients flow through the CAS. In some respects, this is similar to the change that Microsoft made in Exchange 2007 to force every message to move through the transport service by removing direct delivery to mailboxes for messages sent within a database. The new RCA service, implemented in the *MSExchangeRPCAccess* process, is responsible for intercepting all mailbox client connections, including those from MAPI clients, querying Active Directory to locate the mailbox's current location, and proxying the connections to the appropriate mailbox server. This implementation provides the desired separation between mailbox database and server. It removes the code required to process MAPI client connections from the Information Store, which in turn has the added benefit of simplifying the code that executes within the Store and makes it simpler and easier to maintain. At the same time, making sure that all client connections flow through a common point ensures greater consistency in terms of applying business logic during client interaction with data (for example, opening a meeting request with a mobile device while your mailbox is open with Outlook and that client is automatically processing the requests at the same time).

Chapter 11

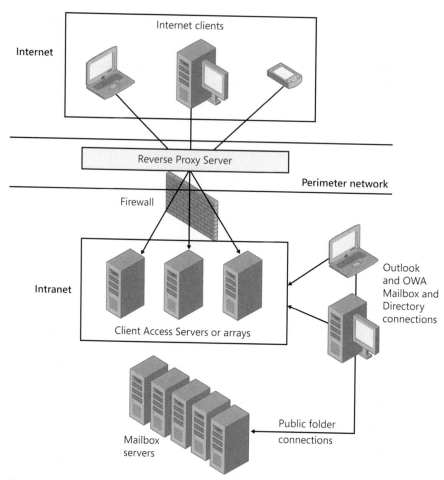

Figure 11-1 The Exchange 2010 Client Access Server architecture.

Clients follow different routes to get to a CAS server, but all end up at the same place:

- Outlook (MAPI) clients connect to CAS servers for mailbox and directory access and mailbox servers to access public folders. Of course, the big difference in Exchange 2010 is that you provide the name of a CAS or CAS array to Outlook instead of a mailbox server when you configure a client to connect to Exchange.

- POP3 and IMAP4 clients connect to a single namespace (for example, mail.contoso.com) that points to a CAS server or array, which then proxies the incoming connection to the correct mailbox server.

- ActiveSync mobile clients connect to the same namespace to synchronize mailbox and calendar data.

- OWA clients connect to the same namespace to retrieve mailbox content that is rendered by the CAS.

A simple picture of a unified connection point for client data access emerges. The CAS is very much a central hub for Exchange clients.

Linking CAS to mailbox databases

Behind the scenes, Outlook clients traditionally access Active Directory to look up the server name where the database that hosts user's mailbox is located. If you look at the LegacyExchangeDN for the database, it will be something like this:

```
legacyExchangeDN: /o=ABC Corp/ou=Exchange Administrative Group
(FYDIBOHF23SPDLT)/cn=Configuration/cn=Servers/cn=ExServer1/cn=Microsoft Private
MDB;
```

In this case, Outlook knows that the database is on the server called ExServer1. As we know, Exchange 2010 breaks the connection between database and server, so the situation is different and Exchange 2010 specifies the name of the CAS server or array that now provides the MAPI endpoint. In simple organizations, the MAPI endpoint might be a server that supports the CAS and mailbox roles; indeed, if a server supports both these roles the endpoint for any database on that server will often be the CAS server on the same server. In more complex environments, the endpoint might be provided by any of the CAS servers in the same site as the mailbox server, or the endpoint might be a CAS array that is created to support connectivity within an Active Directory site.

Exchange 2010 mailbox databases have a new property called *RpcClientAccessServer* that Exchange automatically populates when it creates a database to specify where the MAPI endpoint is hosted. If the server that hosts the database is also a CAS server, Exchange inserts that server in the property. If not, it uses either the name of the site's CAS array (if one is defined) or selects one of the CAS servers that are installed into the site. We discuss how to create a CAS array in the section "Client Access Server arrays" later in this chapter. You can check the current settings with a command like this:

```
Get-MailboxDatabase | Select Name, RpcClientAccessServer, Server | Sort
RpcClientAccessServer
```

Name	RpcClientAccessServer	Server
IT Department	ExServer1.contoso.com	ExServer1
PR	ExServer1.contoso.com	ExServer4
Dublin Users	ExServer1.contoso.com	ExServer1
DB3	ExServer1.contoso.com	ExServer2

Chapter 11

```
DB1                 ExServer1.contoso.com        ExServer1
VIP Data            ExServer2.contoso.com        ExServer4
Operations          ExServer2.contoso.com        ExServer4
DB2                 ExServer2.contoso.com        ExServer2
Sales               ExServer2.contoso.com        ExServer3
```

From the output, we can see that there are two active CAS servers (ExServer1 and ExServer2) present. Simply because of the naming convention, it's likely that ExServer1 was the first CAS server created in the site, but there's no obvious way of telling this from the available information. You can also see that there's no relationship between *RpcClientAccessServer* and the actual server where the database is currently mounted. The property is not updated when a database is moved to another server, a server is down, or a server is removed from the organization. When the preferred CAS server is unavailable for some reason, Exchange will not select the next available CAS server in the site even if another CAS server is available. This is because the mailbox database is associated with a particular CAS server and will continue to attempt to contact that CAS server until instructed otherwise. Outlook users will be unable to connect to Exchange until the CAS server comes online again, in which case Outlook notices that the server is available and will then connect.

Avoiding dependency on a single server is therefore a good reason to consider creating a CAS array even if you only have two CAS servers in a site. We'll discuss CAS arrays shortly.

In the meantime, you can update the *RpcClientAccessServer* property for a mailbox database to point it to a different server. For example, a catastrophic hardware failure might affect a server, in which case you would need to transfer all incoming connections to another CAS server. Make sure that you provide the fully qualified domain name (FQDN) of the CAS server that you want to use. For example:

```
Set-MailboxDatabase –id Sales –RpcClientAccessServer'ExServer1.contoso.com'
```

The *RpcClientAccessServer* property can also be mapped to a Client Access server array. We'll get to that point in just a little while.

INSIDE OUT
You can't have external firewalls between the CAS and mailbox servers

Exchange 2010 does not support the deployment of external firewalls between the CAS and mailbox servers. It is not possible to deploy CAS servers in the perimeter network with a firewall protecting the mailbox servers because Exchange uses too many open ports to make most security professionals happy. You can have Windows Firewall configured on servers, because Exchange will configure it to allow communications automatically, but not a hardware firewall.

See *http://technet.microsoft.com/en-us/library/bb331973.aspx* for a list of ports used by Exchange.

Supporting Outlook 2003 clients

Out of the box, the RCA layer only supports encrypted MAPI connections, which means that only Outlook 2007 and Outlook 2010 clients will connect without intervention. Outlook 2003 clients can connect to an Exchange 2010 CAS server or a CAS array, but you need to enable MAPI encryption on the client or disable it on all of the CAS servers that you use (individually or in arrays) with the Set-RPCClientAccess cmdlet. If Outlook 2003 clients need to access public folders, you'll need to disable the requirement for MAPI encryption on the mailbox servers that host the public folder databases as well.

Clearly the better option is to enable encryption on the client, because that's the default behavior of Outlook 2007 and Outlook 2010 clients and it avoids the need to weaken security, even if the likelihood that someone would intercept packets flowing from Outlook 2003 to a CAS is reasonably low. Although you can enable encryption on individual clients, the more logical and productive approach is to apply this setting through a Group Policy Object (GPO), if this facility exists for you.

You can use the Get-RPCClientAccess cmdlet to check the current encryption setting. For example:

```
Get-RPCClientAccess -Server ExchCAS1 | Format-List Server, *Enc*
```

If you insist on disabling encryption, you can do this with the Set-RPCClientAccess cmdlet:

```
Set-RPCClientAccess -Server ExchCAS1 -EncryptionRequired $False
```

To disable MAPI encryption on a mailbox server that hosts a public folder database:

```
Set-MailboxServer -id ExServer1 -MAPIEncryptionRequired $False
```

Chapter 11

If only because administrators didn't realize the issue and only ran into the problem when the first Outlook 2003 client attempted to connect to Exchange 2010, the encryption requirement proved to be a real problem for Exchange 2010 deployments. Microsoft therefore changed the default configuration for the CAS in SP1 so that encryption is disabled. While this is a solution that enables smooth connections for Outlook 2003 clients, it creates another problem. Older CAS servers deployed with RTM have encryption enabled. This configuration is retained after the upgrade to SP1. New servers deployed using SP1 have encryption disabled. You can then anticipate a situation where a mixture of old and new servers are collected into a CAS array and Outlook 2003 clients become confused because they can connect to the new servers but not to the old. I can imagine that administrators will be confused shortly thereafter as they attempt to debug the problem. With this in mind, best practice remains to force encryption for all client–server communications, even if this means that some Outlook 2003 profiles have to be updated.

CAS access to directory information

The CAS also provides a Name Service Provider interface (NSPI) endpoint for Outlook clients to handle requests for directory information that replaces the DSProxy component used in Exchange 2007. When an Outlook client makes a directory request, the Address Book service in the CAS intercepts it and checks with Active Directory to discover the site in which the client's mailbox is located and the value of the *RPCClientAccessServer* property of the database that hosts the mailbox to know whether to connect to a particular server or array. The selected CAS server then responds to Outlook to tell the client the CAS server to which it needs to connect for directory information, and Outlook proceeds to connect to this server, which communicates with a global catalog server to respond to subsequent client requests for directory information. If a mailbox is located on a legacy server, the CAS is able to redirect the connection to the mailbox server so that it can refer the connection using DSProxy to a global catalog server.

Solving two problems

Channeling directory interaction through the CAS solves two problems for Exchange. First, it resolves a problem for Outlook Anywhere where load balancing SSL-ID solutions found it difficult to handle the split connections required by Exchange 2007 (a Lightweight Directory Access Protocol [LDAP] connection to Active Directory and an RPC connection to DSProxy). Second, it means that all update requests for directory information made by Outlook for group membership, delegate management, or certificate management are handled correctly, even if the client belongs to a different domain from the other objects.

For example, assume that your deployment has two domains in a forest. A user in Domain A is granted management rights over a group owned by Domain B but is unable to manage membership because any update cannot be processed by the domain controller to which Outlook connects the user's domain. This is a problem that has occurred over the years in many large deployments, and it's solved by building logic into the CAS to detect when these cross-domain conditions occur so that Exchange can write to the correct Active Directory server to implement the change.

The Autodiscover service

Microsoft introduced the Autodiscover service in Exchange 2007 as a solution to the perennial problem of how to help users to configure Outlook with the name of their mailbox and the server that hosted the mailbox the first time that they connect to Exchange. Information about the mailbox's location is subsequently held in the Outlook profile. A profile can still be configured manually, but it's a lot easier to let Autodiscover do the work for you. This all works very nicely unless the mailbox for which you are attempting to configure access is hidden from Exchange address lists, in which case Autodiscover won't be able to find the mailbox and you'll have to configure the profile manually. Outlook is also able to requery Autodiscover if it loses connection to the mailbox.

Outlook 2007 and Outlook 2010 clients, any Windows Mobile device running version 6.1 onward, and email clients such as Entourage and Outlook for Mac support Autodiscover. The service is even more valuable for Exchange 2010 because the database where a user's mailbox is located is no longer fixed and is able to move from server to server within a DAG. Outlook 2007 and Outlook 2010 can also connect to mailboxes on Exchange 2000 or Exchange 2003 servers (which do not offer an Autodiscover service), but in these situations the user usually has to configure his profile by inserting full details of his mailbox and server when he first connects to Exchange. After you begin to deploy Exchange 2010, Outlook will be able to find an Exchange 2010 CAS server and fetch its Autodiscover information from this server.

Accessing a Service Connection Point

Clients access Autodiscover in two ways. First, if the client runs on a domain joined workstation, it can execute a lookup against Active Directory to discover the Service Connection Points (SCPs) that Exchange registers when a new CAS is installed. If the client is running outside the domain, it can interrogate the Autodiscover Web site to retrieve the necessary information.

Chapter 11

An SCP is present in Active Directory for every CAS in the organization. An SCP contains an authoritative list of URLs that clients can use to access the Autodiscover service within a forest. An SCP can act as a referral from one forest to another to help clients find Autodiscover information when Exchange is deployed in a multiforest scenario. The URLs returned from the SCPs essentially act as pointers to CAS to which clients can connect to be redirected to whatever mailbox server currently hosts their mailbox. The URLs also point to other Exchange services such as the Availability service.

To determine the SCP it should use, Outlook does the following:

- Retrieves a list of SCPs for available CAS from Active Directory.

- Compares the SCPs to find those that match the Active Directory site to which the workstation running Outlook belongs. If no matching SCPs are found, a separate list is built. The list is ordered by age (the date that the SCP was added to Active Directory).

- Attempts to connect to the Autodiscover service specified in the first SCP in the list. If the first SCP points to an Exchange 2007 CAS (because it is the oldest), and the mailbox is on an Exchange 2010 server, the CAS redirects the request to an Exchange 2010 CAS in the site that hosts the mailbox (this redirect could occur within the same site).

- If the first CAS in the list is unavailable, the client passes to the next CAS, and so on until a successful connection is made or the list is exhausted.

After the client connects to a CAS, it attempts to retrieve the configuration information for its mailbox and the location of the various Exchange services. This step ensures that the profile is kept updated with the latest mailbox settings and that Outlook knows how to find the following:

- Out of Office information

- Availability information from the calendars of other users

- Locations to download the Offline Address Book (OAB) files

- Unified Messaging information (if used)

Another important update that the client receives is the name of the CAS that it should use for future queries. This CAS becomes the MAPI endpoint that replaces the name of the mailbox server that is used in the profile for previous versions of Exchange.

INSIDE OUT   Which server is the CAS server?

This CAS server is not necessarily close to the mailbox server that currently hosts the mailbox where the user's mailbox is located. Remember, this mailbox database can move between servers if multiple database copies are available within a DAG, so Exchange applies the principle of "closest to the client" to select a CAS that is close in network terms to the client computer and uses that as the MAPI endpoint. In most cases, the CAS server and the mailbox server will be in the same Active Directory site, but it is entirely possible that they will be in separate sites.

Things are more complicated when Outlook attempts to connect from the Internet using Outlook Anywhere. In this case, Outlook cannot check against Active Directory to retrieve the list of Autodiscover SCPs.

- Outlook can't resolve the FQDN for the CAS server (or array) that is registered in its profile, so it falls back and attempts to connect to the URL for the external Autodiscover service for the domain using HTTPS (port 443).

  For example, if the user's email address is JSmith@contoso.com, Outlook searches for the Autodiscover Web site by looking for *https://contoso.com/autodiscover* first and then *https://autodiscover.contoso.com* if the first lookup fails. The Autodiscover Web site should be locatable via Domain Name System (DNS) and differs from the one used by OWA users to connect from the Internet, which is usually named something like *https://webmail.contoso.com*. The fact that the names of at least two different Web sites need to be published to the Internet to facilitate external client connectivity is an excellent reason to use Subject Alternative Names (SAN) SSL certificates that contain a list of all the Web site names.

- The result of a successful lookup for Autodiscover is the return of XML-formatted information that tells the client how to contact the RPC proxy service.

- The next step for an incoming connection is when it is serviced by a reverse proxy server (Microsoft Forefront Threat Management Gateway [TMG], Microsoft Internet and Security Acceleration Server [ISA], or a hardware server). Its rule set determines how connections should be processed and directs it to a CAS server that has the RPC proxy component installed to act as the Outlook Anywhere endpoint.

- The RPC proxy component accepts the connection via bridged SSL on TCP port 443 and proceeds to check Active Directory to determine the mailbox database that hosts the user's mailbox; it can then determine the CAS server or array that is associated with the mailbox database.

- The CAS makes RPC calls to the CAS or CAS array configured for the mailbox database to allow the client to complete the connection.

INSIDE OUT How Outlook gathers information

It's worth emphasizing that Outlook gathers the information that it needs for a session in two ways: through its boot process and through a periodic refresh. Every time you start Outlook, it calls the Autodiscover service to fetch information about the Exchange services listed earlier. If Outlook finds this information, it keeps it in a local cache for 60 minutes before attempting a refresh. You can modify this interval on a CAS server by running the Set-OutlookProvider cmdlet to set a new cache lifetime in hours. For example, to set the lifetime to be three hours:

```
Set-OutlookProvider -id 'msExchAutoDiscoverConfig' -TTL 3
```

Outlook also refreshes the data if it is unsuccessful at contacting an Exchange server and will retry at five-minute intervals until it retrieves the data. A background thread is used to refresh the Web services data whenever necessary and users are not aware of this activity.

CAS settings

The Get-ClientAccessServer cmdlet can be used to retrieve information about the settings that Exchange maintains for a CAS to gain some insight into how these data are used.

```
Get-ClientAccessServer -id 'ExchCAS1'
```

```
Name                            : EXCHCAS1
OutlookAnywhereEnabled          : False
AutoDiscoverServiceCN           : EXCHCAS1
AutoDiscoverServiceClassName    : ms-Exchange-AutoDiscover-Service
AutoDiscoverServiceInternalUr   : https://exchcas1.contoso.com/Autodiscover
/Autodiscover.xml
AutoDiscoverServiceGuid         : 77378f46-2c66-4aa9-a6a6-3e7a48b19596
AutoDiscoverSiteScope           : {Dublin}
IsValid                         : True
OriginatingServer               : EXCHCAS1.contoso.com
ObjectCategoryName              : msExchExchangeServer
DistinguishedName               : CN=EXCHCAS1,CN=Servers,CN=Exchange
```

```
Administrative Group (FYDIBOHF23SPDLT),CN=Administrative
Groups,CN=contoso,CN=Microsoft
Exchange,CN=Services,CN=Configuration,DC=contoso, DC=com
```

Two interesting pieces of information are shown here. The first is the site scope (Dublin), which indicates that this CAS is configured to serve requests from clients that belong to the Dublin Active Directory site. You can set a different site scope with the Set-ClientAccessServer cmdlet. The second piece of information is the Uniform Resource Identifier (URI) to the virtual directory for the Autodiscover service. Clients use the Active Directory site scope to discover the best CAS to connect to run the Autodiscover service. If the Active Directory returns a number of servers that are available for the site, Outlook selects one at random and attempts to connect to it via HTTPS. Once connected, Outlook can call the Autodiscover service running on the CAS using the value returned in the *AutoDiscoverServiceInternalUri* property (the URI that points to the Autodiscover service; see the value returned by the Get-ClientAccessServer cmdlet earlier for an example). In fact, the value stored in the *AutoDiscoverServiceInternalUri* property is also the value that is stored in the SCP, as discussed earlier, which connects the two pieces of information nicely.

TROUBLESHOOTING

My Outlook client can't access the mailbox via Outlook Anywhere

A client connecting to a mailbox on an Exchange 2010 server must go through an Exchange 2010 CAS so that it is provided with the Autodiscover information that it needs to access the extended set of Exchange 2010 Web services. Therefore, if you have an Outlook client connecting to an Exchange 2010 mailbox via Outlook Anywhere and the connection is handled by an Internet-facing Exchange 2007 CAS server, the client will not be able to access the mailbox because the Exchange 2007 CAS server is unable to proxy to an Exchange 2010 CAS server in the Internet-facing site. The reason is that Exchange 2007 is totally unaware of the introduction of the RCA service in Exchange 2010. Therefore, its method of calculating where the MAPI endpoint is for a mailbox differs from the mechanism used by Exchange 2010, so any attempt to channel connections through an Exchange 2007 CAS will fail if the destination mailbox is on an Exchange 2010 server. This is the main technical reason why Microsoft strongly recommends that you deploy Exchange 2010 CAS servers to replace Exchange 2007 CAS servers in both Internet-facing and internal Active Directory sites early in your deployment project.

Generally speaking, a new version of Exchange will always allow access to information stored on a server running an earlier version, but it is usually not possible to allow the reverse access because of code changes. This is exactly the situation here and it's really not surprising, given the fundamental nature of the change represented by the movement of the MAPI endpoint to the CAS.

Chapter 11

Site scope

To reduce any potential for network delays, Exchange always attempts to connect client computers to a CAS server that is closest to the client location (in Active Directory terms). As discussed earlier, a site scope is defined for a CAS server to establish the clients that the CAS serves for Autodiscover. If a client computer belongs to the London site, it will look for a CAS server that includes the London site in its scope during the Autodiscover process.

The site scope is created when the CAS server is installed to be the Active Directory site into which the server is installed. If the site scope is set to London, it indicates that the CAS server was installed into the London site and is responsible for servicing Autodiscover requests made by client computers that also belong to the London site. One point of note is that Exchange does not attempt to update the site scope if a CAS server is moved to a different site. There is no notion of autosensing the site within which the CAS currently functions. The consequences of an incorrect site scope include situations where a CAS server services the clients over extended links or where you end up with an overloaded CAS in a site that has to handle a huge number of client connections (because it has the right scope), whereas the other servers don't (because clients ignored them due to an incorrect site scope). Therefore, if you move a CAS or have a practice of building servers from a "gold build" or base configuration, you should check the site scope after the server is installed into its final production site.

A CAS can service client Autodiscover requests for multiple sites. In this example, the site scope for a server is set to cover two Active Directory sites. The limit for site scope is approximately 800 sites. Remarkably, this limit has been encountered in a number of projects where companies have deployed Active Directory access to very many small sites. If you run into this limitation, the only solution is to divide the load across multiple CAS servers by defining a different site scope for each server. You should also set the *AutodiscoverServiceInternalUri* value to the FDQN of a load balancer (see the section "Load balancing and CAS arrays" later in this chapter) so that all available CAS servers share the requests.

```
Set-ClientAccessServer –id ExServer1 –AutoDiscoverSiteScope 'London', 'Dublin'
```

AutoConfiguration

Outlook's AutoConfiguration option combines Autodiscover with another process called GuessSmart to retrieve information about mailboxes by scanning for predictable combinations of server and protocol information. AutoConfiguration can discover settings for POP3 and IMAP4 accounts (with Autodiscover and GuessSmart) or Active Directory (with Autodiscover) to build a profile necessary to connect to Exchange. It also does an excellent job of configuring an Outlook profile to connect to free consumer email services such as Hotmail.

The principles behind GuessSmart are very straightforward. Let's assume that you want to create a new IMAP account. Your Internet service provider (ISP) will allocate you an email address such as James.Seymour@contoso.com. There is a reasonable chance that the IMAP server is called imap.contoso.com or mail.contoso.com and that the Simple Mail Transfer Protocol (SMTP) server will be smtp.contoso.com or mail.contoso.com. Therefore, Outlook can scan for these servers using the ports that the protocols use (like port 25 for SMTP and 110 for IMAP) to see whether these combinations generate a configuration that works. For most ISPs, guessing what the configuration might be works quickly. As you can see from Figure 11-2, the Autodiscover service is able to provide the URLs to allow Outlook to contact Exchange resources such as the Availability service and the Web distribution point for the OAB.

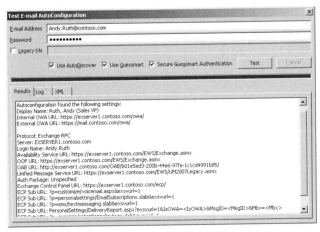

Figure 11-2 Results from the Outlook 2010 AutoConfiguration option.

If you configure a CAS to support Outlook Anywhere, the Autodiscover service will populate the profile with the information necessary for Outlook to connect to Exchange using RPCs over HTTP. The pointers to other services such as Exchange Web Services and the OAB must be configured manually by an administrator by running the Set-WebServicesVirtualDirectory and the Set-OABVirtualDirectory cmdlets to populate the *ExternalURL* property to point to the location where clients can access these services. You can also update the external URL for the OAB through EMC by selecting the Internet-facing CAS server and updating the properties of the OAB virtual directory as shown in Figure 11-3.

Chapter 11

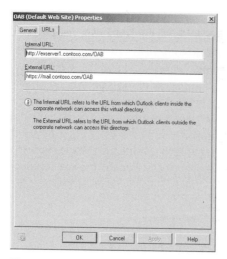

Figure 11-3 Ensuring that the OAB can be accessed outside the firewall.

Alternatively, these values will be populated for Outlook when a client connects to Exchange from within the firewall. Once populated, these values might change on subsequent connection attempts as Outlook reruns the Autodiscover process.

Logging Autodiscover actions

If you encounter difficulties with Autodiscover, you can enable Outlook logging to force Outlook to write details of the actions it performs to *Users\xxxx\AppData\Local\Temp \olkdisc.log*. Figure 11-4 shows how to enable logging with Outlook 2010.

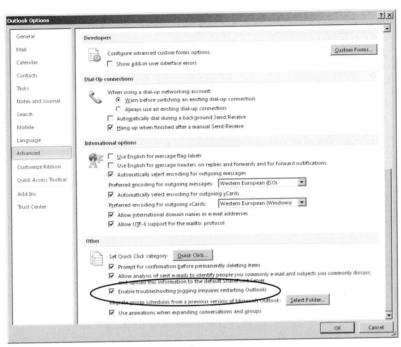

Figure 11-4   Enabling logging with Outlook 2010.

Outlook runs more slowly when it is logging diagnostic information, so you should disable logging as soon as you no longer need to gather data. Some sample logging data are shown next. You can see that the client attempted to contact webmail.contoso.com first and was not able to connect before being redirected to ExServer1.contoso.com, where the Autodiscover XML file containing all the information necessary to connect to Exchange services was found and provided to Outlook.

```
Thread Tick CountDate/TimeDescription
165638897203/03/10 18:38:47Attempting URL https://webmail.contoso.com
/Autodiscover/Autodiscover.xml found through SCP
165638897203/03/10 18:38:47Autodiscover to https://webmail.contoso.com
/Autodiscover/Autodiscover.xml starting
165639265403/03/10 18:38:51Autodiscover to https://webmail.contoso.com
/Autodiscover/Autodiscover.xml Failed (0x800C8204)
165639265403/03/10 18:38:51Autodiscover URL redirection to
https://ExServer1.contoso.com/Autodiscover/Autodiscover.xml
165639267003/03/10 18:38:51Autodiscover to https://ExServer1.contoso.com
/Autodiscover/Autodiscover.xml starting
165639688203/03/10 18:38:55Autodiscover XML Received
```

Chapter 11

```
---BEGIN XML---
<?xml version="1.0" encoding="utf-8"?>
<Autodiscover xmlns="http://schemas.microsoft.com/exchange/autodiscover
/responseschema/2006">
    <Response xmlns="http://schemas.microsoft.com/exchange/autodiscover/outlook
/responseschema/2006a">
        <User>
            <DisplayName>Redmond, Tony</DisplayName>
            <LegacyDN>/o=contoso/ou=Exchange Users/cn=Recipients/cn=TonyR<
/LegacyDN>
            <DeploymentId>146106f8-efb8-4893-9a44-1b2509aa8678</DeploymentId>
        </User>
        <Account>
            <AccountType>email</AccountType>
            <Action>settings</Action>
            <Protocol>
                <Type>EXCH</Type>
                <Server>ExServer1.contoso.com</Server>
                <ServerDN>/o=contoso/ou=Exchange Administrative Group
(FYDIBOHF23SPDLT)/cn=Configuration/cn=Servers/cn=ExServer1</ServerDN>
                <ServerVersion>7380827F</ServerVersion>
                <MdbDN>/o=contoso/ou=Exchange Administrative Group
(FYDIBOHF23SPDLT)/cn=Configuration/cn=Servers/cn=ExServer1/cn=Microsoft Private
MDB</MdbDN>
                <PublicFolderServer>ExServerPF.contoso.com</PublicFolderServer>
                <AD>ADServer-GC1.contoso.com</AD>
                <ASUrl>https://ExServer1.contoso.com/EWS/Exchange.asmx</ASUrl>
                <EwsUrl>https://ExServer1.contoso.com/EWS/Exchange.asmx</EwsUrl>
                <EcpUrl>https://ExServer1.contoso.com/ecp</EcpUrl>
                <EcpUrl-um>?p=customize/voicemail.aspx&amp;exsvurl=1</EcpUrl-um>
                <EcpUrl-aggr>?p=personalsettings/EmailSubscriptions.
slab&amp;exsvurl=1</EcpUrl-aggr>
                <EcpUrl-mt>PersonalSettings/DeliveryReport.aspx?exsvurl=1&amp;IsOWA
=&lt;IsOWA&gt;&amp;MsgID=&lt;MsgID&gt;&amp;Mbx=&lt;Mbx&gt;</EcpUrl-mt>
                <EcpUrl-sms>?p=sms/textmessaging.slab&amp;exsvurl=1</EcpUrl-sms>
                <OOFUrl>https://ExServer1.contoso.com/EWS/Exchange.asmx</OOFUrl>
                <UMUrl>https://ExServer1.contoso.com/EWS/UM2007Legacy.asmx</UMUrl>
                <OABUrl>http://ExServer1.contoso.com/OAB/319318c0-8707-4abb-9e7f-
4e587c0d43e9/</OABUrl>
            </Protocol>
```

If you examine the data returned by the Exchange 2007 Autodiscover, you'll find that they are much simpler than the data returned by Exchange 2010. The Exchange 2007 Autodiscover was the first iteration of a service that provided information to clients to allow them to connect to services without user intervention. Only Outlook and ActiveSync were supported, and the format of the information was plain XML. Now, Exchange 2010 Autodiscover publishes a more comprehensive set of data (still formatted in XML) that is intended for consumption by a much broader set of services that need to access Web services offered by Exchange. For example, Autodiscover now publishes details of a personal archive if this is available to a mailbox. Autodiscover is also version aware, so it understands what has to be returned to clients for Exchange 2007 mailboxes and doesn't confuse them with the increased detail provided to clients that wish to connect to Exchange 2010.

It's a good idea to turn on Outlook logging to collect log files for successful connections under various conditions (internal and Internet) to provide you with a baseline. You can compare these files to log files created for unsuccessful connections to get some idea of where the problems might lie. This technique might not solve your connection problem, but it can certainly give you some insight.

The Exchange Remote Connectivity Analyzer (Chapter 17, "The Exchange Toolbox") is another valuable tool that helps administrators track down problems when Autodiscover and AutoConfiguration don't work as expected. Outlook Anywhere and Autodiscover are two of the tests supported by the Connectivity Analyzer. All you need to provide is a valid email address and account password, and the Analyzer will run tests to determine whether it can connect (with Outlook Anywhere) or configure a profile using AutoConfiguration, and report its results.

You can also select the Outlook icon from the system tray and use the Ctrl+right-click combination to expose the current connection settings used by Outlook. This will give you information such as the servers to which Outlook is currently connected; for example, the CAS server and perhaps a mailbox server if you access public folders. This information is often requested by support personnel when they debug connectivity problems.

Static Autodiscover

Sometimes you need to override the Autodiscover process and provide exact guidance to Outlook so that it knows where to find Exchange services. Let's say that you want to move accounts from an old resource forest running Exchange 2007 into a new forest where Exchange 2010 is present. To prepare for the migration, you create new mail-enabled accounts for Exchange 2010 in the new forest that you'll eventually use as the target for move requests when the users are ready to migrate. The client computers running Outlook are also installed into the new forest. However, some mailboxes remain on Exchange 2007 running in the resource forest. The problem is that when Outlook runs Autodiscover, it automatically looks in the new forest and discovers the new mail-enabled account and attempts to use that rather than Exchange 2007. We therefore need to redirect Outlook and tell it to use Exchange 2007 and ignore Exchange 2010 until the mailboxes are moved. This can be done in three steps:

1. Create an XML file containing the pointer to the Autodiscover location that you want Outlook to use. This file is sometimes called a static Autodiscover configuration.

2. Create a registry entry to tell Outlook where to find the XML file.

3. Create a registry entry to instruct Outlook to use the pointer in the XML file.

The XML file is pretty straightforward. The following code sample illustrates the information that you need to include. The underlined text provides the direction to Outlook, so it needs to include the URL to the Autodiscover that you want Outlook to use.

```
<?xml version="1.0" encoding="utf-8"?>
<Autodiscover xmlns="http://schemas.microsoft.com/exchange/autodiscover
/responseschema/2006">
    <Response xmlns="http://schemas.microsoft.com/exchange/autodiscover/outlook
/responseschema/2006a">
        <Account>
            <AccountType>email</AccountType>
            <Action>redirectUrl</Action>
            <RedirectUrl>https://autodiscover.oldex2007.com/autodiscover
/autodiscover.xml</RedirectUrl>
        </Account>
    </Response>
</Autodiscover>
```

You should place the XML file in a location where clients can access it. For Outlook 2007, create a string entry in the registry at HKCU\Software\Microsoft\Office\12.0\Outlook \Autodiscover*namespace* and enter the full file name there (including the server name, if you locate the file on a file server). The same approach is taken for Outlook 2010, which uses a registry entry at HKCU\Software\Microsoft\Office\14.0\Outlook\Autodiscover *namespace*. In both cases, namespace refers to the domain for which you are redirecting connections, so a fully formed value is something like this:

```
HKCU\Software\Microsoft\Office\14.0\Outlook\Autodiscover\oldex2007.com
```

Finally, we have to instruct Outlook to look for the XML file, read in its contents, and use the instructions found there. This is done with another registry entry. For Outlook 2007, create a new DWORD value at HKCU\Software\Microsoft\Office\12.0\Outlook \Autodiscover\PreferLocalXML; for Outlook 2010, the value is at HKCU\Software\Microsoft \Office\14.0\Outlook\Autodiscover\PreferLocalXML. In both cases, you set the value to 1 (one) to force Outlook to use the local XML file rather than attempting to use network-based Autodiscover.

Of course, this method of configuring Autodiscover requires you to push the registry changes out to all the client computers that need to be updated to use a static Autodiscover configuration. Active Directory Group Policies or another mechanism can be used for this purpose.

SRV pointers to Autodiscover

Non-domain joined Outlook 2007 SP1 and later clients are able to locate Autodiscover settings through SRV records in DNS (in addition to trying fixed domain names as described earlier). This is a useful facility in situations where you want to provide service for a large number of domains. For example, some companies like to use "vanity" domains that are created for different organizations or business groups or for some other special purpose such as running a special event or continued brand recognition following a corporate merger or acquisition. You could provide Autodiscover through a certificate that includes every domain name that you want to use. However, this is an expensive proposition and it's difficult to maintain, especially if domain names tend to change.

For example, contoso.com might want to use contoso-finance.com and contoso-sales.com and continue to maintain its old name, contoso-group.com. As stated earlier, we could simply add the three additional domains to a SAN certificate and point the Autodiscover DNS records for each domain to mail.contoso.com, which is the general-purpose entry point for Outlook Anywhere and OWA. However, other domains might arise and then we'd have to buy a new SAN certificate, so that's why we continue with one certificate for mail.contoso.com and use SRV records to service the other domains. We create an SRV record in the external DNS zone for each of the domains that we want to support. Make sure that any A or CNAME records for the Autodiscover service are removed so the only DNS record that remains is the SRV record that redirects Autodiscover to mail.contoso.com. The SRV record looks like this:

```
Service: _autodiscover
Protocol: _tcp
Port Number: 443
Host: mail.contoso.com
```

When a non-domain joined Outlook client attempts to connect to use Autodiscover for an address in the contoso-group.com domain, the following sequence occurs:

1. Outlook posts to *https://contoso-group.com/Autodiscover/Autodiscover.xml*. This attempt fails because the address is invalid.

2. Outlook posts to *https://autodiscover.contoso-group.com/Autodiscover /Autodiscover.xml*. This attempt also fails for the same reason.

3. Outlook attempts to locate Autodiscover through a redirect check:

   GET http://autodiscover.contoso-group.com/Autodiscover/Autodiscover.xml

   This attempt fails, also for the same reason.

4. Outlook now attempts to lookup DNS to check if it can locate an SRV for _autodiscover._tcp.contoso-group.com. This attempt is successful and DNS returns "mail.contoso.com."

5. Outlook presents a dialog box to request permission from the user to continue with Autodiscover to post to *https://mail.contoso.com/autodiscover/autodiscover.xml*. The warning is this:

   Allow this website to configure user@contoso-group.com server settings?
   https://mail.contoso.com/autodiscover/autodiscover.xml
   Your account was redirected to this website for settings.
   You should only allow settings from sources you know and trust.

6. If permission is granted, Outlook's POST request is successfully delivered to *https://mail.contoso.com/autodiscover/autodiscover.xml* and the Autodiscover information is retrieved.

The request for permission that a user sees in step 5 can be disconcerting, because non-technical users are unlikely to understand exactly what redirection means. You can suppress the request (and stop potential calls to the help desk) by implementing the fix described in *http://support.microsoft.com/?kbid=956528*. Essentially, you need to input a set of domain names into a registry value to let Outlook know that permission to redirect for these domains is in place and it doesn't need to bother the user.

Client Access Server arrays

Because CAS servers now provide the endpoint for MAPI and all other client protocols, it is even more important to provide a resilient capability for client connectivity to CAS servers. As we know, mailbox databases are assigned pointers to CAS servers. This works well until the CAS server assigned to a mailbox database is offline. If the CAS server doesn't come online again quickly, clients will not be able to connect to their mailboxes. This is always an issue when a service depends on a single server. Exchange 2010 introduces a new solution by allowing you to create an array of CAS servers that are linked together by a single network name and IP address that can then be assigned to a mailbox database. Instead of being restricted to a connection to a single CAS server, clients can connect to any CAS server in the array by specifying the FQDN for the array rather than for an individual CAS server. The CAS array therefore removes another hard-coded link along the path from client to mailbox and provides the essence of load balancing by enabling clients to continue working during server outages.

> **Tip**
>
> A CAS array is not a load balancing solution, but if you deploy a load balancer in front of the CAS array, you should see good balancing of client connections across the servers in the array.

You can only have a single CAS array in an Active Directory site, and a CAS array cannot span multiple sites. On the other hand, all of the CAS servers in the site do not have to be in the array, and you can continue to assign individual CAS servers to mailbox databases within the site.

INSIDE OUT   Some limitations for large deployments

CAS arrays are attractive for large deployments, but the limitation of one CAS array per site imposes a restriction on Active Directory design. Consider the situation of a company that has centralized its IT into a number of large sites, each of which provides applications to users around the world. The one CAS array per site limitation creates an issue because it doesn't allow traffic from different user groups to be segregated and managed differently. Creating a link between Active Directory site and CAS array is a good thing for simplicity, but it does remove some flexibility in the largest and most complex deployments.

Another issue to consider is that if you deploy a CAS array, you effectively create a single target for all connections to mailbox databases associated with the array. If the CAS array becomes unavailable for any reason, clients will not be able to connect to those databases.

All of the CAS servers in an array should run the same version of Exchange to the level of the same roll-up release. Although it is acceptable to have different hot fixes applied to individual CAS servers in an array, this situation creates an obvious operational challenge should problems arise in terms of determining whether the problem is due to the presence of a hot fix. Overall, it's best to have exactly the same software versions installed on all servers in an array.

Creating a CAS array

The first step is to create the client access array using the New-ClientAccessArray cmdlet and associate it with the FQDN and the Active Directory site that it serves. There should be a DNS A record for the FQDN that you create:

```
New-ClientAccessArray -Name 'CAS-Array-01' -FQDN 'CASArrayDublin.contoso.com'
-Site 'Dublin'
```

INSIDE OUT   Here's a bad idea

It's a bad idea to publish the FQDN for the array so that it can be resolved by external DNS. The reason is that you don't want Outlook Anywhere clients to attempt to connect to the array with RPC, because they can resolve it in DNS (remember, the array is specified as the MAPI endpoint in their profile) and have to wait up to 30 seconds for the RPC to timeout before attempting to connect to the Outlook Anywhere URL over HTTPS.

The CAS servers that you include in the array should be assigned to the load balancing solution that you want to use. This can be Windows Network Load Balancing (NLB) or a hardware-based load balancer that serves the IP address that you assign to the array. In this context, Exchange 2010 requires access to TCP port 135 (endpoint mapper) and a restricted dynamic RPC port range (6005–65535). The selection of the dynamic port range is influenced by the fact that many Exchange 2007 deployments use ports 6000–6004 to support connections between CAS and mailbox servers. To make things easier, you can assign static ports for MAPI connections and directory access. We'll discuss this point in a little while.

After you create a CAS array, you should amend the settings on the mailbox databases within the site to direct incoming client connections to the client access array. New mailbox databases created after the CAS array is present automatically recognize its existence, but you have to update any mailbox databases that existed previously. To do this, update the mailbox databases in the site with information about the client access array:

```
Set-MailboxDatabase -Identity 'DB1' -RpcClientAccessServer 'CAS-Array-01'
```

> **Note**
>
> You can set the value of the *RpcClientAccessServer* property to either point to an array or to an individual CAS server. The CAS array serves Outlook clients that connect via MAPI. If you also use NLB to provide an array for other client protocols, such as Outlook Anywhere and ActiveSync, you should configure it to use a different FQDN to allow Outlook clients that operate outside your network to revert to Outlook Anywhere immediately if they cannot resolve the FQDN for the CAS array. Thus, if the CAS array has an FQDN of outlook.contoso.com, Outlook Anywhere might use an FQDN of webmail.contoso.com.

The Get-ClientAccessArray cmdlet returns the list of CAS servers in a site. This is inconsistent with the statement that you don't have to include every CAS server in a site in an array. The implementation of the cmdlet creates the inconsistency by outputting the names of all CAS servers in a site rather than just those that are in the array.

If you decommission a CAS server that's part of a CAS array, you also have to take the appropriate steps to remove the CAS server from the load balancer pool, and you will have to update mailbox databases to ensure that they are associated with an individual CAS server or with the CAS array in the site.

If a CAS server in an array fails or is rebooted without connections being drained (gracefully disconnected), Outlook clients will handle the outage properly by establishing a connection to another server in the array. OWA clients aren't quite so elegant, and users will receive a message saying that an unexpected error has occurred and their request couldn't be handled. They will have to go back to the authentication page and log back into OWA.

Managing cross-site connections with the RPC Client Access service

CAS arrays are often deployed to serve DAGs in datacenters. For disaster recovery purposes, you might extend the DAG across a primary and a secondary datacenter. In this situation, you probably have a CAS array in each datacenter. If a disaster happens and you have to activate the secondary datacenter, clients will not automatically switch to the CAS servers in the secondary datacenter, and you will need to update DNS to move the pointer to the CAS array from the array located in the primary datacenter to the array in the secondary datacenter. On the other hand, if a partial failure affected the primary datacenter and you need to bring additional capacity online to replace some failed servers, including some in the CAS array, you might decide to update the array to add CAS servers from the secondary datacenter.

Chapter 11

In general, the recommendation for the original version of Exchange 2010 is not to update the *RPCClientAccessServer* property for databases during failover conditions unless absolutely necessary, such as if the RCA array in the primary datacenter is inaccessible. If the RCA array remains operative, clients will:

- Continue to connect to the RCA array in the primary datacenter.

- Not need to update their profiles and not need to be restarted to make the profile change effective.

The RCA array in the primary datacenter will connect clients to the mailbox servers in the secondary datacenter and will operate in this mode until you can transition service back to the mailbox servers in the primary datacenter.

Although effective, this arrangement is not as effective as it might be. Exchange 2010 SP1 therefore changes how cross-site connections are handled. Four elements should be evaluated to decide what action to take:

1. The cross-site connection setting for the DAG. This is maintained in the *AllowCrossSiteRPCClientAccess* property for the DAG and is set to False by default. See Chapter 8 for more details about how to set DAG properties.

2. The server name registered in the Outlook profile. Unlike early versions of Exchange, which register the name of the mailbox server where the database containing the user's mailbox is located, Exchange 2010 writes the name of the CAS server or CAS array associated with the mailbox database into the Outlook profile.

3. The Active Directory site to which the CAS server or array specified in the Outlook profile belongs. This value is referred to as the preferred database site.

4. The Active Directory site where the active copy of the database holding the user's mailbox is currently mounted. This value is referred to as the active database site.

Table 11-2 illustrates the resulting action following an evaluation of four different scenarios. In all cases, we begin with a datacenter in Dublin that includes an RCA array called ExCASArray1.contoso.com. The first scenario is the norm, where the mailbox database is mounted in its preferred site and client connections flow through the array to the mailbox servers in the same site. An outage forces service to be transitioned to the mailbox servers in the London datacenter. The second and third scenarios describe the outcome dependent on whether the DAG permits cross-site connections. In the fourth scenario, the preferred database is now in the London site, perhaps because the Dublin datacenter has suffered a catastrophic failure and is not going to be online anytime soon, and this forces an update of the Outlook profile to reflect the new circumstances.

Table 11-2 **How Exchange 2010 SP1 handles cross-site connection scenarios**

CAS Server name in Outlook profile	Preferred database site	Active database site	Outcome
ExCASArray1.contoso.com	Dublin	Dublin	Direct connection from Outlook to mailbox database through the RPC Client Access service.
ExCASArray1.contoso.com (site Dublin)	Dublin	London	If cross-site connections are permitted, the RPC Client Access service will allow Outlook to connect to the mailbox database in the London site.
ExCASArray1.contoso.com (site Dublin) Updated to: ExCASArray2.contoso.com (site London)	Dublin	London	If cross-site connections are not permitted, the RPC Client Access server redirects Outlook to the mailbox database in the London site and forces an update of the Outlook profile with the name of a CAS server or array in the London site.
ExCASArray1.contoso.com (site Dublin) Updated to: ExCASArray2.contoso.com (site London)	London	London	The RPC Client Access service redirects Outlook to the mailbox database mounted in the London site AND forces an update of the Outlook profile with the name of a CAS server or array in the London site.

Load balancing and CAS arrays

The combination of Windows NLB and a CAS array provides a low-cost resilient connectivity service for Exchange within an Active Directory site. NLB is an inexpensive solution because it is included in Windows. On the downside, it's an unintelligent load balancer that exhibits a marked lack of service awareness because it does not check ports and services on a server before considering it a suitable candidate for load balancing. Essentially, if a server has a pulse, NLB thinks it is good. In addition, there is no communication between Exchange and NLB, and Exchange makes no attempt to balance client connections across all the CAS servers in the array. In fact, a CAS array is simply an Active Directory object that permits Exchange to make multiple CAS servers available as a single logical point of connection for clients.

Given these limitations, NLB is not a good solution for high-end deployments, which will probably invest in a hardware appliance solution for load balancing across all connectivity layers. However, whatever load balancing solution is deployed, the same principles apply:

- NLB (or another load balancer) presents a single virtual IP address and FQDN for the servers in the client access array to which clients connect. The simplest client access array covers two CAS servers.

- Microsoft's performance team recommends that no more than eight servers are included in a Windows Load Balancing array. If you use Windows Load Balancing, it therefore follows that you can have up to eight CAS servers in the array. On the other hand, if you use hardware-based load balancing, there is no real limit on the number of servers that can be included in the array.

- Incoming client connections are load balanced across all the servers in the client access array.

- The mailbox servers in the site automatically use the client access array as their connectivity point.

A single RCA service can maintain up to 100 concurrent client connections. Microsoft notes that an Exchange 2007 mailbox server can handle 64,000 concurrent connections (assuming that it has sufficient resources to handle that load), whereas they believe that an Exchange 2010 mailbox server should be capable of handling 250,000 RPC connections. These figures have not yet been verified by independent performance testing, but they show the kind of increase in scalability that Microsoft is pursuing within Exchange, largely to make sure that software can keep pace with ever-increasing hardware capabilities.

> **Note**
>
> There is a one-to-one mapping of connections to Outlook sessions, so if a connection is dropped, the Outlook client has to reestablish their session.

Moving the endpoint for connections from the mailbox server to the CAS is not only intended to drive additional scalability. Instead, the more strategic intention is to evolve from the previous position, where a database on a mailbox server represents a single point of failure to function in an environment where the CAS can switch incoming client connections to different databases depending on server availability. This concept persists during ongoing operations; for example, if the Active Manager detects that a database has stopped functioning on a server and decides that it has to switch a passive copy of a database to replace the active copy, it updates the information about the database in the DAG (held in Active Directory) and clients are redirected to the new server.

Upgrading a Client Access Server in an array

Because CAS servers are so important to client connectivity, any time that you want to take a CAS offline to apply a service pack or roll-up update, you run the risk of impacting client connections. Certain impact is guaranteed if you suddenly stop the CAS, because new client connections are no longer possible to Exchange and any existing connections will be abruptly dropped. Outlook clients configured in cached Exchange mode can continue working offline, but other clients will lose access to their mailboxes. In some installations, this situation is unavoidable because you might have only one CAS server for the whole deployment, or one CAS server for a site. In these cases, it is best to schedule maintenance for a time when low client demand is expected.

Many enterprise installations have a farm of CAS servers deployed to handle the connectivity load. The CAS array is usually behind a load balancer. We can therefore take an approach like the one described next to take servers offline, upgrade them, and bring them back into the farm. Again, this work should be scheduled at a time that minimizes any potential effect on clients.

1. Remove some of the CAS servers from the array maintained on the load balancer. This step prevents new connections from being allocated to the CAS servers that are removed while maintaining existing client connections. The number of servers to remove depends on the expected client connectivity load that exists while servers are offline. Some installations prefer to take half their servers offline at one time so that they can complete the upgrades over two scheduled maintenance periods. This might not be possible if you operate in a 24/7 environment where the connectivity load is constant and you are only able to take one or two servers out of the farm at any time. The aim is always to have sufficient connectivity capacity in the remaining CAS servers in the farm to be able to handle the expected load.

2. Wait an hour to allow the existing client connections on the removed CAS servers to reduce. Ideally, the number of client connections should go down to zero, because this means that no clients will be affected when we take the servers offline. Realistically, there will always be some client connections that are forcibly disconnected to take the servers offline. These connections will then need to be reestablished against the CAS servers that remain in the farm.

3. Take the selected servers offline and apply the upgrades.

4. Test the upgraded servers to ensure that the upgrade was successful and has not affected any setting that might prevent a client from connecting to a CAS server. A variety of methods can be used to test an upgraded server, including the Test-ServiceHealth cmdlet and logging into OWA using a URL that points to an upgraded server.

5. Reintroduce the upgraded CAS servers into the farm and update the load balancer so that new connections are now directed to the upgraded servers.

6. Wait for the CAS farm to stabilize. At this point, the upgraded servers should demonstrate that they are able to accept a full load, including connections from Outlook, OWA, and ActiveSync clients.

7. Repeat steps 1 through 6 to apply the upgrades to the other servers.

8. Validate that the fully upgraded farm can accept a full production load. Normally you can't test with a full production load, so this is a matter of careful observation and monitoring of the CAS farm as a full production load is applied during the next period of peak client demand. Of course, users are the best testers to validate that everything is working as expected and you'll hear pretty quickly if anyone has a problem connecting to her mailbox.

The approach described here is a generic method to upgrade servers in an array and must be carefully tested before being used in production. The need for testing is underlined by experience with the Exchange 2010 SP1 upgrade, where a mixture of RTM and SP1 CAS servers in an array can cause ActiveSync to become unreliable. A variation that works well for SP1 is to take one server out of the array, upgrade it, update DNS to point to the upgraded SP1 server and let it take the connection load, then upgrade the other servers in the array before finally bringing the complete upgraded array back online. Clearly, the faster the upgrades are done, the sooner normal service is restored to clients.

CAS and perimeter networks

If you're upgrading from Exchange 2003, you might be tempted to assume that the CAS is a direct replacement for the front-end (FE) servers that you deploy into the perimeter network to handle incoming client connections from the Internet and to block unauthenticated connections. A perimeter network (otherwise known as a demilitarized zone) is deployed between the Internet and a company intranet as part of a defense-in-depth strategy. Servers that are able to handle the threat posed by Internet attacks are placed in the perimeter network to detect and block incoming attack vectors. In these scenarios, a firewall separates the FE servers from the rest of the Exchange organization and sanitizes the traffic that flows from the FE servers into Exchange back-end (BE) mailbox servers. Exchange 2010 does not include FE or BE server roles and Microsoft does not support the deployment of CAS servers into perimeter networks. A change in your deployment plan is therefore necessary as you upgrade Exchange 2003 to Exchange 2010.

First, it's important that you understand how FE servers differ from CAS servers. An Exchange 2003 FE server is an adaptation of a regular Exchange 2003 server that contains all of the code of a regular server, even though it actually executes a very small proportion of this code in its role as an FE server. Microsoft didn't have the time to engineer a purpose-built Exchange 2003 server for perimeter deployments. Although they do not serve the same purpose as FE servers, Exchange 2010 edge servers are purpose-built for perimeter deployments and do a good job of handling SMTP traffic that flows in from the Internet. The other client protocols still have to be handled, and that's where the CAS comes in. Despite the fact that FE servers seem similar at first glance, they don't do the same work as a CAS. For instance, FE servers do no rendering for OWA (this is done by Exchange 2003 mailbox servers), nor do they include any of the middle-tier code that the CAS exploits to process HTTPS, MAPI, ActiveSync, EWS, POP3, and IMAP connections.

Because it handles all the client connections, a CAS is in constant communication with Active Directory to read data about users, servers, and other aspects of Exchange configuration. We don't want to put servers that depend on Active Directory into the perimeter network because this creates the potential for a hacker exploit that might compromise Active Directory. This is one reason why Edge servers don't use or depend on Active Directory. On the other hand, we have to authenticate client traffic just like the Exchange 2003 FE servers do to be able to allow access to mailbox servers. Preauthentication by reverse proxy servers provides the answer.

When Exchange 2003 was introduced, reverse proxy servers weren't all that common and Microsoft's own ISA server was immature. Since then, huge progress has been made in the functionality and capabilities of reverse proxy servers. They are now the obvious answer to the need to position a server in the perimeter that is capable of presenting a single secure interface to a range of applications. Reverse proxy servers usually contain a range of defenses to allow them to resist probes and attacks, and are much more hardened in this respect than a general-purpose email server can ever be. Accordingly, there is no longer a need for an Exchange FE server to authenticate client connections, because this can be left to the reverse proxy server. CAS servers can rely on the reverse proxy to provide a cleansed stream of incoming client connections that represent no threat to Exchange.

When upgrading from Exchange 2003, you therefore need to ensure that you have a dependable and robust reverse proxy server in place in the perimeter network to handle incoming connections. The reverse proxy server will handle preauthentication for clients to replace the BE server and will pass connections through a firewall to the CAS servers sitting inside your intranet. The exact details of how to configure components to support Exchange differ across the software- and hardware-based reverse proxy solutions and firewalls that are available, but the broad concepts remain the same and most vendors have documented specific recommendations that you can follow for different Exchange deployment scenarios.

The article at *http://technet.microsoft.com/en-us/library/bb331973.aspx* documents the set of ports used by different Exchange 2010 server roles.

RPC Client Access logging

By default, Exchange maintains a protocol log for the RPC Client Access service. You can review this log to discover information about incoming client connections and perhaps help in troubleshooting problems with connections. Logging is controlled by settings in the RCA service configuration file (Microsoft.Exchange.RpcClientAccess.Service.exe.config) located in the Exchange binaries directory. Like the other similar configuration files used by other Exchange services, you have to edit the configuration file with a text editor and then restart the service to make the change effective.

If you go through the RCA configuration file shown in the following code sample, you can see the major settings that can be tweaked. As stated earlier, logging is enabled by default. The next setting shows that the logs are captured in \Logging\RPC Client Access\ under the directory where the Exchange binaries were installed. The maximum size that a log can reach before Exchange will create a new log is 10 MB. Exchange will create a new log daily after the first client connects via RPC and will capture 10 MB of data in a log before switching. Logs are named *RCA_YYYYMMDD_x.LOG*, so RCA_20100720_1.LOG is the first log created on July 20, 2010. If Exchange needs to create a second log to accommodate more than 10 MB of data, it will be called RCA_20100720_2.LOG, and so on. Like other protocol logs, Exchange keeps RCA logs for 30 days (720 hours) and will keep up to 1 GB of logs (1048576 KB) before it begins to clean out the log directory using the last-in, first-out principle.

```xml
<?xml version="1.0" encoding="utf-8"?>
<configuration>
    <runtime>
        <gcServer enabled="true" />
        <generatePublisherEvidence enabled="false" />
    </runtime>
    <appSettings>
        <!-- Enables and disables the logging for RPC Client Access. -->
        <add key="ProtocolLoggingEnabled" value="true" />
        <!-- Specifies the folder in which log files will be generated. -->
        <add key="LogPath" value="%ExchangeInstallDir%\Logging\RPC Client
Access\" />
        <!-- Specifies the max size in KB of a single log file can grow to before
a new one is generated. -->
        <add key="PerFileMaxSize" value="10240" />
        <!-- Specifies the max size in KB of the entire directory of logs can
grow to before the oldest log is deleted. -->
        <add key="MaxDirectorySize" value="1048576" />
        <!-- Specifies length of time in hours log files will be retained before
being deleted. -->
        <add key="MaxRetentionPeriod" value="720" />
        <!-- Specifies if we need to switch log file each hour. -->
        <add key="ApplyHourPrecision" value="true" />
        <!--
            Specifies log tags to be logged. The value is comma delimited of
ConnectDisconnect, Logon, Rops, OperationSpecific, Failures, ApplicationData,
Throttling or None.
            ConnectDisconnect - logs connection establishment and close
events.
```

```
            Logon - logs logon events.
            Rops - logs each executed ROP
            OperationSpecific - logs custom trace data
            Failures - logs RPC and ROP layers failures
            ApplicationData - logs data related to the connected application
(mode, process name, etc.)
            Throttling - logs throttling policy-related information
            Warnings - nonfatal conditions that can sometimes be a manifesta-
tion of client-side problems.
     -->
    <add key="LoggingTag" value="ConnectDisconnect, Logon, Failures,
ApplicationData, Warnings" />
</appSettings>
```

You can see the kind of information recorded in Figure 11-5, which shows a log file viewed through Microsoft Excel. Like other Exchange protocol logs, the file format is a slightly modified version of CSV. Among the interesting data that we can see are the following:

- The mailbox that has connected to the CAS (the distinguished name is recorded).

- The version of the client (in this case, it is version 14.0.4760.100, so we know that it's the released version of Outlook 2010).

- Whether the client runs in cached or online mode.

- Details of the connections that Outlook makes to Exchange on an ongoing basis. In this instance we can see multiple connections for a single client. This is explained by the fact that Outlook establishes up to four background threads (each uses a connection) to the server when it is configured in cached Exchange mode. These threads perform the drizzle-mode synchronization to update the replica folders in the OST file with whatever has changed in the master folders on the server. Another thread is created whenever Outlook sends a message.

Administrators don't need to use the RCA Connectivity log except when things are not going well and clients can't connect to the server or are experiencing some instability in their connections. At that point, Microsoft Support might ask for a copy of the RCA Connectivity log to help them determine what's going on.

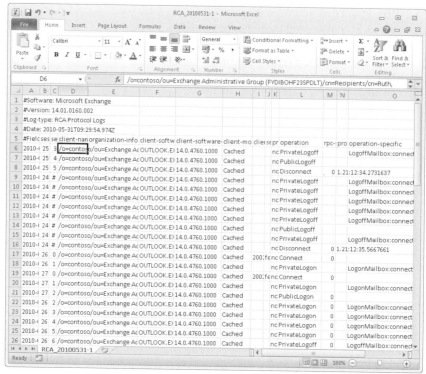

Figure 11-5 Extract from an RPC Client Access log.

Certificates

If you only run Exchange for an internal network and never want to allow access from the Internet, the set of self-published certificates installed on Exchange 2010 servers when they are installed by the setup program is sufficient for your purposes, as long as you're willing to have OWA clients install the self-signed certificates to avoid the nagging warnings from browsers that you're connecting to an untrusted site when you start OWA. To get around the problem, install the self-signed certificate from the Exchange CAS server that you use to connect to OWA in the trusted root certification authorities store on the PC (or use a Group Policy Object to distribute the certificate to multiple PCs around the organization). Afterward the PCs that have installed the certificate, but only those PCs, will then trust that Exchange CAS server for future connections. Of course, if you want to use another CAS server in the future, you'll have to go through the whole rigmarole again to install the self-signed certificate from that CAS server. Multiply the need to install the self-signed certificates for every CAS server that you deploy on every PC used to access OWA (or ECP), and you can see just how much work you might be setting up for yourself to make the self-signed certificates usable in a production environment. On the upside, the self-signed certificates generated by Exchange 2010 CAS servers when they are installed last for five years, whereas those generated by Exchange 2007 CAS servers only last one year, so at least your work will last a reasonable time.

Of course, most organizations don't restrict themselves to internal connectivity and want to deploy a solution that enables secure external connections from the Internet to access internal services such as OWA, ECP, ActiveSync, EWS, and so on. Unless you can persuade other companies to install your self-signed certificates in the trusted root store of their servers, the self-signed certificates created for CAS servers by the Exchange setup program will never be trusted outside your network. The upshot is that these certificates cannot be used to secure client communications from the Internet. You therefore need to buy certificates from a trusted third party and use them to secure SSL communications between clients and servers. Because both the clients and servers trust the third party, they accept the certificates as valid so there's no need to go through the palaver of installing the certificates, providing the certificates come from a well-known certification authority (CA) such as VeriSign, Entrust, DigiCert, or GoDaddy.

When installed, the certificates enable the CAS servers to secure publicly routable connections using protocols such as HTTPS with SSL. An SSL certificate contains a public and a private key that are used to encrypt data exchanged between a server and client. The CAS provides a copy of its public key to clients that connect to it. The clients can encrypt communications with the public key and the CAS is able to decrypt the communications using its private key, so anything sent between client and server is secure. A shared key generated by the client is used to secure data sent from the CAS to the client (see *http://support.microsoft.com/kb/257591* for details on how this connection occurs). The client encrypts the shared key using the CAS's public key and then transmits these data to the CAS. The CAS can then decrypt the shared key to know how it should encrypt communications in such a way that even if someone was to intercept data packets flowing between client and server, he would not be able to break into the data because he doesn't have the shared key.

How many certificates?

The business of deciding which and how many certificates should be deployed can be complex. Here are a number of suggestions to guide the process:

- Minimize the number of certificates in use: The more certificates you use, the more it will cost for their purchase and the more complex the environment becomes.

- Use SAN certificates: Normal certificates contain a single name, but SAN certificates have multiple Subject Alternate Names (SAN), each one of which is a hostname. These are simpler to deploy and reduce the number of required certificates. For example, a SAN certificate might contain SANs for autodiscover. contoso.com, mail.contoso.com, hq-exserver3.contoso.com, and exserver3, thus making that single certificate useful for a variety of purposes. Note that the FDQNs for RCA arrays do not need to be included in certificates, because these names are not used for SSL connections.

- Don't list individual computer hostnames in certificates: Whenever possible, use the names of arrays for Internet and intranet access to services (such as ActiveSync), because these are flexible and expandable.

In Chapter 5, "Exchange Management Console and Control Panel," we discuss the New Certificate Wizard available in EMC. This is new for Exchange 2010 and it greatly simplifies the process of generating a request to a commercial trusted CA to allow it to issue an SSL certificate that meets your needs to secure whatever services you want to secure.

The New-ExchangeCertificate cmdlet allows you to create a request for a certificate that you can send to your preferred certificate vendor. For example, this command creates a request for a SAN certificate that covers three hostnames:

```
New-ExchangeCertificate -GenerateRequest -Path 'C:\Temp\Cert.req' -SubjectName
'c=US;O=Contoso ;CN=Mail.contoso.com' -DomainName 'mail.contoso.com,
autodiscover.contoso.com, legacy.contoso.com' -PrivateKeyExportable $True
```

The private key is generated when the request is made. This key remains on the server that generates the request and is not provided to the third party. However, the *PrivateKeyExportable* flag indicates that you want to allow the private key to be exported and moved to another machine; this allows the single SAN certificate to be used on multiple hosts if mail.contoso.com, autodiscover.contoso.com, and legacy.contoso.com are actually separate machines. When you receive the SSL certificate, you can import it into Exchange with the Import-ExchangeCertificate cmdlet and then assign the certificate to the services that it should support with the Enable-ExchangeCertificate cmdlet. Alternatively, you can use EMC to complete the pending request that you generated with the wizard or the New-ExchangeCertificate cmdlet.

INSIDE OUT   Minimizing the number of hostnames

In addition, it's a good idea to minimize the number of hostnames with which clients have to deal by using split DNS to provide different addresses for the same name for Internet and intranet access. This allows you to have the same name (such as mail.contoso.com) no matter where a client accesses the service from.

Outlook Anywhere

Outlook Anywhere is the component of Exchange 2010 that allows Outlook clients to connect to Exchange from the Internet using HTTPS. Basically, Outlook wraps the RPCs that it usually uses to connect to Exchange in an outer layer of HTTPS that can pass through firewalls. The CAS server strips the HTTPS and redirects the RPCs to the correct mailbox server. This solution avoids the need for clients to use VPNs to communicate with Exchange and the need for administrators to open up additional ports in corporate firewalls.

Outlook Anywhere is not enabled by default. You have to enable it on a CAS server in an Internet-facing Active Directory site to act as the initial entry point for client connections. You also need to enable Outlook Anywhere on at least one CAS server in every internal site. To enable Outlook Anywhere on a server, follow these steps:

1. Go to the Server node in EMC.

2. Select the CAS server.

3. Select the Enable Outlook Anywhere option in the action pane.

Figure 11-6 illustrates the Enable Outlook Anywhere Wizard. The options are very straightforward:

- The external host name is the name that Outlook clients use to connect to the Outlook Anywhere service. Typically, the same name is used for all external points used for email access so that the same SSL certificate can be shared among Outlook Anywhere, ActiveSync, and OWA.

- The client authentication method determines how Outlook clients will authenticate themselves to Exchange when they initiate a connection. The default is basic authentication, meaning that the username and password are transmitted in plain text over an SSL connection. Most deployments use an advanced firewall such as Microsoft Threat Management Gateway that supports NTLM and can therefore enable this authentication method.

- The Allow Secure Channel (SSL) Offloading check box can only be selected if a separate server is used for SSL decryption and encryption. This server will be in front of the CAS server and will terminate the incoming connections and create new connections to send on for processing by the CAS. You'll normally use this option when you have a hardware load balancer or SSL accelerator that terminates or bridges SSL connections itself.

Chapter 11

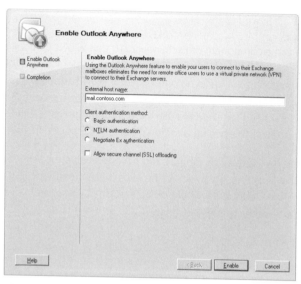

Figure 11-6 Enabling Outlook Anywhere.

The equivalent EMS code used to enable Outlook Anywhere with the same settings shown in Figure 11-6 is:

```
Enable-OutlookAnywhere -Server 'EXSERVER1' -ExternalHostname 'mail.contoso.com'
-DefaultAuthenticationMethod 'Ntlm' -SSLOffloading $False
```

Due to Active Directory replication, it can take up to 15 minutes for the new Outlook Anywhere settings to become effective throughout the organization. After replication has occurred, you can test that Outlook Anywhere works as expected using the Test-OutlookConnectivity cmdlet or the Exchange Remote Connectivity Analyzer (see Chapter 17).

An increased load for the CAS

It's obvious that the relocation of the MAPI endpoint to the RCA layer running on CAS servers has transferred workload from mailbox servers, specifically additional CPU processing. For this reason, Microsoft recommends that Exchange 2010 designs should use a ratio of 3:4 for CAS servers to mailbox cores when you determine server configuration for a site. For example, if the London site has eight mailbox servers, it will need six CAS servers to handle the incoming connections from Outlook clients. This is a very simple calculation and the final number of CAS servers required to handle the load depends on the following factors:

1. The number of mailboxes hosted on each server and the size of an average mailbox.

2. The mix of Outlook (MAPI) clients versus OWA, ActiveSync, POP3, and IMAP4 clients; each client imposes its own unique workload.

3. The distribution of load: A typical office environment might have peaks two or three times during the day.

4. Whether or not you use MailTips: This feature imposes a small performance penalty that will vary from organization to organization depending on the number of clients and how MailTips are used.

Performance advice changes all the time in line with experience, software tweaks, and the availability of new hardware. Microsoft and the hardware vendors will update their suggested configurations for mailbox and CAS servers for you to analyze and determine whether any changes are required inside your environment. Of course, smaller sites might have just one or two multirole servers, in which case the ratio does not apply, because all you need to do is to ensure that the servers are equipped with enough capacity to handle the multirole workload.

See *http://technet.microsoft.com/en-us/library/dd346701.aspx* for more information about understanding server role ratios and Exchange 2010 performance.

Load balancing the CAS

The question of how best to handle load often introduces load balancers into the equation to distribute load over multiple computers. The idea is that by distributing load intelligently you can maximize the use of server resources and minimize the impact of any system downtime. A CAS array is a form of load balancer, but this discussion focuses on hardware- or software-based load balancing systems that sit in front of a set of CAS servers or a CAS array to balance incoming client connections. In this respect, we are concerned about how best to balance connections going to a specific port to access a network service. In all cases, the incoming connection is accepted by the load balancer, which then decides what CAS server will service the connection.

Table 11-3 lists the spectrum of load balancing solutions that are usually considered for corporate Exchange deployments. Implementing a hardware approach using systems often called Application Delivery Network (ADN) devices is required when the connectivity load is generated by tens of thousands of individual clients and creates a volume that requires more than eight ISA/TMG servers to handle. At this level of connections, you start to worry about server scalability, the ability to handle TCP/IP connections, memory usage, and so on. The vendors of these solutions often provide excellent guidelines to assist in the deployment of their technology alongside Exchange (for instance, F5 publishes their advice at *http://www.f5.com/pdf/deployment-guides/f5-exchange-2010-dg.pdf*).

Table 11-3 **Load balancing solutions**

Technology	Comments	Client <-> CAS Affinity	Scalability	Cost
Hardware-based network application system; for example, F5 Big-IP or Citrix NetScaler	Uses different operating system and management components that must be integrated into your management domain; different skills required for administrators.	Several options, including existing cookie, cookie created by load balancer, SSL ID, source IP	Best (hundreds of thousands of connections)	Most expensive
Software-based load balancer running on separate Windows servers; for example, Microsoft TMG or ISA	More Windows servers to manage and license; increased complexity in server infrastructure. In addition, these servers cannot be used to do RPC Client Access array load balancing as they cannot load balance the MAPI endpoint.	Either cookie created by load balancer or source IP, depending on protocol or client	Reasonable (tens of thousands of connections)	Medium

Figure 11-7 illustrates the basic approach to using a hardware-based ADN system with Exchange. HTTP (including Outlook Anywhere), IMAP, and POP traffic flows through the external firewall to the ADN system installed in the perimeter network. The ADN system performs a variety of functions at this point, including SSL termination and reverse proxying, and then round-robins connections through the perimeter firewall to a farm of CAS servers that accept the connections and process them onward to mailbox servers. The CAS servers are individually identified to the server farm for Exchange 2007, but you can use a CAS array instead for Exchange 2010.

Hardware-based solutions are designed for a single purpose and are therefore inherently more scalable and better able to handle massive load than servers that run on top of a general-purpose operating system such as Windows and use commodity hardware sourced from a wide variety of sources. They usually include advanced features such as network optimization and the ability to prioritize application traffic and incorporate sophisticated mechanisms to resist attacks on the network. The downside is that these products are expensive and require specialized skills to deploy and manage. They tend to have their own tools for operations and monitoring and might not fit well in your server monitoring framework. On the other hand, the experience with hardware load balancers in production with Exchange 2007 and Exchange 2010 is that they deliver far higher stability and performance when exposed to very high loads than can be achieved with software-based load balancers.

Software-based load balancing is a good solution for medium to low-end deployments where the connectivity load is measured in thousands of connections. The latest offering from Microsoft in this space is Forefront TMG. In effect, TMG replaces ISA Server 2006, and is the natural option for deployment alongside Exchange 2010 if you don't need the scalability of a hardware solution. The outer limits for software-based reverse proxy solutions were exposed in a number of large-scale deployments of Outlook Anywhere with Exchange 2007. These deployments were characterized by the need to handle traffic generated by more than 40,000 concurrent Outlook Anywhere clients. The initial stages of the deployment are often successful because the full client load is not exposed. However, cracks appear as the load ramps up. When you think about it, ISA Server 2006 is fundamentally restricted by its 32-bit architecture and the limited number of TCP connections that an individual ISA server can handle. TMG is 64-bit software and can be expected to scale better, but this does not remove the need to test any reverse proxy or load balancer with a realistic load to understand where its limits exist.

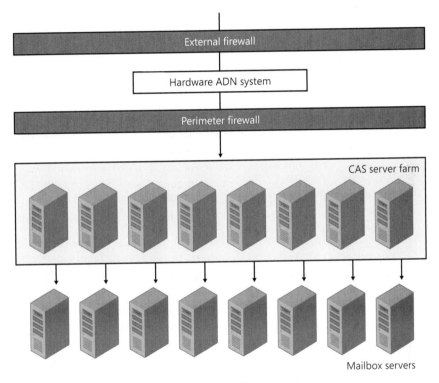

Figure 11-7 Integrating high-end hardware ADN with CAS.

Every deployment is unique in terms of number and types of clients, usage patterns, security requirements, network environment, and so on. For this reason, it is best to consider the positives and negatives of both the software and hardware solutions before you make a definitive choice about how you protect your infrastructure and allow Internet access to Exchange 2010.

Chapter 11

The importance of affinity

Affinity means that a session for a given client remains with the same CAS for the duration of the connection. In other words, once a client connects to a particular CAS, the same CAS will continue to service the connection until the connection is terminated. To do this, session state is maintained so that the load balancer knows which CAS handles which connection and the connections are said to be "sticky." If a load balancer or reverse proxy solution doesn't support affinity, it will break some Exchange services or reduce the performance of others by forcing users to reauthenticate each time the session moves to a different CAS, so this is clearly an area that you need to get right. The services that break are the following:

- OWA and ECP: These applications share the same authentication cookie, so the affinity must persist to the same CAS for a complete session, because only that CAS can decrypt the cookie.

- EWS: At a technical level, some parts of EWS work without affinity, such as requests to the availability service. Others need affinity to work. For best performance, you should consider that all of EWS requires affinity.

- RPC Client Access service: Outlook clients assume that all of the RPC connections that they generate go to the same CAS server, and this cannot happen if affinity doesn't work.

The services that work with reduced performance if affinity is not implemented are the following:

- Outlook Anywhere: When affinity is not used, a component called Network Load Balancing (LBS) attempts to correlate its two RPC_DATA_IN and RPC_DATA_OUT connections (the half-duplex connections used to simulate the full-duplex RPC communication over HTTPS) by checking with all of the CAS servers in a site. The more servers, the higher the inter-CAS traffic and the more server resources are consumed for correlation. Exchange 2010 works better than Exchange 2007, because the DSProxy referrals are replaced by an endpoint on the CAS provided by the Address Book service, so a single LDAP connection goes to the global catalog instead of the two used for the RPC referrals.

- ActiveSync: New mail notifications arrive on an ActiveSync client as the result of notification requests placed by the client to the server. If affinity is not present, the client has to open new notification requests as it moves between CAS servers.

- Address Book service: CAS servers cache Active Directory information to improve responsiveness to client requests. If a client moves between CAS servers he loses access to any cached information that exists as a result of requests made earlier in the session.

- Remote Windows PowerShell: EMS sessions are created with a particular CAS. If affinity does not exist, EMS has to initiate new sessions as it moves between servers.

The following servers work quite happily without affinity:

- Office Address Book: To access the OAB files, a client connects to one of the CAS servers that support OAB distribution and therefore doesn't need affinity.

- Autodiscover: This service makes a one-time request to discover connectivity details for a mailbox and therefore does not depend on affinity.

- POP3 and IMAP4: These protocols continually connect and disconnect to fetch and send messages, so they do not require affinity to function.

Although you might be able to exist without OWA and ECP, you absolutely need to use the RCA service to be able to connect to mailboxes. This need alone should reinforce the importance of affinity for connections to an Exchange 2010 server. Some load balancers are more intelligent than others and use a fall-through scheme whereby the load balancer will attempt to use cookie-based affinity first (existing or cookies created by the load balancer), followed by SSL session ID, and then source IP (the only option supported by Windows NLB). Other issues to resolve are whether or not the load balancer is able to use existing cookies or HTTP headers or needs to generate its own cookies; whether you want to separate traffic based on protocol (with SSL session ID); and some of the edge cases that might occur for specific clients (for example, the Apple iPhone creates new SSL sessions for some parts of its ActiveSync communications with Exchange).

Finally, you need to consider how the load balancer will assign new connections to available CAS servers. Two schemes are often used:

- Least connections: The load balancer uses affinity to track client connections to each server. A client that connects frequently refreshes its affinity record and the load balancer regards it as an active connection that needs to be persisted. However, clients that connect infrequently might have their affinity record expire and therefore be forced to create a new connection when they next want to access data.

- Round robin: The load balancer randomly selects a server and sends the client connection to it. This scheme is usually better for Exchange because it more easily accommodates a mix of active and inactive clients and produces a better distribution of workload across available servers. However, it can take a long time before the workload is well balanced across servers, and you need to be sure that the selected load balancer correctly excludes dead servers from the round-robin process.

Chapter 11

INSIDE OUT This is a topic for the planning phase

Whatever load balancer you use, you should make sure that the topic of affinity is discussed during deployment planning and that you test the selected scheme with all clients that are approved for use in a realistic environment that mimics the expected production workload to arrive at the optimum configuration.

Assigning static ports to the CAS

Exchange uses a number of ports to channel incoming client connections over the MAPI and HTTP protocols to CAS servers. TCP connections are typically assigned dynamic ports. When a service like Exchange that depends on Windows RPC starts up, it registers itself with the RPC service and is dynamically allocated a TCP port for its use. The port number varies over time and is called an endpoint. When a client wants to make a connection to a service, it sends a request to the endpoint mapper service through port 135 and receives the port number to use to find the requested service. The idea is that dynamic allocation makes the best possible use of the limited set of TCP/IP ports that are available. Even though 65,536 TCP/IP ports are theoretically available, the range of available ports is restricted by several factors. If every possible service attempted to insist on using a static endpoint all the time, some collisions between applications would be almost inevitable.

> **Note**
>
> The RPC service allows an exception to dynamic mapping to facilitate connections through firewalls when security reasons would make it impossible for administrators to allow dynamic endpoints.

You can configure static ports on CAS and mailbox servers for MAPI clients to connect to mailboxes and to access directory information. This is commonly done to provide a restricted set of ports to load balancers and so make them easier to manage and secure. Table 11-4 lists the different endpoints used for Outlook client connections. You can't change the static endpoints assigned for Outlook Anywhere, but you can assign static endpoints to replace the dynamic ports that would otherwise be used for internal MAPI and address book connections. Best practice is to make the endpoints all dynamic or all static. In other words, don't change the MAPI endpoint to be static and leave the address book and referral service to be dynamic: Change the three together.

Table 11-4 **TCP Ports used for Outlook client connections**

Connection	Type	Default	Configured
Mailbox (MAPI)	TCP	Dynamic port	Create TCP/IP Port value (DWORD) in system registry
Mailbox (MAPI)	HTTP	Port 6001	Not configurable
Address Book (NSPI)	TCP	Dynamic port	Create RpcTcpPort value (string) in the system registry
Address Book (NSPI)	HTTP	6004	Not configurable; Outlook hard-codes this value
Referral Service (RFR)	TCP	Dynamic port	The NSPI endpoint setting controls this endpoint, too, so the change to the RpcTcpPort setting will have the desired effect
Referral Service (RFR)	HTTP	6002	Not configurable; Outlook hard-codes this value

Internal mailbox connections can be controlled on CAS servers by a registry value called TCP/IP Port that specifies the port number to use. To assign a static port, create a DWORD value for TCP/IP Port under the key HKLM\System\CurrentControlSet\Services \MSExchangeRPC\ParametersSystem (if the key doesn't exist in the registry, you will have to create it). Input the port number to use into this value.

Microsoft made a change in Exchange 2010 SP1 to reduce the number of available ports that can be assigned. In the original version, you can select any port from 6005 to 65535; administrators usually selected values high in the dynamic range to avoid potential clashes with other applications. The SP1 installation reduces the maximum port value to 60554 and limits the dynamic range to between 6005 and 59350. This step creates a value range of between 59531 and 60554 that is purposely set aside to be allocated to static ports. Therefore, you should choose values from this range to use for the static mailbox (MAPI) port and the address book. In this case, I've selected 60001 as the static port number to assign (Figure 11-8).

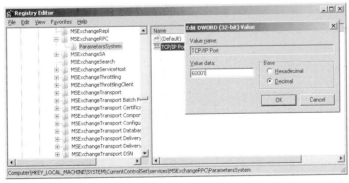

Figure 11-8 Assigning a static port for mailbox connections.

Chapter 11

After you assign a static port for mailbox connections on one CAS server, you should apply the same change on all the other CAS servers in the organization. If you use public folders, you have to make the same change on the mailbox servers that host public folder databases because these connections flow through the mailbox servers rather than the CAS.

INSIDE OUT   A safeguard

The port used for directory connections is controlled by a registry setting for the Address Book service. This is different from the original release of Exchange 2010, in which the Address Book service reads in the settings held in the Microsoft.Exchange .AddressBook.Service.exe.config file. The logic for the change is that moving the setting to the registry avoids the risk that a service pack or update will overwrite an important setting. Components such as configuration files are often completely replaced by a software update.

To assign a static port for the Address Book service, use Regedit to navigate to HKLM\SYSTEM\CurrentControlSet\Services\MSExchangeAB\Parameters and create a new string value called RpcTcpPort. Set the value to the number of the port that you want to use. This port handles connections for both the Address Book Referral interface (RFR) and the NSPI. You can't change the ports assigned for use by Outlook Anywhere, because Outlook is hard-coded to use ports 6002 and 6004.

You need to restart the Microsoft Exchange Information Store service on mailbox servers and the Microsoft Exchange Address Book service and Microsoft Exchange RPC Client Access service on CAS servers to force Exchange to use the static ports. Afterward, you should check that Outlook clients are connecting to the ports that you have configured.

You can use the NetStat program to validate the ports that Exchange is using. Run *NetStat* in a command prompt window on the client PC with the *–na* parameter. When you check the output, you should see TCP connections established to the IP address and assigned port number of the CAS server (or mailbox server if you use public folders). For example, if you decide to assign port 61000 to mailbox connections, 61001 to address book connections, and the IP address of the CAS server is 192.168.50.1, then you will expect to see connections to 192.168.50.1:61000 and 192.168.50.1:61001. Figure 11-9 shows a typical example of static ports as reported by NetStat. You can see that the client computer (192.165.65.60) has connections to ports 61001 and 61002 on the server (192.65.65.50). These are the static ports assigned to the MAPI endpoint and the Address Book service.

Figure 11-9 Using NetStat to check that static ports are in use.

Web services URLs and load balancing

CAS servers publish URLs to allow clients to connect to the various Web services used by Exchange. When you expose these services to the Internet, you typically place one or more CAS servers in an Internet-facing site (behind the perimeter network) and proxy the connections that come into these servers to other servers elsewhere within the organization. It might be convenient to use Windows NLB or another load balancer to create an array to handle a higher volume of connections than a single server can handle, and then the question of how to best publish the various URLs to allow internal and external connections to flow smoothly arises. The basic approach is to configure the URLs according to the guidelines presented in Table 11-5 and to follow these principles:

1. Set the CAS AutoDiscoverServiceInternalURI to the FQDN of the load balancer.

2. Leave the Web Services InternalNLBBypass and OWA InternalURL set to the FQDN of the CAS server.

Table 11-5 **Configuring Web services URLs for load balancers**

Virtual Directory	InternalURL	ExternalURL (Internet-facing Active Directory site)	ExternalURL (internal Active Directory site)
/OWA	Use CAS server or array FQDN	Use FQDN of load balancer	$null
/ECP	Use FQDN of load balancer	Use FQDN of load balancer	$null
/Microsoft-Server-ActiveSync	Use FQDN of load balancer	Use FQDN of load balancer	$null
/OAB	Use FQDN of load balancer	Use FQDN of load balancer	$null
/EWS	Use FQDN of load balancer	Use FQDN of load balancer	$null

As always, some testing is necessary to ensure smooth handling of client connections should a CAS server in the array fail.

Changes to facilitate SSL offloading

SSL offloading is a feature often performed by hardware devices to relieve the workload of SSL encryption and decryption from Web servers in high-demand environments. If you want to use SSL offloading, you have to turn off SSL on the Autodiscover and EWS virtual directories, because the traffic reaching these directories will be plain HTTP rather than HTTPS. Two steps must be taken in Exchange 2010 to turn SSL off for a virtual directory. First, SSL is disabled in Microsoft Internet Information Services (IIS). Second, the relevant web.config file must be edited to remove SSL. Exchange 2010 SP1 makes the task a lot easier by introducing the *–RequireSSL* parameter for the cmdlets used to create and modify the virtual directories. These cmdlets are as follows :

- New-WebServicesVirtualDirectory

- Set-WebServicesVirtualDirectory

- New-AutodiscoverVirtualDirectory

- Set-AutodiscoverVirtualDirectory

If the *–RequireSSL* parameter is set to $True, the virtual directory only supports HTTPS traffic. If set to $False, it supports both HTTP and HTTPS. You do not have to modify IIS, because all the work is done through the cmdlets.

Domain controllers

Handling client connections requires a complex interaction among reverse proxy server, CAS, and domain controller and the root cause for poor responsiveness could be a problem with the domain controller. In situations where domain controllers have to service authentication requests from tens of thousands of incoming client connections, you need to pay attention to two specific aspects. First, it's important that you configure domain controllers with sufficient secure channels to be able to cope with the demand for client connections to be authenticated. The queue for authentication requests is governed by the *MaxConcurrentAPI* setting on domain controllers, and this might have to be adjusted from its default value of two to five or more to increase the ability of the domain controller to handle the demand for client authentications. See TechNet for details about how to make this adjustment. Second, Windows does not automatically load balance secure channels across available domain controllers and you might arrive at a situation where one domain controller is swamped by authentication requests and others are not busy.

The Microsoft Knowledge Base article at *http://support.microsoft.com/kb/167029* explains how to use the Setprfdc utility to address the problem. See *http://blogs.technet.com/b/ad /archive/2008/09/23/ntlm-and-maxconcurrentapi-concerns.aspx* for an excellent blog post about the importance of setting the *–MaxConcurrentAPI* parameter to handle authentication load.

Preparing for transition and interoperability

The easiest deployments are when Exchange is installed for the first time. If you're offering external access to clients via Exchange 2003 BE servers or Exchange 2007 CAS servers, you will have to plan the transition of this service to Exchange 2010. It's difficult to dictate an exact recipe for deployment in projects where legacy FE or CAS servers operate. Basic guidelines can be given, but these have to be adjusted in line with details such as the number of legacy servers, their function (internal, external), the number of sites, the speed of the Exchange 2010 deployment, the time when legacy servers can be decommissioned, and so on. The following two core principles have to be followed.

The first step in the transition is to upgrade your company's external presence so that it is served by Exchange 2010. This means that Exchange 2010 will take over the namespace (such as mail.contoso.com) used by clients to connect to Exchange. Legacy Exchange servers that handle incoming connections (Exchange 2007 CAS servers and Exchange 2003 FE servers) assume a new legacy namespace (such as legacymail.contoso. com) that Exchange 2010 CAS servers can use to refer connections to Exchange 2007 and Exchange 2003 mailbox servers. This approach means that users don't have to change the URL that they use for external access and so avoids the need for them to reconfigure mobile devices, mail profiles, and so on. New SSL certificates will probably be required to incorporate the legacy namespace. Remember not to make any DNS updates until you are ready to switch over to the Exchange 2010 infrastructure and accept user connections. It's best to schedule this kind of switchover for a holiday weekend or some other period when demand is low and any error can be rectified without undue disruption to users.

For a multitude of reasons, including the introduction of the RCA layer and the elimination of WebDAV support, Exchange 2010 CAS servers can't communicate smoothly with Exchange 2007 mailbox servers. ActiveSync, POP3, and IMAP4 access work well, but MAPI and OWA access are problematic. You therefore need at least one Exchange 2007 CAS server in place until you decommission the last Exchange 2007 mailbox server. Incoming connections to Exchange 2007 mailboxes can be proxied by an Exchange 2010 CAS server to the Exchange 2007 CAS.

Therefore, the correct order for deployment is to install Exchange 2010 CAS servers in the site used for external access, followed by the installation of Exchange 2010 CAS servers to replace Exchange 2007 CAS servers in internal sites in conjunction with the roll-out of Exchange 2010 mailbox servers.

Table 11-6 lists a number of work items that should be considered for inclusion in a deployment plan for the transition of external access from Exchange 2003 FE servers or Exchange 2007 CAS servers. This list needs to be carefully reviewed in light of your technical environment and then tested to ensure that everything will run smoothly when the switch occurs.

Chapter 11

Table 11-6 **Work items to prepare for CAS transition**

Work item	Detail
Creation of legacy email namespace	**Exchange 2003/2007:** Create the DNS entries for the legacy email namespace and point them to the Exchange 2003 FE servers, Exchange 2007 CAS servers, or both. Exchange 2010 will use this namespace to serve clients that have mailboxes on legacy servers.
Create link between Exchange 2010 and legacy servers	**Exchange 2003:** Update the OWA virtual directory on the Exchange 2010 CAS servers so that they know where to redirect client connections to Exchange 2003. For example, to instruct the CAS server ExServer1 to redirect Exchange 2003 clients to a server called ExServer2003, we'd use a command like this: ```Set-OWAVirtualDirectory -Identity 'ExServer1\OWA'` ` -Exchange2003URL 'https://ExServer2003.contoso.com/exchange'``` **Exchange 2007:** Update the *ExternalUrl* property on the OWA Virtual Directory on the Exchange 2007 CAS servers so that they point to the legacy namespace. ```Set-OWAVirtualDirectory -Identity 'Ex2007\OWA'` ` -ExternalUrl 'https://legacymail.contoso.com/owa'```
Configure ActiveSync on Exchange 2003	**Exchange 2003:** Turn on Integrated Windows Authentication on the ActiveSync directory on the Exchange 2003 BE servers to ensure that the authenticated connections passing through Exchange 2010 CAS are handled correctly. See *http://support.microsoft.com/kb/937031* for the steps to perform this action.
Update SSL certificates	**Exchange 2003/2007:** The SSL certificates used to secure client connections will not contain the new legacy namespace. Arrange with your certificate vendor for updated certificates and install them on the CAS and FE servers.
Reverse proxy server	**Exchange 2003/2007:** Connect Exchange 2010 CAS servers and test that client connections are able to flow through your external-facing reverse proxy server. Test all aspects of client connectivity, including Autodiscover when configuring a new Outlook installation to connect to mailboxes on Exchange 2010 and legacy mailbox servers.
Switch DNS	**Exchange 2003/2007:** Modify the DNS entries for external email access (for example, mail.contoso.com) to point to the Exchange 2010 CAS servers. Test and monitor client traffic to ensure that connections can be established to mailboxes on Exchange 2010 and legacy mailbox servers.
Reconfigure Outlook Anywhere	**Exchange 2003/2007:** Make sure that the connection point for Outlook Anywhere (RPC over HTTP) is served by Exchange 2010. Disable RPC over HTTP on the Exchange 2003 FE servers and/or Outlook Anywhere on the Exchange 2007 CAS servers as these features are no longer required.

When preparing a transition plan, it's a good idea to scan the Internet for documents published by Microsoft and others that describe different technical aspects of the transition, especially when dealing with topics such as switching external access. TechNet is an obvious source, but the blogs of MVPs and other Exchange experts are also rich hunting grounds for tips and techniques that might solve a problem or accelerate progress.

A matter of manipulation

This chapter reviewed how the CAS server role handles incoming client connections for multiple protocols. Apart from handling MAPI connections, the fundamental nature of this work has not changed much since Exchange 2007. However, Exchange 2010 introduces a whole new range of work for the CAS to do, so let's review how the Mailbox Replication Service, a new service that runs on the CAS, is responsible for manipulating mailboxes. We also need to talk about some other services that support user activity, so that's next on our list.

Mailbox Support Services

MAILBOX *support services* is a loose term that I have coined to describe administrative actions that support ongoing user activity. I've included four broad categories of work in this chapter. We start with two important pieces of functionality managed by the Mailbox Replication Service: how to move mailboxes and how to import and export data to and from mailboxes. We then look at the MailTips service and how it delivers value to users by reminding them about mistakes that they might be just about to make. Finally, we consider the question of the Offline Address Book, a facility used by just about all road warriors to know about the people and groups in their organization.

The Mailbox Replication Service

The Microsoft Exchange Mailbox Replication Service (MRS) is the service that is responsible for processing move, import, and export requests. The MRS runs on every Client Access Server (CAS) server and is able to move information between databases, into databases (import), or out of databases (export). The import and export operations are new functionality for the MRS from Exchange Server 2010 SP1 onward. An Exchange 2010 MRS is only able to process move requests. The name of the MRS process is MSExchangeMailboxReplication.exe. This is sometimes conflated with the database replication used with Database Availability Groups (DAGs; MSExchangeReplication.exe), but they are two separate and distinct processes.

The location of the MRS on the CAS server is an example of how Microsoft has moved all Messaging Application Programming Interface (MAPI) protocol processing to this server role to join the processing of Internet protocols that the CAS took on in Exchange 2007. You can think of import and export operations as another kind of protocol processing or rendering because MRS has to translate the contents of mailbox databases as they are transferred to or from PST files.

MRS configuration file

MRS operation is controlled by settings in the Exchange\Bin
\MSExchangeMailboxReplicationService.exe.config configuration file. You can edit the configuration file using a text editor to alter the operational parameters for MRS. You do not
have to restart the MRS process to pick up any change that you make to these properties
(Table 12-1).

Table 12-1 **Properties to control MRS operation**

Property	Meaning
MaxActiveMovesPerTargetMDB	Controls the number of mailboxes that MRS can move to a single database concurrently. The default is 5 in RTM and 2 in SP1, and the maximum is 100.
MaxActiveMovesPerSourceMDB	Controls the number of mailboxes that MRS can move concurrently from a source database. The default is 5 and the maximum is 100.
MaxActiveMovesPerSourceServer	Controls the maximum number of concurrent moves that a source server can perform. The default is 50 and the maximum is 1,000.
MaxActiveMovesPerTargetServer	Controls the maximum number of concurrent moves that a target server will accept. The default is 5 and the maximum is 1,000.
MaxTotalMovesPerMRS	Controls the total number of concurrent moves that a single MRS instance can process. The default is 100 and the maximum is 1,024.
FullScanMoveJobsPollingInterval	MRS processes move requests when they are initiated and also scans databases looking for move requests to process. The default scan interval is 00:05:00 or five minutes.
RetryDelay	Controls how long MRS will wait to retry an operation in case of tran-sient failures. The default value is 00:00:30, or 30 seconds.
MaxRetries	Controls how many times MRS will attempt an operation in case of transient failures. The default is 60. A move fails when this value is exceeded.
MaxMoveHistoryLength	Controls how many move histories MRS retains for a mailbox. The default is two, meaning that you can extract the last two mailbox his-tory entries for a specified mailbox.

These limits are set on a per-server basis and are regarded as "best effort" limits. In other
words, there might be times when the limits are exceeded. For example, two MRS servers
might access the same source database to process move requests and together exceed
the maximum number of active moves that you have configured the database to support.
However, these will be exceptions rather than the rule, and normal processing will resume
in due course.

> **Note**
>
> If you make a change to the MRS configuration file on one CAS server, you should apply the same change to any other CAS server that is in the site so that every server functions in the same way.

Moving mailboxes

The ability to move mailboxes between databases is a fundamental operational procedure for Exchange. Because you have to install new servers to deploy Exchange 2010, moving mailboxes is the basic method to migrate user data to Exchange 2010 from Exchange 2003 and Exchange 2007 servers. Apart from migration from legacy versions of Exchange, the other reasons why mailboxes are moved include the following:

- Balancing user load across available mailboxes: As users leave and join the company, the number of mailboxes assigned to databases might vary. Some mailboxes might be larger than others. Administrators often seek to rebalance workload across databases by transferring mailboxes so that each database hosts approximately the same number of mailboxes of roughly the same size. With the introduction of personal archives, administrators now have to take the load and storage requirements generated by these mailboxes into account when they rebalance user load. A variation on the theme occurs when administrators decide that, for operational reasons, a database is too large (perhaps the time required to make a backup exceeds the desired period). In this case, the administrators can move mailboxes to other databases. Moving the mailboxes will only create additional white space in the database and won't reduce its size immediately, but it will stop the database from swelling even larger.

- Outsourcing to hosted environments: An Exchange 2010 organization can span a mixture of on-premises and hosted servers. Mailbox moves are used to transfer mailboxes from on-premises servers to hosted servers and vice versa.

- Organizational change: Users might be transferred around the company and change their physical location in such a way that their current mailbox database is now inappropriate (for instance, after the change the database is on a server in a remote datacenter). In this scenario it's common for an administrator to move the user's mailbox to a server that is "closer" to the user.

- Organizational hierarchy: Some companies like to place all of the mailboxes belonging to selected user groups in specific databases so that special policies are applied to these mailboxes (high availability, storage quotas, deleted item retention periods, and so on). For example, all of the company executives might be placed on one database that has four copies to ensure the highest availability, while the mailboxes belonging to transient or part-time employees might be placed in another database that has only two copies.

- Server transition: Before a mailbox server can be decommissioned from the Exchange organization, all of the databases that it hosts must first be removed. Before the databases can be removed, all of its mailboxes must be moved to other databases.

- Mailbox or database corruption: It is possible that corrupt items can occur within a mailbox that causes problems for the database (see the discussion about mailbox quarantine in Chapter 7, "The Exchange 2010 Store"). Moving a mailbox can remove corruption if you set the bad item limit to allow Exchange to discard any suspect items that it encounters as it moves mailbox content.

- Mailbox grouping: Some administrators like to collect all of the mailboxes of a particular type in a certain database (for example, to collect all room mailboxes in one database, to place linked mailboxes in another, and so on). The same approach is often taken to group mailboxes on a department basis so that all of the mailboxes from the Sales Department are in the Sales database.

INSIDE OUT   Using cmdlets for online mailbox moves

Microsoft has made a major change in the way that the move mailbox process works in Exchange 2010. In Exchange 2007, you use the Move-Mailbox cmdlet to move a mailbox from one database to another. Exchange 2010 introduces a series of "move request" cmdlets to manage the process of moving mailbox content from one server to another. The big difference in Exchange 2010 and the reason why new cmdlets are introduced is that mailbox moves now occur asynchronously behind the scenes and do not require the user to log off while the move proceeds. Unlike the Move-Mailbox cmdlet, users can continue to work online while the MRS copies mailbox content in the background. The only interruption users experience is when they switch over to the newly copied mailbox at the end of the move. Microsoft refers to these operations as online mailbox moves. The move request cmdlets are accessed through Exchange Management Console (EMC; the Move Mailbox Wizard) or Exchange Management Shell (EMS).

Microsoft doesn't change the way that Exchange works without good reason. As Exchange 2010 came on the horizon, it was very obvious that the growing size of mailboxes and some problems in previous implementations of the move mailbox feature prompted the change. The Move-Mailbox cmdlet processes mailbox moves synchronously. In other words, once it begins to transfer mailbox contents, Move-Mailbox continues to process items until the full mailbox is successfully moved, a threshold of errors caused by corrupt items in the source mailbox is exceeded, or you abort the move request. If the workstation that runs the move terminates the EMC or EMS session used to perform the move, everything in the new mailbox is lost and the move has to be restarted from scratch, even if several gigabytes of information have been transferred from source server to target server. Last, Exchange 2007 requires users to remain offline and not attempt to access their mailbox while the move is in progress. These limitations are not usually a problem for small mailboxes of less than 500 MB, but the time required to move mailboxes has grown in line with mailbox sizes.

Given that we are heading to an era when mailboxes of 10 GB or even 25 GB will become the norm, it is logical to assume that synchronous moves will take longer to perform and that it will not be acceptable to tie up a workstation waiting for a large move to be complete or to tell a user that she can't access her mailbox for six hours while Exchange transfers items from database to database. The growing popularity of hosted Exchange services is also an influence here, because you might have a situation where some mailboxes are located on servers that you operate within your company's IT infrastructure and some are located on servers "in the cloud." It's likely that bandwidth will be more restricted over the Internet than between two servers in a local network, so synchronous moves from an on-premise server to a hosted server could take even longer than between servers in an on-premise infrastructure.

Asynchronous moving

Mailbox moves between Exchange 2010 servers happen asynchronously. This means that you can start many move requests and go and do something else instead of having your workstation blocked for several hours. The basic flow of processing is as follows:

- A move request is created that identifies the source mailbox and the target database.

- MRS copies the contents of the selected mailbox to the destination database.

- MRS performs a check to determine whether any items have been updated or created in the source mailbox since the move started; if any items are discovered, they are copied across using an incremental synchronization process.

- If a move is interrupted by some error such as a bad item threshold being exceeded, MRS is able to restart the move from the point where it halted.

- After all content has been moved to the new mailbox, MRS completes the move by updating the user's Active Directory account to point to the new mailbox location.

The following are the advantages of this approach:

- Users can continue to work as MRS moves their mailboxes to the target server, a factor that becomes more important as mailbox sizes grow. Although users will be forced to disconnect and reconnect their client after MRS switches the pointer to their mailbox in Active Directory, changes that Microsoft originally planned to implement in Exchange 2010 SP1 (and now due in a future release) will address this issue for moves between Exchange 2010 SP1 databases to produce a seamless move experience. See the section "Preserving the mailbox signature" later in this chapter.

- The load of mailbox moves is automatically spread across all available MRS instances in the Active Directory site. Exchange throttles the load generated by mailbox moves to keep the load from swamping source or target servers. Administrators can adjust these throttles if necessary.

- Personal archives can be moved along with the primary mailbox or left in the source database. You can also elect to move just the personal archive to a different database, which is an option that is useful when you want to relocate personal archives to a dedicated database.

- Dumpster contents (deleted items that have still not exceeded their retention period) are moved with both the primary mailbox and personal archive. This is true for moves from Exchange 2010 servers but, due to the change in dumpster structure implemented in Exchange 2010, dumpster contents are not preserved for moves from legacy Exchange servers.

- Items are incorporated into the content index of the target database as they are moved to ensure that users retain fast search capability. This factor isn't as important if you use Outlook configured in cached Exchange mode, because searches are then performed on the client using Windows Desktop Search. However, it does mean that discovery searches performed by administrators will continue to locate items after the mailbox is switched from source to target database.

- Online moves executed on Exchange 2003 or Exchange 2007 servers don't generate much information to help an administrator understand what has occurred during the move. To enable troubleshooting and debugging, MRS captures comprehensive details about every mailbox move and stores these reports in the mailbox. By default, details of the last two moves are retained for a mailbox. This number can be increased if required.

We explore the details of how MRS delivers these advantages as we go through the remainder of this section.

INSIDE OUT   Legacy mailbox moves

The MRS also manages mailbox moves from Exchange 2003 SP2 and Exchange 2007 SP2 servers to Exchange 2010. In these cases, the moves are initiated from Exchange 2010. Moves from Exchange 2007 are performed online, whereas those from Exchange 2003 are performed offline. In other words, users have to exit their mailbox to allow MRS to pull the data to Exchange 2010 and create the new mailbox in the target database. Moves from earlier legacy versions of Exchange such as Exchange 2000 are not supported. Going the other way, MRS is able to move mailboxes from Exchange 2010 to Exchange 2007 SP2 or Exchange 2003 SP2 and, once again, moves are initiated from Exchange 2010 and the moves are performed offline. In these scenarios, MRS connects directly to the mailbox on the legacy server to move content. MRS is not able to move mailboxes between servers if both the source and target servers run legacy versions of Exchange.

Mailbox Replication Service processing

MRS regularly scans the system mailbox of databases hosted on servers in the site to detect new move requests that are queued there. Apart from the move request queues, the system mailbox also stores details of current move requests that are updated as moves proceed. The data include the current stage of each move, the percentage complete, the bytes transferred, the items transferred, timestamps, any warning information, and so on. As we see later in this section, these data are reported by the Get-MoveRequestStatistics cmdlet.

Figure 12-1 shows the different steps that occur during the process of moving a mailbox with MRS. Move requests are processed in first in, first out (FIFO) order, and once a new move request is detected, one of the MRS instances running on a CAS server in the site takes responsibility for processing the move request by stamping its name into the move request to prevent another MRS instance from attempting to duplicate the move. A number of Active Directory properties are also updated for the account that owns the mailbox to capture information about the move request, including its current status, the source and target databases, the batch name, and some flags.

The responsible MRS then begins to pull data from the source mailbox to populate the new mailbox. Data are moved in a multiphase process. MRS first does an initial seeding pass where it enumerates all of the content in the source mailbox and copies it to the target mailbox. While the initial seeding pass is progressing, MRS tracks changes that occur in the source mailbox and then performs one or more incremental updates to move any content that has been changed or added into the target mailbox to bring it completely up to date.

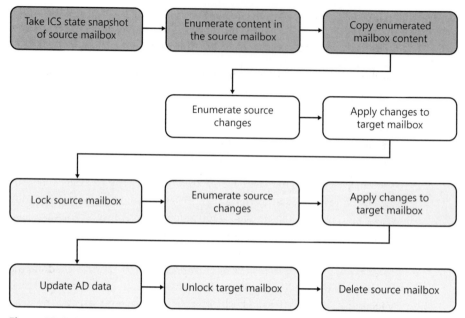

Figure 12-1 Steps in the process of moving an Exchange 2010 mailbox.

Items move from source database to target database continuously unless a high-availability stall condition occurs. This can only happen on servers that are part of a DAG. If the Store reports that the database that holds the target mailbox has fallen behind on log copy (that is, its log copy queues are growing), MRS pauses the move for 30 seconds and then resumes the copy. This is usually sufficient to allow a period of peak demand to pass and to prevent mailbox moves from interfering with the log replication activity within the DAG.

CAUTION

Remember, copying a mailbox from one database to another creates transaction logs that have to be replicated and replayed on servers that host copies of the databases. If the database remains in an unhealthy state for 30 minutes, MRS will fail the move request and it will have to be re-created.

MRS uses Incremental Change Synchronization (ICS) to perform incremental updates. This is the same mechanism used by Outlook to perform background drizzle synchronization when it operates in cached Exchange mode. To complete the move process, MRS locks the source mailbox when it performs the last round of incremental synchronization to make sure that no further change can occur. This step is called the finalization phase and it can last from 10 seconds to five or six minutes, depending on the number of folders in the mailbox. The more folders, the more work MRS has to perform to check that no items arrived or were updated in each folder while the initial seeding occurred.

Mailbox content is indexed on the target server as it arrives to ensure that the new mailbox is functionally complete when MRS finishes moving everything. MRS also moves mailbox metadata, such as views, to provide users with the same experience with the new mailbox as they had with the original. The move request will not fail if the content indexing service is stalled, cannot process items as quickly as they arrive, or is otherwise unavailable. Instead, the content indexing service will have to process the new mailbox when it is next functioning properly.

An MRS instance runs on each CAS server within an Active Directory site. Each instance tracks the work done by the others by examining queued move requests to ensure that the limits for concurrent moves to a target database are respected globally. In other words, if you have two MRS instances running and there are 20 queued move requests for a single database, the first MRS will start to process queued requests by checking the system mailbox of the database and stamping the requests that it accepts for processing. The second MRS process is also active and will process more requests (that have not been stamped by the first MRS) until the global limit for concurrently active moves (five) is reached. At this point, no more requests to the target database will be processed until MRS completes some of the active requests. In addition, if an MRS is halted for any reason, such as a server shutdown, and another MRS is available in the site, that MRS will resume processing of any active moves.

By default, the limits for the processing performed by a single MRS instance are as follows:

- Five concurrent moves to a single target database. The reduction in SP1 is to ensure that better high availability is maintained for target databases.

- Five concurrent moves to a single target server.

- Five (RTM) or two (SP1) concurrent moves from a single source database.

- 50 concurrent moves from a single source server.

- 100 moves across all databases and servers per MRS instance.

The difference in the limit of concurrent moves that MRS will process for a single source server and a single target server gives a good indication of the relative processing load generated on these servers. You can control how MRS operates to increase or decrease the amount of concurrent activity by editing the MRS configuration file (see the section "MRS configuration file" earlier in this chapter).

Preventing loss of data

The last action that MRS performs to finalize a mailbox move is to switch the Active Directory pointer to the active mailbox so that the user will connect to that mailbox and begin using it. MRS in the original version of Exchange 2010 then cleaned up by deleting the source mailbox. This mechanism worked well in situations where the source and target servers were healthy and no server outage happened immediately after the move completed. However, experience demonstrated that it was possible for data loss to occur if the target server hosting the newly moved mailbox suffered a lossy outage caused by a storage failure or other problem.

> **Note**
>
> In this context, a *lossy* failure means that the database is recovered with some loss of data due to missing transaction logs. Often the loss is minor, meaning that just one or two logs containing inconsequential data cannot be recovered, but there have been instances in which mailboxes lost major chunks of information.

The solution introduced in Exchange 2010 SP1 is to take a more cautious approach. Instead of removing the source mailbox immediately following a successfully completed move, Exchange now puts the source mailbox into a SoftDeleted state. This means that the source mailbox—containing all the mailbox content—is retained until the deleted mailbox retention period expires for the database, which is typically anything from seven days to a month, and stored in the *MailboxRetention* property for a database. During this time, data can be recovered from the old source mailbox using a request generated for the New-MailboxRestoreRequest cmdlet. Restore requests are processed by the MRS to recover data from mailboxes in a recovery database (see Chapter 9, "Backups and Restores") or mailboxes that have been soft deleted and retained in a normal database.

You can discover information about soft deleted mailboxes in a database with the Get-MailboxStatistics cmdlet. For example:

```
Get-MailboxStatistics –Database DB3 | Where {$_.DisconnectReason –eq 'SoftDeleted'}
| Format-Table DisplayName, DisconnectReason, DisconnectDate
```

DisplayName	DisconnectReason	DisconnectDate
Peled, Yael (IT)	SoftDeleted	6/3/2010 9:26:42 PM

Although the change to retain old source mailboxes ensures that data can be recovered in case problems happen, it does mean that the age-old practice of moving mailboxes around between databases to balance database sizes needs to be reconsidered. The space occupied by the moved mailboxes is not freed immediately and will only be released when the deleted mailbox retention period expires. If this is an issue, you can force the immediate deletion of a soft deleted mailbox by running the Remove-StoreMailbox cmdlet. To remove the soft deleted mailbox referred to in the last example, we use the following command:

```
Remove-StoreMailbox -Identity 'Peled, Yael (IT)' -MailboxState 'SoftDeleted'
-Database 'DB3'
```

EMS will prompt you to confirm that the action should go ahead and will purge the contents of the soft deleted mailbox if told to proceed.

Moving mailboxes

Figure 12-2 illustrates the Move Mailbox Wizard that is invoked by EMC after you select one or more mailboxes for movement. In this case, a number of mailboxes have been selected to be moved to a different database. Exchange 2010 SP1 allows you to move personal archives along with their primary mailboxes or split the two across different databases during moves. We discuss what happens when you select mailboxes with personal archives in just a little while. The wizard won't show you the options to move archives unless some of the chosen mailboxes have archives.

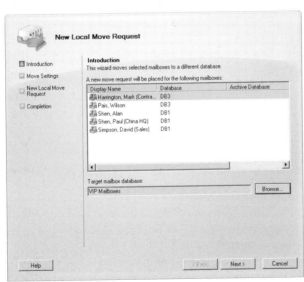

Figure 12-2 Selecting mailboxes to move and the target database to which to move them.

The options presented by the wizard are simple. You have to select a target database and how you want to deal with bad or corrupt items that are encountered in the source mailbox (Figure 12-3). The default value for Skip Corrupted Messages is zero. This means that MRS has a zero tolerance for bad items that it can process in a move. In other words, if MRS meets one bad item in the source mailbox, it fails the move. Using zero is probably too cautious, and in most cases it's best to allow MRS to skip 10 or so corrupt items that are found in the mailbox and go ahead to complete the mailbox move. See the section "Handling move request errors" later in this chapter for more information.

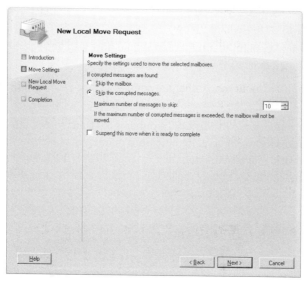

Figure 12-3 Setting the threshold for bad items that can be tolerated during a mailbox move.

Once you complete the wizard, Exchange creates a separate move request for each mailbox and places them onto the MRS queue to be processed. As you'd expect, all of the moves happen in the background, so this is a great way to line up a set of move requests to be processed during lunchtime or overnight.

CAUTION

The wizard does not validate that you select a different database as the destination for the move request. Especially when you process a group of mailboxes, it's quite possible that you will make this mistake. In this situation, EMC will signal an error when it attempts to create the new move request:

```
Mailbox 'contoso.com/Exchange Users/Shen, Paul' is already in the target
database 'IT Department'.
```

As noted earlier, administrators often perform mailbox moves to balance mailboxes across available databases. EMC allows you to include the database in the set of fields displayed for mailbox objects. Including the database field and then sorting by database makes it much easier to select a group of mailboxes from one database to move to another.

You'll notice that EMC does not include the ability to schedule moves in the future. New move requests are put into a queue immediately and will be picked up for processing by one of the MRS instances running in the site (you can assign a move request to a specific MRS instance with the New-MoveRequest cmdlet in EMS, but you cannot when you create a move request from EMC).

You can find information about moves that are currently registered with MRS by clicking the Move Request tree in the Recipient Configuration node (Figure 12-4). The move requests shown by EMC are all those registered in Active Directory for the domain or however the current recipient scope is set for EMC (see the section "How EMC accesses Exchange data" in Chapter 5 for details on how to set the EMC recipient scope). The actual command used by EMC to fetch the move request data is:

```
Get-MoveRequest –ResultSize UnLimited
```

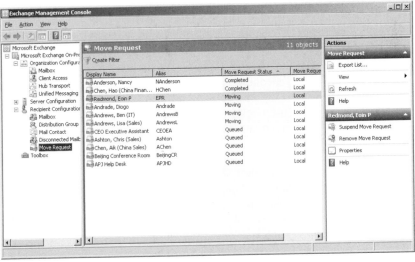

Figure 12-4 Viewing move requests with EMC.

INSIDE OUT   Accessing data for large numbers of move requests

Specifying –*ResultSize Unlimited* means that EMC returns as many move requests as it can find, and you might have to wait a little while EMC fetches these data from Active Directory. For this reason, you might prefer to use EMS to access move request data for a specific set of mailboxes when a large number of requests is present. In EMC, you can view details of a move request by selecting it from the list and then viewing its properties. This is equivalent to running the Get-MoveRequestStatistics cmdlet for a selected mailbox.

The options available to work with move requests are as follows:

- Suspend the request: You can suspend a move request at any time before it completes. EMC will prompt you to enter a reason why you want to suspend the move request (you don't have to enter anything). A suspended move request can be resumed later. The equivalent EMS cmdlet is Suspend-MoveRequest.

- Remove the move request: A move request can only be removed if its status is Queued or Suspended. If you remove a move request, all of the work done by Exchange to set up the move is discarded and you have to create a new request if you want to move the mailbox in the future. The equivalent EMS cmdlet is Remove-MoveRequest.

- Resume the move request: You can resume a suspended move request at any time. MRS will begin processing mailbox contents from the point where it was when the move was suspended. The equivalent EMS cmdlet is Resume-MoveRequest.

- Clear the move request: Once a move request has completed and its status is either Completed or CompletedWithError, you can clear the move request to allow Exchange to schedule another move for the mailbox (running the cmdlet removes the *In Transit* flag for the mailbox). We discuss this topic later in this section. The Remove-MoveRequest cmdlet is also used to process this action.

When you select a move request and view its properties, you have access to three tabs:

- General: Information about the move request. While the move request is in progress, you can see an indication of how much of the mailbox has been moved to the new mailbox, as well as details of the source and target database and the size of the mailbox (Figure 12-5). Note the Suspend The Move When It Is Ready To Complete check box. If you select this check box, MRS will transfer the complete content of the mailbox from the source to the target database and then pause for an administrator to release the move request and allow MRS to perform the final incremental synchronization and update Active Directory to complete the move. You might want to use this option to finalize moves when users are offline, such as in the evening. The next day, the help desk can inform the users of whatever steps are necessary to adjust client settings to connect to the moved mailbox.

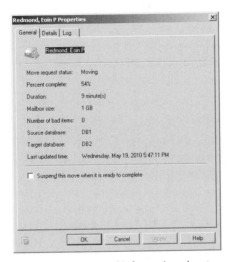

Figure 12-5   General information about a move request.

- Details: The information presented here includes the names of the servers that host the source and target databases and the versions of Exchange that run on these servers. It also shows the date and time when the move request was queued and when MRS started to process the request (and finished if the move is complete).

- Log: MRS maintains a complete log of all of the processing that it performs to move a mailbox to a new database. You can access the report by clicking View. As you can see in Figure 12-6, the move request log is then displayed in a separate window. A move request log contains a lot of information that is very useful for understanding the processing that occurs and also for debugging moves that go wrong for some reason. You can use Ctrl+C to copy the move request log to the clipboard and then paste it into NotePad or another text editor to review or print its contents at your leisure. This feature was introduced to EMC in Exchange 2010 SP1. You can find details about how to access the mailbox move log data with EMS in the section "Accessing move report log data" later in this chapter.

Chapter 12

Figure 12-6 Viewing the move request log.

Clearing move requests

You cannot create another move request for a mailbox until you clear or cancel any previous move request. For example, if you move a mailbox from Database1 to Database2 only to discover that you should have moved the mailbox to Database3, you can cancel the move if the move request is in Queued or Moving status. On the other hand, if the move request has reached the CompletionInProgress stage, you can't cancel it because MRS is finalizing the move at this point and adjusting Active Directory to point to the new mailbox. In this situation, you will have to wait for the first move to complete and then clear the move request by selecting the mailbox under the Move Request node and clicking Clear Move Request in the action pane, and then scheduling a new move request from Database2 to Database3.

It is a nuisance to have to clear requests for successful moves manually, and Microsoft will hopefully provide an automatic mechanism to clear out completed and obsolete move requests in a future version of Exchange.

In addition, you should check periodically if any old move requests are lingering and clear them from time to time because they serve no further purpose once a mailbox has been successfully moved to a target database. Figure 12-7 shows the icons used by EMC to indicate mailboxes with registered move requests and how to clear a group of move requests.

> **Tip**
>
> It's a good idea to check the status of a move request once it is finished to ensure that it finished successfully and not with the CompletedWithWarning status. Moves marked with a CompletedWithWarning status have met a problem that might impact the mailbox, so you should extract a full mailbox move report and examine it to discover the warnings reported by MRS. We review how to create a mailbox move report shortly.

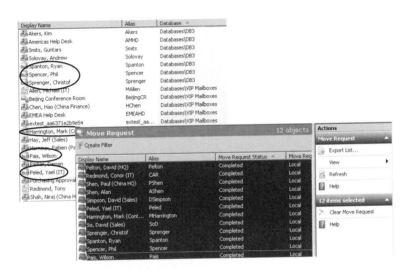

Figure 12-7 Clearing completed move requests.

Managing mailbox moves with EMS

EMS allows you to exert more granular control over move requests than EMC does and is the preferred option to use when you have to manage large quantities of move requests. Both tools use a new set of cmdlets that communicate with the MRS through TCP port 808. The cmdlets are as follows:

- New-MoveRequest: This cmdlet initiates a new move request and performs the processing to ensure that a mailbox can be moved from its existing location to a different database. The request begins in a Queued to Move state and moves through In Progress, meaning that data are being replicated from the source to the target mailbox, and then Ready to Complete, meaning that you can complete the request.

- Get-MoveRequest: This cmdlet provides information fetched from Active Directory about a move request and lets you know how it is progressing.

- Remove-MoveRequest: This cmdlet cancels a move request that is queued or in progress. Any data that have been replicated to the target mailbox are removed. Remove-MoveRequest is also used to remove a completed move request from the list maintained by MRS.

- Suspend-MoveRequest: This cmdlet suspends further processing of a move request until the request is released by an administrator.

- Resume-MoveRequest: This cmdlet resumes processing for suspended move requests, including move requests that are queued with the *SuspendWhenReadyToComplete* flag.

- Get-MoveRequestStatistics: This cmdlet fetches data about move requests from the system mailbox.

You'll also find a MoveMailbox.ps1 script in the Exchange\Scripts directory. The script is intended as a drop-in replacement for the legacy Move-Mailbox cmdlet used in Exchange 2007. The script accepts much the same parameters as the Move-Mailbox cmdlet so it can be used in situations where administrators created code to move mailboxes. Just like the Move-Mailbox cmdlet, the script will continue to process mailboxes until it is finished. There is no notion of background processing! As always, you should test the script carefully before using it in production.

A general description of the script and the available parameters can be found in TechNet at *http://technet.microsoft.com/en-us/library/dd876878.aspx*.

To initiate a move request for a mailbox, we identify the mailbox to move and the target database. In this case, the move is to a database in the same Exchange organization, so it's deemed to be a "local" move.

```
New-MoveRequest -Identity 'Tony.Redmond@contoso.com' -TargetDatabase 'DB1'
```

> **Note**
> If you don't specify a target database, Exchange's database autoprovisioning code will select a target database for you from one of the mailbox databases that are enabled for provisioning. See Chapter 6, "Managing Mail-Enabled Recipients," for more information on database provisioning.

New-MoveRequest initiates the request and puts it into a queued status. As we know, MRS is running on every CAS server. The MRS processes running on the CAS servers "hunt" for new queued move requests for mailboxes within their Active Directory site and will begin to process queued requests soon after they are created. Move requests are shared among all of the MRS instances within the Active Directory site and an individual MRS will handle as many requests as it can up to the throttling limits set in its configuration file.

INSIDE OUT Ensure that the quota is sufficient for the target database

The legacy Move-Mailbox cmdlet offers one advantage over the new move request cmdlets in that you can pass the –*PreserveMailboxSizeLimit* parameter to have Exchange respect the existing mailbox quotas on a mailbox when it is moved. In other words, if the mailbox has a quota of 1 GB in the source database, it will be given a 1 GB quota in the target database even if the default quota for mailboxes is 100 MB. The New-MoveRequest cmdlet doesn't support a similar parameter so you have to ensure that sufficient quota is available in the target databases; if it is not, a move request will fail. Typically this is done by raising the default quota for the database before starting to move mailboxes and making whatever adjustments are necessary afterward. In some instances, you might leave the default database quota as it is; in others, you might set certain elevated quotas on specific mailboxes and reduce the default database quota to control all the other mailboxes.

During a migration to Exchange 2010, mailbox moves are often set up in batches. The –*BatchName* parameter is useful to identify a group of move requests that are scheduled together to allow you to look for those requests later with the Get-MoveRequest cmdlet. For example:

```
Get-Mailbox -Server 'ExServer1' | New-MoveRequest -TargetDatabase 'DB1'
-BatchName 'Transferred Users'
```

We can then check on the progress of these moves with:

```
Get-MoveRequest -BatchName 'Transferred Users'
```

INSIDE OUT Move requests autocomplete

As soon as MRS has moved all the mailbox content to the target database, it updates Active Directory to reflect the new location and to tell the CAS to redirect any future client connections. The exception is when a move request is created with the –*SuspendWhenReadyToComplete* parameter because this instructs MRS to move the mailbox contents but not to switch the mailbox pointer in Active Directory until authorized by an administrator.

Preserving the mailbox signature

Users can continue working online (or in cached Exchange mode) while their mailboxes are moved in the background. On Exchange 2010 servers, after MRS updates the mailbox with any incremental changes and switches the mailbox over to the new database, users will be told that the administrator has made a change that necessitates a restart of Outlook once the move is complete. Restarting allows Outlook to adjust its internal pointers that map data to the old mailbox and allow a connection to the moved mailbox. Outlook Web App (OWA) users will see an error message if they attempt to log on during a mailbox move, but only during the time when the move is being completed by updating Active Directory pointers. It's usually sufficient for the user to wait for a minute or so and then try to connect OWA again.

Interrupting user mailbox access following a move is a small but important irritation that Microsoft removes in Exchange 2010 SP1. Outlook needs to be restarted because it caches information such as MAPI identifiers (or signature), server names, and named properties. Exchange 2010 does not automatically move or adjust these data, so a restart is required to allow Outlook and Exchange to sort things out between themselves and connect the client to the moved mailbox. Any other user who connects to the moved mailbox, such as anyone who has delegate access or shares the calendar, also has to restart Outlook.

Microsoft changed the Exchange 2010 SP1 move mailbox process to allow MRS to copy the MAPI signature and named properties from the source to the target database. These data are moved first, followed by the mailbox contents. The change is sufficient to remove the need for Outlook to restart because all of the data that it needs is preserved during the move. However, you will only see the effect of this change for mailboxes that are newly created on SP1 databases and after mailboxes are moved from an RTM server into an upgraded database. The initial move of a mailbox from RTM to a newer server cannot preserve the signature, so one last restart of Outlook is required after this move.

All of this sounds good, but a bug appeared very late in the development cycle that caused Microsoft to remove the MRS code that preserves mailbox signatures. As shipped, therefore, Exchange 2010 SP1 works in the same way as the RTM version. Microsoft plans to fix the problem and include the upgraded code to preserve mailbox signatures in a roll-up update for Exchange 2010 SP1, which should be available by the time you read this book.

When messages arrive in a mailbox during a move

A complicating factor occurs when a message arrives for the mailbox as it is being moved and forces the promotion of a new named property. A named property is a property in the message header that the client caches when it translates the value to a MAPI identifier. Most common header properties, such as subject and sender, exist in the cache and will be transferred in the first stage of the move process. However, if Outlook discovers a new property that it has not cached in a message header that arrives during the move, it will create a new named property in its cache in the source database. We now have a problem because the range of named properties has already been moved to the target (the range of named properties is also compacted at this point), so the new named property won't exist in the target mailbox. The solution adopted by MRS is to restart the move from scratch if it detects a change in the named properties map for a mailbox. This ensures that named properties are retained even at the expense of some additional overhead to restart the move—but it avoids the need for the user to restart Outlook!

You can force the New-MoveRequest cmdlet to revert to the old behavior and ignore named properties when it moves a mailbox. To do this, include the –*DoNotPreserveMappingSignature* parameter for the move request. For example:

```
New-MoveRequest –Identity 'Jeff Smith' –DoNotPreserveMappingSignature
–TargetDatabase 'DB1'
```

Moving mailboxes between versions of Exchange

The move request cmdlets can be used to manage move requests between Exchange 2010 and legacy Exchange 2003 SP2 and Exchange 2007 SP2 servers. For example, to move a mailbox from a legacy Exchange server to Exchange 2010 (within the same organization):

```
New-MoveRequest –Identity 'Jeff Smith' –TargetDatabase 'B1' –BadItemLimit 10
```

INSIDE OUT   Setting the bad item limit

Note that the bad item limit in the example is explicitly stated to be a reasonably high number. This is because Exchange 2010 is more demanding about correct item format than previous versions and you can run into situations where moves fail when Exchange encounters seemingly corrupt items in the source mailbox on the legacy server. An alternate approach is to start with a lower bad item limit (maybe three) and accept that administrator intervention will be necessary if the move request stalls because it exceeds the bad item limit.

To do the reverse and move from an Exchange 2010 server to a legacy Exchange server in the same organization:

```
New-MoveRequest –Identity 'Jeff Smith' –TargetDatabase 'Exchange 2007 Mbx'
```

Chapter 12

You can also create move requests between forests. For example, let's assume that you create a new forest for Exchange 2010 and want to pull some mailboxes across from an older forest that runs Exchange 2003 SP2 or Exchange 2007. In this scenario, there are no MRS servers in the old forest so all the work has to be done by Exchange 2010. We can set up the move request like this:

```
New-MoveRequest -Identity 'Chris Ashton' -RemoteLegacy -RemoteCredential
(Get-Credential) -RemoteGlobalCatalog 'GC1.contoso.com' -TargetDatabase
'Exchange 2010 Mbx'
```

This code includes the fully qualified domain name (FQDN) of a global catalog server in the other forest to allow Exchange to connect to the Active Directory and retrieve information about the server that hosts the source mailbox. It also contains the *–RemoteLegacy* parameter to indicate to MRS that the move is from a remote forest that doesn't have Exchange 2010 installed. You also need to pass credentials for an account in the remote forest that has access rights to the mailbox. We can collect the credentials with the Get-Credential cmdlet, which displays a dialog box to gather information about the domain, account, and password that we want to use. There's also an assumption here that a suitable account (mail-enabled user) is created in the Exchange 2010 forest to use as the target. In addition, a set of attributes including the *msExchMailboxGuid* and *msExchArchiveGuid* (if you were moving a mailbox from a remote Exchange 2010 forest and had a personal archive) of the source mailbox must be synchronized with the target account using a tool such as GALSync 2007 to allow Exchange to move the mailbox to the correct destination. In addition, to be successful with cross-forest or moves from legacy Exchange organizations, the Exchange 2010 server should be able to resolve the NetBIOS name of the source server as Exchange attempts to connect to the server using the name contained in its *LegacyExchangeDN* attribute, and this is usually just a NetBIOS name.

> **Note**
>
> The work necessary to prepare for and execute cross-forest moves is probably worthy of a separate chapter that unfortunately cannot fit into this book. To begin your investigation, you should consult TechNet for further information about the attribute synchronization requirements, including code to prepare Microsoft Identity Lifecycle Management FP1 to be able to prepare mail-enabled users in an Exchange 2010 organization to which you want to move mailboxes.

Let's assume that we want to move a mailbox back to Exchange 2007, but in this case the other forest includes Exchange 2010 CAS servers:

```
New-MoveRequest -Identity 'Chris Ashton' -Remote -RemoteTargetDatabase 'Exchange 2007
Mbx' -RemoteHostName 'Exch2010CAS.contoso.com' -RemoteCredential (Get-Credential)
```

Because an Exchange 2010 CAS is available, MRS proxies the request to the CAS in the other organization and the CAS server in that organization then processes the move. The major difference between a *Remote* move request and a *RemoteLegacy* move request is that *Remote* moves use a Web service called MRSProxy. MRSProxy is somewhat similar to the RPC over HTTPS connection that Outlook uses for MAPI communication in that it can work across an Internet link. However, MRSProxy is able to update both Store contents and Active Directory, which is what it needs to move a mailbox. By comparison, *RemoteLegacy* moves require direct MAPI and Lightweight Directory Access Protocol (LDAP) access to the remote forest. Different firewall requirements therefore exist for the two scenarios.

All moves between Exchange 2010 and legacy versions (except Exchange 2007 SP2 and later) are offline and the user cannot access his mailbox until the move is complete. You cannot suspend and resume processing of these moves, which also means that any failure that stops the mailbox move will force you to restart from the beginning rather than being able to resume from a checkpoint, as is the case with online moves.

Moving mailboxes with personal archives

The original version of Exchange 2010 always stores a personal archive in the same database as the primary mailbox. Exchange 2010 SP1 introduces more flexibility by allowing a personal archive to be stored in a different database or in a database on a server belonging to the Microsoft Exchange Online hosted service. When you move a mailbox, you normally also move its personal archive. This operation is very straightforward with Exchange 2010, but the additional flexibility introduced in Exchange 2010 SP1 creates some new challenges when you move mailboxes. Things are easy enough when you only have Exchange 2010 SP1 mailbox servers in use because you can then decide to do any of the following moves:

- Mailbox and personal archive to the same target database

- Mailbox to a different database leaving the personal archive in the original database

- Personal archive to a different database leaving the mailbox in the original database

> ### Note
> It's not possible to move the mailbox and its personal archive to two different databases in a single operation (for example, move the mailbox from database DB1 to database DB2 and concurrently move the archive to database DB3). Performing such a split requires two separate move requests.

Figure 12-8 shows what you'll see when you use the New Move Request Wizard on an Exchange 2010 SP1 server. In this case, EMC has detected that two of the mailboxes selected to be moved have personal archives and is offering the administrator the option to do the following:

- Move only the mailbox and leave the personal archive in its current database.

- Move only the personal archive and leave the primary mailbox in its current database.

- Move both the primary mailbox and personal archive to a different database.

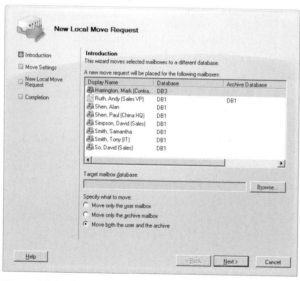

Figure 12-8 The options to move mailboxes that have archives supported by Exchange 2010 SP1.

If the mailboxes selected to be moved do not have personal archives, EMC does not display these options and the administrator can only select the target database.

Things are more complicated when you want to move a mailbox from an SP1 mailbox server to an RTM mailbox server. In this case, some logic checks whether the personal archive is separate from the primary mailbox, and, if this is true, you won't be allowed to move the mailbox until you move the personal archive back into the same database as its primary mailbox.

You might assume that you'll be able to split a mailbox and its archive and move them to two different databases if an Exchange 2010 server is the source and an Exchange 2010 SP1 server is the target. However, this scenario is not supported, because the original version of Exchange 2010 always moves a personal archive along with its mailbox. If you want to separate the two, you have to wait until the mailbox and archive are both located on an SP1 server before you can assign the personal archive to a different database.

Of course, the best way to avoid problems is to make sure that all mailbox servers run the same software version, ideally SP1 (or later).

Checking move request status

To check the status of a move request, we pass the name of the mailbox to the Get-MoveRequest cmdlet:

```
Get-MoveRequest -Identity 'Tony.Redmond@contoso.com'
```

As previously mentioned, move requests are kept after completion, so on a busy system that handles many mailbox moves you probably want to clear requests periodically. One approach is to clear move requests for individual mailboxes when the need arises to move the mailbox again. A command like this will remove a move request:

```
Remove-MoveRequest -Identity 'Tony.Redmond@contoso.com'
```

Alternatively, you can clean everything up with a simple one-line command that looks for all completed requests and then deletes the set of returned objects:

```
Get-MoveRequest -MoveStatus Completed | Remove-MoveRequest -Confirm $False
```

TROUBLESHOOTING

I can't remove a mailbox database
Exchange won't allow you to remove a mailbox database if any move requests for the database have not been cleared. This step prevents the removal of a database if any danger exists that a mailbox move is in progress or a planned move has not completed successfully and requires administrator attention. In addition, every move request is linked to the Active Directory object for the database that holds the associated mailbox, and if a database is deleted while move requests are present (even if complete), Exchange will regard the move requests as invalid and you will not be able to remove them with the Remove-MoveRequest cmdlet; to do this, you'd have to delete the underlying data from Active Directory.

Planning mailbox moves

We've already discussed how to collect move requests into batches that can be processed at one time. It is common practice to initiate a set of mailbox moves to happen overnight when user activity and network traffic are light. You should be careful not to swamp the network with many concurrent move requests for large mailboxes that conflict with other network-intensive activities such as nightly backups. You should also distribute moves across all available servers and databases to avoid the chance of swamping a target server with the load from multiple incoming move requests, all of which generate significant CPU and I/O demand to populate the new mailboxes and update content indexes. Another issue to consider is the limits that MRS imposes on moving information to different mailboxes and servers. For example, if you want to move 1,000 mailboxes to decommission a mailbox server, MRS will process the moves more quickly if you spread the moves across different target servers and databases. By comparison, if you select a single mailbox database as the target, you will be able to queue the 1,000 move requests, but MRS will only process five at a time and the operation is likely to last much longer than you expect.

CAUTION

Ideally, no server should be forced to handle more than five incoming concurrent move requests. The same caution is applied to initiating multiple moves from a single source database. Although the activity level is significantly different, because the source databases stream out information and don't have to adjust their content indexes until mailboxes are finally transferred, it is possible to swamp a source server with multiple requests. Again, moderation is the best policy, and you should schedule moves so that a single database or server cannot become a bottleneck as source or target. The amount of mailbox data that can be moved from server to server is highly dependent on your environment, so some testing is required to determine the optimal number of mailbox moves to schedule for a night or over a weekend. After MRS finishes processing, administrators can review the results of the move operations and mark the successful moves as complete.

You can initiate new move requests with a Suspend status. There are two ways of doing this:

- Use the –*Suspend* parameter.

- Use the –*SuspendWhenReadyToComplete* parameter.

–*Suspend* tells MRS to create a queued move request but do nothing more until the move request is resumed. This is a good way of creating a set of move requests to be processed as a batch, perhaps at night when user demand is low.

–SuspendWhenReadyToComplete tells MRS to perform the initial seeding phase to copy all of the current information from the source mailbox to the target. When an administrator is ready to complete the move, she can release the move request. For example:

```
New-MoveRequest –Identity 'Tony Redmond' –SuspendWhenReadyToComplete
–TargetDatabase 'DB1'
Get-MoveRequestStatistics –Identity 'Tony Redmond' | Format-List
```

```
UserIdentity                       : contoso.com/Exchange Users/Tony Redmond
DisplayName                        : Tony Redmond
Status                             : AutoSuspended
SyncStage                          : IncrementalSync
Flags                              : IntraOrg, Pull, Suspend, SuspendWhenReadyToComplete
SuspendWhenReadyToComplete         : True
QueuedTimestamp                    : 11/17/2010 8:15:26 AM
StartTimestamp                     : 11/17/2010 8:15:31 AM
LastUpdateTimestamp                : 11/17/2010 8:16:52 AM
InitialSeedingCompletedTimestamp   : 11/17/2010 8:16:42 AM
TotalMailboxSize                   : 32.27 MB (33,832,672 bytes)
TotalMailboxItemCount              : 130
BytesTransferred                   : 33.77 MB (35,411,383 bytes)
PercentComplete                    : 95
Message                            : Informational: The move request for mailbox
c612d271-5618-408a-81ef-50f1b3f9a5f7 is ready to complete and has been automatically suspended
because the SuspendWhenReadyToComplete parameter is set to $True.
```

You can see from the output of the Get-MoveRequestStatistics cmdlet that the move is paused at a notional 95 percent of the mailbox (90 percent is used in the original version of Exchange 2010). The last 5 percent is the incremental synchronization that will bring the mailbox completely up to date when we release the move request with the Resume-MoveRequest cmdlet.

```
Resume-MoveRequest –Identity 'John Smith'
```

> **Tip**
> This approach is useful to set up a series of moves for processing by MRS in the background during the working day without any impact on users. Once user demand is low outside normal working hours, the move requests can be released to complete and the users will access their relocated mailboxes the next time that they connect.

Let's assume that you have created a set of suspended move requests that are now ready to complete. To release all of the suspended move requests, you'd use

something like the command shown next (move requests that are created with the
–SuspendWhenReadyToComplete parameter go into a status of AutoSuspended when they
are past the initial seeding phase):

```
Get-MoveRequest –MoveStatus 'AutoSuspended' | Resume-MoveRequest
```

You can use much the same approach to suspend queued move requests that are in progress if you need to stop move requests for some reason, such as to apply a hot fix or to
avoid a backup window:

```
Get-MoveRequest –MoveStatus 'Queued' | Suspend-MoveRequest –SuspendComment
'Paused move to allow application of hot fix'
```

Another way of scheduling moves is to let MRS create the move requests and place them
on the queue but not do anything else until you are ready to proceed. This might be done
when you want to queue a set of move requests that you will release when system load is
low. To do this, specify the *–Suspend* parameter with the New-MoveRequest cmdlet. For
example:

```
New-MoveRequest –Identity 'Tony Redmond' –TargetDatabase 'DB1' –Suspend
```

Because they usually require less processing than other move requests, resumptions receive
a certain priority in that MRS processes them before any other queued requests. However,
they will wait until other move requests that are in progress complete. You can use this
command to retrieve information about moves that are currently in progress:

```
Get-MoveRequest –MoveStatus 'InProgress'
```

You can build on this code to pipe information about the requests to the
Get-MoveRequestStatistics cmdlet to discover which CAS servers are processing current
move requests.

```
Get-MoveRequest –MoveStatus 'InProgress' | Get-MoveRequestStatistics | Format-List
Alias, MoveServerName
```

```
Alias: Epr
MoveServerName: ExServer3.contoso.com
```

The Get-MoveRequest cmdlet retrieves move request data about a mailbox from Active
Directory. This cmdlet only accesses the small set of properties maintained in a mailbox
to describe a move request, whereas the call to Get-MoveRequestStatistics queries the
MRS instance that is responsible for the move to retrieve comprehensive data about the
current status of the move such as the percentage complete, the number of items to move,
and so on.

Move requests are queued in the target database and MRS processes the requests in FIFO order. You can use the Get-MoveRequestStatistics cmdlet to view the move request queue from a database as follows:

```
Get-MoveRequestStatistics -MoveRequestQueue -Database 'DB1'
```

Orphaned move requests

The information returned by Get-MoveRequestStatistics also lists any abandoned or orphaned move requests that it finds in the specified database. These are move requests that don't have matching Active Directory information for some reason. MRS detects orphaned move requests and cleans them up after they are more than 24 hours old. Delaying the cleanup for 24 hours ensures that an orphaned move request does not exist because of a problem with Active Directory replication.

You can use the Get-MoveRequest cmdlet to examine the current moves known to a database.

```
Get-MoveRequest -Database 'DB1'
```

Mailbox moves from legacy versions of Exchange do not move the contents of the dumpster (deleted items awaiting retention time expiry) with their mailboxes. For example, if you move a mailbox from Exchange 2007 to Exchange 2010, no dumpster contents are moved and the moved mailbox starts off with an empty dumpster. As explained in Chapter 15, "Compliance," Exchange 2010 takes a different approach because, to meet legal retention requirements, it moves dumpster contents along with mailboxes when moves occur between Exchange 2010 servers and when moving mailboxes to legacy servers. Legacy Exchange servers don't know anything about the enhanced dumpster used by Exchange 2010 and won't be able to access it. However, if you then move the mailbox back to an Exchange 2010 server, the enhanced dumpster contents become accessible again.

For the same legal retention reason, Exchange 2010 is able to move personal archives and the contents of their dumpster along with primary mailboxes. Clearly, the nature of archives is that they are likely to be larger than the associated primary mailboxes, so if you use Exchange archive mailboxes and force users to move items into the archive with retention policies or manually, you have to expect that mailbox moves will take longer.

Mailbox moves: Speed can vary

The speed of mailbox moves varies depending on system configuration and load. CPU can be a real bottleneck due to the way that mailbox data are indexed as they arrive on a target server. There's no doubt that a lightly loaded server with a fast storage subsystem and multiple CPUs will process moves more quickly than a heavily loaded server running on a virtualized platform. Directing multiple concurrent moves at a single mailbox database will also limit throughput.

Experience to date indicates that the "sweet spot" is to plan for between 5 and 10 concurrent moves per target server, spreading the moves across multiple databases on different disks. Attempting to process more concurrent moves will encounter high CPU usage, usually caused by the context indexing process attempting to handle all the new items as they are transferred into databases. You can expect to process from 4 to 6 GB of mailbox data hourly, so it is realistic to expect that a 2 GB mailbox will take between 15 and 30 minutes to move. Most of the improvement in move mailbox performance is due to the changes made to the Exchange 2010 Store, such as decreased I/O demand. By comparison, Exchange 2007 usually processes mailbox moves at a rate of 600 MB to 800 MB per hour.

A move request can be cancelled at any time before it enters CompletionInProgress status by running the Remove-MoveRequest cmdlet. When you cancel a move request, Exchange stops transferring content to the target mailbox and then deletes the target mailbox. The contents that have been transferred to the point when the move stopped will be cleaned from the target database immediately. The source mailbox is "unlocked" by removing the move request and it reverts to its original condition. The user can continue to use it as before. If you need to move the mailbox again, you have to start from the beginning and cannot pick up from a point reached before.

Ensuring high availability

Mailbox moves performed within a DAG have to take account of the replication activity that underpins the ability of the DAG to deliver high availability. Exchange 2010 SP1 includes two enhancements to reduce the possibility of data loss when mailboxes move between replicated databases on DAG members.

1. At points during the mailbox move, including at the end of the process, before Active Directory is updated with the new mailbox location, MRS queries Active Manager to determine whether transaction log replication is in a healthy state for the target mailbox database and its passive copies. The action taken by MRS depends on the value of the *DataMoveReplicationConstraint* property of the target mailbox database

(you can set this value with the Set-MailboxDatabase cmdlet). The following values are used:

○ None: The move operation continues as if the target database is a standalone (nonreplicated) database and Active Manager is not consulted about replication status.

○ SecondCopy: If the database is replicated, then at least one of the passive copies must have synchronized all the changes made to move the mailbox to date. This is the default action if the value of *DataMoveReplicationConstraint* is not set.

○ SecondDatacenter: If the database is replicated to a second Active Directory site, then at least one of the passive copies in the other site must have replicated the changes.

○ AllDatacenters: If the database is replicated to multiple Active Directory sites, then at least one of the passive copies in each site must have replicated the changes.

○ AllCopies: If the database is replicated, all passive copies must have replicated the changes.

If Active Manager confirms that replication of the new mailbox data is healthy and meets the constraint set for the database, MRS continues the mailbox move. This checking occurs throughout the time required to move a mailbox and, if necessary, MRS will stall for 30 seconds to allow a server that is under load to complete the necessary log replication and then check to see whether the move can continue. MRS will fail the move if the stalled condition is not lifted within 15 minutes. The stalled condition is recorded in the mailbox move history, where you'll see information like this:

```
9/9/2010 4:15:57 PM [ExServer2] Move for mailbox '/o=contoso/ou=Exchange
Administrative Group (FYDIBOHF23SPDLT)/cn=Recipients/cn=Redmond, Tony' is
stalled because DataMoveReplicationConstraint is not satisfied for the
database 'DB1' (agent MailboxDatabaseReplication). Failure Reason:
Database 1ec5194c-90b9-43d8-aae1-01a5374438f2
does not satisfy constraint SecondCopy. There are no available healthy
database copies. Will wait until 9/9/2010 4:30:57 PM.

9/9/2010 4:16:27 PM [ExServer2] Request is no longer stalled and will
continue.
```

The *DataMoveReplicationConstraint* setting is specific to a mailbox database and can obviously vary across the databases in a DAG. In addition, MRS uses two settings in its configuration file to determine how it interacts with Active Manager for all databases. *EnableDataGuaranteeCheck* controls whether MRS interacts with Active Manager to determine the current replication status for databases (the default is True), and *DataGuaranteeCheckPeriod* (default of five minutes with a range from 30 seconds to two hours) controls how often MRS checks with Active Manager. *EnableDataGuaranteeCheck* must be True and a *DataMoveReplicationConstraint* set for a mailbox database before MRS and Active Manager will work together to ensure that mailbox moves do not compromise high availability operations.

2. In the unlikely event that the target server has not generated a log roll because it is waiting for enough data to fill its log buffer, MRS forces the Store to close off the current transaction log and generate a new log. This action then forces the now-closed transaction log that contains the last data for the mailbox move to be replicated to the servers that hold copies of the target database. MRS will force a log roll for each mailbox move if a move request is waiting for more than one minute to complete. This makes sure that a move is treated as a unique transaction. Forcing a log roll should be an extremely rare event, because normal user and background assistant processing on the mailbox server should easily fill the 1 MB log buffer very soon after the last data arrives for the mailbox being moved, so this is strictly a case of being sure and safe.

It's possible that a database transition occurs during a move operation. If this happens, MRS learns from Active Manager where the active database copy is now located and reconnects to that database copy to continue processing the move. If the active copy of the database does not come online within 30 minutes, MRS considers the move to have failed because the database is unavailable.

Reporting mailbox moves

An Exchange 2010 move report includes the size of a mailbox before and after the mailbox is moved. Exchange 2003 mailbox sizes include the dumpster, which could account for a difference between the size (as reported by the management console) and the moved size (as reported in the move request) when mailboxes move from Exchange 2003 to Exchange 2010. The difference will vary depending on the deleted items retention period, and a 10 percent difference is not unusual. For example, you might see a 3 GB mailbox reported by Exchange 2003 end up as a 2.85 GB mailbox when it is moved to Exchange 2010. Exchange 2007 seems to report mailbox sizes more consistently, so there is less observed difference when moving from Exchange 2007 to Exchange 2010 (the difference might be due to the soft-deleted items that are not transferred by MRS to Exchange 2010).

You can use the Get-MoveRequestStatistics cmdlet to view some information about active move requests as data flows from source to target database. For example:

```
Get-MoveRequestStatistics –Identity 'Smith, Jeff' | Select DisplayName, Status,
TotalMailboxSize, TotalMailboxItemCount, PercentComplete, BytesTransferred,
ItemsTransferred, BytesTransferredPerMinute
```

```
DisplayName                 : Smith, Jeff
Status                      : InProgress
TotalMailboxSize            : 379.1 MB (397,473,599 bytes)
TotalMailboxItemCount       : 2837
PercentComplete             : 67
BytesTransferred            : 275.3 MB (288,689,472 bytes)
ItemsTransferred            : 2109
BytesTransferredPerMinute   : 62.06 MB (65,078,175 bytes)
```

The *TotalMailboxSize* property reported by Get-MoveRequestStatistics includes content in the enhanced dumpster. It is the size in which we are most interested because it determines the additional storage required in the target database. It also determines the number of transaction logs that will be generated on the target server during the move. You can antic-ipate that a 200 MB mailbox will generate at least 200 1 MB transaction logs. In contrast, no additional transaction logs are immediately generated on the source server because the old mailbox will be removed during online background maintenance and the delete operations performed then will be interleaved with the other transactions caused by this processing. However, it's possible that you will observe growth in a source database size as mailboxes are moved from it. This seems counterintuitive, but it is explained if the source mailboxes were not used by Outlook configured in cached Exchange mode. In this case, the source mailbox does not contain any indexes or views that are otherwise created by Outlook, and MRS will be forced to create them to perform its incremental synchronization at the last part of the mailbox move. Depending on the available white space in the source database, the creation of these views can cause the database to grow as well as impose some addi-tional I/O demand on the source server.

If you're interested, the split between the storage occupied by items in folders (including items in the Deleted Items folder) and dumpster items in a mailbox can be viewed with the Get-MailboxStatistics cmdlet. For example:

```
Get-MailboxStatistics –Identity 'Smith, Jeff' | Select DisplayName, ItemCount,
TotalItemSize, DeletedItemCount, TotalDeletedItemSize
```

The percentage of move complete reported is an approximation based on the size of moved message rather than the number of items. The reported transfer speed (bytes transferred per minute) is based on a sample taken every second and averaged over the last 20 seconds. Treat this value as a rough guide to how things are moving rather than a very accurate measurement of network speed. After a mailbox move is complete, Exchange reports the total items transferred, the size of the moved mailbox, and the total number of transferred bytes. This value is invariably larger than the actual mailbox size due to a certain amount of transmission overhead involved in the copy plus some metadata about the mailbox that is transferred along with the content.

TROUBLESHOOTING

There was a problem—What happened?

If you encounter a problem with a move, your first step is to run the Get-MoveRequestStatistics cmdlet with the *–IncludeReport* parameter to extract some information about what happened during the move. This is the most common way to find out what kind of problem occurred during a move.

```
Get-MoveRequestStatistics –IncludeReport –Identity 'Tony.Redmond@contoso.com'
```

Accessing move report log data

Unlike Exchange 2007, Exchange 2010 does not maintain separate log files for move mailbox operations. Instead, you can use the Get-MailboxStatistics cmdlet to access this information. Get-MailboxStatistics reads move request information for a selected mailbox from move reports stored in a hidden folder in the non-IPM subtree of the mailbox. During a move operation, you can access a move report with EMC or EMS to gauge progress, in which case Exchange fetches the information from the system mailbox in the target database (for moves between Exchange 2010 servers) or the source database (for moves to legacy servers). Once a move request completes successfully, MRS moves the move history information from the system mailbox into the user's mailbox.

By default, the last two move reports are stored in each mailbox. If necessary, you can change the number of move reports that are stored by updating the value specified in MSExchangeMailboxReplicationService.exe.config, the MRS configuration file stored in the Exchange binaries directory to instruct MRS to hold between 0 and 100 reports. Remember that the MRS configuration file is unique to a CAS server, so if you want to have the same behavior everywhere, you have to make the same change on every CAS server. Before you rush to allow Exchange to store five or six move reports, you should understand that each move report occupies some space in the mailbox that is charged against the mailbox quota. Each report could occupy 200 KB or 300 KB, especially if the move encountered some transient failures along the way. Microsoft originally allowed Exchange to store 10 move reports per mailbox but decreased this number to just two precisely because they were concerned about the storage requirement.

You can extract two types of reports for a mailbox move. Both reports are based on the mailbox move history data and the difference is purely in the amount of detail that each contains.

- Basic history is provided if you pass the *–IncludeMoveHistory* parameter.

- A much more detailed report is generated if you pass the *–IncludeMoveReport* parameter. The SP1 version of EMC uses the *–IncludeMoveReport* parameter to generate the move log that it displays when an administrator views the properties of a move request. However, EMC fetches the data for a mailbox that is being moved from the system mailbox of the target database (for moves between Exchange 2010 servers) or the source database (for moves to legacy servers) rather than the user's mailbox. When the move is completed successfully, MRS updates the user mailbox with the latest move history.

To generate basic history for a mailbox move request, we can use the following code:

```
Get-MailboxStatistics -Identity 'Tony.Redmond@contoso.com' -IncludeMoveHistory
```

INSIDE OUT   Output the move report to a file

Even the basic history report includes a reasonable amount of information and can be difficult to make much sense of on a screen. For this reason, it's best to output the move report to a file that you can then open with a text editor. The following code extracts the history for the most recent move request for a mailbox and pipes the output to a text file that is then opened with the Notepad editor.

```
$BasicReport = (Get-MailboxStatistics -Identity 'Eoin.Redmond@contoso.com'
-IncludeMoveHistory).MoveHistory
$BasicReport[0] | Out-file -FilePath 'c:\Temp\MRS-History.Log' | Notepad
'c:\Temp\MRS-History.Log'
```

In this context, [0] refers to the first (most recent) move report stored in the user's mailbox. If you want to view details of the second (older) move report, you can do so by referencing it as $BasicReport[1]. If the MRS configuration file has been updated to allow for more than two move reports to be kept in a mailbox, you can refer to them as [2], [3], [4], and so on. Now let's generate the full move report.

```
$FullReport = (Get-MailboxStatistics -Identity 'Eoin.Redmond@contoso.com'
-IncludeMoveReport).MoveHistory
$FullReport[0] | Out-file -FilePath 'c:\Temp\MRS-Report.Log' | Notepad
'c:\Temp\MRS-Report.Log'
```

On the surface, Exchange seems to generate much the same file, but using the *–IncludeMoveReport* parameter forces Exchange to output a lot of additional information that helps you to understand exactly what actions MRS performs to move a mailbox.

The following sample shows an edited extract from a move mailbox report. You can see how the progress of the move is reported and how the incremental synchronization is done at the end of the initial move. Earlier in the report (not shown here) you can see details of the moved mailbox being created in the target database and later, after details of actions taken to perform the move, you'll find all of the Active Directory properties for the old and the moved mailbox. The Active Directory information can be invaluable in diagnosing issues such as proxy addresses that are incorrect for the moved mailbox. Other information reported includes the servers that participated in the move and the mailbox sizes before and after the move.

```
5/19/2010 5:41:07 PM [ExServer1] Mailbox Replication Service 'ExServer1.contoso.com'
(14.1.160.2 caps:07) is examining request.
5/19/2010 5:41:07 PM [ExServer1] Connected to target mailbox 'Primary (107738a8-b092-4092-
98d7-d375819b9fa1)', database 'DB2', Mailbox server 'EXSERVER1.contoso.com' Version 14.1
(Build 160.0).
5/19/2010 5:41:07 PM [ExServer1] Connected to source mailbox 'Primary (107738a8-b092-4092-
98d7-d375819b9fa1)', database 'DB1', Mailbox server 'EXSERVER1.contoso.com' Version 14.1
(Build 160.0).
5/19/2010 5:41:07 PM [ExServer1] Request processing started.
5/19/2010 5:41:07 PM [ExServer1] Source Mailbox information before the move:
Regular Items: 7286, 1018 MB (1,067,144,724 bytes)
Regular Deleted Items: 176, 26.99 MB (28,306,004 bytes)
FAI Items: 12, 0 B (0 bytes)
FAI Deleted Items: 0, 0 B (0 bytes)
5/19/2010 5:41:08 PM [ExServer1] Initializing folder hierarchy in mailbox 'Primary
(107738a8-b092-4092-98d7-d375819b9fa1)': 126 folders total.
5/19/2010 5:41:33 PM [ExServer1] Folder hierarchy initialized for mailbox 'Primary
(107738a8-b092-4092-98d7-d375819b9fa1)': 126 folders total.
5/19/2010 5:41:33 PM [ExServer1] Stage: CreatingInitialSyncCheckpoint. Percent complete: 15.
5/19/2010 5:41:37 PM [ExServer1] Stage: LoadingMessages. Percent complete: 20.
5/19/2010 5:41:41 PM [ExServer1] Stage: CopyingMessages. Percent complete: 25.
5/19/2010 5:41:41 PM [ExServer1] Copy progress: 0/7476 messages, 0 B (0 bytes)/1.02 GB
(1,095,450,728 bytes).
5/19/2010 5:41:42 PM [ExServer1] Messages have been enumerated successfully. 7476 items
loaded. Total size: 1.02 GB (1,095,450,728 bytes).
5/19/2010 5:47:00 PM [ExServer1] Stage: CopyingMessages. Percent complete: 42.
5/19/2010 5:47:00 PM [ExServer1] Copy progress: 1987/7476 messages, 260.7 MB (273,347,623
bytes)/1.02 GB (1,095,450,728 bytes).
5/19/2010 5:52:01 PM [ExServer1] Stage: CopyingMessages. Percent complete: 57.
5/19/2010 5:52:01 PM [ExServer1] Copy progress: 4223/7476 messages, 486.3 MB (509,954,232
bytes)/1.02 GB (1,095,450,728 bytes).
5/19/2010 5:57:06 PM [ExServer1] Stage: CopyingMessages. Percent complete: 69.
5/19/2010 5:57:06 PM [ExServer1] Copy progress: 5481/7476 messages, 668.2 MB (700,631,731
bytes)/1.02 GB (1,095,450,728 bytes).
5/19/2010 6:02:06 PM [ExServer1] Stage: CopyingMessages. Percent complete: 75.
5/19/2010 6:02:06 PM [ExServer1] Copy progress: 5985/7476 messages, 759.9 MB (796,797,286
bytes)/1.02 GB (1,095,450,728 bytes).
```

```
5/19/2010 6:09:32 PM [ExServer2] Request processing continued, stage LoadingMessages.
5/19/2010 6:09:34 PM [ExServer2] Stage: CopyingMessages. Percent complete: 77.
5/19/2010 6:09:34 PM [ExServer2] Copy progress: 6122/7476 messages, 776.2 MB (813,954,576
bytes)/1.02 GB (1,095,450,728 bytes).
5/19/2010 6:09:34 PM [ExServer2] Messages have been enumerated successfully. 7476 items
loaded. Total size: 1.02 GB (1,095,450,728 bytes).
5/19/2010 6:14:35 PM [ExServer2] Stage: CopyingMessages. Percent complete: 88.
5/19/2010 6:14:35 PM [ExServer2] Copy progress: 7121/7476 messages, 952.6 MB (998,890,105
bytes)/1.02 GB (1,095,450,728 bytes).
5/19/2010 6:16:21 PM [ExServer2] Initial seeding completed, 7476 items copied, total size 1.02
GB (1,095,450,728 bytes).
5/19/2010 6:16:21 PM [ExServer2] Changes reported in source 'Primary (107738a8-b092-4092-98d7-
d375819b9fa1)': 0 changed folders, 0 deleted folders, 0 changed messages.
5/19/2010 6:16:21 PM [ExServer2] Incremental Sync 'Primary (107738a8-b092-4092-98d7-
d375819b9fa1)' completed: 0 changed items.
5/19/2010 6:16:21 PM [ExServer2] Stage: IncrementalSync. Percent complete: 95.
5/19/2010 6:16:21 PM [ExServer2] Final sync has started.
5/19/2010 6:16:21 PM [ExServer2] Changes reported in source 'Primary (107738a8-b092-4092-98d7-
d375819b9fa1)': 0 changed folders, 0 deleted folders, 0 changed messages.
5/19/2010 6:16:21 PM [ExServer2] Incremental Sync 'Primary (107738a8-b092-4092-98d7-
d375819b9fa1)' completed: 0 changed items.
5/19/2010 6:16:35 PM [ExServer2] Stage: FinalIncrementalSync. Percent complete: 95.
```

Moves and mailbox provisioning

If you move mailboxes between Active Directory forests, you'll discover that the
New-MoveRequest cmdlet requires a fully provisioned Active Directory object to work
against. In the past, you could move a mailbox to a server in another forest (for example, as
part of a migration project from Exchange 2003 to Exchange 2007 when you create a new
forest for Exchange 2007), and Exchange would create the Active Directory account first
and then move the mailbox and update the necessary attributes to establish a fully provisioned user account and mailbox. If your account provisioning procedure depends on this
functionality, you will have to change it to make sure to create the Active Directory account
before attempting to move a mailbox. The reason for the change is that Microsoft found it
too difficult to allow for all of the unique scenarios that exist around account provisioning.
They could have continued to attempt to write code that caters to all these circumstances,
but concluded that it would be easier and more effective to move to a situation where
Exchange takes care of moving mailboxes and Active Directory procedures take care of
everything else. It's up to you to define what those Active Directory procedures should be
to meet the needs of your company.

Chapter 12

INSIDE OUT   A useful script

On the positive side, Exchange 2010 SP1 includes a script called Prepare-MoveRequest.ps1 that provides a prototype structure to move mailboxes to Exchange 2010. This script is a valuable asset in terms of providing a starting point that you can use to build provisioning for your own environment.

Handling move request errors

By default, MRS tolerates up to 60 errors that force it to retry to copy data before it will abort an attempted mailbox move. These errors are different from the declared threshold for bad or corrupt items that MRS encounters in the source mailbox that can be tolerated before MRS is forced to fail a move. Errors that occur during moves must be consecutive. If progress is made between errors, MRS will reset the error count and proceed. You can use the Resume-MoveRequest cmdlet to resume an aborted move and MRS will restart at the point at which it failed. Most errors are transient and are due to conditions such as temporary network glitches between the source and target servers. You can check the event log for event 1101 for MSExchange Mailbox Replication to see if errors occur (bad items are also noted in the move report). The information reported isn't tremendously helpful, but it might indicate a likely cause.

Tip

You should check the event logs on both source and target server. If you do see errors in the event log, you can increase the diagnostic level for Mailbox Replication to high or maximum to increase the amount of information generated in the event log and see if that helps to pinpoint the problem.

Each move request is created with a bad item limit that MRS can tolerate during the move. As explained earlier, the default bad item limit is zero, which means that any problem with an item will force MRS to stop the move. There is no real point in moving corrupt items from database to database and it is good to cleanse a mailbox by removing corrupt content during the move. Any mailbox that has been in use for more than a few years, especially if it was used with Exchange 2000 or Exchange 2003 or was migrated from a foreign email system, has the possibility of some lurking corrupt items. It's true that if you allow MRS to skip the corrupt items you create some potential for data loss, but if an item is corrupt it probably isn't very valuable, hasn't been accessed in some time (otherwise the user would have complained about it), and it could cause a mailbox to be placed into quarantine if the corrupt item causes the Store to consume excessive resources.

We can always check the move request report afterward to determine whether any corrupt items were encountered in a mailbox. If a move fails because it exceeds the bad item limit, you can always restart the move by setting a higher bad item limit with the Set-MoveRequest cmdlet. For example:

```
Set-MoveRequest -Identity 'JSmith' -BadItemLimit 100
```

MRS will then restart the move at the point at which it failed and hopefully go on to complete it. If a large number of items are rejected by the target server, one solution is to identify the problem items from the move report, export them to a PST, and then delete them from the source mailbox. You can then move the rest of the mailbox as normal and later attempt to import the problem items from the PST into the new mailbox.

INSIDE OUT   Use a meaningful bad item limit

You can input a value range from –1 to 2,147,483,647 for the bad item limit. In this instance, –1 means that you don't care how many corrupt items MRS encounters. It is a really bad idea to set the bad item limit to –1, because it means that a move can succeed no matter how many apparently bad items are encountered. It's good to know and better to be able to investigate and deduce a likely reason if you find that a mailbox includes many bad items, so a more measured approach is to set the bad item limit to something reasonable, such as 10, and review the move report afterward to see if any bad items were in fact encountered. Remember that if a move fails because it exceeds its bad item threshold, you can always investigate the problem and then increase the bad item limit to allow MRS to resume the move.

Mailboxes that have high numbers of bad items (more than five or so) are an indicator that the source database has experienced problems in the past and that this is an issue that deserves further investigation. Of course, if you know that a database has had previous problems (usually due to hardware failure) and you don't have a reliable backup copy to restore, you might not care how many corruptions MRS encounters as long as it manages to move the majority of a mailbox to a new database. In other words, you're willing to accept some data loss to recover a mailbox.

The case of the lingering request

It's possible that some move requests will complete successfully but leave a lingering request behind. In this scenario, the mailbox is transferred from the source to the target database and the user can connect to the newly moved mailbox, but the move request remains in the queue. You might see an error similar to the one shown here in the Application Event Log.

```
The Mailbox Replication Service was unable to clean up the source mailbox after
the move. The error was ignored.
Mailbox move: contoso.com/Test/Redmond, Eoin' (Primary (6a144b2e-1b08-412a-
bb1d-f2410db85c9d))
Database: EXCHSVR2\First Storage Group\Mailbox Database
Error: MapiExceptionNotFound: Unable to delete mailbox. (hr=0x8004010f,
ec=-2147221233)
```

The error reports that Exchange was not able to clean up the source mailbox for some reason. It might be that the command to remove the mailbox was not processed by the source server or that some other problem occurred. Problems like this are more common in moves from legacy Exchange servers to Exchange 2010 than between Exchange 2010 servers. If you can connect to the copy of the mailbox on the target server and know that the move was successful, you can flush the move request from the queue with the Remove-MoveRequest cmdlet or with the remove requests option from EMC. The background maintenance performed by the Store will clean things up by removing the now-orphaned mailbox in the source database after the deleted mailbox retention period expires. However, you do need to understand why the problem occurred through further investigation so that you can address any underlying problem before processing future moves.

Moving a mailbox to a database that has a single copy is a straightforward operation. Things are slightly more complicated when you move a mailbox from a database that has multiple copies (in a DAG), because Exchange must ensure that it can recover from a failure that occurs on the primary (active) copy of the database during the move operation. To do this, MRS copies all of the content from the source mailbox to the new mailbox and then checks that at least one of the database copies is healthy (that the –DataReplicationConstraint for the database is satisfied), meaning that there are less than 10 minutes of transaction log files to be replayed and that the queue copy is less than three.

Exchange reports problems with target databases as errors in the event log where you'll see indications such as "some database copies are behind," so it is relatively easy to check for these conditions. A healthy server that is participating properly in log replication will have no difficulty meeting these conditions, because it should be copying logs from active databases and replaying them into its database copies on an ongoing basis. Any buildup of transaction logs to be replayed or logs queued to be copied indicates a potential replication problem or that too much write activity exists for the target server to handle gracefully. Once MRS is convinced that the databases are healthy, it releases the move to continue to completion. These "HA stalls" are treated by MRS as a transient failure, and if a stall lasts for more than 30 minutes the regular MRS failure logic is invoked and the move is marked as failed due to too many transient failures. See the section "Ensuring high availability" earlier in this chapter for more information on this topic.

Mailbox import and export

In the immediate period following the release of Exchange 2010, a great deal of hot air was generated in the Exchange community about the requirement to run a 64-bit version of Outlook 2010 on an Exchange 2010 mailbox server before it is possible to use the Import-Mailbox or Export-Mailbox cmdlets to import or export data to a PST. These cmdlets are also used with Exchange 2007 to work with PST data and they have a dependency on Outlook's client-side MAPI provider to be able to access mailboxes.

The Import-Mailbox and Export-Mailbox cmdlets are obsolete in Exchange 2010 SP1, which replaces these cmdlets with a new mechanism of mailbox import and export requests modeled on the mailbox move model. The new cmdlets are based on a new PST writer library written by the Exchange development group rather than the Outlook MAPI libraries used by the older cmdlets, and there is no requirement to install any Outlook code on any Exchange server to be able to import from a PST or export to a PST. From Exchange 2010 SP1 onward, import and export requests are managed by the new cmdlets, so you need to replace any scripts that depend on the older cmdlets if you want to run them on an Exchange 2010 SP1 server; they can, of course, continue to be used on Exchange 2007 and Exchange 2010 servers. You can only create mailbox import and export requests through EMS because Microsoft did not have the time to integrate the new cmdlets into the EMC user interface.

Like mailbox move requests, mailbox import and export requests are first placed in a queue and are then picked up for processing by an MRS instance running on a CAS server in the site where the requests are created and are processed asynchronously in the background. MRS is able to import data into mailboxes in any database or export data from any mailbox within its site. To facilitate mailbox import–export operations, all the PSTs that MRS reads or writes must be placed in a file share that is accessible by the CAS servers. The file shares are secured against casual browsing by granting access only to the Exchange Trusted Subsystem. As illustrated in Figure 12-9, read/write access is required for export and read-only for import. All exports generate Unicode-format PSTs, and Exchange can read both the older ANSI and Unicode format PSTs when it imports data.

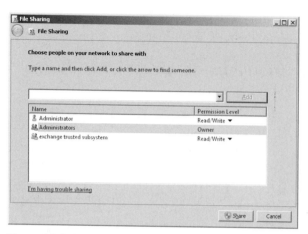

Figure 12-9 Setting the file share to allow access to the Exchange Trusted Subsystem.

> **Note**
> Public folder data cannot be imported or exported using the import–export cmdlets and has to pass through a mailbox before it can be processed. You can copy items from a public folder into a PST and then import the items from the PST into another mailbox.

If you don't want to have administrators use their time to manage mailbox import and export jobs, you can always revert to the time-tested basic method and ask users to move data in and out of their mailboxes by dragging and dropping items between PSTs and mailbox folders (or personal archive folders) and vice versa. However, this is really only an approach that is successful for a small number of items because users quickly become bored with moving data from PST to mailbox and will probably never complete the task.

Removing the requirement to install Outlook on Exchange mailbox servers is a great step forward. More important, the new mailbox import and export request mechanism introduced in SP1 is far more functional than the previous cmdlets. However, setting up mailbox import and export jobs still requires a great deal of administrative intervention. Apart from relocating the fulcrum for import–export operations from the mailbox server to the CAS, Microsoft also announced in October 2009 that they would document the internal format for PST files for the first time. They subsequently have delivered a PST development kit and documentation to allow third-party developers to start the process of developing tools based on the PST file format. This step holds out hope that we will see additional tools in the near future that automate and streamline the import of PST data into Exchange.

You can find the PST development kit and documentation at *http://www.microsoft.com /presspass/press/2010/may10/05-24PSTToolsPR.mspx.*

Gaining permission through RBAC to execute mailbox import and export

Before you can import or export data into a mailbox, your account must hold the Mailbox Import Export role. This role is not assigned by default, even to accounts that hold the Organization Management role. A deliberate administrative action is therefore required to assign the roles to the users or groups that will perform these operations. The logic here is that accessing mailboxes is a sensitive operation that should be restricted to users who really need the permission to be able to import data into someone else's mailbox or export data from someone else's mailbox. Although they don't hold the role by default, holders of the Organization Management role have the right to delegate the Mailbox Import Export role to users, including themselves.

> **Tip**
>
> Like many other instances where you need to delegate a role before someone can perform a task, it's usually better to delegate the role to a group and then manage the group membership because users will inherit or lose the role as they join or leave the group.

You can use a command like this to assign the role to a group:

```
New-ManagementRoleAssignment -Group 'Admins for Mailbox Import Export'
-Role 'Mailbox Import Export'
```

The next time the user initializes an EMS session, role-based access control (RBAC) will inform Exchange that he has the permission to use the import–export cmdlets and the cmdlets will be loaded into the set available to the user during the session. The cmdlets used are described in Table 12-2.

Table 12-2 **Import and Export mailbox cmdlets**

Version	Cmdlet	Purpose
Exchange 2010	Import-Mailbox	Import mailbox data from a PST
	Export-Mailbox	Export mailbox data to a PST
Exchange 2010 SP1	New-MailboxImportRequest	Create a new mailbox import request for processing by MRS
	Set-MailboxImportRequest	Set properties of a mailbox import request

Get-MailboxImportRequest	Retrieve the current status of a mailbox import request
Remove-MailboxImportRequest	Remove a mailbox import request
Get-MailboxImportRequestStatistics	Report detailed information about a mailbox import request
Suspend-MailboxImportRequest	Suspend an import operation from a PST
Resume-MailboxImportRequest	Resume a suspended import operation
New-MailboxExportRequest	Create a new mailbox export request
Set-MailboxExportRequest	Set the properties of a mailbox export request
Get-MailboxExportRequest	Retrieve the current status of a mailbox export request
Get-MailboxExportRequestStatistics	Report detailed information about a mailbox export request
Remove-MailboxExportRequest	Remove a mailbox export request
Suspend-MailboxExportRequest	Suspend an export operation to a PST
Resume-MailboxExportRequest	Resume a suspended export operation

Planning the import of PST data

Before rushing to import data, we need to consider how best to proceed. Among the challenges that are immediately obvious are the following:

- Mailbox quotas might have to be adjusted up to allow the PST data to be imported into the primary mailbox. The increase in quota can be permanent or it can be adjusted downward again after some or all of the data are moved into the user's personal archive. Increasing the quota before an import is a relatively simple procedure to script, but it is indicative of the manual nature of the processing that surrounds PST imports. The size of a PST on disk does not equate to the amount of data that will be imported into the mailbox. The PST file structure imposes a "tax" or overhead of approximately 20 percent over what is required to store items in an online mailbox or archive. Even so, it's still important to ensure that sufficient quota is available in target mailboxes before you begin to import data.

- Every item that is imported creates a transaction that must be captured into a transaction log. I/O demand will spike during the import as the target mailbox databases commit transactions and extend themselves to accommodate the mailboxes now swollen with PST data. Further I/O and CPU activity occurs to add items to the content indexes maintained for the target databases. More I/O will be generated if you move information into personal archives afterward.

- If the import occurs inside a DAG, similar I/O spikes will be experienced on servers hosting database copies due to replication, replay, and indexing activities. This has the potential to create a tsunami of I/O. The same transactional and I/O spikes in demand will occur when the data are moved into the archive mailboxes.

- Mailbox data are imported from PSTs held on file shares. File shares are used because you do not know what CAS server in a site might process the import (or export) requests (unless the site has just one CAS server), so you have to provide access to the data in a location that is accessible by all the CAS servers. Protect the file shares against casual browsing by assigning access to only the Exchange Trusted Subsystem and place the file share on the fastest disk that you can make available to ensure that operations proceed as quickly as possible.

- It's difficult to characterize how efficiently Exchange might be able to handle concurrent import operations, so scheduling the import operations to occur when they do not impact normal day-to-day user activity is often the right approach.

- The speed at which Exchange is able to process mailbox import and export operations will vary from server to server and is highly dependent on current load and system capability (disk throughput is obviously important). As an example, importing a 1.35 GB PST containing 7,450 items took a server under moderate load 15 minutes. Using a more powerful server or scheduling imports to occur at times of lower user demand will increase the throughput, and most servers should be able to import 8 GB per hour.

- MRS uses the *MaxSendSize* transport configuration setting to control the maximum size of item it can import into a mailbox. The default size is 10 MB. If you need to import larger items, you will have to increase the setting. For example:

```
Set-TransportConfig –MaxSendSize 20MB
```

- Make sure that you remove any passwords from the PSTs from which you want to import data because there is no way to provide a password to the cmdlets. Likewise, you cannot place a password on a PST when you create it during a mailbox export operation. Steps therefore have to be taken to protect the PST information held in the file share to ensure that the files cannot be opened by unauthorized clients. Remember, unlike an OST file that can only be opened when a client has knowledge of the mailbox that owns the replica folders inside the OST, any MAPI client can open a PST file. In addition, the presence of a password on a PST does not guarantee its security because there are many utilities available on the Internet that can crack a PST open in a matter of seconds.

Adding to the planning difficulties, before you can start to import anything, you need to understand how much data you're actually going to have to deal with because this knowledge is required to understand the following:

- The resulting size of the mailbox databases after PSTs have been imported

- The quotas you have to set on primary and archive mailboxes to allow the import to occur

INSIDE OUT   Not all information about PSTs is available or reliable

Gathering this information is a challenge because you rely on users to provide you with details such as the number and the size of the PSTs that they currently use. It's hard to scan for this information because PSTs are often inaccessible to centralized tools because they are located on disks installed in workstations or laptops that might not even be connected to the company network. For example, laptops that only sporadically connect to the company local area network (LAN) when frequent travelers are in the office might hold lots of PST information that is invisible to administrators.

Another issue to consider is what data should be imported into online mailboxes or personal archives. You might not want to import everything from user PSTs because some of it is personal and not covered by company data protection guidelines. Some data might simply be too old to worry about. Data protection guidelines often require employees to delete information after a specified period unless it needs to be retained for some reason, such as an impending lawsuit, so a survey of PSTs is a good opportunity to remind users that they should remove any unwanted information from PSTs before they proceed to import data into an online mailbox. Some companies encourage users to delete any PST more than two or three years old and follow this up by implementing blocks to prevent Outlook access to PSTs after the data migration is complete. See the section "Importing into a personal archive" later in this chapter for more information.

Microsoft doesn't have a tool to scan for PSTs on a PC and then import the PSTs that it discovers into mailboxes that match the names of the PSTs or follow some directives contained in a control file. It is possible that the third-party software vendors that already offer tools in this space will recognize the market opportunity that exists to help companies move from a PST-centric environment to online archives and create programs to scan, report, and migrate PST data based on the new import/export cmdlets. Although such a utility seems like a good idea, you might end up importing an immense amount of rubbish into your brand new online archive and have to take on the task of maintaining those data from then on. Once in the archive, it's unlikely that users will spend much time cleaning out old and unwanted material unless they are forced to do so. It is possible that third parties will generate tools that are smarter about how they search for PSTs and extract information to load into the archive.

Importing mailbox data with EMS

To gain a better understanding of what happens when you create a mailbox import request, we need to review how to manage the entire process using EMS. To begin our examples, we can use the New-MailboxImportRequest cmdlet to create a new mailbox import request. For example:

```
New-MailboxImportRequest –Mailbox JSmith –FilePath '\\Exserver1\Imports
\JSmith-Outlook.pst' –Name 'PSTfrom2007' –ConflictResolutionOption KeepLatestItem
–BadItemLimit 5
```

This command creates a new import request for the JSmith mailbox and identifies that the source PST is located on a file share on the ExServer1 server. Once created, the import request is queued and will be processed by the first MRS instance in the site to become aware of the job (you can force a specific MRS to process the request by passing its FQDN in the –*MRSServer* parameter).

By default, Exchange checks for duplicate items when it imports data into a mailbox and doesn't create a copy of an item if it already exists in the target mailbox (the message identifier is used to detect duplicates). In this case, the –*ConfictResolutionOption* parameter specifies that if a duplicate is detected during the import Exchange should keep the latest version of the item. The other options are KeepAll (keep all versions) and KeepSourceItem (keep the version of the item from the import PST).

You can also see that a unique name is provided for the import request. This is an optional parameter and if you don't provide a name, Exchange will use the default *MailboxImport*. If you create multiple import requests for a mailbox, Exchange will use names such as *MailboxImport1, MailboxImport2, MailboxImport3*, and so on to uniquely identify each import operation. The mailbox name and the request name are combined and used to retrieve information about the import request.

Running multiple concurrent imports

Assigning a specific name to an import request becomes important if you want to run multiple concurrent imports for the same mailbox, each of which processes data from a different PST (you can't run concurrent imports from the same PST). In this scenario, the default names assigned by Exchange will work perfectly well, but it's easier to track the progress of each job and troubleshoot any errors that occur if you assign more meaningful names such as the name of the source PST.

You don't have to import everything in a PST because the *–ExcludeFolders* and *–IncludeFolders* parameters allow you to control exactly what folders are imported by Exchange. For example, to import just a few named folders, we can pass their names as follows:

```
-IncludeFolders "Project A", "Project B", "Project C"
```

If you want to include all of the folders under a specific root folder, you would pass the name of the root folder as follows:

```
-IncludeFolders "Projects/*"
```

And if you have to navigate to a specific folder deep in the folder hierarchy, you can pass its name like this:

```
-IncludeFolders "Projects/2010/Secret Project A"
```

PSTs often contain items known as associated items. These are hidden items that are used by Outlook to store data such as rules, forms, and views. Exchange does not import associated items unless you instruct it to do so by setting the *–AssociatedMessagesCopyOption* parameter to Copy. In most cases, you can avoid copying associated items from a PST, because an equivalent associated item might exist in the mailbox. One exception might be when you know that these items include forms required by an application that do not exist in the mailbox.

Retrieving information about import jobs

In the next set of examples, you can see how the name assigned to the import request is combined with the mailbox identifier to retrieve information about a specific import request with which to work:

```
Get-MailboxImportRequest -Identity 'JSmith\PSTfrom2007'
```

The Get-MailboxImportRequest cmdlet supports a number of parameters to allow you to retrieve the status of different groups of jobs.

- The *–BatchName* parameter fetches details of all requests that belong to a named batch.

- The *–Database* parameter fetches details of all requests belonging to mailboxes in a named database.

- The *–Status* parameter fetches details of all requests with a specified status. Valid status codes include Completed, InProgress, Queued, CompletedWithWarning, Suspended, and Failed.

To report the progress of an import, you can use the Get-MailboxImportRequestStatistics cmdlet to discover how much data has been transferred. Initially, you'll see that MRS creates the folder hierarchy in the target mailbox to accept the imported data and then observe an increasing count of transferred items as MRS moves data from the PST into the mailbox. For example:

```
Get-MailboxImportRequestStatistics –Identity 'JSmith\PSTfrom2007' | Format-List
```

A lot of information is revealed by Get-MailboxImportRequestStatistics, so it's a good idea to reduce the properties returned to reveal the essential data about the import operation. Here's what I normally use:

```
Get-MailboxImportRequestStatistics –Identity 'JSmith\PSTfrom2007'| Select Name,
Status, StatusDetail, BytesTransferred, ItemsTransferred, EstimatedTransferItemCount,
BytesTransferredPerMinute
```

```
Name                          : Import 1
Status                        : InProgress
StatusDetail                  : CopyingMessages
BytesTransferred              : 191.6 MB (200,929,681 bytes)
ItemsTransferred              : 2346
EstimatedTransferItemCount    : 4233
BytesTransferredPerMinute     : 75.82 MB (79,505,066 bytes)
```

When the import finishes, you can retrieve a report of everything that MRS did to populate the mailbox with data from the PST with the Get-MailboxImportRequestStatistics cmdlet. Here's how:

```
Get-MailboxImportRequestStatistics –Identity 'JSmith\PSTfrom2007' –IncludeReport |
Format-List
```

The report is dumped to screen, but it is more convenient, contains a lot more information, and is easier to read by piping the output to a text file. The mailbox import report is divided into summary information at the start of the report, followed by detailed information about the processing of each folder from the source PST into the target mailbox. The following example illustrates the typical summary information about a mailbox import. The important information we can see here includes the following:

- The name of the source PST

- The name of the target mailbox and the database where it is located

- The current status of the job (completed, with no warnings)

- The number of bad items encountered during processing (three, below the five-item limit)

- The start and end time for the job and the name of the MRS that processed the job

- The total number of items transferred from the PST into the mailbox and their size

- Whether any folders were explicitly excluded or included

```
Name                          : PSTfrom2007
Status                        : Completed
StatusDetail                  : Completed
SyncStage                     : SyncFinished
Flags                         : IntraOrg, Pull
RequestStyle                  : IntraOrg
Direction                     : Pull
Protect                       : False
Suspend                       : False
FilePath                      : \\exserver1\psts\2007Files.pst
SourceRootFolder              :
SourceVersion                 : Version 0.0 (Build 0.0)
TargetAlias                   : KAkers
TargetIsArchive               : False
TargetExchangeGuid            : 1647709e-61ac-4447-868a-3c8b3bae9839
TargetRootFolder              :
TargetVersion                 : Version 14.1 (Build 160.0)
TargetDatabase                : DB2
TargetMailboxIdentity         : contoso.com/Exchange Users/Smith, John
IncludeFolders                : {}
ExcludeFolders                : {}
ExcludeDumpster               : False
ConflictResolutionOption      : KeepSourceItem
AssociatedMessagesCopyOption  : DoNotCopy
BadItemLimit                  : 5
BadItemsEncountered           : 3
QueuedTimestamp               : 07/05/2010 10:22:10
StartTimestamp                : 07/05/2010 10:22:27
LastUpdateTimestamp           : 07/05/2010 10:37:19
CompletionTimestamp           : 07/05/2010 10:37:19
OverallDuration               : 00:15:09
TotalQueuedDuration           : 00:00:14
TotalInProgressDuration       : 00:14:54
MRSServerName                 : ExServer1.contoso.com
EstimatedTransferSize         : 793.6 MB (832,132,254 bytes)
EstimatedTransferItemCount    : 7450
BytesTransferred              : 1.059 GB (1,137,129,648 bytes)
ItemsTransferred              : 7381
PercentComplete               : 100
```

Our import job encountered some bad items, those that Exchange cannot process for some reason. They could be corrupt or missing some properties that Exchange requires. You can discover details about the bad items by examining the details captured in the import report. The following example shows details reported about a bad item. We can see that it's a reasonably old Microsoft Word document that was first created in a mailbox on an Exchange 4.0 server in August 1996! Apart from its age, there's no apparent reason why this item was deemed bad. To resolve the issue, we can tell the user what items were not processed and ask him to drag and drop these items from the PST into the mailbox if he wants to retain them.

```
07/05/2010 10:36:53 [ExServer1] A corrupted item was encountered during the move operation. It wasn't
copied to the destination mailbox. <baditem errorCode="0x80004005" flags
                ="0x00000000" id="00000000DDFE4E2FABD06C45B4C0A2406BDEBD0E244D2100">
                <folder id="00000000DDFE4E2FABD06C45B4C0A2406BDEBD0EC2870000">
</folder>
                <sender>Tony Redmond</sender>
                <recipient></recipient>
                <subject>The case for SMTP and MIME</subject>
                <messageClass>IPM.Document.Word.Document.6</messageClass>
                <size>59562</size>
                <dateSent>08/23/1996 11:10:47</dateSent>
                <dateReceived>08/23/1996 11:10:47</dateReceived>
                <errorMessage>MapiExceptionCallFailed:
IExchangeFastTransferEx.TransferBuffer failed
                (hr=0x80004005, ec=-2147467259)
                Diagnostic context:
                    Lid: 18969   EcDoRpcExt2 called [length=16476]
                    Lid: 27161   EcDoRpcExt2 returned [ec=0x0][length=71][latency=0]
                    Lid: 23226   --- ROP Parse Start ---
                    Lid: 27962   ROP: ropFXDstCopyConfig [83]
                    Lid: 27962   ROP: ropFXDstPutBufferEx [157]
                    Lid: 17082   ROP Error: 0x80004005
                    Lid: 31329
                    Lid: 21921   StoreEc: 0x80004005
                    Lid: 31418   --- ROP Parse Done ---
                    Lid: 22753
                    Lid: 21817   ROP Failure: 0x80004005
                    Lid: 22630   </errorMessage>
                </baditem>
```

If you want to cancel an import operation, first suspend the import request and then remove it. For example:

```
Suspend-MailboxImportRequest –Identity 'JSmith\PSTfrom2007'
Remove-MailboxImportRequest –Identity 'JSmith\PSTfrom2007'
```

> ## Importing into a personal archive
>
> If a mailbox has a personal archive, you can import PST data directly into the archive without going through the primary mailbox. This is an important functionality because the personal archive is the natural storage location for much of the information that users hold in PST files.
>
> To import PST data into a personal archive, you must specify the *–IsArchive* parameter when you create the import request with the New-MailboxImportRequest cmdlet. For example:
>
> ```
> New-MailboxImportRequest -Mailbox 'Tony Redmond' -IsArchive -FilePath
> '\\ExServer1\ImportData\TR.PST' -Name 'Import-Archive'
> ```
>
> The import request will fail if the mailbox does not own a personal archive.

Exporting mailbox data

There are many circumstances that cause an administrator to need to export information from a mailbox. One example is where a user is transferring responsibility for a project to someone else and wants to provide all the information about the project to that person. For anything but a few items, it would be too onerous and boring to email each item, so it's more convenient to be able to export a complete set of items to a PST. Of course, users can export information to a PST by dragging and dropping the items, but this can be time consuming if there are hundreds of items to transfer. Further problems can then occur if the two users are not in the same geographic location. It's just easier if an administrator (or even better, a help desk representative) can do the work from a central point. Another reasonably common situation is where a company has to provide mailbox data to lawyers as the result of a subpoena.

Exporting mailbox data with EMS

A similar approach is followed to export data from mailboxes on Exchange 2010 SP1 servers as described for import operations, except that we use a different set of cmdlets. We start with the New-MailboxExportRequest to create a new export request. For example, to export a complete mailbox to a PST, you might use a command like this:

```
New-MailboxExportRequest -Mailbox 'Jeff Smith' -Name 'JSmith Export' -BadItemLimit 5
-ExcludeDumpster:$True -FilePath '\\ExServer1\PST\JSmith.PST'
```

This command takes all of the content from the nominated mailbox and writes it out to a PST in the file share location. The contents of the dumpster folders are excluded from the operation. If the PST is not present, Exchange will create a new file; otherwise, if you pass the name of an existing PST, it will write the exported data into it.

Experience demonstrates that it is more common to apply qualifiers to restrict the information exported from a mailbox than it is when you import a PST into a mailbox. Exchange provides a number of parameters to control which information is exported to a PST.

- The –*SourceRootFolder* parameter specifies a folder in the mailbox to use as the base of the export. If this parameter is not passed, Exchange exports the complete content of the mailbox. For example, this command exports only the items that are stored in the Project Athena folder and any of its subfolders. In this instance, the Project Athena folder is a subfolder of the Projects folder.

  ```
  New-MailboxExportRequest –SourceRootFolder 'Projects/Project Athena'
  ```

- The –*TargetRootFolder* parameter specifies a root folder in the target PST to create the folders exported from the mailbox.

- The –*IncludeFolders* parameter specifies one or more folders that are to be exported. For example:

  ```
  New-MailboxExportRequest –IncludeFolders 'Projects', 'Planning/Budgets'
  ```

- The –*ExcludeFolders* parameter specifies one or more folders that are excluded from the export.

- The –*IsArchive* parameter specifies that the export should be done from the user's personal archive rather than the primary mailbox.

Just like import requests, you can trace the status of an export request and fetch information about the work that it is doing. The Get-MailboxExportRequest cmdlet returns the current status of a request to allow you to see it moving from Queued to InProgress to Completed (or to Failed if MRS encounters a problem). For example, we'd use the following command to retrieve the current status of the export request that we created previously:

```
Get-MailboxExportRequest –Identity 'Jeff Smith\JSmith Export'
```

The Get-MailboxExportRequestStatistics cmdlet returns detailed information about an export request. For example, this command fetches slightly different information than the data returned from the example used for an import request:

```
Get-MailboxExportRequestStatistics –Identity 'Jeff Smith\JSmith Export' | Select
Name, Status, StatusDetail, EstimatedTransferSize, EstimatedTransferItemCount,
BytesTransferred, ItemsTransferred, PercentComplete
```

```
Name                           : JSmith Export
Status                         : InProgress
StatusDetail                   : CopyingMessages
EstimatedTransferSize          : 85.24 MB (89,379,213 bytes)
EstimatedTransferItemCount     : 1091
BytesTransferred               : 34.53 MB (36,207,996 bytes)
ItemsTransferred               : 342
PercentComplete                : 41
```

At the end of a job, you can use the *–IncludeReport* parameter to fetch a complete narrative of the export operations.

```
Get-MailboxExportRequestStatistics –Identity 'Jeff Smith\JSmith Export'
–IncludeReport | Format-List
```

As with import requests, the amount of information provided by Exchange about an export to a PST is too much to be viewed comfortably on screen, so it's best to pipe the output from this command to a text file to allow a more leisurely review of the data.

Just like mailbox move requests, it's possible that Exchange will encounter a problem with a corrupt item in a mailbox and won't be able to write it into the PST. The *–BadItemLimit* parameter governs what happens next. If you don't set a value for *–BadItemLimit* when you create the export request, Exchange will abort the export operation after it encounters one corrupt item. The export request is then in a Failed status. To determine what happened, use the Get-MailboxExportRequestStatistics cmdlet to generate a full report and then search the report for errors such as "A bad item was encountered during the move operation." This will tell you exactly which item caused the problem. You could delete the offending item from the source mailbox or you could leave it in place and resume the export from the point at which it failed. To do this, first set a higher tolerance for corrupt items and then resume the export request. For example:

```
Set-MailboxExportRequest -Identity 'Jeff Smith\JSmith Export' –BadItemLimit 10
Resume-MailboxExportRequest -Identity 'Jeff Smith\JSmith Export'
```

Limiting user access to PSTs

Moving data from user PSTs into an enlarged primary mailbox or into a personal archive accomplishes the business goal of making all items available to index and discoverable by Exchange, but it's only a partial solution. Unless you prevent users from putting future items in PSTs, you will end up in a half-and-half situation where some data are online and available and some remain under user control. Even the strongest corporate edict to stop using PSTs will only be respected by some users. Others are likely to ignore it and need some help to do the right thing. You can take the following steps to discourage the use of PSTs.

1. Delete or remove PSTs to a location where they are inaccessible to users after their contents are imported into online mailboxes.

2. Create a new group policy to stop users from adding new content to existing PSTs. Users quickly become frustrated when Outlook reports that they don't have the permission to move items into a PST, including a newly created PST. As shown in Table 12-3, the group policy needs to create a new subkey and set its value to 1.

3. Create a new group policy to disable the AutoArchive menu in Outlook and remove any prompt from Outlook to encourage users to move items from their mailbox into an archive PST (they should keep data in their enlarged primary mailbox or use an archive mailbox instead). In this case, we need to create the six new subkeys listed in Table 12-3 and set all values to 1.

4. Create a new group policy to prevent users from being able to create new PSTs by removing the Outlook Data File option. In this case, set the value of the registry subkey to 5575 for Outlook 2007.

5. All of these registry subkeys are DWORD values and are specific to a version of Outlook. To determine the correct value to use, substitute *xx* with 11 for Outlook 2003 and 12 for Outlook 2007.

For more information on customizing Outlook 2007 with administrative template files, see *http://www.microsoft.com/downloads/en/details.aspx?FamilyID=92d8519a-e143-4aee-8f7a -e4bbaeba13e7&displaylang=en.*

Table 12-3 **Registry values to control PST access (Outlook 2003 and Outlook 2007)**

Function	Registry subkey
Prevent new data from being added to PST	HKCU/Software/Microsoft/Office/*xx*/Outlook/PST/PstDisableGrow
Disable archive option	HKCU/Software/Policies/Microsoft/Office/*xx*/Outlook/Preferences/ ArchiveDelete
Disable archive option	HKCU/Software/Policies/Microsoft/Office/*xx*/Outlook/Preferences /ArchiveMount
Disable archive option	HKCU/Software/Policies/Microsoft/Office/*xx*/Outlook/Preferences /ArchiveOld
Disable archive option	HKCU/Software/Policies/Microsoft/Office/*xx*/Outlook/Preferences /DeleteExpired
Disable archive option	HKCU/Software/Policies/Microsoft/Office/*xx*/Outlook/Preferences /DoAging

| Disable archive option | HKCU/Software/Policies/Microsoft/Office/*xx*/Outlook/Preferences /PromptForAging |
| Disable Outlook Data File option | HKCU/Software/Policies/Microsoft/Office/*xx*/Outlook /DisableCmdBarItemsList/TCID1 |

Because it was designed in conjunction with Exchange 2010, Outlook 2010 is smarter about blocking access to PSTs. A single registry setting controls the ability of users to move data from primary or archive mailboxes into a PST. Create a new multistring value called *DisableCrossAccountCopy* at HKCU\Software\Microsoft\Office\14.0\Outlook. The value holds the Simple Mail Transfer Protocol (SMTP) domain names of messages that you don't want users to move into a PST. You could use the name of your company's domain, in which case Outlook will prevent the movement of any work-related messages into a PST while allowing the user to move messages sent using another service (such as Hotmail). If you want to stop the movement of all messages generated from any account, input * (the asterisk character). A suitable block to stop movement of items originating from contoso. com is shown in the top part of Figure 12-10; the error message seen by users is shown at the bottom.

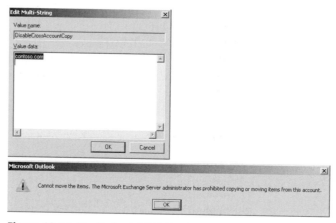

Figure 12-10 The Outlook 2010 block to prevent users from moving email from specific domains into PSTs.

MailTips and group metrics

All of us have stories about an unbelievable but all too common mistake that we have made with email. Maybe you sent a message to the wrong user containing sensitive or other information that they shouldn't have received, or answered a note where you were blind carbon copied and caused the original sender trouble when the other recipients realized that you were copied. Microsoft refers to situations like this as "unfortunate messaging scenarios," whereas administrators might use slightly more robust terms to describe the result of user mistakes that cause system performance to suffer, mail queues to accumulate, or lots of calls to flow to the help desk. It's unfortunate, but humans make mistakes all the time.

Early email systems operated on a simple "send and forget" principle. You dispatched messages into the void and hoped that they'd arrive. As time went by, features such as Out of Office notices (OOF in Microsoft parlance), delivery and read receipts, and nondelivery notifications were incorporated to give users feedback about what happened to their messages after they were sent. Exchange 2010 introduces a variation on that theme with a feature called delivery reports, which allows users to see the path of a message within an Exchange organization, including the expansion of distribution groups into individual members to receive the message, delivery to servers, and delivery to external connectors for transmission to other email systems. However, worthy as these features are, they are all "after the fact." Messages have to be sent before users can be informed that the message has been delivered, that someone is out of the office, or that their email won't be delivered because a recipient's mailbox quota is exceeded.

Enter MailTips, a new feature implemented as an Exchange 2010 Web service and designed to provide users with feedback about common problems before a message is sent. The idea is that warning users that messages might not be delivered or read will make users more productive and less likely to call the help desk to complain that their emails didn't arrive. It will also reduce system resources by eliminating the need to process messages that will fail. Microsoft hopes that MailTips will help people use email more intelligently. The feature works well even if it is only supported by OWA 2010 and Outlook 2010 when connected to an Exchange 2010 mailbox.

MailTips operate on a mixture of data originating from the following sources:

- Active Directory (for example, whether or not a recipient is restricted, and the maximum size of attachments supported by the organization)

- Information Store (mailbox quotas, out of office notices, custom MailTips)

- Group metrics (metadata generated by the CAS, including the total number of recipients and the number of external recipients in a group)

The group metrics data are stored in a cache on Exchange 2010 CAS servers. If MailTips are configured for an organization, on Sunday (you cannot change the day that this operation occurs), the Group Metrics service executes within the Microsoft Service Host process on every mailbox server that is configured to generate group metrics data to count the number of recipients in every group in the organization, including dynamic distribution groups. On the other days of the week, the service generates incremental data for the number of recipients in groups that have been added or changed (event 14024 is logged when this happens). The reason why Offline Address Book (OAB) servers generate group metrics data is that some MailTips data (including group metrics) are distributed with the OAB, so it's obviously necessary to generate the data before it can be included in the OAB.

Exchange automatically configures mailbox servers that generate the OAB to generate group metrics data. Servers other than those that generate the OAB can also be used to produce the group metrics data. Although this won't be important for small organizations, because they likely only need to use the server that generates the OAB for this purpose, larger organizations might want to spread the load, especially if they have highly distributed sites that have limited network connectivity. You cannot control the generation of group metrics data or change its schedule with EMC. Instead, you use the Set-MailboxServer cmdlet. For example, to enable group metrics generation on a server:

```
Set-MailboxServer -Identity ExServer1 -GroupMetricsGenerationEnabled $True
```

The value of this property on a server that generates the OAB is $False unless you change it to $True. The fact that the server generates the OAB overrides the need to enable group metrics generation.

> **Note**
>
> If the server that generates the OAB runs Exchange 2007, you will have to configure another mailbox server to generate group metrics, because Exchange 2007 servers know nothing about group metrics.

When you configure a mailbox server to generate group metrics data, it is added to a list held in Active Directory. The Exchange File Distribution service running on CAS servers queries Active Directory to retrieve the list of mailbox servers that generate group metrics data and copies the data from the closest mailbox server every eight hours. Figure 12-11 shows the contents of the group metrics folder on a mailbox server. The .bin file contains all the data about groups and is named after the date and time when it was generated. The .xml file is used by the Exchange File Distribution service and points to the .bin file that has to be distributed to CAS servers.

By default, Exchange generates group metrics data at a random time within two hours of midnight, but you can set it to occur at a specific time. For example, to generate the data at 21:45:

```
Set-MailboxServer -Identity ExServer1 -GroupMetricsGenerationTime 21:45
```

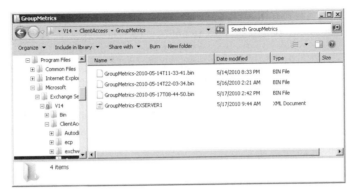

Figure 12-11 Group metrics data.

Client interaction

MailTips-enabled clients request data when a user adds a recipient or attachment to a message or uses the Reply or Reply All command to respond to a message. MailTips are also processed when a draft message is opened. These actions cause the client to invoke a background thread to query the MailTips Web service on a CAS server in the local site and determine whether there are any MailTips that apply to the message. The URL for the MailTips Web service is returned by the CAS server to the client as part of the Autodiscover manifest.

The CAS server is responsible for gathering data from Active Directory and the local group metric cache and responding to the client with applicable data. It also contacts the mailbox servers that host recipient mailboxes to fetch information about mailbox quotas and out of office notices. If some of the mailbox servers are outside the local site, the CAS proxies a request to fetch the data to a CAS server running in the site that hosts the mailboxes.

> **Note**
>
> To avoid unacceptably slow responsiveness, if the CAS is unable to respond to clients within 10 seconds the request will time out and the client proceeds without MailTip data. It's also important to know that you do not have to wait for MailTips processing to finish before you are able to send a message. If MailTips hasn't responded and you need to get the message to its recipients, you can click Send and the message will go without further notice.

To limit the amount of communication with the CAS, Outlook and OWA clients both maintain client-side caches that are populated as messages are processed. For example, if you attempt to send a message containing a very large attachment, the client will check its cache to discover if it exceeds the maximum message size for the organization. If the data are not in the cache, the client retrieves them from the appropriate source (in this case, Exchange configuration data in Active Directory) and caches it locally for future reference. Cached information is aged out of the cache after 24 hours, with the exception of mailbox full and out of office notices, which are likely to change more often and therefore age out after two hours. The MailTips settings used for OWA are contained in the Web.config.xml configuration file. It is possible, but not recommended, to change the cache aging limit and the number of items held in the cache by editing this file. Client-side caches are not persistent and are cleared whenever you exit Outlook or OWA.

Configuring MailTips

From an administrator perspective, the immediate value of MailTips is that they eliminate many of the reasons Exchange has to generate nondelivery reports (for example, destination mailbox is full, message size is too large) and so reduce the strain on the messaging infrastructure. On the downside, the processing required to service client requests for MailTip, data creates an extra load on CAS servers, which Microsoft characterizes as an increase of approximately 5 percent.

All of the management for MailTips is done through EMS. Exchange administrators can configure MailTips on or off, but only at the organization level, by using the Set-OrganizationConfig cmdlet to set the parameters that control MailTips processing. These parameters are as follows:

- *–MailTipsAllTipsEnabled*: Controls whether MailTips are enabled. The default is $True.

- *–MailTipsExternalRecipientTipsEnabled*: Controls whether MailTips for external recipients are enabled. The default is $False. External recipients are determined by reference to the accepted domains list. Any domain in this list is deemed to be internal, whereas any other domain is deemed to be external.

- *–MailTipsGroupMetricsEnabled*: Controls whether MailTips that depend on group sizes are enabled. The default is $True.

- *–MailTipsLargeAudienceThreshold*: Controls the threshold for the number of recipients on a message before MailTips flags it as large. The default value is 25. This value is probably too low for large organizations where big distribution groups are common. In this scenario, it makes sense to increase the value to 50 to stop MailTips from nagging users for no good reason.

- *–MailTipsMailboxSourcedTipsEnabled*: Controls whether MailTips that depend on mailbox data such as out of office notices are enabled. The default is $True.

Table 12-4 lists the common conditions under which MailTips are useful. As you can see, in most cases a MailTip stops a user from doing something that causes frustration (the user's message doesn't get through) or reduces traffic for Exchange (removing the need for nondelivery notifications caused by messages that cannot be processed). Warning users about sending very large distributions is very useful because it is all too easy for a user to address a note to a distribution that she doesn't realize will cause Exchange to deliver the message to thousands of mailboxes. People who receive the message can cause a mail storm by using Reply All to generate a response that goes to everyone and provokes even more responses. The net result is usually a hub transport server that's swamped with traffic, the accumulation of large message queues, and slow delivery of other mail. MailTips won't remove the need for user intelligence, but they can give a hint at appropriate times to stop someone from doing something that he wishes he hadn't.

Table 12-4 **Types of MailTips**

Potential problem	Action
Recipient won't process new email because she is out of the office	If an OOF notice is set for a mailbox, you'll be told that the recipient is away and have the choice to remove her from the message. MailTips displays the first 250 characters of the OOF.
Message addressed to a very large distribution	If you address a message to a group that will result in delivery to more recipients than the large audience size configured for the organization, MailTips tells you how many people will receive the message (per group and in total). Duplicate addressees are not removed, so the overall total might be a little higher than the actual number of messages that are generated, but it's a good guide to stop users from sending messages that result in hundreds of deliveries. Exchange does not attempt to process individual MailTips for messages that are addressed to more than 200 recipients, because this would impose an unacceptable performance overhead on the CAS. For the same reason, when you address a message to a distribution group, Exchange does not evaluate individual MailTips for the members of the group. The exception is that Exchange will show the number of external recipients if there are any in the group.
Message addressed to a nonexistent addressee	Messages can linger in user mailboxes for a long time and might contain addresses that are no longer valid because a recipient has left the company. Invalid addresses can also persist in Outlook's autocomplete list. MailTips detects this condition and lets the user remove the obsolete recipient before sending the message and thereby stops the inevitable nondelivery notification that otherwise results.
Message addressed to an external recipient	If a message is addressed to someone outside the organization or a group that contains an external recipient, MailTips warns the user in case the message contains confidential company information.
Reply to BCC	If you reply to a message where you were on the BCC list, MailTips prompts you that you were BCCd and that if you reply the other recipients will know you received the original message.

Oversized message	If you attempt to send a message that exceeds the maximum message size for the organization or for one of the message recipients, MailTips tells you that Exchange won't deliver the message. Of course, MailTips can't warn you that an external organization will have problems with a message of a certain size.
Message addressed to a moderated group	Messages sent to a moderated group have to be approved by the moderator, so MailTips warns you that there could be a delay before the message is approved. Moderators of the group or anyone explicitly allowed to receive messages addressed to the group do not see this MailTip.
Message addressed to a restricted recipient	Administrators can configure mailboxes and groups so that only certain users can send them messages. If you attempt to send to one of these recipients, MailTips warns you that your message won't be accepted.
Custom MailTips	Administrators and group owners can configure custom MailTips, including the ability to localize the text so that users see the MailTip in their own language. For example, you might want to set up a MailTip for a mailbox used for human resources queries so that users know that any message sent to the mailbox will be dealt with within 24 hours. A recipient's custom MailTip is not displayed if a user does not have the right to send to the recipient.

User experience

Figure 12-12 provides a good illustration of what a user will see if MailTips are configured when he composes a message using OWA. In this case, three conditions have been detected. The user is not allowed to send to the Sales Executives group, so he gets the option to remove the recipient; the number of recipients in the message header exceeds the value of the "large audience" limit as determined in the organization configuration (the default is 25), so the user has the opportunity to consider whether he really wants to send the message; and custom MailTips are displayed for a mailbox.

> **Note**
>
> The exclamation mark shown in the Infobar is red. The user can hide all these warnings by clicking it—the equivalent of the user telling OWA that she really knows what she is doing.

Outlook 2010 is the other client that supports MailTips. If configured in cached Exchange mode, Outlook depends on details of MailTips that are held alongside other recipient attributes in the OAB. However, when it is configured to work online, Outlook fetches MailTips data in the same way as OWA does. In Figure 12-13, you can see that Outlook presents a slightly different view of MailTips to the user. In this case, we have addressed the message to the same three recipients as our previous example. Outlook displays that we can't send a message to the Sales Executives group and also displays the name of the group in a lighter color than the Exchange 2010 Interest List. We can also see the MailTip displayed for the individual EMEA Help Desk mailbox.

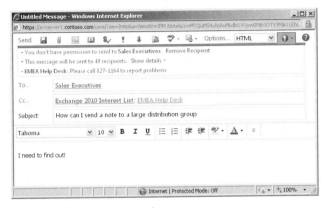

Figure 12-12 MailTips in action.

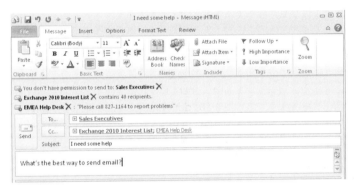

Figure 12-13 Outlook 2010 and MailTips.

However, there's no sign of the warning that we are sending to 50 recipients! This is because Outlook allows a user to configure the MailTips that she wants to see (Figure 12-14), whether to have the MailTips bar available at all times, and whether to expand the MailTips bar if multiple tips are available. OWA does not include any user interface to configure MailTips.

However, if you click the button in the toolbar to collapse the Infobar that contains the MailTips, OWA saves the state across sessions and MailTips will not be revealed again until the user decides to reveal the Infobar again. Behind the scenes, OWA continues to check for MailTips and will change the color of the button to indicate when some MailTips information is available for review. You cannot manipulate the MailTips settings for a mailbox through EMC or EMS.

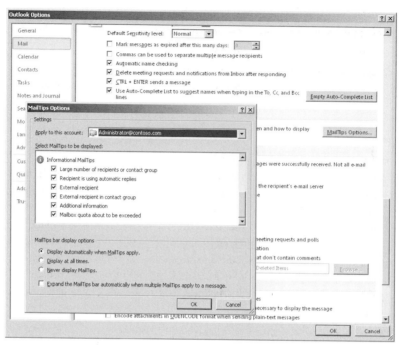

Figure 12-14 The MailTips options available to Outlook 2010.

Custom MailTips

You can add a custom MailTip to any mail-enabled object. Most commonly, this is done for mailboxes that are not monitored, to notify users that their message might not be responded to quickly; to moderated addresses; to restricted distribution groups (including dynamic groups) that don't accept messages from users who aren't on an approved list; and to provide some guidance to users when they send to special mailboxes—such as those used by help desks—to set expectations about when the sender might expect a response. Custom MailTips can be up to 250 characters.

Custom MailTips are configured in exactly the same way as any other property for a mail-enabled object. For example, to create a MailTip for a mailbox, you use the Set-Mailbox cmdlet.

```
Set-Mailbox -Identity 'Help Desk' -MailTip 'Messages to the Help Desk are handled on
a best-effort basis; please call 91184 if you need urgent support'
```

Use the same approach for a distribution group:

```
Set-DistributionGroup -Identity 'Sales' -MailTop 'Only members of the Sales
Executives group can send to this address'
```

MailTips support HTML content. This is useful when you want to include a URL to point users to more information. For example, messages sent to the help desk might include a URL to allow users to log a support call:

```
Set-Mailbox -Identity 'Help Desk' -MailTip 'Please visit the Help Desk site
<A href = "http://help-desk-support.contoso.com" </A> to log a support call'
```

INSIDE OUT   What you cannot do

You cannot edit a MailTip. Instead, you overwrite it with new text. Exchange 2010 only supports simple text in a custom MailTip, meaning that you can't incorporate any form of rule in the MailTip to control when a client might display the MailTip. For example, you can't create a MailTip that scans the message text for a matching pattern such as a Social Security number or even a simple term such as the name of a critical project. In some ways, Exchange 2010 marks the beginning of the ability to offer proactive advice to users to help them use email more efficiently, and it wouldn't be surprising if Microsoft introduced additional rule-based processing capabilities for MailTips in a future version of Exchange.

MailTips are stored as properties of the mailbox in Active Directory. The CAS reads the data hourly, so any change that you make to a custom MailTip can take up to an hour before it is effective. The only way to force a change to become effective earlier is to recycle Microsoft Internet Information Services (IIS), which is difficult in a production environment.

Multilingual custom MailTips

Exchange 2010 accommodates multilingual organizations by allowing you to create custom MailTips in all of the languages you need to support. This is a little more complex than setting a simple MailTip in one language, because you need to first determine the list of languages, translate the string into appropriate text for each language, and then populate the array of translations using the *–MailTipTranslations* parameter for each of the Set-Mailbox, Set-DistributionGroup, Set-Contact, and Set-MailPublicFolder cmdlets as required. You have to create a default MailTip before or when you add the translated values. The default value is used whenever the language specified for a user mailbox does not match a specific value in the list. In this example, we set translated values for four languages in addition to the English default. Each of the languages is separated by a comma.

```
Set-Mailbox -Identity 'Jacky Chen' -MailTip 'Financial Services Manager'
-MailTipTranslations 'NL: Manager van de financiële Diensten', 'IT: Responsabile
di servizi finanziari', 'FR: Directeur de services financiers', 'ES: Encargado de
los servicios financieros'
```

The translated values are stored in the *MailTipTranslations* property as an array of HTML values. To see the values, type:

```
Get-Mailbox -Identity 'Jacky Chen' | Select MailTip* | Format-List
```

The Offline Address Book

The OAB is a snapshot of the Global Address List (GAL) that Outlook clients can download from Exchange to provide a local directory source for address validation and lookup. All recipients in the GAL except those that are marked with the *Hidden From Address Lists* property are included in the OAB (Figure 12-15). You can discover a list of hidden recipients with the following command:

```
Get-Recipient -Filter {HiddenFromAddressListsEnabled -eq $True}
```

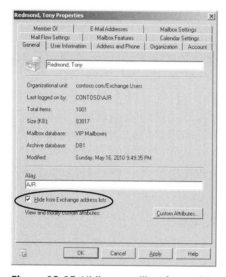

Figure 12-15 Hiding a mailbox from address lists.

Outlook clients need to download a copy of the OAB before they can function fully offline. The OAB contains a subset of the properties held for objects in Active Directory. However, users are seldom aware of this fact because the OAB contains all of the data that they typically need for email or to find recipients. Data that depend on pointers between Active Directory objects are unavailable offline (managers and their reports and group membership are the best examples). The same is true for customized properties that you add to the GAL unless you customize address templates to add them to the OAB.

One problem with the OAB is that new recipients are invisible until Exchange next generates updates for the OAB and clients connect and download and apply the updates to their

OAB. For example, if you add a new mailbox at 11 A.M. on Monday and Exchange generates an OAB update at 4 A.M. on Tuesday, the earliest that a user will see the new mailbox in the GAL is after she downloads the update, which could be the following Thursday or Friday. In reality, this is not usually a problem except when you deal with high-profile users, such as new executives, who want to be visible to the organization as soon as their mailboxes are created. There are two workarounds to the problem. First, you can always use the SMTP address of newly created messages to route email to them. Second, you can use the All Users address list to look for new entries, because this forces Outlook to connect to the server to browse the directory.

OAB download

Outlook clients that are configured in cached Exchange mode download the OAB automatically. The first download occurs after the mailbox folders are replicated to the OST. Thereafter, Outlook checks daily for OAB updates and downloads them from Exchange if available. You cannot vary the daily check, because it is hard-coded into Outlook. In any case, it is a good thing to have an automatic daily update because this keeps the OAB up to date and prevents the situation where the OAB contains a great deal of invalid information because it hasn't been regularly updated.

> **Tip**
> A week-old OAB is usually okay unless the organization is in the middle of a large merger or acquisition or has another reason for directory churn. A month-old OAB is much less satisfactory because of the volume of change that typically occurs in corporate directories.

If an OAB update download fails, Outlook retries hourly until the download succeeds. However, if Outlook needs to fetch a full copy of the OAB, it will only try this operation once in a 13-hour period. Clients can also download the OAB on a demand basis using the Send Receive | Download Address Book option.

You can minimize the amount of data downloaded by selecting No Details, which causes Outlook to download a bare-bones copy of the OAB (basic recipient information and email addresses). These data still allow the OAB to be used to locate recipients and validate email addresses, but this method produces a file that is much less useful than when it contains data, such as phone numbers, that are produced by a Full Details download. Limiting data made sense in an era when networks were less available and slower than they are today. In some respects, the option to download a truncated OAB is of limited use unless you are forced to use something like a dial-up connection.

Like other synchronization operations, Outlook uses a background thread to fetch the OAB files to allow users to continue working while the download proceeds. OAB data used to be made available through a system public folder, but the focus is now on Web-based distribution managed by CAS servers to remove a dependency on public folders. Clients with mailboxes on an Exchange 2010 server have to connect to an Exchange 2010 CAS to fetch OAB files while those with mailboxes on legacy Exchange servers connect to an Exchange 2007 CAS or Exchange public folder server.

After you download the OAB, Outlook creates or updates a set of six files on the PC (Table 12-5). These files vary in size depending on the number of mail-enabled recipients in the organization and can occupy a reasonable amount of space on disk. For example, HP's current OAB requires 383 MB for approximately 450,000 objects, or around 0.85 MB per 1,000 objects. The OAB files and updates are compressed when they are downloaded by Outlook and the compressed files are roughly half the size of the files when they are expanded on disk. However, it can still take a long time to fetch a complete OAB inside a large organization.

Table 12-5 **OAB files**

File	Use
UBrowse.oab	The core index for the OAB. Records contain the object type, display name, and a pointer to the rest of the object's data held in the details file.
UDetails.oab	All of the details (if available) for objects populated through a Full Details download. This is the largest OAB file.
URdndex.oab	An index used to resolve relative distinguished names for recipient objects and to track changes to domain names.
UPdndex.oab	An index for domain names (such as contoso.com).
UAnrdex.oab	An index used to resolve ambiguous names entered by users when addresses are validated.
UTmplts.oab	A file containing language-specific strings used for dialog boxes and any other static items used by OAB templates.

Generally, after the complete OAB is first downloaded, Outlook only needs to refresh it with update files that it fetches from Exchange. These files are generated daily and contain the changes that have occurred since the last update. If Outlook has been offline for several days, it needs to download all of the daily updates that it has missed to update the OAB. A full download is required if Outlook 2003 SP2 (or later) determines that more than a half of the total entries in the GAL have been updated since the last download. Earlier versions of Outlook required a full download when an eighth of the GAL had changed.

Working in a mixed environment

In a mixed environment where Exchange 2003 servers are present, you can provoke a full download for all clients if you add a new administrative group. Other examples of where directory churn might affect a high proportion of OAB records include updating a large number of recipients with new email addresses, changing telephone numbering schemes, moving to a new physical office and updating the office address, and so on. Avoiding the requirement for clients to perform a complete OAB download is important in large organizations where sizable files are involved.

Consider the situation if 10,000 clients had to download 100 MB of OAB data from a single CAS or public folder server. (This is an extreme example to illustrate the point, because no deployment of 10,000 clients would use only a single CAS.) The server has to handle the demand for 1,000 GB of data and could have to do this over a short period, which might stop it from doing much other useful work until the demand for OAB downloads subsides.

For the same reason, it's also a good idea to phase in new versions of Outlook so that you don't create a situation where hundreds of users start up their brand new version of Outlook and immediately begin to synchronize their OST and download the OAB. You can also minimize the impact by providing multiple distribution points for OAB updates by configuring Exchange to distribute the updates to multiple CAS servers (for Web-based distribution) or replicating the OAB public folder to multiple public folder servers.

To offset the potential for server overload, Microsoft uses LZX compression for OAB update files and only distributes binary patches for updated records rather than complete records. Two files are involved. The Data.oab file is a "baseline" file. The Binpatch.oab file is generated daily and contains the differential changes from the previous day (essentially, all the changes in the GAL in the last day). To bring an OAB up to date, Outlook downloads all the versions of Binpatch.oab that correspond to the days since the last update and merges them together into Data.oab. It then generates the new indexes to refresh the OAB. Compression and binary updates are an effective mechanism to manage OAB distribution for all sizes of organizations.

Figure 12-16 shows what you might see if you examine the directory where Exchange holds the OAB files after they are generated. A file called Oab.xml (the OAB manifest) is used to track all of the updates that are available, including the full and differential files, templates used by Windows and Macintosh clients, and metadata such as the compressed and uncompressed file sizes. At the bottom of the list of files you can see Data-24.lzx, the baseline file generated on November 24, 2009. When this file is copied, it becomes Data.oab on the client. The baseline file is generated daily. We can also see the set of daily update files (Binpatch-23.lzx, Binpatch-22.lzx, and so on). A client that has not fetched OAB updates since November 18 would need to copy the set of files from binpatch-19 to binpatch-24 and merge them into Data.oab on the PC to bring its OAB up to date.

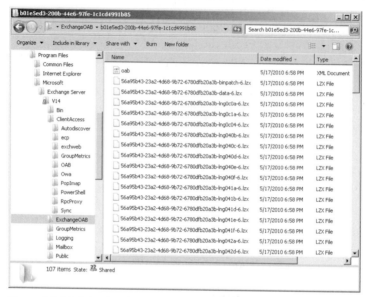

Figure 12-16 OAB data files used for client updates.

When Outlook begins to download the OAB files, it flags this fact as part of its synchronization activity. If you use the Ctrl+Click key combination on the Outlook icon in the system tray to view the client connection status, and then click the Local Mailbox tab, you'll see the OAB download progress.

OAB generation

A specific mailbox server known as the OAB generation server is assigned the responsibility of generating the OAB (the Default Offline Address List) in a job called OABGen that is run as part of the System Attendant process. To generate the OAB, OABGen reads data from Active Directory through Name Service Provider interface (NSPI) queries and creates a set of temporary files that it then compresses and copies to the directory used for Web distribution. If public folder distribution is used, OABGen creates items in the system public folder to hold the OAB updates. One item is used for the full version of the OAB and other items hold the daily difference files.

Usually the server that takes on the OAB generation role is the first mailbox server installed in the organization. To determine which server is currently responsible for OAB generation, go to the Mailbox node under Organization Configuration and then click the Offline Address Book tab. You can then select the Default Offline Address Book and click Properties (Figure 12-17). In this case, we see the following:

- Web-based and public folder distribution methods are enabled. Outlook 2007 and Outlook 2010 clients use Web-based distribution to fetch OAB updates from nominated CAS servers. Outlook 2003 clients access and download the OAB files from a public folder. Web-based distribution occurs from the default OAB Web site. After you decommission the last Outlook 2003 client, you can disable public folder distribution.

- The name of the mailbox server that generates the OAB files daily. If you click the General tab, you can see the schedule used for the generation. The default is to do this at 5 A.M. daily.

- The Address Lists tab specifies the address lists that are included in the OAB. By default, the default OAB is the only address list that is included.

- Exchange is capable of generating OAB files that can be used by different versions of Outlook. In an Exchange 2010–only organization, we really only need the latest version (V4), a Unicode-based version used by Outlook 2003 SP2 and later clients, so we can disable the generation of the V3 version.

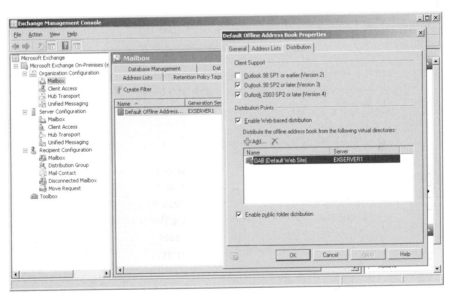

Figure 12-17 Defining how the OAB is distributed to clients.

Naturally, you can manage the OAB generation parameters with EMS. For example, here's how to restrict the versions that are generated to V4 and to disable public folder distribution:

```
Set-OfflineAddressBook -Identity '\Default Offline Address Book'-Versions
'Version4'-PublicFolderDistributionEnabled $False
```

Many interesting details of the OAB are revealed when you use the Get-OfflineAddressBook cmdlet to view OAB properties:

```
Get-OfflineAddressBook -Identity '\Default Offline Address Book' | Format-List
```

```
Server                            : ExServer1
AddressLists                      : {\Default Global Address List}
Versions                          : {Version4}
IsDefault                         : True
PublicFolderDatabase              : PFDatabase1
PublicFolderDistributionEnabled   : False
GlobalWebDistributionEnabled      : False
WebDistributionEnabled            : True
LastTouchedTime                   : 12/3/2009 3:05:42 AM
LastNumberOfRecords               : 455
ConfiguredAttributes              : {OfficeLocation, ANR, ProxyAddresses, ANR,
PhoneticGivenName, ANR, GivenName, ANR, PhoneticSurname, ANR, Surname, ANR, Account, ANR,
PhoneticDisplayName, ANR, DisplayNameUnicode, ANR, ExternalMemberCount, Value,
TotalMemberCount, Value, ModerationEnabled, Value, DelivContLength, Value,
MailTipTranslations, Value, ObjectGuid, Value, IsOrganizational, Value...}
DiffRetentionPeriod               : 30
VirtualDirectories                : {ExServer1\OAB (Default Web Site), ExServer2\OAB
(Default Web Site)}
Identity                          : \Default Offline Address Book
```

The output from the command is edited for clarity, but we can see the following:

- The name of the mailbox server that generates the OAB (ExServer1).

- The address lists included in the OAB. In this case, just the default GAL is included.

- The versions of the OAB that are generated. Because only version 4 is in this OAB, we know that older Outlook clients are not used in the organization.

- The public folder database in which the OAB files are stored and whether public folder distribution is used (it isn't).

- The date and time of the last OAB update.

- The number of records in the OAB (455). This should approximate the number of mailboxes, groups, contacts, and mail-enabled public folders in the organization that are not hidden from address lists.

- The attributes included for each OAB record (configured attributes). Some of these support ambiguous name resolution (ANR), meaning that you can search the OAB based on partial matches of attributes such as Surname and Office name. For example, you can find all of the users in the London office by typing **Lond** into the OAB search dialog box (click the More Columns button to force the OAB to perform more than the default name search). Because it's an ANR search, the OAB will also return users whose surname begins with "Lond." Other attributes contain simple values, such as the MailTips attributes.

- How long (30 days) difference files are kept on the server.

- The virtual directories on servers ExServer1 and ExServer2 that support Web-based distribution of the OAB files.

The list of configured attributes is truncated in this output. To see a complete list, you can do this:

```
$LA = Get-OfflineAddressBook -Identity '\Default Offline Address Book'
$L2 =$LA.ConfiguredAttributes
$L2 | Format-Table -AutoSize
```

Name	Type
OfficeLocation	ANR
ProxyAddresses	ANR
PhoneticGivenName	ANR
GivenName	ANR
PhoneticSurname	ANR
Surname	ANR
Account	ANR
PhoneticDisplayName	ANR
DisplayNameUnicode	ANR
ExternalMember	Value
TotalMemberCount	Value
ModerationEnabled	Value
DelivContLength	Value
MailTipTranslations	Value
ObjectGuid	Value
IsOrganizational	Value
HabSeniorityIndex	Value
DisplayTypeEx	Value
DisplayNamePrintableA	Value
HomeMdbA	Value

```
Certificate                                      Value
UserSMimeCertificate                             Value
UserCertificate                                  Value
Comment                                          Value
PagerTelephoneNumber                             Value
AssistantTelephoneNumber                         Value
MobileTelephoneNumber                            Value
PrimaryFaxNumber                                 Value
otherHomePhone                                   Value
otherTelephone                                   Value
HomeTelephoneNumber                              Value
TargetAddress                                    Value
PhoneticDepartmentName                           Value
DepartmentNameUnicode                            Value
Assistant                                        Value
PhoneticCompanyName                              Value
CompanyName                                      Value
Title                                            Value
Country                                          Value
PostalCode                                       Value
StateOrProvince                                  Value
Locality                                         Value
StreetAddress                                    Value
Initials                                         Value
BusinessTelephoneNumber                          Value
SendRichInfo                                     Value
ObjectType                                       Value
DisplayType                                      Value
RejectMessagesFromDLMembers                      Indicator
AcceptMessagesOnlyFromDLMembers                  Indicator
RejectMessagesFrom                               Indicator
AcceptMessagesOnlyFrom                           Indicator
UmSpokenName                                     Indicator
ThumbnailPhoto                                   Indicator
```

You can customize attributes that are included in an OAB by specifying the desired set with the Set-OfflineAddressBook cmdlet. For example, a really simple OAB that contains just three attributes could be generated as follows:

```
Set-OfflineAddressBook –Identity 'Default Offline Address Book'
–ConfiguredAttributes 'Surname, ANR','GivenName, ANR', 'Account, ANR'
```

Each attribute is defined with its MAPI property name and its type, which must be one of ANR, Value, or Indicator. The correct type for each attribute is listed in the preceding output. If you make a complete mess and want to revert to the default situation, you can do this with:

```
Set-OfflineAddressBook –Identity 'Default Offline Address Book'
–UseDefaultAttributes
```

A small set of attributes are listed to be of type "Indicator." This means that Outlook has to access Active Directory whenever it wants to fetch the attribute data. You might recall from the discussion in Chapter 3, "The Exchange Management Shell," how to use EMS to import a small (sub-10 KB) JPEG image into Active Directory to populate the *ThumbnailPhoto* attribute. The *ThumbnailPhoto* attribute is listed as an indicator and is not downloaded into the OAB; it is therefore not available offline. You can change the attribute type to *Value* to force thumbnail photos to be included in the OAB. This is an acceptable option if you restrict the amount of data added to the overall size of the OAB that subsequently has to be downloaded by clients.

> **Tip**
> You could gradually add thumbnails to user objects to spread the download activity over several weeks or decide that thumbnails should only be added to user objects for people such as board members or other notable individuals. The worst possible option is to collect thumbnails for everyone and script a bulk load into Active Directory over a weekend, because this might generate a burst of activity when clients have to download a newly swollen OAB the next time they connect to Exchange.

Because it's a high-performance database, Active Directory won't be affected by a bulk load of thumbnail data, and the ripple effect of replication across the organization is likely to be slight. Compared to the number of clients, there are relatively few global catalogs to update with the thumbnail data. The sheer number of clients creates a different scenario for Outlook. If you make changes to many objects at one time, you're likely to provoke the need for each client to download the complete OAB. Imagine adding thumbnails to 10,000 user objects. You might only add 9 KB to each object, but that's still an extra 88 MB or thereabouts that Outlook has to download to fetch OAB updates. Add that up for 12,000 clients, and that's about 1,029 GB of data that clients have to download before each client has the newly updated OAB complete with thumbnail data. For this reason, you might prefer to remove the *ThumbnailPhoto* attribute from the set of OAB attributes completely. Here's how you remove the attribute:

```
$NewSet = (Get-OfflineAddressBook "Default Offline Address Book").ConfiguredAttributes
$NewSet.Remove("ThumbnailPhoto,Indicator")
Set-OfflineAddressBook "Default Offline Address Book" –ConfiguredAttributes $NewSet
```

Updating OAB files

You can generate the OAB files manually at any time using the Update option in EMC or with the Update-OfflineAddressBook cmdlet. For example:

```
Update-OfflineAddressBook –Identity '\Default Offline Address Book'
```

Exchange logs event 9107 when the new OAB files are available. If you suspect that some problems are happening in OAB generation, you can increase the diagnostic logging to force Exchange to log additional events in the Application Event Log. For example:

```
Set-EventLogLevel –Identity 'ExServer4\MSExchangeSA\OAL Generator' -Level 'Expert'
```

After the new OAB files are generated, you can force selected CAS servers to poll for updates without waiting for the set poll interval to elapse with the Update-FileDistributionService cmdlet. For example, to force the CAS server called ExchCAS1 to poll for updated OAB files:

```
Update-FileDistributionService –Identity 'ExchCAS1' –Type OAB
```

Moving the OAB generation server

The first mailbox server in the organization might not be the most appropriate server to host OAB generation. You can move this work to any other Exchange 2010 mailbox server in the organization. To do this, select the Move option in the action pane to invoke the Move Offline Address Book Wizard. As Figure 12-18 shows, you will be presented with a picker to select another mailbox server. After you select a new OAB generation server, Exchange copies the current set of OAB files (those shown in Figure 12-16) to it. You can then delete these files from the old server. The task can also be accomplished with the Move-OfflineAddressBook cmdlet:

```
Move-OfflineAddressBook -Identity '\Default Offline Address Book' -Server 'ExServer4'
```

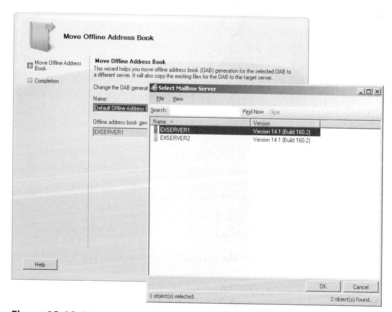

Figure 12-18 Moving the OAB generation server.

Web-based distribution

By default, only the first CAS server in the organization is configured as a Web access point for Outlook 2007 and Outlook 2010 clients to download OAB updates. You can see that a single server is listed in the set of virtual directories under Web-based distribution shown previously in Figure 12-17. You can add more CAS servers to distribute the load across the organization and to make sure that clients can contact a local CAS rather than making an extended connection to a central server. Ideally, you should configure at least one CAS server in every Active Directory site to provide a Web distribution point for OAB files. To add new servers to the list, click Add and select additional CAS servers from the list displayed in the picker. Alternatively, you can do it with EMS:

```
Set-OfflineAddressBook -Identity '\Default Offline Address Book'
-VirtualDirectories 'ExServer1\OAB (Default Web Site)', 'ExServer2\OAB
(Default Web Site)'
```

The OAB updates have to be retrieved by the CAS servers from the OAB generation server. Figure 12-19 illustrates the properties of the OAB default Web site. You can see that the default polling interval is 480 minutes (8 hours). Some deployments feel that a longer polling interval is justified because OAB files are generated daily. To change the polling interval on a server to something like 720 minutes (12 hours), you can set it through EMC or use the following command:

```
Get-OABVirtualDirectory | Set-OABVirtualDirectory –PollInterval 720
```

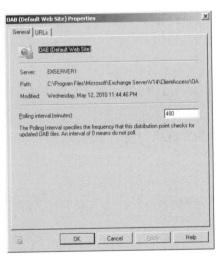

Figure 12-19 Properties of the OAB Web site.

To get the updates, the nominated CAS servers poll the OAB generation server using the defined interval and interrogate the OAB manifest. If new files are discovered, the Microsoft Exchange File Distribution Service (MSExchangeFDS) copies the OAB files using

Background Intelligent Transfer Service (BITS) to the target CAS servers. BITS enables the File Distribution Service to transfer files in small chunks so that even very large files, such as the complete OAB, can travel efficiently across low-bandwidth or high-latency networks, even if the transfer takes several hours.

> **Note**
>
> This ability to transfer files efficiently is an important factor in being able to provide files to CAS servers in sites that might serve remote locations.

The new files are not made available to clients until they are completely copied and verified (the File Distribution Service logs event 1008 at this point). Clients can then connect to their local CAS to fetch the updates. Outlook uses the Autodiscover service to determine the closest CAS server that offers OAB files and uses the OAB manifest to understand what files it has to copy from the Web distribution point. Conceivably, it is possible that clients in different sites use different versions of the OAB simply because temporary problems occur in file distribution. However, over time, these problems should go away and all clients should then use the same OAB.

Public folder distribution

OAB updates have been provided to clients via system public folders since the earliest version of Exchange. However, the era of public folders is drawing to a close and only Outlook 2003 clients are now likely to connect to public folders to fetch OAB updates. If public folder distribution is used, the OAB generation server updates the relevant folders after it creates the OAB files. As shown in Figure 12-20, Exchange maintains separate folders for each OAB version. To ensure the same level of robustness, you can replicate these folders to other public folder databases so that clients can connect to a local replica when they download.

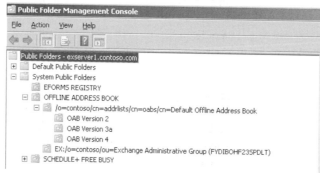

Figure 12-20 Public folders used for OAB distribution.

Creating and using customized OABs

The foundation for the OAB is provided by a set of one or more address lists. The default OAB contains just one address list, the default GAL. This means that any object that is included in the GAL is also included in the default OAB. An address list is nothing more than a convenient way for Exchange to focus on a set of mail-enabled Active Directory objects by applying a filter to locate the objects. The filters are very similar to those used to create the membership of dynamic distribution groups. Each address list has a filter, and when Exchange generates an OAB, it applies the filter for each address list that is included in the OAB. Thus, when Exchange generates the default OAB, it applies the "default GAL" filter to find all the mail-enabled objects in the organization that are not marked to be hidden from address lists.

You can change the OAB that is provided to Outlook clients in two ways. First, you can create a new OAB based on a set of address lists, which is tailored to select the users that you want to include in the new OAB, and then replace the normal OAB by marking the new OAB as the default. Second, you can create one or more OABs and assign these to different sets of users. This can be done by assigning an OAB to a database so that every mailbox in that database uses that OAB, or it can be done on an individual mailbox basis.

If your Exchange organization supports a common set of users about which everyone needs to know, then there is no need to replace the default OAB, because it will serve the purpose of offline access to the directory well. On the other hand, hosting companies that deliver Exchange services to other companies use address lists to provide a customized OAB for each company of the users that belong to each one.

Subsidiaries with a common Exchange infrastrucutre

Large companies that support different subsidiaries with a common Exchange infrastructure often use the same approach as hosting companies so that the users belonging to each subsidiary only see the users from that subsidiary in their OAB (and perhaps users from common shared corporate departments). This is accomplished by creating new address lists to filter out the different user communities and then using the address lists to generate different OABs, which are then assigned to users.

Before we get too far into creating a new OAB, it's worth emphasizing again that OABs are only useful to Outlook clients that work in cached Exchange mode. Clients that work online have access to the complete GAL unless they are constrained by changes to the access controls and other settings maintained in Active Directory. The discussion presented here focuses on the steps that an Exchange administrator has to execute to create a new OAB and does not go into all of the changes that must be applied to Active Directory. These

Chapter 12

changes are comprehensive and in-depth in nature and not for an Active Directory novice to undertake.

Microsoft has published a white paper on how to generate segmented OABs for Exchange 2007, but at the time of writing the same level of detail has not been released by the engineering group for Exchange 2010. With these points in mind, let's consider how to create a new OAB for a scenario where we want to assign an OAB to a group of users in a single location that only includes the mail-enabled objects belonging to that location.

Our first task is to create a suitable address list. We can create a new address list that contains all the mail-enabled objects for the location or an address list for each object type (contacts, rooms, equipment, mailboxes, and groups) that are then combined into the OAB that we eventually generate. Exchange maintains address lists such as All Rooms or All Contacts to make it convenient to locate these objects for different purposes within the product. In this case, multiple address lists would probably overcomplicate matters, so to keep things simple, we create a single address list.

To begin, we go to the Mailbox node under Organization Configuration, click the Address Lists tab and then click New Address List. The first step in the wizard is to name the new address list and to decide whether it is a child of an existing address list (or container) or a top-level address list. A child address list might be something like Contacts in Zurich and be created as a child of the All Contacts address list using a suitable filter to select the contacts located in Zurich. The new object (Figure 12-21) has a name that clearly indicates its purpose as an address list containing Dublin users and its position as a top-level container ("\").

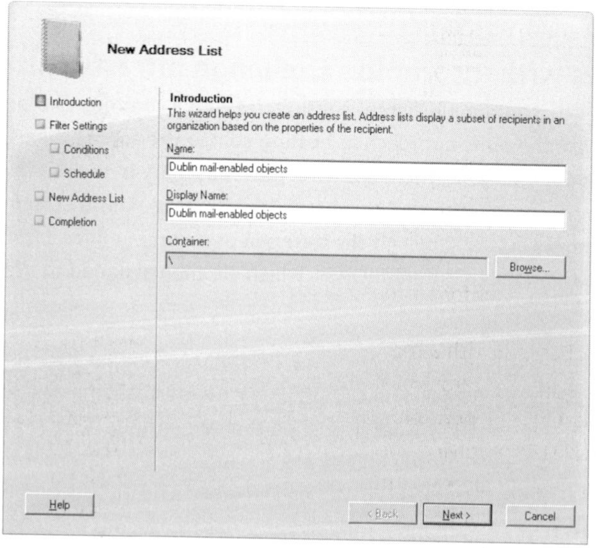

Figure 12-21 Creating a new address list.

The next step is to identify the Active Directory recipient container to which the filter will be applied. It could be that all the target objects are stored in a single organizational unit (OU), in which case you can use this as the recipient container. If not, you'll probably select the root of the directory so that the filter selects all possible matching objects. You also need to indicate whether you want to select all mail-enabled objects or only a specific type.

We then proceed to create the filter by selecting the conditions that it will apply. This is familiar territory for anyone who has created a dynamic distribution group. The filter used for our address list is very simple, because all it does is find any object with "Dublin" in Custom Attribute 2. Figure 12-22 shows the filter being tested to make sure that it accurately identifies the objects that we want to include in the address list. In fact, because similar recipient filters are used by both objects, it is possible to create a new address list based on the filter used by a dynamic distribution group. For example:

```
New-AddressList -Name 'Corporate Functions' -RecipientFilter
(Get-DynamicDistributionGroup 'Corporate Functions').RecipientFilter
```

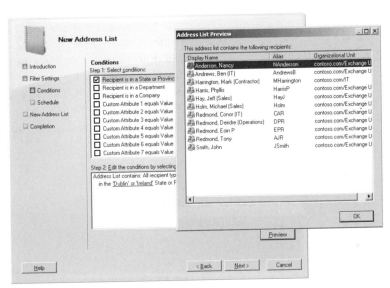

Figure 12-22 Testing the filter for an address list.

If you create an address list with a recipient filter like this, you won't be able to edit the filter conditions using the wizard and will have to apply any updates through the shell. Getting back to creating our new address list, the next step is to define the schedule to update the address list by applying the filter to Active Directory. Typically, you can allow this to occur immediately unless you have a specific reason to wait for a particular time. Updating the address list actually doesn't matter too much because we're going to use the address list with an OAB and Exchange will use the filter to generate the data for the OAB.

Chapter 12

The final step is to allow Exchange to create the new address list object and update the list. The EMS commands will be something like the following code. You can see that a specific OU called Exchange Users is used as the Active Directory location. All mail-enabled recipients found in this OU and any child OUs will be found by the filter.

```
New-AddressList -Name 'Dublin mail-enabled objects' -RecipientContainer
'contoso.com/Exchange Users' -IncludedRecipients 'AllRecipients' -Container '\'
-ConditionalCustomAttribute2 'Dublin' -DisplayName 'Dublin mail-enabled objects'
Update-AddressList -Identity '\Dublin mail-enabled objects'
```

Once the address list is created and updated, the objects that it includes will be available to online users. For example, OWA users who access the GAL normally only see the Default GAL and All Rooms listed in the Address Book (top left of the screen). Other address lists are revealed if you click Show Other Address Lists, including our new address list.

With an address list created, we can move ahead to create a new OAB. Select the New Offline Address Book option to launch the wizard. We have to name the new object, define the mailbox server that will generate the OAB files, and tell Exchange which address lists make up the OAB (Figure 12-23).

Figure 12-23 Creating a new OAB.

Next, we define how we will distribute the new OAB. The available options are Web-based and through public folders. Web-based distribution requires us to define a list of CAS servers to which clients can connect to fetch OAB updates (Figure 12-24). The final step is to create the new OAB with a command like the following code. You can see how the address list that we created is the only one included in this OAB.

```
New-OfflineAddressBook -Name 'Dublin OAB' -Server 'ExServer1' -AddressLists
'\Dublin mail-enabled objects' -PublicFolderDistributionEnabled $True
-VirtualDirectories 'ExServer1\OAB (Default Web Site)','ExServer2\OAB (Default Web
Site)'
```

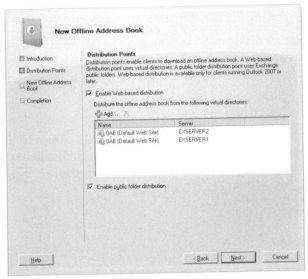

Figure 12-24 Defining Web-based distribution for the new OAB.

The files for the OAB will be generated according to the schedule defined for the nominated server and will not be available to users until the OABGen process runs. You can use the Update-OfflineAddressBook cmdlet to force generation as follows:

```
Update-OfflineAddressBook -Identity 'Dublin OAB'
```

To validate that the new OAB files are available, check the ExchangeOAB share on the server where OABGen runs. Every OAB stores its files in a separate directory, identified by the globally unique identifier (GUID) that Exchange uses to identify the OAB internally. You can match the GUID used to identify a directory with its OAB with this command:

```
Get-OfflineAddressBook | Select Name, GUID
```

Now that we have a new OAB, it can be assigned to individual mailboxes or to all of the mailboxes in a database. Use the Set-Mailbox cmdlet to assign an OAB to a mailbox. For example:

```
Set-Mailbox -id 'David Jones' -OfflineAddressBook 'Dublin OAB'
```

Replace Set-Mailbox with Set-MailboxDatabase to make the assignment for a mailbox database:

```
Set-MailboxDatabase -Identity 'Dublin mailboxes' -OfflineAddressBook 'Dublin OAB'
```

Chapter 12

Alternatively, you can select the database from EMC and access the Client Settings tab to select the OAB there. If an OAB is not explicitly selected for a mailbox database, Exchange uses whatever OAB is the current default. To make a new OAB the default, you'd use a command like that shown here. Only one OAB can be marked as the default at one time.

```
Set-OfflineAddressBook -Identity 'Dublin OAB' -IsDefault $True
```

The steps presented here will create and distribute a new OAB to users, but it won't prevent them from accessing the default GAL when they work online. We need to make the changes to Active Directory referred to earlier to block access to the default address lists.

OAB support for MailTips

The MailTips functionality introduced in Exchange 2010 would be a partial solution if they only worked when users were connected online. Microsoft therefore upgraded the OAB structure to include a new set of MailTips properties for recipients that allow Outlook to process MailTips offline. The properties are as follows:

- Message delivery restrictions

- Custom MailTips

- Maximum receive size

In addition, some new properties are kept for groups:

- Moderation enabled

- Total member count

- External member count

All of these data, with the exception of the membership counts, are extracted from Active Directory. Membership counts come from Group Metrics.

The conditions you can't account for offline

Even with access to the OAB, some conditions exist that are impossible to account for offline. For example, a recipient mailbox might exceed its quota for a short time, a new mailbox might be added to Active Directory and isn't included in the OAB until the next time the client downloads an OAB update, or a user adds an OOF notice. The MailTip for invalid internal recipient (perhaps an address for a mailbox that has recently been deleted) is also unavailable offline.

OABInteg and Dave Goldman's Blog

The OAB can be a complicated feature to troubleshoot. Most of what it does occurs in the background and there's no great amount of detail generated by Exchange or Outlook when something goes wrong, such as a user being unable to download the OAB. Microsoft has a tool called OABInteg to help troubleshoot what's going on with OAB file generation, distribution, and content.

You can get a copy of OABInteg from Microsoft Knowledge Base article 907792 and read all about it at *http://blogs.msdn.com/dgoldman/archive/2005/08/28/oabinteg-and-how-to-use-it-to-troubleshoot-oab-generation-issues.aspx*. The blog belongs to Dave Goldman, an Exchange escalation engineer, and it's an excellent source of information about the many issues that can afflict this feature of Exchange.

Hierarchical address book

The standard address book meets the needs for most companies throughout the world. Presenting users and groups sorted by first name or last name does not work so well in companies where the culture is strongly based on an adherence to a hierarchical structure, especially in East Asian countries. In these situations, the desired result is to present the organization in terms of seniority so that the most important members are listed first. Users can then navigate the address book to walk down through the organization following its structure. For example, they can move from the CEO to the vice presidents who run major departments, to the directors, managers, and then individual contributors.

The combination of Exchange 2010 SP1 and Outlook 2010 or Outlook 2007 (SP2 or later) is required to implement a hierarchical address book (HAB). You can follow these steps to create a new HAB. Steps 1 and 3 are optional insofar as you don't strictly need to use a dedicated OU for the HAB. However, its use allows you to maintain a clear separation between the objects that form the HAB and the other Exchange groups and users. Steps 4 and 5 can be combined into a single set of Set-Group commands. They are isolated here to emphasize the need for the two distinct properties that must be set to allow objects to be included in the HAB.

1. Create an OU in Active Directory to act as container for the groups and user objects that will form the HAB.

2. Configure the organization with the alias of the group that will act as the root of the HAB. In this case, we mark a group containing the CEO's email address as the root of the HAB.

   ```
   Set-OrganizationConfig -HierarchicalAddressBook DG-CEO1
   ```

3. Add the groups and users that will form the HAB into the OU. Again, this is an optional step.

4. Modify each group object that will be in the HAB to set its *IsHierarchicalGroup* property to $True.

```
Set-Group -Identity DG-CE01 -IsHierarchicalGroup $True
```

5. Modify each group and user object that will be in the HAB to set its *SeniorityIndex* property to an integer value that Exchange will use to sort the HAB. An object with a *SeniorityIndex* value of 1 will be at the top of the HAB, so if your CEO represents the top of the organization, you'd set this value to 1 for his user object (or the group object that might contain the CEO and members of his staff). Groups and users that occur further down the hierarchy are assigned higher *SeniorityIndex* values.

```
Set-Group -Identity DG-CE01 -SeniorityIndex 1
Set-User -Identity MyCEO -SeniorityIndex 1
Set-User -Identity DG-SeniorVP1 -SeniorityIndex 2
```

6. Ensure that groups of each level include the groups of the next level down in their membership so that the members of each level are shown when a user navigates through the hierarchy. For example, the HAB shown in Figure 12-25 uses organizational titles from the CEO downward as the basis of its hierarchy. To create this view, the VPs – Level 2 group is a member of the CEO – Level 1 group, the Directors – Level 3 group is a member of the VPs – Level 2 group, and the Senior Managers – Level 4 group shown here is a member of the Directors – Level 3 group. This nesting arrangement continues for the remainder of the hierarchy.

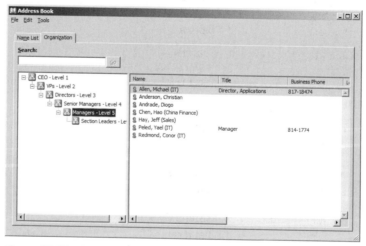

Figure 12-25 Viewing a hierarchical address book.

7. For Japanese HABs, you can also set the *PhoneticDisplayName* property for groups and users. Outlook sorts the HAB first by the *SeniorityIndex* and then by *PhoneticDisplayName*.

```
Set-Group -Identity DG-HAB-Group1 -PhoneticDisplayName 'HAB Group 1'
Set-User -Identity User-HAB1 -PhoenticDisplayName 'User 1'
```

8. Open Outlook 2010 or Outlook 2007 and access the Address Book. Click the Organization tab to reveal the HAB.

Only a single HAB can exist in an organization, and HABs can only be viewed by Outlook clients that are configured to use cached Exchange mode and have successfully down-loaded an OAB that was generated after the properties of the groups that form the HAB were updated (as just described).

Mailbox assistants

Exchange includes a number of mailbox assistants to perform automated processing on different aspects of the data held in mailboxes. An assistant is just another name for a thread that executes within the Microsoft Exchange System Attendant process on a mailbox server. Exchange 2010 uses two types of assistants:

1. Event-based assistants: These respond to events as they occur. For example, the Resource Booking Assistant monitors requests to book rooms and lets users know if a room is unavailable.

2. Throttle-based assistants: These operate all the time to process data and are subject to throttling to ensure that their workload does not impact the responsiveness of a server. The Managed Folder Assistant is the most well-known of these assistants.

Among the more well-known assistants are the following:

- Calendar Assistant: Checks mailboxes for incoming meeting requests and processes the requests according to mailbox settings

- Resource Booking Assistant: Processes meeting requests for room and equipment mailboxes

- Scheduling Assistant: Scans attendee calendars for suitable meeting slots and suggests them to meeting organizers

- Junk E-Mail Options Assistant: Copies safelist data from user mailboxes to their Active Directory accounts so that it can be used by the anti-spam agents

- Managed Folder Assistant: Processes retention policies for managed folders and applies retention policy tags to items in mailboxes

Chapter 12

These assistants are relatively well known because they exist in previous versions of Exchange. For this reason, we focus on a new assistant in the remainder of this section. Exchange 2010 SP1 includes a new test cmdlet to allow administrators to check that the mailbox assistants are functioning properly on a server and to recover from any problem that the test cmdlet detects. For example, this command runs the cmdlet to test that the mailbox assistants are functioning properly on server Exserver1 and then reports the results in list format:

```
Test-AssistantHealth –Server ExServer1 –ResolveProblems | Format-List
```

Calendar Repair Assistant (CRA)

The Calendar Repair Assistant (CRA) is a new component introduced in Exchange 2010 that runs as part of the Exchange Mailbox Assistants service. CRA is designed to detect and correct inconsistencies in calendar data that can be caused by concurrent access from multiple clients to calendars, by software bugs, or by other factors. Many users carry mobile devices today to be able to access their calendar on the move, and they might also leave Outlook open and active on another computer. Both devices process incoming calendar requests and notifications and so create the possibility that each might get in the other's way and introduce inconsistencies and flaws in calendar data.

The idea is that CRA should be able to figure out when calendar items are in an inconsistent state and then fix them so that users don't miss meetings or appointments due to bad calendar data. For example, if CRA finds that a user's calendar is missing a meeting item that she has accepted, it can create the missing item. If the time or location of a meeting is different in an attendee's copy of a meeting, CRA can update the item with the time or location from the meeting owner's copy. CRA is also able to detect variations in recurring meetings where some attendees might be missing entries for some occurrences of an event.

CRA is a "silent" attendant. This means that users are only aware that CRA is active when it performs an action on their behalf and they receive a notification that it has applied a fix to their calendars. Common issues that CRA processes include the following:

- The meeting in an attendee's calendar has an incorrect time or location.

- An attendee's calendar does not have a copy of a meeting even though he accepted an invitation to attend.

- A user has a copy of a meeting in her calendar but her name doesn't appear in the attendee list.

- The tracking status of an attendee's copy of a meeting doesn't match the tracking status of the organizer's copy.

- The copy of a recurring meeting in an attendee's calendar doesn't match the meeting data in the organizer's calendar.

- The calendar of a meeting organizer or an attendee contains multiple items for the same meeting.

> ## How CRA handles a data discrepancy in a meeting attendee's calendar
>
> In most cases, the copy of the item in the organizer's calendar provides the definitive version of where and when a meeting takes place, and the fix that CRA applies is to synchronize the data in an attendee's calendar to match that of the meeting organizer. If CRA finds that a meeting is missing from an attendee's calendar even though he responded with a firm or tentative acceptance to the original invitation, it will re-create the meeting. The fact that CRA re-created the meeting is captured in the meeting description.

By default, CRA scans items 30 days in the future and runs on a schedule that has to be configured on a mailbox server before CRA becomes active. CRA settings can only be manipulated through EMS, because there is no user interface built into EMC for this purpose. Use the Get-MailboxServer cmdlet to retrieve the CRA settings for a mailbox server:

```
Get-MailboxServer -id ExServer1 | Select Name, Calendar*
```

```
Name                                     : ExServer1
CalendarRepairSchedule                   : {}
CalendarRepairMissingItemFixDisabled     : False
CalendarRepairLogEnabled                 : True
CalendarRepairLogSubjectLoggingEnabled   : True
CalendarRepairLogPath                    : C:\Program Files\Microsoft\Exchange Server\V14
\Logging\Calendar Repair Assistant
CalendarRepairIntervalEndWindow          : 30
CalendarRepairLogFileAgeLimit            : 365.00:00:00
CalendarRepairLogDirectorySizeLimit      : unlimited
```

These settings are explained as follows:

- *CalendarRepairSchedule*: Establishes a schedule when the CRA will check user calendars and fix any problems that it finds. If the CRA can't finish during the set time, it will restart at the place where it finished the next time a scheduled window opens up. If no schedule is set, the CRA won't run. The notion of an assistant schedule is replaced with a work cycle in Exchange 2010 SP1 and the CRA is then scheduled by setting its work cycle with the Set-MailboxServer cmdlet, as described in the next section.

- *CalendarRepairLogEnabled*: Determines whether logging is active. The default is $True.

- *CalendarRepairMissingItemFixDisabled*: The default value is $False. If you set it to $True, the CRA will not attempt to fix missing items that it finds in user calendars.

- *CalendarRepairLogPath*: Sets the path to the location where the log files are stored. The default is to store logs in the \Logging\Calendar Repair Agent directory. A log is created for each mailbox that CRA scans. The log captures details of any repairs that CRA makes to the calendar.

- *CalendarRepairLogFileAgeLimit*: Sets the period for which CRA retains logs. The default is 00.00:00:00, indicating no limit, so log files are retained indefinitely.

- *CalendarRepairLogDirectorySizeLimit*: Sets the maximum size of CRA log files that are stored on a server. Once the maximum size is reached, CRA deletes the oldest log file to free space. The default is Unlimited. Each log file typically requires 1 KB to 2 KB of storage, depending on the work that CRA performs on a mailbox. A mailbox server that supports 1,000 mailboxes will generate 1 MB to 2 MB of logs every time CRA runs. If CRA runs weekly, you'll have less than 100 MB of logs generated annually. To be safe, you could allocate 200 KB of storage per mailbox annually.

- *CalendarRepairLogSubjectLoggingEnabled*: Determines whether the subjects of meetings and appointment items are captured in log files. The default is to capture subject data.

The first issue that you have to address is that CRA is not assigned a schedule to run on this server (the value of *CalendarRepairSchedule* is blank). This means that the CRA will never be activated and no processing will occur to detect and fix issues in calendar items in user mailboxes. The first step that we have to take is therefore to create a schedule for CRA processing to occur. This command creates a processing schedule for the CRA between 1 A.M. and 6 A.M. every Sunday. It also limits the size of the log directory to 500 MB, and discards any log over 365 days old:

```
Set-MailboxServer –Identity 'ExServer1'-CalendarRepairSchedule 'Sun.01:00AM-
Sun.06:00AM' CalendarRepairLogDirectorySizeLimit 500MB
–CalendarRepairLogFileAgeLimit 365.00:00:00
```

You should set the same CRA values on all mailbox servers to ensure consistent behavior across the organization. This is easily done by creating a list of mailbox servers and piping them to Set-MailboxServer. For example:

```
Get-MailboxServer | Set-MailboxServer -CalendarRepairSchedule
'Sun.01:00AM-Sun.06:00AM'
```

The names of CRA log files are generated based on the date and time of the run and the alias of the mailbox that is processed. For example, CRA2010031703-1.JSmith.log is the log generated on 3 A.M. on March 17, 2010 for the mailbox with alias "JSmith." The CRA log files contain information about the scan range for items and details of any fixes that CRA performs to calendar items. Apart from the subjects of repaired items, you won't see other details about the item, such as the date and time of a meeting. You can also check the Application Event Log for entries for ID 9018 to see whether any problems are encountered as the assistant processes mailboxes.

All mailboxes on a server are scanned unless they are explicitly excluded. To exclude a mailbox from calendar repair, set its *CalendarRepairEnabled* property to $False. For example:

```
Set-Mailbox -Identity 'Akers, Kim' -CalendarRepairEnabled $False
```

Work cycles

Exchange 2010 SP1 makes an important change to the way that mailbox assistants are scheduled. Up to this point, each assistant had its own method of creating a schedule when it would run. As the number of assistants grew, the lack of consistency became a concern because it was difficult for administrators to know how to schedule each assistant. More important, as servers supported more and more mailboxes, each time an assistant entered a scheduled work window, it created an artificial peak in workload for the server. This is because assistants attempt to get their work done as quickly as possible and process mailboxes consecutively until everything is done. This approach works well, but the window required to complete processing grows and grows as the number of mailboxes and the items to be processed increases.

SP1 moves to a different model, in which the activity of assistants is moderated so that work goes on in the background on a consistent basis to fulfill the conditions set down by a work cycle definition. For example, you might define that the Managed Folder Assistant must process every mailbox on a server at least once every two days. Given the constraints determined in a work cycle, the assistant will work out how much work it has to do over the period and create an internal schedule to allow it to do the work on a phased basis so that a smooth and predictable demand is generated on the server rather than the peaks created by the older model. The assistant monitors system conditions on an ongoing basis to make any required adjustments to achieve its work cycle. If the server is under high demand for a period due to user activity, the assistant can back off its work and then speed up when server load drops.

Table 12-6 **Setting assistant schedules**

Assistant	Work	Method to set schedule
Managed Folder Assistant	Processes mailboxes subject to retention policies and takes action specified in retention policy tags when retention periods expire for items.	Set-MailboxServer −ManagedFolderAssistantSchedule
Sharing Policy	Enforces changes on personal sharing relationships to ensure that they are synchronized with organization policies.	Set-MailboxServer −SharingPolicySchedule
Calendar Repair	Scans user calendars and makes any repairs that are necessary to synchronize the calendars of meeting organizers and attendees.	Set-MailboxServer −CalendarRepairSchedule
Junk Mail	Gathers safelist data from user mailboxes and publishes the data to the users' Active Directory objects so that they can be used for anti-spam checks.	Hard-coded internal schedule not exposed to administrators
Top 'N' Words	Used by the voice mail transcription service to help identify common words spoken in voice mails.	Registry key
UM Reporting	Reports how Unified Messaging is used by Exchange.	

A standard method is introduced in SP1 to establish a schedule for an assistant work cycle. Most of the assistants already use the Set-MailboxServer cmdlet for this purpose, so it makes sense to tweak the cmdlet and make it the common denominator for all. First, let's find out what the current work cycles are for the six assistants:

```
Get-MailboxServer -Identity ExServer1 | Format-List *WorkCycle*
```

```
CalendarRepairWorkCycle                 :
CalendarRepairWorkCycleCheckpoint       :
SharingPolicyWorkCycle                  : 1.00:00:00
SharingPolicyWorkCycleCheckpoint        : 1.00:00:00
SharingSyncWorkCycle                    : 03:00:00
SharingSyncWorkCycleCheckpoint          : 03:00:00
ManagedFolderWorkCycle                  : 1.00:00:00
ManagedFolderWorkCycleCheckpoint        : 1.00:00:00
TopNWorkCycle                           : 7.00:00:00
TopNWorkCycleCheckpoint                 : 1.00:00:00
UMReportingWorkCycle                    : 1.00:00:00
UMReportingWorkCycleCheckpoint          : 1.00:00:00
```

You use the Set-MailboxServer cmdlet to determine the work cycle for an assistant. A work cycle is defined in terms of the total time available for the assistant to process all mailboxes in all databases on the server. The checkpoint specifies when the assistant checks for new objects to process. If no value is set, the assistant uses a default. (In the preceding case, the default work cycle for the CRA is seven days and the default checkpoint is one day.)

For example, to instruct the Calendar Repair Assistant that it has to process all mailboxes daily, you set up a work cycle period of one day as follows:

```
Set-MailboxServer -Identity ExServer1 -CalendarRepairWorkCycle "1.00:00:00"
```

As usual, it makes sense to have the same work cycle settings applied to all mailbox servers in the organization.

Time to transport

We now have everything in place to communicate with internal and external correspondents. This can't happen if we don't have a functioning transport service, so it's time for us to consider the SMTP-centric nature of Exchange's world of transport and how everything fits together to make sure that the mail gets through.

P RIOR to Microsoft Exchange 2007, every previous version of Exchange incorporated all of the components for a fully functional messaging system in a single product. The introduction of server roles allows administrators to assign different roles to individual computers. The hub transport server role is critical to the ebb and flow of messages within an Exchange organization and serves the same purpose as an Exchange 2003 bridgehead server. It also provides a central point where policies can be applied to messages as they pass through the messaging system. Because all messages pass through a hub transport system—even if they are destined for delivery to a database on the same server as the originating mailbox—and because all hub transport servers share common policies defined and distributed through Active Directory, Exchange can offer a guarantee that policies will be respected all the time and in a consistent manner.

In large deployments, hub transport servers are usually deployed on dedicated servers, but in smaller deployments, it is common for a server to support both mailbox and hub transport roles or also include the Client Access Server (CAS) role to provide a complete messaging service. Either type of deployment is as valid as the other; the details of administration and configuration do not change.

In terms of Exchange's transport system, the focus of a messaging administrator is to make sure of the following:

- The default connectors are configured to meet the needs of the organization.

- The messaging system is capable of handling outages gracefully.

- Any safeguards necessary to meet regulatory or legal requirements are in place.

- Any custom connectors required to service connections to clients, applications, or other messaging systems are in place and operational.

- Out-of-the-ordinary situations are handled effectively.

- Data required for monitoring and reporting are gathered and available.

With these points in mind, let's consider how things work inside Exchange's transport system.

Overview of the transport architecture

Exchange 2007 discarded the routing mechanism based on predefined routing groups and connectors used in Exchange 2000 and Exchange 2003. Exchange Server 2010 routing is very similar to Exchange 2007 routing in that direct point-to-point connections between hub transport servers provide the essential foundation for message routing. If a hub transport server has a message addressed to a mailbox on another server, it attempts to make a direct IP connection to the hub transport server that is closest to its final destination to transfer the message. The destination hub transport server could be a multirole server that also hosts the target mailbox database, in which case the message transfer is complete and delivery can be made. On the other hand, the hub transport server could be a transient point in the route and require one or more additional hops before the message can be delivered to the destination mailbox. The Active Directory site topology and site link costs provide Exchange with the essential data to know how best to route messages, but it is important to underscore that Exchange will always use a direct point-to-point connection to transfer messages whenever possible, because the ethos is that messages should avoid intermediate steps when they travel to their destination.

Active Directory sites provide routing boundaries for Exchange 2010. When users send messages, the Microsoft Exchange Mail Submission service on the mailbox server creates a notification event to inform a hub transport server that a message is waiting to be picked up for routing. The notification events are automatically load balanced across the available hub transport servers in the site to ensure that each hub transport server receives an equal number of new messages for routing. You can force a mailbox server to send notifications to a static list of hub transport servers. To do this, use the Set-MailboxServer cmdlet to update the *SubmissionServerOverrideList* property with the list of hub transport servers to use. All of the servers in the list must exist in the same Active Directory site as the mailbox server. For example:

```
Set-MailboxServer -Identity ExServer1 -SubmissionServerOverrideList 'ExHT1', 'ExHT2'
```

Servers that host both the mailbox and hub transport rules within a Database Availability Group (DAG) create a situation that requires special processing to ensure that the shadow redundancy feature has an opportunity to capture copies of messages as they pass through the transport service. Shadow redundancy is a new feature introduced in Exchange 2010 to protect messages by ensuring that the transport system keeps a copy of each message until confirmation is received that the message has been delivered to its final destination. For more information, see the section "Shadow redundancy" later in this chapter.

When messages are submitted from a mailbox server within a DAG that also runs the hub transport role, Exchange prefers to use a nonlocal hub transport server rather than the local server. When the hub transport server attempts to deliver new messages to a database that is replicated and mounted on the local server, it looks for a different hub transport server in the site and attempts to route the messages via that server. These steps force messages to be captured as they pass through the intermediate hub transport server.

Exchange determines the available routing paths for messages by reference to the Active Directory topology and does not use the link state routing algorithm employed by Exchange 2000 and Exchange 2003, and hub transport servers do not send link state update data to keep them abreast of potential connector outages. The routing topology created from routing groups and routing group connectors (and less commonly, Simple Mail Transfer Protocol [SMTP] and X.400 connectors) is replaced by simple point-to-point connections between Exchange hub transport servers. If a point-to-point connection between hub transport servers is unavailable for some reason, Exchange determines how close to the eventual destination it can transport a message by reference to the Active Directory site topology, but only includes sites that include an Exchange hub transport server. To determine the best routing path, Exchange uses the costs assigned to the links that connect Active Directory sites. A lot of intelligence is incorporated to ensure that messages flow efficiently between sites. For example, bifurcation (fan-out) of messages is delayed until it is necessary to generate multiple copies of the messages. Apart from making sure that the Active Directory site topology is accurate, all of this happens without administrative intervention or configuration.

The move to deterministic routing based on point-to-point connections simplified routing behavior and made it more flexible and adaptive to changes in the organization and underlying network. The implementation of routing groups and Exchange site link costs as used in Exchange 2003 works well in most cases, but it calls for more administrative planning, oversight, and maintenance. Exchange 2007 and Exchange 2010 enjoy an automatic configuration that is built out as new hub transport servers are introduced into the organization. The basic fabric created by the hub transport servers and the default receive and send connectors that they include is supplemented by bespoke connectors that are only necessary for external or other dedicated communications. For example, if you want to communicate between Exchange 2010 and Exchange 2003, you'll need a dedicated connector for this purpose. The same is true if you want to use an external smart host relay as the basis for communications with external SMTP servers, including other SMTP-based systems operating behind the firewall. Of course, you'll also need dedicated connectors if you want to communicate with X.400-based systems or systems that use their own messaging protocols.

> **Note**
>
> Connectors built with the old Exchange Development Kit (EDK) such as those used to link Exchange 2003 to foreign messaging systems such as Lotus Notes or Novell GroupWise are not supported by Exchange 2010. If you need to continue to use this functionality, you must retain an Exchange 2003 server in the organization to host the connector or make a transition to SMTP-based routing to connect Exchange to the foreign messaging systems.

The creation of dedicated connectors can be viewed as one-off events that are subsequently managed on an exception basis by administrators while the general day-to-day connections between Exchange servers in the same organization flow automatically without the need for constant intervention.

Microsoft publishes some excellent PDF versions of detailed charts that describe the workings of the Exchange transport system that you can download from TechNet at *http://msexchangeteam.com/archive/2009/12/01/453347.aspx*.

Figure 13-1 is a much simplified view of message flow between Exchange 2010 mailbox and hub transport servers.

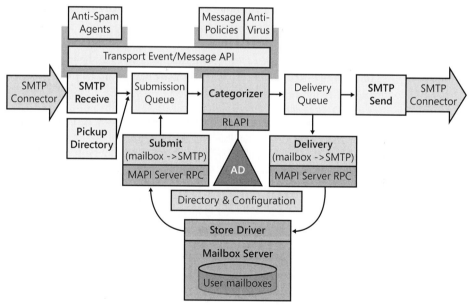

Figure 13-1 Message flow through the Exchange 2010 transport system.

The major points that you need to understand from this diagram are the following:

- Apart from local delivery to a database on the server, mailbox servers never transport mail. Instead, when a mailbox server has a message that it needs to send to a database hosted by another Exchange server or a recipient in another email system, the Microsoft Exchange Mail Submission service running on the mailbox server informs a hub transport server that it has a message to be fetched. The Submission service indicates the database, mailbox, and message identifier to point to where the message is waiting. The transfer of the message between mailbox and hub transport server is the responsibility of the Store driver.

> **Note**
>
> The mailbox server performs the same processing for remote and local deliveries to ensure that all messaging compliance requirements are respected. In effect, outgoing mail goes into an Outbox folder in the Store where it is fetched by the Store driver, which moves the message to the hub transport server, where the message ends up in the submission queue. The transport service retrieves the messages from the submission queue, categorizes them, and then routes the mail by placing the messages onto the appropriate delivery queues for onward transmission.

- Mailbox and hub transport servers within an Active Directory site communicate with each other using server-side remote procedure calls (RPCs). The need to accommodate Exchange RPCs requires the servers to be connected by local area network (LAN)-quality bandwidth because otherwise you run the risk of RPC timeouts and failure.

- If multiple hub transport servers are available in the site, the Mail Submission service selects one on a load-balancing basis. This provides a level of fault tolerance for the transport service. Unless the server is part of a DAG and another hub transport server is available within the site, if a server hosts both the mailbox and hub transport role, Exchange uses the local hub transport server to process messages. An exception is made when a server is part of a DAG because transferring messages off the mailbox server ensures that they are captured by the dumpster of the hub transport server and therefore can be recovered in the case of failure.

- The Active Directory Topology Service is responsible for providing the transport service with information about the current site topology by reference to an Active Directory domain controller/global catalog server.

- Outgoing messages leave via SMTP to other hub transport servers through a routing group connector to legacy Exchange servers, through an SMTP connector to other SMTP email systems, or to a purpose-built gateway for transmission via other means, such as fax.

- Transport events cause various anti-spam agents to fire as messages come into a server. The anti-spam agents can run on hub transport or Edge servers.

- The transport service applies message policies when the categorizer has expanded the set of addresses for messages. The policies are applied through transport rules that can perform processing from the mundane (apply disclaimer text to outgoing messages) to complex (block messages from traveling between different groups of users). The transport service also invokes any journal rules that you define to capture message traffic at this stage.

- Virus scanning products that support the Exchange Virus Scanning API (VSAPI) can inspect incoming and outgoing messages on hub transport and Edge servers.

- All of the hub transport servers in the organization share a common configuration that dictates settings such as the maximum message size that Exchange can transport, the maximum number of recipients on an incoming message, and the connectors that are available to Exchange including connectors hosted by Edge servers. The configuration settings, including details of transport and journal rules, are held in the Active Directory. Edge servers operate as isolated entities that are loosely connected to the organization but do not share configuration settings. If you deploy Edge servers, you have to configure each Edge server separately.

We explore many of these aspects of routing as we progress through the remainder of this chapter.

Active Directory and routing

As we've discussed, Exchange 2010 and Exchange 2007 hub transport servers always attempt to make direct server-to-server connections to send messages. If the destination mailbox is located on a server within the same Active Directory site, the hub transport server makes a direct connection to that server. If the mailbox is located on a server in another site, the hub transport server connects to a hub transport server in that site to exchange the message using a Transport Layer Security (TLS)-secured SMTP link. If the destination server isn't available, Exchange attempts to get the message as close to the destination as possible using a least-cost routing scheme. This is known as queuing at the point of failure.

> **Tip**
>
> Exchange uses Active Directory site costs as the basis for calculating the cheapest cost of transmitting a message. If you're moving from Exchange 2003, you can compare an Active Directory site to a routing group, the Active Directory site link to a routing group connector, and the site link cost to the cost assigned to a routing group connector.

Least-cost routing seems like a simple calculation to perform but it can become a complex exercise in large-scale organizations that span multiple Active Directory sites, especially if the Active Directory administrators haven't paid much attention to site link costs. After all, if replication works, who cares what value the site link costs are? The algorithm used by Exchange is:

1. Determine the target Active Directory site that hosts the destination mailbox.

2. Calculate the cost to the site by adding all of the IP site link costs or connector costs between the source and target sites. Use the separate Exchange cost if it is assigned to a site link. The route with the lowest cost is used.

3. If multiple paths with the same cost exist, the route with the fewest hops is used.

4. If multiple paths still exist, the site with the lowest alphanumeric name is selected.

To queue the message at the point of failure, Exchange goes through the least-cost routing path in reverse order to discover the hub transport server that is closest to the destination. If no hub transport servers outside the home site can be contacted (normally due to a network outage), the message is queued on the local hub transport server and will be retried every minute until it is delivered or it expires from the queue after two days. You can configure these settings with the Set-TransportServer cmdlet. For instance, this command sets the retry interval to five minutes and the timeout interval to three days.

```
Set-TransportServer -Identity ExServer1 -MessageRetryInterval 00:05:00
-MessageExpirationTimeOut 3.00:00:00
```

> **Tip**
>
> You shouldn't change these intervals unless you have good reason to do so. If you do change them, make sure that the same values are applied on all hub transport servers across the organization to ensure consistent behavior.

It's important to understand that least-cost routing determination is not a one-time process that only happens on the originating hub transport server. The same process occurs on each hub transport server through which the message passes to allow further optimization of the route. We discuss how connector scoping can influence routing in the section "Selecting a send connector" later in this chapter.

Overriding Active Directory site link costs

Obviously Active Directory is a very important influence over Exchange 2010 message routing. Any discussion about message routing needs to be informed to make the best possible decisions. One good way to gather the required information is to use the Microsoft Active Directory Topology Diagrammer (downloadable from Microsoft's Web site) to read all the information about the current Active Directory structure and create a graphic representation in Microsoft Visio. The resulting diagrams can be the basis for a discussion about optimum routing paths that takes place between the Active Directory management team and the Exchange administrators (who might be the same people in small to medium-sized companies). Another valuable piece of information is gained by mapping Exchange servers to sites. You can extract a list of servers and their sites with:

```
Get-ExchangeServer | Select Name, Site
```

One possible area of contention is that the IP site link costs that are configured for Active Directory might not represent the best cost for message routing. There are many reasons this could be the case. Active Directory might be in production for a long time and the original IP site link costs have never been updated to reflect the current underlying network connections—and after all, if Active Directory replication works, why worry about revising or updating the site link costs? It's also true that companies might have different teams in charge of Active Directory and Exchange and the two teams might not see eye-to-eye when it comes to assigning the most efficient costs for routing. Such is life. Exchange offers a way around the problem with the ability to substitute an Exchange routing cost for a link to replace the Active Directory IP site link cost. This is done with the Set-ADSiteLink cmdlet. For example, to assign an Exchange cost of 10 to the site link Dublin–London, you'd use a command like this:

```
Set-ADSiteLink -Identity 'Dublin-London' -ExchangeCost 10
```

The Get-ADSite cmdlet reveals all the sites currently defined in Active Directory and the Get-ADSiteLink cmdlet returns a list of current site links. The transport service will begin to use the new cost in its least-cost routing calculations immediately after you configure an Exchange-specific cost for a link. Adding an Exchange-specific cost for a site link does not affect or influence Active Directory replication in any way. Exchange only uses the cost to calculate the optimum routing path for messages.

You can also use the Set-ADSiteLink cmdlet to set a maximum message size for the link. This can be useful if you have a site that sits at the end of an extended link and can't afford to have large messages transmitted across the connection. This might be the case when you have a hub-and-spoke network that connects large datacenters with branch offices or when connections such as satellite links are used to communicate with ships and other locations in hard-to-reach places. The transport service will generate a nondelivery report (NDR) for any attempt to send a larger message across the link. Here's an example of how to set a maximum message size:

```
Set-ADSiteLink –Identity 'Hub to Luton branch' –MaxMessageSize 1MB
```

INSIDE OUT   Do you need another layer of complexity?

Assigning an Exchange-specific routing cost should only be done when absolutely necessary. It might improve the efficiency of routing when first introduced, but moving away from the basic IP site link costs maintained by Active Directory introduces another layer of complexity to manage.

The question of hub sites

Many messaging deployments were designed around hub-and-spoke networks in the days when network bandwidth was expensive, unreliable, and sometimes hard to install into small branch offices or isolated locations. It's a less popular design today now that bandwidth is more plentiful, cheaper, and easier to order and provide almost everywhere. Many companies are exploiting cheap bandwidth to centralize the delivery of IT services and applications in very large datacenters. Some of these projects need to reintroduce elements of hub-and-spoke routing where the datacenter is the hub that hosts the vast majority of computing resources and the spokes go down to a small set of branches that support users who cannot connect to the center to use IT services for one reason or another. Other instances occur where a firewall separates two different parts of a company, each of which has its own Active Directory site, and all communications have to be channeled through a hub site between them.

The Set-ADSite cmdlet is used to mark an Active Directory site as a hub site. For example:

```
Set-ADSite –Identity 'Central Hub Site' –HubSiteEnabled $True
```

You can use the Get-ADSite cmdlet to reveal whether any of the current sites are configured as hub sites.

When hub transport servers calculate the least-cost path for messages, they look to see whether any of the sites in the path are marked as hub sites. If none of the sites are considered hubs, the hub transport server attempts to connect to a hub transport server in the target site to deliver the message. If a hub site is found, the hub transport server attempts to connect to a hub transport server in that site to deliver the message to it for subsequent onward routing to its destination.

Delayed fan-out

Exchange uses a technique called delayed fan-out to optimize the use of network bandwidth to transport messages. After a message goes through the categorizer, Exchange knows the full recipient list and can then calculate the routing path for the message. Once you have a message with multiple recipients, it's likely that different routing paths are necessary to get the message to the destination servers. Typically, email systems fan out and create as many copies of the message as required to travel the different routes. This technique works but it means that all of the copies are created on the originating server and each copy must be processed separately. If some of the recipient mailboxes are in the same database, you end up in a situation where multiple copies of the same message travel across the same connector to the same destination.

To avoid this problem, Exchange examines the routing path for each recipient on a message to determine how it can transfer the fewest copies of the message across common routing paths before it needs to fan out into separate copies. Some copies will have to be generated immediately but in many instances a single copy can be routed across a common link to another hub transport server in another site, which can then create multiple copies for local delivery. The determination of the most efficient delayed fan-out for a message is determined by identifying the hub transport servers that will create multiple copies. Each of these hub transport servers is referred to as a fork in the routing path.

INSIDE OUT   The advantages of delayed fan-out

Delayed fan-out might seem like an esoteric tweak to a well-known routing technique. However, its application can result in substantial savings when messages with large attachments travel across common paths. Consider a message with a 10 MB attachment that's sent to 100 users, 80 of whom are in another site. With normal fan-out, the hub transport server in the local site creates 80 copies of the message and sends them to the hub transport server in the remote site, so a total of 800 MB travels across the network between the two sites. With delayed fan-out, just one copy travels between the hub transport servers in the two sites to achieve a savings of 790 MB. This might not be important if you enjoy unlimited cheap bandwidth, but it can be a critical factor to achieving speedy message transmission across low-bandwidth site connections.

The critical role of hub transport servers

To go deeper into the Exchange transport architecture, it's important to fully understand the work that the hub transport server and the components that collectively form the Exchange transport services do within an Exchange organization. We will get to the details of many of these operations, such as setting up connectors, as we move through the remainder of this chapter.

Hub transport servers are responsible for:

- **Mail flow** Hub transport servers process every message sent inside an Exchange organization before the messages are delivered to mailboxes or routed outside the organization. There are no exceptions to this behavior; Exchange always directs messages through a hub transport server to determine and execute routing. Obviously, this means that you must install a hub transport server inside every Active Directory site that contains a mailbox server.

- **Message submission** Messages flow into hub transport servers in four ways. The first is through SMTP submission via port 25 through a receive connector (or port 587 in the case of POP3 and IMAP4 clients). Connectors handle messages flowing in from other hub transport servers or an Internet connection or through a routing group connector that allows messages to flow in from legacy Exchange servers in a mixed organization. The second method is when applications place properly formatted SMTP messages in the Pickup or Replay directories. The third method is via the Store driver, which handles outgoing messages that the driver fetches when MAPI clients connected to mailbox servers send messages. The Store driver fetches the messages from the Outbox folders in user mailboxes in MAPI format and converts them to

Transport Neutral Encapsulation Format (TNEF) format before submitting them. The last method is when a transport agent creates a message. In all instances, the message ends up on the Submission queue for processing by Transport services. Edge servers accept messages only through a receive connector.

- **Message categorization** The Categorizer performs all address resolution for recipients by checking the addresses for internal recipients in message headers against a global catalog server. It expands distribution groups, which includes making the queries necessary to provide the membership of dynamic distribution groups, and checks these addresses against the global catalog. Once it knows the set of addresses with which it has to work, the categorizer resolves the best routing path for messages and performs any content conversion that is necessary (for example, to ensure that a user receives messages in a preferred format). The categorizer is also responsible for message bifurcation if this is required for efficient message delivery. Every message going through a hub transport server passes through the categorizer. Before the categorizer places a message onto a delivery queue, it checks to see whether the message has to be processed by a transport or journal rule and then performs whatever processing is required. The SP1 version takes user-specified message priority into account when it queues messages to ensure that messages that are of high importance are processed before those of lower importance.

- **Message delivery** When a hub transport server determines that a message is to be delivered to an Exchange mailbox, it either notifies the Store driver (if running on the same server) to effect delivery to a local mailbox (a local mailbox is a mailbox on any server in the same Active Directory site as the hub transport server) or it transfers the message via a send connector to another hub transport server in the Active Directory site hosting the target database, which then takes responsibility for onward delivery to the destination mailbox. If the message cannot be delivered to the hub transport server in that site due to network outages or another reason, the hub transport server will transfer it to another hub transport server in the Active Directory site that is closest to the final destination or queue the message for retry. Messages going to non-Exchange recipients are delivered through an SMTP connector, routed to an Edge server, or routed to an external gateway that has responsibility for transmission to a foreign email system. You don't have to do anything to configure the connectors between hub transport servers in different Active Directory sites because all hub transport servers know about each other through the configuration information held in Active Directory and the connectors are automatically configured by Exchange. You do have to create SMTP connectors for outgoing communications. All communication between hub transport servers is via SMTP and is automatically secured with TLS and Kerberos. Again, you don't have to do anything to configure the secure connections.

- **Protection** Hub transport and Edge servers are the only Exchange servers that can be configured with anti-spam agents to filter and cleanse the messaging stream before messages are routed to recipients. Hub transport servers can host antivirus software to provide a further level of protection. Mailbox servers can also host antivirus software. We discuss how to deploy anti-spam and antivirus software on hub transport and Edge servers later in this chapter.

- **Message recovery** The hub transport server has a facility called the transport dumpster that is used to recover messages that are in transit when a server outage occurs so that they can be redelivered to the mailbox server.

- **Messaging records management** Hub transport servers provide a single point of contact for Exchange to be able to apply transport and journal rules to messages as they flow through the organization. Among other functions, transport rules can apply disclaimers, take selective copies of messages, and stop groups of users from communicating with each other. Journal rules allow Exchange to take full copies of message traffic and move the data to another repository, such as a Hierarchical Storage Management (HSM) system.

Although the Store is often rightly regarded as the heart of Exchange, the message flow capability provided by hub transport servers serves as the lungs because these servers provide the means for Exchange to function and get work done as a messaging system.

Version-based routing

Exchange 2007 made the transition to SMTP-based routing and Exchange 2010 uses the same approach so there should be no problem communicating between servers of the two versions. This theory seems to be proven by the seamless interoperability between Exchange 2007 and Exchange 2010 but, as is so often the case, the devil is in the details. That detail in this case is the change that occurred in the XSO layer due to the massive database schema overhaul for the Store. XSO is an internal managed RPC API that is not documented outside Microsoft (Exchange Web Services [EWS] is now the preferred API for external use). It is used by the Store driver to communicate with the transport service when it needs to send or fetch messages for mailboxes. The Store driver needs to connect to mailbox databases and the schema of those databases is fundamentally transformed by Exchange 2010. The consequence is that the Store driver that runs on an Exchange 2010 mailbox server is very different from the version that runs on an Exchange 2007 mailbox server, which means that an Exchange 2007 mailbox server is unable to communicate directly with an Exchange 2010 hub transport server and vice versa.

The lack of communications seems to create a real challenge for Exchange 2010. Fortunately, there's absolutely no problem with communications between Exchange 2010 hub transport servers and Exchange 2007 hub transport servers because the communications are all based on SMTP. The same is true of intersite routing, because this is also based on SMTP. However, as long as you have one or more Exchange 2007 mailbox servers in a site, you have to retain an Exchange 2007 hub transport server and that hub transport server must run Exchange 2007 SP2 so its routing engine understands the subtle change required to understand different server versions.

The basic routing rule is that messages submitted by or sent to Exchange 2007 mailboxes are handled by an Exchange 2007 hub transport server and messages submitted by Exchange 2010 mailboxes are handled by an Exchange 2010 hub transport server. If an Exchange 2007 mailbox submits a message addressed to an Exchange 2010 mailbox and an Exchange 2010 hub transport server is not available in the site, the routing engine on the Exchange 2007 SP2 hub transport server recognizes that it cannot deliver the message and generates an NDR back to the user; the same process occurs for messages sent along the reverse path. Thus, we need to create the situation shown in Figure 13-2 inside every site that supports a mix of Exchange 2007 and Exchange 2010 servers. You can regard the different hub transport servers as acting as an internal bridgehead between the two versions because messages from an Exchange 2007 mailbox to an Exchange 2010 mailbox must flow through a hub transport server for each version.

> **Tip**
>
> It's a good idea to deploy two hub transport servers of both versions inside large sites that support many mailbox servers to avoid creating a single point of failure. Virtualization is a great way to lower the amount of additional hardware required to maintain the two sets of hub transport servers until you can complete the migration to Exchange 2010.

The requirement to support version-based routing does not compromise the general advice for the order of deployment for Exchange 2010 server roles. You should still deploy CAS servers first, followed by hub transport servers and then mailbox servers. The issue to incorporate into planning is the need to keep at least one Exchange 2007 hub transport server in a site until the last Exchange 2007 mailbox server is removed from that site.

Although it appears complex, the solution of forcing mailbox servers to communicate with a hub transport server running the same version is a good one. The alternative was to force the creation of a separate Active Directory site to support Exchange 2010 servers, which would create a huge amount of complexity within an organization, because you'd need to pair up every existing Active Directory site that contained Exchange 2007 servers with a corresponding site for Exchange 2010 and then install the Exchange 2010 servers into the new sites. After doing all this work, you'd then have to arrange for the old Active Directory sites to be removed after you decommission Exchange 2007.

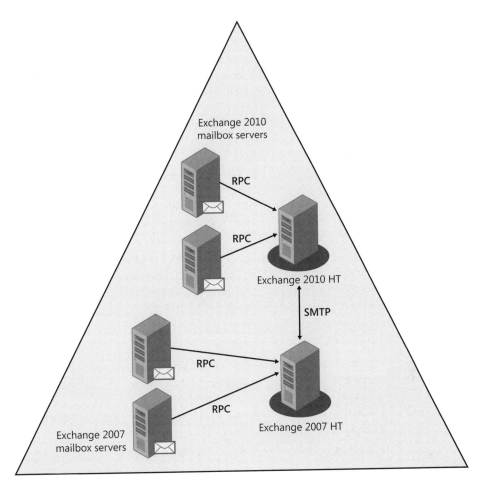

Figure 13-2 Version-based routing.

The X.400 question

If you're migrating from Exchange 2003, you might ask what role the X.400 protocol plays in Exchange 2010. After all, X.400 was the original transport protocol used to connect servers in the days when Exchange still had a tentative relationship with the Internet, a fact that is obvious from the X.400 address stamped on every legacy Exchange mail-enabled object. Although this is all true, the fact is that Exchange has been migrating away from X.400 since Exchange 2000 was released and that process was complete in Exchange 2007. No Exchange 2010 object requires an X.400

address to function and X.400 is never needed for connectivity unless you install an X.400 connector hosted on an Exchange 2003 server to communicate to some legacy email system that still can't talk SMTP.

In the vast majority of cases, once you have moved over to a pure Exchange 2007/2010 environment, you can cheerfully forget all about X.400 and remove any X.400 addresses that linger in the properties of mail-enabled objects. You don't have to delete these addresses if you don't want to. Short of occupying some bytes of storage, they do no harm if left alone.

Transport configuration settings

In Exchange 2000 and Exchange 2003, the Global Message settings define properties such as the maximum message size. Exchange 2007 does not provide the ability to set global messaging defaults through EMC. With Exchange 2010, you can go to the Hub Transport section of the Organization Configuration and click Global Settings to access some of the settings that control how the transport system works. Figure 13-3 illustrates what you will see on the General tab of the Transport Settings Properties dialog box.

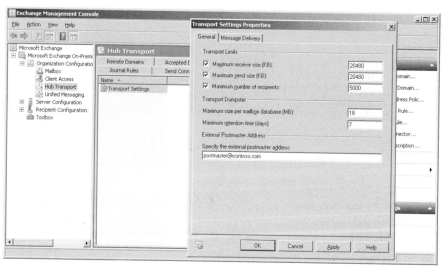

Figure 13-3 Global transport settings.

Inevitably, EMC can only display a subset containing the most commonly altered global transport settings through its user interface. Full access is gained by using the Get-TransportConfig cmdlet to retrieve the settings and the Set-TransportConfig cmdlet to define transport configuration settings for the organization. In a mixed-mode organization, existing settings such as those that govern the maximum size of an incoming message, the maximum size of an outgoing message, and the maximum number of recipients allowed per message are retained, but in a new Exchange organization the value for these parameters is set to be 20 MB. For example, the settings reported by the Get-TransportConfig cmdlet for an organization might look like the output shown next. If you compare this with the output from an Exchange 2007 organization, you'll see that Exchange 2010 has added quite a few additional settings that you can tweak. Some of these properties (for instance, *MigrationEnabled* and *OpenDomainRoutingEnabled*) are reserved for Microsoft internal use when Exchange is deployed in Microsoft's hosted Business Productivity Online Services. Others, such as *ShadowHeartbeatTimeoutInterval*, are used to control new functionality introduced in Exchange 2010 (see the section "Transport pipeline" later in this chapter for more information about shadow redundancy).

```
Get-TransportConfig
```

```
ClearCategories                          : True
DSNConversionMode                        : UseExchangeDSNs
ExternalDelayDsnEnabled                  : True
ExternalDsnDefaultLanguage               :
ExternalDsnLanguageDetectionEnabled      : True
ExternalDsnMaxMessageAttachSize          : 10 MB (10,485,760 bytes)
ExternalDsnReportingAuthority            :
ExternalDsnSendHtml                      : True
ExternalPostmasterAddress                : postmaster@contoso.com
GenerateCopyOfDSNFor                     : {}
HygieneSuite                             : Standard
InternalDelayDsnEnabled                  : True
InternalDsnDefaultLanguage               :
InternalDsnLanguageDetectionEnabled      : True
InternalDsnMaxMessageAttachSize          : 10 MB (10,485,760 bytes)
InternalDsnReportingAuthority            :
InternalDsnSendHtml                      : True
InternalSMTPServers                      : {}
JournalingReportNdrTo                    : Administrator@contoso.com
LegacyJournalingMigrationEnabled         : False
MaxDumpsterSizePerDatabase               : 18 MB (18,874,368 bytes)
MaxDumpsterTime                          : 7.00:00:00
MaxReceiveSize                           : 20 MB (20,971,520 bytes)
MaxRecipientEnvelopeLimit                : 5000
MaxSendSize                              : 20 MB (20,971,520 bytes)
MigrationEnabled                         : False
OpenDomainRoutingEnabled                 : False
Rfc2231EncodingEnabled                   : False
ShadowHeartbeatRetryCount                : 3
ShadowHeartbeatTimeoutInterval           : 00:05:00
ShadowMessageAutoDiscardInterval         : 2.00:00:00
ShadowRedundancyEnabled                  : True
```

```
OrganizationRelationshipForExternalOrganizationEmail :
SupervisionTags
TLSReceiveDomainSecureList                             : {Reject, Allow}
TLSSendDomainSecureList                                : {}
VerifySecureSubmitEnabled                              : {}
VoicemailJournalingEnabled                             : False
HeaderPromotionModeSetting                             : True
Xexch50Enabled                                         : NoCreate
                                                       : True
```

Setting a new value in the transport configuration is easy:

```
Set-TransportConfig -MaxSendSize 50MB
```

Table 13-1 lists the most important properties that you can set with the Set-TransportConfig cmdlet and their meanings. See TechNet or the Exchange help file for more information.

Table 13-1 Global transport settings that can be set through the Set-TransportConfig cmdlet

Parameters	Meaning
−ClearCategories	Controls whether the transport engine clears Outlook categories during content conversion. The default is $True.
−DSNConversionMode	Controls how Exchange handles delivery status notifications (DSNs) that are created by earlier versions of Exchange or non-Exchange messaging systems. The default value is UseExchangeDSNs, which forces a conversion to the DSN format used by Exchange 2010. An alternate is PreserveDSNBody, which converts DSNs to Exchange 2010 format but preserves any customized text that they might contain. You can also specify DoNotConvert, which does exactly what it says.
−ExternalDelayDSNEnabled	Specifies whether Exchange should create a DSN if messages from external recipients cannot be delivered immediately. The default is $True.
−ExternalDSNLanguageDetectionEnabled	Controls whether Exchange attempts to send a DSN in the same language as the original message. The default is $True.
−ExternalDSNMaxMessageAttachSize	Defines the maximum size of the attachments sent with a DSN. The default is 10 MB. If the attachments exceed this value, Exchange sends a DSN that includes the original headers but no attachments.

–ExternalPostmasterAddress	This property specifies the email address that Exchange inserts into the From header field of a DSN sent to an external recipient. The default is $Null, meaning that Exchange uses the default postmaster address from the hub transport or edge server that generates the DSN (postmaster@*defaultaccepteddomain.com*, where *defaultaccepteddomain .com* is the default accepted domain for the organization). If a value is entered in this property, Exchange uses this value instead.
–GenerateCopyOfDSNFor	Defines whether any DSN messages are copied to the Postmaster mailbox (as defined by Set-TransportServer cmdlet). The desired DSNs are defined by their code (for example, 5.1.1). By default, no messages are copied.
–HeaderPromotionModeSetting	Controls whether Exchange creates named properties for values contained in custom X-headers on incoming messages. The default is *NoCreate*, so Exchange does not. You can also set this property to *MustCreate* to force creation or *MayCreate* to allow creation for messages received from authenticated senders.
–InternalDelayDSNEnabled	Determines whether Exchange creates DSNs for messages from internal senders that cannot be delivered immediately. The default is $True.
–InternalDSNMaxMessageAttachSize	Serves a similar purpose to *–ExternalDSNMaxMessageAttach Size* and has the same default value of 10 MB.
–InternalSMTPServers	A list of IP addresses of SMTP servers that the anti-spam agents consider to be internal and therefore ignore as a potential source of spam.
–JournalingReportNdrTo	The mailbox to which the journaling agent will send journal reports if the journal mailbox is unavailable.
–MaxDumpsterSizePerDatabase	Defines the maximum size of the dumpster used by DAG servers to recover in-transit messages in case of "lossy" database transitions failures. Only used when DAGs are active.
–MaxDumpsterTime	Defines the maximum time that messages remain in the transport dumpster. Only used when DAGs are active. To enable the transport dumpster, the size of the dumpster must be greater than zero (it should be something reasonable such as 100 MB) and the dumpster time has to be nonzero. A good standard value is 7.00:00:00, or seven days.
–MaxReceiveSize	The maximum size of message that can be received by the organization.

−MaxRecipientEnvelopeLimit	The maximum number of recipients that can be in the header of an incoming message (including the results of group expansion; groups are counted as 1 even if there are many recipients in the group).
−MaxSendSize	Sets the maximum size of message that can be sent within the organization.
−Rfc2231EncodingEnabled	Specifies whether RFC 2231 MIME encoding is enabled within the organization. The default is $False.
−ShadowHeartbeatRetryCount	Specifies the number of heartbeat intervals that a server waits before assuming that the primary server for a message has failed. In this case, the server assumes ownership of the messages in the shadow queue that are owned by the failed server. The default value is 3.
−ShadowHeartbeatTimeoutInterval	Specifies the time interval that a server waits before it establishes a connection to a primary server to query the discard status of shadow messages. The default is 00:05:00 (five minutes).
−ShadowMessageAutoDiscardInterval	Specifies how long a primary server maintains discard events for shadow messages. If the shadow server doesn't query the events within this interval, the primary server discards them. The default value is 2.00:00:00 (two days).
−ShadowRedundancyEnabled	Specifies whether the shadow redundancy feature us enabled within the organization. The default is $True.
−TLSReceiveDomainSecureList	Contains a list of domains that are configured for mutual TLS authentication through receive connectors.
−TLSSendDomainSecureList	Contains a list of domains that are configured for mutual TLS authentication through send connectors.
−VerifySecureSubmitEnabled	Set to $True to force MAPI clients to submit messages over a secure channel (encrypted RPCs). The default is $False. By default, Outlook 2007 and Outlook 2010 use a secure channel, but previous versions do not.
−VoicemailJournalingEnabled	Defines whether voice mail messages can be journaled by the journal agent. The default is $True.
−Xexch50Enabled	Defines whether backward compatibility should be enabled for Exchange 2000 and Exchange 2003 servers. The default is $True.

Transport configuration settings apply on an organization-wide basis and are respected by all Exchange 2007 and Exchange 2010 hub transport servers. Other commands influence the way that messages are processed by the transport engine. For example, you can configure receive connectors with parameters such as the maximum number of recipients for a message and the maximum number of connections it will accept in total or from one source. For example:

```
Set-ReceiveConnector –Identity 'Internet Connector for Organization'
–MaxRecipientsPerMessage 250
```

After making this change, if the connector is presented with a message that has more than 250 recipients, it accepts the message for the maximum permitted (250) and rejects the rest of the message. Most modern SMTP senders will then resend the message up to the permitted maximum and continue in this loop until all of the message recipients have been processed. After the receive connector has accepted the message (end of data transfer), it checks to see whether the message is too large (size is greater than –*MaxMessageSize*).

Being able to send a very large message is no guarantee that the message will be able to reach its final destination unless the destination is within the Exchange organization because it is very likely that the message will encounter a limit on an external connector or server along its path that will result in a rejection. Even within an Exchange organization, if a user who has the ability to send a 10 MB message sends such a message to a mailbox that is configured with a lower receive limit, then Exchange will reject the message because it is the recipient's limit that governs their ability to receive. In this situation, the sender receives a message similar to that shown in Figure 13-4.

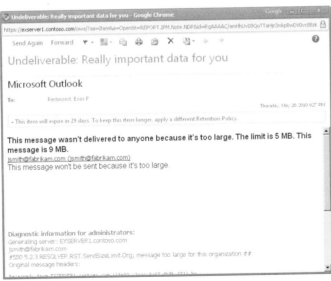

Figure 13-4 Nondelivery notification when a user sends a message that is too large .

The normal default value for the maximum message size for send and receive connectors is 10 MB. To change this value on a send connector:

```
Set-SendConnector –Identity 'Outbound to Legacy' –MaxMessageSize 20MB
```

And for a receive connector:

```
Set-ReceiveConnector -Identity 'Inbound from Fabrikam' -MaxMessageSize 15MB
```

If you don't know the identifiers for the various connectors in the organization, use the Get-SendConnector or Get-ReceiveConnector cmdlets to list all of the current connectors, including those hosted by Edge servers.

It is possible for a message size to fluctuate as it makes its way from initial entry via an Edge or hub transport server to final delivery. Format conversion, encoding, and agent processing are reasons why message size can change. It is undesirable to reject a message just because its original size has swelled due to en-route processing. The first time a message passes through a hub transport server, Exchange stamps a message with an X-header called *X-MS-Exchange-Organization-OriginalSize* and uses this field to store the original message size. Downstream checks performed by hub transport servers in other sites use these data instead of the current message size when they decide whether or not to block a message. Note that some messages bypass checking, including system messages, agent-generated messages, and anything to do with journaling and message quarantining.

The *-MaxRecipientEnvelopeLimit* determines the maximum number of individual recipients that can be in the P1 envelope for a message. Each group in a message header is treated as one recipient for the purpose of checking against the maximum recipient limit.

Limits on user mailboxes

Even when a receive connector is able to accept a message, there are other checks to ensure that Exchange can process an incoming message because you can configure limits on an individual mailbox to reject messages that are smaller than the organization's acceptable maximum size. For example, suppose I did this:

```
Set-Mailbox -Identity Redmond -MaxReceiveSize 2MB
```

Now that the mailbox is confined to a maximum message size of 2 MB, Exchange will reject any message sent to the mailbox that is over that size, even if the receive connector and the global transport settings allow the message to pass. Note that authenticated users can also have a maximum permitted message send size that Exchange will respect even if it blows the limits that apply to connectors. I guess that the logic here is that administrators must know what they are doing when they allow certain mailboxes to send very large messages, so Exchange should treat these situations as exceptions and permit them to pass.

Another point that might be confusing is the meaning of the term "unlimited" when applied to a mailbox. As previously discussed, you can set a maximum size for incoming messages on a mailbox. You can also set a maximum send size on a mailbox. By default, newly created mailboxes have these settings set to Unlimited, so when you examine these settings on mailboxes, you'll probably see output similar to that shown here:

```
Get-Mailbox | Sort DisplayName | Format-Table DisplayName, Max*Size –AutoSize
```

DisplayName	MaxSendSize	MaxReceiveSize
Administrator	unlimited	unlimited
Abrus, Luka	unlimited	unlimited
Adams, Terry	unlimited	unlimited
Alexander, David	unlimited	unlimited
Americas Help Desk	unlimited	unlimited
Anderson, Nancy (Sales)	unlimited	unlimited

Unlimited means that Exchange doesn't apply a specific mailbox restriction when it processes a message. It does not mean that the mailbox is able to send or receive a message of any size and that it can ignore organization-wide or connector-specific limitations. You can set a very large maximum receive size on a mailbox but it will be ignored if the organization and connectors impose lower limits. Likewise, if you set a lower limit on a mailbox than that which applies to the organization and connectors, Exchange will process larger incoming messages until it encounters the mailbox limit, at which point they are rejected.

For trivia fans, the documentation says that the limit for the maximum send and receive properties is 2 GB, but the largest size I could set with EMS is 1.9999 GB. Exchange reported this value as 2 GB. Unfortunately, I could never quite send a 2 GB message to test that it would be delivered!

Transport configuration file

So far we have discussed organization-wide transport settings. Server-specific transport settings for Exchange 2007 and Exchange 2010 hub transport and Edge servers are implemented through a configuration file called EdgeTransport.exe.config located in the \Bin directory. The file is in XML format and the Exchange 2010 version expands to contain many more entries than its Exchange 2007 counterpart and controls settings such as the location of the queue database and various thresholds used to control the performance of the transport system.

Normally, you should not have to access the transport configuration file unless you need to change a parameter that cannot be updated through EMS. For example, if you want to move the location of the transport queue database, you will find that there is no parameter to change through the Set-TransportConfig cmdlet. Instead, you will have to open the transport configuration file with a text editor and edit the default settings to tell the transport service where you want to locate the files. The following lines tell the transport system that the transport queue database and its transaction logs are stored in nonstandard locations on drive D:

```
<add key="QueueDatabasePath" value="D:\Data\TransportQueue" />
<add key="QueueDatabaseLoggingPath" value="D:\Data\TransportLogs" />
```

After making the change to the transport configuration file, you have to stop the transport service and move the queue database and its associated files to the new locations before you restart the transport service.

Another common customization is to include lines in the transport configuration file that affect how the transport service works when hub transport and Edge servers come under load. Exchange 2007 and Exchange 2010 incorporate the concept of back pressure, which means that when a server is under load, it will stop accepting new connections to reduce load on the server. Eventually, the conditions that cause the back pressure to mount will ease and the transport service will resume normal working. Conditions such as free disk space and available memory are used to determine when a back pressure condition exists. For example, if less than 4 GB free (disk and database) space exists on the drive that holds the message queue database, Exchange applies back pressure. Events are logged in the Application Event Log whenever a back pressure condition occurs. For example, the MSExchangeTransport component logs event 15006 whenever available disk space falls below the configured threshold.

You can alter how Exchange responds to back pressure conditions by customizing the transport configuration file. This is quite a complex task to undertake, because you obviously have to understand why the back pressure condition exists before you can proceed to make changes to address the situation. After making a change, you will have to wait until the transport system restarts and stabilizes under load before you know whether the change is successful, so careful monitoring of the server is required until you can be satisfied that the change has the desired effect over the long term.

CAUTION

Another issue to bear in mind is that it is very easy to make a mistake when you edit configuration files with a text editor. An editor like NotePad or WordPad will not flag syntax errors and the first indication that a problem exists will not be seen until the transport service attempts to read the configuration file when it restarts. For this reason, you might want to investigate using an XML-aware editor like Microsoft XML Notepad to reduce the risk of making syntax errors when you edit these files. Be very careful when you make changes and always test each change on a test system before applying it in production.

Caching the results of group expansion

Not all of the available settings are included in the transport configuration file. For example, Exchange allocates some memory to cache the list of members of a distribution group for processing during message categorization. The cached data are examined to detect duplicate addresses that arise as a result of group expansion. A similar cache is used to track any delivery restrictions that might exist for a recipient (for example, whether the message sender is allowed to send to a recipient). Only the Active Directory globally unique identifier (GUID) for each recipient is cached (16 bytes) and the caches are reused for each message, meaning that the available memory is used very efficiently. By default, Exchange allocates both caches 1.6 MB of memory, which is sufficient to hold the GUIDs for up to 100,000 recipients. This should be sufficient to cache the fully expanded recipient list from even the most complex distribution groups formed from many nested groups.

INSIDE OUT   Processing very large distribution groups

If your deployment has to process very large distribution groups, you can alter the cache size by inserting the following keys and providing a value for the number of recipients for the cache:

- MaxResolveRecipientCacheSize controls the memory used to cache recipient GUIDs. Because these GUIDs are unique, duplicate entries are easy to detect.

- MaxResolverMemberofGroupCacheSize controls the memory used to cache the group membership for the sender of the message. Exchange uses the cache to check for any restrictions that might apply to nested groups found when the full recipient list is expanded and thus avoids the need to make multiple lookups against Active Directory.

Exchange 2007 also removes duplicate addressees and tracks restrictions when it expands the membership of groups, but experience proved that performance was slow when Exchange was presented with a very large distribution group that might include many nested groups, some of which had complicated delivery restrictions. To explain the challenge that exists for any email system that has to process a very large set of recipients for a message, consider the case of a group intended to allow users to send to everyone in the company. In any large organization, it's unlikely that you would build such a group from individual recipients or even attempt to create a dynamic distribution group for the purpose. Even if you create a strong integration between the human resources system and Exchange, maintaining the membership of such a list could become a nightmare and the user interface of programs such as EMC isn't designed to deal with lists that contain more than a couple of thousand members. In addition, Windows has its own challenges in dealing with very large groups. Windows 2003 and later versions are much better at handling operations such as membership updates for large groups, but Windows is still not optimized to handle a group that might have 50,000 or 100,000 members.

Accordingly, the usual approach in these circumstances is to build an organization-wide distribution group from many smaller groups, each of which might represent a department or other entity within the organization. By combining all the groups in one "supergroup," you create a much more manageable situation because you can devolve responsibility for maintaining group membership to the department level and also avoid any problems that might arise with software used to list, report, and update group membership. However, Exchange still has to deal with these supergroups when they are used to address messages. Each of the subgroups has to be expanded, each might have its own restrictions (for example, only certain users can send messages to the CEO's office), and there's a fair chance that some duplicate recipients will arise through individuals being associated with multiple departments.

Exchange 2007 is able to expand all the groups in a supergroup and address messages to very large recipient sets but the lack of dedicated caches to track recipient membership and restrictions created a situation where Exchange had to continually access Active Directory as it built the recipient list. Even the fastest servers might take 20 or 30 minutes to process a very large list and the global catalog server used for the Active Directory lookups would be stressed by the queries flowing from Exchange. Adding the caches in Exchange 2010 enables Exchange to resolve group membership much more quickly and dramatically reduces the number of Active Directory queries.

> **Note**
>
> Microsoft has sized the caches to handle all but extreme conditions and you shouldn't need to change the values unless you see evidence that hub transport servers are struggling to process very large groups. For instance, if messages sent to a supergroup are not delivered within five minutes, it might be an indication that Exchange needs to dedicate more memory, especially if the expanded group addresses more than 100,000 recipients.

Routing tables

The routing table contains details of servers, databases, and connectors within the organization and is used by the transport system to determine the best routing for messages. The routing table is cached in memory and is used as the basis for routing decisions. Exchange calculates its routing table every time the transport service is restarted or following a change in the Exchange configuration data held in Active Directory that might affect message routing. These changes include the creation of new connectors, the amendment of connector details to define new address spaces, or the installation of a new hub transport server. The routing table also changes when hub transport and Edge servers renew the Kerberos token that they use to secure communication with Active Directory. The token is renewed every six hours.

Even if no changes occur in the routing configuration, the transport service writes out a snapshot of the current routing table every 12 hours into an XML format log file that you can find in the C:\Program Files\Microsoft\Exchange Server\TransportRoles \Logs\Routing directory. If required, you can amend this interval by changing the *RoutingConfigReloadInterval* variable in the EdgeTransport.exe.config file in the Exchange \Bin directory. The routing log files are named *RoutingConfig#x@mm_dd _yyyy hh_mm_ss.xml*. For example, the routing log created on February 18, 2010 at 05:56:12 am (all times are in UTC) is named RoutingConfig#56@02_18_2010 05_56_12.xml.

By default, Exchange keeps the last seven days of routing tables or up to 50 MB of files. Even in an organization where the routing infrastructure changes all the time, this allocation is usually more than sufficient to store seven days of routing logs, but if the routing tables were to exceed this allocation, Exchange uses a circular logging mechanism to discard the oldest logs to free space for new files. These values can be viewed with the Get-TransportServer cmdlet and updated with the Set-TransportServer cmdlet:

```
Get-TransportServer -Identity ExServer2
```

```
Name                          : ExServer2
RoutingTableLogMaxAge         : 7.00:00:00
RoutingTableLogMaxDirectorySize : 50 MB (52,428,800 bytes)
RoutingTableLogPath           : C:\Program Files\Microsoft\Exchange Server\
V14\TransportRoles\Logs\Routing
```

The routing table is composed of 22 sectors that collectively form Exchange's knowledge of the current routing topology as it exists for the site that hosts the server that generates the table. Each site can have a different routing table because you can create scoped connectors that are only available to hub transport servers within the site and are invisible to hub transport servers outside the site. In this situation, the routing table for the site with the scoped connector will differ from the routing table for the other sites. Therefore, if you ever have to use the routing table to debug a routing problem, make sure that you connect to the server where you suspect the problem exists and use its copy of the routing table as a starting point.

You can access the routing table by opening it with a browser (Figure 13-5) or other XML editor or through the routing table viewer from the Exchange toolbox. Looking through the raw XML reveals some detail about the structure of the routing table. It is divided into sections that describe different aspects of the Exchange routing environment:

- **Routing Tables:** Provides basic information about the routing table such as the date and time of creation plus information about server names (full Active Directory distinguished names are used to distinguish servers), mailbox databases, and legacy servers with server routes.

- **Exchange Topology:** Links server names with topology servers (servers that can participate in routing).

- **Topology Servers:** Lists the Exchange servers that can participate in routing.

- **Topology Sites:** Lists all the Active Directory sites, including those where an Exchange hub transport server is not present.

- **Topology Site Link:** Lists all the Active Directory site links.

- **Active Directory Site Relay Map:** Lists the Active Directory paths to every site containing an Exchange server.

- **Active Directory Topology Path:** Lists routes to every remote Active Directory site.

- **Target Site:** Lists Active Directory sites that contain hub transport servers.

- **Routing Group Relay Map:** Lists the routing groups for legacy Exchange servers.

- **Routing Group Topology Site:** Lists all routing groups and their connectors.

- **Routing Group Topology Link:** Lists the links between routing groups.

- **Routing Group Topology Path:** Links routing groups with connectors.

- **Routing Group Connector Route:** Lists routes to next hop for connectors.

- **Server Routing:** Lists every Exchange server and a route to it.

- **Home Mdb Routing:** Lists every database (including public folder databases) in the organization.

- **Connector Routing:** Lists every connector route in the organization.

- **Connector Route:** Lists every connector in the organization.

- **SMTP Send Connector Configuration:** Lists every SMTP Send Connector in the organization.

- Address space: Lists all the address spaces and types available within the organization.

- Legacy Gateway Connector: Lists every Notes and GroupWise connector used by Exchange 2000 or Exchange 2003 in the organization. As noted previously, Exchange 2010 servers do not support legacy connectors except via an Exchange 2003 server.

- Non-SMTP Gateway Connection: Lists all connectors that use the drop directory.

- Address Type Routing: Maps address types to SMTP connector index.

- SMTP Connector Index: Maps each part of SMTP address space to a node and associates it with a connector. For example, contoso.com will generate nodes for "contoso" and "com."

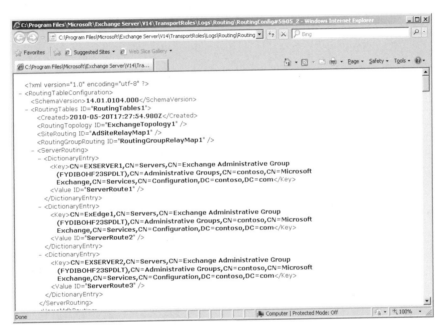

Figure 13-5 Examining an Exchange 2010 routing log.

The raw XML data are interesting but complex to interpret because much of the essential information is hidden in the XML formatting. The Routing Log Viewer (Figure 13-6) interprets the XML to display the routing table. You can select and open a routing log from a hub transport server and browse its contents to discover what connectors are available, the servers that can use the connectors, the address spaces they serve, and so on. Some impediments to routing, such as maximum message size limits, are obvious and you can see details of Active Directory site costs that are used to determine least-cost routes. You'll also see if an Exchange cost has been assigned to an Active Directory site link. As a troubleshooting aid, you can compare one routing log with another to help determine if changes exist between the two configurations. Unfortunately there is no way to create a report of a configuration for record-keeping purposes, but it is easy to take screen shots and paste them into documents if this need occurs.

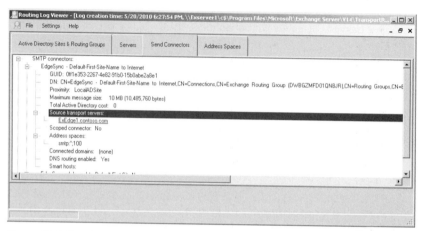

Figure 13-6 Routing Log Viewer.

TLS security

In earlier versions of Exchange, you had to configure TLS manually and install a certificate for TLS to use before servers could encrypt traffic. Exchange 2010 makes the process much easier by enabling TLS by default and automatically securing the communication that flows between hub transport servers with TLS using either the self-signed certificate that Exchange servers generate or the certificate that you install for this purpose. All inbound SMTP sessions can be encrypted and Exchange 2010 will attempt to encrypt all remote sessions, including those to other messaging systems. The existence of self-signed certificates is sufficient to allow Exchange 2010 to negotiate an encrypted connection with other SMTP servers that support a feature called opportunistic TLS. In short, the servers can figure out how to trust each other for the purpose of exchanging protected SMTP traffic.

This is good, except in situations where devices known as WAN Optimization Controllers (WOCs) are used. Typically, these devices are installed to optimize network use between small branch offices and large hub sites so that all of the applications that need to send data between the branch office and the hub are able to use sufficient high-quality network capacity. WOCs accomplish this goal by compressing traffic across the network but SMTP traffic that is secured with TLS cannot be compressed, so this creates a problem.

The solution is to disable TLS. This allows the WOC to compress the SMTP traffic with the side effect that the traffic is then unencrypted.

A full description of the issues involved in this situation can be found at *http://technet .microsoft.com/en-us/library/ee633456.aspx.*

Receive connectors

SMTP has provided the foundation for Exchange's transport system since Exchange 2000 switched from X.400. Exchange has long incorporated SMTP connectors to allow bidirectional email communications with other SMTP-based messaging systems, so the transition to a pure SMTP environment was always on the cards once Internet protocols grew in popularity and replaced X.400 and X.500 as the de facto standards for interoperability. Exchange divides its SMTP communications into receive and send connectors. Receive connectors accept incoming messages from other SMTP servers, including Exchange servers, or POP3 and IMAP4 clients that use SMTP to send their messages. When you install the hub transport role on a server, the installation procedure creates two default receive connectors to allow the server to communicate with other Exchange servers within the organization and to accept messages from authenticated POP3 and IMAP4 clients. In comparison, when you install an Edge server, the installation procedure creates a receive connector that is configured to accept messages from the Internet.

To see the default receive connectors, use the Get-ReceiveConnector cmdlet. For example:

```
Get-ReceiveConnector –Server ExServer1
```

```
Identity                     Bindings                    Enabled
--------                     --------                    -------
ExServer1\Default ExServer1  {:::25, 0.0.0.0:25}         True
ExServer1\Client ExServer1   {:::587, 0.0.0.0:587}       True
```

You'll see two similar receive connectors on any Exchange 2010 hub transport server, so you can regard these connectors as the default set of receive connectors. Each receive connector is configured to listen to a specific port for incoming connections to the server that hosts it. Connectors that handle interserver connections listen to port 25, the standard used by servers to send messages to each other. Connectors that handle messages from POP3 and IMAP4 clients listen to port 587. By default, client connections need to be authenticated, meaning that messages are only accepted from clients who can authenticate themselves with Windows credentials and who have Exchange mailboxes. This is a change from the behavior of Exchange 2003 connectors, which typically allow unauthenticated POP3 and IMAP4 clients to connect and send messages. The default receive connectors accept messages from any IP address, but you can configure them to only accept messages from specific IP addresses.

The properties of the connector establish the servers that can send messages through the connector. One fundamental control is the ability to limit the sources from which the connector will accept messages. This control is exerted by assigning the ability to access the connector to permission groups rather than individual users. A permission group is a predefined set of permissions assigned to an object (in this case, the connector) that is granted to well-known security principals such as a user or group. Exchange uses permission groups to make it easier to configure access to a connector. It is much more convenient to deal with security through groups that represent entities such as "anyone who has an Exchange mailbox" (Exchange users) or "any other Exchange server in this organization" (Exchange servers) rather than having to assign the permission to individual objects. You can find details of all of the permission groups and the permissions that each includes in TechNet online. As an example, Table 13-2 describes the permissions included in the AnonymousUsers and ExchangeUsers permission groups.

Table 13-2 **Example Permission Group**

Permission Group	Security Principal	Included Permissions
AnonymousUsers	Anonymous User Account	Ms-Exch-SMTP-Submit Ms-Exch-SMTP-Accept-Any-Sender MS-Exch-SMTP-Accept-Authoritative-Domain-Sender Ms-Exch-Accept-Headers-Routing
ExchangeUsers	Authenticated User Accounts	Ms-Exch-SMTP-Submit Ms-Exch-SMTP-Accept-Any-Recipient Ms-Exch-Bypass-Anti-Spam Ms-Exch-Accept-Headers-Routing

As you can see in Figure 13-7, the default connector on this hub transport server can handle connections from objects covered by the following permission groups:

- Anonymous users

- Exchange users

- Exchange servers

- Legacy Exchange servers

This configuration differs from the default that Exchange 2010 establishes when it creates a receive connector by including Anonymous Users to permit connections from SMTP servers that don't authenticate themselves, such as Exchange servers in another organization or other SMTP servers operating elsewhere on the Internet.

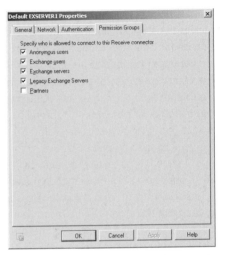

Figure 13-7 Permission groups for a receive connector.

INSIDE OUT   Anonymous connections for receive connectors

It's interesting that Microsoft omits anonymous connections from its default configuration, perhaps due to an assumption that messages flowing into hub transport servers from the Internet flow through Edge servers. Anonymous connections wouldn't be necessary if this was the case because the connection between an Edge server and a hub transport server is always secured with TLS. Edge servers always allow anonymous connections because otherwise they couldn't receive incoming messages from the Internet. The lesson here is that you need to check the permission groups on the default receive connectors created by the Exchange setup program and add the ability to process anonymous connections if you don't use Edge servers. Finally, this receive connector does not include the Partners permission group, which is used when mutual TLS connections are set up with a remote domain. However, the permission groups shown here are sufficient for the vast majority of all Exchange 2007 and Exchange 2010 hub transport servers.

Unless you commit a major security faux pas and expose Exchange hub transport servers directly to the Internet, it is quite safe to update the receive connector to include the Anonymous Users permission group to allow it to handle SMTP traffic generated by other clients and servers within the firewall. Although it might seem like a good idea to configure receive connectors to allow unauthenticated interserver connections, some administrators consider this step to be a security risk. In line with its "secure by default" design principle,

Microsoft decided that it was best if administrators took a deliberate step to configure connectors if they wanted to support anonymous connections on hub transport servers and this is how Exchange 2007 and Exchange 2010 operate. Things are different on Edge servers. In this case, the Edge server role is explicitly designed to accept and process incoming messages from external servers, so it wouldn't make sense if its connectors forced authenticated connections. You can update the connector by selecting the Anonymous Users check box in the Permission Group Properties dialog box, as shown in Figure 13-8, or with EMS:

```
Set-ReceiveConnector -Identity 'ExServer1\Default ExServer1' -PermissionGroups
'AnonymousUsers, ExchangeUsers, ExchangeServers, ExchangeLegacyServers'
```

Remember that receive connectors are scoped to a single server, so if you apply this change to the default receive connector on one hub transport server, you should apply it to all the hub transport servers that are active across the organization. If you don't configure a receive connector to allow anonymous connections, users who send messages from the other email systems will receive nondelivery notifications with an error code of 5.7.1, which means that the sending server was unable to authenticate itself and so the connection was terminated by the hub transport server. If some hub transport servers allow anonymous connections and others don't, you can find yourself in a situation where messages presented at one connector will be accepted whereas they will fail if routed to another connector—an unacceptable situation for a messaging system. Figure 13-8 shows the nondelivery notification generated by an Exchange 2010 organization for a message that it couldn't deliver to a user in another Exchange 2010 organization. In this case, the essential clue is the 5.7.1 Client Was Not Authenticated line in the diagnostic information at the bottom of the message.

Figure 13-8 Undeliverable message because anonymous connections are not allowed.

INSIDE OUT
Best practice for incoming messages from external SMTP servers

Updating the default receive connector to allow anonymous connections is the easy solution to the problem of accepting incoming messages from external SMTP servers. However, this approach means that you use the same configuration for internal and external messages. You might want to treat external messages differently; for instance, you might allow users to send 10 MB messages internally but want to restrict incoming messages to 5 MB. In this circumstance, it is best practice to create one or more dedicated receive connectors to process intranet SMTP traffic and then customize these connectors with appropriate message size limits and to allow anonymous connections. You can then direct internal SMTP traffic for the Exchange organization to the servers that host the receive connectors.

Creating a receive connector

Before you create a new receive connector, you need to understand why it is required and what additional functionality it will provide to the organization over and above that available through the default receive connectors that Exchange creates on all hub transport servers. The questions that you might ask include the following:

1. What hub transport server will host the new connector?

2. What function does the new connector serve? Will it connect two internal Exchange organizations, handle other internal SMTP traffic, connect Exchange 2010 to Exchange 2003, or have another use?

3. What special settings such as the maximum size of inbound messages apply to the connector?

4. What permissions are necessary for clients who will use the receive connector?

Once these answers are clear, you can proceed to the Server Configuration section of EMC. Select the Hub Transport node, then the server that will host the new connector, and then select the New Receive Connector option. EMC launches the New Receive Connector Wizard and asks you to name the new connector and select its purpose from a drop-down list (Figure 13-9).

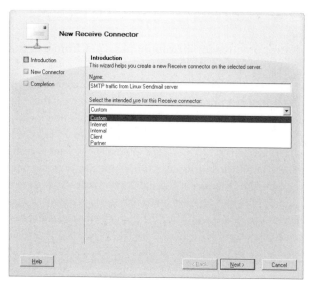

Figure 13-9 Creating a new receive connector.

The selected purpose determines the permission groups and other settings that Exchange applies to the new connector and can be any of the following:

- **Custom:** Allows the greatest flexibility in the use of the connector. A connector of this type can be used for many purposes, including cross-forest connections and connections to other SMTP-based mail systems that operate within the firewall.

- **Internet:** Used to allow unencumbered connections from external SMTP servers. This setting is used by Edge transport servers and should not be used for intranet connections.

- **Internal:** Used for connections between this Exchange organization and other Exchange organizations that operate within the firewall.

- **Client:** Used to support POP3 and IMAP4 client connections.

- **Partner:** Used for TLS-secured connections with specified partner domains (see the discussion in the section "TLS security" earlier in this chapter).

For our purposes, we want to create a new receive connector to handle incoming messages generated by a Linux-based Sendmail system. We don't need to create a specific connector for this purpose, because it would be possible to amend the properties of a default receive connector on a hub transport server to accept anonymous connections, as discussed earlier, and point the Sendmail system to this server as its entry point to the Exchange organization. However, having a dedicated connector allows more control over the messaging flow because we can configure the connector to only accept messages from servers in a certain IP range.

Because it allows for the most control over its settings, the most appropriate type of connector is Custom. After we define the name and purpose of the new connector, the next step is to configure local network settings (Figure 13-10). These control the IP addresses and ports that the connector will monitor for incoming messages. The default values are to monitor all available IP addresses assigned to the server and to use port 25, which are suitable for our purposes. We can also define the fully qualified domain name (FQDN) that the connector will advertise to other servers. The default value is the FQDN of the hub transport server that hosts the connector, but we can change this to something like mail-exchange.contoso.com if we prefer to use a more illustrative name. Of course, we'll need to define an IP address in the Domain Name System (DNS) to resolve this name before the remote servers can connect.

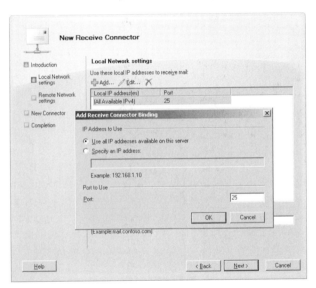

Figure 13-10 Configuring local network settings for the new connector.

The final step is to tell Exchange the IP addresses of remote servers from which the connector will accept messages. The default is to allow all possible IP addresses (from 0.0.0.0 to 255.255.255.255), meaning that any server can connect. Remote servers can also mean POP3 and IMAP4 clients that submit messages via SMTP. For instance, if you want to create a receive connector to send messages on behalf of a set of POP3 and IMAP4 clients, you can specify the range of IP addresses used by the clients to ensure that only these clients can connect to relay their outbound messages. To complete the picture, when creating the receive connector, you'd set it to be of type Client to ensure that Exchange selects the right permissions to allow the clients to connect.

In this case, we know the IP address of our Sendmail server so we can restrict valid connections to just this address, as shown in Figure 13-11. We can then complete the wizard and have it create the new receive connector. The EMS code used will be something like this:

```
New-ReceiveConnector -Name 'SMTP traffic from Linux Sendmail server' -Usage 'Custom'
-Bindings '0.0.0.0:25' -RemoteIPRanges '192.165.70.71' -Server 'EXSERVER1'
```

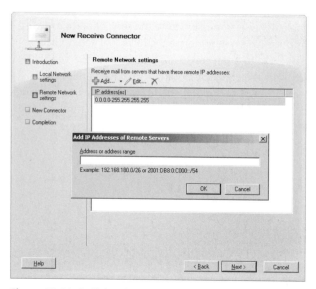

Figure 13-11 Defining the IP range for the new receive connector.

In line with the design philosophy of simplifying the user interface to show options that are necessary and of most use to the vast majority of circumstances (a good application of the 80–20 rule), the settings applied to create the new connector do not represent the complete range of settings that you can use to configure a receive connector. We can explore the available settings by examining the connector's configuration with the Get-ReceiveConnector cmdlet.

```
Get-ReceiveConnector -Identity 'SMTP traffic from Linux Sendmail server'| Format-List
```

```
AuthMechanism                        : Tls
Banner                               :
BinaryMimeEnabled                    : True
Bindings                             : {0.0.0.0:25}
ChunkingEnabled                      : True
DefaultDomain                        :
DeliveryStatusNotificationEnabled    : True
EightBitMimeEnabled                  : True
DomainSecureEnabled                  : False
EnhancedStatusCodesEnabled           : True
```

```
LongAddressesEnabled                          : False
OrarEnabled                                   : False
SuppressXAnonymousTls                         : False
AdvertiseClientSettings                       : False
Fqdn                                          : EXSERVER1.contoso.com
Comment                                       :
Enabled                                       : True
ConnectionTimeout                             : 00:10:00
ConnectionInactivityTimeout                   : 00:05:00
MessageRateLimit                              : unlimited
MessageRateSource                             : IPAddress
MaxInboundConnection                          : 5000
MaxInboundConnectionPerSource                 : 20
MaxInboundConnectionPercentagePerSource       : 2
MaxHeaderSize                                 : 64 KB (65,536 bytes)
MaxHopCount                                   : 60
MaxLocalHopCount                              : 12
MaxLogonFailures                              : 3
MaxMessageSize                                : 10 MB (10,485,760 bytes)
MaxProtocolErrors                             : 5
MaxRecipientsPerMessage                       : 200
PermissionGroups                              : None
PipeliningEnabled                             : True
ProtocolLoggingLevel                          : None
RemoteIPRanges                                : {192.165.70.71}
RequireEHLODomain                             : False
RequireTLS                                    : False
EnableAuthGSSAPI                              : False
ExtendedProtectionPolicy                      : None
ExtendedProtectionTlsTerminatedAtProxy        : False
LiveCredentialEnabled                         : False
TlsDomainCapabilities                         : {}
Server                                        : EXSERVER1
SizeEnabled                                   : Enabled
TarpitInterval                                : 00:00:05
MaxAcknowledgementDelay                       : 00:00:30
AdminDisplayName                              :
ExchangeVersion                               : 0.1 (8.0.535.0)
Name                                          : SMTP traffic from Linux Sendmail server
Identity                                      : EXSERVER1\SMTP traffic from Linux Sendmail server
```

The changes that we might consider include the following:

1. Add some permission groups to the connector. When you create a custom connector, the wizard does not assign any permission groups because it's impossible to know the exact purpose the connector will serve and it's best to force the administrator to consider and then apply the required permission groups. In this case, we need Anonymous Users permission group to allow the Sendmail systems to send messages

through the connector. Changing the permission groups can be done with EMC or EMS.

2. Change the authentication method that the connector advertises and supports. A custom purpose connector is configured to support TLS, which will probably be acceptable for the remote server. Changing the authentication method can only be done with EMS.

3. Change the banner issued in a 220 SMTP command when a connection is made by a remote server. If not set, Exchange 2010 issues Microsoft ESMTP MAIL Service with the current date and time. Some administrators consider this to be a security risk because it tells potential hackers that they have connected to Exchange. A replacement banner must start with 220 and contain only 7-bit ASCII characters. You can change the banner with EMS.

4. Make changes to the other settings such as maximum message size, the number of recipients in a message header, and so on. These changes can only be done through EMS.

Because the majority of the settings we might want to change can only be accessed through EMS, it's convenient to update everything through the shell. Here's a command to update our new connector to allow basic authentication, allow access to anonymous connections, display an updated banner, reduce the maximum message size to 3 MB, and add an administrative comment to indicate what we have done. A comment can be up to 256 characters and if you add one, it is best practice to incorporate your name so that everyone knows who made the changes.

```
Set-ReceiveConnector -Identity 'SMTP traffic from Linux Sendmail server'
-AuthMechanism 'tls, basicauth' -PermissionGroups 'AnonymousUsers' -Banner '220 Hallo
World' -MaxMessageSize 3MB -Comment 'TRedmond 20 May 2010: Added anonymous users'
```

Our connector will now serve to transmit mail from the remote server to Exchange, but one final step is required to enable the connector to support relaying of messages to any destination domain, which is what we might want to do if Exchange acts as the point of external email connectivity to the Internet. To allow relaying, we have to grant a specific permission to anonymous connections before Exchange. Here's how:

```
Get-ReceiveConnector -Identity 'SMTP traffic from Linux Sendmail server' |
Add-ADPermission -User 'NT AUTHORITY\ANONYMOUS LOGON' -ExtendedRights
'ms-Exch-SMTP-Accept-Any-Recipient'
```

This step also forces any messages coming through the connector to pass through anti-spam checking or to resolve P2 addresses in the message header (the SMTP address of the sender will be left intact).

Send connectors

Exchange uses send connectors to send SMTP messages between hub transport servers and outside the organization. Every hub transport server automatically includes a send connector to be able to exchange messages with other hub transport servers. You see no trace of the default send connector if you examine details of a hub transport server through EMC. However, you can gain some insight into the properties used by Exchange to control the default send connector with the Get-TransportServer cmdlet. The following output is an extract of the complete output from the command, which has been edited for clarity. There are a lot of transport configuration settings that you can tweak!

```
Get-TransportServer –Identity ExServer1 | Format-List
```

```
Name                                      : EXSERVER1
AntispamAgentsEnabled                     : False
ConnectivityLogEnabled                    : True
ConnectivityLogMaxAge                     : 30.00:00:00
ConnectivityLogMaxDirectorySize           : 1000 MB (1,048,576,000 bytes)
ConnectivityLogMaxFileSize                : 10 MB (10,485,760 bytes)
ConnectivityLogPath                       : C:\Program Files\Microsoft\
Exchange Server\V14\TransportRoles\Logs\Connectivity
DelayNotificationTimeout                  : 04:00:00
ExternalDNSAdapterEnabled                 : True
ExternalDNSProtocolOption                 : Any
ExternalDNSServers                        : {}
ExternalIPAddress                         :
InternalDNSAdapterEnabled                 : True
InternalDNSProtocolOption                 : Any
InternalDNSServers                        : {}
MaxConcurrentMailboxDeliveries            : 20
MaxConcurrentMailboxSubmissions           : 20
MaxConnectionRatePerMinute                : 1200
MaxOutboundConnections                    : 1000
MaxPerDomainOutboundConnections           : 20
MessageExpirationTimeout                  : 2.00:00:00
MessageRetryInterval                      : 00:01:00
MessageTrackingLogEnabled                 : True
MessageTrackingLogMaxAge                  : 30.00:00:00
MessageTrackingLogMaxDirectorySize        : 1000 MB (1,048,576,000 bytes)
MessageTrackingLogMaxFileSize             : 10 MB (10,485,760 bytes)
MessageTrackingLogPath                    : C:\Program Files\Microsoft\
Exchange Server\V14\TransportRoles\Logs\MessageTracking
IrmLogEnabled                             : True
IrmLogMaxAge                              : 30.00:00:00
IrmLogMaxDirectorySize                    : 250 MB (262,144,000 bytes)
IrmLogMaxFileSize                         : 10 MB (10,485,760 bytes)
IrmLogPath                                : C:\Program Files\Microsoft\
Exchange Server\V14\Logging\IRMLogs
ActiveUserStatisticsLogMaxAge             : 30.00:00:00
```

```
ActiveUserStatisticsLogMaxDirectorySize      : 250 MB (262,144,000 bytes)
ActiveUserStatisticsLogMaxFileSize           : 10 MB (10,485,760 bytes)
ActiveUserStatisticsLogPath                  : C:\Program Files\Microsoft\
Exchange Server\V14\TransportRoles\Logs\ActiveUsersStats
ServerStatisticsLogMaxAge                     : 30.00:00:00
ServerStatisticsLogMaxDirectorySize           : 250 MB (262,144,000 bytes)
ServerStatisticsLogMaxFileSize                : 10 MB (10,485,760 bytes)
ServerStatisticsLogPath                       : C:\Program Files\Microsoft\
Exchange Server\V14\TransportRoles\Logs\ServerStats
MessageTrackingLogSubjectLoggingEnabled       : True
OutboundConnectionFailureRetryInterval        : 00:10:00
IntraOrgConnectorProtocolLoggingLevel         : None
PickupDirectoryMaxHeaderSize                  : 64 KB (65,536 bytes)
PickupDirectoryMaxMessagesPerMinute           : 100
PickupDirectoryMaxRecipientsPerMessage        : 100
PickupDirectoryPath                           : C:\Program Files\Microsoft\
Exchange Server\V14\TransportRoles\Pickup
PipelineTracingEnabled                        : False
ContentConversionTracingEnabled               : False
PipelineTracingPath                           : C:\Program Files\Microsoft\
Exchange Server\V14\TransportRoles\Logs\PipelineTracing
PipelineTracingSenderAddress                  :
PoisonMessageDetectionEnabled                 : True
PoisonThreshold                               : 2
QueueMaxIdleTime                              : 00:03:00
ReceiveProtocolLogMaxAge                      : 30.00:00:00
ReceiveProtocolLogMaxDirectorySize            : 250 MB (262,144,000 bytes)
ReceiveProtocolLogMaxFileSize                 : 10 MB (10,485,760 bytes)
ReceiveProtocolLogPath                        : C:\Program Files\Microsoft\
Exchange Server\V14\TransportRoles\Logs\ProtocolLog\SmtpReceive
RecipientValidationCacheEnabled               : False
ReplayDirectoryPath                           : C:\Program Files\Microsoft\
Exchange Server\V14\TransportRoles\Replay
RootDropDirectoryPath                         :
RoutingTableLogMaxAge                         : 7.00:00:00
RoutingTableLogMaxDirectorySize               : 50 MB (52,428,800 bytes)
RoutingTableLogPath                           : C:\Program Files\Microsoft\
Exchange Server\V14\TransportRoles\Logs\Routing
SendProtocolLogMaxAge                         : 30.00:00:00
SendProtocolLogMaxDirectorySize               : 250 MB (262,144,000 bytes)
SendProtocolLogMaxFileSize                    : 10 MB (10,485,760 bytes)
SendProtocolLogPath                           : C:\Program Files\Microsoft\
Exchange Server\V14\TransportRoles\Logs\ProtocolLog\SmtpSend
TransientFailureRetryCount                    : 6
TransientFailureRetryInterval                 : 00:05:00
AntispamUpdatesEnabled                        : False
InternalTransportCertificateThumbprint        : AB3D032CF097773CC565EE-
41AE8EE5C2C4D2C231
TransportSyncEnabled                          : False
TransportSyncPopEnabled                       : False
WindowsLiveHotmailTransportSyncEnabled        : False
```

```
WindowsLiveContactTransportSyncEnabled           : False
TransportSyncExchangeEnabled                     : False
TransportSyncImapEnabled                         : False
MaxNumberOfTransportSyncAttempts                 : 3
MaxAcceptedTransportSyncJobsPerProcessor         : 64
MaxActiveTransportSyncJobsPerProcessor           : 8
HttpTransportSyncProxyServer                     :
HttpProtocolLogEnabled                           : False
HttpProtocolLogFilePath                          :
HttpProtocolLogMaxAge                            : 7.00:00:00
HttpProtocolLogMaxDirectorySize                  : 250 MB (262,144,000 bytes)
HttpProtocolLogMaxFileSize                       : 10 MB (10,485,760 bytes)
HttpProtocolLogLoggingLevel                      : None
TransportSyncLogEnabled                          : False
TransportSyncLogFilePath                         :
TransportSyncLogLoggingLevel                     : None
TransportSyncLogMaxAge                           : 30.00:00:00
TransportSyncLogMaxDirectorySize                 : 10 GB (10,737,418,240 bytes)
TransportSyncLogMaxFileSize                      : 10 MB (10,485,760 bytes)
TransportSyncHubHealthLogEnabled                 : False
TransportSyncHubHealthLogFilePath                :
TransportSyncHubHealthLogMaxAge                  : 30.00:00:00
TransportSyncHubHealthLogMaxDirectorySize        : 10 GB (10,737,418,240 bytes)
TransportSyncHubHealthLogMaxFileSize             : 10 MB (10,485,760 bytes)
TransportSyncAccountsPoisonDetectionEnabled      : False
TransportSyncAccountsPoisonAccountThreshold      : 2
TransportSyncAccountsPoisonItemThreshold         : 2
TransportSyncAccountsSuccessivePoisonItemThreshold : 3
TransportSyncRemoteConnectionTimeout             : 00:01:40
TransportSyncMaxDownloadSizePerItem              : 25 MB (26,214,400 bytes)
TransportSyncMaxDownloadSizePerConnection        : 50 MB (52,428,800 bytes)
TransportSyncMaxDownloadItemsPerConnection       : 1000
DeltaSyncClientCertificateThumbprint             :
UseDowngradedExchangeServerAuth                  : False
IntraOrgConnectorSmtpMaxMessagesPerConnection    : 20
```

The output contains some interesting additions introduced in Exchange 2010. For example, you can see properties that control the output of the server and user usage statistics logs. These logs can be analyzed to generate reports or provided as input to monitoring products such as Microsoft System Center Operations Manager to provide comprehensive reporting and analysis capabilities over different periods. The documentation for the Microsoft System Center Operations Manager product contains details about how to generate reports from transport data generated by Exchange.

Logically, the Set-TransportConfig cmdlet updates these settings. For example, to update the pickup directory where you can put well-formed SMTP message files to be sent by Exchange, you execute a command like this:

```
Set-TransportConfig –Server ExServer1 –PickupDirectoryPath 'C:\Exchange\Pickup'
```

Exchange will create the directory if it doesn't already exist. Transport settings are specific to a hub transport server, so once again it is best practice to implement the same configuration on all hub transport servers within the organization.

Just like the default send connector, custom send connectors are also SMTP-based. You can create new send connectors to connect Exchange to the Internet (or to transfer messages to foreign SMTP-based email systems) on a hub transport server in much the same way you'd create an SMTP connector hosted on an Exchange 2000 or Exchange 2003 bridge-head server. However, there are some differences that you need to consider:

- You can create custom send connectors on either hub transport or Edge servers. Connectors on hub transport servers are registered in Active Directory and can therefore be managed like any other object known throughout the organization. Connectors on Edge servers are specific to a server and must be managed on that server.

- Unlike receive connectors, which are created automatically when you install a hub transport server and remain bound to that server, send connectors are managed at the organization level. However, before a hub transport server can use a send connector to route messages, you have to add the server as a valid source to the send connector's properties. Figure 13-12 shows that two servers are able to send messages via the Internet Relay Via Smart Host send connector. Both EMC and EMS flag warnings if you add a hub transport server that is not in the same Active Directory site as the hub transport servers that are already registered. The warning is to notify you that you might have created a nonoptimum routing because the transport service always uses deterministic routing and picks one Active Directory site to route messages. Therefore, the transport service cannot load balance messages across two sites. Instead, the transport service selects the first Active Directory site in the list of the connector's source hub transport list and always routes messages via that site.

> **Note**
>
> If you know that the new source server has adequate network connectivity to support routing of messages from other Active Directory sites across the connector, it is acceptable, but not best practice, to add it. Note that even if a hub transport server is not registered as a valid source, it can still send messages across the connector, but it must first route the messages via one of the valid source hub transport servers.

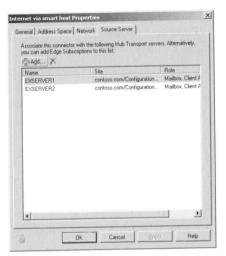

Figure 13-12 Source servers for a send connector.

Creating a send connector

Exchange 2010 hub transport servers contain default send connectors that are used to transport messages within the organization. You do not need to configure these connectors. You therefore only need to create a custom send connector to transport SMTP messages outside the organization. Almost every Exchange organization needs to do this, so it's the rule rather than the exception. In addition, you can configure additional send connectors to handle messages for specific domains.

When you configure a custom send connector, you need to think about the settings to apply to the connector:

- Like a receive connector, the intended usage of the send connector determines the permission groups that you assign to the connector: Internal means that the connector will connect to other Exchange servers; Internet means that anonymous connections will be accepted; Custom means that you will define permissions manually.

- The address space that a connector supports allows you some control over what messages flow across the connector. If you use an address space of "*" (Exchange doesn't support address spaces defined as "*.*" or "@*.*"), then the connector can handle any message to any domain. You might want to establish a connector that routes messages to a specific domain, in which case you would create a new connector and define the appropriate address space on that connector. Let's assume that you had the need to connect to a specific domain in systemx.fabrikam.com and want to be sure that the messages go through a certain connector. You can accomplish this by creating a connector that hosts the exact address of the domain that you want to reach (for example, finance.systemx.fabrikam.com). After you create the connector and establish the address space, Exchange has two available routes that it can use for messages to finance.systemx.fabrikam.com: the default SMTP connector and the one specifically created for this domain. Exchange always routes messages across a connector with the most precise address space, even if choosing this connector incurs a higher routing cost, so any message sent to fabrikam.com will go across the default SMTP connector and any addressed to finance.systemx.fabrikam.com will always travel across the connector that you've just created. This is not new behavior, because this is the way that routing has worked since Exchange 5.0.

- Whether to use DNS MX (mail exchange) records to route email or to send email through one or more smart host servers. A smart host is a server that is able to route SMTP traffic on behalf of other servers. Typically, this is a service offered by your Internet service provider (ISP) or a server that acts as a central point for routing within a company.

- The hub transport servers that are associated with the connector. You can decide to create an association with an Edge subscription at this point so that the connector is published through a hub transport server to become known to an Edge server.

To create a new send connector, go to the hub transport section under Organization Configuration of EMC and select the New Send Connector option. The first step (Figure 13-13) is to name the connector and establish its purpose. An ideal name coveys the use of the connector and requires little additional explanation to any administrator who reviews the messaging configuration.

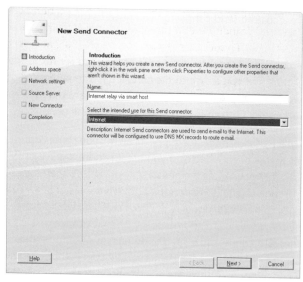

Figure 13-13 The first step in creating a new send connector.

The purpose of the connector determines the permission groups that Exchange applies to the new object and can be one of the following:

- **Custom:** Used for connections to non-Exchange SMTP systems and allows complete control over the configuration.

- **Internet:** Used for connections to Internet SMTP systems, including smart hosts used to relay messages on behalf of the organization.

- **Internal:** Used for connections to send messages to other Exchange hub transport servers within the organization. Because the default send connectors are used for this task, you only need these connectors if you want to exert specific control over message flow.

- **Partner:** Used for connections to partner organizations where TLS-secured links are available.

In this case, we want to create a connection to a smart host server that will relay messages for the organization. This is a reasonably common setup in many companies where a number of different messaging systems are in use. The relay servers usually run UNIX or Linux and are tailored to act as high-performance messaging switches. The Exchange equivalent is an Edge server.

The next step (Figure 13-14) is to define what SMTP domains or address space can be handled by the connector. A smart relay usually handles everything apart from the specific address spaces defined for other connectors. Remember, Exchange will always select the connector with the most specific address space to route a message across, so a smart relay is often the choice at the bottom of the stack that is used when no other connector is available to handle a message. We indicate that this is the case by defining the address space as "*". You can only define SMTP address spaces when you create a new send connector with EMC. However, the New-SendConnector cmdlet allows other address spaces to be defined, such as X.400 or any text string that represents a valid routing address that will be recognized by the messaging system that is eventually charged with the final delivery of a message.

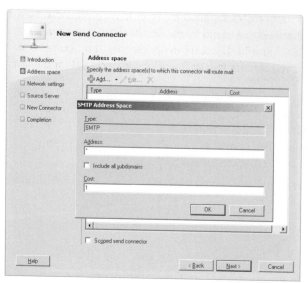

Figure 13-14 Adding the address space for the new send connector.

INSIDE OUT The cost value assigned to an address space

Each address space is given a value for the cost of the connection. One (1) represents the best possible connection value and the range goes up to one hundred (100). The cost allows Exchange to differentiate between two routes. For example, there might be two smart host relays available within an organization: one defined for the America site and one for the Europe site. Servers in the Europe site will have a natural affinity with the smart host relay defined in that site and will ignore the other defined in America even if the address cost is equal. This is logical because of the rule that a connector in the local site is used whenever possible and because the additional site link cost of routing to America always makes that connector more expensive than the one available in the Europe site.

The Scoped Send Connector check box controls whether the connector is available for routing by any hub transport server in the organization. The default is to leave the check box cleared. However, if you select the check box, Exchange will constrain the connector so that only hub transport servers in the same site as the source server can use it for routing. If you run EMC on a hub transport server, Exchange automatically assigns the source server to be that server. If you run EMC on another server that doesn't host the hub transport role, Exchange assigns the source server to be the first hub transport server in the site. As we discussed earlier (see Figure 13-12), you can update the list of source servers for a connector through EMC or you can use the Set-SendConnector cmdlet for the task.

We now have to tell Exchange how to find the smart host. The easiest way to do this (Figure 13-15) is to provide the FQDN or IP address for the server that will relay messages for us. This is a multivalued property, so we can specify a set of FQDNs or IP addresses to give Exchange a choice of available servers. The alternative is to instruct Exchange to use the MX records defined in DNS to find the relay servers.

Figure 13-15 Adding the information about routing through a smart host.

If you opt to use a smart host to route SMTP messages to external destinations, Exchange asks you to specify what kind of authentication mechanism to use when it connects to the smart host. It could be that you have an SMTP server that's set up as an open relay for general use within the company, in which case you won't have to use authentication or you might have to provide a username and password for basic authentication. The smart host can be another Exchange server, in which case you'd use Exchange Server Authentication, or it might support IPsec for encrypted communication between the two servers.

Connections to route messages through a smart host might need to be authenticated. The next step in the New Send Connector Wizard allows us to determine whether authentication is used and, if so, the type of authentication that is used (Figure 13-16).

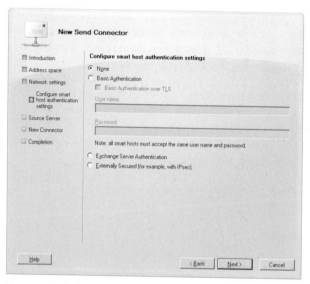

Figure 13-16 Creating the authentication settings for the smart host.

The final step is to make the decision about what source servers are associated with the send connector. You'll have to add at least one hub transport server. This is the logical equivalent of adding a bridgehead server to a routing group connector in Exchange 2003. Exchange will include the name of the local server if you create the new connector on a hub transport server. The command to create the new send connector will be something like this:

```
New-SendConnector -Name 'Internet relay via smart host' -Usage 'Internet'
-AddressSpaces 'SMTP:*;1' -IsScopedConnector $False -DNSRoutingEnabled $False
-SmartHosts 'smtp-relay.contoso.com' -SmartHostAuthMechanism 'None'
-UseExternalDNSServersEnabled $False -SourceTransportServers 'EXSERVER1'
```

As in many other situations, you can tweak the settings for a send connector more comprehensively through EMS. First, let's examine the settings for the new connector after it is created with the Get-SendConnector cmdlet:

```
Get-SendConnector -Identity 'Internet relay via smart host' | Format-List
```

```
AddressSpaces               : {SMTP:*;1}
AuthenticationCredential    :
Comment                     :
ConnectedDomains            : {}
ConnectionInactivityTimeOut : 00:10:00
DNSRoutingEnabled           : False
DomainSecureEnabled         : False
Enabled                     : True
ErrorPolicies               : Default
```

```
ForceHELO                       : False
Fqdn                            :
HomeMTA                         : Microsoft MTA
HomeMtaServerId                 : EXSERVER1
Identity                        : Internet relay via smart host
IgnoreSTARTTLS                  : False
IsScopedConnector               : False
IsSmtpConnector                 : True
LinkedReceiveConnector          :
MaxMessageSize                  : 10 MB (10,485,760 bytes)
Name                            : Internet relay via smart host
Port                            : 25
ProtocolLoggingLevel            : None
RequireOorg                     : False
RequireTLS                      : False
SmartHostAuthMechanism          : None
SmartHosts                      : {smtp-relay.contoso.com}
SmartHostsString                : smtp-relay.contoso.com
SmtpMaxMessagesPerConnection    : 20
SourceIPAddress                 : 0.0.0.0
SourceRoutingGroup              : Exchange Routing Group (DWBGZMFD01QNBJR)
SourceTransportServers          : {EXSERVER1}
TlsAuthLevel                    :
TlsDomain                       :
UseExternalDNSServersEnabled    : False
```

If we need to change any settings, we can do it with the Set-SendConnector cmdlet. Let's assume that we want to reduce the maximum message size that flows across the connector to 5 MB and allow two additional hub transport servers to route directly using the connector. The command is:

```
Set-SendConnector –Identity 'Internet relay via smart host' –MaxMessageSize 5MB
–SourceTransportServers 'ExServer1', 'ExServer2', 'ExServer3' –Comment 'Admin:
Limited size to 5MB 12/31/2010'
```

Selecting a send connector

Several send connectors can exist inside an organization and Exchange has to take them all into account when it determines what connector to use to route a message. The following algorithm is used:

1. Gather a list of all available send connectors.

2. Discard any disabled connectors.

3. Discard all connectors that have a maximum message size less than the size of the message.

4. Select connectors that are available (in scope) for the hub transport server and whose address space accommodates the recipient's domain (an address space of * matches all domains).

5. Select the connector that has the closest address space match. For example, if one connector has an address space of * and a second has an address space of fabrikam.com, any messages addressed to the fabrikam.com domain will be routed to the second connector.

6. If more than one available connector exists, the best choice is determined by the following:

    a. Least routing cost based on aggregated site costs. A connector in the local site will always be preferred over a connector hosted in a remote site.

    b. Whether the connector is hosted by the same hub transport server that is making the routing decision. A connector on the same server is always preferred over a connector on another hub transport server in the same site.

    c. Alphanumerically, meaning that the connector name that comes first in alphanumeric order is used.

Hopefully your messaging environment will be organized in such a way that Exchange never has to resort to alphanumeric selection from a range of connectors hosted by servers in the local site!

The impact of scoping

Scoped send connectors (those with their *IsScopedConnector* property set to $True) are not visible to hub transport servers outside their home site. In other words, hub transport servers in other sites cannot include the connector in their routing tables and therefore will not attempt to route messages across the connector when they calculate the least-cost route for delivery to external recipients.

Routing calculation happens at every hub transport server through which a message passes so that a message follows the optimum path at all times. Therefore, if a message passes through a site that contains a connector that offers a lower cost path, the hub transport server in that site will recompute the route and redirect the message. Any connector hosted in the site is considered when the optimum path is determined, including scoped connectors that were invisible to the hub transport server in the site where the message was originally dispatched. This aspect of Exchange routing might mean that messages pass through a connector when you don't anticipate this happening.

For example, assume that a message is sent to an Internet recipient from a site that doesn't have a connector. To reach the Internet, messages have to pass through a hub site. Let's assume that there are two send connectors in the hub site. One is not scoped and has an address space of SMTP:*. This connector is known throughout the organization and it's the destination connector selected by the hub transport server in the site where the message originates. However, the second connector is scoped and has an address space that is a better match for the message recipients. The hub transport server in the hub site examines the recipient addresses and determines that the scoped connector, which is included in the hub site's routing table, is a better match and therefore puts the message onto the queue for the scoped connector. This is all extremely logical to Exchange but might puzzle administrators if they monitor queues and observe a lack of expected traffic across the general-purpose send connector or an increase in traffic across the scoped connector. It's really not all that important if the two connectors use the same Internet connection, but it could be an issue if you have connection paths with different configurations (such as the maximum message size) and need to force messages along a specific path with scoped connectors.

Because Exchange routing is recalculated in each site through which a message passes, the only way that you can prevent unwanted traffic from going across scoped connectors is to place these connectors in separate sites that don't host other send connectors. If you place scoped connectors in sites that support a lot of traffic going to and from other destinations, the potential for rerouting will always exist for messages as they pass through the site.

Linked connectors

A linked connector is a receive connector that is linked to a send connector in such a way that any message that comes in through the receive connector is immediately transmitted through the send connector. The intention behind linked connectors is to provide a route to redirect messages for processing by a third party before the messages come back to the organization. You'd use this approach to send messages coming in from the Internet for anti-spam and antivirus checking to a company that specializes in this work. There are a couple of prerequisites that you have to understand:

- Only one receive connector can be linked to a send connector; the send connector will be configured to send messages to the SMTP domain for the third party who will process the messages. This is done by making the third party domain a smart host for the send connector.

- The receive connector that you want to use must exist before it can be linked to a send connector. In other words, you need to create the two connectors before you attempt to link them.

- A complementary receive connector is configured to receive the messages that come back from the third-party processor. This receive connector is not linked to the send connector, because otherwise you'd create an endless loop. Its function is to accept cleansed messages back into the organization for routing onward to destination mailboxes by the hub transport servers.

- You'll also need a second send connector to handle outgoing messages generated by users within the organization. This send connector might well use the third-party smart host for cleansing outbound messages.

EMC doesn't allow you to create linked connectors. Instead, you'll use a command like the one shown here to create the linked connectors through EMS. In this instance, we create a send connector that's linked to an existing receive connector called Internet email that's hosted on the ExHT-Dublin hub transport server. Linking the connectors forces any mail that comes in through the receive connector to be sent to a smart host called clean-me. mail-streams-contoso.com:

```
New-SendConnector -Name 'Internet Mail Cleansing' -LinkedReceiveConnector
'ExHT-Dublin\Internet Email' -AddressSpaces $Null -SmartHosts
'clean-me.mail-streams-contoso.com' -SmartHostAuthMechanism ExternalAuthoritative
-DNSRoutingEnabled $False -MaxMessageSize 20MB
```

INSIDE OUT Plan and test carefully to create a linked connector only once

Creating a linked connector is very much a one-time operation that's the result of careful planning and much testing to ensure that mail flows to and from the third party. It's certainly not something that you can expect to do on a regular basis.

Throttling

The nature of email servers that act as the gateways to large companies is that they can be overwhelmed or swamped by large volumes of incoming messages. The servers can either attempt to deal with the volume as best they can and eventually work through the backlog that inevitably accumulates or the software can monitor, recognize, and attempt to take action to manage the condition to maintain an orderly processing regime. Throttling is the mechanism that Exchange 2010 uses to manage peaks in incoming message traffic.

Throttling is a term also used in Exchange 2010 to refer to the control that the CAS server can exert over client connections through throttling policies that you can apply to mailboxes. This kind of throttling aims to restrict the ability of a client to consume large quantities of system resources without good reason and is obviously different from the throttling applied to enable the smooth flow of messages.

You can apply throttling parameters to the following:

- A hub transport or Edge server: This is done with the Set-TransportServer cmdlet (some parameters can be set through EMC). Typically, you only need to apply throttling to servers that deal with external traffic, although it is possible that you might have to apply throttling on hub transport servers positioned in a busy hub site.

- A receive connector: This is done with the Set-ReceiveConnector cmdlet. Again, you usually only need to pay attention to the receive connectors that handle incoming traffic from outside the organization.

- A send connector: This is done with the Set-SendConnector cmdlet.

The default values set by Exchange are usually sufficient for most purposes and only need to be changed if monitoring reveals that hub transport or Edge servers are struggling to cope with incoming traffic. For example, the situation deserves investigation if you see large queues accumulating at peak times that do not reduce when peak times pass. This might be caused by a simple lack of processing capacity or it could be caused by other conditions that you can address by tweaking the throttling parameters. Table 13-3 summarizes the different parameters that you can use to control transport throttling.

Table 13-3 **Available parameters for transport**

Cmdlet	Parameter	Effect
Set-TransportServer	−MaxConcurrentMailboxDeliveries	Sets the maximum number of threads used for concurrent delivery to mailboxes via the Store driver across the entire organization. The default is 20.
Set-TransportServer	−MaxConcurrentMailboxSubmissions	Sets the maximum number of delivery threads that a server can use to accept messages from databases via the Store driver across the organization. The default is 20.
Set-TransportServer	−MaxConnectionRatePerMinute	Sets the maximum rate at which new inbound connections can be created to receive connectors by the hub transport or Edge server. The default is 1,200 connections per minute.

Set-TransportServer (EMC)	−MaxOutboundConnections	Sets the maximum number of concurrent outbound connections that a hub transport or Edge server can open via send connectors. The default value is 1,000. You can set this value to Unlimited to allow the server to create as many connections as resources allow.
Set-TransportServer (EMC)	−MaxPerDomainOutboundConnections	Sets the maximum number of connections that can be opened to a single domain via send connectors. The default value is 20. You can set this value to be Unlimited.
Set-TransportServer	−PickupDirectoryMaxMessagesPer-Minute	Sets the maximum number of messages that the transport service will attempt to load from the pickup and replay directory per minute. The default value is 100 messages per minute per directory. Exchange polls these directories every five seconds, so the value that you set should be divisible by 12 to arrive at the number that Exchange will process each time it polls.
Set-ReceiveConnector	−ConnectionInactivityTimeOut	Sets the maximum idle time that the receive connector will maintain an open SMTP connection with another server. The connection is closed when the period elapses.
Set-ReceiveConnector	−ConnectionTimeOut	Sets the maximum time that an SMTP connection can remain open even if the other server continues to transmit data. The default value is 10 minutes for a hub transport server and five minutes for an Edge server. Logically, this value must be higher than the value of the −ConnectionInactivityTimeOut parameter.
Set-ReceiveConnector	−MaxInboundConnection	Sets the maximum number of concurrent inbound connections that a receive connector can support. The default value is 5,000.
Set-ReceiveConnector	−MaxInboundConnectionPercentage-PerSource	Sets the maximum number of inbound connections that a receive connector permits from a single source. The value is expressed as the percentage of available remaining connections. The default value is 2 percent.
Set-ReceiveConnector	−MaxInboundConnectionPerSource	Sets the maximum number of inbound connections that a receive connector allows from a single server. The default value is 100.
Set-ReceiveConnector	−MaxProtocolErrors	Sets the maximum number of SMTP errors that a receive connector will tolerate before it closes a connection with another server. The default value is five.

| Set-ReceiveConnector | –*TarpitInterval* | Sets the delay parameter that Exchange uses when it suspects that another server is attempting a directory harvest attack. The default value is five seconds. See Chapter 14, "Message Hygiene," for more information. |
| Set-SendConnector | –*ConnectionInactivityTimeOut* | Specifies the maximum time that a send connector maintains an open SMTP connection with another server. The default value is 10 minutes. |

Back pressure

The Exchange transport engine is designed to process extremely large volumes of messages, but circumstances can arise where a server might not have the physical capability to handle incoming or outgoing messages. For instance, a hub transport server might come under load from another source that consumes much of the available memory, or the disk space on some drives might come close to being exhausted. In these circumstances, the back pressure feature allows the transport service to continue running normally and process queued messages while it temporarily rejects incoming connections to stop new messages from being queued. In this scenario, the sending SMTP servers have to queue the messages until the situation that caused pressure on Exchange is relieved. As load on the server reduces to free memory or disk space becomes available because some files are deleted, Exchange will start to accept incoming connections and process new messages.

Table 13-4 shows how hub transport servers react to medium and high back pressure conditions. As you can see, under medium load, basic message flow is preserved because hub transport servers can connect to send mail to each other and are also willing to accept messages from mailbox servers. However, they will not accept incoming traffic from other SMTP servers. As pressure builds, the hub transport server will eventually stop accepting connections and wait until pressure decreases.

Table 13-4 **The effect of back pressure settings on hub transport servers**

Resource utilization	Connections from other Hub Transport servers	Connections from other SMTP servers	Store driver connections from mailbox servers	Pickup and Replay submissions	Internal mail flow
Medium	Allowed	Rejected	Allowed	Rejected	Working
High	Rejected	Rejected	Rejected	Rejected	No flow

How do you know when a back pressure condition exists? The answer is in the Application Event Log, where you will see events such as 15002 from the resource manager component in the Exchange Transport system. This event will tell you what resource is causing Transport to apply back pressure. For example, you might see something like this:

```
Queue database and disk space ("F:\Exchange\TransportRoles\data\queue\Mail.Que") =
81% [High][Normal = 70% Medium High = 72% High = 74%]
```

In this instance, the problem is that the disk that holds the mail queue database is 81 percent full and has exceeded the threshold for high usage of 74 percent. Although there is still 19 percent free space left on the disk, the possibility exists that some other application could take the space or that if Exchange continues to accept messages, the mail queue database could grow to fill the space. Given the size of disks today, you might regard these events as unlikely, but it is best to be cautious when you want to keep a messaging system running. The solution is to move some files off the disk to reduce usage to less than 74 percent.

Another indication is if you see the Mail Submission component report event 1009 on mailbox servers. This event is flagged when Exchange is unable to submit messages to a hub transport server in the local Active Directory site. The hub transport server is down, the transport service is stopped, or Exchange is experiencing a back pressure situation that prevents the transport system from accepting any more messages from mailbox servers. Of course, the mailbox and hub roles might be on the same physical server, in which case the messages will be queued in the Store until the back pressure situation is relieved, unless another hub transport server is available in the same site. Another indication that a hub transport server is throttling itself because of back pressure is when servers receive NDRs when they try to send messages to the server that is under pressure. The sending server will receive NDRs with an error status of "4.3.1 insufficient system resources," and the messages will be queued for redelivery.

INSIDE OUT Settings are being tuned based on real-world experience

Microsoft has tuned some of the back pressure settings in SP1 to reflect real-life experience in production (for example, the available disk space requirement is reduced from 4 GB to 500 MB). You can expect tuning to continue in this space as Microsoft and administrators learn how to better control back pressure situations.

Note

An Exchange mailbox server always prefers to submit messages to the local hub if this role is installed on the same physical server and will only use other hub transport servers if the local server cannot accept messages. In this case, the other hub transport servers are used on a round-robin basis until the local server can accept messages again.

Transport queues

Messages that the transport system is currently processing are held in in-memory queues. To make sure that the messages are reliably captured to disk, they are written into an Extensible Storage Engine (ESE) database called mail.que. When the transport service shuts down, it commits the contents of its in-memory queues to the database to ensure that messages are properly secured. Like other ESE databases, mail.que has a set of transaction logs and reserved logs that allow it to replay messages if a problem such as a server crash prevents the commitment of messages from memory at any point. The current transaction log is named trn.log; Exchange creates a new log generation when 5 MB of message transactions have been captured. Unlike the 1 MB transaction logs used for mailbox databases, mail queue transaction logs are 5 MB. Circular logging is enabled to restrict the amount of storage occupied by the mail queue. Figure 13-17 shows the set of files that make up the mail queue database.

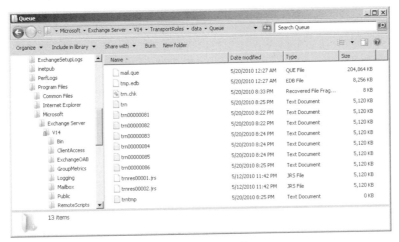

Figure 13-17 Viewing the mail queue database files.

The location of the mail queue database files is set in the EdgeTransport.exe.config configuration file and you can move it to a more suitable location if required. Table 13-5 lists other important parameters relating to the mail queue database that are held in EdgeTransport. exe.config.

INSIDE OUT Consider moving the mail queue database away from the default location

It is a good idea to consider moving the mail queue database away from the default location under the drive used to hold the Exchange binaries on hub transport servers that handle a large volume of messages. Microsoft provides a script called Move-TransportDatabase.ps1 that you can use to move the mail queue database to another location. For example, this command moves the database and its log files to a location called E:\Exchange\MailQueue. The new location must have 2 GB of free space available for the script to work.

```
C:> .\Move-TransportDatabase -QueueDatabasePath E:\Exchange\MailQueue
-QueueDatabaseLoggingPath E:\Exchange\MailQueue
```

Table 13-5 **Parameters influencing mail queue database operation**

Parameter	Meaning
–QueueDatabasePath	Defines the location of the mail queue database. You have to create the directory, stop the transport service, copy the database files, and then restart the transport service.
–QueueDatabaseLoggingPath	Defines the location of the transaction log files for the mail queue database. This does not have to be the same location as the mail queue database.
–QueueDatabaseLoggingBufferSize	Defines the memory in bytes used to cache records before they are committed to a transaction log. The default is 5,242,880 bytes (5 MB).
–QueueDatabaseLoggingFileSize	Defines the maximum size of a transaction log. The default is 5,242,880 bytes.
–QueueDatabaseOnlineDefragEnabled	Defines whether Exchange performs online defragmentation to maintain internal database structures. The default is $True.
–QueueDatabaseOnlineDefragSchedule	Defines the time when Exchange starts online maintenance. The default is 1:00:00 (1 A.M.).
–QueueDatabaseOnlineDefragTimeToRun	Defines how long Exchange is allowed to run online maintenance. The default is 3:00:00 (three hours).

How messages enter the submission queue

Messages enter the Exchange transport service in the following four ways:

- **Store driver:** Messages created by Outlook Web App (OWA) and Outlook clients are first placed into the Outbox folder. The Mail Submission service monitors Outbox folders and the appearance of a message causes it to notify the Store driver to submit the message to the server. Messages are moved from the Outbox to the Sent Items folder on the client after they are accepted for processing by Exchange and have been placed onto the submission queue.

- **Receive connectors:** Messages from other SMTP servers and POP3 and IMAP4 clients that send messages via SMTP arrive through a receive connector. This is the only method that is typically used to introduce messages on an Edge server.

- **Pickup and replay directories:** Messages from foreign email systems or applications can be placed into the pickup directory from which Exchange will fetch them for processing. Messages that need to be replayed as a result of an outage come from the replay directory.

- **System-generated:** Exchange generates messages as the result of actions that occur for messages including nondelivery notifications and delivery receipts. Processing performed by agents such as transport rules can also generate messages. For example, a rule might create a copy of a message and BCC it to a new recipient. Journal reports are another example of system-generated messages.

No matter what their point of entry, all messages eventually arrive into the submission queue. The submission queue is re-created when the transport service starts. It's not a good sign if the submission queue grows constantly and the number of queued messages doesn't decrease, even in times of low overall server demand. This might indicate that the categorizer is under pressure for some reason that deserves investigation.

Moving messages to delivery queues

The categorizer processes messages from the submission queue on a first-in, first-out basis. A message remains in the submission queue until after the categorizer completes all of its processing and makes a decision about how best to route the message. The categorizer on a hub transport server performs three processing steps: The recipient set for the message is determined by validating the addressees and expanding any distribution groups; the optimum routing path for the message is calculated; and any content conversion required before the message can be sent to a user or a domain is performed. By comparison, the categorizer on an Edge server assumes that the full recipient set exists in a message and that the content is suitable for delivery and can therefore pass the message directly to a delivery queue. Although most messages pass through the categorizer very quickly, the expansion of the recipient set for very large dynamic distribution groups is one reason why the categorizer might take a few minutes to process a message.

After the categorizer knows all the routing information for a message, it is able to apply rules and other policies to know on which queue it should place messages. At this point, the categorizer moves the message from the submission queue to either a local delivery queue (MapiDelivery) or a remote delivery queue.

Local delivery queues are serviced by the Store driver for onward delivery to inboxes for recipients in the local site. Exchange 2010 maintains a separate local delivery queue for each mailbox database to which it sends messages, whereas Exchange 2007 uses per-server queues. Local delivery queues only exist on hub transport servers because Edge servers cannot deliver directly to mailbox databases.

Remote delivery queues are serviced by SMTP send connectors or other delivery connectors. A separate remote delivery queue is used for each connector. You'll see queues for the internal SMTP connectors used between hub transport servers and other queues for the connectors created for specific purposes such as routing messages to a partner domain or a smart host.

Viewing queues

One of the joys of Exchange is the speed at which it processes message queues. Messages arrive and depart in the twinkling of an eye and the existence of more than a few messages on a queue indicates that the server is under load or that network conditions are unable to carry the current level of traffic. You can view the current contents of the queues with the Queue Viewer or the Get-Queue cmdlet. The following sample shows the output from the Get-Queue cmdlet on a hub transport server. If you execute this cmdlet without passing a server name, Exchange displays details of the queues on the current server, assuming that it is a hub transport server (you'll see an error if it is not).

```
Get-Queue -Server ExServer1 -SortOrder: -MessageCount
```

Identity	DeliveryType	Status	MessageCount	NextHopDomain
ExServer1\2495	MapiDelivery	Active	2	vip data
ExServer1\2481	MapiDelivery	Active	1	DB2
ExServer1\2503	MapiDelivery	Ready	0	DB3
ExServer1\2516	SmtpRelay...	Ready	0	hub version 14
ExServer1\2527	SmartHost...	Ready	0	smtp1.contoso.com
ExServer1\Submission	Undefined	Ready	0	Submission
ExServer1\Shadow\2285	ShadowRed...	Ready	1	ExServer2

In this instance, we sort the output by the number of messages on the queue. The minus sign in front of the *–MessageCount* parameter means that we want to sort in descending order. Put a plus sign (+) in front of the parameter to sort in ascending order. For example, to sort the queues by status, we can use a command like this:

```
Get-Queue –Server ExServer1 –SortOrder: +Status
```

The *–Filter* parameter is also available to select queues from the full set. For example, here's how to select the queues that hold more than 20 messages:

```
Get-Queue –Server ExServer1 –Filter {MessageCount –gt 20} –SortOrder:
–MessageCount
```

Queue status

A queue status of Ready indicates that the queue is capable of accepting messages for onward processing. You might see a Connecting status that indicates that Exchange is in the process of connecting to a remote server to be able to pass queued messages. An Active status indicates that Exchange is transferring messages from the queue.

The overall appearance of the output looks very much like Exchange 2007, but a number of important differences exist. Whereas Exchange 2007 creates mailbox delivery queues (delivery type of *MapiDelivery*) to hold messages addressed to recipient mailboxes on other Exchange servers as the next-hop destination, Exchange 2010 delivery queues are created for the databases to which the mailboxes belong, so we have queues for Vip data, DAG1-DB2, and DAG1-DB3, all of which are databases on other servers in the same Active Directory site. This change is logical and is due to database mobility. After all, you cannot queue messages to a server and expect to be able to deliver them to a mailbox there if the database that holds the mailbox has been moved to another server following a failover.

Like Exchange 2007, queues are visible on a transient basis. In other words, the transport service creates queues as necessary and tears them down when no messages are queued. If you look at a server during a period of heavy demand you might see queues for every database in the local site (assuming that a message has recently been sent to a recipient in each database) and queues for hub transport servers in all of the other Active Directory sites within the organization. If you look at the queues on the same server at a time of low demand all of the per-database queues might have disappeared and the only queue left is the submission queue used to submit messages to the categorizer. Unlike mail delivery and remote delivery queues, the submission queue is persistent and you will find one submission queue per hub transport server. Exchange also clears queues when messages expire, which occurs by default after a message is more than two days old. The logic here is that a two-day-old message is not very useful to the recipient, so it is better to return it to the sender so that she can contact the intended recipient using another mechanism.

To ensure uniqueness, the transport system builds queue names from the hub transport server name plus a number that it increments over time. The number is reset when the transport service restarts. Among the other queues we can see are the following:

- The SmtpRelay (the full delivery queue type is SmtprelaywithinADSite) holds messages that have to be relayed to another SMTP server within the same Active Directory site. If the message is going to an Edge server, it will be on a queue with a delivery type of SmtpRelayWithinADSiteToEdge.

- The SmartHost queue listed for smtp1.contoso.com (the full delivery queue type is SmartHostConnectorDelivery) is a remote delivery queue that holds messages that are due to be routed to an SMTP smart host for onward delivery. Typically, this queue will hold messages for external SMTP domains that cannot be processed within the Exchange organization.

- The ShadowRedundancy queue is used by the transport dumpster to hold messages until the transport service is sure that the messages have been successfully delivered to the next hop. In this instance, we can see that one message is waiting for server ExServer2 to confirm that it has been successfully processed there. See the section "Transport pipeline" later in this chapter for more information about how the shadow redundancy feature works.

Unreachable and poison queues

You might also see unreachable and poison queues. Only one unreachable queue is ever present to hold messages for which the transport service route is unable to determine a route for some reason. For example, if you have an X.400 connector in the organization and then remove it, Exchange won't be able to route messages addressed to X.400 recipients anymore. Exchange will attempt to clear messages off the unreachable queue by checking periodically to see whether a route can be determined and, if so, will dispatch the message along the route. If a message expires before a route can be determined, Exchange generates an NDR back to the originator.

The poison queue provides a safe place to put messages that Exchange suspects are harmful, and you only see this queue if some poison messages exist. It could be that the message contains malformed SMTP commands or HTML code that could cause problems for the transport system. In any case, if Exchange does not like the look of a message it is placed on the poison queue for review by an administrator. If the message is deemed safe, the administrator can resume routing for the message to force Exchange to put the message back onto the submission queue to go through the categorizer as normal.

Problem queues

Sometimes you'll see that messages start to accumulate on queues and the count does not decrease even when the server is lightly loaded and there are no apparent problems that would cause you to think that messages should fail to be transferred. At this point you might want to investigate further by looking at the messages that are in the queue. For example, this command fetches full details of the current condition of a queue:

```
Get-Queue -id ExServer1\109 | Format-List
```

```
    Identity          : ExServer1\109
    DeliveryType      : SmartHostConnectorDelivery
    NextHopDomain     : smtp121.contoso.com
    NextHopConnector  : f9018e1b-3beb-42eb-8f6b-bf10f09e1157
    Status            : Retry
    MessageCount      : 15
    LastError         : 451 4.4.0 DNS query failed.
    The error was: SMTPSEND.DNS.NonExistentDomain; nonexistent domain
    LastRetryTime     : 3/16/2010 9:19:18 AM
    NextRetryTime     : 3/16/2010 9:20:18 AM
    ObjectState       : Unchanged
```

We can immediately see that the root cause that has caused the queue to build is that DNS has reported that it cannot resolve the name of the smart host that is configured to service the send connector. The NonExistentDomain message is a catch-all error that covers any problem resolving a name through DNS. The domain exists but the name of the server is wrong or cannot currently be resolved for some reason. The solution is to validate the name of the smart host and make sure that it can be resolved by DNS.

Another common problem that you encounter is when a remote server does not respond to a request to connect to exchange messages. In this case, you'll see this error:

```
421 4.2.1 Unable to connect. Attempted failover to alternate host, but that did not
succeed. Either there are no alternate hosts, or delivery failed to all alternate
hosts.
```

The hub transport servers within a site communicate via SMTP. If the transport service isn't running on a hub transport server, Exchange can revert back to a MAPI delivery to have the Store driver on a server pick up a message for a mailbox. You might see this kind of information reported when you interrogate the queue:

```
    Identity          : ExServer1\145
    DeliveryType      : SmtpRelayWithinAdSite
    NextHopDomain     : hub version 14
    NextHopConnector  : 61027a30-e9a9-4c2d-acb5-c1efc96d5d8b
    Status            : Ready
```

```
MessageCount    : 0
LastError       : 451 4.4.0 Primary target IP address responded with: "421
4.2.1 Unable to connect." Attempted failover to alternate host, but that did
not succeed. Either there are no alternate hosts, or delivery failed to all
alternate hosts. Queue will be resubmitted for routing for MAPI delivery
LastRetryTime   : 3/16/2010 9:28:21 AM
NextRetryTime   :
IsValid         : True
```

The *NextHopDomain* property reported is either "hub transport 14" (transfer within a site), the name of an SMTP server such as a smart host, or the name of the Active Directory site to which Exchange is trying to transfer the message. In the latter case, if there is only one hub transport server in the target site, there's a fair chance that the problem is with this server. On the other hand, if more than one hub transport server operates within the site, the problem could be with any of them. Hub transport servers reject connections if they begin to exhaust resources using a feature called back pressure (see the section "Back Pressure," earlier in this chapter), so this is another item for your checklist. If the problem server is a mailbox server, you should verify that the Store is running on the server, because it is possible that the database that hosts the recipient's mailbox is dismounted or inoperative for some reason.

The Get-Message cmdlet reveals details of the messages on the "stuck" queues. For example:

Get-Message

```
Identity              FromAddress         Status    Queue          Subject
--------              -----------         ------    -----          -------
ExServer1\109\1322    Tony.Redmond@con... Ready     ExServer1\109  Really important
ExServer1\109\1324    Tony.Redmond@con... Ready     ExServer1\109  Budget 2010 material
```

If there are more than a few messages queued, it might be more convenient to pipe this output to a text file and review the data using the file. If necessary, you can see the details of an individual message by using its identifier to select the message. In this example, we select the second message in the list.

Get-Message –Identity 'ExServer1\109\1324'-IncludeRecipientInfo | Format-List

```
Identity          : ExServer1\109\1324
Subject           : Budget 2010 Material
InternetMessageId : <DA8443D94CD81648B26E118E7A3A54E6017B4861@ExServer2.contoso.com>
FromAddress       : Tony.Redmond@contoso.com
Status            : Ready
Size              : 3.363 KB (3,444 bytes)
MessageSourceName : FromLocal
```

```
SourceIP          : 255.255.255.255
SCL               : -1
DateReceived      : 3/16/2010 10:44:44 AM
ExpirationTime    : 3/18/2010 10:44:44 AM
LastError         :
RetryCount        : 0
Queue             : ExServer1\109
Recipients        : {tr@gmail.com}
ComponentLatency  :
MessageLatency    : 00:07:02.2280076
IsValid           : True
ObjectState       : Unchanged
```

You can also suspend a message with the Suspend-Message cmdlet by passing the message identifier. In this case, Exchange will keep the message on the queue but will not attempt to process it until an administrator releases the message:

```
Suspend-Message –Identity 'ExServer1\109\1324'
```

To release the message, use the Resume-Message cmdlet:

```
Resume-Message –Identity 'ExServer1\109\1324'
```

The Remove-Message cmdlet deletes a message from a queue. In this example, we send an NDR back to the sender to tell him what's happened. If you set the *–WithNDR* parameter to $False, Exchange deletes the message without sending an NDR:

```
Remove-Message –Identity 'ExServer1\109\1324'–WithNDR $True
```

You do not have to suspend a message before you can delete it.

It might also be possible that some other administrator has suspended a complete queue and suspended processing for all its messages for some reason. If this is the case, the queue status will be Suspended and you will have to determine why the queue was suspended and whether you can resume it. You can resume a queue through the Queue Viewer or with the Resume-Queue cmdlet:

```
Resume-Queue –Identity 'ExServer1\821'
```

Exchange will clear queues automatically and immediately when the underlying problem goes away and will tear down the queue after a couple of minutes if it is no longer required.

Exchange Queue Viewer

You can also use the Exchange Queue Viewer to examine the contents of the transport queues (Figure 13-18). The Queue Viewer is a Microsoft Management Console (MMC) that is part of EMC's toolbox collection. The major advantage of the Queue Viewer is that it provides an easy-to-use method to see what's happening on queues and to examine the properties of messages that are currently in a queue. The transport service is capable of processing even large messages very quickly, so the Queue Viewer refreshes its display every five seconds or so to provide an up-to-date picture of what's happening on a hub transport server.

INSIDE OUT Where the messages are being processed

Remember that if you are operating within a DAG, messages are always submitted to a remote hub transport server if one is available in the site rather than being processed locally, as is the case for "normal" servers. A few administrators have made the mistake of looking at queues on the local server and seeing no activity when all the messages that they were trying to monitor were being processed elsewhere.

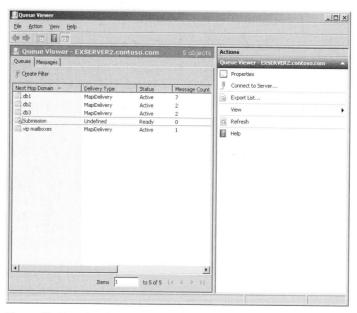

Figure 13-18 Using the Queue Viewer to view transport queues.

All of the actions that we have reviewed in the cmdlets that work with queue contents are supported by the Queue Viewer. Most experienced administrators prefer to use EMS to interrogate message queues because EMS responds more quickly to queries because it doesn't have to allow for the overhead imposed by the Queue Viewer GUI. However, it is nice to have the choice.

Submitting messages through the pickup directory

The pickup directory is typically used to introduce messages created by applications into the transport service. For example, a monitoring agent might detect an application failure and generate a message like the one shown in the following example.

```
To: SystemAdmins@contoso.com
From: AppWarning@contoso.com
Date: 1 March 2011 01:15AM
Subject: Warning - BlackBox Application failure
MIME-Version: 1.0
Content-Type: text/html; charset="iso-8859-1"
Content-Transfer-Encoding: 7bit
<HTML><BODY>
</TABLE>
<h3>
The BlackBox application has experienced a failure on server BBOX188.
Please check!
</h3>
<TABLE>
<TR><TD>Application</TD><TD>Problem Details</TD></TR>
<TR><TD>BBOX Version 2.010</TD><TD>The application is not responding to
prompts</TD></TR>
</BODY></HTML>
```

By default, the pickup directory is located in \TransportRoles\Pickup. You can modify this location with the Set-TransportServer cmdlet. For example:

```
Set-TransportServer –Identity ExServer2 –PickupDirectoryPath
'C:\Exchange\PickupDirectory'
```

The basic idea is that an application creates a text file with an .eml extension that complies with the basic SMTP message format and places the file in the pickup directory. Every five seconds (this interval cannot be altered), Exchange checks the pickup directory and attempts to process any file with an .eml extension that it finds there.

INSIDE OUT   Processing a large volume of messages

Files with any extension other than .eml are ignored. Exchange will process up to 100 files from the pickup directory per minute and will leave the remainder to be processed the next time around if more than this number of .eml files is present. You can instruct Exchange to process more files at one time with the Set-TransportServer cmdlet if you need to accommodate a larger volume of messages generated by applications. For example:

```
Set-TransportServer -PickupDirectoryMaxMessagesPerMinute 250
```

The file is first renamed with a .tmp extension and then examined by Exchange to see if it contains the necessary formatting to allow the file to be converted into a message. If all is well, the message is placed into the submission queue and the .tmp file is removed from the pickup directory. If the file is not properly formatted, Exchange changes the extension to .bad and leaves the file in the pickup directory where hopefully an administrator will find it and deal with it. For example, if you use a mailbox alias rather than the full SMTP address of the mailbox in the From: field, Exchange will reject the file. It's possible that a failure will occur that causes the transport service or the server to stop running when messages are being processed from the pickup directory. In this case, the .tmp files will remain in the directory and Exchange will process them again the next time that it scans for new messages. A slight possibility exists that duplicate messages will be delivered as a result. Administrators won't be aware that duplicates have been delivered but this is unlikely to be of much concern because users are able to detect and eliminate duplicates when these messages arrive in their inboxes.

A message file consists of header fields and text. The basic requirements are as follows:

- Only text files with an .eml extension are processed.

- At least one email address must exist in the To:, CC:, or BCC: fields. All addresses must be in SMTP format.

- Only one email address must be in the From: or Sender: field. If a single address is in both fields, Exchange uses the address in the From: field as the message originator. It is possible to provide multiple addresses in the From: field (separate each address with a comma), but if you do this you also have to provide a single address in the Sender: field that Exchange will then use as the message originator. Outlook displays these messages as if the address specified as the Sender: sent the message on behalf of the first address in the From: list. In all cases, the email address for the message originator should be valid; otherwise the message might be dropped by an anti-spam agent somewhere along its route.

- For plain text messages, a blank line must be between the header fields and the text that forms the message body. A blank line is not required for Multipurpose Internet Mail Extensions (MIME)-format messages.

- The maximum header size is 64 KB and there can be no more than 100 recipients specified in the header.

If present, the Received and Resent header fields are removed by Exchange, as these header fields aren't supported when submitted through the pickup directory. BCC recipients are also removed to preserve their anonymity. If only BCC recipients are present, Exchange replaces them with Undisclosed Recipients in the header. If the date field is missing, Exchange will use the date and time that the file was taken from the pickup directory.

Finally, to help identify messages that come in through the pickup directory, Exchange adds a header like the one shown here.

```
Received: from Pickup by ExServer1.contoso.com with Microsoft SMTP
 Server id 14.0.682.1; Thu, 25 Feb 2010 12:27:49 +0000
```

Replay directory

The replay directory is used to resubmit exported Exchange messages and to receive messages from foreign gateway servers. Like the pickup directory, Exchange checks the replay directory every five seconds and processes any messages that it finds there. The messages that are introduced into the replay directory are formatted by the foreign gateway to comply with Exchange requirements; the gateway performs whatever conversion is required to transform message contents from the original format.

> **Tip**
> You shouldn't attempt to introduce messages through the replay directory. Use the pickup directory when you need to submit a message to Exchange.

Customizable system messages

Exchange 2010 allows you to customize two kinds of system-generated messages: DSNs and quota warning messages. In all versions prior to Exchange 2007, if you wanted to use customized text in system-generated messages, you had to ask Microsoft to supply a custom-built replacement DLL that contained the customized text. Apart from the cost to build the new DLL, you took on two additional problems. First, the customized DLL might compromise support. In practice, if Microsoft supplied the customization, you probably received support for the work. This didn't apply if someone other than Microsoft did the work. Second, the customization had to be tested and deployed to every hub transport server in the organization after Microsoft released a roll-up update or service pack. Exchange 2007 and Exchange 2010 supply the solution with the ability to customize the text used in NDRs and quota warning messages using the New-SystemMessage cmdlet.

Exchange DSNs

Over time, it is inevitable that Exchange will not be able to deliver some of the messages that arrive to a hub transport server for processing. The destination mailbox might be full, the mailbox might have been disabled or deleted, the recipient address might be invalid, and so on. Failed messages cause Exchange to generate nondelivery messages, a form of DSN messages, to inform the sender that something unexpected has occurred with her message. DSN messages fall into five categories:

- **Relayed:** DSNs generated when a user requests a delivery receipt for a message that passes out of the Exchange organization to a remote SMTP server. Tracking the delivery is no longer possible, so Exchange notifies the user that his message has been relayed to the point where it has left the organization. The delivery status for messages sent to another Exchange organization can be tracked successfully, so a relayed DSN is not generated in this case.

- **Delayed:** These DSNs are generated by a hub transport server when queued messages exceed the threshold set for the generation of delay notifications. The default value is 4 hours. You can change the delay threshold with the Set-TransportServer cmdlet. For example, to reduce the delay threshold to 2 hours, you'd use a command similar to that shown below. Note that this setting is server-specific and you therefore have to apply it to all hub transport and Edge servers if you want to impose consistent processing across an organization.

```
Set-TransportServer -Identity ExServer2 -DelayNotificationTimeOut 02:00:00
```

- **Success:** These DSNs are generated when a user requests a delivery receipt for an outgoing message. The DSN is an indication that Exchange has definitely delivered the message to the destination mailbox.

- **Failed:** These are NDRs that state that delivery failed for some reason such as quota exhausted for the destination mailbox or lack of authorization to send to a recipient. The transport service automatically generates these messages and includes the original message for the user to deal with, including the ability to use client-specific features to resend the message after correcting the fault that caused the NDR.

- **Expansion:** A group is expanded and a message is delivered to multiple recipients.

Exchange 2007 greatly improved the quality and readability of the DSNs that it generates when compared to previous versions. The same capability persists and is shared with Exchange 2010 and there usually aren't any problems with the DSNs generated to report message failures or delays. The clarity of the default text in the NDRs is commendable but sometimes you need to amend the text to satisfy organizational requirements or to include some information that is more meaningful to your users. To facilitate this need, Exchange splits the text that it inserts in an NDR into two parts: a brief explanation of the problem in plain language to tell the user why her message failed and a more comprehensive and technical section that contains troubleshooting information for administrators.

The layout of an NDR places the user text first so that it is immediately obvious and can be read even on mobile devices that only download partial messages. As you can see in Figure 13-19, there is a wide section of white space between the user and troubleshooting sections of text. This is by design, to keep the complexities of message routing away from users! The troubleshooting section contains these important pieces of information:

- The FQDN of the hub transport server that generated the NDR.

- The name and email address of the recipient that caused the problem.

- The FQDN for any remote server involved in the message.

- The enhanced DSN status code. These are codes such as 5.5.1 (unknown addressee) or 5.7.1 (unauthorized to send to addressee) defined in RFC 3463 that are generated by SMTP servers to indicate the reason why a message failed.

- Message headers: SMTP message headers for the failed message are included to provide further diagnostic data.

FQDN and the remote server

The example shown in Figure 13-19 doesn't include any details about a remote server because the message was rejected by the hub transport server to which the mailbox server submitted the message. In cases where a hub transport server has a message rejected by a remote SMTP server (for example, the destination address is invalid), the FQDN of that server and the response (such as RESOLVER.RST.NotAuthorized; not authorized) received from the remote server are recorded so that the administrator knows what happened when Exchange attempted to transfer the message.

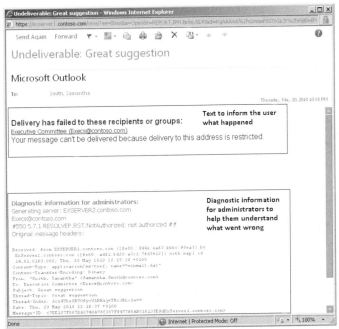

Figure 13-19 Anatomy of a nondelivery notification.

Given the complexities of modern messaging systems, there are numerous reasons why Exchange might not be able to deliver a message to an internal or external recipient. Table 13-6 lists the DSNs for the most common error conditions that you'll encounter.

Table 13-6 Common causes for message delivery to fail

DSN code	Problem
4.4.7 – Message expired	Exchange was not able to deliver the message within two days (the default) so the message expired and has been removed from the delivery queue. Alternatively, an administrator deleted the message from a queue for some reason. The user should resend the message.
5.1.1 – Wrong email address	The intended recipient cannot be found in the directory of the receiving system so the message cannot be delivered. The user might have mistyped the address or even used an outdated message from Outlook's nickname cache. In either case, he will have to fix the address and resend the message.
5.1.3 – Incorrect address format	Exchange believes that the format of the address is incorrect so it can't be delivered. The user has to fix the address and resend.
5.1.4 – Duplicate address	The receiving email system has detected a duplicate address. The user can't do much about this problem, because the remote administrator has to resolve the duplicates before anyone can send to this address.
5.1.8 – Bad sender address	For some reason, a remote server isn't able to accept mail from the sender. The only thing that anyone can do is to read the diagnostic information and attempt to figure out what happened.
5.2.0 – Generic failure to deliver	All sorts of problems with mailboxes can cause this to occur, including a missing SMTP address, an invalid SMTP address, or an invalid forwarding address. The administrator will have to check the recipient's mailbox to verify that everything is correct.
5.2.2 – Mailbox quota exceeded	The recipient's mailbox is full and can't accept incoming messages. The recipient has to reduce the mailbox under quota or have the quota increased to accept new messages.
5.2.3 – Message too large	Either the recipient or the sender is not allowed such a large message.
5.2.4 – Dynamic distribution group query is wrong	Exchange is unable to resolve the query to populate the recipients in a dynamic distribution group. The administrator will have to fix this problem by verifying the query used for the group.

5.3.4 – Message too large to route	Some component along the message path was unable to route the message because of a size restriction. The restriction could be on a connector, imposed by the organization configuration, or imposed by a remote server.
5.4.4 – Unable to route	Normally this is because a user attempts to send a message to a domain that no longer exists, so Exchange is unable to route the message.
5.5.3 – Too many recipients	There are too many recipients in the message header. The only solution is to reduce the number of recipients and resend the message. Remember that distribution groups count as one recipient no matter how many recipients they include, so use distribution groups whenever possible.
5.7.1 – Lack of authorization	The sender doesn't have the necessary authorization to send to a recipient.

Customizing NDRs

You can customize the text presented to users in an NDR or create system messages to associate with new DSN codes that are used with transport rules. As an example, let's assume that you think that the text used by Exchange 2010 in DSNs for error code 5.1.1 can be improved. This code is used when Exchange cannot deliver a message because the recipient is unknown. In other words, Exchange cannot find a mail-enabled group, contact, mailbox, or public folder with the address in the message header. The uncustomized text is:

```
"The email address you entered couldn't be found. Check the address and try resending
the message. If the problem continues, please contact your helpdesk."
```

We use the New-SystemMessage cmdlet to assign customized code to a DSN code. In this case, we want to assign new text to DSN 5.1.1 for English language messages that come from internal senders. Here's what the command looks like. Note that the –*Internal* parameter is set to $False; this instructs Exchange that the message is intended for use outside the organization. If the message was purely for internal use, as in the case of a customized message used with a transport rule, you'd set the –*Internal* parameter to $True.

```
New-SystemMessage –Language en –DsnCode 5.1.1 –Text "Unfortunately our email system
was unable to find your correspondent in our directory so we couldn't deliver the
message. Please check your little black book to validate the email address that you
used or contact the recipient by phone or fax." –Internal $False
```

This is a much more personal message for anyone to receive. Figure 13-20 shows what our customized NDR looks like when it is received by a user. You can see that only the text intended for user consumption is changed and that the diagnostic information provided for administrators remains intact.

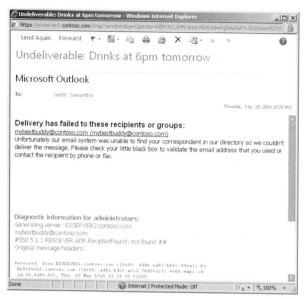

Figure 13-20 Viewing a customized NDR.

For messages intended for internal recipients, we could customize the text further to add a URL that users can click to get more detailed guidance. We can amend the text for a customized message with the Set-SystemMessage cmdlet. Here's an example:

```
Set-SystemMessage –Identity en\Internal\5.1.1 –Text "We couldn't deliver your message
because the email address that you provided was not found in the corporate directory.
Please check <a href='http://contoso.com/directory.html'>Corporate Directory</a> to
find the correct email address to use"
```

Note the way that the identity for the customized message is composed of the language code (en = English), whether it is intended for internal or external use, and the DSN code. Of course, to complete the job, we have to provide customized text for every language in use within the organization and decide whether we need to customize the text seen by external recipients.

Testing the customized text

When you've finished composing the text to use, you can use the Get-SystemMessage cmdlet to check that the customized message is in place and all its properties are as expected:

```
Get-SystemMessage –Identity en\Internal\5.1.1 | Format-List
```

The output is:

```
Text                : We couldn't deliver your message because the email address
that you provided was not found in the corporate directory. Please check <a
href='http://contoso.com/directory.html'>Corporate Directory</a> to find the
correct email address to use
Internal            : True
Language            : en
DsnCode             : 5.1.1
QuotaMessageType    :
AdminDisplayName    :
ExchangeVersion     : 0.1 (8.0.535.0)
Name                : 5.1.1
DistinguishedName   : CN=5.1.1,CN=Internal,CN=9,CN=DSN Customization,CN=Transport
Settings,CN=contoso,CN=Microsoft Exchange,CN=Services,CN=Configuration,
DC=contoso,DC=com
Identity            : en\Internal\5.1.1
```

Customized system messages are stored in the Exchange configuration data in Active
Directory and are replicated throughout the organization to be available to all hub
transport servers. The distinguished name for the system message provides the path to
navigate to the object and we can view its properties in Active Directory using ADSIEdit
(Figure 13-21).

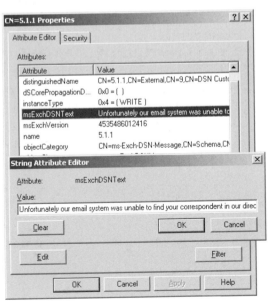

Figure 13-21 Viewing the Active Directory properties of a custom NDR.

You can maintain different sets of customized DSNs for hub transport and Edge servers. You might want to do this to provide additional information in the internal DSNs that you don't want to reveal to external recipients. As discussed in Chapter 14, Edge servers maintain their own configuration that is separate and isolated from the organizational settings stored in Active Directory and used by all hub transport servers. If you want to use customized DSNs for messages that are processed by Edge servers, you have to customize the DSNs on each of your Edge servers using the same technique as explained here.

Customizing quota messages

The New-SystemMessage cmdlet is also used to alter the text of the messages that advise mailbox or public folder owners that mailbox or public folder quotas are approaching their thresholds or have been exceeded. The Exchange Mailbox Assistant checks mailbox and public folder quotas nightly and then sends whatever messages are required. A warning message for a mailbox is sent to the mailbox owner until the user responds to the nagging and reduces her mailbox size under its quota. Warning messages for a public folder are sent to every owner registered for the folder (this could be a distribution group). System-generated messages do not count against mailbox quotas.

Figure 13-22 illustrates the different parts of a typical system-generated quota message. You cannot change the message subject because the values for these fields come from translated strings in Exchange code. You cannot alter or change the graphical comparison of quota against usage. You can customize the text under the graphic that communicates the problem that exists with the mailbox (or public folder) and the action that the user should take. Many companies like to customize this text to point users to a Web site where they can get comprehensive advice about how to clean out old and obsolete items to reduce usage under the quota threshold. Table 13-7 lists the set of message codes for the messages that you can customize together with the default English language text and a note about the circumstances that provoke generation of the message.

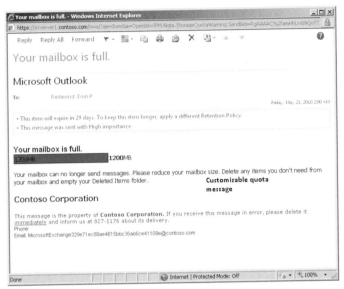

Figure 13-22 Components of a system-generated mailbox quota warning message.

Table 13-7 Customizable quota messages

Message Code	Default subject	Generated when
ProhibitPostPublicFolder	Your public folder is full	A public folder exceeds its prohibit post quota. No further items can be posted into the folder.
ProhibitSendReceiveMailbox	Your mailbox is full	A mailbox exceeds both its prohibit send and receive thresholds. The mailbox can no longer receive or send new messages.
ProhibitSendMailbox	Your mailbox is full	A mailbox exceeds its prohibit send threshold. The mailbox can receive new messages but cannot send new messages.
WarningMailboxUnlimitedSize	Your mailbox is almost full	A mailbox that has no prohibit send or prohibit receive quotas exceeds its warning limit (if set). This is just a warning and the mailbox can continue to send and receive messages.
WarningPublicFolderUnlimitedSize	Your public folder is becoming too large	A public folder that has no prohibit send or prohibit receive quotas exceeds its warning limit (if set). Users can continue to post new items to the public folder.

Chapter 13

WarningMailbox	Your mailbox is becoming too large	A mailbox exceeds its warning threshold. This is just a warning and the mailbox can continue to send and receive messages until it exceeds the send and receive thresholds.
WarningPublicFolder	Your public folder is almost full	A public folder that has a prohibit send quota or prohibit receive quota exceeds its specified warning limit (if set).

Let's assume that you want to change the warning message received by people whose mailboxes are approaching their quota thresholds. We can accomplish our goal with this command:

```
New-SystemMessage –QuotaMessageType WarningMailbox –language En

–Text 'Your mailbox is getting very close to its quota. We recommend that you imme-
diately clean up its content to release space. See <a href="http://tips.contoso.com/
mailboxcontents.html">Mailbox Cleanup Tips</a> for more information' –Internal $True
```

INSIDE OUT   A few tips for working with customized system quota messages

Customized system quota messages are all internal so you do not really need to add the *–Internal $True* parameter. The messages are language specific and if you don't supply customized translated text for a language, Exchange reverts to the default text. If you make a mistake, you can replace the text with the Set-SystemMessage cmdlet. For example:

```
Set-SystemMessage –Identity en\WarningMailbox –Text 'I wish I could tell you
how to clean up a mailbox…'
```

Use the Remove-SystemMessage cmdlet to remove a customized quota message. For example:

```
Remove-SystemMessage en\WarningMailbox
```

Logging

You can configure connectivity and protocol logging for Exchange 2010 hub transport servers. The contents of these logs can help you understand what happens when Exchange sends and receives messages. You won't go looking for these logs on a daily basis, but they are useful whenever you need to understand why messages are not being transported as you expect. Details of logging are exposed with EMC through the Log Setting tab of the Properties dialog box for a server that has the hub or Edge transport role installed (Figure 13-23); the tab is not visible for servers that do not support one of the transport roles. Here you can turn connectivity logging on or off and define where the logs are kept. You can also define locations for the two protocol logs (send and receive) but you can't enable protocol logging through EMC. Protocol logging is controlled through EMS, perhaps on the basis that generation of protocol logs is only necessary on an exception basis. However, it does seem to be slightly inconsistent that Microsoft hasn't included another check box to allow protocol logging to be turned on and off as easily as connectivity logging.

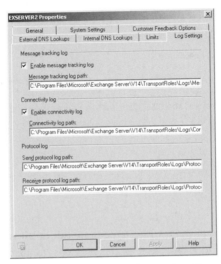

Figure 13-23 Setting logging options for a server.

Controlling connectivity logging

The Exchange 2010 documentation states that connectivity logging is disabled by default. I have not found this to be the case for the servers with which I have worked, but to make sure, we can enable connectivity logging as follows:

```
Set-TransportServer –Identity ExServer4 –ConnectivityLogEnabled $True
```

To reverse this action, you set the parameter to $False. Exchange creates a new connectivity log on a daily basis. The log is created the first time that the transport system processes an outgoing message. The first log created on a day is named using a convention of *CONNECTLOGYYYYMMDD-1.log* where *YYYYMMDD* represents the year, month, and day. For example, the first log created on December 31, 2010 is named CONNECTLOG20101231-1.log. By default, Exchange will create a new log after it captures

10 MB of connectivity data. The second log created on December 31, 2010 would be named CONNECTLOG20101231-2.log, the third CONNECTLOG20101231-3.log, and so on. You can change the size of the connectivity log as follows:

```
Set-TransportServer -Identity ExServer4 -ConnectivityLogMaxFileSize 50MB
```

Exchange keeps 250 MB of connectivity logs. A circular logging scheme keeps the logs in the directory under this size by removing the oldest logs to free up space for new logs. You can increase the amount of storage assigned to connectivity logs by setting the value like this:

```
Set-TransportServer -Identity ExServer4 -ConnectivityLogMaxDirectorySize 500MB
```

Assuming the directory storage threshold is not exceeded, connectivity logs are normally retained for 30 days. Because only the most recent logs are typically used to debug connectivity problems, you might decide to reduce this period. For example, here's how you would set the retention period to 15 days:

```
Set-TransportServer -Identity ExServer4 -ConnectivityLogMaxAge 15.00:00:00
```

The default location for the log files is buried deep under the Exchange root and it's often more convenient to have the logs stored in a more obvious location that's easier to remember. To move the location for the connectivity logs, you can use a command like this:

```
Set-TransportServer -Identity ExServer4 -ConnectivityLogPath 'C:\Logs\Connectivity'
```

TROUBLESHOOTING

How did I get two connectivity logs with the same name?
Exchange will create the directory if the specified path doesn't exist. It will not move the current or any other connectivity logs that already exist to the new location. However, it will begin to use the new location to capture connectivity data immediately after the change is made, which means that you might end up with two logs with the same name if you copy the logs from the original logging directory to the new one. A quick rename of the old log sorts the problem out.

All of these commands are server-specific. It is best practice to apply the same settings to every transport server within the organization so that the servers are consistent with each other. Fortunately, this is easy to do with EMS:

```
Get-TransportServer | Set-TransportServer -ConnectivityLogPath 'C:\Logs\Connectivity'
-ConnectivityLogMaxAge 15.00:00:00
-ConnectivityLogMaxDirectorySize 500MB -ConnectivityLogMaxFileSize 50MB
```

Interpreting a connectivity log

You can open a connectivity log with a text editor or any program that understands the CSV format. I tend to use Microsoft Excel for this purpose. Figure 13-24 illustrates some typical content from a connectivity log. The first five lines tell you that the file was generated by Exchange 2010 (version 14.0.0.0) and declare the date that the log was created and its type. We also see the names of the field written for the remainder of the records in the file.

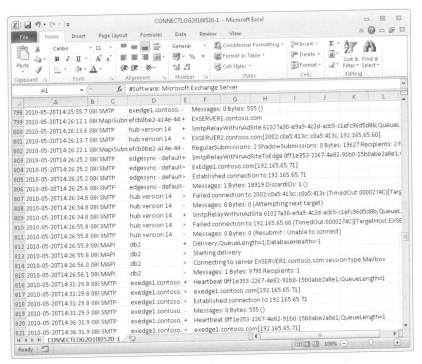

Figure 13-24 Interpreting a connectivity log.

Each transaction with another server to send a message is composed of a number of steps that vary according to the type of transaction and the number of servers that are involved. Some transactions involve a delivery to a mailbox database on another server in the site. The source of the message is clearly indicated as SMTP, meaning that it comes from the remote delivery queue, or MAPI for connections from the mailbox delivery queue to a database. The direction field is used to indicate whether the step is at the start ("+"), middle (">"), or end ("-") of a transaction to allow you to follow the flow.

> **Note**
>
> A transaction can span several sessions. For example, a message that is delivered to multiple databases on other servers requires a separate session for each destination database. If failures occur during transactions, Exchange captures details of the events in the connectivity log.

Figure 13-24 shows the typical detail captured in a connectivity log. A number of connections are captured here. We can see communications between hub transport servers (labeled hub version 14) to transfer messages to each other, a delivery to a database called db2 (the clue is the text "starting delivery"), and connections flowing to and from an Edge transport server called exedge1.contoso.com as messages come into and leave the organization.

Protocol logging

Protocol logging tracks the steps that occur in SMTP conversations to transfer messages between Exchange and other servers. The logging is at a lower level than tracking the connections, because it captures details such as the authentication between servers and the SMTP verbs used in the conversations. The approach taken to the management of protocol logging and the logs that are generated is very similar to connectivity logging. This shouldn't come as a surprise because it wouldn't make sense for the engineering group to create multiple methods for generating and managing logs. Protocol logging is disabled by default, so you have to enable logging on a per-connector basis before Exchange will generate logs. Exchange generates separate logs for SMTP send and for SMTP receive operations.

Like connectivity logging, the output is in CSV format. Figure 13-25 illustrates typical content from an SMTP receive log (some steps have been removed from this extract for the sake of clarity). The example shows how two Exchange hub transport servers set up an SMTP connection to each other to exchange messages. After the normal SMTP interchange of supported verbs, the connection is authenticated with TLS and then the sending server begins to transmit the message header fields, beginning with the sender information (MAIL FROM). The receiving server validates that the recipient is OK by checking that the sender is not blocked (the recipient might be a restricted address that only accepts messages from a defined set of senders). You can also see the new XSHADOW ESMTP (extended SMTP) verb used to send information for the shadow redundancy feature of the transport dumpster. The message content with a binary transfer (BDAT) and the conversation is terminated with a XQDISCARD verb (not shown here). This is another ESMTP verb introduced in Exchange 2010 to support the shadow redundancy mechanism. See the section "Transport pipeline" later in this chapter for more information about how shadow redundancy works. The final step disconnects the link between the two servers.

Chapter 13

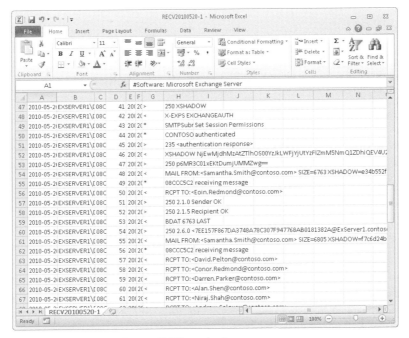

Figure 13-25 Interpreting an SMTP receive log.

The content of a send log is very similar. For example, if you look at the transactions generated to send a message via an external SMTP relay, you will see Exchange identify itself with EHLO, create a TLS-secured connection if this is supported by the relay server, send the message, and close the link.

The first question we must resolve when we decide how to configure protocol logging is what connectors should have logging enabled. Every hub transport server has two default receive connectors: one to monitor port 25 and accept incoming SMTP messages from other servers, and one to monitor port 587 and handle messages sent by clients. We can enable logging for both as follows:

```
Get-ReceiveConnector –Server ExServer1 | Set-ReceiveConnector
–ProtocolLoggingLevel Verbose
```

To turn off protocol logging, we set the logging level to None. Of course, you don't have to set logging for both connectors. To set logging on just the connector that handles SMTP server-based traffic, you'd use a command like this:

```
Set-ReceiveConnector –Identity 'ExServer1\Default ExServer1'–ProtocolLoggingLevel
Verbose
```

Much the same occurs to enable protocol logging for send connectors. There are two types of send connectors: Explicit or normal send connectors are defined to handle traffic to specified SMTP domains; and Exchange also creates a special intraorganization send connector on every hub transport server to send messages within the organization. You can enable protocol logging for a normal connector as follows:

```
Set-SendConnector -Identity 'Smart Relay via contoso.com' -ProtocolLoggingLevel
Verbose
```

Because you don't have an identifier to pass to identify the intraorganization send connector, you can't configure protocol logging for it using Set-SendConnector. Instead, you use the Set-TransportServer cmdlet as follows:

```
Set-TransportServer -Identity ExServer1 -IntraOrgConnectorProtocolLoggingLevel
Verbose
```

The Set-TransportServer cmdlet is also used to specify the location of the send and receive logs, the maximum size of each log (default 10 MB), the overall size of the log directory, and the age limit for the logs. The location for the protocol log directory is the only setting that you can configure with EMC. Just like connectivity logs, Exchange uses a circular logging mechanism to keep the protocol logs under these thresholds. The following command shows how to configure the various settings:

```
Set-TransportServer -Identity ExServer2 -ReceiveProtocolLogPath 'C:\Logs\SMTPReceive'
-SendProtocolLogPath 'C:\Logs\SMTPSend'
-ReceiveProtocolLogMaxFileSize 20MB -SendProtocolLogMaxFileSize 20MB
-ReceiveProtocolLogMaxDirectorySize 500MB  -SendProtocolLogMaxDirectorySize 500MB
-ReceiveProtocolLogMaxAge 15:00.00.00 -SendProtocolLogMaxAge 15:00.00.00
```

As with connectivity logging, it is best practice to use the same settings for all hub transport servers in the organization. This is easily accomplished as described in the last section: Configure the connectivity log settings by using Get-TransportServer to fetch a list of all hub transport servers and use that list as input to Set-TransportServer to implement the settings.

Accepted domains

An email domain or SMTP namespace such as contoso.com must be declared to Exchange before the transport system will accept incoming messages addressed to that domain. Domains for which Exchange accepts messages are called accepted domains. The domain into which Exchange is installed is automatically added to the list of accepted domains during the installation of the first hub transport server in the organization. If you want to use other domains, you have to add them to the list of accepted domains. In essence, you go through the exercise of defining accepted domains to inform Exchange about the SMTP namespace(s) that are used by the organization, the namespaces used by trusted partner organizations, and those for other domains for which Exchange performs some processing.

Exchange supports two types of accepted domains.

- Authoritative domains are those for which the Exchange organization hosts mailboxes. Another way of saying this is that the objects can be found in Active Directory when Exchange looks for them to route incoming messages. For example, if your company is the result of a merger and you want to preserve older email addresses and assign them to mailboxes, you have to make all of the older domains accepted and authoritative. Naturally, external email systems will have to be instructed using DNS MX records to route messages to Exchange for delivery to mailboxes with these addresses.

- Relay domains are those for which Exchange is willing to relay incoming messages. It could be that Exchange serves as a front-end mail server for multiple smaller subsidiaries whose mailboxes are hosted on other email systems. Public MX records for these domains point to Exchange (either an Edge transport server or another front-end server that routes messages to Exchange). In this scenario, you could declare the domains for the subsidiaries to be relay domains to allow Exchange to accept incoming messages and then retransmit the messages to their final destination via a suitable send connector.

A relay domain can be internal or external. Internal relay domains can include recipients who have Exchange mailboxes. In this instance, any incoming message addressed to these recipients can be delivered as normal. Messages addressed to recipients who do not have Exchange mailboxes are routed via a connector that supports the address space. External relay domains have no relationship with Exchange and any incoming messages destined for these domains are simply rerouted via the best possible connector for onward delivery to the destination server. For example, you might have a department that hosts its own SMTP mail server for the dev.contoso.com domain. You can create an accepted domain record for "dev.contoso.com" to allow Exchange to accept messages for the domain and add dev.contoso.com to the address space for a connector so that the transport system can redirect the messages to that connector as soon as they arrive.

Accepted domains can be specific or can include all subdomains. For instance, you can create contoso.com or *.contoso.com as an accepted domain. In the latter case, messages sent to any subdomain of contoso.com will be accepted by Exchange.

CAUTION

Domains must be added to the accepted domains list before they can be included in an email address policy. See Chapter 6, "Managing Mail-Enabled Recipients," for more information about how to create and apply email address policies. An email address policy is rendered invalid if you remove the accepted domain that the policy uses. In this case, users who depend on the email addresses created by the now-invalid policy will be unable to send or receive email until their mailboxes are assigned valid email addresses by a new policy.

Creating a new accepted domain

Let's assume that your company has been bought by the Fabrikam Corporation and you have to assign new fabrikam.com addresses to all users. The first step is to create a new accepted domain for fabrikam.com. To do this with EMC, go to the Hub Transport section of the Organization Configuration node and select the New Accepted Domain option in the action pane. The New Accepted Domain Wizard shown in Figure 13-26 is presented. You can then input the name to identify the domain and the SMTP domain that will be used in messages. You can also select whether the domain is authoritative or a relay domain.

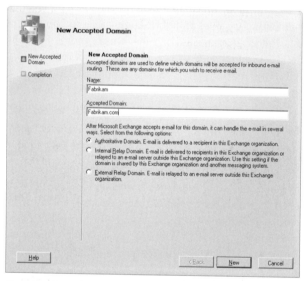

Figure 13-26 Creating a new accepted domain.

The name of the accepted domain has no direct relationship to the SMTP domain. For example, you could use a name such as "Route email to subsidiaries" or "Old premerger domain" to indicate the true use of the domain for messaging purposes. The EMS command to create the new accepted domain is:

```
New-AcceptedDomain -Name 'Fabrikam' -DomainName 'Fabrikam.com' -DomainType
'Authoritative'
```

Once we have defined the new accepted domain, we can update the highest priority email address policy to add new fabrikam.com addresses to mail-enabled recipients. This command should do the trick:

```
Set-EmailAddressPolicy -Identity 'FirstNameLastName'-Priority 1
-EnabledEmailAddressTemplates SMTP:%g.%s@fabrikam.com,smtp:%g.%s@contoso.com
Update-EmailAddressPolicy -Identity 'FirstNameLastName'
```

Updating accepted domains

Apart from creating a new accepted domain, the only other options presented by EMC are viewing the properties of an accepted domain, setting a domain as the default for the organization, or removing the domain from the organization. The first accepted domain in the organization is automatically marked as the default domain and there is usually no need to make a change. EMC indicates the default domain in its list of accepted domains and you can get the same information with the Get-AcceptedDomain cmdlet.

If you delete an accepted domain, Exchange stops accepting email addressed to the SMTP domains covered by the now-deleted domain. For example, if you use the Remove-AcceptedDomain cmdlet to delete the Fabrikam domain, Exchange will no longer accept any messages addressed to *.fabrikam.com.

```
Remove-AcceptedDomain -Identity "Fabrikam"
```

> **CAUTION**
>
> No option is available in either EMC or EMS to update the SMTP domains for an accepted domain. If you make a mistake in the SMTP domains defined for an accepted domain, you have to delete the record for the accepted domain and then re-create it with the correct SMTP domains.

Remote domains

Remote domain entries define the format of messages and the types of automatic messages such as auto-replies that Exchange can send to another SMTP domain. When you install Exchange, a default "catch-all" remote domain (*) is created that is suitable for most purposes. You will only have to create a new remote domain if you know that a foreign SMTP domain has specific requirements. For example, the mail system for that domain might only be able to accept plain text messages with lines wrapped at a particular position. Alternatively, the mail system might be another Exchange 2010 organization that is able to accept any type of message that your Exchange organization generates.

To access the remote domains defined for the organization, select the Organization Configuration node and select Hub Transport. The two Properties dialog boxes shown in Figure 13-27 reveal the default settings for the default remote domain. The General tab controls how Exchange processes out-of-office notices. Up to Exchange 2007, any out-of-office notice generated by a client was passed through by the transport system to any recipient type. Exchange 2007 introduced the ability to differentiate the information in these notices so that you could create one notice for external recipients and another for internal recipients (an internal recipient is any SMTP address that belongs to an accepted domain). The idea is that you probably want a more comprehensive notice to go to internal recipients, one which might contain confidential details about your company that shouldn't be revealed outside. When I travel, I tend to give details such as the contact information of people who might be able to handle questions while I am away. By contrast, the information in my external notice simply says that I am out of the office and will respond to any mail when I return.

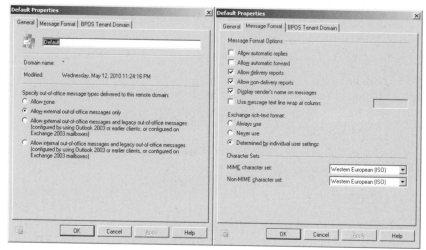

Figure 13-27 Properties of the default remote domain.

The default setting is External, meaning that only external notices generated by Outlook 2007 or later clients will be transmitted to external recipients by the transport system. Outlook 2003 doesn't differentiate between internal and external recipients when it generates OOF notices, so if you still support these clients you should select one of the two options that allow the notices generated by legacy clients to pass. If you trust the remote domain because it belongs to an associated company or another entity to which you are happy to reveal internal information, you can select the last option in the list, which will allow the transport system to send internal notices created by newer clients as well as the notices generated by legacy clients.

The Message Format tab defines the format of messages that Exchange passes to the remote domain. Messages come from user activity or are automatically generated by Exchange or client email programs in response to incoming email. The default settings suppress client-generated automatic responses but allow Exchange to send delivery and non-delivery reports and to include the sender's name in message headers. The default message format setting allows users to control whether they send plain text, rich text, or HTML messages by manipulating client settings. In addition, if you create mail-enabled contacts, you can set a default format to use for messages sent to these recipients. Most clients in use today are capable of handling any message format that Exchange sends so it's quite safe to leave it to clients to determine their preferred format. If necessary, you can force Exchange to send plain text by selecting the Never Use format and then setting a message text wrap position to generate fixed-length lines. This value can be anything up to 132 characters, but 78 is the usual standard for messages. In this case, you could use the Set-RemoteDomain cmdlet to set a remote domain so that Exchange will only send plain text messages:

```
Set-RemoteDomain –Identity 'Gmail' –ContentType 'MimeText' –LineWrapSize 78
–TNEFEnabled $False
```

The Set-RemoteDomain cmdlet also controls whether Exchange generates notifications to meeting organizers when users forward meeting requests to recipients in the remote domain. The default behavior is to generate notifications, but you can disable this setting. For example, the command to suppress notifications when meeting requests are forwarded to Gmail recipients is:

```
Set-RemoteDomain –Identity 'Gmail' –MeetingForwardNotificationEnabled $False
```

Transport pipeline

The Get-TransportPipeline cmdlet can only be executed on a server that has the hub transport or Edge transport role installed to reveal the set of transport agents that have been used since the last time that the transport service was started. Each agent is shown alongside the events for which it is registered. Agents can be attached to connection events, categorizer events, and SMTP receive events. Connection events occur when delivery agents such as the Store driver submit or accept a message. Categorizer events occur as a message is examined to determine its best routing path and to finalize the set of recipients. SMTP events occur when remote servers open up connections to send SMTP messages to a hub transport server or a hub transport server sends an SMTP command to another server. The full set of available events allows great flexibility in designing how and where an agent should intervene in the messaging stream.

More information on how to develop transport agents is available in TechNet.

The following output is typical of what you might see on a transport server. As an example of binding between event and agent, we can see that the Transport Rule Agent is invoked by the *OnRoutedMessage* event. Transport rules are discussed in depth in Chapter 15, "Compliance."

```
Get-TransportPipeline

Event                                    TransportAgents
-----                                    ---------------
OnConnectEvent                           {}
OnHeloCommand                            {}
OnEhloCommand                            {}
OnAuthCommand                            {}
OnEndOfAuthentication                    {}
OnMailCommand                            {}
OnRcptCommand                            {}
OnDataCommand                            {}
OnEndOfHeaders                           {}
OnEndOfData                              {}
OnHelpCommand                            {}
OnNoopCommand                            {}
OnReject                                 {}
OnRsetCommand                            {}
OnDisconnectEvent                        {}
OnSubmittedMessage                       {Text Messaging Routing Agent}
OnResolvedMessage                        {}
OnRoutedMessage                          {Transport Rule Agent}
OnCategorizedMessage                     {}
```

Table 13-8 lists the set of default agents that can be used with hub transport and Edge servers. Other agents can be installed by software products such as antivirus or anti-spam checkers. Agents have complete access to the message stream so it's obvious that these agents have to be tested and validated thoroughly before they are introduced into a production environment.

Table 13-8 Agents used with hub transport and Edge transport

Hub Transport agents	Edge Transport Agents
Transport rule agent	Connection filtering agent
Rights Management Service (RMS) encryption agent	Address rewriting inbound agent
RMS decryption agent	Edge rule agent
RMS prelicensing agent	Content filter agent
Journaling agent	Sender ID agent
Journal report decryption agent	Sender filter agent
Text messaging routing agent	Recipient filter agent
	Protocol analysis agent
	Attachment filtering agent
	Address rewriting outbound agent

The purposes of the default agents are obvious from their names. Most of the agents that operate on an Edge server are there to filter and cleanse an incoming messaging stream. Messages are checked for their content, attachments, recipients, and senders to ensure that messages containing unwanted content do not reach Exchange. Connections are examined to ensure that Exchange only accepts incoming messages from external servers that aren't on block lists. Addresses can be rewritten. All in all, these are agents that tidy and perfect the messaging stream.

The agents that operate on transport servers tend to add more value. As we'll explore when we discuss compliance, transport rules can perform a wide range of operations from adding disclaimers to messages to silently copying messages that meet certain criteria. The RMS agents permit protected messages to pass through the transport system. The journaling agent makes sure that copies are made of any message that needs to be kept while the journal report decryption agent takes care of encrypted messages that are journaled.

Foreign and delivery connectors

The vast majority of messaging communication from Exchange 2010 is conducted using SMTP. However, SMTP is not the only messaging protocol in use and Exchange needs to be able to communicate with systems that don't use SMTP. The growing acceptance of SMTP as the de facto standard for email exchange, plus the addition of other Internet-driven standards such as iCal, permits much better out-of-the-box connectivity between email systems today and has eliminated the need to operate many bespoke gateways. When the need still exists, it is met through either a foreign or delivery connector.

Foreign connectors are the legacy approach to linking Exchange with other messaging systems. Foreign connectors are built using the Exchange 2003 Development Kit (EDK). In the past, Microsoft has provided foreign connectors for email systems such as Lotus Notes and Novell GroupWise, and third-party software vendors have developed connectors for fax, Short Message Service, and so on. The X.400-based routing group connector used to link Exchange 2010 and Exchange 2003 is regarded as a foreign connector.

As mentioned earlier in this chapter, Microsoft has removed support for gateways developed with the Exchange 2003 EDK, meaning that EDK-based connectors cannot be used with Exchange 2007 or Exchange 2010. The biggest impact is usually felt during migration projects from Lotus Notes or Novell GroupWise because you have to maintain an Exchange 2003 SP2 server in the organization for as long as you want to use these connectors. In both cases, it might be a better solution to rely on SMTP connectivity to link Exchange to Lotus Notes or GroupWise, or indeed to any other foreign messaging system that supports SMTP. Basic email is just one part of the interoperability picture when you have to support multiple email systems. It's relatively easy to pass messages between the different systems, but achieving the finer details such as directory synchronization and support for messages that contain meeting requests takes more effort.

Exchange 2010 introduces delivery connectors as a new architecture for non-SMTP messaging connectivity. Both types of connectors perform any bidirectional format conversion required to make Exchange-generated content compatible with the target system.

> ## Foreign connectors versus delivery connectors
>
> The big differences between foreign connectors and delivery connectors are the following:
>
> - Foreign connectors operate by placing messages in a pickup directory; delivery connectors are able to access messages in hub transport server queues and performance is usually better because no overhead is incurred to move files in and out of the pickup directory. Messages for delivery connectors are visible in the transport queues.
>
> - Foreign connectors do not acknowledge the receipt or the transmission of messages; delivery connectors do, which means that you can measure the delivery latency for messages and use these data for service level agreements (SLAs).

Exchange 2010 comes with one delivery connector, which you can see by running the Get-DeliveryAgentConnector cmdlet:

```
Get-DeliveryAgentConnector
```

Name	AddressSpaces	DeliveryProtocol	Enabled
Text Messaging Deliver.	{MOBILE:*;1}	MOBILE	True

The Text Messaging Delivery Agent Connector is registered to handle any message sent to the MOBILE address space and therefore handles text messages sent to mobile devices. A text messaging routing agent is registered with the transport pipeline to route text messages to this connector.

Shadow redundancy

Exchange 2007 introduced the transport dumpster as a method for retaining copies of messages that might be required for recovery purposes following an outage on a clustered (CCR) mailbox server. The idea is to ensure that copies of messages exist that can be replayed if they were in transit when a cluster outage occurred. The implementation worked, but a number of issues were discovered in production. Exchange 2007 maintains a transport dumpster per storage group. This isn't a problem on small servers that host one or two storage groups but complexity and load increases on large servers, especially those that approach Exchange 2007's limit of 50 storage groups. A server failover in these circumstances provokes a huge I/O surge because the transport dumpster cache is accessed by hub transport servers in the site in an attempt to redeliver any waiting messages to the Store. The Store then has the task of sorting out the messages into those that had already been delivered successfully and can be discarded and those that are needed to bring mailboxes up to date. The surge usually causes a spike in I/O demand on the servers and compromises overall server performance until the cache clears and the Store redelivers any outstanding messages.

Exchange 2010 continues to use the transport dumpster and enhances it with a new follow-on feature called shadow redundancy. Microsoft designed shadow redundancy to increase the resilience of Exchange to outages in the transport system and to complement its invest-ment in high availability for other areas of the product. The transport dumpster provides redundancy for messages following a failover and shadow redundancy provides the same capability for messages while they are in transit elsewhere inside the organization. Unlike the transport dumpster, shadow redundancy doesn't depend on clustered servers and works even if you only deploy standard mailbox servers and don't use DAGs. The net effect is that the Exchange transport system gains a form of "near-stateless" operation in terms of its ability to recover messages after a failure.

Shadow redundancy complements the other Exchange features that contribute to high availability, such as database replication, which concentrate on removing databases, disks, and servers as potential single points of failure. The major goal of shadow redundancy is to eliminate transport servers as a single point of failure as SMTP messages come into and flow out of the messaging infrastructure. As long as multiple routing paths exist within the organization, shadow redundancy makes it possible to remove an Edge or hub transport server (or lose a transport server through an outage) without losing any messages. This also means that you can take a transport server offline to apply a software upgrade or perform other maintenance without worrying about any messages that might exist in its queues. It also means that hardware redundancy is less important for hub transport servers and that it is possible to deploy servers with lower cost storage because if you lose a server, you can keep it offline for as long as necessary to fix the problem without worrying that you might lose messages. Of course, all of this is true as long as you have multiple hub transport serv-ers within your organization; if you have only one hub transport server, or even two, they become essential pieces of the messaging infrastructure that have to be protected.

Shadow redundancy depends on three fundamental principles:

1. Whenever a user sends a message from an Exchange 2010 mailbox server, the Mail Submission service retains a hashed copy of the message in the Sent Items folder. The message remains in the Sent Items folder until the hub transport server has accepted ownership for the message and placed it into its transport database. The hub transport server that is currently processing a message is known as the primary

server. If the message is ever lost through an outage somewhere along its route, Exchange can resubmit the copy from the transport database on the primary server and route it to its destination.

2. Hub transport and Edge servers exchange information about the progress of messages until they are finally delivered to a mailbox in the organization or relayed across a connector to a foreign messaging system.

3. When the primary server is sure that a message has been successfully delivered, discard events are generated to inform servers that they can remove any copies of the message that they have. Hub transport servers generate heartbeats to each other in their SMTP communications to indicate that they are available. If a primary server becomes uncontactable based on missing a number of heartbeats over a predetermined interval, Exchange is able to transfer the primary server role to another hub transport server (that has a copy of the message), which can then resubmit the message using the copy in its shadow queue.

Shadow redundancy operates on Edge and hub transport servers to keep copies of messages (called shadow copies) in a special queue until they have been successfully delivered to all of the next hops in the message paths. Basically, servers do not delete a message from their transport databases until they receive conformation (in the form of a discard notification) from all of the receiving servers that the message has successfully arrived. Once a server has received discard notifications for all of the hops in the path of a message it knows that it can remove the shadow copy of the message from its transport database. If any of the hops fail to generate a discard notification, the transport service will queue the message for redelivery.

INSIDE OUT Discard notifications

The discard notifications have a low impact on bandwidth because they are very basic SMTP transactions between servers. Think of something like "Server X: I've received message ID 136146." Servers exchange data about discard notifications during SMTP connections. A server can also establish a separate connection to another server to retrieve data about messages that it had previously sent to allow it to decide whether to discard its copy.

Shadow redundancy is configured on an organization-wide basis by setting the *ShadowRedundancy* property with the Set-TransportConfig cmdlet. For example:

```
Set-TransportConfig –ShadowRedundancy $True
```

The default is true, so Exchange servers insert an XSHADOW ESMTP command into the interaction that they conduct with other SMTP servers to establish whether those servers support shadow redundancy and to provide the heartbeat used to indicate server availability. Discard notifications are also implemented through an SMTP extension called XQDISCARD. Exchange refers to primary and shadow copies of messages and primary and shadow servers. The primary message is the copy that is in transit between an originating server and the other transport servers that should receive copies; the shadow is the copy maintained until the transport service is certain that the primary message has been successfully transferred to everywhere it should go. The primary server is the one that is currently processing the message along its path to eventual delivery. Shadow servers have already processed the message and are waiting to be notified that they can discard their shadow copies.

> **Note**
> The obvious sign that messages are waiting for notifications to come back is their presence on the Shadow Redundancy queue on a hub transport server. Messages stay on this queue until Exchange is sure that they have been transmitted successfully.

Two other transport configuration settings are used to control how shadow redundancy works:

```
Set-TransportConfig –ShadowHeartbeatRetryCount 8 –ShadowHeartbeatTimeoutInterval
00:10:00 –ShadowMessageAutoDiscardInterval 3.00:00:00
```

The first parameter in this command sets the shadow retry count to eight (the default is three), meaning that hub transport servers will try and contact each other up to eight times before concluding that a server is unavailable. If a server is deemed to be unavailable, it can no longer function as a primary server. The next parameter specifies the interval that a hub transport server should wait before attempting to contact another server to see if it is available. The default is five minutes. The net effect of increasing the retry count and timeout interval is to accommodate extended connections between hub transport servers so that they can handle network outages of up to 80 minutes (8 retries at 10-minute intervals). The last parameter increases the discard interval from two days to three days. The discard interval governs how long servers retain discard events for messages in their queue.

> ## Shadow Redundancy Manager: The answer for servers that don't support shadow redundancy
>
> A new component within the transport service called Shadow Redundancy Manager (SRM) monitors the flow of messages, their current delivery status, and the reconciliation of discard notifications that come back from other transport servers to indicate that messages have arrived there. SRM is able to manage transmission to servers that don't support the concept of shadow redundancy and therefore don't issue confirmations back to Exchange when they accept messages. In these instances, a successful SMTP connection and transfer is deemed sufficient confirmation that the message has been moved to the next hop and SRM will mark it as if a confirmation message had been received from the other mail server.

Exchange also attempts to apply the principle of shadow redundancy to incoming messages even if they originate on servers that don't support the feature. In this case, Exchange accepts the message, attempts to deliver it onward, and makes a shadow copy. However, Exchange delays sending an acknowledgment to the originating server until the message has been delivered to all hops within the organization. In an organization that has a complex routing topology or in situations where some connections are not immediately available, it might take some time before a message is delivered to all hops. You do not want the SMTP connection with the other mail server to time out, because this would cause it to resend the message. To get around the problem, Exchange sets a value for the maximum time (in seconds) that it will wait for the message to be processed. The default value is 30 seconds and can be changed by setting the *MaxAcknowledgementDelay* property on receive connectors. If the time delay elapses, Exchange issues an acknowledgment to the originating server. It is possible that this system could result in some messages being lost if a hub transport server fails and loses its transport database. However, in practical terms the risk is not high.

Linking Exchange 2003 to Exchange 2010

During a migration project, you will have to decide how to connect Exchange 2010 servers to the existing routing infrastructure. The detail of how to connect Exchange 2003 to Exchange 2010 is well documented in TechNet and other books and hasn't changed significantly from the situation for Exchange 2007. In brief, the hidden routing group into which Exchange 2010 servers are installed is exposed to Exchange 2003 servers through a routing group connector that links the SMTP-based messaging topology used by Exchange 2010 and Exchange 2007 and the X.400 message transfer agent (MTA)-based approach taken by earlier versions.

The simplest and best approach is to locate the connector in a hub Exchange 2003 routing group. Remember that this will be the message interchange between Exchange 2003 and Exchange 2010 and a lot of traffic will flow across the connector during the migration, so the connector needs to be able to handle the load and the servers in the routing group need to have solid, reliable, and fast network connections with the rest of the Exchange 2003 organization. Picking a nonoptimum routing group isn't a disaster—at least not immediately—but it could have ramifications as you ramp up the message load across the connector as more and more users migrate to Exchange 2010. For example, you might decide to connect the first Exchange hub transport server with a routing group that is not part of the core network, perhaps even a small routing group that occupies a network spoke. Things will work just fine with a small group of users sending mail from Exchange 2010, but as traffic ramps up, it doesn't make sense to funnel all messages from Exchange 2010 down into a network spoke and back up again for delivery to other routing groups. On the Exchange 2010 side, it is equally important that the hub transport server at the other side of the routing group connector is able to handle the traffic, so you should also install this server into a core network site.

The New-RoutingGroupConnector cmdlet creates the bidirectional connectivity between Exchange 2010 and Exchange 2003. For example:

```
New-RoutingGroupConnector –Name "RGC Exchange 2010<-> Legacy"
–SourceTransportServers "ExServer1", "ExServer2" –TargetTransportServers "E2003Svr1"
–Cost 50 –Bidirectional $True
```

This command creates a new routing group connector that links two Exchange 2010 hub transport servers (ExServer1 and ExServer2) with the Exchange 2003 bridgehead server called E2003Svr1. Setting the *–Bidirectional* parameter to $True tells Exchange to create the necessary connectors on both sides. Afterward, you can check the properties of the connector with the Get-RoutingGroupConnector cmdlet (an edited version of the output is shown here):

```
Get-RoutingGroupConnector –Identity "RGC Exchange 2010<-> Legacy" | Format-List
```

```
TargetRoutingGroup            : RG-InterOp
Cost                          : 50
TargetTransportServers        : {E2003Svr1}
ExchangeLegacyDN              : /o=contoso/ou=Exchange Administrative Group
(FYDI
                                BOHF23SPDLT)/cn=Configuration/cn=Connections/cn=
                                RGC Exchange 2010 <-> Legacy
PublicFolderReferralsEnabled  : True
SourceRoutingGroup            : Exchange Routing Group (DWBGZMFD01QNBJR)
SourceTransportServers        : {ExServer1, ExServer2}
Name                          : RGC Exchange 2010 <-> Legacy
Identity                      : RGC Exchange 2010 <-> Legacy
```

The cost of the connector is set reasonably high at 50 instead of the default cost of 1 that is usually assigned to a new routing group connector. The logic here is that you do not usually want to use the routing group connector between Exchange 2003 and Exchange 2010 as a backbone connection, because it's always best to keep messages within their native environment as much as possible. Exchange 2003 servers should only route messages to Exchange 2010 when their final destination is on an Exchange 2010 server. Of course, a time will come during the migration when Exchange 2010 performs the majority of routing or you decide to make Exchange 2010 the backbone mail router for the organization, and in this case you can reduce the connector cost to allow Exchange 2003 servers to transfer messages across the connector more often.

Decommissioning Exchange 2003 routing groups

Eventually, your migration project will come to a point where you can begin to eliminate routing group connectors because the Exchange 2003 servers that used the connectors have been removed from the organization. Another challenge now awaits you: how to decommission servers without creating islands of link state replication. Mail will continue to flow if you remove connectors between Exchange 2003 routing groups and force the Exchange 2003 servers that are left behind to route messages via Exchange 2010. However, Exchange 2003 servers won't be able to send link state updates to each other because Exchange 2010 drops these updates. In terms of routing topology, the Exchange 2003 servers will be frozen in time and will never be aware of any topology changes that occur elsewhere in the organization. This might not be a bad thing if you are decommissioning servers quickly and don't expect the servers to be around for long, but in most cases (especially in large organizations), you can't switch over to Exchange 2010 quickly enough to avoid the potential that messages will be routed ineffectively (or conceivably end up in a black hole because Exchange can't figure out where to send them). For this reason, any time you remove a routing group connector, make sure that the Exchange 2003 servers that are left behind have an alternative connector that they can use to receive link state updates.

Handling Exchange 2003 link state updates

You don't have to care about link state updates if you are in a pure Exchange 2010 organization, but you do have to pay attention to them during migrations from Exchange 2003. Link state updates are a concept that Microsoft introduced in Exchange 2000 where servers that act as routing group masters in an organization send information about the routing topology to each other so that servers know when problems exist in the topology, such as a connector being down or otherwise unavailable, and are then able to adjust message routing to avoid blocks. Dynamic routing made sense as a natural evolution from the static gateway routing table (GWART) used by Exchange 5.5. The problem with using a fixed view of the routing topology is that servers can send messages to a destination where they become stuck until a connector is fixed and brought back into service.

As long as you only have a single routing group connector between Exchange 2003 and Exchange 2010, you don't have to worry about link state information. Exchange 2003 will continue to send link state updates between its routing groups but Exchange 2010 ignores the messages. The two sides operate independently of each other and maintain separate routing topologies. Operating a single connector will be sufficient for small to medium-sized organizations, but things often become more complex with larger organizations because of the need to handle bigger volumes of traffic and to route messages efficiently within geographical network segments. In this situation, you probably need to configure additional routing group connectors between appropriate Exchange 2003 servers and Exchange 2010 hub transport servers.

If you want to stop link state propagation, you have to make a registry change on every Exchange 2003 bridgehead server. To do this, go to HKEY_LOCAL_MACHINE\SYSTEM \CurrentControlSet\Services\RESvc\Parameters and add a new DWORD value called *SuppressStateChanges*. Set the value to 1 (one) and then restart the Exchange Routing Engine, the SMTP service, and the Exchange MTA service. Servers will continue to send link state updates to each other but they will ignore any connector outages that might force a topology change. The change forces Exchange 2003 to always use least-cost routing as the basis for routing messages rather than trying to calculate alternate routes. If a connector experiences an outage, Exchange will either reroute via another available connector or queue messages at that point until the connector is available again.

Changes in Exchange 2010 SP1

The Exchange transport engine is pretty solid and its basics did not need much improvement in Exchange 2010 SP1. Microsoft therefore concentrated on fine-tuning transport in three areas:

- SMTP load-balancing and failover: Making sure that Exchange balances connections most efficiently when an SMTP server fails.

- Submission queue resource monitoring: Making sure that a server that is under stress is not placed under further stress by having to deal with new message submissions. This is a variation of the pressure backoff work that was first introduced in Exchange 2007.

- Mailbox delivery prioritization: Making sure that the general flow of messages isn't slowed down by the email equivalent of slow-moving trucks in the outside lane. In this context, the trucks are represented by messages on which the transport system expends a lot of resources to process.

In addition, SP1 makes some changes to shadow redundancy to improve the capture and retention of messages that come into Exchange from legacy servers and clients that don't support the ESMTP verbs used by Exchange 2010 to implement shadow redundancy.

Better SMTP load balancing

Exchange 2007 and Exchange 2010 attempt to load balance outbound SMTP connections to target servers by distributing messages across all available servers in the next-hop domain or site. For example, take the situation where we have two sites called A and B, each of which has three hub transport servers. The hub transport servers in site A will attempt to distribute messages going to site B across the three hub transport servers in the site. All goes well until one of the servers fails or is taken offline for some reason such as planned maintenance. The hub transport servers in site A still think that there are three valid target servers in site B and attempt to load balance across all three. Of course, one of the servers is unavailable and the servers in site A see failures when they attempt to connect to it. The failed messages are redirected to the next available server in site B, which means that the load balancing is now skewed and uneven with the possibility that one of the hub transport servers in site B will be called on to handle its normal load plus the entire load that usually goes to its missing partner.

The change made in SP1 to improve load balancing when transient outages occur is simple. When an SP1 hub transport server detects a connection error sending to a target server, it adds the FQDN and all associated IP addresses of that server to a list of "down servers." All the hub transport servers in site A can then remove the unavailable servers from the list of available servers in site B for the purpose of load balancing once they detect failure. Thus, taking our example again, when one of the hub transport servers in site B is unavailable, the servers in site A will only attempt to load balance across the two remaining targets in site B. Logic is built in to accommodate three different classes of outages:

- Glitch: Exchange attempts to contact the failed server four times at one-minute intervals. If the server comes back online, Exchange once again considers it a valid target for load balancing and removes the server from the "down server" list.

- Transient: After the glitch tests expire, Exchange moves to a series of six retries at five-minute intervals. The logic is that 30 minutes should be sufficient to apply a software patch or other minor maintenance to a server. Once again, when the server comes back online, Exchange makes it a valid target again.

- Outage: After the transient tests expire, Exchange begins to test the connection at ten-minute intervals until the target server comes online or is removed from the Exchange configuration.

Microsoft's tests show that the new load balancing code performs much better than the original algorithm. You can view the details of the various retry intervals and the "down servers" list with the Get-ExchangeDiagnosticInfo cmdlet. In this example, we look for the information from a server called ExServer1. The output is edited to focus on the most important information:

```
Get-ExchangeDiagnosticInfo –Server ExServer1 –Process EdgeTransport –Component
SmtpOut
```

```
Result      :<Diagnostics>
                <Components>
                 <SmtpOut>
                   <UnhealthyTargetFilter>
                    <Configuration>
                      <Enabled>true</Enabled>
                      <GlitchRetryCount>4</GlitchRetryCount>
                      <GlitchRetryInterval>PT1M</GlitchRetryInterval>
                      <TransientFailureRetryCount>6</TransientFailureRetryCount>
                      <TransientFailureRetryInterval>PT5M</TransientFailureRetryInterval>
   <OutboundConnectionFailureRetryInterval>PT10M</OutboundConnectionFailureRetryInterval>
                    </Configuration>
                    <UnhealthyTargetFqdnFilter>
                      <UnhealthyTargetsCount>0</UnhealthyTargetsCount>
                    </UnhealthyTargetFqdnFilter>
                    <UnhealthyTargetIpAddressFilter>
                      <UnhealthyTargetsCount>0</UnhealthyTargetsCount>
                    </UnhealthyTargetIpAddressFilter>
                   </UnhealthyTargetFilter>
                 </SmtpOut>
                </Components>
               </Diagnostics>
```

Monitoring the submission queue

The categorizer component provides an excellent indication of the overall health of a hub transport server. The categorizer does a lot of work to resolve the addresses on a message and decide its best route forward. If the categorizer is able to process new messages as they arrive, the server is in good health and working without undue strain. Unfortunately the Exchange 2010 transport system is prone to overwork and will continue to accept new messages and will be slow to move them from the submission queue to the categorizer in situations when the categorizer is clearly struggling to keep up with its load. The result is an unacceptable growth in the queue of messages awaiting categorization.

SP1 therefore introduces a monitor to check the categorization queue and detect when the categorizer might be struggling to keep up with demand. A queue of less than 1,000 messages is deemed normal and acceptable but if it grows past this point it can encounter two other thresholds and take action to reduce demand on the server. In this respect, the submission resource monitor behaves in the same way as the other resource monitors used to back off demand at periods of high resource utilization. In general, all resource monitors go through three stages:

1. After the medium threshold is exceeded, the server enters a state of unstabilized resource pressure and invokes a tarpit algorithm to slow further demand until the resource use drops below the normal threshold.

2. If heavy resource use continues, the server stabilizes above the medium threshold but starts to reject work. In the case of the submission queue, message submissions from anonymous clients result in a transient error caused by insufficient system resources. The server will stay in this state until resource use drops below the normal threshold.

3. If heavy resource use continues to a point where resource use stabilizes above the high threshold, submissions of messages from all sources result in an insufficient system resources error. The server stays in this state until resource use drops below the medium threshold.

The thresholds are defined in the Edgetransport.config.exe file.

```
<add key="SubmissionQueueHighThreshold" value="4000" />
<add key="SubmissionQueueMediumThreshold" value="2000" />
<add key="SubmissionQueueNormalThreshold" value="1000" />
```

The submission monitor reviews the queue depth on a continual basis and measures the queue depth against threshold using 300 samples taken at two-second intervals to determine whether action is necessary. This ensures that a spike in load that is cleared by the categorizer won't provoke action. It also means that the submission monitor takes action when a server comes under sustained load and really needs assistance. No one will notice a small peak in load that causes a server to become momentarily less responsive, but users will notice a problem if a server slows down for more than a few seconds.

Mailbox delivery prioritization

All messages are not created equal and some require Exchange to expend a lot more resources to route them to their final destinations. A message sent to a very large distribution group of some 1,000 recipients is more expensive to categorize than another message sent to a single recipient. A message with a 10 MB attachment takes more effort to push through the transport system than another that contains just a couple of sentences in the message body. The problem is that the expensive messages sometimes get in the way of "normal" messages in terms of delivery latency. Everyone will accept that it might take a few seconds for a large message to be delivered, but it's harder to understand when a simple message sometimes takes several seconds to arrive.

The solution introduced in Exchange 2010 SP1 is to assess messages based on the number of recipients and the total size and to then prioritize deliveries based on these parameters. If a message has more than 500 recipients or is larger than 1 MB and it comes from a sender who has recently submitted a lot of similar messages to accumulate a high recent cost of submission, Exchange puts the message in a low-priority queue. Other messages continue to be processed as before but the low-priority queue is processed in such a way that:

- FIFO order is maintained to the next-hop destination. In other words, small messages sent after a very large message won't arrive before the large message because this might confuse users.

- Messages in the normal queue are processed approximately 20 times as often as those in the low-priority queue. This ratio was determined by analysis that showed that "normal" messages are usually 20 times smaller than low-priority messages.

- Messages in the low-priority queue will not be starved. In other words, the transport system will service the queue and take messages off it even when higher-priority messages continue to arrive. There is no intention that the low-priority queue should continue to accumulate messages just because high-priority messages keep slipping ahead of them.

- The queuing behavior only applies to MAPI delivery queues. Messages that come into the transport system via SMTP experience the same queuing process as in Exchange 2007 SP1.

Microsoft's tests show that between 1 percent and 5 percent of total message volume goes onto the low-priority queue, so this change won't affect very many messages. However, it has the effect of smoothing the delivery of messages and making better use of available resources.

In addition to the introduction of the low-priority queue, Exchange 2010 SP1 monitors the health of the mailbox databases to which it delivers to ensure that the transport system does not swamp a mailbox database with a mass of new inbound mail. A mailbox database that is perfectly healthy and capable of handling the current message volume is given a health indicator of 100. This value decreases as the mailbox database becomes busier and less responsive and is measured as deliveries are made by the transport system. The idea is that the transport system will be able to notice when a database becomes less capable and can then back off the deliveries it attempts to the database so that it can continue to accept deliveries and isn't overwhelmed.

The values that control message delivery prioritization are stored in the Edgetransport .config.exe file. In addition, the transport system captures information about messages in the EVENTDATA property of the DELIVER events logged in the message tracking log. You can check these entries to see what messages Exchange puts on the low-priority queue. Here's a sample of the data:

```
EventData           : {[MailboxDatabaseName, db3], [DeliveryPriority, Low],
[PrioritizationReason, AMS:10274739/1048576,ARC:14/500], [DatabaseHealth, 100]}
```

In this instance, we can see that the message was delivered to a database called DB3 but was placed in the low-priority queue because the message size (AMS) was 10,274,739 bytes (9.8 MB), well over the 1,048,576 maximum (1 MB). The number of recipients (ARC) was 14, under the threshold of 500.

Upgraded shadow redundancy

The shadow redundancy feature is designed to protect messages by making sure that they can be recovered if an outage occurs up to the point that they are delivered to their final destination. The feature depends on some new ESMTP verbs that Exchange 2010 servers understand, which means that every message sent between Exchange 2010 servers can be protected. However, legacy Exchange servers and other messaging systems don't know anything about the ESMTP verbs and their messages don't receive the same degree of protection, so the potential exists that some of these messages might be lost if a major outage occurred and servers had to be restored.

To avoid the problem, messages from legacy servers are detected when they arrive at an Exchange 2010 SP1 hub transport server. The transport system then attempts to relay these messages to another hub transport server in the same site. This simple step invokes the ESMTP verbs and gives the messages the same degree of protection that they'd have if they originated on an Exchange 2010 server.

Squeaky-clean email

Email isn't much use if it's ridden with viruses and contains so much spam that you have to wade through hundreds of offers for pharmaceuticals, opportunities to make your fortune, or chances to contact people who want to give you money for nothing. In a world filled with threats, Exchange administrators have to take steps to remove unwanted content before it gets to hub transport servers. Our next topic is how to impose message hygiene for Exchange organizations.

Message Hygiene

ESSAGE hygiene refers to the process by which a stream of messages is cleansed by removing spam, viruses, and other suspicious content. Email-borne viruses took over from viruses transmitted through floppy disks to become the first real threat to companies that deployed Microsoft Exchange. These organizations experienced the effect of rapid infection in incidents such as the famous Melissa (1999) and I Love You (2000) viruses. The growing number of email viruses (and a certain amount of hype in the popular press) accelerated the development of antivirus products. These products initially used MAPI to access mailbox databases to detect and disinfect items and were handicapped by the fact that MAPI is designed for general-purpose messaging and not to be used to scan large volumes of incoming messages. In response, Microsoft produced the Virus Scanning API (VSAPI) for use with Exchange 2003 and this API is used by all modern antivirus products that support Exchange. As more companies and consumers used email systems connected to the Internet, they became targets for spam—unwanted commercial email—which has proliferated and spread at ever-increasing rates since 2000.

Currently, unwanted and unwelcomed email occupies a tremendous percentage of the total message volume circulating across the Internet, much of which contains spam. Given that the vast majority of Exchange servers are connected to the Internet in some way, usually protected by an array of firewalls and perimeter networks, it should be no surprise that the topic of message hygiene is high on the list for Exchange administrators. No one, after all, wants to expose user mailboxes to the more than 80 percent of items removed by anti-spam and antivirus products to cleanse inbound mail.

Some companies such as MessageLabs have reported that over 80 percent of messages contain spam. See *http://www.messagelabs.com/intelligence.aspx* for the latest information.

Two fundamental options are available to companies to achieve good message hygiene. They can do either of the following:

- Outsource the cleansing of inbound mail to a specialized service provider such as MessageLabs, Postini, or Microsoft and accept a cleansed stream for processing by hub transport servers. Exchange Server 2010 supports linked connectors to channel inbound messages to an external service provider. The advantage of outsourcing message hygiene to a specialized third party is that you take advantage of their expertise in combating viruses and spam. Specialized providers have deep probes into the dark side of email and are always able to react quickest to new attacks when they develop across the Internet. In addition, you don't waste valuable administrator, network, and computing resources to deal with the vast amount of unwanted email that appears on your company's doorstep.

- Deploy systems to cleanse inbound mail as it arrives at the company's network. The usual approach is to remove as many obvious problem items as early as possible by dropping any message that is not addressed to a recipient who can be found in Active Directory, and then apply a series of tests to determine whether items are spam, contain viruses, or have attachments with unwanted content. Suspicious items can be dropped or stripped of problematic content, and the cleansed stream is passed through to hub transport servers for delivery. The Exchange 2010 Edge transport server is designed to perform email cleansing, but you do not have to deploy Exchange Edge servers for this purpose, as many other solutions exist for the problem.

Of course, security is best attained through multiple lines of defense. Client-side junk-mail features also make an important contribution to suppressing unwanted content arriving in user inboxes. It's tremendously difficult to protect users to a point where they never see spam or a virus never gets through. Spammers and hackers expend enormous amounts of time and effort to concoct new techniques to mask bad content so that it penetrates the defenses erected by companies to protect users. It therefore follows that user education must provide the final layer of defense, and users must be informed about the danger that spam and viruses represent and the actions that they should take if suspicious messages make it into their inbox. We'll discuss all these questions in this chapter.

To Edge or not to Edge, that's the question

The Microsoft proposition is that you should deploy Edge servers to protect Exchange organizations. This is certainly a valid option, but it's important to understand that alternatives exist that should be considered before you decide to deploy Edge servers.

An Edge server is an attractive proposition to many companies that have a Windows-centric infrastructure. The major advantages of using an Exchange 2010 Edge server as the entry point to the organization are as follows:

- Because it's based on Microsoft Windows 2008 and Exchange 2010, the Edge server is a familiar place for administrators to work.

- The Edge server supports a comprehensive set of transport agents that examine inbound messages in different ways to detect problematic content.

- The Edge server enjoys a close integration with Microsoft Forefront Protection for Exchange 2010 (FPE). If you have paid for enterprise Client Access Licenses (CALs), you can use FPE at no further expense to add sophisticated antivirus processing to the basic antivirus capabilities provided by the Content Filter agent. Automatic updates ensure that the antivirus data are always current.

- The synchronization mechanism allows the Edge server to share configuration and user information with the Exchange organization. Sharing configuration data eases the administrative load and access to aggregated data such as safelists collected from user mailboxes helps to reduce the number of false positives generated during anti-spam checking.

However, some companies might consider it better to deploy a non-Windows server in the perimeter network. This could be because they already have bastion servers deployed to process inbound email; it could be that they outsource message hygiene to a specialized vendor and receive a cleansed message stream from that vendor and so don't need to use a bastion server (a server designed to act as the initial entry point for email into a domain); or they might simply prefer to use a non-Windows platform for all computers deployed in the perimeter network because the company supports heterogeneous email systems that cannot take advantage of the Edge server capabilities. Every company has its own valid reasons for deciding what computers and operating systems to use for different tasks, and although the Microsoft-centric community might prefer to use the Edge server, it simply might not be possible to move along this route.

Edge servers

An Edge server is a peculiar beast that lives in a world of half-complete Active Directory and half-complete Exchange attached by an umbilical cord to its host Exchange organization. Of course, an Edge server is designed to live in a perimeter network, and it's critical to reduce the attack surface presented by the computer so that hackers can't gain access to valuable data by compromising the server. A standard Exchange server would be an attractive target because breaking into an administrator account would allow an attacker to access mailboxes and other data, not to mention the potential to wreak havoc on Active Directory and bring it and Exchange to its knees. An Edge server is therefore a form of truncated stand-alone Exchange system that runs in isolation. Because it is purpose-built to operate on its own to process an incoming messaging stream, it doesn't use sophisticated features of full-blown Exchange such as role-based access control (RBAC) or remote PowerShell. The only data that exist on the server are the mail queue database and the Active Directory Lightweight Directory Service (AD LDS) instance that contains the information synchronized from the host Exchange organization. These data are hashed, so they are of little use to an attacker, even if he gains access to AD LDS. All in all, the Edge server is a locked-down computer that functions more like an appliance than a general-purpose server.

Chapter 14

Apart from the reduced set of prerequisites, installing an Edge server is very much like any other Exchange server role. An external firewall should protect the Edge server, and an internal firewall should isolate the Edge server from the hub transport servers that it connects to when it sends messages into the Exchange organization. A small number of ports need to be open in firewalls to allow an Edge server to function. These ports are described in Table 14-1.

Table 14-1 **Ports used for Edge server communications**

Firewall direction	Port	Use
External	25 (to and from all addresses)	SMTP connections to send and receive messages with external email servers.
External	53	Resolution of domain names via DNS.
Internal	25	SMTP connections to send and receive messages with hub transport servers in the connected Active Directory site.
Internal	50636	Secure Lightweight Directory Access Protocol (LDAP) connections for one-way synchronization of Active Directory information from a hub transport server to the AD LDS instance on the Edge server. This port can be changed by editing the Edge server configuration file.
Internal	3389	Remote Desktop Protocol (RDP) for remote management of the Edge server.

When you install the Edge server role, the setup program also installs the Exchange management tools. However, these are special versions of the tools that operate in the edge environment. EMC (Figure 14-1) fetches and displays data for just the server that it's running on, and there's no evidence of anything other than the functionality required to process messages. The toolbox is limited to tools that are relevant to message processing, such as the tracking log viewer. EMS supports a limited set of cmdlets—there's no evidence of cmdlets like Get-Mailbox or Set-MailboxDatabase on an Edge server because they're not required.

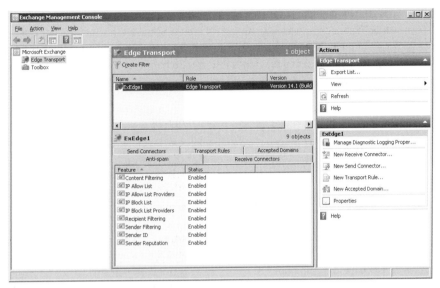

Figure 14-1 EMC running on an Edge server.

INSIDE OUT   A receive connector is created during installation

The installation of an Edge server also creates a receive connector that is capable of accepting SMTP traffic from any server using anonymous connections. This connector is sufficient to allow the Edge server to handle Internet traffic as the Edge synchronization process will assign the different permissions required to allow secure communications with the Exchange organization that is associated with the Edge server. You don't need to create additional receive connectors unless you decide not to use Edge synchronization and instead wish to manually configure connectors to handle communications with Internet servers and Exchange.

Edge synchronization

Edge synchronization is the process that connects an Edge server with Active Directory so that hub transport servers in the site connected to the Edge server can replicate Active Directory information about the organization's messaging configuration to it. The Edge server stores the replicated data in its AD LDS database and uses the data when it examines the incoming message stream to decide what messages should be passed through to Exchange. The connection is known as a site membership affiliation. It allows hub transport servers to relay messages to the Edge server for onward delivery without having to create explicit send connectors.

Multiple edge servers can connect to an Active Directory site, but an Edge server can only be connected with a single Active Directory site. An Exchange 2010 Edge server can connect to an Exchange 2007 hub transport server and vice versa. The only issue that occurs when you connect mixed version servers is that the servers have to perform full synchronization each time they connect. Exchange 2010 servers are able to synchronize the delta changes that have occurred since the last synchronization, a change that reduces the demand on servers and networks. Obviously, all of the servers involved in synchronization must be able to contact each other.

> **Note**
>
> You cannot use the Ping utility to test connectivity to an Edge server because the firewall installed on Edge servers is configured not to respond to ping requests, so the requests will time out.

The basic process of establishing synchronization between an edge server and an Active Directory site is as follows:

1. Create an Edge subscription request by running the New-EdgeSubscription cmdlet on the Edge server (Figure 14-2). Start EMS with elevated permissions by running it as the Administrator, and then use a command like the one shown here to generate the XML file that contains the subscription request:

   ```
   New-EdgeSubscription –FileName "c:\temp\EdgeSyncRequest.xml"
   ```

   When you create a new Edge subscription, the Edge server prepares for synchronization by removing routing configuration objects that will be replaced by new objects synchronized from the hub transport server. These objects include connectors and accepted domains. In addition, because the Edge server will effectively come under the control of the hub transport server that synchronizes configuration data to it on a one-way basis, Exchange disables cmdlets that create or update the routing configuration. The cmdlets include New-SendConnector, New-ReceiveConnector, New-AcceptedDomain, and so on. You can still use the "Get" variants of these cmdlets to view configuration data on the Edge server, but you cannot create routing configuration objects any more.

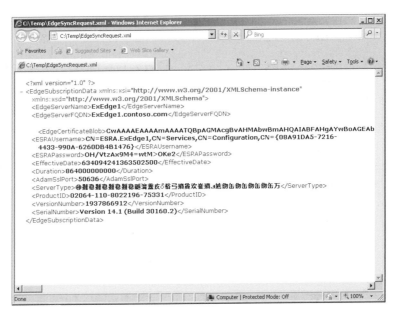

Figure 14-2 Viewing an Edge subscription request.

2. Copy the XML file containing the subscription request from the Edge server to a hub transport server in the Active Directory site that you want to link with the Edge server through synchronization. Typically, the site that you select for this purpose is a hub or central site in terms of Active Directory replication and has good network connectivity with the Edge server through a firewall.

   The subscription request contains credentials to be used during the synchronization process as well as some other information required for synchronization, such as the TCP port to use, the public key for the Edge server's self-signed certificate, and some information about the server, including the version of Exchange that it runs. Creating the subscription request on the Edge server also creates an AD LDS account that's known as the bootstrap replication account (ESBRA). The Edge subscription request contains the credentials to allow synchronization to use the ESBRA to access AD LDS. The bootstrap account expires after 24 hours, so it is critical that you use the request to create the Edge subscription on the hub transport server within 24 hours of its generation. Otherwise, the ESBRA expires, the subscription request is no longer valid, and it will have to be regenerated.

3. Run the New-EdgeSubscription cmdlet on the hub transport server to import the XML file and create the link between the Active Directory site and the Edge server. The syntax for the command appears cryptic because you aren't allowed to pass a simple file name, and you have to pipe its content through the Get-Content cmdlet. The reason for the cryptic input is that you are running in the context of a remote

Windows PowerShell session and cannot, therefore, assume that the file data are local, so you force the Get-Content cmdlet to read the data from the subscription file and provide it to the New-EdgeSubscription cmdlet. Note that the name of the Active Directory site that hosts the hub transport server is specified. Setting the *–CreateInboundSendConnector* and *–CreateInternetSendConnector* parameters to $True requests Exchange to create the send connector to link the Edge server to the Active Directory site and a send connector to connect the Edge server to the Internet.

```
New-EdgeSubscription -FileData ([byte[]]$(Get-Content -Path
"c:\temp\EdgeSyncRequest.xml" -Encoding Byte -ReadCount 0)) -Site
'contoso.com/Configuration/Sites/Dublin'-CreateInboundSendConnector $True
-CreateInternetSendConnector $True
```

After the hub transport server processes the Edge subscription request, it begins the process of synchronization using secure LDAP over TCP port 50656. This port must be open on the firewall between the perimeter and the internal networks. The hub transport server where you run New-EdgeSubscription retrieves the edge server's public key from the subscription request and uses it to decrypt the credentials for the ESBRA. It then updates the Edge server's object in Active Directory with encrypted credentials that can be used to connect to AD LDS during synchronization operations.

Every hub transport server in the site is notified by Active Directory that the site is now connected to an Edge server. All of the hub transport servers use their own public key to store the Edge credentials in their own configuration object. Figure 14-3 shows the Edge credentials stored in the Active Directory object for a hub transport server after a subscription is established.

The hub transport server now connects to the Edge server using ESBRA credentials. After a successful connection is made, the hub transport server sends topology, configuration, and recipient data for the Exchange organization to AD LDS. It also copies the ESBRA credentials so that the Microsoft Exchange Credential service running on the Edge server can use these credentials to authenticate secure future synchronization sessions. Finally, the hub transport server sends a synchronization schedule to the Edge server.

Forcing synchronization

You can also run the Start-EdgeSynchronization cmdlet to force synchronization to occur. Any hub transport server in the site is able to perform synchronization. For example, this command starts synchronization to the Edge server ExEdge1 from hub transport server ExServer3:

```
Start-EdgeSynchronization -TargetServer ExEdge1 -Server ExServer1
```

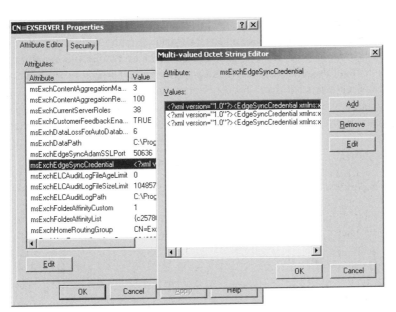

Figure 14-3 Edge credentials stored by a hub transport server.

Validating Edge synchronization

You can check that synchronization has occurred by using EMS on the Edge server to validate that configuration data have been successfully synchronized from the Exchange organization to AD LDS. For example, if you use Get-SendConnector, you should see details of the two send connectors created by the New-EdgeSubscription cmdlet. These send connectors were created on hub transport server and replicated to the Edge server, so you should see the connectors if you run Get-SendConnector on either side of the connection. In this example, we can see that the two connectors are clearly named to indicate their purpose:

```
Get-SendConnector
```

Identity	AddressSpaces	Enabled
EdgeSync – Dublin to Internet	<smtp:*;100>	True
EdgeSync – Inbound to Dublin	<smtp:--:100>	True

The * address space allows the outbound connector to handle messages addressed to any SMTP domain. The "- -" address space for the inbound connector is a special placeholder that instructs the Edge server to route any messages received for domains that are defined as authoritative or internal relay accepted direct to the hub transport servers in the connected site. Any hub transport server in the site can accept messages from the Edge server, including those that are added to the site after the Edge subscription is established. The hub transport servers are regarded as "smart hosts." You don't have to do anything to maintain the list of smart hosts and, indeed, you are prevented from changing the address space or smart hosts for connectors that are automatically created when an Edge subscription is established. If you want to have more control over routing, you can set the *–CreateInboundSendConnector* parameter for New-EdgeSubscription to $False and create a custom send connector afterward. See TechNet for more information on how to create connectors to handle different routing scenarios.

If you run the Get-ReceiveConnector cmdlet on the Edge server, you'll see details of the receive connector created to accept inbound messages from the Internet:

```
Get-ReceiveConnector
```

```
Identity                                      Bindings       Enabled
--------                                      --------       -------
ExEdge1\Default internal receive connector ExEdge1  <0.0.0.0:25>   True
```

Further proof of successful synchronization can be gained by using EMS to interrogate Exchange about known accepted domains or hub transport servers with the Get-AcceptedDomain or Get-TransportServer cmdlets, as these data are also synchronized to the Edge server.

It's also possible to view the data synchronized into AD LDS to see whether it contains the settings for the organization to which the Edge server is connected. Open ADSIEdit on the Edge server and select the Connect To option to specify that you want to connect to the configuration naming context. In the section for the computer name to which you want to connect, enter the name of the Edge server and the port that you want to use. Because AD LDS uses port 50389, we therefore connect using a server name and port number similar to that shown in Figure 14-4.

Once connected, you should be able to browse through the data synchronized to the Edge server from Exchange in much the same way that you would look through the configuration data in Active Directory (Figure 14-5).

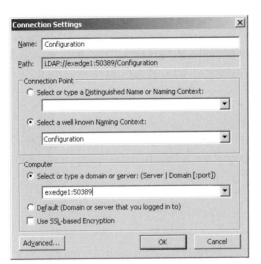

Figure 14-4 Connecting to the Configuration naming context on an Edge server.

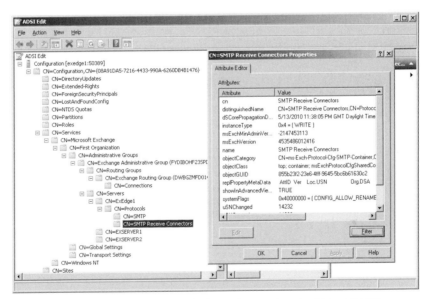

Figure 14-5 Exchange organizational information synchronized into AD LDS.

Chapter 14

INSIDE OUT

Access information in AD LDS about mail-enabled recipients

AD LDS also holds information about mail-enabled recipients in the Exchange organization to be able to validate recipient addresses against incoming messages and access user safelist data to know whether senders are acceptable to recipients. This information is held in a different location in AD LDS. To access this information, you have to connect to an organizational unit (OU) called *MSExchangeGateway* in the default naming context. The LDAP connection is therefore LDAP://server-name:50389 /ou=MsExchangeGateway. Alternatively, you can use localhost:50389 to point to the local server name and port 50389.

Once you are connected, you can navigate to CN=Recipients. This container holds an entry for every mail-enabled recipient (user, contact, group, and public folder) in the organization. However, the entries are obscured so that even if AD LDS is compromised by a hacker who penetrates the Edge server, she will be unable to make much sense of the information. Figure 14-6 shows ADSIEdit positioned in the Recipients container of the MSExchangeGateway OU. You can see the way that AD LDS obscures user information.

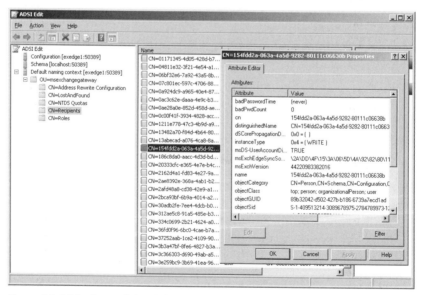

Figure 14-6 Viewing recipient information held in AD LDS.

ADSI is not the only utility that you can use to interrogate AD LDS. Some administrators prefer to use the LDP utility because they believe that it is more precise. You can see the recipient information in AD LDS with LDP by connecting to the MSExchangeGateway OU in much the same way you connect with ADSIEdit.

Finally, you can run the Test-EdgeSynchronization cmdlet on a hub transport server in the connected site to validate that synchronization is running as normal. To perform a full test, specify the *–FullCompareMode* parameter:

```
Test-EdgeSynchronization –TargetServer ExEdge1 –FullCompareMode
```

```
SyncStatus                   : Normal
UtcNow                       : 2/26/2010 12:10:44 AM
Name                         : ExEdge1
LeaseHolder                  : CN=ExServer1,CN=Servers,CN=Exchange Administrative
Group (FYDIBOHF23SPDLT),CN=Administrative Groups,CN=contoso,CN=Microsoft
Exchange,CN=Services,CN=Configuration,DC=contoso,DC=com
LeaseType                    : Option
FailureDetail                :
LeaseExpiryUtc               : 2/26/2010 1:08:59 AM
LastSynchronizedUtc          : 2/26/2010 12:08:59 AM
TransportServerStatus        : Synchronized
TransportConfigStatus        : Synchronized
AcceptedDomainStatus         : Synchronized
RemoteDomainStatus           : Synchronized
SendConnectorStatus          : Synchronized
MessageClassificationStatus  : Synchronized
RecipientStatus              : Synchronized
CredentialRecords            : Number of credentials 6
CookieRecords                : Number of cookies 2
```

After you are satisfed that synchronization is progressing successfully and that the right connectors are in place to handle incoming messages, you can update DNS to create an MX record for the Edge server to allow it to accept new mail for processing.

Ongoing synchronization

It's important that the Edge server receives frequent and ongoing updates to keep abreast of changes to user and configuration data within the Exchange organization. The hub transport and Edge servers are in frequent contact to synchronize updates on a one-way basis to send data from Exchange to Edge. As noted earlier, Exchange 2010 improves synchronization operations by replicating delta changes rather than complete data sets.

Multiple hub transport servers can be present in Active Directory, which connects to an Edge server. Any hub transport server can synchronize with the Edge server, but it's important that the hub transport servers do not contend with each other to create multiple concurrent synchronization sessions. Exchange uses the following algorithm to determine which hub transport server will perform the synchronization:

1. The initial synchronization after running the New-EdgeSubscription cmdlet is performed by the first hub transport server to discover the Edge server through a topology scan of the organization. Discovery occurs because the new Edge server and its connectors appear in the routing topology.

2. The hub transport server that discovers the Edge connection establishes an EdgeSync lease option that sets a lock on the Edge subscription and makes it the preferred synchronization server. The lock prevents another hub transport server in the site from taking the lease option. Only hub transport servers that are present in the site when the Edge subscription is created can participate in synchronization, so if you add new hub transport servers and want them to be able to become the preferred server, you have to recreate the Edge subscription. You can see the hub transport that currently holds the lease by running the Test-EdgeSubscription cmdlet where it is reported as the LeaseHolder. The selection order for the preferred server is to use Exchange 2010 hub transport servers before Exchange 2007 hub transport servers.

3. The EdgeSync lease lasts for an hour. You can still run the Start-EdgeSynchronization cmdlet and specify another hub transport server with the –Server parameter to force a manual synchronization to force that server to connect to the Edge server. If you don't specify a server, the preferred server is used for the manual synchronization.

4. During the lease period, the preferred server will perform all automatic synchronizations unless it is unavailable for some release. If the preferred server is unavailable, its lease lapses after five minutes and another hub transport server takes a new lease to become the preferred server and performs synchronization.

5. The preferred server continues until its lease elapses. At this point, it can renew the lease and continue as the preferred server and stays in this role until it becomes unavailable for some reason.

Automatic synchronization occurs between the preferred hub transport server and the Edge server according to the following intervals:

- Changes to configuration data such as new accepted domains, connectors, and servers are synchronized every three minutes.

- Changes to recipient data such as new mailboxes or groups or updates for user safe-list collections are synchronized every five minutes.

You can alter these intervals with the Set-EdgeSyncServiceConfig cmdlet. First, let's retrieve the default settings to reveal the parameter names and their current values by running the

Get-EdgeSyncServiceConfig cmdlet on a hub transport server in the Active Directory site that is connected to the Edge server:

```
Get-EdgeSyncServiceConfig
```

```
SiteName                    : Dublin
ConfigurationSyncInterval   : 00:03:00
RecipientSyncInterval       : 00:05:00
LockDuration                : 00:05:00
LockRenewalDuration         : 00:01:00
OptionDuration              : 01:00:00
CookieValidDuration         : 21.00:00:00
FailoverDCInterval          : 00:05:00
LogEnabled                  : True
LogMaxAge                   : 30.00:00:00
LogMaxDirectorySize         : 262144000
LogMaxFileSize              : 10485760
LogLevel                    : None
LogPath                     : TransportRoles\Logs\EdgeSync\
Identity                    : contoso.com/Configuration/Sites/Dublin/
EdgeSyncService
```

You can clearly see the synchronization intervals (*ConfigurationSyncInterval* and *RecipientSyncInterval*) and the lease period for the preferred server (*LockRenewalDuration*). You can also see how long Exchange waits for a hub transport server to become available before it attempts to transfer responsibility for synchronization to another hub transport server (*LockDuration*). Finally, this output tells us that synchronization operations are logged into the \TransportRoles\Logs\EdgeSync directory under the Exchange installation directory. However, the default log level is None, and if you want to capture data about synchronization operations, you'll have to increase the logging level to Low, Medium, or High. For example:

```
Set-EdgeSyncServiceConfig –Identity
'contoso.com/Configuration/Sites/Dublin/EdgeSyncService' –LogLevel 'High'
```

With this setting in place you'll see entries logged such as:

```
ExEdge1.contoso.com,50636,TargetConnection,Medium,"Updated: CN=Redmond,
\Eoin,OU=Exchange Users,DC=contoso,DC=com",Succcessfully Updated Entry,,,
```

This entry is for an update to a user mailbox. A property such as an email address might have been added or changed on the mailbox, or the user might have updated his junk email settings and Exchange now needs to synchronize those data to the Edge server for inclusion in anti-spam checking (safelist aggregation). We'll discuss how safelists get to the Edge server shortly.

You can force synchronization to occur immediately with the Start-EdgeSynchronization cmdlet. This has some value in that you can see the results of the synchronization. For example, if you create a new mailbox and then run Start-EdgeSynchronization, you should see that one new recipient is added as shown in this output:

```
Start-EdgeSynchronization
```

```
Result            : Success
Type              : Recipients
Name              : ExEdge1
FailureDetails    :
StartUTC          : 2/26/2010 9:19:29 AM
EndUTC            : 2/26/2010 9:19:30 AM
Added             : 1
Deleted           : 0
Updated           : 0
Scanned           : 1
TargetScanned     : 0
```

INSIDE OUT   Edge server database

The Edge server stores data fetched from the hub transport server through the synchronization process in an AD LDS database. Like other Active Directory databases, AD LDS uses an Extensible Storage Engine (ESE) database that comes complete with transaction logs that use circular logging to reduce the amount of storage required. Because synchronization is now based on delta changes, the number of transaction logs generated by Edge synchronization operations is much reduced in Exchange 2010. The default location of the database is \TransportRoles\Data\Adam. You can change this location by editing the EdgeTransport.exe.config file.

INSIDE OUT   Edge-specific configuration settings

Edge synchronization doesn't configure everything on an Edge server. You still have to input the server license, and you also have to configure settings that are specific to the server, such as transport rules that you want to run for inbound messages, certificates to secure its services, block lists and other anti-spam settings, and details of connectors that are not automatically created through the Edge synchronization process. Microsoft refers to these as user-configured settings because they require administrator intervention, whereas the other settings used by an edge server are maintained through synchronization. Because an Edge server effectively operates in an isolated box and doesn't share the data it stores in AD LDS with any other server, you have to apply user-configured settings separately on every Edge server you deploy by making the change on each server or by cloning a configuration from one server and importing it to others.

Microsoft provides the ExportEdgeConfig.ps1 script to export configuration data from an Edge server to an XML format file and ImportEdgeConfig.ps1 to do the reverse and import configuration settings exported from another Edge server. These scripts are in \Scripts under the Exchange installation directory. See TechNet for more information about the exact steps necessary to perform export and import operations.

Transport rules are an exception as they are not exported or imported using this method and you have to export and import rules separately using the Export-TransportRuleCollection and Import-TransportRuleCollection cmdlets. Remember that Edge servers maintain their own rule collection separate from that shared between hub transport servers in an organization, so when you export and import rule collections on an Edge server, you work only with the rules defined on that Edge server and don't affect or otherwise touch the rule collection used by the organization.

Exchange anti-spam agents

Because the techniques and mechanisms used by spammers are constantly evolving and transforming in an attempt to get past anti-spam defenses, it's impossible to build a single algorithm that will detect all of the spam that occurs in an inbound email stream from the Internet. Exchange 2010 includes a set of anti-spam agents that are designed to work together to process an inbound email stream using a variety of techniques that cumulatively have a very high chance of detecting spam and, conversely, not generating many false positives. You can customize the input data used by the anti-spam agents to refine their processing and Microsoft provides downloadable updates to inform the agents about new spamming techniques that are observed in use.

The Edge server is the natural place to deploy the anti-spam agents. It is the first entry point for the inbound email stream and therefore has the opportunity to detect and block spam before it gets a chance to clutter up user inboxes. The anti-spam agents are installed automatically on an Edge server, and all you need to do is customize their settings to make them appropriate for your organization.

Installing the anti-spam agents on a hub transport server

Some organizations do not deploy Edge servers because they have other anti-spam servers deployed. Typically these servers run Linux or UNIX and like the Edge server are highly optimized for the task. Other organizations are too small to afford the relative luxury of deploying Edge servers in the perimeter network. In these situations, you can install the basic Exchange 2010 anti-spam agents on a hub transport server by running the Install-AntiSpamAgents.ps1 script, which you can find in the \Scripts directory under the Exchange installation directory.

When a best practice isn't a best practice

The Microsoft documentation says that it's not best practice to run the anti-spam agents on a hub transport server. This statement is absolutely true if you run Edge servers. However, it is only best practice if you operate a pure Microsoft environment and is invalid if Exchange is protected by other anti-spam servers that are deployed in the perimeter network. Even if other non-Microsoft anti-spam systems cleanse the inbound stream, you lose nothing and gain through the potential eradication of more spam by running the anti-spam agents on any hub transport server that hosts a receive connector that links the Exchange organization to the Internet (directly or indirectly via an inbound relay).

After you run the script to install the agents on a hub transport server, you'll find that the transport pipeline on the server is populated with a new set of agents that will examine the message stream. If you compare this output to the previous example of Get-TransportPipeline discussed in Chapter 13, "The Exchange Transport System," you'll see that the anti-spam agents are now present in the transport pipeline:

```
Get-TransportPipeline
```

```
Event                      TransportAgents
-----                      ---------------
OnConnectEvent             Connection Filtering Agent, Protocol Analysis ...
OnHeloCommand              {}
OnEhloCommand              {}
OnAuthCommand              {}
OnEndOfAuthentication      {}
OnMailCommand              {Connection Filtering Agent, Sender Filter Agent}
OnRcptCommand              {Connection Filtering Agent, Recipient Filter A...
OnDataCommand              {}
OnEndOfHeaders             {Connection Filtering Agent, Sender Id Agent, S...
OnEndOfData                {Content Filter Agent, Protocol Analysis Agent}
OnHelpCommand              {}
```

```
OnNoopCommand                 {}
OnReject                      {Protocol Analysis Agent}
OnRsetCommand                 {Protocol Analysis Agent}
OnDisconnectEvent             {Protocol Analysis Agent}
OnSubmittedMessage            {Text Messaging Routing Agent}
OnResolvedMessage             {}
OnRoutedMessage               {Transport Rule Agent}
OnCategorizedMessage          {}
```

After you install the anti-spam scripts on a hub transport server, you should restart the transport service and define the set of hub transport servers to the connection filtering agent as "internal SMTP servers" so that the agent knows that any connection from these servers is trusted and therefore can be ignored. To define the servers, use the Set-TransportConfig cmdlet to input their IP addresses in the *–InternalSMTPServers* parameter. For example, if you have two hub transport servers with IP addresses of 192.50.60.1 and 192.50.60.2, the command is:

```
Set-TransportConfig –InternalSMTPServers '192.50.60.1', '192.50.60.2'
```

Apart from attachment filtering, which can only run on an Edge server, all of the anti-spam agents function the same way on a hub transport server as they do on an Edge server. Our upcoming discussion about the different agents is therefore applicable to both server roles.

Order of anti-spam agent processing

Exchange applies a set of tests to determine whether a message is spam. The tests are conducted in the following order. A brief outline of the anti-spam check performed at each step is provided here. We consider how to configure the settings that control the check later on.

- **Connection filtering:** When an external server establishes an SMTP connection to transfer a message, the connection filtering agent examines the source IP address of the external server and compares it against the IP Allow list (known good connections), IP Block list (known bad connections), and a real-time block list (RBL)—if configured—to decide whether the connection should be accepted or dropped. Connections from known or suspected sources of spam are usually dropped to immediately cut off any incoming spam.

- **Sender filtering:** If the connection is maintained, Exchange then compares the sender's SMTP email address against a list of known spammers or unwanted senders (perhaps because they are the source of obscene or otherwise objectionable material). Messages from objectionable sources are dropped.

- **Recipient filtering:** Exchange then examines the recipients listed on the message against a Recipient Block list. Messages sent to addresses for which we don't want to accept mail are dropped. Exchange can also check recipients against Active Directory to determine whether the message is addressed to a valid addressee. Spammers often dispatch literally millions of messages to randomly generated email addresses in an attempt to get some messages through to valid recipients, so companies usually block any message that isn't addressed to a valid recipient.

- **Sender ID filtering:** You can publish special DNS records to inform other domains about the identities of the email servers used by your company. Sender ID processing uses this information to help decide whether a message is coming from the domain that it purports to be. If DNS tells Exchange that the originating server is not a registered email server for a domain, it could be a sign that a spammer is masquerading as the company to try and have their messages accepted as valid. For example, a phishing attack to attempt to convince people to part with their online bank account numbers and passwords involves spam that appears to come from the bank but is sent from the spammer's email systems.

- **Content filtering:** Finally, Exchange compares messages against data provided by users in the form of aggregated safelist information and information gathered by Microsoft about the characteristics of spam to generate a spam confidence level (SCL) rating from 0 to 9 for the message. The lower the SCL, the less likely that the message is spam. Conversely, messages with an SCL rating of 6 or above are suspicious and should be treated with caution. Administrators set SCL thresholds to tell Exchange how to deal with messages after their SCL rating is determined. The messages can be dropped immediately or passed through for delivery to recipient mailboxes, where client-side junk mail processing can make a separate decision about how to handle the message. Exchange also calculates a phishing confidence level (PCL) value for the message, an indicator of how likely the message is to be spam that contains a phishing attack.

> **Tip**
>
> The golden rule of anti-spam checking is that the better the input to the spam checks, the better the results.

X-headers added by anti-spam agents

It would be inefficient if Exchange performed anti-spam checking to determine an SCL rating for a message every time it passed through an Edge or hub transport server that runs the anti-spam agents. Exchange adds X-headers to messages after they go through anti-spam checking to capture the results of the check so that other servers and clients further downstream in the message's path understand what processing has occurred and the results. You can see the X-headers by viewing a message header. In Figure 14-7, we see that the SCL rating for the message is 0, indicating that it has a very low probability of being spam. A full list of the X-headers applied by Exchange is contained in Table 14-2.

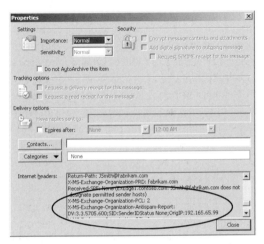

Figure 14-7 Viewing X-headers added by Exchange anti-spam agents.

Table 14-2 X-headers written by Exchange

X-header	Meaning
X-MS-Exchange-Forest-RulesExecuted	Notes all of the transport rules that processed the message.
X-MS-Exchange-Organization-Antispam-Report	Summarizes the results of processing performed by the anti-spam agents.
X-MS-Exchange-Organization-AuthAs	Specifies the authentication source of the message as provided to the receive connector that accepted it. Possible values are Anonymous, Internal, External, or Partner.
X-MS-Exchange-Organization-AuthDomain	Includes the fully qualified domain name (FQDN) of a remote authenticated domain if the message was received through Domain Secure authentication.
X-MS-Exchange-Organization-AuthMechanism	Specifies a two-digit hexadecimal number that indicates the authentication mechanism used when the message was submitted.
X-MS-Exchange-Organization-AuthSource	Specifies the FQDN of the server that evaluated the authentication for the message when it arrived into the organization.
X-MS-Exchange-Organization-Journal-Report	Identifies a message as a journal report.

X-MS-Exchange-Organization-OriginalArrivalTime	Contains the time (in UTC) when the message first arrived in the Exchange organization. If the message passed through another email system, it might contain an X-OriginalArrivalTime header that indicates the time when the message arrived in that system.
X-MS-Exchange-Organization-Original-Sender	Contains the original sender of a quarantined message.
X-MS-Exchange-Organization-Original-Size	Contains the original size of a quarantined message.
X-MS-Exchange-Organization-Original-SCL	Contains the original SCL value for a quarantined message.
X-MS-Exchange-Organization-Original-PCL	Contains the original PCL for a quarantined message.
X-MS-Exchange-Organization-Quarantine	Flag indicating that the message has been redirected into the quarantine mailbox and a delivery status notification (DSN) has been sent. It also indicates when a message was quarantined and has been released for delivery by an administrator.
X-MS-Exchange-Organization-PRD	Contains the purported responsible domain (PRD) if determined by the Sender ID agent.
X-MS-Exchange-Organization-SCL	Contains the SCL for a message. The values range from 0 to 9 with larger values indicating an increasing suspicion that the message is spam. A value of –1 indicates that the message is internal (sent within the same Exchange organization) and has not been processed by the content filter agent.
X-MS-Exchange-Organization-SenderIdResult	Contains the result of the Sender ID agent.

You can also see that the message has a PCL rating of 2. Phishing messages typically invite users to enter confidential data such as their bank account details into a Web site. The user is lulled into a false sense of security because the message seems to have come from a legitimate source such as his bank. However, it's always surprising (and depressing) to hear of instances when users fall for the trick and respond to messages that seem to come from banks with which they have no relationship. Such is the nature of human fallibility. In any case, like an SCL, Exchange calculates a PCL of between 1 and 8 for the message. Anything less than 3 is a neutral value, meaning that the message is unlikely to contain a phishing attack. Values of 4 and over indicate an increasing level of suspicion that the message contains elements such as Web links to suspicious sites that makes Exchange believe that the message is dangerous spam. Outlook's junk mail filter takes the PCL value into account when it scans incoming messages, and anything with a high PCL value is likely to be deleted immediately or end up in the Junk E-Mail folder, depending on user preferences.

After a message passes through the anti-spam agents, Exchange writes an X-header called X-MS-Exchange-Organization-Antispam-Report into the header with a summary result of the processing performed by the agent. In the example shown in Figure 14-7, the report includes the following values:

- **DV 3.3.5705.600:** This is the version of the spam definition data file used by the anti-spam agent.

- **SID:SenderIDStatus:None:** The Sender ID agent reports that the server that sent the message does not have a published Sender Policy Framework (SPF) record.

- **OrigIP:** The IP address of the server where the message originated.

INSIDE OUT   Scouting out suspicious messages

Many other types of information can be included in an anti-spam report, including whether the sender was found in an allowed sender list and the message bypassed anti-spam checking. A suspicious message might have a report like this:

```
SID:SenderIDStatus Fail;PCL:PhishingLevel SUSPICIOUS;CW:CustomList;
TIME:TimeBasedFeatures
```

In this example, the Sender ID check failed, perhaps because the purported sending domain does not exist (spammers commonly masquerade as nonexistent domains); the phishing level is deemed to be suspicious, probably because of embedded Web links in the message; the CW field indicates that a custom blocked word or phrase is present in the message; and the Time field shows that a suspicious delay occurred between the time when the message was apparently sent and when it was received on the server—most messages are delivered very quickly across the Internet, but submissions of millions of spam messages to an email server can create delays.

See *http://technet.microsoft.com/en-us/library/aa996878.aspx* for details of the different fields added by the anti-spam agents.

Header firewalls

Adding X-headers to message headers is usually a good thing because it allows administrators and users to trace the path of messages and see what actions occurred as the message made its way from server to server. However, you might not want to expose information about your messaging infrastructure—such as the name of email servers—to the outside world, as this information might be of use to hackers. It's also possible that a spammer could attempt to get messages past your defenses by inserting headers that seem to testify to their authenticity. Exchange therefore supports "header firewall" functionality to strip X-header information from messages as they pass through a connector.

The header firewall implemented in Exchange 2010 uses Active Directory permissions to know whether header information should be removed or left intact. First, let's review the Active Directory permissions that exist on a send connector. We can retrieve the permissions with a command like this one:

```
Get-SendConnector -Identity 'To Internet via Smart Host' | Get-AdPermission | Select
User, ExtendedRights, Deny | Format-Table -AutoSize
```

User	ExtendedRights	Deny
----	--------------	----
NT AUTHORITY\ANONYMOUS LOGON	{ms-Exch-Send-Headers-Routing}	False
CONTOSO\Exchange Servers	{ms-Exch-Send-Headers-Organization}	False
CONTOSO\Exchange Servers	{ms-Exch-SMTP-Send-Exch50}	False
CONTOSO\Exchange Servers	{ms-Exch-Send-Headers-Forest}	False
CONTOSO\Exchange Servers	{ms-Exch-Send-Headers-Routing}	False
CONTOSO\Exchange Servers	{ms-Exch-SMTP-Send-XShadow}	False
MS Exchange\Partner Servers	{ms-Exch-Send-Headers-Routing}	False
MS Exchange\Hub Transport Servers	{ms-Exch-SMTP-Send-XShadow}	False
MS Exchange\Hub Transport Servers	{ms-Exch-Send-Headers-Forest}	False
MS Exchange\Hub Transport Servers	{ms-Exch-Send-Headers-Organization}	False
MS Exchange\Hub Transport Servers	{ms-Exch-SMTP-Send-Exch50}	False
MS Exchange\Hub Transport Servers	{ms-Exch-Send-Headers-Routing}	False
MS Exchange\Edge Transport Servers	{ms-Exch-Send-Headers-Routing}	False
MS Exchange\Edge Transport Servers	{ms-Exch-SMTP-Send-XShadow}	False
MS Exchange\Edge Transport Servers	{ms-Exch-Send-Headers-Forest}	False
MS Exchange\Edge Transport Servers	{ms-Exch-Send-Headers-Organization}	False
MS Exchange\Edge Transport Servers	{ms-Exch-SMTP-Send-Exch50}	False
MS Exchange\Externally Secured Servers	{ms-Exch-Send-Headers-Routing}	False
MS Exchange\Externally Secured Servers	{ms-Exch-SMTP-Send-Exch50}	False
MS Exchange\Legacy Exchange Servers	{ms-Exch-SMTP-Send-Exch50}	False
MS Exchange\Legacy Exchange Servers	{ms-Exch-Send-Headers-Routing}	False

The output shown here is truncated to focus on the most important permissions for our discussion, and the permission that we are most interested in is listed first. Exchange uses the NT Authority\Anonymous Logon account when it makes unauthenticated connections to external servers. The other accounts that are listed are used for connections within the organization or with Edge servers that are secured with Transport Layer Security (TLS). To remove header information from messages that are going to external servers, we need to deny the *ms-Exch-Send-Headers-Routing* extended right to the account. This is done with a command like this:

```
Add-AdPermission -User 'NT Authority\Anonymous Logon' -ExtendedRights 'ms-Exch-Send-
Headers-Routing' -Deny
```

After you add the new deny permission, you have to restart the Microsoft Exchange Transport service on all hub transport servers that are configured to use the send connector to force them to read in the new permission and respect it. The only information about a server that is retained is the name of the hub transport server that transmitted the message across the send connector.

This is a very simple discussion about how and why you would enable a header firewall. The debate can become a lot more complicated as you factor in receive connectors and dealing with messages from legacy Exchange 2003 organizations (Exchange 2007 servers are not deemed to be legacy in this context because they support header firewalls).

TechNet has a good treatment of the topic at *http://technet.microsoft.com/en-us/library /bb232136.aspx*.

Connection filtering

The Connection Filter agent examines the IP addresses presented by remote SMTP servers that initiate SMTP sessions with Exchange to decide whether to accept the message that the remote server wishes to send. Filtering is applied to all connections that come in from unauthenticated SMTP servers. The Connection Filter agent fires when the *OnConnect* transport event occurs and extracts the underlying IP address that initiates the SMTP session to compare it against IP block lists (to decide whether to drop the session) and IP allow lists (to accept the session). If the IP address is on a block list, Exchange continues to accept data until all recipient information (the RCPT TO data) is received so that it can check if any of the intended recipients are marked to bypass connection checking. You might define bypass recipients to receive spam so that you can analyze the spam and be able to refine your defenses against attack. Bypass recipients are defined with the Set-IPBlockListProvidersConfig cmdlet (or through EMC). For example:

```
Set-IPBlockListProvidersConfig -BypassedRecipients 'Tony.Redmond@contoso.com',
'Kim.Akers@contoso.com'
```

The checks that the Connection Filter agent executes are determined by the IP Allow List configuration and IP Block List configuration, which you can view with the Get-IPAllowListConfig and Get-IPBlockListConfig cmdlets. For example, the settings shown here indicate that the Connection Filter agent is examining external connections but not internal connections. You can also see the messages sent as nondelivery reports (NDRs) in response to blocked messages. You can customize these messages with the Set-IPAllowListConfig and Set-IPBlockListConfig cmdlets:

```
Get-IPBlockListConfig
```

```
Name                          : IPBlockListConfig
MachineEntryRejectionResponse : External client with IP address {0} does not have permissions to
submit to this server. Visit http://support.microsoft.com/kb/928123 for more information.
StaticEntryRejectionResponse  : External client with IP address {0} does not have permissions to
submit to this server.
Enabled                       : True
ExternalMailEnabled           : True
InternalMailEnabled           : False
AdminDisplayName              :
ExchangeVersion               : 0.1 (8.0.535.0)
Identity                      : IPBlockListConfig
```

Most checks of incoming IP connections are performed against lists of IP addresses used by well-known spammers that are maintained by third-party providers such as Spamhaus.org. These RBLs have been in use for years. The accuracy and up-to-date nature of the lists vary from provider to provider so some care has to be taken before you select a provider to use. Apart from satisfying yourself of the accuracy of the information (there is a lot of information about RBLs available on the Web), you need fast response to queries and some guarantee of availability if you are to rely on the chosen provider. If the IP address is found on these lists, Exchange will drop the session as before.

When an IP address is a source of spam

You can configure IP addresses that come to your attention as a source of spam. Exchange always checks the list of IP block entries before it checks an IP address with an RBL. An IP address is added to the block entry list with the Add-IPBlockListEntry cmdlet. You can create an entry for a specific IP address or an IP address range. The following example blocks a range of IP addresses and expires at 23:59 on December 31, 2010. If you don't provide an expiry time, the entry remains on the list until it is removed with the Remove-IPBlockListEntry cmdlet. You can amend the setting of an IP block list entry with the Set-IPBlockListEntry cmdlet.

```
Add-IPBlockListEntry -IPRange 192.168.0.1-192.168.0.10 -ExpirationTime
"12/31/2010 23:59"
```

You can configure IP Block List providers and IP Allow List providers through EMC. Click the Organization Configuration node, select Hub Transport, and then on the Anti-Spam tab, select IP Block List Providers. Figure 14-8 shows how to define an entry for an IP Block List provider. Every provider that you add will slow down processing of inbound messages, so it's important that you balance the need for protection with an equal need for speed. Limiting yourself to two or three (at maximum) providers seems like the right balance. There's also a cost element, as RBL providers charge for their services if your organization generates a large number of queries daily. Typically, the provider will charge a fee to create a regularly updated zone transfer of its data to a local DNS server.

EMC also allows you to define a list of IP Allow List providers, essentially providing the reverse function of the IP Blocked List providers. IP Allow Lists define IP addresses that are known to be safe.

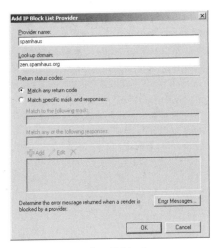

Figure 14-8 Setting IP blocks.

The EMS code to generate this entry is shown here:

```
Add-IPBlockListProvider -Name 'Spamhaus' -LookupDomain 'zen.spamhous.org'
-Enabled $true -BitmaskMatch $null -IPAddressesMatch @() -AnyMatch $True
-Priority '1' -RejectionResponse ''
```

The Test-IPBlockListProvider cmdlet can be used to validate that a Block List provider is working properly. If you have multiple Block List providers, you can test them all in one operation as follows:

```
Get-IPBlockListProvider | Test-IPBlockListProvider -IPAddress xx.xx.xx.xx
```

You'll see a response like this for each provider:

```
RunspaceId     : 3d8ded65-134f-4543-a52f-aaf3e19ea79e
Provider       : Spamhaus
ProviderResult : {208.73.210.27}
Matched        : True
```

A *True* result means that the RBL lookup doesn't reveal that the specified IP address is for a suspected spammer. A *False* result is obviously different, and it is sufficient to block the progress of a message if it was the result of a lookup by the Connection Filter agent.

Sender filtering

Connection filters protect by blocking IP addresses used by well-known spammers. Sender filters add protection by blocking known email addresses and domains that spammers use. The Sender Filter agent fires on the *OnMailCommand* event when the MAIL FROM data are received for a message. The agent works by comparing the sender email address (extracted from both MAIL FROM and the From: field in the message—these are not necessarily the same and are often not in the case of spam) against a list of prohibited addresses that the administrator defines as "bad." You can block individual addresses or a complete domain or even any subdomains. Figure 14-9 shows the general approach to creating a table of blocked senders. You can also see that a rule is defined to block messages that are presented without sender information in their header.

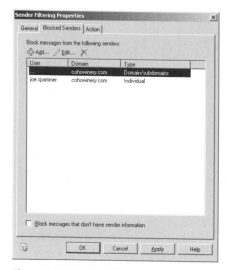

Figure 14-9 Sender Filter agent properties.

After the agent identifies offending messages, it then has to decide how to handle them. The options are to reject the message immediately with a Sender Denied response or to accept the message with the proviso that it comes from a blocked sender. The Content Filter agent will then take this fact into account when it calculates the SCL value for the message. In all likelihood, the message's SCL value will be increased and might lead to it being blocked at a later point in the anti-spam cycle because its SCL value exceeds the threshold for acceptance.

The Get-SenderFilterConfig cmdlet reveals the configuration used by the Sender Filter agent. You can compare the results shown here with the properties visible in Figure 14-9.

```
Get-SenderFilterConfig
```

```
Name                          : SenderFilterConfig
BlockedSenders                : {Joe.Spammer@cohowinery.com}
BlockedDomains                : {}
BlockedDomainsAndSubdomains   : {cohowinery.com}
Action                        : Reject
BlankSenderBlockingEnabled    : True
RecipientBlockedSenderAction  : Reject
Enabled                       : True
ExternalMailEnabled           : True
InternalMailEnabled           : False
```

The Set-SenderFilterConfig cmdlet is used to update the configuration. For example, to add a new domain to the prohibited list, we can use a command like this:

```
Set-SenderFilterConfig -BlockedDomainsAndSubdomains 'cohowinery.com',
'cohovineyard.com','litwareinc.com'
```

Two points are noteworthy. First, there's an obvious difference between *BlockedDomains* and *BlockedDomainsAndSubdomains* because one blocks top-level domains and the other blocks all the subdomains as well. It's easy to miss this subtle but important point when you use tab-complete to cycle through the available parameters for Set-SenderFilterConfig. Second, you have to write out the complete new set of values every time you add or remove an entry for the *BlockedDomains*, *BlockedDomainsAndSubDomains*, and *BlockedSenders* properties. Again, it's easy to miss this and just write the latest domain or sender that you want to block and miss all the values that were present before.

Backscattering

Blocking messages that are presented without a sender is a basic rule of messaging hygiene that has been in place for years. Unfortunately, spammers became wise to this block a long time ago and added sender addresses to messages. This development forced receiving message transfer agents (MTAs) to implement checks with the sender's domain to validate that it is valid (callback verification). If a sender address is invalid, the connection is immediately dropped.

To defeat the callback verification check, spammers began to spoof using legitimate addresses that are harvested and sold between spammers. In turn, this led to another problem called backscattering where the spammer exploits two facts. First, they know that they have a legitimate sender address that will be accepted by an MTA, and second, they know that most reputable MTAs will generate a DSN when a message cannot be delivered because it's addressed to an unknown recipient. Spammers can therefore target an email domain with tens of thousands of messages that appear to come from real people with the intention that these messages will never be delivered but instead result in DSNs that are addressed back to the legitimate addresses! The unwary recipient sees the DSN in her inbox and opens it to find out why she has been notified of the undelivered message—a message that she never sent—and then she reads the content of the undeliverable message. The spammer achieves delivery of content to real users and has circumvented anti-spam protection. The problem for an Exchange organization is that the transport servers have to handle the generation and transmission of the DSNs plus the flood of incoming DSNs that result from spam attacks on other domains.

Sender ID protection helps by forcing verification of email servers for domains, but as we discuss shortly, Sender ID is not implemented universally. The solution is often found through Bounce Address Tag Verification (BATV), a method to suppress backscattering by stamping outbound messages with verifiable tags to attest that these messages come from real users. BATV is generally available across a range of popular MTAs including SendMail, Exim, and Postfix. The Exchange 2010 anti-spam agents do not include BATV, but add-on products such as Microsoft Forefront Protection for Exchange 2010 (FPE) include optional backscatter filters that can be enabled. In the case of FPE, the backscatter filter is implemented as an outbound agent to stamp messages as they pass through the transport categorizer and an inbound agent to examine messages as they are processed through the SMTP pipeline.

Implementing protection against backscattering is not absolutely essential, but the development of filters to suppress the backscattered messages is a good example of the kind of feature that exists in add-on products that isn't available in the Exchange 2010 anti-spam agents that you should consider when you make decisions about how to protect your servers.

Sender reputation

The Sender Reputation Level (SRL) is a value that the Sender Reputation agent calculates based on tests that it performs on incoming messages. The tests include the accuracy of reverse DNS data for a given sender, whether the server that the sender uses appears to be an open proxy (a proxy server that accepts connection requests from any other server and forwards the SMTP traffic as if it originated from the local host), the correctness of the EHLO or HELO connection (senders who use many different and unique EHLO commands are likely to be spammers; regular traffic from nonspammers tends to use the same EHLO command consistently), and the SCL ratings that Exchange has calculated using the Content Filter agent for previous messages from the same sender. A message that comes in with a high SCL rating can cause the sender's SRL to be adjusted downward; a message with a low SCL rating can cause the opposite effect. The resulting SRL is a number between 0 and 9, where a value of 0 indicates less than a 1 percent chance that the sender is a spammer, and a value of 9 indicates that the sender is very likely to be a spammer. An SRL value of 4 indicates that Exchange is neutral about this sender.

The Sender Reputation agent stores the data that it gathers in a database called Pasetting. edb that is located in \TransportRoles\Data\Senderreputation. Over time, a sender's reputation can improve or degrade based on the type of messages sent. All senders start at 0. The agent starts to calculate SRLs for senders after Exchange captures 20 messages from them. The agent actually fires at two points: after the MAIL FROM: command (so that the agent knows who the message is supposedly coming from) and after the end of data command is received, so that the agent knows the SCL that the Content Filter agent has calculated for the message.

Through the Properties dialog box for the Sender Reputation agent (Figure 14-10), you can configure the agent with an SRL threshold to indicate your level of tolerance to spam. The default setting is 9, which means that Exchange takes a cautious approach to deciding that senders' reputations are bad enough to block them. Setting a lower level could cause senders to be blocked when they shouldn't be. If a sender reaches the threshold, the Sender Reputation agent flags the sender to the Sender Filtering agent so that it can add the sender's IP address to the blocked senders list for a temporary period, which is 24 hours by default. You can adjust the blocking period to be shorter or longer as you require, up to a maximum value of 48 hours. Senders whose IP addresses are in Microsoft's own SRL list are automatically added to your blocked list.

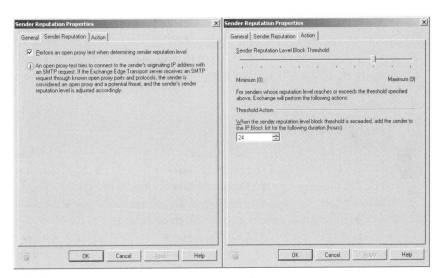

Figure 14-10 Viewing sender reputation properties.

The Get-SenderReputationConfig cmdlet reveals more about the Sender Reputation configuration. You'll notice that the agent is enabled by default for external mail and disabled for internal mail.

```
Get-SenderReputationConfig
```

```
MinMessagesPerDatabaseTransaction : 20
SrlBlockThreshold                 : 7
MinMessagesPerTimeSlice           : 100
TimeSliceInterval                 : 48
OpenProxyDetectionEnabled         : True
SenderBlockingEnabled             : True
OpenProxyRescanInterval           : 10
MinReverseDnsQueryPeriod          : 1
SenderBlockingPeriod              : 24
MaxWorkQueueSize                  : 1000
MaxIdleTime                       : 10
Socks4Ports                       : {1081, 1080}
Socks5Ports                       : {1081, 1080}
WingatePorts                      : {23}
HttpConnectPorts                  : {6588, 3128, 80}
HttpPostPorts                     : {6588, 3128, 80}
TelnetPorts                       : {23}
CiscoPorts                        : {23}
TablePurgeInterval                : 24
MaxPendingOperations              : 100
ProxyServerName                   :
ProxyServerPort                   : 0
ProxyServerType                   : None
Name                              : Sender Reputation
MinDownloadInterval               : 10
MaxDownloadInterval               : 100
SrlSettingsDatabaseFileName       :
ReputationServiceUrl              :
Enabled                           : True
ExternalMailEnabled               : True
InternalMailEnabled               : False
```

You can set properties for the Sender Reputation agent with the Set-SenderReputationConfig command. For example, this command sets the SRL Block Threshold to be 8 and the blocking period to be 36 hours:

```
Set-SenderReputationConfig –SrlBlockThreshold 8 –SenderBlockingPeriod 36
```

Because the result of a sender exceeding the SRL threshold is to be placed on the blocked senders list, the configuration for the Sender Filter determines how Exchange will handle messages from these senders. The default action is to reject new messages, but you can also elect to stamp the messages with a status as coming from a blocked sender and allow them to continue onward.

Recipient filtering

Recipient filters work on the RCPT TO: field in inbound messages to extract and examine recipient addresses. The Recipient Filter agent compares the addresses against administrator-defined Recipient Block lists (Figure 14-11) and Active Directory to determine if any action is necessary on an inbound message. In most cases, Exchange is configured to decline messages addressed to users that it cannot find in the directory.

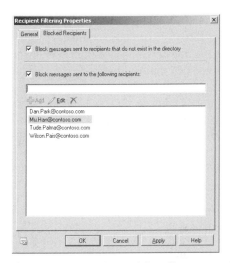

Figure 14-11 Viewing recipient filter properties.

The configuration used by the Recipient Filter agent is very simple and easy to compare against the properties revealed in Figure 14-11. The *Enabled* property determines whether the agent is active. The *InternalMailEnabled* property determines whether the agent examines messages that originate from authenticated domains. The default values are usually good to retain.

```
Get-RecipientFilterConfig
```

```
Name                         : RecipientFilterConfig
BlockedRecipients            : {Dan.Park@contoso.com, Mu.Han@contoso.com,
Tude.Palma@contoso.com, Wilson.Pais@contoso.com}
RecipientValidationEnabled : True
BlockListEnabled             : True
Enabled                      : True
ExternalMailEnabled          : True
InternalMailEnabled          : False
```

You can use the Set-RecipientFilterConfig cmdlet to update any of these settings. For example:

```
Set-RecipientFilterConfig -BlockedRecipients
'Dan.Park@contoso.com', 'Mu.Han@contoso.com', 'Tude.Palma@contoso.com',
'Wilson.Pais@contoso.com'
```

Tarpits

Exchange 2010 includes tarpitting functionality, the ability to throttle back server response after potential spam communication patterns are detected. For example, a remote server might attempt to conduct an address harvest attack whereby it "tests" thousands of addresses against Exchange to see whether Exchange will accept any of the addresses. Normally, the remote server will use a pattern to compose addresses so that it can test multiple possible combinations for potential users. The idea is for spammers to discover what addresses are valid so that they can add these addresses to their lists and either use them for future spam or to sell to other spammers. Tarpitting is designed to slow down the communication process by inserting delays between the request from the external sender and the response from Exchange. The hope is that the remote server will eventually give up because the directory attack takes too long and there are other easier targets to attack.

You can use this command to discover the current tarpit interval on a server:

```
Get-ReceiveConnector | Select Server, TarpitInterval
```

```
Name                                            TarpitInterval
----                                            --------------
Default internal receive connector EXEDGE1      00:00:05
```

In this case, the tarpit interval is five seconds.

Sender ID

The Sender ID agent is enabled by default. The Sender Filter agent that we've just discussed checks the MAIL FROM information in messages to detect spam, but spammers routinely misrepresent themselves by manipulating addresses, so you need another way to detect whether the server that wants to submit a message to your server really belongs to a valid domain. The Sender ID agent does this by attempting to verify the identity of the SMTP server that wants to communicate with Exchange. The check is performed against records held in DNS to identify the IP addresses of the mail servers that are entitled to submit messages on behalf of an SMTP domain. The records used in a Sender ID check are known as SPF records.

How did it evolve?

A movement called the Sender Policy Framework project (*http://www.openspf.org/*) founded by Meng Weng Wong in 2003 provided the initial impetus behind the idea of eradicating email forgery through email sender authentication. At much the same time, Microsoft had launched its own CallerID project, and both efforts seemed to be on the path to merging to the overall benefit of everyone. However, Microsoft's efforts to get their work adopted by the Internet Engineering Task Force through a draft request for comments (RFC) called "MTA authentication records in DNS" (*http://tools.ietf.org/html /draft-ietf-marid-core-01*) foundered and they continue to advocate the use of Sender ID instead of SPF. There are practical differences between the two implementations, and at the time of writing there is no plan to close the gap. However, this shouldn't take away from the central point: It's a good idea to be able to check who is sending you messages whether they arrive by email or by phone.

The Sender ID agent performs the following steps to process a message:

1. The Sender ID agent determines the purported responsible address (PRA) or the supposed sender of the message. This is done by examining the following message attributes in the order of difficulty that these attributes can be spoofed by a spammer (the From header is the easiest to spoof):

    a. Resent-Sender header

    b. Resent-From header

    c. Delivered-To, X-Envelope-To, and Envelope-To headers

    d. Sender header

    e. From header

2. The Sender ID agent then determines the PRD from the email address of the sender. If the message seems to come from John.Smith@contoso.com, then contoso.com is the PRD.

3. The Sender ID agent issues a DNS query to locate the Sender ID "mail policy document" for the PRD (using the IP address of the server that is submitting the message). The mail policy document lists the IP addresses of the servers that are entitled to send messages on behalf of the PRD.

4. If the IP address of the submitting SMTP server matches an IP address for the PRD, Exchange stamps the message with the Sender ID information and passes it to the Content Filter agent.

5. If no match is discovered, Exchange will take the action configured for the Sender ID agent (see Figure 14-12).

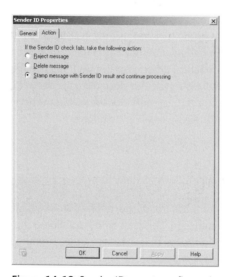

Figure 14-12 Sender ID agent configuration.

Whereas companies like IBM, Microsoft, and Google publish SPF records for their domains in DNS, some major companies (General Electric is a good example) do not. It's quite interesting to look at the format of the SPF records for different companies to see how they publish their Sender ID identity to the Internet and to understand how to format SPF records for your own purpose. You can input the domain name for a company to the Microsoft Sender ID Wizard (Figure 14-13) and have it check whether any SPF records exist for the company or if they use standard A and MX records to identify their email servers. The wizard also displays the SPF records if found, so you can see the different techniques used for this purpose and compare the records that are actually in use with the textbook guidelines for their composition. For example, the SPF record for Google.com is:

```
v=spf1 include:_netblocks.google.com ip4:216.73.93.70/31 ip4:216.73.93.72/31 ~all
```

The SPF record for Gmail.com is a simple redirect to Google.com:

```
v=spf1 redirect=_spf.google.com
```

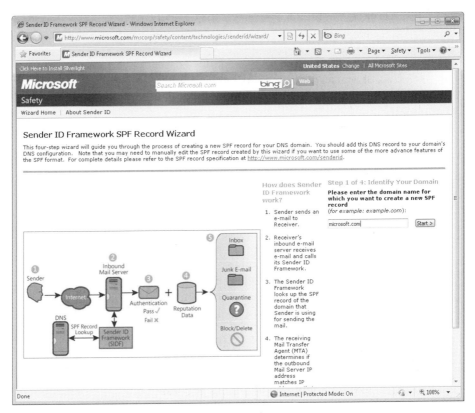

Figure 14-13 Using the Microsoft Sender ID Wizard.

Over time, an increasing number of companies publish SPF records for their domains, but regretfully, as long as some major companies do not, Sender ID checking will remain an incomplete and inexact science.

For more information about creating SPF records for your domain, see the "Sender ID Framework SPF Record Wizard" at *http://www.microsoft.com/mscorp/safety/content /technologies/senderid/wizard/default.aspx.*

Because not all companies publish SPF records yet, it's entirely possible that the result of a Sender ID check will not be possible. The following outcomes can occur:

- **Pass:** The IP address of the sending server is in the authorized set for the PRD.

- **Neutral:** Inconclusive—the company might not have published SPF records in DNS.

- **Soft Fail:** The IP address might be in the NOT permitted set.

- **Fail:** The IP address is in the NOT permitted set and the message is definitely a problem.

- **TempError:** Transient error occurred during the check; for example, it is not possible to contact DNS because of a network error.

- **PermError:** A permanent error occurred; for example, the SPF records are in an illegal format and cannot be properly read.

Looking through the list of potential outcomes, you can realize why the default action for the Sender ID agent is to simply stamp the message with the result and pass it on to the Content Filter agent, which can take account of the Sender ID check result when it calculates the SCL value for the message. For example, a Fail or SoftFail result will increase the SCL value. You can't affect the SCL weighting that Exchange assigns to the different outcomes of a Sender ID check.

Figure 14-12 shows the properties of the Sender ID agent where you define the action to take. You should think through the potential consequences before you move away from the default action to reject or delete messages. When a message is rejected, it is returned to the sender with an NDR. When a message is deleted, it is dropped and no response goes back to the sender. The potential exists that you might delete perfectly good messages because of a transient issue such as a DNS outage. Wise administrators let messages pass to be processed by the Content Filter agent.

Some additional information about the Sender ID configuration can be obtained with the Get-SenderIDConfig cmdlet.

```
Get-SenderIDConfig
```

```
SpoofedDomainAction    : StampStatus
TempErrorAction        : StampStatus
BypassedRecipients     : {}
BypassedSenderDomains  : {}
Name                   : SenderIdConfig
Enabled                : True
ExternalMailEnabled    : True
InternalMailEnabled    : False
AdminDisplayName        :
ExchangeVersion        : 0.1 (8.0.535.0)
DistinguishedName      : CN=SenderIdConfig,CN=Message Hygiene,CN=Transport
Settings,CN=contoso,CN=Microsoft Exchange,CN=Services,CN=Configuration,
DC=contoso,DC=com
```

We can see that there are two actions defined in the configuration. The action revealed by EMC is *SpoofedDomainAction* and we can see that it is set to StampStatus, which is what we expect. The second action is defined in the *TempErrorAction* property and is also set to StampStatus. The Sender ID agent takes this action for messages when TempError is returned from its check.

Three other options are worthy of comment. First, you can define a set of up to 100 recipient addresses that the Sender ID agent will not process. In this example, we define three recipients to be bypassed. Each recipient address is separated by a comma:

```
Set-SenderIDConfig –BypassedRecipients
'TRedmond@contoso.com,ERedmonmd@contoso.com,ARuth@contoso.com'
```

Second, you can also define a set of up to 100 sender domains that the Sender ID agent will ignore. For example:

```
Set-SenderIDConfig –BypassedSenderDomains 'contoso.com,fabrikam.com'
```

CAUTION

It's not a good idea to instruct the Sender ID agent to bypass messages from a domain unless you are very sure that a spammer will never use the domain for its purpose.

Last, all messages generated by authoritative domains within your organization are ignored by the Sender ID agent (because you assume that you know where these messages come from), but you can enable checking for these messages:

```
Set-SenderIDConfig –InternalMailEnabled $True
```

To test that the Sender ID agent is working normally, you can use the Test-SenderID cmdlet. To do this, you pass the IP address that you want to check along with the domain to which the IP address should belong. In this example, we use one of the addresses that we know should work for Google.com as reported by Microsoft's Sender ID wizard:

```
Test-SenderID –IPAddress 216.73.93.70 –PurportedResponsibleDomain Google.com
```

```
RunspaceId    : 3d8ded65-134f-4543-a52f-aaf3e19ea79e
Status        : Pass
FailReason    : None
Explanation   :
```

As we can see, the test succeeded so we know that Google.com really does use the IP address that's registered in its SPF record.

Content filtering

The Content Filter agent executes last in the anti-spam cycle. This agent is a development of the Intelligent Message Agent (IMF) that Microsoft first launched for Exchange 2003 SP1 and was then incorporated into the content filter agent for Exchange 2007. The Content Filter agent and Outlook's junk email agent are both based on Microsoft's SmartScreen technology, originally developed by Microsoft Research to address the problem of how to identify spam. Apart from the algorithms used by the Content Filter agent, Microsoft maintains a database containing elements extracted from billions of messages that Microsoft has processed over the years for its Hotmail service and received from customers. These data have allowed Microsoft to construct a map of the characteristics of both legitimate messages and spam and hone the anti-spam algorithms on an ongoing basis. Microsoft refreshes the SmartScreen database regularly and provides it to customers through Microsoft Update.

The Content Filter adds to the data provided by Microsoft with data gathered from user safelists (see the section "Attachment filtering" later in this chapter) so that the checking can be more tailored to the mail traffic that flows into the organization and reduce the number of false positives that are generated. On an Edge server, the safelist data (the safe senders and blocked senders lists) are provided in aggregated format in the AD LDS database that synchronizes with a hub transport server in the Exchange organization.

When the Content Filter runs on a hub transport server, it can access the safelist data for an intended recipient from Active Directory. All of the SmartScreen data from Microsoft and the aggregated user safelists are considered by the Content Filter agent to determine whether a message contains spam. You know when the Content Agent finds a safelist match for a message because it adds the *SenderOnRecipientSafeSendersList* stamp to the X-MS-Exchange-Organization-Antispam-Report X-header in the message header that you can view if you examine a message's properties.

One of the X-headers that Exchange stamps onto incoming messages contains an SCL value, which is calculated by the Content Filter agent. The SCL value determines the eventual disposition of a message. Figure 14-14 illustrates how different outcomes can result after the Content Filter agent has calculated the SCL. Decision points occur on the hub transport or Edge server that processes the message and on the mailbox server that hosts the database for the recipient mailboxes. Clients can impose further processing as messages arrive into the Inbox to impose user-specific preferences if they include functionality such as the junk e-mail filter that's available in Microsoft Outlook or Outlook Web App. We discuss how you can affect these decision points by setting SCL threshold values shortly.

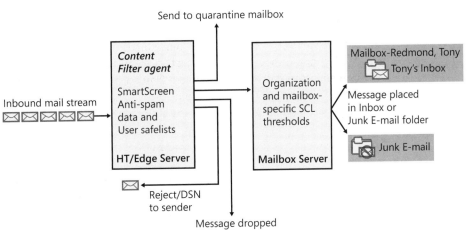

Figure 14-14 How the spam confidence level of a message affects its disposition.

> **Note**
> Because it has to examine many characteristics of a message, the Content Filter agent is the most computationally intense of the anti-spam agents. However, because Exchange executes it last, the load is reduced by the fact that the Content Filter agent only has to process messages that have been passed by other agents such as the Connection Filter and Recipient Filter.

In addition to using Microsoft's SmartScreen spam heuristics to detect suspicious messages, you can add words or phrases that you want to block or allow if they occur in messages by entering them on the Custom Words tab of the Content Filter Properties dialog box (Figure 14-15). You have to be careful with the words that you choose to block, as they might be perfectly valid in some contexts and objectionable in others. International companies have to be very careful in this respect, as they have the added complexity of dealing with multiple languages where words can take on different meanings. This also extends to slang used in different parts of the world. For example, a "sambo" in Ireland is nothing but slang for a sandwich. It has a completely different meaning elsewhere.

Words are checked in both the message subject and body. The allow words take priority over the blocked words, so the Content Filter will allow messages through that contain blocked words if they also contain an allowed word or phrase. Also, the Content Filter will allow a message through that contains blocked words if it is sent by someone on the recipient's safe senders list. The logic here is that the recipient has made an explicit decision to receive email from the sender and should be able to deal with any objectionable content that arrives. However, the message is blocked and will not be delivered to any other recipient. You can also define users whose messages are not checked by the Content Filter agent by inputting their names on the Exceptions tab of the agent Properties dialog box.

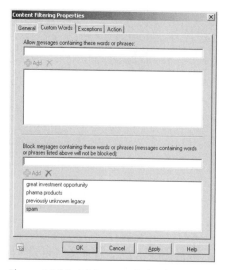

Figure 14-15 Adding words for the Content Filter agent to block.

INSIDE OUT   Content filtering is for messages under 11 MB

Messages larger than 11 MB are not scanned by the Content Filter agent. The logic is that the default maximum size for receive connectors is 10 MB, so an 11 MB message won't be accepted by Exchange unless the organization is configured to handle larger messages. It's also reasonable to assume that people who want to spread viruses and spammers don't send very large attachments because these would slow down message transmission too much.

SCL thresholds

As explained earlier, the output from the Content Filter agent is an SCL value for the message, which is added to the MAPI properties of the message. The value of the SCL ranges from 0 to 9 where 0 means that the message is absolutely not spam and 9 means that it absolutely is spam. A value of –1 indicates that the message came from a trusted internal source. You control the action that the Content Filter agent takes for a message after its SCL value is determined by adjusting three different thresholds on the Action tab of the agent Properties dialog box (Figure 14-16).

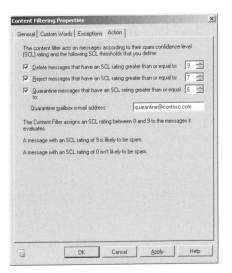

Figure 14-16 Determining actions for the Content Filter agent.

- **Delete:** The message is deleted when its SCL value equals or exceeds this threshold. No notification is sent to the originating email server. If the SCL value is lower than the Delete threshold, compare it to the Reject threshold.

- **Reject:** The message is deleted, and Exchange sends a rejection response (DSN) to the originating email server when the SCL value equals or exceeds the Reject threshold. The intention behind returning a DSN to the sender is to advise him that his message seems to be spam and so allow a legitimate sender to adjust the content and resend (or ask for his name to be added to a safe senders list). If the SCL value is lower than the Reject threshold, it is then compared to the Quarantine threshold.

- **Quarantine:** The message is quarantined by sending it to a special quarantine mailbox if its SCL value equals the quarantine threshold. The address does not have to be an Exchange mailbox; the only requirement is that Exchange has to be able to route messages to the address, as otherwise the messages will be dropped. Administrators can review the messages that are deposited in this mailbox from time to time (daily is suggested) to establish whether the SCL thresholds are appropriate. Note that the messages that arrive into the quarantine mailbox look like NDRs. To see the content of a quarantined message, use Outlook to open the message and select the Send Again option. It is obvious that the messages that arrive into the quarantine mailbox might contain confidential and sensitive information, so you have to exercise care over who is able to access the quarantine mailbox as well as provide some direction as to how they should handle the content.

INSIDE OUT   It's a balancing act

Setting effective SCL thresholds is a balance between achieving a high level of protection against spam (users complain very quickly when they begin to receive large volumes of spam) and avoiding false positives. In addition, it does not make sense to set the quarantine threshold so high that vast quantities of messages end up in the quarantine mailbox waiting for an administrator to review and decide whether to pass the message on to the addressee. Some trial and error is likely before you arrive at a balance that makes sense for the organization.

Per-mailbox SCL thresholds

At a more granular level, you can dictate SCL thresholds on a per-mailbox basis with the Set-Mailbox cmdlet. You might want to do this for users who complain that they receive a large volume of spam. For example, let's assume that you want to set more rigorous thresholds for a mailbox than the default thresholds set for the Content Filter agent of 9 (Delete), 8 (Reject), and 7 (Quarantine) by reducing these values to 8, 6, and 5. The command looks something like this:

```
Set-Mailbox -Identity TRedmond -SCLDeleteEnabled $True -SCLDeleteThreshold 8
-SCLRejectEnabled $True -SCLRejectThreshold 6
-SCLQuarantineEnabled $True -SCLQuarantineThreshold 5
```

All of the thresholds discussed to date apply to processing that occurs within the Content Filter agent. Messages with SCL values that are lower than the quarantine threshold emerge from the hub transport or Edge server and are routed onward to the destination mailbox. The next step in the anti-spam process is for the mailbox server to decide whether the message goes into the Inbox or the Junk E-Mail folder. Exchange has an organization-wide SCL threshold that tells mailbox servers how to deal with potential spam if a specific threshold is not set for a mailbox. The default threshold is 4, meaning that any message that has an SCL value of 5 or above will be redirected to the Junk E-Mail folder rather than the Inbox. This value is maintained through the Set-OrganizationConfig cmdlet. For example, after this command is executed, mailbox servers will move any message with an SCL value greater than 5 into the Junk E-Mail folder:

```
Set-OrganizationConfig -SCLJunkThreshold 5
```

It's possible to set a specific threshold for a mailbox using the Set-Mailbox cmdlet. For example:

```
Set-Mailbox -Identity TRedmond -SCLJunkEnabled $True -SCLJunkThreshold 6
```

INSIDE OUT   Strategies for handling executives' mailboxes

It's also possible to mark a mailbox to be ignored during anti-spam process-ing by enabling its *AntiSpamBypassEnabled* property. Any message addressed to a mailbox with this property set to $True bypasses the Content Filter agent. To avoid a deluge of spam arriving into the mailbox, administrators often set the *RequireSenderAuthenticationEnabled* property, which means that the mailbox won't accept messages from senders who do not authenticate themselves to Exchange. This can be an effective way of blocking spam from mailboxes used by company execu-tives at the expense that messages from third parties that might be of interest to the executive won't be delivered if they are not authenticated. One way around this is to create two mailboxes per executive, one with a public email address that is monitored by an assistant, and one for internal communications that is moderated and won't accept messages from nonauthenticated senders. Here's the command to lock down a mailbox:

```
Set-Mailbox –Identity CEOMailbox –RequireSenderAuthenticationEnabled $True
–AntiSpamBypassEnabled $True
```

Managing the Content Filter agent with EMS

Like elsewhere in Exchange, you can access and manipulate the properties of the Content Filter agent through EMS. Here's how to list the current properties for the Content Filter agent. Remember, these are organization-wide settings when viewed on a hub transport server and specific to the server if you check on an Edge server:

```
Get-ContentFilterConfig
```

```
Name                                     : ContentFilterConfig
RejectionResponse                        : Message rejected as spam by Content
Filtering.
OutlookEmailPostmarkValidationEnabled    : True
BypassedRecipients                       : {}
QuarantineMailbox                        : Quarantine@contoso.com
SCLRejectThreshold                       : 8
SCLRejectEnabled                         : True
SCLDeleteThreshold                       : 9
SCLDeleteEnabled                         : True
SCLQuarantineThreshold                   : 7
SCLQuarantineEnabled                     : True
BypassedSenders                          : {}
BypassedSenderDomains                    : {}
Enabled                                  : True
```

```
ExternalMailEnabled                     : True
InternalMailEnabled                     : True
AdminDisplayName                        :
ExchangeVersion                         : 0.1 (8.0.535.0)
DistinguishedName                       : CN=ContentFilterConfig,CN=Message
Hygiene,CN=Transport Settings,CN=contoso,CN=Microsoft Exchange,CN=Services,
CN=Configuration,DC=contoso,DC=com
Identity                                : ContentFilterConfig
```

By default, the Content Filter agent only operates on messages that come into the organization from external senders. You can force it to operate on internal messages, too, by setting the –*InternalMailEnabled* property with the Set-ContentFilterConfig cmdlet.

```
Set-ContentFilterConfig –InternalMailEnabled $True
```

Another common example of customization for the Content Filter agent is to change the
rejection response sent in reply to messages that are dropped during filtering. The DSN
code is 5.7.1 and you can instruct Exchange to include whatever text you like (up to 240
characters). For example:

```
Set-ContentFilterConfig –RejectionResponse 'Message is obviously spam; why would you
send it to us?'
```

Blocked words and phrases used by the Content Filter agent can be accessed with the Get-
ContentFilterPhrase cmdlet:

```
Get-ContentFilterPhrase
```

```
RunspaceId : 3d8ded65-134f-4543-a52f-aaf3e19ea79e
Influence  : BadWord
Phrase     : Great Investment Opportunity
Identity   : Great Investment Opportunity
IsValid    : True
```

You can add new words or phrases with the Add-ContentFilterPhrase cmdlet or remove
them with the Remove-ContentFilterPhrase cmdlet. There's no cmdlet to update an existing blocked word or phrase so you have to remove the old entry first and then add the
amended version. For example:

```
Remove-ContentFilterPhrase –Identity 'Great Investment Opportunity' –Force
Add-ContentFilterPhrase –Identity 'Fanastic new investment opportunity' –Influence
BadWord
```

Using SCL values in transport rules

You can build transport rules that perform processing based on the SCL value assigned to a message. For instance, you might want to prefix the message subject with something like "SPAM>>>" to make the recipient realize that a message could contain spam. However, to be effective, the rule agent has to execute after the Content Filter has completed its evaluation of messages and stamped them with SCL values. By default, the Transport Rule agent executes before the Content Filter agent on an Edge server, so the transport rule is never exposed to an SCL value. The solution is to switch the two agents around so that the Content Filter agent has a higher priority in the transport pipeline than the Transport Rule agent. You can do this with the command:

```
Set-TransportAgent 'Content Filter Agent' -Priority 3
```

Attachment filtering

The Attachment Filter agent only runs on Edge servers to intercept suspicious attachments that are identified by their extension, MIME type, or file name. There's no obvious reason why the Attachment Filter agent couldn't run on internal hub transport servers apart from the potential that an overzealous application of the filter might strip a lot of attachments on messages circulating between internal recipients.

This agent is different from its peers in that it can only be managed through EMS using the Get-AttachmentFilterEntry and Add-AttachmentFilterEntry cmdlets. In addition, it does not log its activities in the agent log. Microsoft's default list of blocked attachments is long because many attempts have been made by hackers to exploit the unwary. You can see the list of attachment types that the agent currently intercepts (the output is edited, as it's a very long list) with the following command:

```
Get-AttachmentFilterEntry | Format-List Type, Name -AutoSize
```

```
        Type Name
        ---- ----
 ContentType application/x-msdownload
 ContentType message/partial
 ContentType text/scriptlet
 ContentType application/prg
 ContentType application/msaccess
 ContentType text/javascript
 ContentType application/x-javascript
 ContentType application/javascript
 ContentType x-internet-signup
 ContentType application/hta
    FileName *.xnk
    FileName *.wsh
```

```
FileName *.wsf
FileName *.wsc
FileName *.vbs
FileName *.vbe
FileName *.vb
```

This extract shows that Exchange won't pass messages with attachments that could contain executable code. The Attachment Filter agent is able to detect file types even if they have been renamed (for example, from .vbs to .tmp). The agent also checks compressed files (such as a ZIP) to detect whether any of the files contained within should be blocked.

You can update the list of blocked files with the Add-AttachmentFilterEntry cmdlet to add blocks for specific file names, all files of a specific type, or all files of a specific MIME content type. For example, to block the file ILoveYou.docx, you'd use this command:

```
Add-AttachmentFilterEntry –Name 'ILoveYou.docx' –Type FileName
```

To block all files of a specific type:

```
Add-AttachmentFilterEntry –Name '*.ttx' –Type FileName
```

The command is slightly different when you block attachments using MIME content types. This example creates a block for MPEG video files.

```
Add-AttachmentFilterEntry –Name 'video/mpeg' –Type ContentType
```

You can get a complete list of MIME content types from *http://www.iana.org/assignments /media-types/index.html*.

The Remove-AttachmentFilterEntry cmdlet is available if you want to remove an entry from the block list. For example:

```
Remove-AttachmentFilterEntry –Name 'video/mpeg'
```

The Get-AttachmentFilterListConfig cmdlet reveals some other information about the Attachment Filter, including the default action to take when the filter detects a problem attachment. In the following output, we can see that the action is "Strip," meaning that Exchange will remove the attachment and pass the message through with an indication to the user of what happened.

```
Get-AttachmentFilterListConfig
```

```
Name             : Transport Settings
RejectResponse   : Message rejected due to unacceptable attachments
AdminMessage     : This attachment was removed.
Action           : Strip
```

```
ExceptionConnectors : {}
AttachmentNames    : {ContentType:application/x-msdownload,
ContentType:message/partial, ContentType:text/scriplet, ContentType:application
/prg, ContentType:application/msaccess, ContentType:text/javascript,
ContentType:application/x-javascript, ContentType:application/javascript,
ContentType:x-internet-signup, ContentType:application/hta, FileName:*.xnk,
FileName:*.wsh, FileName:*.wsf, FileName:*.wsc, FileName:*.vbs, FileName:*
.vbe...}
```

You can amend this option to be "Reject" (delete the message and send a DSN) or "SilentDelete" (delete the message without sending a DSN). If you choose the latter option, you might want to update the *RejectResponse* property to provide your own explanation to the sender in up to 240 characters. For example:

```
Set-AttachmentFilterListConfig –Action 'SilentDelete' –RejectResponse
'Contoso Corporation does not accept attachments of this type'
```

> **Note**
>
> Stripped or dropped attachments are removed immediately and cannot be accessed, even by an administrator, to validate the effectiveness of the block.

Two other properties are of interest. The *AdminMessage* property contains the text that Exchange includes in a message if an attachment is stripped and sent on to the recipient. The *ExceptionConnectors* property contains the globally unique identifier (GUID) of any connector that you want to exclude from attachment filtering. You could use this to exclude a connector that handles mail from a trusted partner that contains information in a format (such as video files) that you otherwise want to reject.

Address rewriting

The Address Rewrite agent can only run on an Edge server. Its purpose is to intercept inbound and outbound messages and rewrite the RCPT TO addresses on incoming messages or the MAIL FROM addresses on outgoing messages. This functionality is broadly similar to the token replacement capability offered by U*X-based email systems such as SendMail. Organizations might decide not to reveal internal email addresses to the outside world and provide users with addresses that are sufficient to route messages to the edge of the organization but no further. The Address Rewrite agent then rewrites the outbound message headers so that when the messages pass outside the organization, the headers have outward-facing addresses. In the same way, addresses can be intercepted by the Address Rewrite agent en route into the organization and rewritten into addresses that are suitable for internal routing.

The first step is to enable the Address Rewrite agent. There are two forms of the agent: One handles inbound messages, the other outbound. You can enable either or both:

```
Enable-TransportAgent –Identity 'Address Rewriting Inbound Agent'
Enable-TransportAgent –Identity 'Address Rewriting Outbound Agent'
```

After enabling the agents, you have to restart the Microsoft Exchange Transport service. You can then begin to add the address rewrite entries to control how the agents work. An address rewrite entry identifies a single email address or a complete domain for processing and specifies how addresses are to be rewritten. There is no GUI to maintain address rewrite rules, so everything has to be done through the set of New/Get/Set/Remove-AddressRewriteEntry cmdlets. Unless otherwise specified, address rewrite rules operate on both inbound and outbound message streams.

For example, let's assume that you provide users with outward-facing addresses like:

```
John.Smith@contoso.com
```

Internally, however, the mailbox is identified as Smith-JohnA@Exchange.Email.contoso.com. Clearly, the first form is much easier for people to remember or to include on business cards. To instruct the Address Rewrite agent to deal with the message, we create an address rewrite entry:

```
New-AddressRewriteEntry –Name "John Smith External" –InternalAddress
'Smith-JohnA@Exchange.email.contoso.com' External@contoso.com"
-ExternalAddress John.Smith@contoso.com
```

The internal address that you specify must exist for a mail-enabled recipient within the Exchange organization to allow Exchange to route the message onward. Creating address rewrite entries like this is clearly a laborious process to set up and maintain if you have more than a few address rewrite entries to look after. You can therefore create address rewrite entries to handle complete domains. This might be required if a company is acquired and its users continue to use the email address for their old company. You want to strip these addresses off outbound messages and replace them with the domain name for the amalgamated company. Here's an example:

```
New-AddressRewriteEntry 'Transform Contoso to Fabrikam' –InternalAddress
'*.contoso.com' –ExternalAddress 'fabrikam.com' –Outbound $True
```

In this example we specify that the address rewrite entry only applies to outbound messages (*Outbound* is $True) and that any of the subdomains under contoso.com are covered by the rule. If you need to exclude certain domains from the effect of the rewriting rule, you can do so by including their name in a list stated in the *–ExceptionList* parameter and passed to the New-AddressRewriteEntry cmdlet.

> **Tip**
>
> Remember that any change made to a configuration on an Edge server has to be copied to other Edge servers that are deployed. This is especially important when you process settings such as user addresses.

It's possible that the Address Rewrite agent will be unable to update an address on some messages because they are encrypted, digitally signed, or rights-protected. The problem is that updating the message could compromise its digital integrity or just be impossible, as it would render the resulting message unreadable. In these instances, the Address Rewrite agent will not attempt to update the message and pass it through unaltered.

Agent logs

Exchange captures the results of agent processing in a set of log files called AgentLogYYYYMMDD-1.log in the \Program Files\Microsoft\Exchange Server\V14 \TransportRoles\Logs\AgentLog directory. Logs are created daily and Exchange keeps logs for up to 30 days, or until the directory holds 250 MB of logs. A new log is generated after 10 MB of data are captured. Entries are written into the agent log by the Connection Filter agent, the Content Filter agent, the Edge Rules agent, the Recipient Filter agent, the Sender Filter agent, and the Sender ID agent.

Like the other logs generated by Exchange 2010, the agent log is stored in comma-separated value (CSV) format. Figure 14-17 shows Microsoft Excel being used to open an agent log and you can see the kind of information captured in the log. In this instance, the data come from the Content Filter agent and refer to a number of messages that have been marked as spam (their SCL value is set to 9), some that have been passed as unlikely to be spam (their SCL values are 2 and 1), and some where the checking done by the Content Filter agent has been bypassed because of mailbox settings (for example, the *AntiSpamBypassEnabled* property is set). You can also see the action taken by the Content Filter agent to delete one message and to remove one or more recipients from another. The latter happens when the Content Filter agent is able to deliver a message to one recipient even when it is above the spam threshold because the sender is in the recipient's safe senders list. The message goes through to that recipient but all other recipients are stripped from the message.

Chapter 14

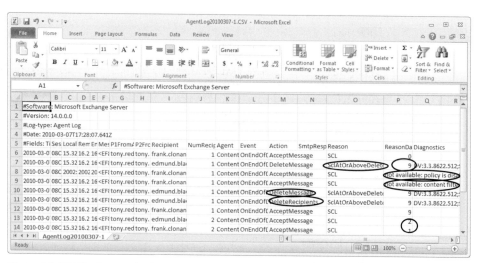

Figure 14-17 Viewing entries in an agent log.

You can use EMS to interrogate the agent log with the Get-AgentLog cmdlet to form an idea of the steps taken by the agents when they process mail. For example, to discover what messages are being dropped because they have exceeded the SCL threshold to be deleted, you can scan the agent log as follows. The output is the message identifier, the P1 (header) information for the sender, and the recipients: It's important to provide a start and end date for the search, as otherwise you will have to wade through an entry for every message that has been dropped in the last 30 days:

```
Get-AgentLog –StartDate '03/10/2011 07:00AM' –EndDate '03/10/2011 09:00AM' | Where
{$_.Reason –eq 'SCLAtOrAboveDeleteThreshold'} | Select MessageId, P1FromAddress,
Recipient
```

The Get-AgentLog cmdlet does not provide great filtering capabilities. To find out what happened to a particular message, you have to set a date scope to limit the number of records that might be searched and then filter using the message identifier or another unique value. For example, you might be looking for a message sent by someone that has been reported as never delivered. In this case, you can filter based on the P1FromAddress field.

```
Get-AgentLog –StartDate '01/01/2011 03:00PM' –EndDate '01/01/2011 03:15PM' | Where {$_.P1FromAddress
–eq 'tony.redmond@contoso.com'}
```

Here is an example of a message sent from a specific address that successfully passed through the Content Filter agent:

```
Timestamp         : 10/7/2010 10:10:48 AM
SessionId         : 08CC8C3823463F3F
IPAddress         : 16.228.9.186
MessageId         : <EF806EB1F8A19642B316B86DFA23C58B15E337E5@GWServer@fabrikam.com>
P1FromAddress     : John.Smith@fabrikam.com
P2FromAddresses   : {john.smith@fabrikam.com}
Recipients        : {David.Pelton@contoso.com, Andy.Ruth@contoso.com}
Agent             : Content Filter Agent
Event             : OnEndOfData
Action            : AcceptMessage
SmtpResponse      :
Reason            : SCL
ReasonData        : 1
Diagnostics       :
```

To compare, here's a log entry that captures the deletion of a message because its SCL value is 9. The probable reason for such a high value is indicated by the presence of "CW:CustomList" in the anti-spam report captured in the diagnostics field. This means that the Content Filter agent detected the presence of one of the custom blocked words or phrases.

```
Timestamp         : 10/7/2010 9:55:27 AM
SessionId         : 08CC8C35250120E3
IPAddress         : 16.228.9.186
MessageId         : <EF806EB1F8A19642B316B86DFA23C58B15E337AA@GWServer.fabrikam.com>
P1FromAddress     : John.Smith@fabrikam.com
P2FromAddresses   : {John.Smith@fabrikam.com}
Recipients        : {Andy.Ruth@contoso.com}
Agent             : Content Filter Agent
Event             : OnEndOfData
Action            : DeleteMessage
SmtpResponse      :
Reason            : SclAtOrAboveDeleteThreshold
ReasonData        : 9
Diagnostics       : DV:3.3.8622.512;SV:3.3.4604.600;SID:SenderIDStatus None;CW:CustomList
```

Few administrators have the time or patience to go through agent logs unless it's absolutely required, as in the case of tracking down the reason for messages being blocked. The agent logs contain some interesting data from an analytical perspective and Microsoft provides a number of scripts (stored in the \Scripts directory) to analyze the data and report anti-spam activity. Table 14-3 lists the scripts and their intended use. The scripts depend on the data held in the agent logs so their output covers the period for which the logs are available. As they are scripts, you can always tweak the code to meet your own requirements.

Chapter 14

Table 14-3 **Scripts to report anti-spam activity**

Script	Use
Get-AntispamFilteringReport.ps1	Generates the top-ten list of spam sources as identified by rejected connections or messages that were eventually deleted or quarantined. Valid parameters are "connections," "commands," "messagesrejected," "messagesdeleted," and "messagesquarantined."
Get-AntispamSCLHistogram.ps1	Analyzes the entries written by the Content Filter agent and groups them according to the SCL values assigned to messages.
Get-AntispamTopBlockedSenderDomains.ps1	Reports the top ten domains that have been blocked by anti-spam agents.
Get-AntispamTopBlockedSenderIPs.ps1	Reports the top ten blocked sender IP addresses.
Get-AntispamTopBlockedSenders.ps1	Reports the top ten senders that have been blocked.
Get-AntispamTopRBLProviders.ps1	Reports the top ten reasons for rejection by block list providers.
Get-AntispamTopRecipients.ps1	Reports the top ten recipients for messages that have been blocked by anti-spam agents.

INSIDE OUT   Enabling anti-spam updates

Spammers evolve and develop new techniques in a constant battle to disguise their messages and have them accepted by email systems. Applying frequent and timely updates to the SmartScreen data that the Content Filter uses to detect spam is a critical part of maintaining an effective anti-spam defense. Microsoft makes updates for SmartScreen available through Microsoft Update. If you have bought Enterprise CALs and use Microsoft Forefront Protection for Exchange, it will download and apply its own updates automatically. You do not have to download any updates manually as in Exchange 2007 or Exchange 2010 and the Enable-AntiSpamUpdates cmdlet that was used previously is deprecated in Exchange 2010 SP1.

Safelist aggregation

Safelist collections are formed as users create safe sender, safe recipient, and blocked sender lists as they process incoming messages. These lists are stored as hidden items in the root folder of user mailboxes. External contacts are also included in a safelist collection if the user elects to trust email from their contacts. OWA and Outlook clients use these data to examine incoming messages that have passed through server-based anti-spam processing to make the final determination of what items will stay in the Inbox and what will be deleted or moved to the Junk E-Mail folder. Up to 1,024 unique entries can exist in a safelist collection for a mailbox.

Safelist aggregation means that Exchange collects and formats the safelist data created by users so that the data can be used by the Content Filter agent to filter out spam as it arrives on an Edge or hub transport server. The Content Filter agent is disabled if you run Forefront Protection for Exchange 2010 because Forefront has its own content filtering capability. Nevertheless, Forefront also uses the aggregated safelist data so nothing is wasted.

The value of safelist data provided by users is that this information can reduce the number of false positives generated during anti-spam checking. A false positive is a bad thing because it means that the server has blocked a message that a user is perfectly willing to accept. Aggregating the safelist collections from users across the organization and making those data available to anti-spam processing can substantially reduce the number of false positives and ensure that users receive "good" messages while "bad" messages are blocked by the server. The fact that the data that Exchange uses to make decisions come from users and are based on real-life interactions that they have with correspondents in other companies is good; the fact that users can contribute these data without administrator intervention or with no additional work required by the administrator is even better.

To aggregate the safelist data, a mailbox assistant called the Junk E-Mail Options Assistant monitors changes that users make to their junk email options. If a change is detected, the assistant updates the user's Active Directory object with a one-way hashed (SHA-256) version of the safelist data. The data are hashed to protect them from examination if they are replicated to AD LDS running on an Edge server. Even if a hacker is able to penetrate the Edge server and AD LDS, she won't be able to turn the 4-byte entries into usable email addresses.

INSIDE OUT
Hashing and safe list collections

Hashing also reduces the amount of data to 4 bytes for each entry to limit the resources required to store and replicate the data. A complete safelist collection therefore requires just 4,096 bytes of storage. The entries equate to SMTP addresses and Exchange is able to very quickly compare the SMTP addresses on incoming messages against the hashed safelist entries to decide whether a message is good or not. If a sender's address matches against the safe sender hash, it bypasses content filtering, whereas if the sender address matches against the blocked senders hash, it is blocked by the server.

Active Directory stores the safelist collection in three binary objects (blobs) called the *msExchSafeSendersHash*, *msExchSafeRecipientsHash*, and *msExchBlockedSendersHash* attributes. You can view these attributes with ADSIEdit. Figure 14-18 shows how the *msExchSafeRecipientsHash* attribute appears when you view the properties of a mail-enabled account that has populated some data. The nonprinting characters obscure the blob so you can make no sense of what the hashed values might represent.

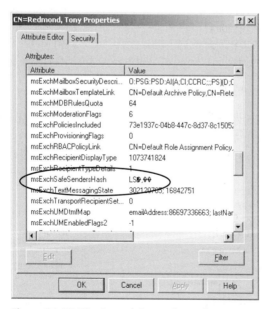

Figure 14-18 Viewing safelist attributes for an Active Directory account.

Exchange 2007 forces administrators to use the Update-SafeList cmdlet to collect safelist data from user mailboxes and prepare the data for synchronization with an Edge server. The Junk E-Mail Options Assistant takes over this responsibility in Exchange 2010 and ensures that Active Directory is updated with safelist data on an ongoing and constant basis, so you don't have to worry about running regular jobs to perform this function.

Two other differences exist in how Exchange 2007 and Exchange 2010 compose safelist data. The first is that Exchange 2010 only includes individual sender email addresses rather than sender domains. In Exchange 2007, it is possible for a user to inadvertently open a hole by including a sender domain in his safelist. The sender domain is aggregated and used for anti-spam checks, but if a spammer attempts to get email through by impersonating users from a domain that is in the safelist, the spam will get past the check because the domain is in the safelist. Restricting aggregation to sender addresses closes this hole. The second is that the Junk E-Mail Options Assistant ignores entries for any of the authoritative domains for the organization when it copies safelist data from mailboxes to the Active Directory. This stops a user from inadvertently allowing spam that seems to come from one of the authoritative domains through. In addition, even if a user does add internal domains to her safelist data, as a further protection against spam, the store process that moves spam into the Junk E-Mail folder does not skip messages that appear to come from an authoritative domain when it examines messages after they have been delivered to a user's mailbox.

The Update-SafeList cmdlet still exists in Exchange 2010 and you can use it to force Exchange to retrieve the safelist data in one or more mailboxes, convert the data to hashed values, and perform any required updates to Active Directory accounts. For example, to update safelist data for a selected mailbox, you pass the mailbox identity to the cmdlet:

```
Update-SafeList –Identity JSmith
```

Of course, you can pipe a set of mailboxes to the Update-SafeList cmdlet to force updates for all of the selected mailboxes:

```
Get-Mailbox –Database 'VIP Data' | Update-SafeList
```

> **Tip**
>
> It's safe to leave updates to the Junk E-Mail Options Assistant unless you have a good reason to force manual updates. In all cases, the updated information held in Active Directory won't be used for anti-spam checking by an Edge server until the next time Edge synchronization runs. If you've installed the anti-spam agents onto a hub transport server, the information is used immediately.

Choosing an antivirus product

Exchange's anti-spam agents do a reasonable job of applying basic anti-spam techniques to remove unwanted email from the inbound mail stream. Its antivirus capabilities are rudimentary and cannot be guaranteed to deliver the same level of protection as a dedicated antivirus solution can. You should therefore supplement this layer of defense by deploying a good antivirus product that is built to support Exchange on the edge of hub transport servers that process inbound email from the Internet. The choice is often between Microsoft FPE and a non-Microsoft product. You could make the assumption that the easy decision is to select FPE because its development group works alongside the Exchange team and must therefore create a tighter and more integrated defense. In addition, if you already pay for enterprise Exchange CALs, you also license FPE.

It's certainly true that FPE is worthy of consideration, if only because of its integration with Exchange, but a wider and more considered assessment of antivirus products should be undertaken before you make a final decision. Among the aspects that you should consider to select the antivirus product to deploy alongside Exchange are the following:

1. VSAPI support: All modern antivirus products that support Exchange use VSAPI. You should not select a product that attempts to access Exchange data structures in any other way.

2. Support for all types of Exchange deployment: Make sure that the antivirus product supports all kinds of deployment from simple mailbox servers to servers in a Database Availability Group (DAG) to multirole servers.

3. Centralized management and deployment of new antivirus updates: Unless you only support one or two servers, it's much easier if the antivirus product allows you to manage all servers from a central console, including the reporting of alerts and the ability to download and distribute updates for antivirus signatures to servers. It's also good if the product creates reports that analyze virus activity and attacks so that you understand the degree of threat that the email servers face.

4. Support for multiple antivirus engines: A single antivirus engine can deliver a high level of protection against incoming viruses. However, it can also be regarded as a potential single point of failure for protection. Multiple antivirus engines usually deliver a higher degree of protection, especially after the outbreak of a new virus. This is because each engine has its own strengths in terms of detection, and a virus that slips by one engine is likely to be detected by another. It should be possible to run the different engines on mailbox and hub transport/Edge servers. You don't need to run an antivirus program on Client Access Servers (CAS) servers because messages are not processed on these computers.

5. Support for single intervention: The antivirus product should stamp a message after it is processed so that performance is not affected by messages being scanned by the same engine at multiple points in your organization.

6. Speedy release of upgrades: Antivirus signatures must be upgraded and made available speedily (preferably automatically) to let you protect the organization when new types of viruses appear. In addition, new releases of the antivirus product should be available to support roll-up upgrades and service packs of Exchange soon after they are released by Microsoft.

Apart from these Exchange-specific criteria, your choice could be influenced by a corporate product selection for antivirus protection across all platforms. The cost of protecting tens of thousands of client PCs is usually large enough to make it an important consideration during product selection. If you secure a great deal to protect client PCs and Windows servers, you might have to compromise and go with a "not quite optimal" choice for Exchange antivirus. However, it's fair to say that all of the major antivirus products available for Exchange today are solid and will protect systems.

If you deploy FPE on Edge servers, should you also deploy Microsoft Forefront Threat Management Gateway (TMG) on the same computer? TMG is designed to provide front-line protection against threats coming into perimeter networks from the Internet. TMG can perform URL filtering, anti-malware inspection, HTTP/HTTPS inspection, and intrusion prevention. It can also act as an application and network-layer firewall. The idea is that obvious detectable threats are removed from the connections that arrive to an Edge server through a defensive layer that is installed at the outer edge of the perimeter network.

Microsoft has done a good job of combining TMG, FPE, and the Edge server so that the complete security regime for the Edge server, including its subscription to the Exchange organization, can be managed from the email policy section of the TMG console. The level of integration means that the combination is worth considering, if only to set a baseline for the kind of joined-up approach to security that makes it more difficult for attackers to penetrate networks. However, some commentators have reported that it takes more work than they expect to make all of the components work together smoothly. Other products can provide a similar level of protection, and the final selection might come down to aspects such as cost (acquisition, deployment, support, and ongoing licensing), integration with non-Microsoft platforms, and scalability (hardware appliances are more scalable and are usually a more appropriate choice to protect large networks).

Client defense

Even with the best possible array of bastion and anti-spam Edge servers arranged to suppress incoming spam before it penetrates your network, it is inevitable that some percentage of spam will get through to user mailboxes. For this reason, client-side spam suppression is an important part of the overall defense mechanism against spam. Every version of Outlook includes some rule processing capability to allow users to create some degree of automation in handling incoming messages. In the early days, rules took care of tasks such as filing messages into appropriate folders and we never really had to deal with the electronic version of junk mail, unless the messages from some of our regular correspondents fell into that category. The typical approach taken with rules is to look for a keyword in the message subject and use its presence to decide whether the message should be deleted. However, as spam became more pervasive, Outlook rules just couldn't handle the complexity of detecting the many variations of spam that got past corporate anti-spam filters to arrive in user mailboxes. The need therefore arose for an intelligent client-side anti-spam filter. Microsoft delivered the first version of client-side junk mail processing in Outlook 2003 and has continued to enhance it since. Junk mail processing is also available in OWA and both Outlook and OWA respect the same user preferences, albeit working in a slightly different manner. For example, you can only use Outlook's junk mail filter when you work in cached Exchange mode because Outlook must download messages before it can process them through its filter.

Outlook's junk mail filter

Some junk mail is very easy to detect, and that's why rules were able to do the job when junk mail was reasonably uncommon. The earliest spam was crude and unsophisticated. Examples include in-your-face invitations to buy drugs or notifications that you have the opportunity to work with someone you have never met in your life before to extract vast sums of money from an African country, and so on. It always interests me that so many people fall prey to invitations to part with their money when the invitations are badly written, only use uppercase letters, and contain lots of misspellings. As discussed earlier in this chapter, anti-spam software relies on a variety of techniques to detect unsolicited commercial email. Microsoft originally developed its SmartScreen technology to protect the consumer Hotmail servers. SmartScreen depends on exposure to a vast collection of spam to learn and recognize the characteristic signs that indicate potential spam. Outlook's junk mail filter uses a version of the SmartScreen spam heuristics that Microsoft adapted to run on a PC and to take user preferences into account when messages are examined. You can also use rules to block messages from specific senders but general-purpose rules are slow to execute and are therefore unsuited to handle the rate of incoming email that busy mailboxes receive. Outlook's junk mail filter runs as compiled code and executes quickly enough to avoid any perceivable delay in the delivery of new mail.

The raw data that allow Outlook to filter messages are contained in a file called Outfldr.dat, which holds a large dictionary of keywords and phrases that the junk mail filter uses. You cannot add to the filter file so you cannot train Outlook to respect your preferences. Instead, Microsoft issues regular updates for the filter file as part of its update service for Office (*www.microsoft.com/officeupdate*), so as long as you download and install the updates, you will benefit from the latest ways to detect spam.

Assuming that you opt to use the junk mail filter, Outlook checks new messages as they arrive. The default protect level is Low, but I prefer to run at High, as experience with the filter has shown me that it does a pretty good job. The difference between Low and High is that the first setting filters only the really obvious spam, whereas the second does a much more thorough filtering job. You have the option to delete any mail that the filter catches immediately or have Outlook put these messages in your Junk E-Mail folder. I usually opt to delete messages immediately, but from time to time I capture messages just to see what kind of spam is arriving. OWA doesn't offer quite the same control over junk mail filtering as Outlook does, but you can still input lists of safe senders and recipients (Figure 14-19) and opt to always accept email from your contacts. Outlook and OWA both share the same junk e-mail settings, as these are stored in the root folder of the user's mailbox.

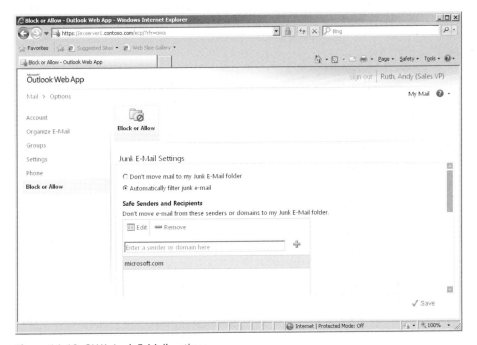

Figure 14-19 OWA Junk E-Mail options.

Although you can't update the filters that Outlook uses to detect spam, you can help Outlook improve its accuracy when it comes to filtering the incoming message stream to your Inbox by indicating who you think are safe senders (people that you always want to receive email from) and users and domains that you regard as nuisances (those that have sent you spam). Outlook uses this information when it runs its checks to filter messages. The order that Outlook performs checks is as follows:

- Check the sender against your contacts. Any message from a contact is assumed to be safe because you have taken an explicit action to mark someone as a contact, and you would not do this if you didn't want to receive email from her.

- Check the sender against the Global Address List. Outlook assumes that you are willing to read a message sent by another user in the same organization (note that you cannot use the filter to block messages from another user in the organization; to do this, you have to create a rule).

- Check the sender against your Safe Senders list. If you add someone to this list, you tell Outlook that you always want to receive email from him, and Exchange will publish these data to Active Directory so that they can be used in anti-spam processing.

- Check the sender against your Safe Recipients list. If you add an address to this list, you tell Outlook that it's OK to accept any message that contains the address.

- Check the sender against your Blocked Senders list. Outlook blocks any message from anyone on this list. The junk mail filter also checks for incoming messages that are from any blocked domains or contain specific character sets. For example, because anyone I know in Russia sends me email in English, I block any other message that arrives in the Russian Cyrillic character set. Figure 14-20 shows a typical example of a message that ended up in my Junk E-Mail folder for this reason. As it happens, this message is pretty innocent because (according to Yahoo! Babel Fish translation), it's an invitation for me to use some professional bookkeeping services. However, even if the message isn't dangerous, I can't read Russian and don't need Russian email in my Inbox, so that's why messages using this character set are blocked.

- Run the junk mail filter to detect messages that have gotten this far but might still be spam.

The result of the filter is a ranking (think of a number between 1 and 100, where 100 means that the message is absolutely spam) that Outlook uses to determine whether a message is spam. If you opt for Low protection, Outlook is cautious, and the ranking has to be very high before Outlook regards a message as spam. If you opt for a High level of protection, Outlook is more aggressive and moves the ranking bar downward.

As you can see in Figure 14-20, information in the message header informs you about the actions that Outlook took to remove potentially dangerous content from messages that end up in the Junk E-Mail folder. Messages are converted to plain text and all links to Web sites are disabled. This prevents users from accidently clicking live links in messages when they review messages in the Junk E-Mail folder and being brought to sites that they probably don't want to visit. Removing links also prevents "Web beacons" from working. These are invisible links that spammers use as a form of "phone home" signal to let them know when messages have been received by a live address. Because they know that a live address is in use, these addresses are much more valuable to spammers than addresses made up in an attempt to batter their way into a company. If a user attempts to use a link, Outlook signals the warning shown in Figure 14-21. The user can ignore better judgement and move the message back to the Inbox if he really wants to use the link, but hopefully good sense will prevail.

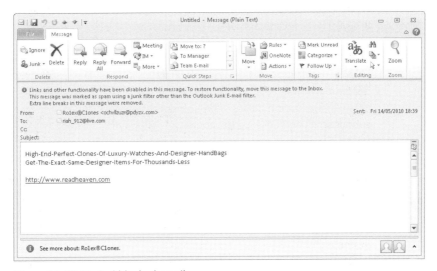

Figure 14-20 Typical blocked email.

Figure 14-21 Warning about disabled links.

Outlook's junk mail filter is pretty effective at blocking spam that gets through the Exchange anti-spam agents and gets better with each version. It even works when you attempt to recover a message from the deleted items cache; if Outlook thinks that the message is spam, it will not recover the message. If you use BlackBerry or Windows Mobile handheld, you get an idea of how much spam is suppressed by Outlook because the spam that gets through the server-side anti-spam agents is delivered to the handheld. It is annoying that you receive the spam on the handheld, but this demonstrates that Outlook has to download messages before it can detect junk email; you then realize how effective the junk mail filter is because the spam you see on the handheld does not appear in Outlook's Inbox.

Although Outlook's junk mail filter works well most of the time, occasionally you will find that Outlook moves messages into the Junk E-Mail folder when you think that the message is perfectly legitimate. The opposite situation also occurs and spam ends up in the Inbox, despite being totally obvious spam to the human eye. Either situation might cause you to question the effectiveness of the junk mail filter. Here are some reasons why these situations occur:

- Messages generated by applications are regarded as spam: Examples include expense reports, notifications from Microsoft SharePoint Portal Server, subscription updates, distributions from newsgroups, and so on. Messages like this are often generated when an application makes an unauthenticated SMTP connection to a server to submit email and because the connection is unauthenticated, they are suspicious because spammers might have attempted to hijack what seems to be a perfectly valid internal email address and use it for their purposes. In addition, the content of automatically generated messages might contain little text context, have URLs for pointers to application data, and lack a From: field specified in their header, all of which are indications that a message might be spam. The solution is to add the sending address to the Safe Senders list or have the administrator of the application change it to use an authenticated SMTP connection.

- Obvious spam that is not caught by the filter: This might simply be due to a new tactic created by a spammer to outwit filters; unfortunately spammers succeed in this respect all the time. In a company that operates a comprehensive anti-spam defense, you can expect to see one or two messages a week sneak through. Anything more is an indication that the defenses need to be updated. For example, you might need to download and install the latest version of the Outlook junk mail filter data file.

- Illogical message moves between folders: If you still use mailbox rules to process incoming messages, you can encounter a condition where Outlook downloads message headers (to provide sufficient data for rules to process messages) and then proceeds to download the full content (required for the junk mail filter to process messages), only to find that rules move some messages to specific folders followed by a subsequent move to the Junk E-Mail folder after Outlook has run the junk mail filter. The behavior is logical in computer terms, but the result can baffle users.

Given that spammers invent new techniques to get past filters all the time, even the best anti-spam defenses let some messages through. You can capture addresses from messages that you know to be spam and add these addresses or complete domains to the Blocked Senders list to gradually build up your own list of spammers. You can export any of the Safe Sender, Blocked Sender, and Safe Recipients lists to a text file that can then be imported by another user.

The use of the Blocked Senders and Safe Senders list is apparent, but the purpose of the Safe Recipients list is less so. Essentially, a safe recipient is a way to identify messages sent to a particular destination, often a distribution list or newsgroup that you are part of and from which you want to receive messages. You do not control the membership of the list or group, but you assume that whoever administers the list will make sure that it is not used for spam and that therefore any message that is addressed to the list is safe. If you couldn't mark the list as being safe, then Outlook might assume that its messages are spam and so suppress them. By marking the address of the list or any other similar address as a Safe Recipient you tell Outlook that it can ignore messages from this address when it applies its filters.

Exchange uses the contents of a user's Blocked Senders and Safe Senders lists in tandem with the SCL and PCL values set by the Content Filter agent as it process messages. As discussed earlier, the SCL indicates how strongly Exchange believes that the message is spam, and the PCL indicates whether it might be a phishing message. If a message gets to Outlook, it means that Exchange considers it to be reasonably safe, as otherwise Exchange will have suppressed the message either at a transport server or when it arrived into the mailbox store. The Store checks the Blocked Senders list for each mailbox as it delivers messages and suppresses messages if it matches the address of the sender against the list, so Outlook never gets to process these messages (suppression at this point saves Outlook the overhead of having to download the messages to process them locally). The Store uses the Safe Senders list to check messages with a high SCL to see whether the user wants to receive messages from the originator, and if the Store finds that an address is on the Safe Senders list, it passes the message and Outlook can pick it up the next time it synchronizes the Inbox.

Outlook's Automatic Picture Download setting (available through Outlook's Trust Center) controls whether Outlook downloads pictures and other graphics automatically in email. The default is not to download, and there is no good reason to change this setting. You can control whether to download from sites in specific Internet zones or for messages from trusted senders, so if you expect to get lots of email from a graphically rich site like eBay, you can always add it to your Safe Senders list. The Automatic Picture Download setting is supported in Outlook 2003, Outlook 2007, and Outlook 2010. See TechNet for the latest advice about how best to accomplish this task using Group Policies and the Office Customization Tool.

Chapter 14

INSIDE OUT   No more postmarks

Outlook 2007 introduced the ability to stamp messages with computationally intense postmarks to signal to recipients that a message is not spam, even if it exhibited some of the signs commonly seen in spam. The idea was that adding postmarks would slow down operations too much for spammers to send millions of messages on the basis that they are happy if a small percentage get through and cause a response. Outlook stored its postmarks in X-headers containing a computational puzzle and a hashed version of the answer generated by the client. Microsoft has removed the postmark capability from Outlook 2010, mostly because the initiative received slim support elsewhere in the industry. However, postmarks generated by Outlook 2007 clients are processed by the Exchange 2010 content filter agent, and the presence of a properly solved puzzle causes the agent to reduce the SCL rating for the message.

Cleansed email, but compliant?

The transport service is happy to process as many squeaky-clean messages as you care to send its way. Some of those messages will be of interest to those charged with the responsibility of ensuring that a company complies with whatever regulatory or legislative requirements it has to meet. Exchange 2010 offers a broad range of features that you can use to enforce compliance and to investigate and prove compliance (or lack of it) after the fact. Compliance is the next stop on our odyssey through Exchange 2010.

T HE need to achieve compliance with legal and regulatory requirements is a fact of corporate life today. Legislation such as the Sarbanes-Oxley Act in the United States has influenced many other countries to introduce similar requirements to keep records that show when something was done and by whom. Microsoft started on the process to build records management capability into Microsoft Exchange Server 2007 with the introduction of managed folders. However, users (and many administrators) didn't really understand the purpose of managed folders and compliance was weak. To address these issues and to provide a true basis for compliance, Microsoft Exchange Server 2010 introduces its own features, including the following:

- The ability to audit administrator actions

- The provision of archive mailboxes

- The ability to create and apply retention policies to items and folders

- The ability to recover items even if a user has deleted them from the dumpster

- The ability to place mailboxes on retention hold or litigation hold

There is a big difference between retention hold and litigation hold (also referred to as legal hold) that we need to be clear about when we discuss compliance. Retention hold means that any retention policies that are in force on a mailbox are suspended, normally when the mailbox owner is unable to process messages for a period. Litigation hold is a totally different feature that is designed to capture all edit and delete operations for a mailbox inside the dumpster so that a user cannot affect or eliminate data that might be required by a discovery action. If you put a mailbox on litigation hold, you nullify the effect of retention hold because the effect of any retention policies is suspended. Wise administrators take advice and guidance from the company's legal department before they place a mailbox on retention or litigation hold to ensure that the action complies with any legal requirements that are in force and does not compromise any document retention policies that are in effect. There's no point in enabling a feature that collects unneeded or unwanted data.

The features just listed are not exhaustive, as other Exchange features can be associated with compliance. For example, transport rules allow a disclaimer to be appended to every outgoing message that can limit liability by complying with rules that say that messages from a company must contain specific contact or other information about the company. The point is that compliance is an area that continues to evolve. There is no doubt that Microsoft will update the Exchange feature set over time to satisfy the broadest possible set of requirements. However, it is unreasonable to expect any software to deliver a complete answer. For example, although you can place mailboxes on litigation hold or establish an extended deleted item retention period to ensure that important information is not deleted, you also need to figure out the administrative procedures to handle situations such as mailbox retention following the death of an employee. Handling situations like this is reasonably straightforward (disable the account, hide the user's mailbox from the Global Address List [GAL], and keep it and any archives—including PSTs that you recover from the user's PC—until any legal hold period is passed) as long as you think everything through.

With that cheerful thought in mind, let's review the new compliance features in Exchange 2010 and explore the updated functionality available for older compliance features such as transport rules and journaling.

The joy of legal discovery

Legal discovery actions have been around for centuries. Over the last two decades, we have seen the focus of discovery or searches for information pertinent to a legal case begin to shift from paper evidence to electronic evidence. This shift reflects the different manner in which organizations store data today. We still have filing cabinets stuffed full of paper, but much of the correspondence that companies conducted by letter, fax, and telex is now sent by email, so the focus for discovery has to accommodate both paper and electronic media.

Discovery actions for email systems first began in the mid-1980s. At that time messages were recovered from backup tapes and printed for lawyers to review. The process was dreadfully expensive and time consuming. The only mitigating factor was that it was much easier to determine who might have sent an incriminating message because relatively few people in a company had email and the overall volume of email was low. Messages were text only and tended to be short. It was therefore possible to satisfy a judge's order to retrieve all messages for ten specific users over a month without running up an extraordinarily high bill.

Today's environment is obviously different. Many more users are typically hosted on each server, they send and receive an ever-increasing volume of messages, and those messages contain many different types of attachments, including video and audio files. The result of living in the age of electronic communication is that the cost of legal discovery is higher because there is more information to process. In March 2009, Fortune Magazine reported that the court-appointed trustee of bankrupt Lehman Brothers, Inc. had captured 3.2 billion email and instant messages occupying 1.4 TB. This isn't an unusual amount, as the FBI investigation of Enron in 2001 reviewed 31 TB of data and ended up using 4 TB as evidence. Email is a critical means of business communication that has replaced telexes, faxes, and written letters in many respects, so legal discovery of email has moved from an out-of-the-ordinary situation to something that is extremely common, whether it is to satisfy a legal or regulatory requirement, respond to a subpoena, or deal with an internal matter concerning employee ethics, harassment, or discipline.

The first generation of Exchange offered no way to keep mail around after it was deleted, which meant that you had to restore a database from a backup if you wanted to recover a message, whether it was needed to satisfy a legal order or because a user had deleted it in error. Gradually Microsoft began to add new features to Exchange to help. The original version of the "dumpster" as implemented in Exchange 2000 through Exchange 2007 provides a two-phase delete process where messages are marked as deleted but kept in the database until their retention period expires, at which time they are removed. The initial operation is a "soft delete," the latter is a "hard delete." Note that folder structures are not respected in the dumpster, as messages are "flattened" into a single repository. In other words, if you delete ten folders, each of which holds 2,000 items, and then realize that you should not have deleted one of the folders, you will have to recover the 2,000 items for that folder from the 20,000 items that are put into the dumpster. As we will see in the section "Dumpster 2.0 arrives" later in this chapter, Exchange 2010 includes an enhanced dumpster with some useful new features.

Journaling made its appearance in Exchange 2003 and was upgraded in Exchange 2007. However, the functionality offered by Exchange was basic, and most companies that invested in products to capture and archive messages went for purpose-designed products such as Symantec's Enterprise Vault, Mimosa Systems' (a division of Iron Mountain) NearPoint, or the HP Information Archive. Microsoft added managed folders in Exchange 2007 with the idea that administrators could create folders that are distributed to mailboxes for users to store important items. The contents of these folders are managed through policies, and it is possible to create procedures to harvest information from these folders on a regular basis. Not many companies used managed folders, and it is an example of a reasonable idea with a good purpose that collapsed when it was exposed to the acid usability test of real-life deployment outside Microsoft.

The compliance features in Exchange 2007 were a start and provided useful feedback from the companies that deployed managed folders. However, the overall experience was not compelling enough to generate widespread usage of the compliance features, which then led Microsoft to deliver a new set of features in Exchange 2010 and then further enhance the features in SP1. At TechEd and other events, Microsoft presenters acknowledge that many vendors have been actively selling archive solutions for Exchange for nearly a decade and that some offer much more developed functionality than Exchange 2010, especially in areas such as workflow, their ability to archive information taken from other sources, and the experience that companies have with these products in integrating the archival process with regulations. They go on to characterize the target market for Exchange 2010 archiving as the vast majority of the installed base that:

- Does not use archiving today.

- Depends on PSTs as a "relief valve" for restrictive mailbox quotas.

- Relies on tape/disk backups to respond to requests to recover data from users or to respond to discovery actions; this is obviously a very costly and time-intensive method.

Microsoft has to convince customers that having integrated archiving and search incorporated into an email server is a better solution than dedicated archiving and search applications that have been in use and developed over many years. It can be argued that cost is one key Microsoft advantage because archiving is available at the price of an enterprise Client Access License (CAL) that might be already acquired. The cost of an enterprise CAL for each user will often be lower than the cost of dedicated archiving software plus any additional hardware that is required to run the archiving software. This argument works if the functionality available in Exchange 2010 meets your requirements but fails if it doesn't. Microsoft makes the point that they work closely with third-party software developers to ensure that the widest possible choice is available to customers, and it will be interesting to see how vendors such as Symantec and Mimosa cooperate and compete with Microsoft in this area over the next few years.

Personal archives

A personal archive is an extension of a user's primary mailbox that provides an online archive facility. It is also referred to as an archive mailbox. The name might cause some confusion with the personal archives that users create with PST files for Outlook. The big difference is that the Exchange archive is integrated into the Information Store, and the data held in the archive are therefore accessible using all the features available to mailboxes, including discovery searches. By comparison, PST archives are confined to a PC, and the data that they contain are inaccessible to server-based processing. Indeed, Outlook's AutoArchive feature can be argued to conflict with the archiving functionality now available in Exchange because it focuses on moving items from server-based folders into PSTs, whereas a central point of Exchange-based archiving is the elimination, whenever possible, of PSTs. For that reason, you might want to consider using group policy settings to disable the use of AutoArchive.

Exchange 2010 originally restricted the location of the personal archive to the same database that hosts the primary mailbox. From Exchange 2010 SP1 onward you can elect to have the archive in a separate database that can be on a completely different server, provided that the database is located on a server in the same Active Directory site as the primary mailbox. The archive can be in a database managed by a different Database Availability Group (DAG) if the Active Directory site supports multiple DAGs.

> **Note**
>
> The archive can also be on a mailbox server that is not part of a DAG, although in this case you should be concerned about data protection because only one copy exists of the database that holds the personal archive.

Finally, if you use the Microsoft Exchange Online service (part of the Office 365 suite), the personal archive can be stored "in the cloud," an option that might prove increasingly attractive as companies gain more experience and confidence with cloud-based services (this feature will be made available after Microsoft upgrades its Exchange Online service to use Exchange 2010 , expected in early 2011). It is attractive to be able to hive off personal archives to a cloud-based service because this allows you to remain focused on the care and maintenance of production mailboxes while the hosting provider takes care of the archives. Whatever option is chosen, a mailbox can have just one personal archive, and each personal archive requires that the mailbox has an enterprise CAL.

Microsoft views personal archives as the natural replacement for PSTs, which were never designed to function as user archives. The growth of messages and the reluctance of administrators to increase mailbox quotas—coupled with the inability of Exchange and its clients to deal elegantly with very large mailboxes (5 GB and upward)—meant that most organizations were forced to use PSTs to offload data from the online store. Users do like to behave like human pack rats and keep messages, even if they never look at them again (some estimate that a message filed into a PST has a 99 percent chance of never being looked at again after six months). Other problems with PST management typically cited in corporate messaging deployments include the following.

- **Reduced security** PSTs are personal stores, but users keep just about anything in them, including sensitive and usually unencrypted corporate information ranging from budgets to presentations about new products to performance reviews. If someone loses a laptop—or even a USB device that has a PST on it—that information is immediately exposed and potentially available to anyone who finds the device and accesses it. Even if protected by a password, the PST file structure is insecure and can be quickly cracked using utilities commonly available on the Internet. Once the password is bypassed, a PST can be opened using any Microsoft Outlook client.

- **Inability to respond to discovery actions** Information held on a PST is usually invisible to searches that a company performs to respond to discovery requests. This is fine if the information is personal or irrelevant to the discovery request, but it could be very expensive if required information is not disclosed to a court and is subsequently discovered.

- **Inability to apply policy** Many companies have a data retention policy that requires users to delete documents and messages after a certain period. The period may vary depending on the type of information contained in different items. In any case, the company loses any ability to apply policy centrally once a user moves an item from his mailbox into a PST.

- **Exposure to data loss** Laptop disks are notoriously prone to failure. If users don't back up their data, any disk crash exposes them to potential data loss, and that information might be important.

The alternative solution to increasing disk quota for mailboxes in previous versions of Exchange was to buy and deploy a dedicated third-party archiving solution such as Symantec Enterprise Vault. Using PSTs is obviously far cheaper for a company. It's also easier for users because they control how many PSTs they create and how they use them. Some create a separate PST for each year; some create a PST for each major project. However, the big downside is that PSTs then expose the company to the risks previously described. Even so, it will take time to pry user fingers from their beloved PSTs.

Exchange personal archives are not perfect, and a number of limitations exist that could hinder deployment, including the following.

- Exchange 2010 does not support delegate access to a personal archive. Users can delegate access to their primary mailbox, but the same delegation does not carry through to the archive. This is an issue for assistants who support executives. You can impose retention policies to force items to move into the archive, but the mailbox owner is the only person who can manage the items afterward (and few executives will have the time or interest for this work). Exchange 2010 SP1 supports delegate access to the personal archive; when you enable delegate access to a mailbox, delegates are automatically granted access to the mailbox's personal archive.

- You cannot transfer an archive to another mailbox. If a user leaves and you delete her mailbox, the archive disappears, too. You can save data by exporting items from the archive (and the primary mailbox) to a PST and then importing them back into the personal archive of another user, but it would be more elegant to be able to transfer the archive intact.

- You cannot copy or move sections of the archive to transfer it to another user. For example, a user who wants to transfer responsibility for a project to another user has to extract and provide the folders and other items relating to the project from his archive and provide them to the other user. Again, the workaround is to export selected folders from the personal archive to a PST and provide the PST to the other user (or import the PST into her archive).

- You cannot assign permissions on a folder level within the archive to allow users to give access to parts of their archive to other users. In fact, there is no permissions model for the archive yet.

These are examples of areas where Microsoft will doubtless consider enhancements in the future. It's likely that they will wait to see how archives are used in practical terms within customer deployments before they plan how archives will evolve in future releases of Exchange.

Enabling a personal archive

Before you can create and use personal archives with Exchange 2010, you have to deploy clients that support the feature. When first introduced, Microsoft Outlook 2010 (Figure 15-1) and Outlook Web App were the only clients that supported personal archives. The need to deploy a new version of Outlook proved to be a significant deployment blocker for many companies, so Microsoft announced their intention to provide an upgrade for Outlook 2007 with the code necessary to detect that a mailbox had an associated personal archive and then display it in the list of available mailbox resources. At the time of writing, Microsoft has not yet released the upgraded code for Outlook 2007, but it is expected to work in much the same way as Outlook 2010 interacts with personal archives.

The easiest way to assign a personal archive to a mailbox is when you create the mailbox (Figure 15-2). The SP1 version of Exchange Management Console (EMC) allows you to select a different database to host the personal archive, providing that the database is not mounted on an Exchange 2010 RTM server. Interestingly, if you place the personal mailbox in a different database, Exchange automatically transfers the dumpster to the personal archive to minimize the size of the primary mailbox.

Chapter 15

Figure 15-1 Archive mailbox in Outlook Web App.

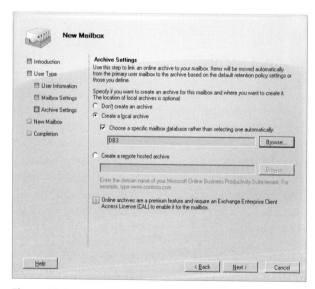

Figure 15-2 Creating a personal archive with a new mailbox.

INSIDE OUT
You won't lose access to personal archives if there is a server failure

EMC restricts the databases that you can choose to hold the personal archive to those that are mounted on servers in the same site. However, Exchange supports an exception to this rule when a database transfers to a server in another site following a failure. In this case, the CAS will redirect clients to the personal archive in the database in the other site using a cross-site connection for as long as the database is hosted in that site. You won't want to use cross-site connections for an extended period, and normal connections will resume after you switch the database that contains the personal archive back to a server in its original site. You can also see the option displayed by EMC to allow the personal archive to be hosted by Office 365 when this feature is supported by Microsoft for their Exchange Online service.

To enable an archive when you create a mailbox with EMS, you simply add the *–Archive* parameter to the New-Mailbox cmdlet. See Chapter 6, "Managing Mail-Enabled Recipients," for a full discussion about how to create new mailboxes.

You can also enable a personal archive for existing mailboxes by selecting a mailbox in EMC and then selecting the Enable Archive option in the action pane. EMC warns you that enabling this feature requires an enterprise CAL, and if you click OK, the mailbox is enabled. You can also enable a personal archive for an existing mailbox with Exchange Management Shell (EMS). For example:

```
Enable-Mailbox –Identity 'Tony Redmond' –Archive
```

You cannot archive mailboxes that use managed folders

You can enable an archive for room and equipment mailboxes, which seems a little strange. However, you cannot enable an archive for a mailbox that has been assigned a managed folders policy (Figure 15-3). Managed folders provide the basis for messaging records management in Exchange 2007, but they are superseded by retention policies in Exchange 2010. Retention policies work closely with archive mailboxes and are the future basis for Exchange messaging records management. Given these facts, the developers decided not to support archives for mailboxes that use managed folders.

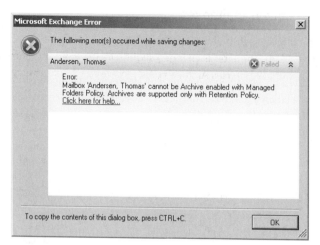

Figure 15-3 Exchange can't enable a personal archive because the mailbox uses managed folders.

Scanning mailboxes that are in managed folders

As part of your preparation for the deployment of personal archives, you can scan for mailboxes that are assigned a managed folders policy. On the surface, you'd expect that using some code to look for any mailbox that doesn't have a null value in its managed folders mailbox policy property would do the trick. For example:

```
Get-Mailbox -Filter {ManagedFolderMailboxPolicy -ne $Null} | Select Name,
ManagedFolderMailboxPolicy
```

This code returns a list of mailboxes, but it's flawed because it includes any mailbox that was assigned a managed folders mailbox policy in the past, even if the managed folders policy was subsequently removed from the mailbox and replaced by an archive mailbox. Better code that produces the right results by filtering out archive-enabled mailboxes is:

```
Get-Mailbox -Filter {ManagedFolderMailboxPolicy -ne $Null -and ArchiveName -eq $Null}
| Select Name, ManagedFolderMailboxPolicy
```

You can remove the MRM 1.0 policy from a mailbox with a command like this:

```
Set-Mailbox -Identity 'Andersen, Thomas' -ManagedFolderMailboxPolicy $Null
```

> **Note**
> It is possible to enable a personal archive for a room or resource mailbox. I cannot quite think of why anyone might want to maintain an archive for a room or resource mailbox, but I'm sure that someone will come up with a good reason in time.

Filtering for archived mailboxes

EMC includes a canned filter to allow you to see the mailboxes that already have archive mailboxes (Figure 15-4). The filter is changed slightly in SP1 from the one used in the original release of Exchange 2010 (Has Archive = Yes) because SP1 can host personal archives on an on-premise or hosted service.

You can also use the Get-Recipient or Get-Mailbox cmdlets to search for mailboxes that have an archive. For example:

```
Get-Mailbox –Filter {ArchiveName –ne $Null} | Select Name, ArchiveName
```

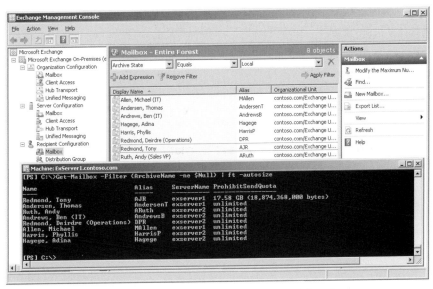

Figure 15-4 Displaying the list of personal archives in EMC and EMS.

Enabling the archive and its properties

Behind the scenes, EMC calls the Enable-Mailbox cmdlet to enable an archive. These commands first enable the personal archive for a mailbox and then retrieve the properties that Exchange maintains for an archive.

```
Enable-Mailbox –Identity 'Andy.Ruth@contoso.com' –Archive
Get-Mailbox –Identity 'Andy.Ruth@contoso.com' | Select Name, Arch*
```

```
Name               : Ruth, Andy
ArchiveGuid        : f7552939-8185-4634-824e-d4cd6241d674
ArchiveName        : {Online Archive –Ruth, Andy)}
ArchiveQuota       : unlimited
```

```
ArchiveWarningQuota : unlimited
ArchiveDomain       :
ArchiveDatabase     :
ArchiveStatus       : none
```

The first four properties listed here are always present for a mailbox after its archive is enabled. The globally unique identifier (GUID) identifies the archive mailbox within the database where it is stored. The default name for the archive is derived from the prefix "Online Archive" plus the mailbox's display name and can be changed afterward to whatever name you prefer. The archive quotas are inherited from the default values set for the database and reflect the values that Exchange uses to limit the amount of information in the archive and the point when it starts to issue warning messages.

You can alter these values with the Set-Mailbox cmdlet. For example:

```
Set-Mailbox -Identity 'Andy.Ruth@contoso.com' -ArchiveName "Andy's Splendid Online
Archive" -ArchiveQuota 2GB -ArchiveWarningQuota 1.9GB
```

The last three of the archive properties listed for the mailbox are introduced in Exchange 2010 SP1.

- *ArchiveDomain* is only used if the personal archive is stored on an Exchange Online server (Office 365). If used, the property holds the Simple Mail Transfer Protocol (SMTP) name of the hosted domain.

- *ArchiveStatus* contains a status value to indicate whether the personal archive has been created on an Exchange Online server.

- *ArchiveDatabase* is blank if the personal archive is stored in the same mailbox database as the primary mailbox; otherwise the property contains the name of the mailbox database that holds the archive.

Checking space usage

The amount of space used in an archive mailbox can be checked with the Get-MailboxStatistics cmdlet, which supports the –*Archive* parameter to tell it to report details of the archive mailbox rather than the primary mailbox. For example:

```
Get-MailboxStatistics -Identity 'John Smith' -Archive | Select DisplayName,
ItemCount, TotalItemSize, LastLogonTime
```

```
DisplayName                    ItemCount  TotalItemSize              LastLogonTime
-----------                    ---------  -------------              -------------
Online Archive - Smith, John... 128        31.51 MB (33,037,293 bytes) 4/14/2010 3:30:26 AM
```

Updating the name of an archive mailbox

You can also update the name of the archive mailbox through EMC. To do this, select the mailbox, click Properties, select Mailbox Features, and then select Archive from the list of mailbox features. However, although you can update the name (Figure 15-5), you can't update archive quotas through EMC, nor can you view details of the items stored or quota used in the archive mailbox.

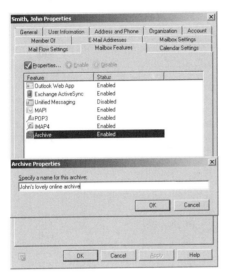

Figure 15-5 Updating the name of a personal archive through EMC.

Default archive policy

When you enable a personal archive for a mailbox, Exchange assigns a retention policy called Default Archive and Retention Policy to the mailbox to help the mailbox's owner use the archive by automatically moving items from the primary mailbox into the archive as their retention period expires. The retention period applied by the default tag in the policy is two years, so the effect of applying the policy is that any item that is not stamped with another tag will be moved into the archive after it is two years old. The retention policy assigned to the mailbox becomes effective the next time the Managed Folder Assistant processes the mailbox. The default policy is not assigned if the mailbox is already under the control of another retention policy. We discuss how to manipulate retention policies and tags in the "Messaging Records Management" section later in this chapter.

Originally, the RTM version of Exchange 2010 applied a different retention policy called Default Archive Policy that only contained archive tags. You'll find both policies are available, but Exchange 2010 SP1 now only uses the Default Archive and Retention Policy. As the name implies, the big difference between the two retention policies is that the Default Archive and Retention Policy contains both retention tags (those that affect how long an item is kept by Exchange) and archive tags (those that affect when an item is archived). Table 15-1 describes the retention and archive tags that are included in the default archive policy. You can add or delete retention and archive tags to the default archive and retention policy if required. You do not need to delete the older default archive policy. However, after upgrading an organization to Exchange 2010 SP1, you can check for mailboxes that have the older policy assigned to them and replace these assignments with the new default archive and retention policy.

Table 15-1 Tags included in default archive policy

Tag name	Type	Purpose
Default 2 year move to archive	Default	Automatically move items to the personal archive when they are two years old. This tag is applied to any item in the mailbox that does not have an explicit tag applied by the user or is inherited when an item moves into a folder that has a default policy.
Personal 1 year move to archive	Personal	Tag that the user can apply to items to instruct the Managed Folder Assistant to move the items into the personal archive after they are one year (365 days) old.
Personal 5 year move to archive	Personal	Tag that the user can apply to items to instruct the Managed Folder Assistant to move items into the personal archive after they are five years (1,825 days) old.
Personal never move to archive	Personal	Tag that the user can apply to items to block the Managed Folder Assistant from ever moving the items into the personal archive.
Recoverable Items 14 days move to archive	Recoverable Items folder	Move items placed in the Recoverable Items folder to the personal archive after 14 days.
1 Month Delete	Personal	Move items into the Recoverable Items folder after one month.
1 Week Delete	Personal	Move items into the Recoverable Items folder after one week.
6 Month Delete	Personal	Move items into the Recoverable Items folder after six months.
1 Year Delete	Personal	Move items into the Recoverable Items folder after one year.
5 Year Delete	Personal	Move items into the Recoverable Items folder after five years.
Never Delete	Personal	Disabled tag that prevents the Managed Folder Assistant from processing the item; the effect is to stop the item from ever being deleted.

The major impact of the application of the Default Archive and Retention Policy is that the Managed Folder Assistant will begin to move items into the personal archive after they are two years old. This leads to the "disappearing items" syndrome where users log problem reports that their mailbox is missing items. In the vast majority of cases, the missing items are found safe and sound in folders in the archive mailbox. It just takes time for users to realize that Exchange will move items automatically after they reach a certain age, so this underlines the importance of communication with the user community as you implement archive mailboxes.

Don't delete the default policy! Change it or create a custom retention policy.

You should not delete the Default Archive and Retention policy, because this will impact the processing performed by the Managed Folder Assistant for the mailboxes to which the policy is assigned. It's a better idea to create a custom archive and retention policy tailored to the needs of the company or to different groups of users and apply that policy to their mailboxes. In this case, the custom retention policy replaces the default archive policy. We discuss how to manipulate retention policies and tags later in this chapter.

Disabling a personal archive

You can disable an archive with the Disable-Mailbox cmdlet. For example:

```
Disable-Mailbox -Identity 'Smith, John' -Archive
```

EMS prompts for a confirmation before it proceeds unless you add the *–Confirm:$False* parameter. This is not a good idea unless you are absolutely sure that you want to disable the archive. When it disables an archive mailbox, the Store disconnects it from the primary mailbox and keeps it in the database until the deleted mailbox retention period expires.

Using a personal archive

Assuming that a personal archive is in place and a suitable client is at hand, working with items in a personal archive is just like working with items in the primary mailbox. You can create new items, reply to messages, move items around, and so on. After the archive mailbox is created, it is up to the user to populate it, most likely by using drag and drop to move folders or items from his primary mailbox. Administrators can import the complete contents of PSTs into a mailbox, but there are some limitations with this approach, as we discussed previously.

Exchange doesn't support offline access for data held in personal archives. In other words, when Outlook is configured to use cached Exchange mode, it has access only to the offline copies of the folders from the primary mailbox that are stored in the OST and uses background synchronization to keep those folders updated. This arrangement allows Outlook to continue to work through transient network interruptions. Outlook has to be able to connect to the server before it can work with a personal archive.

TROUBLESHOOTING

I can't access my personal archive when I'm offline.

If you want something to be available offline, you have to store it in the primary mailbox. The personal archive is designed to hold information that isn't always required immediately and you can wait until you can get back online to access it, so if you need something from the archive and know that you have to work offline (for example, on a road trip), then you have to plan ahead and move the desired items from the personal archive into the primary mailbox beforehand.

INSIDE OUT   Some personal archive issues

Exchange 2010 marks Microsoft's first venture into archive mailboxes, and it's inevitable that there will be some issues that implementers have to understand as they plan deployments.

The first and most obvious issue is the need for archive-aware clients to gain full advantage of the archive. If you have a large population of Outlook 2003 or Outlook 2007 clients, you need to plan for client upgrades to Outlook 2010 or decide whether Outlook Web App is a viable workaround for users who want to access an archive. As mentioned earlier, Microsoft has announced their intention to provide code that allows Outlook 2007 clients to access archive mailboxes, but nothing will be done for Outlook 2003.

Archive mailboxes require enterprise CALs. This might not be a problem if you use other features that require the enterprise CAL, but it can be an additional and unexpected cost if you only use standard CALs today. As noted in Chapter 5, "Exchange Management Console and Control Panel," you can use the Get-OrganizationConfig cmdlet or the EMC option to collect Organization Health information to report on the number of enterprise CALs that you require.

Microsoft has no client that can currently perform a client-side search across the contents of both primary mailboxes and archive mailboxes. Both Outlook and Outlook Web App limit the user to searching in either the primary or archive mailbox. This is somewhat more understandable in the case of Outlook that performs searches on the PC, especially when the client is configured in cached Exchange mode, as the contents of the archive mailbox are not replicated to the OST and are therefore not available when the user works offline. However, I cannot understand why a client like

Outlook Web App, which works online all the time and has access to the Exchange content indexes, cannot perform a search across both repositories. The logic might be that such a search could require access to two different servers if the primary and archive mailbox are located in separate databases, but it's not something that will make much sense to users.

The RTM version of Exchange 2010 does not support delegate access to archive mailboxes. This issue is addressed in SP1.

Messaging records management

Exchange 2007 introduced the messaging records management (MRM) system as its "business email" strategy to help users comply with regulatory and legal requirements. The idea is to provide a method for users to retain messages and attachments that are required business records. Another way of thinking about MRM is that it helps users keep control over mailboxes by automating the retention process; marked items are kept as long as required, whereas others can be automatically discarded when their retention period (otherwise known as the expiration limit) expires.

The key to success for any scheme that aims to alter user behavior is to make it as simple as possible while achieving maximum functionality. Exchange 2007 didn't quite meet this goal. Its version of MRM uses a set of managed folders that have policies attached to them. The folders can be one of the default mail folders (Inbox, Sent Items, and so on) or a specially created folder that can be used to store items that the business wishes to control. The Managed Folder Assistant (MFA) is responsible for the application of the policies attached to the folders. The MFA runs on a regular basis to process items in managed folders. Items are stamped with the retention policy that applies to the folder, and this dictates what happens to the items in the future. For example, if a policy is set on the Inbox to delete any item older than 60 days, the MFA will move items older than this limit to the Deleted Items folder.

Exchange 2007 MRM works if users are disciplined in their filing habits and understand the concept of managed folders. Some people like the structure imposed by managed folders because it creates a structured approach to work. The problem is that the vast majority of Exchange users are relatively undisciplined when it comes to filing, and they do not wish to spend time moving items around unless it's necessary to delete items or move them into a PST to get their mailbox size under quota so that they can send or receive new messages. Indeed, the radically better search facilities that are available in recent versions of Exchange and Outlook encourage users never to refile anything because they can always search for an item when required. In addition, Exchange is able to handle very large folders that hold tens of thousands of items, so the imperative to refile items to achieve acceptable performance does not exist. The combination of human nature and better software conspired to make Exchange 2007 MRM ineffective in real terms. Microsoft therefore needed to change its tactics to provide a workable implementation of MRM for Exchange 2010.

The new approach to messaging records management in Exchange 2010

Managed folders persist in Exchange 2010, but only for backward compatibility. The future of Exchange-based MRM lies in a structure created by retention tags and policies. Retention tags can be applied to any item in any folder to specify what action Exchange should take for the item when its retention period expires. Supported actions include the hard (permanent) or soft (recoverable) deletion of the item, moving the item to a personal archive, or flagging the item for user attention. Retention policies group retention tags together in a convenient manner to allow administrators to apply policies to mailboxes rather than having to assign individual retention tags to folders. Retention tags and policies are organization-wide objects that are stored in Active Directory and can therefore be applied to any mailbox in the organization after they are created. Just like Exchange 2007, the MFA is responsible for checking mailbox contents against policy and taking whatever action is determined by policy for items that exceed their retention period.

This all sounds like a workable solution. The only issue is that Microsoft didn't ship any GUI to allow administrators to set up and manage retention tags and policies in the RTM release of Exchange 2010. Instead, you have to perform all management of retention tags and policies through EMS until you deploy Exchange 2010 SP1, which includes the necessary GUI in its version of EMC. In addition, Exchange 2010 SP1 includes a set of retention and archive tags such as "1 Month Delete" (items stamped with this tag are moved into the Deleted Items folder after one month) that you can use as a starting point to develop your own retention policies.

Types of retention tags

Table 15-2 describes the three types of retention tags supported by Exchange 2010. The "type" shown in the third column is a value passed to the *–Type* parameter when you create a new tag with the New-RetentionPolicyTag cmdlet. Exchange uses this value to understand the scope of the items in a user mailbox to which it can apply the tag.

Table 15-2 **Types of retention tags**

Tag type	Context	Type
Retention policy tags (RPT)	Administrators can apply these tags to default mailbox folders such as the Inbox, Sent Items, and Deleted Items. In Exchange 2010 SP1, tags cannot be applied to the Tasks and Contacts folders. If an RPT is assigned to a default folder, all items in the folder automatically come under the control of the tag unless the user applies a personal tag to the item. Only one RPT can be assigned per default folder.	DeletedItems Drafts Inbox JunkMail Journal Notes Outbox SentItems All
Default policy tags (DPT)	A catch-all tag that the MFA applies to any item that does not inherit a tag from its parent folder or has not had a tag explicitly applied to it by the user. In other words, if no other tag applies to an item, Exchange will respect the instructions contained in the default tag. A retention policy only includes a single DPT that is used to delete items; you can specify another to control the default movement of items into the personal archive. It's logical but sometimes overlooked that if you specify two DPTs in a policy, the tag that moves items into the archive must have a shorter retention period than the tag that deletes items.	All
Personal tags	Users can apply these tags to nondefault folders and individual items in a mailbox. Personal tags that move items into the archive can also be applied to default folders. Personal tags mark an item with an explicit retention, usually to comply with a business requirement. For example, you might use an "Audit" tag to mark items that users are compelled to retain for audit purposes. A retention policy can include many different personal tags.	Personal

You'll notice that some default folders that you expect to find in every mailbox are excluded from the list of folders that support retention policy tags. The RTM version of Exchange 2010 doesn't allow retention policy tags to be applied to the Calendar, Contacts, Journal, Notes, and Tasks folders. However, items in these folders were covered by the default retention policy and so could be removed unexpectedly.

INSIDE OUT   There is a way to create retention policy tags for calendars

Microsoft's thinking on the subject evolved in Exchange 2010 SP1, and you can now use the New Retention Policy Tag Wizard to create retention policy tags for almost all of the default folders. Although the wizard interface allows you to select the Contacts folder and create a tag, this is really a bug, and the MFA ignores any tag placed on

Contacts. Somewhat bizarrely, the wizard interface does not allow you to select the Calendar folder to create a retention policy tag for it, but you can create a retention policy tag for the Calendar with the New-RetentionPolicyTag cmdlet. Perhaps the logic here is that you should be careful when applying a retention policy to user calendars because users often want to keep the items stored in these folders for longer than items in other folders, so you are forced to do more work to create a retention policy tag for the calendar. After all, no one will thank you if you clean out the CEO's calendar after 120 days! Once you create the retention policy tag for the calendar with EMS, you can manage it as normal with EMC, and you can include it in retention policies and apply it to mailboxes.

Overall, the set of default folders covered by Exchange 2010 SP1 is much broader than before and includes those where items often accumulate without users noticing, such as the Sync Issues and RSS Feeds folders, so you can now create and apply retention tags that clear out these folders for users automatically. You can see the list of folders for which you can create retention policy tags in Exchange 2010 SP1 in Figure 15-6. The All Other Folders In The Mailbox choice is used when you create a default policy tag.

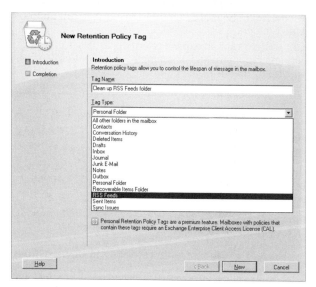

Figure 15-6 Listing of folders for which you can create retention policy tags.

INSIDE OUT   Some items are timeless

Items in some of these folders tend to be more "timeless" than general-purpose messages, so you should be careful to think through the potential consequences when you create retention policy tags for folders such the Journal or RSS Feeds. For example, how long do users reasonably want to keep items in the Drafts folder? Some users like to keep drafts for a long time because it's their practice to create a message and compose it through multiple edits over time before they decide whether they want to send it. Others view the Drafts folder as strictly transient and never keep items there for longer than a day or so. For this reason, it might be best to create retention policy tags that mark some items to "never expire." This is done by setting the tag to be disabled rather than giving it a retention period. When an item is stamped with a disabled retention tag, it tells the MFA that it should ignore the item and the item will therefore never be processed.

Retention tags cannot be applied to items directly. They first have to be assigned to a retention policy and the retention policy assigned, in turn, to the mailboxes that you want to manage. A retention tag can be reused several times in different policies. Although there is no practical limit to the number of retention tags that you can define for an organization, it makes sense to create a set of tags that can be shared and reused between retention policies rather than creating separate tags for each policy.

Exchange can only apply one retention policy tag and one archive tag to an item. Two simple rules are used when Exchange evaluates policies that it can apply to an item. The first rule states that the policy with the longest retention period always wins and is intended to ensure that Exchange never deletes an item before its time truly expires. The second rule is that an explicit policy is always respected ahead of an implicit or default policy. In other words, if you apply a personal tag to an item to retain it for six years and the default retention policy for the folder requires deletion after 12 months, the item will be kept for six years. Retention tags can be placed on items, conversations, or complete folders, and they are transferred with items if you move them between folders.

> **Note**
> When you apply a tag to a conversation, you really just apply the tag to the items that make up the conversation at that point in time. Exchange knows that the items are part of the conversation and is able to apply the tag, but it won't look for and tag new items as they arrive and join the conversation. This is because a conversation is not a real storage container within a mailbox and therefore cannot be tagged permanently. In short, tags only exist in a persistent manner for folders and individual items.

Chapter 15

Of course, to make any sense of retention policies, you also need to deploy clients that include the necessary intelligence and user interface. At the time of writing, the only clients in this category are Outlook 2010 and Outlook Web App. As we'll see when we review how retention policies function from a user perspective, Outlook's user interface provides the richest views of retention policies and tags. Outlook Web App is less capable, but still highly usable.

System tags

Exchange 2010 supports two types of retention tags: system tags and nonsystem tags. System tags are used by Exchange for its own purposes and are not shown when you run the Get-RetentionPolicyTag cmdlet unless you specify the *–IncludeSystemTags* parameter. By default, Get-RetentionPolicyTag only lists nonsystem tags (those created to be used with normal retention policies). To see the system tags defined in an organization, you can execute this command (nonsystem tags will be listed afterward):

```
Get-RetentionPolicyTag -IncludeSystemTags | Format-Table Name, Type, SystemTag
```

Name	Type	SystemTag
AutoGroup	Personal	True
ModeratedRecipients	Personal	True
Personal 1 Year move to archive	Personal	False
Default 2 year move to archive	All	False
Personal 5 year move to archive	Personal	False
Personal never move to archive	Personal	False

The first two entries (AutoGroup and ModeratedRecipients) are system tags that are used by Exchange to prevent items from accumulating in arbitration mailboxes. The tags instruct the MFA to clean out these mailboxes as items expire. To see details of the retention policy used for arbitration mailboxes and its links to the two system tags, run these commands:

```
Get-RetentionPolicy -Identity 'ArbitrationMailbox'
Get-RetentionPolicyTag -Identity 'AutoGroup'
Get-RetentionPolicyTag -Identity 'ModeratedRecipients'
```

The last four entries are nonsystem tags that belong to the Default Archive and Retention Policy. Exchange automatically applies this policy after a personal archive is enabled for a mailbox. The idea is to provide a set of tags to allow users to control how items are moved into the archive. The tags are revealed by clients after the user's mailbox is processed by the next run of the MFA. The default archive policy is replaced when another retention policy is applied to a mailbox.

> **CAUTION**
>
> You cannot add system tags to a retention policy that's applied to user mailboxes. Deleting a system tag is also a bad thing as you have no idea of what potential consequences might follow from this event.

Designing a retention policy

Many different retention policy tags can exist within an organization. This allows great flexibility in creating appropriate policies for different groups that work within a company. For example, the finance department might want Exchange to permanently delete everything in the Deleted Items folder more than three days old (the shred principle), whereas users in other departments are not concerned if items survive in the Deleted Items folder for 30 days or more. You can apply a retention policy to members of the finance department that includes a retention policy tag for the Deleted Items folder that instructs the MFA to remove items after three days. The same policy might include a personal tag that allows members of the finance department to mark items that have to be archived for audit purposes after a month in the primary mailbox. The MFA will move items with this tag to the archive mailbox when it processes the mailbox.

Chapter 15

> **Why are you creating this retention policy?**
>
> Before you rush to create a retention policy for anyone—even the finance department—you should sit down and determine the why, when, and how for the policy:
>
> - Why you are implementing the policy? What business need will the policy serve?
>
> - When will you implement the policy? What mailboxes will the policy be applied to? How will you communicate the policy to end users so that they understand the purpose of the policy and how it will affect the contents of their mailboxes?
>
> - How will you implement the policy? What tags and types of tags are required? What actions will you enforce through tags and what retention periods are used? Do any restrictions exist as a result of other aspects of your deployment? For example, if you use an archiving product from another vendor, you cannot deploy tags to move items into an archive mailbox after a designated period.

The design for a retention policy might be captured in a simple table format that makes it clear what tags are included in the policy, their purpose, and the folders that are processed by the MFA. Apart from its other advantages, capturing the design like this makes it easier to communicate the policy to users. Table 15-3 lays out a simple policy that could be applied to help managers cope with overloaded mailboxes.

Table 15-3 **Laying out a retention policy**

Retention Policy Name:	***Management retention policy***		
Applies to:	***Mailboxes with CustomAttribute7 = "Management"***		
General purpose:	*Automatic clean-out of Inbox and Sent Items folders to encourage users to keep these folders tidy. Items in all other folders can remain in place for a year. Removal of items from the Deleted Items folder after a week and permanent removal of anything filed into the Junk Mail folder after two days. A tag is provided to allow users to mark items for retention for five years.*		
Tag name	*Tag type*	*Applies to*	*Action*
RPT-Inbox	RPT	Inbox folder	Move items to Recoverable Items after 30 days
RPT-SentItems	RPT	Sent Items	Move items to Recoverable Items after 30 days
RPT-Deleted	RPT	Deleted Items	Permanently remove items after 7 days
RPT-JunkMail	RPT	Junk Mail	Permanently remove items after 3 days
DPT-General	DPT	All folders	Move items to Recoverable Items after 365 days
PER-Retain	PER	All folders	Move items to Recoverable Items after 1,825 days (5 years)

Logically, you can only have a single RPT for each default folder within a retention policy. It would be very confusing to have two retention policies compete within a single folder! In addition, a retention policy can only have one default retention policy that applies to all folders.

INSIDE OUT   Keep it simple

Exchange allows you to create and apply as many retention policies as you want, but the question of long-term supportability arises. You should also consider the question of how many retention policies are really required for the organization as a whole and attempt to restrict the number to the minimum necessary to meet business needs. A couple of well-designed, logical policies that satisfy the vast bulk of requirements will be easier to create, deploy, and manage on an ongoing basis than a mass of granular policies generated to meet the specific needs of a department or other business group that might disappear following the next corporate reorganization. The more policies that exist, the more potential there is to confuse administrators and users alike.

Exchange uses the date and time when an item is created in a user's mailbox as the baseline to calculate the age of the item for retention purposes, so an age limit of 30 days for the Inbox default retention tag essentially means that items become eligible for processing by the MFA 30 days after they are delivered into the Inbox. The creation date is used for retention purposes even for modifiable items such as posts. You can create a tag to mark items never to be processed by the MFA. Such a tag will have no value set for its *AgeLimitForRetention* property, and its *RetentionEnabled* property will be set to $False.

The MFA is responsible for implementing the actions specified in retention and archive tags when it processes a mailbox. For example, if the retention period for the Inbox is 30 days, the MFA will tag any item aged up to 30 days and take the specified action for items aged 30 days. Therefore, before you implement a policy that potentially will affect thousands of items in user mailboxes, it is critical to clearly communicate what is going to happen, when it will happen, and how users can prepare for the implementation of the retention policy and respond to its actions afterward. You might have to communicate several times before the retention policies are implemented to avoid a deluge of calls to the help desk the morning after the MFA runs.

Naming retention tags

The tags described in the example management retention policy that we created follow a specific naming scheme. Retention policy tags are prefixed with "RPT," default policy tags are prefixed with "DPT," and personal tags are prefixed with "PER." The tag name is then completed with some text to convey its meaning and to associate it with the retention policy where it is used. Thus, DPT-General makes sense in an administrative sense because the name conveys that the tag is a default policy tag used generally across the organization. Of course, the last sentence means nothing to end users, especially if they have never coded and have not been exposed to the cryptic (but always logical) naming schemes beloved by programmers.

The problem that has to be solved when you determine a tag naming scheme is that the retention policy menu displayed by Outlook 2010 and Outlook Web App lists tag names and their retention period (such as "6 months") to end users but doesn't display any other detail such as the action that will be taken when the tag's retention period expires. Tags can have a variety of associated actions, from permanent deletion to merely warning that the retention period has expired. Outlook 2010 users can view the actions for the default tag on a folder by viewing the folder properties, but this information is not available to Outlook Web App, and they are the only two clients that expose retention tags today. It can be argued that the tags used in an archive policy and displayed in the archive menu are an exception because users should know that the purpose of these tags is to move items into the personal archive when their retention period expires, but that's still no reason to use cryptic tag names.

The question, therefore, has to be asked whether you should use a more user-friendly naming scheme for retention tags. For example, would "RPT-Inbox" be better named "Inbox retention policy" and should "PER-Retain" be called "Retain for five years"? Some prefer the structure of the first approach, but users probably find the second approach easier to understand.

Another approach that is often taken is to use names that give clear business directives for retention tags. For example, you might use names such as these:

- Business Critical

- Partner Negotiations

- Legal Retention

Tags named like this are usually more specific to departments or groups than more generic names such as "Keep for five years" or "Required for Annual Audit," so you might end up defining a set of retention tags for each department to match their work practices.

It's impossible to give a definitive answer about a naming convention that is suitable for all deployments. Some organizations are happy with cryptic tags because they are a standard that is valid no matter what language is used to connect to Exchange; others will elect to use more user-friendly names because it's easier to communicate the purpose of a retention policy to users and they feel that this will both ease the introduction of retention policies within the organization and avoid some calls to the help desk. The important thing is to make a decision before you start to design and implement retention policies, as changing the names of tags halfway through a deployment is guaranteed to cause maximum confusion.

Creating retention tags

Retention tags can only be created using EMS with Exchange 2010 RTM. With SP1, you have the choice of working with EMC or EMS. EMC is easier to deal with, so we'll begin with it. Under Organization Configuration, go to the Mailbox section and select the New Retention Tag option to launch the New Retention Policy Tag Wizard. As you can see from Figure 15-7, this wizard is very straightforward, and all we need to do is input the settings laid out for each tag in the policy described previously in Table 15-3.

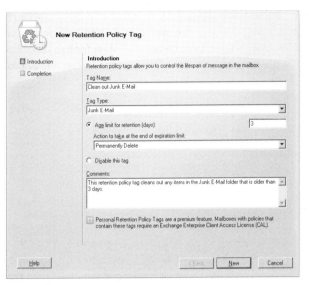

Figure 15-7 Creating a new retention policy tag.

After creating all of the retention policy tags that we need, we should end up with something like the situation illustrated in Figure 15-8. This is the complete set of the retention policy tags defined for the organization, and you can immediately see the advantage of following a well-thought-out naming convention for tags, as this set contains both structured and free-form names. In addition, you can see how it is possible to quickly accumulate a large number of tags that are used by different retention policies in an organization. With some forethought, it is possible to reduce the total number of tags by designing some utility tags that are included in every policy, which then means that the only additional tags that you need to define are those specifically required by a policy. For example, you can probably define utility tags to clean out folders such as Junk E-Mail and RSS Feeds that apply the same retention period and action for every policy. You might not be as successful in defining utility tags for default folders, such as the Inbox or Sent Items, as different sets of users might need to keep items in these folders for different periods.

Chapter 15

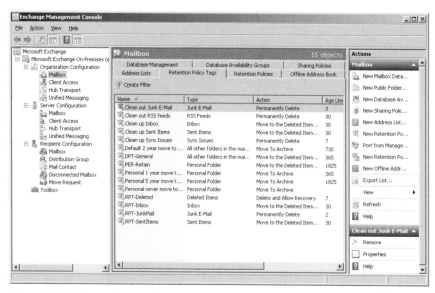

Figure 15-8 Viewing the set of retention policy tags defined for the organization.

As an example of how to accomplish the same task with EMS, let's create the four retention policy tags for the Inbox, Sent Items, Junk Mail, and Deleted Items folders.

```
New-RetentionPolicyTag -Name 'RPT-Inbox' -RetentionAction DeleteAndAllowRecovery
-AgeLimitForRetention
30 -Type Inbox -Comment 'Inbox items are automatically deleted after 30 days'
-RetentionEnabled $True

New-RetentionPolicyTag -Name 'RPT-SentItems' -RetentionAction DeleteAndAllowRecovery
-AgeLimitForRetention 30 -Type SentItems -Comment 'Sent Items are deleted
after 30 days' -RetentionEnabled $True

New-RetentionPolicyTag -Name 'RPT-JunkMail' -RetentionAction PermanentlyDelete
-AgeLimitForRetention 2 -Type JunkEmail -Comment 'All junk mail is permanently
removed after two days'
 -RetentionEnabled $True

New-RetentionPolicyTag -Name 'RPT-Deleted' -RetentionAction DeleteAndAllowRecovery
-AgeLimitForRetention 7 -Type DeletedItems -Comment 'Deleted Items are removed after
7 days; they can be recovered if necessary'    -RetentionEnabled $True
```

We can check the properties of our new retention tags with the Get-RetentionPolicyTag cmdlet. For example:

```
Get-RetentionPolicyTag -Identity 'RPT-Inbox' | Format-List
```

```
IsPrimary                        : False
MessageClassDisplayName          : All Mailbox Content
MessageClass                     : *
Description                      : Managed Content Settings
RetentionEnabled                 : True
RetentionAction                  : DeleteAndAllowRecovery
AgeLimitForRetention             : 30.00:00:00
MoveToDestinationFolder          :
TriggerForRetention              : WhenDelivered
MessageFormatForJournaling       : UseTnef
JournalingEnabled                : False
AddressForJournaling             :
LabelForJournaling               :
Type                             : Inbox
SystemTag                        : False
LocalizedRetentionPolicyTagName  : {}
Comment                          : Inbox items are automatically deleted after 30 days
LocalizedComment                 : {}
MustDisplayCommentEnabled        : False
LegacyManagedFolder              :
AdminDisplayName                 :
Name                             : RPT-Inbox
Identity                         : RPT-Inbox
```

The output from Get-RetentionPolicyTag confirms that the tag can cover any class of item (MessageClass = *, the default for Exchange 2010), that it is for the Inbox folder (Type = Inbox), and that items tagged with this RPT will be moved to the Deleted Items folder after 30 days (indicated in the *RetentionAction* and *AgeLimitForRetention* properties). In fact, unlike managed folders, retention tags don't accommodate the notion of item segregation. In other words, you cannot build a retention tag that only applies to items of a certain class in a folder (such as apply the policy to items of class *IPM.Note* but ignore those of class *IPM.Contact*).

INSIDE OUT   Voice mail is an exception

Voice mail is a noted exception to this rule because you can create a specific tag for voice mail. Along the same lines, you can't define different actions for different item types such as moving expired messages to an archive folder while deleting any other item type. Some observers consider these shortcomings to be a retrograde step in messaging records management.

Let's now create the other tags that are required for the management retention policy. This time a personal tag (type = personal) is needed to allow users to mark items to be kept in their mailbox for five years (1,825 days), after which the items will be automatically moved into the Recoverable Items folder. Exchange gives the action and retention period defined in a personal tag priority if a user applies it to an item in a folder that's already under the control of a retention policy tag. In other words, if a user applies the PER-Retain tag on an item in the Inbox, Exchange will not move it to the Recoverable Items folder after 30 days as called for by the retention policy tag associated with the Inbox. Instead, Exchange will respect the action and retention period defined in the personal tag because the rule is that an explicit policy always trumps an implicit policy. In addition, you should also remember that Exchange will keep a personal tag on an item even if the item moves to another folder that has an associated retention policy tag.

We create the new personal tag with the following command:

```
New-RetentionPolicyTag –Name 'PER-Retain' –RetentionAction PermanentlyDelete
–RetentionEnabled $True –AgeLimitForRetention 1825 –Type Personal –Comment 'Item to
be kept forfive years before it is moved to Recoverable Items'
```

Setting the *Type* parameter to Personal is the critical thing here because it makes the tag personal and explicit rather than the implicit tags applied to all items in a folder. To create a personal tag with EMC, select Personal Folder as the tag type.

TROUBLESHOOTING

I created a retention tag with the wrong type. What do I do?

If you make a mistake and create a retention tag of the wrong type, you aren't able to change the type with the Set-RetentionPolicyTag cmdlet. Instead, you will have to delete the tag with the Remove-RetentionPolicyTag cmdlet and then re-create it afterward with the correct type.

To complete the design, the policy needs to provide managers with a default retention tag that forces any items older than a year (365 days) to be moved into the Recoverable Items folder. As you'll recall, a default tag is used when no other tag has been applied to an item.

```
New-RetentionPolicyTag -Name 'DPT-General' -RetentionAction DeleteAndAllowRecovery
-RetentionEnabled $True -AgeLimitForRetention 365 -Type All -Comment 'Items older
than a year are moved to Recoverable Items unless otherwise tagged'
```

You'll have noticed that all of the tags that we created specify *–RetentionEnabled $True*. This means that the tag is active and should be processed by the MFA. To disable a tag, you set *–RetentionEnabled $False*. A tag in this state is ignored by the MFA.

Most of the tags that we have created so far use the DeleteAndAllowRecovery action. The other actions are as follows:

- *PermanentlyDelete*   Immediately deletes the item in such a way that it cannot be seen using the Recover Deleted Items option. If the mailbox is on retention or litigation hold, the item is retained and still available to discovery searches.

- *MoveToArchive*   Moves the item to a folder of the same name in an archive mailbox. Clearly this action is only possible if the mailbox has a personal archive. If not, the action is ignored. Moving to the archive is analogous to the Outlook Auto-Archive option that moves items into a PST on a regular schedule to help keep a mailbox under quota. The big difference is that users don't get to vote whether they want to use the option, as Exchange moves items into the personal archive automatically without asking for user opinion. Policies that move items into an archive mailbox are known as archive policies. Exchange will ignore the archive tags if you create a retention policy that includes tags to move items into the archive and apply it to a mailbox that doesn't have a personal archive. If the mailbox is subsequently assigned a personal archive, the MFA will apply the archive tags for the mailbox the next time that it runs.

To check that we have all of the required tags in place to build the retention policy, we can review the set of tags through EMC or execute the following EMS command:

```
Get-RetentionPolicyTag | Format-Table Name, Type, RetentionAction, RetentionEnabled,
AgeLimitForRetention -AutoSize
```

Name	Type	RetentionAction	RetentionEnabled	AgeLimitForRetention
RPT-Inbox	Inbox	DeleteAndAllowRecovery	True	30.00:00:00
RPT-SentItems	SentItems	DeleteAndAllowRecovery		30.00:00:00
RPT-JunkMail	JunkEmail	PermanentlyDelete	True	2.00.00.00
RPT-Deleted	DeletedItems	PermanentlyDelete	True	7.00:00:00
PER-Retain	Personal	DeleteAndAllowRecovery	True	1825.00:00:00
DPT-General	All	DeleteAndAllowRecovery	True	365.00:00:00

Chapter 15

All seems correct in this case, but if you make a mistake, you can remove a retention policy tag with the Remove-RetentionPolicyTag cmdlet. If the tag has already been applied to mailbox items, the MFA will clean up by removing any reference to the removed tag from items as it processes mailboxes.

Creating a retention policy

Now that we have created the necessary retention tags to help managers impose order on their mailboxes, we can proceed to create a new retention policy. In EMC, under Organization Configuration in the Mailbox section, select the New Retention Policy option to launch a wizard to help guide us through the process. We have two tasks to accomplish:

1. Select and add the retention tags that we want to include in the new policy. Figure 15-9 shows that the six tags that we created have been selected for inclusion in the new policy.

2. Select the mailboxes that we want to apply the new retention policy to after it is created (Figure 15-10). This is an optional step, and you are not required to select any mailboxes now. A retention policy can be added to mailboxes at any time after it is defined.

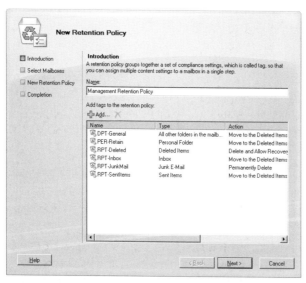

Figure 15-9 Creating a new retention policy with EMC.

Figure 15-9 illustrates a retention policy containing a number of tags that specify actions that have been removed in Exchange 2010 SP1. Microsoft no longer supports the use of the Move to the Deleted Items and Mark as Past Retention Limit actions. Although these actions are still respected by the MFA, they might cease to work in a future release of Exchange. The policy shown here was created with Exchange 2010 RTM and needs to be updated to use the set of retention actions available in SP1. It is possible that Microsoft will reintroduce a more expansive set of retention actions in a future version of Exchange.

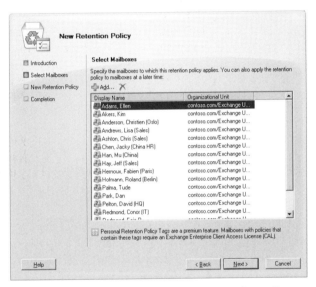

Figure 15-10 Adding mailboxes to a new retention policy.

When you click Finish to complete the wizard, Exchange first reviews the set of retention policy tags that you have assigned to the policy to validate that you are not including multiple tags for the same folder.

TROUBLESHOOTING

I created multiple tags for the same folder.

This is a common error, and if it is detected, Exchange flags the error as shown in Figure 15-11. Fixing the error is easy: Note the problem tag reported by Exchange and then check it against the set of tags that you have included in the policy to determine which of the duplicate tags you want to retain in the policy. Once you've addressed the problem, go through the wizard pages again to finish and create the new retention policy.

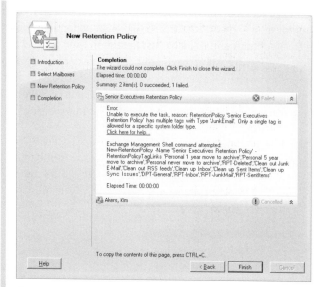

Figure 15-11 Encountering an error in creating a new retention policy.

Assuming that everything goes according to plan, Exchange will create the new retention policy and then apply it to any mailboxes that you selected. The MFA will stamp the tags defined in the retention policy on items in the mailboxes the next time that it processes the mailboxes.

Exchange 2010 only allows you to create retention policies through EMS using the New-RetentionPolicy cmdlet. In this command, we create the policy and associate the six tags that we want to use with the new policy.

```
New-RetentionPolicy –Name 'Management retention policy'
–RetentionPolicyTagLinks 'RPT-Inbox', 'RPT-SentItems', 'RPT-Deleted',
'PER-JunkMail','PER-Retain', 'DPT-General'
```

We can examine details of the new retention policy with the Get-RetentionPolicy cmdlet:

```
Get-RetentionPolicy –id 'Management retention policy'
```

```
RetentionPolicyTagLinks : {DPT-General, Per-retain, RPT-Deleted, RPT-SentItems, RPT-Inbox}
AdminDisplayName        :
ExchangeVersion         : 1.0 (0.0.0.0)
Name                    : Management retention policy
```

```
DistinguishedName      : CN=Management retention policy,CN=Retention Policies Container,
CN=contoso,CN=Microsoft Exchange,CN=Services,CN=Configuration,DC=contoso,DC=com
Identity               : Management retention policy
ObjectClass            : {top, msExchRecipientTemplate, msExchMailboxRecipientTemplate}
```

A six-tag policy is a reasonably simple retention policy, as other policies can incorporate a lot more tags to create a very exact retention environment for a user to operate within. Obviously, you might have more tags than this if you decide to include a retention policy tag for every default folder. Using retention policy tags to clean out items that otherwise accumulate and are never cleared out in default folders such as Sync Issues, Junk E-Mail, and RSS Feeds is a good example of where you can gain real value from a well-designed retention policy. Figure 15-7, shown previously, is a good example of such a "good folder health" retention policy tag.

INSIDE OUT   Good reasons to limit the number of tags in a policy

Microsoft recommends that you have no more than 10 personal tags in a policy, as otherwise you might confuse users with too much choice. This is reasonable advice, but as with most advice, there will be edge cases where you need to incorporate more tags in a policy to meet specialized business needs. A more sophisticated policy for a department might have separate retention tags for many of the default folders, a set of personal tags developed specifically to suit the retention needs of the department, and a default retention tag for everything else. User interface constraints are another good reason for limiting the number of tags in a policy. If you have 10 tags or fewer in a policy, there's a reasonable guarantee that Outlook Web App and Outlook will be able to display all the tags in their user interface. On the other hand, if you have 20 tags in a policy, you'll find that Outlook Web App is unable to list all of the tags and some will simply drop off the end of the available list. Outlook has a separate dialog box that users can navigate to if they want to discover all of the tags available in a policy, but this requires many separate clicks and additional knowledge of where to go to find the tags. For all these reasons, it's just a bad idea to go crazy and create a tag-filled policy.

Applying a retention policy to mailboxes

The Set-Mailbox cmdlet is used to apply a retention policy to an existing mailbox. The New Mailbox Wizard available in the original release of Exchange 2010 does not allow you to set a retention policy on a mailbox when it is created, but this problem is addressed in the SP1 version. The policy becomes active the next time the MFA processes the mailbox. SP1 also allows you to select a retention policy from the Mailbox section of Organization Configuration and add one or more mailboxes to it. Because you can use the mailbox picker to browse and select from all the mailboxes in the organization, this is the easiest way to add a large number of mailboxes to a retention policy in one operation.

INSIDE OUT Only one retention policy—ever

A mailbox can only ever have one retention policy, so when you assign a retention policy to a mailbox, the action overwrites any policy that might already be in place. You can change retention policies multiple times on a mailbox, but this isn't a good idea unless you really need to switch policies because the effect of the different policies might confuse users, as the MFA responds to different retention settings in the different policies. Setting a value for the *RetentionURL* parameter is not compulsory, but it is a useful way to communicate where a user might go to find additional details about the company's retention policy. This URL is only visible through Outlook 2010 and isn't displayed by earlier clients or Outlook Web App.

```
Set-Mailbox -Identity 'JSmith' -RetentionPolicy'Management retention policy'
-RetentionComment 'Management retention policy applies to this mailbox'
-RetentionURL'http://Intranet.contoso.com/RetentionPolicies.html'
```

Exchange will warn you that clients earlier than Outlook 2007 don't support retention policies. More correctly, this should be Outlook 2010. Of course, if you're setting a policy for a group of users, you'll probably do it in one operation by selecting the mailboxes with the Get-Mailbox cmdlet and piping the results to Set-Mailbox. For example:

```
Get-Mailbox -Filter {CustomAttribute7 -eq'Management'} | Set-Mailbox
-RetentionPolicy 'Management retention policy'
-RetentionComment 'Management retention policy applies to this mailbox'
```

The new policy will be applied to the mailboxes the next time that the MFA processes the mailboxes. See the section "How the Managed Folder Assistant implements retention policies" later in this chapter for more information about the processing performed by the MFA.

To discover the set of mailboxes that have retention policies in place, you can use a command like this:

```
Get-Mailbox -Filter {RetentionPolicy -ne $Null} | Format-Table Name, RetentionPolicy
-AutoSize
```

> **The value of $Null**
>
> When you want to remove a retention policy from a mailbox, you simply set the policy to *$Null*. For completeness, it's a good idea to set the other properties associated with retention policies to null as well. Here's the command:
>
> ```
> Set-Mailbox –Identity 'JSmith' –RetentionPolicy $Null –RetentionComment $Null
> –RetentionURL $Null
> ```

Of course, after you begin to deploy retention policies to mailboxes, the question arises of how to integrate the assignment of retention policies with any user provisioning process that your company has in place. Exchange doesn't have a default retention policy that can be assigned automatically, so an explicit administrative action is always required to allocate a retention policy to a mailbox. This action is not difficult to code with EMS, but it is something that needs to be considered as part of your deployment plan.

Modifying a retention policy

Policies can evolve over time by the addition or removal of tags. As we've discussed, you add multiple retention tags to a policy by separating the entry for each tag with a comma. You can add new tags to the policy afterward with the Set-RetentionPolicy cmdlet. To add a new tag, you need to include it in the full list of tags submitted to Set-RetentionPolicy in the *–RetentionPolicyTagLinks* parameter. It is not sufficient to merely specify the new tag on its own, as this will update the policy to only include the new tag.

You can use two approaches to including a new tag in a retention policy. The first approach is best for simple policies that only include a few tags and requires you to write the complete list of tags into the policy to overwrite the existing list. For example:

```
Set-RetentionPolicy –Identity 'Audit Department'
–RetentionPolicyTagLinks 'RPT-Audit-Inbox', 'RPT-Audit-SentItems'
Get-RetentionPolicy –Identity 'Audit Department'
```

The second approach is best when dealing with complex policies that have six or more tags, and the potential exists that you might forget to input one of the tags. *RetentionPolicyTags* is a multivalued property, so to add a new tag to an existing list, you first extract the existing tags into a variable, then add the new tag to the variable, and finally write the new set back into the policy. Here's code that updates a complex policy with a new tag:

```
$TagList = (Get-RetentionPolicy –Identity
'Management Retention Policy').RetentionPolicyTagLinks
$NewTag = Get-RetentionPolicyTag –Identity 'Per-New-ArchivePolicy')
$TagList += $NewTag
Set-RetentionPolicy –Identity 'Management Retention Policy' –RetentionPolicyTagLinks
$TagList
```

```
Get-RetentionPolicy -Identity 'Management RetentionPolicy' | Select Name,
RetentionPolicyTagLinks
```

The second approach requires a little more typing on the part of the administrator, but it absolutely guarantees that all existing tags are preserved.

To remove a tag from a policy, you have to write a replacement list into the policy as in the first approach previously described. If you remove a tag from a policy, users covered by the policy cannot apply the tag to any items to their mailbox, but existing items that have been stamped with the tag continue in place and will be processed by the MFA.

Changing a retention tag: An exception to the rule

Changing the retention period in a tag is similar to removing a tag. All items stamped with the retention period up to the point where you made the change will continue to use that retention period; items that are stamped with the updated policy will have the new retention period. The exception to this rule is when you set the *RetentionEnabled* property of a tag to $False, as this value instructs the MFA to leave the tags in place but ignore them when it processes items. For example:

```
Set-RetentionPolicyTag -Identity 'Keep Items Forever' -RetentionEnabled $False
```

This situation continues until the user explicitly assigns a replacement tag to an item or you remove the tag from Active Directory using the Remove-RetentionPolicyTag cmdlet. When this happens, the next time that the MFA runs, it will remove the deleted tag from any items where it was used.

Customizing retention policies for specific mailboxes

You can tailor the retention policy for a specific user by assigning personal tags on a per-mailbox basis. This can only be done if a retention policy already applies to the user's mailbox. For example, let's assume that you want to assign a new personal tag to a user to allow him to mark an item to be moved into the archive after a year. You can do this as follows:

```
Set-RetentionPolicyTag -Mailbox JSmith -OptionalInMailbox 'Per-Move-Archive'
```

Exchange adds the optional tag to the set of tags covered in the retention policy that already applies to the mailbox and makes the expanded set available the next time that the user connects. Unfortunately, no cmdlet is available to report whether a mailbox has been assigned optional tags. If you examine a mailbox with Get-Mailbox, it tells you if a retention policy is assigned, but nothing else. Therefore, if you want to change the list of optional tags assigned to a mailbox, you have to write the complete list with Set-RetentionPolicyTag.

For example, to add an additional tag to the one that has already been assigned, we use this command:

```
Set-RetentionPolicyTag –Mailbox JSmith –OptionalInMailbox 'Per-Move-Archive',
'Per-Keep-LongTime'
```

EMS doesn't validate that the tags that you assign to a mailbox will be effective. For example, you can assign a new archive tag to a mailbox that doesn't have a personal archive. This is really a null operation because neither Outlook Web App nor Outlook displays archive tags if the mailbox doesn't have a personal archive.

To remove all optional retention tags from a mailbox, you set the list to *$Null* as follows:

```
Set-RetentionPolicyTag –Mailbox JSmith –OptionalInMailbox $Null
```

INSIDE OUT   Accessing personal tags in Exchange 2010 SP1

Exchange 2010 SP1 makes the process of accessing personal tags easier by allowing users to see a list of available personal tags through Exchange Control Panel (ECP) to decide what personal tags they would like to use. Figure 15-12 shows the option exposed through the Organize Email section of ECP.

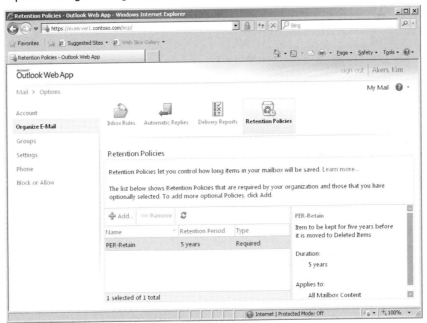

Figure 15-12 User access to personal retention tags through ECP.

A retention policy must be in effect for a user's mailbox, and the MyRetentionPolicies policy must be included in the role assignment policy for the mailbox before ECP reveals personal tags. If shown, the user sees the personal tags that she can already use because they are included in the retention policy (these tags are listed as Required) and the other personal tags that are defined for the organization that she can choose to use (these tags are listed as Optional). The user cannot remove any of the Required tags because their presence is mandated by the retention policy that is applied to the mailbox. A user can begin to apply personal retention tags to items immediately after adding the tags to her mailbox.

User interaction with retention policies

The first evidence that users see that their mailbox has been assigned a retention policy is when they see indications in message headers that start to appear 30 days before an item expires. These warnings are visible when a message is opened or shown in the message preview. Figure 15-13 shows how Outlook Web App advises that a message has 27 days before it expires as the result of a retention policy tag placed on the Inbox. The user now has the choice to either leave the message to expire, in which case the MFA will process whatever action is defined in the tag (Move to Deleted Items, Permanently Delete, and so on) or apply a different tag to the item.

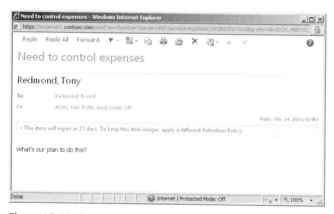

Figure 15-13 Outlook Web App warns that an item is approaching its expiry deadline.

Users have two options to apply a different tag to an item in their Inbox. First, they can move the item to a different folder and so remove it from the influence of the retention policy tag that applies to Inbox items. After it is moved, the item is governed by the default policy tag defined in the retention policy that applies to the mailbox, if one exists, or by an explicit policy that is applied to the folder and therefore inherited by all items that are added to the folder. If neither of these conditions exists, the item is left untagged and therefore will not be subject to processing by the MFA.

The second option is to place an explicit tag on the item. Users can choose from any of the personal tags defined in the retention policy applied to their mailbox by right-clicking an item and then selecting the personal tag to apply. Figure 15-14 shows how Outlook 2010 (left) and Outlook Web App (right) display retention and archive tags included in a single retention policy in the list of options that can be taken for a message. If a tag specifies *MoveToArchive* as its action, clients list it under Archive Policy rather than Retention Policy. Logically, archive tags can only be used with mailboxes that have personal archives. Outlook provides a richer set of options, even if you can argue that Outlook Web App's user interface is less confusing for the novice user. You won't see the user interface for retention policies unless a policy is applied to your mailbox.

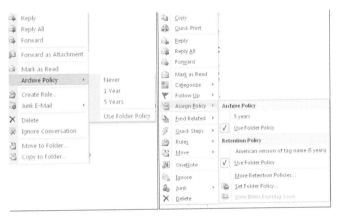

Figure 15-14 How Outlook and Outlook Web App display the list of available retention and archive tags.

After a personal tag has been applied to an item, the item is no longer subject to the provisions of either the folder policy or the default policy, as an explicit tag always takes precedence over a tag placed on a folder. The personal tag also remains with the item if it is moved to another folder or into the personal archive. If users want to impose a different retention policy on the item, they will have to replace the existing tag with a new personal tag.

Outlook keeps users updated about the retention policy that applies to an item by displaying details as part of the message header. The retention information displayed by Outlook 2010 when a message is read is shown in Figure 15-15. Users can see quite clearly how long it will be before the item expires, and they can also see details of the retention policy that is applied to the item.

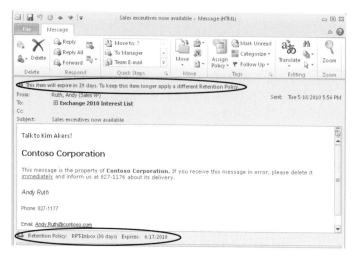

Figure 15-15 Outlook 2010 displays retention information.

Managed Folder Assistant automatically applies the retention policy

Although most retention policies will include a default policy tag to provide retention instructions for items held in nondefault folders, Outlook and Outlook Web App support the use of personal retention tags to set a different retention policy on a folder. In effect, this means that Exchange will apply the policy defined in the personal retention tag to items held in the folder, much in the same way that it applies the retention policy tags placed on default folders such as the Inbox. In some respects, you can use this approach to create a roughly equivalent situation to the functionality provided by Exchange 2007 managed folders. However, the big difference is that you have to create the folders and apply the retention policies manually, whereas the MFA does the work to push out new folders to user mailboxes and apply the retention policy automatically for managed folders.

To set a new default policy for a folder with Outlook, select the folder and click Assign Policy on the toolbar, then select Set Retention Policy from the drop-down menu. Outlook then displays the folder properties positioned on the Policy tab (Figure 15-16). You can select any personal tag to use as the new default retention policy for the folder, and items subsequently created in the folder will inherit the default tag. The same inheritance occurs when an item is moved into the folder unless an explicit tag has already been applied to the item, in which case the existing tag is retained. To set a default policy on a folder with Outlook Web App, select the folder from the folder list under the mailbox root, right-click to select the Retention Policy option, and then select the retention policy to apply to the folder.

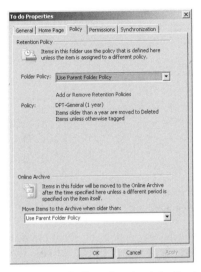

Figure 15-16 Changing the default retention policy for a folder.

Figure 15-17 shows how Outlook 2010 is able to display some information about retention policy in its backstage area. In this example, if we look at the mailbox, we'll see that its properties are as follows:

```
Get-Mailbox –Identity 'Ruth, Andy' | Select Retent*
```

```
RetentionComment   : The management retention policy applies to this mailbox
RetentionUrl       : <a href="http://intranet.contoso.com/retentionpolicies.html"> Retention
Policy Information</a>
RetentionPolicy    : Management retention policy
```

The *RetentionComment* property provides the text that you can see beside "Account Settings," and the *RetentionUrl* property is used to provide a URL to a Web site where the additional information resides. These properties are usually set when you place a mailbox on retention or litigation hold. We will come to these topics shortly. For now, although you don't have to set these properties to impose an effective retention regime, they are helpful to communicate information to users about what's going on in their mailbox. Experience of many projects demonstrates that anything that assists in effective communications with users is likely to reduce help desk calls. Apart from the two properties that we can set on a mailbox, Outlook tells the user that the default archive policy for the mailbox will move items out of the primary mailbox after they are two years old.

Chapter 15

Figure 15-17 Viewing retention information in Outlook's backstage area.

Figure 15-18 shows that you can provide localized versions of retention tags that Outlook will display to users based on the client language setting.

Figure 15-18 Viewing a localized retention policy tag.

> **Note**
>
> Clearly you don't have to go to the trouble of creating local language versions of tags if you operate a mono-language environment, but once again this is a useful thing to do when you have to support users who operate in different languages. Just be sure that you get accurate translations that clearly convey the meaning of the tag, and don't be tempted to cut corners and use school-quality translations or even those that you might be able to procure free of charge from the Internet.

If we examine the tag that generates the output, we can see this output:

```
Get-RetentionPolicyTag -Identity 'Per-Retain' | Select Local*, Comment
```

```
LocalizedRetentionPolicyTagName : {En-IE: Irish version of tag, En-US: American
version of tag name}
LocalizedComment                : {En-US: General five year tag (US), En-IE:
General five year tag (IRL)}
Comment                         : Item to be kept for five years before it is
moved to Deleted Items
```

Notice that the *LocalizedRetentionPolicyTagName* property has two values for "En-IE" (Ireland variant of English) and "En-Us" (U.S. variant of English). The screen shows that Outlook displays the U.S. version, so you know that Outlook is running in that language version. An example of the command to provide localized text for a retention tag is:

```
Set-RetentionPolicyTag -Identity 'Per-Retain' -LocalizedRetentionPolicyTagName
'EN-US: American version of tag name', 'EN-IE: Irish version of tag name'
-LocalizedComment 'EN-US: US text comment', 'EN-IE: Irish text comment'
```

Removing a retention policy

The Remove-RetentionPolicy cmdlet is used to remove a retention policy from the organization. For example:

```
Remove-RetentionPolicy -Identity 'Retention Policy - PR Department'
```

Removing a retention policy has the effect of removing the policy from any mailboxes to which it is currently applied. If any mailboxes are associated with the policy, EMS will prompt you to confirm its removal. If you proceed, Exchange removes the reference to the now-deleted policy from the mailboxes. Exchange can't decide what retention should replace the one that has just been removed, so no policy is applied. Locating the mailboxes to which a retention policy is applied is therefore a proactive step that you should take before you remove the policy. You can scan mailboxes to discover where a retention policy is applied with a command like this:

```
Get-Mailbox | Where {$_.RetentionPolicy -eq "Retention Policy - Audit Department"} |
Select Name
```

A similar set of commands can be run to locate mailboxes with a specific retention policy and assign a new retention policy to the mailboxes. For example:

```
Get-Mailbox | Where {$_.RetentionPolicy -eq "Retention Policy - Audit Department"} |
Set-Mailbox -RetentionPolicy 'New Retention Policy for Auditors'
```

Chapter 15

Upgrading from managed folders

You can upgrade a managed folder to a retention tag by using it as the template to create a new tag. For example, let's assume that you have a managed folder called Never Delete that acts as a repository for items that users never want to have removed from a mailbox because they are so important. You could argue the case that these items could be equally stored in an archive mailbox. However, archive mailboxes didn't exist in Exchange 2007, and it takes time for people to change their behavior. We can use a command like the one shown here to create a new retention policy tag from the Never Delete managed folder:

```
New-RetentionPolicyTag –Name 'Mark item to never expire' –ManagedFolderToUpgrade
'Never Delete' –Comment 'Tag created from old Never Delete managed folder'
```

Of course, to complete the process, we have to associate the new tag with a retention policy and assign it to a user. After this is done, the user will be able to apply the new tag on any item in his mailbox rather than just the items placed in the managed folder.

How the Managed Folder Assistant implements retention policies

After you apply a retention policy to a mailbox, you can either wait for the next scheduled run of the MFA or start it manually so that the new policy is applied immediately. When the MFA runs, it performs the following tasks:

- It applies the tags specified in retention policies to the mailboxes covered by these policies and stamps the items in the various folders covered by the policies with the appropriate tag name and expiration date.

- It populates new managed folders into mailboxes that are under the control of a managed folder policy.

- If a policy defines a retention or expiry period for items, it stamps a Messaging Application Programming Interface (MAPI) property (*ElcMoveDate*) on the items indicating the date and time from which the retention period will start. A future run of the assistant can then use this date and time to calculate when to delete an item or mark it as expired.

- It locates items in folders that are past their expiration date and takes whatever action is defined in the policy (delete, age out, move to another folder).

- If required by policy, it journals new items that have been placed in managed folders. In this context, journaling is different than that performed by transport rules because items are only processed when the MFA is active rather than immediately when they arrive into the folder. The MFA does not use the transport engine to journal items because there is no guarantee that the transport role is installed on the mailbox server that hosts the managed folders.

The default schedule for the MFA on Exchange 2010 mailbox servers extends from 1 A.M. to 9 A.M. daily. On small servers that host a few hundred mailboxes, the MFA invariably has plenty of time to complete processing of all mailboxes during its scheduled timeslot. On large servers where several thousand mailboxes might need to be processed, a run of the MFA might not complete during its timeslot, especially if this is the first time that policies are applied and many items have to be deleted or moved into an archive.

> ## Behind the scenes: When a timeslot expires before processing is complete
>
> The work done by the MFA to process mailboxes, stamp items with retention tags, and action items whose retention period has expired is resource-intensive in terms of server resources and might also create a lot of network traffic within a DAG to replicate all of the store transactions created as items are processed. If the timeslot expires before the MFA completes processing, it will stop and will resume processing at the point where it was forced to stop when the next timeslot becomes available. You can alter the default schedule on the Messaging Records Management tab of the server Properties dialog box, but only on Exchange 2010 servers, as the tab doesn't exist on Exchange 2010 SP1. When the job starts, the MFA begins multithreaded (concurrent) processing of all of the databases on a server.

As discussed in Chapter 12, "Mailbox Support Services," Exchange 2010 SP1 introduces a new method to schedule and perform the work done by mailbox assistants, including the MFA. When the scheduled window for the MFA opens on an Exchange 2010 RTM server, the Assistant begins to process all mailboxes one after another as quickly as possible. In effect, the MFA sprints through all its work in an attempt to reach the finish line as quickly as possible. This creates a high processing load on the server, and this could occur at the same time that other housekeeping activities happen, such as background maintenance and backup jobs. The fact that the MFA does more work than ever before to stamp new items and process items according to the conditions specified in retention policies is also of concern, as this drives additional server load.

Instead of sprinting to the finish, the Exchange 2010 SP1 version of the MFA assesses the expected workload in terms of the number of mailboxes that it has to process and then spreads out its processing across the complete window. For example, if 600 mailboxes are to be processed over three hours, the MFA will create its own internal schedule to process 200 mailboxes per hour, or roughly three mailboxes per minute. In addition, there is a checkpoint defined for the work cycle, at which time the MFA will look for new mailboxes that should be added to its list for processing. The default values for the work cycle and checkpoint are both one day, meaning that the MFA will attempt to process every mailbox in its list daily and will check for new mailboxes daily. Overall, the work cycle mechanism makes more effective use of server resources in an easy and relaxed manner throughout the day and doesn't create potential spikes in demand.

You might find that you want to run the MFA immediately, perhaps to apply a policy to a group of users for the first time. To force a nonscheduled run of the MFA on an Exchange 2010 server, connect to the server that hosts the database where the mailboxes are located, start EMS, and enter this command:

```
Start-ManagedFolderAssistant
```

Exchange 2010 SP1 will still process the mailboxes if you force an immediate run, but the mailboxes will be processed as described earlier.

> **Note**
>
> The *–Identity* parameter is no longer used by the Start-ManagedFolderAssistant cmdlet to refer to a server in SP1. Instead, it replaces the previous use of the *–Mailbox* parameter and is used to identify a mailbox that you want the Assistant to process immediately.

Forcing immediate execution for a selected mailbox is a useful thing to do when you start to apply policies to mailboxes and want to gauge the effect of the policy by examining the output of a log file, which might be easier than asking users what happened to the contents of their mailboxes (especially if you've made a mistake with the policy and just removed half of the items from the mailbox). To force processing for a selected mailbox, we specify its name with the *–Identity* parameter:

```
Start-ManagedFolderAssistant –Identity 'Akers, Kim'
```

To process a group of mailboxes, we either provide a set of mailbox identifiers as input or use the Get-Mailbox cmdlet with a filter to retrieve a set of mailboxes and pipe it as input to Start-ManagedFolderAssistant. In the first example, two mailbox identifiers are provided as input. In the second, we process all the mailboxes in a database, and in the third, we use a filter to find all the mailboxes from a particular office.

```
"Redmond, Tony", "Akers, Kim" | Start-ManagedFolderAssistant
Get-Mailbox –Database 'VIP Data' | Start-ManagedFolderAssistant
Get-Mailbox –Filter {Office –eq 'Dublin'} | Start-ManagedFolderAssistant
```

The time required for the MFA to complete its run depends on the number of mailboxes and the number of items to which it has to apply retention policies. A run on a small server that hosts a few hundred mailboxes will complete in a couple of minutes unless the mailboxes hold thousands of items. On the other hand, processing 7,000 mailboxes, each of which holds an average of 20,000 items, could take several hours, especially if the server is loaded with other tasks or the policies cause a heavy I/O load because many items are permanently removed or moved from primary to archive mailboxes. You should monitor the first runs of the MFA on a server to gauge the scope of the activity and how long a "normal" run takes to complete. Equipped with this information, you'll be able to quickly assess whether future runs are progressing as expected.

After the MFA has applied a new policy to a mailbox, the next time that the user connects to the mailbox with a client that supports retention policies, she will see that retention tags are shown on items and the retention policy options are visible. Another important point that you should understand is that if you apply a retention policy that contains a default policy tag, the MFA will stamp the default tag on every item in the mailbox. This action will force Outlook to download the complete contents of the mailbox the next time the client connects and synchronizes with Exchange. Clearly, such a massive synchronization has the potential to flood a network and keep clients fully occupied for a long time. Including a default archive tag in a policy does not have the same effect, as the MFA does not stamp every item with this tag.

Putting a mailbox on retention hold

When you put a mailbox on retention hold, you tell Exchange to suspend the processing of any retention policies that apply to the mailbox. For example, if a user is away for an extended period and will not be able to process the items in his mailbox, you could put his mailbox on retention hold to prevent Exchange moving from items to his archive mailbox. You can set retention hold on a mailbox through EMC or EMS. To do this with EMC, select the mailbox and view its properties. Click the Mailbox Settings tab and select the Messaging Records Management option. You can then select the start and end date for the retention hold period (Figure 15-19). Setting any hold on a mailbox—retention or litigation—could take up to 60 minutes to become effective because the hold is respected after Exchange refreshes the cache that it uses to hold account information.

The equivalent command to set retention hold on a mailbox as executed through EMS is shown next. You'll see that we have also added a retention comment in this command. The retention comment does not appear in versions of Outlook before Outlook 2010 as there is no user interface exposed for this purpose. Outlook Web App does not display the retention comment either, for the same reason. The retention comment will appear in Outlook after the MFA next runs and processes the mailbox.

```
Set-Mailbox -Identity 'Andrews, Lisa (Sales)' -RetentionHoldEnabled $True
-StartDateForRetentionHold '7/20/2010 8:00:00 AM' -EndDateForRetentionHold
'8/11/2010 8:00:00 AM'
```

Chapter 15

```
-RetentionComment 'This mailbox is on retention hold while the user is on vacation
between July 20 and August 11, 2010'
```

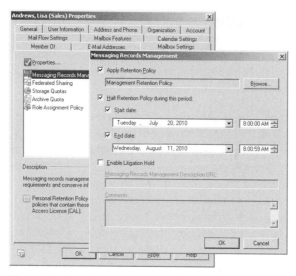

Figure 15-19 Setting retention hold through EMC.

To remove the retention hold and restore the normal processing of retention policies, set the property to $False:

```
Set-Mailbox -Identity 'Andrews, Lisa (Sales)' -RetentionHoldEnabled $False
-RetentionComment $Null
```

Putting a mailbox on litigation hold

When you place a mailbox on litigation hold (sometimes referred to as "legal hold"), Exchange stops removing items when their deleted items retention period expires, and any attempts by the user to delete or change items are retained in the dumpster. Items remain in the dumpster indefinitely until the litigation hold is released and are not subject to any quotas. Because items are retained, they remain available to be indexed and can be retrieved by discovery searches (see the section "Discovery searches" later in this chapter).

Exchange 2010 RTM only supports placing a mailbox on litigation hold using the Set-Mailbox cmdlet. For example:

```
Set-Mailbox -Identity 'Ruth, Andy (VP Sales)' -LitigationHoldEnabled $True
-RetentionComment 'Mailbox placed on litigation hold on 16 May 2010'
-RetentionURL 'http://intranet.contoso.com/LegalHold.html'
-LitigationHoldDate '4/1/2011 09:00'
-LitigationHoldOwner 'Legal Department'
```

With Exchange 2010 SP1, you can set litigation hold on a mailbox with EMC in much the same way as you set retention hold on a mailbox (Figure 15-20).

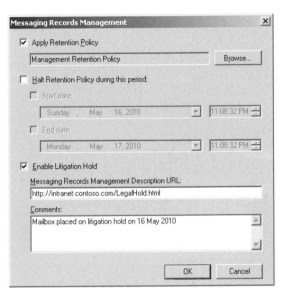

Figure 15-20 Setting litigation hold on a mailbox with EMC.

The *RetentionComment* and *RetentionURL* properties are used to populate the Account Settings section of Outlook 2010's backstage area to inform users that their mailbox has been placed on hold. The *–LitigationHoldDate* and *–LitigationHoldOwner* parameters are only available with Exchange 2010 SP1 and are used to hold the date and time when the hold was enforced and the account that enforced the hold. Exchange completes these details automatically when you place a mailbox on litigation hold using EMC or ECP, so if you put a mailbox on hold with EMS you should also provide these details.

Litigation hold: What about the user?

Exchange doesn't automatically inform users that their mailbox has been placed on litigation hold, and unless they visit the backstage area and notice the retention comment, they will be unaware that their mailbox is in a hold status. Indeed, if they don't use Outlook 2010, users might never be aware of this fact. For this reason, you might want to incorporate a step in the hold process where whoever authorizes the litigation hold is responsible for sending users an email notification to inform them why the hold is being placed on their mailbox and provide some information about what being on litigation hold means for a mailbox.

Releasing the mailbox from litigation hold is done by reversing the process:

```
Set-Mailbox -Identity 'Akers, Kim' -LitigationHoldEnabled $False
-RetentionComment $Null
```

To set litigation hold through ECP, select the mailbox and scroll down to the Mailbox Features section to reveal the option (Figure 15-21). You can then enable the hold and input an appropriate retention comment and URL for users to access more information about what this new status means for them. After you save the new setting, Exchange updates the mailbox properties (as previously) and advises you that it might take up to 60 minutes before the hold becomes effective.

Figure 15-21 Putting a mailbox on litigation hold with ECP.

The exact delay depends on your Active Directory infrastructure and how quickly updated mailbox settings are replicated. Two influences are in play. First, Active Directory must replicate the updated litigation hold property to all global catalog servers before you can be assured that the setting applies across the forest. Second, the Store caches Active Directory data about mailbox properties for performance reasons and therefore will not know that the litigation hold setting has changed for the mailbox until the next time that the Store refreshes its cache. The updated litigation hold setting will be fetched from Active Directory and become effective the next time that the Store refreshes its cache. The complete cycle of Active Directory replication and Store cache refreshes could take up to an hour. For this reason, it is a good idea to implement litigation holds, if possible, at a time when users are not actively using their mailboxes.

The very valuable dumpster

Two dumpsters operate in Exchange. The transport dumpster functions on hub transport servers and acts as a repository for in-transit messages that might have to be replayed after a server outage, so although it functions on an ongoing basis, an administrator shouldn't have to rely on the transport dumpster too often. The Store dumpster is much more useful on a day-to-day basis because it works for every mailbox and saves administrators from the need to restore mailbox databases to recover items that users have deleted in error. Of course, not every user can justify the expense of going through a full database recovery—and even the most important users probably can't justify the expense for every item that they delete in error—but mailbox restores for item recovery were quite a common practice before the dumpster first appeared in Exchange 2000. The elimination of these restore operations is of huge value to administrators, and that's why the dumpster is one of the high-value, low-cost features in Exchange.

Dumpster basics

Before we consider the changes that have occurred in Exchange 2010, we should review some dumpster basics. By default, the dumpster holds an item for a retention period after a user deletes it from a folder. The default retention period is 7 days in Exchange 2003 and 14 days in Exchange 2007 and Exchange 2010. Items in the dumpster are "soft deleted" in that users have deleted them from their original folder and emptied the Deleted Items folder. The items still remain in the database. In previous versions of Exchange, soft deleted items are kept in the Deleted Items folder but are hidden from the user's view. In Exchange 2010, when users empty their Deleted Items folder, Exchange moves the items into a new subfolder under Recoverable Items called Deletions. The items in this folder are what Outlook and Outlook Web App show when a user selects the Recover Deleted Items option. Non-MAPI clients that use protocols such as Post Office Protocol 3 (POP3) and Internet Message Access Protocol 4 (IMAP4) do not include the user interface or the basic support in the protocols to enable recovery from the dumpster, and that's why you don't find the feature in these clients.

When you select the Recover Deleted Items option, Outlook displays a list of all of the items in the dumpster. For example, Figure 15-22 shows a list of deleted items from my mailbox as displayed through Outlook Web App. (Outlook Web App is a little more functional than Outlook because it allows you greater flexibility about where to recover items, including the ability to create a new folder for the purpose.) The list includes items deleted from all folders, including those that have transited through the Deleted Items folder and those placed directly into the dumpster by being hard deleted with the Shift+Delete key combination.

Figure 15-22 Recovering deleted items from the dumpster.

Recoverable items expire when the dumpster's retention period passes, at which time the items will be hard deleted or permanently removed from the database. Items can also be hard deleted immediately as the *PermanentlyDeleted* action required by a retention tag. In this case, the MFA is responsible for removing the items stamped with the tag from the database and these items are deleted the next time that the MFA runs after the item's retention period expires. Deleted items that are still recoverable don't count against the user's normal mailbox quota, so an extended retention period won't make any difference to users, except that they can recover items at any time up until the retention period passes.

> **Experience says: Use longer deleted items retention periods**
>
> By contrast, once removed from the database, items can only be made available again by an administrator after considerable effort to restore the database that contains the mailbox from a backup and then exporting the recovered items to a PST to provide to the user. It is for this reason that experienced Exchange administrators prefer to use longer rather than shorter deleted items retention periods. The default 14-day period is a good starting point, but 28 days might be even better. After all, if someone can't remember that she made a mistake in deleting an item within 28 days, maybe the item isn't important enough to warrant administrator intervention.

By default, Outlook 2003 only supports recovery of items that were originally removed from the Deleted Items folder, whereas Outlook 2007 allows recovery of items from any folder, including those that have been hard deleted. You can force Outlook 2003 to support recovery of deleted items from any folder by inserting a new DWORD value set to 1 in the following location:

HKEY_LOCAL_MACHINE\Software\Microsoft\Exchange\Client\Options\DumpsterAlwaysOn

Dumpster 2.0 arrives

From a user perspective, the experience of working with the Exchange 2010 dumpster is similar to previous versions. Behind the scenes, the introduction of new features to meet legal and regulatory requirements has had a massive influence on the dumpster. If users are under litigation hold, it's obvious that they shouldn't be able to affect the content in the dumpster, as deleted items could form part of the legal record. This requirement prompted Microsoft to look at how the dumpster works and led to the design of an enhanced dumpster ("dumpster 2.0") for Exchange 2010. Among the major changes are the following:

- Items in the dumpster are included when you move a mailbox from one database to another rather than being purged as in previous versions of Exchange. This prevents the loss of any item that should be retained as a consequence of normal rebalancing of server load.

- Items in the dumpster are indexed so that they can be discovered by searches.

- The Store maintains a quota for the dumpster.

- Versions are maintained of changes made to items in the mailbox.

- Users cannot purge data by using the Recover Deleted Items option to view the contents of the dumpster, selecting one or more items, and then deleting them (with the "X" option shown previously in Figure 15-22).

- The dumpster is maintained on a per-mailbox rather than a per-folder basis.

The Exchange 2007 version of the dumpster is based on a hidden view maintained on a per-folder basis. As items are deleted, the Store sets a MAPI flag (ptagDeletedOnFlag) and starts the retention time countdown. The deleted items stay in the folder but are hidden from clients. They cannot be indexed or searched because Outlook and other clients don't see these items. This mechanism works, but it can't accommodate the requirements for indexing to allow discovery searches. The new dumpster is implemented as a hidden folder called Recoverable Items located in the non-IPM subtree of user mailboxes. No client interface ever exposes this subtree, so the folder remains invisible to users. The Recoverable Items folder contains three subfolders called Deletions, Versions, and Purges used to hold items at different points in their journey toward eventual removal from the Store. Using folders instead of views enables indexing and searching and also makes sure that dumpster data are moved along with the rest of the mailbox.

The Deletions folder replaces the MAPI flag and hidden view. When a user deletes an item as normal (soft delete) by emptying the Deleted Items folder, the Store moves the item into the Recoverable Items\Deletions folder. The Recover Deleted Items option accesses this folder, even when accessed by older Outlook clients, as the RPC Client Access Layer interprets client requests that were previously satisfied using the hidden view through items retrieved from the Deletions folder. If the user has a personal archive, a separate set of dumpster folders is maintained in the archive to handle the deletions that occur for archived items.

The Dumpster does not preserve the folder context for deleted items. In other words, you don't see the folder from which an item was deleted when you view the contents of the dumpster. This isn't usually an issue unless you have a very large number of items in the dumpster and therefore have to peruse a long list to find the right item to recover or a user deletes a complete large folder by accident and is faced with the need to find and recover all of the items from the deleted folder from among the mass of other items in the dumpster.

Some observers have commented that this situation happens often enough to keep them busy restoring deleted folders from backup copies, in turn meaning that the thought of ever going to a "no backup" regime for Exchange is impossible until the dumpster captures folder information, too. For now, the default sort order used in the dumpster is the date and time when an item is hard deleted (removed from the Deleted Items folder). Sometimes it is easier to find items if you click the appropriate column heading to sort by message subject or author. Microsoft is considering how best to improve matters in future versions of Exchange, perhaps by supporting the preservation of the folder structure for deleted items, which potentially would allow you to find items based on the folder from which they were originally soft deleted.

If you enable auditing for a mailbox (see the section "Auditing mailbox access" later in this chapter), Exchange stores the audit data in the Audit subfolder of the Recoverable Items folder in the dumpster. Audit entries age out after 90 days by default, so this folder can contain many items if a high degree of audit settings is enabled on the mailbox.

> **Note**
>
> The dumpster does not retain information if you delete a mailbox. The dumpster only handles deleted items from active mailboxes, so if you delete a mailbox, its content is no longer visible to Exchange for functions such as discovery searches. You can't suspend the final removal of a mailbox and retain it indefinitely or for a specified period, either, as the Store will remove a deleted mailbox permanently from its database when the deleted mailbox retention period expires. If you need to retain information for mailboxes used by people who leave the organization so that the items in the mailboxes can be found by discovery searches, you can disable the mailbox and keep it for as long as the items might be required. You could also import any PSTs that you want to retain into the mailbox to make them available to searches.

Single item recovery

From a user perspective, everything discussed so far works as in previous versions. The foundation is different but the effect remains the same. The Versions and Purges subfolders, which are never exposed to clients, provide additional functionality by allowing Exchange to preserve data even if a user attempts to change or purge deleted items. Microsoft calls this feature Single Item Recovery.

As we know, deleted items are now held in the Recoverable Items\Deletions folder and remain there until the deleted items retention period elapses, at which time the MFA permanently removes them from the database. Mailboxes that are placed on litigation hold do not respect the deleted items retention period, and items will remain in the folder until the litigation hold is released. Note that calendar items are always retained for 120 days, the logic being that the calendars of those under investigation are usually highly interesting to the teams working on legal discovery.

It is possible that a user might seek to change or remove items while they are in the Deletions folder. For example, if users receive a message containing some incriminating information, they can delete it with Shift+Delete to force the item into the Deletions folder. They can then use the Recover Deleted Items option to view the items in the Deletions folder, select the offending item, and delete it. In previous versions of Exchange, the item would be immediately removed from the database and a database restore would be required to retrieve it thereafter. Administrators will probably not be aware that the item was deleted, the database recovery will probably never be performed, and the item is lost for good.

However, for Exchange 2010 mailboxes that are enabled for single item recovery, the Store moves the item into the Recoverable Item\Purges folder. Users are unaware of this fact because the Purges folder is invisible to any client, and they probably don't know that their mailbox is enabled for single item recovery. As far as the users are concerned, the evidence has been buried, but the Purges folder is indexed so a discovery search performed by an administrator will locate the item in the Purges folder as long as it is within the deleted items retention period. The items identified by a search are extracted and placed into the selected discovery mailbox in a folder named after the user and the date and time of the search. The administrator or other authorized user with access to the discovery search mailbox can then export the discovered items to provide the evidence to the legal team.

The Versions folder comes into play if users attempt to alter an item. Let's assume that a user is worried about a document attached to a message in the Inbox. She opens the message, removes the attachment, and saves the change. To the user's eyes, the item no longer has an attachment, but in reality the Store has saved a copy of the original message complete with the attachment in the Versions folder. Technically speaking, any action that changes an item generates a new version through a copy-on-write operation. Changes to subjects, message bodies, attachments, sender and recipient details, and date information are all examples of actions that generate a new version. Table 15-4 lists the actions that cause Exchange to retain a new version of an item in the Versions subfolder.

Table 15-4 Actions that cause item versions to be generated

Item	Actions that cause versions to be retained
Messages and posts	Updates to: Subject Item body Attachments Sender or recipient data Send or received dates
Other item types	Changes to any property visible to a client except: The folder in which the item is stored Item read status Retention tag status

Draft items are the only exception to dumpster processing. A draft item is one that has the "unsent" bit set in the MAPI message flags. If this bit is set, the dumpster does not capture updates in the versions folder. There are two reasons for this: First, a draft item typically goes through multiple revisions that might be captured by a client's auto-save process before it is eventually sent. Second, a draft item is not really interesting for discovery until it is sent and becomes a full-fledged communication to another person. After all, it's not a problem if a user thinks about doing something wrong, such as making an illegal recommendation to someone else to engage in insider trading, and captures the thought in a draft message. The thought only becomes a problem and consequently of interest for discovery purposes if the user sends the message to another person.

INSIDE OUT   **Keeping items indefinitely through a litigation hold**

Items captured through single item recovery remain in the Purges and Versions folders until their normal retention period expires. When this happens, the MFA removes the items as normal. If you need to keep items for an indefinite period, you should enable litigation hold for the mailbox as this instructs Exchange to keep everything until the hold is eventually lifted.

Knowing what's in the dumpster

A user can view the items in the dumpster at any time by using the Recover Deleted Items option in Outlook or Outlook Web App. Administrators can't access items in the dumpster unless they open a user's mailbox, but they can get a sense of how much data are held there and what type of data they are by using the Get-MailboxFolderStatistics cmdlet and pointing it at the dumpster with the *–FolderScope* parameter. For example:

```
Get-MailboxFolderStatistics –Identity TR –FolderScopeRecoverableItems |
Select Identity, ItemsInFolder, FolderSize, FolderType
```

Identity	ItemsInFolder	FolderSize	FolderType
tr\Recover	6	15.1 KB (15,466 bytes)	RecoverableItemsRoot
tr\Deletions	75	6.905 MB (7,240,761 bytes)	RecoverableItemsDeletions
tr\Purges	9	40.59 KB (41,562 bytes)	RecoverableItemsPurges
tr\Versions	3	269.7 KB (276,174 bytes)	RecoverableItemsVersions

You can see references to the different types of items captured by the dumpster. As we know from the description in the previous section:

- The Root folder holds stripped versions of calendar items.

- The Deletions folder stores any soft deleted items.

- The Purges folder stores any hard deleted items.

- The Versions folder stores any previous versions of deleted items that have been edited.

Calendar items are held in the dumpster for 120 days. "Stripped" versions of calendar items have no attachments. Exchange creates these copies from calendar items that are purged or updated in the dumpster to use as logs to track these changes. The stripped items are stored in the Root folder of the dumpster. Full copies of items that are changed or purged are also stored in the Versions or Purges folders, respectively.

Managing dumpster parameters

Single item recovery is not enabled for any mailbox by default. You can enable a mailbox as follows:

```
Set-Mailbox -Identity 'John Smith' -SingleItemRecoveryEnabled $True
```

In a scenario where executives or other users who need to use single item recovery are gathered into a single database, you can enable all the mailboxes by piping a list of mailboxes into the Set-Mailbox cmdlet. In this example, we also set the period for the Store to maintain the deleted items to 28 days (the default is 14).

```
Get-Mailbox -Database 'DB1' | Set-Mailbox -SingleItemRecoveryEnabled $True
-RetainDeletedItemsFor 28
```

Exchange doesn't provide a method to configure every mailbox in an organization for single item recovery through a global setting. It's easy (but slow in large organizations) to find all mailboxes with the Get-Mailbox cmdlet and set single item recovery for each, but you then face the task of ensuring that any new mailboxes are enabled for single item recovery thereafter, meaning that you have to run jobs to locate mailboxes that haven't been enabled regularly. This is an annoyance that Microsoft is aware of and one that they are considering addressing in a future release.

Moving on from single item recovery, you can set a default deleted items retention period for a database with the Set-MailboxDatabase cmdlet:

```
Set-MailboxDatabase -Identity 'DB1' -DeletedItemRetention 15
```

Like many other settings, these are held in Active Directory and cached by the Store for faster access. The exact time when a mailbox is enabled for single item recovery depends on how quickly Active Directory replicates the new setting around the organization and when the Store cache is refreshed after replication.

Items in these folders do not count against the mailbox quota. You can set separate quotas for the dumpster folders on a per-mailbox or per-database level. For example:

```
Set-Mailbox -Identity 'John Smith' -RecoverableItemsWarningQuota 1GB
-RecoverableItemsQuota 1.5GB
```

In this case, we set a warning point at 1 GB and an absolute quota at 1.5 GB for the dumpster folders in the specified mailbox. The default values used if these parameters are not explicitly set are 20 GB and 30 GB, which seems excessive unless a mailbox is placed under litigation hold and needs to maintain a large amount of deleted items for a significant period. Increasing the retention quota does not affect the mailbox quota, but it does have an impact on the calculation of database size as the Store keeps the deleted items in the same database.

When the total size of the folders reaches the warning point, the Store issues warnings in the event log. Litigation hold disables expiry of items from the dumpster, so they will be held until the litigation hold is released. More important, Store background maintenance will begin to delete the oldest items in the Deletions folder to free up space and to accommodate newly deleted items. If the absolute quota is reached, the Store flags the error and will not preserve newly deleted items until some quota is released.

Table 15-5 summarizes the different data retention states that an Exchange 2010 mailbox can be in from the default position where the mailbox essentially operates much like Exchange 2003 or Exchange 2007—through the enabling of single item recovery—which provokes the use of the Purges and Versions folders, to a point where litigation hold freezes the mailbox and prevents any data from being removed until the hold is released.

Table 15-5 **The different data retention states for Exchange 2010 mailboxes**

Mailbox status	Deleted items kept in dumpster	Versions and purges kept in dumpster	User can delete items from the dumpster	When message management removes items from the dumpster
Default—Single item recovery not enabled on a mailbox	Yes	No	Yes	After deletion item retention period expires (120 days for calendar items)
Single item recovery enabled	Yes	Yes	No	After deletion item retention period expires (120 days for calendar items)
Litigation hold enabled for mailbox	Yes	Yes	No	Items retained until litigation hold is released

Initial measurement of the effect of single item recovery on mailbox sizes indicates a growth of 3 to 5 percent for a 14-day retention period. It's not usual to enable every mailbox in a database for single item recovery unless you have dedicated databases for VIPs or other users affected by legal proceedings, so the overall effect on a mailbox database is usually less.

Discovery searches

Discovery searches are performed through ECP by users who hold the Discovery Management role. ECP reveals the options to initiate mailbox searches under the Reporting node (Figure 15-23) to mailboxes that hold the Discovery Management role. This feature is a good example of functionality that is available through ECP and doesn't appear in EMC.

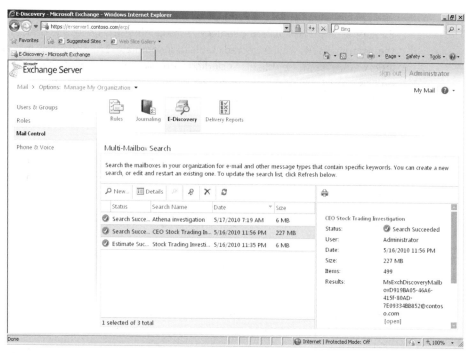

Figure 15-23 Viewing the ECP options for mailbox searches.

It is a quirk of Microsoft licensing policy that you need an enterprise CAL to be able to use the Discovery options included in ECP, but a standard CAL suffices if you conduct searches using the Search-Mailbox cmdlet as described later on in this section. You can therefore save a few dollars by executing all searches through EMS, which seems to be a strange situation!

Exchange is able to search across items stored in primary mailboxes, archive mailboxes, and the dumpster. It is not able to search through mailboxes that are deleted, even if the mailbox content is still in the database, because it hasn't exceeded the deleted mailbox retention period.

INSIDE OUT Discovery search policy for exiting employees

If your company commonly needs to conduct discovery searches, it's wise to have a policy of disabling mailboxes for a month or so after someone leaves the company rather than rushing to delete mailboxes. This is especially true for mailboxes that belong to company officers or other executives, where you might need to keep a mailbox for up to a year after an employee leaves the company.

The content index catalogs that are maintained for mailbox databases are critical to Exchange's ability to perform searches: If the catalogs are unhealthy or not fully populated, then search results will be unpredictable or incomplete. Exchange uses the same content indexes for searches by clients, including Outlook Web App and Outlook. However, Outlook only uses the Exchange content indexes when it is configured to work in online mode. Most Outlook clients are now configured in cached Exchange mode, in which case they use local search indexes created with Windows Desktop Search to be able to conduct searches even when they are not connected to a server.

Microsoft introduced the current system of content indexing in Exchange 2007 and improved the performance and throughput of the content indexing component in Exchange 2010 in the following areas:

- Content indexing uses fewer system resources such as CPU, memory, I/O, and disk space.

- Items are typically indexed within 10 seconds of their creation on a server. Query results are much faster.

- You don't need to configure Exchange Search. It is automatically installed and configured on all mailbox servers.

- Attachments are indexed (see the "Unsearchable items" discussion next).

- Indexing throttles back automatically in periods when mailbox servers experience heavy load. Again, administrators don't have to take any action for this to happen.

Administrators tend to forget about content indexing because it hums away in the background and doesn't make their lives difficult.

Unsearchable items

As shown in the left screen in Figure 15-24, all item types are discoverable, including voice messages, drafts, attached documents of various formats, and IM conversations (if stored in mailboxes). Before Exchange can include a document, usually an attachment to a message, in its content indexes, it must be able to extract the content. Exchange includes a set of content filters for this purpose. Unlike the RTM version of Exchange 2010, Exchange 2010 SP1 registers the IFilters for Office 2010 with Exchange Search. However, if you want to use other IFilters, such as the one for Adobe PDF, you have to install them separately.

See *http://technet.microsoft.com/en-us/library/ff622320.aspx* for more information.

You can see the list of default filters installed on mailbox servers by looking in the system registry at HKLM\SOFTWARE\Microsoft\ExchangeServer\v14\MSSearch\Filters. The list includes formats that you would expect, such as Microsoft Office, text attachments, HTML files, and so on.

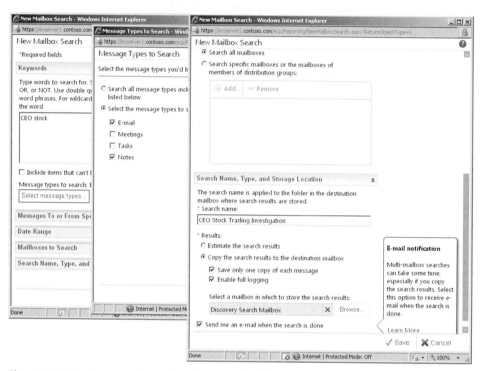

Figure 15-24 Determining the options for a multimailbox search.

If Exchange meets content that it doesn't understand, it marks the item as unsearchable. For example, if you use an application that generates files of a type that are only understood if the application is installed on a client workstation, the content indexing agent running on a mailbox server won't be able to open and index the files. Other items that Exchange deems as unsearchable include items encrypted with Secure Multipurpose Internet Mail Extensions (S/MIME). However, messages protected with Active Directory Rights Management Services remain searchable for discovery purposes.

You can see a list of unsearchable items with the Get-FailedContentIndexDocuments cmdlet. When you run the cmdlet, you can pass it the name of a server to see all items on a server, or just a mailbox database to see the unsearchable items in the content index for that database. For example, here's how to run the cmdlet followed by an extract of the information returned for an unsearchable item (pipe the results to the Format-List cmdlet to see this information). As you can see, the item shown couldn't be indexed because a filter wasn't found for the attachment type.

```
Get-FailedContentIndexDocuments -MailboxDatabase DB1
```

```
RunspaceId        : 5de022fc-bd60-4b22-8f5e-e983550a4f8a
DocID             : 21847
Database          : DB3
MailboxGuid       : ab83c57b-d51c-4527-8f99-5609e0ee96c8
Mailbox           : Ruth, Andy
SmtpAddress       : Andy.Ruth@contoso.com
EntryID           : 000000002BA4E1B5193C7441BCD9110F91902C5A0700A0EAF17663EEB9429D-
934943C3A2409300000000002000005036EA2334225B46B46EA1623061B2A40000017803030000
Subject           : Designing Secure Multi-Tenancy into Virtualized data center (Secure Cloud
Architecture)
ErrorCode         : 2147749142
Description       : Filter not found
IsPartialIndexed  : True
Identity          :
IsValid           : True
```

Should you be worried if many unsearchable items exist for your database? The answer is, "It depends." First, it depends on the percentage of unsearchable items. If 0.0002 percent of items are unsearchable, then it's probably acceptable because any search has a very high chance of discovering information that's required. Second, it depends on the items that are failing to be indexed. If they are all of the same type and a filter is available, you can install that filter to solve the problem. However, if the items are of a type for which a filter is not available or known to be unsearchable (such as S/MIME encrypted items), then you might have to live with the situation.

See *http://technet.microsoft.com/en-us/library/ff354976(EXCHG.80).aspx* for information about how to install a new filter.

Normally, a relatively small number of items turn out to be unsearchable. In addition, you should remember that item properties (sender, recipients, subject, and so on) and message bodies are always indexed and searchable, so the fact that a small percentage of attachments can't be searched is probably not going to be of great concern in a legal search. After all, if people are doing something that they shouldn't, it's likely that they will leave some trace of their activity in a searchable property that will be discovered. After this happens, the next step is often for investigators to take a complete copy of the suspect's mailbox to conduct a detailed search to discover what it contains, and any lurking unsearchable items can be reviewed at that time.

Creating and executing a multimailbox search

A mailbox search can cover every mailbox in the organization (rightmost screen in Figure 15-24) or a select set formed of individual mailboxes or the members of specific distribution groups (but not dynamic distribution groups). You can include other search criteria such as date ranges and specific words or phrases in message bodies and subjects. You can update the search criteria multiple times; each time you do, Exchange will restart the search and discard any items found using the previous criteria. However, if you want to change the criteria for a search while it is being processed, you have to stop the search before you can make any changes.

After you input all the search criteria and click Save, Exchange stores the criteria as search metadata in the default discovery mailbox. At this point, the original version of Exchange 2010 proceeds to execute a full search and will copy any results that it finds into the selected discovery mailbox. Exchange 2010 SP1 offers you the option of running either an estimate or the search. A search estimate is a scan of the content indexes to determine how many hits are likely if you initiate a search with the criteria as provided. You can see these options revealed under the Search Name And Storage Location section of the right-most screen in Figure 15-24.

An estimate does not actually retrieve the located items and copy them into the discovery mailbox, so it runs much faster than a "copy" search. After Exchange completes its scan to determine the estimate, the number of hits and the mailboxes that contain items are shown in the results pane (Figure 15-25). Because estimates run faster, you can afford to run a number of estimates to refine the search criteria to meet your exact needs. You don't have to run an estimate before you conduct a full search. If you want to search and copy items without an estimate, just select the Copy Results To The Selected Mailbox option and save the search. However, it makes sense to run an estimate to see just how much data might be found and test the efficiency of the search criteria.

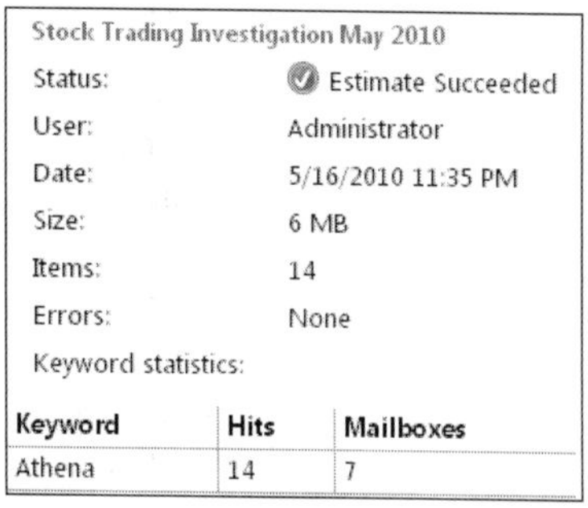

Stock Trading Investigation May 2010		
Status:	✅ Estimate Succeeded	
User:	Administrator	
Date:	5/16/2010 11:35 PM	
Size:	6 MB	
Items:	14	
Errors:	None	
Keyword statistics:		
Keyword	**Hits**	**Mailboxes**
Athena	14	7

Figure 15-25 Viewing a search estimate.

As you refine a search, you'll probably experiment with the query that lies at the heart of the search. The query is passed in Advanced Query Syntax (AQS) format. Table 15-6 lists the most important query terms that you are likely to use in discovery searches.

http://www.microsoft.com/windows/products/winfamily/desktopsearch/technicalresources/ advquery.mspx provides further information about how to construct AQS queries.

Table 15-6 AQS terms that can be used in search queries

Property	Example	Search results
Attachments	Attachment:BadReport.ppt Attachment:Bad*.pp*	Return any items that have an attachment called BadReport.ppt. The second example shows how to use wildcards to conduct a less specific search.
CC	CC: Joe Healy CC: JoeH CC: JoeHealy@contoso.com	Return any message with Joe Healy listed as a CC recipient in the message header. The second and third examples show how to specify a search for an alias or an SMTP address.
From	From: Tony Redmond From: Tony.Redmond@contoso.com	Return any message sent by Tony Redmond using different forms of his address.
Keywords	RetentionPolicy:Critical	Returns any item that has the Critical retention tag applied to it.
Expiration	Expires: 10/10/2010	Returns any item that expires on October 10, 2010.
Search message recipients	Person: Tony Redmond Person: TR@contoso.com	Returns any item that has the recipient included as a To:, CC:, or BCC: in the message header. You can pass the display name, alias, or SMTP address.
Sent	Sent: yesterday	Returns messages sent yesterday.
Subject	Subject: "Trading Tip"	Returns all items that include the words "Trading Tip" in the subject.
To	To: Tony Redmond To: TR@contoso.com	Returns any message that has Tony Redmond listed as a To: recipient. You can use the display name, alias, or SMTP address.

You can run as many search estimates as you want. To change the search criteria, click the Details icon and amend details such as the mailboxes to search or the phrases for which you are looking. It's entirely possible that your first attempt to create a search could result in an estimate of thousands of hits across hundreds of mailboxes when you expect to find just a few items. This might force you to narrow (or sometimes widen) the search criteria. For example, you might exclude some mailboxes from the search or include some new terms that you think will help to locate just the right information. On the other hand, you might be happy that you've found so much data. From Exchange 2010 SP1 onward, ECP and EMS both default to deduplicated searches.

Once you're happy that the search will find the data that you're interested in, you can click the Details icon to change the type of search and instruct Exchange to copy the matching items. You also need to decide whether Exchange should save a copy of each matching item in the discovery mailbox or if it should reduce the number of items that it copies by only capturing the first copy found. After you save the updated search parameters,

Exchange will then conduct the full search and copy any items that it locates into the discovery mailbox.

Mailbox searches are performed in the background. You can wait for the search to be complete or have Exchange notify you with an email (Figure 15-26). The next step is then to access the discovery mailbox where Exchange has copied the items found by the search.

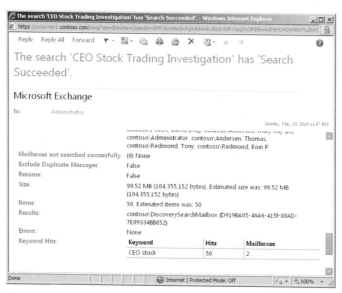

Figure 15-26 Notification message after a successful search.

Accessing search results

By default, there is a single discovery mailbox in an Exchange organization. As described in Chapter 6, you can create additional discovery mailboxes to use to hold search results, and you have to select a discovery mailbox to use when you create a new search. The results of the search, including copies of all items that match the search criteria, will be placed in the selected discovery mailbox. If you have the necessary permission to access the discovery mailbox, you can enter its name in the in the Switch Mailbox control (Figure 15-27). The name of the default discovery mailbox is long, but you can enter the first few characters and then press Ctrl+K to have Outlook Web App validate the mailbox name. Thereafter, Outlook Web App will remember the mailbox and you can select it easily from a drop-down list of mailboxes if you need to access the discovery mailbox again. Of course, you can also use Outlook to open the discovery mailbox by configuring a suitable profile.

Figure 15-27 Switching to the discovery mailbox.

Within the discovery mailbox, Exchange inserts the items located by a search into a set of folders called after the name that you gave to the search. For example, if you call the search "Illegal stock trading investigation," Exchange will create a root folder of this name in the discovery mailbox and then create a child folder underneath for each mailbox where a matching item was found. The date and time of the search (the date and time of the server rather than the client workstation that starts the search) is appended to the mailbox name to clearly identify different searches that have occurred and to provide a solid time line for when evidence is gathered for an investigation. If you open the folder for a mailbox (Figure 15-28), you see all of the folders from which items have been copied in both the primary mailbox and the personal archive (if the mailbox has one). You can then click on the items to review their content and decide whether they are of real interest to your investigation. Incriminating evidence can be retained and any useless thoughts of idle minds discarded.

Figure 15-28 Viewing search results in a discovery mailbox.

If you use Active Directory Rights Management Services (see the section "Protecting content" later in this chapter), searches might uncover items that are protected because a user has applied an Information Rights Management (IRM) template to them. When an item is protected, its content can only be read by the sender, the intended recipients, and members of the Active Directory Rights Management Services (AD RMS) Super Users group; the team that is reviewing the contents copied into the discovery mailbox won't be able to see anything but the message header data (Figure 15-29). This information might be enough to eliminate an item from the list of those that an investigator wants to see, but more often it's an indication that makes an item even more interesting to an investigator.

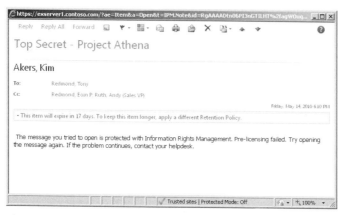

Figure 15-29 Viewing a protected message uncovered by a mailbox search.

Typically, the AD RMS Super Users group only contains the federated system mailbox, as its membership allows Exchange to decrypt protected messages as they pass through the transport system and apply transport and journal rules as required. In the RTM version of Exchange 2010, to allow investigators to view protected content, we therefore have to make the discovery mailbox a member of the AD RMS Super Users group for as long as the investigators need to review items uncovered by the search. The discovery mailbox uses a disabled account, and this also has to be enabled. These actions will allow the AD RMS server to provide the necessary credentials to the discovery mailbox to reveal the hidden content to the investigators. It seems strange to insist that the discovery mailbox account must be enabled to allow access to protected content, but AD RMS can only provide credentials to enabled accounts. The act of enabling the discovery mailbox should be approved and audited by some authority within the company because enabling the account creates a higher risk that someone could have unauthorized access to its contents.

Enabling accounts that should remain disabled is clearly an unacceptable workaround to a problem that should be fixed in software. Microsoft addressed the issue in Exchange 2010 SP1 by introducing a new parameter for the IRM configuration cmdlet to instruct Rights Management to allow access to protected content for legal investigators. To make everything work, you have to run the Set-IRMConfiguration cmdlet as follows:

```
Set-IRMConfiguration -EdiscoverySuperUserEnabled $True
```

Search access to dumpster content

All searches launched by ECP automatically examine the contents of the dumpster (you can exclude the dumpster contents with a search created with EMS) to ensure that any items that are of interest are captured even if a user has attempted to remove all traces of their existence. As shown in Figure 15-30, if an item is found in the dumpster, it will be shown under the Recoverable Items folder within the user's primary mailbox or personal archive.

Figure 15-30 Dumpster items retrieved in a discovery mailbox.

Deduplication of search results

An item that you are searching for might exist in multiple mailboxes. You don't necessarily want to copy every single occurrence of the message from every mailbox in which Exchange finds it. Apart from the system overhead that is incurred to copy and store every instance of a message found in the searched mailboxes, providing extra copies of messages will drive up the cost of responding to legal discovery actions if the lawyers or other individuals who review the search results are paid on a per-item basis. Deduplication is therefore a very useful feature, with the only drawback being that storing the first discovered copy of an item sent to a distribution group does not prove that an individual received the item. You'd need to find the item in their mailbox to prove this.

> **Note**
> Because Exchange does not expand the membership of a group into a message header, seeing that a message was delivered to a group doesn't tell you whether someone received a copy because there's no way of proving what the membership of the group was at the point when the transport service expanded the group membership and delivered the message.

You instruct Exchange to deduplicate search results by selecting the Copy Only One Instance Of The Message option under the Search Name And Storage Location section. When Exchange copies items for a deduplicated search, it places a single copy of each unique item in a single folder called "Results" and the date and time of the search under a root folder for the search name (Figure 15-31). The message identifier, which is a unique value established when items are first created, is used as the basis of deduplication.

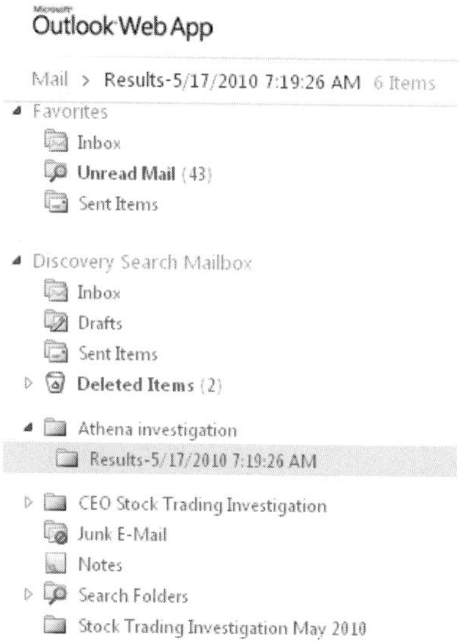

Figure 15-31 The folder structure created by a deduplicate search.

The users who perform discovery searches are not necessarily those who can access the results of the searches that are placed in discovery mailboxes. As discussed in Chapter 6, you need to assign full access permission to the discovery mailbox to a user before he will be able to open it to access the search results. By default, members of the Discovery Management role group should be able to access the default discovery mailbox, but you have to explicitly grant full access to any other discovery mailboxes that you create for use in mailbox searches.

A clear separation therefore exists between the following:

- Membership of the Discovery Management role group, which is required to be able to create and execute mailbox searches.

- Full access to the discovery mailbox used for a mailbox search, which is required to be able to open the discovery mailbox and review the items copied there by the mailbox search.

The separation in the two requirements allows for a division of responsibilities between those who are responsible for responding to requests for information (often the IT department) and those who will review the retrieved information forensically to look for evidence or other information that is important to an investigation (often the legal department). You might therefore create discovery mailboxes to hold information retrieved for different types of searches so that you can restrict access to those mailboxes to ensure that confidential material is always treated in a correct and legally defendable manner. Some discovery mailboxes might be used for straightforward legal discovery actions and be under the control of the legal department, whereas others might be used for the pursuit of internal complaints against an employee for something like sexual harassment and be restricted to selected members of the HR department.

CAUTION

Access to content held in discovery mailboxes should be carefully controlled so that only the people who need to be able to review and work with the data have access. You also need to be sure that the users do not interfere with the search results in an unauthorized manner. For example, it would not be a good situation if someone attempted to cover up illegal activities by appearing to conduct a search for suspicious items and then deleted a selected group of the discovered items to remove evidence. To address this situation, you can enable auditing for discovery mailboxes to force Exchange to capture information about the actions that these users take when they work with items. More information about how to set up mailbox auditing is available in the section "Auditing mailbox access" later in this chapter.

Search logging

Exchange generates a log for every mailbox search unless you suppress it by setting the *–LogLevel* parameter for the search to Suppress. By default, the search log captures basic information about the parameters used for the search as well as the results of the search. You can also increase the logging level to Full, in which case Exchange captures information about the items that are captured by the search in an attachment. The search report and any attachment are stored in the top-level folder created for the search in the discovery mailbox. Figure 15-32 shows a typical search report. You can see that it has an attachment, so this indicated that the logging level was set to full (you can also see this in the search parameters).

You can conduct a search and copy results multiple times. However, if you do this without creating a new search, Exchange removes the previous search results from the discovery mailbox before it copies items as a result of the new search. Therefore, you have to create and execute a new search if you want to keep the results of a previous search.

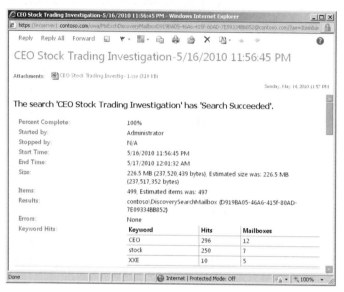

Figure 15-32 Viewing a search log report.

Search annotation

The ability to annotate search results is a new feature in Exchange 2010 SP1. Basically, the idea is that the people who look through search results should be able to mark the items that are of interest. Exchange accomplishes this through some special user interface that Outlook Web App exposes whenever a user logs into a discovery mailbox.

Figure 15-33 shows how annotation works. The Open Message Annotation option is exposed in the shortcut menu. This opens a simple text box to allow users to input whatever text they deem fit to mark the item. For example, they might mark items with a case reference or other indicator. Later on, they can search the mailbox for the marked items to see the collection of items of interest. There's no feature provided to export annotated items from the discovery mailbox if you need to provide copies for use elsewhere, but it's easy to copy the items to a folder and then use the New-MailboxExportRequest cmdlet to export the folder to a PST. Alternatively, you can open the discovery mailbox with Outlook and drag and drop the copied items into a PST.

The annotation is only visible through Outlook Web App and can't be accessed with other clients.

Figure 15-33 Annotation of search results.

Executing searches with EMS

ECP is a very convenient interface to create and initiate searches, but you can also do the same through EMS using a set of cmdlets that are only exposed if you are a member of the Discovery Management role group. These cmdlets are as follows:

- **New-MailboxSearch** Creates and initiates a new mailbox search.

- **Get-MailboxSearch** Retrieves details of a mailbox search.

- **Set-MailboxSearch** Changes the search criteria for a search that has already been created.

- **Start-MailboxSearch** Restarts a mailbox search.

- **Remove-MailboxSearch** Removes a mailbox search. This action also removes all of the items found by a search from the discovery mailbox.

For example, a new search to look for information about potential illegal stock trading by company officers could be initiated with this command:

```
New-MailboxSearch -Name "Stock Trading Discovery 2" -SourceMailboxes 'Company
Officers' -TargetMailbox 'DiscoveryMailbox@contoso.com' -StartDate '10/01/2010'
-EndDate '11/30/2010' -SearchQuery "XXE Stock tip"
-StatusMailRecipients 'LegalSearch@contoso.com' -SearchDumpster -DoNotIncludeArchive
-EstimateOnly
-IncludeUnsearchableItems -ExcludeDuplicateMessages:$False -LogLevel Full
```

Table 15-7 lists the most important parameters that you are likely to use with the New-MailboxSearch cmdlet and their meaning.

Table 15-7 **Important parameters for the New-MailboxSearch cmdlet**

Parameter	Meaning
Name	A unique identifier for the search that should be something meaningful, such as "Illegal stock trading review."
SourceMailboxes	Specifies the mailboxes that Exchange will search. If you have more than a few mailboxes to search, it is more convenient (and probably more accurate) to create a distribution group to identify the mailboxes to include in the search. If you don't specify the –SourceMailboxes parameter, Exchange searches all mailboxes.
TargetMailbox	Specifies the SMTP email address of the discovery mailbox where you want to store the search results. The default discovery mailbox has a rather long and complicated email address so I usually assign a new and shorter secondary email address to the mailbox to make it easier to type. In fact, this mailbox doesn't have to be a discovery mailbox, as Exchange is happy to place search results in any mailbox that you select.
SearchQuery	An AQS-format query that Exchange will execute to locate items in the target mailboxes. In the example shown, Exchange will match any of the words in the search query. This search query is a very simple one and some trial and error is probably required to arrive at the best query. If you omit the search query, Exchange will find every item in every mailbox that you include in the search and store copies of all those items in the discovery mailbox. This kind of search can swamp a server with work.
StatusMailRecipients	Tells Exchange the recipients who should be notified by email after the search is complete. No message is sent if you don't provide a value for this parameter. You can provide one or more recipient SMTP addresses to receive notifications, separating each address with a comma. It's often more convenient to use a distribution group for this purpose.
SearchDumpster	Forces Exchange to include the contents of the dumpster in the search. All searches executed through ECP include this parameter. As shown in Figure 15-30, any items from the Dumpster that are found by a search are placed in the Recoverable Items folder in the discovery mailbox.
DoNotIncludeArchive	Instructs Exchange to ignore items stored in any personal archives that are assigned to mailboxes.
EstimateOnly	Tells Exchange that it is to run a search estimate only rather than to copy items that match the search criteria to the discovery mailbox.
ExcludeDuplicateMessages	Tells Exchange how to deal with duplicate items that it encounters in mailboxes. Set the parameter to $True to force Exchange to deduplicate (only copy a single instance of an item) or $False to copy every copy of an item that it finds.
LoaLevel	Dictates the level of logging that Exchange performs for the search. Valid options are Suppress, Basic (default), and Full. If Basic or Full are chosen, Exchange creates a search report in the root folder for the search in the discovery mailbox.

The Get-MailboxSearch cmdlet tells us what happened to a search. All known searches are revealed. For example:

```
Get-MailboxSearch | Format-Table Name, Status, PercentComplete, ResultSize,
ResultNumber -AutoSize
```

Name	Status	PercentComplete	ResultSize	ResultNumber
Review Dumpster content	InProgress	39 112.8 MB	(118,262,783 bytes)	395
Deduplicated search	Failed	9 3.061 MB	(3,209,944 bytes)	20
XXE Investigation March 2010	InProgress	87 1.132 GB	(1,214,974,519 bytes)	730
CEO Discovery	Succeeded	100 136.1 MB	(142,687,323 bytes)	161
XXE Investigation Feb 2010	Succeeded	100 134.8 MB	(141,344,252 bytes)	156
Stock Trading Discovery 3	Succeeded	10020.42 MB	(21,413,083 bytes)	536
Stock Trading Discovery 2	Succeeded	1005.269 KB	(5,395 bytes)	2
Illegal stock trading investigation	Succeeded	100 9.008 KB	(9,224 bytes)	2

The information we are interested in here is the status (this will be Estimate Succeeded, Succeeded, InProgress, or Failed) and the number of items found by the search. The size of the items is interesting if we expect to find a large attachment. As you can see from the search called "XXE Investigation March 2010," a search can generate a lot of information. In this case, the search located a number of very large objects (730 objects for 1.132 GB at 87 percent complete), so it will be interesting to check the contents of the discovery mailbox to find out just what these objects are.

INSIDE OUT   Running concurrent searches

You can run concurrent searches as long as each search has a different name. The searches proceed a little slower because of contention when writing found items into the discovery mailbox. If you need to run concurrent searches on an ongoing basis, it would be a good idea to spread the load by creating several discovery mailboxes and locating them in different databases.

Auditing administrator actions

As even a brief reading of this book reveals, an administrator has the ability to change many settings or create many new objects that influence the way Exchange operates. Up to Exchange 2010, there was no facility available to be able to track who did what and when at an administrative level. The addition of Windows PowerShell and its ability to affect many objects with relatively simple commands reinforced the need to be able to log what happens within an Exchange organization.

Exchange 2010 includes the ability to audit actions taken by administrators in EMC and EMS. This is intended to allow organizations to maintain records of who did what and when to execute the cmdlets used to manage Exchange. Apart from providing definitive proof about what account was used to add a mailbox, change properties on a connector, set up a new domain, or any of the myriad day-to-day operations that occur in an Exchange organization, maintaining an audit log can help satisfy legislative requirements by demonstrating that strict controls are imposed on the work that administrators do with Exchange.

Some administrators will not welcome this development and will view it as yet another example of big brother looking over their shoulder as they struggle to keep the email system up and running. Others will consider increased oversight as part of modern life, much in the same way that we all seem to be under the eyes of video surveillance wherever we go. Auditing is not enabled by default. The Set-AdminAuditLogConfig cmdlet controls how administration logging functions across the organization.

```
Set-AdminAuditLogConfig -AdminAuditLogEnabled $True
```

When logging is enabled, administrators see no indication that their actions are being captured in the audit log unless they search the audit log.

Enabling administrative logging instructs the Admin Audit Log agent, one of the standard set of cmdlet extension agents shipped with Exchange 2010, to begin capturing details of administrative events. The admin audit agent runs on all Exchange 2010 servers to monitor the running of all cmdlets and record details of the cmdlets that you configure to be audited. As described in Chapter 3, "The Exchange Management Shell," the execution of all business logic in Exchange 2010 flows through cmdlets so the agent is able to monitor all administrative operations.

INSIDE OUT   Disabling administrative auditing

To disable administrative auditing, you run the same command and set the parameter to $False. Remember that this setting has to be replicated across the organization before it is effective on all servers, so it might take an hour or so before you can be sure that all administrative actions are being captured.

A number of other configuration settings are used to control the finer details of administrator audit logging. You can view the current audit configuration settings for the organization with the Get-AdminAuditLogConfig cmdlet. For example:

```
Get-AdminAuditLogConfig | Format-List
```

```
AdminAuditLogEnabled      : True
TestCmdletLoggingEnabled  : False
AdminAuditLogCmdlets      : {*}
AdminAuditLogParameters   : {*}
AdminAuditLogAgeLimit     : 90.00:00:00
AdminDisplayName          :
ExchangeVersion           : 0.10 (14.0.100.0)
Name                      : Admin Audit Log Settings
DistinguishedName         : CN=Admin Audit Log Settings,CN=Global
Settings,CN=contoso,CN=Microsoft Exchange,CN=Services,CN=Configuration,DC=contoso,DC=com
Identity                  : Admin Audit Log Settings
```

Auditing is performed on a cmdlet basis and can be further refined to select specific parameters to audit. By default, the use of every cmdlet and every parameter is audited, so the preceding configuration has values of "{*}" (asterisk). In fact, Exchange ignores auditing for cmdlets beginning with "Get," "Search," and "Test" so as not to clutter up the audit log with entries for cmdlets that simply retrieve or read information. The purpose here is to audit operations that create or manipulate objects. Enabling the audit of every cmdlet is a bad idea because it will generate a huge mass of audit entries, including entries for actions that are probably not of great concern such as a user updating her OOF.

To focus on a specific set of cmdlets, we define the cmdlets in a list passed in the –AdminAuditLogCmdlets parameter for the Set-AdminAuditLogConfig cmdlet. For example, this command tells Exchange that we want to audit any use of the New-Mailbox and New-DistributionGroup cmdlets and any cmdlet that has "Transport" in its name.

```
Set-AdminAuditLogConfig –AdminAuditLogCmdlets 'New-Mailbox, New-DistributionGroup,
*Transport'
```

Exchange now captures details about any creation of new mailboxes and distribution groups plus any action taken with the cmdlets used to manage the transport service. Let's assume that you only want to capture certain details about new mailboxes. This command captures details of the name, display name, and custom attributes for new mailboxes.

```
Set-AdminAuditLogConfig -AdminAuditLogParameters Name, DisplayName, *Custom'
```

Clearly, you have to arrive at a balance to capture the required auditing data but not so much as to make it difficult to find an instance when necessary. It is likely that some trial and error will be required to settle on the right list of cmdlets and parameters to audit.

Chapter 15

The audit mailbox

On Exchange 2010 RTM servers, you have to create and configure a mailbox to act as the repository for the audit reports that Exchange creates every time that one of the cmdlets within the audit scope is run. Exchange 2010 SP1 removes the requirement to configure an audit mailbox. Instead, SP1 uses a folder called AdminAuditLogs in the special arbitration mailbox with the display name "Microsoft Exchange" as the repository for audit reports. This is a more secure location because administrators can't simply grant themselves access to the audit mailbox and log on to remove any audit reports that they don't want others to see. On the other hand, the change in audit mailbox location means that any audit reports collected in the audit mailbox that you define for Exchange 2010 are ignored for the purposes of the audit reports that you can view through ECP. This shouldn't be a real problem in practice and you can delete the original audit mailbox after you have deployed Exchange 2010 SP1 throughout the organization.

In addition to the change of audit mailbox, SP1 introduces an aging mechanism for audit reports to prevent an unwanted accumulation of data. By default, audit reports are held for 90 days and the MFA removes audit logs after their retention period expires. If you want to change the retention period, you can update it with the Set-AdminAuditLogConfig cmdlet. This command sets the audit log retention period to 182 days (approximately six months):

```
Set-AdminAuditLogConfig -AdminAuditLogAgeLimit 182.00:00:00
```

The audit configuration applies to administrator activity on an organization-wide basis so all of the reports generated across the entire organization go to the one mailbox. As you can imagine, it is all too easy to fill this mailbox with audit reports if you use settings that enable auditing of an extensive set of cmdlets and keep the reports for extended periods.

How administrator auditing happens

Auditing is performed by the Admin Audit Log agent, which evaluates cmdlets as they are run against the audit configuration to decide whether the use of the cmdlet needs to be logged. If so, the agent creates an item containing details of the cmdlet in the Inbox of the audit mailbox. Table 15-8 lists the data that are captured in the audit reports.

Table 15-8 Data captured in audit reports

Field	Description
CmdletName	The name of the cmdlet that was executed
ObjectModified	The object that the cmdlet was used to access (for example, a mailbox)
CmdletParameters	The parameters and values specified for the cmdlet
ModifiedProperties	The properties that were modified by the cmdlet

Caller	The user account that ran the cmdlet
Succeeded	True or False to indicate whether the cmdlet succeeded
Error	Details of any error message that was generated
RunDate	Date and time when the cmdlet was executed in UTC format

The audit agent creates separate reports for each object if you execute an action that is performed against several objects. For example, if you use Get-Mailbox to fetch a list of mailboxes from a database and then use Set-Mailbox to set a new storage quota for each mailbox, the audit agent creates a separate report for each mailbox as it is updated.

You can also write your own entries into the audit log. For example, if you wanted to document a script being run or to take note of a particular administrative operation that you performed to solve a problem, you can capture it with the Write-AdminAuditLog cmdlet as shown here. You can insert up to 500 characters of text into the comment parameter, which is captured in the *CmdletParameters* property of the log entry:

```
Write-AdminAuditLog –Comment 'Server acting up; cleared by increasing HeapSize to
30000'
```

Only one audit mailbox is used for the organization. This can pose some difficulties in widely distributed organizations where actions performed in one part of the network might have difficulty being registered in the arbitration mailbox. Even in highly centralized environments where a small set of administrators perform all actions for the organization, it is still possible to see errors caused by the unavailability of the database that hosts the arbitration mailbox. For example, Figure 15-34 shows what happens when the database containing the audit mailbox is unavailable. Exchange is unable to capture audit entries until the database becomes available again. While the database containing the audit mailbox is unavailable, Exchange writes event 5000 from the msExchange Management Application into the application event for each instance when it is unable to log an audit entry.

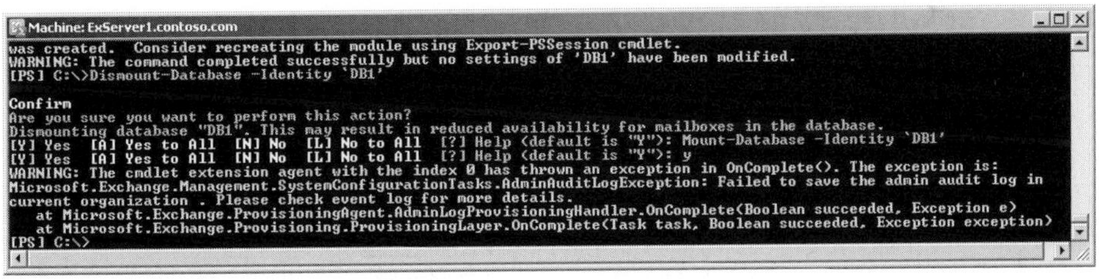

Figure 15-34 EMS flags an error accessing the audit mailbox.

Exchange 2010 doesn't provide facilities to interrogate the audit reports and create analysis of the management activity within an organization. Exchange 2010 SP1 addresses the lack in two ways.

- A set of precanned audit reports that cover the most common needs for an organization (as determined by the Exchange developers) are available through ECP (Figure 15-35). The reports cover both mailbox audit data and administrator audit data.

- The new Search-AdminAuditLog cmdlet is provided to allow administrators to create their own analysis of the administrator audit logs.

The reports provided through ECP depend on the Search-AdminAuditLog and other cmdlets to generate their data. For example, the litigation hold report is created by examining the ligitation hold property set on mailboxes that are on hold and the role groups report examines changes made to role groups to grant permission to users to perform different administrative operations. I'll discuss what happens with mailbox audits and how you can search audit data in the next section.

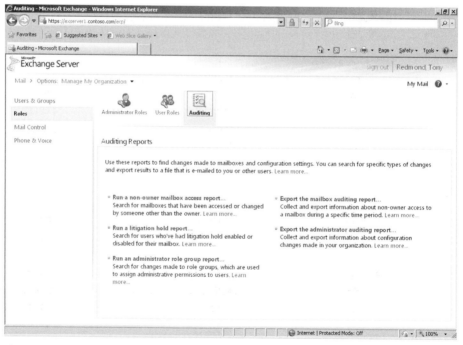

Figure 15-35 Audit reports available in ECP.

Interrogating the audit reports with the Search-AdminAuditLog cmdlet is straightforward. Here are a few examples that illustrate the possibilities that exist to discover just what administrators are doing within the organization:

1. Search for actions performed by one or more users. Each of the users that you want to look for is identified by alias, email address, display name, or distinguished name. Separate the names with commas:

```
Search-AdminAuditLog –UserIds Administrator, 'Tony.Redmond@contoso.com' |
Format-Table Rundate, Caller, CmdletName
```

RunDate	Caller	CmdletName
4/5/2010 7:45:56 PM	contoso.com/Users/Administrator	Set-Group
4/5/2010 10:18:11 PM	contoso.com/Users/Administrator	Set-OrganizationConfig
4/6/2010 1:50:38 AM	contoso.com/Users/Administrator	Set-Mailbox
4/6/2010 1:55:07 AM	contoso.com/Users/Administrator	New-MailboxImportRequest
4/6/2010 1:55:55 AM	contoso.com/Exchange	Users/Redmond, Tony Set-CalendarProcessing
4/6/2010 2:22:21 AM	contoso.com/Users/Administrator	Set-Mailbox
4/6/2010 2:56:57 AM	contoso.com/Users/Administrator	Start-ManagedFolderAssistant
4/8/2010 3:10:16 PM	contoso.com/Users/Administrator	New-Mailbox
4/8/2010 3:10:17 PM	contoso.com/Users/Administrator	Set-User
4/8/2010 4:23:17 PM	contoso.com/Exchange	Users/Redmond, Tony Remove-MailboxSearch

2. Search for specific actions. In this example we want to know who has recently mounted or dismounted mailbox databases. To locate the audit records, you specify the cmdlets that are used for these purposes. The *ObjectModified* property returned in each audit log tells you the name of the database that was operated on.

```
Search-AdminAuditLog –Cmdlets Dismount-Database, Mount-Database | Format-Table
RunDate, Caller, CmdletName, ObjectModified -AutoSize
```

RunDate	Caller	CmdletName	ObjectModified
3/19/2010 6:06:47 PM	contoso.com/Users/Administrator	Mount-Database	Managers
3/19/2010 6:07:49 PM	contoso.com/Users/Administrator	Dismount-Database	Managers
3/19/2010 6:07:58 PM	contoso.com/Users/Administrator	Mount-Database	VIP Data

3. Search for audit records within a particular date range. In this case we want to find out who has been creating new mailboxes over a specified period. Note that we include the *Succeeded* property in the output because it is possible that some

attempts to run the New-Mailbox cmdlet were unsuccessful, which is, in fact, what we can see in the results.

```
Search-AdminAuditLog –StartDate "04/01/2010 00:00" –EndDate "04/15/2010 23:59"
–Cmdlets New-Mailbox | Format-Table RunDate, Caller, ObjectModified, Succeeded
```

RunDate	Caller	ObjectModified	Succeeded
4/8/2010 3:10:16 PM	contoso.com/Users/Administrator	contoso.com/Users/extest_3a8609984	True
4/8/2010 4:24:20 PM	contoso.com/Users/Administrator	contoso.com/Users/Legal Searches	True
4/9/2010 9:47:33 AM	contoso.com/Users/Administrator	contoso.com/Users/Leitrim Room	False
4/9/2010 9:47:58 AM	contoso.com/Users/Administrator	contoso.com/Users/Leitrim Room	False
4/9/2010 9:48:21 AM	contoso.com/Users/Administrator	contoso.com/Users/Leitrim Room	False
4/9/2010 9:48:34 AM	contoso.com/Users/Administrator	contoso.com/Users/Leitrim Room	True
4/9/2010 3:58:16 PM	contoso.com/Users/Administrator	contoso.com/EMEA/Pelton, David	True
4/9/2010 3:59:01 PM	contoso.com/Users/Administrator	contoso.com/EMEA/Ruth, Andy	True

4. Analyze the cmdlets that are being run by administrators. These data are really just for interest's sake, but they do reveal what are the most commonly used cmdlets.

```
Search-AdminAuditLog | Sort CmdletName | Group CmdletName | Format-Table Count,
Name –AutoSize
```

Count	Name
26	Add-DistributionGroupMember
2	Add-MailboxPermission
1	Dismount-Database
1	Enable-Mailbox
2	Mount-Database
1	Move-DatabasePath
1	Move-OfflineAddressBook
4	New-ActiveSyncDeviceAccessRule
1	New-ActiveSyncMailboxPolicy
9	New-DistributionGroup

INSIDE OUT   Accessing comments from the audit log

One small quirk with the Search-AdminAuditLog cmdlet is that it doesn't return the comments inserted into the audit log with the Write-AdminAuditLog cmdlet. As you'll recall, the comments store the administrator-specified information that they want to write into the audit log, so these are data that you will want to be able to access. The data are held in the cmdlet parameters property of the audit entry, but if you include this property in the output set, all you will see is the string value "comment". The data are in the audit log but must be extracted by directing the output of the Search-AdminAuditLog cmdlet into an array and then looking at the appropriate record in the array. For example, these commands create an array and then examine the cmdlet parameters data in the first record in the array:

```
$AuditArray = Search-AdminAuditLog –StartDate '11/1/2010 00:00'
–EndDate '11/1/2010 23:59'
$AuditArray[1].cmdletparameters
```

Capturing audit data for administrator actions does not replace the need for operational discipline in the careful recording of changes made to server and organization configuration, including the following:

- Hotfixes and roll-up updates tested and applied, including any updates for add-on products

- Service packs for Windows and Exchange tested and applied

- Major network updates (for example, the introduction of a new DNS server)

- Installation of new Windows and Exchange servers

- Installation of any software on an Exchange server

- Changes to transport configuration such as the addition of a new connector or a change to transport settings

In this context, audit reports are helpful to record administrator actions, but they are not a complete solution.

Auditing mailbox access

Users gain access to mailboxes in different ways:

- Users log on and use their mailboxes as normal.

- An administrator can delegate full access to a mailbox to another user. See Chapter 6 for more information on this topic.

- Administrators can grant themselves access to a user's mailbox and then log on to it.

Normally administrators do not concern themselves about what happens inside user mailboxes. However, there are mailboxes that contain sensitive information that might need to be protected against attempts to conceal or remove items that are required by the company, typically to justify actions that the company or its employees took in a particular situation such as discussions with other companies relating to a merger, sale, or acquisition. Internally, sensitive information is often captured in discovery search mailboxes that must be monitored to detect any attempt to interfere with the data.

Best Practice: Protecting information by restricting access

Best practice in protecting information is to restrict access to people who can justify their access. In other words, you wouldn't open up your CEO's mailbox to all, but the CEO might delegate access to her executive assistant. In the same way, if a human resources (HR) investigation uses a specific discovery mailbox to capture information relating to potential harassment of an employee, you only grant Full Access to the discovery mailbox to the members of the HR department who absolutely need that access. Another best practice is to always remove access from users as soon as they no longer can justify the access.

Mailbox auditing is a feature introduced in Exchange 2010 SP1 that backs up best practice by allowing administrators to configure mailboxes so that details of specified actions are captured by Exchange. Audit entries are captured in the Audit subfolder of the Recoverable Items folder (the dumpster) and can be interrogated with the Search-MailboxAuditLog cmdlet. Mailbox actions are divided into three categories:

- **The mailbox owner** It is not normal to audit user actions, as they typically have full control over their mailbox contents. In addition, because mailbox owners use their mailboxes on a consistent and ongoing basis, the volume of audit entries is highest when auditing is enabled for the mailbox owner. For these reasons, when you compare the mailbox audit configuration for owners against the other categories, you'll see that the list of audit actions for owners is blank.

- **Delegates** Other users who have been assigned the SendAs, SendOnBehalf, or FullAccess permission can access some or all of a mailbox and take actions to affect its contents.

- **Administrative operations** These are operations such as mailbox moves, mailbox imports from PST, and mailbox discovery searches that are performed by administrators and affect mailbox contents in some way, if only to open folders.

Table 15-9 lists the various actions that Exchange can audit for a mailbox. Those marked with an asterisk (*) are part of the default set of actions that are marked for auditing when you enable auditing for a mailbox. For example, if you enable auditing for a mailbox, then Exchange will record details of all instances when a delegate sends a message using the *SendAs* permission. On the other hand, instances when delegates access the mailbox and send a message using *SendOnBehalf* permission are not captured unless you specifically mark this action for auditing. The decision to include one action over another in the default set of logged actions is probably explained by the fact that a message sent using the *SendAs* permission represents a higher degree of impersonation than one sent using the *SendOnBehalf* permission. We will discuss how to configure actions for auditing in a little while.

Table 15-9 Actions that can be audited for a mailbox

Action	Description	Admin	Delegate	Owner
BulkSync	Synchronization of a mailbox by an Outlook client configured in cached Exchange mode.	Yes*	Yes*	Yes
Copy	A message is copied to another folder in the mailbox or personal archive.	Yes	Yes	Yes
FolderBind	A mailbox folder is accessed (opened) by a client.	Yes*	Yes	Yes
HardDelete	A message is deleted permanently from the database (removed from the Recoverable Items folder).	Yes*	Yes*	Yes
MessageBind	A message is opened or viewed in the preview pane.	Yes	Yes	Yes
Move	A message is moved to another folder.	Yes*	Yes	Yes
MoveToDeletedItems	A message is deleted and moved into the Deleted Items folder.	Yes*	Yes	Yes
SendAs	A message is sent from the mailbox using the SendAs permission.	Yes*	Yes*	Yes
SendOnBehalf	A message is sent from the mailbox using the SendOnBehalf permission.	Yes*	Yes	Yes
SoftDelete	A message is deleted from the Deleted Items folder (and moved into the Recoverable Items folder).	Yes*	Yes*	Yes
Update	The properties of an item are updated.	Yes*	Yes*	Yes

Enabling mailboxes for auditing

The first step in the process is to enable the mailboxes that you want to audit by running the Set-Mailbox cmdlet. You cannot configure mailbox auditing with EMC or ECP. In this example, we enable auditing for the default discovery search mailbox.

```
Set-Mailbox -Identity 'Discovery Search Mailbox' -AuditEnabled $True
```

Chapter 15

We can then check that the audit setting is in place with the Get-Mailbox cmdlet:

```
Get-Mailbox –Identity 'Discovery Search Mailbox' | Format-List Name, Aud*
```

```
Name               : DiscoverySearchMailbox {D919BA05-46A6-415f-80AD-7E09334BB852}
AuditEnabled       : True
AuditLogAgeLimit   : 90.00:00:00
AuditAdmin         : {Update, Move, MoveToDeletedItems, SoftDelete, HardDelete, FolderBind,
SendAs, SendOnBehalf}
AuditDelegate      : {Update, SoftDelete, HardDelete, SendAs}
AuditOwner         : {MoveToDeletedItems, SoftDelete, HardDelete}
```

You can see that the act of enabling auditing for the mailbox has also assigned the default set of actions to be audited for the different categories of users who log onto the mailbox. You can also see that a property called *AuditLogAgeLimit* is present. This controls how long Exchange retains audit entries in the mailbox and the default value is 90 days. Once audit entries expire, they are removed from the mailbox by the MFA the next time it processes the mailbox.

You can set the value of *AuditLogAgeLimit* to anything up to 24,855 days. This amounts to just over 68 years, which should be sufficient for even the most retentive administrators. Oddly, for whatever reason, the actual coded maximum is 24,855 days, 3 hours, 14 minutes, and 7 seconds, which produces an audit age limit like this:

```
AuditLogAgeLimit : 24855.03:14:07
```

You can clear out all existing audit entries by setting the *AuditLogAgeLimit* property to 00:00:00. If you do this, Exchange will prompt you to confirm that all of the entries should be deleted and will proceed if you confirm that this is what you want to do.

You can decide to include or exclude audit actions for administrators, delegates, or owners by writing out the required actions into the *AuditAdmin*, *AuditDelegate*, and *AuditOwner* properties. For example, the owner of the default discovery search mailbox folder will never log onto it, so we can set the audit settings for the owner to "null". On the other hand, we might want to tweak the settings applied when administrators access the mailbox. Here's how we can make the change:

```
Set-Mailbox –Identity 'Discovery Search Mailbox' –AuditOwner $Null –AuditAdminUpdate,
Move, MoveToDeletedItems, SoftDelete, HardDelete,SendAs, SendOnBehalf –AuditEnabled
$True
```

To reverse the process and turn off auditing for a mailbox, we set the *AuditEnabled* flag to $False as follows:

```
Set-Mailbox -Identity 'Discovery Search Mailbox' -AuditEnabled $False
```

Accessing mailbox audit data

Mailbox audit information is written into the Audit subfolder of the Recoverable Items folder. However, this folder is invisible to any client so you cannot simply log onto the mailbox and browse through the audit entries. Instead, you have to submit a search with EMS and have Exchange retrieve and display the found entries to you. Searches are performed in two ways:

- The Search-MailboxAuditLog cmdlet performs a synchronous search for one or more mailboxes and returns the results on screen.

- The New-MailboxAuditLogSearch cmdlet can search across one or more mailboxes asynchronously in the background and return the results via email.

First, let's perform a simple search for audit entries for a single mailbox. In this example, we are looking for entries for a particular day, so we pass a start and end date. We then select a number of fields to be output for each entry that is found. Specifying the *-ShowDetails* parameter instructs Exchange to output details for each audit entry that it locates and passing "Delegate" to the *-LogonType* parameter restricts output to entries performed by a user who has delegate access to the mailbox. If you search many mailboxes for entries from an extended period, it is more than likely that Exchange might return thousands of entries. In this situation, you can use the *-ResultSize* parameter to specify how many entries you want to be returned. By default Exchange will output 1,000 entries.

```
Search-MailboxAuditLog -Identity 'Ruth, Andy' -ShowDetails -StartDate '5/12/2010
00:01'
-EndDate '5/18/2010 23:59' -LogonType Delegate -ResultSize 100 |
Format-Table Operation,
OperationResult, LogonUserDisplayName, ItemSubject, LastAcccessed
```

Operation	OperationResult	LogonUserDisplayName	ItemSubject	LastAccessed
SendOnBehalf	Succeeded	Executive Assistant	Travel Requests	11/05/2010 15:52:31
SendAs	Succeeded	Andrews, Lisa	Note from Peter	11/05/2010 15:54:41
SoftDelete	Succeeded	Smith, John		11/05/2010 15:58:46
SendOnBehalf	Succeeded	Executive Assistant	Business directives	11/05/2010 16:05:09

This output is what you'd expect from a mailbox that has granted access to different users to perform actions on their behalf, which we see in the *SendOnBehalf* and *SendAs* entries.

Chapter 15

Full access is obviously available to user John Smith because this user has been able to delete an item in the mailbox.

If you change the value passed to the *–LogonType* parameter to "Admin" you will see any operations performed against the mailbox as a result of administrative activity. For example, if a mailbox search is performed, you will probably see entries like this:

```
FolderBind      Succeeded      Administrator          11/05/2010 18:24:13
```

Of course, if you find something of interest, there is a lot more detail in an audit entry that can reveal additional information. For example, entries for a mailbox move will show detail like that shown here, whereas the *ClientInfoString* property for a mailbox search will contain *"Client=Management; Action=E-Discovery (mailbox search)"*, so it's relatively easy to determine what administrative process accessed the mailbox.

```
FolderPathName          : \MailboxReplicationServiceSyncStates
ClientInfoString        : Client=MSExchangeRPC
ClientIPAddress         : 2002:c0a5:4134::c0a5:4134
ClientMachineName       : EXSERVER2
ClientProcessName       : MSExchangeMailboxReplication.exe
ClientVersion           : 14.1.160.2
InternalLogonType       : DelegatedAdmin
```

The New-MailboxAuditLogSearch cmdlet is designed to operate behind the scenes to fetch audit entries for perhaps many mailboxes on servers across the organization and respond with an email with an XML attachment that contains the search results. The XML data are complete but need to be poured through a formatter to make sense of them, or at least, to make sense for those of us who are not fluent in interpreting raw XML. The command to create a typical background mailbox audit log search looks like this:

```
New-MailboxAuditLogSearch –Name 'Unauthorized Delegate Access review' –LogonTypes
Delegate
-Mailboxes 'CEO Assistant', 'CEO', 'Senior VP-Finance' –StartDate '1/1/2010'
-EndDate '12/31/2010'
-StatusMailRecipients'ComplianceAuditMailbox@contoso.com'
```

Figure 15-36 shows how EMS acknowledges the submission of a new mailbox audit log search. The command that is run creates a search through the audit entries for delegate access that are stored in the three specified mailboxes between the start and end date. If you don't specify any mailboxes, Exchange will return audit data for every mailbox on an Exchange 2010 server in the organization that has been enabled for auditing.

When the search is complete, Exchange records the fact in event 4003 in the Application Event Log and sends an email containing the results to the email address or addresses specified in the *–StatusMailRecipients* parameter. Figure 15-37 shows an example of the type of email delivered to these recipients. The text of the message contains the search criteria and the attached XML file contains the actual results. The recipients for mailbox audit reports must be mail-enabled objects known to the organization. Normally, they will be mailboxes or groups, but you can arrange for the email reports to go to external recipients such as your auditors, providing that you create a mail-enabled contact that contains their address.

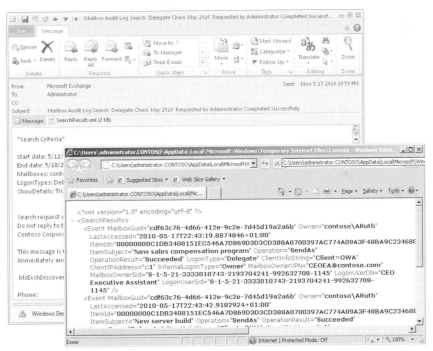

Figure 15-36 Launching a mailbox audit log search with New-MailboxAuditLogSearch.

Figure 15-37 Viewing the message with details of a mailbox audit log search and the XML file containing the results.

Chapter 15

No one could pretend that mailbox auditing is complete in terms of functionality or presentation. Forcing all interaction through EMS is acceptable if the output was easier to extract and interpret, but that's not the case. Eventually, Microsoft might do the work in a future version or service pack to integrate mailbox auditing into ECP and make this interesting and worthwhile functionality more accessible to administrators.

Message classifications

Microsoft introduced message classifications in Exchange 2007 in an attempt to allow users to apply business-specific labels to messages. The labels are stored as properties of the messages and can be acted on by transport rules. Users can also react to the classifications when they see them on messages through Outlook or Outlook Web App. For example, if a message is labeled "Super Critical," a user might be less likely to delete it and more likely to quickly respond to the request that the message contains.

The problems with message classifications are threefold. First, you rely on senders to apply classifications and receivers to respond appropriately to the classifications when messages arrive. Second, there's no automated method to distribute and publish message classification data to clients such as the approach used by Outlook protection rules, so you have to make an arrangement to distribute the necessary classification information to Outlook clients. By comparison, Outlook Web App picks up classifications direct from the server. Third, only Outlook 2007 and Outlook 2010 clients and Outlook Web App support classifications. Any other client simply ignores their presence.

Even with the acknowledged limitations, there are customers who find message classifications a very useful and worthwhile facility. The characteristics of these customers usually include the following:

- A requirement to classify messages in terms of their sensitivity, content, or intended audience that is well understood by the user population.

- A well-structured classification scheme for information that makes sense to users and the business. Ideally, email shares the same classification scheme as applied to documents and other information. Multiple classification schemes invariably cause confusion and result in a lesser degree of compliance by users.

- The ability to deploy updates to Outlook clients in a reliable manner.

- A population of Outlook 2007 and Outlook 2010 clients.

Typical classifications include labels such as Personal, Secret, Business Critical, Audit Retention, and so on. The diversity of businesses is reflected in the diversity of classifications that are created and applied to material. However, within an individual company, it is a good idea to keep the number of classifications to a minimum to avoid user confusion and to encourage compliance.

INSIDE OUT   Message classifications have value but are of limited use

It's important to understand that message classifications are purely indications of the importance of content in one way or another. Apart from being recognized as an actionable condition by transport rules, there is no other way to use a message classification to force Exchange to do anything. In short, message classifications are an inert and passive component of the overall MRM environment.

Creating a message classification

You can't create a new message classification using EMC or ECP. All manipulation of message classifications is performed through EMS. Before creating any message classifications, it's worthwhile to sit down and chart out the various classifications that you think are needed by the business. Too many classifications are likely to confuse users if they don't know which classification to apply in a given circumstance, whereas too few might not achieve the granularity of classification required by the business. Each classification therefore should be justified by business logic and its application should be easily explainable to a user. In other words, the use and purpose of every message classification must be blindingly obvious if it is to succeed.

Let's assume that we have done the necessary due diligence and have decided to create a new message classification called "Top Secret." We can do this with the New-MessageClassification cmdlet:

```
New-MessageClassification -Name 'Top Secret' -DisplayName 'Top Secret: Eyes Only'
-SenderDescription 'This message contains Top Secret information that must not be
shared outside the company' -RecipientDescription 'This message contains Top Secret
information that must not be shared outside the company: Do not forward!'
```

Table 15-10 explains the parameters that you can use with the New-MessageClassification cmdlet and their meaning.

Table 15-10 **Parameters used with the New-MessageClassification cmdlet**

Parameter	Description
Name	The internal name of the message classification that identifies the object to Exchange.
DisplayName	The name of the message classification that is visible to Outlook 2007 and Outlook 2010 and Outlook Web App clients when they select a classification to apply to a message. You can create a name of up to 64 characters.
SenderDescription	Text that describes the purpose of the message classification displayed by clients after a user adds the classification to a message.
RecipientDescription	Text displayed to recipients to help them understand what they should or should not do with a message bearing a particular classification. If this parameter is not set, clients use the value of the *SenderDescription* instead.
Locale	A parameter indicating that the message classification is for a particular language. If omitted, the message classification is created with the default locale, meaning that it is used by mailboxes of any language where a localized classification is not available.
RetainClassificationEnabled	Specifies whether the message classification persists with the message if it is forwarded or replied to. The default value is $True.
UserDisplayEnabled	Controls whether users see the *RecipientDescription* or *DisplayName* information for a message classification on a message that they receive. The default value is $True, meaning that recipients see this information. You can suppress it by setting the parameter to $False. In this case, Exchange carries the classification but doesn't reveal it to recipients. However, the classification can still be operated on by a transport rule.
DisplayPrecedence	Outlook and Outlook Web App only allow users to select a single message classification for a message but a transport rule can apply another classification. This parameter controls the order in which the classifications are displayed to users. The default is medium, but you can set other values: Highest, Higher, High, MediumHigh, Medium, MediumLow, Low, Lower, and Lowest.

Our new classification is now registered in Active Directory and is replicated throughout the forest. Users will be able to use the new classification the next time they connect to Exchange. We can retrieve the details of the classification with the Get-MessageClassification cmdlet. For example:

```
Get-MessageClassification –Identity 'Top Secret'
```

```
ClassificationID       : 7387906a-20fe-49e9-bedf-6a637f104b93
DisplayName            : Top Secret: Eyes Only
DisplayPrecedence      : Medium
Identity               : Default\Top Secret
```

```
IsDefault                 : True
Locale                    :
RecipientDescription      : This message contains Top Secret information that must not be
shared outside the company: Do Not forward!
RetainClassificationEnabled : True
SenderDescription         : This message contains Top Secret information that must not be
shared outside the company
UserDisplayEnabled        : True
Version                   : 0
```

Localized message classifications

The message classification that we just created will work for all languages, but let's assume that we have to support a group of French users. We can create a separate message classification for French that includes translated or localized text that Exchange will provide to clients connected to mailboxes that have French listed as a supported language. When we create the French version of the "Top Secret" message classification, we identify it as a localized version by including the locale parameter. For example:

```
New-MessageClassification –Name 'Top Secret' –DisplayName 'Top Secret: Eyes Only'
–SenderDescription "Ce message contientl'informationextrêmementsecrète qui ne doit
pas êtrepartagée en dehors de la compagnie"
–RecipientDescription"Ce message contient l'information extrêmement secrète qui ne
doit pas être partagée en dehors de la compagnie : N'expédiez pas !" –Locale 'fr-FR'
```

If you use the Get-MessageClassification cmdlet to list the message classifications known to Exchange after creating the localized version, you won't see the localized version listed because the cmdlet only returns classifications for the default language. To retrieve details of a localized classification, you have to pass its identifier. For example, in this instance we need:

```
Get-MessageClassification –Identity 'fr-FR\Top Secret'
```

Client access to message classifications

Because Outlook Web App reads in message classification data each time it creates a new session, assuming that Active Directory replication is working smoothly, new or updated message classifications are available to Outlook Web App clients the next time that they connect to a server. The situation is less satisfactory for Outlook because you have to instruct Outlook to read in classification data from a location with registry keys. Because of the difficulty of distribution of updates to all clients in a reliable and robust manner, it is bad news for administrators any time that you have to customize Outlook through registry keys.

Access to message classifications from Outlook Web App is very straightforward. When you create a new message, you can click the Restriction icon (envelope overlaid with a red Access Denied sign) to see the set of classifications available within the organization. The top screen shown in Figure 15-38 shows four available classifications. The No Restriction classification is the default value that Exchange applies to message if the user doesn't select an explicit classification. The Do Not Forward classification is in fact the default AD RMS template. We discuss AD RMS in detail very soon.

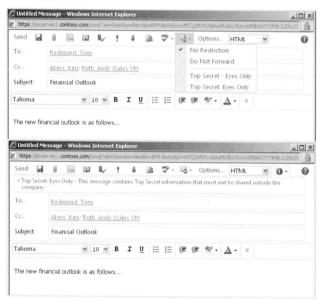

Figure 15-38 Using message classifications with Outlook Web App.

The important point that comes through here is that if you use AD RMS and message classifications, you have to make sure that you use a naming convention that clearly identifies message classifications and templates to users. The problem here is that we have an AD RMS template called "Top Secret – Eyes Only" and a message classification called "Top Secret: Eyes Only". The poor users won't know what to choose without clear direction and some help through the naming convention. Let's assume that this is a very clever user, so he knows that the "Top Secret: Eyes Only" classification is the one he wants. When you select a classification, Exchange displays the text defined in the classification's *SenderDescription* property. The bottom screen in Figure 15-38 shows how the text for the message classification is displayed. Much the same happens when the message is delivered except that the text is taken from the *RecipientDescription* property (Figure 15-39).

Figure 15-39 Recipient text displayed by Outlook Web App for a message classification.

Making message classifications available to Outlook 2007 and Outlook 2010 clients is a multistage process. You have to do the following:

1. Export the message classifications from Active Directory to an XML file. Exchange provides the Export-OutlookClassification.ps1 script for this purpose. Run the script to output the XML file as follows:

```
Export-OutlookClassification.ps1 > c:\Temp\Classifications.XML
```

2. The XML file contains information about the message classifications that are currently known to Exchange and establishes the set of classifications that are available to Outlook. It must be regenerated each time you make changes to classifications or add or delete classifications. The XML content for a classification looks like this:

```
<Classification>
<Name>Top Secret: Eyes Only</Name>
<Description>This message contains Top Secret information that must not be
shared outside the company</Description>
<Guid>7387906a-20fe-49e9-bedf-6a637f104b93</Guid>
<AutoClassifyReplies />
</Classification>
```

3. Each Outlook client must be separately enabled to use message classifications. This is done by updating the system registry to instruct Outlook to enable classifications and where to find the XML file that describes the available classifications. A suitable registry update file for Outlook 2010 is shown here. Change "14.0" to "12.0" in the first line to create an update file for Outlook 2007 clients. The three values instruct Outlook where to find the XML file, enable message classifications, and assert that the classifications placed on messages are trusted by the Exchange organization. Exchange 2003 supports a different form of message classification so you should

set this registry value to 0 (zero) for users who still have their mailboxes on an Exchange 2003 server.

```
[HKEY_CURRENT_USER\Software\Microsoft\Office\14.0\Common\Policy]
"AdminClassificationPath"="\\ExServer1\Outlook\Classifications.xml"
"EnableClassifications"=dword:00000001
"TrustClassifications"=dword:00000001
```

4. The next time Outlook starts it discovers that classifications are enabled and attempts to read in the XML file. If the XML file is unavailable for some reason (for example, the server that hosts the share is offline or Outlook is working offline and can't contact the server), Outlook won't be able to add classifications to messages. If you want classifications to be available all the time, you can either distribute the XML file to every PC so that it is available locally or you can put it in a network share and use the Windows offline files feature to synchronize the file so that it is in the local files cache and therefore available even when offline.

All of the steps just described are reasonably straightforward to accomplish on a single computer. Things get messy when you have to ensure that every computer in a large organization has access to the XML file and receives updates after they are made available in a reasonably guaranteed manner. Once this is done, probably through a mixture of group policies and offline file synchronization, you are ready to use message classifications with Outlook clients.

> **Note**
>
> If an Outlook client uses an outdated classifications file, it will not be able to add new classifications to messages, but it will be able to see new classifications if they have been added by a client that has access to an updated XML file.

See Chapter 16, "Rules and Journals," for an example of how to use the Top Secret message classification in a transport rule that stops messages marked with this classification from going outside the organization.

Protecting content

Message classifications are useful to a point. They don't impose any restrictions on users and apart from providing some advice as to how important information contained in a message is, users can blissfully ignore their invocation to deal with the information in any particular way. Another approach is necessary if you want to impose restrictions on users as to what they can and cannot do with content. This isn't a new requirement. For almost 20 years, companies have attempted to protect sensitive information that users transmit in email. The first attempts were based on message encryption and required the sender and recipient to share common (public) keys. The first versions of Exchange-based message encryption used the Windows Public Key Infrastructure (PKI). Some companies experienced success with message encryption but others found that PKI-based systems require a lot of administrative knowledge and intervention (at times) and users often didn't use encryption when they should. In addition, software and hardware upgrades for server and clients had to be carefully managed to ensure that keys were preserved. The result was often disappointing in terms of the degree of protection achieved across the organization.

Software vendors began to explore different approaches to content protection toward the end of the 1990s. These solutions typically required users to explicitly protect a message by invoking a client add-in and relied on communication with specially designated servers. It was difficult to achieve true protection across a range of Web, mobile, and desktop and laptop clients working in offline and online modes. Costs were high because of the need to buy, deploy, and manage additional client and server software and achieving interoperability with partners was tricky. Needless to say, mergers and acquisitions posed even more challenges.

Apart from the ability to send S/MIME protected messages, Exchange 2010 supports two more sophisticated mechanisms to protect content:

- **Information Rights Management (IRM)** IRM relies on templates that describe different sensitivity levels for content and the actions that users can take when they receive protected contents. IRM depends on AD RMS and is now well-integrated throughout Exchange 2010 in terms of client support (Outlook Web App, Outlook, Windows Mobile, and BlackBerry), its support for federation, and the ability to apply IRM through transport rules. Exchange is able to decrypt IRM protected content to inspect it during transport rules processing and discovery searches and can journal protected content in a satisfactory manner. In short, IRM is the approach most suitable for enterprises that are willing to dedicate sufficient resources to achieving a sophisticated and comprehensive level of protection.

- **Outlook protection rules** An Exchange 2010 administrator can create rules that are pushed out to Outlook 2010 clients, which then use the rules to automatically apply AD RMS templates to protect content as users create and send messages. For example, a rule might say that any message sent to a specific distribution group must be protected. Outlook protection rules are in their first iteration and have a major dependency in that they cannot be used without first deploying Outlook 2010 clients.

Planning for the deployment of protected content within an enterprise is not just a matter of selecting and deploying technology. User education is often the biggest obstacle to overcome, especially in large, multinational, and highly distributed companies. It's also not a matter that the Exchange administrators can decide on alone. The Active Directory management team has to be involved if you want to use AD RMS and the corporate security team and legal group need to be involved to ensure that content protection is aligned with other security initiatives and complies with any legal or regulatory regime to which the company is exposed. The topic is therefore complex at many levels and the best idea is to research the information available on TechNet and other sources before you progress too far along toward a decision to deploy.

Active Directory Rights Management Services

Active Directory Rights Management Service (AD RMS) is a new version of Windows Rights Managment Service (RMS) that allows companies to protect sensitive information by applying policies that dictate how that information can be accessed and shared by users. In an email context, AD RMS can be used with Exchange 2010 to stop users from sending or forwarding messages to unauthorized recipients or otherwise sharing contents by printing, cutting and pasting into other messages, and so on. RMS had a somewhat checkered history because it is very Windows-centric and didn't meet the needs of companies that had heterogeneous environments. AD RMS runs on a Microsoft Windows 2008 server and leverages Active Directory extensively, so it still poses some issues for companies that don't depend on Microsoft for large sections of their IT infrastructure. However, the latest implementation does offer some new features in conjunction with Exchange 2010 that make it more interesting to a messaging administrator. One major advance is the fact that Outlook Web App now supports protected messages for non-Microsoft browsers running on non-Windows platforms, so it is now possible to deploy rights management in a heterogeneous multiplatform infrastructure and expect that users will be able to read protected information. (In addition, Microsoft Outlook for Mac OS X supports AD RMS, as do Windows Mobile 6.1 and later.)

Every message that flows through Exchange passes through the transport service. It is therefore sensible to use this choke point as the place to impose restrictions on email content. Transport protection encryption is an integration that allows you to use AD RMS with Exchange transport rules to apply AD RMS templates to messages as they are processed by the transport service. For example, you could apply the standard Do Not Forward AD RMS template to outgoing messages sent by your senior management team to members of the board of directors to stamp the messages as highly confidential and to ensure that they cannot be forwarded. A key part of making this feature work is that the Exchange 2010 transport system can read protected messages so that journaling and transport rules can be applied. In response to user demands, Exchange 2010 Unified Messaging also supports protection for voice mail messages by marking private messages with the Do Not Forward AD RMS template before they are submitted to a hub transport service.

AD RMS is supported by Outlook 2010, Outlook Web App, Windows Mobile, and some non–Windows Mobile devices. Windows Mobile clients depend on the AD RMS prelicensing agent that was first shipped in Exchange 2007 SP1. The agent runs on hub transport servers and proactively requests licenses to allow Outlook 2007 (and later) and Windows Mobile 6.0 (and later) clients to read protected content without having to first submit credentials. The idea is to make protected content less onerous to deploy and use.

CAUTION

It's worth emphasizing that technology is one part of the solution for information leakage. Many projects have announced their intention to deploy technology to protect information, only to run into the two rocks of user discontent and heterogeneous systems. If users don't buy into the idea that information must be protected and accept the technology that is deployed for this purpose, they will attempt to get around the strictures and information will continue to leak. And if the chosen technology cannot accommodate all the platforms used within an organization, including all varieties of mobile devices, the same lack of success is firmly on the project's horizon.

Installing Active Directory Rights Management

There's plenty of information available in TechNet to help guide you through the detail of installing and configuring Active Directory Rights Management Service so we do not provide a detailed step-by-step guide here. Essentially, the following are the headline steps.

1. Decide on the server that will host the AD RMS cluster (the server that will control the licenses that underpin rights protection within the organization). The server can run Windows 2008 SP2 (a hotfix is required for this version of the operating system) or Windows 2008 R2. It is not best practice to install AD RMS on the same server as Exchange 2010.

2. Install the Active Directory Rights Management Services role on the server (Figure 15-40). The installation wizard leads you through many screens and you might want to perform an installation on a test server before you attempt to introduce AD RMS into the production environment.

3. Perform the postinstallation steps to configure Exchange 2010 to use IRM.

4. Validate that everything is running properly and that users can protect and access content using IRM.

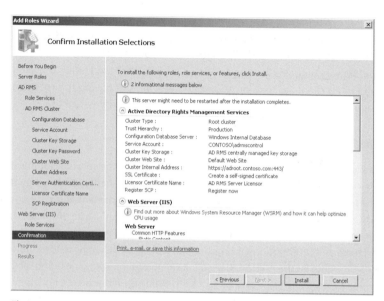

Figure 15-40 Installing Active Directory Rights Management Services on a Windows 2008 R2 server.

After a successful installation of Active Directory Rights Management Service, there are still some steps that must be performed before AD RMS is ready to support Exchange:

- The certificate specified for use by the installation (or created by the installation) must be installed on Exchange mailbox and hub transport servers. You can export the certificate from the server that supports the AD RMS cluster that will be used by Exchange and import it into the Exchange mailbox and hub transport servers. The certificate is required to provide Secure Sockets Layer (SSL) communications between Exchange and the AD RMS server.

- The Exchange Servers security group must be granted read and write permission to the AD RMS cluster certification pipeline. This is a file called \inetpub\wwwroot\ _wmcs\certification\ServerCertification.asmx located on the AD RMS cluster. Exchange hub transport servers need to be able to access this file to be able to use the AD RMS prelicensing agent to request licenses to access protected content pro-actively on behalf of clients.

- The account for the federated delivery mailbox must be added to the super users group for the AD RMS cluster. This step allows Exchange to decrypt protected messages as they pass through the transport system (to apply rules based on mes-sage content), to journal protected messages, to incorporate protected items into Exchange content indexes, and to allow Outlook Web App users to use IRM.

- IRM features must be enabled for messages sent to internal recipients (within the same Exchange organization) to allow them to access AD RMS templates. To perform this step, run the Set-IRMConfiguration cmdlet as follows:

```
Set-IRMConfiguration -InternaLicensingEnabled $True
```

You can check the IRM configuration with the Get-IRMConfiguration cmdlet.

After taking these steps, you can verify that the IRM configuration is valid by running the Test-IRMConfiguration cmdlet. In this example we use two email addresses to verify that prelicensing and journal encryption works:

```
Test-IRMConfiguration -Recipient TRedmond@contoso.com -Sender epr@contoso.com
```

```
Results : Checking Exchange Server ...
             - PASS: Exchange Server is running in Enterprise.
          Loading IRM configuration ...
             - PASS: IRM configuration loaded successfully.
          Retrieving RMS Certification Uri ...
             - PASS: RMS Certification Uri: https://adroot.contoso.com/_wmcs/certification.
          Verifying RMS version for https://adroot.contoso.com/_wmcs/certification ...
             - PASS: RMS Version verified successfully.
          Retrieving RMS Publishing Uri ...
             - PASS: RMS Publishing Uri: https://adroot.contoso.com/_wmcs/licensing.
          Acquiring Rights Account Certificate (RAC) and Client Licensor Certificate (CLC) ...
             - PASS: RAC and CLC acquired.
          Acquiring RMS Templates ...
             - PASS: RMS Templates acquired.
          Retrieving RMS Licensing Uri ...
             - PASS: RMS Licensing Uri: https://adroot.contoso.com/_wmcs/licensing.
          Verifying RMS version for https://adroot.contoso.com/_wmcs/licensing ...
             - PASS: RMS Version verified successfully.
          Creating Publishing License ...
             - PASS: Publishing License created.
          Acquiring Prelicense for 'tredmond@contoso.com' from RMS Licensing Uri
(https://adroot.contoso.com/_wmcs/licensing)
          ...
             - PASS: Prelicense acquired.
          Acquiring Use License from RMS Licensing Uri
(https://adroot.contoso.com/_wmcs/licensing)
             - PASS: Use License acquired.

          OVERALL RESULT: PASS
```

After you are sure that the basic AD RMS configuration is working, you can consider the finer details of your deployment. By default, AD RMS installs a template called Do Not Forward that users can apply to messages to mark them as confidential. A template defines the rights that users have over items to which the template is applied and you might want to create some additional templates to meet business needs within the company. For example, Figure 15-41 shows the properties of a template called Top Secret – Do Not Share as viewed through the AD RMS console. This template is purposely restrictive because we don't want to allow users to do much except view its contents and reply to the messages that are marked with the template. Behind the scenes the AD RMS server distributes new and updated templates to clients so that they are available for use.

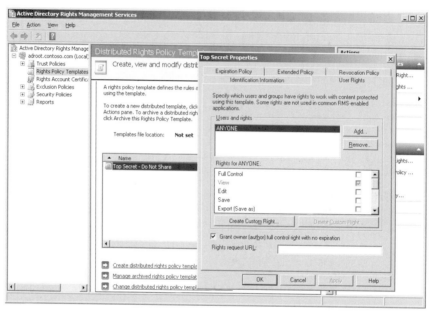

Figure 15-41 Viewing the properties of the "Top Secret" AD RMS template.

You can discover the set of templates that are currently defined with the Get-RMSTemplate cmdlet. For example:

```
Get-RMSTemplate
```

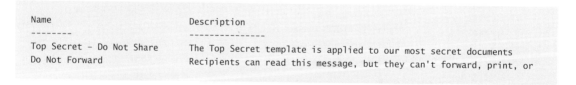

Name	Description
Top Secret – Do Not Share	The Top Secret template is applied to our most secret documents
Do Not Forward	Recipients can read this message, but they can't forward, print, or

Using AD RMS to protect content

Figure 15-42 shows the Top Secret template being applied to a new message with Outlook Web App. The same drop-down menu is used for message classifications, which we discussed earlier in this chapter, so if you define some message classifications, you'll see them listed here along with AD RMS templates. Once again, this reinforces the necessity for a good naming convention to help users do the right thing.

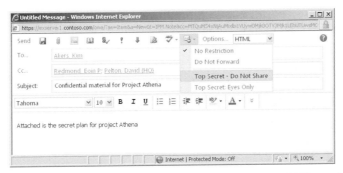

Figure 15-42 Marking a message with the Top Secret AD RMS template.

Once a template is applied, it remains with the message no matter where it passes through the messaging system. The transport system is able to decrypt protected content. Decryption occurs first in the transport pipeline to ensure that subsequent agents can process the content to apply transport and journal rules. Protected messages can be discovered by mailbox searches so that any relevant protected items are included in the content captured in a discovery mailbox.

The first time that a client accesses protected content during a session, it contacts Exchange and the AD RMS server to fetch the credentials that are necessary to access protected items. The understandable need to retrieve credentials can slow down access to protected content, especially when the client is separated from the AD RMS server by an extended network connection. Outlook Web App is a lot less obvious than Outlook is when it comes to configuring itself for rights management, as the user will probably be unaware of the work going on behind the scenes. As you can see from Figure 15-43, Outlook 2010 provides the user with a lot more insight about the configuration process.

The user interface of clients also adjusts to take account of the rights defined in the template. As you can see in Figure 15-44, Outlook Web App has disabled the Forward and Print options because these rights are not allowed for items marked with the Top Secret template. In addition, if you reply to a message the client will not be able to include the text of the original message, as it is protected, so the original message will be added as an attachment to the reply.

You can also see evidence that the transport system has processed the message because the corporate disclaimer has been appended. We will develop the topic further when we discuss transport rules in Chapter 16 and see how the transport system can automatically apply AD RMS templates to protect confidential information in messages as they pass from user to user.

Chapter 15

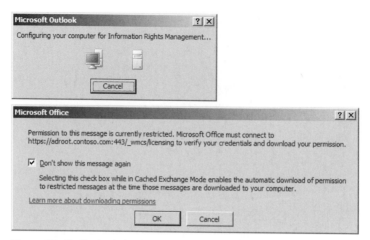

Figure 15-43 Outlook 2010 is configured for rights management.

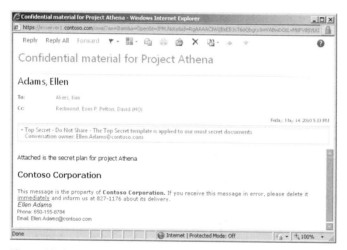

Figure 15-44 Viewing a message marked with the Top Secret AD RMS template.

Figure 15-45 shows how Outlook 2010 displays a protected message (all versions from Outlook 2003 SP2 are able to access protected content). The View Permissions option is accessed by clicking the highlighted bar that shows details of the template that protects the item. When selected, Outlook displays the permissions defined in the template. As you can see from the list, the template applied to this item does not allow users to do much except view or reply to the item. They cannot print, save, export, or even copy the item (and the restriction on copying goes so far as to prohibit any attempt to save a view of the content with a screen capture tool).

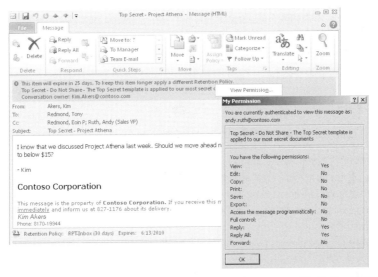

Figure 15-45 Viewing permissions on a protected message with Outlook 2010.

Unless they can access the necessary credentials, external recipients won't be able to access protected content if a user forwards a protected message outside the organization. This is the biggest value of applying protection to messages because it stops users from being able to share confidential or other sensitive information either by accident (forwarding the wrong message or sending it to the wrong recipient) or deliberately. Information leakage is deemed by some companies to be a form of corporate sabotage and carries severe consequences for the responsible employee.

Protecting information on Windows Mobile clients

The ability to protect content also extends to Windows Mobile clients as long as they run Windows Mobile 6.1 or later. As with many advanced features for mobile devices, the newer the operating system, the easier it is to use advanced features like rights management.

The ability to support rights management for Exchange is accomplished by having ActiveSync prefetch the credentials necessary to view protected content as it downloads items to the mobile device. All of the necessary decryption and encryption is performed by the Client Access Server (CAS) during synchronization after the CAS recognizes that the client is capable of handling protected content. Part of the synchronization process downloads the list of available rights templates to the device for local storage and access. A protected item that arrives on the mobile device is decrypted and the processing to display the template and respect the rights that it describes becomes the responsibility of the mobile device.

Chapter 15

Outgoing messages are processed by the CAS to ensure that template restrictions are applied before new items are transmitted to recipients. However, this is an implementation that might not be supported by all ActiveSync clients, so it's something that you need to verify as you test mobile devices to include in your deployment.

Rights management enhancements in Exchange 2010 SP1

A number of changes are made in Exchange 2010 SP1 to improve the effectiveness of rights protection. Protected attachments can now be read using the Outlook Web App WebReady document viewer. Also, Microsoft now supports IRM between on-premise servers and Exchange running in its Office 365 hosted service. This is accomplished through the Trusted Publishing Domain (TPD) feature that allows the RMS cluster running in the on-premise deployment to trust and use the licenses issued by the Office 365 servers and vice versa. Much the same approach can be taken to deploy federated IRM between two organizations.

After a rough start, Microsoft has improved the implementation and capabilities of its rights management solution to a point where it is very usable, providing that you deploy the latest clients. However, the success or failure of any solution that aims to protect confidential material is not dependent on technology alone; it is much more important to achieve strong user buy-in and appreciation of the need to protect the material. Unless this aspect of the project is achieved, it will eventually fail because users will find other ways to share information with each other, maybe by pasting it into Facebook!

Outlook Protection Rules

If you use Outlook 2010 clients and have AD RMS deployed, you can use a complementary function called Outlook Protection Rules that allows Exchange administrators to create new rules and distribute them to Outlook users to have protection automatically applied at the client rather than waiting for messages to be transmitted to Exchange. Although it adds another layer of security for messages in corporate email systems, this feature is also intended for use in scenarios where companies use Exchange in hosted services and want to ensure that content is protected against snooping or other unauthorized access by the managers of the hosted service. Outlook Protection Rules require you to install an add-on to Outlook 2010 before they work. After that, the administrator creates and distributes new rules using the set of cmdlets described in Table 15-11. You need to be an organization administrator to be able to use these cmdlets.

Table 15-11 **Outlook Protection Rule cmdlets**

Cmdlet	Use
New-OutlookProtectionRule	Create a new Outlook Protection Rule
Enable-OutlookProtectionRule	Enable an Outlook Protection Rule and make it available to clients
Get-OutlookProtectionRule	Return information about a selected Outlook Protection Rule or all of the rules within the organization
Set-OutlookProtectionRule	Set properties of an existing Outlook Protection Rule
Remove-OutlookProtectionRule	Remove an Outlook Protection Rule from the organization
Disable-OutlookProtectionRule	Disable an Outlook Protection Rule

Essentially, an Outlook Protection Rule establishes the conditions for when to apply the rule, states the scope of recipients for whom the rule applies, and tells Outlook what AD RMS template it should apply when the conditions and scope are satisfied. Outlook monitors new messages as they are created and will load the necessary templates when it first detects that it might need them during a session. The scope can be internal recipients, all recipients, or specific recipients.

To take a practical example, let's assume that we have been told that we need to protect any message sent to the CEO's staff. This EMS command creates a new rule that applies the default Do Not Forward AD RMS template to any message sent to the SMTP address specified in the rule (in this case, the address is for the distribution group used to map all of the CEO staff):

```
New-OutlookProtectionRule -Name "CEO Staff Communications" -SentTo
CEOStaff@contoso.com -ApplyRightsProtectionTemplate "Do Not Forward" Priority 1
```

After an Outlook protection rule is defined, it is distributed to clients using Exchange Web Services. If you make a change to a rule, it will take about an hour to redistribute the rule as they are cached for better performance. You can force a rule to be distributed by recycling the Microsoft Internet Information Services (IIS) process. In addition, you have to restart Outlook to make new rules available to the client.

For the rule to work properly, Outlook must have access to the AD RMS template. The default Do Not Forward template is automatically made available to clients when they contact the AD RMS server for the first time. If you create new templates, they will have to be distributed so that the client can access the XML that describes the template. To check that a template is available to Outlook, create a new message and click the Options tab to view the list of templates available through the Permission list. If the template doesn't appear here it means that it has not yet been distributed to the client computer.

For advice about how best to distribute templates, see the AD RMS Template Deployment Step-by-Step guide at *http://go.microsoft.com/fwlink/?LinkID=153712*.

Chapter 15

Rules help compliance, too

Exchange supports transport and journal rules. These could be considered to be part of the compliance landscape, but because they are capable of solving so many more problems for a hard-pressed Exchange administrator they deserve their own chapter. Let's go and talk about rules, and we will see how some of the topics presented in this chapter reoccur in that domain.

O NE of the most important architectural changes made in Microsoft Exchange 2007 was the positioning of the transport service as the single point en route from sender to recipient through which every message had to flow. With a single transport pipeline in place, Microsoft was able to create the ability to insert agents to perform specific processing as messages traveled through. In this chapter, we discuss how anti-spam agents operate on messages, so you should have a good idea of how powerful and flexible the transport pipeline is. Transport rules and journal rules are implemented through agents as well. The purpose of these agents is to process messages created within the organization to help users comply with whatever regulations are in force. As we'll see, transport rules serve a wide range of purposes, whereas journal rules are singular in focus because they simply capture copies of information that might be needed in the future. Together, transport and journal rules are a good example of how Exchange has developed well beyond its original scope as a functional email server to become a well-rounded information management platform.

Transport rules

Exchange 2007 was the first version to include transport rules, which allow administrators to create conditional processing for messages as they pass through the transport service. Rules can be applied to messages that remain within the organization and to those that enter or leave the organization. Many rules are designed to ensure that users comply with company or legal regulations. The same kind of intervention and examination of en-route messages was possible with earlier versions of Exchange, but only at the cost of developing expensive installation-specific "event sinks" that could only be written by developers with substantial knowledge of Exchange internals. Event sinks were not for the fainthearted, but as the complexity of the tasks that messaging systems were called on to perform increased, it became more obvious that a simple method to introduce conditional processing was required. Exchange 2007 therefore provides a set of cmdlets and EMC wizards to allow administrators to create and deploy transport rules across an organization.

Microsoft Exchange Server 2010 builds on the foundation established by Exchange 2007 by giving administrators the ability to use a much wider set of actions, predicates, conditions, and exceptions in transport rules. The new functionality in Exchange 2010 does not mean that you will never be forced to write code to create an event sink, because conditions exist that cannot be handled by transport rules. For example, you cannot call your own code from a transport rule to access directories other than Active Directory. Nonetheless, the developments in Exchange 2010 are very welcome and allow transport rules to deal with the vast majority of conditions that occur in corporate messaging systems. To provide some insight into the comprehensive range of predicates available to Exchange 2010 transport rules, Table 16-1 lists some of the most common predicates that you'll encounter. Details about the full set can be found in the Exchange documentation in TechNet. We'll see how many of these predicates are put to use in the example transport rules described in this chapter.

Table 16-1 Examples of transport rule predicates

Predicate type	Predicates
Identify the sender	From a specific person From a member of a distribution list From users inside or outside the organization From a sender with a specific value in an *Active Directory* property
Identify the recipient	When a recipient is a specific person (To, CC, or BCC) When any of the recipients is a member of a distribution list (To, CC, or BCC) When the recipient is inside or outside the organization or in a partner domain When a message is sent from one distribution list to another When a recipient has a specific value in an *Active Directory* property
Message characteristic	When the message has an attachment with a size greater than or equal to a limit When the message is marked with a specific importance When the message is of a specific type When the message has a Spam Confidence Level (SCL) that is greater than or equal to a limit When the message is marked with a specific classification When the message subject contains specific words When the message's attachment contains specific words

The transport rules developed for Exchange 2007 continue to work with Exchange 2010. However, Exchange 2007 transport rules are very much a subset of the enhanced rules that you can deploy with Exchange 2010. Upgrades such as the ability to make decisions about email processing based on Active Directory attributes for both senders and recipients make transport rules more powerful and flexible.

INSIDE OUT   Another reason to upgrade hub transport servers early in your deployment

Transport rules created under Exchange 2007 and Exchange 2010 share the same object version number (8.0.535.0), so you'd expect to be able to edit Exchange 2010 transport rules from an Exchange 2007 server. In fact, this isn't possible because Exchange 2010 stores its transport rules in a different location in Active Directory, so its rules are invisible to Exchange 2007. When you install the first Exchange 2010 hub transport server into an organization that contains Exchange 2007 servers, the setup program checks for transport rules and copies any rules that it finds to make them available to the Exchange 2010 hub transport servers. However, if you make a subsequent change to an Exchange 2007 transport rule, the change is not automatically synchronized with Exchange 2010, creating an obvious opportunity for confusion. This is one of the reasons Microsoft recommends that you replace Exchange 2007 hub transport and edge servers with Exchange 2010 equivalents very early in a deployment project.

Examples of transport rules

The best way to understand the value that transport rules bring is to walk through a number of examples of how to apply transport rules to provide answers to common requirements in corporate deployments. The examples are as follows:

1. Apply a disclaimer to outgoing messages.

2. Use a rule to create basic workflow through moderation.

3. Evaluate messages by examining Active Directory attributes of senders and recipients.

4. Create an ethical firewall to block communications between two user communities.

5. Block certain users from sending email outside the organization.

6. Scan attachments for confidential information.

7. Look for messages classified as Top Secret and stop them from leaving the organization.

8. Protect confidential information by applying an Active Directory Rights Management template.

The idea is that you should be able to take these rules and use them as the basis for creating solutions to requirements that arise in your own deployment. Although they work, these rules are not complete solutions in themselves, but rather can be used as the basis for fully developed solutions that address real business needs. Other examples that you might consider include rules that do the following:

- Restrict the transmission of specific message types (such as out-of-office notifications) so that these messages never go outside the organization. The important predicates for this rule are MessageTypeMatches = "OOF" and SentInScope = "NotInOrganization."

- Defend against the spread of a virus by checking the message subject for a specific text pattern such as "I Love You." This rule requires a simple check against "SubjectContainsWords" and the action might be DeleteMessage $True. Obviously you have to be careful to create conditions that do not block and delete valid messages when using this rule.

Because of the complexities involved in setting many of the conditions used by transport rules, it's likely that you will use EMC instead of EMS to work with rules and that this work will be done by a small number of administrators who are familiar with their concept and implementation. It's important that any rule is tested extensively in a realistic environment before it is introduced into production. In particular, you need to make sure that rules complement rather than interfere with each other and that they are processed in the correct priority order.

It's also a good idea to create rules with Windows PowerShell scripts becasue this allows you to recreate rules easily if an accident occurs, such as if an administrator deletes a rule in error. The scripts can contain comments to explain the business purpose served by the rule and therefore act as a form of primitative documentation. The alternative is to take a series of screen shots to document the different sections of every rule and paste the screen shots into a document. However, this approach is unwieldly and it is all too easy to miss an important detail that won't be overlooked in the EMS code used to create a rule.

If you want to use EMS to work with transport rules, the following cmdlets are available:

- New-TransportRule: Creates a new rule.

- Set-TransportRule: Amends the properties of an existing rule.

- Get-TransportRule: Retrieves the properties of one or more rules.

- Remove-TransportRule: Removes a transport rule from the organization.

The EMS code to create the rules is listed with each example.

Rules and ECP

The Exchange 2010 SP1 version of ECP (Figure 16-1) allows administrators to work with transport and journal rules without EMC. Some will find this user interface to be more approachable than EMC and it's certainly a good thing to have the ability to deploy the responsibility for creating and maintaining rules via a browser without the accompanying need to deploy the Exchange management tools. However, in most large organizations I believe that the maintenance of rules will be done by a small group of administrators who will continue to use EMC for most issues associated with rules, with an occasional foray into EMS.

> **Note**
>
> Because a badly implemented rule can wreak so much havoc on the transport service, the last thing you want is to have administrators experiment with rules.

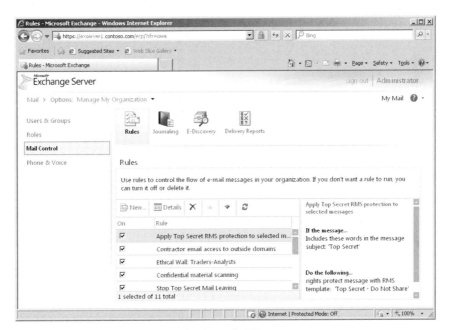

Figure 16-1 Accessing transport rules through ECP.

Basic structure of transport rules

All transport rules share a basic structure. A rule is composed of three separate parts: conditions, actions, and exceptions. The EMC Wizard leads you to the specification of each part when you create or modify a transport rule.

- The conditions of the rule are established to tell the transport service when it should intervene and select a message. For example, "apply this rule to all outgoing messages" or "apply this rule to members of a specific distribution group."

- The actions to apply to the message are determined. For example, append some disclaimer text to the end of the message body or forward the message to a particular address for moderation.

- Any exceptions are declared. For example, don't apply the rule if the sender is in a specified distribution group.

Apart from naming the rule and providing some comments so that other administrators know the rule's purpose and perhaps who created the rule and when it was implemented, all you need to do is go through these three steps to create a rule. As such, the three steps provide a useful framework for designing a rule. After all, if you cannot say what conditions will invoke the rule, what the rule will do, and whether any exceptions exist, you will never be able to define the rule for Exchange.

Transport rules are applied to messages by the transport rules agent after the full recipient list is determined by the categorizer.

Edge versus hub rules

You can create transport rules to run on either Edge or hub transport servers. However, it's important to understand that the two types of servers operate in completely different contexts, which influence how transport rules are processed. Edge servers handle incoming message streams from external sources, so the priority is to remove unwanted spam and potential virus-laden messages. Hub transport servers process messages within the organization, between organizations, and into and out of the organization. As such, hub transport servers have to handle a much broader range of circumstances. Each type of server therefore runs a slightly different version of the transport rules agent. Table 16-2 summarizes the differences in the rules agent running on Edge and hub transport servers.

Table 16-2 Differences for the rules agent running on Edge and hub transport servers

	Hub transport server	Edge transport server
Storage	Stored in the configuration naming context of Active Directory and replicated throughout the forest to be available to every hub transport server.	Stored in the unique Active Directory Lightweight Directory Services instance running on the Edge server and only available to that server. Rule collections can be exported from an Edge server and imported into another.
Events	Hub transport rules fire when the *OnRoutedMessage* event occurs for a message.	Edge transport rules fire when the *EndOfData* event occurs for a message.
Disclaimers	Can apply disclaimers (plain text and HTML) to messages sent internally and externally.	Edge transport rules cannot apply disclaimers to messages.
Messages	Processes all messages except system messages (such as nondelivery reports [NDRs]).	Processes all messages including system messages.
Predicates	Very wide range of predicates available to identify messages that should be processed by a rule.	Limited set of predicates available, some of which deal with recipient addresses and are only available on an Edge server.
Active Directory access	Can access Active Directory to execute rule conditions that depend on group membership or user properties.	No access to Active Directory.
Access to protected content	Can inspect Information Rights Management (IRM)-protected messages and take action based on its content (this requires the enabling of the transport decryption feature).	No access to protected content.

The example rules examined in the remainder of this chapter have been developed for and are intended for use on a hub transport server.

Setting transport rule priority

Transport rules are shared among all hub transport servers in an organization. Each rule has a priority from 0 (zero, the highest) downward to instruct the transport service what order to use when it processes the rules. When you open EMC and go to the Hub Transport section of Organization Configuration, EMC lists the current set of transport rules in priority order. You can amend the priority of a rule by selecting it and setting a new value, as shown in Figure 16-2. The new priority becomes effective immediately.

Chapter 16

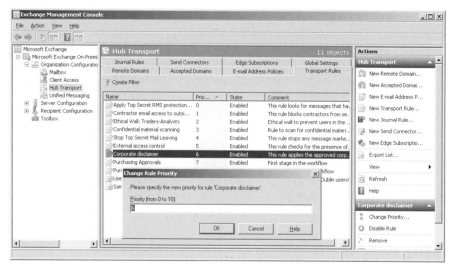

Figure 16-2 Setting priority for a transport rule.

The same effect can be achieved with EMS by first retrieving a list of rules with Get-TransportRule cmdlet and then setting the required priority. For example:

```
Get-TransportRule
```

Name	State	Priority	Comments
Ethical Wall: Traders-Analysts Traders	Enabled	0	Ethical wall to prevent users in the
Contractor email access to outside sending email	Enabled	1	This rule blocks contractors from
Confidential material scanning and	Enabled	2	Rule to scan for confidential material
External access control	Enabled	3	This rule checks for the presence of
Stop Top Secret Mail Leaving the Top	Enabled	4	This rule stops any message marked with
Company disclaimer company	Enabled	5	This transport rule applies the approved
Purchasing Approvals workflow	Enabled	6	First stage in the purchasing approvals
Purchasing Sanctions workflow	Enabled	7	Second stage in the purchasing approvals
Users in Dublin who are	Enabled	8	This rule prepends some text to users
Test rule	Disabled	9	

```
Set-TransportRule -Identity 'Contractor email access to outside domains'
 -Priority 2
```

Apart from establishing a clear order of precedence for rule execution, priority can some-times provide a workaround to a limitation that exists in transport rules. Many rule condi-tions evaluate a property of a message but can only examine that property for one value. For example, a rule can check for an SCL value determined for a message but only look for one value because the predicate applies that restriction. Thus, if you want to check for two SCL values (say, 5 and 6), you need multiple rules. You could have one rule to check for an SCL value of 5, another to check for an SCL value of 6, and have both apply an update action to write a value into the message header. A third rule that follows the other rules could then check for the value in the message header and take whatever action is required. It's an imperfect but effective way of extending transport rule functionality to work around a small limitation.

See *http://technet.microsoft.com/en-us/library/aa995960(EXCHG.80).aspx* for information on transport rule predicates.

Creating a corporate disclaimer

Creating a corporate disclaimer that's appended to every outgoing message is a com-mon requirement in messaging deployments, so it's a good example to illustrate how to go about creating a transport rule. To begin, click the Hub Transport section of the Organization Configuration section in EMC and click the Transport Rules tab. Click Create New Transport Rule to launch the wizard.

The first step (Figure 16-3) is to name the new rule and provide a description. The descrip-tion is only available to administrators and it's a good idea to include an explanation of what the rule is intended to do, who created it, and when the rule was implemented.

INSIDE OUT   Don't forget that you forget

Although it might seem tiresome to input this amount of information when you're creating a rule, memories fade and it is extremely valuable to understand the whys and wherefores of a rule collection when the time comes to move to a new version of Exchange (at which time you might have to upgrade rules) or a new administra-tor joins the team and has to be brought up to speed on the details of the Exchange organization.

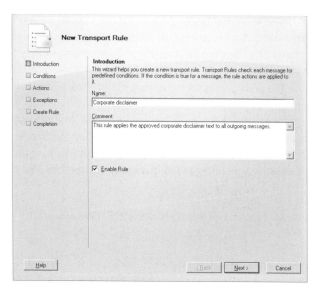

Figure 16-3 Creating a new transport rule.

The next two steps in the wizard allow you to configure the conditions under which Exchange will apply the rule and the actions taken to apply the rule. For a disclaimer, the conditions are usually straightforward. We can do the following:

- Apply the disclaimer to all messages.

- Apply the disclaimer only to messages that go to external recipients.

- Apply different disclaimers for different destinations.

The *SendToScope* property for the rule is the most useful for our purpose. If this property is not set, the rule will be applied to all messages. Otherwise, the scope can have these values:

- *InOrganization*: Internal recipients in an accepted domain for the Exchange organization

- *NotInOrganization*: External recipients that aren't in an accepted domain

- *ExternalPartner*: Recipients in external domains that are configured to use Transport Layer Security (TLS)-secured connections

- *ExternalNonPartner*: Recipients in external domains that do not use secured connections

If we want to apply the disclaimer to messages to external recipients, we set the scope to be *NotInOrganization*, which the wizard displays as "Outside the organization." Some companies create different rules for external and internal recipients and specify different disclaimer text in each rule. The disclaimer text for external recipients tends to be longer and more legalistic. Disclaimers for internal recipients are usually shorter and might contain pointers to internal information that is not useful outside the firewall.

The rule description in Figure 16-4 shows that the scope for external recipients is selected. We can also see that the action to append the disclaimer text is selected. Exchange 2007 allows the creation of disclaimers using simple, unformatted text. Exchange 2010 improves matters by supporting the use of an HTML-formatted disclaimer of up to 5,000 characters.

Before implementing an HTML format disclaimer, know the restrictions

There are some restrictions to take into account before you rush to use an HTML formatted disclaimer.

- First, the HTML text is only respected if users send messages in HTML or Rich Text Format. If a user composes a message in plain text, the disclaimer is appended in plain text so the recipient sees all the HTML tags and coding in the disclaimer instead of a nicely formatted corporate disclaimer. Most Outlook and Outlook Web App users send messages in HTML or Rich Text but Post Office Protocol 3 (POP3) and Internet Message Access Protocol 4 (IMAP4) clients often generate plain text messages.

- Second, applying a corporate disclaimer with a transport rule doesn't stop user-generated autosignature text inserted into outgoing messages by clients. When you introduce a corporate disclaimer, you should tell users what is included in the disclaimer and what they should include (if anything) in their personal auto-signature. For example, you could tell them that the disclaimer will include user details extracted from Active Directory (we'll describe how to do this later on) and that the only thing that they should put into the autosignature is a personal motto or something similar.

The dialog box presented to input the disclaimer text is a very basic text editor. You can input and edit text but there's no context-sensitive in-line recognition of HTML tags and syntax, so it is best to prepare and test the disclaimer text using an HTML editor and then cut and paste the result into the text box.

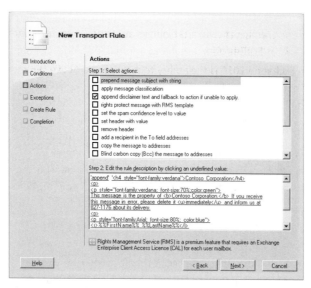

Figure 16-4 Defining actions for a transport rule that applies a company disclaimer to outgoing messages.

Figure 16-5 illustrates some HTML code for a disclaimer that generates some bold and underlined words in a certain size and color. It's easy to add images such as corporate logos here with a reference to an image that's available on a public Web site that both internal and external recipients can access when they open messages. For example:

```
<IMG src="http://webserver.contoso.com/images/contosocompanylogo.gif">
```

If you include an image in a disclaimer, make sure that the image file is as small as possible; otherwise you will fill up mailboxes with duplicate images and slow down access to email.

Figure 16-5 Editing HTML text for the disclaimer.

INSIDE OUT   A transport rule that eliminates the need for users to create autosignatures

A nice change in Exchange 2010 is the ability to incorporate Active Directory information about the message sender to personalize the disclaimer and avoid the need for users to create their personal autosignature text. You can find full details of the available Active Directory fields in the Exchange 2010 help file. The advantage of this feature is that users don't have to create their own autosignature files that invariably differ across the organization. You also avoid situations where users do silly things like including a large graphics file in their autosignatures. Using a transport rule allows the creation of an autosignature that meets organizational requirements, looks good, and is consistent across the organization.

In this example, we'll add some basic details such as a user's name, phone number, and email address—all fields often incorporated into personal autosignature text. Exchange extracts the information from the sender's account and inserts it into the disclaimer text when the rule is processed by the hub transport server. No intelligence is available to handle situations when a value such as the user's phone number is blank. In these situations you'll see the template text followed by the blank. To round things out and make our text stand out, some HTML formatting is used to differentiate the personal information from the legal disclaimer text (Figure 16-6).

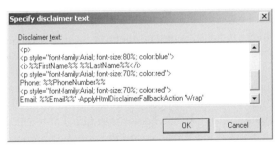

Figure 16-6 Adding Active Directory data to a disclaimer.

There are no exceptions for this transport rule, because we want it applied to every outgoing message sent from every mailbox, so we can move the wizard to the point where the rule is created (Figure 16-7). This screen shot does not include the Active Directory references that we've just discussed, because I wanted to show a complete rule. Adding the HTML to incorporate the Active Directory information would overflow the available display space.

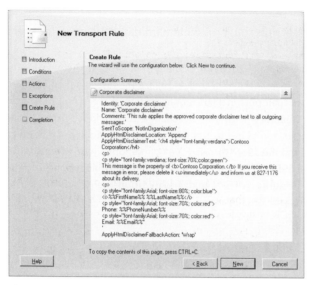

Figure 16-7 Completing the transport rule to apply a corporate disclaimer on outgoing messages.

Figure 16-7 shows the final stage in the process when we complete the wizard and create the new transport rule. The EMS code that creates the transport rule is shown next. There you can see the HTML text for the disclaimer; that we want to apply the disclaimer at the end of messages (Location = "Append"); and that the default action to take if Exchange can't add the disclaimer is "Wrap." This means that if Exchange can't access the original text of the message (because it is encrypted or in a format that Exchange doesn't support) to append the disclaimer, it creates a new envelope to include the original message and the disclaimer. Rules that can create new envelopes should therefore be placed at the lowest priority so that all other rules processing occurs beforehand. You can also see that we've chosen to enable the rule immediately. Finally, we've included an exception (in the –*ExceptIfSubjectOrBodyContainsWords* parameter) to force the rule to check messages for the presence of the corporate disclaimer. This check makes sure that the rule doesn't insert the disclaimer each time a message in a thread passes through the transport system. One corporate disclaimer is probably sufficient for every message thread.

```
New-TransportRule -Identity 'Company disclaimer' -Name 'Company disclaimer'
-Comments 'This transport rule applies the approved company disclaimer to every
outgoing message' -Priority '0' -Enabled $true -SentToScope 'NotInOrganization'
-ApplyHtmlDisclaimerLocation 'Append' -ApplyHtmlDisclaimerText
'<h4 style="font-family:verdana">Contoso Corporation</h4>
<p>
<p style="font-family:verdana; font-size:70%;color:green">
This message is the property of <b>Contoso Corporation.</b> If you receive this
message in error, please delete it <u>immediately</u> and inform us at 827-1176 about
its delivery.
```

```
<p>
<p style="font-family:Arial; font-size:80%; color:blue">
<i>%%FirstName%% %%LastName%%</i>
<p style="font-family:Arial; font-size:70%; color:red">
Phone: %%PhoneNumber%%
<p style="font-family:Arial; font-size:70%; color:red">
Email: %%Email%%' -ApplyHtmlDisclaimerFallbackAction 'Wrap'
-ExceptIfSubjectOrBodyContainsWords 'This message is the property of Contoso
Corporation'
```

Figure 16-8 brings everything together as viewed by a user in a mail message. Our disclaimer is built from some Active Directory properties (first name, last name, phone number, and email address) shown in a different font and size to differentiate this information from the legal disclaimer text that follows. If the user has created his own disclaimer using Outlook Web App or Outlook, his personal text is inserted first (by the client) and is then followed by the text inserted by the transport rule, which can get a little confusing at times. Copies of messages in the Sent Items folder will not show the disclaimer because these copies have not been processed by a hub transport server.

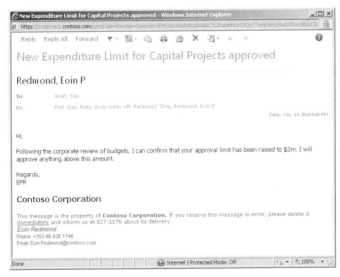

Figure 16-8 Viewing the corporate disclaimer as applied to a message.

Basic moderated workflow

One of the more interesting possibilities created through the increased functionality in transport rules implemented in Exchange 2010 is to combine mailbox moderation with rules. As you'll recall from the discussion in Chapter 6, "Managing Mail-Enabled Recipients," about how to apply moderation for messages sent to distribution groups, the transport system checks for conditions that force it to redirect messages to a mailbox for approval before they can be delivered to the intended recipients. In this case, we can leverage a rule to impose moderation and also take advantage of the fact that Exchange is able to track the progress of a message through a set of rules so that it imposes the correct moderation at the right stage. This ability is used to create rules to impose a primitive form of workflow that takes a message from mailbox to mailbox in an approval process.

Our scenario calls for messages sent to a central purchasing department mailbox that contain requests for approval to be redirected to two other mailboxes in sequential order to receive approval before the messages are delivered to the purchasing department mailbox. In other words:

- Messages sent for approval to Purchasing Department mailbox

- First go to Purchasing Approvals to seek approval

- Then go to Purchasing Sanctions to complete the approval process

We need two rules to create the workflow. A single rule that requests moderation from Purchasing Approvals or Purchasing Sanctions is insufficient because either mailbox could approve a request. We want approvals from both. We therefore create two rules in the correct order of priority to first direct messages to Purchasing Approvals and then, if approval is granted, to Purchasing Sanctions. You could improve the rule by adding extra conditions or exceptions, such as exempting messages from specified mailboxes from the approval process, but this basic rule serves to illustrate the point.

The second rule is very similar to the first with the exception that messages go to Purchasing Sanctions for moderation. The second rule has a lower priority than the first so that it is only invoked after the first rule has completed processing. This will occur after the message has been delivered to Purchasing Approvals and has received approval. The second rule then fires and the transport system redirects the message to the Purchasing Sanctions mailbox. If approval is received from this mailbox, the message will finally be delivered to the Purchasing Department mailbox. A small weakness now reveals itself: No evidence that moderation has occurred appears in the message when it arrives in the Purchasing Department mailbox, because it is not possible to force the rule to prepend any text to indicate progress through the approving mailboxes. (If you create a rule to enforce moderation, it can only contain the moderation action.) It's also not possible for the approving users to manually insert any text, because they are not allowed to edit the message content. However, assuming that the workflow functions as it should, the users who process items that arrive in the Purchasing Department mailbox might be entitled to assume that moderation has occurred and the necessary approvals have been granted. Again, this is primitive workflow!

The EMS code that creates the two rules used to create simple two-stage message moderation is:

```
New-TransportRule -Name 'Purchasing Approvals'-Comments 'First stage in the workflow'
-Priority '1' -Enabled $True -SentTo 'PurchasingDepartment.Mailbox@contoso.com'
-SubjectContainsWords 'Purchase','Request','Sanction' -ModerateMessageByUser
'Purchasing.Approvals@contoso.com' -ExceptIfFrom 'Purchasing.Sanctions@contoso.
com','Purchasing.Approvals@contoso.com'

New-TransportRule -Name 'Purchasing Sanctions' -Comments 'Second stage in the
workflow' -Priority '2' -Enabled $True -SentTo
'Purchasing.DepartmentMailbox@contoso.com' -SubjectContainsWords
'Purchase','Request','Sanction' -ModerateMessageByUser
'Purchasing.Sanctions@contoso.com' -ExceptIfFrom
'Purchasing.Sanctions@contoso.com','Purchasing.Approvals@contoso.com'
```

After the rules are created, we need to make sure that they are placed in the correct order of priority so that approvals are sought in the right order. As discussed previously, we can check this in EMC (Figure 16-9).

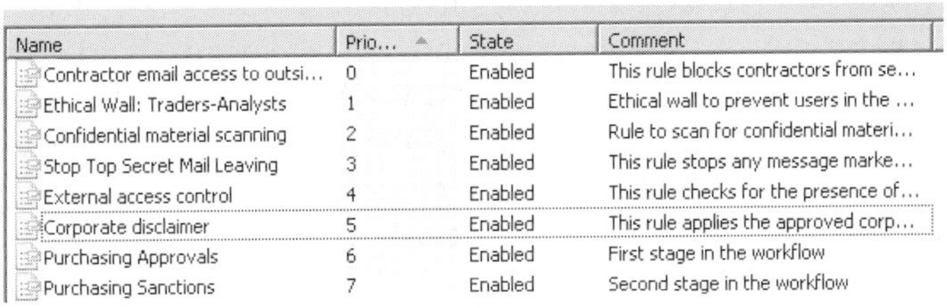

Name	Prio...	State	Comment
Contractor email access to outsi...	0	Enabled	This rule blocks contractors from se...
Ethical Wall: Traders-Analysts	1	Enabled	Ethical wall to prevent users in the ...
Confidential material scanning	2	Enabled	Rule to scan for confidential materi...
Stop Top Secret Mail Leaving	3	Enabled	This rule stops any message marke...
External access control	4	Enabled	This rule checks for the presence of...
Corporate disclaimer	5	Enabled	This rule applies the approved corp...
Purchasing Approvals	6	Enabled	First stage in the workflow
Purchasing Sanctions	7	Enabled	Second stage in the workflow

Figure 16-9 Making sure the rules are in the correct order.

Evaluating Active Directory attributes in transport rules

Exchange 2010 allows you to evaluate Active Directory attributes of senders and recipients to decide whether to apply rules to messages. You can check the following conditions:

- *RecipientADAttributeContainsWords*: One or more recipient attributes contains a word.

- *RecipientADAttributeMatchesPatterns*: One or more recipient attributes matches a predetermined pattern.

- *SenderADAttributeContainsWords*: One or more sender attributes contains a word.

- *SenderADAttributeMatchesPatterns*: One or more sender attributes matches a predetermined pattern.

Chapter 16

Here's a trite example that illustrates how such a test might be conducted. In this case, the rule looks for "Dublin" in the CustomAttribute1 of message recipients and, if it is found, prepends the message subject with some text:

```
New-TransportRule -Name 'Users in Dublin'-RecipientADAttributeContainsWords
'customattribute1:Dublin' -PrependSubject 'User in Dublin:'
```

When working through EMC, you can select conditions such as "when a recipient's properties contains specific words" and then enter the attributes against which you want to check and the values for which you are looking. Figure 16-10 shows that a comprehensive range of attributes are available to be checked. You can create rules that check against multiple attributes, although you have to be careful that the different values do not clash with each other.

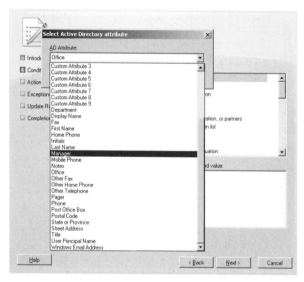

Figure 16-10 Selecting an Active Directory attribute for use in a transport rule.

Exchange 2010 also supports rules based on a comparison between the values of an Active Directory attribute for a message's sender and recipient. Again, a simple example rule illustrates this concept. The first important point to note is the *–ADComparisonAttribute* parameter, which specifies the attribute that we want to compare. In this case, we use "Office," but all of the attributes discussed before are available for checking (see TechNet for an exhaustive list). The second point is the *–AdComparisonOperator* parameter, which will be Equal or Not Equal depending on the comparison we want to make.

```
New-TransportRule -Name 'Same Office' -ADComparisonAttribute 'Office'
-ADComparisonOperator 'Equal' -PrependSubject 'User in same office: '
```

Ethical firewalls

An ethical firewall is a software block that prevents users in one part of the company from sharing information with users in another part of the company. The classic example is the need to prevent information from flowing between traders and analysts in a financial services company so that the traders can never be accused of being in receipt of information from analysts that affects their trading behavior. Exchange transport rules make it reasonably easy to build an ethical firewall that meets most requirements. The basic requirement is to be able to identify both sets of users so that a rule can detect when individuals are attempting to communicate with someone that they shouldn't and then define what happens. The easiest approach is to look for messages that flow between two distribution groups because groups are easy to maintain and can be used for other purposes such as legitimate communication, controlling access to resources, and so on. The condition for which we need to check is therefore internal communication between two groups.

The action we want to take is to reject the message and send back a nondelivery notification to the user to tell her what we've done. We will exploit the functionality we explored in Chapter 13, "The Exchange Transport System," to create a custom system message with a new enhanced status code (5.7.100) to use with our NDR. We'll use the custom system message to communicate some specific text to the user to inform her about the problem. We don't absolutely need to use a customized NDR, because the ethical firewall will function with the default enhanced status code for rejection messages (5.7.1). However, the customized text underlines the gravity of the situation to the user whose message is rejected. You cannot combine other actions when you create a rule to reject a message. The code to create the new rule is as follows:

```
New-TransportRule -Name 'Ethical Wall: Traders-Analysts' -Comments 'Ethical wall to
prevent users in the Traders and Analysts departments communicating.'
-Priority '0' -Enabled $True -BetweenMemberOf1 'Analysts@contoso.com'
-BetweenMemberOf2 'Traders@contoso.com'-RejectMessageReasonText 'Message in violation
of ethical firewall'-RejectMessageEnhancedStatusCode '5.7.100'
```

Figure 16-11 shows the message generated by Exchange after it detects an attempt to communicate between the two groups. The text specified in our customized delivery status notification (DSN) is clearly shown under the email address of the recipient with whom the user attempted to communicate. We can also see that the text defined for the customized system message specified in the rule is included in the diagnostic information for administrators at the bottom of the message.

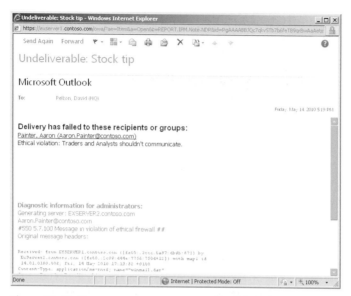

Figure 16-11 The message sent to users who violate the ethical firewall.

Blocking certain users from sending external email

User communities can cover a diverse set of individual users. We might want to exert control over the communications of certain users. It's common to find that companies want to ensure that contract workers are restricted to internal communications and aren't allowed to use their time to send messages to outside domains. This kind of restriction is easily accomplished with a transport rule.

Figure 16-12 shows the basic conditions that we need for our rule. The first condition is that we are only concerned with messages that go outside the organization. The second is that we check for some indicator that marks the user as worthy of our attention. In this instance we check against Active Directory and look for the Contractor string in CustomAttribute10. This is a good example of how you can use one of the custom attributes to locate specific individuals. You could also check other Active Directory attributes such as Title or even look for members of a distribution group. The action taken by the rule is to reject the message and send a custom NDR back to the user. We've added one exception to allow members of a distribution group to send messages to external recipients.

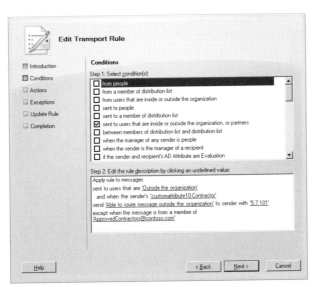

Figure 16-12 Creating a transport rule to block contractors from sending external email.

The EMS code for the new rule is shown here:

```
New-TransportRule -Name 'Contractor email access to outside domains' -Comments 'This
rule blocks contractors from sending email to outside domains. The rule looks for
"Contractor" in the CustomAttribute10 of user accounts.' -Priority '0' -Enabled
$True
-SentToScope 'NotInOrganization' -SenderADAttributeContainsWords
'customattribute10:Contractor' -RejectMessageReasonText 'Able to route message
outside the organization' -RejectMessageEnhancedStatusCode '5.7.101'
-ExceptIfFromMemberOf 'ApprovedContractors@contoso.com'
```

Users who fall afoul of the rule receive a message similar to that illustrated in Figure 16-13. Creating the custom NDR uses a technique that we have explored before so there is no need to comment further.

We can improve the rule by adding more exceptions to allow contractors to communicate with "safe" domains. For example, let's assume that your company has just taken over another company and you're in the middle of the work required to merge the two companies. In these circumstances, it's likely that the acquired company will have its own email domain and it is reasonable to expect that you will want to allow contractors to communicate with users in that domain. You might have other safe domains that you want to add to allow contractors to communicate with suppliers or other companies that they have legitimate reasons to contact. Exchange 2010 transport rules support a wide range of exceptions that can be combined in an additive fashion, so we can amend our rule with the

Chapter 16

Set-TransportRule cmdlet to add another exception. This command allows our contractors to send email to recipients in microsoft.com and cohowinery.com:

```
Set-TransportRule -Identity 'Contractor email access to outside domains'
-ExceptifRecipientAddressMatchesPatterns '@Microsoft.com', '@cohowinery.com'
```

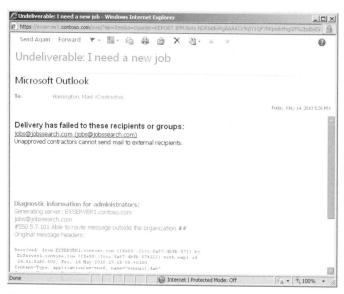

Figure 16-13 A contractor's message is blocked.

The full rule therefore allows two exceptions: Contractors in a special distribution group can send to any external domain and any contractor is allowed to send to the two domains that we have specified in the rule.

Two new features: Message moderation and access to Active Directory data

A variation on the theme that illustrates the rich set of conditions and actions that you can deploy in transport rules is solving the problem of controlling access to external recipients by creating a rule that redirects any message sent by a contractor to an external address to the contractor's manager for moderation. The manager can check the message and approve it to allow it to proceed or reject it and send the message back to the originator with some text to explain why it was rejected. Such a rule depends on two new features for transport rules introduced in Exchange 2010: message moderation and access to Active Directory data. Of course, it also depends on the accurate population of Active Directory with management information for users. If Active Directory doesn't hold any management information for a user, a rule that depends on these data fails. The transport system can't apply moderation and will therefore pass the messages through for delivery.

Assuming that we have the necessary information populated in Active Directory, a transport rule to enforce message moderation by managers might look something like this:

```
New-TransportRule –Name 'External access control' -SentToScope 'NotInOrganization'
-SenderADAttributeMatchesPatterns 'customattribute12:NoExternalAccess'
–ModerateMessageByManager $True -ExceptIfFromMemberOf
'ApprovedContractors@contoso.com' -Priority '3' -Enabled $True -Comments 'This rule
checks for the presence of "NoExternalAccess" in CustomAttribute12. If detected, the
message is sent to the manager of the sender for moderation. An exception is allowed
for members of the Approved Contractors group.'
```

An example of the kind of message that you might want to intercept is shown in Figure 16-14. I'm sure that you can think of a witty response!

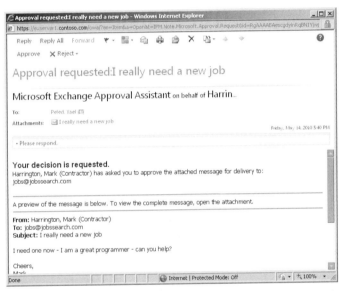

Figure 16-14 Moderation provoked by a transport rule.

Scanning attachments with transport rules

Exchange 2007 transport rules can scan message subjects and bodies for words, but the ability to build transport rules to scan attachments for words or text patterns is new in Exchange 2010. Rules can check the complete body of an attachment, including headers and footers, but not document metadata to look for pattern matches. The most basic example is to check for documents that contain a company confidential notice to prevent them going to external recipients. You might check for strings such as Company Confidential or Company Private, always making sure that the string that you select isn't so general as to block attachments that should be permitted to pass.

There are probably a few users who are allowed to communicate confidential material to the outside world, so we could create a distribution group and make messages from this group an exception. Transport rules depend on IFilters to be able to access attachment content. The set of IFilters installed with Exchange 2010 include Microsoft Office, email messages, and HTML/XML (only rendered content). PDF is a major exception, which means that an easy way to send confidential material without detection is to render it in PDF and send that file—unless you download and install Adobe IFilter for PDF using the instructions provided in Chapter 2, "Installing Exchange 2010," or implement a condition in a transport rule to check for attachments of an unsupported file type and take an appropriate step such as blocking the message.

> ### Note
>
> The set of IFilters is held in the system registry because it is shared with the MSSearch component. This means that you have to update every transport server in the organization with a new IFilter before it is effective globally. Similar to other data used by transport rules, information about IFilters is cached and refreshed every 30 minutes, so you need to restart the transport service if you want to impose scanning for a new attachment type immediately.

After we have specified a few secret code words and figured out any exceptions, the final rule might look something like this:

```
New-TransportRule -Name 'Confidential material scanning'
-Comments 'Rule to scan for confidential material and remove it from outgoing
messages.' -Priority '3'
-Enabled $True -SentToScope 'NotInOrganization' -AttachmentContainsWords
'Boggle','Truffles','Maxia','Confidential' -RejectMessageReasonText 'Confidential
data should not be discussed with anyone outside the company'
-RejectMessageEnhancedStatusCode '5.7.1' -DeleteMessage $False
-ExceptIfFromMemberOf 'COs@contoso.com'
```

Exchange 2010 also includes the ability to check for regular expressions within messages so that you can stop people from sending content that you can identify through a specific pattern of characters. The TechNet documentation describes the regular expressions supported by Exchange 2007 and Exchange 2010 with a U.S. Social Security number (SSN) being the commonly cited example. An SSN is of the form 999-99-9999, so the regular pattern is "\d\d\d-\d\d-\d\d\d\d" (the \d pattern matches any single numeric digit). You can imagine checks for other examples such as looking for a project code name such as "Project Fabrikam Merger."

```
$Condition = Get-TransportRulePredicate SubjectMatches
$Condition.Patterns = @("\d\d\d-\d\d-\d\d\d\d")
$Action = Get-TransportRuleAction RejectMessage $Action.RejectReason =
```

```
"The transmission of Social Security Numbers is prohibited."
New-TransportRule -Name "Social Security Number Block Rule" -Conditions $Condition
-Actions $Action
```

Once a rule detects a pattern match, you have a range of options to apply through the rule:

- Apply an AD RMS (Rights Management System) template to the message and its attachments so that only authorized recipients can read it. Note that Exchange 2010 supports integration with AD RMS to allow transport rules to inspect the contents of protected messages and attachments. For example, you might decide to amend the rule that scans for confidential material and apply an RMS template to it rather than bounce the message back to the user. To do this, you'd remove the commands to bounce the message and replace it with a direction to apply an RMS template, as shown here:

  ```
  -ApplyRightsProtectionTemplate "Confidential material"
  ```

- Forward the message to a reviewer to make a decision whether the content can be sent.

- Apply a disclaimer to the message.

- Copy the message to an address so that a record is kept or appropriate people are advised that content has left the organization.

- Silently delete the message.

All of these options present their own difficulties. The most obvious is cultural: You don't want users to attempt to get around a block by simply deleting the strings that the rule looks for from their document because it's usually important to have appropriate disclaimers or indications of confidential material included in sensitive documents. You don't want users to feel that "big brother" is watching their every move, but you do want them to understand that it's important to handle confidential material appropriately to protect the interests of the company. You don't want to impose a block that might slow the transmission of material to authorized parties such as confidential documents that users might want to send to your company's external legal advisors or auditors. If you copy the message to a mailbox, some mechanism is required to check the mailbox on a regular basis—a task that could become very onerous if a high volume of messages is intercepted by the rule.

It's also worth remembering that the ability to process attachments can be combined with any of the other conditions that are available to process messages with transport rules. For example, you can include an exception to allow members of the legal or accounting departments or senior management to send company confidential material to external recipients on the basis that they should know what they are doing. You can block attachments of more than a certain size or of a certain file type to ensure that users don't send each other large video files. The full set of conditions available to transport rules creates a great deal of flexibility to handle different business requirements.

Using message classifications and rights management templates in transport rules

The steps required to create and enable message classifications are discussed in Chapter 15, "Compliance." Once users have applied classifications to messages, you can create transport rules that take action if a particular classification is found. The example message classification discussed in Chapter 15 is "Top Secret" and is intended to mark messages that should not go outside the organization. The transport rule that implements such a block is very straightforward.

"Marked with classification" is one of the conditions that you can select for a transport rule. This condition instructs the transport system to look for a classification attribute on a message. As usual, you then specify the actions that you want to take—an appropriate action seems to be to reject the message and send a DSN. You then add any exceptions. For example, senior executives might be allowed to circumvent the restriction because they presumably know how to protect intellectual property and other secret information.

The basic EMS code to create the transport rule is shown here. This code doesn't include an exception—adding one is an exercise for the reader!

```
New-TransportRule -Name 'Stop Top Secret Mail Leaving' -Comments 'This rule stops any
message marked with the Top Secret classification leaving the organization.'
-Priority '0' -Enabled $True -HasClassification 'Default\Top Secret'
-RejectMessageReasonText "You can't send Top Secret messages out of the organization"
-RejectMessageEnhancedStatusCode '5.7.900'
```

A simple example of how to apply an AD RMS template to protect confidential information is to look for the presence of some text in a message subject and then apply a template if the text is found. In this example, our rule looks for "Top Secret" in the subject to decide whether to apply the "Top Secret—Do Not Share" template discussed in Chapter 17, "The Exchange Toolbox." As obvious from Figure 16-15, the rule is very straightforward and the only difference from any rule that we have seen before is the need to pick an AD RMS template to apply. The EMS code for the rule is as follows:

```
New-TransportRule -Name 'Apply Top Secret RMS protection to selected messages'
-Comments 'This rule looks for messages that have Top Secret in the message subject
and applies the Top Secret AD RMS template to these messages to protect them.'
-Priority '5' -Enabled $true -SubjectContainsWords 'Top Secret'
-ApplyRightsProtectionTemplate 'Top Secret - Do Not Share'
```

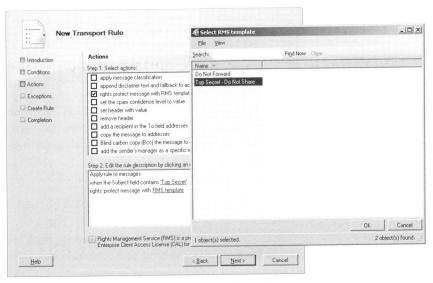

Figure 16-15 Specifying an AD RMS template for a rule.

Evidence that the rule is applied and has an effect is easily seen by creating and sending a message that includes "Top Secret" in its subject. Fortunately our fears are lifted when we check a message (Figure 16-16) to find that the template has been applied and our confidential information has been protected without any intervention on the part of the user.

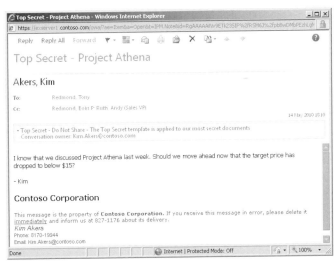

Figure 16-16 Checking that top secret information has been protected by a transport rule.

Caching transport rules

To reduce the number of calls Exchange must make to Active Directory to resolve members of distribution groups that are specified in transport rules, hub transport servers cache these data and refresh them from Active Directory every four hours. The cache is populated when the first message is processed after the transport service is started by scanning the set of transport rules for the *IsMemberOf* condition and resolving the membership of all groups found by this check. The use of cached data speeds performance but it also creates a difficulty because transport rules can function while blissfully unaware of important changes to distribution groups.

An example: Blocking communication between two business units

For example, let's assume that you have a rule that blocks specific users in one part of the business from contacting users in another part to maintain an ethical firewall. The relevant users are identified through distribution groups. If you add a new user to the group, it could be up to four hours before the block is active for that user. This might not be important if the ethical wall isn't there because of regulatory requirements, but you can see the danger that exists. In Exchange 2007 the only solution was to recycle the Microsoft Exchange Transport service to force repopulation of the cache. Exchange 2010 includes a more elegant solution because you can configure the cache population interval through settings in the *AppSettings* section of the transport configuration file (EdgeTransport.exe.config). The change is not replicated within the organization and must be applied to every hub transport and Edge server.

Table 16-3 lists the settings that you can manipulate to meet the needs of your organization. The default values work reasonably well and should only be justified when you have good reason to do so. Microsoft suggests that any change to the *ExpirationInterval* is matched with a similar change (that is, similar in order of magnitude) to *CleanupInterval* to synchronize the internal processing of cache entries. You can make the change with any text editor but you have to recycle the Microsoft Exchange Transport service afterward to force it to pick up the new settings.

Table 16-3 Settings to control transport service caching of Active Directory data

Setting	Type	Def. value	Min	Max
Transport_IsMemberOfResolver_ResolvedGroupsCache _ExpirationInterval	TimeSpan	3 hours	5 seconds	1 day
This entry governs the expiration period for cached entries. Items (members of groups) are marked as expired after they have been in the cache for this period.				
Transport_IsMemberOfResolver_ResolvedGroupsCache _CleanupInterval	TimeSpan	60 minutes	5 seconds	4 hours
The transport service automatically cleans up its cache by removing expired entries after the cleanup period. For example, if items expire after 3 hours and the cleanup interval is 1 hour, they are removed after 4 hours. If an expired entry is accessed before it is removed, the transport service refreshes it by querying Active Directory with a background thread. Entries that linger in the cache past their cleanup interval (waiting to be removed) are not returned as a result of a request, which is satisfied through a new query to Active Directory.				
Transport_IsMemberOfResolver_ResolvedGroupsCache _PurgeInterval	TimeSpan	5 minutes	5 seconds	4 hours
This entry specifies how often the transport service checks its cache for expired entries that should be purged.				
Transport_IsMemberOfResolver_ResolvedGroupsCache _MaxSize	File Size	32 MB	0 MB	128 MB
The maximum size of the cache used to hold Active Directory data.				

Remember that each hub transport server caches data. Therefore, if you send a message inside a site that has four hub transport servers, your message could be handled by any of those servers. Accordingly, if you decide to restart the transport service to flush and reload the cache on one server, you should perform the same operation on all servers to ensure that all the caches are consistent.

Transferring rules between Exchange versions

You don't need to transfer transport rules when Exchange 2007 and Exchange 2010 servers operate in the same organization because the servers will share a common set of rules and understand how to process them. As mentioned at the start of this section, Exchange 2007 hub transport servers won't be able to access rules created by Exchange 2010 and will

Chapter 16

therefore ignore them. Exchange 2010 hub transport servers can access rules created by both versions.

There might be the need to transfer an existing set of transport rules from an Exchange 2007 organization to a new Exchange 2010 organization that is set up for test purposes or to be the future deployment platform. Apart from the Export-TransportRuleCollection and Import-TransportRuleCollection cmdlets, there is no built in-facility to transfer transport rules from one Exchange server to another. These cmdlets are intended to export rules from an Exchange organization and import them into Edge servers. The Import-TransportRuleCollection cmdlet is able to import a set of transport rules exported from an Exchange 2007 organization, so it's the one that you should use to get your old rule set across to Exchange 2010.

INSIDE OUT   Exchange 2010 and delete and bounce actions

One slight problem that you might encounter is that Exchange 2010 is more exact about the use of the delete and bounce actions. These actions are terminal in that a transport rule will perform no more processing after it encounters an instruction to delete a message or to bounce it to another user. Exchange 2007 wasn't quite so picky and it allows transport rules to combine these actions with another. For example, a rule might copy a blocked message to an administrator's address at the same time as it deletes it. In this scenario, the administrator gets a chance to review the content of blocked messages to ensure that the rule is operating properly and to coach users who receive blocked messages as to why they have been dropped by Exchange. It might be possible to work around the problem by building one rule to apply whatever processing is necessary for a message and have another rule that deletes or bounces the message. As long as the "delete or bounce" rule has a lower priority than the other rule, the two should work happily together to accomplish the goal.

Transport rule actions

Transport rule priority provides the obvious framework for rule execution. Internally, Exchange maintains a table of available actions for transport rules. Different sets of actions are available on hub transport and Edge servers, largely because hub transport servers can access Active Directory information whereas Edge servers cannot. You examine the available action set with the Get-TransportRuleAction cmdlet. We have encountered many of these actions as we worked through the different examples of transport rules, from adding a disclaimer to sending a message to a manager for moderation. The set available on a hub transport server is:

```
Get-TransportRuleAction
```

```
Name                        Rank  LinkedDisplayText
----                        ---   -----------------
PrependSubject              0     prepend message subject with <a id="PrependSubject">string</a>
ApplyClassification         1     apply <a id="ApplyClassification">message classification</a>
ApplyHtmlDisclaimer         2     <a id="ApplyHtmlDisclaimerLocation">append</a><a
RightsProtectMessage        3     rights protect message with <a id="ApplyRightsProtectionTemplate">RMS
SetSCL                      4     set the spam confidence level to<a id="SetSCL">value</a>
SetHeader                   5     set <a id="SetHeaderName">header</a> with <a >
RemoveHeader                6     remove <a id="RemoveHeader">header</a>
AddToRecipient              7     add a recipient in the To field <a id="AddToRecipients">addresses</a>
CopyTo                      8     copy the message to <a id="CopyTo">addresses</a>
BlindCopyTo                 9     Blind carbon copy (Bcc) the message to <a >
AddManagerAsRecipientType   10    add the sender's manager as a <a
ModerateMessageByUser       11    forward the message to <a id="ModerateMessageByUser">addresses</a>
for
ModerateMessageByManager    12    forward the message to the sender's manager for moderation<a
RedirectMessage             13    redirect the message to <a id="RedirectMessageTo">addresses</a>
RejectMessage               14    send <a id="RejectMessageReasonText">rejection message</a> to sender
DeleteMessage               15    Delete the message without notifying anyone<a id="DeleteMessage"></a>
```

The rule actions are listed in the order in which they are processed by transport rules. You can see more detail by specifying the name of the rule action you want to examine:

```
Get-TransportRuleAction -Name ApplyHtmlDisclaimer
```

```
Location          : Append
Text              :
FallbackAction    : Wrap
Name              : ApplyHtmlDisclaimer
Rank              : 2
LinkedDisplayText : <a id="ApplyHtmlDisclaimerLocation">append</a>
<a id="ApplyHtmlDisclaimerText">disclaimer text</aand fallback to
<a id="ApplyHtmlDisclaimerFallbackAction">action</a> if unable to apply.
```

Developing custom transport agents

If you've been using Exchange 2003, you might have some custom code written in a language such as C# that's known as a transport sink or Store event that runs on mailbox servers to process messages as they are sent to and from users. Exchange 2003 is not like Exchange 2007 or Exchange 2010 in that Exchange 2003 lacks a single point through which all messages must pass. Deploying code for something like an ethical firewall is more complex and costly, if only because the programmers who were experienced at writing this code were relatively difficult to find. Microsoft introduced transport rules in Exchange 2007 as a solution for many of the common situations that forced customers to write transport sinks and indeed, the experience is that Exchange 2007 succeeds in this aspect.

Exchange 2010 expands the capabilities of transport rules, but even so, the current abilities of transport rules might not satisfy your requirements. The solution is to write your own code to process messages as they pass through the message pipeline. Transport rules are agents that Exchange loads into the categorizer pipeline when the transport service initializes. You build these agents using the interfaces defined in the Exchange Software Development Kit, along with Microsoft Visual Studio, and the .NET Framework.

http://msexchangeteam.com/archive/2006/12/04/431755.aspx **provides a short guide to how to approach writing a custom transport agent and detailed instructions are available in MSDN. Another example can be found at** *http://gsexdev.blogspot.com/2009/01/from-address -rewriting-in-transport.html.*

Transport rule priority

The Get-TransportAgent cmdlet reveals the set of transport agents that are installed on a hub transport or Edge server. For example:

```
Get-TransportAgent
```

Identity	Enabled	Priority
Transport Rule Agent	True	1
Text Messaging Routing Agent	True	2
Text Messaging Delivery Agent	True	3

On an Exchange 2007 server you'd expect to see the journal rule agent listed here and indeed, some deployments increased the priority of the journal agent over the transport rule agent in an effort to ensure that even messages that are rejected by a transport rule would be captured by journaling. This is not necessary in Exchange 2010 and you cannot assign a new priority to the transport rule agent because of the potential to interfere with the integrity of the transport system. If custom agents or other agents (such as antivirus scanners) are installed, you might be able to change their priority using the Set-TransportAgent cmdlet if you have good reason to do so and are sure that switching agent priority won't break anything.

Journaling

If you review the actions available to transport rules, you'll see that you can create a rule that copies messages that meet stated conditions. For example, a rule could check for messages that contain certain phrases and copy any that are detected to a BCC or other addressee. Copying certain messages to a destination sounds much like the functionality that journaling delivers, so why does Exchange consider journaling to be different from transport rules?

As we've seen, transport rules allow for many different conditions and help organizations to manage the message stream in many different ways, including the interception and copying of selected messages. However, interception by a transport rule is intended to allow organizations to supervise and validate messages that are sent by users. Journal rules, which the journaling agent executes after the transport rules agent runs, cover a smaller range of conditions but do a far more comprehensive job of capturing messages in such a way that the copies are suitable for regulatory or compliance purposes. In other words, a message intercepted and copied by a transport rule can provide a pointer to bad user behavior that can be used for internal purposes. A message copied by a journal rule is a high-fidelity copy in the form of a journal report that will stand up as evidence in a court of law. The difference between the two rule sets is therefore a matter of scope and depth, so it's important that you understand what journal rules are designed to do and how to apply them to capture and archive messages.

Journaling only became important to enterprise email systems after two developments occurred in large corporations. First, email became the de facto mechanism for internal and external communication to a point where people naturally gravitated to email instead of the phone or traditional letters when they needed to share information with others. Second, investigations of corporate scandals revealed emphatically just how email could serve as a conduit for the misuse of commercially sensitive information. The requirement that email join the corpus of corporate data retained for audit purposes gathered pace steadily from the late 1990s onward and is now firmly ensconced in laws in various jurisdictions around the world. The Sarbanes-Oxley (SOX) and SEC Rule 17A-4 are two examples of U.S. legal and regulatory requirements that corporations have to meet that could cause a company to have to introduce message journaling.

When journaling happens

Immediately after you enable a journal rule, the journal agent running within the transport service begins to examine the message stream to identify messages that should be journaled. Journal reports are created for these messages, and the reports are sent to the journal recipient. The journal agent runs on every hub transport server and is registered for the *OnSubmittedMessage* and *OnRoutedMessage* events within the transport categorizer. Registering for events that fire when messages are submitted and routed allows the journal agent to detect whether any new addressee has been added during message processing. It does this by comparing the recipient list available for both events to determine whether a change has occurred. If this is the case, the journal agent runs its rules again.

When a message is submitted to the journal agent, it checks for the presence of the *X-Microsoft-Exchange-ProcessedByJournaling* header in the message. The presence of this header indicates that the message has already been processed by another hub transport server. If the header is not found, the journal agent runs its rules and stamps the header onto the message. All of the journal rules are concatenated together to allow the journal agent to evaluate all possible conditions at one time. The journal agent will also run its rules again if the recipient set for the message has changed as a result of distribution group expansion or a transport rule. If any condition is determined to be true, the journal agent generates a journal report.

Journaling options

Exchange 2010 supports two options for journaling.

- Standard journaling is configured on a per-mailbox database basis. When configured, the journaling agent captures all messages sent to and from mailboxes in a database. Therefore, to capture every message in an organization you need to enable journaling on all mailbox databases.

- Premium journaling is available when you hold enterprise Client Access Licenses (CALs) and provides more granular control, because it allows you to implement journal rules to establish exact conditions for journaling. We'll explore exactly what you can do with journal rules later in this section.

By default, Exchange 2007 does not journal voice mail messages and missed call notification messages created by a Unified Messaging server. Exchange 2010 enables journaling of voice mail messages by default. You can use this command to check the current status of voice mail journaling:

```
Get-TransportConfig | Select VoiceMailJournalingEnabled
```

Voice mail messages are journaled if the property is set to $True. You can change this setting with the Set-TransportConfig cmdlet:

```
Set-TransportConfig –VoiceMailJournalingEnabled $False
```

Journal reports

The first journaling features built into Exchange were rudimentary and focused on the simple capture of messages delivered to target mailboxes or databases so that they could be examined later if deemed necessary. This kind of journaling is known as *message-only journaling*. Exchange 2007 introduced a more comprehensive kind of journaling known as *envelope journaling* along with the ability to build and deploy granular journal rules that are executed as messages pass through the transport system. Envelope journaling captures all of the information contained in message envelopes along with the message body, including details of all recipients including BCC recipients and members of distribution groups. All of this information is captured in journal reports in such a way that these data can be used as the basis for forensic investigation of email communications. Journal reports meet legal evidentiary requirements and allow investigators to understand the full life cycle of a message.

The body of a journal report (Figure 16-17) includes data such as sender information, message identifier, addressee list (including BCC), content, group membership, and so on. All of the recipient metadata for the message are recorded in the journal report, including the complete recipient set from the Simple Mail Transfer Protocol (SMTP) envelope (as defined as the P1 recipient list in RFC 2821) as well as how each recipient was added to the message. Some recipients are explicitly added to a message by the sender, whereas others might be added by the transport system when a distribution group is expanded or when a transport rule adds a recipient, as in the case when a message is BCC'd to a sender's manager. The journal report also captures whether the message was forwarded and, if so, who received copies. In addition to the message header information, the original message is attached to the journal report. Attaching a copy of the original message ensures that all of the original message headers and properties are fully retained.

> **Note**
> This is an important difference from transport rules that forward copies of messages to recipients because these copies are not intended to be faithful replicas of the original message and can have some information removed from the header.

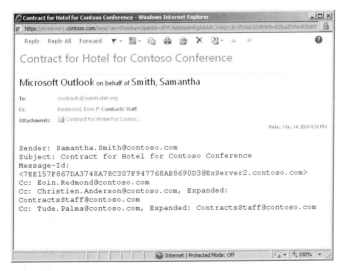

Figure 16-17 Viewing a journal report.

Exchange 2007 and Exchange 2010 journal reports are in Summary Transport Neutral Encapsulation Format (S/TNEF). S/TNEF is a richer form of the simpler TNEF format that allows more information (for instance, Outlook voting buttons) to be transported with messages. S/TNEF parts can be carried within a Multipurpose Internet Mail Extensions (MIME) message. Technically, journal reports are MIME-encoded with their content-transfer-encoding field set to binary. Exchange has used S/TNEF format to transport messages between servers since Exchange 2000 and converts this format to standard MIME when messages are transferred across an SMTP connector to an external email system. If you use an external archive system via SMTP, you can configure its domain to accept messages in MIME or S/TNEF.

The data written into journal reports are structured according to Augmented Backus-Naur Form (ABNF), a definition language often used for Internet Engineering Task Force (IETF) communication protocols. Data are written in pairs of fields and value separated by colons. The data captured include the following:

- Sender: The SMTP address of the message sender.

- Subject: The subject of the message being journaled.

- Message-id: The internal message identifier created by Exchange when the message is first submitted to the transport service. The message identifier is unique and remains with the message for its entire life cycle.

- Recipient list: Each recipient is listed as a To:, CC:, BCC:, or "Recipient" (undetermined type) together with the SMTP address. Extra information is given if the recipient is included in the message as the result of an action such as group message, address rewriting, or transport rule intervention.

The journal reports generated for messages internal to an Exchange organization differ from those created for messages that come into Exchange from SMTP connectors. Internal messages have access to a much richer set of information about message recipients (referred to as extended fields). Figure 16-17 is a journal report for an internal message. Exchange can verify that the message came from the mailbox shown as the sender. Because the message has been categorized by the transport system, many data about the recipients are available so we know that most of the recipients were added as a result of group expansion. The journal report in Figure 16-18 is for a message coming in from an external SMTP domain. It contains more basic information, because Exchange doesn't know who the sender really is and can report that a mailbox received the message but can't say whether it was a To:, CC:, or BCC: recipient. Finally, the attached message is in MIME format, whereas messages attached to journal reports for internal messages are in S/TNEF.

Figure 16-18 A journal report for a message from an external domain.

Once generated, the journaling agent submits the journal reports for delivery via SMTP to the journal destination. Exchange treats journal reports differently from other messages in that they do not generate NDR reports and do not expire on message queues. Not expiring on queues means that journal reports will not be dropped due to messaging outages and will be delivered to the journal destination when the outage is resolved. This is important because the ability to track communications forensically depends on the availability of all reports and would be compromised if some reports expired.

When multiple journal reports are generated

A single journal report is normally generated per message. However, there are circumstances when Exchange is forced to generate multiple reports. In large organizations, you might see a situation where messages are addressed to a very large number of recipients and exceed the "chipping size" defined for the hub transport server. The chipping size is defined in the *ExpansionSizeLimit* setting in the EdgeTransport.exe. xml configuration file. The default value is 1,000, so if Exchange processes a message that has more than 1,000 recipients, it splits the message into multiple copies so that no copy of the message has more than 1,000 recipients. When this happens, a separate journal report is created for each copy.

Multiple journal reports are also created any time that Exchange has to bifurcate a message. Let's assume that you send a message addressed to a distribution group that is set to be expanded on a hub transport server in a remote site. The message is also addressed to a set of individual CC: recipients. Exchange will create one journal report for the CC: recipients because the message can be routed to these addresses by the first hub transport server. Another journal report will be generated by the second hub transport server after it has expanded the membership of the distribution group and routed the message to those recipients. The second journal report contains information about the members of the distribution group. Both journal reports contain a copy of the original message and the two can be reconciled because both contain the message identifier of the original message.

Even encrypted messages protected by IRM can be intercepted and copied by journaling. However, you need to enable journal report decryption to allow this. Messages copied by transport rules remain encrypted.

Exchange 2010 is more efficient at generating journal reports. Exchange 2007 generates a separate journal report for each recipient, which isn't a problem until distribution groups are factored into the equation. Distribution groups are very popular, but when the transport system expands group membership to route messages, it has a knock-on effect of creating a journal report for each group member. In some deployments, up to 40 percent of all journal reports are duplicates generated after group expansion. Exchange 2010 therefore applies a deduplication step to generate just one journal report per message to reduce the number of journal reports (while still maintaining the integrity of the journal archive). This step also reduces demand for system resources and storage.

Alternate journal recipient

If Exchange encounters a problem when it attempts to deliver a journal report to the journal destination, its default behavior is to requeue the message for another attempted. This is sufficient to handle transient issues such as a temporary network outage. However, it can become an issue if a fundamental problem occurs, such as a catastrophic failure of the server that hosts the mailbox serving as the journal recipient. Depending on the kind of journaling being performed, these outages can result in large queues and you might prefer to redirect journal reports while the problem exists. You can configure an alternate journal recipient for this purpose to which Exchange will redirect journal reports if it detects an NDR condition for the primary journal recipient. You configure the alternate journal recipient with the Set-TransportConfig cmdlet by setting the *–JournalingReportNdrTo* parameter to the SMTP address of the alternate. For example:

```
Set-TransportConfig –JournalingReportNdrTo 'AlternateComplianceMailbox@contoso.com'
```

When an NDR condition occurs for a journal report, Exchange checks to see whether an alternate recipient is available. If not, the journal reports are requeued, but if an alternate is available, Exchange sends the NDR containing the journal report to the alternate recipient and removes the journal report from its queue. The advantage here is that removing items from message queues reduces the load on hub transport servers by avoiding the need to continually retry messages that cannot get through. The NDRs arrive in the alternate mailbox and can be accessed there to be re-sent once the problem is addressed and the normal journal recipient becomes available again.

INSIDE OUT   Potential issues with alternate recipients

Although an alternate recipient provides an immediate fix for a problem that allows Exchange to continue to process journal reports during an outage, there are a few issues that need to be considered before you can implement an alternate recipient.

First, if the alternate recipient is unavailable for any reason, Exchange will delete the NDRs and some journal reports will be lost. For example, if the alternate recipient is a mailbox and its quota is exceeded due to a flood of incoming NDRs, it will reject further messages and cause them to be dropped. Therefore, the alternate recipient has to be able to cope with the load generated by journaling during the outage.

Second, a considerable amount of effort might be required to process the NDRs after the outage is over. You will have to open the mailbox, select each NDR, and re-send the journal report to have Exchange redeliver the reports to the journal recipient. This is fine for 10 or 20 NDRs, but opening and resending NDRs can quickly become boring.

Last, your legal team has to be satisfied that routing to an alternate recipient does not compromise any requirements that your company has to satisfy. They might be concerned that potential exists for interference with journal reports during the recovery operation and want to know who will recover journal reports from NDRs, how the recovery will proceed, and how to be sure that no journal reports are missed.

Even if an alternate recipient is a viable option for your company, if you use a mailbox as the journal recipient it might be a better approach to minimize the possibility that an outage will interfere with processing by locating the mailbox on a database that is protected by multiple database copies within a Database Availability Group (DAG). In the event of a database failure, the transport service will reroute journal reports to the mailbox in the newly activated copy and continue processing. This approach avoids any of the potential problems discussed previously.

Standard journaling

Standard journaling is very much a blunt instrument because it captures every single message generated by and received into every mailbox in a database. To enable journaling on a per-database basis, you select the database, open its Properties dialog box, and click the

Maintenance tab. Select the Journal Recipient check box and input the name of a journal recipient, as shown in Figure 16-19. The journal recipient can be any mail-enabled object. Most often it is a mailbox or a mail-enabled contact that points to the SMTP address of an external archiving product. It is less common to use a public folder as a journal recipient, and it is unheard-of to use a distribution group.

Figure 16-19 Adding a journal recipient for a mailbox database.

The EMS command to enable journaling for a mailbox database is:

```
Set-MailboxDatabase -Identity 'DB1'-JournalRecipient 'Journal Mailbox'
```

You can discover whether any mailbox databases have journal recipients defined with this command:

```
Get-MailboxDatabase | Where {$_.JournalRecipient -ne $Null} | Format-Table Name,
JournalRecipient
```

Journal rules

Journal rules allow administrators to set conditions for the journaling agent to use when it checks for messages flowing to and from specific users or groups of users. Journal rules and details of any journal recipients configured for mailbox databases are stored in Active Directory in the Exchange configuration data and are therefore shared by all hub transport servers to create a common journaling regime across the organization. The journal agent is registered for Active Directory notification events to allow it to know when a new journal rule is added or a journal rule is modified. When this happens, the journal agent reloads the set of journal rules. This arrangement allows journal rule updates to take effect quickly across an organization, assuming that Active Directory replication is functioning normally.

Although you can design rules to impose journaling for a single recipient, this is not an effective approach unless there is something unique about the recipient. For example, you might decide that any message sent to the CEO will be journaled to a particular mailbox or archive system. However, if you wanted to journal messages sent to the CEO's staff, you probably would not create a separate journal destination for every recipient. It would therefore be inefficient to have a separate journal rule for each member of the CEO's staff, because it would be an administrative nightmare to maintain the rules as people leave and join the staff. It is much more efficient to create a single journal rule and use a distribution group to identify the recipients.

Because they are easy to manage, distribution groups are often used for journaling within large organizations. Similar to transport rules, Exchange caches distribution group membership to avoid the need to make constant Active Directory queries. The cache is automatically refreshed every four hours, so if you add a new member to a distribution group it could take up to four hours before Exchange begins to journal that person's messages. The only way to force the repopulation of the cache is to restart the transport service. For this reason, it might be better to use database-based journaling for groups of users that change frequently. In this scenario, you'd create a separate database for the group, move all the group's mailboxes to the new database, and apply journaling for the database. Exchange also caches information about databases that are journaled. This cache is refreshed every 10 minutes, so journaling for new users that join a group is effective more quickly.

You can also create a journal rule that affects every user in the organization. To do this, do not specify a recipient when you create the rule with EMC or the New-JournalRule cmdlet. Clearly the sheer volume of journal reports that such a rule will create means that this is a fundamental step to take for all but the smallest organizations.

Creating a journal rule

A journal rule states the following:

- Who is being monitored?

- What is the scope of the monitoring? This can be Global (all messages), Internal (only messages generated within the Exchange organization), or External (only messages with an external recipient or sender).

- Where should journal reports be sent? Again, this can be any SMTP address.

To create a new journal rule, go to the hub transport section of Organization Configuration and click New Journal Rule to invoke the New Journal Rule Wizard. There's only one screen to complete. Figure 16-20 illustrates the creation of a typical rule. As you can see, the rule applies to messages sent to or received from external addresses for a recipient identified by its SMTP address. As it happens, this is the address of a distribution group. Reports for

Chapter 16

any messages that meet the journal criteria are sent to another SMTP address, in this case a mailbox.

The EMS code to create the rule is as follows:

```
New-JournalRule -Name 'Capture external email sent by Contracts staff'
-JournalEmailAddress 'Contracts.Compliance@contoso.com' -Scope 'External'
-Enabled $True -Recipient 'ContractsStaff@contoso.com'
```

Immediately after the rule is created, the transport system reloads its journal rule configuration from Active Directory and begins to use the new rule.

Figure 16-20 Creating a new journal rule.

A journal rule is a much simpler entity than a transport rule, but this is understandable when you consider that a journal rule fulfills a single-purpose function that doesn't have to span the set of conditions that you can configure for a transport rule. The relative starkness and simplicity of a journal rule is captured when you examine the output of the Get-JournalRule cmdlet:

```
Name                 : Capture external email sent by Contracts staff
Recipient            : ContractsStaff@contoso.com
JournalEmailAddress  : Contracts.Compliance@contoso.com
Scope                : External
Enabled              : True
```

A further set of cmdlets is available to manipulate journal rules after they are created. You can update the properties of a journal rule with the Set-JournalRule cmdlet. For example, we could change the email address of the journal recipient and set the scope of the rule so that every message is journaled with this command:

```
Set-JournalRule -Identity 'Capture external email sent by Contracts staff'
-JournalEmailAddress 'NewJournalAddress@contoso.com' -Scope Global
```

If you want to disable journaling for a while, you can do this with the Disable-JournalRule cmdlet:

```
Disable-JournalRule -Identity 'Capture external email sent by Contracts staff'
```

And to enable the rule again, use the Enable-JournalRule cmdlet:

```
Enable-JournalRule -Identity 'Capture external email sent by Contracts staff'
```

Finally, to remove a rule completely:

```
Remove-JournalRule -Identity 'Capture external email sent by Contracts staff'
```

Assessing journal load

It is critical that the journal destination is capable of handling the expected load and have sufficient storage to be able to store copies of all of the messages that it receives. This shouldn't be an issue if you use an external archiving service as the journal recipient, but it could be if you opt to use a mailbox. You can attempt to estimate the volume of messages that the journal recipient will handle by analyzing the message tracking logs (it's easier to do this with a product designed for this purpose; see Chapter 17) and by tracking the growth of a mailbox database over time. These will give you rough ideas, but the real volume will only be revealed when you begin journaling.

```
Timestamp              EventId Source Recipients                      MessageSubject
---------              ------- ------ ----------                      --------------
5/20/2010 12:23:15 PM  RECEIVE AGENT  {Contracts.Compliance@contoso.com} Fabrikam contract
5/20/2010 12:25:59 PM  RECEIVE AGENT  {Contracts.Compliance@contoso.com} Fabrikam Follow-up
5/20/2010 12:38:00 PM  RECEIVE AGENT  {Contracts.Compliance@contoso.com} New contract procedures
```

Journal activities are captured in the message tracking logs. As messages are submitted from the mailbox database to the transport system by the Store Driver, the journal agent is invoked to dispatch a journal report to the journal recipient, so you can track the capture of journal messages by searching the message tracking logs for entries such as those just shown. Even nondelivery notifications are captured by journaling, as are other system messages, including messages rejected by moderation. Transport rules do not process system messages.

Securing a mailbox used as a journal recipient

If you use a mailbox to receive journal reports, you need to secure the mailbox so that only journal reports generated by Exchange are stored there and that a user cannot "spoof" or create a false journal report to disguise some illegal activity or compromise the integrity of the repository so that it is not reliable for investigative purposes. In addition, it's important to emphasize that some confidential information can accumulate in the journal mailbox, so the first step is to restrict the number of users who can open the mailbox to the bare minimum, all of whom are authorized by the legal department as needing access to the mailbox.

After securing basic access, three steps are usually taken to lockdown a mailbox used as a journal destination:

- Prevent unwanted messages from cluttering up the mailbox by restricting access to authenticated users. Senders outside the organization are blocked.

- Prevent internal users from inadvertently attempting to send messages to the mailbox by not listing it in the Global Address List (GAL). People can still send messages to the mailbox using its SMTP address, but this would be a deliberate action, so:

- Prevent anyone but the journal agent from sending messages to the mailbox by restricting acceptable senders to the special "Microsoft Exchange" address.

We can enforce these restrictions as follows:

```
Set-Mailbox 'Compliance Monitoring Mailbox' –HiddenFromAddressBookEnabled $True
–RequireSenderAuthenticationEnabled $True -AcceptMessagesOnlyFromSendersOrMembers
'Microsoft Exchange'
```

If you open a mailbox that's used as a journal recipient, you'll see that all of the journal reports are waiting in the Inbox. Although Exchange 2010 is much better at dealing with large quantities of items in a single folder, it's also true that a busy journal recipient will rapidly accumulate items and could easily surpass 100,000 items in the Inbox if left alone. Some mechanism is therefore required to clean out the journal recipient on a regular basis. Unless the mailbox database contains just a few mailboxes that generate a relatively light load, having someone review and clean out the contents of the journal recipient's mailbox is probably unworkable if thousands of new items arrive daily. A more automated approach is usually required, which accounts for the popularity of using a mail contact pointing to the SMTP address of an archiving product that processes new journal items as they arrive.

Interversion and interorganization journaling

Exchange 2007 and Exchange 2010 share the same journaling mechanism, so no problems should be encountered with journaling inside an organization using these servers. Journaling is also supported when Exchange 2003 servers are present and between multiple Exchange organizations. The routing topologies, connectors, and security and journaling requirements vary greatly in these conditions, so it's impossible to give detailed advice about how best to proceed. One general recommendation that makes sense is to move mailboxes that you need to journal off legacy mailbox servers as quickly as you can to simplify the flow of journaling. Apart from this, you should read the advice available on TechNet on how to approach various scenarios and consult an expert in journaling if you need more help, especially if an external archiving system is involved.

To the toolbox

Not everything fits snugly into a product. There are utility programs and other useful pieces of code that just don't seem to fall neatly into place in the structure established by a management framework that splits items up into organization, servers, and recipients. The solution is to sling anything that doesn't fit into the toolbox. This description might seem to imply that the toolbox is the graveyard of unwanted programs, but it's actually a very productive place for any Exchange administrator to be. Let's continue on our way to consider why.

The Exchange Toolbox

T HE Exchange toolbox provides administrators with convenient access to a set of utilities that they can use to analyze, manage, and understand different components of an Exchange organization. The intention of the Exchange development group is that they will add items to the toolbox as they become available. Not all of the tools come from the development group. Some, like the Remote Connectivity Analyzer, are generated by other Microsoft teams such as those who support Exchange. To some degree, the tools that come from outside the development group are the most interesting and worthwhile tools because they have been built to address real problems that occur during implementations.

Table 17-1 lists the contents of the Exchange 2010 toolbox. As you can see, the utilities in the toolbox do not share a common interface. Some use the framework created for the Exchange Best Practice Analyzer (ExBPA); others have their own unique interface, are integrated into ECP, or call a Windows utility. Two are provided as Microsoft Management Console (MMC) snap-ins. The lack of a unifying interface is explained by the bolted-on nature of the toolbox, the various histories behind the development of each program, and the fact that the toolbox is really just a convenient location to provide interesting and useful tools to Exchange administrators.

Table 17-1 Exchange 2010 Toolbox contents

Tool	Purpose	User Interface
Best Practice Analyzer	Checks the configuration of the current Exchange organization against a set of best practices maintained by Microsoft and generates a report that administrators can use to improve their organization by addressing obvious problems or amending settings to enhance performance. Microsoft used to provide updates for the best practice rules used by ExBPA via the exbpa.com Web site. The use of this site has now been discontinued, and best practice updates are provided along with other roll-up updates for Exchange.	BPA

Details Templates Editor	Amends the language-specific detail templates used to present directory (Global Address List) information to Outlook users.	Own
Public Folder management console	Manages the public folder hierarchy and settings (but not the content) for individual public folders.	MMC
Remote Connectivity Analyzer	Validates that connection points such as Simple Mail Transfer Protocol (SMTP) and ActiveSync work correctly.	Web
Role Based Access Control (RBAC) user editor	Management of role assignment to users by placing users in role groups.	ECP
Mail Flow Troubleshooter	Validates that the transport system is working properly.	BPA
Message Tracking	Access ECP and use the Delivery Reports feature to check the status of messages sent by users that they log on as over the last two weeks.	ECP
Queue Viewer	View and manage messages in the transport queues.	MMC
Routing Log Viewer	Views the contents of transport routing logs and allows an administrator to compare the configurations from two routing logs.	Own
Tracking Log Explorer	Browses the contents of message tracking logs to track their progress from server to server to the boundary of the organization.	BPA
Performance Monitor	Launches a customized version of the standard Windows Performance Monitor utility that measures a set of preloaded counters important to the overall health of an Exchange server.	PerfMon
Performance Troubleshooting Assistant	Attempts to identify the root cause of common performance issues on an Exchange server.	BPA

We've already encountered some of these tools such as the transport queue viewer elsewhere in the book, so this section focuses on the tools that have not yet been covered.

Display or Details Templates Editor

Outlook uses detail (otherwise called display) templates to format and display directory information when users view details about objects in the Global Address List (GAL). You can customize the templates to add or remove fields or change the text descriptions (labels) used for the fields. Customizing display templates is a relatively common occurrence in large organizations but less common in smaller organizations, which typically stay with the default versions shipped with Exchange.

Figure 17-1 illustrates a simple customization of a display template. The top screen is the standard *Organization* property page and the bottom is the customized version. Outlook 2010 is used in both cases, but the same techniques apply to Outlook 2003 and Outlook 2007 as well. Two new attributes about the mailbox are visible in the customized template:

- Contoso Accounting Code: Most large organizations assign employees to cost centers or similar accounting structures. Users might want to access this information to know what they should enter into documents such as expense reports. You can adapt one of the standard Exchange properties for this purpose by renaming it, but it is usually better to use one of the 15 extended properties provided by Exchange for customizations like this.

- Employee type: Again, depending on the culture of the organization, you might want to display information about a user's employment status (permanent, part-time, contractor, or in this case, executive) to other users.

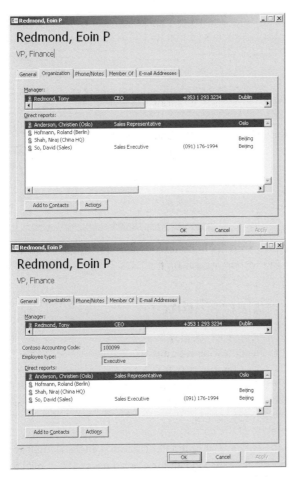

Figure 17-1 Viewing standard (top) and customized (bottom) display templates.

You can modify display templates through the Toolbox section of EMC. Click Details Templates Editor and then select Open Tool from the action pane. The tool is a new instance of MMC that reads in the information about available details templates from Active Directory and loads them into the console as shown in Figure 17-2. You can use the tool to modify templates in any of the languages supported by Exchange. If you operate in a multilingual organization, you should be consistent and make the same changes to the details templates for each language version of Outlook client that you deploy. For example, if you deploy the Swedish, Finnish, German, and English versions of Outlook, then you should update the details templates for these four languages.

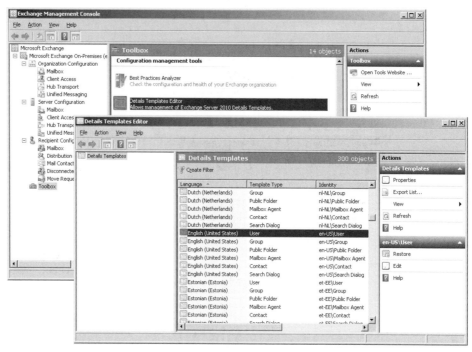

Figure 17-2 EMC and the Details Templates console.

The user template is the most commonly customized template. As we have already used it as an example in Figure 17-1, I will explain how to apply the customizations described before. To work with a template, select it from the list and double-click, at which point Exchange fetches the details of the current template from Active Directory. The template we are interested in is the en-US\User template. This is the English language—U.S. variant— of the user details template. Despite the fact that Exchange is used in English in many other places such as the United Kingdom, Ireland, and Australia that often do not share the same spelling or usage of words, you only have one English language details template to work with. The same is true of one Spanish template, one Portuguese template, and so on. The rule, therefore, is that whatever changes you make have to apply to the broadest possible user population that access Exchange in whatever language you choose.

> **Note**
> You can also see that the console includes a Restore option. This is your get-out-of-jail-free card in case you make an absolute mess of editing a template, as the option restores a template back to its original version as shipped in the Exchange kit. Of course, if you select this option, you will lose all work that you have done on a template, but it's sometimes the best and only choice.

The template editor provided with Exchange 2010 is the same as that used with Exchange 2007. It is still basic by comparison to most layout editors, but it gets the job done. Figure 17-3 shows the Organization tab of the user details template loaded, and you can see that the added accounting code field is selected.

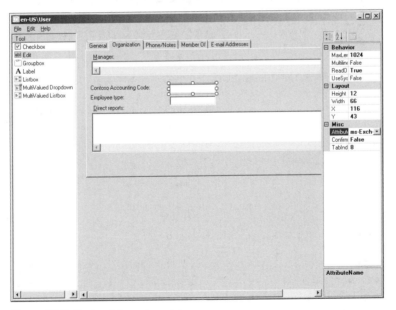

Figure 17-3 Customizing a template.

The toolbox on the far left allows you to select different types of controls for the various properties that you want to display. To add a new field, select the type that you want and drag it to the position on the page, then set its properties, such as the attribute that you want to display. In this case, the Contoso Accounting Code is displayed in a simple edit box that is linked to the ms-Exch-Extension-Attribute15 mailbox attribute (otherwise known as CustomAttribute15). You can click a drop-down list of available attributes for the mailbox object.

The control types that you can choose from are the following:

- Checkbox: Used for on–off or yes–no fields such as flags indicating that an object has a particular status.

- Edit: Displays only one value for an attribute. For example, users only have one first name, which comes from the Given-Name attribute. In our example, the edit box is the best option because our accounting codes and employee type are single-value attributes.

- Listbox: Displays data for a list of attributes that come from different objects. For example, a user can be a member of many distribution groups, so the Member Of page has a listbox that is populated from the Is-Member-Of-DL attribute.

- Multivalued Listbox: Displays data for an attribute that can have multiple values. For example, user objects can have multiple email addresses, so the Email Addresses page has a single multivalued listbox that is populated from the Proxy-Addresses attribute.

- Label: Holds a language-dependent text string and typically appears alongside another control that holds data. You will notice that some characters in the label fields are underlined to indicate that users can navigate to these fields using the Alt+letter key combination. For example, the Supervisor: field has the S underlined, so you can move to it with an Alt+S combination. You include the ampersand (&) character in the label control value to set this up, so the value in the label field in this case is &Supervisor.

- Group box: Specifies a group of fields that Outlook draws a line around when it displays the template. For example, the General page of the user template has a line around the First, Last, Display, and Alias fields.

Once you've saved the customized template, Exchange makes it available immediately to any Outlook client that connects in online mode. Outlook clients that connect in cached Exchange mode won't be able to see the customized template until the next time that they connect and download the Offline Address Book (OAB).

INSIDE OUT   Points to consider

Customizing details templates is easy, but you have to ask the question whether a customization adds any value before you rush to change something, and there are some minor points that you need to consider. Remember that you will have to revalidate the customization after each upgrade of Exchange because there is no guarantee that Microsoft will not overwrite your customization or make a change to the templates that is not compatible with your changes in a new version or service pack. As it happens, the transition from Exchange 2003 to Exchange 2007 and then on to Exchange 2010 was very smooth for template customizations, but this might not be the case in the future. If you operate multiple organizations, you will not be able to share template customizations directly between the organizations. Instead, you will have to export them using a tool like LDIFDE from the organization where you make (and test) the customizations and import them into the Active Directory instances that support the other organizations.

Message tracking

The ability to track messages by reference to logs that contain details of the path that messages take through different components of Exchange has been in the product since its first release and has been used for many purposes, including the determination of overall end-to-end performance of the messaging infrastructure and forensic tracking of messages to establish that someone definitely sent or received a message. The details of message tracking have varied from version to version, but the functionality and operation presented in Exchange 2010 is similar to that available in Exchange 2007. The difference now is that the introduction of user-accessible delivery reports (see Chapter 5, "Exchange Management Console and Control Panel") might reduce the number of requests going from users to system administrators to ask about the fate of sent messages. Delivery reports are generated from the content of message tracking logs, but they contain a subset of the information available to administrators.

Exchange begins to collect information about messages as clients submit them via the Store on mailbox servers. More data are then collected when the transport service retrieves messages from the Store submission queue and then categorizes and dispatches messages to their final destination on a server within the same Exchange organization or across a connector to another mail system. The data in message tracking logs provide an insight into all of the activity that occurs on a server, including incoming messages, public folder replication, nondelivery notifications, and so on. The tracking data also include system-generated messages such as nondelivery notifications, warnings about approaching problems with mailbox quotas, expiry notifications for moderated messages, and so on. The amount of data generated on a hub transport server varies according to the traffic from a couple of megabytes to hundreds of megabytes daily.

> **Note**
>
> Many companies use the data captured by these logs to analyze message traffic so that they can predict future demand or for forensic purposes if they need to validate that a message went from one user to another.

By default, Exchange hub transport, mailbox, or Edge servers are configured to generate message tracking logs. Dedicated Client Access Server (CAS) or Unified Messaging (UM) servers do not generate message traffic logs because these server roles do not participate in message transport. Exchange 2007 and Exchange 2010 share the same CSV-style log format that is similar to the format used for other transport logging (for example, SMTP protocol logging). The shared log format means that you can track messages across these servers. However, Exchange 2003 servers generate message tracking logs in Internet Information Services (IIS) format, so you cannot track messages from Exchange 2003 to Exchange 2007 or Exchange 2010 and vice versa. If you need to track a message that originated on an Exchange 2003 server and was then transferred to Exchange 2007 or Exchange 2010 or followed the reverse route and was delivered to an Exchange 2003 server, you will need to perform a search on Exchange 2003 followed by a search on Exchange 2007 or Exchange 2010 and then combine the results manually.

Tracking is performed by submitting requests to the Microsoft Exchange Transport Log Search service, a service introduced in Exchange 2007. Obviously, this service must be running on all servers that might have processed a message before you can track a message from initial submission to final delivery or transmission outside the organization. You can discover where message tracking logs are stored on a hub transport server by finding the server under the Servers node in EMC and then viewing the Log Settings section of its properties. The default settings are to enable message tracking logs and to create them in a folder called C:\Program Files\Microsoft\Exchange Server\V14\TransportRoles\Logs \MessageTracking. Because searches are performed by the Transport Log Search service, the location for the message tracking logs does not have to be exposed as a file share, as is the case with Exchange 2000 and Exchange 2003.

Because their contents require a constant stream of append operations to add details of new messages to sequential logs, the generation of message tracking logs does not impose a significant load on even a busy hub transport server. The advice given by Microsoft for Exchange 2007 was that log generation created no more than 2 percent additional overhead for a server, and the increase in server performance and decrease in I/O demand in Exchange 2010 means that the overhead created by other system components is now lower. Server hardware performance has also improved greatly over the last few years. Consequently, there is no good reason to disable message tracking logs on any server.

Curiously, even though Exchange maintains message tracking logs on mailbox servers that don't have the hub transport role installed, you won't be able to view the location of the message tracking logs through server properties. Instead, you will have to use EMS to manipulate the properties that enable the gathering of message tracking logs and their location on mailbox servers. For example, you can use this command to find out the mailbox servers in the organization that have enabled the generation of message tracking logs:

```
Get-MailboxServer |Where {$_.MessageTrackingLogEnabled -eq $True} | Select Name,
MessageTrackingEnabled
```

The equivalent to check for hub transport servers with message tracking enabled is:

```
Get-TransportServer |Where {$_.MessageTrackingLogEnabled -eq $True} | Select Name,
MessageTrackingEnabled
```

If you need to, you can enable message tracking logs on a mailbox server with a command like this:

```
Set-MailboxServer -Identity ExServer1 -MessageTrackingLogEnabled $True
```

As we've seen, the default location for message tracking logs is on the same disk that hosts the Exchange binaries. This location is acceptable for a small or lightly loaded server, but you should consider relocating the logs to another disk on large or heavily trafficked servers. This is easily done by amending the location through server properties or with EMS with a command like this:

```
Set-MailboxServer -Identity ExServer4 -MessageTrackingLogPath 'D:\Logs\
MessageTracking\'
```

This command will create the new directory if it doesn't already exist. However, it will not move any log files, and you'll have to relocate them manually by copying them to the new location. If you don't copy the current log, Exchange will re-create it the next time that a message is presented for processing on the server.

We can investigate message tracking log settings on a mailbox server with this command (use the Get-TransportServer cmdlet on a hub transport or Edge server):

```
Get-MailboxServer -Identity ExServer4 | Select MessageTracking*
```

```
MessageTrackingLogEnabled                 : True
MessageTrackingLogMaxAge                  : 30.00:00:00
MessageTrackingLogMaxDirectorySize        : 1000 MB (1,048,576,000 bytes)
MessageTrackingLogMaxFileSize             : 10 MB (10,485,760 bytes)
MessageTrackingLogPath                    : c:\Temp\MessageLogs
MessageTrackingLogSubjectLoggingEnabled   : True
```

You'll notice that only two of these properties are revealed through EMC (enabling and log location). The other properties can be manipulated only through EMS. You'll also notice that the properties that control the retention period for the message tracking logs (*MaxAge*), the maximum size of logs retained (*MaxDirectorySize*), and the size of an individual log (*FileSize*) are very similar in concept and implementation to the commands that control the configuration of the transport protocol logs that we covered in Chapter 13, "The Exchange Transport System," so no further comment is required here.

INSIDE OUT A useful tool with few associated risks

The *MessageTrackingLogSubjectLoggingEnabled* parameter controls whether Exchange writes information about message subjects into the logs. This parameter has created some debate in the past with people worrying that capturing message subjects might compromise user privacy because administrators have access to the data and might be able to understand the topics that users send email about by reading the logs. It's true that an obsessive administrator might well take the time to analyze message traffic for an individual user or even between two users, but this is unlikely to happen in practice and is therefore regarded as a small risk. In any case, normal data protection regulations in force within companies should seek to prevent this kind of administrative activity and provide for appropriate sanctions if someone is silly enough to misuse tracking data. The real point here is that the subject data are enormously useful to administrators when they are asked to track a message for a user.

Tracking and Mailbox Servers

Some administrators ask why they should enable message tracking on mailbox servers. After all, if Exchange routes everything through hub transport servers to provide a single consistent point to apply features such as transport rules, isn't it sufficient to enable message tracking only on the hub transport servers? The answer is that messages originate on mailbox servers, and if you want to build a complete picture of the life cycle of a message, you have to capture all of the events that occur. In detail, three specific items that don't occur on hub transport servers are of interest in constructing a message's life cycle:

1. The initial Submission event when a user sends a message. This event can be matched against a Receive event on the hub transport server that processes the message.

2. The final Deliver event after the transport system has fully processed the message and handed it to the mailbox server that currently hosts the user's mailbox. This event indicates whether any Inbox rules fired to cause the message to be moved to a different folder.

3. The Read Status of the message as shown in the message properties after all processing is complete.

For these reasons, it simply makes sense to enable message tracking on all mailbox servers.

Message tracking log files generated on servers

You can find three separate logs on a server:

- **MSGTRK**YYYYMMDD-N.LOG: This log stores information about routing operations that occur for messages, such as the expansion of distribution group membership and routing to other SMTP servers.

- **MSGTRKA**YYYYMMDD-N.LOG: The data in this log capture information about events that occur to moderated messages that flow through an arbitration mailbox.

- **MSGTRKM**YYYYMMDD-N.LOG: The data in this log relate to processing that occurs for the mailbox role, such as client submissions from the Store Driver to a hub transport server.

YYYYMMDD is the date and N is the sequential number of the log generated on the date. Thus, MSGTRK20100720-1.LOG is the first message tracking log containing data about routing operations created on July 20, 2010. The default size for message tracking logs is 10 MB. Once a log is filled, Exchange creates another log and begins to append transactional data to the end of the new log. Logs are kept for 30 days or until the configured size of the log directory is exceeded, in which case Exchange applies a circular log management mechanism and removes the oldest logs until the directory size drops under the threshold. You can increase the size of a message tracking log, the log retention period, or the threshold for the directory size with the Set-MailboxServer (on mailbox servers) or Set-TransportServer (on hub transport servers) cmdlets. The growth in logs depends on the volume of messaging traffic on a server and the operations performed to route messages.

Chapter 17

INSIDE OUT   Preparing mailbox and hub transport servers

A simple message sent between two users will create less than 1 KB of message track-ing data, whereas a message sent to a large distribution group with more than 100 recipients, some of whom are unreachable or generate out of office (OOF) messages, could create 30 KB or more. Some large hub transport servers that handle a large vol-ume of traffic for an organization might generate 300 MB or more of message tracking logs daily or up to 2 GB weekly. Clearly this won't be the situation for every server, but you do need to measure and validate the configuration applied to mailbox and hub transport servers to ensure that Exchange doesn't delete valuable data to keep under an undersized threshold before you get the chance to analyze it.

Like transport protocol logs, message tracking logs store their data in CSV format and you can open logs with editors as diverse as NotePad and Microsoft Excel. Figure 17-4 shows what you can expect to see when you open a log. The first three lines declare the version, log type, and date and time when the log was created. The fourth line provides the header information for the data written for messaging log entries. Table 17-2 lists the fields in the data entries and their meaning.

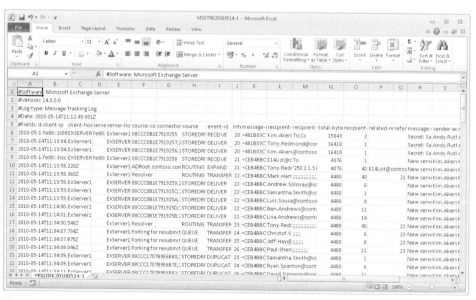

Figure 17-4 Viewing the raw data in a message tracking log.

Table 17-2 **Fields in message tracking logs**

Field	Meaning
Date-time	The date and time of the messaging event in ISO 8601 or UTC format given down to fractions of a second.
Client-ip	The IP address of the server or client that submitted the message.
Client-hostname	The name of the server or client that submitted the message.
Server-ip	The IP address of the Exchange server that processes the message.
Server-hostname	The name of the Exchange server that processes the message.
Source-context	Field to capture additional information about an operation. For example, the domain controller used by the transport service to expand the membership of a distribution group.
Connector-id	The name of the connector associated with the event. This field is not populated for every event.
Source	The transport component that generated the event. Valid components are: ADMIN: Replay of messages from the transport dumpster AGENT: Processing by a transport agent DSN: Generation of a Delivery Service Notification message GATEWAY: Submission of a message from a foreign email system via a connector PICKUP: Acceptance of a message from the pickup or replay directories ROUTING: Processing of a message through the routing engine SMTP: Transit of a message through an SMTP connector STOREDRIVER: MAPI interaction with the Store on mailbox servers
Event-id	See Table 17-3 for a list of valid events.
Internal-message-id	A number that uniquely identifies the message on the server that generated the tracking log. The internal message identifier for an individual message varies across all the servers that process a message.
Message-id	A constant identifier that remains with a message throughout its life cycle and is carried in the header of the message.
Recipient-address	A list of recipients for the message separated by semicolons. The names of distribution groups are written into this field until their membership is expanded by the transport service.
Recipient-status	This field is only populated after the message is transmitted to another SMTP server, in which case the success or failure of the recipient check is captured.
Total-bytes	The size of the message in bytes including all attachments.
Recipient-count	The count of recipients for the message. A distribution group counts as one recipient until their membership is expanded.
Related-recipient-address	Field to capture additional information for EXPAND, RESOLVE, and REDIRECT events. For example, the name of the distribution group that is expanded into individual addresses is written into this field for EXPAND events. RESOLVE events note when the transport service has to resolve a non-SMTP address in a message header. In this case, the field stores the resolved address.

Reference	Field to capture additional information for DSN, SEND, and TRANSFER events. For example, when Exchange sends a DSN for a message, it stores its message identifier in this field and writes the reason for the DSN in the Source-context field.
Message-subject	If configured on the server, this field captures the message subject.
Sender-address	The email address of the message sender as stored in the Sender field in the message header. If this field is blank in the message header, Exchange takes the value from the From: field.
Return-path	The return address for the message based on the MAIL FROM: field in the message envelope. Many events write "<>" into this field where it doesn't make sense to include a return path.
Message-info	Contains the message origination time for DELIVER and SEND events. The origination time is when the message first enters the Exchange organization. The time is in UTC.
Message-latency	The message latency time in seconds as calculated by Exchange.
Message-latency-type	The baseline used to measure message latency. For example, EndtoEnd means that the message latency represents the complete cycle from submission to delivery.

The Get-MessageTrackingLog cmdlet is used to interrogate message tracking logs and merges the different logs together into a coherent whole with events ordered by time when it retrieves data in response to queries. If you run the cmdlet without providing any parameters, Exchange opens the latest log and begins to list the entries and will continue to list data out until it reaches the end of the last available log or EMS exceeds its ResultSize setting, which usually allows the retrieval and listing of 5,000 entries.

Interpreting entries in message tracking logs

You use the Get-MessageTrackingLog cmdlet to interrogate the contents of message tracking logs. Because of the quantity of data in the logs on any production server, it's important to provide the cmdlet with fairly specific parameters to narrow its search and return data that are of interest. A general trawl through message tracking logs is an invariably frustrating experience and will lead to the output of multiple entries.

> **Tip**
>
> Another issue to remember is that whenever you run the Get-MessageTrackingLog cmdlet without specifying the –*Server* parameter to indicate the server that you want to interrogate, Exchange will return entries from the server on which you are running Exchange Web Services (EWS). This could be a dedicated CAS server that has no function in message transport, in which case you'll execute an unproductive search.

To begin to work with message tracking logs efficiently, we need to understand what entries in the message tracking log contain. Exchange stamps each entry with an event identifier to indicate the processing stage that the message is at during its life cycle. Table 17-3 provides a full listing of all of the event identifiers generated by Exchange in message tracking log entries.

Table 17-3 Event identifiers used in message tracking logs

Event identifier	Meaning
AGENT	A transport or journal agent processed the message.
BADMAIL	The transport service took a message from the Pickup or Replay directory that cannot be processed or returned to the sender.
DELIVER	The message was delivered to a mailbox and the life cycle of the message is complete.
DEFER	Message delivery was delayed.
DSN	The transport service generated a delivery status notification (DSN).
DUPLICATEDELIVER	The transport service discovered a duplicate address in a message header after all the addresses are resolved. The duplicate address is removed.
EXPAND	A distribution group was expanded to determine its membership and allow routing to proceed.
FAIL	A failure occurs in the routing of a message. For example, a transport rule condition causes a message to be rejected.
INITMESSAGE	The transport service initiates the next step for a moderated message.
NOTIFYMAPI	A mailbox agent submitted a MAPI notification message to the Store Driver to be delivered to an end user; for example, messages to indicate that the mailbox quota is almost exhausted. These events are only seen on mailbox servers.
POISONMESSAGE	The transport service determined that the message contains some "poison" content and therefore put it onto the poison message queue. The event is also logged when the transport service takes a message from the poison message queue to resume processing.
PROCESS	The transport service processes a moderated message.
RECEIVE	A message was received and committed to the transport service database.
REDIRECT	A message was redirected to an alternate recipient after the original recipient was checked in Active Directory.
RESOLVE	The addresses for one or more recipients on a message were resolved to different email addresses after checking with Active Directory.
SEND	The transport service transferred a message via SMTP to another server.
SUBMIT	A mailbox server submitted a message for processing to a hub transport server.
TRANSFER	Recipients were moved to a forked message because of content conversion, message recipient limits, or some processing needs to be performed by an agent such as a transport rule.

Chapter 17

Here are the entries for a simple messaging transaction where one user sends a message to another. The databases containing these mailboxes happen to be on the same server. Some of the content has been removed for clarity. The output from the Get-MessageTrackingLog cmdlet broadly matches the fields described in Table 17-3 with some extra formatting applied to make the output more readable. For example, the timestamp is the UTC format time in the log converted to local server time. The first entry that we'll look at is from the mailbox server where the user submits the message, so we know that we have to look for a SUBMIT entry. We might retrieve these data with a command like the one shown here. It's enough to provide just the first few characters to search using the message subject and searching does not depend on an exact case match. If you input a start date and time to use in a search, you have to provide an end date, as otherwise EMS will signal an error:

```
Get-MessageTrackingLog -Server ExServer1 -MessageSubject 'Fantastic news'
-Sender 'Andy.Ruth@contoso.com' -Start '5/20/2010 11:30' -End '5/20/2010 11:59'
-EventId 'SUBMIT' | Format-List
```

```
Timestamp                   : 5/20/2010 11:54:30 AM
ClientIp                    : fe80::3ccc:8a87:db9b:87%12
ClientHostname              : EXSERVER1
ServerIp                    :
ServerHostname              : EXSERVER1
SourceContext               : MDB:86137325-d162-4655-a3f6-f9ddf4ccbd4a,
Mailbox:dcca82c0-10b7-4337-8dab-7bcc6a7ed54f, Event:88401, MessageClass:IPM.Note,
CreationTime:2010-05-20T10:53:45.095Z, ClientType  :OWA
ConnectorId                 :
Source                      : STOREDRIVER
EventId                     : SUBMIT
InternalMessageId           :
MessageId                   : <481B03C78D4B494BB59FB7F3E48B4108013AC16D@ExServer1.contoso.com>
Recipients                  : {}
RecipientStatus             : {}
TotalBytes                  :
RecipientCount              :
RelatedRecipientAddress     :
Reference                   :
MessageSubject              : Fantastic news
Sender                      : Andy.Ruth@contoso.com
ReturnPath                  :
MessageInfo                 : 2010-05-20T10:53:45.095Z;LSRV=EXSERVER1.contoso.
com:TOTAL=45|MSSN=2|MSSFA=42
MessageLatency              : 00:00:45.1410000
MessageLatencyType          : LocalServer
```

From this entry, we can see:

- The names of the mailbox server (client host name) where the user creates the message (ExServer1) and the hub transport server (server host name) that the Store on the mailbox server is connected.

- Some information (source context) about the mailbox database and mailbox from where the message originates (globally unique identifiers [GUIDs] identify the mailbox and database), the message type (IPM.Note), and the client type used (Outlook Web App).

- The source of the message is STOREDRIVER, so we know that this message is being introduced into the transport service by the Store Driver on the mailbox server. The Store Driver is responsible for all interaction between mailbox databases and the transport service. Remember, Exchange directs every message through a hub transport server to allow transport rules and other policies to be applied on a consistent basis, even if the databases involved in the transaction are both located on the same server.

- The internal message identifier is unique and is used to track all of the transactions for the message. You can input this value to the Get-MessageTrackingLog cmdlet to select all of the entries in the message tracking logs that chart the path of the message.

- The sender is clearly identified by their SMTP address.

- At the end of the entry, some information about the message is gathered to help track the performance of message routing. We'll see how to use this information in a little while.

The next stage in the message's life cycle is to be fully accepted by the transport service so that it can end up on a queue for processing. This stage is marked by a RECEIVE entry when the transport service commits the message into its database. The entry comes from the hub transport server that processes the message and is as follows:

```
Timestamp            : 5/20/2010 11:54:30 AM
ClientIp             : fe80::3ccc:8a87:db9b:87
ClientHostname       : EXSERVER1.contoso.com
ServerIp             : fe80::3ccc:8a87:db9b:87%12
ServerHostname       : ExServer1
SourceContext        : 08CCC5C2F0411286
ConnectorId          :
```

```
Source                    : STOREDRIVER
EventId                   : RECEIVE
InternalMessageId         : 174
MessageId                 : <481B03C78D4B494BB59FB7F3E48B4108013AC16D@ExServer1.contoso.com>
Recipients                : {CEOStaff@contoso.com}
RecipientStatus           : {To}
TotalBytes                : 4159
RecipientCount            : 1
RelatedRecipientAddress   :
Reference                 :
MessageSubject            : Fantastic news
Sender                    : Andy.Ruth@contoso.com
ReturnPath                : Andy.Ruth@contoso.com
MessageInfo               : 04I:
MessageLatency            :
MessageLatencyType        : None
```

We can see the following:

- The client and server involved in the transactions remain as we expect. The Store Driver on ExServer1 acts as a client to submit the message to the transport service, which is also running on server ExServer1.

- The event identifier is RECEIVE, so we know that the hub transport server has received the message for processing.

- The TotalBytes and RecipientCount fields are updated with content after the transport service accepts the message.

Our message is accepted and processed by a hub transport server. After the hub transport server completes the categorization and routing decisions for the message, it returns the message back to the original mailbox server to be delivered to the database that holds the recipient's mailbox. On the hub transport server, we see the following entry:

```
Timestamp                 : 5/20/2010 11:55:12 AM
ClientIp                  :
ClientHostname            : ExServer1
ServerIp                  :
ServerHostname            : EXSERVER1
SourceContext             : 08CCC5C2F041128A;2010-05-20T10:55:12.533Z;0
ConnectorId               :
Source                    : STOREDRIVER
EventId                   : DELIVER
InternalMessageId         : 175
MessageId                 : <481B03C78D4B494BB59FB7F3E48B4108013AC16D@ExServer1.contoso.com>
Recipients                : {Andy.Ruth@contoso.com}
```

```
RecipientStatus         : {}
TotalBytes              : 5014
RecipientCount          : 1
RelatedRecipientAddress :
Reference               :
MessageSubject          : Fantastic news
Sender                  : Andy.Ruth@contoso.com
ReturnPath              : Andy.Ruth@contoso.com
MessageInfo             : 2010-05-20T10:53:45.095Z;SRV=EXSERVER1.contoso.com:TOTAL=44|MSSN=2|
MSSFA=42;SRV=EXSERVER1.contoso.com:TOTAL=42|QD=42
MessageLatency          : 00:01:27.5630000
MessageLatencyType      : EndToEnd
EventData               : {[MailboxDatabaseName, db1], [DatabaseHealth, -1]}
```

We can see that the data is different from the original entry:

- The source for the entry remains STOREDRIVER, but the event identifier is now DELIVER to indicate that the Store Driver has accepted the message from the transport service for delivery to the database that holds the recipient's mailbox.

- The internal message identifier remains the same, as do the recipients, sender, and so on.

- The total bytes value reported for the message has changed. This indicates that the transport system has performed some processing that affected message content. In this case, we know that a transport rule applied an autosignature to the message and this accounts for the changed size.

- Because the message has reached the end of its routing, Exchange has updated the message information fields to indicate the routing steps and the latency for the message transfer. This information can be analyzed and reported by products such as Microsoft System Center Operations Manager to provide an overall picture of routing performance within the organization.

- The information in the EventData field (which is also logged for the other routing entries) is introduced by Exchange 2010 SP1 to allow it to distinguish between different classes of messages. In this case, the data report the database that the message was delivered to and a flag showing that the database is healthy.

By walking through these entries, we conclude that the simplest path for a message from one user to another recipient in the same Exchange organization is recorded by three message tracking log entries:

- SUBMIT: Logged on the mailbox server to indicate transmission to the hub transport server

- RECEIVE: Logged on the hub transport server when it has accepted the message

- DELIVER: Logged on the hub transport server when it delivers the message to the mailbox server that holds the recipient's mailbox

Clearly, messages that go from one mailbox to another represent a minority of those that occur on a production server. Let's see what the message tracking log entries hold for other common operations. First, let's send a message to a distribution group and see the entries that are logged on the hub transport server that processes the message after it is submitted by a mailbox server:

```
EventId   Source      Sender                      Recipients
-------   ------      ------                      ----------
SUBMIT    STOREDRIVER Samantha.Smith@contoso.com  {}
RECEIVE   STOREDRIVER Samantha.Smith@contoso.com  {ContractsStaff@contoso.com, Kim.Akers@contoso.com}
EXPAND    ROUTING     Samantha.Smith@contoso.com  {Christen.Anderson@contoso.com, Samantha.Smith@co..
TRANSFER  ROUTING     Samantha.Smith@contoso.com  {Tude.Palma@contoso.com, Samantha.Smith@contoso.com,
DELIVER   STOREDRIVER Samantha.Smith@contoso.com  {Kim.Akers@contoso.com}
DELIVER   STOREDRIVER Samantha.Smith@contoso.com  {Tude.Palma@contoso.com, Samantha.Smith@contoso.com,
```

The entries are different and more numerous:

- The message is submitted by the sender.

- As before, the hub transport server accepts the message from the mailbox server and commits it into its database for processing (RECEIVE).

- Because the message is addressed to a distribution group, the first event that occurs is the expansion of the distribution group membership so that the message can be routed (EXPAND). If we examine the EXPAND entry in detail, we will discover the total number of recipients in the group after expansion.

- A TRANSFER event then occurs. We know from Table 17-3 that this event is logged when the transport service has to fork a message for some reason. A forked message means that the transport service needs to create additional copies of the message because specific processing needs to occur for one or more recipients. For example, some recipients might have defined that they only wish to receive a message in a certain format that differs from the format of the original message. It is also possible that the message will be processed by a transport rule such as the one described in Chapter 16, "Rules and Journals," which prepend some text to the message subject for some but not all recipients. If this happens, you'll see the message subject changed for some recipients.

- A DELIVER event is logged for every mailbox database that hosts recipients for the message.

The EXPAND event tells us the domain controller used by the hub transport to retrieve group membership as well as the number of recipients after resolution and a list of some of the returned addresses:

```
Timestamp                 : 5/20/2010 12:09:00 PM
ClientIp                  :
ClientHostname            :
ServerIp                  :
ServerHostname            : ExServer1
SourceContext             : ADRoot.contoso.com
ConnectorId               :
Source                    : ROUTING
EventId                   : EXPAND
InternalMessageId         : 186
MessageId                 : <7EE157F867DA3748A78C307F947768AB01813380@ExServer1.contoso.com>
Recipients                : {Christen.Anderson@contoso.com, Samantha.Smith@contoso.com,
Tude.Palma@contoso.com}
RecipientStatus           : {250 2.1.5 RESOLVER.GRP.Expanded; distribution list expanded}
TotalBytes                : 4679
RecipientCount            : 3
RelatedRecipientAddress   : ContractsStaff@contoso.com
Reference                 :
MessageSubject            : Fabrikam contract
Sender                    : Samantha.Smith@contoso.com
ReturnPath                : Samantha.Smith@contoso.com
MessageInfo               :
MessageLatency            :
MessageLatencyType        : None
EventData                 :
```

Much the same processing occurs for messages sent to dynamic distribution groups, and the EXPAND event occurs when the transport service executes the OPATH query against Active Directory to determine the group membership.

Incoming messages that are processed by a hub transport server and delivered to a mailbox server are captured by a RECEIVE event to log the incoming message and a DELIVER event when the message is delivered to the server hosting the mailbox database. The entry that records the RECEIVE event also captures some information about the remote server that sent the message and how the incoming message is processed by Exchange. We can see this by reviewing the full entry as shown here:

```
Timestamp                 : 5/20/2010 12:09:00 PM
ClientIp                  : fe80::3ccc:8a87:db9b:87
ClientHostname            : EXSERVER1.contoso.com
ServerIp                  : fe80::3ccc:8a87:db9b:87%12
ServerHostname            : ExServer1
```

```
SourceContext           : 08CCC5C2F0411297
ConnectorId             :
Source                  : STOREDRIVER
EventId                 : RECEIVE
InternalMessageId       : 186
MessageId               : <7EE157F867DA3748A78C307F947768AB01813380@ExServer1.contoso.com>
Recipients              : {ContractsStaff@contoso.com, Kim.Akers@contoso.com}
RecipientStatus         : {To, Cc}
TotalBytes              : 4679
RecipientCount          : 2
RelatedRecipientAddress :
Reference               :
MessageSubject          : Fabrikam contract
Sender                  : Samantha.Smith@contoso.com
ReturnPath              : Samantha.Smith@contoso.com
MessageInfo             : 04I:
MessageLatency          :
MessageLatencyType      : None
EventData               : {[MailboxDatabaseGuid, 86137325-d162-4655-a3f6-f9ddf4ccbd4a],
[ItemEntryId, 00-00-00-00-3F-B3-69-A2-69-A7-FC-4B-BC-C6-8D-C2-2D-FD-EE-41-07-00-7E-E1-57-F8-
67-DA-37-48-A7-8C-30-7F-94-77-68-AB-00-00-00-85-AD-95-00-00-7E-E1-57-F8-67-DA-37-48-A7-8C-30-
7F-94-77-68-AB-00-00-01-81-33-83-00-00]}
```

Outgoing messages that are transmitted outside Exchange travel across an SMTP or other connector to their destination. This example shows a SEND event logged for an SMTP message sent across a connector named Intra-Organization SMTP Send Connector to the exedge1.contoso.com (Edge transport) server. Again, because the message is leaving the Exchange organization, the message information fields at the end of the entry capture some information about how long the message took in transit.

```
Timestamp               : 5/20/2010 12:16:04 PM
ClientIp                : 192.165.65.50
ClientHostname          : ExServer1
ServerIp                : 192.165.65.71
ServerHostname          : ExEdge1.contoso.com
SourceContext           : 08CCC5C2F041129F;250 2.6.0 <7EE157F867DA3748A78C-
307F947768AB01813590@ExServer1.contoso.com> [InternalId=20] Queued mail for delivery
ConnectorId             : Intra-Organization SMTP Send Connector
Source                  : SMTP
EventId                 : SEND
InternalMessageId       : 192
MessageId               : <7EE157F867DA3748A78C307F947768AB01813590@ExServer1.contoso.com>
Recipients              : {JSmith@fabrikam.com}
RecipientStatus         : {250 2.1.5 Recipient OK}
TotalBytes              : 4706
RecipientCount          : 1
RelatedRecipientAddress :
Reference               :
```

```
MessageSubject      : RE: Fabrikam contract
Sender              : Samantha.Smith@contoso.com
ReturnPath          : Samantha.Smith@contoso.com
MessageInfo         : 2010-05-20T11:16:03.955Z;LSRV=EXSERVER1.contoso.com:TOTAL=0
MessageLatency      : 00:00:01
MessageLatencyType  : LocalServer
EventData           :
```

Measuring message latency

Exchange 2010 introduces latency measurement into the transport service to allow products such as Microsoft System Center Operations Manager to generate reports about server performance that can be used to compare against service level agreements (SLAs). Exchange captures latency data as messages pass through the transport service and writes the information into the message tracking log entries. If you look back at the message tracking log entries we have just reviewed, you can see the latency data in the MessageLatency and MessageLatencyType fields of the log entries.

It's difficult to make sense of the data from individual entries because they don't make much sense until the full picture is assembled to measure the path of a message or messages from submission to final delivery. You can get some idea of how the data might be used by running the Get-MessageTrackingLog cmdlet to select some messages and piping the output to the ConvertTo-MessageLatency.ps1 script in the \Scripts directory. It's best if you do this with some messages that you send so that you can put your knowledge of the messages and their recipients into context with the results reported by the script. For example, here's a command to illustrate how to feed some tracking log data into the script and some edited highlights of the resulting output:

```
Get-MessageTrackingLog -Sender 'andy.ruth@contoso.com' -Start '05/20/2010 12:30'
-End '05/20/2010 13:30' | .\ConvertTo-MessageLatency.ps1
```

```
InternalMessageId   : 206
MessageId           : <7EE157F867DA3748A78C307F947768AB018135A8@ExServer1.contoso.com>
MessageLatency      : 00:00:01.9840000
MessageLatencyType  : LocalServer
ComponentServerFqdn : EXSERVER1.contoso.com
ComponentCode       : CAT
ComponentName       : Categorizer
ComponentLatency    : 00:00:01

InternalMessageId   : 206
MessageId           : <7EE157F867DA3748A78C307F947768AB018135A8@ExServer1.contoso.com>
MessageLatency      : 00:00:48.4370000
MessageLatencyType  : EndToEnd
ComponentServerFqdn : EXSERVER1.contoso.com
```

```
ComponentCode        : TOTAL
ComponentName        : Total Server Latency
ComponentLatency     : 00:00:47

InternalMessageId    : 206
MessageId            : <7EE157F867DA3748A78C307F947768AB018135A8@ExServer1.contoso.com>
MessageLatency       : 00:00:48.4370000
MessageLatencyType   : EndToEnd
ComponentServerFqdn  : EXSERVER1.contoso.com
ComponentCode        : SDD
ComponentName        : Store Driver Delivery
ComponentLatency     : 00:00:04

InternalMessageId    : 206
MessageId            : <7EE157F867DA3748A78C307F947768AB018135A8@ExServer1.contoso.com>
MessageLatency       : 00:00:48.4370000
MessageLatencyType   : EndToEnd
ComponentServerFqdn  : EXSERVER1.contoso.com
ComponentCode        : QD
ComponentName        : Delivery Queue
ComponentLatency     : 00:00:41
```

The first entry reports the time that the message spent in the categorizer. The next shows it going onto a local delivery queue. (The knowledge of the message pays off here because I know the message was sent from a mailbox on the ExServer1 server.) The third entry reports the message transit through the Store Driver to be delivered to a mailbox database on the same server, and the last entry gives details of transmission to another hub transport server in the same site. The message latency data are clearly reported in terms of seconds. We know that the first three records all relate to delivery on the same server, so the end-to-end delivery time from submission to delivery is just fewer than six seconds. The message takes a little longer to be delivered to the second hub transport server.

All of this is very well, but you can't expect administrators to wade through tens of thousands of message tracking log entries to determine how their servers are performing in terms of message delivery. Exchange therefore processes the message tracking logs automatically on each hub transport server to generate a set of statistics that can be used for analysis and reporting purposes. These data are captured as follows:

- Every hour, latency data about interserver message traffic are captured in log files in the \TransportRoles\Logs\ServerStats directory. No file is created if the server is inactive.

- Every eight hours, latency data about messages sent from and delivered to mailboxes are captured in log files in the \TransportRoles\Logs\ActiveUserStats directory.

The log files are in CSV format and can be opened with Microsoft Excel to browse their contents.

The Exchange Management Pack for Microsoft System Center Operations Manager accesses the log files and imports them into the System Center data warehouse to generate reports about hourly and daily server statistics, active users, and distribution group usage (captured from categorizer expansion of group membership).

Using the Tracking Log Explorer

The Get-MessageTrackingLog cmdlet is powerful and very capable of extracting useful information from message tracking logs. However, using the cmdlet can be a somewhat cumbersome and demanding exercise, especially if you are not familiar with the parameters and how to use them to conduct successful searches. The Tracking Log Explorer is designed to address this issue by providing an easy-to-use interface that leverages the same framework as the Exchange Troubleshooting Assistant. In effect, message tracking is another task that you can perform using the Troubleshooting Assistant. This feature has not changed since Exchange 2007.

You can think of the Tracking Log Explorer as a funnel on information. When you start a search at the top of the funnel, you provide some general information about the message in which you are interested. As the search progresses through the mass of message tracking data, the funnel narrows to locate the desired message. Once you have found the message, you can then narrow the search further to track the progress of the message from sender to recipient within the organization, from mailbox server to hub transport and back to a mailbox server or perhaps across a connector to a foreign email system.

With this analogy in mind, the first order of business is to provide the log explorer with clues to help it find the message that you are looking for. The sender's address is an obvious item to provide, as is some or the entire message subject, the time span when the message was sent, and the name of the server where the search should commence. Exchange uses the SMTP address of the sender when it searches message tracking logs, so you can input the SMTP address for an external or internal sender into this field. The Resolve Recipient and Resolve Sender buttons look up the GAL using whatever you input into the fields and will successfully resolve addresses if you provide enough data to locate a unique entry. However, it's not so successful if you input an ambiguous address that matches multiple entries in the GAL. For example, if you input **Smith** and multiple users named Smith exist in the GAL, Exchange returns the first matching entry. There's a fair chance that this is not the person that you want to search for, so you need to be careful and check the returned value when you resolve addresses using these options.

INSIDE OUT

Start from the server that hosts the mailbox

If you input a valid internal address for a sender, you should also click Server From Sender to have Exchange insert the server name that hosts the sender's mailbox, because this will ensure that Exchange begins the search on the server where messages from the sender originate. Best practice is to always start from the server that hosts the mailbox and follow a message from point of submission by the Store Driver and work forward.

Figure 17-5 shows the screen that is used to establish the initial search parameters. In this case, we've entered the name of the sender and provided a start and end time. The screen shot shows the list of events from which we can select. As we want to track the path of a message sent by a known individual, we select the SUBMIT event to be able to track the message from its initial submission. Notice that the Tracking Log Explorer generates EMS code in the last field. You can copy this code to reuse or just use it as a learning aid. When you have provided enough information (three or four fields) to create an effective filter that won't return hundreds of messages, click Next to execute the initial search.

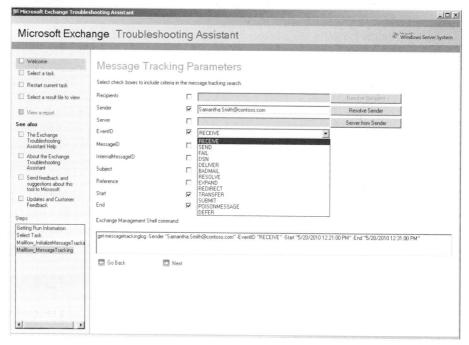

Figure 17-5 Setting up the initial search parameters with the Tracking Log Explorer.

The Tracking Log Explorer presents its search results in a grid (Figure 17-6), which shows the set of messages sent by the selected user within the specified timeframe. You can move up and down in the grid to select a message that you want to track further. Once you've selected a message, click Next to continue with tracking.

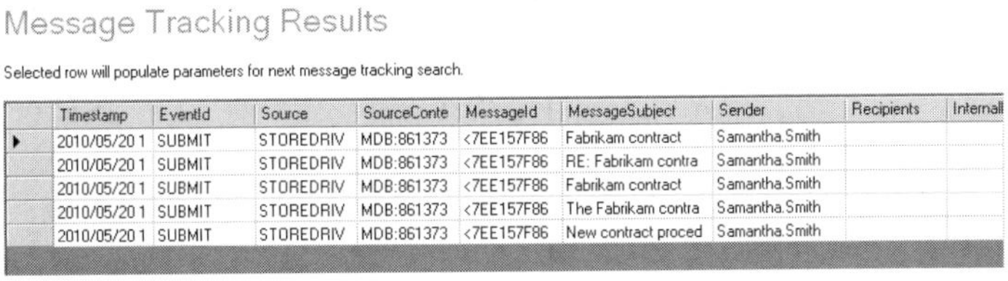

Message Tracking Results

Selected row will populate parameters for next message tracking search.

Timestamp	EventId	Source	SourceConte	MessageId	MessageSubject	Sender	Recipients	Internall
2010/05/20 1	SUBMIT	STOREDRIV	MDB:861373	<7EE157F86	Fabrikam contract	Samantha.Smith		
2010/05/20 1	SUBMIT	STOREDRIV	MDB:861373	<7EE157F86	RE: Fabrikam contra	Samantha.Smith		
2010/05/20 1	SUBMIT	STOREDRIV	MDB:861373	<7EE157F86	Fabrikam contract	Samantha.Smith		
2010/05/20 1	SUBMIT	STOREDRIV	MDB:861373	<7EE157F86	The Fabrikam contra	Samantha.Smith		
2010/05/20 1	SUBMIT	STOREDRIV	MDB:861373	<7EE157F86	New contract proced	Samantha.Smith		

Figure 17-6 Viewing the initial search results.

The Tracking Log Explorer presents the search dialog box again (Figure 17-7) with the search fields prepopulated with data for the message that you selected. In particular, you can see that the internal message identifier is now filled in because we have selected a particular message.

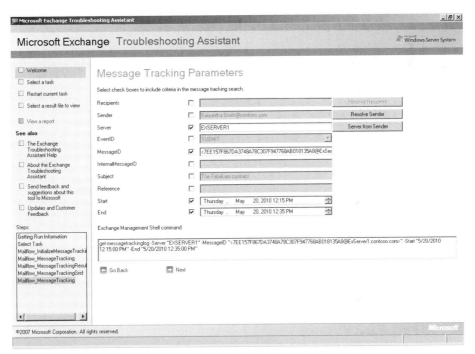

Figure 17-7 Viewing the parameters used to continue the search for a selected message.

All further searches will be executed using this identifier so that the Tracking Log Explorer only returns results applicable to this message. The EMS code that is used to locate this message shows how the message identifier is passed:

```
Get-MessageTrackingLog -Server 'EXSERVER1' -MessageID
'7EE157F867DA3748A78C307F947768AB018135B9@ExServer1.contoso.com' -Start '5/20/2010
12:27:00 PM' -End '5/20/2010 12:47:00 PM'
```

To proceed with the search, click Next. The Tracking Log Explorer now extracts all of the detailed events for the specific message that we are tracking. The set of events is shown in Figure 17-8. We can track the message through:

1. Initial submission (SUBMIT).

2. Acceptance by the Store Driver (RECEIVE).

3. Expansion of a distribution group membership (EXPAND).

4. Execution of a transport rule (AGENT).

5. Routing for the message (ROUTING). Several events are recorded, as there are multiple recipients for the message (both local and remote).

6. A failure to route a message is logged (FAIL). This is likely because the recipient (my mailbox!) only accepts messages from a restricted list of senders.

7. Routing to a connector for delivery to the external recipient (SEND).

8. Deliveries to local mailbox databases (DELIVER). Although there is no facility to generate a nicely formatted report, we can make a screen capture of the results to prove that the message really was delivered to any skeptical users.

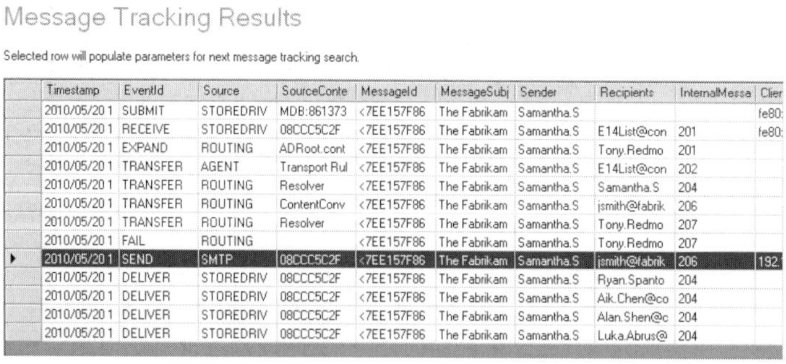

Message Tracking Results

Selected row will populate parameters for next message tracking search.

Timestamp	EventId	Source	SourceConte	MessageId	MessageSubj	Sender	Recipients	InternalMessa	Clien
2010/05/201	SUBMIT	STOREDRIV	MDB:861373	<7EE157F86	The Fabrikam	Samantha.S			fe80:
2010/05/201	RECEIVE	STOREDRIV	08CCC5C2F	<7EE157F86	The Fabrikam	Samantha.S	E14List@con	201	fe80:
2010/05/201	EXPAND	ROUTING	ADRoot.cont	<7EE157F86	The Fabrikam	Samantha.S	Tony.Redmo	201	
2010/05/201	TRANSFER	AGENT	Transport Rul	<7EE157F86	The Fabrikam	Samantha.S	E14List@con	202	
2010/05/201	TRANSFER	ROUTING	Resolver	<7EE157F86	The Fabrikam	Samantha.S	Samantha.S	204	
2010/05/201	TRANSFER	ROUTING	ContentConv	<7EE157F86	The Fabrikam	Samantha.S	jsmith@fabrik	206	
2010/05/201	TRANSFER	ROUTING	Resolver	<7EE157F86	The Fabrikam	Samantha.S	Tony.Redmo	207	
2010/05/201	FAIL	ROUTING		<7EE157F86	The Fabrikam	Samantha.S	Tony.Redmo	207	
2010/05/201	SEND	SMTP	08CCC5C2F	<7EE157F86	The Fabrikam	Samantha.S	jsmith@fabrik	206	192.
2010/05/201	DELIVER	STOREDRIV	08CCC5C2F	<7EE157F86	The Fabrikam	Samantha.S	Ryan.Spanto	204	
2010/05/201	DELIVER	STOREDRIV	08CCC5C2F	<7EE157F86	The Fabrikam	Samantha.S	Aik.Chen@co	204	
2010/05/201	DELIVER	STOREDRIV	08CCC5C2F	<7EE157F86	The Fabrikam	Samantha.S	Alan.Shen@c	204	
2010/05/201	DELIVER	STOREDRIV	08CCC5C2F	<7EE157F86	The Fabrikam	Samantha.S	Luka.Abrus@	204	

Figure 17-8 Discovering all the events recorded for a message.

The grid allows us to select an event for the message and continue the search. The success of the search depends on the route that the message has taken from this point:

- Local delivery: The DELIVER event indicates that the message has completed its route to the destination mailbox, so no further tracking data are available.

- Routing to another Exchange hub transport server in the organization: The Tracking Log Explorer will request message tracking log data from the hub transport server that accepts the message and will continue to track from that point.

- Routing to an SMTP connector for delivery to an external recipient: The Tracking Log Explorer will be unable to track the message further because the message has left the Exchange organization and is now under the control of another messaging system en route to its final destination.

- Routing to an Edge transport server: The Tracking Log Explorer will not be able to access message tracking data on an Edge server, so no further events can be uncovered.

There's no doubt that tracking some messages can be more problematic. One of the servers in the path might be unavailable when you attempt to track through it; others might not be running the Transport Log Search service and are unable to respond to search requests. Users might not provide sufficient data to conduct efficient searches or give you inaccurate data that lead to ineffective and frustrating searches. However, given time and persistence, you should eventually be able to locate a message using the Tracking Log Explorer and perhaps some hand-tooled searches created with EMS.

You can execute an equivalent EMS command to search for all events in the life cycle of a message by looking for all instances of events logged for a particular message identifier. Assuming that you capture the message identifier in the variable *$MsgId,* the command to look for events across all hub transport and mailbox servers in the organization is:

```
Get-ExchangeServer | Where {$_.IsHubTransportServer -or $_.IsMailboxServer} |
Get-MessageTrackingLog -MessageId $MsgId | Sort TimeStamp | Format-Table TimeStamp,
EventId, Source, MessageSubject, Sender, Recipients -AutoSize
```

Another example of using the Get-MessageTrackingLog cmdlet to satisfy a common request is to search the logs for traces of messages being sent to an external domain. This code looks through the logs on a server for any message sent to a recipient in the fabrikam.com domain in a 90-minute period and reports out the time, sender, recipients, and message subject:

```
Get-MessageTrackingLog -Start "5/20/2010 8:00AM" -End "5/20/2010 9:30AM" -Server
'ExServer1' -Eventid "SEND" | Where-Object {$_.Recipients -Match ".*@fabrikam\.com"}
| Sort TimeStamp | Format-Table TimeStamp, Sender, Recipients, MessageSubject
-AutoSize
```

Chapter 17

> **Tip**
>
> The trick with commands like this is to limit the time period that you scan to be as short as possible to restrict the amount of work that Exchange has to do to locate log entries. A search based on matching text patterns in a field that has to process hundreds of megabytes of tracking log won't complete quickly.

Other options for analyzing messaging tracking logs

The Tracking Log Explorer allows you to focus in on selected messages, but it doesn't give you an insight into the overall traffic patterns that an Exchange server processes, nor does it deliver the kind of information that is valuable to administrators to help understand server workload. Measurements such as average daily message volume (raw numbers, senders, bytes processed, and so on), who are the top senders and receivers of email, what distribution groups are in constant use and which never receive messages, and the percentage of messages that fail to be delivered are all indicators that can help you to understand whether your messaging infrastructure is in good health. The options to gain a better understanding of message traffic include the following:

- Build your own analysis framework leveraging available tools.

- Buy a commercial product.

- Integrate messaging tracking analysis into a broader management framework.

The cost to procure and implement a solution increases as you progress through the list.

Building your own analysis framework

One well-known option is to build an analysis framework with available tools. Three tools in particular have a good track record.

- LogParser: A number of presentations have been given at TechEd and the Exchange Connections conference over the years that explain how to extract and analyze data with LogParser, a free utility that does an excellent job of parsing out the contents of log files generated by many different applications, including Exchange and IIS (where you can mine some useful information about ActiveSync activity). You can also search the Internet to discover the procedures that other administrators are using to analyze data about their Exchange servers based on message tracking logs. Although written for Exchange 2007, the suggestions posted at *http://msexchangeteam.com /archive/2007/11/12/447515.aspx* provide an excellent starting point for administrators who want to "roll their own."

- Process Tracking Log Tool: You can also investigate the Process Tracking Log Tool for Exchange 2007 (downloadable from *http://msexchangeteam.com/archive/2008 /02/07/448082.aspx*), created by the members of the Exchange development team. The tool works for Exchange 2010, too, so you could use and amend it to suit your own purposes.

- ExLogAnalyzer: This tool is another contribution from Microsoft to the Exchange community that is able to generate reports and graphical analysis from message tracking logs. ExLogAnalyzer is also able to analyze the data contained in connectivity and SMTP receive logs. You can download this tool from *http://msexchangeteam. com/archive/2010/01/20/453843.aspx*.

Buying a commercial product

The benchmark in this space for many years was set by Promodag Reports (*http://www .promodag.com*), which extracts data from message tracking logs and stores them in SQL or Microsoft Access databases to be able to provide a comprehensive analysis of the essential characteristics and workload of an Exchange server. Promodag also provides a freeware version that you can test before buying. In the recent past, other products have appeared to challenge Promodag. Sirana AppAnalyzer (*http://www.sirana.com*) is another highly capable product that analyzes messaging tracking logs to extract information about trends and to enable features such as the ability to charge back departments for their use of Exchange.

Integrating messaging tracking analysis into a broader framework

Alongside its other capabilities, Microsoft System Center for Operations Manager can use message tracking log data to report email traffic statistics. If you're already using this as your management framework for Windows, you can explore its ability to report on Exchange.

Performance Monitor

Although you can launch the Performance Monitor from Windows, the version included in the Exchange toolbox is provided as a preconfigured console that includes the most important counters necessary to monitor the performance of an Exchange server. You can retrieve a listing of all of the Performance Monitor counters for Exchange with the following command:

```
$FormatEnumerationLimit = -1
Get-Counter -ListSet 'MSExchange*' | Format-List CounterSetName,
Paths > C:\Temp\MSExchangePerf.txt
```

Setting $FormatEnumerationLimit$ to –1 tells Windows PowerShell that you do not want to truncate the output values. This is important because many of the counter sets provided by

Exchange, especially those for the Information Store, include a large number of counters. To understand the output, the *CounterSetName* is a collection of counters for individual areas of the product, and Paths gives you the names of the individual counters. The output for the MSExchange Mail Submission *CounterSetName* is shown here:

```
CounterSetName : MSExchange Mail Submission
Counter        : {\MSExchange Mail Submission(*)\Successful Submissions,
\MSExchange Mail Submission(*)\Successful Submissions Per Second, \MSExchange
Mail Submission(*)\Failed Submissions, \MSExchange Mail Submission(*)\Failed
Submissions Per Second, \MSExchange Mail Submission(*)\Temporary Submission
Failures, \MSExchange Mail Submission(*)\Temporary Submission Failures/sec,
\MSExchange Mail Submission(*)\Hub Servers InRetry, \MSExchange Mail
Submission(*)\Hub Servers, \MSExchange Mail Submission(*)\Hub Transport Servers
Percent Active, \MSExchange Mail Submission(*)\Aggregate Shadow Queue Length,
\MSExchange Mail Submission(*)\Shadow Queue Auto Discards Total, \MSExchange
Mail Submission(*)\Shadow Re-submission Length, \MSExchange Mail Submission(*)\
Shadow Message Re-submissions Total}
```

Every Exchange performance expert has her own set of favorite Performance Monitor counters that she uses to analyze the performance of an Exchange server. Table 17-4 provides a good set to start you off. You can add or subtract to the counters used here based on your own experience and knowledge of the servers that you operate.

INSIDE OUT   Understanding the information

In all cases, it is a good idea to have a solid view about what values you should see from Performance Monitor when a server is operating properly and what indicates a variance that requires your attention. This view forms your baseline for acceptable performance, and it's an essential part of understanding your systems and knowing when something isn't right.

Table 17-4 **Important Performance Monitor counters for Exchange 2010**

Object	Counter	Meaning	What to look for
MSExchange Database	\<Information Store> I/O Database Reads (Attached) Average Latency	Average time to read data from the active database file.	Should be below 20 milliseconds on average with spikes restrained to less than 100 milliseconds.

MSExchange Database	I/O Database Reads (Recovery) Average Latency	Average time to read data from a passive database file (only in a Database Availability Group [DAG]).	Can be more than the values observed for an active copy because it's not providing service to users, but shouldn't be excessively different.
MSExchange IS	RPC Requests	Reports the number of remote procedure call (RPC) requests currently executing within the Store process.	Should remain under 70.
MSExchangeIS	RPC Averaged Latency	Reports the averaged RPC latency in milliseconds as calculated for all operations in the last 1,024 packets.	Should remain under 10 milliseconds.
MSExchangeIS Client (*)	RPC Averaged Latency	As above, except that the latency is reported for client RPC requests.	As above. Note that (*) will add a counter for each Exchange component that generates RPC requests, including all client protocols.
Database	Database Page Fault Stalls/sec	Reports the rate of page faults that Windows cannot service because no pages are available in the cache.	Should be zero. Anything above this value might indicate that the write latency for databases is too high (the database can't keep with demand).
MSExchangeTransport Queues (total)	Aggregate Delivery Queue Length (All Queues)	Reports the total messages in all queues that are waiting to be delivered.	The figure will fluctuate on hub transport servers. It deserves investigation if there are more than 5,000 items awaiting delivery at peak times.
MSExchangeTransport Queues (total)	Active Remote Delivery Queue Length	Reports the total messages in active queues for remote delivery.	Another fluctuating figure that becomes a concern when it grows above 250 and remains there for some time, as this might indicate that mail can't flow off the server.
MSExchangeTransport Queues (total)	Submission Queue Length	Reports the total messages in the Submission queue.	This queue should remain less than 50. If it grows to 100, it could indicate that a bottleneck exists on either the Active Directory global catalog servers (responding to requests for Active Directory data during categorization) or the mailbox servers (submitting the messages).

Chapter 17

Performance experts talk about the need to maintain good health of the four basic elements of system performance: CPU, memory, disk, and network. This is a good list to review when you are concerned about server performance, and it will guide you to ask questions and look for data to confirm that the server is running properly. The data will guide you through symptoms such as disk saturation or memory starvation to the fundamental problem and an eventual solution.

Exchange Performance Troubleshooter

The Exchange Performance Troubleshooter Assistant was created as an offshoot of ExBPA. It functions by collecting some performance data from a server to compare against known problem conditions and then works out some remedial action that an administrator can take. It's possible that this utility will provide the essential insight to allow you to solve a performance problem on a server, but the truth is that technology is now so complex that we are past the point where a utility that covers only a small number of potential issues can add real value when a server suffers performance problems. You are far more likely to use Windows Performance Monitor to log the essential performance counters on the problem server and then turn over the performance data to experts to figure out what the problem is, if it's not apparent when you review it.

INSIDE OUT   Taking a server offline

Of course, one of the problems that every administrator has to face when confronted by a server that is apparently exhibiting abnormal performance is to decide if and when to take the server offline to see whether a reboot cures whatever is causing the server to perform poorly. No one wants to take a server offline during the day, as this can have a huge impact on users (even a slow server can provide access to data that users need), and in most cases administrators attempt to hang on until user demand slows and server downtime has less of an impact. That time can be usefully occupied by running some performance tests in an attempt to determine where the root cause might lie.

ExPerfWiz

If you experience performance problems on a server and involve help from a group such as Microsoft PSS to understand where the root of the issue might lie, you will probably be asked to gather data for analysis. The classic way to approach this task is to configure the Windows Performance Monitor utility to track a number of critical counters generated by Exchange and perhaps other Windows components such as IIS. Indeed, the toolbox includes a configured version of Performance Monitor that captures the most important counters for Exchange and serves as an excellent starting point for any data gathering exercise.

Another approach to gathering essential performance data for Exchange is to leverage the set of Exchange Performance Wizard (ExPerfWiz) XML PerfMon template files published by Microsoft. These files are designed to gather the data necessary to analyze performance for the different Exchange server roles. Versions are available for Exchange 2007 and Exchange 2010. The combination of the templates and the Performance Monitor replaces PerfWiz.exe, the performance wizard utility provided as part of Exchange 2003.

The XML templates specify the performance counters that collectively form a data collector set. To collect data, you do the following:

- Download the latest ExPerfWiz templates and store them on the server.

   The blog at *http://blogs.technet.com/mikelag/* contains good pointers to the latest templates; it's also an excellent source for information about many aspects of Exchange 2007 and Exchange 2010 performance.

- Open Performance Monitor.

- Click Data Collector Sets and then select User Defined.

- Right-click and select New to launch the wizard to create a new data collector set. Browse to select the template.

- Click Finish to create the data collector set.

As shown in Figure 17-9, you can then start the data collector by selecting it and clicking Start. Performance Monitor then begins to gather information for all of the counters specified in the template and will continue this process until you stop collection by clicking Stop. The reports generated by ExPerfWiz are stored under the User Defined section of the Reports node. Figure 17-9 shows one report (named 000001) for the Exchange Performance Wizard. Each run of the wizard creates a separate report. The next report is called 000002, the one after 000003, and so on.

Select and click a report to view its contents. By default, Performance Monitor presents the results of a data collection as a graph. However, the ExPerfWiz templates contain so many counters that the graph is tremendously busy and essentially unreadable, and so it is useless for performance analysis (Figure 17-10). It's therefore best to switch to report mode, as you can then browse the report to review the reported results and focus on counters that indicate where performance problems might lie.

Chapter 17

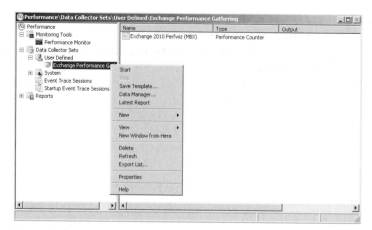

Figure 17-9 Starting the ExPerfWiz data collector set.

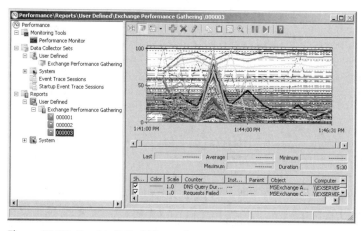

Figure 17-10 Graphic ExPerfWiz results.

ExPerfWiz limitations

Even the Performance Wizard has its limits. Understanding the impact of applications that are linked to Exchange but not directly accessible to Exchange is an excellent example of how such a situation might occur. The two best examples of this are the following:

- RIM BlackBerry Enterprise Server (BES)

- Desktop indexing tools

BES links BlackBerry mobile devices, Exchange, and the mobile operator whose service is used to connect BlackBerry devices to the network. BES uses Messaging Application Programming Interface (MAPI) to communicate with Exchange when it needs to fetch or deliver messages to mailboxes. MAPI clients impose a heavier load on an Exchange server than other protocols, and the general rule of thumb is that a BlackBerry client exerts roughly four times the I/O load of a client that runs ActiveSync (such as Windows Mobile, Android, iPhone, and Palm devices). Therefore, if you use BlackBerry devices, you have to make sure that you deploy sufficient computers running BES to handle the connectivity load, and you have to distribute the BlackBerry users across available mailbox servers so as to avoid creating a "BlackBerry hot spot" consisting of many BlackBerry users concentrated in one mailbox database. Apart from keeping a close eye on the number of BlackBerry devices that connect to Exchange, you should consult the information available on RIM's Web site (*http://na.blackberry.com/eng/services/business/server/full/*) for the latest tuning and performance information for BES connected to Exchange 2010 and make sure that this tremendously useful communications system doesn't turn into a problem for your deployment. Third-party tools such as Zenprise Mobile Manager (*http://www.zenprise.com*) can be helpful to track BlackBerry usage and to debug any connectivity problems that you might run into.

Desktop indexing tools such as Google Desktop for Windows or Xobni (*http://www.xobni .com*) are powerful user productivity tools that allow users to index everything in their mailbox. Windows Desktop Search does the same thing, but the other tools offer other features that make them popular with users. Xobni, for instance, supported threaded conversations and social connections before Microsoft built these features into Outlook 2010. The problem with desktop indexing tools is that they have to gain access to data to be able to index it, and sometimes these tools exert a very heavy load on an Exchange mailbox server when they access online data; at this point, it seems like the server is under load from a mass of hyperactive users who have a tad too much coffee on board. Not all desktop indexing tools access data online (Windows Desktop Search stopped online access from version 3.01 onward) and instead use the data cached on the PC in OST and PST files. This is the preferred behavior, so it's something that you should look for when you select approved desktop indexing tools for your users. Of course, we should acknowledge here that it is entirely possible for users to download and install a new desktop indexing tool without administrator knowledge and the only way to detect that this has happened is if you notice an unexpected spurt in resources consumed by a particular user.

Exchange Load Generator 2010

Exchange Load Generator 2010 (LoadGen) is the only supported load generator for Exchange and replaces the older Loadsim and Exchange Server Stress and Performance (ESP) utilities. LoadGen uses the same interface as ExBPA and also offers a command-line

Chapter 17

interface that you can use to create performance simulations for clients running the following protocols:

- Outlook (online and cached); the tests are based on Outlook 2003 and Outlook 2007, but can be used to represent Outlook 2010

- Internet (POP3 and IMAP4)

- Outlook Web App

- ActiveSync

- SMTP

LoadGen is designed to run in an environment that represents the production environment that you want to deploy. The idea is that LoadGen should be able to stress test the environment to show whether it will be able to support a certain client population. Because LoadGen creates the mailboxes it uses for its tests, you shouldn't attempt to run it in a production environment. Apart from cluttering up Active Directory with test accounts, running LoadGen will cause an obvious and measureable performance degradation for any other application that's running on the same systems.

LoadGen controls its testing from a client computer, which can run Vista, Windows 7, or Windows Server 2008 SP2 or R2. You do not need to install the Exchange management tools on this computer.

A LoadGen test runs for a specified period and uses a configuration that you create. The configuration mimics the client population that you expect to support in a production environment in terms of the numbers of mailboxes, the clients that they use, and other conditions such as the distribution lists used in the environment. A single client computer can control the simulation of up to 1,500 users. You'll need to run the test using multiple clients if you want to create a test that uses more than this number of users. Creating and managing a large-scale test (more than 10,000 users) can be quite a task that requires careful coordination and planning. Some experienced commentators believe that you don't need to go to this trouble, as you can take the result of a test based on, say, 1,000 users and predict the result for the target population from these numbers. The point that they make is that it's easy to spend an excessive amount of time and energy running tests to a point where you lose sight of the need to do other things, such as manage the operational environment!

After a test has been set up, you initialize the environment to create the mailboxes and other objects that LoadGen will use during its tests. Once this is done, you can start the test and LoadGen will run to the end of its test period.

INSIDE OUT How to use the LoadGen summary report

Don't expect to see a detailed printout at the end of a LoadGen test to provide results. Although it generates a summary report to indicate that the test ran successfully, LoadGen doesn't rate Exchange servers with something like a user experience index like you get with Windows 7. Instead, you have to be prepared to monitor the servers under load during the test period to determine whether the stress that LoadGen is placing onto the servers is being handled in an acceptable manner. You can use your tools of choice to review performance during this period, including Performance Monitor. The performance counters described in Table 17-4 are a good set to observe and measure during a LoadGen test.

No performance test will generate results that 100 percent reflect what you will see in production. Simulated users don't behave like human beings, and tests, by their very nature, are designed to create situations that can be replicated over and over again to allow their results to be compared. It's difficult to integrate business requirements into performance testing, and it can be difficult to incorporate any sense of the culture of the organization (for example, are users allowed to send video files as email attachments, or do their voice mail messages tend to be short and curt or long and rambling?). Performance testing gives you a baseline, something that you can assess different configurations against to understand what setup is likely to be best for your company. Performance testing also gives confidence that your deployment is based on a solid foundation. But it's not a silver bullet and no amount of testing will guarantee results, especially for a system that will evolve and flex to accommodate user demands, software updates, and potentially new hardware. Good performance for an Exchange organization can therefore only be achieved over a sustained period through hard work and ongoing attention to detail by the system administrators.

Remote Connectivity Analyzer

The Exchange Remote Connectivity Analyzer (RCA) was developed as a Web site that customers could use to test Outlook Anywhere connectivity. RPC over HTTP connections can be problematic to configure, and the site delivered real value in providing an external point that could "ping" a server to test the end-to-end connection from client to mailbox. Over time, Microsoft has enhanced the RCA site (*https://www.testexchangeconnectivity.com/*) to support connectivity tests for the following:

- Exchange ActiveSync (including Autodiscover for mobile devices)

- Outlook Anywhere (including Autodiscover for Outlook)

Chapter 17

- Exchange Web Services (for example, availability and out of office services)

- Inbound and outbound SMTP (Figure 17-11)

Figure 17-11 The Exchange Remote Connectivity Analyzer.

INSIDE OUT   Every Exchange administrator needs to know RCA

Microsoft included the RCA in the Exchange 2010 toolbox to gain more visibility for the tool and because it is the most valuable connectivity test tool available today. There is nothing else that can perform the same tests as RCA, so it is something with which every Exchange administrator should become familiar.

You can access RCA through the toolbox or by typing its URL into a browser. Best results are achieved with Microsoft Internet Explorer, as this is the browser used by the developers.

To use RCA, you'll need credentials for an account on an Exchange server connected to the Internet that supports the feature you want to test. Ideally, the account should be created for test purposes, as it is a bad idea to provide the credentials for your own account to a system over which you have no control. Microsoft is quite clear that you take full responsibility for using the RCA facility.

After you connect to the RCA site, you select the test that you want to perform and then provide the necessary information to allow RCA to execute the test. Figure 17-11 shows the information required to test that a system can send SMTP outbound messages. In this case, you have to provide the IP address of the SMTP server and an email address to address a test message. When RCA conducts a test, it uses the provided information to mimic a user interaction with Exchange to establish that the functionality works as expected.

When things don't go so well, RCA reports the actions that it took and why the problem occurred. In Figure 17-12, an ActiveSync test failed because the test was unable to contact the Autodiscover service for the domain that was being tested. If the RCA test doesn't work, either the test parameters are incorrect (for example, incorrect credentials were provided for the test account) or some other fundamental problem exists that will stop real users from connecting. This kind of feedback provides the administrator with an immediate pointer to a problem that has to be solved before a feature such as ActiveSync can be placed into production.

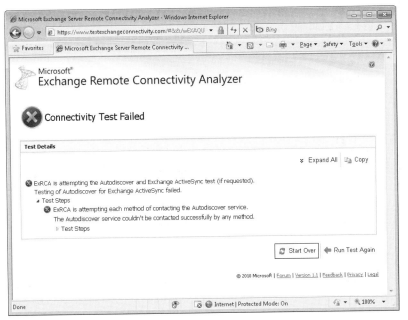

Figure 17-12 An ActiveSync test fails with RCA.

Chapter 17

Searching for more information

This is the end of the book, but it's certainly not the end of the quest for knowledge about Exchange 2010. Every book is constrained by factors such as page count, production time, and not least the time required to research the technology and to then write the text. I freely admit that there are lots of topics that I have not covered in-depth or that I have ignored completely. Other books have been written about Exchange 2010 or the associated technologies that are fundamental prerequisites or are often deployed alongside Exchange 2010. I encourage you to continue your reading on topics including the following:

- Windows Server 2008 R2

- Active Directory

- SharePoint 2010

- Outlook 2010

- Office Communications Server 2010

I maintain a list of technical books that I like on my blog at *http://thoughtsofanidlemind. wordpress.com/*. Please check out my list but don't regard its contents as the only books that are worthwhile. New books appear all the time to advance our collective knowledge about technology and to reinforce best practice.

I also encourage you to be frequent visitors to the Exchange development group's blog (EHLO) at *http://msexchangeteam.com/*. The development group has become much better over the years at writing about their product and their blog is an excellent and worthwhile resource of which you need to be aware. Apart from all of the other information from EHLO that I refer to elsewhere in the book, you'll definitely want a copy of the Exchange 2010 Architecture posted at *http://msexchangeteam.com/archive/2010/10/18/456643.aspx*.

Now on to the next version of Exchange—whenever that might be!

Index to Troubleshooting Topics

Error	Description	Page
setup program	A failure occurs during setup.	49
synchronization	I changed the schema and now Exchange isn't synchronized with Active Directory.	35
WS-Management services	Can't connect to the remote host because WS-Management service is not running.	89

Index

About the Author

 Before retiring in March 2010, **Tony Redmond** spent 26 years at Digital Equipment Corporation, Compaq, and HP, ending up as the Vice-President and Chief Technology Officer for HP Services. Throughout that time, he maintained a close interest in enterprise email and worked on products such as ALL-IN-1, MailWorks, and TeamLinks at Digital, and then formed a group to work on Microsoft Exchange Server 4.0 in 1996. Over the next 14 years, Tony stayed interested in Exchange and wrote extensively about the technology. This is his tenth book covering Exchange.

Although Tony now runs his own consulting company, his range of other interests limits the time he spends doing real work. You can track his activities on his blog at *http://thoughtsofanidlemind.wordpress.com/*.

Resources for Microsoft Exchange Server and Forefront

**Microsoft®
Exchange Server 2010
Best Practices**

Siegfried Jagott and Joel Stidley
with the Microsoft Exchange
Server Team

ISBN 9780735627192

Apply real-world best practices, field-tested
solutions, and candid advice for administering
Exchange Server 2010 and SP1—and optimize
your operational efficiency and results.

**Microsoft Forefront®
Threat Management
Gateway (TMG)
Administrator's Companion**

Jim Harrison, Yuri Diogenes,
and Mohit Saxena from the
Microsoft Forefront TMG Team
with Dr. Tom Shinder

ISBN 9780735626386

Help protect your business from Web-based
threats with this essential administrator's reference
to planning, deploying, and managing Forefront
TMG—successor to Microsoft ISA Server.

**Microsoft
Exchange Server 2010
Inside Out**

Tony Redmond

ISBN 9780735640610

Pre-order now
This supremely organized reference packs all
the details you need to deploy and manage
your Exchange Server 2010–based system—
from the inside out. Covers SP1.

**Microsoft
Exchange Server 2010
Administrator's
Pocket Consultant**

William R. Stanek

ISBN 9780735627123

Portable and precise, this pocket-sized guide
delivers ready answers for the day-to-day
administration of Exchange Server 2010.

Microsoft®
Press

microsoft.com/mspress

Windows Server 2008—
Resources for Administrators

Windows Server® 2008
Administrator's Companion

Charlie Russel and Sharon
Crawford

ISBN 9780735625051

Your comprehensive, one-volume guide to deployment, administration, and support. Delve into core system capabilities and administration topics, including Active Directory®, security issues, disaster planning/recovery, interoperability, IIS 7.0, virtualization, clustering, and performance tuning.

Windows Server 2008
Administrator's
Pocket Consultant,
Second Edition

William R. Stanek

ISBN 9780735627116

Portable and precise—with the focused information you need for administering server roles, Active Directory, user/group accounts, rights and permissions, file-system management, TCP/IP, DHCP, DNS, printers, network performance, backup, and restoration.

Windows Server 2008
Resource Kit

Microsoft MVPs with Microsoft
Windows Server Team

ISBN 9780735623613

Six volumes! Your definitive resource for deployment and operations—from the experts who know the technology best. Get in-depth technical information on Active Directory, Windows PowerShell® scripting, advanced administration, networking and network access protection, security administration, IIS, and more—plus an essential toolkit of resources on CD.

Internet Information
Services (IIS) 7.0
Administrator's
Pocket Consultant

William R. Stanek

ISBN 9780735623644

This pocket-sized guide delivers immediate answers for administering IIS 7.0. Topics include customizing installation; configuration and XML schema; application management; user access and security; Web sites, directories, and content; and performance, backup, and recovery.

Windows PowerShell 2.0
Administrator's
Pocket Consultant

William R. Stanek

ISBN 9780735625952

The practical, portable guide to using *cmdlets* and scripts to automate everyday system administration—including configuring server roles, services, features, and security settings; managing TCP/IP networking; monitoring and tuning performance; and other essential tasks.

ALSO SEE

**Windows
PowerShell 2.0
Best Practices**

ISBN 9780735626461

**Windows® Administration
Resource Kit:
Productivity Solutions
for IT Professionals**

ISBN 9780735624313

**Windows Server 2008
Hyper-V™
Resource Kit**

ISBN 9780735625174

**Windows Server 2008
Security Resource Kit**

ISBN 9780735625044

microsoft.com/mspress

Get Certified—Windows Server 2008

Ace your preparation for the skills measured by the Microsoft® certification exams—and on the job. With 2-in-1 *Self-Paced Training Kits*, you get an official exam-prep guide + practice tests. Work at your own pace through lessons and real-world case scenarios that cover the exam objectives. Then, assess your skills using practice tests with multiple testing modes—and get a customized learning plan based on your results.

EXAMS 70-640, 70-642, 70-646

MCITP Self-Paced Training Kit: Windows Server® 2008 Server Administrator Core Requirements

ISBN 9780735625082

EXAMS 70-640, 70-642, 70-643, 70-647

MCITP Self-Paced Training Kit: Windows Server 2008 Enterprise Administrator Core Requirements

ISBN 9780735625723

EXAM 70-640

MCTS Self-Paced Training Kit: Configuring Windows Server® 2008 Active Directory®

Dan Holme, Nelson Ruest, and Danielle Ruest

ISBN 9780735625136

EXAM 70-647

MCITP Self-Paced Training Kit: Windows® Enterprise Administration

Orin Thomas, et al.

ISBN 9780735625099

EXAM 70-642

MCTS Self-Paced Training Kit: Configuring Windows Server 2008 Network Infrastructure

Tony Northrup, J.C. Mackin

ISBN 9780735625129

ALSO SEE

Windows Server 2008, Administrator's Pocket Consultant, Second Edition

William R. Stanek

ISBN 9780735627116

EXAM 70-643

MCTS Self-Paced Training Kit: Configuring Windows Server 2008 Applications Infrastructure

J.C. Mackin, Anil Desai

ISBN 9780735625112

Windows Server 2008 Administrator's Companion

Charlie Russel, Sharon Crawford

ISBN 9780735625051

Windows Server 2008 Resource Kit

Microsoft MVPs with Windows Server Team

ISBN 9780735623613

EXAM 70-646

MCITP Self-Paced Training Kit: Windows Server Administration

Ian McLean, Orin Thomas

ISBN 9780735625105

microsoft.com/mspress

What do you think of this book?

We want to hear from you!

To participate in a brief online survey, please visit:

microsoft.com/learning/booksurvey

Tell us how well this book meets your needs—what works effectively, and what we can do better. Your feedback will help us continually improve our books and learning resources for you.

Thank you in advance for your input!

Stay in touch!

To subscribe to the *Microsoft Press® Book Connection Newsletter*—for news on upcoming books, events, and special offers—please visit:

microsoft.com/learning/books/newsletter